Twentieth-Century Literary Criticism

Topics Volume

Guide to Gale Literary Criticism Series

For criticism on	Consult these Gale series
Authors now living or who died after December 31, 1959	*CONTEMPORARY LITERARY CRITICISM (CLC)*
Authors who died between 1900 and 1959	*TWENTIETH-CENTURY LITERARY CRITICISM (TCLC)*
Authors who died between 1800 and 1899	*NINETEENTH-CENTURY LITERATURE CRITICISM (NCLC)*
Authors who died between 1400 and 1799	*LITERATURE CRITICISM FROM 1400 TO 1800 (LC)* *SHAKESPEAREAN CRITICISM (SC)*
Authors who died before 1400	*CLASSICAL AND MEDIEVAL LITERATURE CRITICISM (CMLC)*
Authors of books for children and young adults	*CHILDREN'S LITERATURE REVIEW (CLR)*
Dramatists	*DRAMA CRITICISM (DC)*
Poets	*POETRY CRITICISM (PC)*
Short story writers	*SHORT STORY CRITICISM (SSC)*
Black writers of the past two hundred years	*BLACK LITERATURE CRITICISM (BLC)*
Hispanic writers of the late nineteenth and twentieth centuries	*HISPANIC LITERATURE CRITICISM (HLC)*
Native North American writers and orators of the eighteenth, nineteenth, and twentieth centuries	*NATIVE NORTH AMERICAN LITERATURE (NNAL)*
Major authors from the Renaissance to the present	*WORLD LITERATURE CRITICISM, 1500 TO THE PRESENT (WLC)*

ISSN 0276-8178

Volume 86

Twentieth-Century Literary Criticism

Topics Volume

**Excerpts from Criticism of Various Topics
in Twentieth-Century Literature, including Literary
and Critical Movements, Prominent Themes and
Genres, Anniversary Celebrations, and Surveys
of National Literatures**

Jennifer Baise
Editor

Thomas Ligotti
Associate Editor

GALE GROUP

Detroit
San Francisco
London
Boston
Woodbridge, CT

STAFF

Jennifer Baise, *Editor*

Thomas Ligotti, *Associate Editor*

Maria Franklin, *Permissions Manager*
Kimberly F. Smilay, *Permissions Specialist*
Kelly A. Quin, *Permissions Associates*
Sandy Gore, *Permissions Assistant*

Victoria B. Cariappa, *Research Manager*
Andrew Guy Malonis, Barbara McNeil, Gary J. Oudersluys, Maureen Richards, Cheryl L. Warnock, *Research Specialists*
Patricia T. Ballard, Tamara C. Nott, Tracie A. Richardson, *Research Associates*
Phyllis Blackman, Corrine Stocker, *Research Assistant*

Mary Beth Trimper, *Production Director*
Cindy Range, *Buyer*

Gary Leach, *Graphic Artist*
Randy Bassett, *Image Database Supervisor*
Robert Duncan, Michael Logusz, *Imaging Specialists*
Pamela Reed, *Imaging Coordinator*

Library of Congress Catalog Card Number 76-46132
ISBN 0-7876-2747-X
ISSN 0276-8178

Printed in the United States of America
10 9 8 7 6 5 4 3 2 1

Contents

Preface vii

Acknowledgments xi

Preface

Since its inception more than fifteen years ago, *Twentieth-Century Literary Criticism* has been purchased and used by nearly 10,000 school, public, and college or university libraries. *TCLC* has covered more than 500 authors, representing 58 nationalities, and over 25,000 titles. No other reference source has surveyed the critical response to twentieth-century authors and literature as thoroughly as *TCLC*. In the words of one reviewer, "there is nothing comparable available." *TCLC* "is a gold mine of information—dates, pseudonyms, biographical information, and criticism from books and periodicals—which many libraries would have difficulty assembling on their own."

Scope of the Series

TCLC is designed to serve as an introduction to authors who died between 1900 and 1960 and to the most significant interpretations of these author's works. The great poets, novelists, short story writers, playwrights, and philosophers of this period are frequently studied in high school and college literature courses. In organizing and reprinting the vast amount of critical material written on these authors, *TCLC* helps students develop valuable insight into literary history, promotes a better understanding of the texts, and sparks ideas for papers and assignments. Each entry in *TCLC* presents a comprehensive survey of an author's career or an individual work of literature and provides the user with a multiplicity of interpretations and assessments. Such variety allows students to pursue their own interests; furthermore, it fosters an awareness that literature is dynamic and responsive to many different opinions.

Every fourth volume of *TCLC* is devoted to literary topics. These topic entries widen the focus of the series from individual authors to such broader subjects as literary movements, prominent themes in twentieth-century literature, literary reaction to political and historical events, significant eras in literary history, prominent literary anniversaries, and the literatures of cultures that are often overlooked by English-speaking readers.

TCLC is designed as a companion series to Gale's *Contemporary Literary Criticism,* which reprints commentary on authors now living or who have died since 1960. Because of the different periods under consideration, there is no duplication of material between *CLC* and *TCLC*. For additional information about *CLC* and Gale's other criticism titles, users should consult the Guide to Gale Literary Criticism Series preceding the title page in this volume.

Coverage

Each volume of *TCLC* is carefully compiled to present:

- criticism of authors, or literary topics, representing a variety of genres and nationalities

- both major and lesser-known writers and literary works of the period

- 6-12 authors or 3-6 topics per volume

- individual entries that survey critical response to each author's work or each topic in literary history, including early criticism to reflect initial reactions; later criticism to represent any rise or decline in reputation; and current retrospective analyses.

Organization of This Book

An author entry consists of the following elements: author heading, biographical and critical introduction, list of principal works, reprints of criticism (each preceded by an annotation and a bibliographic citation), and a bibliography of further reading.

- The **Author Heading** consists of the name under which the author most commonly wrote, followed by birth and death dates. If an author wrote consistently under a pseudonym, the pseudonym will be listed in the author heading and the real name given in parentheses on the first line of the biographical and critical introduction. Also located at the beginning of the beginning of the introduction to the author entry are any name variations under which an author wrote, including transliterated forms for authors whose languages use nonroman alphabets.

- The **Biographical and Critical Introduction** outlines the author's life and career, as well as the critical issues surrounding his or her work. References to past volumes of *TCLC* are provided at the beginning of the introduction. Additional sources of information in other biographical and critical reference series published by Gale, including *Short Story Criticism, Children's Literature Review, Contemporary Authors, Dictionary of Literary Biography,* and *Something about the Author,* are listed in a box at the end of the entry.

- Some *TCLC* entries include **Portraits** of the author. Entries also may contain reproductions of materials pertinent to an author's career, including manuscript pages, title pages, dust jackets, letters, and drawings, as well as photographs of important people, places, and events in an author's life.

- The **List of Principal Works** is chronological by date of first book publication and identifies the genre of each work. In the case of foreign authors with both foreign-language publications and English translations, the title and date of the first English-language edition are given in brackets. Unless otherwise indicated, dramas are dated by first performance, not first publication.

- Critical essays are prefaced by **Annotations** providing the reader with information about both the critic and the criticism that follows. Included are the critic's reputation, individual approach to literary criticism, and particular expertise in an author's works. Also noted are the relative importance of a work of criticism, the scope of the essay, and the growth of critical controversy or changes in critical trends regarding an author. In some cases, these annotations cross-reference essays by critics who discuss each other's commentary.

- A complete **Bibliographic Citation** designed to facilitate location of the original essay or book precedes each piece of criticism.

- Criticism is arranged chronologically in each author entry to provide a perspective on changes in critical evaluation over the years. All titles of works by the author featured in the entry are printed in boldface type to enable the user to easily locate discussion of particular works. Also for purposes of easier identification, the critic's name and the publication date of the essay are given at the beginning of each piece of criticism. Unsigned criticism is preceded by the title of the journal in which it appeared. Some of the essays in *TCLC* also contain translated material. Unless otherwise noted, translations in brackets are by the editors; translations in parentheses or continuous with the text are by the critic. Publication information (such as footnotes or page and line references to specific editions of works) have been deleted at the editor's discretion to provide smoother reading of the text.

- An annotated list of **Further Reading** appearing at the end of each author entry suggests secondary sources on the author. In some cases it includes essays for which the editors could not obtain reprint rights.

Cumulative Indexes

- Each volume of *TCLC* contains a cumulative **Author Index** listing all authors who have appeared in Gale's Literary Criticism Series, along with cross references to such biographical series as *Contemporary Authors* and *Dictionary of Literary Biography.* For readers' convenience, a complete list of Gale titles included appears on the first page of the author index. Useful for locating authors within the various series, this index is particularly valuable for those authors who are identified by a certain period but who, because of their death dates, are placed in another, or for those authors whose careers span two periods. For example, F. Scott Fitzgerald is found in *TCLC,* yet a writer often associated with him, Ernest Hemingway, is found in *CLC.*

- Each *TCLC* volume includes a cumulative **Nationality Index** which lists all authors who have appeared in *TCLC* volumes, arranged alphabetically under their respective nationalities, as well as Topics volume entries devoted to particular national literatures.

- Each new volume in Gale's Literary Criticism Series includes a cumulative **Topic Index,** which lists all literary topics treated in *NCLC, TCLC, LC 1400-1800,* and the *CLC* year-book.

- Each new volume of *TCLC,* with the exception of the Topics volumes, includes a **Title Index** listing the titles of all literary works discussed in the volume. In response to numerous suggestions from librarians, Gale has also produced a **Special Paperbound Edition** of the *TCLC* title index. This annual cumulation lists all titles discussed in the series since its inception and is issued with the first volume of *TCLC* published each year. Additional copies of the index are available on request. Librarians and patrons will welcome this separate index; it saves shelf space, is easy to use, and is recyclable upon receipt of the following year's cumulation. Titles discussed in the Topics volume entries are not included *TCLC* cumulative index.

Citing Twentieth-Century Literary Criticism

When writing papers, students who quote directly from any volume in Gale's literary Criticism Series may use the following general forms to footnote reprinted criticism. The first example pertains to materials drawn from periodicals, the second to material reprinted from books.

[1]William H. Slavick, "Going to School to DuBose Heyward," *The Harlem Renaissance Re-examined,* (AMS Press, 1987); reprinted in *Twentieth-Century Literary Criticism,* Vol. 59, ed. Jennifer Gariepy (Detroit: Gale Research, 1995), pp. 94-105.

[2]George Orwell, "Reflections on Gandhi," *Partisan Review,* 6 (Winter 1949), pp. 85-92; reprinted in *Twentieth-Century Literary Criticism,* Vol. 59, ed. Jennifer Gariepy (Detroit: Gale Research, 1995), pp. 40-3.

Suggestions Are Welcome

In response to suggestions, several features have been added to *TCLC* since the series began, including annotations to critical essays, a cumulative index to authors in all Gale literary criticism series, entries devoted to criticism on a single work by a major author, more extensive illustrations, and a title index listing all literary works discussed in the series since its inception.

Readers who wish to suggest authors or topics to appear in future volumes, or who have other suggestions, are cordially invited to write the editors.

Acknowledgments

The editors wish to thank the copyright holders of the excerpted criticism included in this volume and the permissions managers of many book and magazine publishing companies for assisting us in securing reproduction rights. We are also grateful to the staffs of the Detroit Public Library, the Library of Congress, the University of Detroit Mercy Library, Wayne State University Purdy/Kresge Library Complex, and the University of Michigan Libraries for making their resources available to us. Following is a list of the copyright holders who have granted us permission to reproduce material in this volume of *TCLC*. Every effort has been made to trace copyright, but if omissions have been made, please let us know.

COPYRIGHTED EXCERPTS IN *TCLC*, VOLUME 86, WERE REPRODUCED FROM THE FOLLOWING PERIODICALS:

COPYRIGHTED EXCERPTS IN *TCLC*, VOLUME 86, WERE REPRODUCED FROM THE FOLLOWING BOOKS:

American Autobiography

INTRODUCTION

Following a model established by the spiritual self-examination of the *Confessions of St. Augustine* in the late fourth century, a work of autobiography typically comprises a prose exposition of the significant experiences in an individual life as recalled by its subject. In American literature these tales have taken such forms as slave narratives, stories of religious conversion, memoirs of successful political and commercial figures, and the self-analyses of prominent writers and thinkers. Reflecting the changing mood of the American national culture over time, these various forms have emphasized the individual's outward experiences, spiritual life, public achievements, or intellectual development. In the twentieth century, American autobiography has evolved into an acknowledged imaginative art, which is characterized as much by the use of the forms and techniques of fiction as by the candid rendering of genuine emotions and events.

The main current in American autobiography stems from the *Autobiography of Benjamin Franklin* (1868) and extends through Henry David Thoreau's *Walden; or, Life in the Woods* (1854) and *The Education of Henry Adams* (1918) to *The Autobiography of Malcolm X* (1966). An early example of the "rags to riches" theme in American autobiography, Franklin's memoir was originally published in installments between 1791 and 1798 and covers his many intellectual pursuits in addition to detailing his early life as a printer's apprentice and his ascent to political office. *Walden,* although it focuses only on Thoreau's life at Walden Pond from 1845 to 1847 rather than providing a historical account of his life, exemplifies the introspective nature of autobiography and is considered among the seminal works in American literature for its keen observations of nature, perceptive social commentary, and compelling prose style. Henry James, in such volumes as *A Small Boy and Others* (1913), *Notes of a Son and Brother* (1914), and *The Middle Years* (1917), discussed the shaping influences on his aesthetic development and his decision to pursue a literary career, and in his *Education,* Henry Adams focused on intellectual development as the most meaningful aspect of the story of one's life. In the mid-twentieth century, Gertrude Stein effectively created a new form in her *The Autobiography of Alice B. Toklas* (1933), reflecting herself through the ostensible autobiography of her secretary and companion. Initiating the subgenre of mock-autobiography, Stein's volume gave rise to numerous experiments in the genre, including Frank Conroy's highly-regarded *Stop-Time* (1967), an impressionistic account of the early life of a thirty-year-old writer of no particular significance. Considered one of the most important works of autobiography in American literature, *The Autobiography of Malcolm X* synthesizes various facets of the genre by combining religious, political, and race issues while utilizing the forms and techniques of fiction.

Among the key critical issues surrounding American autobiography in the late twentieth century is the difficulty distinguishing autobiography from fiction, a situation caused in part by such blended forms as the autobiographical novel and by the trend toward the impressionistic exploration of emotions rather than the accurate depiction of events. As a result of experiments in the genre, the unique, defining characteristics of autobiography have become more difficult to delineate. For some critics, autobiography no longer signifies anything more than a work whose subject is also its author, with no reference to scope, narrative form, or historical accuracy. Since the early 1970s, critics have argued for the acceptance of autobiography as an imaginative art that can be discussed in terms of critical criteria in much the same manner as drama, poetry, and fiction. These commentators view such issues as the selection (or omission) of material and the presentation of a "persona" in a work as two literary aspects of autobiography that strongly affect the work that results. In addition, such previously marginalized works as women's and Native American autobiography have begun gaining recognition from critics of the genre.

REPRESENTATIVE WORKS

Henry Adams
The Education of Henry Adams, 1918

Maya Angelou
I Know Why the Caged Bird Sings, 1970
Gather Together in My Name, 1974
Singin' and Swingin' and Gettin' Merry Like Christmas, 1976
The Heart of a Woman, 1981

Russell Baker
Growing Up, 1982

Henry Bibb
Narrative of the Life and Adventures of Henry Bibb, an American Slave, 1849

Black Elk and John G. Neihardt
Black Elk Speaks: Being the Life Story of a Holy Man of the Oglala Sioux, 1932

William Wells Brown
Narrative of the Life and Escape of William Wells Brown, 1852

Stephen Burroughs
The Memoirs of the Notorious Stephen Burroughs of New Hampshire, c. 1800s, reissued 1924

Eldridge Cleaver
Soul on Ice, 1968

Ciyé Cochise [with A. Kinney Griffith]
The First Hundred Years of Niño Cochise, 1972

Frank Conroy
Stop-Time, 1967

Malcolm Cowley
Exile's Return, 1934

Frederick Douglass
Narrative of the Life of Frederick Douglass, an American Slave, Written by Himself, 1845, reprinted, 1960

W. E. B. Du Bois
Dusk of Dawn: The Autobiography of a Race Concept, 1940, reprinted, 1968

Charles Eastman
Indian Boyhood. 1902, reissued, 1971

Olaudah Equiano
The Interesting Narrative of Olaudah Equiano, or Gustavus Vassa, The African, 1789

F. Scott Fitzgerald
The Crack-Up, edited by Edmund Wilson, 1945

Benjamin Franklin
The Autobiography of Benjamin Franklin, 1868

Hamlin Garland
A Son of the Middle Border, 1917

Geronimo
Geronimo: His Own Story, edited by S. M. Barrett, 1906, rev. ed., 1970

Lillian Hellman
An Unfinished Woman: A Memoir, 1969
Pentimento: A Book of Portraits, 1973
Scoundrel Time, 1976
Maybe: A Story, 1980

Ernest Hemingway
A Moveable Feast, 1964

John Dunn Hunter
Memoirs of Captivity among the Indians of North America, 1824

Henry James
A Small Boy and Others, 1913
Notes of a Son and Brother, 1914
The Middle Years, 1917

Maxine Hong Kingston
The Woman Warrior: Memoirs of a Girlhood among Ghosts, 1977

Lame Deer, John (Fire), and Richard Erdoes
Lame Deer: Seeker of Visions, 1972

Lucy Larcom
A New England Girlhood, 1889

Norman Mailer
The Armies of the Night, 1968

Malcolm X and Alex Haley
The Autobiography of Malcolm X, 1966

Mary McCarthy
Memories of a Catholic Girlhood, 1957

Vladimir Nabokov
Speak Memory: An Autobiography Revisited, 1966

Solomon Northrup
Twelve Years a Slave, 1854

Philip Roth
The Facts: A Novelist's Autobiography, 1988

Gertrude Stein
The Autobiography of Alice B. Toklas, 1933

Henry David Thoreau
Walden; or, Life in the Woods, 1854

Mark Twain
Life on the Mississippi, 1883
Mark Twain's Autobiography. 2 vols., edited by Albert Bigelow Paine, 1924

John Updike
Self-Consciousness: Memoirs, 1989

Booker T. Washington
Up from Slavery, 1901

George Webb
A Pima Remembers, 1959

Tobias Wolff
This Boy's Life: A Memoir, 1989

Richard Wright
Black Boy: A Record of Childhood and Youth, 1945
American Hunger, 1977

OVERVIEWS

Albert E. Stone

SOURCE: "Autobiography and American Culture," in *American Studies*, Vol. XI, No. 2, Winter, 1972, pp. 22-36.

[*In the following essay, Stone identifies major works of American autobiography, offers a definition of the genre, and discusses some leading critical approaches to the subject.*]

One of the striking and promising developments in recent American studies is the new exploration of autobiography. This concern, a product largely of the past decade, is currently being pursued with an energy and sophistication which virtually constitute a rediscovery of the manifold possibilities of the genre. As a cultural document providing unique insights into history, social and individual experience and identity, and cultural change, the autobiography has, of course, long been used by social scientists and historians. As a prime form of the American imagination also, autobiography engages the attention of literary critics and scholars for whom Franklin, Thoreau, Henry Adams, and Gertrude Stein are distinctive names, among others, in the history of American consciousness. Both groups find in the 6377 items listed in Kaplan's *A Bibliography of American Autobiographies* (1), as in its more selective predecessor, Lillard's *American Life in Autobiography, A Descriptive Guide* (2), a wealth of cultural information quite literally unparalleled in other sources. Moreover, the number of autobiographies increases astronomically; it has been estimated that more than 10,000 life stories by Americans have now been published in the United States. Hardly a week passes but the newspapers announce that another American like Frank Sinatra or Gwendolyn Brooks has written his or her story.

"This most democratic province in the republic of letters," as William Dean Howells called it in 1909, is open to all; nearly anyone, it seems, who writes "the sincere relation of what he has been and done and felt and thought" (3) is assured of an audience. To this genre have been drawn public and private figures: poets, philosophers, prizefighters; actresses, artists, political activists; statesmen and penitentiary prisoners; financiers and football players; Quakers and Black Muslims; immigrants and Indians. The range of personality, experience, and profession reflected in the forms of American autobiography is as varied as American life itself. Barriers of literacy, education, and taste which usually divide a culture into "low" and "high" seem almost to disappear in this case. As Lillard reminds us, "autobiography is as near as mankind gets to a unified, lasting, prima facie version of what happens in an individual's lifetime."

PAPERBACKS AND AUTOBIOGRAPHY

Because of the natural and widespread interest in a form of literature thus varied, personal, and illuminating, paperback publishers thrive on autobiography. The availability of classic, new, and neglected autobiographies in inexpensive editions is one factor in the increased attention paid by readers, teachers, and scholars. Sales of such works have so increased of late that traditional estimates of readership as a reflection of cultural significance or influence have been upset. Thus it is probably more dangerous to cite sales figures as meaningful indices of the importance of autobiographies than is the case for most other documents. Benjamin Franklin's *Autobiography* (4), the book that begins the American tradition in autobiography and which remains one of the most famous works in American literature, may never have sold as many copies as *The Autobiography of Malcolm X* (5), the most impressive of recent autobiographies and, as Carol Ohmann has pointed out, a literary descendant in important respects of Franklin's masterpiece. (6) Both, however, may be eclipsed by autobiographies riding the crest of a purely temporary popularity.

Memoirs and autobiographies like footballer Jerry Kramer's *Instant Replay* (7) or entertainer Sammy Davis, Jr.'s *Yes I Can* (8) have an apparent appeal but actually offer limited insights to the cultural critic. How to distinguish the permanently valuable from the Madison Avenue product of the moment, how to establish, for instance, the immense superiority of an Indian autobiography like *Black Elk Speaks* (9) over an imitation like *The Memoirs of Chief Red Fox* (19), or of Shirley MacLaine's *Don't Fall Off the Mountain* (11) over *Yes I Can*, calls not only for familiarity with the range of American autobiographies now available but also for an awareness of essential definitions, distinctions, and standards in this fast-changing field. These criteria—not all of which are highbrow or academic—are now being established by a number of scholars who approach autobiography freshly from a variety of fruitful perspectives, including traditional English and European literary criticism, historical American Studies, social psychology and psychoanalysis, and Black Studies.

WHAT IS AUTOBIOGRAPHY?

Before any distinctively American emphases or aspects of autobiography can be described or accounted for, some general definitions are needed. These may be found in abundance in the classic discussions of autobiography by Georg Misch (12), André Maurois (13), Arthur Melville Clark (14), Wayne Shumaker (15), Georges Gusdorf (16), Roy Pascal (17), Jean Starobinski (18), and James Olney (19). Among these critics—most of them European or British in origin or concern—there is wide agreement that autobiography, as roughly distinguished from journal, diary, memoir, or reminiscence, is the retrospective account of an individual's life, or a significant part thereof, written by that person with the avowed intent of telling the truthful story of his or her public and private experience. Autobiography thus describes a content not a form. Three hazy areas can at once be detected in this consensus definition, each of potential importance for American autobiography. These are: "a significant part thereof"; "written by that person"; and "avowed truth." Given the pace of modern experience and the still widely shared belief that ordinary individuals can participate meaningfully in extraordinary events, many topical autobiographies or memoirs appear. Sometimes it is difficult to see any generic difference between, for instance, two contemporary works like Kramer's *Instant Replay* and Norman Mailer's *The Armies of the Night* (20). Both chronicle brief portions of the authors' recent lives. Yet Kramer's subtitle, *The Green Bay Packer Diary,* justly removes it from the category of autobiography, whereas Mailer's even more restricted narrative of the October, 1967 peace march on the Pentagon is true autobiography. Two critics who argue Mailer's case most persuasively are Richard Gilman (21) and Warner Berthoff (22).

A second problem for the student of American autobiography is authorship. Many modern autobiographies, though not "written by that person," still make available the experience of inarticulate lives. Are their efforts invariably to be denied the status of "true autobiography"? So many slick and superficial fabrications of pseudo-identity and experience have been published that one is tempted to reply categorically yes—until one turns to *The Autobiography of Malcolm X* or *Black Elk Speaks*. Both were written in collaboration yet create vividly and powerfully the personality of a man. Other instances of similar triumphs over the ghostwriter suggest that readers should proceed case by case and not by rule.

A brilliant essay by F. R. Hart takes precisely this empirical, inductive approach in discussing the knotty problem of "truth" in autobiography. (23) Taking issue with Shumaker and others who insist that autobiographers always want to be taken as writing nothing that is not literally and factually true, Hart quotes Renan ("ce qu'on dit de soi est toujours poésie") and cites many autobiographers who acknowledge the necessarily fictive element in the genre. In reference to Nabokov's *Speak, Memory* (24), perhaps the most poetically evocative of all immigrant or emigré autobiographies, Hart properly observes, "The historicity of the recreation is imperative, *even though* the autobiographer knows the terrible elusiveness of that historicity." Autobiography *is* a species of history but it is also a form of fiction; like history, it is descriptive and subject to verification, but like fiction it is inventive and lays claims to veracity. The reader of autobiography knows that he can never wholly separate the two. What he must learn is a sophisticated reality-testing, a point argued by Norman Holland in an important psychoanalytic essay on non-fiction. "Any given paragraph could be fiction or non-fiction—it is our different expectations

from fiction and non-fiction rather than the texts as such that differentiate our degrees of involvement. Nonfiction usually asks us to do more reality-testing than fiction." (25) Though all readers may not share Holland's belief in Freudian reality, most recognize that autobiography overlaps history, literature, and psychology and can be properly understood only by reference to the coinciding concerns and criteria of all three disciplines. Thus it is a natural interdisciplinary study.

AUTOBIOGRAPHY AND AMERICAN HISTORY AND MYTH

One of the first historical dimensions of autobiography as an American act is a fact James M. Cox emphasizes in an important essay (26): the very term "autobiography" in its modern sense was coined only in 1809, and the new phenomenon to which Robert Southey applied it was a product of what R. R. Palmer calls the Age of the Democratic Revolutions. Franklin shares with Rousseau the honor of creating modern autobiography. The two classical forms of autobiography—the memoir and the confession—persist in their original titles but were transformed into secular, private, democratic, and psychological modes by the American and the Frenchman. Each invented the literary analogue to the revolutionary changes in their respective societies. Even earlier than Franklin, however, the spiritual autobiographies composed by Puritan and Quaker colonists had assumed a subtly different content if not a different form from their European prototypes. In *Spiritual Autobiography in Early America* (27), Daniel B. Shea, Jr. examines a number of the colonial followers of Bunyan and Fox, including Thomas Shepard (28), Jonathan Edwards (29), and John Woolman (30). Shea concludes that these Americans departed very early from the narrow narrative of conversion; their autobiographical accounts often include a very wide range of experience that bore on their spiritual condition. The same inclusive approach can be seen in the first great black autobiography associated with American literature, *The Life of Olaudah Equiano, or Gustavus Vassa, The African* (31). Conversion, adventure, and abolitionist propaganda are almost equally prominent themes in this remarkable Nigerian's story.

Cox's thesis that America and autobiography arose together and under the stimulus of similar forces suggests that this democratic literary genre has much closer, more immediate links to political and historical events than do fiction, poetry, or drama. Light on this hypothesis comes by checking in Kaplan the publication dates for a number of important autobiographical works. An unusual clustering does seem to occur at the time of the American Revolution (Woolman, Franklin, Crèvecoeur (32), Vassa); in the pre-Civil War years (slaves' narratives, Thoreau (33), Whitman (34)); just before or after World War I (Henry Adams (35), Mark Twain (36), Henry James (37), Alexander Berkman (38), Mary Antin (39), Andrew Carnegie (40), Theodore Dreiser (41), Louis Sullivan (42)); during the Great Depression (Gertrude Stein (44), Black Elk, Lincoln

Steffens (43), Clarence Darrow (45), W. E. B. DuBois (46)); and in the post-World War II era (Richard Wright (47), Conrad Aiken (48), Nabokov, Whittaker Chambers (49), Malcolm X, Claude Brown (50), Mailer, Eldridge Cleaver (51)). Periods of relative social or political calm—pre-Stamp Act America, the early nineteenth century, the Gilded Age—seem to have been times when fewer important autobiographies appeared. Yet Robert Cantwell, in an essay on the spate of autobiographies that appeared around 1938, warns of the dangers of making such simple connections between parts and ages of a culture. (52) Because autobiography is, in Starobinski's terms, both past history and present discourse, it is necessarily a double reflection of attitudes and values. Thus *Personal Memoirs of Ulysses S. Grant* (53), which appeared in 1885, is a far more significant document of the Civil War than of the Gilded Age, to which Grant scarcely makes a single reference. Conversely, Lucy Larcom's *A New England Girlhood* (1889) (54) chronicles family life in the New England of the 1820s and 30s, but her nostalgia reflects more properly emotional values shared with Howells and Thomas Bailey Aldrich.

An alternate way to relate autobiography and history is proposed in a pioneering essay by William C. Spengemann and L. R. Lundquist. (55) These critics assert that because autobiography is an imaginative art it "has nothing to do with factual truth," so cannot be used descriptively to illuminate historical events or eras. The truth, and therefore the use, of autobiography is mythic; "the writer explains his life by depicting himself according to culturally evaluated images of character. As he turns his private experience into language he assumes one of the many identities outlined in the myth and so asserts his connection with his culture."

Spengemann and Lundquist describe "the" American myth as "a pilgrimage from imperfection to perfection." An adaptation of Christian mythology to the changing problems and possibilities of American life, this increasingly secular myth defines roles for Americans which are assumed and acted out in the exemplary autobiographies of our culture: the Prophet (Whitman, Norman Mailer); the Hero (Franklin, Carnegie); the Villain (P. T. Barnum (56), Whittaker Chambers); the Outcast or Outsider (Mae West (57), Caryl Chessman (58); the Disenchanted (Fitzgerald (59)). Thus autobiographical form is controlled by cultural belief in "an integrated, continuing personality which transcends the limitations and irregularities of time and space and unites all of one's apparently contradictory experiences into an identifiable whole. This notion of individual identity, in fact, may well be the central belief of our culture. With all its ramifications—personal responsibility, individual destiny, dissent, vocation and so forth—it forms the core of our being and the fabric of our history."

This is a broad and challenging thesis, but rests upon the prescriptively narrow assumption that all significant autobiographers settle upon a central self or an accepted role. For Spengemann and Lundquist, the writer "must adopt some consistent, overriding view of himself and his part. He must identify the 'I' which unites all his past experiences." A critic like Hart might reply that writing autobiography is often a far more protean act of self-discovery, many of whose American monuments display discontinuities and fragmentations of self and society more clearly than consistent identities and clearly defined roles.

AUTOBIOGRAPHY AND AMERICAN LITERATURE

At present there is no critical history of American autobiography as a branch of American literature. Several recent books and a number of essays offer partial views of the whole landscape or detailed looks at particular works, but no comprehensive survey has yet been written. (Both Robert F. Sayre and Spengemann and Lundquist are apparently at work on such a project; there are no doubt others.) James M. Cox's essay (26) is presently the best brief discussion, but treats only Franklin, Thoreau, Whitman, and Henry Adams, with a final glance at Gertrude Stein.

A far fuller treatment of Franklin, Adams, and Henry James is provided by Sayre's excellent work, *The Examined Self* (60). Sayre rejects the reduction of autobiography to biography and history and attempts instead what he terms proper "autobiographical criticism." This means not merely tracking "fictional" episodes back to their "real life" sources, but, more importantly, relating each part of an autobiography to the writer's changing need for appropriate form and image. Sayre's literary analysis draws illuminating parallels between the forms of fiction and autobiography (in the picaresque Part One of Franklin's *Autobiography*) and suggests themes and techniques shared by the novels and autobiographies of an artist like James or by the histories of Henry Adams and his *Education*, probably the greatest of American autobiographies. Sayre's approach offers many possibilities for viewing representations of American experience in terms more purely literary than Spengemann and Lundquist employ. Thus works like James's *A Small Boy and Others* and *Notes of a Son and Brother* might be seen as imaginative rediscoveries of childhood and youth to be stylistically and structurally compared to similar stories by Lucy Larcom, Louis Sullivan, Richard Wright, or James Baldwin (61) but also to novels like *The Adventures of Tom Sawyer* and *What Maisie Knew*.

This imaginative and comparative approach is carried even further by David L. Minter in *The Interpreted Design* (62). Here Minter traces a recurrent theme, design, and metaphor in American fiction and autobiography—the juxtaposition of two characters, a man of bold design who acts and a man of interpretation through whose consciousness the story of the other comes to us. In fiction the classic examples are *The Blithedale Romance, The Great Gatsby,* and *Absalom! Absalom!* In autobiography

Jonathan Edwards, Franklin, Thoreau, and Henry Adams model their life-stories on this pattern. This emphasis upon design in life and art leads Minter to read Part Two of Franklin's *Autobiography,* in which the plan for moral perfection is recounted, as the work's core. Through the eyes of the older, observing Franklin we see both the idealism and the naive egotism of the younger Franklin who tries on one active role after another in search of both worldly success and the humility of Jesus and Socrates. Similarly, Adams as an older writer looks back on the little manikin who is his historical self, and in recording the failure of his attempts to master history and nature makes of the *Education* a work of art, a "supreme no to chaos and disorder."

Aside from Cox, Sayre, and Minter, however, there remains chiefly a growing list of individual essays, chapters, and introductions which treat American autobiographies as separate works of art. Many of these criticisms are couched in cultural rather than narrowly aesthetic terms; in this their authors reflect the influence of American Studies training as well as the inevitably interdisciplinary nature of autobiography itself. What follows is a selective sampling of useful commentaries on certain of the best-known American autobiographies.

Of the many studies of Franklin published in recent years those by Charles Sanford (63), David Levin (64), and John William Ward (65) should prove helpful, but no reader can afford to neglect the riches of the Yale Paperbound edition with its extensive historical and biographical materials. Significant criticism of the eighty-odd slave narratives published in pre-Civil War America has been contributed by Arna Bontemps (66), Gilbert Osofsky (67), C. H. Nichols (68), and John F. Bayliss (69). Certain of these narratives stand out for their imaginative recreation of the horrors of slavery, the excitement of escape, the achievement of freedom and manhood. Historians and critics, both black and white, return most often to the narratives of Gustavus Vassa, Frederick Douglass (70), Henry Bibb (67), Solomon Northup (67), Father Josiah Henson (71), and Harriet Jacobs. (72)

No one has contributed more than J. C. Levenson to our appreciation of *The Education of Henry Adams* (73). A brilliant recent study of Gertrude Stein and her two autobiographies is Richard Bridgman's *Gertrude Stein in Pieces* (74). Richard Wright's *Black Boy,* the most poetically powerful of all black autobiographies, has been perceptively discussed by Ralph Ellison (75), George E. Kent (76), and Robert Bone (77). The triple nature of Conrad Aiken's *Ushant* as autobiography, essay and novel is sensitively traced by Jay Martin. (78)

Though *The Autobiography of Malcolm X* is now widely appreciated as the imaginative equal of *Black Boy,* its literary form and relation to earlier black writing have not been fully established. Warner Berthoff (22) has written of it from a white perspective, but Richard Gilman (21) has argued that proper criticism of works

like *Malcolm X* and Cleaver's *Soul on Ice* must come from black critics. Materials for such appreciation of *The Autobiography* may be found in J. H. Clarke's *Malcolm X* which contains an interesting essay by the young Egyptian-American scholar, A. M. Elmessiri (79). One reason why we have not had more literary discussions of autobiographies like *Malcolm X* may be that many militant black intellectuals remain profoundly suspicious not only of formal literary criticism but also of autobiography as a traditional European genre explicitly committed to individualism—all can be seen as white cultural threats to black consciousness and community. V.S. Pritchett, the English critic, has commented on a similar ideological attack on Western autobiography by Communist critics. Such works, in this view necessarily enhance the private ego and thus are proof of bourgeois social decay. Pritchett disagrees, asserting instead that autobiographies are significant expressions of a "revolutionary" egoism and "the necessary civilising force in mass society." (80) Thus literary analysis of autobiography shades imperceptibly into ideology and the cultural critic can refine his awareness of the inevitability of this fact by reading Frederick Crews' thoughtful essay "Do Literary Studies have an Ideology?" (81)

AUTOBIOGRAPHY AND THE SOCIAL SCIENCES

Psychology, psychoanalysis, anthropology and sociology are the social sciences most directly involved in the study of the subjective dimension of culture. The proper use of human documents in the discovery and testing of social data has been an issue at least since the publication of Thomas and Znaniecki's *The Polish Peasant in Europe and America* (82), one part of which is the analysis of an autobiography by Władek a Polish immigrant to the United States. Thomas and Znaniecki's famous description of autobiography as "the *perfect* type of sociological material" has since been criticized, most acutely by Herbert Blumer (83). Despite their fullness of detail about the personal experience of social process, autobiographies never can fully meet, either singly or in collection, the three criteria for scientific evidence: representativeness, adequacy, reliability. Moreover, as Blumer points out a personal document as individual and imaginatively self-contained as an autobiography bears a double relationship to any scientific theory. Speaking of Thomas and Znaniecki's theory of "social becoming" in light of Władek's narrative Blumer observes "while the experiences have a tough independent character which enables them to be a test of a theoretical conception, at other times they seem, metaphorically speaking, to be helpless before the imposition of a theoretical view." Blumer concludes that while personal documents lend themselves to diverse interpretations they grow less satisfactory as the interpretation grows more abstract. "At best, these materials only enable one to make a *case* for the theoretical interpretation."

Gordon W. Allport accepts Blumer's critique but still vigorously defends the use of autobiography as a legitimate and necessary idiographic tool. In *The Nature of Personality* (particularly in the challenging final essay "Personality: A Problem for Science or a Problem for Art?") (84), Allport counters arguments of scientific objectivists and urges the use of various quantitative and non-quantitative methods of validation of theory by means of autobiographies. Allport extends his case in *The Use of Personal Documents in Psychological Science* (85). Here he concludes: "Acquaintance with the particular case, a sense of its patterned character and its individualized laws of action, stand at the gateway of generalized knowledge and at its terminus at the point of application . . . The positivist who dreads the subjectivity of the process of understanding needs as much as does the intuitionist to settle down to the task of finding out how his own mind, the most sensitive recording machine in existence, is capable of registering multiple variables and discerning relationships between them."

A promising technique for doing this which has developed since Allport and Blumer first wrote is value analysis. The pioneering study is Ralph K. White's examination of Richard Wright's *Black Boy* (86) by means of alternating impressionistic and statistical analyses. White redraws the picture of Wright's personality in the light of both kinds of reading, in comparison to eight very different white life-stories, within a Freudian framework. Like Blumer, White accepts *Black Boy*'s imaginative integrity which by turns, fits, and tests, evades his hypotheses. His analysis has, however, limitations for the cultural critic looking for help from the social scientist. Thus White downplays the issue of fundamental differences in identity and psychosocial development between blacks and whites. (This important area is currently being explored, through insights derived in part from black autobiographies, by Erikson (87), Silberman (88), Hauser (90) and others.) Also, White tends to ignore the historical dimensions of Wright's autobiography. For example, he underestimates the influence of Wright's Communist experiences in the 1930s as a factor affecting the narrative treatment of family, black community, and self in *Black Boy*.

Although anthropology is also a biographically-based science, many American anthropologists once neglected life-histories as idiographic instruments. With the recent emphasis on culture-and-personality interpretations, however, anthropologists are following the lead of Kardiner, Hallowell, Lewis and others in using biographies and autobiographies as significant sources in the study of internalization and motivation. L. L. Langness presents the best case for the relevance of autobiography in *Life History in Anthropological Science*. (89)

In this interface of history and psychology within autobiography the most significant recent work has been done by Erik Erikson, whose *Childhood and Society* (91) provides one of the most flexible neo-Freudian contexts for studying American autobiography. Erikson's later studies of Luther and Ghandi are built upon a deep and sensitive awareness of individual experience as somatic, social, and historical and of individual expression as conditioned by form, language, and convention. "There is always some naive self-revelation in any outpouring of autobiographic data," he writes of Ghandi's *Autobiography*. "Yet each given medium (diary, conversation, or autobiography) has its own formal laws and serves tradition and personal style. As to unconscious motivation, we must always remember that the autobiographer has not agreed to a therapeutic contract by which he promises to put into words his 'free associations,' so that we may help him to compare them with inner and outer 'reality.'" (92) Erikson enumerates the factors to be considered in "helping" an autobiographer; one must keep in mind "the *stage of the recorder's life*," and "*the course of his whole life history*" and the "*historical process*" of which any moment is but a stage. Moreover, the interpreter must never forget that he himself is subject to the "*mood of his own life*" and is heir to a given "*lineage of conceptualization*." *Ghandi's Truth* (93) demonstrates how well Erikson has balanced these factors to illuminate both a man and his autobiography.

Finding links between individual and group experience is as much the historian's task as the social scientist's, and many American historians today find Erikson the most stimulating exemplar of new ways to "do history" in relation to psychoanalysis. H. Stuart Hughes summarizes in *History as Art and as Science* (94) the coinciding concerns of the two disciplines: history and psychoanalysis both "believe in the radical subjectivity of human understanding"; both seek for systematic generalizations for dealing with individual consciousness as the "final datum, the bedrock of what we know." Hughes concludes that historians and psychoanalysts "have finally realized that the individual can be understood in his full cultural context only if his spiritual biography is viewed in relation to the lives of others with whom he has deep-seated emotional affinities; . . . . the path to the fuller understanding of the individual lies through the group—and vice versa. In both cases, the explanation of motive runs from the single human being to others comparable to him, and then back to the individual once more, as the ramifying thought and action of both are gradually illuminated. This reciprocal method is the ultimate concern that history and psychoanalysis share." Hughes' reference to the importance of "spiritual biography" in tracing this process suggests the role that autobiography may continue to play in the future development of American history as a social science and an art.

SUGGESTED READING

Author's Note: In addition to the traditional journals serving the disciplines of literature, history, and social sciences, there are several others which the student of American autobiography should consult. Besides those with an obvious interdisciplinary focus (e.g. *American Quarterly, Literature & Psychology, Phylon*), there are two new journals of special interest: *New Literary History,* published at the University of Virginia, and *Journal of Interdisciplinary History*, published at MIT. The following documents are referred to in the essay. Soft cover editions (*) are listed in all instances where they are available.

(1) Louis Kaplan, *A Bibliography of American Autobiographies* (Madison, Univ. of Wisconsin Press, 1961).

(2) Richard G. Lillard, *American Life in Autobiography, A Descriptive Guide* (Stanford, Stanford Univ. Press, 1956).

(3) William Dean Howells, "Editor's Easy Chair," *Harper's Monthly* 119 (October, 1909), p. 798.

*(4) *The Autobiography of Benjamin Franklin*, eds. L. W. Labaree, R. L. Ketcham, H. C. Boatfield, H. H. Fineman (New Haven, Yale Univ. Press, 1964).

*(5) Malcolm X and Alex Haley, *The Autobiography of Malcolm X* (New York, Grove Press, 1966).

(6) C. Ohmann, "*The Autobiography of Malcolm X*: A Revolutionary Use of the Franklin Tradition," *American Quarterly* 22 (Summer, 1970), pp. 131-49.

*(7) Jerry Kramer, *Instant Replay: The Green Bay Packer Diary*, ed. Dick Schaap (New York: New American Library, 1968).

*(8) Sammy Davis Jr. and Jane and Burt Boyar, *Yes I Can, The Story of Sammy Davis, Jr.* (New York, Pocket Books, 1966).

*(9) *Black Elk Speaks, Being the Life Story of a Holy Man of the Oglala Sioux*, as told through John G. Neihardt (Lincoln, Univ. of Nebraska Press, 1961).

*(10) *The Memoirs of Chief Red Fox* (Greenwich, Conn., Fawcett, 1971).

*(11) Shirley MacLaine, *Don't Fall Off the Mountain* (New York, Bantam, 1970).

(12) Georg Misch, *The History of Autobiography in Antiquity* (Cambridge, Harvard Univ. Press, 1951), Vol. I, chap. 1.

(13) André Maurois, *Aspects of Biography* (tr. S. C. Roberts) (New York, Ungar, 1966).

(14) Arthur Melville Clark, *Autobiography, Its Genesis and Phases* (Edinburgh, 1935; reprinted Folcroft Press, 1969).

(15) Wayne Shumaker, *English Autobiography: Its Emergence, Materials, and Forms* (Berkeley, Univ. of California Press, 1954).

(16) Georges Gusdorf, "Conditions et limites de l'autobiographie," in *Formen der Selbstdarstellung*, eds.

G. Reichenkron and E. Haase (Berlin, Duncker & Humblot, 1956), pp. 105-23.

(17) Roy Pascal, *Design and Truth in Autobiography* (Cambridge, Harvard Univ. Press, 1960).

(18) Jean Starobinski, "The Style of Autobiography," in *Literary Style, a Symposium*, ed. S. B. Chatman (New York, Oxford Univ. Press, 1971), pp. 285-96.

(19) James Olney, *Metaphors of Self: The Meaning of Autobiography* (Princeton, Princeton Univ. Press, 1972).

*(20) Norman Mailer, *The Armies of the Night: History as a Novel, The Novel as History* (New York, New American Library, 1968).

*(21) Richard Gilman, *The Confusion of Realms* (New York, Random House, 1970).

(22) Warner Berthoff, "Witness and Testament: Two Contemporary Classics," in *Aspects of Narrative*, ed. J. H. Miller (New York, Columbia Univ. Press, 1971), pp. 173-98.

(23) Francis R. Hart, "Notes for an Anatomy of Modern Autobiography," *New Literary History*, I (Spring, 1970), pp. 485-511.

*(24) Vladimir Nabokov, *Speak, Memory, An Autobiography Revisited* (New York, Pyramid Books, 1966).

(25) Norman N. Holland, "Prose and Minds: A Psychoanalytic Approach to Non-Fiction," in *The Art of Victorian Prose*, eds. G. Lavine & W. Madden (New York: Oxford Univ. Press, 1968), pp. 314-37.

(26) James M. Cox, "Autobiography and America," in *Aspects of Narrative op. cit.*, pp. 143-72.

(27) Daniel B. Shea, Jr., *Spiritual Autobiography in Early America* (Princeton, Princeton Univ. Press, 1968).

(28) Thomas Shepard, "The Autobiography of Thomas Shepard," ed A. B. Forbers, *Publications of the Colonial Society of Massachusetts* Vol. 27 (1932) pp. 345-400.

*(29) Jonathan Edwards, *Personal Narrative in The American Tradition in Literature*, eds. S. Bradley, R. C. Beatty, and E. H. Long (New York, W. W. Norton, 1967) I, pp. 124-36.

*(30) John Woolman, *The Journal of John Woolman* (New York, Corinth Books, 1961).

(31) *The Life of Olaudah Equiano, or Gustavus Vassa, the African. Written by Himself* in *Great Slave Narratives*, ed. A. Bontemps (Boston, Beacon Press, 1969).

*(32) M. G. St.-John de Crèvecoeur, *Letters from an American Farmer and Sketches of XVIII-Century America,* ed. A. E. Stone (New York, New American Library, 1963).

*(33) H. D. Thoreau, *The Varlorum Waldan,* ed. W. Harding (New York, Washington Square Press, 1968).

*(34) W. Whitman, *Song of Myself,* in *Leaves of Grass* (New York, W. W. Norton, 1968); *Specimen Days,* ed. A. Kagin (New York, D. R. Godine, 1971).

*(35) Henry Adams, *The Education of Henry Adams* (Boston, Houghton Mifflin, Sentry Ed., 1961).

(36) *Mark Twain's Autobiography,* ed. A. B. Paine (New York, Harper, 1924). *Mark Twain in Eruption,* ed. B. DeVoto (New York, Putnam, 1968). *The Autobiography of Mark Twain,* ed. C. Neider (New York, Harper, 1959).

(37) Henry James, *Henry James Autobiography,* ed. F. W. Dupes (New York, Criterion Books, 1956).

*(38) Alexander Berkman, *Prison Memoirs of an Anarchist* (New York, Schocken Books, 1970).

*(39) Mary Antin, *The Promised Land* (Boston, Houghton Mifflin, Sentry Ed., 1969).

(40) Andrew Carnegie, *Autobiography of Andrew Carnegie* (Boston, Houghton Mifflin, 1920).

*(41) Theodore Dreiser, *Dawn* and *A Book About Myself* (Greenwich, Fawcett Premier Books, 1965).

*(42) Louis H. Sullivan, *The Autobiography of an Idea* (New York, Dover Pub., 1956).

*(43) Lincoln Steffens, *The Autobiography of Lincoln Steffens* (New York, Harbrace Book, 1968), 2 vols.

*(44) Gertrude Stein, *The Autobiography of Alice B. Toklas* (New York, Random Vintage Book, 1960).

*(45) Clarence Darrow, *The Story of My Life* (New York, Scribner's, 1960).

*(46) W. E. B. DuBois, *Dusk of Dawn: An Essay Toward an Autobiography of a Race Concept* (New York, Schocken Books, 1968).

*(47) Richard Wright, *Black Boy, A Record of Childhood and Youth* (New York, Harper & Row, 1966).

*(48) Conrad Aiken, *Ushant, An Essay* (Cleveland & New York, Meridian Books, 1962).

*(49) Whittaker Chambers, *Witness* (Chicago, Regnery, 1969).

*(50) Claude Brown, *Manchild in the Promised Land* (New York, New American Library, 1965).

*(51) Eldridge Cleaver, *Soul on Ice* (New York, Dell, 1970).

(52) Robert Cantwell, "The Autobiographers," *New Republic* 94 (27 April, 1938), pp. 354-56.

*(53) Ulysses S. Grant, *Personal Memoirs of Ulysses S. Grant* (New York, Grosset & Dunlap, Universal Library, 1962).

*(54) Lucy Larcom, *A New England Girlhood* (New York, Corinth Books, 1961).

(55) William C. Spengemann & L. R. Lundquist, "Autobiography and the American Myth," *American Quarterly* 17 (Fall, 1965), pp. 92-110.

(56) Phineas T. Barnum, *The Life of P. T. Barnum, Written by Himself* (Buffalo, Courier Co., 1888).

(57) Mae West, *Goodness Had Nothing to Do With It* (Englewood Cliffs, N. J., Prentice-Hall, 1959).

(58) Caryl Chessman, *Call 2455, Death Row* (New York, Prentice-Hall, 1954).

*(59) F. Scott Fitzgerald, *The Crack-Up,* ed. E. Wilson (Norfolk, Conn., New Directions, 1956).

(60) Robert F. Sayre, *The Examined Self: Benjamin Franklin, Henry Adams, Henry James* (Princeton, Princeton Univ. Press, 1964).

*(61) James Baldwin, *Notes of a Native Son* (Boston, Beacon Press, 1957).

(62) David L. Minter, *The Interpreted Design as a Structural Principle in American Prose,* (New Haven, Yale Univ. Press, 1969).

(63) Charles L. Sanford, *The Quest for Paradise: Europe and the American Moral Imagination* (Urbana, Univ. of Illinois Press, 1961), chap. 7.

(64) David Levin, *In Defense of Historical Literature* (New York, Hill & Wang, 1967), chap. 3.

(65) John William Ward, "Who Was Benjamin Franklin?," *American Scholar* 32 (Autumn, 1963), pp. 541-53.

*(66) Arna Bontemps, "The Slave Narrative: An American Genre," in *Great Slave Narratives* (Boston, Beacon Press, 1969).

*(67) Gilbert Osefsky, *Puttin' On Ole Massa, The Slave Narratives of Henry Bibb, William Wells Brown, and Solomon Northup* (New York, Harper Torchbooks, 1969), introduction.

(68) C. H. Nichols, Jr., "Slave Narratives and the Plantation Legend," *Phylon* 10, No. 3 (1949), pp. 201-09.

————, "Who Read the Slave Narratives?" *Phylon* 20, No. 2 (1959), pp. 149-62.

*(69) John E. Bayliss, *Black Slave Narratives* (New York, Macmillan, 1970), introduction.

*(70) Frederick Douglass, *Narrative of the Life of Frederick Douglass, An American Slave, Written by Himself,* ed. B. Quarles (Cambridge, Harvard Univ. Press, 1960).

*(71) Josiah Henson, *Father Henson's Story of His Own Life* (New York, Corinth Books, 1962).

(72) Harriet Jacobs, *Incidents in the Life of a Slave Girl, Written by Herself* (Miami, Mmesnosyne Pub. Co., 1969).

*(73) J. C. Levenson, *The Mind and Art of Henry Adams* (Stanford, Stanford Univ. Press, 1968).

(74) Richard Bridgman, *Gertrude Stein in Pieces* (New York, Oxford Univ. Press, 1970).

*(75) Ralph Ellison, *Shadow and Act* (New York, Random House, Vintage Books, 1972).

(76) George E. Kent, "Richard Wright: Blackness and the Adventure of Western Culture," *CLA Journal* 12 (1969), pp. 322-43.

*(77) Robert Bone, *Richard Wright* (Minneapolis, Univ. of Minnesota Press, 1969).

(78) Jay Martin, *Conrad Aiken, A Life of His Art* (Princeton, Princeton Univ. Press, 1962).

(79) *Malcolm X: The Man and His Times,* ed. John H. Clarke (New York, Macmillan, 1969).

(80) V. S. Pritchett, "All About Ourselves," *New Statesman & Nation* 51 (26 May, 1956), pp. 601-02.

(81) Frederick C. Crews, "Do Literary Studies Have an Ideology?" *PMLA* 85 (May, 1970), pp. 423-28.

(82) W. I. Thomas & F. Znaniecki, *The Polish Peasant in Europe and America* (New York, A. A. Knopf, 1927), 2 vols.

(83) Herbert Blumer, *Critiques of Research in the Social Sciences: I An Appraisal of Thomas and Znaniecki's The Polish Peasant in Europe and America* (New York, Social Science Research Council, 1939).

(84) Gordon W. Allport, *The Nature of Personality: Selected Papers* (Cambridge, Addison-Wesley Press, 1950).

*(85)————, *The Use of Personal Documents in Psychological Science* (New York, Social Science Research Council, 1942).

(86) Ralph K. White, "*Black Boy:* A Value-Analysis," *Journal of Abnormal and Social Psychology* 42 (October, 1947), pp. 440-61.

(87) Erik Erikson, "The Concept of Identity in Race Relations: Notes and Queries," *Daedalus* 95 (Winter, 1966), pp. 145-71.

(88) Charles Silberman, *Crisis in Black and White* (New York, Vintage Books, 1964).

*(89) L. L. Langness, *The Life History in Anthropological Science* (New York, Holt Rinehart & Winston, 1965).

(90) Stuart T. Hauser, *Black and White Identity Formation: Studies in the Psychosocial Development of Lower Socioeconomic Class Adolescent Boys* (New York, John Wiley, 1971) chap. 1.

*(91) Erik Erikson, *Childhood and Society,* rev. ed. (New York, W. W. Norton, 1963).

(92)————, "Ghandi's *Autobiography:* The Leader as a Child," *American Scholar* 35 (Autumn, 1966), pp. 632-46.

*(93)————, *Ghandi's Truth* (New York, W. W. Norton, 1969).

*(94) H. Stuart Hughes, *History as Art and as Science: Twin Vistas on the Past* (New York, Harper & Row, 1964).

Robert F. Sayre

SOURCE: "The Proper Study—Autobiographies in American Studies," in *American Quarterly,* Vol. XXIX, No. 3, 1977, pp. 241-58.

[In the following essay, Sayre assesses the relevance of autobiographical writings to the discipline of American Studies.]

Autobiographies, in all their bewildering number and variety, offer the student in American Studies a broader and more direct contact with American experience than any other kind of writing. For they have been written in almost every part of the country by presidents and thieves, judges and professors, Indians and immigrants (of nearly every nationality), by ex-slaves and slave owners, by men and women in practically every line of work, abolitionists to zookeepers, by adolescents and octogenarians, counterfeiters, captives, muggers, muckrakers, preachers, and everybody else. The catalogue is as great as one of Walt Whitman's own . . . or greater. It is the true Song of Myself. And Ourselves.

The bibliographies listed at the end of this essay are a partial verification. Louis Kaplan's *Bibliography of American Autobiographies* lists 6,377 titles, and it covers only works published before 1945, the year in which he and his associates began to assemble them. Its forty-five-page subject index also breaks the entries down according to occupations, regions, and (where applicable) the foreign countries from which the writers came or in which they later lived. The defects in the book are that its subject descriptions are often vague and that it excludes several kinds of writing about which many people might be most curious: slave narratives; Indian captivity narratives; travel, sporting, and adventure narratives "in which the autobiographical element is insignificant"; and journals, diaries, and collections of letters. Some of these defects are made up by Russell C. Brignano's *Black America in Autobiography* and will be further remedied by the works of Mary Louise Briscoe, Patricia Addis, Delores K. Gros-Louis, and Carolyn Rhodes. Richard G. Lillard's *American Life in Autobiography* is a selection of 400 books which Lillard read and summarized in a paragraph each. However, it mainly covers works printed or reprinted since 1900, listing them according to the authors' occupations. Thus, there is still a need for annotated bibliographies of earlier American autobiographies.

Yet until quite recently, autobiographies have not received very much scholarly attention. The English departments of the 1950s and early '60s generally scorned them as an inferior kind of literature. They were not works of imagination, not *belles lettres*. They did not seem to demand the ingenious analysis of structure, theme, image, and myth which one devoted to a Donne poem or a Faulkner novel. To say that a novel was "autobiographical" was to show knowing disapproval. *Redburn* and *This Side of Paradise* were autobiographical; *Moby-Dick* and *The Great Gatsby* were art. History departments, meanwhile, believed that autobiographies were too subjective. As the author's own account of his life and work, an autobiography was sure to be biased and one-sided. A serious historian or biographer was duty-bound to correct such incomplete accounts of things. As a result, a student in American Studies, getting most of his teaching from professors of English and history, was not likely to hear many good words about autobiographies. They were attacked from both sides, bastards whom neither parent would defend.

Ironically, the American Studies student has or had a similar curse. He has sought his own legitimacy by getting literature and history to marry, and autobiographies already represent an indissoluble common-law marriage. They are history in that they are source materials, containing facts and interpreting facts, preserving the past, and drawing lessons from it. They are literature in that they must please and entertain as well as teach. And like both history and literature, they have to select and narrate. They have to organize their materials, address an audience, and, in more subtle ways, create audiences, find links between the actor-writers who are in them and the readers, then or generations later, who are outside and must be engaged, drawn in. To legitimate himself, the student of American culture might seek to understand these other literary-historical crossbreeds.

The oldest and in some respects still most fundamental theoretician of autobiography was the nineteenth-century German philosopher of history, Wilhelm Dilthey. Regrettably, only a fraction of his work has been translated, but the selections made by H. P. Rickman in *Pattern and Meaning in History* show that understanding of the individual, through the individual's own understanding of himself and his time, in autobiography, was at the center of Dilthey's conception of history. To Dilthey there were no Zeitgeists, philosophical essences, or other monolithic interpretations of history. For him "there was no one 'meaning of life,'" Rickman says, "but only the meaning which individuals perceived in, or attributed to their own lives." So the autobiographer or, in Dilthey's words, the "person who seeks the connecting threads in the history of his life" is the primary historian, and the later historian seeking meanings as another age knew them should begin with autobiographers. They tell us what life was, as they conceived it and organized it in their living and as they then put it into retrospective language.

Dilthey's few paragraphs on Augustine, Rousseau, and Goethe are too brief for one to tell what his own methods of analysis might have been, but his ideas lay behind his student Georg Misch's *History of Autobiography in Antiquity*. Misch's book is dull Germanic scholarship, but it is important in at least two ways. It shows that there was no "autobiography," in a modern sense, until St. Augustine. (The very word was not coined until the early nineteenth century.) But it also shows that personal expressions of the meaning of life, in Dilthey's sense, certainly did exist and that a study of them, in whatever forms they took, is rewarding. Indeed the forms and conventions are as interesting as the content. They reveal the relationships of the writer or speaker to his culture, how the individual could speak about himself.

Misch's work, therefore, might persuade students of American autobiography to make their definitions broad enough to take in all forms of self-history. Yet definition is difficult, and controversial. Most people who wrote about autobiography in the last ten or twenty years (including the present writer) adopted definitions more or less like those of Georges Gusdorf and Roy Pascal. Autobiography, said Pascal, "involves the reconstruction of the movement of a life, or part of a life, in the actual circumstances in which it was lived. . . . It imposes a pattern on a life, constructs out of it a coherent story. It establishes certain stages in an individual life, makes links between them, and defines, implicitly or explicitly, a certain consistency of relationship between the self and the outside world. . . . " Pascal considered letters and diaries to be autobiographical but not autobiography, because they did not have a single point of view and were not written from a single point in time. Memoirs were too external, self-portraits too static, and autobiographical fiction was also generally excluded from pure autobiography because the author had license, whether he took it or not, to change and invent. Thus the major precursor of modern autobiography, according to this definition, was the religious conversion narrative. Its authors looked back from a single, organizing perspective and told a fairly coherent story of a sizeable portion of their lives. John Morris' *Versions of the Self: Studies in English Autobiography from John Bunyan to John Stuart Mill* is a very instructive history of this tradition of autobiography and of its contributions to modern literature and modern concepts of the self.

Yet recent books and articles have had trouble with this definition and, along with it, the related standards of evaluation. In *Metaphors of Self,* James Olney begins by making some Jungian refinements of it—distinguishing between autobiographies "simplex" which tell the one story of a career, conversion, or achievement and the autobiographies "duplex" which attempt to portray a whole person. But Olney's last chapter on Eliot's *Four Quartets* stretches the definition to the breaking point. If the *Four Quartets* are autobiography, what isn't? If it is legitimate to include Eliot as an autobiographer, aren't there many other authors who should be included too, by making the definition less restrictive? Previously, in "Autobiography as Narrative," Alfred Kazin had implied a broader definition in saying that "autobiography, like other literary forms, is what a gifted writer makes of it." Kazin was most interested in the large number of modern books like Hemingway's *A Moveable Feast* and Robert Lowell's *Life Studies* which use fictional techniques yet "deliberately retain the facts behind the story in order to show the imaginative possibilities inherent in fact." That kind of writing, which, as Kazin said, is "very characteristic of our period," is hard to approach as traditional autobiography. It doesn't tell the same kind of story; its chronology is likely to be fragmentary or shuffled, inventive and exploratory; it approaches fiction.

Barrett John Mandel, however, was disturbed by Kazin's implications that autobiography could take such liberties and should therefore be judged according to the supposedly higher aesthetic standards of fiction. In "The Autobiographer's Art" he insisted on the reader's right to know whether he was reading fiction or fact and the autobiographer's right to be judged as an autobiographer and not a novelist. Francis Hart, as another participant in this debate, attempted to find his answers in the actual practice of some forty autobiographers since Rousseau. Scholarly and theoretical answers to the questions of the interplay of fiction and history, form, and authorial intention were, Hart said, "prescriptive" and "premature."

The debate over definitions arose in yet another way when Richard Gilman, reviewing Eldridge Cleaver's *Soul on Ice,* wrote "that white critics have not the right to make judgments on a certain kind of black writing." Cleaver, Malcolm X, and other angry black writers wrote with an immediacy and sense of purpose and mission which white critics, accustomed to *The Education of Henry Adams* or Newman's *Apologia,* could not appreciate. Reading Gilman's reviews, republished in

The Confusion of Realms, brings back the raging arguments of the 1960s when his position was taken, for varying reasons, by both black and white, activist and conservative. But Gilman was answered convincingly by Warner Berthoff. Writing mainly about *The Autobiography of Malcolm X* and Norman Mailer's *Armies of the Night,* Berthoff argued that critics did have a responsibility to assess this literature of "Witness and Testament" and to recognize its precedents in autobiographical traditions. "The open letter, the preachment, the apology, the parable or representative anecdote, the capitulatory brief, the tirade, the narrative or polemical expose, the public prayer, the appeal to conscience, the call to arms" was Berthoff's list of the genres which Cleaver and other black writers had used. Not to recognize these as sometimes the most important forms of autobiography would be like throwing away half the tools (and weapons) of survival.

To add my own testimony and tabulations to the question, I can only say that in the last fifteen years or so I have read about 400 American autobiographies (very broadly-defined), and that they have been like a private history, in several senses, of the amazing crimes, achievements, banalities, and wonders of American life. Orthodox history is, by contrast, a bland soup. This history is unorthodox, heterodox. For example, take the impostor's tale. This is a story where the author either is or has been an impostor, or where his tale is so improbable that he has been charged with being one and must tell the tale to authenticate himself. The rogues' biographies and autobiographical fictions and non-fictions of Defoe and Fielding were the immediate European predecessors, and Ebenezer Cooke's pre-Barthian *Sot-Weed Factor* was an early American approach to it. But *The Memoirs of the Notorious Stephen Burroughs of New Hampshire* is the masterpiece. Burroughs, who flourished between about 1780 and 1810, was an impostor-clergyman (he stole his uncle's sermons), a counterfeiter (he decided that he believed in a large money supply), a schoolteacher on Long Island, and later a salesman of western lands. His book was apparently very popular in the early 1800s, but was almost forgotten until Robert Frost persuaded the Dial Press to republish it in 1924. It is a stunning revelation of American gullibility and sure-enough social mobility.

An even more remarkable case is John Dunn Hunter, author of *Memoirs of Captivity among the Indians of North America* (1824). Hunter was called an impostor because his tale of having been captured as an infant and raised among the Kansas and Osage tribes simply seemed incredible—and because his pro-Indian attitudes challenged government policy. Richard Drinnon has recently vindicated Hunter in the biography *White Savage,* but the charge that he was an impostor prevented his influencing the policies he attacked.

The sagas of Burroughs and Hunter also suggest that in those ages before transcripts, identity cards, and rapid communication, impostors were indeed more frequent.

The ones in *Huckleberry Finn* and *The Confidence Man* were not mere inventions. But perhaps Americans were also less sure of each other because they were so profoundly unsure of themselves. At one moment they bragged like fighting cocks; at another they were dour and insecure. An impostor with confidence and determination could escape with a lot, as William and Ellen Craft did in *Running a Thousand Miles for Freedom.* By Ellen's dressing as a white master and William's pretending to be "his"/her body servant, these slaves escaped with their lives. Yet we shouldn't be too sure that such escapades are over. The falsified lives of Chief Red Fox and Howard Hughes and the purportedly true underground lives of Abbie Hoffman and Patricia Hearst are ample proof that lies are still told and truth still uncertain.

Susan Kuhlmann's *Knave, Fool, and Genius* is among the several studies of the fictional confidence man in America. But no book, to my knowledge, has investigated his autobiographical and biographical real-life origins (or replicas) in books like Burroughs' *Memoirs* and *Ringolevio: A Life Played for Keeps,* by Emmet Grogan. Grogan, legendary founder of the Diggers in San Francisco in the 1960s, resembles Burroughs in some ways. You never know whether he is lying and putting you on or not. Thus one further value in studying these books is that they make the sometimes nitpicking aesthetic questions of "pose" and persona a life-and-death matter. Is Grogan right that only thieves and revolutionaries play for keeps? Does the artist and "straight" merely play for fun?

Another subject for study is the secret diary, which has immense contemporary significance because of the still-secret Nixon tapes. Diaries, we have assumed, are only source material for biographers and historians. We think that they are not literature because diarists cannot fully anticipate and arrange the events they record and because they are supposedly only talking to themselves. But these problems never reduced the interest which we find in some great ones like Samuel Sewall's, those of the Adams family, George Templeton Strong's, and Thoreau's *Journal.* Privacy—a person's right to keep and record things to himself—has encouraged some people to write as they otherwise could not. Secrecy, too, may be necessary when the thoughts or facts are about other people and could damage them, the recorder, and still larger groups. But both privacy and secrecy are relative. William Byrd's *Secret History of the Dividing Line* was not for publication but was apparently read to Byrd's friends. *The Journal of Charlotte L. Forten* was private primarily because Charlotte, as a wealthy black Philadelphian, had no friendly listeners to whom she could express her sense of frustration and isolation. White girls at pre-Civil War New England academies were often required to keep diaries and also required to show them to their teachers! Anäis Nin's diaries became destined for publication; as Robert Fothergill shows in *Private Chronicles,* they became the fulfillment of her literary ambitions. James J. Fahey's *Pacific War Diary,* not published until 1963, had to be secret because naval

regulations forbade it and because the things he wrote about some officers might have gotten him in trouble. Yet he kept it devotedly, despite his utter exhaustion after long hours at battle stations, and it is one of the most vivid accounts of World War II which I have read. There are other diaries and letters from every war, and one suspects that they may still be "secret," in the sense of forgotten or suppressed, because we still do not think of war from the ordinary soldier's or sailor's viewpoint. (The modern Russian scholars of American literature, by contrast, show great interest in such a work as Philip Freneau's "Prison Ship," and one wishes to hear more of their reasons.[1]) When we say a prison diary or war diary is merely boring or illiterate, repetitious and inconsequential, we need to ask ourselves what we really mean, and why we say it. For these can be the words of consciousness suppressing bad dreams and the unwanted messages of history and the unconscious. We need no more dramatic evidence of the efforts to which a supposedly rational and governing consciousness will go in such suppression—and the tireless energy necessary to dig out the truth—than the stories of White House tapes and *All the President's Men.* We may guard the "tapes" to our own personal and collective transgressions just as fiercely as Nixon "stonewalled" his critics.

The whole matter of secrecy in diaries and autobiographies obviously needs discussion. Bruce Mazlish's "Autobiography and Psycho-analysis—Between Truth and Self-Deception" does an inadequate job of showing how modern autobiography has been influenced by Freudian theory. Jeffrey Mehlman's *A Structural Study of Autobiography* concentrates too much, for the American reader, on French autobiographers. Moreover, Mehlman's implications that because he is following questions in the later works of Freud he is therefore more serious than other scholars is cult nonsense, a mixture of vanity and exclusiveness. But his initial questions are basic. How does one become "alive *(bio)* to oneself *(auto)* in the exclusive realm that the French call *écriture (graphie)*"?

But the issue of secrecy is just one part of the overall question of what autobiography *reveals.* However secret or open, what can be learned from it which cannot be so readily learned from drama, fiction, history, and other forms of expression? Or to put the question pedagogically, what does it teach? The existence and planning of many courses in American autobiography, taught in both American Studies and English departments, makes the question very pertinent. What are the organizing themes in its history?

For thoughtful answers we may turn to Karl J. Weintraub's essay on "Autobiography and Historical Consciousness." Like Dilthey, Weintraub is interested in autobiography's "very special function in elucidating history." And the greatest value in autobiography, he feels, is in the basic conceptions of self and personality which it reveals. People have written different kinds of autobiography in different times and cultures because of their different self-conceptions. He also hastens to insist that "one can study self-conception without having to be a Freudian, Jungian, Skinnerian, or what have we," for the point is to realize how an autobiographer conceived of his own life and not just what one discipline of psychologists or economists would perceive in it. Self-conceptions have a history and a full humanistic range of interest, and while they can be read most intensely in the history of autobiography, that reading must be further informed by as much additional historical knowledge and insight as the reader possesses. The latter part of Weintraub's essay is a short but brilliantly illustrated outline of such autobiographical self-conceptions from classical antiquity to the nineteenth century.

Some other readers, I realize, might prefer to organize their study along more specifically ideological lines. One could after all read autobiographies as a Marxist, an Eriksonian, or with great interest as an historian of ethnic and sexual oppression and liberation. But the greater advantage in Weintraub's approach is that it encourages a wider view, without necessarily excluding these others. It therefore has considerable suggestiveness to students in American Studies, most of whom would like to use such particular ideologies or disciplines and at the same time not be constricted by them. But be that as it may, I have found Weintraub's relation of the history of autobiography to the history of concepts of self to be so useful that I would like to follow it. It suggests what might yet be done with American autobiography, while still allowing one to talk about what has been done in recent (and not so recent) scholarship and criticism. My only modification will be to accept a broader definition of autobiography than his. Instead of saying "*that form* in which an author undertakes a retrospective vision over a significant portion of his life, perceiving his life as a process of interaction with a coexistent world," I would like to say "*those forms. . . .* " As should already be clear, I don't think we can have an adequate history of American autobiography which is not as plural in genre as it is pluralistic in subject matter. When there is so much to say and so little space, being so inclusive may be all the more presumptuous. But we cannot talk about concepts of self (and selves) without realizing that the concepts inevitably take different literary forms as well as different social and cultural ones.

This history begins, obviously, with the Indians. And a course in autobiography is perhaps better prepared to deal with this fact than most others, even though the recording of Indian "autobiographies" did not begin until the nineteenth century and writing by Indians themselves until the twentieth century. But Lynne Woods O'Brien's pamphlet, *Plains Indian Autobiographies,* shows that Native Americans clearly did have their own forms of autobiography such as coup stories and visions (which still exist in pictographs) and the stories later recorded by white collectors developed from them. L. L. Longness' *The Life History in Anthropological Science* has a long bibliography of the dictated autobiographies and a professional discussion of the collectors' methods. So Indian autobiography clearly can

be taught in American Studies classes and makes more than just a "token." It reveals, for one thing, a set of self-conceptions in which, as in *Black Elk Speaks,* self-history is impossible to separate from tribal welfare and a collective conscious and unconscious life.

Yet the Puritans also had a sense of their lives unfolding within a grand cosmic drama, and this has long made the study of autobiographies one of the most rewarding approaches to them. Perry Miller's books and essays on the New England mind are, in a way, an extended treatment of Puritan self-history. Sacvan Berkovitch's *Puritan Origins of the American Self,* which moves beyond Miller's intellectual history to a complex study of Puritan typology, promises to be a successor to Miller's work in both its density and, unfortunately, its obscurity. The chapters on personal narratives in Kenneth Murdock's *Literature and Theology in Colonial New England* are still a more available and pleasing introduction. Daniel Shea criticizes both Miller and Murdock, however, for limiting their studies of autobiography to conversion narratives and the not very typical autobiography of Thomas Shepard. The conversion narrative, Shea shows, was such a fixed form that one reads pretty much like another. Not even Edward Taylor could depart from it and tell a recognizably individual story. Shea's comprehensive reading of both the conventional and the unconventional early American spiritual autobiographies makes his book currently the best. It has excellent chapters on the Quakers and John Woolman, on the Mathers, and on Jonathan Edwards.

The early American concept of self may emerge most clearly, however, in the narratives of Indian captivity. There the writer's or scribe's sense of being a white Christian European is in bold relief against the supposed horrors and temptations of the wilderness and another culture. Only recently have we begun to realize their importance. In the late 1940s and early '50s, Roy Harvey Pearce treated them as a sub-literary genre whose interest was in their prejudices about Indians and their contributions to the themes and situations of later fiction. Richard Slotkin has shown that their significance is greater, because their prejudices and archetypes have been more influential. James Axtell, on the other hand, has used them for what they can be relied upon to tell about Indian life and to explain why so many captives preferred Indian life to white. Richard Vanderbeets attributes their popularity to their ritualistic patterns of a person's "Separation, Transformation, and Return."

That Benjamin Franklin secularized spiritual autobiography is a familiar point, but the result is not the smug and artless little guide to riches which the Wanamakers cherished and D. H. Lawrence loathed. Franklin, as John William Ward showed in "Who Was Benjamin Franklin?", artfully used the *Autobiography* to compose himself. In *The Interpreted Design,* David L. Minter has gone on to examine the narrative techniques of Franklin the writer. John Lynen's *Design of the Present* also has a very good chapter on Franklin's relation to his own past and its meaning. Opposing views of the *Autobiography*'s contribution to the success myth are in John Cawelti's *Apostles of the Self-Made Man* and William Spengemann's and L. R. Lundquist's "Autobiography and the American Myth." But we also can't forget that the *Autobiography* was addressed to Franklin's son, and Claude-Anne Lopez's and Eugenia W. Herbert's biography, *The Private Franklin,* is of special interest because it studies him in his role as father and famous relative to dozens of dependent siblings, nephews, and nieces. Lopez and Herbert bring out Franklin the bourgeois family man, who tried to aid and promote his relatives but also had to recognize their limitations. Their book illustrates the advantages of biography as a supplement to autobiography.

In the early nineteenth century, autobiography united the struggle to develop an indigenous literature with the even more fundamental motive to define and create an American character. The tacit second question after Crevecoeur's "What then is an American?" is, "And who am I?" It was asked in a book which represented several autobiographical forms—the epistle, the travel narrative, and the idealizing pastoral ecologue, all of which were common in the early national literature. Epistolary forms, both signed and pseudonymous, personal and political, were common in the pamphlets and literature of controversy. Travel books, in which the writer had the opportunity to define himself as an American against the backgrounds of Europe, the sea, and the American West, were continued by Dana, Irving, Margaret Fuller, Parkman, and many later writers, famous and obscure.

It was in the 1840s and '50s, however, that American autobiographical writing became most diverse and original. The most uniquely American, we now see, was the slave narrative, created *sui generis* by the conditions of a racially and politically divided country. Where the convention of many later white autobiographies was the success story, the convention of the slave narrative was the escape from bondage to freedom, or a degree of it. This looked back, in some ways, to the pattern of early Pilgrim and settler literature. It also looked forward to later black autobiography, as Gilbert Osofsky, Stephen Butterfield, Sidonie Smith, and many others have said. Butterfield, in addition, makes a very strong case for black autobiography as the "heart of autobiography in American literature," because personal experience there so closely unites history and art. But the autobiographies of any oppressed people make conceptions of self peculiarly important. A necessary step in anyone's liberation from stereotypes and injustice is the moment when he or she asserts his or her own rights and values against those imposed from without. This *is* the discovery of self, and it is what has made autobiography such an important ideological weapon, not only in the abolitionist era but in the civil rights era, and to many other groups and causes. James Olney's *Tell Me Africa,* though not about American autobiography at all, still shows vital recognition of this in his opening chapters

on the value of autobiography to an American trying to understand modern African artists and political leaders. Moreover, as Albert E. Stone says in his essay on Frederick Douglass' *Narrative,* the ex-slave (or ex-colonial, we can add) turned to autobiography because he wished to make his story an example to other people and a justification of his continued fight. He had urgent answers to the question any autobiographer is asked, "Why am I writing the story of my life?" Scratch the surface of an American autobiography, James Cox noted in his essay on Franklin, Thoreau, Whitman, and Henry Adams, and somewhere inside is a revolution or a revolutionary.

The self-assertive white writers of the American Renaissance are, nevertheless, a somewhat more difficult group to place in an autobiographical framework than their black contemporaries. They cannot be left out, because their philosophic sympathies were so strong, approaching exhortation. Where was the American Dante, demanded Emerson, who would "write his autobiography into colossal cipher, or into universality"? But their practices were so idiosyncratic and diverse, ranging from Hawthorne's guarded but profoundly revealing auto-bibli-ography to *The Scarlet Letter* to Whitman's brash but profoundly shifty and anonymous *Song of Myself.* One can agree with Lawrence Buell in *Literary Transcendentalism* that "the most egotistical movement in American literary history produced no first-rate autobiography, unless one counts *Walden* as such." The reasons, Buell feels, are that the Transcendentalists (and the same could probably be said of Hawthorne and Melville) had both historical and personal reasons for making a paradox of their self-preoccupation and their desire for self-transcendence. Their democratic, romantic, and Protestant values all demanded self-examination but also proscribed it and redirected it towards universals. Democracy, as Tocqueville perceived, restricted freedom of opinion and made Americans fond of general ideas. Romantic thought in America turned even more to nature than it had in England and France. Protestant spiritual autobiography became "more complex, more literary, and less intimate."

On the other hand, we could invert Buell's evidence and say that these same influences actually provoked Emerson, Thoreau, Whitman, and Melville into expansions and improvements on autobiographical forms rather than evasions of them. The old forms were inadequate, as might be proved by a closer examination of the botches made by such contemporaries as Orestes Brownson. Margaret Fuller, as Bell Gale Chevigny shows in her new collection of Fuller's writing and the writing about her, was a person whose need for liberated self-conceptions in both literature and life was tragically intense. But finding new literary metaphors of the self required the greatest American audacity. When they began writing, none of the major writers of the American Renaissance, with the possible exception of Melville, had met one of the major requirements of autobiography: they hadn't done anything. Spiritual autobiographies had been open to the less famous because they emphasized what had *happened to* the writer more than what he had achieved. But Rousseau and Franklin and an increasingly broad, secular society had reduced the importance of narrowly religious histories. A great autobiography had to come from a great man like Franklin or an infamous egotist like Rousseau (a figure most Americans then despised). In England similar restrictions made Wordsworth and Mill refrain from publishing their masterpieces, while Carlyle went through his charade with a tailor. So when Whitman published his *Leaves of Grass* in 1855 it contained very little that can be called "personal experience." It was a vicarious national autobiography, with democratic general ideas and long lists of everybody's business. Thoreau, meanwhile, had found his outlet by doing something so cranky, going out to *be* instead of *do,* that an accounting was justified. Melville, having fitted his earlier experiences in the formulas of captivity narratives and sea stories, eventually universalized his autobiography also. The self was at once a daring cosmic revolutionary and a pantheistical and calm solitary observer.

The Civil War seems to have brought a return to more traditional forms of autobiography, just as it reawakened some of the other ghosts of old Calvinist righteousness and later a business conservatism. Like all wars it was an occasion for military memoirs (not to bury Caesar but to revive him); of these, Grant's is a classic. In its modesty and firm resolution, its realistic language and ever-increasing epic range, it is a great monument of both Grant the man and the armies he led. Two other classics of the Civil War are John William de Forest's partially autobiographical novel *Miss Ravenel's Conversion from Secession to Loyalty* and Whitman's hospital notes in *Specimen Days.* From the Southern side, the greatest work is Mary Boykin Chesnut's *Diary from Dixie.* Yet with the exception of Edmund Wilson's absorbing chapters in *Patriotic Gore,* which examines these and other works mainly for their documentary value, very little has been written about them as autobiographical literature. They are, to be sure, military memoirs, novel, journal, and diary. They are not within the narrow limits of what Gusdorf called *"autobiographie proprement dite."* But this only indicates again that the definition is what may be wrong. We need to ask why writers chose these genres as proper, as their own.

In contrast to this neglect of Civil War autobiography is the enormous current interest in Henry Adams. He is mentioned in nearly every book and article on American autobiography as a whole and studied in detail in many other places. But as I look at him and his associates and contemporaries in this rapid and yet long-range historical perspective, what is most striking is a new conception of the self as defined not by nature or religion or specific events and achievements but by family, history, and civilization. He resembles Gibbon in this respect, but Gibbon in America, where civilization had simultaneously just triumphed and just become terrifying, a machine, a dynamo of vast and uncertain potential.

James, Howells, and even Mark Twain give the same sense in their autobiographies of being proudly civilized men of the world who had travelled and seen great change, but their responses are different from his. To a greater degree than Adams, they looked backward, enveloped themselves in the lyrical joys of childhood. They were closer than Adams to the explicitly nostalgic autobiographies of the late nineteenth century—Lucy Larcom's *A New England Girlhood,* Edward Everett Hale's *A New England Boyhood,* and Charles Eastman's *Indian Boyhood.* Yet these too illustrate the coming of an adulthood which was vastly enlarged and chaotic. Adulthood was so different it required a second book. Eastman's second life—perhaps the most altered one of all—was in *From the Deep Woods to Civilization.* James' later reflections are in *The American Scene.* And Mark Twain, sometimes recoiling from his civilized world as desperately as Adams, gave up altogether on a unified autobiography. As Jay Martin has suggested in *Harvests of Change,* Mark Twain's consequent experiments in autobiography look ahead to Gertrude Stein and Conrad Aiken.

What I am rather hastily and tentatively suggesting is that from about 1900 onwards the concept of self in America is very closely related to the concept of civilization and that the forms and structures of autobiography reflect this, inevitably also reflecting different personal and generational responses to the promises and perils of modern civilization. For the writers of Adams' generation wrote what Thomas Cooley has suggestively called *Educated Lives.* Education, in both the formal and the larger senses, plays an enormous part in these lives. Education, in Adams' many senses, became the necessary preparation for a new civilization, the only possible means of regaining control over it, and so also the unifying (or dis-unifying?) theme of autobiography. The identity of modern man was in his relation to the rewards and demands, hopes and horrors of the complex civilized society in which he lived. Travel, religion, nature, and even personal success in this society had ceased to be individually important; they had been swallowed up in it. We can outline modern responses to this civilized multiverse, as Adams called it, by looking briefly at three generations of twentieth century autobiographers. Those in the first generation, on the whole, were journalists, progressives, and professionals. They were born in the 1860s and '70s and reached the active period of their careers between about 1895 and 1920: Edith Wharton, Jane Addams, Teddy Roosevelt, Lincoln Steffens, Frederic C. Howe, S. S. McClure, Charlotte Perkins Gilman, Ray Stannard Baker, Ida Tarbell, Upton Sinclair, Hamlin Garland, Richard Ely, William Allen White, Booker T. Washington, Jacob Riis, Edward Bok, Mabel Dodge Luhan, Louis Sullivan, the Hapgoods, Tom Johnson, Clarence Darrow. Some were aristocrats, some prairie farmers; some became socialists, some solid Republicans. Yet in the form of their autobiographies, they are astonishingly alike. Many came from small towns in western Pennsylvania or the Middle West, a few from mansions in California and

New York, but the latter part of their lives were *in* the new industrial civilization—writing for newspapers, travelling on Pullman trains and ocean liners, lecturing, organizing, and vacationing in some summer cottage or cabin. All these activities were a function of their work, their jobs. (Thus they justify the assumption behind Richard Lillard's *American Life in Autobiography* that classifications of autobiography should be made according to careers or professions.) But careers became important because the new industrial civilization offered such a variety of interesting ones. It also had such a variety of problems on which critics and reformers could work—monopolies, immigration, the shame of the cities, modern marriage, the color line, and so on. Understandably, a great deal of history has since been written about their work, their origins, points of view, and motives. But they have not been studied very much as autobiographers. Milan James Kedro's "Autobiography as a Key to Identity of the Progressive Era" and Robert Stinson's "S. S. McClure's *My Autobiography:* The Progressive as Self-Made Man" are the best essays on them which I know. Christopher Lasch's *The New Radicalism in America,* though not specifically about their autobiographies, is very incisive about their personalities and self-images. But their similar autobiographies are an amazing picture of their collective identity. They wrote the first large group of American autobiographies to be entitled *The Autobiography of . . . ,* and the definition was simply a biography written by one's self. The books usually cover the full range from youth to middle or old age, and they self-consciously stand in their firm big bindings as monuments to the life and work of the author. Thus, despite these authors' many criticisms of their society, their books still reveal their thorough involvement in it. The building of new institutions, the reform of old ones, and the realizing of new careers had absorbed the writers' lifelong energies and enthusiasms.

The next generation, which came of age in the 1920s and '30s, had a much more serious quarrel with the civilization into which they were born. Gertrude Stein's name for it, the Lost Generation, still holds, for its leaders were not people who found meaningful work in causes and professions; they were writers and artists who rebelled. Yet even their rebellion had uncertain direction. Thus these autobiographers—Eugene O'Neill, Sinclair Lewis, Sherwood Anderson, Conrad Aiken, Dos Passos, Hemingway, Fitzgerald, James T. Farrell, Gertrude Stein, Hart Crane, Hilda Doolittle, Edmund Wilson, E. E. Cummings, Henry Roth, Thomas Wolfe—chose much less traditional, discreet, and clearly organized forms. Their most traditional genre, perhaps, was the *Bildungsroman,* which not only described their anguished coming of age, in small towns or Eastern colleges, but also gave the child's vision of the sickness and terror of the adult world. Another revealing genre was the autobiographical war novel. In it, civilization was E. E. Cummings' foul French prison or Hemingway's battlefields and hospitals. In such places, how is one day different from another? Time therefore became an individual and obviously arbitrary matter. Temporal

structure changed, place became more important, and the self seemed more anarchistic and precious, less civilized and more instinctual. The self was not identified with the gratifications of work or the luxuries of ocean liners but with the simple, minimal pleasures of a clean, well-lighted place or the sweet and special individuality of the other victims, the "delectable mountains."

The best book on this generation's autobiography is still Malcolm Cowley's *Exile's Return,* perhaps because Cowley wrote his "criticism" from his own experience just as Fitzgerald, Hemingway, Wolfe, and Dos Passos wrote their "fiction" from theirs. Other critics, with the exception of the biographers who have documented these autobiographical novels and short stories, have instead praised the aesthetic, mythic, or inventive aspects of their achievements. But their contributions to autobiography are surely as great as their contributions to "fiction." They liberated it from the lock-step of chronology and the recitation of the insignificant. Why tell of birth and ancestry or anything else unless it immediately matters? Why wait to write about one's experience until one is celebrated, when one can become celebrated by writing? One might live so long. Why not write and examine while the memories are hot? And why keep the taboos against sex and bad behavior, against gossip and the exposure of one's friends? One need only substitute some fictional names, change dates and places. The novels of the Russian and French realists had already done many of these same things, but the explosion of autobiographical "fictions" by American writers in the 1920s and '30s was more inspiringly personal. It affected the tastes and behavior of its readers like no other books since *Childe Harold* and *The Sorrows of Young Werther.* The writers reported life; the readers imitated art.

Yet, as Malcolm Cowley noted, these writers were spectators. They resisted identification with the civilization in which they lived and so with few exceptions, did little to try to change it. They preferred to experiment and document and thus alter their world, if at all, through "art." No matter how autobiographical or biographical and documentary their "art," "art" was still above politics and propaganda. And the position of the "artist," even in the 1930s, was still somehow detached. To report, he had to come out as someone detached as well as concerned. So there is detachment and experimentation even in the most explicit autobiography. Gertrude Stein's self-portrait through the eyes of Alice B. Toklas and Conrad Aiken's *Ushant,* where fantasy and history merge in a timeless dream voyage, are two examples. But by these means the avant-garde leaders of this generation certainly did change autobiography just as they changed prose and poetic "fiction," often in the same works.

Full appreciation of more recent American autobiography, by the third generation since Adams, is impossible without recognition of this deep plowing and harrowing and planting. It is, to be sure, the work of a diverse group of writers (as I here lump them together): from Norman Mailer to Alex Haley and Malcolm X, from

Jack Kerouac and Allen Ginsberg to Robert Lowell and James Baldwin, and including Sylvia Plath, Mary McCarthy, Scott Momaday, Frank Conroy, Vance Bourjaily, Willie Morris, Lillian Hellman, and many others. But it is the very diversity of their work and the difficulty of assimilating it into one coherent tradition which has frustrated many readers and forced us to look at the history of autobiography, instead of just the history of the novel. Very few of their books—perhaps only *The Autobiography of Malcolm X*—could have been written without the innovations of the preceding generation. As John W. Aldridge testified in *After the Lost Generation,* the writers of this generation grew up in the shadow of giants. But the conclusive evidence of the giants' influence is in Norman Mailer's *Advertisements for Myself* (even though it is now out of print and displaced by *Armies of the Night* and Mailer's other later works of personal journalism). Mailer could not best Hemingway as a "novelist" for the simple reason that the full title was for the "novelist" as person, as autobiographical hero and clown and performer. The concept of the self as independent critic and adversary of modern civilization could not be articulated in "fiction" alone. It required stances, self-display, and the many other rhetorical devices of the public man. Thus *Advertisements for Myself* is almost a textbook of autobiographical forms—apologias, personal essays, interviews (including self-interviews), reflections on earlier work, political manifestos, letters, gossip, and so on. It outraged many of Mailer's fellow writers, but it seems eventually to have helped promote and unify their generation. It broke the ice. Many other kinds of self-disclosure have since become more possible.

Another kind of disclosure in this generation (especially in books published in the last ten or fifteen years) is the experience of people whose ancestors were not within the pale of "civilization" as the earlier generations recognized it. The black, ethnic, and feminist autobiographies have broken through the walls of race and sex which so invidiously defined the old "civilization." In doing so they revived the tradition of autobiography and protest and the use of autobiography to establish the writer's self-concept. Autobiography as history and documentary has an ultimate value no novel or drama, no fiction can ever have. Behind is a person, a living or once-living woman or man. It says, to adapt Whitman's well-known words, "I am the woman, I suffered, I was there." And the person, as opposed to the necessary but dangerous imitations of fiction, will not be a "convention." The "person" uses "convention" as a synonym for "stereotype," for all the non-persons "I" am not. But beyond protest is the joy of being able to say "I am" and who I am. *I Know Why the Caged Bird Sings, A Different Woman, An Unfinished Woman, Manchild in the Promised Land*—the delight and sorrow, the ironies and humor of self are in the very titles of these autobiographies. A person who has found his or her self has, in fact, found something like the *humor* of old medical theory: one's special combination of elements, of blood and history, earth and fire, of which one is made.

So self-advertisement and disclosure are not the only purposes of these autobiographies. Public figures though they be, the authors have not been mere good, honest political candidates obediently revealing all their holdings before assuming public trust. For writers, fortunately, that is not required. It might rob writers, as private persons, of the mysteries which still exist in themselves and which are still lurking in even the most open autobiographies. The paradox of vision is that it cannot be used, cannot change and cure until it is shown; but if it is fully shown, the possessor may lose all personal power. So it may be more appropriate to characterize these autobiographers as having widened the areas of public trust, as having broken the old restrictive civilization, and its dangerous assumption that it alone offered a rewarding life. They have extended concepts of self and of society at the same time. They have made their personal dreams and nightmares a part of the public discourse. Rather than consult the statistics and opinion surveys, they have counseled with their own pasts and personal needs. In an age of threatening depersonalization, when, paradoxically, everyone wants to find his/her "identity," the autobiographer is a hero . . . or another one of the anti-heroes.

NOTES

[1] A. N. Nikolyukin, "Past and Present Discussions of American National Literature," *New Literary History,* 4 (1973), 575-90.

William C. Spengemann and L. R. Lundquist

SOURCE: "Autobiography and the American Myth," in *American Quarterly,* Vol. XVII, No. 3, Fall, 1965, pp. 501-19.

[*In the following essay, Spengemann and Lundquist relate American autobiographical writings to the development of the American cultural myth that "in its most general form, describes human history as a pilgrimage from imperfection to perfection."*]

Like all of our imaginative writers, American autobiographers have traditionally drawn their materials from the fund of metaphors which grow out of our shared experiences, assumptions and beliefs—the American myth. The main difference between American autobiographers and writers of fiction is that the autobiographers have employed these metaphors in self-scrutiny and self-portrayal rather than in the presentation of fictional characters, but the resulting creation lends itself to cultural analysis as readily as purely fictional characters do. The created character in both cases represents values that are recognized by the reading audience at large. A consideration of several American autobiographers as cultural types may provide some new ways of viewing this special genre in our literature and suggest that autobiography in general is, in Georg Misch's words, "not only a special kind of literature but also an instrument of knowledge."[1] By regarding the creation of autobiographical character in America as a cultural act, we may suggest some of the ways in which Americans shape their views of themselves by attending closely to the dominant patterns of our culture. In addition, by noting the similarities between the fictional and autobiographical processes, we may offer an explanation of the striking coalition which these two genres have formed in our own time.

Before going on to examine specific cases, we should understand what we mean by "autobiography" and by "the American myth." We must recognize, first of all, that the term "autobiography" implies only that the author is writing specifically about himself; it has nothing to do with factual truth. Autobiography does not communicate raw experience, for that is uncommunicable. It presents, rather, a metaphor for the raw experience. The language of autobiography stands in symbolic relation to both author and subject. As an author translates his life into language he creates for himself a symbolic identity and sees himself through the focusing glass of language. Since the language of the autobiographer is the common possession of his culture, it is not only subject to his personal manipulation, but it is filled with the assumed values of his society. The act of writing about oneself brings together the personal, unassimilated experiences of the writer and the shared values of his culture. The act of recollection becomes an act of creation and an act of self-evaluation at the same time.

When a man writes his autobiography he translates a unique view of himself into the language of his culture, subjecting some part of his private self to public evaluation. In doing so, he creates a fictive character who undergoes adventures drawn from the author's memory and a narrative persona who reports these experiences and evaluates them according to their place in the cultural pattern. The narrative persona stands between the created character and the body of cultural value that the author recognizes and describes an evaluative relationship between the two. Any autobiography, then, may be described according to the attitude of the narrative persona toward the behavior of the created character, in relation to the evaluated beliefs of the society as the author sees them. As Georg Misch puts it, "The spirit brooding over the recollected material is the truest and most real element in autobiography."[2]

As for the meaning of "the American myth," it is almost impossible to talk about *the* myth of any culture, since cultural values will undergo continual change as long as individuals have experiences and translate them into social belief. Even when communal assumptions take the form of a concrete story, that tale must remain sufficiently flexible and suggestive to allow for repeated interpretation. When it can no longer be reinterpreted to depict contemporary belief and to explain present problems it must fall into disuse and interest only the antiquarian. It is doubly difficult, furthermore, to define

the myth of a democratic society such as ours, which at least purports to allow free competition among its individuals and its institutions for the allegiance of the people. In the United States, institutions rise to power and fall into impotence, and each describes national or cultural value in its own voice and its own terms. For the very reason that no single institution ever enjoys complete power, however, our cultural beliefs must be larger than their formulation by any one voice.

The more or less orderly shift in dominant institutions in America suggests that the entire process occurs within a single system of values, which, compared to the forms it takes at different times, remains relatively constant. Social change in the United States is never more than apparently radical, it seems. An abiding and slowly shifting cultural pattern bridges all gaps and softens all shocks, no matter how deep or severe. Each new aspirant to social dominion must capitalize on values already a part of the tradition, even though he may intend to change them once he is in power. Indeed, the necessity to subscribe to these traditions at the outset limits his ability to change them in the long run. Our broadest values and traditions, then, either remain intact through all subsidiary change, or they alter so gradually that their movement may be charted and explained. Dissidence and competition do not deny the existence or power of a cultural myth; on the contrary, they serve to define it.

The American myth, in its most general form, describes human history as a pilgrimage from imperfection to perfection; from a dimly remembered union with the Divine to a re-establishment of that union. Within these very broad outlines, Americans have continually reinterpreted the several terms of the myth. For the Puritans, imperfection meant the natural depravity of human nature as exemplified by Adam; perfection referred to ultimate salvation through God's grace. For the Rationalists of our eighteenth century, the two terms meant, respectively, intellectual backwardness and worldly happiness through reason. For the Transcendentalists, they meant separation from and union with the spirit that is alive in Nature. For some later nineteenth-century reformers they denoted predatory individualism and collective Utopian harmony. For all of these groups the two terms were absolutely inseparable from the belief in America as a moral idea.

Whatever the particular form in which the myth has presented itself, it remains, as Charles Sanford has shown,[3] an adaptation of Christian mythology to the particular problems of American life, for which it has been both a source and a means of solution. As a Christian myth, it has concerned itself mainly with reconciling human life with divine law; as an American myth it has combined, and often confused, the religious ideas of sin and atonement with the political issues of democracy. Just as the religious life attends to the task of reconciling the finite many with the infinite one, the political life works to reconcile the particular individual with the general group.

Like all myths, this one directs individual energies toward a common goal, by evaluating forms of behavior, delineating appropriate roles, and making it generally possible for individuals to relate their lives to a larger pattern of value and purpose, to transcend their existential limitations and to extend beyond their proper selves their sphere of influence. Acts are evaluated in this case primarily according to how well they contribute to "progress," however that term is defined at any time. The primary roles described by the myth, similarly, arise out of this notion of progress. They receive their specific lineaments from previous objectifications of the myth, in sacred scripture and in secular literature. Every myth has its heroes and its villains, its victors and its victims.

This function of myth is particularly important for our purposes, since in autobiography the writer explains his life by depicting himself according to culturally evaluated images of character. As he turns his private experiences into language he assumes one of the many identities outlined in the myth and so asserts his connection with his culture. Given the millennial cast and the pervading futuristic spirit of the myth, we are not surprised to find the main character types to be the Prophets (those who interpret the complex relationship between present and future), the Heroes (those who successfully enact the prophecies), the Villains (those who throw up obstacles to fulfillment) and the Outcasts (those who fail to make a place for themselves in the great cultural program). There are, in short, a whole range of stances available to autobiographers, whether they choose to affirm the values stated in the myth or to deny the "truth" of the myth and define themselves by an act of negation. A very brief look at some characteristic American autobiographers in the act of portraying themselves should serve to illustrate a few of the available stances and some of the specific images and ideas that the myth has encompassed as it has influenced the lives of individual Americans.

Properly enough, the first man to relate his personal experience to the American myth was Columbus, who by grounding Christian prophecy in the New World soil became our first Prophet. "God made me the messenger of the new heaven and the new earth," he said, "of which He spoke in the Apocalypse by St. John, after having spoken of it by the mouth of Isaiah; and He showed me the spot where to find it."[4] Columbus learned to see himself as a Prophet—spiritually descended from Isaiah and John—after absorbing the Medieval and Renaissance mythology of the western paradise.[5] Considered as a part of European intellectual history, this self-image has wide and complex significances; considered as a part of American mythology, it is a crude beginning. Five centuries of American life have carried the myth in many directions from this starting point. Yet, this short passage marks the first autobiography to explain the life of the writer by relating it to a body of belief which may be called American.

The right to connect personal experience with great destinies is not vouchsafed to discoverers of continents alone. The true Prophet must work constantly to find a place in history for *all* his acts. His job, after all, is to teach the faithful how they may make their lives part of the great program, and he learns from his own life the wisdom he gives them. Cotton Mather judged all things according to their place in the divine plan. In the following passage from his diary he attempts to elevate the meanest concerns to that high degree of significance he elsewhere assigned to the New England settlements.

> There are with me, in common with all the Children of Men, the usual Evacuations of Nature, to be daily attended. I would not only improve the Time which these call for, to form some Thoughts of Piety, wherein I may differ from the Brutes, (which in the Actions themselves I do vary little) and this I have usually already done; but I would now more particularly study that the Thoughts I form on these Occasions, may be of some abasing Tendency. The Actions themselves carry Humiliations in them; and a Christian ought alwayes to think humble of himself, and be full of self-abasing and self-abhorring Reflections. By loathing of himself continually, and being very sensible of what are his own loathsome Circumstances, a Christian does what is very pleasing to Heaven. My Life (above any Man's) ought to be filled with such Things: and now I contrive certain Spotts of Time, in which I shall be by Nature itself invited unto them.[6]

This hierophantic voice descends from Augustine by way of Luther, proclaiming, as it does, that human nature impedes the progress of divine history and delays the journey to the Heavenly City.

A more sanguine Prophet, Walt Whitman, indicates how humanized the divine plan had become in a century and a half. Celebrating his transcendent self, he wrote:

> I do not press my fingers across my mouth,
> I keep as delicate around the bowels as around
> 　　the head and heart,
>
> Copulation is not more rank to me than death is.
>
> I believe in the flesh and the appetites,
> Seeing, hearing, feeling, are miracles, and each
> 　　part and tag of me is
> a miracle.[7]

Even while these vaunts mark an important change in the American self-image since Edward Taylor wrote the humbly supplicatory *Sacramental Meditations,* the prophetic aim—to define the mythic significance of daily activity—has not altered. A century after Whitman, we detect the same tone in Norman Mailer: "A phallic narcissist she called me. Well, I was phallic enough, a Village stickman who could muster on the head of his will enough of the divine It to call forth more than one becoming out of the womb of feminine Time."[8] Mather debased himself in order to be exalted; Whitman sought to exalt the base;

Mailer seems to enjoy debasing the exalted. All three saw that men must discover some way to align secular life with a fundamentally religious idea of destiny.

Because these passages illustrate so clearly how an individual may assimilate mythical themes in forming his autobiographical personality, they may seem to be extreme cases. When we compare these self-portraits to those of such beloved culture-heroes as Thomas Paine and Theodore Roosevelt, however, we see that Americans often employ rather crude, although effective, metaphors in defining themselves and their world. What is more, these men display considerably more sophistication in distinguishing rhetorical metaphor from observable fact than do men like James J. Strang, who was king of the Mormon settlement at Beaver Island; Lorenzo Dow, the great revivalist; and John Humphrey Noyes, founder of the Utopian colony at Oneida. These men were as little able to separate metaphor from fact as were Coronado and the seekers for the Seven Cities of Cibola. Noyes, for instance, recounting past prophecy, present torment and future hope, shows how absolutely he identified American expectation with the Biblical images which had conventionally expressed it. "Between the present time and the establishment of God's kingdom over the earth," he said, "lies a chaos of confusion, tribulation and war such as must attend the destruction of the fashion of the world and the introduction of the will of God as it is done in heaven. God has set me to cast up a highway across this chaos, and I am gathering out the stones and grading the track as fast as possible."[9]

Similarly possessed by the myth was Bronson Alcott. Instead of looking for a material enactment of spiritual prophecy, however, he propelled himself entirely into the world of spirit and passed off the physical world as a snare and an imperfect delusion. He was possessed by a millennial strain in American mythology which traces its ancestry back through Protestant history to the Gnostics and the Pelagians, and forward to Mary Baker Eddy. In the never-never land of his imaginings, evidences of imperfection and trouble passed away, and all his hopes became imminent possibilities. Walking in his garden on the Fourth of July 1846, he mused on the meaning of true freedom:

> I cast my silent vote for the emancipation of the human soul, amidst the plants I love. The aroma of the buckwheat, eloquently humming with the winged freemen of the hives, disturbed now and then by the gunner's crack aiming death to the joyous songsters of the air and groves. They ventured not, these monstrous boys, into my coppice of protecting boughs, not into my peaceful glebes. Ah me! War rages near me, and the fields of this my Concord are beleaguered round with armed ruffians. Happy for myself if I am as yet a freeman, and a soul at peace . . . Alone in my benefice, why should I not rejoice in that freeness that cheapens all conventions, and makes me, in thought if not in deed, independent of the States and times, an honest and upright man in the midst of my age.[10]

The more obsessed of these prophetic figures usually undergo a violent self-transformation of some sort. This experience creates the intensified self-consciousness which prompts them to write autobiography in the first place, and it usually appears in the narrative itself as a "calling." The subject may feel himself wrenched out of an unsatisfactory, commonplace or misguided existence and swept up in the rush of divine history, as do so many of the converts who described their experiences in our great revival movements. One of these, an obscure and uncommonly endearing zealot from Kentucky named John Hinkle, explains that, after several uncertain inklings that God wanted him to give up farming and become a preacher, he went through long torment ("The flames of hell pierced my mouth and nose"), then transfiguration: "I fell asleep for a short time and when I awoke I was happier than I ever was in all my life. All my troubles were gone, and I felt as helpless as a little child; did not think I could move my hands or feet, but soon I moved, and saw that I had physical strength . . . I felt that I never would commit another sin and that I could soar in the air shouting and praising God for the great love He had made manifest to me. I think that was January 1, 1886."[11] Elder Hinkle, as he calls himself, also shows how the autobiography of the assumed stems from the experience of assumption, when he says in his first sentence, "I have had a desire to tell the dealings of the Lord with me."[12]

Political callings may dictate a similarly religious expression, particularly when the assumed one's party embodies the utopian or millennial aspirations peculiar to religious prophecy. John Reed's metamorphosis from aristocrat to proletarian follows the pattern and employs the language of religious conversion at times, as does this account of Emma Goldman's response to the death of the Chicago anarchists:

> I was in a stupor; a feeling of numbness came over me, something too horrible even for tears . . . I was entirely absorbed in what I felt was my own loss . . . I was put to bed, and soon I feel into a deep sleep. The next morning I awoke as from a long illness, but free from the numbness and the depression of the final shock. I had a distinct sensation that something new and wonderful had been born in my soul. A great ideal, a burning faith, a determination to dedicate myself to the memory of my martyred comrades, to make their cause my own, to make known to the world their beautiful lives and heroic deaths.[13]

Once again, we seem to be concerned with extreme cases; and it is true that not all autobiographers who describe self-transformation become Prophets in their reincarnations. Many have simply undergone some experience that has changed their cultural status, and, consequently, their self-image. These write autobiographies to assess the mythical significance of their new selves, to re-establish the cultural contact which the change interrupted. They may have risen from relative anonymity to national importance, as did U. S. Grant because of his part in the Civil War. They may have abandoned a troublesome identity for one culturally even more precarious, like the controversial jazz musician Mez Mezzrow, when he decided to become a Negro. Or, they may have had their culture forcibly stripped from them and been hurled by accident into a new life, as was Cabeza de Vaca when, cut off from his countrymen in the primitive Southwest, he found himself becoming more an Indian than a Conquistador. In each case, the autobiography serves, among other ends,14 to articulate the experience of transformation and so make sense of it.

This first group of autobiographers is comprised of restless types, searching for truth, undergoing personal metamorphosis, interpreting the holy mysteries of their tribe, forecasting the collective destiny. A second variety of autobiographer has seen the elephant; he has taken the journey prescribed by the myth; and he looks back with some satisfaction on events which seem to have fulfilled his initial expectations. His real life, he says, corresponds significantly to the mythical ideal; it has enacted the values his society holds sacred. Benjamin Franklin introduces his autobiography with these words: "Having emerged from the poverty and obscurity in which I was born and bred, to a state of affluence and some degree of reputation in the world, and having gone so far through life with a considerable share of felicity, the conducing means I made use of, which with the blessing of God so well succeeded, my posterity may like to know, as they may find some of them suitable to their own situations, and therefore fit to be imitated."15

The mythical elements are all here: the progress from penury to wealth, the religious overtones of secular success, the identification of affluence and worldly reputation with happiness. Furthermore, the sense of personal fulfillment, characteristically, makes the subject feel that he has the right to teach and so to perpetuate a viable tradition. His teaching was well heeded, as we know; a whole nation of entrepreneurs has found him a model of success, perfectly "fit to be imitated."

Franklin's optimism is legendary; it caused him to view his personal past as the fulfillment of earlier prophecy and the foreshadowing of greater things to come in the general history of mankind. A somewhat similar figure, Andrew Carnegie, concerned himself more with his personal career and less with universal history, but he worked equally hard to depict his past as an enactment of divine commandment. God spoke to Carnegie, as He did to Franklin, through natural law, but the law had become more severe in one hundred and fifty years. At one period in his life, Carnegie tells us, he was "all at sea":

> All was chaos. I had outgrown the old [religion] and had found no substitute . . . Here came to me Spencer and Darwin, whom I read with absorbing interest, until laying down a volume one day I was able to say, "That settles the question." I had found at last the guides which led me to the temple

of man's real knowledge upon the earth. These works were revelations to me: here was the truth which reconciled all things as far as the finite mind can grasp them, the alembic which harmonized hitherto conflicting ideas and brought order out of chaos . . . I was on firm ground, and with every year of my life since there has come less dogmatism, less theology, but greater reverence.16

The similarity between Franklin and Carnegie has not gone unnoticed; D. H. Lawrence read back into Franklin the excesses, the selfishness and meanness which his ideals bred in the nineteenth century. In Carnegie's autobiography, a shrill note of protestation seems to replace the natural optimism sounded by Franklin, and that work marks a mid-point between eighteenth-century hope and twentieth-century nostalgia. Latter-day Heroes who write these autobiographies of fulfillment are apt to locate the golden age in the past rather than in the future. The past offered grand opportunities for successes like mine, they tell us, but those days will never come again. Striking an unusually docile pose, H. L. Mencken recalls the "gaudy life that young newspaper reporters led in the major American cities at the turn of the century. I believed then," he goes on, "and still believe today, that it was the maddest, gladdest, damndest existence ever enjoyed by mortal youth."17 The nostalgia evident here resembles that which tints all American writing in the local-color tradition. But the mood is less pervasive in this urban piece than it is in its pastoral counterparts—Mark Twain's *Roughing It,* for example. The city, after all, was to move steadily into the thematic center of American mythology and to push the farm and the frontier farther and farther onto the periphery. By the twentieth century, the autobiographer who wished to characterize his life as a fulfillment of agrarian values and still sound optimistic about the future of those values, had to perform some startling gymnastics to do so. Leland Cutler, in *America is Good to a Country Boy,* portrays Henry Kaiser (and, by strong implication, himself) as a man who has succeeded in commerce and industry because he possesses the rustic virtue of a love for nature.18 Despite specific changes in the meaning of optimism we see, a single stance unites all the autobiographers who choose to explain their lives as fulfilling cultural and personal expectation. Each merely adapts the general characteristic of the stance to his particular purposes.

So far, we have looked at several Prophets and some autobiographers whom we call Heroes. The third main group includes all those who, for some reason, find themselves outside the limits of culturally approved behavior. They may be distinguished by the way they react to the realization that their lives have failed to assert and demonstrate the established values and beliefs of their world. To review the several stances included in this group, we may pass from the most contrite to the most unregenerate, looking first at the man who writes his autobiography to confess his sins and to make an example of himself, to get back into the social family.

One of the most typical, and least lovable, of these confessions to appear in recent years is Whittaker Chambers' *Witness,* which chronicles a life of political sin followed by an awakening to grace. "What I had been," Chambers writes, "fell from me like dirty rags. The rags that fell from me were not only Communism. What fell was the whole web of the materialist modern mind—the luminous shroud which it has spun about the spirit of man, paralyzing in the name of rationalism the instinct of his soul for God, denying in the name of knowledge the reality of the soul and its birthright in that mystery on which mere knowledge shatters and falters at every step."[19] Chambers elects here to describe his passage in the language of evangelical anti-intellectualism, which has been an integral part of American mythology since the eighteenth century, at least. Such a tone was guaranteed to reunite him with those from whom he felt most exiled.

Our next type adopts a considerably different tactic as he works to insinuate himself into a state of social grace. Instead of repenting his past misdeeds, P. T. Barnum argues that they were not misdeeds at all, but virtues in disguise. Dedicating his autobiography to the "Universal Yankee Nation of which I Am Proud to Be One," Barnum refutes charge after charge that he is a humbug, a cheat and a thief. What have been called his avarice and guile, he insists, are the Yankee virtues of thrift and ingenuity—all of which he learned from Ben Franklin.[20] Indeed, by the time he has finished reporting his life in the jargon of American commerce, it is hard to distinguish between his career and that of any respectable entrepreneur. Of his early genius for business, he tells us: "Always looking for the main chance . . . I had sheep of my own, a calf of which I was the sole proprietor, and other individual property which made me feel, at twelve years of age, that I was a man of substance."[21] Such a career would have to please even so secure an insider as Leland Cutler, who suggested that great men in America succeeded because they learned at an early age "what money meant."[22]

Moving farther along a scale marked off in degrees of commitment to established belief, we come to the socially condemned autobiographer who feels that his apparent social failures are actually insignificant, since he was following a higher and truer law than that espoused by his society. Such men portray themselves as condemned by a blind or unregenerate society, and they use their autobiographies to show that *they* know the true way. Mary Austin, criticized for her feminist agitation and her oddly emancipated ways, explains, "Since the pattern of my adult behavior was in no sense a made-up pattern, but one that rose through the surface index of Mary, myself, out of a deeper self, of which the umbilical cord which bound it to the source of selfness had not been cut, it in a measure justified all its behaviors, rid me of the onus of responsibility for those which failed to coincide with the current standards of success."[23] No apologetic tone marks this stance, only a certain lingering pity for the uninitiated multitude.

More rational and less subjective is the self-exiled critic who has found a high ground on which to stand and survey the inconsistencies, hypocrisies and injustices of the myth. Whittaker Chambers denigrated his intellect to make himself morally acceptable to the American public; the critic will often assert his intellect in order to emphasize the degree of his detachment from popular belief. After excoriating all the minions of American know-nothingness—"the prohibitionists of Kansas, the lynchers of Georgia, the hardheaded businessmen in the chambers of commerce in a thousand cities, the members of the National Security League, The American Legion, the Loyal American League . . . all these self-appointed inquisitors and Black Hundreds"—Ludwig Lewisohn underscores his position by refusing to adopt one of his country's most cherished attitudes: "Shall I say now, in order to end agreeably: It is always darkest before the dawn? No; for that kind of professional optimism is precisely one of our national vices. The hour is dark."[24]

Interestingly enough, both Chambers and Lewisohn regard their lives as morally symbolic and, like Franklin's, "fit to be imitated." Lewisohn says, "There are thousands of people among us who can find in my adventures a living symbol of their own and in whom, as in me, this moment in history has burned away delusion to the last shred."[25] And Chambers, seeking an altogether different end, intones, "On a scale personal enough to be felt by all, but big enough to be symbolic, the two irreconcilable faiths of our time—Communism and Freedom—came to grips in the persons of two conscious and resolute men . . . The Great Case would end in the destruction of one or both of the contending figures, just as the history of our times . . . can end only in the destruction of one or both of the contending forces."[26] Whether he agonizes over his exile or seeks to ensure it, it seems, the Outsider is often moved to enlist a following by capitalizing on the myth which defines his stance. As he cleanses his soul, Chambers becomes another Cotton Mather, struggling with the devil and purifying the Commonwealth; Lewisohn assumes the guise of Tom Paine, ridiculing superstition and preaching the true, enlightened freedom.

The reason that these two men betray this similarity despite their obvious differences, of course, is that, outcasts or not, they both care deeply about American life and its future. Our next type, however—the last of those whom we call the Outsiders—deserves that name most of all. While Chambers, Barnum, Lewisohn and Mary Austin adopt attitudes actually provided for by American mythology, and so are, in a sense, acceptable Outsiders, the most abandoned type cares nothing for acknowledged American values. Like Mae West, who attacks American sexual hypocrisy in *Goodness Had Nothing to Do With It,* this autobiographer mentions our values only to expose what he considers their idiocies, and he does so with unmistakable detachment, finding some sort of unique, individual balance. As Miss West says, "I have held firmly to my ideas and my values . . .

I have made a peace, or at least an armed truce, with myself and with the universe. I am in key with my world as I know it and have seen it."[27]

Very few of these renegades manage to maintain their defiant attitudes throughout their autobiographies, however. Even Mae West felt impelled by the public nature of the form to intone, irrelevantly, "I have done what I set out to do, which was to review . . . a life that goes down deeply into the human enigma, the problems of man (and woman) in relation to the godhead and the yet unopened secrets of the universe,"[28] and to mention the importance of religion (unspecified) in sexual education. Caryl Chessman, although he operated all his life well outside the bounds of acceptable behavior, offers his life as a constructive criticism of his society, which he hopes will make the necessary legal alterations and prosper. An autobiographical statement like William Burroughs introduction to *Naked Lunch,* which depicts the writer's total withdrawal from the forms of belief which Americans cherish, is rare, even in this age of dissident memoirs. No American autobiographer, Henry Miller included, has assumed the stature and notoriety of Sade.

All these stances, with the possible exception of the last, derive partly from the traits of character and forms of behavior prescribed by the American myth and partly from the subject's knowledge of previous autobiographies. Misch has discussed how much any autobiographer may learn from his predecessors, revising earlier modes of self portrayal to suit his own needs. Columbus learned to see himself and to interpret his experience by following the lead of St. John. Cotton Mather modeled his self-image on Luther, just as Luther seems to have emulated Augustine. Franklin tells us that Bunyan and Mather were his teachers; but since he aimed to represent his life as an earthly pilgrimage, we see how earlier forms may be adapted to present demands. Barnum shows us still another application of the basic form when he legitimizes otherwise reprehensible conduct by reporting it in the manner of Franklin. Autobiography does not merely follow the cultural pattern, it is clear; it contributes to that pattern by developing and formulating the very structure of individuality.

We must always remember that these stances are forms of self-knowledge and self-portrayal assumed for literary and cultural purposes. Obviously, no man maintains the same stance throughout his life, nor does he usually take the same attitude toward all problems at any one time in his life. His journals and his letters may show him taking on a number of these personae over time. But when he comes to write his autobiography—whether he seeks to discover himself through it or to publicize what he has already found out—he must adopt some consistent overriding view of himself and his past. He must identify the "I" which unites all his past experiences. If he does not, his life will seem to him fragmented and incoherent, and its story will appear to us pointless and confused. Mencken, for example, presents himself throughout his long career in a variety of guises—irascible

critic, learned scholar, champion of human dignity, irresponsible bad boy. But when he was faced with the task of organizing his recollections into a single volume, he recognized the need to come to some decision about what they all amounted to. He says of his life:

> My days of work have been spent . . . in recording the current scene, usually in a far from acquiescent spirit. But I must confess, with sixty only around the corner, that I have found existence on this meanest of planets extremely amusing, and taking one day with another, perfectly satisfactory. . . . The Gaseous Vertebrata who own, operate and afflict the universe have treated me with excessive politeness, and when I mount the gallows at last I may well say with the Psalmist (putting it, of course, in the prudent past tense): The lines have fallen to me in pleasant places.[29]

Any stance, then, is a cultural convention, formulated first by a particularly daring and imaginative analyst of the self, like Augustine or Rousseau, and then imitated by a host of autobiographical followers. But what happens when none of the conventions satisfies an autobiographer's need to order the details of his life? What happens to the man whose faith in the myth has led him to ruin? The autobiographer in this predicament either invents some new way of giving meaning to his experience or records his *anomie* in what we may call the autobiography of the Disenchanted. This man no longer draws strength from his culture, and having nothing to substitute for it, he can neither criticize it nor flout its mandates with any satisfaction. When F. Scott Fitzgerald realized that his life was not leading to paradise, he described his sense of loss:

> This was something I could neither accept nor struggle against, something which tended to make my efforts obsolescent, as the chain stores have crippled the small merchant, an exterior force, unbeatable. . . . There was not an "I" any more— not a basis on which I could organize my self-respect. . . . It was strange to have no self—to be like a little boy left alone in a big house, who knew that now he could do anything he wanted to do, but found that there was nothing that he wanted to do.[30]

Fitzgerald strikes here at some of the fundamental tenets of American faith which have gone to define many of the stances we examined earlier: the efficacy of the individual will, the infinite resources of the spirit, the joys of freedom. This stance, among all those we have discussed so far, seems to have the most to tell us about those autobiographical forms which we recognize as being distinctly modern.

We have seen that autobiographical form is inextricably bound up with cultural belief, that civilization prescribes fairly specific roles for its citizens to adopt when portraying themselves in writing. In Western civilization, these roles share a common quality: they all express an integrated, continuing personality which transcends the limitations and irregularities of time and space and unites all of one's apparently contradictory experiences into an identifiable whole. This notion of individual identity, in fact, may well be the central belief of our culture. With all its ramifications—personal responsibility, individual destiny, dissent, vocation and so forth—it forms the core of our being and the fabric of our history. Ever since St. Augustine wrote his *Confessions* and turned autobiography into a literary act of spiritual self-consciousness, it has retained an unswerving belief in the individual as a definable entity, linked to the divine, which reveals itself through self-analysis.

Although this belief in the integrated consciousness continues to inform large areas of public activity at the present time, it has become the object of increasing critical examination during the past century—especially in those places where social and institutional forms which express and support it have been disrupted by ideological upheaval, revolution and war. Self-consciousness, it seems, will recommend itself only as long as the world allows some fruitful occupation for the liberated individual. When it only thwarts and dismays him, he may seek to escape from identity, into selflessness, anonymity and rest. Or, on the other hand, the anxieties which attend purposeless and corrosive self-awareness may prompt the subject to go back and find some new basis upon which to establish his being, and so create a new order of life. Although the impulse to escape from being is antithetical to the very meaning of autobiography, we should expect to find written records of those individuals who are searching for new forms of identity.

And so we do, but not in conventional autobiography, which grew out of a very special idea of individuality and so is unfit in its traditional form to examine new possibilities of being. The ideals of spiritual identity gave autobiography its subject and its form; new ideals must seek new forms appropriate to them. The modern autobiographer needs an especially flexible form, one that can always outrun attempts to define it, one notably amenable to innovation and experiment. Unable to identify himself within the conventional framework, the modern autobiographer seems to have taken to the novel to find the freedom he needs to conduct his experiments with self.

Traditional autobiography can satisfy only those self-analysts whose identities are clear enough and whose lives seem coherent enough to be expressed in conventional form. The teleology implied in the convention of a narrator surveying his past in terms of the present, rules out all autobiographers who perceive no such purposeful progression or continuity in the events of their lives. Although he wrote no formal autobiography, Emerson exhibited the frame of mind most amenable to it. In a letter to Margaret Fuller, F. O. Matthiessen tells us, he stated that "he could discern no essential difference between the experience of his boyhood and that of his maturity . . . 'A little more excitement now

[Emerson said] but the fact identical, both in my consciousness and in my relations.'"[31] The inviolable, transcendent self provided him with a sense of identity, apparently, which survived all temporal change.

Wright Morris, on the other hand, feeling no such assurance about his identity, describes how he has sought other forms to chronicle his conceptions of self. "Before coming of age," Mr. Morris writes,

> . . . I had led, or rather been led by, half a dozen separate lives. Each life had its own scene, its own milieu; it frequently appeared to have its own beginning and ending, the only connecting tissue being the narrow thread of my *self*. I had been there, but that, indeed, explained nothing. In an effort to come to terms with the experience, I processed it in fragments, collecting pieces of the puzzle. In time, a certain overall pattern *appeared* to be there. But this appearance was essentially a process—an imaginative act of apprehension—rather than a research into the artifacts of my life.[32]

Unable to adopt one unifying attitude, the autobiographer in this uncertain condition substitutes for exposition an examination of the details of experience. The process of review takes the place of the consistent, evaluative point of view as a unifying principle. Since that process may adopt such non-narrative modes of unification as symbolism and imagery, the surface of the work may appear discontinuous and fragmented. The writer speaks here as an individual, whose unwillingness to assume one of the identities prescribed by his culture prevents him from speaking as a public figure and from employing the extended, continuous forms appropriate to those roles.

When the novel abandoned its original function of evaluating social behavior from an increasingly clear point of view and began to devise ways to escape the moral smugness which its bourgeois origins had thrust upon it, it turned away from history to the lyric for less explicit, more symbolic modes of expression. In so doing, it recoiled from society and directed its gaze inward, searching for some surer experiential basis for reality and judgment. This, it seems, is that point where autobiography and the novel begin to merge. Under the pressures and anxieties of social dislocation, the novel became increasingly autobiographical. Disenchanted with the conventional roles which society offered, the autobiographer found in the new novel the chance to examine personal experience without having to assume some ill-fitting social guise. Although conventional autobiographies and novels continue to be written by people who have no quarrel with tradition, those works which we recognize as being significantly of our time have made the terms "novel" and "autobiography" very often indistinguishable.

This entire problem of the purpose and limits of the organizing judgment has generated some of the most important critical studies of the twentieth century. And yet we too often assume that the heavily subjective novel has been restricted to Europe, at least until the twentieth century. We concentrate on the German line of development from Goethe to Hesse, or the even more popular English evolution of Joyce out of Butler, forgetting that nineteenth-century America produced a group of writers who experimented continually with autobiographical forms to solve their problems of spiritual alienation from a society whose myths failed to satisfy their personal demands. Poe's *Narrative of Arthur Gordon Pym* adopts the conventions of autobiographical travel narrative to explore the labyrinths of the disoriented psyche. Herman Melville and Mark Twain arrived at their respective masterpieces by way of the same autobiographical form, the exactly opposite narrative modes of *Moby-Dick* and *Huckleberry Finn* reflecting their respective authors' very similar conclusions about the value of personal experience. Furthermore, the works which follow these two great novels—that is, *Pierre* and *The Mysterious Stranger*—examine the psychic disintegration which results when the self recoils altogether from established norms of judgment.

Wherever we choose to study it, however, the fact remains that autobiography can elucidate for us those central issues which have brought literature to its present state, inform its present concerns and chart its future course. Certainly, modern writers must find their way out of the apparent impasse into which attention to the self has brought them; but just as certainly, they cannot go back to the older forms. Regarding the formal problems of his own autobiography, Henry Adams said in his "Editor's Preface" that "his great ambition was to complete St. Augustine's 'Confessions,' but that St. Augustine, like a great artist, had worked from multiplicity to unity, while he, like a small one, had to reverse the method."[33] The way back to unity is closed off, obstructed by the wreckage of a hundred philosophies. The new directions can come only from present attempts to find in experience new forms, new myths, new roles for the self, which the writer can adopt to speak once again as an integral part of his culture.

[1] *A History of Autobiography in Antiquity* (2 vols: Cambridge, 1951), I, 10.

[2] *Ibid.*

[3] *The Quest for Paradise: Europe and the American Moral Imagination* (Urbana, Ill., 1961), esp. chaps. i-v.

[4] *Four Voyages to the New World: Letters and Selected Documents,* trans. and ed. R. H. Major (New York, 1961), p. 148.

[5] See Sanford, chap. iv.

[6] *The Diary,* "Collections of the Massachusetts Historical Society" (2 vols.; Boston, 1911), I, 357.

[7] "Song of Myself," in *Walt Whitman, Representative Selections* rev. ed. Floyd Stovall, "The American Writers Series" (New York, 1961), pp. 26-27 (ll. 519-23).

[8] *Advertisements for Myself* (New York, 1959), p. 496.

[9] G. Wallingford Noyes, *Religious Experience of John Humphrey Noyes* (New York, 1923), p. 308. Columbus never considered it irrational to look in the Western Hemisphere for the Earthly Paradise of Christian mythology. In his letter from the New World written during his third voyage, he said, regarding a river he had seen, "I hold that if this river does not issue from the Earthly Paradise, it must come from an immense country that lies to the S., of which there has been no knowledge until now: but I am well assured in my own mind that there, where I have declared, lies the Earthly Paradise, and I rest my opinion on the arguments and authorities which I have given above." *Narratives of the Discovery of America,* eds. A. W. Lawrence and Jean Young (New York, 1931), p. 300.

[10] *The Journals of Bronson Alcott,* ed. Odell Shepherd (Boston, 1938), p. 183.

[11] *I Saw My Savior* (New York, 1953), p. 15.

[12] Hinkle, p. 1.

[13] *Living My Life* (New York, 1931), p. 10.

[14] Grant wrote his memoirs to be sure that his family would be solvent after his death; Cabeza de Vaca's recollections appear in an official report to his king.

[15] *Autobiography,* ed. Dixon Wecter (New York, 1948), p. 1. For a very important analysis of this work as a social myth, see Charles Sanford, chap. vii.

[16] *Miscellaneous Writings,* ed. Burton J. Hendrick (2 vols.; Garden City, N. Y., 1933), II, 297. How little the specific matter under consideration by the writer in any autobiography may dictate the stance may be illustrated by a comparison of the widely divergent metaphorical uses of Darwin in the autobiographies of Carnegie, Henry Adams and Hamlin Garland.

[17] *Newspaper Days* (New York, 1941), p. ix.

[18] About Kaiser, Cutler says, "Great builder that he is, I think he has not ever crushed a flower half hidden in the grass that he did not wish he might have walked some other way." *America is Good to a Country Boy* (Stanford, Calif., 1954), p. 156.

[19] *Witness* (New York, 1952), p. 83.

[20] *Barnum's Own Story* (New York, 1961), p. 8.

[21] Barnum, p. 6.

[22] In explanation of the success of certain construction magnates, Cutler says, "The mothers and fathers of these boys . . . did the best they could, unconsciously training them for their later roles: to work unceasingly . . . to know what money meant . . . to love the land of their birth . . . Because these boys grew to manhood honoring their fathers and their mothers, their days were many in the land and the name of the Six Companies is a name to reckon with." *America is Good to a Country Boy,* pp. 154-55.

[23] *Earth Horizon* (New York, 1932), p. viii.

[24] *Up Stream: An American Chronicle* (New York, 1922), pp. 236, 248.

[25] Lewisohn, p. 10.

[26] Chambers, p. 4.

[27] *Goodness Had Nothing to Do With It* (Englewood Cliffs, N. J., 1959), p. 257.

[28] Mae West, p. 256.

[29] H. L. Mencken, *Happy Days* (New York, 1940), p. ix.

[30] *The Crack Up,* ed. Edmund Wilson (New York, 1956), pp. 78, 79.

[31] F. O. Matthiessen, *American Renaissance* (New York, 1941), p. 58.

[32] *The Territory Ahead* (New York, 1963), p. 15.

[33] *The Education of Henry Adams* (New York, 1931), pp. vii-viii.

James M. Cox

SOURCE: "Autobiography and America," in *The Virginia Quarterly Review,* Vol. XLVII, No. Winter-Spring, 1971, pp. 252-77.

[In the following essay, Cox describes the development of autobiographical writing in American literature—from Benjamin Franklin through Henry David Thoreau and Henry Adams to Gertrude Stein—as a reflection of American political life.]

Autobiography and confessional writing are now receiving much more critical attention than they used to, and not merely because criticism has exhausted the other genres and is now moving in on a relatively virgin field. For something has happened to the whole idea of literature in the last ten years. To remember that novelists such as Truman Capote and Norman Mailer have in "In Cold Blood" and "The Armies of the Night" challenged the distinction between non-fiction and fiction; to be reminded that biography and autobiography are more marketable products than fiction; to realize that "The Autobiography of Malcolm X" is somehow one of the great imaginative works of the last decade; to recall that Michel Butor told an MLA audience in Denver that there is no real difference between fiction and non-fiction, between a novel and an autobiography—to reflect upon all this is to begin to acknowledge that much more has happened than a mere opportunistic exploitation of a neglected field.

Much of this change is, I think, a result of and a response to the revolutionary political attitudes and feelings which have fully emerged in the last five years. For when politics and history become dominant realities for the imagination, then the traditional prose forms of the essay and the autobiography both gain and attract power and the more overtly "literary" forms of prose fiction—the novel and the short story—are likely to be threatened and impoverished. As such a process takes place—as politics and history tend to claim dominion over the imagination—then the literary imagination tends to respond by denying the generic distinctions which are both powerful and convenient categories in periods of stability and peace. Of course, the problem is much more complicated, but these remarks may provide some sense of a present which can be related to my sense of the past importance of autobiography in America.

For autobiography has been important in this country. As I shall suggest, the very idea of autobiography has grown out of the political necessities and discoveries of the American and French revolutions. It is no mere accident that an astonishingly large proportion of the slender shelf of so-called American classics is occupied by autobiographies. Certainly "Walden" and "The Education of Henry Adams" would rank in almost anybody's list of the ten major American prose works, novels included. I would also include Franklin's "Autobiography" though there would doubtless be dissenters as well as adherents to such a choice. Even so, I have chosen Franklin, Thoreau, and Adams primarily because they are central and not peripheral writers, are indeed classic American writers in the sense that their acts of imagination in the form of autobiography are unforgettable imaginative experience. Whitman offers a problem which I shall face when I reach him.

II

So much for preliminaries. There remains the question of just what autobiography is—and despite the present tendency to blur generic distinctions, I want to try to keep them, and not simply as a convenience but as a necessary means of clarifying the whole subject. Strictly speaking, of course, autobiography is not a genre at all in the sense that poetry, fiction, and drama are. It is a term designating a sub-class of that hopelessly confusing variety of writing we place under the heading of non-fiction prose. Yet of all the sub-classifications in that inchoate group, autobiography and biography are probably the clearest in our minds. We at least think we know what we mean when we speak of autobiography and biography and we are equally sure that others mean the same thing when they speak of them. Thus, in answer to the question, "What is autobiography?" I want to hold to the definition I believe we all know: a narrative of a person's life written by himself. Autobiography is in this sense the story of a life, but here there is a problem. It is not the story but the history of a life, for it is history and not fiction—which raises the further issue of distinguishing between history and fiction. Without rushing to or yearning for conclusive definitions of the two, we can at least see that both history and fiction are at base narratives, the distinction being that one narrative is based on fact, the other on invention. The one tells a story of what did happen, the other of what didn't; the one can be corroborated by public and private record, the other has to protect itself against the possibility of being taken literally. All this is of course commonplace, but it is often forgotten by critics of autobiography who begin to exercise the poetics of fiction in the analysis of autobiography.

There is another striking difference between the nature of historical and fictive narrative. In historical narrative the beginning and the ending are by necessity arbitrary and unreal (perhaps untrue would be the better term), for history has no beginning and no end. Thus the historian has to set up a principle of organization which will justify a beginning and an ending, concealing his intrusion into the irreversible historical stream. He therefore writes of the history of nations, of wars, of movements, of ideas, of governments, of decades, of explorations, always segmenting the continuous narrative line of history. His exit and entrance are the two sure fictive aspects of his form, and though he may achieve freedom of interpretation along the way, he is bound to the fact and the sequence of past events. The writer of fiction, on the other hand, has to begin and he has to end, for fiction is all invention, and its sure truths are that it does begin and does end. That is the inescapable necessity for the novelist and his whole effort is to realize that truth—to make the beginning and the ending as fatal and as final as they truly are.

Now autobiographical narrative falls between history and fictive narrative in this respect. If it is clearly historical in nature, it at least does have a beginning: the birth of its subject. True, the autobiographer, unless he has a prodigious memory, cannot remember his birth without becoming Shandyan, but at least he can chronicle it from hearsay or he can begin with his first memory. In any event he has a point of beginning which is logical and incontrovertible, though of course he can deviate from such a point, beginning with a history of his parents, as if he were a biographer, or at an arbitrary point in his life almost as if he were a novelist. He cannot, however, write about his death. Thus that great event, which is the goal of the biographer, is forever inaccessible to the autobiographer, though he may establish a kind of pattern of

his life which will enable him to treat it as if it were ended. There is another point which relates autobiography to fiction: it is the life of a person, and both it and biography have subject matter which likens them to fiction, which is dependent on characters, *i.e.* representations of persons.

These reflections, though they by no means define autobiography, put us in a position to see rudimentary issues of autobiographical form. But there is also an historical problem about autobiography which is directly related to the subject of American autobiography. We are prone to think that autobiography preceded America, for if we know anything we know that there were great autobiographers before the American nation existed. St. Augustine, Cellini, Montaigne, and Casanova come quickly to mind. But it is a fact worth recording that autobiography as a term did not exist at the time of the American revolution. It was first used, according to the OED, by Robert Southey in a review of Portuguese literature in 1809. Before the emergence of the term, there were two categories of people's lives written by themselves: the confession and the memoir. The confession was an account of a man's private life, centering on his emotions, feelings, secrets, frustrations—essentially his private world. The memoir was more on the order of chronicle, relating the individual's rôle upon the stage of history. The confession bared the inner thoughts; the memoir recounted the career. It is impossible to say just why autobiography should have emerged as a term to include both confession and memoir, but it may be helpful to note its appearance just after the age of revolution when the modern self was being liberated as well as defined. For the American and French Revolutions, whatever else they did, were the convulsive acts which released the individual as a potent political entity and gave us what we are pleased to call modern man. And each nation produced in this revolutionary period a classic account of the self: Rousseau's "Confessions" and Franklin's "Memoir" (for Franklin had only the old term with which to name his book).

In this connection, it is worth noting that the corresponding classic in English literature of the period is a biography, Boswell's "Life of Johnson." Thus, while America and France were readying for revolution, Franklin and Rousseau at almost the same moment in history were embarking on decisive accounts of themselves, while in England (which was desperately staving off revolution) Boswell was devoting himself to a biography of Johnson. Moreover, his relationship to his subject was constructed in terms of hierarchy. Yet if Boswell submitted to Johnson, Johnson in turn submitted himself to biography, and the completed work resulted in fulfillment for both men, since Boswell's remarkable revelation and recording of Johnson's talk raised Johnson's stature in English literature from a position of nobility to one of monarchy.

III

But Franklin and Rousseau were very great revolutionaries, and while Johnson was writing his pamphlet against the American revolution (an act which Boswell regretted), they were engaged in liberating themselves in accounts of their own lives. These accounts were no mere records of their past, but genuine acts of life, not mere ways of saying but essential acts of being. Thus, Rousseau, after showing talent in a host of ways—as musician, social philosopher, pamphleteer, and novelist, at last liberated the self which stood behind yet could not be released by all the forms of expression he had tried. "I felt before I thought," he announced near the beginning of his "Confessions," and his entire book was devoted to the generative life of feeling. The self which emerges in his pages is, with all its contradictions, something new and powerful in literature.

Instead of recording shame and later conversion in the manner of St. Augustine, Rousseau gives a nearly shameless revelation of himself, prefaced by a dare to all men to say whether they are better than he. Such a dare would be mere rhetoric if Rousseau in the course of his confessions did not exceed the wildest expectations of what an inner self might be. Thus, if his perversity and his revelations about his thwarted, devious, deviant, and frantic sexuality evoke surprise, his defenses of himself evoke outrage, and his pleas for justice by posterity are likely to provoke judgment and suppression on the part of those who wish for order. Small wonder that Johnson deplored Rousseau, for the self which Rousseau releases is the very self which Johnson's whole life was bent upon checking. Indeed, Rousseau's release of such a self was the promise of the revolution which Johnson could feel in his very bones and which his whole style was both continuously and precariously subduing.

How different is Franklin's life. Johnson himself would have been hard put to disapprove it. Whereas Rousseau had released his inner life in the form of confession, Franklin chronicled his public life. Yet just as Rousseau had transformed the confession, Franklin transformed the memoir. Although Franklin chronicles his rise from obscurity to prominence, he does not suppress his emotional life so much as he shows the process of converting, using, and incorporating his desires, inner conflicts, doubts, and frustrations into a model life which in its turn can also be used by posterity. Thus, having organized a philosophical society, a university, a hospital, a lending library, an efficient postal system, and having invented the stove, the smokeless streetlamp, bifocals, electrical conduction, the harmonica, and a host of other items too numerous to mention, Franklin at the age of sixty-five embarked upon what one wants to call his great invention—the invention of himself, not as fiction, but as a fact both of and in history.

What is truly interesting is that Franklin's act of conceiving, discovering, or inventing himself almost exactly coincides with the birth of America. For Franklin began his biography in 1771 in England, just as he was becoming fully involved in the emerging separation from England, came back to work on it in France in 1784, worked on it again in 1788, and was once more

involved with it months before his death in 1791. When he died, he had brought the record of his life forward to 1757—to that point when he was at the threshold of the professional diplomatic life, the life of his country, which would both occupy and preoccupy him for the rest of his days.

But Franklin is a true writer, and, like Rousseau, is as interested in the act of writing as in what he writes about. Thus he states at the outset that he is writing because he has a moment's time free from his diplomatic duties. He is therefore writing not simply out of leisure but as leisure, and that celebrated simple style of his with its even tenor equals the motive and act of leisure with which he begins. More than that, he sees his act of writing as the next best thing to living his life over again and he thus sees his memoir not as a record but as a second edition in which the sins of his life (which would have enormous emotional weight in the confessional form) become the mere errata of the first edition which he can point to and playfully wish to remove.

Even more important, he dates the time of his writing so that the dates of composition I referred to are not biographical information but textual reality. Thus the "life," which is to say Franklin's account of his early years, is placed between the years 1771 and 1788, the years of the American revolution, confederation, and constitution. What literally happens in the form of Franklin's work is that the history of the revolution, in which Franklin played such a conspicuous part, is displaced by the narrative of Franklin's early life, so that Franklin's personal history *stands in place of the revolution.* Now the personal history which Franklin puts in place of revolutionary history recounts Franklin's rise from political anonymity and impotence to the position of agent for his colony, representing the people of Pennsylvania against the proprietors who reside in England. Thus, his life begins in Boston where freedom of the press is threatened by the crown and where freedom of impulse is threatened by his older brother; it ends in London where he is defending the colony from the attempted encroachments of the proprietors. But this represented history was not the actual revolution. There still remained the form which would realize the revolution and thus stand for it. That form was the autobiography—the life of a self-made, self-governing man written by the man himself. Though Franklin had only the term memoir, it is not difficult to see why in the light of what both he and Rousseau were doing to memoir and confession, a new term would be possible as well as necessary.

It is now possible to turn to the structure of Franklin's autobiography to see how Franklin's history reveals the man. For Rousseau life is total crisis; his life is defined in terms of one intense feeling after another. For Franklin there is no crisis. For Rousseau, all life is a turning point, and he thus finds himself time after time insisting that such and such an event fixed his fate. For Franklin, there is no turning point; all events are essentially equal and that equality is not the mere inertness of a chronicle but a way of being which both reveals and reflects Franklin the man. Everything being essentially equal, Franklin is never trapped in or attached to events but free to see them with detachment and curiosity. Thus, because Franklin sees street drainage and street lighting as being equal to law making and political theory, he is free from self-absorption as he walks home from assembly sessions to think about the possibility of inventions. His detached vision objectifies ideas, equalizes all concerns, and frees him to experiment with and concentrate upon a whole variety of probabilities.

Similarly, he is free in his form, for he makes use of the very limitations of the memoir. Thus he converts the limitation of being unable to catch up with his life and write of his death into the freedom of stopping his account whenever he wants to. After all, whenever he wants to or has to stop for whatever reason—whether business or death—will be the end. That of course is Franklin's freedom of form, and we don't find ourselves dissatisfied or wishing for more when Franklin does stop. He could have stopped with the first section of the book written in 1771 (he actually did stop and continued at the request of two Philadelphia friends, publishing their letters as a kind of advertisement of himself and his life) because he is not seeing his life in terms of turning point or finale, but as usable history—usable for others as a record of converting private desires into public life and private passions into rigorous self-government; usable for himself as leisure and amusement during a time of preoccupation with revolutionary duties. For the life he was able to recount in those few leisure moments was precisely that life which both brought him to the fate of a career yet remained the old free experience in which he retained the possibility of doing everything or anything. Writing that life during the period when his career was fixed was not to recapture or relive the old free life (Franklin, unlike Rousseau, does not recall or remember or yearn for his past) but to assert that life as fact and put it in place of revolutionary history.

All this may seem like far-fetched speculation to those who wish to think that Franklin was just writing away on his life without any notion of writing a revolutionary book. Surely these speculations would at best amuse Franklin, but it is well in dealing with Franklin's consciousness to try to be as shrewdly calculating as he himself was. For Franklin knew he was going to be a revolutionary not only before the revolution but before he began his autobiography. Two weeks before he embarked upon the autobiography he wrote to James Otis, Thomas Cushing, and Samuel Adams one of the most visionary letters of the eighteenth century. Acquainting them with the repressive attitude of Parliament and the crown, he forecast the steps of the revolution which was to come:

> I think one may clearly see, in the system of customs to be exacted in America by act of Parliament, the seeds sown of a total disunion of the two countries, though as yet that event may be at a considerable distance. The course and

natural progress seems to be, first, the appointment of needy men as officers, for others do not care to leave England; then, their necessities make them rapacious, their office makes them proud and insolent, their insolence and rapacity make them odious, and being conscious that they are hated, they become malicious; their malice urges them to a continual abuse of the inhabitants in their letters to administration, representing them as disaffected and rebellious, and (to encourage the use of severity) as weak, divided, timid, and cowardly. Government believes all; thinks it necessary to support countenance to its officers; their quarrelling with the people is deemed a mark and consequence of their fidelity; they are therefore more highly rewarded, and this makes their conduct still more insolent and provoking.

> The resentment of the people will, at times and on particular incidents, burst into outrages and violence upon such officers, and this naturally draws down severity and acts of further oppression from hence. The more the people are dissatisfied the more rigour will be thought necessary; severe punishments will be inflicted to terrify; rights and privileges will be abolished; greater force will then be required to secure execution and submission; the expense will become enormous; it will then be thought proper, by fresh exactions, to make the people defray it; thence the British nation and government will become odious, and subjection to it will be deemed no longer tolerable; war ensues, and the bloody war will end in absolute slavery to America or ruin to Britain by the loss of her colonies; the latter most probable, from America's growing strength and magnitude.

So Franklin not only saw the coming revolution; he calculated the probable outcome. It may make him an unglamorous revolutionary to have had such vision, since one doesn't seem much like a revolutionary if he has seen so much and calculated so shrewdly. It is also worth remembering that Franklin was sixty-five when he determined upon revolution, an old age to begin such an enterprise, but the fact may serve as a model of possibility, a reminder that one doesn't have to be young, or desperate, or hopeless to engage in a great revolution.

So of course Franklin's act of art in the "Autobiography" doesn't seem revolutionary; it seems even and easy and simple. But it is there in the path, and the best one can do to those professors of English who condescend to it is to say simply and innocently that it is the first book we have. For before Franklin there was no American literature; there was only English Colonial literature. With Franklin came consciousness, total consciousness in the form of autobiography—a history of a self-made life written by the man who made it. It is not a fiction but a cultural fact of life and we have to make the best of it.

IV

To make the best of it is to see the great American autobiography which followed, not only in relation to

Franklin's initial act but in relation to the history of the country. Here it is worth noting that Thoreau's "Walden," by all admission the next great American autobiography, appears in 1854, at just the moment the nation was moving toward Civil War, reminding us that autobiography becomes more possible when history and politics seem to possess the very drama we seek for in stage and fictive experience in periods of equanimity and peace. In any event, "Walden" did appear in 1854, and it was much concerned with the issues of slavery and abolition which were splitting the nation apart. But it was also autobiography, and Thoreau, like Franklin and Rousseau before him, was both revolutionary and writer. Thus, writing for him was as it was for them, not simply the record of experience but an act of life, a making of experience. Moreover, Thoreau, for all his differences from Franklin, does not turn inward upon himself or his feelings but looks out upon a world of natural fact. He too proposes a model life, and though it is not presented as a model to follow but one to equal, it is a life which Thoreau like Franklin before him has made for himself.

Yet it is much more than a making or recording of experience. It was for Thoreau a finishing of experience, and Thoreau's experiment in form is most dramatically evident in his determination to reach a conclusion, thereby completing his life—just what Franklin and Rousseau, by virtue of their choice of form, cannot do. There is a cost, of course, for Thoreau in order to complete his life has to take a part of it—the two years he spent at Walden Pond ten years earlier—and make them stand for the whole. He went much further. He compressed the two years into one, letting the cycle of the seasons stand for the completed circle of the self. In order to make his style realize such a conception of the self, Thoreau sought a language at once metaphoric and concise. Yet for all the wit and concision of his language, there is always the fact of Walden Pond, a fact which lies outside himself and outside language as both a seal and promise of his own reality. Much as Thoreau may play upon the analogies of the pond to his own life, its existence as a natural fact is as important for him as it is for us. That is why we cannot imagine Walden being a fiction, even though when we visit it today we inevitably realize that we did not really have to go there.

What Thoreau aimed to do was to translate the particular fact of Walden into the possibilities of being himself. Working steadily along analogical lines with that startling clarity of his, he saw himself as much a metaphor of Walden as it was of him. Because it was a pond, because it was self-contained, because it had the purity and clarity to reflect his image against the heavens, it became the reservoir of possibilities he could realize only in relation to it. The cycle of the seasons brooding over it was the natural time in which he determined to cast his life. And the hut he began to construct along its shores in the spring, occupied on July 4, and closed in with the coming of the ice upon Walden, gains significance always in relation to the pond which Thoreau, true surveyor that he was, maps and scrutinizes even as it reflects the self.

The self which emerges from the analogy is a far cry from the selves Franklin and Rousseau had discovered. Franklin, in concentrating on the externality of his past, had shown largely by implication in his style and structure the conversion of his inner self into a social and political self. Thus his "success" is an exemplary narrative implicitly depicting the sublimation of private energies into social action. Rousseau's experiential narration is almost the inverse of Franklin's. He discloses his progressive alienation from society—the long process by which he withdrew by stages from society to his island in a lake. His island is a perfect equivalent of the embattled, moated, insular, present consciousness which at once generates and releases the past which has grown inside him.

For all their difference in self-conception, however, both Rousseau and Franklin realize themselves narratively and chronologically. In "Walden," both narration and chronology tend to disappear, for just as a single year is being made to stand for a whole life, essence is always taking precedence over existence. Thoreau is neither taking over nor withdrawing from society. He stands between it and the pond in a constant attitude of seeing in Walden—Earth's Eye—an image of himself austerely and severely against society. That severity becomes Thoreau's fierce irony and makes the reading of "Walden" a humiliating as well as an exhilarating experience. The exhilaration comes from the kind of joy and independence Thoreau achieves in his insular solitude beside the pond. The humiliation comes from his almost savage criticism and exposure of the condition of man in his own time and, by ruthless implication, in all time to come. For Thoreau challenges his reader like a persecuting conscience. He says at the beginning that he writes not for the strong and self-reliant souls, if such there be, but for those who find themselves somehow unhappy with their lot. He shows in the course of his revolutionary life the possibilities which lie near at hand—as near and as familiar as Walden—but he also exposes the shabby lot society has made of life, revealing in a way that no other book has revealed not only that we can do what we want but that, alas!, we have already done what we wanted—that as Americans we are always free to be free but that also as Americans we always choose to be slaves. That is why he brilliantly begins with the chapter on economy, showing the minimal requirements not simply for survival but for fulfillment. For Thoreau, writing almost on the eve of Civil War, sees freedom not as Franklin's self-making but as self-possession. And he sees the self not as a means but as an end. Thus, unlike Franklin and Rousseau, he does indeed have a conclusion in which the self is completed in an ecstasy of possibility, a radiance and radiation of analogy and metaphor.

Yet Thoreau does not reach a conclusion so much as he is all conclusion, and his language is not a means to relate his history so much as it is itself his very essence—the literal translation of his being into symbol. That is why his whole direction is not to naturalize himself but to spiritualize nature, to overcome and subdue it, thereby becoming an ideal which will both afflict and elevate his reader. His language, his whole act of writing, is bent always toward a finish, a refinement, and a purity (in the full and not the genteel meaning of those words). In order to achieve a representative life, one which will stand for a complete life, Thoreau accentuates his individuality. The tension in his consciousness and his style is thus always between universality and eccentricity, for in order to dramatize the universality of the individual, Thoreau emphasizes the uniqueness of the self. His equivalent act in language is to take such a personal hold of it that its abstractions are bent to his will and wit. Insofar as he determines to represent man he means to render a concrete life different from the lives of others. The very burden of being an individual is to discover one's own way which of necessity must take the individual to a land as distant, as austere, and as self-contained as the Walden Pond he keeps discovering. These are the terms as well as the burden of Thoreau's self-possession.

All this is of course self-evident, and I would not think of claiming freshness of insight into Walden. To approach such insight I need the presence of Whitman. I know that his presence in my list of autobiographers must seem anomalous. It is anomalous, for Whitman is a poet if he is anything, and to begin to play fast and loose with categories is to begin to play the devil. If autobiography is narrative and history, then it is not poem and prophecy. So my chief aim is not to claim Whitman as autobiographer, but to use him to gain a perspective on Thoreau. Yet, I can't forbear a few defenses of having included him. After all, he did write a poem entitled "Song of Myself," which, considered in relation to Wordsworth's "Prelude" and Coleridge's "Biographia Literaria," reminds us how pervasive the autobiographical form in literature became after the American and French Revolutions. Moreover, Henry James, Jr., in reviewing Whitman's poetry, said that whatever Whitman's medium was, it wasn't poetry, though he went on to observe that it wasn't prose either. As far as James could make out in that early review (he happily lived to revise his opinion), Whitman's poetry was an incredibly vulgar offense against the muse herself, a blatant exhibition of self which no one concerned with the craft and glory of art could condone. Art for James was a subduing of the self through form and language. James's criticism is still remarkably apt for anyone who hasn't genteelized Whitman with respectability, for Whitman is and should be hard to take. Instead of the fine economy we find in Thoreau's language, the wit, the intelligence, the precision, the exactness, there is a great deal of wind, flatness, and abstraction. There is much, much more, to be sure, but one of the feelings that Whitman's poetry inspires and clearly means to inspire is that we the readers could do as well—that, indeed, if this is poetry then what isn't.

Thoreau had sought to create a sharply individualized consciousness which would stand for the possibilities of self-possession and had announced at the outset that though the first person pronoun was dropped in many a personal narrative he would retain it. Whitman went another way. Seizing upon the crucial fact that in the pronominal system of the English language there is no distinction in form between the second person singular and plural, he was able to address his reader as *you* and be at once personal and general. He added to that radical formal discovery an audacious democratic program of asserting an identification between the I of the poet and the you—both singular and plural—of all whom his poetry would prophesy. Whereas Thoreau's direction had been to translate his flesh into spirit and himself into concrete metaphor, Whitman's inspiration was to speak the word of himself, thereby creating the reader as poet. The reader would be the concrete emotional self, the embodiment of the word. Thus Thoreau's austerity and solitude; thus Whitman's constant emphasis upon love and union.

Considered in relation to their time, Whitman is the poet of union, Thoreau the voice of secession, the most powerful voice of secession in our literature. I do not mean that Thoreau was a Southerner at heart. He wasn't. He was a Yankee, but Yankees had been old revolutionaries, and revolution had meant separation from authority. It took the genius of Lincoln to transform the old revolutionary impulse toward separation, which was as deep a part of American identity as the wish for union, into a national will for union, and it took a bloody Civil War to establish the Union as an irrevocable reality. It is hardly surprising in this connection that Thoreau should have died quietly while the war raged in the South and that Whitman, who was totally prepared for Civil War, could go to the battlefields and hospitals as a male nurse, could kiss the soldiers of the South as well as those of the North, could—best of all—write letters home for the wounded and dying, could fully see Lincoln from the moment he took the stage (even Emerson could hardly see him), and could write "When Lilacs Last in the Dooryard Bloom'd" almost the moment Lincoln was assassinated. If Milton had moved from elegy through losing Civil War toward epic, Whitman moved from epic through victorious Civil War toward elegy, translating the dead bodies of all his brave soldiers into the leaves of grass whose roots (as he had epically promised in 1855) came out of the faint red roofs of the mouths of the dead. The leaves of grass were nothing less than the living tongues of the dead. For if love was the impulse which would create the future reader, death had to be the event which Whitman had to translate. How else could there be immortality of the flesh? For it is not immortality of the spirit which interests Whitman—any Baptist preacher could indulge that argument—but immortality of the flesh. Thus, that magnificent line near the end of "Song of Myself":

I effuse my flesh in eddies and drift it in lacy jags.

And thus the pun on leaves of grass as leaves of the book.

To face that pun fully is to remember Walden once more. For in Thoreau's chapter on Spring, just before his conclusion, he describes the breaking up of the ice on Walden and the thawing of the frozen earth. Standing before the railroad bankside which man has cut in nature, Thoreau sees the spring rivulets tenderly eroding the fresh earth and forming miniature alluvial fans whose shape takes the forms of primordial leaves. Playing upon the analogy, Thoreau sees earth's whole excretory process as a purification into and a promise of the leaves to come. Almost like a savage, he tries to make a language from the very word leaf, expanding it into lobe, gutterally evolving it further into globe, and at last wishing that Earth's primal form will be translated into the leaves of his book so that he can turn over a new leaf at last. Just as the excretion of the world's body becomes the delicate leaf above the earth, Thoreau wants his words and pages to be the purification of his flesh into pure spirit, a resurrection of the body. Whitman, on the other hand, seeks to say and be the word which will descend into the body, and his urge as well as his vision is literally to embrace the world and become it, to embrace reader and readers and become them, to be the tongue which invades every part of the body and gives every part an equal voice—a radical democratization of both body and body politic and an immortal union of himself with the world of readers he is creating, so that "Song of Myself" will, when we begin to grasp it, be true to its title—the song of ourselves, the instantaneous miracle which makes us poets, putting us at the threshold of a living faith that, lo and behold, we are the living poem which Whitman's new Biblical verse has created.

V

It is a long way from Thoreau and Whitman to Henry Adams, largely because Adams himself sought to make the space in time as wide as possible. Yet differently as he saw and created his life from theirs, like them he eschews the confessional element in autobiography. He does not remember, explain, or defend his past in the manner of Mill and Newman anymore than he wishes to confess, reveal, and justify it in the manner of Rousseau, but, like Franklin and Thoreau, he makes use of it and makes it useful. His too is a model life, but not a paradigm like Franklin's or a challenge like Thoreau's, for his whole notion of a model life is that of a mannikin—a figure in which clothing, outline, and pattern are everything, the life nothing but plaster and sawdust, an elusive and ironic joke at the center of education, which is at once history, the thought into which life has died, and art, the narrative upon which life is spent. Being an historian, Adams saw life as history; being an autobiographer, he knew he had to make life art. Being these and being an Adams too, he dared to identify his history with that of his country. Comprehending these strands of being in a single narrative, he left an autobiography which drew life from the autobiography that had gone before him and abundantly gave meaning back to it, as I shall try to demonstrate.

There are two striking facts of form in Adams's "Education." First, it is written in the third person and therefore guarantees the possibility of completeness. Second, it has a gap in the center, a vacuum of twenty years about which Adams hardly speaks. We know—and such a fact of form forces us to wonder if we don't know—what happened during those twenty years. He taught at Harvard (he touches upon this fact) and was therefore not a student of life. He wrote history (he alludes to this at points along his way) and was thus an historian instead of being a part of history. And he married, only to experience the tragedy of his wife's suicide (he alludes only once to that harrowing event, telling of watching in Rock Creek Cemetery the people who came to see St. Gaudens' great sculpture of grief which monumentalized his wife's grave). These three acts are the silence in the midst of life, and the autobiography which surrounds them is the act of mind converting them into their opposite. The teacher is converted into the student Henry Adams; the historian is converted into the victim and expression of history. And the grief-stricken husband is converted into the pleasure seeker of the mind whose whole act of play is to convert his past into a third person in an act of joyful suicide.

To see these paradoxes is to begin to grasp the consequences of Adams's third person narration, consequences which Adams embraces with almost dismaying enthusiasm. Thoreau had retained the "I" but in order to achieve a completed self was forced into the synechdochic strategy of making a part stand for the whole. Adams however, by converting himself into the third person was able to treat himself not as character—for characters are in fiction and drama, not in autobiography—but as history. The consequences of such a strategy are enormous. For if the self is truly history, then it is somehow past, and Adams would become merely the biographer of himself. Yet Adams is not a biographer but an autobiographer, and of all things the "Education" is not, one is surely biography. It is rather a division of the self into two parts, two poles—a past and a present—in which the present self generates the past self as history. The new Henry Adams, the present generative consciousness, which in conventional historical terms grew out of the past, is by virtue of Adams's inversion actually releasing and attracting the old Henry Adams (he would be the young Adams in conventional terms) toward his source. Adams fully realizes these inversions by means of a style which can best be described as a series of paradoxes riding upon a narrative current.

The new Adams, the present Adams, who is as much the source as the end of the past, constantly exposes the descent of the old Adams, who, born too late into history from a line of Presidents and fated for success and power, steadily failed. The old Adams, always unprepared for contingency, is drawn forward—not recorded or chronicled—through the resistance of history toward the moment of the present which is the hidden "I" that he can never reach. That is the fate of Adams's form which casts the self as history. The old Adams's approach to the present is as a victim of forces beyond his control, a child amid theory, politics, technology, and above all, accelerating history. Everything he is made to learn merely unprepares him for the past through which he is drawn. He is the great grandson and the grandson of Presidents only to feel himself cast aside from the sources of power; he goes to Harvard only to discover himself a fool in Europe; he faces Civil War as a loyal Union man only to discover that the real treason was the betrayal of his father by Charles Sumner, the most trusted family friend; he goes to England as secretary for his father the ambassador in an effort to secure the balance of power they think England holds only to discover that the Civil War has already shifted the power to America and that England by remaining neutral has actually fallen behind history; he learns evolution only to return to America and find Grant in the White House; he attempts to expose the economic scandals of the Grant era only to find himself in touch with the energy of capital—which defies all his calculations; he teaches medieval history at Harvard only to discover his total ignorance of all history; he writes the history of the early years of the Republic only to recognize that the ideas of humanistic history are completely negated by the laws of physical energy. And so at last he attempts to learn the laws of science in an effort to plot force and energy in time, thereby making the art of history a science possessing predictive force, only to realize that acceleration is the law of history. Having made his predictions and seen the law of acceleration, he steps aside.

This series of belated recognitions constitutes the history and the failure of the old Adams, but it is failure generated by the polarity of the new Henry Adams in relation to the old. Indeed, the new Adams is literally *educating* the old Adams, giving the title an active and present sense which is often overlooked. Moreover, he is educating him all the time, at every instant of the narrative. For the education is nothing less than the act and vision whereby the new Adams ironically objectifies the old as a victim of history. If the old Adams is being educated by the new, the discovery is not simply one of gloomy personal failure but of the failure of all the history he has lived through—the dissolution of an old order of causation into a new energy. Thus the nineteenth century dissolves into the twentieth, exposing in the process that the men of power—thinkers, politicians, and diplomats—were not simply wrong but did not even know what they were doing, were indeed victims of the power and drift of history. Their ignorance was but one more mass of energy for the historian to measure in terms of its force.

As the old Henry Adams is attracted toward the new, his life is taken, not as a loss or grief but as a conversion, and not the conversion of confessional form—the conversion of man into God as in Augustine, or into feeling as in Rousseau—but a conversion into historical force, so that autobiographical narrative does not displace history, as in Franklin, but becomes an ironic vision of history. The moment of conversion is, as everyone

knows, Adams's vision of the dynamo in the gallery of machines at the Paris exposition of 1900, six hundred years after Dante's vision of Beatrice. The dynamo is the beautiful objectification of Adams's act of form, for it comes into being at precisely the moment when the old Henry Adams has been attracted to the present source of his energy. True to his form at this moment when he envisions the dynamo as the end of the old Adams, the new Adams is able to see an opposite force, not forward in time but backward in history; he sees the Virgin.

These then become the poles of past and future which the old and new Adams generate as they meet at the beginning of twentieth century; they are at the same time the poles of energy which constitute Adams's conversion, for they make possible his dynamic theory and act of history. Because it is at once theory (an analytic formulation about past and future) and act (a literal attraction of the old Adams to the source which has generated him) it can become a genuine vision, but a vision in Adamic not in Augustinian terms, for it is a conversion of the self not into divine but into historical lines of force. That is why Adams's vision of the future is not so much prophetic as it is speculative.

Happily for us, the poles of dynamo and Virgin are also beautifully conclusive as a vision of autobiography and America. For Adams's discovery of the dynamo takes us directly back to our point of departure. After all, Franklin not only invented American autobiography; he also discovered—fathered might be the better term—electricity, and those Promethean acts bind him deeply to Adams's form and substance. More than that, there was an old family score for Adams to settle, and though Adams was terribly ironic about himself and his progenitors, he *was* an Adams through and through and had a way of dealing with the Jeffersons and Randolphs who had thwarted his great grandfather. Franklin in Paris during the American Revolution had driven John Adams to distraction with his social ease, detachment, and wit. While John Adams toiled, Franklin seemed to play and yet reap all the praise. The whole miserable contrast so piqued Adams that he confided his exasperation to his Journal. So in disclosing the dynamo as the essence of America and the future which would be American, Henry Adams was settling old scores even as he was being utterly true to his form. If Franklin had seen autobiography as self-generation, Adams would show the end of self-generation. Instead of seeing his life as the rise from obscurity to prominence, Adams saw it as the descent from prominence into obscurity and utter posthumous silence. Instead of treating life as a chronicle of success, Adams showed it as both the history of failure and the failure of history. Thus at the moment of his conversion, the old Adams feels like worshiping the dynamo, but the new Adams generates the opposite of the dynamo—the Virgin of a deeper, more primal past. For what autobiography as self generation perforce left out was woman, the force which had moved the medieval world in Adams's illuminated vision of the past, and yet the force which had been rendered irrelevant by American autobiography and revolution. There were no women in Franklin's world of the self-invented self—only the wife as helpmeet in the most practical sense and as a practical object for excess sexual energy. There were no women at all in Thoreau. Although there was a feminine principle in Whitman, he hermaphroditically absorbed it as he absorbed Kanada and Missouri and Montana.

And so Adams delightfully chose the Virgin, not at all as a converted Catholic, possibly as atonement and love for the wife who had killed herself, certainly as a pleasure seeker in history where he could be a tourist to his heart's desire.

All this is much, but it is not all. Adams declared an end to education, autobiography, and history in 1905, the year John Hay concluded the treaty between Russia and Japan. That marked the end of Adams's old eighteenth-century provincial America, the America of Franklin's invention. That America had moved from peripheral and provincial entity to become *the* treaty-making power in the West, and thus a line of force to meet the inertia of Russia and China in the East. Thus, the city which had drawn his ancestors from Quincy and Boston and which Adams, having failed to occupy as President, had occupied as historian was now the center of power in the West—the point from which Adams could let the energy of his mind run its own lines of force into the past and future.

But there is still more. 1905 was the date of Einstein's equation and the beginning of all that it has meant. Though Adams may not have known the equation, who, after reading "The Education," can say that he could not have imagined it? Even to ask the question is to answer it, for the fact is that Adams's "Education" is the heroic act of the imagination unifying history and science in an act of mind and art. To read it is to recognize the genuine pathos of C. P. Snow's cry of alarm, some fifty years later, at the perilous division between the two cultures of science and the humanities. Whatever its content, the form of Snow's "scientific" vision is, like his forms of fiction, still in the age of Howells. Adams had not only seen and measured the division between the two cultures but had imagined them as the poles of attractive force which, converting the inertia of life and history into energy of mind, would transform the self into a unifying consciousness—a third force in a new magnetic field. That is why his book is genuinely true to its title, remaining to this day an education for *any* twentieth-century reader. Of all American literature, it alone deserves to be required reading for all *students,* which is far from saying that it should be required reading for everyone or that it is the "best" American autobiography.

VI

This, however, is an essay not about education but about American autobiography, and Adams's achievement puts me in a position to conclude the subject, which does not mean to summarize my argument. A conclusion, it seems to me, ought to evoke an American writer after Adams who somehow extended the American autobiographical tradition along the lines of force I have tentatively sketched out.

For me, that writer is Gertrude Stein. She is the woman whom Adams had tried to imagine emerging from the American scene. She drops out of medical school and the world of philosophy and science to become a dictatorial force in the world of art. She realizes almost from the beginning that America is not the newest but the oldest country in the world, since, immediately following its own Civil War, it was the first country fully to enter the modern world of steam and electricity. She leaves America to occupy Paris, the city of art, there to become an esthetic dictator of the new art which, emerging from the nineteenth-century dissolution of image and representation into impression, asserted clarity of line in an instantaneous perspective of abstraction. And she was, inevitably, an autobiographer. But where Adams had, by doubling himself, succeeded in retaining a narrative past at once generated by and attracted to a present consciousness, Gertrude Stein sought an absolute present in which not the life would be everything, the words nothing—as in Whitman—but the words everything and the life nothing. The abstraction of language would be the total present, and the achievement of the writer would lie in disconnecting language from referential reality, thereby making the words upon the page not true but real, not possessed of but possessing total reality in and of themselves. They would, in her words, be "being existing."

The only way that Gertrude Stein could even acknowledge narrative perspective was to write through her companion Alice B. Toklas speaking about herself, Gertrude Stein. Thus, like the other American autobiographers she could only reach herself by going outside. In reaching herself by being, not imagining, her intimate companion, she was not at all trying to gain an objective perspective on herself. Rather, she united both autobiographical and biographical consciousness in a single creative act, annihilating their priority and leaving only anecdotal perception upon the page as pure act and pure fact—not a new life in time, but a new thing in space. It has been said that she became her own Boswell, and in a sense she did, but it might be truer to say that, after writing "The Making of Americans," she at last became one. Perhaps it was right that she should have settled in Paris, the city where Franklin had gone—in D. H. Lawrence's vision—to cut a hole in the Old World through which Europe would eventually bleed to death. Lawrence, at the end of his essay on Franklin written between the wars when Hitler was waiting in the wings of history, had cried out for Europe to let hell loose and get its own back from America. But when Hitler finally did let hell loose, it was certainly right that Gertrude Stein, who had been in Paris all these years, should have been waiting there to receive the victorious American soldiers when they liberated the city in 1945. She—as

American, as man-woman, as new Buddha—seems to me to be both the fact and the mystery at the end of American autobiography. Her life in time, which ended in 1946, a year after the atomic bomb, is a good place to end this glimpse of the subject. Her life in words, a total present, would be the living fact on which to base a genuine vision of American autobiography as American history. That is why she is my conclusion.

AMERICAN AUTHORS AND AUTOBIOGRAPHY

Marc Dolan

SOURCE: "The (Hi)story of Their Lives: Mythic Autobiography and 'The Lost Generation'," in *Journal of American Studies,* Vol. 27, No. 1, April, 1993, pp. 35-56.

[*In the following essay, Dolan discusses the influence of autobiographical writings—particularly Malcolm Cowley's* Exile's Return *(1934), Ernest Hemingway's* A Moveable Feast *(1964), and F. Scott Fitzgerald's* The Crack-Up *(1945)—in establishing popular views of American expatriate writers in Paris during the 1920s.*]

Of what use is autobiography to history? At first glance, autobiographies would seem invaluable to historians. After all, no attempt to reconstruct or understand the past would seem complete without a sprinkling of quotations from some form of "eyewitness account." Among the various forms of such accounts available to historians, the formal autobiography often provides the most comprehensive and comprehensible account extant of the personal experience of historical events.[1] Yet even so strong an admirer of the genre as Allan Nevins was forced to admit that very few autobiographies were ideally suited to the traditional historian's purpose. Most, he conceded, were "imperfect" historical documents at best and could prove "far more deeply misleading" than many other historical sources.[2]

Considered schematically, there are five frequently-raised, formal objections that twentieth-century historians like Nevins have made to the indiscriminate use of formal autobiographies as primary sources of historical evidence. All five objections are variations on some fairly standard historiographical problems; and while none of these objections is damaging enough in its own right to rule out any and all evidentiary use of formal autobiography, taken together these five objections are enough to give us pause. For example, one standard objection—the limited, distorting perspective provided on history by the evidence of a single consciousness—is clearly part of the ongoing historiographical debate over the relative merits of so-called "objective" and "subjective" approaches to history. This debate is also sometimes configured as a conflict between the study of "historical

events" and the study of "historical experience," or as the conflict between "scientific," "quantitative" history and "artistic," "qualitative" history. At base, the problem is fairly simple. Which is more valuable to historical studies: historical knowledge that concerns itself with objectively verifiable political, sociological, and economic "events" (occurrences or trends that can be reasonably demonstrated by recourse to valid documentary and/or statistical evidence); or historical knowledge that concerns itself with the ultimately unverifiable, inner "experience" of the past as lived by its individual citizens (the internal, subjective knowledge that G. M. Young once delineated as "not what happened, but what people felt about when it was happening")?[3]

Even if this first objection to formal autobiography may be surmounted fairly easily (by declaring that "historical events" and "historical experience" are both equally important to historical studies), a second, related objection—to the genre's overall emphasis on a single life, rather than the "collective life" or interconnected lives of a community, a nation, or an age—proves slightly more difficult to elude. Ultimately, this second problem comes down to a question of priority: how do we go about integrating these two separate, very different types of historical knowledge? Do we, as David Hackett Fisher suggests, first use statistical evidence to determine what he calls "modal tendencies" in a given era, and then select individual accounts of that experience that provide us with statistically confirmed "modal characters"? Or do we, as David Levin proposes, begin with the subjective account of historical experience, and then work outward from these insights to the collateral evidence that confirms those individual tendencies that are characteristic rather than idiosyncratic in a given period? This may seem like hairsplitting, but if we seek out a particular life story for closer study, have we not already decided that it is in some way "representative," i.e., that it shores up the historical knowledge that we have already determined to be important?[4]

Ultimately, neither of these problems of "subjectivity" and "objectivity" can ever be satisfactorily resolved, nor will we find a satisfactory resolution to the historiographical controversy that lies behind a third objection—the genre's near-axiomatic recourse to linear narrative. Theoreticians like Karl Popper and Carl Hempel have advanced shrewd, cogent arguments regarding the essential falsity of narrative form, while historical philosophers like Michael Oakeshott and J. H. Hexter have made equally compelling cases for the Bergsonian view that history is experienced as continuity rather than segmentation and should consequently be represented as such. "Change in history," as Oakeshott observed in 1933, "carries with it its own explanation; the course of events is one, so far integrated, so far filled in and complete, that no external cause or reason is looked for or required in order to account for any particular event." History, in other words, resides in contingency as much as in more obvious, overdetermined causes. To remove contingency—to remove the continuity of narratively rather than analytically organized historiography—is thus to simplify the true causality of historical events.[5]

Opposing camps in all three of these historiographical debates have been active for some time. (Certainly, no thinking historian of the last century and a half would have taken any of these issues for granted.) But the historiographical problems that lie behind the two remaining objections to formal autobiography—to its obscuring literariness and its frequent distance from the events described—remained dormant until quite recently. Historians of all stripes, from R. G. Collingwood to E. H. Carr, from Allan Nevins to Marc Bloch, could all agree that a published memoir written decades after the fact needed to be regarded more skeptically than a deed-register, a census-report, or even a contemporaneous account taken from a diary or letter. "[T]here can be no doubt," Bloch wrote in the posthumously published *The Historian's Craft* (1953), a historiographical "bible" for several generations of historians, "that, in the course of its development, historical research has gradually been led to place more and more confidence . . . in the evidence of witnesses in spite of themselves." "Even in the present," Bloch observed, writing in 1942, "who among us would not prefer to get hold of a few secret chancellery papers or some confidential military reports, to having all the newspapers of 1938 or 1939?"[6]

Such historiographical unanimity has disappeared, however, with the recent rise of the so-called "new cultural history." Eschewing many of the evidentiary rules honored by professional historians from Leopold von Ranke forward, cultural historians of the 1980s and 1990s have adopted a historiographical practice that frequently falls halfway between anthropology and literary criticism, drawing on the insights and methodologies of both fields. As Lynn Hunt has observed, this new form of historiographical practice is increasingly interested in the oddly *textual* nature of historical knowledge; in the ways in which the historian's notions of evidence and its value inevitably hinge on acts of interpretation not unlike those of the ethnographer or literary critic. In considering the problem of representativeness alluded to above, for example, cultural historian Robert Darnton freely admits that he "[cannot] see a clear way of distinguishing idiom from individuality," but asserts that "[t]o proceed . . . by first establishing an idiom and then explaining the individual expression [i.e., as David Hackett Fisher proposed doing when selecting a "modal character"] does not seem workable." "We never meet pure idiom," Darnton notes, "[w]e interpret texts."[7]

It would be comforting for our purposes to take Darnton's last statement as gospel—to assert that, since all historical knowledge comes to us by way of textual evidence, there can be no valid unique objections to employing formal autobiography any way we want to—but such an easy assertion would be ill-advised. Yet the ideas of contemporary cultural history do suggest a possible means of minimizing our five objections, even if

we cannot eliminate them altogether. What if we treated the *rhetoric* of a formal autobiography as "historical fact" rather than as its content? Darnton, Dominick LaCapra and the other practitioners of the "new" cultural and intellectual history do have a point: the one thing that we do know exists is the text. Rather than reading a formal autobiography as a documentary account of factual events and judging its dubious veracity accordingly, perhaps we should read it instead as a rhetorically constructed account of the relation of narrated past to narrating present within the life of a particular individual. In line with the foregoing discussion, we may most reliably posit that such accounts often betray their "true" historical information less through their manifest content than through their rhetorical devices, their dialogic relations with the past, and their discernible traces of subjectivity. They also reveal similarly valuable historical traces both through their narrative form and discourse and through their signs of post facto revision via a particular, self-justifying consciousness.[8]

Another way of putting this would be to say that, in order to employ formal autobiographies as historical evidence, we must read them as myth, not fact; as simultaneously personal and tribal myths; as myths not just of the self or the age, but myths of the relation between the two. Consequently, just as each autobiographical myth constitutes a separate historical "fact," any *pattern* of autobiographical mythology—any shared, near-contemporaneous re-imagining of the past that travels across and among autobiographical texts—is a "fact" of paramount historical significance. Such "facts" may be found, not in instances of the same, repeatedly retold anecdote, nor even in multiple accounts of the same "event" from different angles, but rather in the inclusion of similar sets of experiences or patterns of experiences. Viewed in this light, formal autobiographies become most important to the study of history as indications of *projection* and *mood,* of what participants might have thought happened around them and of how they might remember feeling while it was occurring.

A case in point is posed by the numerous memoirs of Americans in Paris in the 1920s. These volumes have proved extraordinarily influential in shaping popular views of the period, even though professional literary and social historians of the era have spent much of their time demonstrating how nonfactual so many of them are. Taken as a whole, such volumes as Sylvia Beach's *Shakespeare and Company* (1956), Morley Callaghan's *That Summer in Paris* (1963), and Kay Boyle's skillful revision (1968) of Robert McAlmon's already classic *Being Geniuses Together* (1938)—not to mention such lesser known but no less striking memoirs as Harold Stearns' *The Street I Know* (1935), Matthew Josephson's *Life Among the Surrealists* (1962), and Gorham Munson's *The Awakening Twenties* (1985)—present a remarkably coherent myth of American writers in the 1920s, a myth commonly designated in popular discourse by the phrase "The Lost Generation."[9]

A full account of the myth of "The Lost Generation" and its relation to the nonfictional and fictional writings of those who participated in its construction and dissemination demands a thorough, book-length study. For the purposes of this essay, however, I would like to suggest the outlines that such a full-length treatment might take by focusing more narrowly on the three formally autobiographical volumes that have proven the most influential in forming popular notions of the period: Malcolm Cowley's *Exile's Return* (1934; 1951); Ernest Hemingway's *A Moveable Feast* (1964); and *The Crack-Up* (1945), a posthumous collection of pieces by and about F. Scott Fitzgerald that was edited by Fitzgerald's old college friend Edmund Wilson.[10]

These three volumes are more responsible than any other nonfictional works for the popular myth of "The Lost Generation." In tracing where this myth came from and how these three writers co-opted it and made it their own, I will attempt to demonstrate how their three nonfictional/nonfactual memoirs provide a valuable, mythic testimony of their own experience of the 1920s. After examining how these three particular tests participate in the construction of this myth, I will end by sketching a theory of the myth's wider cultural implications: implications not only for the relatively insignificant segment of the society that may be legitimately grouped under the rubric of "The Lost Generation," but also for the allegedly "unwritten" mass of American society in this period.

In so doing, I will be "working," as Darnton proposes cultural historians should do, "back and forth between texts and contexts,"[11] although I intend eventually to place the undeniable "fact" of these memoirs' textuality in the foreground of my analysis. As relatively privileged young men who were born just before the turn of the century, Hemingway, Cowley, and Fitzgerald witnessed the birth of modern American politics, culture, and society. In their personal testaments, they tell us about the dawn of a new age in literature, a new age of social and political organization, and the birth of a modern, consumer-oriented mass culture. They speak, however, as writers and mythmakers and not as eyewitnesses for the prosecution or defense. They communicate their true autobiographical selves more through "lies" and "distortions" than "facts," capturing their experience of the early twentieth century more in a borrowed plotline, a string of semes, or a switch in focus or point-of-view than in their manifest eyewitness accounts of Paris, New York, or the Charlestown Prison.

I

The phrase "lost generation" was first employed by the German Expressionist Franz Pfemfert in *Die Aktion* in 1912 and was used extensively in Britain and France in the first years after the war to describe the literal age cohort that had been severely reduced by the fighting of 1914-18.[12] After the publication of *The Sun Also Rises*, however, with its famous paired epigraphs, the term "lost generation" could never again be employed in so broad or international a sense. Today, even if the phrase makes a non-specialist think of Britons or Frenchmen, most likely the images conjured up are of Montparnasse or the Cap d'Antibes rather than of a row of gravestones in Flanders. These are images of presence, not absence. All that is left of the phrase's original connotation is the vague notion that the well-known "disillusionment" of the generation had "something to do with the war." Why? Why did the American version of this symbol become so popular? Why has the 1920s become, in the popular imagination, the decade of the Lost Generation?

First, let us consider the words. "In the slogan," Malcolm Cowley tells us at the beginning of *Exile's Return*, "the noun was more important than the adjective" (*ER*, p. 4). The realization of a shared narrow identity ("generation") was more important than the implied absence ("lost") of an established, culture-wide identity. When Gertrude Stein greets young Ernest Hemingway with the same harsh slogan in "'Une Génération Perdue,'" the third sketch in the published version of *A Moveable Feast,* he offers an almost identical reaction, wondering "about the boy in the garage and if he had ever been hauled in one of those vehicles when they were converted to ambulances." In other words, Ernest[13] feels a common bond with a young man around his own age and in almost the same breath denies the significance of the term "lost generation." What he explicitly denies is the adjective: "I thought that all generations were lost by something," he writes, "and always had been and always would be" (*MF*, p. 30). As for F. Scott Fitzgerald, although he never employed the full term in his public writings, he had been speaking and thinking of "generations" in his writing since his first published novel, with its famous final reference to "a new generation . . . grown up to find all Gods dead, all wars fought, all faiths in man shaken."[14] "[M]y point of vantage," he tells us of this period of his writing in "Early Success," "was the dividing line between the two generations, and there I sat—somewhat self-consciously" (*CU*, p. 87).

Notwithstanding Hemingway's assertion that all generations were "lost by something," it is still worth asking why this "generation" was so aware of itself. If we examine the historical record, we see that the sense of common identity they discovered in age sprang from their demographic uniqueness. As Paula Fass has demonstrated, the years from 1870 to 1930 showed a steady decline in the national birth rate and consequently in the size of the family unit. The early 1920s (the time of Fitzgerald's "younger" generation and Cowley's "youngest" generation) witnessed an unprecedented interest in youth and their "moral situation" precisely because the young segment of the population was steadily declining. "Whereas," Fass observes, "in 1870 there were two persons 24 to 64 years of age to every one 15 to 24 years, there were three older persons to every one youth in 1930."[15]

In other words, the members of the "Lost Generation" felt the full weight of the noun in that slogan precisely because they stood at the beginning of an obviously growing demographic trend. They were the first generation to represent a declining proportion of youth, and that decline would continue throughout the 1920s, the first years of which they certainly dominated. Because of these developments, not only did they become the focus for a great deal of public commentary, they also became the pundits of the era. This is the shrewd truth behind Fitzgerald's comment about his "peculiar vantage point," not to mention the vignettes that dominate the second chapter ("War in Bohemia") of Cowley's narrative. Among the popular arts of the period, from "Bernice Bobs Her Hair" to *Gentlemen Prefer Blondes* and from *Flaming Youth* (both novel and film) to *The Sun Also Rises,* the works that focused on "youth" or "generation" were inevitably engaged in the dramatization of a popular type.

To be sure, "youth" had started being a prominent topic of American writing before the war, just as "The American girl" had been a popular topic for American writing throughout the latter half of the nineteenth century. But what distinguished these postwar writings from prewar texts by Booth Tarkington and others was the sense, initiated by the publication of *This Side of Paradise* (and books like it) and driven home by the publication of *The Sun Also Rises* (and its many literary imitators) that "youth" was now speaking for itself. In their memoirs of the 1920s, both Cowley and Fitzgerald directly address the issue of what it meant to be "young" then, while Hemingway rather noticeably ignores it, save for the instance quoted above. But all three authors carry their youth like a badge of honor. Only Cowley is not wholly wistful about it. By 1951 he could characterize the 1920s as "easy, quick, adventurous . . . [and] good to be young in," all the while insisting that "on coming out of [them] one felt a sense of relief" (*ER*, p. 309).

So, according to their autobiographical testimony, the word "generation" had powerful significance for these three writers and their contemporaries almost from the moment they came of age. "Lost," however, came later. Because of the low rate of mortality among American soldiers in the war (relative to European casualties), it is difficult to find any usage of the term "lost generation" in America before 1926, the year of Hemingway's celebrated first novel. After that point, as Cowley notes, the phrase became a fetish, even "a craze—young men tried to get as imperturbably drunk as the hero, young women of good families took a succession of lovers in the same heartbroken fashion" (*ER*, p. 3). The phrase had stuck and finally made the moral baggage of the term "younger generation" explicit. Such young men and women were "lost"—they had lost their moral bearings.

In essence, what Hemingway had done was to give an Anglo-European name ("lost generation") to an American phenomenon (the rise of a noticeable and noticeably anti-traditionalist youth cohort), but that was not the end of the story. The phrase "lost generation," like any mythic signifier, contains many meanings. If Cowley's report about the reception of Hemingway's novel and its

paired epigraphs may be believed, then a second shift in dominant meaning occurred between 1926 (when the term was first applied in its moral/American sense) and 1931 (when both Fitzgerald and Cowley began their cultural and ideological inquiries into the recent past). In the late 1920s, the term "lost generation," captured for Americans by Hemingway, shifted from a moral to a cultural connotation. In the process of moving from "a lost generation" at the opening of Hemingway's novel to "the lost generation" on the first page of Cowley's narrative of ideas, the phenomenon of loss came to mean less "moral looseness" and more "deracination." The suggestion of deracination was there in *The Sun Also Rises,* to be sure, but it was overpowered by the issue of problematic morality among the exiles.

By the time Cowley sat down to write the first installments of the serialized text of *Exile's Return* in the spring of 1931, and Fitzgerald "Echoes of the Jazz Age" later that summer, there was no longer any question of blaming the members of this generation for their loss, as there had been in the earlier moral formulation. Now there was the alternative notion that these men and women were victims of history. The term had undergone a subtle change in the years surrounding the apocalyptically perceived Wall Street Crash, and in so doing it had also acquired an implicit mythic narrative as well. Writing to Max Perkins in May of 1931, Fitzgerald declared that the Jazz Age was now "over." It had "extended," Fitzgerald wrote, "from the suppression of the riots on May Day 1919 to the crash of the stock market in 1929—almost exactly one decade."[16] As the essay that grew out of these comments subsequently demonstrated, Fitzgerald saw the historical narrative of that decade chiefly as the transit of his own generation from ebullience to dissipation. This even influenced him to the extent of placing the zenith of the decade's characteristic behavior as early as 1922. "That was the peak of the younger generation," he wrote, "for though the Jazz Age continued, it became less and less an affair of youth . . . like a children's party taken over by the elders" (*CU*, p. 15).

Even in his prior, off-the-cuff assertion to Perkins, the mythic narrative that Fitzgerald perceived in the decade and presented in his auto-biographical writings had a clear protagonist (his own generation), a clear beginning (the heady days after the War), and a very clear end (the despondent time just after the Crash)—but the middle stretches of that mythic narrative remained oddly murky. In general, this may be said of Cowley's and Hemingway's historical/autobiographical narratives as well. The so-called "Lost Generation" is absent from our three texts during the middle years of the decade. What we find in the autobiographical writings of Hemingway, Cowley, and Fitzgerald are thick descriptions of the generation in the early 1920s (visions of heady youth) and then in the late 1920s (images of doom and self-destruction). We very seldom see the transformation between these two stages, the necessary intermediary stage between honest enjoyment and self-indulgence. The reasons for Ernest's infidelity in *A Moveable Feast,* for example, are implied, not stated; we see Kenneth Burke at the beginning of *Exile's Return* and Harry Crosby at the end but are only given a suggestion as to how Malcolm Cowley is a link between these two icons; F. Scott Fitzgerald describes both his early success and his crack-up a number of times in Edmund Wilson's posthumous collection), but he never shows us the connections between these two phases of his life.

When any of these three authors speaks of the events of the mid-1920s, he widens the story so that he need not dwell on its more personal elements. In the central passage of these tales, the individual and group centers of generational consciousness to which we have grown accustomed vanish for the middle stretches of the decade, leaving us to investigate a more widely conceived version of the postwar period than any we have seen in the narrative so far. Thus the middle third of *A Moveable Feast* depicts the world of literary memoir and the celebrated cafés; this world provides the implied causal link between Ernest the devoted husband and Ernest the adulterer. Likewise, the years between *Broom* and the Crash pass in *Exile's Return* in a blurred summary of "Mass Production, Babbittry, [and] Our Business Civilization" (*ER,* p. 217), which is, one supposes, intended to explain why poets like Hart Crane and Harry Crosby killed themselves. And it is in the middle of "Echoes of the Jazz Age" that Fitzgerald provides his frequently cited analysis of popular films and novels, leaving aside for the moment his crucial group protagonist of rich young people. That, Fitzgerald's text almost suggests, is how they got from the productive atmosphere of postwar New York to the seductive surroundings of the Cap d'Antibes.

What we have in each of these three formal autobiographies, then, is a journey from the initial realization of "generation" to the eventual realization of "lost." What is significant about this symbolic pattern is that in all three cases we must pass through an area of wider focus (Modernist writers, business civilization, popular culture) in order to get from the noun to the adjective that is supposed to modify or describe it. The journey out in all three narratives begins with the realization of unique identity ("generation"). In the separate texts, this is signified by the act of writing the first good story ("A Good Café on the Place St.-Michel" in *A Moveable Feast*); the eye-opening experience of the war and Greenwich Village ("Mansions in the Air" and "War in Bohemia" in *Exile's Return*); and the liberating *Zeitgeist* of prewar college and postwar New York (described in three different forms in Fitzgerald's "Echoes of the Jazz Age," "My Lost City," and "Early Success"). This feeling of uniqueness lasts a while and then fades, as it becomes apparent that what is unique about the generation is what they lack rather than what they possess. This is the final realization of "lost," the realization of the late 1920s, whose two separate stages we have already examined. To admit one was "lost" was to wish to be "found," and so

the early 1930s were a sort of homecoming, as Cowley contends in *Exile's Return,* just as the early part of the decade was a sort of departure.

Cowley articulates this perception of a real-life arrival/departure motif even better in the Epilogue to the second edition of his memoirs when he notes, on rereading them seventeen years after their initial composition, that their story "seems to follow the old pattern of alienation and reintegration, or departure and return, that is repeated in scores of European myths . . ." (*ER,* p. 289). What it follows—what all three texts follow, in fact—is Joseph Campbell's famous outline of the "protomyth," the general narrative line of mythic adventure that cuts across most of the world's cultures, especially post-agricultural ones.[17] But what these three historical autobiographers were trying to do was slightly more sophisticated than a run-of-the-mill, Eliotesque variation on the "blighted land"/"Holy Grail" theme. By merging their own personal histories with those of the perceived "generation," they were telling two mythic narratives (a personal story and a generational story) by blending them into a third mythic narrative (a "representative" story of "the lost generation").

This implied heroic narrative explains a number of stylistic and tropical peculiarities that traverse the three texts. For one thing, there is the matter of shifting personification, particularly in the writings of Cowley and Fitzgerald. In the first chapter of *Exile's Return,* for example, the antecedent of the first person plural shifts from each subsection to the next: from the contemporary grouping of Cowley and his dialogically inscribed reader(s) in "Blue Juniata"; to the historical grouping of Malcolm and his teenage friends in "Big-Town High School"; to just Malcolm and young Kenneth Burke in "Apprentice of the Arts"; to anyone who attended college in the prewar period in "American College, 1916"; to all young Americans who served in noncombatant roles in the war in "Ambulance Service." Each shift in antecedent is accomplished through a transitional excursion into either the cool, historical third person plural or the direct, anecdotal first person singular. The ambiguous, generational, active "we" is constantly mediating between these two passive antecedent poles; the potential polysemy of the first person plural thus makes it the perfect pronoun for the protagonist of a text that attempts to merge public history and personal memoir. In reality, almost no single individual had the precise set of historical experiences attributed to this protean first person plural protagonist—not even Malcolm Cowley.

Beyond this implicit, generational narrative, there are also the symbolic activities ("dissipation," "exile," "self-destruction," and "youth") that we normally associate with that grouping. It should not surprise us that these symbolic activities help reinforce the larger narrative pattern that we have already uncovered. An activity like alcoholic consumption, as it is used in these stories, can convey the shift in mood from honest enjoyment in the former part of the decade to pure self-indulgence in the latter phase, merely by its impenetrable symbolism; the versatility of drunkenness as a seme for the era is that it may be employed as either a seme of Joy or a seme of Dissipation depending on the context in which it is placed. Like Chanel's famous little black dress, it goes with everything: immaturity, exhilaration, fanciful visions, obsessive behavior, sudden violence, and the depths of despondency. Like the shifting antecedent of the personal pronoun, the pure signifier of alcoholic consumption allows these three authors to tell a personal, metaphorical "story" about public, metonymical "history." In other words, the point of the prominence of alcohol in "A Good Café on the Place St.-Michel" or "Echoes of the Jazz Age" or Cowley's "Significant Gesture" is not to convey the specious "fact" that everyone drank their way through the 1920s, but rather to make readers understand that the closest group of analogous experiences to the feeling of living through the period are the variety of ways that one can react to alcohol.

Like the symbolic field of alcoholic consumption, the words, types, experiences, and settings (Paris, the Riviera, and New York City) that we commonly associate with Hemingway, Fitzgerald and Cowley belong to the domain of "narrative truth" that Donald Spence describes, rather than to the parallel domain that he delineates as "historical fact." Taken as a whole, all these common mythic tropes constitute the symbolic field of "the Lost Generation" and add up to a common historical "mood" evoked through constant incantation and repetition of tropes. This "mood" is the chief historical "meaning" conveyed by all these stories—in the sense that Spence speaks of "meaning" intertwined with "interpretation"—whether they emphasize youth (like Hemingway), cooptation (like Cowley), or middle-aged generativity (like Fitzgerald). In all the stories, the mood is the message; and the message is true, whether or not "the facts" are verifiable.[18]

In many ways, the transit of the phrase "the Lost Generation," like that of the mythic symbol and mythic narrative it embodies, reflects this gradual shift in mood. So does the possibly erroneous etymology that Fitzgerald traces early in "Echoes of the Jazz Age":

> The word jazz in its progress toward respectability has meant first sex, then dancing, then music. It is associated with a state of nervous stimulation, not unlike that of big cities behind the lines in a war (*CU*, p. 16).

As parochial as this passage might seem as a factual description of 1920s popular culture (especially popular music),[19] it is a shrewd encapsulation of the mythic narrative of the Lost Generation: from sex to dancing to music and on; from youthful exuberance to group activity to public performance and stylization. Writing in the spring and summer of 1931, this was how both Fitzgerald and Cowley saw their mythic journeys of the previous decade—as a jerky "progress toward respectability." Looking back on the same period from the

vantage point of the late 1950s, even willful Ernest Hemingway probably would not have disagreed.

II

We could carry our mythic reading of these three texts farther still, but the general outlines of such a reading have been sufficiently established. In reading *Exile's Return, A Moveable Feast,* and the Fitzgerald essays in *The Crack-Up* as literary and mythic rather than documentary texts, we have discovered a number of things about their authors' perception of how and why America changed during the 1920s; as well as about their perceptions of their own relation, both to that perceived change and to contemporary Americans of similar ages, backgrounds, and interests. Most important, we have discovered that all three authors shared a common notion of the narrative transit of the 1920s, the tripartite structure that I have outlined above.

Now all this is very interesting, but is it historically valuable? After all, we can dismiss objections as to literariness by scrutinizing a text's rhetoric rather than its disputable and possibly even irrecoverable referent; we can read a narrative's linear shape as a form of hypothesis and not as fact; we can be fully alert to textual traces of self-justifying consciousness and the relation of narrated past to narrating present (two topics I have not had sufficient time to treat in their necessary depth here)—but, after all that, we are still left with the most nagging objection of all: putative representativeness. Why these three lives? Even if we had the time to perform the same sort of analysis for the three dozen or so other formal autobiographies of "The Lost Generation," what would that tell us in the end? Simply what three dozen people who had more education, time, and money than they knew what to do with *thought* was going on in the 1920s? Where's the historical value in that?

We may find a suggestion of an answer to this question in the extratextual resonances of several topics raised and dropped earlier in our analysis. For example, we theorized that what the myth of the Lost Generation most clearly stood for was a sharply demarcated narrative transit of mood: from joy to dissipation; from "generation" to "lost." It is in this purely affective sense—in the idea that the decade began with exhilaration and ended in deflation—that our three autobiographical texts may be able to lay their most convincing claims to representativeness.

According to many contemporary observers, technological innovation and the expansion of the consumer-oriented aspects of the economy combined to make the earlier part of the 1920s particularly memorable for most Americans. In such influential works as *Middletown* (1929) and *Only Yesterday* (1931), authors like Robert and Helen Lynd and Frederick Lewis Allen observed that the pace of life in these years strongly reflected the sort of "nervous energy" that Fitzgerald implicitly ascribed to the era in his fiction and would subsequently describe explicitly in the essays collected in *The Crack-Up*. In *Middletown,* the Lynds characterized the 1920s in passing as "[a] period of rapidly changing standards of living, irregular employment . . . [and] increasing isolation and mobility of the individual family. . . . " Inevitably, Allen subscribed to a similar but less restrained version of this view of the early 1920s as a nexus of volatile "modernizing" forces. The legendary first chapter of *Only Yesterday*—published, like "Echoes of the Jazz Age" and the first fragments of Cowley's autobiographical narrative, in the fall of 1931—details a veritable explosion of brand-new consumer goods and faddish concerns (e.g., short skirts, bobbed hair, rouge, beauty parlors, vitamins, tabloids, radio, sound movies, and crossword puzzles), all of which owe their first significant period of popularity to the years between 1919 and 1929.[20]

We are, of course, familiar with these aspects of the decade. They are the ones featured by Cowley and, more notably, Fitzgerald, in those "crowded" middle sections of their narrative lines. Symbolically, then, the Lynds' "rapid changes" and Allen's "faddishness" supply us with the missing narrative link between *Broom* and Harry Crosby in *Exile's Return,* and between New York City and the Cap d'Antibes in "Echoes of the Jazz Age." The implications of the covert plotline of *A Moveable Feast* are even more significant in this regard: by the same token, this covert plotline would seem to suggest that the commercialization and commodification of literary modernism (via the café set and the state apparatus of publishing) is the true implicit cause of Ernest's seemingly unseen transformation. Narrative logic dictates that this blurring of aesthetic and commercial cultures implicitly transforms Ernest the sincere young man into Ernest the two-timing weasel.

One could object that contemporaneous sociological and journalistic accounts like those offered in *Middletown* and *Only Yesterday* are no more immune to charges of privilege and exclusivity than are the autobiographical narratives of Hemingway, Cowley, and Fitzgerald. Indeed, a highly convincing case might be made for the position that the Lynds and Allen, as well as such other postwar journalists and intellectuals as Charles and Mary Beard, Walter Lippmann, Joseph Wood Krutch, and Charles Merz, played as large a role in "creating" the mythic 1920s as did the three authors featured here. Intellectual historian John Thomas has recently taken this argument even farther, holding that the "apocalypse" of the 1929 Crash had been heralded throughout by preceding decade by intellectuals like Lewis Mumford and Van Wyck Brooks. To a great extent, the post-Crash myth of the 1920s was thus "built into" the historical experience of the 1920s through precisely the sort of prior narrative projection and expectation that David Carr has theorized inheres to all historical events. If this is true, though, then the myth sketched above may be only a myth of the intelligentsia, not of the American people at large.[21]

However, we need not rely solely on contemporaneous accounts for validation. The attention of such subsequent

historians of the period as William E. Leuchtenberg, Roland Marchand, George Marsden, Lary May, George Mowry, Robert Sklar, and Warren Susman has been equally drawn to precisely these sorts of "mass-cultural" developments. For such historians, those "middle years," in which "nothing happened" to Ernest, Malcolm, and Scott, often loom as the most important years of the decade, containing as they do such crucial events as the passage of the immigration restriction act and a notable surge of religious fundamentalism that came to its well-publicized climax in the Scopes trial. If we widen the scope by just one year at either end, we encounter the emergence of Babe Ruth at the beginning of the decade and the production of the last Model T at the end. If we add the Lindbergh flight and the popular novels, films, and leisure crazes that Fitzgerald mentions, we are talking about perhaps the first decade in American history in which groups and not individuals dominated public discourse.[22]

Everywhere you turned in the mid-1920s, you encountered another group: movie audiences, target audiences for advertising, immigrants, motorists, sports fanatics, and religious zealots. In earlier ages one could speak of particular groups that focused the public's attention (farmers, speculators, workers, abolitionists, etc.) but in the 1920s it sometimes seemed that there had never before been so many distinct, overlapping groups, never so many all at once. One could argue that the 1920s was less an age of group identity than of hero worship— after all, it was this decade that essentially created the parallel phenomena of the modern movie star and the modern sports hero—but as both May and Susman show in their parallel analyses of these phenomena, these were less cults of exemplary, ideal heroism (in which the celebrity was held up as a distant object of love and adoration) than cults of personality and identification (in which the celebrity's public identity was seen as an extension of the fan's sense of self). In both cases, as in most mass cultural phenomena and epiphenomena of the 1920s, it was the cult that drove its object, and not the other way around.[23]

The ultimate cultural significance of the myth of the Lost Generation may lie in this phenomenon of pervasive attention to group activity that is so characteristic of the factual 1920s. In their journey from joy to dissipation, from the new realization of uniqueness ("generation") to the later realization of diminished commonality ("lost"), the Lost Generation turned its attention to the culture at large, just as the attention of American popular culture turned away from this "youngest generation" after the first years of the decade. In noting other people's fads and quirks in those impersonal middle sections of their narratives, Hemingway, Cowley, and Fitzgerald (as well as Ernest, Malcolm, and Scott) all come to realize by implication their own status as "types," and thus discard the bad, immature part of their youthful pride and retain the good part, the mature sense of mollified identity. In this way, Ernest moves from the uncertain journalist of "Miss Stein Instructs" to the self-important author of "Birth of a New School" to the humbled, "tamed" novelist of "There Is Never Any End to Paris." So too does Malcolm's generational "we" move from deracinated young men to individualistic purveyors of significant gestures to the resigned Americans that wake up ready for work on "New Year's Day." Both protagonists are, in their turn, following the historical pattern posed by F. Scott Fitzgerald—from success to celebrity to the comeuppance of crack-up.

In other words, the signified journey of all these narratives is from the false perception of cultural homogeneity through an illusive sense of cultural uniqueness to a renewed commitment to cultural pluralism. This is the journey that so many cohorts of Americans made in the crowded years between the two World Wars, the same transformation that Susman alludes to when he speaks of a shift from an overwhelming interest in "civilization" in the 1920s to an almost mystical belief in "community" in the 1930s. It is also the transition, which Walter Benn Michaels has recently noted in this period, away from the polarities of political identity and biological identity toward the radical ambiguity of cultural identity, a "model" that, as Michaels notes, "has turned out to be—for better or worse—the greatest cultural contribution of the classic American literature of the '20s."[24]

Throughout the decade following World War I, this pattern was repeated over and over in American cultural life: first, a number of individuals discovered they had something in common (an interest in mah johng, a type of product they all liked to buy, or an aesthetic philosophy that seemed tempting at the moment). Then, the group was suddenly "discovered" by the culture at large and analyzed at length (by feature journalists, by advertising agency employees, or by pundits in the literary reviews). Finally, the group seemed to burn itself out, but its residue was added to the larger picture (of game players, consumers, or American writers). This cycle of discovery, analysis, and dissipation played itself out hundreds of times over the course of the decade. The Lost Generation was just one example of this phenomenon; miniature golf was another.

III

Even after augmenting our analysis with more conventionally derived historical information, however, the issues examined in the beginning of this essay still nag. Never wholly dissolved, our five objections persist; suggesting that, no matter how architectonic a picture we may construct of the period, we are still begging the larger historiographical question. Even considering this newly uncovered resonance between wider American cultural developments of the 1920s and the narrower myth of the Lost Generation, we must still ask whether our reconstituted knowledge of these three (textualized) lives contributes anything new and valuable to our knowledge of America in the 1920s. Have we simply discovered three mythically modal characters, whose lives recapitulate a symbolic pattern already discovered elsewhere in the period? Or have we instead reversed this process, seeking out the requisite previously established historical knowledge that validates our initial interest but does so only after the fact?

As I suggested above, there are no easy answers to these sorts of questions. The key issues—subjectivity vs. objectivity, priority of data vs. priority of methodology, narrativity vs. analysis, historical events vs. historical experience—will never be sufficiently established for anyone's purposes, certainly not for ours.

Yet, despite all these doubts, the perception of resonance persists. "The Younger/Youngest/Lost Generation" did experience that three-part cycle, just like so many of the other publicly identified "groups" of the 1920s. The entire decade may have been, as literary critic Walter Benn Michaels and historian George Marsden have both suggested, an "immigrant experience" for all Americans, even those whose families had arrived on the *Mayflower* and the *Arbella*: in the 1920s, they "arrived," like young Malcolm Cowley, in an America they did not recognize. Like Michaels' Native Americans and Marsden's fundamentalists, the Lost Generation enjoyed a highly public moment of simultaneous elevation and dissipation in the 1920s, with both processes firmly anchored in their sense of cultural uniqueness. Culturally constructed as admirable Other, they rose to prominence, only to discover in the end that they were just another mass media fad.

If "historical experience" exists, and if it is possible for subsequent scholars to recover it, then it exists in resonances such as these; in the sorts of shared patterns of textually inscribed subjective experience, as well as objectively demonstrable events and demography, that New Historicist literary critics like Stephen Greenblatt and Louis Montrose have dubbed "the poetics of culture." As Raymond Williams suggested nearly a quarter of a century ago, it is not at all uncommon for "a unique life, in a place and a time, [to speak] from its own uniqueness and yet [to speak] a common experience." In other words, the elements of this sort of cultural discourse—what we have analyzed here as the metaphors and mythic narratives of historical experience—often transcend the economic and sociological categories used to classify the writers who produced them. Such categories are occasionally more suited to the study of "historical events" than to the parallel study of "historical experience." After all, if it is by no means certain that canonical writers possessed greater access to "representative" historical experience of their own time, then it is similarly unproven that they possessed *less* access to it. As not only Williams but most New Historicists would contend, it may very well be that these common metaphors and narrative patterns point to larger historical shifts, which transcend such material categories and point to "structural" changes that traverse the superstructures of modern society.[25]

In the end, there is no such thing as a "representative," "typical," or "modal" man or woman in a given historical period. There are only millions of individuals, many of them undocumented, most of them irrecoverable. Given those odds, "historical experience" may prove, in practice, to be as much of a myth as "the Lost Generation." But if it is not a myth, and if we seek to know what a given historical period like the 1920s "felt like while it was happening," then we must recover each of the mythic life-stories of that period, one by one, from low to high, from unfortunately forgotten to seemingly well-known. Once we have gathered these myths, we must measure them against each other, in the hopes of discovering palpable, resonant, historically significant patterns.

NOTES

[1] In speaking of "the formal autobiography," I seek to distinguish, à la Marc Bloch, between those autobiographical texts clearly intended for a public and frequently posterior audience, hereafter "formal autobiographies"; and those eventually published texts that were originally intended for more private purposes. (Postmodernist critics should note that my use of the word "formal" is not to be considered identical to current usage of the word "performative." For what it's worth, I consider all texts performative.)

[2] Allan Nevins, "The Autobiography," collected in *Allan Nevins on History,* compiled and introduced by Ray Allen Billington (New York: Scribners, 1975), 237-38. For a good example of Nevins' earlier praise of the genre, see Nevins, *The Gateway to History* (1938; rept. New York: D. Appleton & Century, 1938), 323.

[3] G. M. Young, *Victorian England: Portrait of an Age* (1936; rept. London: Oxford University Press, 1960), vi. On the idea of "historical experience," also see: Peter Gay, General Introduction to *The Bourgeois Experience from Victoria to Freud,* in Gay, *Education of the Senses* (New York: Oxford University Press, 1984), esp. pp. 9-16; Bernard Bailyn, "The Challenge of Modern Historiography," *American Historical Review,* 87 (1982), 1-24, esp. pp. 18-22; and Raymond Williams, *The English Novel from Dickens to Lawrence* (London: Hogarth Press, 1984), 185-92.

[4] David Hackett Fisher, "The Braided Narrative: Substance and Form in Social History," in Angus Fletcher, ed., *The Literature of Fact: Selected Papers from the English Institute* (New York: Columbia University Press, 1976), esp. 123-26; and David Levin, *In Defense of Historical Literature: Essays on American History, Autobiography, Drama, and Fiction* (New York: Hill & Wang, 1967), esp. Chs. 2 and 3. On these issues and their relation to the current vogue of cultural history discussed below, cf. Dominick LaCapra, "Is Everyone a Mentalité Case?" in *History and Criticism* (Ithaca: Cornell University Press, 1985), 71-94.

[5] Michael Oakeshott, "Historical Continuity and Casual Analysis," collected in William H. Dray, ed., *Philosophical Analysis in History* (New York: Harper & Row,

1966), 207. On this point, also see the essays by Carl Hempel and Alan Donagan in Dray's anthology, as well as J. H. Hexter, "The Rhetoric of History," in *The Rhetoric of History* (Bloomington: Indiana University Press, 1971), 15-76.

[6] Marc Bloch, *The Historian's Craft,* tr. Peter Putnam (New York: Vintage Books, 1953), 61, 62. For further illustrative examples of these objections, see: Nevins, *Gateway,* 318-32; R. G. Collingwood, *The Idea of History* (1946; rept. London: Oxford University Press, 1956), 295-96; and E. H. Carr, *What Is History?* (New York: Vintage Books, 1961), 16-20.

[7] Robert Darnton, *The Great Cat Massacre and Other Episodes in French Cultural History* (1984; rept. New York: Vintage Books, 1985), 262. For a full account of the complicated origins of these recent movements, see Lynn Hunt, "Introduction: History, Culture, and Text," in Hunt, ed., *The New Cultural History* (Berkeley: University of California Press, 1989), 1-22.

[8] For LaCapra's ideas on the historical uses of rhetorical analysis, see "Rhetoric and History," in *History and Criticism,* 15-44; and *History, Politics, and the Novel* (Ithaca: Cornell University Press, 1987), passim.

[9] Sylvia Beach, *Shakespeare and Company* (New York: Harcourt, Brace, 1956); Morley Callaghan, *That Summer in Paris* (New York: Coward, McCann, 1963); Robert McAlmon and Kay Boyle, *Being Geniuses Together* (1968; rept. San Francisco: North Point Press, 1984); Harold Stearns, *The Street I Know* (New York: Furman, 1935); Matthew Josephson, *Life Among the Surrealists* (New York: Holt, 1962); and Gorham Munson, *The Awakening Twenties* (Baton Rouge: Louisiana State University Press, 1985).

[10] Malcolm Cowley, *Exile's Return* 2nd edn. (1934; rept. New York: Viking Press, 1951); Ernest Hemingway, *A Moveable Feast* (New York: Scribners, 1964); and F. Scott Fitzgerald, *The Crack-Up,* ed. Edmund Wilson (New York: New Directions, 1945). These texts will hereafter be cited parenthetically within the text as *ER, MF,* and *CU,* respectively.

For more on the problematic state of these three texts, and how it has affected several of my readings, see Marc Dolan, "'True Stories' of 'The Lost Generation': An Exploration of Narrative Truth and Literary Meaning in Three Memoirs of the Lost Generation" (Ph.D. thesis, Harvard University, 1988), 171-72, 199-206, 282-93.

[11] Darnton, 262.

[12] On this general point, see Robert Wohl, *The Generation of 1914* (Cambridge, MA: Harvard University Press, 1979), passim. The translation of the phrase "lost generation" from Pfemfert's *Aktion* article of 11 December 1912 is Wohl's (p. 45).

[13] To avoid confusion, I have adopted the device throughout this essay of referring to protagonists by their given names and authors by their surnames. Thus, in this case, *A Moveable Feast* is a book by "Hemingway" about "Ernest."

[14] Fitzgerald, *This Side of Paradise* (New York: Scribner's, 1920), 282.

[15] Paula Fass, *The Damned and the Beautiful* (New York: Oxford University Press, 1977), 58.

[16] Fitzgerald to Maxwell Perkins, [ca. 15 May 1931], in John Kuehl and Jackson R. Bryer, eds., *Dear Scott/Dear Max* (New York: Scribners, 1971), 171.

[17] The classic summary of the "protomyth" is in Campbell, *The Hero with a Thousand Faces* (Princeton: Princeton University Press, 1949), 245-46. For the extent to which temporal and regional variations can affect its narrative contours, see also Campbell, *The Masks of God,* 4 vols. (New York: Viking Press, 1959-69); and Campbell, *Historical Atlas of World Mythology,* 5 vols. (New York: Harper & Row, 1988-89).

[18] It should be noted that all three authors provide their readers with explicit warnings that their texts should not be taken at face value. The most blatant of these is Hemingway's posthumously edited remark, in the Preface to the published edition of *A Moveable Feast,* that "If the reader prefers, this book may be regarded as fiction" (*MF,* p. ix). The author is even blunter in most of the surviving manuscript drafts of this passage, simply writing "This book is fiction" and leaving it at that. Less overt but no less significant are Fitzgerald's admission that "it all seems rosy and romantic" in his account of the period (*CU,* p. 22), as well as Cowley's climactic invocation in the revised text of *Exile's Return* of "the children in Grimm's fairy tales" (*ER,* p. 288) as analogues to his protagonists.

On "narrative truth" vs. "historical truth," see in particular Donald Spence, *Narrative Truth and Historical Truth* (New York: W. W. Norton, 1982), 292 and passim.

[19] See, for example, LeRoi Jones, *Blues People* (New York: William Morrow & Co., 1963), Chs. 6-10; and Gunther Schuller, *Early Jazz: Its Roots and Musical Development* (New York: Oxford University Press, 1968), passim.

[20] Robert and Helen Lynd, *Middletown* (New York: Harcourt, Brace, & World, 1929), 125; Frederick Lewis Allen, *Only Yesterday* (New York: Harper's, 1931), Ch. 1.

[21] Charles and Mary Beard, *The Rise of American Civilization* (New York: Macmillan, 1927), 2 vols; Joseph Wood Krutch, *The Modern Temper* (New York: Harcourt, Brace, & World, 1929); Walter Lippman, *A Preface to Morals* (New York: Macmillan, 1929); and Charles Merz, *The Dry Decade* (New York: Doubleday, Doran, 1931).

For Thomas' argument, see "The Uses of Catastrophism: Lewis Mumford, Vernon L. Parrington, Van Wyck Brooks, and the End of American Regionalism," *American Quarterly,* 42 (1990), 223-51.

[22] On these points, see: Ellis W. Hawley, *The Great War and the Search for a Modern Order* (New York: St. Martin's, 1979), Chs. 4-9; John Higham, *Strangers in the Land,* 2nd edn. (1955; rept. New York: Atheneum, 1963), Chs. 10 & 11; William E. Leuchtenberg, *The Perils of Prosperity* (Chicago: University of Chicago Press, 1958), Ch. XI; Roland Marchand, *Advertising the American Dream* (Berkeley: University of California Press, 1985), passim; George M. Marsden, *Fundamentalism and American Culture* (New York: Oxford University Press, 1980), passim; Lary May, *Screening Out the Past* (New York: Oxford University Press, 1980), Chs. 6-8; George E. Mowry, *The Urban Nation* (New York: Hill & Wang, 1965), Ch. 1; Robert Sklar, *Movie-Made America* (New York: Random House, 1975), Part II; and Warren Susman, *Culture As History* (New York: Pantheon, 1984), passim.

[23] For these specific issues, see Susman, "Culture Heroes: Ford, Barton, Ruth," in *Culture,* 122-49; and May, Ch. 5.

[24] Walter Benn Michaels, "The Vanishing American," *American Literary History,* 2 (1990), 238. For Susman's interpretation of the interwar years, see the essays in Part III of *Culture,* especially "Culture and Civilization: The Nineteen Twenties," "The Culture of the Thirties," and "Culture and Commitment," pp. 105-21 and 150-210.

[25] Stephen Greenblatt, "Towards a Poetics of Culture" and Louis A. Montrose, "Professing the Renaissance: The Poetics and Politics of Culture," both in H. Aram Veeser, ed., *The New Historicism* (New York: Routledge, 1989), 1-36; Williams, *Novel,* 192.

Lynn Z. Bloom

SOURCE: "Gertrude Is Alice Is Everybody: Innovation and Point of View in Gertrude Stein's Autobiographies," in *Twentieth Century Literature,* Vol. 24, No. 1, Spring, 1978, pp. 81-93.

[*In the following essay, Bloom focuses on Stein's innovative use of point of view in* The Autobiography of Alice B. Toklas.]

Gertrude Stein's major innovations as an autobiographer pertain to the creation of the alleged autobiography of another person to tell the story of the author's own life. Related to this are her variations on three major uses of point of view, to perform egotistical, interpretive, and objective functions within the autobiography.

Let us consider the autobiographical persona first.

> About six weeks ago Gertrude Stein said, it does not look to me as if you [Alice B. Toklas] were ever going to write that autobiography. You know what I am going to do. I am going to write it for you. I am going to write it as simply as Defoe did the autobiography of Robinson Crusoe. And she has and this is it.[1]

As an epilogue for *The Autobiography of Alice B. Toklas,* this passage, which illustrates a number of Gertrude Stein's innovations as an autobiographer, is *fitting* but *misleading.* Defoe, of course, created a fictitious character, Robinson Crusoe. Then, through Crusoe's alleged words, Defoe created and manipulated situations, language, and interpretations to suit his own authorial aims. For the purposes of the first volume of Gertrude Stein's own autobiography, *The Autobiography of Alice B. Toklas,* Alice B. Toklas is no more of an independently functioning person than is Robinson Crusoe.

This is true even though, unlike Robinson Crusoe, Alice Toklas not only read but typed the manuscript and provided occasional corrections, interpretations, and cancellations.[2] Among the most significant of her editings was her refusal to be made to proclaim enthusiasm for *The Making of Americans:* "She cancelled the italicized phrases in the following . . . : 'Mildred was very fond of Gertrude Stein and took a deep interest in the book's ending *and so did I.* It was over a thousand pages long and I was typewriting it *and I enjoyed every minute of it.'*"[3] Yet, to a large extent, Alice B. Toklas functions throughout the *Autobiography,* if not as the ventriloquist's dummy, then certainly as the ventriloquist's smart-ie, but as the ventriloquist's versatile tool nevertheless, skillfully performing a myriad of functions essential to the work's success.

Narration of one's own autobiography through the persona of the individual about whom the biography was supposedly written is, to the best of my knowledge of autobiographies in English, completely innovative and utterly unique. By the very nature of its form, autobiography-by-*Doppelgänger* veritably precludes repetition or imitation. The wit intrinsic in the initial endeavor becomes a joke progressively more stale with each repetition, guaranteed to annoy the readers of successive works, even though they are in the joke because they are cozily in league with the author, who has made the *real* subject of the autobiography unmistakable from the third page on.[4] Imagine the third volume of Stein's autobiography, *Wars I Have Seen,* rewritten as *Wars Alice B. Toklas Has Seen!* Once is genius; twice is gimmickry; thrice is boredom. The form itself is almost self-destructing.

Let us see why this is so, for the form has a number of advantages both literary and autobiographical which should surely have tempted imitators if the imitations were feasible.

In conventional autobiographies the form is usually quite commonplace—either a chronological or a topical presentation of its author's life. In these numerous instances, the reader's familiarity with the form breeds indifference or oblivion to it. As a result, he is much more likely to concentrate on the content and perhaps on the style.

Such cannot be the case when the form is so compellingly unique. It obliges attention, which is to Stein's advantage, for her skill and innovative craftsmanship warrant notice. The reader wonders what Gertrude will have Alice will have Gertrude say or do next; what Alice will reply; how Gertrude will react in this dialogue spoken by a monologist.

This unique form provides a persona—real or not (even though Toklas is, of course, a real person independent of the *Autobiography*)—to express the real Gertrude Stein's point of view. It allows the author much greater latitude of expression than she might have had if she'd been speaking in the first person, for she has two people speaking for one. Sutherland observes that Stein used

> as a sounding board her companion. . . . It has been said that the writing takes on very much Miss Toklas' conversational style, and while this is true the style is still a variant of Miss Stein's conversational style, for she had about the same way with an anecdote or a sly observation in talking as Miss Toklas has. . . . it is part of the miracle of this little scheme of objectification that she could by way of imitating Miss Toklas put in writing something of her own beautiful conversation. So that, aside from making a real present of her past, she re-created a figure of herself, established an identity, a twin. . . . [5]

This ventriloquistic persona performs a number of functions which may be grouped into three major categories with several subtle variations on each: the egotistical, the interpretive, and the objective. These overlap and blend to produce a work far more interesting than one without such variety would be. One of the most important aspects of the *egotistical function* is to *disarm* or *distract* the reader from the egotism inherent in conventional autobiography. By consistently employing "Gertrude Stein" or "Miss Stein" when referring to the *Autobiography*'s real subject, and by using third-person pronouns less often than expected, *The Autobiography of Alice B. Toklas* escapes the egotism of the consistent first-person usage that is otherwise inevitable in conventional autobiography. This is an extraordinarily clever way to eliminate a plethora of *I*'s; "I" here refers to Alice B. Toklas and her persona uses it sparingly.

The forms of these references to Gertrude Stein serve an *honorific function* as well, for they give her dignity and authority that the plain, familiar "Gertrude" or the flippant "Gerty" would not sustain. Stein, through Toklas, thereby flouts the convention that has persisted in women's biographies throughout the centuries, of addressing women subjects by their first names, regardless of their age, rank, or social status.[6]

Yet paradoxically, removal of the first-person pronoun from the real subject of the autobiography permits Stein to be even more conspicuously egotistical than she might appear if she used the first person consistently. By putting references to herself in the third person instead of the first, Gertrude Stein as autobiographer gives herself the advantage of allowing Alice B. Toklas' persona to perform the *egotistical function* of referring to Gertrude Stein by her proper name many more times than are necessary for either clarity, emphasis, or stylistic grace. Characteristically, Stein has Toklas say:

> But to come back to Roché at Kathleen Bruce's studio. They all talked about one thing and another and Gertrude Stein happened to mention that they had just bought a picture from Sagot by a young spaniard named Picasso. Good good excellent, said Roché, he is a very interesting young fellow, I know him. Oh do you, said *Gertrude Stein,* well enough to take somebody to see him. Why certainly, said Roché. Very well, said *Gertrude Stein,* my brother I know is very anxious to make his acquaintance. And there and then the appointment was made and shortly after Roché and *Gertrude Stein's* brother went to see Picasso.
>
> It was only a very short time after this that Picasso began the portrait of *Gertrude Stein,* now so widely known. . . . (p. 55)[7]

In all the italicized portions "she" or "her" could be substituted with no loss of meaning, but with considerably less emphasis on the name of the autobiographer. Thus the *self-advertising function* of the first person is omnipresent, but cleverly, with the appearance of being eliminated in favor of the third-person reference. Moreover, once Gertrude has been introduced (on p. 5), the other members of the Stein family are not mentioned anywhere in the autobiography by name, but only in their relation to the writer—"Gertrude Stein's older brother and his wife" (p. 5), "Gertrude Stein's mother" (p. 89). Thus her prominence is enhanced both within her family circle and throughout the autobiography.

Gertrude Stein's prominence within her own circle is augmented by a corollary manifestation of this technique, *the enhancement function of the selective inclusion of proper names,* not invented by Stein but certainly refined by her. When discussing habitués of her salon, or people to whom she gave literary advice or artistic encouragement, or other associates, Stein refers to the famous, the talented, and the notorious by name, and generally without identifying explanations. But except for a few close personal friends, she leaves anonymous most of the more innocuous persons. Since all are seen in relation to Gertrude Stein, rather than in relation to the autobiography's ostensible subject, and since Stein's name is, naturally, mentioned more frequently than the others, this technique has the repeated effect of making Gertrude Stein seem to be the focus of a coterie of luminaries. For the purposes of Stein's autobiographical books the relationships of various celebrities to one another are subordinate, however important they may actually have been, but perhaps this is the inevitable consequence of any autobiography.

The innovative device of a ventriloquizing persona of Alice B. Toklas in the *Autobiography* also performs a number of functions related to *interpreting* Gertrude Stein. A common aspect of this function is that of *reporter*. The persona of Alice can quote Gertrude Stein secondhand or refer (and defer) to Stein's opinions. This allows Stein-as-autobiographer much greater freedom and latitude of expression, with greater literary tact than she might have had if she had been speaking in the first person. For instance, Alice-as-reporter observes, "The young often when they have learnt all they can learn accuse her [Gertrude Stein] of an inordinate pride" (p. 94), and then quotes Stein indirectly:

> "She says yes of course. She realizes that in english literature in her time she is the only one. She has always known it and now she says it.
>
> She understands very well the basis of creation and therefore her advice and criticism is invaluable to all her friends. (p. 94)

This sort of self-congratulation, even if true, would appear insufferably egotistical if spoken directly by a first-person autobiographer, and as such would be likely to antagonize most readers, if it would not alienate them completely. So Stein's strategy is sound. *Alice-as-intermediary* softens the direct thrust, blunts the egotism, evades the hubris, and communicates her own appreciation of the rightness of Stein's opinion of herself. Judging from Toklas' own autobiography, *What Is Remembered,*[8] and from the critics referred to in this essay, this appreciation represents Alice B. Toklas' genuine attitude in real life and is not a posture Stein has forced her into for autobiographical purposes. *Alice-as-reinforcer* then supplements her own implied or stated judgments with the opinions of recognized masters, whose own confidence in Stein's judgments corroborates Toklas' views and validates those of Stein herself.

For example, immediately following "therefore her [Stein's] advice and criticism is invaluable to all her friends," *Alice-as-reinforcing-reporter* explains,

> How often have I heard Picasso say to her when she has said something about a picture of his and then illustrated by something she was trying to do, racontez-moi cela. In other words tell me about it. These two even to-day have long solitary conversations. They sit in two little low chairs up in his apartment studio, knee to knee and Picasso says, expliquez-moi cela. And they explain to each other. They talk about everything, about pictures, about dogs, about death, about unhappiness. (p. 95)

Thus through such solidly specific details, the "little low chairs" in Picasso's studio, the intimate conversation about "everything"—dogs, death, unhappiness—Toklas' unobtrusive view (even though created or re-created by Stein) leavens Stein's manifest egotism and subtly aligns the reader with Toklas' own pleasant and pleasured perspective.

On other occasions, though less frequently, Alice functions more overtly as an *interpreter:* "Gertrude Stein was in those days a little bitter, all her unpublished manuscripts, and no hope of publication or serious recognition" (p. 241). Commonly, Alice's alleged interpretations are mingled more directly with Gertrude's. For instance, Alice begins: "Now as for herself she [Gertrude Stein] was not efficient, she was good humoured, she was democratic, one person was as good as another, and she knew what she wanted done." Then Gertrude, quoted by Alice, continues, "If you are like that she says, anybody will do anything for you. The important thing, she insists, is that you must have deep down as the deepest thing in you a sense of equality" (p. 215). Thus Stein the innovator transforms the monologue form of conventional autobiography into a pseudo-dialogue between Alice B. Toklas as pseudo-author and Gertrude Stein, real though covert author and real autobiographical subject. Again, because Alice illustrates her interpretations with such intimate, specific knowledge of her subject, the reader is likely to accept the perspective of Alice-as-interpreter as valid, even though he may suspect Gertrude of breathing rather heavily down Alice's neck at times.

Yet Alice's persona appears more independent-minded than the conventional yes-woman. She occasionally interjects her own opinions: "I always say you cannot tell what a picture really is or what an object really is until you dust it every day and you cannot tell what a book is until you type it or proof-read it" (pp. 138-39). Despite Alice's self-assertiveness, I have searched the *Autobiography* in vain for instances where Alice-as-narrator contradicts Gertrude Stein or provides a corrective of her views, except in a jesting manner which is apparently not meant to be taken seriously, as in: "Gertrude Stein was born in Allegheny, Pennsylvania. As I am an ardent californian and as she spent her youth there I have often begged her to be born in California but she has always remained firmly born in Allegheny, Pennsylvania" (p. 85).

So, whether or not the correspondence of opinions is explicitly stated, the views of Alice-as-narrator, whether reporter, intermediary, reinforcer, or interpreter, would seem to be those of Gertrude Stein. But so insinuatingly does Alice manifest her point of view that it is almost impossible to react to Stein on terms other than those imputed to and imposed by the created Alice. So Stein, both through selecting and revealing the real Alice's real views and through creating the persona of Alice-as-narrator-of-Stein's-autobiography, remains fully in control not only of her material but of her readers' reactions as well.

In imposing such control, Stein also imposes *objectivity,* the third major function of her autobiographical point of view. Gertrude Stein as autobiographer, of course, has absolute control not only over the literary image and personality of Alice B. Toklas but over the persona and personality of herself that she chooses to present to the readers. This in itself, being germane to autobiography as a genre, is not particularly innovative, but Stein's apparent objectivity in that presentation is highly unusual and innovative in autobiography.

It is hard for the autobiographer to be objective in conventional autobiography, when the self is talking directly about the self. But Stein-the-writer has created both the ventriloquist, Alice Toklas, and Stein-the-puppet, who actually though subtly controls the ventriloquist. The continuous presence of two personages in action and interaction enables Stein to *appear* to present Gertrude Stein from the *outside,* rather than from the autobiographer's almost inevitable *inside,* perspective, for the reader sees her as she is allegedly seen by Toklas. "Sentences not only words but sentences and always sentences have been Gertrude Stein's life long passion" (p. 50) is much more external, impersonal than the conventional alternative, "I have always loved long sentences passionately." Likewise, secondhand fury is somewhat milder than firsthand wrath in such observations as: "Gertrude Stein used to get furious when the english all talked about german organisation. She used to insist that the germans had no organisation, they had method but no organisation" (pp. 187-88). As a result, Stein appears as solid and as foursquare as Jo Davidson's seated, washerwomanlike sculpture of her, and, like the sculpture, a human entity visible essentially from the outside.

That this objectivity is Stein's contrivance and not merely a re-creation of Toklas' actual mode of expression is evident throughout Toklas' own autobiography. In *What Is Remembered* Toklas' own comments about Stein, though understated, are much more evocative than Stein's own, as is evident in Toklas' account of their first meeting.

> In the room were Mr. and Mrs. Stein and Gertrude Stein. It was Gertrude Stein who held my complete attention, as she did for all the many years I knew her until her death, and all these empty ones since then. She was a golden brown presence, burned by the Tuscan sun and with a golden glint in her warm brown hair. She was dressed in a warm brown corduroy suit. She wore a large round coral brooch and when she talked, very little, or laughed, a good deal, I thought her voice came from this brooch. It was unlike anyone else's voice—deep, full, velvety like a great contralto's, like two voices. She was large and heavy with delicate small hands and a beautifully modeled and unique head.[9]

Toklas' passage emanates the warmth she sees in Stein and feels for her—warm sights, warm sounds, the warm and dignifiedly uninhibited, moving reactions of an exposed personality who is not afraid to acknowledge the fullness of life with a beloved friend and the emptiness of life without her. In her own autobiography Toklas discloses, among other selves, a private, vulnerable self of the sort which Stein-as-autobiographer rarely reveals.

The advantages of Stein's autobiographical objectivity are numerous, despite some loss of warmth. Stein-as-autobiographer keeps control of her material—content, self-image(s), tone, mood—at all times, rather than self-indulgently letting it control her. Thus she is, and can be, nonsentimental, and devoid of maudlinity, self-pity, self-flagellation, false modesty, hypocrisy, and other demeaning, self-denigrating attitudes and images of self.

Her objectivity permits her to treat even the presumably painful with a certain detachment:

> Life in California came to its end when Gertrude Stein was about seventeen years old. The last few years had been lonesome ones and had been passed in an agony of adolescence. After the death of first her mother and then her father she . . . came to Baltimore and stayed with her mother's people. There she began to lose her lonesomeness. (p. 92)

Stein's dispassion avoids the self-pity that a conventional biographical point of view on unpleasant personal matters might encourage. And, for better or worse, it permits the reader to respond to the presentation of personal pain with an objectivity equal to the presenter's.

Stein's objectivity also avoids the confessional mode common to autobiography. She doesn't tell anything she doesn't want to, and because of Toklas as the intermediary persona, the reader doesn't *expect* Stein to be more revealing than she is. She leaves finances, personal conflicts (such as her estrangement from her brother Leo), and griefs vague, and never discusses her own sexuality, spinsterhood, or loves—except for dogs. The closest she comes to verging on the intimately sexual is a reference to a short first novel she had written during a gloomy, postadolescent period and then forgotten about until she accidentally discovered the manuscript some years later: "She was very bashful and hesitant about it, did not really want to read it. Louis Bromfield was at the house that evening and she handed him the manuscript and said to him, you read it" (p. 104). Yet she never reveals the novel's title or content, and does not discuss it again. Clarification of this enigma took nearly forty years, when Richard Bridgman, in *Gertrude Stein in Pieces,* identified the work as "Things as They Are," a tale written in 1903 of "three young women in passionate stalemate . . . based upon Gertrude Stein's frustrated romance with May Bookstaver, a Baltimore friend."[10]

Of course, one can raise the question of why Stein made even so oblique an allusion to a painful past. Evidently the *Autobiography* is full of numerous allusions meaningful to Stein and her immediate circle but inaccessible to the general public.[11] This may be yet another example

of her "split-level" autobiographical technique of talking to two audiences, private and public, on two levels.

At other times Stein remains objective on personal matters by generalizing. She does not talk specifically about stresses with her own father, but instead, in *Everybody's Autobiography,* remarks of fathers in general: "Fathers are depressing. . . . Mothers may not be cheering but they are not as depressing as fathers."[12] She then shifts to the personal—not about her own father, but rather, remarking on Bennett Cerf and Thornton Wilder in father roles. After that she gives the generalities a political bite:

> There is too much fathering going on just now and there is no doubt about it fathers are depressing. Everybody nowadays is a father, there is father Mussolini and father Hitler and father Roosevelt and father Stalin and father Lewis and father Blum and father Franco is just commencing now and there are ever so many more ready to be one.[13]

Then Stein generalizes again: "Fathers are depressing."[14]

Stein's prevailing detachment and nonsentimentality permit her to treat herself and her milieu with considerable humor. Her somewhat self-indulgent laughter sets the tone for the readers' reaction as well. She can laugh at herself, as she does in recounting the anecdote when her servant drove Stein to profanity by pretending to have broken the writer's treasured black Renaissance plate—and thereby cured her hiccups, which was the maid's intention (pp. 106-07). Stein can also engage the reader in the laughter of rightness vindicated. She tells of a visit from the "very nice very american young" (p. 83) vanity publisher's emissary concerning *Three Lives,* who said,

> slightly hesitant, the director of the Grafton Press is under the impression that perhaps your knowledge of English. [Here Stein lets the reader supply the devastating omission.] But I am an american, said Gertrude Stein indignantly. Yes yes I understand that perfectly now, he said, but perhaps you have not had much experience in writing. I suppose, said she laughing [as Stein's mood brightens, so does the reader's], you were under the impression that I was imperfectly educated. He blushed [we laugh], why no, he said, but you might not have had much experience in writing. (p. 84)

As both the humor and the tension build, Stein delivers her good-natured *coup de grâce:*

> Oh yes, she said, oh yes. Well it's alright. I will write to the director and you might as well tell him also that everything that is written in the manuscript is written with the intention of its being so written and all he has to do is print it and I will take the responsibility. The young man bowed himself out. (p. 84)

We appreciate the young man's polite discomfiture, but more particularly we appreciate Stein's astute awareness and defense of her talent. Thus Stein creates a prevailing mood of good humor and good-naturedness which enhances the *Autobiography*'s zest and charm.

Moreover, by letting the reader in on the joke of the real authorship of the *Autobiography* right from the start, instead of publishing it anonymously or pseudonymously, Stein's strategy is to take the reader into league with her. Once she has him on her side as a participant in her joke, it's hard to turn against the perpetrator of it. Thus the reader is more inclined to accept Stein's image of herself (as seen by Toklas and by herself) as true than he might if he had the judgment of a bona fide intermediary biographer to question. Again Stein, through Toklas, controls the reader as well as her material.

If the subject's personality or psyche were suppressed, flattened, distorted, or falsified, some of the advantages of autobiography-by-indirection would be lost. But none of these occur in *The Autobiography of Alice B. Toklas,* in which both Gertrude Stein and Alice B. Toklas are very much alive and very well. All in all, the advantages of this innovative form are manifold, and as practiced by Stein it has no conspicuous disadvantages—except unrepeatability.

Another innovative aspect of *The Autobiography of Alice B. Toklas* is that, despite its intense focus on Gertrude Stein, a biographical portrait of the alleged autobiographical subject does emerge quite clearly. The work is a double portrait, of Stein and of Toklas. The *Autobiography* is further unusual in that Stein deliberately wrote it to emulate the oral speech mannerisms of another person—in choice of words, level of language, syntax, speech rhythms—rather than precisely her own, though the two are not incompatible.[15] Indeed, she succeeded very well, judging from Toklas' own style in *What Is Remembered* (see above), even allowing for the possibility that in the latter volume Toklas could have imitated Stein's imitation of herself. Stein always treats Toklas-as-narrator the way she evidently treated Toklas-as-intimate-lifelong-friend, with the respect that maintains Toklas' integrity and never makes her feeble or foolish, never jokes at Toklas' expense (unlike Boswell's sometimes silly sycophancy, with which Toklas is occasionally wrongly compared). Thus Alice, like her biographical creator, is a vivid, witty, personable, tartly gracious presence in her own pseudo-autobiography, an enduring tribute to a friend and to a friendship, among other things.

A comparison of the *Autobiography* with Stein's other autobiographical works, *Everybody's Autobiography* and *Wars I Have Seen,* throws the advantages of *The Autobiography of Alice B. Toklas* form into even sharper relief. With the narrative persona of Alice B. Toklas missing, these other autobiographies are subject to some of the problems germane to the conventional first-person autobiographies. Alice, even as a created persona, functions effectively as an *editor* in the *Autobiography.* Her narrative presence provides control over the material, for in the *Autobiography* Stein fairly successfully overcomes the difficulties inherent in the associative technique she employs throughout all three autobiographical volumes. In the *Autobiography* Alice-as-narrator more or less sticks to the subject in an essentially chronological progression, and so some overall pattern of Stein's life and growing personality emerges clearly. In the other volumes, with Alice's editorial presence removed, Stein as narrator in her own persona is more discursive, more eclectic, less controlled. Space limitations prevent detailed demonstration of this; suffice to say that the *Autobiography,* representing fifty-eight years of Stein's life, is 310 pages long; *Everybody's Autobiography,* representing essentially five years, has only 8 more pages but about 20 percent more words; and *Wars I Have Seen,* covering essentially the years of World War II, is of comparable length to *Everybody's Autobiography.* The more frequent the rambling, somewhat self-indulgent excursions and the higher the number of first-person references (in *Everybody's Autobiography* they average twenty-eight per page, versus eight per page in the *Autobiography*), the greater the impression of autobiographical self-indulgence, despite Stein's ingenuous claim that "everybody" wrote *Everybody's Autobiography.*[16]

Thus like a grandiose firework *The Autobiography of Alice B. Toklas,* autobiography-by-*Doppelgänger,* can be set off only once. Its innovative strategy and form and variations on point of view exhibit the uniqueness, innovativeness, and memorability of its creator. It leaves a dazzling afterglow against the more somber sky of conventional autobiographies.

NOTES

[1] Gertrude Stein, *The Autobiography of Alice B. Toklas* (New York: Harcourt, Brace, 1933), p. 310. All future references to this work appear in the text.

[2] Richard Bridgman, *Gertrude Stein in Pieces* (New York: Oxford Univ. Press, 1970), pp. 212-13. After exploring the question of whether Toklas may have composed a preliminary autobiography, which might have influenced the *Autobiography*'s striking departure from Stein's customary style, Bridgman states that "[t]he physical evidence indicates that *The Autobiography of Alice B. Toklas* was written by Gertrude Stein alone, with few hesitations or changes" (p. 212).

[3] Ibid., pp. 212-13.

[4] Donald Sutherland disagrees, claiming that "[t]he scheme of the second autobiography, *Everybody's Autobiography,* is an extension of the first. Having created her twin or reflection in the first autobiography and committed it to the public, she had to watch this second 'Gertrude Stein' get entirely away from her, as it was elaborated upon by the enormous publicity it received during her tour of America in 1934-35. So that now she could discover her past and present as reflected by 'everybody' just as before they had

been reflected by Miss Toklas." *Gertrude Stein: A Biography of Her Work* (New Haven: Yale Univ. Press, 1951), p. 153. Since even in this view "everybody" speaks in the first person of Gertrude Stein herself in these later autobiographical works, I maintain that in them the advantages of the ventriloquized form of *The Autobiography of Alice B. Toklas* are absent (passim but see especially pp. 16-17).

[5] Sutherland, pp. 148-49.

[6] Men in biographies are much more often addressed by their last names and titles. A random sample reveals that in biographies of men, last names outnumber first four to one; in biographies of women, first names outnumber last nine to one. The exceptions are either feminist biographies or works written prior to the twentieth century, when modes of address were more formal anyway. Interestingly, biographies of women which call their subjects by their first names also tend to call the men in those works by their first names; the reverse is not often the case.

[7] Emphasis mine.

[8] Alice B. Toklas, *What Is Remembered* (New York: Holt, Rinehart and Winston, 1963).

[9] Ibid., p. 23.

[10] Bridgman, p. 40. In *Gertrude Stein: Her Life and Work* (New York: Harper, 1957), Elizabeth Sprigge treats the understated relationship in *Things as They Are* more delicately and ambiguously, claiming that Adele (Gertrude Stein's alias) was "using Helen as a subject for psychological experiment" and concludes, "Thus, through the pages of *Things as They Are* one watches Gertrude Stein developing from a raw girl to a mature young woman, and realizes that she had to break away from what she called 'the general American sisterhood'" (p. 49). Two years later John Malcolm Brinnin is equally discreet, referring only to "Gertrude Stein's ability to keep the forbidden subject muted" concerning "emotions . . . of a nature rarely hinted at in the literature of the time." *The Third Rose: Gertrude Stein and Her World* (Boston: Little, Brown, 1959), p. 46.

[11] See Bridgman, p. 227.

[12] Gertrude Stein, *Everybody's Autobiography* (New York: Random House, 1937), pp. 132-33.

[13] Ibid., p. 133.

[14] Ibid.

[15] Sutherland, p. 148, quoting Carl Van Vechten, introduction to *Selected Writings* (New York: Random House, 1946), pp. xii-xiii.

[16] In the first edition, "anybody" is identified as the author in the first sentence: "Alice B. Toklas did hers and now anybody will do theirs" (p. 3). This was an error that Toklas had made in transcribing the manuscript. Neither she nor Stein realized it when they corrected the proofs for the first American edition. It was corrected in the English edition published by William Heinemann in 1938. In the Random House Vintage Books edition (1973) "anybody" has been changed to "everybody."

William Hoffa

SOURCE: "The Final Preface: Henry James's Autobiography," in *The Sewanee Review,* Vol. LXXVII, No. 2, Spring, 1969, pp. 277-293.

[*In the following essay, Hoffa examines the motivation, method, and mood underlying Henry James's* Autobiography.]

Though we today readily place the two and one-third volumes about his youth which Henry James published in the late years of his life in the genre of autobiography, it is clear from the few records which James has left us that his intentions for the project underwent a considerable shift before and even during the time of its composition. James had always been wary of the "devilish art of biography", in spite of his two full-length biographies—of Hawthorne in 1879, and William Wetmore Story in 1903—and his numerous biographical-critical sketches of other writers. Thus he did not even subtitle the work "Autobiography", though, as F. W. Dupee has suggested, this is the "simplest, the most nearly appropriate, or at any rate the least misleading of several possibilities". James's references to the work in his letters, moreover, present a decidedly ambivalent attitude toward it. To some correspondents he deprecated his efforts as "reminiscential twaddle", "printed divagations", and a "jumble of childish memories". Yet to others he expressed the loftiest hopes: to Edith Wharton he described it as "extremely special, experimental and as yet occult", to Auguste Monod, a "fond experiment", and to Mrs. William James, "difficult and unprecedented and perilous—but if I bring it off it will be exquisite and unique . . .". Such vacillation is indeed perplexing. But, at the same time, nearly everything James said about the *Autobiography* is in some way true; for it is, taken as a whole, a "jumble of childish memories", "reminiscential twaddle", and something "difficult and unprecedented", "exquisite and unique".

James's original idea was to write a "Family Book", a desire occasioned by the death in 1910 of William. It is now apparent that this plan was supplanted, as he worked, by the desire to write a "final Preface" which would, he hoped, do for his life what his "Prefaces" had tried to do for his fiction: to uncover certain "formative" principles. The resulting autobiographical Preface, moreover, can be seen to have developed into a book which shares many of the themes and techniques of his

"Major Phase" novels, and it is thus, in a sense, the "American novel" he had hoped to write after his trip to the United States in 1904-05. In addition, the *Autobiography* is perhaps James's most eloquent plea for the values of art to civilization and, in his words, "the personal history . . . of an imagination".

I

In September, 1911, James returned to England from America. Soon afterwards he wrote to William's widow, Alice, that the illness which he had suffered from in America had subsided and that "the conditions [of work] were what [he] needed." He felt that he could work his way "back to an equilibrium" and desired "to get, more surely and swiftly now, up to [his] neck into the book about William and the rest of us". The idea of the "Family Book" had come, he admitted later to his nephew, Henry James II, in conversation with Alice in the "dark days" following William's death, and now in England he was beginning to dictate the book to his amanuensis, Theodora Bosanquet. Working from memories mostly, but also from assorted letters he had brought back with him to England, he was apparently very concerned about "proprieties"; not wanting to be too "intensely domestic, private and personal", he nevertheless reserved for himself final judgment in such matters. He told Alice:

> I am writing to him [H. J. II] in a very few days, and will then tell him how I am entirely at one with him about the kind of use to be made by me of all these early things, the kind of setting they must have, the kind of encompassment that the book, as *my* book, my play of reminiscence and almost of brotherly autobiography, and filial autobiography not less, must enshrine them in.

There is little or no indication at this point that he planned the book to be about himself nearly exclusively—as it turned out to be. Later, in the next year, however, to his nephew, James began to stress more "the 'literary and artistic,' the technical, side of the matter".

> . . . In doing this book I am led, by the very process and action of my idiosyncrasy, on and on into more . . . ramification of old images and connections, more intellectual and moral autobiography . . . than I shall quite know what to do with. . . .

The phrase "intellectual and moral autobiography" is revealing because in it James seems to be admitting for the first time that his narrative was centering more on his own life than on the collective life of the James family, and also that he was trying to present his own life in such a way that it would embody a "moral". The precise final nature of the moral is not difficult to determine, since it is restated in varying forms throughout the *Autobiography;* perhaps its most simple expression comes at the end of Chapter Two of *Small Boy:*

> . . . No education avails for the intelligence that doesn't stir in it some subjective passion, and . . .

on the other hand almost anything that does so act is largely educative, however small a figure the process might make in a scheme of training. Strange indeed, furthermore, are some of the things that *have* stirred a subjective passion—stirred it, I mean, in young persons predisposed to a more or less fine inspired application.

Miss Bosanquet has reported that "no preliminary work was needed" in writing the *Autobiography;* that James "dived" right into the past and came up with "handfuls of memories". But, as the above excerpt reveals, after the process of dredging, there came the process of selecting, ordering, and molding. James wrote in the same letter to his nephew that, as in the composition of his novels, the real task was one of shaping the raw material into "significant" form: " . . . I have to project and *do* a great deal in order to choose from that, after the fact, what is most designated and supremely urgent." It is, he admits, "a costly way of working, as regards time, material etc.—at least in the short run"; but "in the long run, and 'by and large'", it "justifies itself". While the process of dictation no doubt gave additional length and breadth to the work, there can be no doubt that, as ever with James, the processes of "selection" and "discrimination" were the more essential.

In another letter to his nephew in 1913 it becomes apparent that Uncle Henry had occasionally, in the eyes of his family, "refashioned" his material too liberally. In reply to the objection that he had altered certain parts of William's letters, Henry argued that he had done "no violence . . . to his [*i.e.,* William's] real identity"; he then defended his prerogative to reshape his "material" into its own "realized" solidity:

> . . . I daresay I did instinctively regard it at last as all *my* truth, to do what I would with. . . . I have to the last point the instinct and the sense for fusions and interrelations, for framing and encircling . . . every part of my stuff in every other. . . .

Nevertheless, James did feel a certain somewhat resentful responsibility to the factual material with which he was working; he realized the "danger when the frame and circle play over too much upon the image". And at times this "danger", this responsibility to be objective and thereby sacrifice his subjective vision, made him resent straying from his "proper work", the writing of pure fiction, "the one in which that danger is the reverse of one and becomes a rightness and a beauty". What "framing" and "encircling" he gave his memories was apparently not done in an attempt to distort the truth, but to give perspective and dimension to his own development as an artist.

It was this subjective task rather than the completion of a family history which primarily motivated James during 1912 and 1913. The unimpaired "uncanny interest" in and "zeal" for the *Autobiography* which he reports in 1913, after setting to work on *Notes,* attest to the strength of his motivation. At this time he reports that *Small Boy* is about "to burst upon the world", in spite of "months of hampering and baffling illness". This volume seemed to him "good", the "proof of [his] powers". Though he yearned to get back to his long-postponed "American novel", *The Ivory Tower,* he first desired "to complete" *Notes* "with the last perfection".

Thus "through all sorts of discomfitures and difficulties—and disillusionments", the "light" which the idea of a "Family Book" had led to, inspired James to sustain his composition; the "spirit" and "vision" of his project which had begun when Alice James had "dropped the seed" became, as Henry later told his nephew, "as far removed as possible from my mere isolated documentation of your Father's [*i.e.,* William's] record". Yet not even to his nephew did James disclose completely the full intention he had for his "fond experiment".

James's letter to Auguste Monod in 1913 begins to express what the fuller aspirations of his "fond experiment" had been:

> . . . I found the experiment succeed, from my own point of view, as soon as all sorts of dimnesses of far past began to *like* to wake up again at pressure of the spring. They kept waking and waking and I grew more and more touched and amazed by their doing so, and thus my rather fatuous emotions became *un gros volume.* . . . The new volume will . . . express for me how much I feel that in a literary work of the least complexity the very form and texture are the substance itself and that the flesh is indetachable from the bones! Translation is an effort . . . to *tear* the hapless flesh, and in fact to get rid of so much of it that the living thing bleeds and faints away! . . . But without having in the least sought the effect, it does interest me, it does even partly exhilarate me to recognise that the small Boy, while yet so tame and intrinsically safe a little animal, is locked fast in the golden cage of the *intraduisible!*

This satisfaction is the satisfaction of the artist, not the biographer. It emphasizes how much the medium of the *Autobiography* is actually its subject; how much James's thickly textured prose was able to capture the true subject of his book: his own dramatized consciousness of the past as it lived in the present.

Verification of this comes in two other letters, one to Howells in 1908, long before James had actually started consciously considering an autobiography, the other to Henry Adams, after he had finished *Notes.* To Howells he wrote that he would some day like to furnish his just completed Prefaces to the New York Edition of his works with "a final Preface". Considering that he saw the Prefaces as representing "over a considerable course the continuity of an artist's endeavor, the growth of his whole operative consciousness", his remark to Howells would seem to suggest that he hoped to trace that "growth" farther back in his own personal history.

Moreover it suggests James's continual fascination with his present "operative consciousness", with the way the mind could intuitively turn up nuances of emotion and insight hitherto hidden. To Adams, six years later, James's remarks confirm that he felt he *had* written his "final Preface" and that the process itself had been exhilarating. This famous letter responds to Adams's *Education* and to his nihilistic letter which had attempted to undermine James's project. James admitted that they both seemed "lone survivors" of the past and that there was "no use talking unless one particularly *wants* to". Then he went on to say that the purpose of his "printed divagations" was to show Adams that he *did* want to "talk":

> Behold me therefore so behaving—and apparently capable of continuing to do so. I still find my consciousness interesting—under *cultivation* of the interest. . . . *Why* mine yields an interest I don't know that I can tell you, but I don't challenge or quarrel with it—I encourage it with a ghastly grin. You see I still, in presence of life (or of what you deny to be such), have reactions—as many as possible—and the book I sent you is a proof of them. It's, I suppose, because I am that queer monster, the artist, an obstinate finality, an inexhaustible sensibility. Hence the reactions—appearances, memories, many things, go on playing upon it with consequences that I note and "enjoy" (grim word!) noting. It all takes doing—and I *do.* I believe I shall do yet again—it is still an act of life.

This letter convincingly reinforces the dominant mood of the *Autobiography,* which is celebrative and affirmative far more than reminiscential and nostalgic. It celebrates and affirms not only the vividness of the past but the present *re*-creation of it. At the core of the *Autobiography* we find not a yearning lament for the lost beauty of the past but a present "act of life", a labored but obviously pleasure-giving attempt to discover "significance" and meaning in the past. The *Autobiography* is not, therefore, about the past as historical sequence, and it is only tangentially about William, about the James family, or about mid-nineteenth-century America. These personages and experiences only "matter" as they impinge upon Henry James's awareness of his development into that "queer monster, the artist, an obstinate finality, an inexhaustible sensibility". Moreover, the unity of the *Autobiography* comes from James's awareness that the process of writing his autobiography is itself an experience of the same nature as the process of growing into manhood and artistic maturity. It is this awareness which constitutes the "uniqueness" of James's "experiment".

II

Like all autobiographies James's is about the early life of its author, but it is just as much about the autobiographer's reaction to the process of telling his story, about the present re-experiencing of his early life. James's achievement encompasses this double dimension in the sense that it incorporates the method of the "central" or "registering" consciousness into the more traditional modes of autobiography, wherein the autobiographer tells his story entirely from a static and omniscient point of view. In James's *Autobiography,* to be sure, we do find in abundance this traditional narrative manner and pose. He does present himself as the expatriated "Master of Lamb House", the literary lion, the author of novels and short stories, drama, and literary and social criticism. He does, from the secure vantage point of age, attempt to assess the sequence of events in his early life which formed his basic aspirations and character. At times he becomes the "passionate pilgrim" of his early travel essays or the "restless analyst" of *The American Scene;* at others he is the painter of social and natural panorama. Not infrequently he is the omniscient narrator of some of his short stories and novels, the psychological portrait painter and caricaturist. His desire for detached narration at times even leads him to see the "small boy" as someone else, a little hero with an adventure all his own, though one with which the older man is sympathetic:

> I at any rate watch the small boy dawdle and gape again, I smell the cold dusty paint and iron as the rails of the Eighteenth Street corner rub his contemplative nose, and, feeling him foredoomed, withhold from him no grain of my sympathy. He is a convenient little image or warning of all that was to be for him, and he might well have been even happier than he was. For there was the very pattern and measure of all he was to demand: just to *be* somewhere—almost anywhere would do—and somehow receive an impression or an accession, feel a relation or a vibration.

The mood is retrospective and meditative, as in nearly all autobiographies, and James's "late manner" prose style provides a perfect medium for its expression; it is a beautifully evocative and richly textured tapestry of words which more than adequately suits the richness of feeling and thought of James's reflections. Had James been satisfied to tell his story entirely in this traditional manner and mode, the *Autobiography* would still remain a moving and satisfying work. But as a novelist, he must have realized that there were nuances and intensities in his "story" which could not be divulged by the usual methods of the autobiographer. And it is for this reason that he decided to incorporate into the narrative medium the added drama of his own "registering" intelligence.

It is this added dimension to usual autobiographical narrative method in the *Autobiography* which brings out the drama of the storyteller as he discovers more in his story than he had hitherto realized was inherent in it. We watch over the shoulder of the "Master of Lamb House" as he watches his younger self march before him. Phrases, sentences, even whole paragraphs, which express his reaction to newly discovered "significance" or something hitherto hidden in the past, punctuate the entire book. Such exclamations as the following—which are not so much a part of the story as of the telling of the story—could have easily been struck out when James was revising his dictated manuscripts: "I taste again," "as I reconsider", "I hear it again," "I insist on yielding to it," "I seem to

remember," "there were occasional figures that I now recover," "these opposed glimpses hang before me," "so far do I let myself go," "I see that *there* was the American spirit," etc., or finally this sentence, typical in sentiment:

> I find bribes to recognition and recovery quite mercilessly multiply, and with the effort to brush past them more and more difficult; with the sense for me at any rate (whatever that may be worth for wisdom or comfort) of sitting rather queerly safe and alone, though as with a dangle of legs over the edge of a precipice, on the hither side of great gulfs of history.

But James did not edit out such apparent asides. Expressing astonishment and wonder, delight and helplessness, recognition and confusion, such phrases keep the reader aware of the "struggle" with the past which he describes on the first page of the *Autobiography:*

> . . . Aspects [of the past] began to multiply and images to swarm, so far at least as they showed, to appreciation, as true terms and happy values; and that I might positively . . . rejoice in my relation to most of them, using it for all that, as the phrase is, it should be worth. To knock at the door of the past was in a word to see it open to me quite wide—to see the world within begin to "compose" with a grace of its own round the primary figure, see it people itself vividly and insistently.

James presents himself as a kind of bewildered but delighted spectator, a gratified eavesdropper, a curious dreamer whose dream has been real and whose vision is being fulfilled. This nearly Proustian recovery of the past takes the form of a dialectical probing and analyzing of his memories; his "vibrations" and impressions ebb and flow in "significance" and intensity. Whether they depend on the concrete fact or a flickering memory, they use the known as a springboard to the unknown. It is as Percy Lubbock has said of James, that "he never took anything as it came":

> His life was no mere succession of facts, such as could be compiled and recorded by another hand; it was a densely knit cluster of emotions and memories, each one steeped in lights and colours thrown out by the rest, the whole making up a picture that no one but himself could dream of undertaking to paint. . . . The thing that happened to him was merely the point of departure for a deliberate, and . . . more masterly, creative energy, which could never leave a sight or sound of any kind until it had been looked at and listened to with absorbed attention, pondered in thought, linked with its associations, and which did not spend itself until the remembrance had been crystallised in expression, so that it could then be appropriated like a tangible object.

Moreover, it is the display of this energy, more than anything he says about the past, which makes this autobiography.

James had said in 1884, in "The Art of Fiction", "experience is never complete, and reality has a myriad of forms"; his *Autobiography* is a further manifestation of this same ontological perspective. This makes it, in essence, a kind of extended and usually leisurely dramatic monologue. It is, as he says, a "tale of assimilations, small and fine", whose "apparently dispersed and disordered parts" are strung upon a "silver thread". However, while he insists that his story is "no plotted thing at all", he himself seems to discover near the end of *Notes*—in a moment of self-awareness similar to those he gives many of his characters—the "principle" on which his "recording and figuring act" is based: a "long-sought occasion" to trace "the personal history . . . of an imagination, a lively one of course". This quest, he realizes, had been "haunting" him through a good portion of his life. He wanted therefore to "catch" this "man of imagination" and show him as the "creature of that force or the sport of that fate or the wielder of that arm, for the hero of a hundred possible fields". In a remarkable passage of self-revelation James goes on to account not only for the inception and nature of the *Autobiography* but also for its connection with his fiction:

> What was *I* thus, within and essentially, what had I ever been and could I ever be but a man of imagination at the active pitch?—so that if it was a question of treating *some* happy case, any that would give me what, artistically speaking, I wanted, here on the very spot was one at hand in default of a better. It wasn't what I should have preferred, yet it was after all the example I knew best and should feel most at home with—granting always that objectivity, the prize to be won, shouldn't just be frightened away by the odd terms of the affair.

Whether or not such a moment of insight actually came to James when he was dictating his book to Miss Bosanquet, we can never say for certain. But it is obvious that James uses this climactic epiphany to give drama to his narrative, and that the drama focuses on the reflecting mind of the storyteller rather than on the story he tells. Throughout James's "tale of assimilations" supplementary moments of illumination occur. Sometimes they concern what the "small boy" or the "son and brother" learned; more often, they concern what James, as autobiographer, discovered about his past or about the relation between events past and events present. Despite the assurance, calm, and perspective of most of the book, "the reminiscential twaddle", these frequent emotional moments of self-discovery which trace "the growth of a poet's mind" dominate our interest. Yet that growth, as in Wordsworth's *Prelude,* is not merely recounted as a past occurrence; it is, as well, *demonstrated* as a present principle of consciousness. In Jamesian terms, it is a matter of both "telling" and "showing". Seen in this way, James's *Autobiography* is more than ever *his* book and it is decidedly the "final Preface" he had hinted at to Howells. Moreover, its theme and technique, its vision, aligns it with James's late fiction and, conversely, provides us with a way of interpreting that fiction.

III

In most of the late fiction, the real focus of James's story is on the effect experience has upon a "registering consciousness", upon what this sensitive observer and participant can make of what he slowly, gropingly "sees" happening to him. However, though many readers of James fail to grasp this, "seeing" is never enough; the Jamesian hero, to be a hero, necessarily utilizes his newly gained insight in some kind of ethically meaningful action. Thus, in *The Ambassadors,* it is not enough for Strether to be aware that he has not "lived"; he must initiate certain actions—refusing to "profit", scolding Chad for his callousness, rejecting an easy return to America—which demonstrate what he has learned. In a like manner, in *The Wings of the Dove,* Milly Theale decides to leave her fortune to Merton Densher "for Love" after she realizes that she has been betrayed by him; and in *The Golden Bowl,* having discovered her husband's adultery, Maggie Verver arranges a marriage between her father and Charlotte, so that she can love him as his wife. These positive actions which occur after awareness has been achieved counter a common view that James's heroes are "trapped spectators" of their fate. Correspondingly the *Autobiography* argues that as both artist and man James did not consider himself a passive victim of his intelligence.

Like the novels, moreover, the *Autobiography* traces a journey—indirect, groping, intuitive—of increasing perceptions. In *A Small Boy and Others* James sees his childhood as a "riot of the senses, a revel of the mind"; he wanders aimlessly, nourished by "impressions", "vibrations", and "accessions"; he senses his alienation, his "otherness", but he does not know what it "means". In *Notes of a Son and Brother* James recalls the excitement of beginning to "discriminate" and "differentiate" between "impressions"; yet he notes that he had only a faint idea of the "use" to which they could be put; his intellect awakens, his social horizon broadens; he reads more, meditates more, and worries more—especially about his place within the social order. Finally, in *The Middle Years* James recalls how he began to "harvest" his "impressions", to put them to use in his art; like Joyce he shows how he realized the necessity of cutting himself off from his family, his country, and his friends. Meaningful action becomes synonymous with artistic creation, which in terms of outward action showed little, but for the artist was everything.

By the end of the finished portion of *The Middle Years* James had brought himself to the age of twenty-seven, a time of self-imposed exile in Europe and full dedication to the art of fiction. Though in fact his break with America was not so abrupt—Leon Edel has shown us that it took *two* trips to Europe to convince James that he should live abroad—James makes it seem so; this last, incomplete volume, then, constitutes a celebration of the discovery of his "calling". Though we now know that he had published numerous short pieces of fiction and criticism by 1870, this fact is purposely underplayed in the *Autobiography*. James apparently wanted to dramatize the suddenness of his self-discovery, of his new-found inspiration and application. It seems also probable that James scarcely mentions his early writing because he wants the overriding emphasis to be upon the development of the inner artistic consciousness rather than his public achievement. Moreover, though there are well-documented reasons for the incomplete state of this final volume—James's illness, his concern over the war, his other writing obligations—it can be argued that he instinctively knew that he had said as much as he had to say. Throughout his life he had insisted, time and again, that the successful artist disappears into his work; that his life was interesting only up to the point where his art became the dominating concern of his existence; after this point the artist has *no* personality and is not therefore interesting as a subject for fiction. As many of his stories of artists and writers urge (*i.e.,* "The Figure in the Carpet", "The Death of the Lion", "The Author of Beltraffio"), the artist's essential "life" is to be found in his work and nowhere else.

Thus, the real conclusion to James's *Autobiography* is to be found in his novels and stories. They, like it, follow the idealistic quest of a hero capable of learning from his experience and converting what he has learned into an ethically meaningful action. They are all—as James admits in his *Autobiography*—about the "man of imagination" who lives at an "active pitch", discovers himself, and then works out a personal salvation. In the *Autobiography* this "hero" happens to be a developing artist rather than an aging editor, a dying heiress, or the rich American wife of an Italian prince. The problems which fate presents are similar in all cases; the modes of perception, reflection, and resolution identical. The Realistic necessities of life—physical, social, and economic—are largely de-emphasized in order to emphasize the intensely idealistic search for identity; the corresponding rewards are found not within the social order but within the self. James's interest in his *Autobiography* is thus not with his "career" but with his "subjective passion" and his "inexhaustible sensibility". Like his "Major Phase" novels, which are not "novels" in quite the same way that *Washington Square, Portrait, Bostonians, Princess Casamassima,* and *Tragic Muse* are, his *Autobiography* is a kind of "poetic drama" which depicts an altered consciousness in a largely nontemporal, non-spatial world. James consciously underplays the emotional and social involvements of his life in order to bring out more sharply the correlative, the intensity and necessity of his detached observation of the world swarming around him. He seems to know well that it was only this quality, the joy of observing and recording, of giving Form to dissociated experience, which redeemed the "queer monster" within himself.

IV

Late in his life James wrote to H. G. Wells that "it is art that *makes* life, makes interest, makes importance, for our consideration and application of these things, and I know

of no substitute whatever for the force and beauty of its process." This statement does seem to describe the primary emphasis of James's *Autobiography*. For art did "make" his life, in the sense that no other passion, intellectual or personal, ever threatened his consciousness, and his *Autobiography* is a step-by-step account of his seduction by the artistic muse. "The force and beauty of its process" is the real subject of his narrative; it began when he was a "small boy" and continued the rest of his life without abatement. The labored and dramatized act of writing the *Autobiography* is ample proof that James's powers of discrimination and analysis were still at an active pitch late in his long life. The careful reconstruction of the "significant" events of his life argues for his continuing desire to convert and refashion experience into something with formal and therefore realized value. His generalized abstracted concentration on himself as a "man of imagination", his wide range of reference, and his highly analytical and figurative language, furthermore, argue for a way of "taking life", not merely a way of taking Henry James.

As a "final Preface" it is neither a vain nor superficial nor especially "intimate" account of his life. Instead it is more an appeal, a plea, a demonstrated pattern of "reacting" to life, to put against the ignorance, tastelessness, despair, and impermanence which James felt were threatening to obliterate civilization as he knew it. It is especially appropriate that this "final Preface" about the value of art and the imaginative life is itself a highly "formed" work of art. James said, in a letter to George Bernard Shaw:

> Works of art . . . are capable of saying more things to man about himself than any other 'works' whatever are capable of doing—and it's only by saying . . . , as nearly as we can, all there is, and in as many ways and on as many sides, and with a vividness of presentation that 'art', and art alone, is an adequate mistress of, that we enable him to pick and choose and compare and know, enable him to arrive at any sort of synthesis that isn't, through all its superficialities and vacancies, a base and illusive humbug.

Thus, by its poetic method and by the particular aesthetic pleasures it gives—reflective, meditative, affirmative, celebrative—the *Autobiography* of Henry James is a significant literary document with a deserved place all its own in James's literary achievements.

Louis A. Renza

SOURCE: "Killing Time With Mark Twain's Autobiographies," in *ELH,* Vol. 54, No. 1, Spring, 1987, pp. 157-82.

[*In the following essay, Renza discusses various critical responses to the random and repetitious presentation of events in Mark Twain's* Autobiography *and* Life on the Mississippi.]

> Persons attempting to find a motive in this narrative will be prosecuted; persons attempting

to find a moral in it will be banished; persons attempting to find a plot in it will be shot.

—*Adventures of Huckleberry Finn*

I

Not unexpectedly, Mark Twain's autobiographical writings still provoke critical tall tales. It is well known by now that in his 1924 edition of approximately half of Twain's extant autobiographical papers, Albert Bigelow Paine followed Twain's directive in printing them in the exact sequence of their composition.[1] The result is also well known. Twain's *Autobiography* renders events in a "casual and repetitious and disorderly" manner (Carl Van Doren); Paine's omission of the other papers conceals the anxious and misanthropic Mark Twain "in eruption" (Bernard DeVoto); both the omitted and included papers show the promise of an artistic or at least a conventional autobiographical coherence, but in their present state lack an organizational principle that could have excised the "trivia," the "embarrassing" mélange of "fragmentary notations on news stories of the day, exchange of letters, opinions of the moment" (Charles Neider).[2]

One could easily cite other apparent faults in Twain's forty-year, periodically produced *Autobiography,* such as detailed descriptions of places that lack the barest semblance of metaphorical edge, unmemorable anecdotes of memory, and repetitiously self-conscious references to Twain's very construction of this work. Only a stretched critical imagination, it appears, could make these papers evince even a simple American story of literary or social success, the ideological *telos,* for example, that minimally justifies Benjamin Franklin's otherwise trivial, self-congratulatory, or simply neutral listing of achievements that appears towards the end of his autobiographical memoirs. In short, perceived in terms of established literary criteria, Twain's autobiography seems to request the revisionary selections and narrative reorganizations later attempted by the DeVoto and Neider editions. For Paine to have published these papers in literal-minded obedience to Twain's wishes, Neider suggests, only does "injury to his literary reputation," a reputation which at least in this instance Twain's critical guardians tend to regard as canonically precarious.[3]

Of course, one could regard the *Autobiography* as simply a minor aberration within Twain's literary career. His canonical status, after all, surely rests secure on the evidence of his published fiction and more successful forays into autobiographical writing such as *Life on the Mississippi.* Yet even the reader of *Life* confronts a work in a state of narrative dishabille. There, too, one encounters a loose narrative series of chapters comprised of miscellaneous conventional genres, whimsically inserted digressions, episodes, anecdotes, jokes, newspaper excerpts, letters, geographical and economic "facts," and even an arbitrarily thrown in chapter from *Adventures of Huckleberry Finn.* Inscribed within the second part of this commissioned travel-book about his return to the Mississippi, such textual confusion tends to dilute the more tightly focused narrative of "Old Times on the Mississippi," the narrative of Twain's youthful experiences as a steamboat pilot, which had appeared earlier in the *Atlantic* and which now formally constitutes only the first part of *Life.*

Still, there exist more critically exegetical perspectives than DeVoto's or Neider's to recuperate the aesthetic force and value of the *Autobiography* and *Life on the Mississippi.* For example, why not regard the very compositional praxis of the *Autobiography,* a praxis to which Twain continually draws his and our attention, as the self-referential center of this work? From this perspective, Twain's "disorderly" references to past and present events function as pretexts for a mode of narration that one could characterize as a forerunner of stream of consciousness prose. Moreover, by situating this compositional thematic within the postbellum American era, one could also argue that this apparently free-associational procedure of writing expressionistically dramatizes what Jay Martin describes as Twain's turn from "the terror of drift," his sense of encroaching worldly chaos and "despair" that began to surface in his later fiction, "into a principle of pleasure."[4] At the very least, Twain's mode of writing his *Autobiography* has all the honorific traits of an "experiment" in which, according to Marilyn DeEulis, he seeks to transcend "conventional autobiographical idiom" and thus destroy time or, in his words, "deliver the past whole." On the one hand, as a collage of discrete verbal activities, the *Autobiography* distinguishes itself "from the mainstream of American personal narrative"; on the other, precisely because it enacts a "sensitivity to the potentials of medium," it not only "connects [itself] to the bulk of Twain's literary efforts," but also, we could say, here as well engages a protomodernist or ideologically universal project: to "kill" time by spatializing it—to make the past become present through the mediation of the text.[5]

But in making such claims, critics like Martin and DeEulis tend to overlook the phenomenological datum and/or trope of referentiality that at once defines any autobiographical project and, particularly in the case of Twain's topically myriad references to his experiences in the *Autobiography,* mitigates the immanent drama of temporality imputed to its written performance. Conceived as a project before he was to write his major fiction, Twain's autobiographical writings may always have existed alongside his fictional works as ongoing options for writing according to what Martin terms a "principle of pleasure." Thus it is Martin's own critical perspective, his wish to trace the drama of historical change in Twain's later mode of writing, that generates the *Autobiography*'s putative dramatic tension, or its manifest conversion from "terror" to "pleasure."[6] To the same effect, DeEulis cites the various means by which Twain strives to realize the "innovative" autobiographical goal of making his past present, his "uniquely ambitious attempt to discover a means of cheating the page into charting a life": when first writing autobiography, for example, Twain employs alliterative, incantative or prose-poetic repetition; when writing it later, he juxtaposes oral dictations to printed newspaper clippings.[7] But in citing these strategies, DeEulis effectively reconstructs the *Autobiography* in terms of an ambitious attempt it itself only occasionally traces through its verbal operations. In other words, she locates the textual value of the Autobiography in its critically deducible intention rather than in its dominant mode of representing past events. Suggestive as it is, then, this critical recuperation of Twain's text ironically reduces it to a failed experiment, for whether as an autobiographical record of Twain's life or as an autobiography of his attempt to write this record, the *Autobiography* by itself lacks the communicative power ("cheating the page into charting a life") with which DeEulis seeks to endow it.

Unquestionably, these critical stretchers regarding Twain's *Autobiography* derive from the mixed, literarily ambitious signals emanating from Twain's autobiographical writings, especially when, as in the case of *Life on the Mississippi*, this ambition indeed seems to constitute the work's dramatic, self-referential subtext. James M. Cox flatly states that as opposed to the "chaos of his *Autobiography*," Twain's "real autobiography, which is say the *myth* of Mark Twain, ended with 'Old Times on the Mississippi.'" For Cox, the very act of writing these sketches effectively converts Samuel Clemens into "Mark Twain," the legendary writer of "a tall tale which an entire nation would come to believe." Cox thus maintains that in "Old Times," Twain metaphorically yokes his past as a riverboat pilot with his present as a writer: "The past which [Twain] was reconstructing involved learning to be a pilot; the act of reconstruction involved learning to be a full-fledged artist".[8] Adding that the river itself "gave Clemens a metaphor that he apparently unconsciously adopted for his method of writing," Edgar J. Burde also perceives this internalized but recoverable symbolic equation of pilot-becoming-writer in the first part of *Life*. Burde specifically regards Twain's depiction of his relation to Bixby, the master pilot and authority-figure in this section, as a figurative pretext through which Twain imagines his own mastery of writing.[9]

But such psychodynamic, symbolically enriching recuperations remain partial at best. If they do not dismiss it outright, they rationalize even as they seek to accommodate the cumbersome facticity of the second part of Twain's *Life*. Thus, Cox sees a fall from humor, a fall from Twain's sense of "having been born . . . out of humiliation inflicted upon him" in "Old Times," to his "nostalgia and sentimental guilt fantasies of *Life on the Mississippi*," and Burde suggests that the second part of *Life* tells the story of Twain's own sense of vocational regression.[10] In fact, this later section ironically enacts the autobiographical principle Twain satirizes in his initial depiction of Brown in "Old Times": "And so on, by the hour, [Brown's] tongue would go. He could *not* forget anything. It was simply impossible. The most

trivial details remained as distinct and luminous in his head, after they had lain there for years, as the most memorable events."[11]

In contrast to *Life*, the variety of topical concerns in the *Autobiography* lacks even a provisionally symbolic autobiographical vehicle (rehearsing one's past experiences through a narrative figuratively synonymous with a journey on a once familiar river) without which it also lacks a recuperable psychodramatic topos that could signify Twain's progressive (or regressive) sense of vocation. Indeed, when writing this later autobiographical work, Twain himself seems to recognize his reliance on the operational ideal of, if not actual ability to effect, a Brown-like screed of details: "When I was younger I could remember anything, whether it happened or not; but my faculties are decaying now, and soon I shall be so I cannot remember any but the things that never happened" (1:96).

But couldn't we regard this ironic repetition of Brown's "casual and repetitious and disorderly" memory in Twain's later *Autobiography* as an instance of his self-evident desire to differentiate its writing from prevailing standards of literary narrative? And is this desire adumbrated even in the way he sets aside *Huckleberry Finn* to write *Life?* Or mitigates in *Life* the metaphor of self he had inscribed in "Old Times"? Or in writing his unpublished *Autobiography*, employs an unalleviated digressive praxis that all but guarantees future injury to his public literary career? Of course, Twain's statements on writing his *Autobiography* hardly exhibit signs of literary anxiety, let alone of a masochistic or perversely deliberate effort to sabotage the very canonical career his textual bookkeepers would preserve. On the contrary, he admits to looking for a way to write his *Autobiography* that would make his "labor . . . mere amusement, play, pastime, and wholly effortless" (1:233). In other words, he seeks to write it with pastoral ease: by simply allowing his "narrative [to] flow as flows the brook down through the hills and the leafy woodlands, its course changed by every bowlder it comes across . . . always *going*, and always following at least one law . . . the law of *narrative*, which *has no law*" (1:237).

At the same time, however, these methodological remarks clearly betray a certain self-consciousness. As with fiction, for example, nineteenth-century autobiographical narratives conventionally tend to follow the "law" of teleological coherence rather than the quixotic (non-)principle of pastoral "play."[12] Twain himself recognizes this demand for narrative coherence—a demand that would convert his writing into a species of concentrated and patient literary "labor"—even as he writes his autobiographical papers: "There is only one right form for a story, and if you fail to find that form the story will not tell itself. You may try a dozen wrong forms but in each case you will not get very far. . . . " (*E*, 199). Paradoxically, then, he must at least unconsciously labor to keep from writing his *Autobiography* as a "story" necessitating his consciousness of "right form." Moreover,

Twain's sense of narrative law derives from a tradition of past autobiographical narratives that, by an inescapable if subliminal analogy, invokes a *textual* past that can always interrupt his attempt to convert his recollections of the past into the self-present substitutive play of his "always going" narrative praxis. For example, the *Autobiography* clearly recognizes its own affiliation with at least one textual precedent: "This autobiography of mine differs from other autobiographies—differs from *all* other autobiographies, except Benvenuto's, perhaps" (2:311). But if this passage's last-minute qualifying "perhaps" suggests Twain's self-confidence about the unique self-presence of his project, his adoption of Cellini as his sole autobiographical precursor clearly works to neutralize the force field of other potential claimants to autobiographical originality. It inversely confesses, in other words, his sense of textual precedents—especially closer-to-home American autobiographical precedents like Franklin's—which he here conspicuously reduces to one monolithic entity: "*all* other autobiographies."[13]

In short, Twain's desire to write autobiography in a pastoral or time-lessening mode of composition encounters the immanent problem of his writing autobiography autobiographically, or in his own radically original style or signature:

> all our phrasings are spiritualized shadows cast multitudinously from our readings: . . . no happy phrase of ours is ever quite original with us; there is nothing of our own in it except some slight change born of our temperament, character, environment, teachings, and associations; . . . that this slight change differentiates it from another man's manner of saying it, stamps it with our own special style, and makes it our own for the time being.

> (1:241)

Just as he claims that his writing differs from "all other autobiographies," Twain here notably "cast[s]" prior textual "phrasings" as "multitudinously" indeterminate—as virtually unspecifiable precedents whose influence on his project he thus momentarily neutralizes. Only by "*always* going" or continuously losing himself through the act of writing, then, can he effectively outrace the "spiritualized shadows" of these other texts in order to achieve his "own special [autobiographical] style."

But to write continuously also precludes the possibility of self-consciously registering the "slight change" that putatively differentiates his writing (and by extension, the experiences it traces) from these same shadowy and shadowing texts. And what happens when he perforce stops writing and in fact discerns his autobiographical imprimatur or stamp in the residual text that this writing has ineluctably produced? For one thing, he can come face to face with the temporality generated by the precedent of his own textual activity. In one place in his *Autobiography,* he (correctly) surmises that a then popular event in the newspapers, "the Morris incident," will inevitably lose its status as an interesting event for his future readers. In the process, it will also lose its power as a signifier of his ongoing narrative present. In other words, Twain's anticipation that this event will become purely past or lack its referential vitality beyond the historical moment effectively contaminates his narrative's substitutive project to evoke its own radical self-presence: "It may be some years yet, but . . . I am confident that by that time the nation, encountering the Morris incident in my autobiography, would be trying to remember what the incident was, and not succeeding" (1:285).

The sheer act of writing autobiography, then, at once facilitates and frustrates his project to write it in the mode of pastoral play. Even in *Life,* Twain can only incompletely sustain his attempt to forget, paradoxically by thematically staging, the textual precedents his writing inevitably invokes. The writer Walter Scott, for example, becomes his scapegoat in *Life* for an impotent or "old inflated" Southern prose beholden to "the past, not the present" (241). Yet as James Cox points out, Twain's own writing, even in one of the most famous passages from "Old Times" referring to how "the romance and beauty were all gone from the river," itself occasionally lapses into "conventionalized pretentiousness" or else "hovers along the borderline of two or three grandiose clichés." Far from catching Twain in an egregious contradiction, however, Cox argues that in the context of "Old Times" such a passage demonstrates Twain's awareness of the need to "slough off" by here "recreating . . . the whole sentimental tradition of art" in order "to learn the *art* of piloting" or, metaphorically speaking, the art of writing.[14] But since Twain, a lapsed Southern writer himself, explicitly introduces the issue of Scott's influence in the second part of *Life,* we can also infer that his metaphorical revision of the "sentimental tradition" in "Old Times" fails to prevent the latter's resurgent influence when writing his later narrative, hence his revisionary recourse there to an explicit conceptual belittlement of this influence.

Textuality, in short, inevitably becomes synonymous with the very past he wishes to regard as inviting the self-present play of autobiographical signification. But if this text-congealing past threatens to frame his present scene of writing as one of labor rather than pastoral play, it does soonly after his having written: in the ebb from each performative instance of discourse. Thus, if only in the moment of writing forwards, Twain can still intentionalize the act of autobiographical writing per se as a recuperable and repeatable site of a text-evading, self-present play of discourse: "the idea of blocking out a consecutive series of events which have happened to me, or which I imagine have happened to me—I can see that that is impossible for me. The only thing possible for me is to talk about the thing that something suggests at the moment . . ." (1:269). At the same time, we have already seen how Twain must also intentionalize this writing as always in the process of evading the immanently present narrative demand for the "one right form" associated with the writing of fiction and traditional autobiography. His anarchic narrative praxis in *Life* and the *Autobiography* can thus effectively displace the pastness signified by his own as well as other texts. Because it is distracted by the need to evade "right form," Twain's writing can again recover itself as a self-referential signifier of a present that reduces such influences to inconsequential or merely epiphenomenal pressures.

Needless to say, this last mode of recovery has indisputable canonical consequences. Assiduously defined as an endless exercise in play, Twain's autobiographical writing in effect defines him as a childlike or "minor" authorial persona. And in no less assiduously construing this writing precisely as a continual evasion of narrative law and/or the pressures of marketplace or serious literary production, Twain indeed deliberately seeks to define such writing, at least to himself, as an ongoing, purely recreational activity without any literary consequences—in short, as a radically minor literary project.

II

But it turns out that even this would-be enabling conception of the autobiographical project as a species of minor literary play ironically engages another unexpected American precedent: that of Poe's secret autobiographical project as subliminally expressed through his tales.[15] This connection between Poe and Twain as intentional practitioners of a minor autobiographical literature at first, of course, seems as bizarre as one of Poe's tales or as tall as one of Twain's. Yet just as we saw Twain explicitly acknowledge in order to minimize the influence of Scott, so we find Twain resorting to a series of textual strategies in part 2 of *Life* as well as his *Autobiography* to distance himself from or neutralize Poe so as to gain his freedom to write autobiography in his own original *and minor* literary terms.

The most obvious such strategy is humor, humor here understood as a narrative trope rather than as an identifiable aspect of his style or thematic proclivities. That is, through humor and parody Twain can bring Poe consciously into his text in a manner that avoids the issue of influence. For example, he writes quite literally of a "Captain Poe" in *Life* who commits a deed very much like that of the narrator in Poe's "The Black Cat." His boat snagged and filling with water "in the head of Kentucky Bend" (the Southern ambience of Poe's tales?), this Captain Poe "cut into his wife's stateroom from above with an ax; she was asleep in the upper berth, the roof a flimsier one than was supposed; the first blow crashed down through the rotten boards and clove her skull" (167). In the same way, Twain's humorous exposé of spiritualist seances in *Life* (247-49) also doubles as a parodic framing and reduction of Poe's "Mesmeric Revelation" and "The Facts in the Case of M. Valdemar." *Life* also contains spoofs of Poe's tales of criminal-alias-textual detection: Karl Ritter's Pudd'nhead Wilson-like discovery of a murderer by means of a thumbprint (174-75); or Twain's own preposterous decipherment of an epistolary forgery—a text

also referred to as "literary machinery" (270-72).[16] Indeed, we could claim that this equally Poe-esque association of mechanism with text also informs Twain's concern with the visual or printed format of his *Autobiography*, a format that not only includes literal collocations of other texts like actual newspaper stories (not unlike Poe's "Marie Roget"), but more generally refers us to his experiments with writing on the typewriter and his half-humorous advocacy of a "simplified alphabet."[17]

To be sure, like his apparent sense of alienated literary labor, Twain's association or blurring of text with mechanism undoubtedly bespeaks the pressures incurred by his specific ideological as well as literary-historical scene of writing. Doesn't his enthusiastic if doomed investment in the Paige typesetter, a quintessential example of his wish to convert text into mechanism, suggest Twain's endorsement of his postbellum America's wholesale commitment to industrial capitalist expansion, especially as abetted by a marked technological progress? But in the first place, critics like John Kasson have noted Twain's critical or at least ambivalent relation to the American postbellum "technological sublime."[18] More important, the necessarily asymmetrical relation between discernible historical and literary-historical influences on a writer's specific scene of writing complicates our ability to decide which influence takes priority over the other as regards a particular text. In either case, Twain's visualist-mechanistic sense of textuality effectively defines the autobiographical text as a marginal allegory rather than as a fully self-present symbol of the autobiographer's consciousness. Since it is not organically but mechanically, that is, arbitrarily, related to its writer's sense of referring to his past, or since it only appears as a "thing" comprised of interchangeable parts, such a text belongs to no one in particular and to anyone in general.[19] Moreover, to construe one's text as a mechanism is also to license an explicitly plagiaristic procedure—the construction of any text in terms of preestablished or non-author-ized parts. This procedure clearly manifests itself in Poe's obsessive concerns with detecting plagiarisms in the works of other writers, a charge of self-conscious literary concealment, of course, to which his own works remain liable. Not surprisingly, we also find Twain resorting to similar procedures throughout his autobiographical papers. There he not only collects news accounts, letters and other texts written by others (including his daughter Susy's biography of him), but like Poe with his contemporary "literati" he also de-author-izes Shakespeare, for example, in a long and putatively serious essay he wanted included among these papers.

Because this plagiaristic praxis appears explicit or self-evidently signifies itself as such, however, we could equally surmise that Twain here registers a "slight change" from Poe's more concealed mode of plagiarism. Thus, he all but confesses his plagiaristic procedures in part 2 of *Life on the Mississippi* when he names "Rob Styles" as the character who "explodes" his self-adopted "incognito" in the pilot's cabin after first returning to the river (129-33). From this perspective the second part of *Life* reads less like a composite miscellany of various literary genres than a nonteleological series of pilfered ad hoc "styles" of writing. These overexposed styles, moreover, perform at least two strategic functions. First, their obtrusive appearance interferes with the reader's conventional demand for a representationally thematic autobiographical story of self-progression or regression. Second, they also effectively transform the journey-topos itself into a mere pretext for an apparently stylistic exhibitionism that Twain would have the reader easily rationalize as a series of mere literary jokes.

Thus, if his Poe-esque allusions at once strive and fail to decisively separate his text from Poe's precedent, they also double at a distance Poe's own humorous, parodic, pun-ridden and plagiaristic strategies. Moreover, the melting-pot inclusion of largely incompatible genres and styles in *Life,* akin to Poe's inscribed overexposures of his period's literary-generic practices, fortuitously serves to conceal Twain himself, the writer of these autobiographical texts, from their would-be reader. For besides textual precedents, textuality also entails the sociality indigenous to the very act of writing. Despite the fact that he dictates or writes much of his *Autobiography* explicitly in terms of a public witness like Paine, and although, as we shall see, Twain desires to postpone the transformation of his writing per se into a public text (the reason he projects its publication "a century hence" [1:322]), this very writing ceaselessly invokes a public readership as he writes these papers. The sheer public semiosis of writing, then, best accounts for his association of the literary profession with slavery and his (former) piloting with freedom in another well-known passage from the first part of *Life:*

> I loved the [pilot's] profession far better than any I have followed since, and I took a measureless pride in it. The reason is plain: a pilot, in those days, was the only unfettered and entirely independent human being that lived on the earth. . . . Writers of all kinds are manacled servants of the public. We write frankly and fearlessly, but then we "modify" before we print.
>
> (77-78)

This nostalgic diminution of his vocation as a writer clearly assumes that writing quintessentially publishes or makes public what it refers to and thus becomes prone to censorship, that is, to the juridical, moral and/or aesthetic demands of a public at large: the others coterminously invoked in his acts of writing, and more specifically of persons whom he intimately knows and whom his autobiographical narrative could still offend or who could still offend him.

Thus, the deaths of Brown and Sellers in *Life* eventuate in his freedom to take revenge on them precisely through a now "unfettered" act of autobiographical writing. Conversely, writing about an incident in his *Autobiography* after his wife's death—he had allowed and

even encouraged Olivia to expurgate morally questionable passages from his other written works—now frees him to confess responsibility for his son's death, which occurred when she was alive: "I was the cause of the child's illness. . . . I have always felt shame for that treacherous morning's work. . . . I doubt if I had the courage to make confession at the time. I think it most likely that I have never confessed until now" (2:230-31). Other shameful incidents he cannot "consent to [have] go on paper yet. . . . [If] I should put in all those incidents I would be sure to strike them out when I came to revise this book" (2:331). Yet the conditional ("if I should") and indefinite aspect of these confessions about the incidents not confessed ("fifteen hundred to two thousand" of them), not to mention the conditional and indefinite confession ("I doubt if I had the courage at the time") about another confession that still only *might* have occurred ("most likely . . . I have never confessed until now"), clearly exemplifies Twain's fugitive mode of producing texts that readers might otherwise apprehend as minimally consistent with conventional autobiographies. In this sense, the autobiographical project enables Twain to at least imagine a mode of literary production free from the competitive ideology of his postbellum American environment; or equivalently, it serves as a pretext for entertaining the possibility of a purely narcissistic relation to his act of writing. And here again we can detect Poe's autobiographical influence on Twain, this time revealing itself not only in the uncannily similar words they respectively use to describe the autobiographical project, but also in their similar views of it as little more than an idea:

> Once written, [men] would laugh at the notion of being disturbed by [an autobiography's] publication during their life . . . [or] after their death. But to write it—*there* is the rub. No man dare write it. No man ever will dare write it. No man *could* write it, even if he dared. The paper would shrivel and blaze at every touch of the fiery pen.[20]

> What a wee little part of a person's life are his acts and his words! His real life is led in his head, and is known to none but himself. . . . The mass of him is hidden—it and its volcanic fires that toss and boil, and never rest, night nor day. These are his life, and they are not written, and cannot be written.
>
> (1:2)

For both writers, the disturbing aspect of writing autobiography lies not in its imagined (im)moral content, even less in the publication of such content, but rather in the "fiery" and "volcanic" *intentionality* of simply writing it. Poe and Twain, that is, construe the autobiographical project itself as a radically narcissistic or antisocial epistemological activity. To write autobiography is to violate the conventional social norms of knowing and thus of expressing oneself insofar as such writing reveals the impossibility of representing one's thoughts to others. Preexisting and coming after each imagined instance of writing them down, these thoughts *become* "hidden" precisely through such writing. For Twain, writing autobiography only makes one aware of "the storm of thoughts that is forever blowing through one's head. . . . Therefore a full autobiography has never been written, and it never will be" (1:283). To Twain, writing autobiography thus entails a kind of suicide, an imaginary occlusion of its reading by others—"I am not interested in getting done with anything. I am only interested in talking along and wandering around as much as I want to, regardless of results to the future reader" (1:327)—and an imaginary posthumous writing that expels any imagined reading of his text (including his own) as he writes it: "In this Autobiography, I shall keep in mind . . . that I am speaking from the grave. . . . [The] writer gets his limitless freedom of statement and expression from his sense that no stranger is going to see what he is writing" (1:xv). Bordering on social pariahhood, such grave-like writing (itself Poe-esque) insists on repressing what these very passages show gets continually regenerated: the continual reification of his own acts of writing; their constant phenomenological transformation into a finishable or objectified text that self-referentially signifies to him their displacement into a de facto past tense.[21] At the very least, if autobiographical narrative at first seems to license limitless or uninhibited acts of writing, it also tends to become "too literary" for him, already, as he confesses at one point, too much like a text that reinvokes the "stranger" reading that can inhibit his autobiographical performance: "Within the last eight or ten years I have made several attempts to do the autobiography . . . with a pen, but the result was not satisfactory; it was too literary. With the pen in one's hand, narrative is a difficult art. . . . " (1:237).

In this sense, one can argue that Twain willingly accepts rather than intentionally evades the moral or aesthetic ("right form") censorship of his writing. Shifting genres, robbed styles, censored or "manacled" writing: these clearly decenter Twain as *Life*'s main narrative consciousness as well as the work's foregrounded autobiographical focus. In the same way, Twain's explicitly intertextual constructions of *Life* and the *Autobiography* show his tendency to frame "writing" within his own writing in order to destabilize the locus of his authorial voice and to promote a textual confusion that doubly displaces the otherwise unproblematically accessible autobiographical tenor of these works to their reader. Both as theme and act of narration, the autobiographical self here turns into an intersection, a nonself-centered conduit, of other texts that contaminate the autobiographer's putatively dominant narrative with contingency. And besides projecting his writing as being always on the verge of disappearing from its reader, such framing also exemplifies another internalization of Poe, namely a structural as well as thematic deployment of doubling.[22] As we have seen, for example, *Life* clearly constitutes a two-part or bifurcated text about two times in his life and, because of the historical marker of the Civil War, two times in the life of the Mississippi region.[23] But the most telling and well-known example of narrative doubling in *Life* concerns Twain's representation of his own

vocational identity: not only his nominal differentiation of himself as former pilot and present writer, "Samuel Clemens" and "Mark Twain," but also his ambivalent allusions to the origins and significance of his nom de plume. Did Mark Twain take his literary name, as Cox suggests, in reparation for a guilty deed he had done to Isaiah Sellers?[24] Or did he take it out of nostalgia for an innocent time in his life when "mark twain!" could metonymically signify his youth—precisely when as an inexperienced steamboat pilot he could become the butt of Bixby's joke (*L*, 75-77)?

Such doubling here and elsewhere in Twain's autobiographical writings functions to retroactively revise the referential events of his past life by exposing their incomplete status, their capacity to be narrated in a different register of discourse or from a different moment of memory. This incompleteness in turn undoes their standing as conventional autobiographical referents. In the *Autobiography,* for example, Twain's confession of his dream, censored in *Life,* about Henry's death (he can now confess it because of his mother's death [1:306-12]) has the effect of converting *Life* into a palimpsest or provisional autobiographical text. Once made, moreover, this conversion also inevitably redounds to the *Autobiography*'s own referential events, including the very one which licenses such speculation. Similarly, *Life* doubles to undo the latent vocational metaphoricity of "Old Times." Besides markedly diluting this metaphoricity, the generic reifications of autobiographical narrative in the second part of *Life* also enact by signifying a marked change of passing textual time, which in turn metonymically marks a separation between the two vocations in his life. If "Old Times" narrates his past experience on the river in a way that yokes his past and present vocations, Twain's writing of *Life* again disjoins them by making "Old Times" a narrative about himself before he became the well-known writer he is when he comes to write *Life*. *Life* converts "Old Times," already a story about apprenticeship rather than professional expertise, into a pre-vocational story about a textually incognito Samuel Clemens, the self as writer-yet-to-be. When Rob Styles "explodes" his "incognito" in part 2 of *Life,* he discloses Twain's identity as "Samuel Clemens," ex-pilot, not as "Mark Twain," the writer who, were we to regard this scene as metaphorical at all, here figuratively represents himself as still incognito, that is even as he writes this very narrative.

Twain's textual doubling thus effectively blocks out past acts of autobiographical writing and substitutes in their place a merely propaedeutic scene of writing wherein he positions himself as about to write the autobiography others, therefore, will never come to read. In the manner of Poe with his tales, Twain paradoxically never "writes" the autobiographical texts he of necessity actually produces. Moreover, textual doubling also allows Twain to write such texts in terms of a hidden persona that enables him to determine his own private relation to this writing in the face of anticipated literary communities or codes, morally, commercially, or canonically defined, which would place it in the public domain even as he writes it. It is in this sense that Twain so casually places an unfinished work of fiction, *The Mysterious Stranger,* in his *Autobiography,* and inserts a chapter from *Huckleberry Finn,* his great novel about the Mississippi region which he was then in the process of writing, into *Life,* an autobiographical narrative even less associated with literature than the Mississippi sketches of "Old Times." Writing *Huckleberry Finn,* that is, no doubt calls up to him a variety of overdetermined literary pressures and ambitions. At the very least, it reminds him of his need to find the "only one right form," in other words, of his difficult literary labor within the commercial marketplace as well as the precincts of literary history.

The intertextual doubling of fiction by autobiography in *Life* and the *Autobiography* thus separates—appropriately marks in twain—two modes of textual production or scenes of writing: one publicly and intimately communicable through imagination and requiring narrative care; the other restricting such access by virtually becoming, like the later *Autobiography,* a deliberately careless and Poe-esque self-indulgent tall tale devolving on Twain's private autobiographical relation to autobiographical writing itself. This relation requires the no less fantastic demand that Twain continually evade the psychodramatic demands posed by the inevitable placement of this writing in a competitive field not only comprised of past texts but also of future as well as contemporary codes of reading, and not least those critical responses we have seen striving to redeem or censor his autobiographical writings precisely as psychodramatic or serious literary events. In short, Twain's autobiographical writings ironically confess his desire to produce texts that will appear radically contingent to others, which is to say free from any and all inspections associated with any and all regnant criteria of major literature.

III

Needless to say, the foregoing critical fantasy of Twain's autobiographical fantasy could still point to his representative American resistance to whatever privileged criteria would not only deny original status to his work, but also in effect preclude his original relation to its very production. Not just in his autobiographies but even in his fiction we can discern doubling functioning as a strategy to neutralize such criteria. His "talking," vernacular, or humorous prose constantly undercuts serious or teleologically coherent narrative projects, most notably in the last, "Tom Sawyer" chapters of *Huckleberry Finn.* In a metaphorical mood, one could even construe Twain's stated preference in *Life* for cremation over burial in graveyards (for even "the children know that a dead saint enters upon a century-long career of assassination the moment the earth closes over his corpse" [221]) as a latent or underdetermined image of his heroic desire to burn away or explode dead literary monuments, including his own, and destroy the very idea of canonical uniqueness itself. Or, clearly echoing

with American democratic vistas, Twain's stated principle of narrative anarchy in his *Autobiography,* his mode of representing important and unimportant events side by side so that "nobody will be able to tell one [incident] from the other by difference of size" (1:238), or simply his desire not to be "interested in interesting [the] reader" of his narrative (2:312), could easily disguise an aggressive democratic theory of writing that seeks to evade arranging autobiographical references according to an ideologically privileged *telos* or a hierarchical scale of human values. Twain thus thinks his *Autobiography* will be interesting precisely because it "deals merely in the common experiences which go to make up the life of the average human being . . ." (2:245). Even those (in this context) merely inferred narcissistic maneuvers of both *Life* and the *Autobiography* perhaps mask Twain's critical relation to a postbellum America's anti-democratic ideology; that is, at the level of autobiographical style they effectively duplicate the confidence-man role he more representationally assigns to Huck Finn as "a figure of survival in a confidence [postbellum American] culture. . . . "[5] At the very least, couldn't one easily maintain that the second part of *Life* thematically expresses Twain's continuing nostalgic desire for his former innocent relation to a Mississippi region whose synecdochal river—no less than Thoreau's Walden Pond—itself synecdochally represents an original nature in the Emersonian American grain? Moreover, both Twain's avowed pastoral topos in *Life* (his return to this river, after all, invokes another pastoral American myth in its taking place after a Rip Van Winkle-like twenty years) and his avowed pastoral process of writing the *Autobiography* (a process he continually invokes as such by a paradoxically focused and self-conscious anarchic mode of referentiality) work to preserve his autobiographical materials from becoming as stale or commonplace to him as they become, for instance, to that Vicksburg couple in *Life* who experienced war bombardments for six successive weeks: "Left to tell their story in their own way, those people told it without fire, almost without interest" (192). For the same reason, Twain cannot use "skeleton notes . . . as texts in writing . . . chapters" in his *Autobiography,* for "if I left them unused for several weeks, or several months, their power to suggest and excite had usually passed away" (1:326).

Yet such ideological redemptions of Twain's democratic or anarchically original autobiographical intentions suspiciously resemble canonical apologies for his literarily embarrassing *Autobiography.* Rather than evincing aggressive or inversely ambitious anti-canonical postures, this writing consistently resorts to what we could more accurately depict as a virtually endless series of *de-*canonical verbal maneuvers. If *Life* explicitly invites its readers to make ideologically serious connections or closures, their recurrent, even pervasive, and so always possibly operative veto by humor continually casts doubt on them ahead of time. At best, this humor forces the reader into a self-conscious relation to their merely latent operational presence within Twain's narrative. His provocative cremation of canonicity, for example, remains a recalcitrant or deadpan metonym, no more than a latent metaphor of his anti-canonical desires—a defiguration, then, of what could ideologically redramatize the very process or scene of his writing.

Thus, if Twain undoubtedly seeks to intentionalize the past as an endlessly open present, to bring "the past and the present . . . constantly . . . face to face, resulting in contrasts which newly fire up the interest all along" (2:245), this quest for continual narrative originality gets no less continually aborted by the residual narrative that the reader will in fact confront. Writing an allegory of an autobiography that he never quite wants to become public, Twain also seeks to postpone the placement of his texts in both literary-historical and marketplace settings. In this light, for example, his recurring self-conscious ruminations on the nature of his autobiography function as tropes that, in relation to the prospective reader of his *Autobiography,* conceptualize and thus block this reader's actual or active participation in the present process of writing. For Twain alone, then, this continual and solely experimental process "fire[s] up [his] interest all along."

For this reason, he also internalizes strategies of reading within his *Autobiography* to ensure its incomplete status in relation to how he wants to imagine others will only be able to read it. Rather than offering a model of an ideal reading others should adopt with his text, Twain on occasion explicitly inscribes this hermeneutical *mise en scène* to project his own ideal or posthumous reading of it, that is, as if when his text will have become a published or finished metonym of his life to others. Even in this imagined future, as this staged proleptic reading seeks to demonstrate, his text will remain incomplete and thus fugitive to any ideological demand. In his *Autobiography,* for example, he incorporates his daughter Susy's biography of him in narrative fragments interspersed with his own present commentary. Besides serving to postpone his literal memory of her death, this narrative as fragmented through his writing in effect slows down both his reading of her biographical narrative and his autobiographical recollections of himself in relation to what she in fact wrote about him. Through his *Autobiography,* Susy's biography, an unpolished, fragmentary as well as non-literary narrative of his life (an account written, after all, by a child) literally takes time to read. As such, it also doubles and serves to define the unpolished, non-literary and still unfinished status of the *Autobiography* he himself is presently writing.

Yet insofar as such strategies threaten to surface as strategies, they also threaten to reinvoke Twain's sense of writing a public or other-directed text. And so the best strategy for killing time lies in his accepting and even promoting the inevitable textual reification of his writing. Once written, that is, Twain's signified experiences function as *post factum* markers of a private autobiographical space which his writing has yet to traverse:

"[An autobiographer's] acts and . . . words are merely the visible, thin crust of his world, with its scattered snow summits and its vacant wastes of water—and they are so trifling a part of his bulk! a mere skin enveloping it" (1:2). Readers, then, will perceive a "visible" textual account of the autobiographer's memories that will seem relatively complete or finished. But as Twain imagines their reception, these memories become simultaneously framed as residually "trifling" signifieds, "a mere skin" of references, thus also becoming mere pretexts for other memories within or beyond the former ones. As such they can only appear to him alone with the promise of autobiographical transcriptions endlessly yet to occur or with the Chicago-like novelty he praises at the end of *Life:* "She is always a novelty, for she is never the Chicago you saw when you passed through the last time" (316).

In this sense, too, Twain reversibly tries to accelerate rather than slow down the transformation of private writing into public text. His experiments in writing his *Autobiography* with the typewriter and later by stenographic dictation performatively spatialize narrative time, that is, rapidly convert the temporality synonymous with writing into a finished or printed—a public—text. But they do so first in the mode of a privately published document, and second in a way that makes recorded memories seem superficially present or displaced as memories by their visible objectification. On the one hand, Twain's experiments in textual spatialization through dictation free him from the "difficult art" of writing narrative "with the pen in one's hand." As with his association of textual production with mechanical reproduction, they liberate his memories from the literary constraints he associates with writing autobiography. On the other hand, these devices for spatializing his text paradoxically induce his veritable amnesia about such memories even when he records and thus manifestly remembers them.[26] In other words, they exempt Twain from registering the loss of time as determined by the always possible discrepancy between the pastness of a remembered event and its present autobiographical transcription. For example, if in the process of writing he sometimes remembers a "forgotten event [by employing] another forgotten event for its resurrection" (1:239), he clearly cannot forget forgetfulness or the sense of lost time itself. Even as he writes his narrative, text-spatializing procedures reproduce its ersatz fate as a public text. They afford him a way to peruse how others will peruse his text, so see and thus define it as it will be seen, hence to grasp it as a pretext for securing his private or incognito relation to his act of writing autobiography. In the end, doesn't even the commodified status of *Life* constitute such a pretext? If the commodification of "Old Times" through *Life* exemplifies Twain's alienation or enslavement within the American literary and/or economic marketplace, this very situation ironically propagates his wish to realize a private and totally free relation to his act of writing. Producing it as a commodity, Twain can regard his writing while writing as if through the eyes of others expecting a narrative without canonical literary value. Through this semiotic self-alienation—an active exploitation rather than reflexive sublimation of literary-economic alienation—Twain's writing of *Life* here again imaginatively positions itself as a superficial or minor literary activity. Assured of its status as a devalued commodified activity, Twain can read his own narrative at once like and unlike those pilots that "Old Times" depicts as "gazing at the water and pretending to read it *as if* it were a book"—a superficial narrative, that is, "which told [Twain] nothing" (48; my emphasis). Yet even as "nothing," this commodified narrative again intimates a private space of writing, a symbolic autobiographical writing still to take place or be expressed.

But what about his *Autobiography?* There Twain's unconventional writing and refusal to publish it during his lifetime suggest his attempt, as DeVoto notes, to "outwit the copyright law" and avoid "economic exploitation" (*E*, xv). Yet if he resists conceiving his *Autobiography* as a public commodity, he still envisions it as a private enterprise, if only in the sense of a private or paradoxically vacant scene of writing. Writing autobiography thus induces a dialectical situation in which Twain can narcissistically promote himself into a valuable commodity to himself. Not only does he write this work as "a mirror, and I am looking at myself in it all the time," he uses "the people that pass along my back" as he writes it to "help advertise me and flatter me and raise me in my own estimation . . ." (2:312).

Thus, whether as a spatialized text, a self-inscribed public or private commodity, or a teleologically unredeemed and virtually interminable series of anecdotes or memories, Twain's autobiographical writing assiduously seeks to insulate itself from even the desire for literary or ideological rereadings. For this reason, Twain self-consciously defines his autobiography's "apparently system-less" procedures as "a complete and purposed jumble—a course which begins nowhere, follows no specified route, and can never reach an end while I am alive" (2:246). For this reason, too, he keeps seeking to clear a space for beginning to write the autobiography he literally keeps beginning to write: "I resolved to begin my autobiography at once. I did begin it, but the resolve melted away and disappeared in a week and I threw my beginning away. Since then, about every three or four years I have made other beginnings and thrown them away" (1:236-37). Such repetitive autobiographical beginnings clearly suggest the arbitrary textual status the *Autobiography* possesses for Twain himself. A text in the potential state of perpetual beginning remains a private text since others can only read it as having already begun. Far from indicating his psychosymbolic attempts through autobiographical writing either to delay his death or to achieve a representatively free, constantly original and inalienable relation to his life, this autobiography of autobiographical beginnings (not to mention its very advertisement in the *Autobiography*) thus serves to remind Twain of the contingency of his project, or of its inevitable misapprehension by others as wholly

equivalent to this project's objectification as a definitively public text. Moreover, this inscribed memo about his contingent scene of autobiographical writing has for him the further strategic effect of deferring the textual appearance of "Mark Twain," the immediately recognizable public literary figure whose writing, as even these marginal psychosymbolic understandings of this sense demonstrate, would no less immediately become public property—not his own.

In short, one could argue that the narrative as well as generic "jumble" comprising both *Life on the Mississippi* and Twain's *Autobiography* has no other ostensible intention than to kill time: to waste one's time in the writing or reading of these works. Of course, public by definition although sufficiently jumbled as to resist actual publication, these texts cannot fully repress their inherited ideological charges to have produced a democratically available, original, marketable, or even ideologically self-alienated American literature. And Twain no doubt revealingly protests too much about the "systemless" method of his *Autobiography*. In spite and perhaps because of its evasive textual strategies, his autobiographical writing keeps turning into "no holiday excursion" for him but "a journey"—a serious literary journey, after all, which he thus "hate[s] to get at" or "begin" (1:269), and which will invite his critical guardians to refine and redeem.

But at the same time, the autobiographical texts which he leaves behind, texts which he projects as postscripts of their scene of writing, in fact manifest little more than "vacant [verbal] wastes" with only occasional—and even then only reluctant—symbolic gestures that like "scattered snow summits" still seem to resist rather than to invite further hermeneutic exploration. At best, they remain unfinished texts, a concessionary series of narratives telling us nothing except that they begin to be autobiography, and so can only begin to execute whatever literary or ideological charge readers may assign to them. Faced with the public and published residues of this writing, which tempt us to construct critical tall tales about their motives, morals and plots, we too can only "kill time" (but never kill *time*) by reading Mark Twain's autobiographies.

NOTES

[1] Mark Twain, *Mark Twain's Autobiography,* ed. Albert Bigelow Paine (New York: Harper and Brothers, 1924), 2 vols. Further references to this edition will be made parenthetically by volume and page.

[2] Carl Van Doren's as well as Charles Neider's remarks on Paine's edition of the *Autobiography* appear in Neider's introduction to his own edition of Twain's autobiographical papers, *The Autobiography of Mark Twain* (New York: Washington Square Press, 1961), xviii. References to Bernard Devoto's edition of Twain's autobiographical papers, *Mark Twain in Eruption* (New York: Harper & Brothers Publishers, 1940), will be

made parenthetically by page and identified as *E*. In these editions of Twain's papers, both DeVoto and Neider try to rearrange the latter according to "a more coherent plan than Mark Twain's (*E*, x) or to a notion of "true autobiography" (Neider, x). Besides excising as well as including materials not published in Paine's edition, both editors modernize Twain's spelling and correct his grammar and erratic punctuation. In large and small matters, then, Twain's textual guardians tend to censor his autobiographical writing; yet such censorship, I argue, constitutes an integral aspect of these disarrayed papers and their inconsistent mode of composition. In his *Mark Twain: The Fate of Humor* (Princeton: Princeton Univ. Press, 1966), 293-310. James M. Cox gives another "strategic" view of Twain's "autobiography" in its various editions. In particular, Cox argues that Twain's papers in effect provoke censorship for a more existentially motivated reason than I propose: "The freedom and the self [Twain] spoke of had meaning only in relation to censorship and approval. Neither form nor self even *existed*, except in relation to publication" (305).

3 Neider, xxii.

4 Jay Martin. *Harvests of Change: American Literature 1865-1914* (Englewood Cliffs: Prentice-Hall, 1967), 199. All but using the phrase 'stream of consciousness," Martin maintains that "Twain's book marks a new stage in the autobiographical form" since it exemplifies "the new conditions of consciousness [after the Civil War] that would come to restructure mental process and shape the modern mind": at the very least, Twain's *Autobiography* actively reflects the growing psychological interest in what "men, for the first time, simultaneously thought and thought about their thought" (199).

5 Marilyn Davis DeEulis, "Mark Twain's Experiments in Autobiography," *American Literature* 53 (1981): 205, 203.

6 On the conception of Twain's autobiographical project, see DeEulis, 204-5. Doubtless even the inertness of Twain's autobiographical narrative could be critically recuperated as a precursor to modernist writing (see Martin, 197-201), especially to the experimental prose of Gertrude Stein. But one only has to think of Twain's contemporary, Henry Adams, who was also in the process of writing an unpublished autobiography, to see an example of autobiographical writing predicated on a principle of dynamic form which Twain's writing assiduously avoids. Thus, in a famous passage from *The Education*, Adams inscribes his own process of writing this work as a drama between personal and impersonal forces: "The pen works for itself, and acts like a hand, modelling the plastic material over and over again to the form that suits it best. The form is never arbitrary, but is a sort of growth like crystallization . . . for often the pencil or pen runs into side paths and shapelessness, loses its relations. . . . Then it has to return on its trail, and recover, if it can, its line of force." *The Education of Henry Adams*, ed. Ernest Samuels (Boston: Houghton Mifflin, 1974), 389.

7 DeEulis, 204, 212-13, 208, 211.

8 Cox, 105, 120.

9 Edgar J. Burde, "Mark Twain: The Writer as Pilot," *PMLA* 73 (1978): 882, 883.

10 Cox, 166: Burde, 885-89.

11 Mark Twain, *Life on the Mississippi* (New York: Amsco School Publications, n.d.), 73. Further references to this edition will be made parenthetically by page and identified, when necessary, as *L*.

12 Of course, many critics have noted the problem of narrative coherence even in Twain's fictional works. Martin regards the deviation from such coherence in Twain's early as opposed to late works of fiction as expressing a positive rather than pejorative "dream of drift" to which the later *Autobiography* returns (193 ff.). John Carlos Rowe (*Through the Custom-House, Nineteenth-Century American Fiction and Modern Theory* [Baltimore: The Johns Hopkins University Press, 1982]. 141 passim) also tries to view Twain's deviant narrative fictional behavior in a positive light. Such deviations. Rowe suggests, tell us more about the egregious critical demands for "order, coherence, consistency, and unity"— and Twain's resistance to such logocentric ideals—than they prove Twain's failure as a literary artist. Still, Twain's sense of the need to find the "one right form for a story" (see pp. 161 and 164 above) shows both his awareness of and tendency to acquiesce to the teleological pressures endemic to conventional narrative writing.

13 As historically, culturally and linguistically distanced, Cellini's autobiography could serve as the very means by which Twain denies the influence of American textual precedents like Franklin's. One could easily argue that Franklin's well-known work renders his past experiences in as casually an idiomatic and unpressured narrative manner as Twain's supposedly innovative *Autobiography* advertises itself as doing. Franklin's represented experiences, moreover, resemble Twain's in the way they conspicuously avoid sensational narrative contexts, that is, do not confess risqué private desires or his life as a revolutionary. Twain's autobiographical project, then, his attempt to abjure self-consciously traditional or teleologically constrained modes of autobiographical narrative, refers itself willy-nilly to an established and even founding American precedent which, although it effectively legitimizes an unpressured mode of autobiographical writing, paradoxically constrains this project to misrecognize its own temporality within American literary history. And although less eccentrically conceived and written than the *Autobiography*, even *Life on the Mississippi* inevitably requires Twain to write within an American tradition of nonconventional personal and pastorally motivated narratives. Like *Life*, for example, Thoreau's no less generically eclectic *A Week on the Concord and Merrimack Rivers* also metaphorically blurs the topos of an American river-journey with the writer's

narrative quest to signify his own and his region's more youthful and pastorally resonant past.

[14] Cox, 112-13, 114.

[15] This view of Poe appears in my essay, "Poe's Secret Autobiography" collected in *The American Renaissance Reconsidered: Selected Papers from the English Institute, 1982-83,* ed. Donald E. Pease and Walter Benn Michaels (Baltimore: The Johns Hopkins Univ. Press, 1985), 58-89. In essence, the essay maintains that Poe deploys a series of strategies in his tales (such as his promotion of his texts as mechanisms and his use of structural as well as representational doubles—matters I invoke in discussing Twain here) to induce his narcissistic relation to the very act of writing them. In other words, Poe writes fiction in such a way as to stage its virtual unreadability to others and/or its reserving a self-referential significance for himself alone. In my discussion here, I only touch upon these matters as they pertain to Twain's (to be sure) more conventionally identifiable autobiographical writing in *Life* and the *Autobiography.* Although critics have generally accepted Twain's statements to the effect that he "abhorred" Poe's fiction (see, for example, Sydney J. Krause, *Mark Twain as Critic* [Baltimore: The Johns Hopkins Univ. Press, 1967], 14), I am arguing that Twain's relation to Poe in writing autobiography remains as secret as the relation between Poe's hidden autobiographical project and his writing of fiction. For further critical references on this issue of Twain's view of Poe or the connections between some of their works, see Alan Gribben's *Mark Twain's Library: A Reconstruction* (Boston: G. K. Hall, 1980), 2: 551-53.

[16] Twain's interest in literary detection surfaces most explicitly—and after an initially humorous debunking of the topic—in another piece that he wanted to publish with his autobiographical papers, his long essay "Is Shakespeare Dead?", collected in Charles Neider's edition of *The Complete Essays of Mark Twain* (Garden City: Doubleday & Company, 1963), 407-54.

[17] Resembling Poe's practice in his "Autography" collection and especially his demonstrations of "secret writing" in "The Gold Bug" and "Some Words on Secret Writing," Twain's proposal for a simplified alphabet in another essay intended for his autobiographical papers (*Complete Essays,* 544-50) not only iconographically illustrates such an alphabet but humorously offers to reduce the "*labor* in writing," yet actually ends up proposing "for acceptance and adoption . . . not shorthand, but longhand, written with the *shorthand alphabet unreduced*"—in other words, recommends an unreadably chaotic, heterogeneous phonetic writing.

[18] John F. Kasson, *Civilizing the Machine: Technology and Republican Values in America, 1776-1900* (New York: Penguin Books, 1977), 205-15.

[19] Twain's construction of *Life* and especially the *Autobiography* on the basis of interchangeable parts could easily be made to reflect yet another aspect of the technological infrastructure of postbellum America. Such construction can again call our attention to the possible influence of social modes of commodity production on a writer's sense of his literary production. Especially after the 1880's, American manufacturing—for example, of the Singer sewing-machines—increasingly began to use machine-made, interchangeable and thus uniform or homogeneous parts to make products more mass reproducible. See David A. Hounshell, *From the American System to Mass Production 1800-1932* (Baltimore: The Johns Hopkins Univ. Press, 1984), 116, 121-23 and passim. In this context, Twain's strangely depersonalizing (or what I term "plagiarizing" and intertextual) procedures in writing autobiography betray an ideologically induced sense of homogeneous identity—a loss of personality, which his anarchic narrative praxis simultaneously functions to resist. But here again, I would argue that Twain's relation to Poe, or simply the aleatory factor of literary history, complicates any attempt to see Twain's autobiographical writings from *Life* through his unpublished papers as a simple reflection of a lived American ideological contradiction. Moreover, I would suggest that Twain effectively accepts and even desires rather than resists the textual fallout of such ideological anonymity. And he does so, paradoxically, in order to secure an ideal space for himself as beyond the illusion of a commodified (and only putatively separate) American individualism and its dialectical alternative, that of writing about himself as if he were a kind of American metaphor of self or autobiographical *vox populi.*

[20] Edgar Allan Poe, *Marginalia,* ed. John Carl Miller (Charlottesville: Univ. Press of Virginia, 1981), 150.

[21] Twain actually writes about the "desolation" he feels when finishing a work *(Joan of Arc)* in a brief essay entitled "The Finished Book" (*Complete Essays,* 624-25), an essay that was also meant to be included in his autobiographical papers.

[22] As many critics have noted, Twain's thematic exemplification of Poe-esque doubling explicitly appears in his fictional work, *Pudd'nhead Wilson.* There one could argue that it functions as a means to expose the egregiously arbitrary basis of the social distinction between master and slave (see Rowe, 148 and 157). But I am arguing here that there also exist purely textual instances of doubling in Twain's autobiographical writings.

[23] One could easily add to the kind of doublings that occur within the topos and very texture of *Life.* The narrative clearly gives us double characterizations: the humorously rendered, memory-compulsive Brown of "Old Times" versus the mean Brown whom Twain "often wanted to kill" (109); or the earlier dramatized Bixby, the master pilot, versus the barely mentioned Bixby in the second part of *Life.* Economically speaking, the narrative encompasses two Mississippi Rivers and two functions of steamboating, one essential, the other essentially recreational. As regards Twain's personal

experience of time, of course, two Hannibals appear and, thanks also to the Civil War, two versions of other cities and towns along the River. *Life* even depicts two extremities of the River at the time Twain revisits it. As American cities, New Orleans is older and more known than the relatively new Minneapolis; but when compared with the Indian legends included in the text and identifying Minneapolis's pre-American regional past, New Orleans comes to represent the newer city.

24 Cox, 166.

25 Gary Lindberg, *The Confidence Man in American Literature* (New York: Oxford Univ. Press, 1982), 200.

26 Thomas M. Walsh and Thomas D. Zlatic evince a different understanding of Twain's use of these devices in their jointly written essay, "Mark Twain and the Art of Memory," *American Literature* 53 (1981): 214-31. They argue that Twain's "visualist conception of words and knowledge" (227), aided by devices that "rapidly, clearly, and errorlessly arrange words in space so as to fix truth in a typographic tableau" (229), essentially performs a mnemonic rather than amnesiac function for him. They further maintain that this view of memory serves to "reinforce the spatialized, mechanistic, deterministic, and cyclical view of history of [Twain's] later years," eventually leading to his "cynicism toward human freedom and originality."

Marilyn Moss

SOURCE: "The Child in the Text: Autobiography, Fiction, and the Aesthetics of Deception in 'Without Stopping'," in *Twentieth Century Literature,* Vol. 32, No. 3/4, Fall/Winter, 1986, pp. 314-33.

[*In the following essay, Moss attempts "to locate the aesthetic strategies of (Paul) Bowles's aversion to introspection in* Without Stopping."]

Paul Bowles's autobiography, *Without Stopping,* has received relatively little attention since it appeared in 1972. What slight attention it has received is critical. Paul Metcalf has recently called *Without Stopping* "a disappointment" and "an emptiness," saying that "It is hard to imagine how a man who can write as well as he [Bowles] does . . . could indulge in so much unrevealing personal trivia. One can only assume that it must be for money? . . . or Fame? . . . or, simply, notice?"[1] On a more generous note, Gore Vidal, in his introduction to Bowles's *Collected Stories,* while calling "the memoir . . . pleasurable for those who can read between the lines," admits also that "we don't learn very much about what the subject had in mind."[2] *Without Stopping* is an autobiography that some Bowles admirers would not only dismiss as unsatisfactory, but even excise entirely from the Bowles canon. Given its author's acute aversion to introspection as well as the seemingly offhanded style of reportage that characterizes this text, these comments are understandable.

However, the failure of *Without Stopping* to win more than such passing critical attention is at the very least unfortunate. An autobiography by Bowles, one of our prominent contemporary American writers, should invite careful consideration, not only for the means by which it contributes to an understanding of our national literary psyche, but for the way that the unique presentation of its author's psychology teaches us to read other autobiographical writing. More specifically, as I mean to demonstrate here, a close investigation of *Without Stopping* will prove instrumental to our continued discourse on the relatedness of autobiography to fiction, an alliance, as it were, that figures prominently in Bowles's text. With the reissue of *Without Stopping* now at hand[3]—thirteen years after its initial publication, and for a number of those years out of print—it is now time to reevaluate this problematic text, and in so doing to reexamine this most curious of contemporary American writers—a writer, who, now in his seventy-sixth year, while he has continued to produce an abundance of fiction and poetry, has chosen nevertheless to keep himself, for the better part of his life, both psychologically and literally on the margins of mainstream American letters.

The misunderstanding between reader and text in the case of Bowles's *Without Stopping* is essentially a simple one: while readers of his autobiography have clearly responded to Bowles's self-proclaimed aversion to introspection in the text, they have failed to understand this aversion as a troubled response to the threat of self-exposure that autobiography poses for Bowles—a threat that he means to push down by inventing for himself various fictive poses in the text, from the pose of author-as-victimized-child to the attempted fiction of the adult-now-turned-reporter who, as autobiographer, must then stand back from the text, and, in Bowles's own words, "tell a good story." The intention of this study is to locate the aesthetic strategies of Bowles's aversion to introspection in *Without Stopping,* strategies which lead overwhelmingly to the fictive-making impulses of this autobiographer—and fiction here for Bowles means little other than a device for concealment, a means of avoiding meeting his reader head on. Even as he exposes himself, he protects himself against the threat of such direct confrontation with a multiplicity of diversionary tactics: to disappear into the text and reemerge concealed as a subject of his own invention so as to render himself unsusceptible to the scrutiny of his reader.

As current discourse on autobiography teaches us, autobiographical texts, not unlike fictional texts, embody a unique and cogent aesthetic structure; what is more, they embody what we might term a *psychoaesthetics*—a system of textual strategies that exhibit the autobiographer's psychological attitude toward re-creating his or her life in the text. We can locate this psychoaesthetics only if we attend to the *way* an autobiographer remembers and re-creates that life in the text as well as *what* he or she chooses to remember.[4] I would suggest here that we can locate the integrity of Bowles's aesthetic in *Without Stopping* only if we attend to the way he attempts to fictionalize—and thus conceal—himself in this autobiography.

On the surface of this text, it *looks* as if Bowles is not telling us much about himself. Thus, he will write, characteristically, of events in the latter part of the text, "It is precisely at this point where memory becomes less distinct. The recall is not blocked, it is simply that I was busy living."[5] To this his readers have responded that *Without Stopping* indeed stops short of being much other than a travelogue of names and dates in Bowles's life. However, if we look closer at the *way* such diversions are organized, we find that Bowles is indeed telling us a great deal about himself; moreover, that he is telling us a great deal about his anxiety in being an autobiographer. Yet, we can locate Bowles's psychology in *Without Stopping* only if we can accept this text on Bowles's own terms and accept that the terms of his aesthetic are deeply situated in *deception*—deception as a style of functioning with the burden and threat of self-exposure, deception, learned early and successfully as a child, that leads ultimately to the shelter of Bowles's own fictive-making impulses.

Early on in *Without Stopping*, Bowles writes that, as a child, "I became an expert in the practice of deceit. I could feign enthusiasm for what I disliked and, even more essential, hide whatever enjoyment I felt." In deceiving others, he tells us, he meant to deflect attention away from himself, a skill he came to regard early in his life as "a great victory." Bowles reminds us within the first few pages of his autobiography that he urgently attempted to release himself from the constant surveillance of his family that he felt left him powerless. He writes that he did not know other children until the age of five, leading him to feel subjected to a world of adults—one that included his grandparents and his extended family—"each," he writes, "eager to try out his favorite system on me and study the results" (*WS*, p. 22).

Yet Bowles's experience of family, he maintains, rested fundamentally with his experience of his father, Claude, a man whose persistent intrusion into his son's life, scrupulously and strategically recorded in the text, was experienced by the young Bowles at times as nothing less than life-threatening. In an attempt to control the threat his father posed, Bowles records also that he learned early in his young life to deceive—thus, defy—his father, a maneuver that resulted in a growing hostility between the two. Bowles writes of the time his father beat him for his refusing to relinquish to Claude Bowles the secret notebooks Bowles kept in his room. "It began a new stage in the development of hostilities between us," he writes, "I vowed to devote my life to his destruction, even though it meant my own—an infantile conceit, but one which continued to preoccupy me for many years" (*WS*, p. 45). Bowles's great preoccupation in his childhood, we are led to conclude, became then a means of successfully shielding himself from his father. One possible means of protection, he tells us, was to *look* as if he were not thinking, thereby he could escape his

father's censorship of his thoughts. This is a method he would later incorporate into fiction through his heroine, Aileen, in the short story, "The Echo"—clearly an autobiographical moment for Bowles.

> As a child she had convinced herself that her head was transparent, that the thoughts there could be perceived immediately by others. Accordingly, when she found herself in uncomfortable situations, rather than risk the dangers of being suspected of harboring uncomplimentary or rebellious thoughts, she had developed a system of refraining from thinking at all. (*CS*, p. 55)

Aileen does eventually reveal herself to Prue, her mother's lover in "The Echo," and is able, at the story's conclusion, "to utter the greatest scream of her life." Yet Bowles could resolve in fiction a conflict that in his personal life he intimates he was never able to achieve. In reading *Without Stopping* we come to learn that the one great subject of his autobiography, of his life, was and is his inability to resolve the conflict resulting from his struggle with his father—a struggle for authority stemming from his inability to gain control over and achieve autonomy from his father.

This conflict presented special problems for Bowles when he came to write *Without Stopping*. The prospect of self-exposure that autobiography poses for Bowles causes him, the text implies, much anxiety, thus triggering once again the fear he experienced as a child of being susceptible to his father, Claude. In this regard, the childhood strategies for self-concealment—of making fictions in the face of this father—now resurface in the text of *Without Stopping* in relation to his audience. Moreover, I suspect that Bowles perceives the reader of this autobiography to *be* the father. Thus he remains emotionally absorbed in defending himself against—*defying*—this reader-father, likewise triggering the impulse to conceal the text, his very life, within the aesthetic strategies of deception. That is to say, he now reconstructs his life deeply narrativized within the layers of a fiction—a fiction that renders him now a creature of his own device and making. Thus he can conceal himself from the authority that the reader represents. To protect himself from the authority of the reader is tantamount to protecting himself from the structuring absence of the father.[6]

While Normal Holland has stated that all autobiographies are fictions, Erik Erikson has said that a man writes his autobiography to verify a myth of himself. In this regard, Bowles constructs in *Without Stopping* first and foremost a myth of himself as the child victimized by the hand of the father. James Olney writes that in autobiography the self is revealed through metaphorical structures. In Bowles's text, his re-creation of himself lies deeply rooted in the metaphors of the archetypal adolescent. Patricia Meyer Spacks has written of adolescence as an organizing principle in autobiography, saying that we see the subject then "ever finding objects of defiance, locating novel experiences,"[7] *and* for Bowles, ever resisting self-exposure. Two specific fictive forms or styles of functioning operate in *Without Stopping*— first, the fiction that gives Bowles the greatest sense of pleasure and control—the conception of himself as the victimized and emotionally abused child. Second, however, as Bowles relinquishes his "childhood" to the presentation of the "adult" in this text, the coherence of this first fiction curiously dissolves and dissipates, transforming itself instead into a narrative seeped in anxiety, thus aversion, deception, and defiance of the reader. That is, in the latter part of *Without Stopping*, a less successful and cogent fiction emerges: the fiction of the autobiographer who, as "objectified reporter," paradoxically emerges and remains fully absorbed in those childhood strategies of defiance in which Bowles's identity is so deeply situated.

In reconstructing his childhood in *Without Stopping*, Bowles centers his narrative around his father, Claude. It was this father, he informs us, from whose constrictive New England forms of self-discipline Bowles urgently attempted to extricate himself, and whose presence he reexperiences in the autobiographical act. His father, we are told, became for Bowles the prototype of male dominance that led him to identify early in his life with the women in his extended family. To escape the authority of male discipline, Bowles's first literate fictions, written while he was still a child, depicted heroines who traveled perilous roads before landing safely on exotic soil. We are led to assume that it was Claude Bowles's attempt to dominate his young son's life that also led Bowles to seek out the femaleness of exotic and erotic landscapes in North Africa later in his life. Bowles experienced his father as an intrusive force who could not be controlled. He was ultimately nothing less than the force that drove Paul Bowles into his own fictions.

As a young child, Bowles writes, he had already experienced episodes of anxiety and depersonalization. He felt himself to be at odds with his body as well as with his physical environment. "The best way of describing it," he writes of one of these episodes, "is to say that the connection between me and my body was instantaneously severed" (*WS*, p. 59). Words whose meaning he knew well could suddenly become unfamiliar to him. "This astonished me," he writes, "it also gave me a vague feeling of unease" (*WS*, p. 9). Bowles began early on to feel an undefined sense of menace in his life, one which he associates with his father. The first recollection of Claude Bowles in the autobiography is linked to Paul's mother's illness, which originated from his breach-birth delivery. "Your mother is a very sick woman," Bowles recounts his father telling him when he was a young child, "and it's all because of you, young man. Remember that" (*WS*, p. 10). Bowles remarks that he was "bewildered and resentful" at the accusations that "I was the cause of my mother's continuing illness." Yet, he writes that by the age of four he already took for granted his father's "constant and alloyed criticism . . . it was one of the inalterables of existence" (*WS*, p. 10). Bowles's maternal grandmother,

he adds, was never at a loss to unleash her spleen for Claude Bowles, and he credits her with a narrative recounting the attempts of the father to kill Bowles when he was an infant.

> When you were only six weeks old he did it. He came home one terrible night when the wind was roaring and the snow was coming down—a real blizzard—and marched straight into your room, opened the window up wide, walked over to your crib and yanked you out from under your warm blankets, stripped you naked, and carried you over to the window where the snow was sailing in. And that devil just left you there in a wicker basket on the windowsill for the snow to fall on. And if I hadn't heard you crying a little later, you'd have been dead inside an hour. (*WS*, p. 39)

While Bowles "recalls" his "excitement" as a child at learning of this "dramatic confrontation," this is in fact a narrative detailed, not by a child but by Bowles the adult autobiographer who relives his fear and hatred of the father in this narrative. Moreover, he reexperiences, in the present, the delight the child would soon learn to take in making fictions. This narrative is indeed mediated by the autobiographical act, so that what may have been historical truth has now been transformed into a "fictive" truth—a narrative dealing with the integrity of the childhood that Bowles so urgently wants to see for himself and present to his reader. Bowles surmounts a multitude of such narratives in describing his childhood in *Without Stopping*—a childhood that he impels his reader (no less than himself) to understand as an imprisonment dealt to him by the power of the father. He spent his days as a child, he writes, "playing by myself in the house except for the occasional hour when I was turned out in the backyard" (*WS*, p. 14). Of one of these occasions, he recounts:

> on one side there were nine windows, looking out at me like nine eyes, and from any one of them could come a sudden shout of disapproval. If I stood still and watched the clock that was always placed in the window so I would know when the hour was up, I heard taps on a third-story window and saw my mother making gestures exhorting me to move around and play. But if I began to gallop around the yard, my father would call from the second story: "Calm down, young man!" (*WS*, p. 14)

Again with great detail and inventiveness, Bowles constructs this narrative to reinforce the undefined sense of entrapment he experienced as a child. What is more, he tells us, he came to regard his privacy as a tenuous matter, subject at any given time to his father's appropriation. In his bedroom, he says, he kept a toy chest which, "by Daddy's edict," had to be "locked up by six in the evening, all of its contents in order. Whatever remained outside would be confiscated and I would never see it again" (*WS*, p. 14). Bowles tells us that he began to lock his bedroom door, a move which inspired his father's wrath. When Claude Bowles beat his son for being denied access into this bedroom, the hostilities between father and son escalated to reach "new proportions." With this in mind, it would be no coincidence that years later, Bowles would explore and attempt to resolve this conflict with his father in the short story, "The Frozen Fields," through his fictional yet autobiographical self, Donald, the hero of the story.

> Before Donald knew what was happening, his father had seized him with one hand while he bent over and with the other scooped up as much snow as he could. . . . As he felt the wet icy mass sliding down his back, he doubled over. His eyes were squeezed shut; he was certain his father was trying to kill him.
>
> An unfamiliar feeling had come over him: he was not sorry for himself for being wet and cold, or even resentful at having been mistreated. He felt detached; it was an agreeable, almost voluptuous sensation which he accepted without understanding or questioning it. (*CS*, p. 274)

Earlier in the story—a "fictionalization" of Bowles's own move toward the "voluptuousness" of disengagement, and placed in a fictional representation of his grandparents' farm in Connecticut—Donald had dreamed of a wolf who came into the woods, grabbing the father by the throat and carrying him off as his prey. At the story's conclusion, Donald once again dreams of the wolf, thus becoming imaginatively one with the animal to signify his dominance over his father and the resolve of his separation from him. Yet, in this wish-fulfillment story, Bowles, even at a much later period in his life, could once again resolve such a conflict only in fiction.[8] He writes in *Without Stopping* that after his father beat him, he would fantasize devoting his life to Claude Bowles's destruction, insisting that this fantasy preoccupied him for a great portion of his life. He understood, he tells us, that he would always "be kept from doing what I enjoyed and forced to do that which I did not," and thus he concentrated on any means possible by which to deceive and escape his father. This feeling of helplessness, thus the hunger to defy his father, has now become the organizing psychology and textual strategy of the autobiography, a psychology coupled with Bowles's early—and persistent—infatuation with the written word. "I could not make myself lie," he writes, "inasmuch as the word and its literal meaning had supreme importance" (*WS*, p. 17). Yet he could "feign" enthusiasm through facial expression and what is more could appear to have no thoughts whatsoever. He could, if necessary, he insists, deceive his father by presenting to Claude Bowles a fiction of himself entirely divorced from the self that he hid in his "real" fictions: the secret notebooks and diaries he kept locked in his room.

It was Bowles's mother, Rena, this autobiographer tells us, who also taught her son the powers of escaping the real world of the father for the shelter of his own mind—a skill that Bowles insists he never forgot. Rena Bowles taught her son a means of retreating into the "blankness" of his own thoughts, a powerful weapon that enabled Bowles to render himself "unsusceptible" to the hostilities he felt his father leveled at him. Again, Bowles constructs a narrative to explain this game between mother and son.

> Did you ever try to make your mind a blank and hold it that way? You mustn't imagine anything or remember anything or think of anything; not even think: "I'm not thinking anything" . . . I do it sometimes when I'm just resting in the afternoon, and I've got so that I can hold on to it for quite a while. I just go into the blank place and shut the door. (*WS*, p. 43)

Bowles writes that he began to practice this game secretly and eventually managed to attain a desired "blank state." He could then disappear from two worlds at once: the world of adults, which he experienced as one of "distrust and intrigue," feeling fortunate "to be a child so as not to have to take part in it"; and he could protect himself from the world of children his own age, which he soon found to be "a world of unremitting warfare." He remembers that "my intuitions warned me that everything must be hidden from them; they were potential enemies" (*WS*, p. 27).

It becomes clear then that Bowles learned quickly and exquisitely the power that "making fictions," making himself disappear from the world, could give him. In *Without Stopping* he poses himself and *invents* himself as a child who learned by necessity to depend on the usefulness of his own imagination, as well as the tools of language, as a means of receding into his own safely concealed world. He could posture himself as speechless—hidden behind a wall of silence—when he needed to conceal himself; yet he could also invent a fictive world of imaginary characters through which he sublimated expression and desire. He writes that in school he took notes in a secret code of his own devising so that his classmates could not read them. Similarly, he would hand in class assignments to his teacher "written backwards . . . so that she could not interpret them." To interact with others on their own terms, insists Bowles, meant that he could be subjugated to them. "Vaguely I understood that laws were invented to keep you from doing what you wanted," he writes, and his intention was to rebel against the authority that made him so miserable.

It would seem that Bowles came to regard others as he regarded his own father, thus he anticipated that *any* adult or child was a potential enemy. As such, he organizes the narrative of his childhood in this autobiography as one of a child who, by necessity, learned to divorce himself from his social world instead of expressing himself in "secret diaries and notebooks . . . so heavy that I could hardly lift them to the center of my room." He recounts that "I made daily entries in the diary of several imaginary characters and continued to add books of information to my fictitious world." In short, he chose a world of interiority in the face of the social world around him, coming to think of himself as "nothing more and nothing less than a registering consciousness. . . . My nonexistence was a *sine qua non* for the validity of the invented cosmos" (*WS*, p. 53). He writes that he once invented a series of childlike fictions—again, identifying himself as a woman, and certainly as omnipotent—writing a sequence of stories in his notebooks about a female spy named Bluey Laber Dozlen who "sails from an unidentified European country to survive several marriages and divorces, as well as influenza and pneumonia from which everyone else dies" (*WS*, p. 35). What is more, by the age of thirteen Bowles found "an even more satisfactory way of not existing as myself," thus being able "to go on functioning":

> This was a fantasy in which the entire unrolling
> of events as I experienced them was the invention
> of a vast telekinetic sending station. Whatever I
> saw or heard was simultaneously being experienced
> by millions of enthralled viewers. They did not
> see me or know that I existed, but they saw
> through my eyes. (*WS*, p. 45)

This narcissistic, borderline fantasy, fictionalized as a remembrance from childhood, reflects Bowles's present attitude toward the reader of *Without Stopping* no less than it speaks of his childhood feelings. It is an expression, recalled with amazing precision, as it were, of Bowles's desire always to retreat from this world: to subvert scrutiny of himself—first as the child and now as the adult autobiographer—to the point of becoming *invisible*. He adds, furthermore, that this childhood fantasy enabled him "to view rather than participate in my own existence." To secure this necessary posture before his reader, it is not surprising that his concluding statement regarding this childhood fantasy should be a declaration that by the time he entered high school he had found a multitude of ways to convince himself that "the world was not really there."

Bowles then tells us that, unknown to his father, he left the United States and sailed for Europe before reaching his twentieth birthday. Yet, despite this statement declaring his autonomy, his emotional independence, we see also his continued need to remain the child paradoxically tied to the father. Bowles immediately writes that, while in Europe, he initiated two close relationships with adults who figured as parental surrogates: he lived and traveled with his mentor, Aaron Copland, for several years after arriving in Europe; there he soon developed an ongoing intimate relationship with Gertrude Stein, who he indicates often reminded him of his grandmother. Stein renamed him, he adds, "because she insisted that I was really a Freddy and not a Paul" (*WS*, p. 106). This, he writes, seemed to him "the most personal kind of relationship."[9]

Bowles never successfully separates himself from his father in *Without Stopping,* even as he relinquishes the constructed narrative of his childhood to the presentation of his adult life. While he refers to Rena Bowles as "Mother," he continues to call Claude Bowles "Daddy," thereby continuing to perceive himself as the child in

the text. Bowles remains emotionally absorbed in his infantile and adolescent idea of the father. That is to say, he demonstrates his continual remerging with the father in the very self-protective rhetoric and textual maneuvers manifested to deceive the father-now-turned-reader. In constructing his adult life in the autobiography, Bowles wishes to shed the authority figure, a desire that paradoxically only reflects his remaining fixation with the father. Bowles is an autobiographer whose psychology is so deeply situated in the conception of himself as the defiant, concealed child that the move toward emancipation and adulthood in the text triggers enough panic in him now to re-create the father in a *new* fictive context and construct. As Claude Bowles disappears from the text as an actual presence in the life of Bowles the child, now to become a structuring absence for Bowles's defiance, Bowles transfers his need for self-protection onto the reader. Thus the latter part of *Without Stopping* is immersed in such rhetoric as, "Since nothing was real, it did not matter too much" (*WS*, p. 105).

Bowles attempts, with much anxiety—yet with safety in that anxiety—to absolve himself of the responsibility for telling of his adult life. This is the safety of concealment in which Bowles's identity is likewise so deeply rooted. Yet, as the construction of himself as a child, abused by the "presence" of the father, afforded him great fictive and narrative possibilities, no such possibilities are available to Bowles as the "adult" here. Thus his narrative dissolves and transforms into a much less successful fictive pose of Bowles, who, if finding himself anxious and exposed at the prospect of his reader's ability to scrutinize him, quickly attempts to avert this reader by "fictionalizing" himself as the objectified reporter of the life of Paul Bowles. In this way, he speaks his adult life while simultaneously remaining deeply submerged in the defiance—hence the textual strategies of deception—that he impelled us to attend to in the construction of his childhood, the first part of the text. While these strategies now become an unsuccessful means of concealment, they are nonetheless an extension of the child and are central to an understanding of the psychology of Paul Bowles the autobiographer.

Bowles's overriding means of disavowal, of attempted deception, in the latter part of *Without Stopping* is "consciously" to deny the autobiographical act. He "denies" being the author of his own text, thereby disclaiming ownership of its contents and similarly disclaiming "ownership" of Paul Bowles, autobiographer. "Writing an autobiography is an ungratifying occupation at best," he writes. "It is not the kind of work one would expect most writers to enjoy doing" (*WS*, pp. 369-70). Bowles would like his reader to believe that autobiography is, at best, an unreliable means of knowing a man, of knowing a life. In enshrouding or inventing himself now as an objective and removed "reporter," he can write of autobiography, "It is the sort of journalism in which the report, rather than being an eyewitness account of an event, is instead only a memory of the last time it was recalled" (*WS*, p. 370). Bowles puts up stumbling blocks to his life and text here, a maneuver intended no less for his reader than for himself. As Lawrence Stewart reports, while Bowles was writing *Without Stopping,* he would say that "I work each day on the autobiography, but it gives me no pleasure as yet, perhaps because I am trying to remember things which are almost forgotten."[10] This admission would signify a perhaps unconscious move on Bowles's part to disengage himself from feelings that are painful—no less, conflicting—and would erupt during the autobiographical act. To protect himself, he now constructs his own "Platonic" hierarchy of untruths—a hierarchy that before anything signals once again the emergence of the child who wants desperately to shield himself from the father-reader. Hence, Bowles signifies that autobiography is "the telling of a good story," and what is more, that "a good story" may not necessarily denote the truth. Bowles wants his reader to believe that *this* reporter's means of storytelling may in fact be truth *or* fiction.

> My first intention is to give a bare report of the principal events and nothing more and eventually allow an extension of that material. It must become increasingly obvious to the listener that I am withholding information; this can hardly be an endearing characteristic to observe in a friend. In the end I suppose a story told backwards out of uncertainty as to how much need be told could be indistinguishable from a story told backwards out of sheer perversity. (*WS,* p. 189)

In suggesting to his reader that his "uncertainty" might be masked by and become indistinguishable from "sheer perversity," Bowles evokes the conflicts of his childhood: while he might expose himself to his father-reader and thus be able to have his needs met by this authority figure, this fantasy poses too great a threat, and to ease the anxiety of this conflict he then maneuvers a strategy whereby he warns his reader that he may elude him.

Since Bowles's first impulse is always to defy the authority figure, he continues to represent his adult life through the metaphors of the rebellious child. As a means by which to function with the fear of his reader's scrutiny of him, Bowles constructs a text of himself as a man (yet a child) absorbed with his own uprootedness, wanting to appear as elusive and unwilling to be pinned down by the particulars and the restrictions of any specific place or event in the text. Where readers of *Without Stopping* have criticized this autobiography as little more than a travelogue of names and events in Bowles's life, they are in truth witnessing Bowles's strategy to present his life as one lived through rebelliousness. Writing of his "nomadic" existence in Europe and North Africa in his adult years, Bowles's need to be seen as rebellious impels him to organize his text also around the metaphors of travel. He would have us believe that he intended always to leave America behind him: to shed the father by shedding the fatherland. Clearly, Bowles represents his appetite to deny America as inexhaustible.

> Each day lived on this side of the Atlantic was one more day spent outside prison. I was aware of the paranoia in my attitude and that with each succeeding month of absence from the United States I was augmenting it. Still there is not much doubt that with sufficient funds I should have stayed indefinitely outside America. (*WS,* p. 165)

The fatherland, and so the father, becomes a significant object of defiance in Bowles's re-creation of his adult years. Though he records that he returned to the United States with some frequency before settling permanently in Tangier in 1947, he remains staunchly committed to his desire to escape anything America had to offer him. He insists that "a constantly changing life" was "the most pleasant of all possible lives"—and one, of course, that would require as little commitment as possible. Writing that he and his wife, Jane Bowles, lived in New York during the 1940s—admittedly for him a time of great productivity as a writer—he tells us nonetheless that he consistently suppressed the impulse "to get as far away as possible" from that city. America is clearly the nightmare from which Bowles seeks to awaken. He recalls that his curiosity about alien and primitive cultures—a curiosity and geography that pervade the novels and short stories written during these years—was "avid and obsessive . . . I had a placid belief that it was good for me to live in the midst of people whose motives I did not understand" (*WS,* p. 297). Yet, such an admission is likewise a warning to the reader of *Without Stopping:* it signals Bowles's expressed though perhaps unconscious desire that the reader of his autobiography will fail to understand the motives of Paul Bowles, and that reading this text will itself be not unlike traveling through an alien country.

Bowles writes also that, while traveling through Spanish Morocco to Tangier in the late 1930s, he wished to experience, "consciously, the ill-defined sensation" that "inexplicably" came upon him as he moved "toward unfamiliar regions." He wanted to find "that magical place which, in disclosing its secrets would give me ecstasy and wisdom—perhaps even death" (*WS,* p. 125). In rebelling against the felt oppressiveness of his childhood, Bowles now reconstructs his adult life in the autobiography as one that was subject to chance and lived "without conscious intervention." As an aesthetic strategy here, he would like, ultimately, to absolve himself of any responsibility for the course this life would seem to take. As Bowles would express this desire through his fictional self, Port, in the novel, *The Sheltering Sky:* "He had long since come to deny all purpose to the phenomena of existence." Thus Bowles describes how he came eventually to settle permanently in Tangier—not by conscious choice, he insists, but rather in response to a dream he had once had, a dream of a city in whose "magical streets" he had once wandered.

If Bowles is the traveler, no less the objectifying reporter, who uproots himself from the responsibility for and participation in the events in this text, this uprootedness once again manifests the earlier fiction of the displaced and depersonalized child. The aesthetic strategy of the adult Bowles is to represent himself as the displaced narrator of this text, posing himself as little other than the witness to events that have simply *happened*. In this fictive yet necessary pose, he attempts to shield himself from accountability for the life in this autobiography—a maneuver he plays out by dodging introspection. Yet, in doing so, he creates gaping holes in his narrative, holes into which he mysteriously disappears. His telling of how he came to write the short story, "Pages from Cold Point," is a stellar example of the style by which Bowles copes with, not only his persistent fear of intimacy with his reader, but also the anxiety of disclosing intimacy with others in his life who are integral to all episodes in the text. Bowles tells us that he wrote the short story, "Pages"—a fiction concerning a father and son remerging through a sexual encounter—in 1947 while on board ship to Tangier where he intended to settle. He writes that, the night previous to his departure, his anxious wife, Jane, had "misplaced" his passport, an unconscious expression that she disapproved of his leaving without her.

> Jane earnestly claimed to know nothing about it. Yet no one else had come into the apartment. We looked at her accusingly. She laughed, "You know I don't want you to go," she said. "So I must have hidden it."
>
> I merely left the apartment, as though I were going away for the weekend (a very poor idea, as things turned out) and with far too much luggage boarded the ship. The stateroom was big, and the sea was calm all the way across. During the voyage I wrote a long story about an hedonist; it had been vaguely trying to get born for six months, ever since my visit to Jamaica. I finished it the day before we got to Casablanca and called it "Pages from Cold Point." Then we landed and Morocco took over. (*WS*, p. 276)

In this narrative, representative of Bowles's ability to shift, meteorically—and unconsciously—from feeling to action throughout this text, what he chooses to censor exhibits his enormous need to veil any access to his inner life. While implying that Jane's behavior did affect him on some level, he refuses to explore his *own* response to her behavior. He writes that "I merely left the apartment as if I were going away for the weekend," signifying that the feelings he experienced at the time of the incident, as well as during the autobiographical act, are suppressed in the service of concealment. Moreover, we do not know to whom the "we" refers ("We looked at her accusingly"), yet the "we" is significant, as throughout this autobiography Bowles implies that he and Jane infrequently lived alone and without other intimate companions, and this incident raises once more Bowles's hesitancy in identifying these other companions. Bowles "the reporter" sincerely believes that he is telling his life, and telling it as "a good story." Yet Bowles the autobiographer fears the consequences of intimacy with his reader. His means of coping with this conflict is to shift his attention abruptly here to having

taken "too much luggage aboard ship," and to focus on his recalling that "the stateroom was big."

It is Bowles the objectified reporter who feels he must link the specifics of this incident chronologically, to report simply that Jane misplaced his passport, he boarded ship and wrote a short story called "Pages from Cold Point." Yet it is Bowles the reticent and fearful autobiographer who suppresses the emotions that, during the process of writing this autobiography, link these incidents with one another and hence trigger one another. For clearly, autobiography has less to do with sequential truth-telling than it does with the psychological import of recall. Yet the power that this narrative—this moment of recovery—presents to Bowles, and the anxiety it triggers, impels him to *appear* unaware of the relationship between these instances. We should, moreover, attend to his indirect and brief reference to his short story, "Pages from Cold Point," here. He calls it simply "a story about an hedonist," saying little more. Yet, considering the importance that the father plays in this autobiography, the importance that Bowles has consciously and unconsciously given this father, it would seem likely that the memory of having written this short story—of a father's sexual imposition on his son—would carry with it significant meaning for Bowles in the present. Yet Bowles denies the reader access to the genesis of "Pages." What is more, he relinquishes any further claim to being the author of this story, a strategy that is characteristic of Bowles's references to his fictions in this latter half of *Without Stopping*. Here, Bowles is impelled simply to relinquish himself to "the sea" that "was calm," and to write that "We landed and Morocco took over." His need to obstruct both his *and* his reader's path toward interiority is an act of denial in the face of self-exposure. Bowles clearly does not want to trust his reader, nor does he wish his reader to trust him.

While Bowles is able, more often than not, to recall or construct events microscopically (and it is here that we may witness the relationship of recall to invention), he chooses, nonetheless, to aim vision outward, not interiorily to investigate Bowles in the text. He does, indeed, move rapidly and "without stopping," his sequential narratives now perpetuating themselves on their own volition as if stopping to reflect would pose a clear and present danger, and *as if* the catalog of those names that postulate his life and text were, for the most part, not integral to these narratives. Where he might clarify relations with others, thereby exposing more of himself, he represents others instead as objects of defiance.

When he writes of how he came to adapt the theatrical production of *Huis Clos*, he focuses our attention to director John Huston's "ideological distortions" and ultimate "mutilation" of the play. In recounting how he came to orchestrate the ballet, *Dans un vieux parc solitaire et glace*, from the poem by Verlaine, Bowles records with great precision and great irony only that the ballet's producer, the Marques de Cuevas, was "an eccentric in the grand tradition," a man who ultimately "did not believe any of what he was saying," and a man by whom Bowles "was royally duped." Thus, Bowles's means of defining himself in these narratives is to be proudly, defiantly, what others are not. Of his wife, Jane's, writing fiction, clearly experienced by Bowles in this text as a threat to his own capabilities as a writer, he emphasizes—with almost childlike wonder—that for Jane, writing was often a painful confrontation with herself. He writes, for example, of her difficulty in "constructing" an imaginary bridge for a passage in her novella, *Camp Cataract:*

> We talked for a while about the problem, and I confessed my mystification. "Why do you have to *construct* the damn thing?" I demanded. "Why can't you just say it was there and let it go at that?" She shook her head. "If I don't know how it was built, I can't see it," she answered.
>
> It never occurred to me that such considerations could enter into the act of writing. Perhaps for the first time I had an inkling of what Jane meant when she remarked, as she often did, that writing was "so hard." (*WS*, p. 287)

Bowles confesses his "confusion," not only that writing could be so "difficult" for someone, but that it could also become so conspicuous. This might be Bowles's most abject defiance of Jane in the autobiography, not simply that writing could be painful for her—*unlike* for himself, he makes clear—but that it could become a subject for discussion. For, if Bowles has learned anything from his childhood, it is that one's fictions, not unlike one's thoughts, are matters of the strictest secrecy and confinement. Throughout this autobiography, and this is the perception he held as a child, Bowles insists that the artist is someone who ought to be—who *must* be—inconspicuous. The writer is a criminal, as it were, and not unlike the way Bowles experienced himself through his father as a maker of fictions, this criminal is the child who still harbors secret thoughts and secret notebooks from that father. Moreover, this is the perception of himself that he has most adamantly presented to his reader. "My own conviction," he writes, "was that the artist, being an enemy of society, for his own good must remain as invisible as possible and certainly should be indistinguishable from the rest of the crowd" (*WS*, p. 67). The position and aesthetic strategy Bowles has maintained throughout *Without Stopping* is that art and crime are indissolubly linked: the greater the art, "the more drastic the punishment for it."

It is understandable, then, that Bowles is the most hesitant—the most anxious and therefore ambiguous—in confronting his relationship to his own novels and short stories in *Without Stopping*. He had published four novels and three collections of short stories before the time he wrote this autobiography, yet he refuses to investigate and present to his reader, in any satisfactory way, the interiority of his fictional world during his adult years. No doubt he fears, as the child learned to fear, that to admit to a relationship with his fictions will

certainly result in their confiscation. Bowles does not mention his writing fiction until late in the autobiography. When he does so, he writes that, "Long ago I had decided that the world was too complex for me ever to be able to write fiction; since I failed to understand life, I would not be able to find a point of reference which the hypothetical reader might have in common with me" (*WS*, p. 263).

This admission of course is a rhetorical strategy on Bowles's part, one born out of anxiety and thus aversion. What Bowles means to say (and must not say) here is that it is the *reader* of his autobiography who shares nothing with him. Thus he conceals his fictions from the reader by "dismissing" his writing as a gratuitous occupation. "During the five week sea-voyage I wrote a piece for *Holiday* and a short story, "The Frozen Fields," which I sent off to *Harper's Bazaar* the day I arrived in Colombo," he characteristically will write (*WS*, p. 334). "I had finished *The Sheltering Sky* and sent it off to Doubleday," he similarly recalls, wanting his reader to believe that he wrote fiction to satisfy a publisher rather than himself, and that his intentions always were to send off his fictions—get rid of them— not write them. These fictions are, as they were for the child, the most vulnerable part of himself. As this child would feel the urgency to protect himself, thus to minimize and veil the importance of his fictions to the father, Bowles means still to protect this fictional life against a world that he expects to be rejecting and hostile.

Bowles's most deeply felt fear, a fear he can acknowledge neither to himself nor his reader, is that he remains the artist-criminal who, if he is to survive as the child learned to survive, must invent for himself a pose and therefore an aesthetics of deception to keep himself permanently safe and separate from others. Bowles has said that, "Relationships with other people are at best nebulous; their presences keep us from giving form to our life."[11] In *Without Stopping* he has given textual form to his life by shaping this sentiment into an aesthetic—an aesthetic that is deeply situated in the conflict between his desire to speak and represent his life to his reader and his enormous aversion to intimacy with this reader. Bowles's style of functioning with this burden is to attempt to elude his reader by posing, fictionalizing himself behind layers of deception. Yet, for all his attempts to narrativize and conceal himself, Bowles has paradoxically created a cogent and, what is more, an exquisitely intimate representation of his own psychology. In this text, he has permanently sutured deception to the act of autobiographical writing. If deception leads to fiction, as it did for Bowles the child, then *Without Stopping* is Bowles's greatest fiction to date, and his greatest fiction of himself.

NOTES

[1] Paul Metcalf, "A Journey in Search of Paul Bowles," *The Review of Contemporary Fiction: Paul Bowles/ Coleman Dowell Number* (Elmwood Park, Ill.), 2, No. 7 (Fall 1982), 40.

[2] Gore Vidal, Introduction to *Paul Bowles: Collected Stories 1930-1976* (Santa Barbara, Calif.: Black Sparrow Press, 1979). All references to Bowles's short stories are hereafter cited as *CS*.

[3] Newly retitled as *Paul Bowles, An Autobiography, Without Stopping* (New York: Ecco Press, 1985).

[4] I refer here to R. Victoria Arana's use of the term psychoaesthetics. Arana convincingly argues for an aesthetic unique to autobiographical writing in her insightful article, "The Psychoaesthetics of Autobiography" in *biography,* 6, No. 1, pp. 53-67.

[5] Paul Bowles, *Without Stopping* (New York: Putnam's, 1972), p. 17. All references to *Without Stopping* are hereafter cited as *WS*.

[6] I use the term "structuring absence" here to mean that material in the writer's unconscious that is too painful, fearful, or dangerous to be given expression in the "logical" conscious text. Yet this repressed material paradoxically not only breaks through to erupt into the logical text but more often than not actually *determines* the text's underlying structure. The term comes from the psychoanalytical model of the visible text as a "revision" of the writer's unconscious. For a detailed analysis of this term, see The Editors of *Cahiers du Cinema,* "John Ford's 'Young Mr. Lincoln'" (*Cahiers du Cinema,* No. 223, 1970), who locate in Ford's cinematic text signifiers of such repressed material, adding to this psychoanalytical model Althusser's expression of "the internal shadows of exclusion" in the text. With specific reference to Bowles here, we may say that the unconscious feelings toward the father inform the logical flow and organization of the text, whether or not these feelings are consciously expressed. In short, this text exhibits an aesthetic both consciously *and* unconsciously determined.

[7] Patricia Meyer Spacks, "Stages of Self: Notes on Autobiography and the Life Cycle," cited in *American Autobiography,* ed. Albert E. Stone (Englewood Cliffs, N.J.: Prentice-Hall, 1981), p. 54.

[8] If we look further at Bowles's short story, "The Frozen Fields," we see the extent to which he contrasts the anxiety associated with the father to the "safety" of the landscape of his maternal grandparents' farm. Bowles writes (*CS,* p. 262):

> Everything connected with the farm was imbued with magic. The house was the nucleus of an enchanted world more real than the world that other people knew about. During the long green summers he had spent there with his mother and the members of her family he had discovered that world and explored it, and none of them had ever noticed that he was living in it. But his father's presence here would constitute a grave danger, because it was next to impossible to conceal anything from him, and once aware of the existence of the other world he would spare no pains to destroy it.

[9] Lawrence D. Stewart elaborates on the special relationships between Bowles and Stein in his *Paul Bowles: The Illumination of North Africa* (Carbondale: Southern Illinois Univ. Press, 1974).

[10] *The Review of Contemporary Fiction, Paul Bowles/ Coleman Dowell Number,* p. 68.

[11] Millicent Dillon, *A Little Original Sin: The Life and Works of Jane Bowles* (New York: Holt, 1981), p. 44.

Peter J. Bailey

SOURCE: "'Why Not Tell the Truth?': The Autobiographies of Three Fiction Writers," in *Critique: Studies in Modern Fiction,* Vol. XXXII, No. 4, Summer, 1991, pp. 211-23.

[*In the following essay, Bailey focuses on autobiographical works by John Updike, Philip Roth, and Tobias Wolff in a discussion of a late twentieth-century trend toward merging fiction and autobiography.*]

American writers often have found themselves, late in their careers, resorting to the writing of autobiographical narratives. Theodore Dreiser, Sherwood Anderson, F. Scott Fitzgerald, Ernest Hemingway, and Lillian Hellman all succumbed to the lure of recording their actual experiences. Consequently, it is not surprising to find a number of contemporary American fiction writers—Annie Dillard, Reynolds Price, John Gregory Dunne, Richard Ford, John Updike, Philip Roth, and Tobias Wolff among them—turning to autobiography in recent months. What is, perhaps, surprising is that only half of these writers could, even remotely, be described as being late in their careers; and fewer still seem to acknowledge that what they are doing in turning to autobiography is qualitatively different from writing fiction. In discussing three of these autobiographies—those of Updike, Roth, and Wolff—I am proposing that their authors have attempted the genre out of varying allegiances to the fiction from which they have taken a hiatus and that the coincidental, nearly simultaneous appearance of these books has much to do with a literary climate in which the distinction between autobiography and fiction has been sufficiently diluted so as to facilitate their melding into a form that might be called *autobiografiction.* Because Updike, Roth, and Wolff are very different writers, their levels of commitment to this hybrid form are not the same: Updike's *Self-Consciousness,* for instance, closely resembles earlier literary autobiographies in everything save the lush extravagance of its language. Updike is, nonetheless, responding to a literary atmosphere in which there is a strong impulse toward affirming contingent, unaestheticized, and unliterarily synchronized experience as well as a marked skepticism of the contrivances of fiction. Unlike Roth and Wolff, who seize the opportunity to escape from the archetectonic imperatives of fictional construction and to find new literary possibilities in autobiographical narrative, Updike indulges the autobiographical impulse very warily, insisting that he should be writing fiction instead. Arguably, the greatest difference among the three writers is that Roth and Wolff never fully acknowledge that in writing autobiography they are not doing exactly that.

In his foreword to *Olinger Stories: A Selection,* Updike discussed the relationship between those stories and his youth and young manhood in Shillington, Pennsylvania, concluding that, "Not an autobiography, they have made one impossible" (vi). What seemed impossible in 1964, clearly, no longer seemed so by the late 1980s when sections of *Self-Consciousness* began appearing in *The New Yorker, Granta,* and *The Boston Review.* More interesting than Updike's change of mind twenty years later is that in the interval the distinction between autobiography and fiction has hardened for him. The final story in *Olinger Stories,* "In Football Season," reads like a personal memoir and includes characters bearing names identical to those of Shillingtonians that Updike recalls in *Self-Consciousness.* The autobiographical basis of other stories he was writing in the early 1960s allowed him to publish as autobiographical essays in *Assorted Prose* stories that *The New Yorker* had accepted but had not printed. In his foreword to *Self-Consciousness,* he acknowledges that forgetfulness has "eroded the raw material of autobiography into shapes scarcely less imaginary, though less final, than those of fiction" (xi). It is the finality that fictional rendering confers upon lived experience that Updike sees as the primary differentiation between the genres of fiction and autobiography and that most clearly distinguishes his more traditional literary autobiography from the more genre-blurring ones of Roth and Wolff.

Updike admits that he began his autobiographical task defensively, as a response to learning that someone wanted to write his biography, an act he perceived as an attempt to "take my life, my lode of ore and heap of memories, from me!" Therefore, he commenced writing "always with some natural hesitation and distaste" for the task. His autobiographical chapters "record what seems to me important in my own life, and try to treat this life, this massive datum which happens to be mine, as a specimen life, representative in its odd uniqueness of all the oddly unique lives in this world. A mode of impersonal egoism was my aim: an attempt to touch honestly upon the central veins, with a scientific dispassion and curiosity" (xi). So dispassionate is the inquiry, that Updike hastens to let his fiction gloss the autobiography before the reader can jump in and do so first; the text has footnotes quoting passages from Updike's stories, novels, and poetry in which the material he is discussing autobiographically was first addressed. If this seems a trifle punctilious, as though Updike were trying to be writer and critic of his autobiography at the same time, he disclaims any intention of exhausting or achieving a kind of authoritative last

word on this material. "A life-view by the living," he writes, "can only be provisional. Perspectives are altered by the fact of being drawn; description solidifies the past and creates a gravitational body that wasn't there before. A background of dark matter—all that is not said—remains, buzzing" (xii).

Which is not to say that a good deal does not get said in *Self-Consciousness.* Updike lyrically revisits his boyhood home of Shillington, Pennsylvania, evoking in his description of this small middle-class town the personal significances, the resonances within the ordinary, which are perhaps his fiction's greatest claim to literary pre-eminence. In the subsequent two chapters, Updike speaks with candor and characteristic eloquence about the twin crosses of his life: psoriasis and stuttering. He characterizes his experience of psoriasis as "the sense of another presence co-occupying your body and singling you out from the happy herds of healthy, normal mankind" (42) and attributes to the affliction a primary impetus for his having become a writer, the pages he produced having represented a "surrogate presence," "a signature that multiplies even as it conceals" (48). "What was my creativity, my relentless need to produce, but a parody of my skin's embarrassing overproduction?" he asks himself rhetorically and locates in his infirmity a key to the sort of fiction he came to write: "I had no trouble with the duplicity that generates plots and surprises and symbolism and layers of meaning; dualism, indeed, such as existed between my skin and myself, appeared to me the very engine of the human" (75). Stuttering, he suggests, "is a kind of recoil at the thrust of your own voice, an expression of alarm and shame at sounding like yourself, at being yourself, at taking up space and air" (87). The assumption of a vocal mask—singing, affecting a strange voice—often unblocks speech and alleviates the impediment, Updike argues. The literary corollary to this notion arises naturally from it, writing representing "words to be printed, as smooth in their arrangement and flow as repeated revision could make them, words lifted free of the fearful imperfection and impermanence of the words we all, haltingly, stumblingly, speak" (102). Clearly for Updike, the meticulously sculpted sentences of his massive literary output represent an ideal counter-self, a corrective to the psoriatic, stuttering one that lives in the world with so much less lyrical grace. However little sympathy he claims to feel for some of his previous selves, Updike nonetheless acknowledges in all of them one shared, absolute value: "a belief in print, in ink, in a sacred realm of publication that will redeem them" (222).

Chapters 4 and 5 of *Self-Consciousness* present Updike in an uncharacteristically argumentative posture; the former, "On Being a Dove," revisits his publically proclaimed support for America's involvement with Vietnam,[1] and the latter explains the white, Anglo-Saxon genealogy of the Updike family to the author's grandsons, whose heritage is partly African. If these chapters initially seem like exercises in special pleading, they gradually reveal themselves to be courageous acts of self-confrontation, representing Updike's attempts to answer the unanswerable objections that have been raised against his work and himself—that he is a middle-class, privileged, white, American male whose fiction embodies the relative lack of tension and want of experience of cultural antagonism or conflict that has been his life. He admits that his anti-Dove stance was inextricably linked to his sense of gratitude to a nation that had let him be the Shillington boy who grew up "out of harm's way" so that he could mature into the writer he became; he confesses, too, that as a writer interested above all in seeking "for nuances within the normal" (146), the war could seem nothing but a national distraction and one that he was content to let others carry out as they saw fit. Finally, he acknowledges that his support of the war coincided with his Christian beliefs:

> My undovishness, like my battered and vestigal but unsurrendered Christianity, constituted a refusal to give up, deny and disown, my deepest and most fruitful self, my Shillington self—dimes for war stamps, nickels for the Sunday-school collection, and grown-ups maintaining order so that I might be free to play with my cartoons and Big Little Books. I was grateful to be exempted from the dirty, dreary business of maintaining the overarching order, and felt that a silent non-protest was the least I in gratitude owed those who were not exempted. (141)

This stance, he candidly admits, renders his work vulnerable to the charge of preciousness and insularity, and he even cites one such critical indictment: Alfred Kazin's description of his fiction as "profoundly untroubled" and of Updike as a writer who can "brilliantly describe the adult world without conveying its depths and risks," one "wholly literary, dazzlingly bright, the quickest of quick children" (149). In rejoinder, Updike points to the thoroughly adult themes of his work and his willingness to probe relentlessly into the seamy underside of American middle-class life. And yet, he never completely refutes the challenge to his vision that Kazin's comments represent. It is indicative of the honest self-examination enacted in *Self-Consciousness* that Updike never utterly disclaims the presence of his "Shillington self"—the privileged and protected author-to-be—in his work's development nor disavows the analogy he implicitly draws between his literary profession and his childhood preoccupation with "cartoons and Big Little Books."

In the final chapter of *Self-Consciousness*, "On Being a Self Forever," Updike offers a series of informal, eloquent meditations upon the self and its conflicted impulses toward expansion and protection, toward the things of this world and those things as shadows of another. As he concludes his autobiographical musings, he confesses that his memoirs feel to him "shabby" and forced because they are written "at the behest of others, of hypothetical 'autobiography' readers." They expose,

he suggests, "what should be *behind:* behind the facade, the human courtesies, my performance, my 'act'" (232). It is, clearly, the expository nature of *Self-Consciousness* that Updike is worrying here, the absence in this book of "the duplicity that generates plots and surprises and symbolism and layers of meaning." Despite having undertaken the 250-page *Memoirs*, Updike remains convinced of the superiority of fictional narrative in conveying human truth, acknowledging that "What I have written here strains to be true but nevertheless is not true *enough*. Truth is in anecdotes, narrative, the snug, opaque quotidian" (234). Still, *Self-Consciousness* allows him a freedom of meditation and exposition that fiction and poetry do not and allows him his extensive articulation of the aesthetic that underlies his work, an aesthetic that is, by turns, deeply spiritual and remarkably self-protective. "Imitation is praise," Updike writes,

> Description expresses love. I early arrived at these self-justifying inklings. Having accepted that old Shillington blessing, I have felt free to describe life as accurately as I could, with especial attention to human erosions and betrayals. What small faith I have has given me what artistic courage I have. My theory was that God already knows everything and cannot be shocked. And only truth is useful. Only truth can be built upon. From a higher, inhuman point of view, only truth, however harsh, is holy. The fabricated truth of poetry and fiction makes a shelter in which I feel safe, sheltered within interlaced plausibilities in the image of a real world for which I am not to blame. Such writing is in essence pure. Out of soiled and restless life, I have refined my books. (231)

Despite the fact that his work—the Rabbit trilogy in particular—has probably done as much to build bridges between literature and the accents of daily American life as the fiction of any non-Jewish American writer, Updike, in *Self-Consciousness,* remains staunchly Modernist in his insistence on the absolute divisibility of literature and life and in his assumption that the former represents an improvement upon, or refinement of, the latter. Consequently Updike offers *Self-Consciousness* as a work of literary exposition distinct from his other literary efforts; and, in addition, one that comments only in the most glancing ways upon his stories, poems, and novels. The absence of such commentary reflects, in part, Updike's characteristic diffidence about making claims for his own work ("my success," he admits at one point, "was based on a certain calculated modesty . . ."), but it dramatizes as well his sense of the difference between literary and expository projects and his feeling that using the *Memoirs* to gloss the literature would be to conflate inappropriately discontinuous genres. "Until the 20th century," he argued in his introduction to *Writers at Work: The Paris Review Interviews, Seventh Series,*[2] "it was generally assumed that a writer said what he had to say in his works," and Updike's *Memoirs* reflect on every page their author's mindfulness of the risk that the book's autobiographical assertions "will be taken as a worthy substitute for the words he or she has written with such labor and love and hope of imperishability written down and seen into print." *Self-Consciousness* is highly revealing and surprisingly candid about Updike the man; about his specific works (many of his best-known titles are not even mentioned) it has next to nothing to say. These, their mechanics, their secrets must remain "behind," concealed beneath the sacred cloak of Modernist contrivance, leaving undisclosed the craft through which the artificer refines life into literature.

Whereas Updike's memoirs create their own occasion and represent an explicit divergence on the author's part from fiction writing, Roth's approach to autobiography involves, quite characteristically, an intermingling of fictional and nonfictional modes and evolves out of more personal, extreme, and conflicted impulses. In his introductory letter to Nathan Zuckerman, Roth's self-proclaimed artistic alter-ego, the protagonist of the Zuckerman trilogy and of Roth's most recent novel, *The Counterlife,* Roth explains that the Zuckerman books "were probably what made me sick of fictionalizing myself further, worn out with coaxing into existence a being whose experience was comparable to my own and yet registered a more powerful valence, a life more highly charged and energized, more entertaining than my own." "This manuscript," Roth informed his protagonist, "embodies *my* counterlife, the antidote and answer to all those fictions that culminated in the fiction of you." If *The Facts: A Novelist's Autobiography* conveys Roth's "exhaustion with masks, disguises, distortions and lies," it also represents his attempt to "get back what he'd lost" as a consequence of fictionalizing his experience, through embellishing and rearranging and exaggerating it so as to make it significant in a different, literary way. Roth acknowledges that *The Facts* is the product of a personal and professional crisis he suffered in 1987 in which all sense of who he was seemed ambiguous, questionable, and to which he responded by writing a book dedicated not to fabrication but to autobiographical actualities. "Here, so as to fall back into my former life, to retrieve my former vitality, to transform myself into *myself,* I began rendering experience untransformed" (6).

The crisis that necessitated the composition of *The Facts* is anticipated in the closing chapter of *The Counterlife.* Although that novel is, among other things, a cautionary fable discouraging readers from confusing novelistic contrivance with authorial autobiographical fact, its highly self-conscious narrative strategies and its insistence upon undermining every fictional situation it establishes by immediately intruding upon it a counter- or contradictory-narrative culminate in a reading experience whose final effect on the reader is in no small degree like the sense of disaffection and disorientation that inspired Roth to seek a personal regrounding of self in the facts of his life. In the final chapter of *The Counterlife,* Zuckerman assures his British fiancée, Maria, that her finely constructed English sense of self is pure illusion. "There is no you, Maria, any more than

there's a me," he insists. " . . . It's all impersonation—in the absence of a self, one impersonates selves, and after a while impersonates best the self that gets one through. . . . All that I can tell you with certainty is that I, for one, have no self, and that I am unwilling or unable to perpetrate upon myself the joke of a self" (320). Zuckerman's disorientation (or the reader's parallel case of it) is largely the result of his having survived a narrative in which, in serial chapters, he (1) watches his brother, rendered impotent by medication for a heart ailment, seek surgical relief and die on the operating table; (2) suffers the same affliction and brings upon himself the identical fate through surgery; (3) becomes involved in the hijacking of an El Al airliner and is threatened with castration by the Israeli secret police for his role in it; (4) discovers that in marrying Maria he is marrying into a family of rabid anti-Semites. Nor do these self-canceling counterplots exhaust the novel's commitment to vertiginously accumulating recastings and reinterpretations of its materials: *The Counterlife* abounds with documents—Zuckerman's self-inscribed eulogy, his posthumous interview with Maria concerning her relationship with him, a farewell letter from Maria that he writes to himself imagining her response to his response to her family's anti-Semitism—all of which have the effect of endlessly complicating the book's central issues (self-gratification versus community and social commitments, the repeated attempts of the characters to create alternate existences for themselves and thus achieve "redemption through the recovery of a sanitized, confusionless life" [323]) while seriously undermining the "reality" of the characters as well. Little wonder, then, that Zuckerman, the product of so many disparate and contradictory experiences, should write off identity as impersonation; and little wonder, too, that the creator of this compendium of postmodernist narrative deflection and self-referentiality would proceed subsequently to embrace enthusiastically a project subsumable under the title *The Facts.*

Roth's "Novelist's Autobiography" is as concerned as Updike's with describing his formative experiences as a writer, but in it he proves significantly more willing than Updike to speculate about the sources of his fiction and to provide personal interpretations of his works' germinations. He sketches briefly his childhood in Newark, his experiences at Bucknell, the relationship that inspired the novella *Goodbye, Columbus,* and the charges of anti-Semitism, which the collection of stories of that title elicited from some Jewish readers and which have continued to arise in response to his subsequent novels. But the centerpiece of *The Facts*—because it represents one of Roth's central preoccupations—is the description of his relationship with his first wife, "Josie." Drawn to her initially because her turbulent lower-class WASP origins contrasted so markedly with his own comfortable Jewish middle-class background, Roth became trapped with her in a destructive marriage that they were helpless to improve or to dissolve. Her allure for him was perversely augmented by his realization that she had lied her way into their marriage, and

Roth rhetorically asks himself "how could I be anything *but* mesmerized by this over-brimming talent for brazen self-invention, how could a half-formed, fledgling novelist hope ever to detach himself from this undiscourageable imagination unashamedly concocting the most diabolical ironies?" (111). Excoriate her as he might, Roth finally pays "Josie" the ultimate compliment of ascribing to her the inspiration for his metamorphosis from Jamesian realist to Kafkaesque fabulist. Describing the deception through which she gained him as husband, Roth explains that

> What may have begun as little more than a mendacious, provincial mentality tempted to ensnare a good catch was transformed, not by weakness but by the strength of my resistance, into something marvelous and crazy, a bedazzling lunatic imagination that—everything else aside—rendered absolutely ridiculous my conventional university conceptions of fictional probability and all those elegant, Jamesian formulations I'd imbibed about proportion and indirection and tact. It took time and it took blood, and not really until *Portnoy's Complaint* would I be able to cut loose with anything approaching her gift for flabbergasting boldness. Without doubt she was my worst enemy ever, but, alas, she was also nothing less than the greatest creative writing teacher of them all, specialist par excellence in the aesthetics of extremist fiction. (112)

So strong was the hold "Josie" had on Roth's imagination that she came to permeate his fiction, becoming the model, as he freely admits, for Lucy Nelson in *When She Was Good* and for Lydia and Maureen, the wives of Nathan Zuckerman and Peter Tarnopol in the fiction-within-a-fiction that is *My Life as a Man.* What Roth does not mention in *The Facts* is that the fictional character Peter Tarnopol in that 1974 novel had attempted to do very much what Roth attempts to do in his 1988 autobiography. At the beginning of "My True Story," the third part of *My Life as a Man,* we are told

> Presently Mr. Tarnopol is preparing to forsake the art of fiction for a while and embark upon an autobiographical narrative, an endeavor which he approaches warily, uncertain as to both its advisability and usefulness. Not only would the publication of such a personal document raise serious legal and ethical problems, but there is no reason to believe that by keeping his imagination at bay and rigorously adhering to the facts, Mr. Tarnopol will have exorcised his obsession [with ex-wife Maureen] once and for all. It remains to be seen whether his candor, such as it is, can serve any better than his art . . . to demystify the past and mitigate his admittedly uncommendable sense of defeat. (100-01)

Fourteen years after he had ascribed the same symptoms to and prescribed the same antidote for his protagonist, Roth in *The Facts* rehearses the malady and opts for the identical cure, attempting to "demystify the past" by defictionalizing it and, as a result, seeking relief from a sense of alienation and defeat. In the final chapter of *The Facts,* Roth presents Nathan Zuckerman's critique of his creator's autobiography; the contrivance allows Roth to spin out a highly ironic—because articulated by a fictional character—defense of fiction over autobiography, while dramatizing the fact that Roth is recovered from "his sickness with fictionalizing himself" and is once again embellishing and exaggerating that life through imposing new conflicts on his favorite literary persona. Whereas in *My Life as a Man* Tarnopol's attempts to define himself through both fiction and autobiographical narrative—as Roth put it, to "realize himself through the right words"[3]—fail, Roth has revisited this strategy in *The Facts* and manages to make the standoff between fiction and autobiography emblematic of the impossibility of extricating the literary from the actual, the fictional from *The Facts.*

Tobias Wolff's *This Boy's Life: A Memoir* is not a literary autobiography in the same sense that Updike's or Roth's books are, largely because it is limited to Wolff's childhood and nowhere explicitly refers to his having become a fiction writer as an adult. Nonetheless, just as the Updike and Roth autobiographies arrive at their own definitions of the relationship between an author's life and his fiction and enact the conclusions drawn about that relationship, Wolff's book similarly represents an attempt to re-examine the prevailing assumptions about the differences between fact and fiction and to create a literary work in the interstices between the two.

That Wolff's childhood provided a store of material for autobiographical treatment is the most obvious point dramatized by *This Boy's Life.* Although the reader occasionally suspects the presence of dramatic heightening in the recalling of specific scenes, Wolff expressly disavows any such manipulation of his material. In the brief prefatory remarks that are his only extratextual comment on the narrative, Wolff acknowledges that he has been "corrected on some points, mostly of chronology. Also my mother thinks that a dog I describe as ugly was really quite handsome. I've allowed some of these points to stand, because this is a book of memory, and memory has its own story to tell. But I have done my best to make it tell a truthful story" (i).

That story begins with Wolff at the age of ten traveling with his mother from Florida to Utah in search of better fortune, a new start. When her marriage dissolved five years earlier, Wolff's mother gained unsupported custody of him; her ex-husband took the older son, Geoffrey, who in later years would memorialize his father in his own autobiography, *The Duke of Deception.* Responsibly taking on menial secretarial jobs to support herself and her son, Wolff's mother experiences her downfall through her attraction to feckless, authoritarian, and sometimes brutal men with whom she futilely tries to create new families for herself and Wolff. Growing up with such makeshift, transient households is the subject of much of *This Boy's Life;* but rather than presenting himself as a victim of the contingency and marginality of lower class American life, Wolff concentrates instead on his boyhood strategy for dealing with his circumstances. In moving from Florida to Salt Lake City, Wolff resolved to transform himself from Tobias to Jack (after Jack London, one of a very few writers the boy Wolff admits to any familiarity with), a decision that represents the first of his many attempts to recreate himself through imagination, to contrive fictitious versions of himself as a substitute for the one whose childhood his mother's unhappy attractions had brutalized, leaving him with no one to be. (The protagonist is but one of a number of characters in this work who feel themselves "betrayed into an inferior version of life" and who believe that the life they imagine for themselves is more actual than "the real lie . . . told by our present unworthy circumstances" [158].)

Wolff never explains what inspired him to put aside the short fiction with which he had been so conspicuously successful in favor of autobiography, but the book he wrote—significantly, his first full-length narrative—is itself answer enough. *This Boy's Life* is an extended meditation upon selfhood, upon the disparity between ideal and actual selves that is a potential product of a deprived childhood, if not a necessary consequence of being human. Because his father and brother both attended prep schools, Jack is encouraged to do so despite his complete lack of academic qualifications. Undeterred by his high school C average and an extensive record of delinquency, Jack contrives for himself a fictitious transcript in which his grades are magically transformed into A's and his teachers sing his praises. Wolff understands that he was lying, but he saw his fabrications as containing a greater truthfulness: "I wrote [the letters of recommendation] without heat or hyperbole," he recalls, "in the words my teachers would have used if they had known me as I knew myself. These were their letters. And on the boy who lived in the letters, the splendid phantom who carried all my hopes, it seemed to me I saw, at last, my own face" (160).

Whereas Updike dilates expositorily on the self and Roth approaches the complexities of the self by embroiling it within the ironies of contradictory, mutually annulling narratives, Wolff presents the developing self as a fiction that is occasionally transformed into actuality, only to be exposed subsequently as a fraud. Thus Jack is accepted at the Hill School with the help of an interested, unsuspecting alumnus who plays the role of kindly benefactor to Jack's ersatz Horatio Alger, buying the boy an entire wardrobe and preparing him for his new life. At the tailor shop where he is being outfitted, Jack stares in the mirror at the "elegant stranger" wearing an expensive overcoat and silk scarf and feels himself regarded

> with a doubtful, almost haunted expression. Now that he had been called into existence, he seemed to be looking for some sign of what lay in store for him.
>
> He studied me as if I held the answer.

> Luckily for him, he was no judge of men. If he had seen the fissures in my character he might have known what he was in for. He might have known that he was headed for all kinds of trouble, and, knowing this, he might have lost heart before the game even started.
>
> But he saw nothing to alarm him. He took a step forward, stuck his hands in his pockets, threw back his shoulders and cocked his head. There was a dash of swagger in his pose, something of the stage cavalier, but his smile was friendly and hopeful. (276)

Perhaps the greatest accomplishment of *This Boy's Life* is that it manages to keep both of Jack's selves—the cocky, endlessly fabricating "stage cavalier" and the friendly, hopeful, well-meaning American boy—before the reader simultaneously, and it is Wolff's ability to maintain this tension that made autobiography for him not so much an alternative to fiction as an extension of fiction's capacities and possibilities. Adopting a strategy opposite to that of Frederick Exley and Frank Conroy, who in the late 1960s wrote autobiographical novels with projections of themselves as protagonists,[4] Wolff wrote an autobiography that reads like a novel because of his control over the material and his conviction that the dividing line between fiction and autobiography is a tenuous, ethereal one. The point Roth makes through an accumulation of self-canceling texts Wolff makes through the simple, direct presentation of autobiography that reads like fiction. His book evokes the same sense of the interpenetrability of autobiography and fiction one finds in the work of his friends and fellow neorealists, Raymond Carver and Richard Ford.[5] Wolff's autobiography illuminates his short fiction—especially stories like "The Liar" and "Coming Attractions," in which a protagonist's tendency toward lying is central—but it also competes with and even surpasses those stories in substance and resonance. In his depiction of a boy whose life is dedicated to blurring the distinction between actual and ideal selves, to living a lie of success because the truth of growing up amidst so much transience and defeat is intolerable, Wolff has created a moving parable about the necessary lie that is autobiography. *This Boy's Life* is a "truthful story" told by an autobiographer who, in his youth, was devoted to the lie that conveyed a deeper truth; and it is in the unresolved tension between truth and lie, self and imposture, autobiography and fiction, that the book finds a structuring dichotomy worthy of and concordant with the finest literary fiction.

For Updike, the division between fiction and autobiography remains inviolate, firm; his *Self-Consciousness* dictates that the "private throes of imagination" generative of works of fiction and poetry remain private and that the act of writing memoirs be an act apart, a work of exposition different from that of literary creation. What connects them to each other is Updike's eloquence, the stylistic brilliance and linguistic precision that often make *Self-Consciousness* read like the best of his self-proclaimedly literary work. For Roth and Wolff, the interdependencies of fact and fiction become the subject and substance of their autobiographical projects, the lies of life providing the inspiration for the truths of fiction. Rather than concealing the author's "private throes of imagination," *The Facts* and *This Boy's Life* expose and examine the process that culminates in the transformation of life into literature and that closely parallels the process by which masquerade is transformed into selfhood. These books posit no irreducible "Shillington self," no psychological cornerstone upon which a career or an autobiographical narrative can be constructed;[6] they simply affirm the inexhaustible capacities of writers, boys, and other human beings to fabricate selves—and books to be.

NOTES

[1] Updike expressed qualified support for U.S. involvement in Vietnam in Cecil Woolf and John Bagguely, *Authors Take Sides on Vietnam* (New York: Simon, 1967) 73 and expanded upon his position in a letter to the *New York Times* 24 Sept. 1967 when a *Times* review of *Authors Take Sides* identified him as the only American writer included who defended America's presence in Vietnam.

[2] This introduction first appeared as "Writers on Themselves: Working Secrets," *New York Times Book Review* 17 Aug. 1986: 1.

[3] Quoted in Judith Paterson Jones and Guinevara A. Nance, *Philip Roth* (New York: Ungar, 1981) 100.

[4] See Albert E. Stone, *Autobiographical Occasions and Original Acts* (Philadelphia: U of Pennsylvania P, 1982) 291-304, and Peter J. Bailey, "Notes on the Novel-as-Autobiography," *Genre* XIV, 1 (1981): 79-95.

[5] Compare, for instance, the account of the death of the narrator's father in Carver's "Mr. Fixit and Mr. Coffee" in *What We Talk About When We Talk About Love* with the conclusion of Carver's "My Father's Life," *Esquire* 102, 3 (1984): 68; compare Ford's "My Mother, In Memory", *Harper's* 275, 1647 (1988): 45-57, with "Great Falls" and "Communist," two stories in *Rock Springs* that address a similar mother-son relationship but come to different conclusions. The style and tone of *This Boy's Life* occasionally recall Ford's stories, in part because the social settings and familial circumstances of these works are remarkably parallel.

[6] Revisiting Shillington, Updike finds that "The street, the house where I had lived, seemed blunt, modest in scale, simple; this deceptive simplicity composed their precious, mystical secret, the conviction of whose existence I had parlayed into a career, a message to sustain a writer book after book" (*Self-Consciousness,* 24).

WORKS CITED

Roth, Philip. *The Counterlife.* New York: Farrar, 1987.

————. *The Facts: A Novelist's Autobiography.* New York: Farrar, 1988.

————. *My Life as a Man.* New York: Holt, 1987.

Updike, John. *Olinger Stories: A Selection.* New York: Vintage, 1964.

————. *Self-Consciousness: Memoirs.* New York: Knopf, 1989.

Wolff, Tobias. *This Boy's Life.* New York: Atlantic Monthly, 1989.

AFRICAN-AMERICAN AUTOBIOGRAPHY

William L. Andrews

SOURCE: "Richard Wright and the African American Autobiography Tradition," in *Style,* Vol. 27, No. 2, Summer, 1993, pp. 271-84.

[*In the following essay, Andrews identifies Richard Wright's* Black Boy (American Hunger) *as a defining work in the tradition of African American autobiography.*]

To tell the whole truth in the name of complete honesty or to conceal part of the truth out of deference to white readers' sensibilities—this dilemma and the anxiety it spawned have haunted African-American autobiography since its beginnings. The earliest black American autobiographers frequently commented on their unique dilemma: speak forthrightly and be thought a liar or censor oneself in the hope of being believed. Antebellum slave narrators introduced what Robert Stepto has called "distrust of the reader" into African-American autobiographical discourse by admitting, in the classic formulation of Harriet Jacobs, "I have not exaggerated the wrongs inflicted by Slavery; on the contrary, my descriptions fall far short of the facts" (1). By assuring her white reader that she has not told the whole truth, Jacobs paradoxically seeks to confirm the first and most important statement she makes in her autobiography: "Reader, be assured this narrative is no fiction" (1).

One way to chart the development of African-American autobiography is to track the gradual replacement of a discourse of distrust and self-restraint that relies on white-authored prefaces and appendices to authenticate and authorize black writing by a discourse that avows frank self-expression as a sign of authenticity and independent self-authorization. We know, of course, that much nineteenth-century black autobiography was structured and to some extent governed by internal rhetorical strategies and external documents designed to confirm the sincerity (i.e., the genuineness and good character) of the narrator and the sincerity (i.e., the truthfulness) of her or his story (Andrews 3-7, 19-22). What is not so well understood, perhaps, is the role that discourses of sincerity and autobiographical acts of authentication have played in the evolution of black-American autobiography into the modern era. My purpose is to situate Richard Wright's *Black Boy (American Hunger)* in the context of African-American autobiography's long-standing concern with sincerity and authenticity in order to show how *Black Boy (American Hunger)* redefined these crucial parameters and thus signaled the arrival of a new kind of discourse in the history of black autobiography in the United States.

Most antebellum slave narrators were sufficiently distrustful of, or deferential to, the sensibilities of whites that they and/or the whites who introduced their texts felt obliged to assure their readers that credibility, not self-expression, was their watchword in narrating their stories. Frederick Douglass's 1845 *Narrative* carries a preface by William Lloyd Garrison, promising the reader that while "essentially true in all its statements," Douglass's story "comes short of the reality, rather than overstate a single fact in regard to SLAVERY AS IT IS" (38). Douglass also understood how useful the discourse of sincerity could be, as is clear when he professed not to care whether some might consider him egotistical in judging his boyhood removal to Baltimore "a special interposition of divine Providence in my favor." "I prefer to be true to myself, even at the hazard of incurring the ridicule of others, rather than to be false, and incur my own abhorrence" (75), Douglass claimed. Yet in stating that he cared less about the ridicule of others than about telling the truth, Douglass indirectly promised that his reader could believe him because he had openly declared his dedication to truth, regardless of whether it placed him in a less than admirable light. By stating that he would rather be true than credible, Douglass subtly bears witness to how seriously he takes his own credibility. Only a writer who wants very much to be believed will claim to be more sincerely dedicated to truth than to credibility. A further indication of Douglass's espousal of the discourse of sincerity comes up in the appendix to his *Narrative,* where he announces that, despite all appearances to the contrary in his autobiography, he is not "an opponent of all religion." He wants his reader to understand that he means to denounce only "the hypocritical Christianity of this land" so that it will not be confused with "the pure, peaceable, and impartial Christianity of Christ," which "I love" (153). In this instance Douglass is sufficiently worried about white "misapprehensions" of his religious views that he feels obliged to declare himself a sincere Christian so that the hard truths he has told will not be dismissed by those whom he believes are still capable of moral reform.

During the crisis decade of the 1850s, occasionally a black autobiographer, most notably Harriet Jacobs, would hint at or complain of the tension between a sense of obligation to self and to the white reader's expectations.[1]

This attempt to be honest about what it meant not to be fully honest in telling one's story was fairly short-lived, however. Post-Reconstruction autobiographies such as the *Life and Times of Frederick Douglass* (1881), John Mercer Langston's *From the Virginia Plantation to the National Capitol* (1894), and Booker T. Washington's *Up from Slavery* (1901) had nothing to say about the question of sincerity versus credibility in black-American autobiography. By implication, this postbellum breed of successful, progressive black autobiographer had little difficulty following Polonius's advice to Hamlet: "to thine own self be true/And it doth follow, as the night the day,/Thou canst not then be false to any man." In these lines, which represent the epitome of the traditional idea of sincerity according to Lionel Trilling (3-4), we learn that truth to self naturally and inevitably leads one to do right by everyone else, an idea that Washington espoused in *Up from Slavery* not only for himself but for all progressive-minded people, black and white.[2] Like Washington, the most famous turn-of-the-century black autobiographers represented themselves as so much in agreement with what white Americans already believed that the old anxieties about truth to self versus believability to others seemed no longer an issue.

With the rise of the so-called "New Negro" in the 1920s, the problem of self-expressiveness versus self-restraint returned to center stage in the well-known battles that black artists and intellectuals fought over what blacks should write about in general and how they should represent themselves in particular. To those, white as well as black, who prescribed any agenda, any standard of discrimination and value other than that emanating from within the artist, Langston Hughes retorted defiantly: "We younger Negro artists who create now intend to express our individual dark-skinned selves without fear or shame" (694). Despite his black critics' shame or his white critics' fears, Hughes defended himself and his frankly "racial" jazz poetry by stating: "I am sincere as I know how to be in these poems" (693). Hughes's New Negro supporters, such as Wallace Thurman and Claude McKay, championed a similar creed of artistic sincerity that granted any black writer the right, in effect, to call them as he saw them as long as he did not pander blatantly to white prejudices.

Yet while New Negro critics egged on their fellow novelists, dramatists, and poets toward greater self-expressiveness, the question of how much an autobiographer should feel free to expose about himself or herself or about the relationships of actual blacks and whites in the recent past or immediate present did not get much attention. In part this is attributable to the fact that few critics in the 1920s, black or white, are likely to have thought of autobiography at all when they considered the kinds of African-American literary "art" that needed policing or protecting. The New Negro era was a time of comparatively few noteworthy autobiographies. Those that did get a hearing were mostly by men of traditional values and outlook: successful members of the black clergy, such as Bishop William Henry Heard, author of

From Slavery to the Bishopric in the A. M. E. Church (1924), or protégés of Washington, such as Robert Russa Moton, whose *Finding a Way Out* (1920) preached the message of the great Tuskegeean in a manner calculated to leave an image of the African-American leader as a man of "unemotional business-like self-control" (213).

During the 1920s almost all the literary New Negroes were too busy working in the more traditional belletristic genres to take the time to write personal reminiscences. One significant exception, William Pickens, who published his autobiography, *Bursting Bonds,* in the same year as *Cane,* evoked the familiar parameters of nineteenth-century narrative when he stated in his preface: "If I am frank, it is only to be true" (Foreword n. pag.). For Pickens, though very much the New Negro with the New Negro's determination to speak his mind, the traditional Shakespearian formulation of sincerity was still applicable: frankness about oneself was a necessary condition to telling white people the truth. Frankness was in fact the sign of truthfulness rather than, as it had often seemed to whites reading blacks, a warning flag that something unpleasantly "bitter" was about to come up. Nevertheless, even Pickens acknowledged that aspects of his experience as a New Negro in the South would defy his white reader's credibility. Thus, when recounting a year he spent in east Texas just before the outbreak of World War I, Pickens prefaced his remarks by stating that he would "not strain credulity too far by endeavoring to tell the whole truth" about the "savage treatment of colored people in this section of the civilized world," but would instead "relate only some of the believable things" (57).

Some white readers of the 1920s, particularly the more "liberal" and trendy of the white literati, seem to have been prompted by the cult of primitivism to embrace and indeed assume that black personal narratives would bare the soul of their authors. Muriel Draper's introduction to Taylor Gordon's *Born to Be* (1929) promised the white reader that this celebrated black entertainer had composed his story "with rare candor," attributable, she suggests, to his inherent "honesty, humor and complete freedom from vulgarity" as well as to his lack of both "racial self-consciousness" and "literary self-consciousness" (1). In Draper's assessment of Gordon, we find a curious resolution of the conflict between candor and truthfulness: only let the black autobiographer be "unfettered" from consciousness of himself as a black person writing, and the result will be a prodigy at liberty simply to be himself, which in fact, Draper implies, is what this Negro was "born to be." Draper's notion that an identification of selfhood with race must inhibit a black autobiographer's ability to speak fully and fairly gives us an early instance of a presumption invoked by many white critics during the first half of the twentieth century: namely, that if blacks would start writing as "people" rather than as Negroes, their (white) readers would find them more interesting and more believable. Ironically, however, in his foreword to

Draper's introduction to Taylor Gordon's autobiography, Carl Van Vechten could not help raising doubts about Draper's reading of Gordon as an unself-conscious, freely expressive black autobiographer. Van Vechten applauded Gordon for his writing especially "frankly" about blacks, but of Gordon's recollections of his dealings with whites Van Vechten warned: "constantly you suspect him of concealing the most monstrous facts" (xlvi). Thus even the "new kind of personality" that Van Vechten saw in this remarkable New Negro could not be fully trusted. Van Vechten could not believe that the traditional mask of the black autobiographer had been abandoned.

The decade and a half after the New Negro Renaissance saw the publication of a number of important autobiographies by James Weldon Johnson (*Along This Way,* 1933), Claude McKay (*A Long Way from Home,* 1937), Angelo Herndon (*Let Me Live,* 1937), Mary Church Terrell (*A Colored Woman in a White World,* 1940), Langston Hughes (*The Big Sea,* 1940), W. E. B. Du Bois (*Dusk of Dawn,* 1940), Zora Neale Hurston (*Dust Tracks on a Road,* 1942), J. Saunders Redding (*No Day of Triumph,* 1942), and of course, Richard Wright (*Black Boy,* 1945). Significantly, only four of these autobiographies—Terrell's, Du Bois's, Redding's, and Wright's—have prefaces at all. Those by Johnson, McKay, Herndon, Hughes, and Hurston enter directly into the narration without so much as a hint of whether their authors have negotiated or simply ignored the old problem of self-expressiveness versus self-restraint. One might think from reading the majority of these remarkable life stories that the old problem had been rendered passé by virtue of the liberation of consciousness and expression enacted by the New Negro Renaissance. Only Terrell harked back to the hesitancy of the past when she introduced her life story with the caveat: "In relating the story of my life I shall simply tell the truth and nothing but the truth—but not the whole truth, for that would be impossible. And even if I tried to tell the whole truth few people would believe me" (n. pag.). In the "apology" that prefaces *Dusk of Dawn* Du Bois depreciated what he called "mere autobiography," but he did not attribute to black autobiography the "reticences, repressions and distortions which come because men do not dare to be absolutely frank" (1). He implied instead that selective truthfulness and lack of candor were inherent in autobiography as a form, regardless of the ethnicity of the author. For Du Bois, the solution to this problem lay in writing the sort of narrative that transcended personality altogether. His autobiography would subsume the whole vexed question of the individual's obligation to the truth under a larger, historically verifiable rubric: the Truth of a race's experience.[3] Hence the subtitle of *Dusk of Dawn* is *An Essay toward an Autobiography of a Race Concept.* By making himself a spokesman and exemplar of a supposedly desubjectivized Truth of history rather than of the self, Du Bois tried, in effect, to claim for his autobiography the ultimate sincerity of which he felt himself and his form capable: the sincerity of the historian-sociologist impartially dedicated to recovering the Truth of his era.

Du Bois's bid for ultimate sincerity did not, however, turn the tradition of African-American autobiography in a new direction with regard to the relationship of narrator, narratee, and narrative. Most of Du Bois's contemporaries in black autobiography in the 1930s and '40s showed little interest in modeling themselves on any historically verifiable idea of representativeness or typicalness. Instead of this traditional, nineteenth-century way of conceiving selfhood,[4] the likes of Hurston, Hughes, McKay, and Redding argue that they were sufficiently different—that is, temperamentally resistant to the models of their predecessors and atypical of their peers as well—that they could appeal to nothing more valid than the example of their own individuality as a standard for judging the credibility of what they said about themselves.

In *Dust Tracks on a Road,* for instance, Hurston describes herself as having felt impelled from her earliest school days "to talk back at established authority" (95). Yet even Hurston admitted that she concealed her "feeling of difference from my fellow men" out of fear that telling the truth about what she saw and felt would bring her ridicule as well as the reputation of being "a story-teller": that is, a liar (58-59). Similarly, when McKay recalled his decision not to follow the example of William Stanley Braithwaite, the most successful African-American poet of his time, the West Indian claimed with pride that his own poetic expression was "too subjective, personal and tell-tale" (28) to suit the expectations of traditionalists. Yet McKay, in the spirit of Hurston, confessed later in *A Long Way from Home* that there had been limits to his often-professed creed of full romantic self-expression. He had deliberately omitted "If We Must Die," a poem of revolutionary candor, from his first widely read volume of poetry, *Spring in New Hampshire* (1920), and it had taken a white man, Frank Harris, to sting him into full recognition of the sort of betrayal this act of self-censorship had entailed. Harris had called McKay "a traitor to [his] race" for implicitly disavowing "If We Must Die." But, wrote McKay in his autobiography, "I felt worse for being a traitor to myself. For if a man is not faithful to his own individuality, he cannot be loyal to anything" (99).

In this statement, McKay iterates once again the sentiments of Shakespeare's Polonius, affirming the long-standing Euro-American ideal of sincerity as a truth to, and of, self that ensures inevitably a communal bond of right dealing with the other. As I have tried to show, Douglass, Washington, Pickens, and Du Bois gave McKay ample precedent for believing that a black autobiographer could find a way to reconcile truth to self with a credible, socially constructive relationship to the white reader. On the other hand, as I have also tried to illustrate, from Jacobs to Hurston to Terrell, important African-American women autobiographers called attention to the gender-specific problems that arose whenever a black woman tried to speak frankly in order to expand her white reader's horizon of belief with regard to the realities of the color line. I do not want to make too much of this gendered distinction in African-American

autobiography; one could easily point to black women autobiographers who do not allude in any way to the problem of sincerity as I have tried to outline it here, for instance.[5] What is more significant for the history of this tradition is the way that Richard Wright in *Black Boy (American Hunger)* tried to dispose of the whole question of whether or at what cost a black autobiographer could or should adopt the discourse of sincerity in addressing whites.

In her "Introductory Note" recommending the 1945 edition of *Black Boy* to all "morally responsible Americans," Dorothy Canfield Fisher characterizes with only three adjectives Wright's "story of a Negro childhood and youth." Fisher labels the story "honest," "dreadful," and "heart-breaking" (*Black Boy,* n. pag.). Like many white liberals before her, Fisher was proud to put her name on the line in testimony to a black autobiographer's honesty. But refusing to claim more for *Black Boy* than that it was "dreadful" and "heart-breaking" and in particular refusing to speak of how the book could enlighten the reader or help to change the social order—this failure, in other words, to attest to any desire in Wright to have an ameliorative effect on the world that his autobiography describes constitutes a significant change in the purpose to which prefaces by whites had been traditionally put in the tradition of black American autobiography. In this sense, Fisher's preface hints at a move away from sincerity in Wright's discourse and toward a new kind of self-authentication.

We find Wright articulating this new standard of selfhood most explicitly in chapter 9 of his autobiography, wherein he discusses his last months in Jackson, Mississippi, before he left for Memphis at the age of seventeen. The aloof, defensive, and yet unyielding teenager who refused to give in to his principal over the content of his ninth-grade valedictory speech has to begin his first sustained dealings with whites in order to get a job. He plays the part of black supplicant so awkwardly that his friend Griggs takes him aside to explain the rules of the game. "Dick, look, you're black, black, *black,* see? . . . You act around white people as if you didn't know that they were white. And they *see* it." Wright retorts, "I can't be a slave." But Griggs reminds him, "[Y]ou've got to eat." Therefore, he continues, "When you're in front of white people, *think* before you act, *think* before you speak. Your way of doing things is all right among *our* people, but not for *white* people" (*Black Boy (American Hunger)* 176-77). Wright's response to this advice has often been quoted by scholars as a key to the mind of the man.

> What Griggs was saying was true, but it was simply utterly impossible for me to calculate, to scheme, to act, to plot all the time. I would remember to dissemble for short periods, then I would forget and act straight and human again, not with the desire to harm anybody, but merely forgetting the artificial status of race and class. It was the same with whites as with blacks; it was my way with everybody.

Wright's "way," put simply, was that of personal authenticity, not sincerity. From Douglass forward, the way of sincerity required representing oneself in such a way as to try quite deliberately not to offend whites but rather to try to show them how sincere discourse from a black autobiographer could give the white reader a truth that would set him or her free. Autobiographers like Jacobs foregrounded the calculatedness, the insincerity, of adopting a discourse of sincerity in African-American autobiography, but neither Jacobs nor Hurston nor any other black autobiographer before Wright would claim that he or she simply could not adopt that autobiographical act even though it seemed the only way to keep from alienating whites predisposed to be distrustful. What Wright suggests in his analysis of his inability to conform to Grigg's advice is that by the time he was ready to go out on his own, he was constitutionally incapable of being anyone or anything other than himself. He was, and could not help but be, authentically and inescapably himself, regardless of whom he was around, regardless of what would seem to be in his best interest or anyone else's.

The hallmark of Wright's personal authenticity in *Black Boy* is not his refusal to conform to social demands; rather, it is his constitutional *inability* to conform though he is told repeatedly by blacks and whites who he is to be and how he is to act in order to get along. The more people, black as well as white, judge him strange, intractable, offensive, and threatening, the more Wright encourages his reader to conclude that he was the only truly authentic person in the oppressive world in which he grew up. Every time the black boy is told to shut up or is slapped on the mouth, every time he shocks someone with his writing or is punished by someone in power for refusing to censor himself, Wright, in effect, authenticates himself as the quintessentially authentic modern writer, devoted absolutely to expression of self, indifferent to any external standard, especially that of pleasing or improving the reader. Instead of arguing that being true to himself was for the good of others and indeed made community possible, the usual justification of the discourse of sincerity, Wright's autobiography shows how truth to the self led to ruptures with every community the black writer tried to join.

Cast out by southern blacks and northern whites, hated by Dixie rednecks and Yankee reds, Wright turns his alienation from community into a badge of his intellectual and ultimately his artistic integrity. To identify himself as the supremely authentic man, he must render the entirety of society, black as well as white, profoundly inauthentic, pervasively false. This tactic, it seems to me, is why from the outset of *Black Boy (American Hunger)* Wright is at such pains to condemn the black southern community, to deny that black people even had a community or had the capacity for community, as is evidenced in his famous denunciation of "the cultural barrenness of black life" and his complaints about "how lacking we were in those intangible sentiments that bind man to man" (*Black Boy (American*

Hunger) 37). Individual authenticity is not measured in the modern era by the degree to which the social order recognizes and endows one with authenticity but by the extent to which one can claim to have asserted one's self in direct opposition to that which the social order recognizes and respects. Thus from his struggles with the Seventh-Day Adventists through his disillusionment with the Communist Party, Wright fashions an image of himself as uniquely and authentically "human" by showing how every community had failed him, how "my country had shown me no examples of how to live a human life" (*Black Boy (American Hunger)* 365), how in the end he would have to go on alone with nothing but his inner "hunger for life" to guide him.

The discourse of authenticity pioneered in Wright's autobiography introduced a new mode of authentication for African-American autobiography in the post-World-War-II era. Not until the 1960s, however, did Wright's call provoke a response in the writings of an unprecedentedly bold group of black autobiographers who not only regarded autobiography as an important means of telling white America the truth about itself but also portrayed themselves as messengers unmuzzled by past forms of racial etiquette, as tribunes whose militant dedication to telling it like it is constituted vocal confirmation of the authority and authenticity of the selfhood they claimed. Eldridge Cleaver's opening proclamation in *Soul on Ice* (1968) about the necessity of "speaking frankly and directly" about the most volatile of personal topics—such as the attraction and repulsion of black men for white women—was designed to demonstrate the black man's commitment to "individuality" and the "salvation" of his manhood (16-17), two hallmarks of authenticity in Wright's autobiography. One of the central themes of *Coming of Age in Mississippi* (1968) is Anne Moody's accelerating alienation from family in general and her mother's expectations in particular because of an awakening of "discontent" and "rebelliousness" that cause her to behave "as if I should please myself doing whatever pleased me" (350). Others in her family may be able to stifle their sense of oppression, but as Moody comes of age, she takes pride in her inability to suppress her "discontent" with the status quo. "It had always been there. Sometimes I used to try to suppress it and it didn't show. Now it showed all the time" (351). Autobiographical writings of the 1960s by people like Cleaver and Moody testify to a process of self-discovery very much reminiscent of Wright's search for personal authenticity, except that in the 1960s the expression of such authenticity often finds its fulfillment in a sociopolitical radicalization about which Wright at the end of his autobiography seems distinctly ambivalent. While personal authenticity and radical politics dovetail in many "revolutionary" black autobiographies of the 1960s, in the Wright model the authentic man is cast out by his fellow radicals for being, in effect, too radically committed to telling everyone (even the radicals) the truth as he sees it. In considering this difference between Wright and his 1960s successors, one should remember that the second half of Wright's autobiography

(*American Hunger*), which records the author's disillusionment with radical politics, did not get into print until 1977, well after the heyday of the militant black autobiographer of the 1960s.

On the verge of his death in 1963, Du Bois, the archradical among twentieth-century African-American intellectuals, would not deceive himself or his reader with the claim of having achieved full truthfulness in his final *Autobiography* (1968). The author of *Dusk of Dawn* still thought autobiography was "always incomplete, and often unreliable." His last book, therefore, would be at best "the Soliloquy of an old man on what he dreams his life has been as he sees it slowly drifting away; and what he would like others to believe" (12-13). But Du Bois's skepticism about what a black autobiographer, even with the most authentic of intentions, could say did not cause the readers of *The Autobiography of Malcolm X* (1965) to doubt Malcolm when he insisted, "I'm telling it like it *is!*" (273). A man who went through as many name changes and revisions of identity and political persuasions as had Malcolm had great need of the discourse of authentication, which he invoked without qualification throughout his autobiography in such statements as, "You *never* have to worry about me biting my tongue if something I know as truth is on my mind. Raw, naked truth exchanged between the black man and the white man is what a whole lot more of is needed in this country" (273). Even more explicitly than Wright, Malcolm predicates his authenticity as a black man on the fear he instills in whites every time he tells them the "raw, naked truth" about the racial scene in the United States. Those he labels contemptuously as "ultra-proper-talking Negroes" (284) betray their racial inauthenticity, their lack of genuine solidarity with black people, in every word of integrationist reconciliation they utter. Only by working separately toward the eradication of racism and defeatism in their separate racial groups, Malcolm concludes in the last chapter of his autobiography, can "sincere white people and sincere black people . . . show a road to the salvation of America's very soul" (377). The implication of Malcolm's words is that only authentic black and white people have a chance to become sincerely socially redemptive. While the pursuit of integration would abet more role playing and pretense, racial separatism dedicated toward a common antiracist goal could foster an unprecedented "mutual sincerity" (377) between the races. In light of Polonius's classic formulation of sincerity, Malcolm might be read as applying Polonius's advice to a racial group, rather than an individual self, and promising that truth to one's race is the only way to guarantee an end to falseness to those of any other race.

The Autobiography of Malcolm X is one of the last African-American autobiographies to be introduced by a white person, in this case the journalist M. S. Handler, who, very much in the spirit of such introductions, represents Malcolm among the ranks of those "remarkable men who pulled themselves to the summit by their bootstraps" (xiv) and championed "Negroes as an integral part of the American community" (xiii). Such a testimonial, with its concluding image of Malcolm as a disillusioned separatist and a protointegrationist, calls attention to a crucial disjunction between Handler's notion of what ultimately qualified Malcolm as a sincere black writer (a perception of Malcolm's emerging acceptance of integration) and what Malcolm himself implied was the basis of a black writer's sincerity (his rejection of integration as inevitably inauthentic and self-abnegating). Like abolitionist introducers and reviewers of slave narratives, Handler betrays a lingering desire to measure a black autobiographer's sincerity according to the palatability of his or her politics and personal style; hence Handler attempts to rehabilitate Malcolm X by promising that the private Malcolm of the autobiography had outgrown the "diabolic dialectic" (xii) of his public persona and was moving toward a more revealing and less polarizing style of self-representation.[6] Maybe Handler's well-meaning but unthinking recapitulation of the traditional role of the white introducer as "handler" in effect, as manager and manipulator of first impressions, as character reference for the sincerity of the black autobiographer—especially when contrasted with Malcolm's own powerful rhetoric of self-authentication—crystallized in an unprecedented and unmistakable way the problematic function of the white introducer and his or her discourse of sincerity. In any event, after *The Autobiography of Malcolm X,* the few whites who were asked to introduce African-American autobiographies made little attempt to adduce the sincerity of the autobiographer in question. Instead these introductions, usually written by academics, concentrate on matters of authenticity relating to the text (not the autobiographer), such as how the text came into being, how it has been edited, and what its value is to a reliable understanding of literary, cultural, or social history.[7]

In surveying the evolution of discourses of sincerity and authenticity in African-American autobiography, we need to be careful in gauging the impact of Wright's mode of self-authentication on black autobiography of the last forty years. Wright was virtually unique in predicating authenticity on the alienation of the individual from any community, black as well as white. When we celebrate Wright's contribution to African-American autobiography, we should remember that his myth of the individual could not have given us narratives of self-discovery through, rather than in spite of, community, narratives such as Maya Angelou's *I Know Why the Caged Bird Sings* (1969), Ned Cobb's *All God's Dangers* (1974), or John Wideman's *Brothers and Keepers* (1984). Wright's example of personal authenticity was sufficiently magnetic to draw the pendulum of tradition toward the polar opposition he represented, but his significance may ultimately depend more on the force that he exerted on the pendulum's swing than on the arc it has followed since his death.

If recent African-American autobiographers have felt little need to authenticate themselves in Wright's manner, the fact that they (and their publishers) have felt little need of an introducer (white or black) to testify to their sincerity or credibility may evince sufficiently their debt to Wright's conviction that an African-American autobiography could be, and had to be, self-authenticating in every sense of the term. Nowadays it is not impossible to find an African-American autobiographer invoking the old conventions of sincerity and authentication, but when such discourse turns up, as in Itabari Njeri's *Every Good-Bye Ain't Gone* (1990), we ought not be surprised to see the terms of that discourse ironically exploited. "What follows on these pages," Njeri writes in her preface to her autobiography, "began as a novel and ends up the literal truth; many might not have believed the portrayals otherwise. . . . But the characters in my family only seem made up. At times both comical and tragic, they *have* been too large for life" (6-7). In acknowledging that her African-American reality may seem "too large for life" (7) and hence for life story as well as too incredible for fiction, Njeri takes her reader back to Jacobs's dilemma in which neither telling "the literal truth" nor resorting to the subterfuge of fiction could satisfy a black woman autobiographer's need to be read as sincere and credible. Like Jacobs, Njeri wants her reader to "be assured this narrative is no fiction," but the changing status of the discourses of sincerity and authenticity enables Njeri to escape Jacobs's trap, the trap of promising to be credible by not telling the whole truth. Njeri has come to realize that fiction, for so long the bogeyman of the black autobiographer, the presumed refuge of the insincere black narrator, need not be a diversion from the truth, but may serve as the means to her ultimate autobiographical end, the telling of "literal truth."

Since this is so, Njeri need not try to prove her sincerity or demonstrate her credibility by rejecting fiction or by subscribing to the simple oppositions of fact versus fiction, authenticity versus credibility that have bedeviled African-American autobiographers for so long. Njeri can simply point out that her attempt to encompass her African-American reality in fiction brought her to the outer boundaries of probability. To break through those limits she had to make a commitment to a radical concept of autobiography. She had to reject the anxieties of African-American autobiographers who felt that their form, more than anything else, had to read credibly in order for them to be regarded as sincere. Once Njeri realized that the only way to *seem* sincere or credible was to write "the literal truth" of autobiography, acknowledging that such truth was almost inevitably "too large for life," she had in effect got the monkey of sincerity off her back and thrust it into her reader's lap. Is her reader prepared to accept autobiography as the closest thing to an adequate means of reconstructing a personal and family history inherently "too large" for the house of fiction or any other narrative model except autobiography itself? If so, then we as readers can join Njeri as autobiographer and put anxieties about sincerity and authenticity far enough behind us when we read texts like *Every Good-Bye Ain't Gone* so as to confront African-American life first and fully before trying to decide how to accommodate our sense of truth to it.

NOTES

[1] See Samuel Ringgold Ward's acknowledgment of his bitterness toward whites, though he is aware of the danger to his credibility that such open expression of feeling entails, in *Autobiography of a Fugitive Negro.*

[2] Washington contends repeatedly in *Up from Slavery* that the ambition and effort based on mere self-seeking yield neither long-term nor deeply felt success. True success comes only when one decides "to lose himself in a great cause. In proportion as one loses himself in this way, in the same degree does he get the highest happiness out of his work" (311). Thus the truest and most complete act of self-interest occurs when dedicating oneself to others.

[3] "Thus very evidently to me and to others I did little to create my day or greatly change it; but I did exemplify it and thus for all time my life is significant for all lives of men" (*Dusk of Dawn* 4).

[4] See, for instance, James McCune Smith's introduction to Douglass's *My Bondage and My Freedom,* in which Douglass is presented as a "representative man."

[5] Most of the autobiographies reprinted in the Schomburg Library of Nineteenth-Century Black Women Writers (Oxford UP, 1988) and its Supplement (1991) do not allude to this problem.

[6] Handler's attitude toward Malcolm X in his introduction to *The Autobiography* takes the approximate stance of Ephraim Peabody in his 1849 review of five slave narratives, including that of Frederick Douglass. Peabody takes Douglass to task for "extravagance," "sweeping denunciations," and "violent declarations"—just the sort of rhetoric for which Malcolm X was censured—because Peabody believes such rhetoric is likely to antagonize whites while making even Douglass's friends doubt his "real earnestness" about achieving "any great reform." By contrast the "tolerant, calm, benevolent, and wise" character of Josiah Henson's narrative demonstrates that he does not wish to alienate whites (Peabody 24-26).

[7] See the introductions by Herbert Aptheker to *The Autobiography of W. E. B. Du Bois* (1968), Theodore Rosengarten to Ned Cobb's *All God's Dangers: The Life of Nate Shaw* (1974), and David J. Garrow to Jo Ann Gibson Robinson's *The Montgomery Bus Boycott and the Women Who Started It* (1987).

WORKS CITED

Angelou, Maya. *I Know Why the Caged Bird Sings.* New York: Random House, 1969.

Andrews, William L. *To Tell a Free Story: The First Century of Afro-American Autobiography, 1760-1865.* Urbana: U of Illinois P. 1986.

Aptheker, Herbert. Introduction. *The Autobiography of W. E. B. Du Bois.* By W. E. B. Du Bois. New York: International, 1968. 5-6.

Cleaver, Eldridge. *Soul on Ice.* New York: Dell, 1968.

Cobb, Ned. *All God's Dangers: The Life of Nate Shaw.* Ed. Theodore Rosengarten. New York: Knopf, 1974.

Douglass, Frederick. *My Bondage and My Freedom.* Ed. William L. Andrews. Introd. James McCune Smith. Urbana: U of Illinois P, 1987.

————. *Narrative of the Life of Frederick Douglass, An American Slave.* Ed. Houston A. Baker, Jr. 1845. New York: Penguin, 1982.

Draper, Muriel. Introduction. *Born to Be.* By Taylor Gordon. Seattle: U of Washington P, 1975. xlix-liv.

Du Bois, W. E. B. *The Autobiography of W. E. B. Du Bois.* Introd. Herbert Aptheker. New York: International, 1968.

————. *Dusk of Dawn: An Essay toward an Autobiography of a Race Concept.* New York: Schocken, 1968.

Fisher, Dorothy Canfield. "Introductory Note." *Black Boy.* By Richard Wright. New York: Harper, 1966. n. pag.

Garrow, David J. Introduction. *The Montgomery Bus Boycott and the Women Who Started It.* By Jo Ann Gibson Robinson. Knoxville: U of Tennessee P, 1987. ix-xv.

Gordon, Taylor. *Born to Be.* Ed. Robert Hemenway. Seattle: U of Washington P, 1975.

Handler, M. S. Introduction. *The Autobiography of Malcolm X.* By Malcolm X. New York: Grove, 1965. ix-xiv.

Heard, William Henry. *From Slavery to the Bishopric in the A. M. E. Church.* Philadelphia: A. M. E. Book Concern, 1924.

Hughes, Langston. "The Negro Artist and the Racial Mountain." *Nation* 23 June 1926: 692-94.

Hurston, Zora Neale. *Dust Tracks on a Road.* Ed. Robert E. Hemenway. 2nd ed. Urbana: U of Illinois P, 1984.

Jacobs, Harriet. *Incidents in the Life of a Slave Girl.* Ed. Jean Fagan Yellin. Cambridge: Harvard UP, 1987.

Malcolm X. *The Autobiography of Malcolm X.* Introd. M. S. Handler. New York: Grove, 1965.

McKay, Claude. *A Long Way from Home.* New York: Arno, 1969.

————. "A Negro to His Critics." *New York Tribune Books* 6 March 1932: 1, 6.

Moody, Anne. *Coming of Age in Mississippi.* New York: Dell, 1968.

Moton, Robert Russa. *Finding a Way Out.* Garden City: Doubleday, 1920.

Njeri, Itabari. *Every Good-Bye Ain't Gone.* New York: Random, 1990.

Peabody, Ephraim. "Narratives of Fugitive Slaves." *The Slave's Narrative.* Ed. Charles T. Davis and Henry Louis Gates, Jr. New York: Oxford UP, 1985. 19-28.

Pickens, William. *Bursting Bonds.* Ed. William L. Andrews. Bloomington: Indiana UP, 1991.

Robinson, Jo Ann Gibson. *The Montgomery Bus Boycott and the Women Who Started It.* Ed. DavidJ. Garrow. Knoxville: U of Tennessee P, 1987.

Rosengarten, Theodore. Introduction. *All God's Dangers: The Life of Nate Shaw.* By Ned Cobb. New York: Knopf, 1974. xiii-xxv.

Smith, James McCune. Introduction. *My Bondage and My Freedom.* By Frederick Douglass. Ed. William L. Andrews: Urbana: U of Illinois P, 1987. 9-23.

Stepto, Robert B. "Distrust of the Reader in Afro-American Narratives." *Reconstructing American Literary History.* Ed. Sacvan Bercovitch. Cambridge: Harvard UP, 1986. 300-22.

Terrell, Mary Church. *A Colored Woman in a White World.* Washington, D.C.: Ransdell, 1940.

Thurman, Wallace. "Negro Artists and the Negro." *New Republic* 31 August 1927: 37-39.

Trilling, Lionel. *Sincerity and Authenticity.* Cambridge: Harvard UP, 1971.

Vechten, Carl Van. Foreword. *Born to Be.* By Taylor Gordon. Seattle: U of Washington P, 1975. xlv-xlvii

Ward, Samuel Ringgold. *Autobiography of a Fugitive Negro.* London: Snow, 1855.

Washington, Booker T. *Up From Slavery: The Booker T. Washington Papers.* Ed. Louis R. Harlan. Vol. 1. Urbana: U of Illinois P, 1972. 14 vols. 1972-1989.

Wideman, John. *Brothers and Keepers.* New York: Holt, 1984.

Wright, Richard. *Black Boy.* Introd. Dorothy Canfield Fisher. 1945. New York: Harper, 1966.

————. *Black Boy (American Hunger).* 1977. New York: Library of America, 1991.

William E. Cain

SOURCE: "W. E. B. Du Bois's 'Autobiography' and the Politics of Literature," in *Black American Literature Forum*, Vol. 24, No. 2, Summer, 1990, pp. 299-313.

[*In the following essay, Cain discusses W. E. B. Du Bois's political ideology as revealed in his autobiography.*]

During the course of his long career, W. E. B. Du Bois produced superb work in many genres. His Harvard dissertation *The Suppression of the African Slave Trade* (1896) was a pioneering, minutely detailed analysis of the growth and eventual elimination of the slave trade to the Unites States; his absorbing rendering of African culture and African-American history *The Negro* (1915) served as "the Bible of Pan-Africanism" (Rampersad 234); and his later historical book *Black Reconstruction* (1935) bitingly challenged the traditional view of the post-Civil-War period as a time of white suffering and Negro abuses and abominations. His studies of the black family and community, especially *The Philadelphia Negro* (1899), remain valuable; his countless essays and reviews, not only in *The Crisis* but in other academic journals and popular magazines and newspapers, are impressive in their scope and virtuosity; and his numerous articles on education, labor, and the Pan-African movement further testify to his national and international vision of the development of colored people. He also wrote novels, stories, and poetry, and invented mixed genres of his own, as the sociologically acute and lyrical *The Souls of Black Folk* (1903) demonstrates. Du Bois's many autobiographical writings, notably *Dusk of Dawn* (1940) and his posthumous *Autobiography* (1968), are also rewarding texts that situate the life of the writer within the complex trends of the late-nineteenth and twentieth centuries.

As a premier man of letters, Du Bois has few rivals in this century. Yet with the exception of *The Souls of Black Folk,* his writings are infrequently taught and rarely accorded in literary history the credit they deserve. In part this results from the fertile ways in which Du Bois's writings cross and exceed generic and disciplinary categories. Who should teach him? Where should he be taught? Du Bois's astonishing range has possibly worked to his disadvantage, particularly in the academy, leaving the majority of his books unstudied because it is unclear to whose departmental terrain they belong. "His contribution," concludes Arnold Rampersad, "has sunk to the status of a footnote in the long history of race relations in the United States" (291).

Another, more commanding reason for Du Bois's uneven and troubled reputation is that he wrote politically: He always perceived his writing, in whatever form or forum, as having political point and purpose. As he noted in a diary entry on his twenty-fifth birthday, "'I . . . take the world that the Unknown lay in my hands and work for the rise of the Negro people, taking for granted that their best development means the best development of the

world'" (*Autobiography* 171). Du Bois assembled knowledge, fired off polemics, issued moral appeals, and preached international brotherhood and peace in the hope of effecting differences in the lives of the lowly and oppressed. He stood for equality and justice, for bringing all men and women into "the kingdom of culture" as co-workers (*Souls* 4). So much was this Du Bois's intention that he was willing to use the explosive word *propaganda* to accent it. Viewing himself as, in everything, a writer and an artist, he affirmed that "all art is propaganda and ever must be, despite the wailing of the purists. I stand in utter shamelessness and say that whatever art I have for writing has been used always for propaganda for gaining the right of black folk to love and enjoy" ("Criteria for Negro Art" 288).

Du Bois's blunt deployment of art as "propaganda" makes plain the reason that he has proved an awkward figure for literary historians, yet it still remains curious that he is undertaught and undervalued. William James, Nathaniel Shaler, Albert Bushnell Hart, George Santayana, and others praised Du Bois during his student days at Harvard. Hart later said that he counted him "'always among the ablest and keenest of our teacher-scholars, an American who viewed his country broadly'" (cited in *Autobiography* 269). Some of America's most gifted novelists, poets, and playwrights admired him. Eugene O'Neill once referred to Du Bois as "ranking among the foremost writers of true importance in the country" (Tuttle 52). Van Wyck Brooks commended him as "an intellectual who was also an artist and a prophet," a man "with a mind at once passionate, critical, humorous, and detached" and "a mental horizon as wide as the world" (548). Even earlier, no less an eminence than Henry James termed him "that most accomplished of members of the Negro race" (418). It was William James who sent his brother a copy of *The Souls of Black Folk,* referring to it as "a decidedly moving book" (196).

The Souls of Black Folk is indeed a landmark in African-American culture. James Weldon Johnson, in his autobiography, stated that the book "had a greater effect upon and within the Negro race in America than any other single book published in this country since *Uncle Tom's Cabin*" (203). Rampersad has summarized its significance even more dramatically: "If all of the nation's literature may stem from one book, as Hemingway implied about *The Adventures of Huckleberry Finn,* then it can as accurately be said that all of Afro-American literature of a creative nature has proceeded from Du Bois's comprehensive statement on the nature of the people in *The Souls of Black Folk*" (89).

But while *The Souls of Black Folk* has loomed large within the African-American intellectual community and, to an extent, within the white one as well, it has not generated a more extensive interest in Du Bois's autobiographies and writings in other genres. In part, Du Bois has received relatively little scrutiny because his race has worked against him in the dominant culture: His black skin bars him from reaching the stature that he had, by rights, attained through his publications and activities. But Du Bois remains an outcast as much, if not more, for ideological reasons. His standing has suffered—and he suffered literally in his life—because of his leftist/socialist sympathies and eventual membership, in 1961, in the Communist Party. As not only a black man but, by February 1963, a Communist citizen of Nkrumah's Ghana, Du Bois has been excluded from the main literary and historical register of scholarship and canon formation.[1]

The *Autobiography,* the last of Du Bois's works, is crucial not only for its review of the formidable span of his career, but also for the ideological positions that it conveys, positions that help account for Du Bois's problematical reputation inside and outside the academy. The *Autobiography* begins with an intense account of Du Bois's extremely favorable impressions of the Soviet Union and China, and it concludes with ample sections on his "work for peace," indictment and trial for allegedly subversive behavior (he was eventually acquitted), and zealous support for Pan-Africanism and Communism. To be sure, we must attend carefully to the *Autobiography* as an interestingly structured work of autobiographical art. But at this juncture, we need particularly to engage and reexamine the ideologically charged parts of Du Bois's book, acknowledging his errors and misjudgments where these exist but also perceiving how his Communist views, as he understood them, stemmed from his lifelong commitment to brotherhood and peace. His decision near the end of his life to become a Communist seemed treasonous during the Cold War, and it strikes many as luridly aberrant today, as the Communist countries of Eastern Europe and the Soviet Union undergo sweeping transformations. But this decision was one that Du Bois weighed carefully. It is important to grasp its origins and not allow it to blind us to his achievement, integrity, and intellectual conscience. The basic case for Du Bois as an exemplary intellectual and one of America's major writers has yet to be satisfactorily made, and the place to begin, artistically and politically, is with the *Autobiography.*[2]

Not all readers, it should be noted, have felt comfortable about the status of the *Autobiography* as a text. The editor of the book, Herbert Aptheker, tells us that Du Bois wrote the first draft in 1958-59 (when he was 90 years old), and then revised it somewhat in 1960. According to Aptheker, Du Bois took the draft with him to Ghana in late 1961, and it was first published, in an abbreviated form, in China, the USSR, and the German Democratic Republic in 1964-65. Shirley Graham Du Bois, the author's widow, fortunately managed to rescue the manuscript after the military coup that occurred in Ghana in late 1966; and Aptheker reports that he prepared it for publication in its entirety, making only a few minor corrections such as fixing a date or providing a complete name. But when the *Autobiography* appeared in 1968, some scholars testily wagered that Aptheker had probably played a more active role. Truman Nelson, for example, queried the inclusion of the long opening

section on Du Bois's travels in, and enthusiastic support for, the Soviet Union and the People's Republic of China. Maintaining that this section did not appear in a carbon copy of the manuscript in his own possession, Nelson implied that it might have been stitched into the manuscript by Aptheker.[3] Rayford Logan and others have similarly questioned Aptheker's involvement, noting many resemblances between passages in the *Autobiography* and much earlier writings by Du Bois (Logan and Winston 196). Aptheker has steadfastly denied that he significantly modified or adjusted the manuscript. In his 1973 *Annotated Bibliography* of Du Bois's writings, he repeated that he had merely made "technical" changes (561).

For the literary and historical record, it is obviously imperative to know as best we can the condition of the manuscript that Du Bois himself wrote. One needs also to tally the affinities between parts of the *Autobiography* and material previously published in *The Souls of Black Folk, Dusk of Dawn, In Battle for Peace,* and other texts. Yet, in another sense, the controversy about the text of the *Autobiography* simply dramatizes issues of authorship and authority familiar to us from many African-American autobiographies. Who is the real author of the text? Was it actually produced, in part or whole, by a black or white author, co-author, or editor? What is the relation between the manuscript and the published book? These questions, often raised about slave narratives in the nineteenth century, have also figured in discussion of autobiographical writings by Booker T. Washington, Zora Neale Hurston, Richard Wright, and Malcolm X. Such questions, and the difficulty of answering them cleanly, constitute a vexed central feature of the tradition of African-American autobiography.

Often such questions arise because some readers frankly doubt or object to what the text itself says. They do not readily believe in a text that advances a self-representation that is at odds with their own understanding of the author's self and with the historical and political truths that they have embraced. In the case of Du Bois's *Autobiography,* many readers have doubtless discounted this text as much on political as on scholarly and bibliographical grounds. They would prefer, it sometimes seems, to regard the ardently pro-Communist thrust of the book, and its hugely uncritical attitude toward Soviet state power, to be somehow not "really" present in Du Bois's text—as though these sentiments were more a faithful reflection of Aptheker (a Communist Party member himself) than of Du Bois, who, a tired old man of 90, could not have deeply meant his own words even if he did indeed write them.

The *Autobiography* is a flawed and disappointing book in certain respects, but we can only make sense of it (and of the life and career to which it attests) if we confront how its words—however much we might disapprove of them—tellingly accord with crucial facts about Du Bois. By the mid-1940s, he was adamantly hostile to the conduct of American foreign policy, and, in the midst of Cold War repression in the United States, he sought to establish connections to and alliances with the Soviet Union. In 1958-59, when he drafted the *Autobiography,* he traveled extensively in the Soviet Union and China; and, in 1961, his manuscript now finished, Du Bois joined the Communist Party of the United States.

As the *Autobiography* reveals, the foundations for Du Bois's decisive act of 1961 were laid even earlier than the 1940s. He first became absorbed in Marxism at the time of the Russian Revolution, journeyed to the Soviet Union in 1926, and, after his resignation from the NAACP and return to Atlanta University in 1934, began to teach a graduate course there on Marxism. In *Dusk of Dawn,* published in 1940, Du Bois speaks skeptically about Communism, rebuking the misguided forays of the Party in America and declaring, "I was not and am not a communist" (302). Yet he also boldly praises Marx, touts the extraordinary importance of the Russian Revolution, and aligns himself with the struggle for socialism in his statement of the "Basic American Negro Creed." Though he claims that he spurns the revolutionary pitch of Communism, he also says openly that "Western Europe did not and does not want democracy, never believed in it, never practiced it and never without fundamental and basic revolution will accept it" (170). Du Bois's belief in Communism did not descend upon him suddenly, nor did it result from world weariness. He knew where he stood—he was not "mindless" (Duberman 38)—and clearly gauged what he was doing when he at last became a Party member.

The *Autobiography* not only contains explicit statements of Du Bois's homage to Communism, but also furnishes prophetic signs of the emergence and development of the views he came devoutly to hold in his last years. When he first visited the Soviet Union in the 1920s, what impressed him about the Russian people was their vital, energizing "hope." All of life, he states, "was being renewed and filled with vigor and ideal" (290). Everywhere he looked, he approvingly noticed a dedicated striving to modernize education, abolish poverty, and end the reign of destructive myth and superstition. Nowhere did he detect evidence of race hatred. Returning to the Soviet Union in 1958-59, he saw that the hopes of the Russian people (and his own as well) had taken inspiring form: "The Soviet Union which I see in 1959 is power and faith and not simply hope" (39). Once again, too, he did not sight in the Soviet Union the harrowing fact of bigotry that informed his excruciating vision of America and Europe: "The Soviet Union seems to me the only European country where people are not more or less taught and encouraged to despise and look down on some class, group or race. I know countries where race and color prejudice show only slight manifestations, but no white country where race and color prejudice seems so absolutely absent" (39). Free from the scarring presence of race hatred, the Soviet Union seeks always, Du Bois insists, to lend its support to liberation movements and the world-wide fight against racism, imperialism, and colonialism.

Du Bois's celebration of the Soviet Union is difficult to appraise because it complicatedly blends the country (and ideology in action) that Du Bois actually glimpsed with the country he longed to locate, one that would be constructed according to reason and scientific principle and that would foreground a better, and manifestly attainable, alternative to the oppressive situation in America. The *Autobiography* can hardly be said to supply readers with a rounded, dispassionate account of the Soviet system. For Du Bois, intolerance and injustice, brutality, imprisonment, and murder do not exist under Communism. To allege that these do exist, or to fasten upon the apparent immorality and human price for converting Communist theory into rigorous, coherent practice, signals political blindness and bad faith, Du Bois believes. Such a critique of the Soviet Union misleadingly and unfairly stresses the "ethics" of the "methods" employed to secure Marxist socialism rather than sympathetically observing the workings of the thing itself.

Du Bois's perspective on the Soviet Union is skewed, but it does reflect an honorable, if exasperating, consistency. It derives from his own bitter disappointment in, and alienation from, the American scene. which seemed to him in the 1950s still to be ravaged by racism despite his own and others' decades of struggle. From one angle, his strangely distanced remarks about the Soviet purge trials of the 1930s (290), his affirmation of the rightness of the Soviet invasion of Hungary (28), and similarly meager, muted statements about the limits of Communism likely strike us as absurd. Yet it may be missing the point somewhat to label Du Bois in his *Autobiography*—as does Irving Howe—a dismal apologist for Stalinism "whose final commitment was soiled both morally and intellectually" (179). In large measure, Du Bois's grand endorsement of Communism represents his own implacable verdict upon America; and his refusal or inability to articulate the evils of Communism bears unremitting witness to his desire to preserve a leftist point of view untainted by the U.S.'s Cold War rhetoric. Like Howe, we are inescapably drawn to indict Stalinism, as are now the Soviet people themselves, encouraged by Mikhail Gorbachev's new spirit of openness and reexamination of the past. But Du Bois, in the 1940s and 1950s, regarded attacks on Stalinist Russia as always deflecting the gaze away from America's own history and crimes in the present and, furthermore, as weakening the already marginalized American left. Du Bois judged, I think, that when people on the left assailed Communism under Stalin, they recklessly played into the hands of the McCarthyite right; by so self-righteously criticizing an apparently pro-Stalinist left, they threatened to discredit the left in general.[4]

The *Autobiography* therefore places exacting political pressure on its readers, who face a potent array of pro-Soviet claims. But the book does provide rewards not tied to the ideological strife of the Cold War, including precise accounts of Du Bois's boyhood in Great Barrington, Massachusetts; his education at Fisk, Harvard, and the University of Berlin; his work as a teacher and scholar at Wilberforce, the University of Pennsylvania, and Atlanta University; and his opposition to Washington's program for Negro uplift, his leadership of the Niagara movement, and his leading role in the organization of the NAACP. The *Autobiography* is, however, regrettably silent or restrained on many key aspects of Du Bois's life. He says nothing at all about his five novels and very little about his other written works, especially such historical studies as the epic volume *Black Reconstruction.* While he mentions his estimable labor for *The Crisis,* the NAACP magazine he edited from 1910 to 1934, he offers few details. He omits altogether his relation to the writers and artists of the Harlem Renaissance, and refers in a sketchy manner to his ferocious feud with Marcus Garvey (273-74).[5] With so much of the beginning of the book taken up with an account of Du Bois's travels to the Soviet Union and China, and with so much space toward the end occupied by Du Bois's work for peace and his indictment and trial in the 1950s, there are inevitably missed opportunities, and much personal, professional, and sociopolitical material is left unexamined.

Du Bois is also guarded about his inner life. He refers to his "habit of repression" (93), hints at the "self-protective coloration, with perhaps an inferiority complex," that marked his life at Harvard (136), and alludes to his reserve and inhibitions (253, 281). But these statements are few and fleeting, and do not serve as occasions for deeper probing and meditation. Even the chapter titled "My Character" (277-88), though surprisingly candid about Du Bois's own sexual disappointment during his first marriage, is rather formal and stiff. Du Bois does not seem at ease with sustained self-scrutiny, finding a chapter on his "character" to be necessary to certify the autobiographical "picture" as a "complete" one (277) but not meeting the assignment with real curiosity or earnest intent.

The cost of Du Bois's relative inattention to his inner life bears upon the politics of his book. It is not just that many readers have heatedly disputed Du Bois's Communism, but that they also cannot clearly perceive its intellectual, emotional, and psychological appeal for him. He exhibits the external conditions in the Communist state that gratify him, yet fails to clarify the human needs that such a state functions to fulfill. When one reads Richard Wright's *American Hunger* or his essay in *The God That Failed* (Crosman 103-46), one can apprehend why Communism so attracted Wright and crucially assisted him in forging his identity as a writer. Even as he recants his affiliation with the Party, his prose still testifies compellingly to his gratitude to it for its constructive lessons. In their different ways, the autobiographies of the African-American Communists Hosea Hudson and Harry Haywood also achieve something that Du Bois's book does not. Filled with detail about arduous educational and organizational work, these texts enable readers to appreciate the concrete meaning of Communism for many black Americans, particularly during the 1930s, as they dramatize the powerful feelings of solidarity along race and class lines that both men experienced.

Du Bois's own proud, prickly temperament partially explains the absence of personal inquiry in his *Autobiography;* he did not view this potential of the genre as one that kindled his writerly interest. In this respect, his term for his autobiographical act in this book—he calls it a "soliloquy" (12, 13)—is admittedly absorbing on a theoretical level but is an inappropriate guide to the nature of what he has actually achieved. *Soliloquy* implies a 'speaking to oneself,' a disclosing of one's innermost thoughts and feelings unmindful of an audience. It connotes, too, a theatricalized or dramatic posture and pose, a vividly prosecuted, intellectually dense and complex form of speech that highlights self-reflection and risks unanticipated kinds of self-exposure. Du Bois's *Autobiography* does not really take such a cast or tone. It is less a soliloquy than an elaborate lecture or, better still, the prolonged testimony of an unyielding conscience that accosts America with truths that this nation, in Du Bois's appraisal, was too imprisoned in Cold War defensiveness and guilt to discern itself: "I sit and see the Truth. I look it full in the face, and I will not lie about it, neither to myself nor to the world. . . . I see this land not merely by statistics or reading lies agreed upon by historians. I judge by what I have seen, heard, and lived through for near a century" (415).

Du Bois suggests that he has earned the right to pronounce this stern sentence through long years of demanding, systematic, progressive "work." *Work* is, in fact, the key word of the *Autobiography.* Du Bois uses it many times, nearly always in the context of the building or shaping of a whole "life" in terms of a carefully chosen, determinedly pursued form of work. Preparing to begin his studies at Harvard, Du Bois stresses that he "above all believed in work, systematic and tireless" (124). Later, having finished his advanced training at the University of Berlin, he returned to America to earn his living as a scholar and teacher: "I just got down on my knees and begged for work, anything and anywhere. I began a systematic mail campaign" to find work (184). Seizing upon an opportunity for an appointment at the University of Pennsylvania, he avidly professes that he was "ready and eager to begin a life-work, leading to the emancipation of the American Negro" (192).

These passages and others similar to them show that Du Bois conceives of his life, as represented in his *Autobiography,* as highly dedicated "work." He undertakes work with a mission, and according to a specific plan: "The Negro problem was in my mind a matter of systematic investigation and intelligent understanding. The world was thinking wrong about race, because it did not know. The ultimate evil was stupidity. The cure for it was knowledge based on scientific investigation" (197). The word *work* is aligned with a group of related words—system, knowledge, fact, basis, truth, plan, organization—, and the *Autobiography* as a whole contains a number of proposals and schemes for mammoth research projects on the condition of the Negro. Writing in his ninetieth year, Du Bois realizes the limitations of his vision of work, especially as he formulated it in his early years as a scholar and educator. Everything he did, he now understands, presumed the willingness of Americans to ponder the conclusions that his work unequivocally disclosed and to *do* what the true facts mandated (22). Du Bois concedes that he was naïve about the ability of accumulated knowledge to speak for itself and impel certain reforms. But this by no means lessens his staunch conviction that one's life only matters when "work" defines it.

Du Bois's concern for "work," for visible achievement that ratifies the worth and rightness of life, possibly accounts for the reticence about personal feeling in his *Autobiography.* Deeds matter more than feelings, in Du Bois's calculation. The self knows how it feels by looking back upon and confidently reckoning what it has done. Though commendable in most ways, such a program has its dangers, and, as Du Bois describes it, it is unduly abstract and theoretical. Indeed, one wonders whether Du Bois's extreme emphasis on resolutely organized work, systematic investigation, highly controlled scientific inquiry, and centralized authority and administration indicates to us why the Soviet state struck him so positively. Accenting everywhere its admirable central planning and scientific efficiency, he does not comprehend, let alone grapple with, the pain and devastation among the masses of men and women that Stalin's work of economic overhaul entailed.

Du Bois admits that his *Autobiography* is not an altogether reliable record of his life. It is, he observes, "a theory of my life, with much forgotten and misconceived, with valuable testimony but often less than absolutely true, despite my intention to be frank and fair" (12). If the *Autobiography* fails or disappoints us, it may do so because of the intriguing inadequacy of the very "theory" of Du Bois's life and career that it propounds. Du Bois says clearly that he "believe[s] in socialism" and seeks "a world where the ideals of communism will triumph—to each according to his need, from each according to his ability. For this I will work as long as I live. And I still live" (421-22). Even as he states his loyalty to the Communist ideal, however, and unflinchingly affirms the model for nationhood that he perceives in both the Soviet Union and China, he adheres to a myth of American exceptionalism and does not recognize the tension and conflict that he thereby introduces into his book—and into his theoretical conception of his life.

"I know the United States," Du Bois concludes. "It is my country and the land of my fathers. It is still a land of magnificent possibilities. It is still the home of noble souls and generous people. But it is selling its birthright. It is betraying its mighty destiny" (419). Du Bois swears that he still loves America, yet how can his profession of faith in this nation stand alongside his passionate fidelity to Communism and the Soviet experiment? To put the question even more pointedly: What does Du Bois mean by his invocation of American destiny? This seems to be a puzzling term for him to employ at this stage of his

book (and his career), since he had powerfully sought in his painstaking historical research to demonstrate how America's destiny, and its power and wealth, has been terribly entwined with slavery and racism. It is not as though Du Bois has forgotten these hard facts in his *Autobiography,* for he refers in his final pages to the tragic legacy of slavery in America (418, 422). But he appears momentarily to need to lose sight of these facts in order to retain his sense of America as essentially a land of freedom and opportunity that has strayed from its destined path.

Some have said that Du Bois idealizes the Soviet Union, but he may idealize America just as much. In his final paragraph, he states that "this is a wonderful America, which the founding fathers dreamed until their sons drowned it in the blood of slavery and devoured it in greed" (422). Yet Du Bois himself had noted, several pages earlier, that George Washington "bought, owned, and sold slaves" (418); he knows that the founding fathers compromised their "dream" from the very beginning, and that they, not their sons alone, carry the burden and guilt of slavery.

In his first book, *The Suppression of the African Slave Trade,* Du Bois spoke words that reverberate against the position to which he clings in these final pages of his last one. "We must face the fact," he stated in 1896,

> that this problem [of slavery] arose principally from the cupidity and carelessness of our ancestors. It was the plain duty of the colonies to crush the trade and the system in its infancy: they preferred to enrich themselves on its profits. It was the plain duty of a Revolution based upon "Liberty" to take steps toward the abolition of slavery: it preferred promises to straightforward action. It was the plain duty of the Constitutional Convention, in founding a new nation, to compromise with a threatening social evil only in case its settlement would thereby be postponed to a more favorable time: this was not the case in the slavery and slave-trade compromises; there never was a time in this history of America when the system had a slighter economic, political, and moral justification than in 1787; and yet with this real, existent, growing evil before their eyes, a bargain largely of dollars and cents was allowed to open the highway that led straight to the Civil War. (198)

Though the *Autobiography* announces its acceptance of Marxist-Leninist ideology, it is *The Suppression of the African Slave Trade* that arguably shows greater insight into the relationship between politics and economics, and that more resourcefully demystifies pure notions of American destiny.[6] Audaciously pro-Soviet and highly critical of American policies at home and abroad, the *Autobiography* nevertheless gives evidence of Du Bois's deep attachment to America and his inclination to idealize his native land even as he sagely and sometimes savagely criticizes it.

At one point, for example, Du Bois commends the "democratic" theory and practice of Soviet society, citing the frequent debates, consultations, and discussions of common events current there, and he adds that life under Communism thereby resonates with the same democratic rhythms as small-town America. The Soviet people, he says, "sit and sit and talk and talk, and vote and vote; if this is all a mirage, it is a perfect one. They believe it as I used to believe in the Spring Town Meeting in my village" (35).

There is more detail about these town meetings in Du Bois's chapter on his boyhood in Great Barrington, where he tells of his respect for them. There was one old man who regularly attended these meetings, using them as an opportunity to rail against funds for the local high school.

> I remember distinctly how furious I used to get at the stolid town folk, who sat and listened to him. He was nothing and nobody. Yet the town heard him gravely because he was a citizen and property-holder on a small scale and when he was through, they calmly voted the usual funds for the high school. Gradually as I grew up, I began to see that this was the essence of democracy: listening to the other man's opinion and then voting your own, honestly and intelligently. (92)

On the next page, Du Bois concedes that the democracy he admired was not truly democratic: "of course our democracy was not full and free. Certain well-known and well-to-do citizens were always elected to office—not the richest or most noted but just as surely not the poorest or the Irish Catholic" (93). Du Bois shrewdly exposes the limits of the ideal he reveres, and he incorporates other de-idealizing devices elsewhere in his book, as when he observes that the "golden" river of his birth (61) was golden "because of the waste which the paper and woolen mills poured into it and because more and more the river became a public sewer into which town and slum poured their filth" (83). Yet he safeguards his exaltation of America's "dream" from irony, despite his own mustering of evidence that would seem to make the irony inescapable for him. In a word, Du Bois exempts America from the indictment that his own reading of our history would appear to demand. This pro-Soviet, anti-American text is, then, confusedly, movingly, and eloquently patriotic—a jeremiad that simultaneously blasts America for its contemptible sins and hymns its magnificent, if not yet achieved, destiny.

Near the center of his *Autobiography,* Du Bois reflects that his "thought" has long been characterized by a "dichotomy": "How far can love for my oppressed race accord with love for the oppressing country? And when these loyalties diverge, where shall my soul find refuge?" (169). One could conceivably maintain that by the close of his life, as he sums it up in his book, Du Bois had chosen his race and rejected his country, becoming a believer in Communism and a supporter of the Soviet Union because America had come, for him, to stand for sheer intolerance, repression, and militaristic sponsorship of colonialism. But Du Bois never lost his fervent

affection for his country. Even at the end, he declared his belief in a distinctive American message and mission, curiously suspending the ironic demystifications of the American dream that he had defiantly undertaken for many decades and that he had reiterated in the *Autobiography* itself. To say that Du Bois was a Stalinist apologist and, eventually, a Communist Party member registers truths about the life that he led and wrote about. But these explicitly recorded truths perhaps count for less than the queer beauty of Du Bois's lingering love for the America he told himself he had momentously abandoned.

NOTES

[1] Recent books by Horne, Marable, and Andrews indicate that a new day may be dawning for Du Bois scholarship. The Library of America has also devoted a volume to Du Bois (1986). This work, along with Rampersad's superb earlier study and Williamson's cogent account, in *The Crucible of Race,* of Du Bois's Hegelianism (399-413), should foster lively interest in Du Bois's writings. But it remains to be seen whether readers are at last ready to regard him as more than the author of *The Souls of Black Folk.* Du Bois himself was given to remark ruefully that people sometimes assumed that he had died or disappeared after his dispute with Booker T. Washington, or, if he had survived beyond that era, that he had surely passed away shortly after 1934, when he resigned from the NAACP and stopped editing *The Crisis.*

[2] For a valuable "Checklist of Du Bois's Autobiographical Writings," see Andrews (226-30).

[3] See also the exchange of letters between James S. Allen, the president of International Publishers, and Nelson ("A Question of Inference").

[4] My effort at a sympathetic understanding of Du Bois's stance admittedly becomes harder to sustain in light of some of his periodical pieces from the 1950s. See, for instance, his Mar. 1953 tribute to Stalin, whom he honors as a "great man" and hero beloved by common people everywhere ("On Stalin"). For Du Bois's statement of his belief in Communism, see his 1 Oct. 1961 letter to Gus Hall applying "for admission to membership in the Communist Party of the United States" (*Correspondence* 439-40).

[5] Readers can acquire a better sense of Du Bois's response to the Harlem Renaissance from the chapter "High Harlem" in his 1959 novel *Mansart Builds a School,* volume two of *The Black Flame* trilogy. For a crisp overview of the Du Bois-Garvey feud, one that is frequently critical of Du Bois, see Martin (273-343).

[6] See also *The Negro* (194) and *The Gift of Black Folk* (136-39). In *The World and Africa,* Du Bois refers to Marx as having made "the great unanswerable charge of the sources of capitalism in African slavery" (56).

WORKS CITED

Andrews, William L., ed. *Critical Essays on W. E. B. Du Bois.* Boston: Hall, 1985.

Aptheker, Herbert. *Annotated Bibliography of the Published Writings of W. E. B. Du Bois.* Millwood: Kraus-Thomson, 1973.

Brooks, Van Wyck. *The Confident Years, 1885-1915.* New York: Dutton, 1952.

Crosman, Richard, ed. *The God That Failed.* 1950. New York: Bantam, 1965.

Du Bois, W. E. B. *The Autobiography of W. E. B. Du Bois.* 1968. New York: International, 1980.

———. *The Correspondence of W. E. B. Du Bois.* Ed. Herbert Aptheker. Vol. 1. Amherst: U of Massachusetts P, 1978.

———. "Criteria of Negro Art." 1926. *W. E. B. Du Bois: "The Crisis" Writings.* Ed. Daniel Walden. Greenwich: Fawcett, 1972. 279-90.

———. *Dusk of Dawn.* 1940. Millwood: Kraus-Thomson, 1985.

———. *The Gift of Black Folk.* 1924. Millwood: Kraus-Thomson, 1987.

———. *Mansart Builds a School.* 1959. Millwood: Kraus-Thomson, 1976.

———. *The Negro.* 1915. Millwood: Kraus-Thomson, 1975.

———. "On Stalin." *Newspaper Columns by W. E. B. Du Bois.* Ed. Herbert Aptheker. Vol. 2. Millwood: Kraus-Thomson, 1986. 910-11. 2 vols.

———. *The Souls of Black Folk.* 1903. Millwood: Kraus-Thomson, 1985.

———. *The World and Africa.* 1947. Millwood: Kraus-Thomson, 1976.

———. *Writings.* New York: Library of America. 1986.

Duberman, Martin. "Du Bois as Prophet." *New Republic* 23 Mar. 1968: 36-39.

Horne, Gerald. *Black and Red: W. E. B. Du Bois and the Afro-American Response to the Cold War, 1944-1963.* Albany: State U of New York P, 1986.

Howe, Irving. *Celebrations and Attacks: Thirty Years of Literary and Cultural Commentary.* New York. Horizon, 1979.

James, Henry. *The American Scene.* 1907. Bloomington: Indiana UP, 1969.

James, William. *Letters.* Ed. Henry James, Jr. Vol. 2. 1920. New York: Kraus, 1969.

Johnson, James Weldon. *Along This Way.* 1933. New York: Viking, 1961.

Logan, Rayford and Michael R. Winston. "W. E. B. Du Bois." *Dictionary of American Negro Biography.* Ed. Logan and Winston. New York: Norton, 1982. 193-99.

Marable, Manning. *W. E. B. Du Bois: Black Radical Democrat.* Boston: Twayne, 1986.

Martin, Tony. *Race First: The Ideological and Organizational Struggles of Marcus Garvey and the Universal Negro Improvement Association.* 1976. Dover: Majority, 1986.

Nelson, Truman. "A Life Style of Conscience." *Nation* 29 Apr. 1968: 574-75.

"A Question of Inference." (An exchange between James S. Allen and Truman Nelson.) *Nation* 24 June 1968: 810, 834.

Rampersad, Arnold. *The Art and Imagination of W. E. B. Du Bois.* Cambridge: Harvard UP, 1976.

Tuttle, William M., ed. *W. E. B. Du Bois.* Englewood Cliffs: Prentice, 1973.

Houston A. Baker, Jr.

SOURCE: "The Problem of Being: Some Reflections on Black Autobiography," in *Obsidian*, Vol. 1, No. 1, 1975, pp. 18-30.

[*In the following essay, Baker focuses on* The Narrative of the Life of Frederick Douglass *as one of the best examples illustrating the African American autobiographer's "quest for being," or self-definition.*]

> It was a severe cross, and I took it up reluctantly. The truth was, I felt myself a slave, and the idea of speaking to white people weighed me down. I spoke but a few moments, when I felt a degree of freedom, and said what I desired with considerable ease.
>
> Frederick Douglass

Benedetto Croce called autobiography "a by-product of an egotism and a self-consciousness which achieve nothing but to render obvious their own futility and should be left to die of it." And one of the most important critics of the Black American Renaissance of the twenties expressed some of the same reservations when he wrote: "admittedly, the autobiography has limitations as a vehicle of truth. Although so long an accepted technique towards understanding, the self-portrait often tends to be formal and poised, idealized or purposely exaggerated. The author is bound by his organized self. Even if he wishes, he is unable to remember the whole story or to interpret the complete experience."[1] A number of eighteenth- and nineteenth-century American thinkers would undoubtedly have appreciated the wit and felicity of style manifested by these observations, but at the same time, they would have taken issue with the content. Egotism, self-consciousness, a deep and abiding concern with the individual are at the forefront of the American intellectual tradition, and the formal limitations of autobiography were not of great concern to men who felt all existent literary forms inadequate to encompass their unique experiences.

Envisioning themselves as God's elect and imbued with a sense of purpose, the Puritans braved the seas on a mission into the wilderness. The emptiness of the New World, the absence of established American institutions and traditions, reinforced their inclination to follow the example of their European forebears and brothers in God. They turned inward for reassurance and guidance. Self-examination became the *sine qua non* in an uncertain world where some were predestined for temporal leadership and eventual heavenly reward and others for a wretched earthly existence followed by hell's fires. The diary, the journal, the meditation, the book of evidences drawn from personal experience were the literary results of this preoccupation with self, and even those documents motivated by religious controversy often took the form of apology or self-justification. A statement from the *Personal Narrative* of Jonathan Edwards offers a view of the entire tradition:

> I spent most of my time in thinking of divine things, year after year: often walking alone in the woods, and solitary places, for meditation, soliloquy, and prayer, and converse with God; and it was always my manner, at such times, to sing forth my contemplations.[2]

The man alone, seeking self-definition and salvation, certain that he has a God-given duty to perform, is one image of the American writer. Commenting on Edwards and on the inevitable growth of autobiography in a land without a fully articulated social framework, Robert Sayre writes: " . . . Edwards could and had to seek self-discovery within himself because there were so few avenues to it outside himself. The loneliness and the need for new forms really go together. They are consequences of one another and serve jointly as inducements and as difficulties to autobiography."[3] This appraisal must be qualified, of course, since the form employed by Edwards does not differ substantially from John Bunyan's, and his isolated meditations fit neatly into a Calvinistic spectrum. Sayre is essentially correct, however, when he specifies a concern with solitude and a desire for unique literary expression as important facets of the American experience.

Despite the impression of loneliness left by Edwards's *Personal Narrative* and the sense of a barren and unpromising land for literature left by such comments as those of Hawthorne in his "Preface" to *The Marble Faun* or those of Henry James in *Hawthorne,* there were certain *a priori* assumptions available to the white American thinker. They developed over a wide chronological span (the original religious ideals becoming increasingly secularized) and provided a background ready to hand. First, there was his sense that he was part of a new cultural experience, that he had gotten away from what D.H. Lawrence calls his old masters and could establish a new and fruitful way of life in America. Second, there was the whole panoply of spiritual sanctions. As one of the chosen people, he was responsible for the construction of a new earthly paradise, one that would serve as a Godly paradigm for the rest of the world. Third—growing out of the liberal, secular thought of Descartes, Locke, and Newton—was his belief that the individual was responsible for his own actions. A man was endowed with certain inalienable rights, and one of these was apparently the right to educate himself and strive for commercial success. Fourth, was his feeling that America offered boundless opportunities for creative originality. A unique culture with peculiar sanctions should produce a *sui generis* literature and art.

Thus, while James's "extraordinary blankness—a curious paleness of colour and paucity of detail" characterized the early American scene, leading many toward introspection, there were also more substantial aspects. The white American writer could look to the Puritan ontology and sense of mission, to the conception of the self-made man, or to the prevailing American concern for a new aesthetic as pre-shaping influences for his work. The objective world provided philosophical and ideological justification for his task. When Emerson wrote "Dante's praise is that he dared to write his autobiography in colossal cipher, or into universality," he optimistically stated the possibilities immanent in the situation of the American author. The writer of comprehensive soul who dared to project his experiences on a broad scale could stand at the head of a great tradition. According to Emerson, the world surrounding such a person—that supposedly void externality—offered all necessary support. The permanence and importance of works such as Edwards's *Personal Narrative,* Franklin's *Autobiography,* Whitman's *Leaves of Grass,* and Adams's *The Education of Henry Adams* in the American literary tradition confirm his insight. As the American autobiographer turned inward to seek "the deepest *whole* self of man," he carried with him the pre-existent codes of his culture. They aided his definition of self and are fully reflected in the final artifact—the self-conscious, literary autobiography.

This perspective on the situation of the white American autobiographer highlights the distinctions between two cultures. Moved to introspection by the apparent "blankness" that surrounded him, the Black American had no *a priori* assumptions to act as stays in his quest for self-definition. He was part of the African Diaspora, a displaced man set down among alien gods in a strange land. For him, the white externality provided no ontological or ideological certainties; in fact, it consciously denied him the grounds of being. The seventeenth- and eighteenth-century black codes defined him as a slave in perpetuity, taking away his chance to become a free and participating citizen in the American city of God. The Constitution reaffirmed his bondage, and the repressive legislation of the nineteenth century categorized him as "chattel personal." Instead of the ebullient sense of a new land offering limitless opportunities, the Black American slave—staring into the heart of whiteness around him—must have felt as though he had been flung into existence without a human purpose. The white externality must have loomed like Heidegger's "Nothingness" (the negative foundation of being). Jean Wahl's characterization of Heidegger's philosophy of existence succinctly captures one point of view the slave might justifiably have held:

> Man is in this world, a world limited by death and experienced in anguish; is aware of himself as essentially anxious; is burdened by his solitude within the horizon of his temporality.[4]

There were at least two alternatives to this vision. First, there was the recourse of looking romantically back to Africa as a point of reference, and Sterling Stuckey has adequately demonstrated that a small but vocal minority employed this strategy.[5] Second, there was the possibility of adopting the God of the enslaver as a solace. A larger number chose this option and looked to the apocalyptic day that would bring release from captivity and vengeance on the oppressors. Finally, though, the picture that emerges from the innumerable accounts of slaves is charged with anguish—an anguish that reveals the bondsman to himself as out in the world, forlorn, without refuge.

And unlike the white American who could assume literacy and a familiarity with existing literary models as norms, the slave found himself without a written language—"uneducated" in the denotative sense of the word. His task was not simply one of moving toward the requisite largeness of soul and faith in the value of his experiences. He first had to seize the word. In a sense, his being erupts from nothingness. By grasping the word, he is able to engage in the speech/act that defines his self-hood, and he is more concerned with creating a human and liberated self than with projecting one that reflects a peculiar landscape and tradition. His problem is not to answer a question like Crevecoeur's: "What then is the American, this new man?" It is the problem of being itself.

The *Narrative of the Life of Frederick Douglass,* one of the finest slave narratives, serves as an illustration of the Black autobiographer's quest for being. The recovered past that emerges from the work is a sparse existence characterized by uncertainty and brutality:

> I have no accurate knowledge of my age.[6] The opinion was . . . whispered about that my master was my father; but of the correctness of this opinion, I know nothing. . . .   (pp. 21-2)

> My mother and I were separated when I was but an infant. (p. 22)

> I was seldom whipped by my old master, and suffered little from any thing else than hunger and cold. (p. 43)

> Our food was coarse corn meal boiled. This was called *mush.* It was put into a large wooden trough, and set down upon the ground. The children were then called, like so many pigs, and like so many pigs they would come and devour the mush. . . .
> (p. 44)

Unlike David Walker who, in his *Appeal to the Colored Citizens of the World,* attempts to explain why Blacks are violently held in bondage, the young Douglass finds no explanation for his condition. And though he describes the treatment of his fellow slaves (including members of his own family), the impression left by the first half of the *Narrative* is one of a lone existence plagued by anxiety. The white world rigorously suppresses all knowledge and action that might lead the Black man to a sense of his humanity.

Mr. Hugh Auld, whom Douglass is sent to serve in Baltimore, offers a case in point. Finding that his wife—out of an impulse to kindness rare among whites in the *Narrative*—has begun to instruct the slave in the fundamentals of language, the husband vociferously objects that "Learning would *spoil* the best nigger in the world." Not only is it illegal to teach a slave to read, but also folly, since it makes him aspire to an exalted position. The slave's reaction to this injunction might be equated with the "dizziness" which, according to Heidegger, accompanies the perception of possibilities that lie beyond anguish:

> These words sank into my heart, stirred up sentiments within that lay slumbering, and called into existence an entirely new train of thought. It was a new and special revelation, explaining dark and mysterious things, with which my youthful understanding had struggled, but struggled in vain. I now understood what had been to me a most perplexing difficulty—to wit, the white man's power to enslave the black man. (p. 49)

He has come to understand, by "the merest accident," the power of the word. His future is determined by this moment of revelation: he resolves "at whatever cost of trouble, to learn how to read." Douglass begins, in other words, to detach himself from the white externality around him, declaring:

> What he [Mr. Auld] most dreaded, that I most desired. What he most loved, that I most hated. That which to him was a great evil, to be carefully shunned, was to me a great good, to be diligently

sought; and the argument which he so warmly urged, against my learning to read, only served to inspire me with a desire and determination to learn. (p. 50)

Much of the remainder of the *Narrative* counterpoints the assumption of the white world that the slave is a brute against the slave's expanding awareness of language and its capacity to carry him toward new dimensions of experience. The entirety of chapter seven (the one following the Auld encounter), for example, is devoted to Douglass's increasing command of the word. He discovers *The Columbian Orator* with its practical exemplification of the virtue of fine speaking and its striking messages of human dignity and freedom. He learns the significance of that all-important word, "abolition." Against these new perceptions, he juxtaposes the unthinking condition of slaves who have not yet acquired the same language skill. At times, he envies them since they (like the "meanest reptile") are not fully and self-consciously aware of their situation. For the narrator, language brings the possibility of freedom and renders his enslavement even more tormenting. But it also gives rise to his decision to escape as soon as his age and the opportunity are appropriate. Meanwhile, he is content to bide his time perfecting his writing, since (as he says in a telling act of autobiographical conflation) "I might have occasion to write my own pass." (p. 57)

Douglass's description of his reaction to ships on the Chesapeake illustrates that he did, effectively, write his own pass. "Those beautiful vessels," he says, "robed in purest white, so delightful to the eye of freemen, were to me so many shrouded ghosts to terrify and torment me with thoughts of my wretched condition." (p. 76) He continues with a passionate apostrophe that shows how antithetical are his own and the condition of these white, "swift-winged angels." When clarified and understood through language, the deathly and terrifying nothingness around him reveals the grounds of being. Freedom, the ability to choose one's own direction, makes life beautiful and pure. Only the man who is not held in thrall has a chance to obtain the farthest reaches of humanity. From what appears a blank and awesome backdrop, Douglass has wrested significance. His subsequent progression through the roles of educated leader, freeman, abolitionist, and autobiographer mark a firm sense of being.

But while it is the fact that the ships are loosed from their moorings that intrigues Douglass, he also drives home their whiteness and places them in a Christian context. And it is here that certain added difficulties for the Black autobiographer reveal themselves. For the acquisition of language, which leads to being, has ramifications that have been best stated by the West Indian novelist George Lamming. Lamming draws on the relationship between Prospero and Caliban to illustrate:

> Prospero has given Caliban Language; and with it an unstated history of consequences, an unknown history of future intentions. This gift of language meant not English, in particular, but speech and

concept as a way, a method, a necessary avenue towards areas of the self which could not be reached in any other way. It is this way, entirely Prospero's enterprise, which makes Caliban aware of possibilities. Therefore, all of Caliban's future—for future is the very name for possibilities—must derive from Prospero's experiment, which is also his risk.[7]

Mr. Auld had seen that language could lead to the restiveness of his slave; he had not understood that it was possible to imprison him even more thoroughly in the manner described by Lamming. The angelic Mrs. Auld—in accord with the best evangelical codes of her era—however, has given Douglass the rudiments of a structure that eventually incarcerates him. True, the slave is only able to arrive at a sense of being through language. But it is also true that his conception of the pre-eminent form of being is conditioned by white, Christian standards.

To say this, however, is not to level a charge of treachery, or myopia. Stripped of his African modes of cultural adaptation and subjected to slavery, the Black American could only arrive at a sense of self by a rigorous and selective process of resistance and accommodation. Unable to transplant the institutions of his homeland in the soil of America, he had to seek means of survival and fulfillment in a world where he was made to stand in fear. He had to seize whatever weapons came to hand in his struggle toward self-definition, and the range of instruments was extremely limited. Evangelical Christians and committed abolitionists were the only easily discernible groups who placed themselves squarely in the path of a nation's hypocrisy and inhumanity. The dictates of these groups, therefore, seemed to provide a way beyond servitude. They were the only signs and wonders in a bleak environment where Black men were deemed "things." Determined to move beyond his subservient role, cut off from most of the alternatives held out to whites by the surrounding society, and, like Arna Bontemps's Gabriel Prosser, endowed with the feeling that freedom is the natural condition of life, Douglass adopted a conceptual structure that would enable him to avoid mortification. Once he had acquired language and a set of codes that viewed freedom and equality as norms, a meet posture became less problematical. The roles that he projects for himself in the latter part of the *Narrative* are in harmony with a white, Christian, abolitionist framework.

During his year at Mr. Freeland's farm, he spends much of his time "doing something that looked like bettering the condition of my race." (p. 90) His enterprise is a Sabbath school devoted to teaching his "loved fellow-slaves" so they will be able "to read the will of God." (p. 89) His endeavor combines the philanthropic impulses of the man of sympathy with a missionary zeal akin to Uncle Tom's. Of course, he insists that literacy and freedom are the ultimate goals.

Having returned to Mr. Auld's house after an absence of three years, he undertakes a useful trade and earns the right to hire out his time. All goes well until he attends a religious camp meeting on a Saturday and fails to pay his wages to the master. When Auld rebukes him, the demands of the "robber" are set against a man's right to freely worship God. Once again, freedom is placed in a Christian context. Infuriated by this occurrence, he decides that the time and circumstances are now conducive to his escape. When he arrives in New York, he feels like a man who has "escaped a den of hungry lions" (a sort of new-world Daniel), and one of his first acts is to marry Anna Murray in a Christian ceremony presided over by the Reverend James W.C. Pennington. One would not overstate the case at this point if one insisted that the liberated self portrayed by Douglass is Christian in orientation, having adopted some of the most cherished values of the white world that held him in fee. It is not surprising, therefore, that one witnesses this figure moving rapidly into the ranks of the abolitionists— that zealous body of men and women bent on putting America in harmony with its professed ideals. Nor is it striking that Douglass concludes his work with an appendix justifying himself as a true Christian.

In recounting his tale, then, the autobiographer shows his movement from the position of a baffled and isolated existent to that of a Christian abolitionist lecturer and writer. The self in the autobiographical moment (the present, the time in which the work is composed), however, seems unaware of the subtle limitations that have accompanied his progress. Even though the writer seems certain (given the integrity of the *Narrative*) how he is going to picture his development and how the emergent self will appear to most readers, he seems to ignore the fact that one cannot transcend existence in a universe where there is only existence. One can realize his humanity through "speech and concept," but one cannot distinguish the uniqueness of the self if the "avenues towards areas of the self" exclude individualizing and humanistic definitions of that self.

Douglass grasps language in a Promethean act of will, but he leaves unexamined its potentially devastating effects for himself and his fellow slaves. One reflection of this is the *Narrative* itself, which was written at the urging of those white abolitionists who had become the fugitive slave's employers. The work was written to prove that he had indeed been a slave. And while the necessary autobiographical commitment to truth forced him to portray accurately the existentiality of his original condition, the kindly-leading light of abolitionism is never far behind the supposedly dense veil concealing meaning. The issue here is not simply one of intentionality (how the author wishes to portray the self, or selves). It is one that combines Douglass's understandable desire to keep his job with the more complex concerns surrounding "privacy," in the current philosophical sense of the word.

Unwilling to tackle the speculations of Hobbes, Locke, and Wittgenstein in detail, one might simplify privacy by saying that language is a public institution like all other social institutions, and it is the only means we have of arriving at the philosophical "other." Moreover, since it is the only way we become aware of anything (thoughts, feelings, and sensations included), it is possible that there is no "private" domain. By adopting language as his way of extracting meaning from nothingness, a sense of being from an anguished existence, Douglass becomes a public figure. He is reassured, but also restricted by the conventions of the institution he chooses.

The results are manifested in the concepts that finally serve as a basis of value in the *Narrative,* and they are even closer to the surface when the style of the book is indistinguishable from the sentimental-romantic oratory and creative writing that marked Douglass's age. Elsewhere, I have attempted to demonstrate that there were unstated codes the autobiographer drew on and reflected in his work.[8] Had there been a unique Black language available, he might have set forth these peculiar aspects of Black oral culture without encountering the liabilities just discussed. What stands out here, however, is that the nature of the Black autobiographer's situation seems to force him to move to a public version of the self—one molded by the values of white America.

Of course, there are tangible, historical reasons for the image Douglass projects, since the feeling of larger goals shared with the white majority culture has always been present among Black Americans, e.g., the sharing of the same God and the accommodation mentioned earlier. From at least the third decade of the nineteenth century this feeling has been reinforced by the efforts of whites like William Lloyd Garrison and Wendell Phillips, by constitutional amendments, civil rights legislation, and repeated assurances that the American dream is the Black man's as well. Furthermore, what better support was there than the palpable achievements of a man like Frederick Douglass?

When Douglass revised his original *Narrative* for the third time in 1893, therefore, it represented the end of a process that began at the home of Hugh Auld, and its form and content make it a fitting example of the issues raised heretofore. The work is public, rooted in the language of its time, and considerably less existential than the 1845 version. What we have is the somewhat verbose and hackneyed story of a life written by a man of achievement. The white externality has been transformed into an arena where sterling accomplishments are possible and where the "old master" receives a convivial embrace. It is significant that this volume was reprinted in 1895, the year that saw its author's death and the emergence of Booker T. Washington as one of the most influential men Black America has produced.

Six years later, Washington's *Up From Slavery* appeared, and it offers a perfect illustration of the Black autobiographer's assumption of a public mantle. Unlike Douglass's developmental *Narrative,* Washington's work is primarily a life-and-times account that views the self against a broad social current. Instead of apology or justification for rebellion against this current, one finds gratitude—even joy—that the self has been swept along and acknowledged for aiding its progressive flow. Moral uplift and financial success quickly run together as Washington accepts *Homo Economicus* as the starting point in his ascent from ignorance, poverty, and vice to property ownership and a sound bank account. He cannot be immediately denounced for portraying himself in this manner, since his condemnation would require a general censure of the age in which he lived. Situated in America's "Gilded Age" and surrounded by the racial oppression so welcome to a number of its citizens, he adopted a public mask that displayed a self in accord with its era. The problem with his strategy, however, was that it forced him to commit the inexcusable sin of the autobiographer—insincerity. He simply ignored facts that did not agree with his image. He, thus, failed as a historian. Moreover, since autobiography is always closely tied to the social class and intellectual attainments of its author, he failed in the second domain of the genre. He cared little for imaginative literature, and his work has few fictive analogues that can redeem it from classification as a tract for the times. In this sense, it does not even possess the virtues of a good Horatio Alger story. Hence, *Up From Slavery* demonstrates some of the major pitfalls that confront the Black autobiographer.

The book is repetitious because the terms at hand for the author's materialistic portrait are so scarce. A self distinguishable from Huntington, Carnegie, and Vanderbilt never emerges, and the sense that being can only erupt through a white nothingness is contradicted by the countless white friends who aid Washington on his way to language, education, and a clean Yankee self. Rebecca Chalmers Barton has defined the entire school of Washingtonian autobiographers as "accommodators": self-seeking, pseudo-idealists who hide their ambitiousness and feelings of inferiority behind religious rhetoric and oratory dedicated to a cause.[9] Given the nature of *Up From Slavery,* this assessment seems just, and it is difficult to understand how one more recent writer[10] has set such store by those turn-of-the-century autobiographers who, time and again, show themselves drawn helplessly into the linguistic and emotional traps of the white world.

To end here, however, would be a disservice to the accomplished tradition of Black American autobiography. The number and diversity of slave narratives are sufficient to show the Black American self in its prototypical form, emerging from an existential barrenness and moving into being through language. Though the movement into the white, public sphere has claimed "many thousands," recent works such as *The Autobiography of Malcolm X* and George Cain's *Blueschild Baby* reveal a countermovement. Both take the city as setting, and both are products of a time that has witnessed rigorous attempts by Black Americans to detach themselves from a white externality.

A northern, urban existence and the urge for cultural autonomy have resulted in a new autobiographical self

that is public, but also undeniably Black and gifted with its own unique language—"Black English," the reforged language of white America. The time may yet come, therefore, when one will no longer encounter such ironical statements in Black autobiographies as the quotation from Douglass that serves as an epigraph for this discussion. Black Americans will derive their freedom from the speech/act without feeling "weighed down" by the idea of speaking to whites. And they will hardly employ an image like "a severe cross" in recovering their singular past.

NOTES

[1] Quoted from Rebecca Chalmers Barton, *Witnesses for Freedom* (New York: Harper, 1948), p. xii.

[2] Quoted from George McMichael, ed., *Anthology of American Literature* (New York: Macmillan, 1974), I, 228.

[3] *The Examined Self* (Princeton: Princeton University Press, 1964), p. 39.

[4] *A Short History of Existentialism* (New York: The Philosophical Library, 1949), p. 31.

[5] Sterling Stuckey, *The Ideological Origins of Black Nationalism* (Boston: Beacon, 1972).

[6] *Narrative of the Life of Frederick Douglass An American Slave Written by Himself* (New York: Signet, 1968), p. 21. All citations from the *Narrative* in my text refer to this edition.

[7] Quoted from Janheinz Jahn, *Neo-African Literature* (New York: Grove, 1969), p. 240.

[8] "Revolution and Reform: Walker, Douglass, and the Road to Freedom," in *Long Black Song* (Charlottesville: University Press of Virginia, 1972), pp. 76-9.

[9] Barton, *op. cit.*

[10] John W. Blassingame, "Black Autobiographies as History and Literature," *Black Scholar,* V (1973-4), 2-9.

Joseph Bruchac

SOURCE: "Black Autobiography in Africa and America," in *Black Academy Review,* Vol. 2, No. 1&2, Spring-Summer, 1971, pp. 61-70.

[*In the following essay, Bruchac discusses similarities between* Black Boy *by Richard Wright and* The Dark Child *by Camara Laye and places these works in the tradition of black autobiography that begins with* The Interesting Narrative of Olaudah Equiano or Gustavus Vassa, The African *(1789).*]

Autobiography has always been one of the most important of forms in black writing, both in Africa and in the Americas. And though there are often great differences between the life stories of such men as Richard Wright, whose tale of his childhood in the Delta south, *Black Boy,* has become an American classic since its publication in 1945 and Camara Laye, whose nostalgically idealized recounting of his youth in Guinea, *The Dark Child,* has also become a classic in its own right since its first publication in French under the title *L'Enfant Noir* in 1954. If we examine these works closely we are struck by the similarities between them—especially when we take note of the historical context which has produced them. Moreover, each book broadens our outlook on the other. But let us first look at the background.

For the past five hundred years or so, the Western world and those nations and peoples unfortunate enough to be in a subservient relationship to it have been in an age of a very near-sighted and unusually color-conscious colonialism. We might mark the beginning of this period, as does John Henrik Clarke, at 1492, a year distinguished not so much by a bad Genoan navigator stumbling into the Caribbean islands of the New World while using maps made years before by Jewish traders, as by the marriage of Ferdinand and Isabella, an event which united Christian Spain and signalled the true end of a long and prosperous period of what we now must recognize as African colonialism. For several centuries, the dark Moors of North Africa had occupied large parts of Europe, bringing to the more ignorant natives such advances as mathematics and new ideas in medicine and architecture. Shakespeare's picture of Othello was drawn from the experience of his times, when Moorish emissaries were contacting Queen Elizabeth in the hopes of establishing an alliance with Britain which would allow them to reconquer Spain. Later writers than Shakespeare would not present a black character so straightforwardly again. As John Pepper Clark expressed it in his essay "The Legacy of Caliban" which appeared in the February, 1968 volume of *Black Orpheus:* "After Shakespeare, the treatment by English writers of the speech habits of the savage or black man becomes less original and imaginative, approaching (a) stereotype . . ."

We have lived in this age and perhaps it is unnecessary for me to spell out once more those characteristics of attitude which have made this age so tragic a one for the non-white. Perhaps, but then again, these characteristics are so much a part of our culture and our everyday lives that despite the work of men who have gone down to martyrdom in North America, in South Africa, in the Congo and elsewhere and despite the writings of those particular men I wish to focus on in this paper, these characteristics of a colonial age are to some degree still accepted, merely glossed over here and there by euphemisms.

The first of these characteristics is the assumption that the black man is bad because of the color of his skin, that his blackness is evil. The plantation owners of the ante-bellum South and the Boers of South Africa were not above using the Bible to justify both slavery and this view by referring to Noah's curse on Canaan in Genesis 9, 20-27. The reactions of contemporary law-enforcement officers in this country to the Black Panther Party may well have some connection with this deeply ingrained historical assumption in Western culture about blacks.

The second characteristic, which is closely linked to the first, is the assumption that black people in general, whether in America or Africa, are something less than human, are savages or the descendents of savages, unable to take care of themselves or run their own affairs without the benevolent guidance of a European. This assumption, like the first, neglects the wealth of African culture which existed before the disruptive coming of the Europeans to Africa. As the German Africanist, Jahnheinz Jahn, who is best known for his penetrating though somewhat over-simplified survey of neo-African culture *Muntu,* expresses it in the title of one of his books: *Wir Nennten Ihm Savagen*—"We Named Them Savages." The many arguments which are still heard in many quarters of government today about the inability of African nations to run their own affairs is only one example of this second characteristic assumption of Western culture.

These assumptions and others, of course, were quite convenient to justify the evils of slavery and colonialism. Not only were they believed in by the colonial master, but sometimes they were accepted by the enslaved or the colonized—not completely, for there have always been men like the Maroons of Jamaica, Toussaint L'Ouverture, Marcus Garvey, and W. E. B. DuBois, men who would see through the lie and pierce the veil. Phyllis Wheatley's poem "On Being Brought From Africa To America," though a plea for the humanity of the black, still looks at the Negro through a Western lens:

> 'Twas mercy brought me from my *Pagan* land,
> Taught my benighted soul to understand
> That there's a God, that there's a Saviour too:
> Once I redemption neither sought nor knew.
> Some view our race with scornful eye,
> "Their color is a diabolic dye."
> Remember, Christians, Negroes, black as Cain,
> May be refined, and join th' angelic train.

Key words in this poem are "refined," "benighted" and "pagan." The phrase "Negroes, black as Cain" indicates that the poet was accepting the old idea of the implicit evil of black, and the entire major assumption of the poem seems to be not so much that Negroes are human as it is that Negroes can be made human if they are taught Christianity. Moreover, slavery is implicitly, for Phyllis Wheatley at least, a blessing in disguise.

Phyllis Wheatley, however, was a young girl when she was taken from Senegal and brought to America in 1761. Perhaps she had little memory of an Africa quite different from a benighted land of savage pageantry. It was the picture of a quite different Africa which would make the first major autobiography written by an African slave so unlike Phyllis Wheatley's writing in its portrayal of the dark mother. But then again, autobiography is by its very nature self-assertion, and the man who wrote in 1789 *The Interesting Narrative of Olaudah Equiano or Gustavus Vassa, The African* was a most unusual one.

Olaudah Equiano, born in 1745 in the kingdom of Benin, now a part of the present day nation of Nigeria, was kidnapped at the age of ten, through luck and perseverance was able to buy his way out of slavery, and became an active abolitionist and world traveller. His words about his early days in Eboe, his home village include many such evocative passages as the following:

> We are almost a nation of dancers, musicians and poets. Thus every event such as a triumphant return from battle or other cause of public rejoicing is celebrated in public dances, which are accompanied with songs and music suited to the occasion.

and

> Agriculture is our chief employment, and everyone, even the women and children, are engaged in it. Thus we are all habituated to labour from our earliest years. Everyone contributes something to the common stock, and as we are unacquainted with idleness we have no beggars.

and

> As to religion, the natives believe that there is one Creator of all things.

The picture which begins to emerge, we hardly need stress, is quite different from one of benighted and ignorant savagery.

One of the most ironic parts of Equiano's autobiography, by the way, is his description of his emotions on being taken on board the slave ship. It illustrates both his sensitivity and that the role of savage was not, in this case, being played by black men:

> When I looked 'round the ship too, and saw a large furnace of copper boiling and a multitude of black people of every description chained together, every one of their countenances expressing dejection and sorrow, I no longer doubted my fate; and quite overpowered with horror and anguish, I fell motionless on the deck and fainted. When I recovered a little I found some black people about me. . . . I asked them if we were not to be eaten by those white men with horrible looks, red faces, and loose hair.

Olaudah Equiano's narrative marks the beginning of what was to be a long line of autobiographical works by African and Afro-American writers, all of which would have in common one great point—that they were written with a knowledge of the dehumanizing assumptions of

Western culture about African and African-American peoples and that they would, in one way or another, endeavor to prove the falseness of these assumptions.

The black American equivalent of Olaudah Equiano was William Wells Brown, an unusually versatile man who was America's first real black man of letters. He later would write both plays and novels, including the famous book which Union soldiers carried with them into battle along with *Uncle Tom's Cabin, Clotelle, or, The President's Daughter,* but it was in 1842 that his autobiography was published, ushering in an era of narratives, often partially written or at least edited by Abolitionists working with escaped slaves, which would present to the American public horrifying tales of bondage and escape. From 1840 to 1860 dozens of such book-length accounts were published, including, in 1845, the *Narrative of The Life of Frederick Douglass, An American Slave, Written By Himself.*

The number and the importance of the works of autobiographical nature written by Africans and African Americans since those first books by Brown and Equiano, make it impossible to go into them in any real depth at this time. One possible way of looking at them in terms of classification, however, might be of interest. It seems to me that we might be able to pick out three distinct patterns in terms of the autobiographical theme in Black writing: the Political Autobiography, the Personal and more Literary Autobiography, and the Autobiographical Novel.

The first of these is generally a work written by a person who is of considerable political importance. This, rather than the literary quality of the work (which may also be quite considerable) seems to be the main interest for the reader. Such works as Booker T. Washington's *Up From Slavery, The Autobiography of Malcolm X,* Chief Albert Luthuli's *Let My People Go,* and Kwame Nkrumah's *Ghana* are prominent examples of this type. So, too, are the celebrity biographies such as those of Dick Gregory, and Sammy Davis Jr.

The second is usually the work of a person whose first profession is writing. In many cases it states the experiences and themes which that writer has used in his other works. Generally, as a work of literature, it is more substantial and better written than the political autobiography. Wright's and Laye's books, as well as such books as Langston Hughes' *The Big Sea,* Ezekiel Mphalele's *Down Second Avenue* and *The Autobiography of W. E. B. DuBois* are examples of this second type.

(There is also a possible fourth category which seems to fit between these first two. It is the sensational autobiography, a work which may be a one-shot deal for its author and presents the writer as a sort of Ishmael character—though all black autobiographers are, in a sense, Ishmael. Prince Modupe's *I Was a Savage* and Claude Brown's *Manchild in the Promised Land* might be given as examples of this type.)

The last category, the Autobiographical Novel, is a work of fiction which either presents a character who is relating the story of his life or, in some way creates a character who is a mask of the author and lives the writer's own experience. James Weldon Johnson's *The Autobiography of An Ex-Colored Man* (which many people do not recognize as a work of fiction—Johnson's real autobiography, *Along This Way* was published in 1933, twenty-one years after the novel mistaken for his autobiography), Ayi Kwei Armah's powerful *Fragments,* Ferdinand Oyono's tragic *Boy* and even Ellison's *Invisible Man* might be placed in this category which, we find, includes a large percentage of all the writings done by African and Afro-American writers.

With these ideas in mind, let us now turn to those two major works which are, in a sense, the quintessence of the black autobiographical tradition.

At first glance, it might seem that apart from the similarity in their titles, *Black Boy* and *The Dark Child* have little in common. The first is a story of a childhood spent in the crushing poverty and inhuman brutality of a viciously color-conscious society. The second is almost a poem in its lyricism. It recounts in near-ideal terms the growing up in a strongly traditional society charged with principles of compassionate humanism of a boy who has none of the doubts about himself and his future which so haunted the young Richard Wright.

If we look again, however, we begin to see a similarity in pattern and motive between the two books.

Both Wright and Laye write of the forces which shape a man who, because he was born into a society and a time affected in one way or another by Western culture, must assert his own integrity against the dehumanizing assumptions of that society. *The Dark Child* was written while Laye was working in an automobile factory in France. Far behind him was the childhood which is so vividly described in his book. He was a member of the working class of France, France the great mother of art and culture, yet like the poets of negritude he was not satisfied with being a black Frenchman. He knew that he never could be that, partially because of the elitist nature of the French policies of assimilation, partially because his own cultural heritage was so rich and so true. To find himself, to define himself to both the Western world and himself he returned to childhood. His story does not begin when he was rescued from the savagery of a primitive Africa and it does not end with his becoming an honored citizen of France. It is not a success story, and though it may seem charged with happiness and satisfaction when compared to the agonies of the Delta South Wright pictures, one of the most real elements of *The Dark Child* is a sense of loss. It begins:

> I was a little boy playing around my father's hut. How old would I have been at that time? I can not remember exactly. I must have been very young: five, maybe six years old. My mother was in the workshop with my father, and I could just hear their familiar voices above the noise of the anvil and the conversation of the customers.

After this picture of a secure world, surrounded by the presence and voices of family and friends, the agony of the last few pages of the book is much clearer. Because of his success in trade school Laye is to go to France. It is the dark child's mother who reacts the strongest to his forthcoming departure, knowing full well that more than mere miles will separate them:

> "Am I never to have peace. Yesterday it was the school in Conarky; today it's the school in France; tomorrow . . . what will it be tomorrow? Every day there's some mad scheme to take my son from me. . . . Have you already forgotten how sick he was in Conarky? But that's not enough for you. Now you want to send him to France. . . . What are they thinking about at the school. Do they imagine I'm going to live my whole life apart from my son? Die with him far away? Have they no mothers, those people? They can't have. They wouldn't have gone so far away from home if they had."

To be sure, the contrast is very real with Richard Wright's separation from his family. When Richard Wright headed north, he was not leaving a world of security and order. In fact, his family wished to flee with him:

> The accidental visit of Aunt Maggie to Memphis formed a practical basis for my planning to go north. . . . My mother, Aunt Maggie, my brother and I held long conferences, speculating on the prospects of jobs and the cost of apartments in Chicago. And every time we conferred, we defeated ourselves. It was impossible for all four of us to go at once; we did not have enough money.

But both Wright and Laye are heading into the unknown, forced to leave the life which has formed them by pressures from outside, pressures exerted by Western culture. When Laye ends his story with these words:

> Later on I felt something hard when I put my hand in my pocket. It was the map of the *metro.* . . .

We should not have to stretch our imagination too far to realize that in a very real sense he is about to enter the metro, the subway, the underground world of white civilization, to descend into hell. And from Wright's other books, we should be able to see clearly that what awaited the young Richard in the cities of the north was also far from a promised land.

There are other facets of these two books in addition to their concluding flights to centers of Western civilization which can be meaningfully compared. One of these areas is education.

Both books, dealing with the coming of age of a young man, center on the education which is a major aspect of that maturity. Where Richard Wright's formal education is haphazard and often capricious, as in the case of his experiences as a pupil of his Aunt Addie's in religious school, Laye's is planned and structured. Yet it is structured in such a way as to draw him inevitably further from his own heritage, as his mother so wisely sees. The formal education of each of the young protagonists, however, is not so important as another kind of education having to do with society. And it is at this point that we see the greatest contrast between the lives of Wright and Laye. Wright is taught, by beatings from his family, by painful example, and by the often threatening attitudes of his white employers that he must not aspire to rise above his place in the Jim Crow South. When he refuses to read the valedictory speech written by his 9th grade principal instead of his own he is well on his way to a final rejection of that society.

Laye, on the other hand, is taught in the meaningful rituals of manhood and circumcisions what it is to be a man in an ordered and humane African society. His ritual of passage is one of acceptance.

Another area which is important in both books is that of family. There are obvious differences. Richard Wright's family is fatherless and most of his descriptions of family life seem to focus on the terrible conflicts he had with mother, grandmother, and various aunts and uncles. In *The Dark Child* we see a closely knit family with a father and mother both of whom are not only figures of pride to the young Laye, but even figures of magic. His father has a guardian spirit in the form of a small black snake which visits him at his forge. His mother is familiar with all of the mysteries of his country and has mysterious powers. To say, however, that Wright's family cared less for their child than did Laye's seems to me to be a misinterpretation. Their actions to chasten the indomitable spirit of a very proud and extremely sensitive youth were actions taken to save him from the lynching which was usually the regard for the sort of individuality he was showing. It is in council with his relatives and with their very direct help that Wright makes the decision to leave the Delta. Even further, if we note the closeness of uncles, aunts, cousins and so on to Wright's immediate family, we realize that we are witnessing the American equivalent, even after years of slavery and degradation, of the African extended family.

Ralph Ellison, in an essay on *Black Boy* has called Wright's autobiography blues, defining the blues as:

> an impulse to keep the painful details and episodes of a brutal experience alive in one's aching consciousness, to finger its jagged grain, and to transcend it, not by the consolation of philosophy but by squeezing from it a near-tragic, near-comic lyricism.

We can hear this blues note in the passages when Wright finds himself wakening to the mystery and beauty of the ambiguous world around him:

> The days and hours began to speak now with a clearer tongue. Each experience had a sharp meaning of its own.
>
> There was the breathless anxious fun of chasing and catching flitting fireflies on drowsy summer nights. . . .
>
> There was the excitement of fishing in muddy county creeks with my grandpa on cloudy days. . . .
>
> There was the fear and awe I felt when Grandpa took me to a sawmill to watch the giant whirring steel blades whine and scream as they bit into wet green logs. . . .

And we hear it most clearly of all in the last paragraphs of the book when Wright says:

> Yet, deep down, I knew that I could never really leave the South. . . . I was taking a part of the South to transplant in alien soil, to see if it could grow differently, if it could drink of new and cool rains, bend in strange winds, respond to the warmth of other suns, and perhaps, to bloom. . . . And if that miracle ever happened, then I would know that there was yet hope in that southern swamp of despair and violence, that light would emerge even out of the blackness of the southern night.

If Wright's *Black Boy* is the blues, then Camara Laye's *The Dark Child* is the music of the praise singer, the muted balafong and drum, a music which may be soft yet is as strong and deep as the beat of the human heart.

Both blues and praise song are African forms, and as a symbol of the strength of human dignity Africa lives in the writing of both Laye and Wright. Wright's Africa is deep within himself, it is the tough strength of a persevering descendent of African slaves. Laye's is the Africa his incomplete Europeanization has drawn him away from. And in reading their works and the books of other African and Afro-American autobiographers, we see that it is that Africa of human compassion and dignity to which we must all return.

Michael G. Cooke

SOURCE: "Modern Black Autobiography in the Tradition," in *Romanticism: Vistas, Instances, Continuities,* edited by David Thorburn and Geoffrey Hartman, Cornell University Press, No. 1973, pp. 255-80.

[*In the following essay, Cooke discusses the autobiographical writings of Richard Wright, Malcolm X, and Eldridge Cleaver, three African American writers who have made "evolutionary contributions to the form of western autobiography."*]

INTRODUCTION: AUTOBIOGRAPHY

In terms of literature, Jung's antinomian law, "that the real picture consists of nothing but exceptions to the rule,"[1] may have been framed for autobiography. Paradox inheres in the form, which calls for personal uniqueness and yet depends on a cogent general category—the definition of self achieved by one autobiographer must be both genuine and inimitable, and cannot lend itself to use by others without leading to a certain forgery. Critically speaking, we can be sure when generality has been taken too far, as in Gibbon's refusing to discuss "the first consciousness of manhood" on the grounds that this "very interesting moment of our lives" "less properly belong to the memoirs of an individual, than to the natural history of the species."[2] But we are equally sure that generality cannot be wished away. Even the prototypal professor of uniqueness, Jean-Jacques Rousseau, continually ascends to generality, though he finds it shaky ground. Rousseau's example provides a vivid instance of the paradox of autobiography: that in its presumption of uniqueness it is frustrated by the demands of philosophy, while remaining impotent in its conceptual and expository needs unless it has the philosopher's tools at its command. It is this state of being at odds with itself that I would like to study here, with a view to showing that at least three modern black writers have achieved happy resolutions of the autobiographical paradox, making evolutionary contributions to the form of western autobiography.

It is important to maintain a distinction between what may be autobiographical and autobiography proper, akin to the distinction between the poetical and poetry. In another context, a recent writer on spiritual autobiography addresses himself to this point: "Donne's record of his illness in *Devotions upon Emergent Occasions* is a splendid example of autobiographical material essential yet subordinate to a work's main scheme; personal experience is assimilated into what is, in effect, an extended homily" on the human condition.[3] Perfect obedience to memory and candor would yield something richly autobiographical, but less than autobiography, just as the most eloquent profession of the meaning of one's life or reflections upon it would constitute more of a credo than an autobiography. The form entails simultaneous, if conflicting, obligations to narrative and to analysis and exposition. The essential thing in realizing this form is that the work of memory, the material truth, not only must contain an essential informing truth as an available element, but must convey it as an explicit and active one. (The lack of an informing truth as a principle of coherence keeps such modes as the diary or journal or travelogue or memoir at the level of the autobiographical, and has the same effect on many poems and novels, from Byron and Gottfried Keller to Conrad, Proust, and Joyce.)

The skepticism usually aimed at the autobiographer's reliability will not take us very far.[4] At least not if autobiography, as a literary form, incorporates an honorable selection and proportion of facts, and a plausible (not definitive) human judgment, *without being defined by them*. Individualizing articulation is the very spirit of the form. Barring a selection of data or an interpretive bias so flagrant as to involve autobiographer and reader in a cynical disregard of literary integrity, the point of autobiography is how shape and significance can be found in, or given to, the amorphousness of experience, how the abstraction of the "I" can be identified and realized.

And the overriding concern comes to center on the style of the autobiography, taking style to mean not sentence structure and vocabulary, as Roy Pascal seems to do,[5] but the whole complex of resources, of selection, proportion, sequence, and recurrence, as well as those verbal, rhetorical, logical, structural resources whereby the work at once apprehends and expresses its subject. In spite of his best efforts, then, Gibbon's treatment of the first consciousness of manhood, by its very idiom and its obliqueness, becomes as perspicuous as that of Rousseau or Yeats or Dylan Thomas. For in effect style in autobiography distinctively entails not just the representation of the self in language, but the giving over of the self to language. Anyone with enough energy and reflection to do an autobiography goes beyond a reporting into a realization of the self through the instrumentality of language.

It is no mere coincidence that autobiography first cuts its own stream in the literary landscape toward the end of the eighteenth century, or as a sign of the Romantic movement. Formally, or generically speaking, autobiography may be associated with the dissolution or permutation of genres in the romantic period: *The Prelude* is a lyrical-epical-philosophical-mystical-descriptive-travelogue-autobiographical poem. Further, autobiography feeds on the experimental or deferential arrogance of the age; the self is the source of the system of which it is a part, creates what it discovers, and although (as Coleridge realized) it is nothing unto itself, it is the possibility of everything for itself. Autobiography is the coordination of the self as content—everything available in memory, perception, understanding, imagination, desire—and the self as shaped, formed in terms of a perspective and pattern of interpretation. Autobiography readily engrafts itself on, or insinuates itself into what once had been generically simpler statements. The result of such multiplicity is both great hazards and great possibilities, the event again depending least on the intention of the writer, something shared equally by Gibbon and Rousseau. De Quincey poignantly indicates the autobiographer's anxiety in his *Autobiographic Sketches,* where he deprecates the mere "amusement which attaches to any real story," while remaining uncertain how to blend "intellectual impulses" and "absolute frankness" so as to produce the "deep, solemn, and . . . even . . . thrilling interest" which should bind together all the elements of the work.

What De Quincey is concerned about (and it should be observed that he is not speaking as a novice autobiographer) is the difficulty of finding a definition of his subject, *and* a congruent form. This indivisible difficulty may be taken as the essential one for autobiography. The way it is met, by the same token, would go far toward establishing the essential quality of an autobiography or of an era in autobiography.

The problem of establishing a subject and form gives special interest to the rewriting of autobiographies. Rewriting has been taken up on stylistic grounds, as in Ian Jack's study of De Quincey,[6] but unaccountably not as a characteristic or essential issue for autobiography, not even in John Morris' *Versions of the Self.*[7] For whether the restlessness that brings a man back to recast his image and form be psychic or critical, the stages of his self-presentation have to be tied up with a question of identity; the autobiographer loses clarity and authority even as he multiplies himself. One's autobiograph*ies* constitute an anomaly, though autobiography, as Wordsworth and Malcolm X in different ways have shown, may be generated out of a subject's knowing struggle for identity, by stages, or his undergoing a conscious evolution of self-conception.

The problem of the self and time is paramount for autobiography.[8] It compounds the problem of conceptual unity if the "self" alters in time, or alters its formulation. And yet no autobiography can be exempt from the force of its moment. As the selection of material can raise questions as to content, so the choice of time implies questions as to conception. How and what is written depends on the *when* of the writing. It is of particular interest, then, to see Edward Gibbon, habituated to neo-classical discipline and elegant practicality, going through the labyrinth of self-description. Both the tidiness of hand and the polished statement of each of the six versions of his *Autobiography* profess a clear decision and power as regards the portrayal of "the historian of Rome"; but the succession of versions, so obscure in its patternlessness, critically weakens the foundations of assurance on which the individual versions seem to rest. Indeed, *Memoir C,* which describes itself most impersonally as "the narrative of my literary life" (257), exhibits an unusual, if not uniform, degree of frankness and copiousnes concerning a host of subjects: his "estate," as to which he is so reticent in *B;* the misdemeanors on his second visit to Lausanne; his desire for power and authority, especially in relation to his father, whose death is used as a motif and epoch here; his relationship with Deyverdun and his attitude toward women; and the predominance of pragmatism over affection in his makeup.

It seems at least statistically clear that the form of autobiography proved for Gibbon more recalcitrant than the form of his immortal history, for which he needed no more than three revisions of the initial chapters to hit his stride. The problem was in part one of settling on the attitude to take toward his subject and his audience, but it was probably first a problem of identifying his subject and his purpose. In short, the problem of autobiography unwittingly experienced by one whose habits of assurance, while evidently baffled, were strong enough to withstand the radical threats conveyed by the very form he adopts in what one may call his composed

egotism. It is possible to extrapolate from the whole set of Gibbon's autobiographies, or would-be autobiographies, a basic concern with survival and security, generated by an ill-concealed intuition of the precariousness of life, personal freedom, and social expectations. But none of this is explicit or reliable, and it is not, by way of anticipation, till we come to Richard Wright's *Black Boy* that we find an achieved autobiography dealing centrally with these issues.

If Gibbon willy-nilly demonstrates the perennial problem of autobiography, it will be profitable to glance at the terms of success discovered by various exponents of the form, as a background for the scrutiny of Wright, Malcolm X and Eldridge Cleaver. For this purpose I should like to consider the original version of De Quincey's *Confessions of an English Opium Eater,* Newman's *Apologia pro Vita Sua,* and Yeats's *Reveries over Childhood and Youth,* as somehow typifying the periods in which they were written, and yet also as necessarily singular illustrations of the possibilities of success in autobiography.

DE QUINCEY, NEWMAN, YEATS

Things were to change by the time he got to the revised version, but De Quincey in 1822 had had neither time nor occasion to think better of the adventure of the original *Confessions of an English Opium-Eater.* A half-jocular hubris marks the work, which is ultimately less a confession than an exploration and appropriation of uncharted psychological territory. The revised version is more informative, but at the cost of becoming prolix, choppy and either sermonizing or polemical;[9] the original seems genuinely coherent and philosophical, provided we recognize the perversity of its confession. The sense of guilt, of reconciliation with the community, works only as an opening ploy to indulge the reader's self-importance and tranquilize his fear. The sense of avowing a position is the implicit one, and becomes salient in two ways. The first of these is negative, in the impugning of standard authorities and orthodoxies in the academy, in medicine, in a system of morality which has become "inhuman," and even in the social assumptions concerning wine; the second is positive, and takes the form of establishing his own credentials and authority as a philosopher of the "inner eye and [the] power of intuition for the vision and mysteries of human nature." The language of the text suggests that the vision is both apocalyptic and natural; opium is associated with Eden at its best and at its worst (it is ambiguously described as "insufferable splendour"), and again with dreams which are themselves associated with infinity, with childhood, and with unexceptionable figures like Dryden and Fuseli; so that myth and memory and art alike sanction it. In this respect the *Confessions* become an informal or dramatic trial of De Quincey's aborted *magnum opus, De Emendatione Humani Intellectus.*

No one needs to be reminded of De Quincey's incessant concern with the reader's reactions in the original

Confessions. A note De Quincey added to the original preface gives a clear indication of why this is so:

> I feel [our own age] to be, more emphatically than any since the period of Queen Elizabeth and Charles I, an intellectual, a moving, and a self-conflicting age: and inevitably, where the intellect has been preternaturally awakened, the moral sensibility must soon be commensurately stirred. The very distinctions, psychologic or metaphysical, by which, as its hinges and articulations, our modern thinking moves, proclaim the subtler character of the questions which now occupy our thoughts. Not as pedantic only, but as suspiciously unintelligible, such distinctions would, one hundred and thirty years ago, have been viewed as indictable.[10]

It is necessary to stress the way De Quincey's manner, while it involves playing up to the reader, intrinsically serves as a way of playing on him. The author's pious protestations that the will to be "useful and instructive" alone has made him remove the "decent veil of drapery" from his miserable experience is pious equivocation. The veil is really removed from unknown and hence uncomfortable regions of the human mind, of which De Quincey by "chance" or "accident"—key terms recurring throughout—has been the Columbus. The function of the autobiography is to map out this region, authenticate it, and annex it to the kingdom of humanity. The articulation of the life takes place in terms of the personal capacities and external circumstances which have equipped De Quincey for the task of emending the picture of the human mind. In this sense, the *Confessions* modulate into apologia and beyond that into radical missionary work for "the church of opium."

The peculiar interplay of chance and teleology in the career exhibited in the *Confessions,* and the temper of self-seeking and apostolic self-justification which informs it (De Quincey founds the "church of opium") bear a strong enough resemblance to Rousseau's *Confessions,* Wordsworth's *Prelude,* and Coleridge's *Biographia Literaria* to be thought of as Romantic. A certain buoyancy in the face of a situation problematical on the subjective as well as public levels marks all of these works, and is especially striking in the case of Coleridge, who, in the autobiographical context, surpasses himself in personal and philosophical daring.[11] In this light one is tempted to say that a concentration on the collapse of certitudes as a stimulus to Romanticism goes awry; a degree of courage and resiliency and resourcefulness in coping with incertitude seems to merit stronger emphasis. Certainly an almost evolutionary change can be recognized in the way autobiographers like Newman or Mill or Gosse or Pattison or F. W. H. Myers or even Tennyson, in the Victorian era, see themselves and the world in terms of the need for authority, with the self-generating philosophy of High Romanticism fading into improbability.

To deal in particular with Newman, it is hard to agree with Pascal that the *Apologia* does not enable us "to

perceive and feel the driving forces in the man, the genetic sources of the personality, the numerous potentialities in him which ultimately led to [the] great decision of Newman's life" (*Design and Truth,* p. 100). The very contrary would seem true, unless one can indifferently pass by such lines as the following:

> If I looked into a mirror, and did not see my face, I should have the sort of feeling which actually comes upon me, when I look into this living busy world, and see no reflexion of its Creator. . . . I am far from denying the real force of the arguments in proof of a God, drawn from the general facts of human society and the course of history, but these do not warm me or enlighten me; they do not take away the winter of my desolation, or make the buds unfold and the leaves grow within me, and my moral being rejoice.[12]

A salient feature of Newman's apologetics, for all its institutional and analytical tendencies, is its saturation with his "private thoughts and feelings," or, to use another phrase of his, his capacity for "identifying" himself (p. 229) with authority. The pattern of the book follows a progression from personal to institutional authority, from national to catholic authority, from legitimate to infallible authority, where finally and alone true rest is possible. But Newman's impulse toward identifying himself with authority goes hand in hand with an impulse toward "vindicating it," so that the liveliest communication exists continuously between the poles of personalty and logic, and indeed, though Newman declares "it is not . . . easy . . . to wind up an Englishman to a dogmatic level," between personality and dogma when the dogma will not let him down and leave him, as did the Anglican divines, "in a humour" to "bite off [somebody's] ears." The crystallization of Newman's need for authority and dogma seems to have occurred around a typically nineteenth-century trauma: the humiliation and bafflement of death.

> The truth is, I was beginning to prefer intellectual excellence to moral; I was drifting in the direction of the Liberalism of the day. I was rudely awakened from my dream at the end of 1827 by two great blows—illness and bereavement.

The "influence of a definite Creed," and "impressions of dogma" which were never "effaced or obscured" had been felt more than a decade before, in 1816, and "the doctrine of Tradition" had been grasped as a principle from Dr. Hawkins five years before, in 1822; but the critical point arrives in 1827, as just described. The crisis, of course, is not one of mutual exclusion as between intellectual and moral excellence, but of "preference." Intellectual excellence becomes more of an instrument than an ideal. If the *Apologia* exhibits Newman's need for authority, it also exhibits a true fastidiousness about the subject in the all but scrupulous deliberations which attended his acceptance of authority. Newman himself observes that "to reconcile theory and fact is almost an instinct of the mind," and it seems proper to treat his description of one change as normative:

> The process of change [from liberalism] had been slow; it had been done not rashly, but by rule and measure, "at sundry times and in divers manners," first one disclosure and then another, till the whole evangelical doctrine was brought into full manifestation.

I would only suggest that not intellectuality but the subjective importance of authority is the ground of these deliberations, a paradox only compounded when Newman, quite justly, links acceptance of authority with "bold unworldliness and vigorous independence of mind." The phrase is applied to Thomas Scott of Aston Sandford, but Scott is used as a model by Newman, and his "independence," which takes the form of just acts of obedience to the right institution—"he followed truth wherever it led him"[13]—must be set against the independence of the man who, "at an unseasonable time," tries to carry "a reformation of an abuse, or the fuller development of a doctrine, or the adoption of a particular policy (p. 244). Newman's suspicion of such unqualified independence is noteworthy and may be treated in his own words:

> Knowing that there is no one who will be doing anything toward [his objective] in his own lifetime unless he does it himself, he will not listen to the voice of authority, and he spoils a good work in his own century, in order that another man as yet unborn, may not have the opportunity of bringing it happily to perfection in the next. He may seem to the world to be nothing else than a bold champion for the truth and a martyr to free opinion, when he is just one of those persons whom the competent authority ought to silence; and, though the case may not fall within that subject-matter in which that authority is infallible, . . . it is clearly the duty of authority to act vigorously in the case. [p. 245]

The introduction of the purpose clause—*in order that* another man . . . may not have the opportunity of bringing it happily to perfection"—where a result clause might seem more fitting, perhaps strikes an ominous note, but the argument for authority in terms of prudence or pragmatism is too gracious to arouse suspicion on that score. Basically it extends, and does not define Newman's position. Its prime effect is to deepen our understanding of Newman's panoptic devotion to authority, the quest for which almost comes to seem the essential feature of his "history of [him]self." I have suggested that such a quest marks him as a man of his time. What singles him out withal is the consciousness of the quest, the intricacy of its articulation, its eloquence, and the achievement of personal authority by the expression and satisfaction of his greatest needs and powers in terms of Authority.

If in retrospect the creation or discovery of spontaneous authority might seem to characterize De Quincey as a Romantic autobiographer, and dedication to formal authority to characterize Newman as Victorian, nothing could be more telling for twentieth-century developments than the way Yeats circumvents the awful authority of "God," whom he takes his Grandfather for, in *Reveries over Childhood and Youth*.[14] This is not to suggest that Yeats is taking a stand in direct relation to Newman; rather his stand freely lends itself to comparison with Newman's and furnishes important help toward understanding the evolution of autobiography.

On the surface, the *Reveries over Childhood and Youth* would seem to be little more than random "recollections of relatives and friends,"[15] but there are good grounds for taking it as an integral work following quite original lines of organization. It is true that the opening statement as it were helplessly confesses a lack of order or relation in memory, and hence the impossibility of ordering and understanding experience. But this statement turns out to work more as a symbol than as description: "My first memories [Yeats writes] are fragmentary and contemporaneous. . . . "[16] But he immediately adds a metaphor of intellection: "as though one remembered some first moments of the Seven Days." In this way he makes the experience available to us by an imaginative act that seems to be widely possible; it is "one" who remembers, not "I." Further elaborating and, let me stress, interpreting this obscure experience, Yeats writes: "It seems as if time had not yet been created, for all thoughts connected with emotion and place are without sequence." In fact, time signals are plentiful enough in the writing, though occurring at random and not in such a way as to provide or permit the kind of assurance we are likely to feel about a work where we can set up its narrative progression (I mean, it is easier to think one knows *The Faerie Queene*, Bk. I, than *The Prelude*, Bk. I, simply in terms of ease of narrative connection). But the nullifying of time is not just incidental to Yeats's "first memories"; it informs *all* his memories, the *Reveries* being organized in discontinuous sections to reveal the fact that his entire experience, or perhaps his grasp of his experience, is "fragmentary and isolated and contemporaneous."

On the whole this might seem to describe only the effect and not the thesis of the presentation; but I would suggest that the final paragraph of the *Reveries* functions as a retroactive thesis, which carries us irresistibly back to the sense of aboriginal beginning, making this sense endless and explaining the absence of narrative progression and the nullifying of time:

> When I think of all the books I have read, and of the wise words I have heard spoken, and of the anxiety I have given to parents and grandparents, and of the hopes that I have had, all life weighed in the scales of my own life seems to me a preparation for something that never happens.[17]

In effect, the replication of the Seven Days in his own world, Yeats's version of the primary imagination, has not come about, so that we are left with an uncreated, and hence in literary terms an unorganized world, but also at the same time an adequate conception of this uncreated state, and even a sort of representation of it.

Yeats is clear about his unclarity. Indeed, the number of sections in the *Reveries,* thirty-three, seems to me meant to suggest the Christological age, with the revealing difference that for Yeats whatever is in preparation "never happens." This suggestion in fact appears to be strengthened by the title of the second part of Yeats's *Autobiography,* namely "The Trembling of the Veil." The analogy may be considered as clear, and as obscure, as the answer to the question: And what rough beast . . . slouches toward Bethlehem? Yeats assembled his *Autobiography* with a running spontaneity but also with a retrospective calculation; and it is one of the happy effects of his agnosticism that leaving the final section on "The Bounty of Sweden" unshaped fits both his whimsy and his design. For the "autobiographical muse," far from "betraying" Yeats and "abandoning him to ultimate perplexity as to the meaning of his experiences" (Ellman, *Yeats: Man and Masks,* p. 2), seems instead to have clarified for him the elusiveness of any such meaning, no matter how diligently he sought it.

Yeats's achievement in autobiography, a considerable one, is to have invented a sort of mosaic or pointillist form which both represents and controls incertitude of mind, and futility of action. From H. G. Wells to Bertrand Russell and Norman Podhoretz one still finds more or less plausible pretensions to philosophy or to power, but what Yeats implies and Wells himself declares, a sense of "planless casualness" in the modern world, feels truer in the first place, and proves stronger and deeper in literary experience: one may quickly cite, for example, Frank Budgen's *Myselves When Young* and Goronwy Rees's *A Bundle of Sensations.*[18] In this regard, the work of modern black autobiographers emerges with singular force. In this work, the sense of a perennially emergent or explosive universe is made palpable, the sense of personal encumbrance urgent and ubiquitous, while the sense of the self as not only finding itself but somehow thriving (not just making it) in the flux also comes through. The presence of Yeats by itself will indicate that this is a cultural, and not just a black pattern; anyone who recalls Hemingway's *Green Hills of Africa* or H. M. Tomlinson's *The Sea and the Jungle* will find this point driven home.

WRIGHT, MALCOLM X, CLEAVER

The three writers, Richard Wright, Malcolm X, and Eldridge Cleaver, at once become the environment it has been my concern to outline, and become their own men. They demand to be read for something more than what Gottfried Keller deigned to praise Rousseau for, a certain confessional shock-value. With *Black Boy,*[19] Wright, who does not fail to suggest the high security he attained in terms of "the external drama of life" (*BB,* 112), surpasses all writers I know in the naturalistic, non-Kafkaesque evocation of the physical dimensions of incertitude, its simple separation from the operations of interpretive reason and purposive will. Accident becomes substantive almost; as Wright says, "anything might happen" (224). Flogging, fighting, theft, death or

threats of death, and above all the endless disorientation of moving and flight spread through the narrative so far as to become symbols, and finally round into the status of things, comparable to the litanies of objects that dot the early pages of the work. They are part of Wright's world, like trees. He breathes the atmosphere they exude, and escapes from them only by a kind of homeopathic experiment. "The thirst for violence . . ." he says, "was in me, for intrigue, for plotting, for secrecy, for bloody murders," but it is his first calculated, as opposed to reflexive, wrongdoing, stealing for money, that breaks him free.

This act, though, seems rather instrumental than essential to Wright's freedom. What saves him from the fascination of the physical is first his intuition of "the drama of human feeling," the inquisitive shaping mind and sensitivity of the artist whose external story (how and when I wrote what, and what then) is never told. Appropriately enough, this inner self is continually represented by Wright in metaphors, and particularly in metaphors of a journey marked by an obscure destination and a threatening fate (187).

A spontaneous conviction of the essential being and the coercive impress of the physical state form two main threads of which *Black Boy* is woven. It is significant that Wright does not finally take in the coercive physical state until well past the mid-point of the work, where he calls himself "a black boy in Mississippi"; the phrase may be glossed, for posterity: a black boy in Mississippi is as good as a born slave, and at that a difficult rather than a quiescent one, to be carefully excluded from every good but work. And by this point Wright's personal metaphor, the leitmotif of travel, is well enough established to oppose this formula and suggest that he will have his "own strange and separate road" (140).

The personal and the public definitions do not meet without some turbulence, reflected in the continual revision of their relationship. Wright gives his life the character of something externally "shaped" (124) and determined, while also fluid and as it were arising by a creative capacity and response in himself. Perhaps a basic doubtfulness finds expression in the presence of a crepuscular light at key moments: the shopping episode, the selling of KKK papers, the threatened flogging by his Uncle to put him in his place. Certainly the definiteness with which Wright summarizes his existence in the light of his "mother's suffering" or "the white death"—his blinding phrase for the social syndrome which used to culminate in lynching—is of more local than general validity. The two do not chime together, a fact which provokes a distracting curiosity about the relation of his home life to the effect of Mississippi on him (111, 112, 165, 181, 190, 192); and neither allows for the reality of his "undreamed-of shores." A genuine duality arises here, I think, and it picks up Wright's knowing presentation of his swings between wild activity and paralysis, as well as his consciousness of being "strongly tender and cruel, violent and peaceful" (112). The principle of reconciliation in this case does not appear. What Wright gives us instead is a distillation from the very solidity and at the same time disorder of his experience. Twice, at points of wide survey, he sets up the issues of his life in abstract terms. "At the age of twelve," he tells us, he formed "a conviction that the meaning of living came only when one was struggling to wring a meaning out of meaningless suffering" (112). And then the grown man writing his autobiography, pronounces that men "if . . . lucky . . . might win some redeeming meaning for their having struggled and suffered here beneath the stars" (285). Even if the similarity in idiom is an accident of the time of writing, the similarity in situation remains to give weight to the problem of knowledge in the text. The bombardment of the mind by multifarious data stands out in *Black Boy,* and that may indicate the upshot of the mind's learning to struggle toward *the* definition which will comprehend this or that definition arising along the way. One struggles with everything or risks getting caught off guard. But by the same token the struggle, oblique or dormant as it can be, in part limits the possibilities for ultimate resolution of particular issues. There comes to mind the picture of Wright threatened with a more or less arbitrary flogging and refusing to give in. The threat, you will recall, is common in the book, and is never really overcome; one source of hope appears, as Wright's reaction, at first hysterical, modulates toward the cold resentment and clear-eyed strength of the clash with his uncle. This scene, unlike, say, Wordsworth's hike toward sunrise on Mt. Snowdon, does not furnish any kind of practical-symbolic solution to a basic question of being. But a solution need not preoccupy us. The emergence of the question against enormous odds is itself noteworthy, and Wright's portrayal of its ubiquitous physicality appears both cogent and distinctive.

The Autobiography of Malcolm X,[20] because of the circumstances under which it was produced, does not entirely lend itself to the stylistic approach I have been following. But the rhythm of the work gives legitimate grounds for comment on Malcolm X's response to changeableness, and his capacity for definition, two of the very issues which Wright so graphically raises. Though he is not above interpreting particular events in what might seem an arbitrary light (Allah made him fight Bill Peterson a second time, to end his "fight career"), the distinctive feature of the *Autobiography* is its naturalistic use of time, the willingness to let the past stand as it was, in its own season, even when later developments, of intellect or intuition or event, give it a different quality. It is, I would surmise, on such grounds that C.W.E. Bigsby calls Malcolm "a naif of stunning integrity."[21] Malcolm goes through a series of virtual incarnations, starting with the name Malcolm Little, and becoming delinquent, prize student, Shorty's "homeboy," Detroit Red, Satan, convert to Muslimism and so Malcolm X, ex-Muslim founder of the Muslim Mosque, Inc., and finally the follower of the orthodox Islam, El-Hajj Malik El-Shabazz. But not quite finally. The changes at first take place ad lib, but by the end it

is clear that, though he does not seek change, Malcolm, seeking truth and his own best humanity, will not flinch from its demands. He may not have a stable position, but the interview with Africa's most respected American ambassador (who is white) clearly images a deeper stability of intellect and of spirit. The atmosphere in which the *Autobiography* operates is remarkably practical and quick-moving; its genius springs from being so and at the same time remarkably responsive to crystallizations of meaning, as Malcolm X avoids Richard Wright's anxieties without trying to evade his problems. In historical terms, a measure of this performance can be gained by reference to Bunyan and Wordsworth, since Malcolm X has written a distinctively modern conversion narrative without, like Bunyan, subordinating the intensity of particular stages of his life, and has depicted a wholeness of personality which accommodates unpredictable turns, like Wordsworth, but which does not suggest even an inscrutable teleology.[22]

On the surface Cleaver's *Soul on Ice*[23] seems as thoroughly given over to analysis as *The Autobiography of Malcolm X* to narrative. But I would propose that Cleaver's is really a highly eclectic style which, combined with an ingenious organization of diversified elements, produces in effect the autobiography of a mind, from the birth of an almost savage self-consciousness ("Prior to 1954 we lived in an atmosphere of novocain") to the spiritual projection of a wide human contact founded on self-sacrifice, self-understanding, compassion, reverence, and hope. In the sequence of items, political, sociological, psychological, epistolary, dramatic, analytical, narrative, journalistic, critical, we may be equally encountering a raw source of experience and knowledge ("The Allegory of the Black Eunuchs"), the highly formal or formulaic product of experience and reflection ("The Black Man's Stake in Vietnam" or "The Primeval Mitosis"), the account of participation in typical social patterns and the discovery of their implications ("A Day in Folsom Prison"), or soul-searching love-letters. The thing to recognize here is that each is part of Cleaver's "adventure in discovery," as record, or as stage. Cleaver explicitly identifies political and autobiographical concerns from the start:

> Nineteen fifty-four . . . is held to be a crucial turning point in the history of the Afro-American— for the U.S.A. as a whole—the year segregation was outlawed by the U.S. Supreme Court. It was also a crucial year for me.

The identification gets even clearer later on: "We are a very sick country—I, perhaps, am sicker than most" (p. 16). But that identification is not complete, or at least not deterministic. In substance *Soul on Ice* develops Cleaver's knowledge that "instead of simply *reacting* [he] could *act*" (p. 5), and beyond that his knowledge of the way to act with strength and grace, so as to benefit others. In *Soul on Ice* we see combined two major possibilities of autobiography isolated by James M. Cox: Franklin's model act of self-making, and Thoreau's model act of self-possession.[24]

The title of the opening chapter, "On Becoming," sets the keynote of the work, reducing to the status of details, rather than implicit laws of being, the facts Cleaver cites at the beginning of the second letter from prison:

> I'm perfectly aware that I'm in prison, that I'm a Negro, that I've been a rapist, and that I have a Higher Uneducation. . . . [But] I could just as easily . . . [mention] that I'm tall, that I'm skinny, that I need a shave, that I'm hard-up. [pp. 18-19]

Obviously Cleaver does not anticipate becoming an elected official, or even a registered voter; his commitment to becoming may in fact prolong his stay in prison. What he has in mind is the kind of man he is "going to be," and his response to Thomas Merton's *The Seven Storey Mountain* makes plain his attempt to digest everything, books, people, ideas, events, toward this end of becoming:

> I was tortured by that book because Merton's suffering, in his quest for God, seemed all in vain to me. At the time I was a Black Muslim chained in the bottom of a pit by the Devil. Did I expect Allah to tear down the walls and set me free? . . . I wished that Merton had stated in secular terms the reasons he withdrew from the political, economic, military, and social system into which he was born, seeking refuge in a monastery.
>
> Despite my rejection of Merton's theistic world view, I could not keep him out of the room. . . . Most impressive of all to me was [his] description of . . . Harlem. [p. 34]

The passage Cleaver goes on to cite from *The Seven Storey Mountain* graphically and poignantly sets forth the repression and waste of "inestimable natural gifts, wisdom, love, music, science, poetry" in Harlem. Its value to Cleaver is manifold. Even where he "rejects" it, it helps to solidify his own political bent. And he candidly uses it to replenish his "flame of indignation," in that Merton confirms all he himself knows of the formidable threats to becoming, and so gives as much of an impetus to Cleaver's aims as Muhammad Ali or the Biblical story of Lazarus.

It is, we may observe, this "flame of indignation" which swells to illuminate the "fundamental revolution and reconstruction" posited and promoted in "Rallying Round the Flag," "The Black Man's Stake in Vietnam," and "Domestic Law and International Order." By the same token, with a reversal of perspective the political generalities of these chapters yield to the "Prelude to Love," where the erotico-spiritual way to "renew and transform" society (p. 190) is initiated. If anything is straightforward, simple and clear about "The Allegory of the Black Eunuchs," it is that Cleaver dramatizes in it the elimination of the old Negro, the Infidel as to the future, from the "sight" and "lives" of the "young, strong, superlative Black Eunuchs" (taking Eunuch as antithesis of the degraded stud). The new man, then, meets the present problems elaborated in "The Primeval

Mitosis" and "Convalescence," and the positive forward movement of the section comes to its culmination in the solemn address "To All Black Women, from All Black Men," which combines a moving immediacy with an almost religious sense of assembly, a grave theory of history, and a sacred principle of action to create an atmosphere of atonement and exalted promise. If this falls short of loving "all mankind," it yet achieves a great deal; Cleaver's ability to speak so profoundly for all black men gives a fair measure of how far he has come, or how much larger he has become, since awaking to himself in felonious rage. And *Soul on Ice,* formally so singular, seems impeccably designed to show not so much the process as the elements of this becoming. Read just as Cleaver's opinions, it loses much of its life, because his opinions are infused with his autobiography, and practically inseparable from it.

"The self," Wallace Stevens has written,

> is a cloister full of remembered sounds
> And of sounds so far forgotten . . .
> That they return unrecognized. The self
> Detects the sound of a voice that doubles its own.
> In the images of desire, the forms that speak,
> The ideas that come to it with a sense of speech.

And autobiography, on this reading, must be something like a means of gaining access to the cloister, gaining knowledge of its lines of communication, its manners and laws and ideals, gaining perspective on these, and having withal the gift to tell the story justly both as to content and form. Generically, it seems to me, autobiography makes exceptional demands of originality, though remaining susceptible to the spirit of periods, and though subject to the pull of generality. Limits can be recognized for it; at least the idea of a surrealist painting as a "symbolic autobiography"[25] at best confuses the object autobiographical with autobiography proper, and perhaps actually mistakes the autobiographical implications of any personal gesture for a finished, reflective autobiography.

But if, instead of wondering where the genre might go, one asks about its recent history, there arises a legitimate question that nevertheless can only be answered by conjecture: why has the black writer so far flourished in the field of autobiography? First, I conjecture, as a part of a broad literary advance, encompassing the essay, the novel, drama, poetry. Second, because the genre of late seems peculiarly answerable to the explosive patterns of modern life, and the black writer may, by nature of his historical disadvantages, have a singular advantage in handling these patterns. Third, because the ubiquity of technology (as of institutional formulas) seems to have threatened to deface our humanity, and autobiography lends itself so well to a rediscovery that proceeds from the ego out—here the genre stands in opposition to a positive threat of individual nonentity, where in the Romantic period it worked to offset a negative effect in the environment, a vacancy resulting from the removal of an external cosmos of thought and value. And fourth, perhaps, because critical expectations and endeavors in relation to the black writer seem to be changing for the better. But when all is said and done, it may be only because such factors constellated for a handful of exceptional individual black writers. Autobiography after all calls for the individual who adheres to the category even as he changes its definition.

[1] Carl Jung, *The Undiscovered Self,* trans. R. F. C. Hull (New York: Mentor Books—New American Library, 1958), p. 17.

[2] Edward Gibbon, *The Autobiographies,* printed verbatim from hitherto unpublished mss., ed. John Murray (London: J. Murray, 1896), *Memoir B,* p. 150.

[3] George Starr, *Defoe and Spiritual Autobiography* (Princeton: Princeton Univ. Press, 1969), pp. 33-34.

[4] Dr. Johnson, of course, thinks the "subjective" individual more, not less, reliable than the "objective" observer in matters of information and interpretation of his life. So does De Quincey. The mistrust of the autobiographer's motives and judgment seems to have sprung up in our century, but it is worth noting that it does not pass unchallenged; in his essay on "Finding a Poem" W. D. Snodgrass writes: "the only reality which a man can ever surely know is that self he cannot help being, though he will only know that self through its interactions with the world around it" (*Partisan Review,* 26 [Spring 1959], 283). Besides individual witnesses, there is an essential argument against skepticism, in that autobiography is both objective and subjective, and allows the autobiographer to turn the outsider's skepticism upon himself with the genuine possibility of a balanced view embodying the best of both perspectives. Otherwise, we must suppose him proceeding from subjectivity to objectivity, which is in turn subjectivity, and so on endlessly, in a maze of multiplying reservations that baffle expression and response.

[5] *Design and Truth in Autobiography* (Cambridge, Mass.: Harvard Univ. Press, 1960), p. 79f.

[6] "De Quincey Revises His *Confessions,*" *PMLA,* 72 (1957), 122-46.

[7] New York: Basic Books, 1966. See in particular p. 10, where the question is rather narrowly conceived, and set aside.

[8] That is, with the exception of one suspicious subcategory, utilitarian or applied autobiography, exemplified by Bunyan, Franklin, Vico, and perhaps St. Augustine, who show little susceptibility to the internal material doubts which autobiography as such has been heir to.

[9] See John Jordan's judicious summary in his introduction to *The Confessions* (New York: Everyman's Library,

1960), pp. x-xii. As a *book,* rather than a storehouse, I think the first version merits the palm.

[10] "De Quincey's Additions in 1856 to his Original Preface of 1822," *Confessions of an English Opium-Eater,* rev. and enl. ed. of 1856, in *The Collected Writings of Thomas De Quincey,* ed. David Masson, III (Edinburgh: A. & C. Black, 1890), 216.

[11] This point is developed by M. G. Cooke, *"Quinsque Sui Faber:* Coleridge in the *Biographia Literaria,"* *Philological Quarterly,* 50 (April, 1971), 208-229.

[12] *Apologia pro Vita Sua,* ed. A. Dwight Culler (Cambridge, Mass.: Riverside ed., Houghton Mifflin, 1956), p. 230.

[13] *Apologia,* p. 25.

[14] The course of autobiography, though it encourages the recognition of time boundaries, may be rather evolutionary than otherwise, with various stages of development occurring together, and without loss of validity or viability for precedent forms, because others subsequently come to the fore. H. G. Wells may be regarded as Victorian in his "idea of the modern world-state," but modern in his sense of "the planless casualness of our contemporary world." And Edwin Muir shows what can still be done with autobiography in explicitly religious terms.

[15] Pascal, *Design and Truth in Autobiography,* p. 8.

[16] *The Autobiography of William Butler Yeats,* (New York: Collier Books, 1971), p. 1.

[17] Richard Ellmann, pointing out that *At the Hawk's Well* ends on the same note as the *Reveries,* insists on the biographical fact that "a great deal had happened" (*Yeats: The Man and the Masks* [New York: E. P. Dutton, 1948], p. 216). But this ignores the difference between "happening" and "becoming," between experienced event and conceived or identified reality. By the same token, Joseph Ronsley's stress on "self-assertion" in the *Reveries* seems to ignore the indecisive and inconsequential quality of the gestures of self-assertion (*Yeats's Autobiography: Life as Symbolic Pattern* [Cambridge, Mass.: Harvard Univ. Press, 1968], pp. 50 f).

[18] Well treated by Morris, *Versions of the Self,* p. 11.

[19] Richard Wright, *Black Boy: A Record of Childhood and Youth* (Cleveland and New York: World, 1945).

[20] Malcolm X, *The Autobiography . . . With the assistance of Alex Haley,* intro. by M. S. Handler (New York: Grove Press, 1965).

[21] "The Black American Writer," in *The Black American Writer,* ed. C.W.E. Bigsby, Vol. I, *Fiction,* (Baltimore: Pelican Books, 1971), p. 21.

[22] In these terms one finds little basis for Richard Gilman's judgment of the *Autobiography:* "Its way of looking at the world, its formulation of experience, is not the potential possession . . . of us all; hard, local, intransigent, . . . it remains in some sense unassimilable for those . . . who aren't black" ("White standards and Negro Writing," in Bigsby, *Black American Writer,* p. 35). To the contrary, as James M. Cox observes, "'The Autobiography of Malcolm X' is somehow one of the great imaginative works of the last decade" ("Autobiography and America," *Virginia Quarterly Review,* 47 [Spring, 1971], 252).

[23] Eldridge Cleaver, *Soul on Ice,* intro. by Maxwell Geismar (New York: McGraw-Hill, 1968).

[24] "Autobiography and America," p. 265.

[25] The conception implied here has been espoused by James Olney in *Metaphors of Self: The Meaning of Autobiography* (Princeton: Princeton Univ. Press, 1972). Various objections to it have already been raised in this essay. One more may be touched on, in the fact that "autobiographical" novelists like Conrad, Wolfe, and Gide have such difficulty coping with the demands of autobiography proper. What one does to express oneself is not tantamount to how one tries to define oneself. The distinction between the autobiographical and autobiography is at once theoretical and real. Instead of a "symbolic autobiography" we should probably speak of an "autobiographical symbol."

FURTHER READING

Secondary Sources

Abbott, H. Porter. "Autobiography, Autography, Fiction: Groundwork for a Taxonomy of Textual Categories." *New Literary History* 19, No. 3 (Spring 1988): 597-615.
> Refines the meaning of autobiography "to include . . . what can be called the reader's autobiographical response; to accommodate at the same time the formal variety that usually threatens definition of autobiography; and to establish a clear distinction between the larger set, autography, and other fundamental textual categories."

Adams, Timothy Dow. *Telling Lies in Modern American Autobiography.* Chapel Hill: University of North Carolina Press, 1990, 205 p.
> Focuses on the autobiographical works of Gertrude Stein, Sherwood Anderson, Richard Wright, Mary McCarthy, and Lillian Hellman, in an attempt to "resolve some of the paradoxes of recent autobiographical theory and to reconcile those paradoxes by looking at the classic question of design and

truth in autobiography from the underside—that is, with a focus on lying rather than on truth."

Andrews, William L., ed. *African American Autobiography: A Collection of Critical Essays.* Englewood Cliffs, N.J.: Prentice Hall, 1993, 231 p.
> Includes essays on the autobiographical works of Frederick Douglass, Ida B. Wells, Richard Wright, Malcolm X, and Maya Angelou, among others.

Bell, Robert. "Autobiography and Literary Criticism." *Modern Language Quarterly* 46, No. 2 (June 1985): 191-201.
> Identifies strengths and weaknesses of modern critical approaches to autobiography, in particular the views advanced by A. O. J. Cockshut in *The Art of Autobiography in Nineteenth- and Twentieth-Century England* and Susanna Egan in *Patterns of Experience in Autobiography.*

Blasing, Mutlu Konuk. *The Art of Life: Studies in American Autobiographical Literature.* Austin: University of Texas Press, 1977, 193 p.
> Considers the autobiographical writings of Henry David Thoreau, Walt Whitman, Henry James, Henry Adams, William Carlos Williams, and Frank O'Hara.

Culley, Margo, ed., *American Women's Autobiography: Fea(s)ts of Memory.* Madison: University of Wisconsin Press, 1992, 329 p.
> Collection of essays covering numerous autobiographies by American women beginning with the conversion narratives of Puritan settlers.

Dudley, David L. *My Father's Shadow: Intergenerational Conflict in African American Men's Autobiography.* Philadelphia: University of Pennsylvania Press, 1991, 218 p.
> Traces "a kind of Oedipal conflict" from the slave narratives of the eighteenth and nineteenth centuries to the autobiographies of civil rights activists in the 1960s and 1970s "wherein each rising writer faces and overcomes his predecessor in the tradition."

Fowlie, Wallace. "On Writing Autobiography." *Southern Review* 22, No. 2 (April 1986): 273-79.
> Offers an informal discussion of the process of writing autobiography. According to Fowlie: "The use of memory, indispensable to autobiography, is a recycling of memories, both conscious and subconscious aspects of living, by means of which a life story may be transformed into a personal myth. Images persistently return in this recycling, and typical scenes or episodes return. These images and patterns reveal the identity of the writer, to himself first, and then to a reader."

Grossman, Anita Susan. "Art Versus in Autobiography: The Case of Lillian Hellman" *CLIO: A Journal of Literature, History and the Philosophy of History,* Vol. 14, No. 3 (Spring 1985): 289-308.

Examines the issue of reliability in the autobiographical works of Lillian Hellman.

Miller, Ross. "Autobiography as Fact and Fiction: Franklin, Adams, Malcolm X." *The Centennial Review*, Vol. XVI, No. 3 (Summer 1972): 221-32.
  Traces the use of fiction devices in the American autobiographical tradition that extends from Benjamin Franklin through Henry Adams to Malcolm X.

Rosenblatt, Roger. "Black Autobiograpy: Life as the Death Weapon." *Yale Review*, Vol. 65 (June 1976): 515-27.
  Investigates shared characteristics of black autobiography.

Smith, William F., Jr. "American Indian Autobiographies." *American Indian Quarterly* 2, No. 3 (Autumn 1975): 237-45.
  Assesses the literary merit of *The Autobiography of a Winnebago Indian, Jim Whitewolf: The Life of a Kiowa Apache Indian, Black Elk Speaks, Two Leggings: The Making of a Crow Warrior, Geronimo: His Own Story, The First Hundred Years of Niño Cochise, A Pima Remembers, Indian Boyhood,* and *Lame Deer: Seeker of Visions.*

Spengemann, William C. *The Forms of Autobiography: Episodes in the History of a Literary Genre.* New Haven: Yale University Press, 1980, 254 p.
  Includes American works in a broad study of the evolution of the genre beginning with the *Confessions of St. Augustine.*

Stepto, Robert B. *From Behind the Veil: A Study of Afro-American Narrative.* Urbana: University of Illinois Press, 1979, 203 p.
  Offers extended discussion of such works as Henry Bibb's *Narrative of the Life and Adventures of Henry Bibb, an American Slave,* Solomon Northrup's *Twelve Years a Slave,* Frederick Douglass's *Narrative of the Life of Frederick Douglass, an American Slave, Written by Himself,* William Wells Brown's *Narrative of the Life and Escape of William Wells Brown,* Booker T. Washington's *Up from Slavery,* W. E. B. Du Bois's *The Souls of Black Folk,* James Weldon Johnson's *The Autobiography of an Ex-Coloured Man,* Richard Wright's *Black Boy,* and Ralph Ellison's *Invisible Man.*

Wong, Hertha Dawn. *Sending My Heart Back across the Years: Tradition and Innovation in Native American Autobiography.* New York: Oxford University Press, 1922, 246 p.
  Traces "the changes in Native American autobiography from pre-contact oral and pictographic personal narratives through late-nineteenth- and twentieth-century life histories to contemporary autobiographies."

Zinsser, William. *Inventing the Truth: The Art and Craft of Memoir.* Boston: Houghton Mifflin Company, 1987, 172 p.
  Compilation of lectures by Russell Baker, Annie Dillard, Alfred Kazin, Toni Morrison, and Lewis Thomas sponsored by the Book of the Month Club and held at the New York Public Library in 1986.

Folklore and Literature

INTRODUCTION

The concept of folklore in literature may seem problematic on first glance: folklore, being a set of stories, sayings, beliefs, and traditions passed down orally, is in its purest form an essentially nonliterary medium. Nonetheless, its uses in literature—particularly in the period since the Romantic era, which saw a flowering of interest in folklore—are many. A short but certainly incomplete list of folk forms would include the following: yarns, fairy tales, tall tales, beast epics, and some kinds of myth; sermons, incantations, and mystical teachings; ballads, folk songs, blues songs, spirituals, and chants; proverbs, folk sayings, riddles, and jingles.

Folklore in literature appears both in the direct recounting of folktales by folklorists and in a variety of embellished or muted forms, translated through the work of a novelist, short story writer, or poet. Between these two poles is a range of forms, exemplified by the work of one of the preeminent folklorists in American literature, Joel Chandler Harris. In the stories collected in *Uncle Remus* (1880), and in other of his collections, Harris recreates traditional African-American stories using animal characters that include Brer Rabbit and Brer Fox, with the storyteller Uncle Remus providing a "frame" for the tales.

The adaptation of black traditions by the white Southerner Harris has not been without controversy, particularly in the latter part of the twentieth century. Indeed, a number of African-American writers have penned their own interpretations of narratives that evolved as an inevitable response to the hardships of slavery and segregation. Thus James Weldon Johnson used the unique form of the "Negro sermon" in *God's Trombones* (1927); Zora Neale Hurston employed folktales in *Mules and Men* (1935); and Richard Wright and Ralph Ellison respectively implemented a variety of folk elements in *Black Boy* (1945) and *Invisible Man* (1952).

Likewise there is a body of Native American folklore, often referred to as the first American literature, which dates back thousands of years before the arrival of European settlers on the North American continent. These tales were often appropriated by white storytellers, who used them for their own purposes; and later a European American mythology of the West, which focused on the cowboy and the settler, evolved in works such as Owen Wister's *The Virginian* (1902). Native American writers of the late twentieth century have celebrated their ancestral traditions in works that include N. Scott Momaday's *House Made of Dawn* (1968), Leslie Marmon Silko's *Storyteller* (1981), and others.

Folklore clearly serves a political purpose, in that it exemplifies aspects of a national myth; but it likewise appears in literature as a means of illustrating qualities of the human condition which change little with place or time. Thus, for example, the uses of folklore in Southern literature by non-black writers: sometimes folklore has been put to work with the aim of demonstrating white cultural superiority, but as often as not, works with folkloric elements have served exactly the opposite purpose. Indeed, one of the most significant works of American literature, *The Adventures of Huckleberry Finn* (1884) by Mark Twain—a novel which certainly contains elements of folklore—illustrates the fundamental oneness of humankind and the cruel absurdity of slavery. At its heart, however, *Huckleberry Finn* is not a political tale, but simply an engaging and compelling yarn—as is a later American epic that uses folklore, John Steinbeck's *The Grapes of Wrath* (1939).

Folklorists such as Richard M. Dorson have busied themselves with gathering folktales from a variety of peoples and locales, their aim being to preserve the traditions of a group before those traditions are overtaken by the expansion of a mass popular culture. In so doing, they identify types, both in character and narrative, which transcend ethnicity. Conversely, folklorists as diverse as Lafcadio Hearn and Constance Rourke have helped to preserve specific folkways of distinct groups: Hearn's work on the Orient, where he spent much of his life, helped introduce American readers to the distinct cultures of Japan and China, whereas Rourke's *American Humor* (1931) explored a seemingly familiar topic and made it new by identifying varieties of typology within the realm of American humor.

Humor has often proved the most accessible medium for the presentation of folklore in literature, as for instance in one of the first notable works by a European American, Washington Irving's *The Sketch Book* (1835). Similarly, humor animates the narratives of Mark Twain and Harris; but Nathaniel Hawthorne's *The Scarlet Letter* (1850) or Herman Melville's *Moby-Dick* (1851) illustrate the ways in which writers explore the darker side of the collective folk memory. Folklore also employs the supernatural, whether in the mystical work of Carlos Castaneda, or in the re-creations of African-American sermons in writings by Johnson, Ellison, and others. It can appear in the form of the short story, as used by Irving; or in poetry, as in Henry Wadsworth Longfellow's *Evangeline* (1847). It is at once universal and particular, adaptable to a variety of forms and situations, but likewise exemplifying the traditions of a specific group, whether European, African, Asian, or Native American.

REPRESENTATIVE WORKS

Maya Angelou
I Know Why the Caged Bird Sings (autobiography) 1970

James Baldwin
Go Tell It on the Mountain (novel) 1952

Donald Barthelme
Snow White (novel) 1965

Stephen Vincent Benet
John Brown's Body (poetry) 1928

Thomas Berger
Little Big Man (novel) 1964

Carlos Castaneda
Teachings of Don Juan (nonfiction) 1969
Journey to Ixtlan (nonfiction) 1972

Willa Cather
Death Comes for the Archbishop (novel) 1927

Walter van Tilburg Clark
The Ox-Bow Incident (novel) 1940

James Fenimore Cooper
The Last of the Mohicans (novel) 1826

Robert Coover
The Public Burning (novel) 1977

Richard M. Dorson
Jonathan Draws the Long Bow: New England Popular Tales and Legends (short stories) 1946
American Negro Folktales [editor] (anthology) 1950
American Folklore and the Historian (criticism) 1971
America in Legend (criticism) 1973
Folklore and Fakelore (essays) 1976

W. E. B. Du Bois
The Souls of Black Folk (essays and short stories) 1903

T. S. Eliot
The Waste Land (poetry) 1922

Ralph Ellison
Invisible Man (novel) 1952

William Faulkner
The Sound and the Fury (novel) 1929
The Hamlet (novel) 1940

Ernest J. Gaines
The Autobiography of Miss Jane Pittman (novel) 1971

Zane Grey
Riders of the Purple Sage (novel) 1912

Joel Chandler Harris
Uncle Remus, His Songs and His Sayings (folklore) 1880
Nights with Uncle Remus (folklore)1883
Uncle Remus and His Friends (short stories, songs, and poetry) 1892

Nathaniel Hawthorne
The Scarlet Letter (novel) 1850

Lafcadio Hearn
Some Chinese Ghosts (short stories) 1887
Two Years in the French West Indies (essays and sketches) 1890
Glimpses of Unfamiliar Japan. 2 vols. (essays and sketches) 1894

Chester Himes
If He Hollers Let Him Go (novel) 1945

Langston Hughes
The Weary Blues (poetry) 1926
The Best of Simple (short stories) 1961

Zora Neale Hurston
Mules and Men (folklore) 1935
Their Eyes Were Watching God (novel) 1937

Washington Irving
The Sketch Book (short stories) 1835*

James Weldon Johnson
The Book of American Negro Poetry [editor] (anthology) 1922
The Book of American Negro Spirituals [editor] (anthology) 1925
God's Trombones: Seven Negro Sermons in Verse (poetry) 1927

Gayl Jones
Corregidora (novel) 1975

Alain Locke
The New Negro [editor] (anthology) 1925

Henry Wadsworth Longfellow
Evangeline (poetry) 1847
The Song of Hiawatha (poetry) 1855

Carson McCullers
The Ballad of the Sad Cafe (novella) 1943

Herman Melville
Moby-Dick; or, The Whale (novel) 1851

N. Scott Momaday
House Made of Dawn (novel) 1968

Toni Morrison
Sula (novel) 1973

Frank Norris
The Octopus: A Story of California (novel) 1901

Constance Rourke
American Humor: A Study of the National Character (criticism) 1931

Leslie Marmon Silko
Storyteller (poetry and short stories) 1981

John Steinbeck
The Grapes of Wrath (novel) 1939

Harriet Beecher Stowe
Old Town Fireside Stories (short stories) 1871

Frederick Jackson Turner
The Frontier in American History (essays) 1920

Mark Twain
The Celebrated Jumping Frog of Calaveras County and Other Sketches (short stories) 1865
The Adventures of Huckleberry Finn (novel) 1884

Elliott Wigginton
The Foxfire Book [editor] (interviews, essays, and sketches) 1972

Owen Wister
The Virginian (novel) 1902

Thomas Wolfe
The Hills Beyond (novel fragment, drama, and short stories) 1943

Richard Wright
Native Son (novel) 1940
Black Boy (autobiography) 1945
Lawd Today (novel) 1963

*Includes "Rip van Winkle" and "The Legend of Sleepy Hollow."

OVERVIEWS

Daniel R. Barnes

SOURCE: "Toward the Establishment of Principles for the Study of Folklore and Literature," in *Southern Folklore Quarterly,* Vol. 43, Nos. 1 & 2, 1979, pp. 5-16.

[*In the following excerpt, Barnes takes issue with prevailing attitudes in folklore criticism.*]

In their more melancholic moments, academics are often inclined to admit that the pursuit of scholarship is at best a kind of game. Such a pursuit does (to invoke the textbook definition of a true game) involve "the element of competition, the possibility of winning or losing [one's academic future is often literally at stake], and a measure of organization with some kind of controlling rules."[1] When judged even by such minimally demanding criteria as these, however, the formal study of folklore in its relation to literature seems, with few and notable exceptions, never to have developed beyond the level of *pastime* (defined, we recall, in an appropriately circular fashion as "a traditional recreation performed simply to pass the time away").[2] The cavalier manner with which we go about our work has undoubtedly confirmed the worst suspicions of our colleagues among both professional folklorists and literary scholars. Both groups (who seem otherwise incapable of reaching agreement on any subject) are, I suspect, at least of a single mind concerning what Roger Abrahams has designated as "the lore-in-lit people": we are a kind of lunatic fringe entertaining some half-cocked notions of bridging the gap between folklorists and literary scholars, huddled in small rooms at the annual meetings of the MLA and AFS. We are, in short, like the bastard who persists in showing up at every family reunion: we are commonly supposed to have some vague right to be present, but that right could hardly be considered legitimate.

It is precisely the absence of "a measure of organization with some kind of controlling rules" that must finally disqualify from competition most of the extant scholarship on folklore and literature. As yet there is available to us no generally recognized theory from and through which our scholarship may proceed, by whatever methodological means, to genuinely useful and valid observations. Instead, we remain content to cite again and again in our own introductory paragraphs the same handful of articles: Taylor's "Folklore and the Student of Literature" (1948); Dorson's "The Identification of Folklore in American Literature" (1957); Hoffman's "Folklore in Literature: Notes Toward a Theory of Interpretation" (1957); Dundes's "The Study of Folklore in Literature and Culture: Identification and Interpretation" (1965); and Cohen's "American Literature and American Folklore" (1968). As valuable as each of these is in its own right, not one of them represents a generally accepted view, if we are to judge from the widely varying practices of those who claim to be following them in published criticism. More serious than this, however, even the best of these essays fails finally to offer much more than a rudimentary methodology, one which is more often than not at odds with those that have gone before. The position assumed in nearly every case is not unlike the one described and defended some years ago by Henry Nash Smith in an assessment of American Studies scholarship: "Method in scholarship grows out of practice, or rather out of repeated criticism of practice intended to remedy obvious shortcomings."[3] This position, as Richard E. Sykes has pointed out, is typical of those who would have us "wait for a discipline to define itself through practice" rather than provide beforehand (as Sykes would have us do) a clearly articulated theory to govern our methods:

While those who suggest that practice must come before theory deserve our respect, especially because of their outstanding practical successes, it seems doubtful to me whether anything is to be gained from the neglect of theory, provided that theoretical suggestions are treated as just that, as suggestions, and not as dogmatic attempts to circumscribe a new and developing field. Theory and definition have the value of clarification, of suggesting useful distinctions and possibly fruitful hypotheses.[4]

Though I find significantly fewer practitioners of "lore-in-lit" as having produced outstanding practical successes, I am nonetheless in general agreement with Professor Sykes's argument. Unlike him, however, I find it profitable—indeed, necessary—to begin working toward the establishment of principles by offering precisely that "criticism of practice" Smith sees as central to the development of any scholarly methodology. As a result, the tone of what follows may seem at times relentlessly negative, even destructive; be that as it may, my intentions are finally positive and I hope constructive. My remarks are offered as nothing more than attempts to clarify, to suggest useful distinctions and possibly fruitful hypotheses. I propose simply to examine a few common assumptions about folklore-and-literature which I find to be invalid, or dubious, or at best incapable of demonstration. Insofar as I adopt an identifiable critical position, it is one influenced by the writings of W. K. Wimsatt, Jr., in particular his essays on critical fallacies;[5] but I am no less concerned about the more common logical fallacies I see operating in much of our scholarship. My focus, for the purpose of this essay, will be primarily upon the relation of oral and written *narrative,* the most complex of oral-literary relations and in many ways the most confusedly handled.

. . . . .

Despite a growing tendency among professional folklorists to de-emphasize, if not openly deplore, "item-centered" conceptions of and approaches to their materials, this approach continues to dominate the scholarship concerned with the relationship of folklore to literature—largely, I suspect, because both folklorists and literary scholars assent to the notion that each in his chosen field is dealing finally with "texts" and that such texts may legitimately be compared *qua* texts. Yet as folklorists we yield the victory to the literary scholars almost before the first shot is fired when we consent to—even encourage—an item-centered basis for comparison. We *reduce,* as it were, folklore to the level of literature by tacitly acquiescing to the assumption that the legend or tale in question is a text to be collated against the text of a novel or story. Our perennial complaint against the literary scholar—that when compared with its literary counterpart the oral narrative is inevitably left with the short end of the artistic stick—actually speaks more to our own failure to demand a more rigorous discrimination of the "items" for comparison than to the often alleged snobbery and myopia of the literary scholar.

To be sure, there are many reasons why we persist in so operating. Some are historical and in fact connected to the history of folklore scholarship itself. Many of the most eminent names in the field were (and still are) first of all literary scholars, and more often than not literary historians. Their interest in folklore was an outgrowth of their study of literary history. Kittredge is a typical example, and it must not be forgotten that among his many great gifts was that of a textual critic. While we should not presume to minimize the contributions of such men as he, yet neither should we ignore the consequences of their particular mode of emphasis.[6] We must always remember that, while the study of the relationship of folklore and literature is comparative, it is also interdisciplinary. The tools—even the very conceptions—of one discipline do not necessarily have application or validity for another. (One would no more subject a body of oral texts to collation by the Hinman machine than he would apply the Finnish method to a study of Shakespeare's text.) As a result, we cannot to any significant degree understand such a relationship until we are able to recognize the fundamental differences between the two traditions. While folklore-and-literature scholarship has almost without exception recognized and emphasized the apparent similarities (based upon a "comparison of texts"), seldom has a scholar addressed himself to that fundamental difference in *kind* (discipline) which defines the limits within which we may operate as comparatists.

Surely the most distinctive feature of oral narrative—that which immediately differentiates it from literary narrative—is the simple, self-evident fact that it *is* "oral" and *not* "written." The "text" of a folktale is not "the folktale," but the transcription of an oral performance. This would hardly deserve repeating, were it not for the fact that the distinction seems so seldom to be observed in our scholarship. Literature, as the object of scholarly inquiry, has traditionally been conceived of as precisely that: an *object,* an *artifact.* M. H. Abrams's influential triad—

—is explicitly set forth as an "artifact-centered" model.[7] However useful this paradigm may be when adapted as a model for the study of material culture remains to be seen, but it should be immediately apparent that it will not have general applicability to the study of verbal folklore, just as it has none for literary drama, because it posits a clear distinction between the artist-as-creator and the work-as-creation.[8] Such a conception must of necessity ignore the "ontological *situs*" of oral narrative: the act of performance.[9]

A more satisfactory model (though one not without its own peculiar limitations) seems to me that provided by

Northrop Frye in *Anatomy of Criticism.* "The basis of generic distinctions in literature," according to Frye (literature here meant to include oral narrative as well as written), "appears to be the radical of presentation. Words may be acted in front of a spectator; they may be spoken in front of a listener; or they may be written for a reader. . . . The basis of generic criticism in any case is rhetorical, in the sense that the genre is determined by the conditions established between the poet and his public."[10] The importance of Frye's generic model to the student of folklore and literature seems to me to lie in its more inclusive conception of "literature" as a domain inhabited by both oral and written narrative, among others; and what he has to say concerning the differences in "radical of presentation"—the differences between *"epos"* (words spoken in front of a listener) and "fiction" (words written for a reader)—can be of considerable use to us. For it we are to move beyond and perhaps away from the notion of oral narrative as a text, as I think we must, Frye's observations may best serve by holding us to a kind of scrupulous adherence, a recognition of those differences as differences in *kind.*

If we accept Frye's distinction between *epos* and fiction—oral narrative and written narrative—as a valid and useful one, then we must accordingly rule out the possibility of any such thing as a "transitional text."[11] That is to say, we must accept a given narrative as *either* oral *or* written, and never somehow a combination of both (or, as it is occasionally represented in the scholarship, an oral narrative on-its-way-to-becoming a written narrative). Our fuzzy and uncritical acceptance of "transitional texts" as real phenomena has impeded our advancement as scholars in several ways. In a sense, this acceptance is reflected in the impulse of late to construct typologies to describe "the ways in which writers use folklore." Though they would have us believe that they are concerned *only* with "literature" which "contains" folklore, these typologists really posit, either directly or implicitly, the existence of a vast middle ground between folklore and literature that is both supra-traditional and sub-literary—more than folklore, but somehow less than literature. In nearly every instance, the typologist posits a bi-polar spectrum, extending from "close-to-oral" to "remote-from-oral" literary works—useful enough as a system for rating literary texts—only to fall victim to this same schematic model when, in classifying various literary works, he has recourse to such confusing concepts as "the pseudo-transcriptive use of folklore," "close replicas of oral texts" (one of which is described as "so like the collected version that it could qualify as a told tale"), "the altered folklore level," and so on.[12] Not only do typologies like these sacrifice philosophical precision on the altars of taste (compare, for example, the clear connotations of "subliterary"); they have the unfortunate effect of forcing us to accept highly questionable if not false generalizations as principles to guide our research. I do not think it too extreme to say that individual works constitute unique cases, that there are as many and complicated "ways of using folklore" as there are works or

even parts of works. Like Dorson (or at least the Dorson of one paragraph of a recent essay),[13] I cannot offer any "easy generalizations about the relation of folklore to literature" (from which statement Dorson goes on, in several pages following, to offer just that); but more important, I am unable to offer or accept any easy generalizations about even a *single writer* who thus employs folklore, be he Mark Twain or Hawthorne or whoever. The Mark Twain who uses folklore in "The Celebrated Jumping Frog" is not the same Mark Twain at work in "The Dandy Frightening the Squatter" or in *Huckleberry Finn*; nor are the Hawthornes of "Young Goodman Brown" and *The Scarlet Letter*. Once again, individual works present individual cases.

In short, if we agree with Alan Dundes that "There can be no rigorous typology without prior morphology,"[14] then we must recognize that we have had as yet no serious attention paid to those morphological distinctions which provide the only sound basis for a typology of "the uses of folklore in literature."[15]

There are other equally fundamental assumptions about our field of study that deserve closer scrutiny than they have as yet received. One of these is the widely shared notion that literature is a "repository" or "source" for folklore. In his recent essay on "The Use of Printed Sources," Dorson devotes considerable attention to literature, which, he asserts, "itself must be regarded as a bountiful source for folklore." After invoking the now-familiar litany of the "many ways in which a writer may employ folk materials," Dorson wisely qualifies his earlier assertion by admitting that "we cannot offer any easy generalizations about the relation of folklore to literature, except to say that literature offers an invaluable, if ambiguous, source for the folklorist."[16] Yet is this not the crux of the issue: just how "invaluable" *is* an "ambiguous source"? And in what sense, or to what extent; may literature be properly considered a "repository" or "source" for folklore at all? I should answer: *only insofar as a given literary work is conceived as denotative and expository*—as, if you will, *a reference work.* To be sure, many literary works thus conceived have yielded the kinds of practical successes that have made our study possible and viable; one has only to think of the work of Taylor and Whiting on the proverb in literature to provide eminent defense for the legitimacy of such a conception. But it is worth remembering that almost without exception these scholars and others were dealing with non-narrative elements—with proverbs, beliefs, and riddles for the most part. Indeed, Taylor's influential essay on "Folklore and the Student of Literature"—an essay to which all of us return often for moral support, if not for methodological defense—is typical of most of our scholarship in its neglect of folk *narrative* as it relates to literary narrative.

It is in the realm of narrative that the potentially dangerous consequences of this view of "literature-as-repository" have become actualized, posing a number of related problems which are manifested in any of several ways. For one thing, such a view often leads to the common confusion of writers with their works. One simply may not assume that a given work reflects in an unmediated fashion the values and beliefs of its author. To assume this is as if by fiat to disallow the possibilities of any "rhetoric of fiction." The potential for distance between an author and his work is always present in literature; the possibility of that potential's being actualized increases accordingly as the work approaches the condition of fiction.[17] To accept any literary narrative—but especially a fictional narrative—as documentary evidence of a writer's beliefs and attitudes is to do real violence to that very characteristic that distinguishes literary from oral narrative: its potential distance relative to the author.[18] And to assent, finally, to the proposition that a Hardy novel or a Hawthorne tale is a "repository" for folklore—a place where one may find "the faithful recording of folkways" or "accurate transcriptions of life"—is in effect to deny that it is a work of art at all.[19]

All of this speaks to one of the most curious and lamentable ironies of our scholarship: that, while as folklorists we have with growing frequency insisted upon the vital importance of context, as students of folklore in its relation to literature we have persisted in ignoring literary contexts.[20] We are, I take it—or at least we should be—aware of the effect and contextual function of literary frameworks, from Chaucer to Mark Twain (and there is, as we know, in the case of both writers considerable evidence to suggest the influence of oral tales upon their work). Yet how many of us in our scholarship have been willing to concede that traditional material in *any* literary work is *de facto* "framed"?[21] Why is it that in our endless essays on "Folklore in the Fiction of _____" we so seldom pay serious attention to what it is that the folklore is "in," or more importantly, what it is that folklore is an integral *part* of?

Of the validity of yet another assumption—namely, that folklore may properly be considered a source for the creative artist—I have no doubt. But that this is either readily or even potentially demonstrable in the case of a given literary work, not to mention a writer's corpus, I find highly questionable. It would be an easy matter to cite a long list of essays in which folklore scholars, one after another, have committed what logicians term the fallacy of the undistributed middle—or even more commonly, the fallacy of false cause. That we persist in arguing in this manner is symptomatic of our refusal to abide by the rules of a very demanding scholarly game. There are among us, myself included, those who have openly rebelled against what we take to be the excessively rigid criteria of biographical, internal, and corroborative evidence first outlined by Dorson in 1957; yet, for all our grumbling and dissatisfaction with his method, Dorson alone has recognized what all of us should have been aware of from the start: that to argue the direct influence of oral tradition on literary works is to engage in one of the most taxing of all scholarly activities. I would urge those of us who feel compelled

to pursue what John W. Ashton once called "the dubious pleasures of source-hunting"[22] to read what is still, after half a century, the wisest and most definitive of essays on "The Investigation and Interpretation of Sources" in Andre Morize's *Problems and Methods of Literary History*. "We must," as Morize warns, "avoid what I call the 'hypnotism of the unique source.' Take warning from those authors of monographs who, having devoted themselves largely to the study of one person [he later extends this to include "an idea or a theory"], are as a result obsessed with a tendency to detect his influence on every side." Morize has much to say as well concerning "the danger of reasoning from a resemblance to a direct dependence"—that is, through ignorance of possible intermediaries. Finally, in addition to warning against the literary scholar's "obsession for the written source," Morize addresses the issue of "*Oral and indefinite sources,*" describing this as "a class as important as it is difficult to trace. . . . Is it necessary to say that, in most cases these sources are bound to elude us, and that we must be resigned? It would be absurd to grasp the intangible: we should risk obtaining for our pains only worthless and ridiculous results."[23]

Now all of us, I take it, have enjoyed the exhilarating experience of discovering in an avowedly literary work—be it poem, play, or novel—something we know to be "in oral tradition." I should be the last person to deny the real importance and value of such an unique opportunity as is our own to make known these discoveries to the literary scholar. But whence this compulsion among us to construct elaborate demonstrations of Hardy's or Hawthorne's or Faulkner's or Frost's *direct* link to oral tradition? Is it not sufficient—not to mention philosophically more sound—to avoid the route that leads inevitably to "worthless and ridiculous results" and turn instead to other matters of more pressing importance that give promise of a more profitable yield?[24]

The foregoing are, as I have suggested earlier, among the most commonly assumed propositions about folklore and literature; indeed, one or the other (most often a combination of several) lies at the heart of most of our arguments. If this is what most of us have been doing and if, as I suggest, we should *not* be doing it, what *can* and *should* we be doing instead? To put it plainly, we must guard against being seduced by apparent "similarities" and attend rigorously to those aspects of our data that speak to differences—in kind, no less than in function. Even some of the basic distinctions between oral and literary narrative I have cited bear further scrutiny. What, for instance, of the assertion of Scholes and Kellogg that authorial distance (one's awareness of the presence of an "author-in-the-modern sense") is wholly foreign to traditional narrative? Does this need qualification in light of the folklorist's distinction between, say, legend and folktale? If, for example, the presence of opening and closing formulae in *Märchen* affects the degree of belief in an audience—and, indeed, makes it possible for us to identify the genre as being that of the folktale—then it would appear that clearly we have some kind of authorial distance at work. To be sure, it may certainly not be what Scholes and Kellogg represent as an "author-in-the-modern-sense"—yet it may hardly be said to describe a situation in which teller and tale are one in the sense that the *histor* of legend is one with his narrative. In this connection one might also wish to examine humorous local character anecdotes (most of which reflect the teller's distance) or tellers of tall tales, many of whom are known for miles around as "the biggest liar in these parts"—even though the tales they tell may be third-person accounts of another person's lies (that is, in effect "framed" by the teller and rendered thus).

Or consider the distinctions between function in an oral context and function in a literary context. If, as Frye suggests, it is possible to distinguish generically between oral and written narrative, is it not necessary as well to examine these phenomena more closely? If the teller of a legend, for example, assumes the pose of *histor* to his audience and the teller of a tale the pose of *fictor,* what if anything happens to those poses as manifested in literary versions? My own researches with legendary materials in Hawthorne's fiction suggest that he for one takes great liberties with the distinguishing feature of that oral genre—the "belief factor"—by impugning its veracity. Is Hawthorne's manipulation of legend typical of other writers? Does something similar happen when a writer, or writers in general, appropriate the folktale to fiction? What, for that matter, is the possible relation of belief in oral narrative to belief in literature generally? Is the kind of assent one finds in legend what Newman would refer to as "real assent" and belief in fiction only "notional"?

These are the kinds of questions that we can and must answer if we are ever to make any significant progress as students of folklore and literature. It will no longer do for us to invoke those hoary, time-worn, and finally circular arguments ("X uses folklore to provide an air of realism to his writing") that have for so long characterized our scholarship. Neither should we waste our efforts in pursuit of nebulous or unattainable goals. Instead, we must ever remain aware that the discipline of folklore and the discipline of literature has each its own distinctive nature and function; that, though it is possible for us to make legitimate comparative studies of their relationships, we always run the risk of oversimplifying, even falsifying their essential differences. Above all, we must recognize that before we may speak with authority about folklore-*in*-literature we need to understand folklore-*and*-literature more thoroughly than we have so far, each for itself and for what each has to teach us.

NOTES

[1] Jan Harold Brunvand, *The Study of American Folklore: An Introduction* (New York, 1968), p. 228.

[2] Brunvand, p. 228.

[3] "Can 'American Studies' Develop a Method?" originally published in *American Quarterly* (1957); reprinted in *The American Experience: An Approach to the Study of the United States,* ed. Henning Cohen (Boston, 1968), pp. 338-349; passage cited appears on p. 348.

[4] "American Studies and the Concept of Culture: A Theory and Method," originally published in *American Quarterly* (1963); reprinted in Cohen, pp. 392-410; passage cited appears on p. 392.

[5] Cf. especially "The Intentional Fallacy" and "The Affective Fallacy," in *The Verbal Icon* (Lexington, Ky., 1954), pp. 3-18, 21-39, and "Genesis: A Fallacy Revisited," in *The Disciplines of Criticism,* ed. Peter Demetz, Thomas Greene, and Lowry Nelson, Jr. (New Haven, 1968), pp. 193-225.

[6] This issue is explored at some length in a forthcoming essay on "Textual Criticism and the Study of Folklore."

[7] See *The Mirror and the Lamp: Romantic Theory and the Critical Tradition* (New York, 1953), esp. pp. 3-29.

[8] Despite its inapplicability, Abrams's model has been adopted (with slight modification) by Roger Abrahams in "Introductory Remarks to a Rhetorical Theory of Folklore," *Journal of American Folklore,* 81 (1968), 143-158. See also Giles B. Gunn, "Literature and Its Relation to Religion," *Journal of Religion,* 50 (1970), 268-291.

[9] The term "ontological *situs*" is appropriated from René Wellek and Austin Warren, *Theory of Literature* (New York, 1956), p. 129.

[10] *Anatomy of Criticism* (Princeton, 1957), pp. 246-247.

[11] This is not, however, to deny the existence of transitional *periods* in cultural history (see, for example, Robert Scholes and Robert Kellogg, *The Nature of Narrative* [New York, 1966], esp. pp. 17-56; Eric A. Havelock, *Preface to Plato* [Cambridge, Mass., 1963], pp. 115-133; Walter J. Ong, S.J., "Oral Residue in Tudor Prose Style," *PMLA,* 80 [1965], 145-154; and Larry D. Benson, "The Literary Character of Anglo-Saxon Formulaic Poetry," *PMLA,* 81 [1966], 334-341).

[12] The citations are taken, respectively, from Henning Cohen, "American Literature and American Folklore," in *Our Living Traditions,* ed. Tristram P. Coffin (New York, 1968), pp. 238-247; Richard M. Dorson, "The Use of Printed Sources," in *Folklore and Folklife: An Introduction,* ed. Richard M. Dorson (Chicago, 1972), pp. 465-477; and Angus K. Gillespie, "Teaching Folklore in the Secondary School: the Institutional Setting," *Journal of the Ohio Folklore Society,* 2 (1973), 17-31.

[13] "The Use of Printed Sources," p. 471.

[14] "Structural Typology in North American Indian Folktales," *Southwestern Journal of Anthropology*, 19 (1963), 121-130; reprinted in Dundes, *The Study of Folklore* (Englewood Cliffs, N.J., 1965), pp. 206-215.

[15] The continuing controversy over the lengths—or limits—to which structural analysis may be applied is a case in point: see Butler Waugh, "Structural Analysis in Literature and Folklore," *Western Folklore*, 24 (1966), 153-164; see also Benson, "The Literary Character of Anglo-Saxon Formulaic Poetry," for a lucid discussion of some of the limits of the Parry-Lord thesis. Both Waugh and Benson are critical of the misuse of tools from one tradition in examining another.

[16] "The Use of Printed Sources," p. 471.

[17] See Wayne Booth, *The Rhetoric of Fiction* (Chicago, 1961).

[18] See Scholes and Kellogg, pp. 51-56.

[19] More than one scholar in recent years has seemed clearly to view literary works in precisely these terms—as books which are "built" out of scraps culled and skimmed from anthologies and collections of oral materials—and thus misconceiving them has accordingly misused them as evidence. See, for example, Donald M. Winkleman, "Three American Authors as Semi-Folk Artists," *Journal of American Folklore*, 78 (1965), 130-135; David J. Winslow, "Hawthorne's Folklore and the Folklorists' Hawthorne: A Re-examination," *Southern Folklore Quarterly*, 34 (1970), 34-52; and Robert C. Ferguson, "Folklore References in Faulkner's *The Hamlet* and *As I Lay Dying*," *Journal of the Ohio Folklore Society*, I (1972), 1-10.

[20] Dundes has spoken of the need for contextual study of folklore in literature in "The Study of Folklore in Literature and Culture: Identification and Interpretation," *Journal of American Folklore*, 78 (1965), 136-142.

[21] I have discussed this further in a forthcoming paper on "Oral Tales and Literary Frameworks."

[22] "Folklore in the Literature of Elizabethan England," *Journal of American Folklore*, 70 (1957), 12.

[23] *Problems and Methods of Literary History* (Boston, 1922), pp. 88, 90, 113.

[24] For what I take to be some legitimate alternatives to source study in folklore-literature scholarship, see "The Bosom Serpent: A Legend in American Literature and Culture," *Journal of American Folklore*, 85 (1972), 111-122.

Carlos C. Drake

SOURCE: "Literary Criticism and Folklore," in *Journal of Popular Culture*, Vol. V, No. 2, Fall, 1971, pp. 289-97.

[*In the following essay, Drake distinguishes the work of the folklorist from that of his or her colleagues in a typical English department.*]

That folklorist would have to be very insensitive who was unaware of the suspicion held by many of his colleagues in English departments that his scholarly activities, at least as compared with theirs, hardly warrant the label of scholarship. Of what real use to the study of major literary texts is the collecting of comparatively crude material from oral tradition? What critical concepts do his students employ when comparing motifs in legends or describing harvest festivals? If the work of the literary critic consists mainly in the analysis and judgment of works of fiction and poetry, does not an activity which treats most of its texts at the same level of discrimination, as if all of the same worth, tend to just the opposite end, namely a debasement of critical standards? These are some of the doubts; is it any wonder that the folklorist may at times feel rather isolated in an English department, a pariah among the initiates?

This situation is not overstated, and it represents, I suggest, a pervasive misunderstanding of folklore and of the folklorist's role as teacher and scholar, a misunderstanding probably owing in the first instance to a confusion of ends. I want to discuss this and also the usefulness of folklore and folklore methods to literary criticism.

An assumption usually made by those who criticize folklore for not making aesthetic judgments of texts is that it has the same end as literary criticism, essentially the appreciation of particular literary works. Although the folklorist should make such judgments where they are important to what he is doing, he does not seek these as an end, in the sense, say, that the literary critic does or that the scientist seeks the formulation of general laws as the end of his research. The end of folklore research is retentive and descriptive; that is, it seeks to make a record of its material, and doing this may involve an example of the object itself, verbatim texts, tape recordings, photographs—those things, in short, necessary to understand and preserve the item or items. To this end the folklorist will borrow theoretical formulations from a variety of disciplines, including literary criticism, without at the same time also borrowing their ends. This point is crucial to understanding what folklorists are doing: essentially they seek to know, to describe, and to preserve, and this is not the same thing as appreciating in the sense of evaluating. The objects of their investigations are limited to those in or from oral tradition, presumably products of a "folk"; that is, any homogeneous group in which such traditions may arise. Traditional material may be found among doctors and nurses in a hospital, rural whites in an urban ghetto, trainmen in a railroad yard—any place where oral traditions can develop among individuals having something in common.

Such material may also be found in innumerable works of fiction.[2] For the most part, folklorists have restricted themselves to pointing out the use of traditional material in these, and have cited various kinds of evidence in support of their assertions.[3] Just how useful to the literary critic such discoveries may be depends on the material used, how it functions in the particular work, and whether or not, or to what extent, the use of the material was a conscious appropriation on the part of the author. For the folklorist, questions of source and meaning would be more important than the critic's judgments of function and style, though an examination of how the author used a certain item would be essential to any comparative study he might undertake.

If, for example, the folklorist were interested in studying certain mythological themes used in a novel, he would probably attempt to find other uses of the same themes, but he would not restrict himself to the world of letters. His other sources would probably include various indexes and other reference helps that folklorists have compiled for comparative research;[4] his own or other fieldwork collections, including those by anthropologists, on deposit in archives in this country and abroad; and other genre, such as folk beliefs, festivals, and other cultural expressions of mythological motifs. The critic, on the other hand, would probably confine himself exclusively to literary sources. This difference in approach to the same material by the folklorist and the literary critic underscores again not only the difference in ends, but also a difference in the way the material is viewed in time. The critic approaches a work in terms of his critical presuppositions, which relate to the world of letters and a tradition that constantly looks to the past; his judgments are always of the past. His comparative material, usually confined to notable literary examples, is also of the past. The folklorist's view, on the other hand, is not wholly or necessarily confined to the past or to a certain theoretical tradition; he sees folklore as a living process that can embrace past, present, and future.

If a good deal of the material collected by folklorists is crude by literary standards, it is also free of the detached and labored quality of much fiction; there is immediacy to it, however fumbling or boring the informant. The heart of many introductory folklore courses is the collecting project, and students are often surprised to discover suddenly when face to face with an informant that instead of critical concepts to rely on, or a set of categories, they have to make do with themselves: exactly what they are. Each collecting situation is different, and many are devoid of intellectual stimulation; they are nonetheless personal. Even if the folklorist's collecting project does not involve particular informants—he might, for example, be doing an inventory of tombstone carvings, house types, or place names—he is obliged to collect and analyze his own material; he is not drawing his conclusions on the basis of someone else's interpretation. As any field collector knows, the tricky part of many projects is the rapport established with an informant. On the success of this may hinge days of preparation and long waiting hours. It is far from an assured thing that the informant will gladly sing his ballads for your tape recorder or tell you his superstitions about his

crops; he may give a little or a great deal or nothing; the rapport between the informant and the folklorist determines in large measure what will be collected.

Rapport is partly a feeling state between individuals and though it involves conscious awareness, irrational and nonverbal factors are important to it. These can be extremely subtle—a gesture, a touch, a smile, a momentary change in the atmosphere—and it takes sensitivity to spot and understand them when they occur. This can be developed in only one way: by field experience. If collecting folksongs, for example, the folklorist will want to note the relationship between the folksinger and his audience, since many singers respond in particular ways to cues from their audiences, ways that may be reflected in their manner of performance and also in material added to or left out of their songs. The cues can be so subtle that the performer himself may be only partially aware of them. It is generally the case that we will all respond in some degree to emotionally charged events and situations, and these responses may not involve words at all. Everyone has some command over a range of nonverbal means of communication, assertion, and reaction. From his collecting experiences the folklorist is led to an awareness of some of the typical projections that his informants are likely to make on him. As projections have emotional content and are frequently unconscious, one has to be very alert to catch them; and as most people infrequently encounter unfamiliar projections, they remain mostly unaware of them. Of necessity, however, the folklorist encounters a wide range of projections when collecting, and must learn how to handle them. For instance, an informant in the course of a long collecting session with a folklorist may experience a sudden dislike for the folklorist. The negative rapport resulting from this could ruin the interview if the folklorist were unable to take in this particular projection from his informant, understand that it was natural and to be expected, and consequently be able to dissipate it.

From this description of the collecting process, it should be obvious that the folklorist occasionally works at a different level of reality than his other colleagues in the English Department, whose encounters with authors occur on the printed page. The literary critic's research rarely carries him beyond the library, and the reality he deals with is mostly at secondhand, as seen, experienced, and expressed by someone else. For his students he is obliged to interpret descriptions of feeling states, emotionally charged events, and archetypal situations of which his own experience may be very limited. Naturally, he is also obliged to maintain rapport, collectively and individually, with his students and also with his colleagues. Most of these individuals, however, have assumptions and life plans not too different from his own; their projections on him are balanced by his on them; and all of these are maintained, usually at about the same level of emotional intensity. The folklorist in the field has no such expectation; he is likely to meet individuals whose assumptions and objectives in life are very different from his own; and he must meet them on an equal basis. The professional persona is an effective crutch for many people in academic life, but the folklorist who attempts to use his on his informants quickly discovers that he is as likely to be resented—because he seems to feel more important than his informant—as he is to be welcomed and admired.

English majors often find a collecting project an intellectually invigorating change from their other course work. Instead of confining themselves exclusively to printed examples of literary devices, they may have the opportunity to hear various ones used directly in folk speech; instead of only reading about symbolic behavior, they may observe it at first hand. Collecting routinely includes recording life histories of informants by way of trying to provide a cultural context for the material collected, and these reflect in various ways time problems, successes and failures, of particular human beings. Talk of relevance, of lack of concern for problems outside of the university by students who feel their studies somehow unrelated to current events, evaporates quickly in a folklore course, and not only because of experience in the field. Students discover in the interdisciplinary and cross-cultural approach of folklore a sense of personal involvement, in many cases leaving more room for their own initiative than work, say, on a novel which has already produced a large amount of criticism. The sheer mass of critical material, books and articles, generated by some novels can be overwhelming to the student who is asked to come up with his own fresh interpretation.

The most serious doubt entertained about folklore among literary scholars is that the subject matter, because of its often qualitatively debatable nature, and the field of study itself, because it lacks a coherent theoretical structure, has little intellectual depth; indeed, that it amounts to not much more than a loose agglomeration of various kinds of "lore" and ideas about it. The suspicion is that a folklorist, however otherwise well qualified he may be, is simply a curio hunter, a preserver of the quaint, the folksy, the nostalgic.

There is some justice to this attitude. In the past, folklorists have spent a great deal of time collecting material and relatively little time in trying to understand it. Some folklorists have undoubtedly been inspired by sentimental yearnings and have tended to exaggerate, even glorify, the worth of material they have collected; having few critical presuppositions, they have often accepted at face value obvious fakes.[5] And it is to some extent still the case that folklorists are not agreed among themselves as to what their field is really about—whether, for example, it should be more properly classified among the social sciences than the humanities.

Paradoxically, a great strength of the field is found in its diversity of approaches and professional orientations. Folklorists are found in anthropology, comparative literature, English, linguistics, psychology, sociology, and a number of other fields in addition to their own departments and programs in a few universities. In their journals and conferences they regularly exchange ideas and report on research from a variety of perspectives. The level of scholarship currently demanded is at least as high, and in some cases higher, than that found in other disciplines. While some fields do pay lip service to interdisciplinary approaches, this usually means that an occasional professor incorporates material in one of his courses from another field; in folklore, it also reflects a critical attitude of mind; the folklorist has to be interdisciplinary to understand what many of his colleagues are even talking about.

There is also the general awareness among folklorists that if they adopt concepts and terminology from another field, they can expect a critical evaluation by experts in that field; loose or incorrect usage is quickly pointed out. In contrast, for example, psychological terms are frequently used in literary criticism in such a manner as to suggest that the critic has only a very slight knowledge of the theoretical framework from which they were taken and what, indeed, their present status is in psychology. The risk seems minimal that a psychologist is going to pick them up on their faulty usage. How much more careful a good deal of criticism might be if its authors knew that professionals from other fields might likely read it. This is the situation in folklore.

Although the subject matter of the field varies in quality, and few folklorists would argue over the intrinsic value of much of it, there is no dispute among folklorists over the importance of collecting folklore and trying to understand it. Unlike practically every other field, folklore does not posit a set of assumptions through which it regularly views and preserves its material; it tries to see the thing itself. Thus of all fields, it is much closer to the elusive thing called reality, and its objects of study are their own justification, not some set of concepts which allows the investigator to abstract and simplify them. If some folklore is ugly or stupid or obscene (and much of it is beautiful), then that is the truth of it; a critical abstraction in terms of one or another set of concepts only distorts this.

Literary fashions change, but for the folklorist the question of meaning demands the use of any critical tools that can serve his ends. In comparative mythology courses, for example, students are introduced to a variety of critical approaches to mythology from a number of disciplines, including anthropology, comparative religion, and literary criticism, which the English major could use in the explication of mythological themes and motifs in fiction. How important this is for the student of literature often depends on the attitude of his professors, but increasingly teachers of English are encouraging the study of mythology (and not just the classic myths of Greece and Rome) as an essential background for criticism itself. For many it is no longer good enough to simply point out examples of the mythic in poems or plays or novels. Where did the motif come from? How was it originally used? Does this author's use of it differ, and in what ways, from the way it has been used in the past? Is it found in tradition today?

Of the major academic disciplines, English remains one of the most conservative by its nature and reflects social change the least. Ironically, innumerable works of literature reflect and were inspired by cultural changes, but the study of these is conducted, as it were, in a fishbowl where outside realities impinge the least. In a constantly quickening number of discoveries and innovations, particularly in the sciences, scholars have gone beyond the ability of many of their colleagues in the humanities to understand what they are doing. Similarly, society itself is undergoing changes that will soon outstrip much of the literature that might eventually reflect them, coming only years later to the attention of the critic. It may be supposed that many individuals in English will, in their personal lives, stay attuned to major time problems, but unless these can be made relevant to their students and can be reflected in their criticism, they will not matter much to the field as a whole. If English majors, as well as their teachers, were required to go out into the field and collect children's rhymes, or examples of dialect patterns, or local legends, or place names, or descriptions of crafts, they would hear and experience oral literature directly and realize that it does exist as a living process and is not just a product of the past. In this way the field techniques of the folklorist could be useful to his colleagues in English; similarly, his interdisciplinary approach to his research is already providing for many English majors a broader and often richer perspective on their literary studies than the critical theories of their field alone. Writing in 1912 and referring specifically to the would-be psychiatrist or psychologist, C. G. Jung spoke of the need to experience life directly oneself:

> . . . Anyone who wants to know the human psyche will learn next to nothing from experimental psychology. He would be better advised to put away his scholar's gown, bid farewell to his study, and wander with human heart through the world. There, in the horrors of prisons, lunatic asylums and hospitals, in drab suburban pubs, in brothels and gambling-halls, in the salons of the elegant, the Stock Exchanges, Socialist meetings, churches, revivalist gatherings, and ecstatic sects, through love and hate, through the experience of passion in every form in his own body, he would reap richer stores of knowledge than textbooks a foot thick could give him, and he will know how to doctor the sick with real knowledge of the human soul. He may be pardoned if his respect for the so-called cornerstones of experimental psychology is no longer excessive. For between what science calls psychology and what the practical needs of daily life demand from psychology there is a great gulf fixed.[6]

Literary critics and folklorists are in some sense interpreters of life for their students, and it simply makes sense that they should have real experience of the reality they presume to interpret.

NOTES

[1]Delivered at the Midwest Modern Language Association Annual Meeting, Detroit, November 1971.

[2]See especially the symposium "Folklore in Literature," *Journal of American Folklore,* 70 (1957); chapters 11 and 12 of Richard M. Dorson, *American Folklore and the Historian* (Chicago: Univ. of Chicago Press, 1971), entitled "The Identification of Folklore in American Literature" and "Folklore in American Literature: A Postscript"; and John T. Flanagan and Arthur Palmer Hudson, eds., *Folklore in American Literature* (Evanston: Row, Peterson, 1958).

[3]In addition to the two articles by Richard M. Dorson cited above, discussion of ways of spotting folklore and evaluating its usage in literature have been considered by Hennig Cohen, "American Literature and American Folklore" in Tristram P. Coffin, ed., *Our Living Traditions* (New York: Basic Books, 1968); Daniel Hoffman, *Form and Fable in American Fiction* (New York: Oxford Univ. Press, 1961, 1965); Archer Taylor, "Folklore and the Student of Literature," in Alan Dundes, ed., *The Study of Folklore* (Englewood Cliffs, N. J.: Prentice-Hall, 1965); and Ronald L. Baker, *Folklore in the Writings of Rowland E. Robinson* (Bowling Green, Ohio: Bowling Green Popular Press, in press).

[4]The best known of these are Antti Aarne and Stith Thompson, *The Types of the Folktale,* Folklore Fellows Communications, No. 184 (Helsinki, 1961) and Stith Thompson, *Motif-Index of Folk Literature,* 6 vols. (Bloomington, Ind.: Indiana Univ. Press, 1955-58), but there are many others.

[5]For one folklorist's fight to make his field more scholarly, see "Fakelore" in Richard M. Dorson, *American Folklore and the Historian.*

[6]C. G. Jung, "New Patterns in Psychology," in *Collected Works of C. G. Jung,* vol. 7, *Two Essays on Analytical Psychology,* trans. R. F. C. Hull (London: Routledge & Kegan Paul, 1953), pp. 244-45.

Stella Brewer Brookes

SOURCE: "Folklore and Literary Art," in *Joel Chandler Harris: Folklorist,* The University of Georgia Press, 1950, pp. 22-40.

[*In the following excerpt, Brookes makes a case that Joel Chandler Harris was a literary artist rather than a mere recorder of others' tales.*]

American folklore began with Uncle Remus, some literary historians declare. Although one may not be able to accept so sweeping a verdict, for in a sense Franklin and Irving were folklorists, the claim for Harris is authentic enough to afford a convenient introduction to this section of the discussion. It is true that Harris's Tar-Baby story, published in *The Atlanta Constitution* in 1879 and widely read, antedates the organization of the American Folklore Society by nine years. It is true that Joel Chandler Harris was a charter member of the Society when it was founded. Furthermore, the first president of the Society stated in the first issue of its journal: ". . . to Joel Chandler Harris belongs the credit for introducing to the public the type of story known as the 'Uncle Remus' story."

For at least a decade Harris's voice, nationally and internationally, was one of the most arresting. It seems safe to speculate that the Uncle Remus stories, published in 1880, if not the first of this distinctive type of literature, were at least prominently the means of creating a vogue which swept the country in the early 1880's. Pattee says: "With the success of the first 'Uncle Remus' book, there came the greatest flood of dialect literature that America has ever known. The years 1883 and 1884 mark the high tide of this peculiar outbreak, and to Georgia more than any other locality may be traced the primal cause."[1]

Harris called himself "an accidental author"; his surprise at the flood of inquiries which came to him mark him as also "an accidental folklorist." The numerous letters which he received with regard to this element in his stories first amazed, then amused, but finally aroused and interested him. The Uncle Remus stories we know from his own statement were not written as folklore. To answer the correspondence with regard to the folklore element he had no more knowledge than "the man in the moon." He says:

> To be frank, I did not know much about folk-lore, and I didn't think that anybody else did. Imagine my surprise when I began to receive letters from learned philologists and folklore students from England to India, asking all sorts of questions and calling upon me to explain how certain stories told in the ricefields of India and on the cottonfields of Georgia were identical, or similar, or at least akin. Then they wanted to know why this folklore had been handed down for centuries and perhaps for thousands of years. They wanted to know, too, why the negro makes Brer Rabbit so cunning and masterful. These letters came from royal institutes and literary societies, from scholars and from travelers. What answer could I make to them? None—none whatever. All that I know— all that we Southerners know—about it, is that every old plantation mammy in the South is full of these stories. One thing is certain—the negroes did not get them from the whites: probably they are of remote African origin.[2]

By December 8, 1880, the first Uncle Remus book had passed through the fourth edition. It had been noticed in every paper of importance in the country. Scientific journals devoted columns to it as a contribution to folklore. The stress laid upon this aspect of the stories sometimes annoyed Harris. He had occasion to write a review of some folk tales of the Southwest, and in this connection, he said: "First, let us have the folk-tales told as they were intended to be told, for the sake of amusement— as a part of the art of literary entertainment. Then, if the folklorists find in them anything of value to their pretensions let it be picked out and preserved with as little cackling as possible."[3]

With respect to the effect of the folklore interest upon him, Julia Harris comments:

> The aftermath of the appearance of "Uncle Remus: His Songs and His Sayings," demonstrated to father with peculiar force, one thing: that he was to be educated in the subject of folklore whether he willed it or not! I am certain that when "Uncle Remus" received his first greeting from the English-speaking public, his creator was ignorant of the fact that variants of the legend were to be found among so many of the primitive people.[4]

Again, she writes:

> Whether or not father had anything more than a passing interest in folklore *before* the stories were published, he certainly made some study of the subject later on. He was a subscriber to the "Folk-Lore Journal" published in London, and his library was well stocked with folklore of different nations; but never for one instant did the humorist and imaginative writer separate himself from his "bump of locality" and get lost in the complicated mazes of ethnic or philologic investigation. . . .[5]

Further evidence of his interest in the folklore aspect of the stories is furnished by a letter which he wrote to an Englishman in 1883, referring to one of the stories in *Uncle Remus: His Songs and His Sayings*. David Bogue brought out an English edition of the book in 1881. The name of the Englishman to whom the letter is written is not given.

> Atlanta, Georgia, U.S.A.
> 1883: 28 June
>
> Dear Sir:
>
> A note from Mr. Brander Matthews informs me that you are interested in at least one of the Uncle Remus legends—the Crayfish and the Deluge. The history of that legend, as far as my knowledge of its genuineness extends, is this: I heard it told a number of times from 1862 to 1865 on the Turner Plantation (Putnam County—Middle Georgia) each time by a negro. The Remus legends, it should be said here, were not written with an eye to their importance as folklore stories. I had no more conception of that than the man in the moon. The first one was written out almost by accident, and as a study in dialect. It was so popular that I at once began to ransack my memory for others. My friends ransacked their memories, and the result was the book as it is printed—and another volume still to be printed, specimens of which you will

find in the July "Century Magazine." But in order to make assurance doubly sure, I took the pains to verify every story anew, and, out of a variety of versions, to select the version that seemed to be most characteristic of the negro: so that it may be said that each legend comes fresh and direct from the negroes. My sole purpose in this was to preserve the stories dear to Southern children in the dialect of the cotton plantations.

To return: The crayfish story was told me by negroes on the Turner Plantation many times during the war period. It was recalled to me by a suggestion from the Editor of the "Savannah Daily News," who overheard it on the coast, and by other friends, and I then searched for it until I found it among the negroes of this—the Northern—section of the state. Since the publication of the book I have found a variant in which the Mud Turtle is substituted for the Crayfish.

I enclose with this a letter written some weeks ago to Mr. Laurence Gomme. I had decided not to post it for fear that the gentleman might be disposed to regard it as a presumptuous effort to intrude the Remus book upon his attention—notwithstanding the fact that my relation to the stories is that of compiler merely. Pray consider the letter as a postscript to this.

I shall be glad to give you any information you may desire in regard to the negro legends, or to serve you in any way, not merely because I am interested in the study of comparative folklore, but because the enjoyment I have obtained from some of your poems has made me your debtor.

Very truly yours
Joel Chandler Harris

The Constitution, Atlanta, Ga.
Editorial Rooms
Atlanta, Georgia, United States
9 June, 1883

Dear Sir:—

I have just been reading in the "Folk-Lore Journal" "The Hare in Folk-Lore," by William George Black, F.S.A., and his treatment of the subject has suggested to me the propriety of calling your attention to my little book "Uncle Remus and his Legends of the Old Plantation." (London: David Bogue, 1881.)

It is a misfortune, perhaps, from an English point of view, that the stories in that volume are rendered in the American negro dialect, but it was my desire to preserve the stories as far as I might be able, in the form in which I heard them, and to preserve also if possible, the quaint humor of the negro. It is his humor that gives the collection its popularity in the United States, but I think you will find the stories more important than humorous should you take the trouble to examine them. Not one of them is cooked, and

not one nor any part of one is an invention of mine. They are all genuine folklore tales.

Since the publication of that book, I have interested myself in the matter, and, with the assistance of friends and correspondents in various parts of the Southern states, I have been enabled to gather seventy or eighty new ones. Pardon this letter. I am interested in the negro stories only as their compiler.

Very truly yours
Joel Chandler Harris

G. Laurence Gomme, F.S.A.

Editor Folk-Lore Journal, London.[6]

After Harris's interest had been aroused in the folklore element of his stories, he persistently held that the stories were "uncooked"—that they were "pure folklore." The stories which appeared in the first book bear greater evidence of pure folklore than those which appeared in subsequent books. Perhaps the most convincing evidence that is offered in proof of the folklore element throughout the series is the inclusion in many of the stories of "Miss Meadows an' de gals." Of this subtle, whimsical creation—so intimately a part of the stories and existing in natural relationship with the animal creatures—Harris seems to have had no definite conception. In the story called "Mr. Rabbit Grossly Deceives Mr. Fox" the Little Boy asks Uncle Remus, "Who was Miss Meadows?" Uncle Remus replies: "Don't ax me, honey. She wuz in de tale, Miss Meadows en de gals wuz, en de tale I give you like hi't wer' gun ter me."[7] It seemed as if that was intended to end the inquiry.

The illustrations for the first edition of *Uncle Remus: His Songs and His Sayings* were to be done by Frederick Church and James Moser. Mr. Church's job was the delineation of the animals. Puzzled as to what he should do with "Miss Meadows an' de gals," he wrote Harris: "What is your idea of 'Miss Meadows an' de gals'? . . . perhaps they mean just *Nature*, in which case I should depict them as pretty girls in simple costumes, making a charming contrast to the ludicrous positions of the animals."[8]

Mr. Harris seemed pleased with the suggestion, but re-emphasized the idea that he was merely the "compiler" of the stories. He replied:

The Constitution, Atlanta, Ga.
Editorial Rooms, June 11, 1880

My Dear Mr. Church:—

My relations toward the sketches you are illustrating are those of compiler merely; consequently I cannot pretend to know what is meant by Miss Meadows. She plays a minor part in the entire series, as you will perceive when the concluding numbers have been sent you. Why she is there, I cannot say, but your conception will give to the sketches a poetical color (if I may say so) which will add vastly to whatever interest they may have for people of taste. By all means let Miss Meadows figure as Nature in the shape of a beautiful girl in a simple but not unpicturesque costume. As it is your own conception, I know you will treat the young lady tenderly. . . .

Yours very truly
J. C. Harris[9]

Kipling's curiosity was similarly aroused. Harris had written an appreciation of Kipling's *Jungle Book*; at the conclusion of a letter of appreciation dated December 6, 1895, which Kipling sent Harris, he said: "One thing I want to know badly (you must loathe the people who pester you with this kind of thing), but from what nature-myth or *what* come 'Miss Meadows and the girls?' Where did they begin—in whose mind? what do you think they are?"[10]

An examination of the Introductions to the first three volumes of the Uncle Remus stories (*Songs and Sayings,* 1880; *Nights,* 1883; *Friends,* 1892) is enlightening with regard to Harris's developing and then apparently waning interest in the folklore element. Evidently Harris had received many letters with regard to the folklore in stories which had appeared in newspapers and magazines prior to 1880. In the Introduction to the first book he refers to the correspondence and tells his amazement at the interest manifested in this particular phase of the tales. It is significant that the Uncle Remus sketches began appearing in the columns of *The Atlanta Constitution* as early as 1878, and that the Tar-Baby story (which was extremely popular at home and abroad) appeared in 1879. In the Introduction to the first book he tells of his method of collecting, of variants of the stories included in the volume, and insists that his aim is to preserve the stories in their "original simplicity." A portion of this Introduction is sufficiently important to be given in Harris's own words:

With respect to the Folk-Lore series, my purpose has been to preserve the legends themselves in their original simplicity, and to wed them permanently to the quaint dialect—if, indeed, it can be called a dialect—through the medium of which they have become a part of the domestic history of every Southern family; and I have endeavored to give the whole a genuine flavor of the old plantation.

Each legend has its variants, but in every instance I have retained that particular version which seemed to me to be the most characteristic, and have given it without embellishment and without exaggeration. The dialect, it will be observed, is wholly different from that of the Hon. Pompey Smash and his literary descendants, and different also from the intolerable misrepresentations of the ministrel stage, but it is at least phonetically genuine. Nevertheless, if the language of Uncle Remus fails to give vivid hints of the really poetic imagination of the negro; if it fails to embody the

quaint and homely humor which was his most prominent characteristic; if it does not suggest a certain picturesque sensitiveness—a curious exaltation of mind and temperament not to be defined by words—then I have reproduced the form of the dialect merely, and not the essence, and my attempt may be accounted a failure. At any rate, I trust that I have been successful in presenting what must be, at least to a large portion of American readers, a new and by no means unattractive phase of negro character. . . .

A number of the plantation legends originally appeared in the columns of a daily newspaper— The Atlanta Constitution—and in that shape they attracted the attention of various gentlemen who were kind enough to suggest that they would prove to be valuable contributions to myth-literature. It is but fair to say that ethnological considerations formed no part of the undertaking which has resulted in the publication of this volume. Professor J. W. Powell, of the Smithsonian Institution, who is engaged in an investigation of the mythology of the North American Indians, informs me that some of Uncle Remus's stories appear in a number of different languages, and in various modified forms, among the Indians; and he is of the opinion that they are borrowed by the negroes from the red-men. But this, to say the least, is extremely doubtful.[11]

In 1870, Professor C. F. Hartt of Cornell University[12] heard at Santaren, on the Amazon, a story in *lingua geral* of "The Tortoise that Outran the Deer," a version of which he afterwards published in the *Cornell Era* (January 20, 1871) and which attracted the attention of a writer in *The Nation* (February 23, 1871) who gave a variant of the same myth as found among the Negroes of South Carolina. Harris tells the same story in *S. and S.,* "Mr. Rabbit Finds His Match at Last."

The curious resemblance between the Amazonian story told by Professor Hartt and the one found among the Negroes of South Carolina, a version of which Harris recounted was not noticed again until Mr. Herbert Smith, in his *Brazil, the Amazons and the Costa* (1879) in a chapter on "The Myths of the Amazonian Indians" gave a number of animal fables, merely noting the resemblances which had already attracted the attention of Professor Hartt and others. The proof-sheets of this chapter were sent to Mr. Harris, who at once saw that almost every story quoted by Mr. Smith had a parallel among the stories of the Southern Negroes, and some were so nearly identical in his opinion to point unmistakably to a common origin. Puzzled, Mr. Harris asks: "When did the negro or the North American Indian ever come in contact with the tribes of South America?"[13]

The tales in the first book, published in 1880, had delighted so large a circle that there was a growing demand for more stories. In October of 1882, Harris had been in correspondence with Mr. Osgood of the firm of Boston publishers regarding a second book. It seems that to supply the demand, Harris had sought the aid of a former newspaper associate, Mr. R. W. Grubb of Darien, a Georgia coast town.[14]

3 February, 1883

Dear Grubbs:—

Isn't there some one connected with your office who would be willing to piroot around among the negroes of Darien and gather me the outlines of the animal and alligator stories that form the basis of African mythology? I have a whole raft of stories current among the cotton plantation negroes, but there is another whole raft current among the coast negroes. Can't you get some one, who has the knack, to get in with some old negro, male or female, and secure me a dozen or more specimens? There are a number of stories in which the alligator figures, which I would like to have. All I want is a reasonably intelligent outline of the story as the Negroes tell them, and for such outlines I would be glad to pay what the collector may consider reasonable and fair. The only way to get at these stories is for the person seeking them to obtain a footing by telling one or two on his own hook—beginning, for instance, with the tar-baby. There are few negroes that will fail to respond to this.[15]

As a result of this letter, Mr. Grubb introduced Harris to Mrs. Helen Barclay who had gathered many stories on the Pierce Butler estates in the neighborhood of Darien. Others from whom Mr. Harris obtained outlines of tales were Mr. Charles C. Jones, who later compiled some of the stories he had heard into a book,[16] and Mr. John Devereux, who had been living in North Carolina. Mr. Devereux wrote: "I had been familiar with these stories from childhood and I sent Mr. Harris the bare outlines of several leaving it to his genius to make 'these dry bones live.'"[17]

In Harris's second book, *Nights with Uncle Remus*, (1883) the new type of interest both in the folklore element and the method of collecting is indicated in the prefatory material. In the earlier book, the author devotes eight pages of the Introduction to the discussion of this question; in the second book, he devotes twenty-nine pages to this aspect. He gives details about methods of collecting, comparative studies with Kaffir folk-tales, parallels of the Remus stories and Amazonian myths, similarities among Negro plantation proverbs and Kaffir proverbs, and a comparative study of the stories in his book with a volume of Negro stories of South Africa, translated by W. H. I. Bleek.[18] He also includes a dialect vocabulary, and the reprint of a French story, which brings out the Creole's use of dialect and the explanation that the Miss Meadows of the Georgia negro is Mamzel Calinda of the Creoles.[19] He was "folklore conscious" to the extent that he wrote his publishers "I think I shall come to Boston to write the introduction, so as to take advantage of the folklore collection in the Harvard library. . . ."[20]

A detailed examination of some of the changes is enlightening: for instance, in the Introduction to the first book, he says very little about methods of collecting. Only a few lines are required to express his views on this subject: "Curiously enough, I have found few negroes who will acknowledge to a stranger that they know anything of these legends; and yet to relate one is the surest road to their confidence and esteem. In this way, and in this way only, have I been able to identify the folklore included in this volume."[21]

In the Introduction to the second book, *Nights with Uncle Remus,* he remarks that the thirty-four legends in the first volume were easy to verify because they were the most popular among the Negroes and were easily remembered, but many of the stories in the second volume were known only to a small group "who have the gift of story-telling,—a gift that is as rare among the blacks as among the whites."[22]

From the folklore point of view, he realized that the importance of the stories depended upon their verification, therefore, he let no opportunity pass that would aid him in the authentication. In the first book he had spoken of the diffidence of Negroes in releasing the stories; in the next book he relates in detail one instance in which he was successful in gaining the confidence of a group which was extremely valuable in verifying the legends. He wrote:

> One of these opportunities occurred in the summer of 1882, at Norcross, a little railroad station, twenty miles northeast of Atlanta. The writer was waiting to take the train to Atlanta, and this train, as it fortunately happened, was delayed. At the station were a number of negroes, who had been engaged in working on the railroad. It was night, and, with nothing better to do, they were waiting to see the train go by. Some were sitting in little groups up and down the platform of the station, and some were perched upon a pile of cross-ties. They seemed to be in great good-humor, and cracked jokes at each other's expense in the midst of boisterous shouts of laughter. The writer sat next to one of the liveliest talkers in the party; and, after listening and laughing awhile, told the "Tar Baby" story by way of a feeler, the excuse being that some one in the crowd mentioned "Ole Molly Har'." The story was told in a low tone, as if to avoid attracting attention, but the comments of the negro, who was a little past middle age, were loud and frequent. "Dar now!" he would exclaim, or, "He's a honey, mon!" or "Gentermen! git out de way, an' gin 'im room!"[23]

This brought the other Negroes near and they began to listen attentively. Harris next told the story of "Brer Rabbit and the Mosquitoes," with all the accompanying gestures. The group was so delighted that all began telling stories and for almost two hours a crowd of thirty or more vied with each other to see which could tell the most and best tales. Among the stories, Harris recognized many that he had already heard; a few were new.

Thus, the stories included in the volume, *Nights with Uncle Remus,* embody legends heard by the author supplemented by those collected by his friends. Furthermore, they were rendered more with an eye to their ethnological importance.

Nine years elapsed between the printing of *Nights with Uncle Remus* and the appearance of *Uncle Remus and His Friends,* (1892). During these years, Harris's interest in the folklore element seems to have waned. As for the collecting of the stories for this volume, he seemed to have relied primarily upon two sources. In the Introduction to this volume, he wrote:

> The stories here gathered have been caught for me in the kitchen. Some of them are discoveries, many are verifications of stories that have been sent me by friends, and others are the odds and ends and fragments from my notebooks which I have been able to verify and complete. This work of verification and putting together has been going on since 1884, but not in any definite or systematic way. There has been a general understanding in my household for a dozen years or more that preference was to be given in the kitchen to a cook of the plantation type,—the type that we have come to call here the "old-timey" negro. Naturally, it has sometimes happened that digestion was sacrificed to sentiment, but the special result is to be found in the pages that follow.[24]

The other source for the fathering of these stories was also a "home source"; namely, his children. He states that there was a general agreement that the children should use all their arts to discover a new story or to verify one already in hand. The plan was to give the children a cue word or phrase from a story that needed verification or from an interesting fragment that lacked completion. Harris relates one particular instance in which this plan had excellent results. His rehearsal of it is worth noting:

> The cook in charge had a son-in-law named John Holder, who had shown a tendency to indulge in story-telling in his hours of ease. This was in 1886. Mr. Richard Adams Learned of Newton, Sussex County, New Jersey, had sent me the story about the man who, with his two dogs, harassed the wild cattle. (See p. 91). One of the youngsters was told to ask about this story, and his cue was "a man, two dogs, and the wild cattle."[25] But the child's memory was short. He asked about a boy and two dogs, and the result was the story of "The Little Boy and his Dogs," to be found in the supplementary part of "Daddy Jake, the Runaway" (page 76). Some months afterwards the child remembered the wild cattle, and got the story from John Holder substantially as it had been sent me by Mr. Learned. The variations are not worth taking into account. I have referred to this matter because it has been made interesting by an article which Mr. David Dwight Wells contributes to the "Popular Science Monthly," for May, 1892. Mr. Wells embodies the wild cattle story, which differs in no essential particular from the version sent me by Mr. Learned. Mr. Wells had the story from

a gentleman who was born about the beginning of this century in Essequibo, British Guiana, South America. The story was told to Mr. Learned by his grandfather (born in 1802), who had it from his old "mammy" nurse in Demarara. In John Holder's story the names of the dogs are changed to Minny-minny-morack and Follamalinska; in Mr. Learned's story the names are Yarmeàroo and Gengamoroto, in Mr. Wells's, Ya-me-o-ro and Cen-ga-mo-ro-to. The Georgia negro had the story pat, and out of it grew the tale of the "Bull that went a-courting . . . " which the wild cattle story seems to be the sequel of. Thus, we have a series that ought to be of some interest to students of folklore.[26]

However, he hastens to add that he is unable to handle the folklore branch of the subject. In fact, he devotes but three pages to the discussion of this element in the book as compared to eight pages in the first volume and twenty-nine in the second. He seems definitely convinced that he knows less now about folklore than he has ever known. He says:

> But the folklore branch of the subject I gladly leave to those who think they know something about it. My own utter ignorance I confess without a pang. To know that you are ignorant is a valuable form of knowledge, and I am gradually accumulating a vast store of it. In the light of this knowledge, the enterprising inconsequence of the Introduction to "Nights with Uncle Remus" is worth noting on account of its unconscious and harmless humor. I knew a good deal more about comparative folklore then than I know now; and the whole affair is carried off with remarkable gravity. Since that Introduction was written, I have gone far enough into the subject (by the aid of those who are Fellows of This and Professors of That, to say nothing of Doctors of the Other) to discover that at the end of investigation and discussion Speculation stands grinning.[27]

We may presume that Harris was also "grinning" at many of the folklorists and their deductions. An excerpt from a letter published in the *Critic* in September, 1882, regarding a collection of American Indian myths reveals that Harris regarded lightly his reputation in the field of folklore:

> I am not specially well versed in folklore, but I presume this collection will possess scientific value. . . . It would be a wonder if any contribution to myth-literature could be made that would not be promptly traced, historically or psychologically, to the Aryan sun-myth—as, for instance, if a South American cotia creeps in at one end of a hollow log and out at the other, or if Brer Fox runs Brer Rabbit into a hollow tree, we have the going down and the rising of the sun typified. And really the sun-myth does nobody any harm; if it is quackery it is quackery of a very mild kind.[28]

Not only did he treat lightly his reputation as a folklorist, but he also discounted the literary value of his productions and his own art of re-telling. In a letter to William Baskervill, dated March 18, 1895, he wrote:

> I have tried to keep Joel Chandler Harris as much out of my work as possible and I think I have succeeded in the sense that so many others have failed—that is to say, what I have written was for its own sake, and not for money nor for the glorification of the man who was accidentally behind it all. And yet the man is there somewhere—standing for lack of cultivation, lack of literary art, and lack of all the graces that make life worth living to those who affect culture; but I hope that honesty, sincerity, and simplicity are not lacking. . . . I should be delighted to see you seize hold of the manifold defects in my stuff, deal with them generously but candidly, and so point out to the younger writers that all this talk, this silly chatter, of making a literary reputation in an hour is nonsense. I have tried hard to get at the secret of literary art, and have failed. I have had the knack of hard work, but the gift has somehow been lacking.
>
> Nobody knows better than I do how far below the level of permanence my writings fall. . . . [29]

In his Introduction to *Gabriel Tolliver,* he further enlarged upon the absence of any "idea of art" in his writings:

> Let those who can do so continue to import harmony and unity into their fabrications and call it art. Whether it be art or artificiality, the trick is beyond my powers. I can only deal with things as they were; on many occasions they were far from what I would have had them be; but as I was powerless to change them, so I am powerless to twist individuals and events to suit the demands or necessities of what is called art.[30]

Of the Uncle Remus stories he said:

> But there is no pretense that the . . . poor little stories are in the nature of literature, or that their re-telling touches literary art at any point. All the accessories are lacking. There is nothing here but an old negro man, a little boy, and a dull reporter, the matter of discourse being fantasies as uncouth as the original man ever conceived of.[31]

Despite the persistent refusal to acknowledge his art, Harris's correspondence and the productions themselves point to the fact that he did have skill, that he did, in some instances, consciously develop the art of writing through deliberate self-discipline. His awareness of the differentiating qualities of style and diction is noted in a letter to his daughter; in the same letter, he also sets forth the secrets of good writing.

May Day, Sunday, 1898

Dear Lillian:—

The Gleanings came to hand, and I read your account of the pottery tour with great pleasure. It is particularly well done, and the reason is very plain. You had something to write about, you knew what you wanted to say, and you said it, briefly and clearly. There are two secrets of good writing that I will whisper in your ear. One is to write about something that interests you because you know it; the other is to be familiar with and believe in the ideas you propose to write about. One secret refers to description, and the other to views, feelings, opinions. Combined, or separate, they relate to everything that has been or can be written in the shape of literature. So far as merely correct diction is concerned, that can easily be acquired, especially by those who have a knack or gift of expression.

In nearly all the books and magazines that I read, diction is called style. Why, I don't know, for the two come together and combine only in the works of the very greatest writers, as, for instance, Hawthorne—or, to name a greater still, Cardinal Newman. I have just been reading some of the Cardinal's works, and I am simply amazed at the beauty, power, fluency and vividness with which he uses the English tongue. In discussing the dryest subjects, he frequently thrills the mind with passages of such singular beauty as almost to take one's breath away. In these passages you cannot separate the style from the diction, for they are fused.

Nevertheless, style is one thing and diction is another. If some one should compel me by force to explain the difference between the two my answer would be something like this: Diction is the body—the flesh and bone—and style is the spirit. But some years ago, that able Heathen, Mr. Herbert Spencer, had something he wanted to say about diction, and so he wrote it out and called it An Essay on Style, and ever since then the Heathens, the Pagans, and not a few who call themselves Christians, have persisted in referring to diction as style—just as our Northern scholars refer to the "provincialism of the South," when they mean the *provinciality* of the South. Dear me! I hope I am not wearying you with all this; more than all, I hope I have made myself understood. It is so easy to be vague and hazy when talking about writing as a gift and as an art. A person who has the gift must acquire the art, and that is to be done only by long practice.[32]

Perhaps Joe Harris was not conscious of the ability of Joel Chandler Harris. He always insisted upon his dual personality. The letter which follows was written to his daughter; in this, he offers an explanation of himself as a writer:

> As for myself—though you could hardly call me a real, sure enough author—I never have anything but the vaguest ideas of what I am going to write; but when I take my pen in my hand, the rust clears away and the "other fellow" takes charge. You know all of us have two entities, or personalities. That is the reason you see and hear persons "talking to themselves." They are talking to the "other fellow." I have often asked my "other fellow" where he gets all his information, and how he can remember, in the nick of time, things that I have forgotten long ago; but he never satisfies my

curiosity. He is simply a spectator of my folly until I seize a pen, and then he comes forward and takes charge.

Sometimes I laugh heartily at what he writes. If you could see me at such times, and they are very frequent, you would no doubt say, "It is very conceited in that old man to laugh at his own writing." But that is the very point; it is not my writing at all; it is my "other fellow" doing the work and I am getting all the credit for it. Now, I'll admit that I write the editorials for the paper. The "other fellow" has nothing to do with them, and, so far as I am able to get his views on the subject, he regards them with scorn and contempt; though there are rare occasions when he helps me out on a Sunday editorial. He is a creature hard to understand, but, so far as I can understand him, he's a very sour, surly fellow until I give him an opportunity to guide my pen in subjects congenial to him; whereas, I am, as you know, jolly, good-natured, and entirely harmless.

Now, my "other fellow," I am convinced, would do some damage if I didn't give him an opportunity to work off his energy in the way he delights. I say to him, "Now, here's an editor who says he will pay well for a short story. He wants it at once." Then I forget all about the matter, and go on writing editorials and taking Celery Compound and presently my "other fellow" says sourly: "What about that story?" Then when night comes, I take up my pen, surrender unconditionally to my "other fellow", and out comes the story, and if it is a good story I am as much surprised as the people who read it. Now, my dear gals will think I am writing nonsense; but I am telling them the truth as near as I can get at the facts—for the "other fellow" is secretive.[33]

To discover Harris's art one has only to examine one of the "uncooked" stories as sent him by a Negro correspondent and compare it with the finished version. An exact report of a correspondent from Senoia, Georgia was:

Mr. Harris I have one tale of Uncle Remus that I have not seen in print yet. Bro Rabbit at Mis Meadows and Bro Bare went to Bro Rabbit house and eat up his childrun and set his house on fire and make like the childrun all burnt up but Bro Rabbit saw his track he knowed Bro Bare was the man so one day Bro Rabbit saw Bro Bare in the woods with his ax hunting a bee tree after Bro Rabbit spon howdy he tell Bro Bare he know whare a bee tree was and he would go an show and help him cut it down they went and cut it an Bro Rabbit drove in the glut [wedge] while Bro Bare push his head in the hole Bro Rabbit nock out the glut and cut him hickry. Mr. Harris you have the tale now give it wit I never had room to give you all you can finish it.[34]

This tale was the source of the story which appeared in *Uncle Remus: His Songs and His Sayings,* under the title "The End of Mr. Bear."[35] One has only to read the tale as given by Harris to recognize the craftsman's art.

A comparison of the two versions proves that Harris was no mere copyist. Despite his stubborn insistence that the stories were "pure folklore," they seem "folklore somewhat embroidered."

One of the best appraisals in connection with the respective literary and folklore elements is that given by Mark Twain. On August 4, 1881, Harris had written in a letter to Mark Twain:

Everybody has been kind to the old man, but you have been kindest of all. I am perfectly aware that my book has no basis of literary art to stand upon; I know it is the matter and not the manner that has attracted public attention and won the consideration of people of taste at the North; I understand that my relations toward Uncle Remus are similar to those that exist between an almanac-maker and the calendar; but at the same time I feel grateful to those who have taken the old man under their wing.[36]

Mark Twain realized his friend's modest valuation of his talents, and in his reply stated:

You can argue *yourself* into the delusion that the principle of life is in the stories themselves and not in their setting, but you will save labor by stopping with that solitary convert, for he is the only intelligent one you will bag. In reality the stories are only alligator pears—one eats them merely for the sake of the dressing. "Uncle Remus" is most deftly drawn and is a lovable and delightful creation; he and the little boy and their relations with each other are bright, fine literature, and worthy to live. . . . [37]

NOTES

[1] Fred Lewis Pattee, *American Literature Since 1870* (New York, 1915), p. 306.

[2] *Life and Letters,* p. 162.

[3] *Ibid.,* p. 153.

[4] *Ibid.,* p. 161.

[5] *Ibid.,* p. 154.

[6] *Ibid.,* pp. 155-158.

[7] *Songs and Sayings,* p. 25.

[8] *Life and Letters,* p. 149.

[9] *Ibid.,* p. 150.

[10] *Ibid.,* p. 334.

[11] *Songs and Sayings,* pp. vii-ix.

[12] Professor of Geology at Cornell University.

[13] _Songs and Sayings,_ p. xi.

[14] _Life and Letters,_ p. 192.

[15] _Ibid.,_ pp. 192-193.

[16] Mr. Jones' book was _Negro Myths of the Georgia Coast,_ published in 1888.

[17] _Life and Letters,_ p. 195.

[18] W. H. I. Bleek, _Reynard, the Fox, in South Africa; or Hottentot Fables and Tales._

[19] Joel Chandler Harris, _Nights with Uncle Remus_ (Boston, 1883), p. xxxv.

[20] Caroline Tichnor, "Glimpses of the Author of Uncle Remus," _Bookman,_ XXVII (August, 1908), p. 554.

[21] _Songs and Sayings,_ p. 10.

[22] _Nights with Uncle Remus,_ p. xiv.

[23] _Ibid.,_ p. xv.

[24] Joel Chandler Harris, _Uncle Remus and His Friends_ (Boston, 1892), p. iv.

[25] Youngster referred to was Julian La Rose Harris.

[26] _Uncle Remus and His Friends,_ p. vi.

[27] _Ibid.,_ p. vii.

[28] _Life and Letters,_ pp. 299-300.

[29] Hubbell, "Letters of Uncle Remus," pp. 216-223.

[30] _Life and Letters,_ p. 455.

[31] _Uncle Remus and His Friends,_ pp. 10-11.

[32] _Life and Letters,_ pp. 393-395.

[33] _Ibid.,_ pp. 384-386.

[34] _Ibid.,_ p. 197.

[35] _Songs and Sayings,_ p. 119.

[36] _Life and Letters,_ p. 168.

[37] _Ibid.,_ pp. 169-170.

Gene Bluestein

SOURCE: "Constance Rourke and the Folk Sources of American Literature," in _Western Folklore,_ Vol. XXVI, No. 2, April, 1967, pp. 77-87.

[_In the following essay, Bluestein examines the methodology of, and resulting themes in, Constance Rourke's_ American Humor.]

With one exception, very little analysis of the method and approach of Constance Rourke has appeared since her death in 1941.[1] In an otherwise sympathetic essay, Stanley Edgar Hyman finds her work flawed because, unlike Jane Harrison, Miss Rourke did not follow the clues in her materials to their ultimate source in myth and ritual. It is a little like criticizing Mark Twain because he was not William Shakespeare. Her interests lay in other directions, and, with the publication of _American Humor, A Study of the National Character_ (1931), Miss Rourke focused her attention on two major issues: the folk sources of an American literary tradition and the function of humor in its development. Much has been written on the nature of the American identity since _American Humor,_ and I feel that Miss Rourke's contributions to our understanding of the subject and its reflection in our literature are of the first importance.

Constance Rourke's first preoccupation in _American Humor_ was to offset the assertion by many of her contemporaries that American civilization had little to offer in the fine arts. The history of this assumption is long and complicated, but one of its major formulations (reinforced from time to time by native as well as foreign critics) is based on the notion that the United States was brought into existence under circumstances that denied it the period of gestation necessary for the creation of a mature and richly textured culture. Miss Rourke's response to this point of view is one of the best measures of her accomplishments as a scholar and a critic. The argument that America was too young a nation to have a literature of its own, she knew, reflected a major but unexpressed assumption in Western literary criticism. What it really meant to say was that no nation can create a fine art literature unless it has a folk culture to build it upon. If there is a distinctive literary tradition in this country, she argued, there must have been a matrix of folk and popular materials behind it.

Later, in _The Roots of American Culture_ (1942), Miss Rourke correctly identified this view with the philosophy of Johann Gottfried von Herder.[2] Herder first developed fully the idea that a nation's literature is truly national and legitimately its own when it arises from the folklore of its people. Denied a feudal era, America apparently lacked just such a crucial period of folk accumulation which, in Herder's conception, was necessary to the building of an indigenous literature. As a result, Miss Rourke pointed out, the idea that America was a derivative (and therefore inferior) culture

was inevitably accepted in the colonial era and has been further defined, elaborated and added to explicitly or otherwise until it stands as a main approach to the study of our culture and even of our political, social and economic history.[3]

What small reservoir of folklore might be found here was the result of emigration from the Old World, the colonists naturally bringing with them the forms of their native folk traditions. But this would provide little in the way of nourishment for an American folklore. As Miss Rourke explained:

> The arts would spread much as water is passed in buckets at a country fire—spilled along the way no doubt, with much of it lost and perhaps acquiring a peculiar tang or flavor, if one should taste it. What we might hope eventually to possess was an extension of European culture, that is, if the process of diffusion was not too greatly impaired by forces peculiar to American life.[4]

Here was the rub, for not only was it asserted that America had not created its own folk tradition, it was also suggested that any meaningful importations would be vitiated by the American experience.

The first task in any correction of this view was to establish the nature and significance of those materials and conditions in America which could provide the basis for a national literature. In an earlier work, Miss Rourke had employed folklore decoratively to enliven the basic outlines of her story.[5] But in *American Humor* she developed a method of literary and cultural analysis which was, in the strictest sense, neither folkloristic nor historical but a unique combination of both disciplines. She wrote in the foreword:

> This book has no quarrel with the American character; one might as well dispute with some established feature in the natural landscape. Nor can it be called a defense. . . . This study has grown from an enjoyment of American vagaries, and from the belief that these have woven together a tradition which is various, subtle, sinewy, scant at times but not poor.[6]

Despite its own relatively short existence, Miss Rourke insisted, America had its own tradition, unique in its development and rich enough to control and to color the flow of fine art which issued from it.

In the first of what was to be a trio of characterological studies, Miss Rourke discerned the lineaments of the American as they emerged in the figure of the Yankee. By the end of the eighteenth century, she noted, he was easily identified as the peddler, a lone, shrewd figure who had already become more than regional, taking on aspects of myth and fantasy. It was an image fashioned, as it is to this day, by New England, the West, and even the South. The emphasis on the finagling, calculating merchant (strangely analogous to the stereotype of the Jew) obscured origins that were complex and variegated. During the Revolutionary War era, when the Yankee began to emerge as a national symbol, Miss Rourke noted also the emergence of a major theme in American cultural history. The tension between Europe and America, which later critics have identified as the "international theme," is apparent from the very beginning

of our national history. Miss Rourke is rarely a polemicist, but in a bibliographical note at the end of *American Humor* she criticized Van Wyck Brooks for not recognizing that "the international scene is a natural and even traditional American subject. . . . " The insight was a crucial one, for it illuminated a problem that many critics had not known how to handle. The contrast between Europe and America (especially between England and the United States) in politics, manners, and literary productions led some scholars to place the conflict outside the configurations of American experience. The nature as well as the significance of the antagonism were, thus, easily misread as manifestations of American chauvinism or British pomposity. By placing the opposition of Old World and New squarely in the main stream of American thought, Miss Rourke skirted the pitfalls of either extreme position, at the same time affirming its significance as an American rather than a strictly regional antagonism. Much of the criticism leveled by both sides was accurate. But the important point, she insisted, was that the American character was formed under the pressure of criticism from abroad, a circumstance which helped to explain some of its special qualities. In a later section of *American Humor,* she identified this theme as a major one in the work of Henry James and Mark Twain.

The Yankee's major virtue was adaptability, his main accomplishment the creation of a subtle humor, couched not so much in a new dialect as in a new "lingo." (The distinction is Lowell's, and Miss Rourke interpreted it to mean that the "oddities of language were consciously assumed.") Yet the Yankee remained a highly complex character who operated most effectively on the level of fantasy, a stratagem which managed to keep secretive the innermost qualities of his mind and personality. In the process the figure of the Yankee foreshadowed the American. His basic qualities of adaptability, self-confidence, and vitality were the result of a hybridization of diverse forms. The Yankee presented an outline which was filled in during the course of American development.

The second major phase of this steady accretion of national characteristics bore the clear imprint of the backwoodsman. Miss Rourke noted the interesting fact that, as the Yankee had emerged from the embroilments of the Revolutionary War, so the frontiersman made his appearance during the War of 1812. In both cases, the pressure of a military and political conflict demanded a forceful image capable of fusing diverse aspects of the national imagination. But a more significant insight is her insistence that the backwoodsman's ancestry was similar to the Yankee's, rooted in Calvinism and drawing upon the same ethnic stocks. His response to the wilderness was more extreme than the Yankee's reaction to the New England frontier, but the movement was toward the same goal marked out by the Yankee, the process consisting mainly of filling in the earlier outline. Miss Rourke's emphasis here is upon the influence of the new land upon an already identifiable new man. He created a new bestiary, including mythical animals, drawing freely upon the lore and legend of Indians and Negro slaves. Indeed, a new folk music arose through his "mixing Negro breakdowns with Irish reels and jigs" and his singing "his rough improvisations mingled with the older songs." But the crowning accomplishment was the backwoodsman himself, "a new beast" spawned by the rivers and forests of the West. Miss Rourke was fully aware of the implications held by her descriptions of this new stage in the synthesis of old and new elements. There was a dark stain at the heart of this development. Horror, terror, and death were ever present in the frontier experience; the tales and legends of the frontiersman repeated an earlier motif which mingled magical outcroppings of birth with clear intimations of terror and death, resulting often in a middle ground that Miss Rourke identified as the grotesque. In all this, however, the comic sense functioned as before, providing a resilience which "swept through them in waves, transcending the past, transcending terror, with the sense of comedy itself a wild emotion."

The backwoodsman "emerged as a full-bodied figure," but in him there was also discernible the earlier character of the Yankee. Neither alone seemed capable of sustaining the weight of national consciousness, but the

> two figures seemed to join in a new national mythology, forming a striking composite, with a blank mask in common, a similar habit of sporting in public the faults with which they were charged, both speaking in copious monologues, both possessing a bent toward the self-conscious and theatrical, not merely because they appeared on the stage but because of essential combinations in mythical character (p. 67).

The third major figure whose character became permanently etched into the emerging portrait of the American was the Negro. Other ethnic types had appeared briefly, and, though some were destined to persist on the stage (the Dutchman and the immigrant Irishman, for example), none exerted so strong a hold on the popular imagination—and this despite his slave status. The attempt to determine the relationship of Negro culture to our national life has permeated every field of American scholarship. Sociologists, political scientists, historians, musicologists, and literary critics have juggled the issues concerning the Negro's special status in our society. They are far from being decided, as contemporary agitation throughout the country reveals, but, even when the discussion has been heated by special pleadings or obscured by deep-rooted prejudices, the result has always been a clarification of our national aspirations. It is as if, when we talk about the Negro, we inevitably uncover some basic truths about Americans as a whole. (As William Faulkner has shown us, to pursue the problem fully is to illuminate the condition of mankind.)

Despite some general interest in the Negro's religious music, it was the vogue of minstrelsy, which first brought his music and lore to the attention of mass audiences.[7] Miss Rourke saw in minstrelsy a major

source of several important elements which added to the still unfinished portrait of the American. The first was satirical humor that often blossomed into full-scale burlesque. White minstrels, including Dan Emmett, the most famous of them all, clearly borrowed fables and tunes from Negro tradition, but, even when their intention was to glorify the plantation South, the minstrels provided a strange and exotic effect which gave their caricatures a wider meaning. Negro folklore abounded in animal fables and nonsense songs that introduced a "bolder comic quality" than had been expressed in earlier American humor. But Miss Rourke identified in Negro tradition something more than a simple primitivism. Beneath the careless and often preposterous humor, there was a tragic substratum which filled a gap in the configuration of American traits. The Negro had known defeat, and it "could be heard in the occasional minor key and in the smothered satire" of his music and song. Like the earlier prototypes of the American, the Negro wore a mask, but, unlike them, his conscious satire was rooted in a vision of the human condition which the flourishes of his fantasy never fully obscured. The sense of the limitation and ultimate defeat of man, which might have been the contribution of Calvinism to the American character, Miss Rourke's argument suggests, came rather through the experience of the Negro, though blunted and refracted for the popular mind by white minstrelsy. Indirectly, though forcefully, a third figure was added to the Yankee and the Backwoodsman, merging like the earlier ones into the generic type.

White minstrelsy was a "double mask" which seemed to arouse "an instinctive response" among American audiences. Folklorists such as John and Alan Lomax have established beyond much doubt the germinal power of Negro folksong in the development of a distinctly native folk tradition in the United States. Throughout the 1930's and 1940's, and quite independently of Miss Rourke's research, the Lomaxes developed a remarkably similar view of the sources of an American folksong tradition, emphasizing the gradual but unmistakable mixing of Negro and British folk motifs in a deceptively unself-conscious amalgamation. Despite the surface tensions which have always characterized Negro-white relationships, Alan Lomax wrote,

> Negroes and whites have swapped tunes, tales, dances and religious ideas. And in the even more basic areas of speech and motor behavior this meeting of minds between the two groups is clearer still. White Americans, perhaps at first attracted by the exotic rhythms and earthy poesy of Negro song, have been deeply stirred by the poignant sorrow, the biting irony, and the noble yearning for a better world implicit there.[8]

Miss Rourke's formulation brought into sharp relief the deep imprint of Negro styles on popular rather than folk tradition, and it is an impact still discernible in our most recent experiences. Minstrelsy lasted long after the Civil War, and the vogue of the blackface comedian persisted even longer. Periodically, however, Negro folk styles have penetrated popular song traditions and reached incredibly large audiences: after minstrelsy there was the development of several varieties of jazz, from the distinctly Negro New Orleans style to the more widely dispersed white imitation which became known as "Dixieland"; in the period after World War II there emerged the highly popular vogue of "rock and roll," which was itself a commercialized version of "rhythm and blues"; and most recently as a result of the interest in American folksong there is the wide influence of a group of traditional Negro singers and instrumentalists, among them Huddie Ledbetter (Leadbelly). In all these cases, the ultimate source of influence is Negro, but its main force flows through white performers and is received by white audiences. However masked and indirect this influence is, Miss Rourke was accurate in her assertion that it was widespread and persistent. And, despite the generally flippant tone of the surface, there was always the tragic undercurrent: "The young American Narcissus had looked at himself in the narrow rocky pools of New England and by the waters of the Mississippi; he also gazed long at a darker image" (p. 90). It was an image, we can add now with the perspective of more than thirty years, that has sharpened and intensified rather than blurring and diffusing out of the picture of American life.

The first part of *American Humor* concentrated on a typological study of the sources of American character. After establishing her triptych, Miss Rourke turned to environmental and institutional forces which helped to shape the larger patterns of American literature. Her central concern was the theater, especially as it was developed on the frontier.

Each of the three character types had strong associations with theater, a term which Miss Rourke opposed to the drama. The theatrical, she pointed out,

> is full of experiment, finding its way to audiences by their quick responses and rejections. On the stage the shimmer and glow, the minor appurtenances, the jokes and dances and songs, the stretching and changes of plots, are arranged and altered almost literally by the audience or in their close company; its measure is human, not literary (p. 93).

The last phrase contains the major insight, for it helps to explain the curious resistance in American literature to the classical and neoclassical conception of the sublime. As she noted later in connection with our novelists and poets, the movement is away from traditional forms which emphasize a high style and the hegemony of tragedy. The center of gravity was comic, and, as in earlier experiences, it was a levelling agent with marked antagonism toward "highbrow" traditions. The theater is an especially sensitive gauge of this tendency.

> [It] took a place which in a civilization of slower and quieter growth might have been occupied almost altogether by casual song and story; even the comic

tale was theatrically contrived, with the teller always the actor, and the effect dependent upon manner and gesture and stress of speech (p. 93).

No drama in the literary sense emerged from the nineteenth-century American theater, yet the theatrical was a native mode, and, especially in the West, it "was a composite of native feeling."

The major theme of these early stage writers "was the false romanticism of American sentiment for the Indian." Their favorite form was the burlesque with its inevitable edge of satire. Fantasy, in their hands, became a source of lethal ridicule with a subject matter that ranged from obvious barbs in the direction of Longfellow to burlesques on the theories of free love, feminism, or political scandals. These were native themes, and the mode of representing them led toward an essentially comic art which helps to define not only Mark Twain (who drew heavily and consciously upon these motifs), but such makers of the modern theater as Tennessee Williams. "This lawless satire" of the 1930's and 1940's "was engaged in a pursuit which had occupied comedy in the native vein elsewhere. . . . Comedy was conspiring toward the removal of all alien traditions, out of delight in pure destruction or as preparation for new growth" (p. 110).

Miss Rourke did not make this frontier hypothesis in an articulate formulation, but it is so close to the main lines of Turnerian speculation that it merits attention. Over and over again, the frontier has been defined by important critics and writers as the area in which the legacy of the Old World was wiped clean and the meaning of America written afresh. For Miss Rourke, it was comedy which purged the old traditions and provided the basis for the new. As in the classical formulation by Frederick Jackson Turner, it was a process by stages through repeated contact with an unsophisticated but vital frontier existence. But, where Turner emphasized the pragmatic and anti-intellectual propensities of the frontiersman, Miss Rourke saw a new mythology springing from the depths of the American wilderness. The difference is perhaps that, as a historian, Turner was too often unaware that he had shifted his ground to typological or mythical approaches. Miss Rourke's approach was almost always folkloristic, and she was consequently sensitive to categories of analysis which were only implied in Turner's formulation. Moreover, frontier religion submerged the individual in a communal passion that was expressed in fantasy and legend. Though traditions associated with the theater as well as with revivalism had foreign sources, they soon "took on a native extravagance." These were the conditions of America's childhood, "extended and spatially widened by the opening of wilderness after wilderness, the breaking down of frontier after frontier."

As I pointed out earlier, one of Constance Rourke's main tasks was to provide evidence of a rich source from which an American literary tradition could be seen to flow. By exploring both folk and popular developments, she more than made her point. "Far from having no childhood," she could argue, "the American nation was having a prolonged childhood. . . ." What she had shown was that, despite its lack of a feudal or antique past, America had its own period of primitive accumulation upon which, and in general accordance with Herderian theory, a fine art tradition could be built. All of its preparation, however, led American literature to a unique expression "derived from the life out of which it sprang." If its natural level was not the sublime, even its comedy demanded special definition. Quoting Meredith's declaration that the comic poet can be produced only in a "society of cultivated men and women," Miss Rourke described the emergence of American humor from an unsophisticated and almost barbaric people. "To know comedy," Meredith had insisted, "you must know the real world." But the main forms of America's comic spirit were in the realm of fantasy and legend, in the extravagance of folk speech, and the unbridled satire of popular theater. Its function, moreover, was not related to the traditional comedy of manners. If America's comic fantasies

> failed to exhibit subtlety, fineness, balance, they had created laughter and had served the ends of communication among a people unacquainted with themselves, strange to the land, unshaped as a nation; they had produced a shadowy social coherence (p. 129).

Although its central function was to unify the heterogeneous elements of our experience, its technique was poetic, "keeping that archetypal largeness which inheres in the more elementary poetic forms, with the inevitable slide into figure and that compact turn with unspoken implications which is the essence of poetic expression."

Here, it seems to me, the most valuable of Miss Rourke's critical observations comes into clearest focus. It is essentially a revision of Herderian theory which, on the one hand, avoids a mechanical application of the idea to American conditions and, on the other, helps to explain the distinct configurations of our native tradition. The materials brought together during our period of germination, she maintains, existed on several levels. Hence

> this comic poetry could not be called folk-poetry, but it had the breadth and much of the spontaneous freedom of a folk-poetry; in a rough sense its makers had been the nation. Full of experiment and improvisation, it did not belong to literature; but it used the primary stuffs of literature, the theater that lies behind the drama, the primitive religious ceremony that has been anterior to both, the tale that has preceded both the drama and the novel, the monologue that has been a rudimentary source for many forms (p. 129).

The primary phase in America was never, in Herderian terms, "purely" folk but already a hybrid concatenation of folk and popular. Jane Harrison had suggested that every great period in art must have the same circumstances

of "a new spirit seizing or appropriated by an old established order." But that dictum seemed inappropriate for an evaluation of American development where "the American had cut himself off from the older traditions; the natural heritage of England and the continent had been cast away so far as a gesture could accomplish this feat." Where the tendency persisted it was in the direction of romantic nostalgia for the Indian, but, as Miss Rourke has shown, that quickly became a source of burlesque and satire.

In a more traditionally Herderian vein, Miss Rourke agreed that the outlines of an American literature proceeded from this substratum. She maintained:

> Such preludes have existed for all literatures in songs and primitive ballads and a folk theater and rude chronicles. Great writers have often drawn directly from these sources; . . . From them literature gains immensely; without them it can hardly be said to exist at all.

Like most literatures, the productions of America are related to an "anterior popular lore that must for lack of a better word be called a folk-lore." But no direct relationships can be drawn from this set of circumstances, "no simple, orderly completion." Behind the formal accomplishments of our writers, there lay the ground work which had been fashioned by the comic trio, as well as the "strollers of the theater and of the cults and revivals, the innumerable comic story-tellers and myth makers. . . ." The comic spirit had been lawless and irreverent, concerned with the generic image rather than close observation of the individual character or of "society." Indeed, the American literary tradition veered always toward the

> inner view, the inner fantasy, which belonged to the American comic sense. Genius necessarily made its own unaccountable revelations. Many external influences were at work. But the basic patterns, those flowing unconscious patterns of mind and feeling which create fundamental outlines in expression, had been developed in a native comic lore. The same character was at work on both levels (p. 132).

Mr. Hyman has criticized Constance Rourke's method for what he conceives to be a simple-minded manipulation of the relationships between folk and fine art traditions. It results in a "certain distortion—Hawthorne becomes a teller of folk tales, *Moby Dick,* with its comic Biblical names and nautical puns, a cousin to the jokebooks of the day—but sometimes the distortion is a brilliant restoration, like the recognition of Lincoln as a literary figure."[9] The left-handed compliment, I submit, does little justice to the breadth or subtlety of Miss Rourke's accomplishments in *American Humor.* In the closing sections of the book, she does provide a somewhat sketchy analysis of the main lines of our literary tradition which flow from the sources she was the first to identify as crucial to our literary development. As I have tried to show, she does not conceive of our literary figures as "outgrowths of folk culture." To the contrary, her comment was that

Though he drew upon traditional material, Hawthorne could not rest at ease as the great English poets have rested within the poetic tradition that came to them through the ballads and romances, or as the great English novelists have drawn upon rich local accumulations of character and lore (p. 151).

What she could explain was Hawthorne's predilection for the "romance," which led him to transmute "regional legends into inner moods" or, as in *The Scarlet Letter,* to slip "into an irreverent rude comedy far from the conscious Puritan habit." (Miss Rourke may have had in mind that truly humorous scene, redolent with hints of Elmer Gantry and other lecherous clerics, in which Dimmesdale, fresh from his forest encounter with Hester, almost seduces the most virginal of his parishoners.)

Her comments about Melville, Whitman, Poe, Twain, James, and later writers are brief, but perceptive, insights which justify the nature of her approach to the special but identifiable sources of a native tradition. She developed a rich and sophisticated method of dealing with the full range of the American experience and its manifestation in a variety of significant though not always prestigious forms. But, aside from these accomplishments, we owe Constance Rourke a large debt for her insights into the way that folk and popular traditions have merged to create the characteristic modes of American expression. The more remarkable for being stated so long ago, it is a point of view that provides rich possibilities for the work that still needs to be done on the level of folk popular and fine arts.

NOTES

[1] The only extended criticism is in Stanley Edgar Hyman, *The Armed Vision* (New York: 1948), chap. five. Brief appreciations of Miss Rourke's pioneering efforts appear in F. O. Mathiessen, *American Renaissance*; Richard Chase, *The American Novel and its Tradition*; and Henry Nash Smith *Virgin Land,* as well as in numerous works devoted more directly to American folklore or closely related studies.

[2] I have discussed Herder's conceptions and their relation to native literary traditions in "Herder and Whitman's Nationalism," *Journal of the History of Ideas,* XXIV (1963), 115-126.

[3] *The Roots of American Culture,* p. 45.

[4] *Ibid.,* p. 46.

[5] *Trumpets of Jubilee* (New York: 1927).

[6] *American Humor,* p. 10. Henceforth, page references to this work, Anchor edition, appear in parentheses following quotations.

[7] A recent definitive study is Hans Nathan, *Dan Emmett and the Rise of Early Negro Minstrelsy* (Norman, Oklahoma: 1962).

[8] *Folk Song: U.S.A.* (New York: 1947), pp. viii-ix.

[9] Hyman, *op. cit.,* p. 128.

Arthur Palmer Hudson

SOURCE: "The Impact of Folklore on American Poetry," in *A Tribute to George Coffin Taylor: Studies and Essays, Chiefly Elizabethan, by His Students and Friends,* edited by Arnold Williams, The University of North Carolina Press, 1952, pp. 132-47.

[*In the following excerpt, Hudson examines the folkloric roots of works by an array of American poets from Henry Wadsworth Longfellow to Wallace Stevens.*]

At Cairo, Illinois, the Ohio joins the Mississippi. It is said that for some miles below the junction point, one can distinguish the Ohio by its clear stream from the muddy Father of Waters. Yet who could speak accurately of the "impact" of the Ohio on the Mississippi? They are both basically water, H_2O, with various organic and inorganic matter in solution or afloat. So with folklore and poetry. They are both creations of the human fantasy or imagination operating upon the material of human experiences. In primitive ages they are indistinguishable, so that your *Iliad* and *Odyssey,* your *Beowulf* and *Kalevala* are at the same time your magazine of folklore and your supreme poems. It is only when imagination grows conscious of itself and of its materials, aims, and methods that folklore in a substantial sense becomes art poetry. So it falls to me to try to show the point at which American poetry grows conscious of itself as American and of its subjects, its aims, and its art as American, and to survey some of the results.

I cannot fix that point precisely in time-space. It is approximately established, however, in Robert Frost's "The Gift Outright." We came to this land as British, Irish, French, German, Scandinavian, Spanish, African, et cetera, bearing with us the folksongs, folktales, legends, myths, proverbs, riddles, games, customs, beliefs, et cetera, of our homelands. Here we found another race and another folklore, both alien and incomprehensible, and at first both horrendous and unassimilable. For a hundred years "we were England's still, still colonials," singing our babies to sleep with "Froggie Went a-Courting" and "Old Bangum," making love with "Lord Randal" and "Bonny Barbara Allan's Cruelty," twitting our women with the proverb of the leaky roof and the scolding wife, celebrating our heroes with ballads about Robin Hood, entertaining the chimney corner with the Wives of St. Ives. And we still do, for that matter. But as the shores of the old homelands receded in distance and time, we grew restless and uneasy—

> Possessing what we still were unpossessed by,
> Possessed by what we now no more possessed.

And our people, long before the poets, were possessed by this land, and possessed it. We unconsciously adapted the old folk-lore to the new scene. The English and Scottish ballads "have become as American as anything not Red Indian can be."

> Songs of my people, the cuckoo's voice
> 　Dies out, faint and forlorn,
> And louder caws the garden thief
> 　That pecks the farmer's corn.
> The raven's now an old black crow;
> 　He spies no knight new-slain—
> Merely the carcass of a horse
> 　A-lying in the lane.

We learned to paddle our own canoe. Also, we observed that "The bigger they are, the harder they fall." And often, too often perhaps, we went

> All the way to Arkansaw
> To eat cornbread and possum jaw.

From the beginning of American literature until the early years of the Romantic Period, connections between art poetry and folklore were incidental and more or less consistent with British precedent.[1] Until well into the nineteenth century broadside and newspaper ballads were staple reading provender. Franklin and, later, Bryant and Cooper wrote ballads for newspapers and itinerant singers and peddlers. Royall Tyler's "Ode Composed for the Fourth of July" (1786) gives a gusty list of folk customs, including game songs and dances. Freneau occasionally used folksong patterns, as in the come-all-ye "Barney's Invitation" and "The Battle of Stonington." His "The Indian Student" and "The Indian Burying Ground" show sympathetic interest in Indian character, custom, and belief. Joel Barlow's *The Hasty Pudding* is a mock-heroic but savory treatment of the folklore of native food—Polanta, Polante, mush, Suppawn, and Hasty Pudding. Bryant's "The Little People of the Snow" is a tedious attempt to tell a fairy tale in blank verse. His "Monument Mountain" (1824) more successfully treats a local legend. It is one of the earliest poetic handlings of the lover's-leap story, with Indian characters and setting. Bryant's "The Prairies" contains an extensive account of the mysterious Mound-Builders. His "Song of Marion's Men" (1831), a ballad celebrating the exploits of the South Carolina Swamp Fox and his band, had the ironical fate of becoming a favorite song around Confederate campfires during the Civil War. "The Adventures of the Green Mountain Boys" treats heroic material belonging to New England. Though Poe's fiction utilizes American folklore to some extent, his poetry owes little to folklore except the form and technique of the Romantic ballad, as in "The Raven" and "Annabel Lee."

In Longfellow and Whittier treatment of American folklore goes somewhat beyond the conventions established by British Romantics. In them we begin to see the workings of the yeast which animates Emerson's "Phi Beta Kappa Address."

Whittier's *Snowbound* makes rich allusive use of folklore in painting the picture of the humble life of a New England family. Childish fancy

> Whispered the old rhyme, *Under the Tree*
> *When fire outdoors burns merrily,*
> *There the witches are making tea.*
>
> 　．．．．．
>
> We sped the time in stories old,
> Wrought puzzles out, and riddles told.

In a later couplet with the same rhymes he recalls "tales of witchcraft." The father remembers the violin "which did the village dancers sway" in the French towns. The mother

> Told how the Indian bands came down
> At midnight on Cocheeco town,
>
> 　．．．．．
>
> Recalling in her fitting phrase,
> 　So rich and picturesque and free
> (The common unrhymed poetry
> Of simple life and country ways),
> 　The story of her early days.
>
> 　．．．．．
>
> We stole with her a frightened look
> At the grey wizard's conjuring-book.

The schoolmaster is a well-drawn folk character, versed in the rustic party games, skilled on the merry violin and adept at retelling the "classic legends rare and old" which he had learned in Dartmouth's college halls, in "mirth provoking version." When time dragged the family re-read the Almanac and conned the village paper for "jest, anecdote, and love-lorn tale." Whittier's "Songs of Slaves in the Desert" suggests the old spirituals, especially in the refrain, "Where are we going, Rubee?" "The Wreck of Rivermouth" is based on the legend of a seventeenth-century witch who cast a spell on a fishing boat, and upon her death was buried with a stake through her body. "Telling the Bees" treats "a remarkable custom brought from the Old Country, formerly prevalent in the rural districts of New England." "The Huskers" is a pleasing picture of a characteristically American rural festival, with its "husky ballad" sung by the schoolmaster. The familiar "Maud Muller" is an idyllic ballad. Whittier's most successful short efforts are his ballads treating American historical or traditional themes. "Brown of Ossawatomie," in fourteeners, is a worthy forerunner of fine poems by Carl Sandburg and Stephen Vincent Benét. "Barbara Frietchie" is known to most schoolboys as a spirited treatment of an incident in the Confederate invasion of the North. Whittier's finest achievement in the ballad is "Skipper Ireson's Ride," with its swift and violent action and its tarry and salty folk speech.

Longfellow is the most systematic exploiter of American folklore. Three of his major poems would alone offer material for a substantial study. *Evangeline,* besides utilizing much historical material, owes a great deal to legend and other types of folklore. Not content with the main traditional outlines of his story, he carefully worked up the Acadian folk beliefs. The old notary of Grand Pré was beloved of the children,

> For he told them tales of the Loup-Garou in the
>   forest,
> And of the goblin that came in the night to water
>   the horses
> And of the white letiche, the ghost of the child
>   who unchristened
> Died, and was doomed to haunt the unseen
>   chambers of children;
> And how on Christmas eve the oxen talked in the
>   stable,
> And how the fever was cured by a spider shut up
>   in a nutshell,
> And of the marvelous powers of four-leaved
>   clover and horseshoes,
> And whatsoever was writ in the lore of the village.

In the Ozark Country Evangeline and Basil listened to the Shawnee woman's "tale of the fair Lilinau who was wooed by a phantom," until she felt "That, like the Indian maid, she too, was pursuing a phantom." *Hiawatha* (1855), based on Henry R. Schoolcraft's monumental studies of the American Indians, is the earliest successful effort at an American epic. Taking his verse form from the Finnish epic, *The Kalevala,* Longfellow tried to make *Hiawatha* "This Indian Edda—if I may so call it." The measure of his success is suggested by Stith Thompson's remark that "it is through *Hiawatha* that most Americans even now learn what little they know about the American Indian story."[2] *The Courtship of Miles Standish* (1857-58) was based on traditions well known before Longfellow took up the story. These three long poems, drawing in part from folkloristic sources, in turn "did something to stay if not to satisfy America's hunger for a past, a legendry, a body of myth of her own."[3] Such were the origins and such the effects of Longfellow's *Tales of a Wayside Inn* and his other short poems. If his subjects were not already folklore, he sought to make them such, in the manner of eighteenth-century English Romantics, who, if they did not have medieval ruins on their estates, carefully constructed ruins, or the University of Chicago, which is alleged to have smoked and dusted its brand-new Gothic to give it the proper patina. "Thus, in writing 'The Wreck of the Hesperus,' less than two weeks after the incident it describes and within fifty miles of its scene, he made it sound as much as possible like a medieval popular ballad." A recent critic has complained that "The scenes of his three long narrative poems with an ostensible American setting might almost have been laid in Arcadia, so devoid they are of sharp factual detail and contemporary reference."[4] In "The Village Blacksmith," "The Building of the Ship," and "The Shoemakers" Longfellow attempts a gentlemanly

treatment of the folklore of American labor. Whatever its errors as to fact, "Paul Revere's Ride" is one of America's best historical ballads, not any too well known even by graduate students and upperclass collegians. And we have had need to remember it. We have need now to remember it, in the faith that

> borne on the night-wind of the Past,
> Through all our history, to the last,
> In the hour of darkness and peril and need,
> The people will waken and listen to hear
> The hurrying hoof-beats of that steed,
> And the midnight message of Paul Revere.

Of the other two members of "The New England Triumvirate," we have space for only a few illustrations. Oliver Wendell Holmes's use of folklore was in the tongue-in-the-cheek mode. "The Stethoscope Song, a Professional Ballad" (1848) and "The Deacon's Masterpiece" are *jeux d'esprit* using the ballad form and some ballad tricks to tell tall tales of a profession and a trade. "The Ballad of the Oysterman" is a barefaced burlesque of the balladeering of his friend Longfellow and others. Holmes would have relished the fact that the folk have taken it seriously, subjecting it to the perils of oral transmission, and that it turns up in some American collections as a "folksong"! "The Broomstick Train; or the Return of the Witches" recalls a formidable amount of New England superstitions and legends to account for the modern black magic of the electric trolley-car. The witches are brought back with their broomsticks to pull the cars:

> As for the hag, you can't see her.
> But hark! you can hear her black cat's purr.
> And now and then, as a car goes by,
> You may catch a gleam from her wicked eye.

(In view of advances in modern urban transportation, one wonders how soon electric trolley cars will seem to us as quaint as witches riding broomsticks!) Holmes's friend Lowell, who admired such "electrical tingles of hit after hit," is significant for his artistic use of folk speech. *The Biglow Papers* (1846 ff.) represent the cracker-barrel philosophy applied to current national issues. They are studded with folk sayings like "I heern him a thrashin round like a short-tailed bull in fli-time" and

> Tain't a knowin kind of cattle
> That is ketched with such moldy corn.

It has been noted that "The humor of Birdofredum, the unmoral trickster and rascal, has deep origins in folklore and appears often in the humor of the Southwest."[5] "The Courtin" is a lovely New England idyl in ballad form and style.

Walt Whitman declared, "I hear America singing, the varied carols I hear"—of mechanics, carpenters, masons, boatmen, shoemakers, wood-cutters, ploughboys, and housewives. Though he did not use the independent folk patterns, he is the Homer of the American folk, absorbing into his epic of self, in allusive form, the stuff of American folklore: "such folk references as the murder of the young men at Goliad, the Western turkey-shooting, coon-seekers going through the regions of the Red River, wooly-pates hoeing in the sugar field, the Missourian crossing the plains toting his wares and his cattle."[6] He records, as part of himself, his being

> At he-festivals, with black-guard jibes, ironical
> license,
> bull-dances, drinking, laughter,
> At the cider-mill tasting the sweets of the brown
> mash,
> sucking the juice through a straw,
> At apple-peelings wanting kisses for all the red
> fruit I find,
> At musters, beach-parties, friendly bees,
> huskings, house-raisings.

He works into his tapestry little ballad-like vignettes of such episodes as "an old-time sea-fight . . . as my grandmother's father the sailor told it to me." Furthermore, his style is marked by such folk devices as the catalogue, parallel structure, incremental repetition, refrain, and folksong echoes like "It was good to gain the day" and "I will go back to Tennessee and never wander any more."

Author of one of the most eloquent tributes to the old ballads, Sidney Lanier wrote two fine imitations, "The Revenge of Hamish" and "A Ballad of Trees and the Master." His dialect pieces, such as "Uncle Jim's Baptist Revival" and "Thar's More in the Men than Thar Is in the Land," though inferior, are closer to current American folksong.

With Bret Harte and John Hay, vernacular poetry in the United States plants its feet solidly on the ground of American folksong. Tickled by "Joe Bowers," they established the vogue of the Pike County ballad with such pieces as "The Heathen Chinee," "Jim Bludso," and "Little Britches." Shortly after this innovation, Irwin Russell, a young Mississippian, showed the possibility of a more authentic poetic treatment of Negro life and character than had hitherto appeared in pseudo-Negro poetry, even at its best in the songs of Stephen Collins Foster. Such poems as Russell's "Christmas Night in the Quarters" owed a part of their effectiveness to the undertones of Negro song and dance. Dialect verse exhibiting the inspiration of folksong and affinities with it constituted an important part of the local color movement. Among the chief practitioners were Will Carleton, James Whitcomb Riley, Eugene Field, and the Canadian Robert W. Service. Coming from the folk, Riley's stuff has gone back to the folk in surreptitiously circulated broadsides.

At the turn of the nineteenth century American scholars were busily collecting folklore and publishing it in more or less popular form. Child and Kittredge at Harvard and Kittredge's pupils were making the results of their labors available to the creative writers.

In the most successful twentieth-century poetry, folklore exploitation is seldom a program. The greatest exception is John S. Neihardt, whose two lays, *The Song of Three Friends* and *The Song of Hugh Glass,* tell hero tales of the American fur trade. Though important, folklore for most contemporary poets is only one of many streams which the poet draws on for inspiration and creation. But its quieter simplicities and its creative power can be traced in much of the best that we read today.

Edwin Arlington Robinson used the ballad form in "Miniver Cheevy" and "Clavering," created authentic folk characters in "Isaac and Archibald," and used both the ballad form and some devices of ballad style in "Mr. Flood's Party." Edgar Lee Masters, though adapting form and technique suggested by the Greek anthology, vividly realizes a whole gallery of folk characters, of whom "Fiddler Jones" is perhaps closest to a recognizable type:

> I ended up with forty acres;
> I ended up with a broken fiddle—
> And a broken laugh, and a thousand memories,
> And not a single regret.

Lucinda Matlock recalls the dances at Chandlerville, when in a change of partners at snap-out she "found Davis," with whom she was to live for seventy years, learning that "It takes life to love life." The humor of "Barney Hainsfeather" turns upon the mistake that occurred after the wreck of the excursion train to Peoria—

> John Allen . . . was sent to the Hebrew Cemetery
> At Chicago,
> And John for me, so I lie here.
> It was bad enough to run a clothing store
> in this town
> But to be buried here—*ach!*

Robert Frost has played with both folk material and form in such pieces as "Brown's Descent or the Willy-Nilly Slide," characterized by Louis Untermeyer as "a tart New England version of 'John Gilpin's Ride,'" and "Paul's Wife," a bit of apocryphal Bunyaniana. To a folk proverb in circulation as early as 1856 Frost owes the most memorable line in "Mending Wall."

Nursed on *Uncle Remus,* Negro songs, and pioneer traditions, Vachel Lindsay reflected his heritage in such poems as "The Congo," "General Booth Enters into Heaven," "My Father Came from Kentucky," "The Statue of Old Andrew Jackson," and "Preface to 'Bob Taylor's Birthday.'" His "Bryan, Bryan, Bryan," derives one of its most effective descriptive stanzas from a catalogue of real, fabulous, and mythological American critters:

> Oh, the longhorns from Texas,
> The jay hawks from Kansas,
> The plop-eyed bungaroo and giant giasiccus,
> The varmint, chipmunk, bugaboo,
> The horned-toad, prairie-dog and ballyhoo,
>
>   . . . . .

The fawn, prodactyl and thing-a-majig,
The rakaboor, the hellangone,
The whangdoodle, batfowl and pig

. . . . .

Against the way of Tubal Cain, too cunning for
   the young,
The longhorn calf, the buffalo, and wampus gave
   tongue.

Lindsay's "The Apple-Barrel of Johnny Appleseed" is a vision of one of the few saints in American hagiology.

Carl Sandburg, singing minstrel, distinguished folksong anthologist, skillful weaver of folk proverbs, owes little to the forms but much to the feeling and the phrase of folk poetry. Of old John Brown he wrote:

They said: You are the fool killer
   You for the booby hatch
   and a necktie party

. . . . .

They laid hands on him
And the fool killers had a laugh
And the necktie party was a go, by God.

Mr. Sandburg once told me that when he was young he wrote many ballads in the folk style, and that in his opinion this was the best sort of exercise to attain mastery of poetic technique.

The best illustrations of the influence of all elements are to be found in the poetry of Stephen Vincent Benét. *John Brown's Body* begins with an "Invocation" that complains of the attempts of previous poets who had sought to capture the spirit of America and tell its stories in the old molds and words.

They tried to fit you with an English song
And clip your speech into the English tale.
But, even from the first, the words went wrong,
The catbird pecked away the nightingale.

. . . . .

Never the running stag, the gull at wing,
The pure elixir, the American thing.

Of his poem the poet declares:

This flesh was seeded from no foreign grain
But Pennsylvania and Kentucky wheat,
And it was soaked in California rain
And five years tempered in New England sleet.

Recognizable grains of wheat are such folksong adaptations as "Blow the Man Down," the spiritual "Oh Lordy Je-sus," the lyric "Since I Was Begotten," the political song of "Thirteen Sisters beside the Sea," "John Brown's Prayer," snatches from "Dixie," "We'll Hang Jeff Davis on a Sour-Apple Tree," recurrent lines from "Foggy Foggy Dew," and dance tunes of Wingate Hall, the exquisite ballad "Love came by from the river smoke," allusions to "The Castle Thunder Men" (which cost me many hours when I was editing a "Deserter's Song" about it in *The Frank C. Brown Collection of North Carolina Folklore*), Stonewall Jackson's dying words, the "Jubilo" song "Sherman's buzzing along to the sea," the various dialects of America, and a hundred anecdotes of the war as they were told by the fireside. These and a thousand more details of the sort enrich the harmonies and color the texture of *John Brown's Body*. Among his shorter pieces, Benét's "The Ballad of William Sycamore" is the incarnation of the pioneer spirit set to a perfect American transposition of the old ballad music. "The Mountain Whippoorwill . . . (A Georgia Romance)" is a capital ballad on a fiddler's contest.

A glance at the work of poets still publishing or but recently dead shows a more oblique and sophisticated handling of folk elements. Wallace Stevens, in "The Comedian as the Letter C," begins:

Nota: Man is the intelligence of the soil,
The sovereign ghost.

Further:

Nota: his soil is man's intelligence.
That's better. That's worth crossing seas to find.

Thus:

The man in Georgia walking among pines
Should be pine-spokesman. The responsive man,
Planting his pristine cores in Florida,
Should prick thereof, not on the psaltery,
But on the banjo's categorical gut,
Tuck, tuck, while the flamingoes flapped his bays.

Thus, too, Stevens resorts to a folk saying to label the meaning of one of his most desolate and despairing poems—"No Possum, No Sop, No Taters." E. E. Cummings' "'All in green went my love riding,'" without using the regular ballad stanza, recaptures, as did Keats and Scott in the traditional form, the glamor of the old chivalric world in the same way as, but more completely than, the ancient fairy ballads like "Tam Lin" and "Thomas Rymer and Queen of Elfland." John Crowe Ransom's "Captain Carpenter" is a macabre *Don Quixote* in ballad measure, with phrasal echoes of "The Twa Corbies" and "Edward." This story of the slowly expendable but hardly educable idealist obtains a dash of its bitter irony from the simplicities of the old ballad. Hart Crane's "The Harbor Dawn" makes its nostalgia and its satire effective with "the sin and slogans of the years," "There's no place like Booneville, though Buddy," and "The myths of her fathers"—

As though the waters breathed that you might
   know
Memphis Johnny, Steamboat Bill, Missouri Joe,

and "Casey Jones" and "Deep River."

Two recent examples will indicate what is being done with the local legend and the ballad. Phelps Putnam's "Ballad of a Strange Thing" tells a story somewhat like the old Pan and Syrinx myth, or, as Shelley told it,

> Singing how down the vale of Maenalus
>   I pursued a maiden and clasped a reed.
> Gods and men, we are all deluded thus.
>   It breaks in our bosom and then we bleed.

But the setting is New England, a bonfire with a ring of cider-drunk Yankees listening to Jack Chance, a "lucid fool" who has drifted "into the township of Pollard Mill" to "sing his bawdy songs" and enchant "A dozen foolish farmers." And the denouement when autumn comes and

> From the black trees, choking the ditches
> And over the seas came sons-of-bitches
> With a hollow quarrel, the talking rats
> Of England and of Europe,

is as strange and remote in time as the girl's turning into a "Shivering graceful sheaf of reeds." The ballad in "A Strange Thing" moves into and out of the authentic setting as naturally as the grace notes on a fiddle. The same casual, easy technique characterizes Robert Penn Warren's "The Ballad of Billie Potts." The story Warren says he heard "from an old lady who was a relative"; and "The scene . . . was in the section of Western Kentucky known as 'Between the Rivers' . . . the Cumberland and the Tennessee." It is a gruesome story of how a rascally couple who keep a backwoods tavern and rob their guests bring up a son to be a highwayman and unwittingly murder him when, years after he has left home in disgrace, he returns boasting of his swag and pretending to be a stranger. The purely narrative part is told with the forthrightness and the brutality of the old murder ballads. But into the simple tale the poet has infused the tragic irony and frustration of man's life "on a doomed and derelict planet":

> You came, weary of greetings and the new
>   friend's smile,
> Weary in the art of the stranger, worn with your
>   wanderer's wile,
> Weary of innocence and the husks of Time,
> Prodigal, back to the homeland of no-Time
> To ask for forgiveness and the patrimony of your
>   crime.

Thus, material and form are only incidental and subordinate to a deeply-realized meaning, as they doubtless were to the Greek tragedians who told the old Oedipus story of how a son killed a father.

These examples, I trust, are sufficient to establish my thesis. From the beginning, folklore has been one of the main ingredients of American poetry. First, it was used in a conscious, conventional, somewhat decorative way, in line with older precedents. Then, as Americans began to think of themselves as Americans, and to feel the need of a mythology, a legendry, and a tradition of their own, they set about their task of inventing or adapting folklore and incorporating it in a synthetic way—they made a cult of it, with results of varying though on the whole inferior merit. Meanwhile, scholars were gathering and publishing American ballads, songs, and tales. It was only when creative artists steeped themselves in the living stream or turned to it as an aspect of their own deeply-realized experience that they achieved complete and successful transmutation. Folklore has been and will continue to be indispensable to most poets, particularly to those who seek to interpret us and our lives to ourselves. Chaucer stated an old truth that he demonstrated in his own art:

> For oute of olde feldys, as men sey,
> Comyth all this newe corn from yere to yere,
> And out of old bokis in good fey,
> Comyth all this newe science that men lere.

As Thomas Mann makes Mai-Sachem, Joseph's wise old jailor, say: "There are, so far as I can see, two kinds of poetry; one springs from folk-simplicity, the other from the literary gift in essence. The second is undoubtedly the higher form. But in my view it cannot flourish cut off from the other, needing it as a plant needs soil."

NOTES

[1] In this and several following paragraphs, I am indebted to the Macmillan Company for permission to make considerable use of my article "Folklore" in *Literary History of the United States,* ed. Robert Spiller, Willard Thorp, *et al.,* 3 vols. (New York: The Macmillan Company, 1948), 715-16, 727.

[2] "The Indian Heritage," *Literary History of the United States,* II, 694.

[3] Odell Shepard, "The New England Triumvirate," *Literary History of the United States,* II, 593.

[4] *Ibid.*

[5] Harold W. Thompson, "Humor," *Literary History of the United States,* II, 736.

[6] Ernest E. Leisy, "Folklore in American Literature," *College English,* VIII (December 1946), 127.

NATIVE AMERICAN LITERATURE

Bernard A. Hirsch

SOURCE: "'The Telling Which Continues': Oral Tradition and the Written Word in Leslie Marmon Silko's 'Storyteller'," in *The American Indian Quarterly,* Vol. XII, No. 1, Winter, 1988, pp. 1-26.

[In the following essay, Hirsch provides an in-depth examination of Leslie Marmon Silko's Storyteller, *a collection of writings in several genres which, the critic suggests, constitutes a piece drawn from a vast, ever-regenerating Laguna Pueblo oral tradition.]*

"I was never tempted to go to those things . . . ," said Leslie Marmon Silko of the old BAE reports. ". . . I . . . don't have to because from the time I was little I heard quite a bit. I heard it in what would be passed now off as rumor or gossip. I could hear through all that. I could hear something else, that there was a kind of continuum. . . . "[2] That continuum provides both the structural and thematic basis of *Storyteller.* Comprised of personal reminiscences and narratives, retellings of traditional Laguna stories, photographs, and a generous portion of her previously published short fiction and poetry, this multigeneric work lovingly maps the fertile storytelling ground from which her art evolves and to which it is here returned—an offering to the oral tradition which nurtured it.[3]

Silko has acknowledged often and eloquently the importance of the oral tradition to her work and tries to embody its characteristics in her writing. This effort, as she well knows, is immensely difficult and potentially dangerous, and this awareness surfaces at several points in *Storyteller.* She recalls, for instance, talking with Nora, whose "grandchildren had brought home / a . . . book that had my 'Laguna coyote' poem in it":

> "We all enjoyed it so much [says Nora]
> but I was telling the children
> the way my grandpa used to tell it
> is longer."
>
> "Yes, that's the trouble with writing," I said.
>
> You can't go on and on the way we do
> when we tell stories around here (p. 110).[4]

"The trouble with writing," in the context Silko here establishes for it, is twofold: first, it is static; it freezes words in space and time. It does not allow the living story to change and grow, as does the oral tradition. Second, though it potentially widens a story's audience, writing removes the story from its immediate context, from the place and people who nourished it in the telling, and thus robs it of much of its meaning.[5] This absence of the story's dynamic context is why, in writing, "You can't go on the way we do / when we tell stories around here."

But Nora does a wonderful thing. She uses Silko's poem to create a storytelling event of her own. In this sense Silko's poem itself becomes a part of the oral tradition and, through Nora's recollection of her grandfather's telling, a means of advancing it as well. The conversation with Nora is important in *Storyteller* because it reminds us of the flexibility and inclusiveness of the oral tradition.[6] Even writing can be made to serve its ends.

Storyteller helps keep the oral tradition strong through Silko's masterful use of the written word, and the photographs, to recall and reestablish its essential contexts. The photographs are important because they reveal something of the particular landscape and community out of which Laguna oral tradition is born, and of specific individuals—of Aunt Susie, Grandma A'mooh, Grandpa Hank, and all those storytellers who have accepted responsibility for "remembering a portion . . . [of] the long story of the people" (p.7). The photographs, however, as Silko uses them, do more than provide a survival record. As we shall see, they involve the reader more fully in the storytelling process itself and, "because they are part of many of the stories / and because many of the stories can be traced in the photographs" (p. 1), they expand the reader's understanding of individual works and also suggest structural and thematic links between them.

The photographs also are arranged to suggest the circular design of *Storyteller,* a design characteristic of oral tradition. The merging of past and present are manifest in the book's design, as is the union of personal, historical, and cultural levels of being and experience, and through such harmonies—and their periodic sundering—the ongoing flux of life expresses itself. The opening photograph, for instance, is of Robert G. Marmon and Marie Anayah Marmon, Silko's great-grandparents, "holding [her] grandpa Hank" (p. 2, 269). The second picture, three pages later, is of Aunt Susie—of whom Silko is the "self-acknowledged, self-appointed heir"[7]—and Leslie Silko herself as a child. These photographs do not merely locate Silko within a genealogical context or even that of an extended family, but within a continuous generational line of Laguna storytellers as well. The last three photographs in the book bring us full circle. The first of these comes at the end of the book's written text; it is of the adult Silko and was taken among the Tucson Mountains where she now lives. The second is of Grandpa Hank as a young man after his return from Sherman Institute, and the third is of three generations preceding her, including her father as a boy, Grandpa Hank's brother, and her great-grandfather. Though there is clearly an autobiographical dimension to *Storyteller,* Silko's arrangement of photographs at the beginning and end of the book subordinates the individual to the communal and cultural. Her life and art compels us, as does the literature itself, to acknowledge the ongoing power of Laguna oral tradition in her writing.

This cyclic design, of course, is not merely a function of the arrangement of photographs. It derives primarily from the episodic structure of *Storyteller* and the accretive process of teaching inherent in it. Each individual item is a narrative episode in itself which relates to other such episodes in various ways. Oral storytelling, Walter J. Ong tells us, "normally and naturally operated in episodic patterning . . . episodic structure was the natural way to talk out a lengthy story line if only because the experience of real life is more like a string of episodes than it is like a Freytag pyramid";[8] and it is real life, "the long story of the people," that is Silko's concern. Moreover, the telling of her portion of the story, and of the individual stories which comprise it, involves, like all oral storytelling, a teaching process, one in which the varieties of genre and voice Silko uses are essential.

In *Storyteller,* the reader learns by accretion. Successive narrative episodes cast long shadows both forward and back, lending different or complementary shades of meaning to those preceding them and offering perspectives from which to consider those that follow. Such perspectives are then themselves often expanded or in some way altered as the new material reflects back upon them. This kind of learning process is part of the dynamic of oral tradition. Silko uses it in *Storyteller* to foster the kind of intimacy with the reader that the oral storyteller does with the listener. Such a relationship is born of both the powerful claims of the story, in whole and in part, on the reader's attention and the active engagement by the accretive process of the reader's imagination. This process in effect makes the reader's responses to the various narrative episodes a part of the larger, ongoing story these episodes comprise while simultaneously allowing the episodes to create the contexts which direct and refine these responses. In this way the stories continue; in this way both the story and the reader are renewed.

It is impossible within the limits of this paper to explore the workings of this process over the entire length of *Storyteller,* yet the interrelationships between the various narrative episodes and photographs throughout is so rich and intricate that any attempt to formally divide the work into sections or categories would be arbitrary at best, of necessity reductive, and at worst misleading. Still, there are groups of narrative episodes that seem to cluster around particular themes and cultural motifs which I believe can be meaningfully seen as representative of the overall design and method of the book.

II

N. Scott Momaday has said: "We are what we imagine. Our very existence consists in our imagination of ourselves. . . . The greatest tragedy that can befall us is to go unimagined."[9] It is apparent throughout *Storyteller* that Silko would agree, and she reminds us that in the oral tradition, "sometimes what we call 'memory' and what we call 'imagination' are not so easily distinguished" (p. 227). In "The Storyteller's Escape," the old storyteller's greatest fear as she waits for death is that she will go unremembered—unimagined. *Storyteller* itself is a self-renewing act of imagination/memory designed to keep storytellers as well as stories from so tragic a fate. The book's opening section, which I will arbitrarily call the "Survival" section (pp. 1-53), establishes this particular concern.[10] Embracing 5 reminiscences, 4 photographs, 2 traditional Laguna stories, the short stories "Storyteller" and "Lullaby," and the poem "Indian Song: Survival," this section explores

from various angles the dynamics and meaning of survival, both personal and cultural, for tribal people in contemporary America.

Silko visually establishes continuity through the photographs. The first two, described earlier, reveal in their depiction of three generations of Silko's family genealogical continuity, but especially important in primarily the second and third photos is the idea of cultural transmission. Such transmission involves more than the passing of stories from generation to generation, essential as that is. It involves the entire context within which such passing occurs, and this includes both the land and the relationship, beyond blood ties, between teller and hearer. That is why, to tell the story correctly, Silko must bring us into the storytellers' presence, to let us somehow see them, learn something of their histories, and most of all, to hear them tell their stories.

These elements are certainly present in the book's title story, "Storyteller," which is at the hub not only of the "Survival" section but of the book as a whole. Explaining, in Silko's words, "the dimensions of the process" of storytelling, this tale, set not in Laguna but in Inuit country near Bethel, Alaska,[11] is at once dark and hopeful, embracing all that has come before it in the book and establishing both the structure and primary thematic concerns of what follows. It is a tale of multiple journeys that become one journey expressed through multiple stories that become one story. At its center is a young Eskimo girl, orphaned, living with a lecherous and dying old man, the village storyteller, and his wife, victimized by Gussuck and "assimilated" Eskimo men, and determined to avenge herself against the Gussuck storekeeper responsible for her parents' death.

Speaking of his use of "three distinct narrative voices in *The Way to Rainy Mountain*—the mythical, the historical, and the immediate"—Momaday says: "Together, they serve, hopefully, to validate the oral tradition to an extent that might not otherwise be possible."[12] A similar mix of voices occurs in "Storyteller"—indeed, throughout the book as a whole—and to similar effect. Against the backdrop of the prophesied coming of a "final winter," the girl comes of age and the old man, the mythic voice, begins his story of the great bear pursuing the lone hunter across the ice.

He tells the story lovingly, nurturing every detail with his life's breath, because it is the story that makes his death meaningful. The story is an expression of sacred natural processes, ancient and unending, of which his death is a part, processes Silko will treat later in the book in such works as "The Man to Send Rain Clouds" and the poem "Deer Song." But most importantly the story, in the intensely beautiful precision of the old man's telling, becomes the girl's legacy, a powerful vision by which she can unify the disparate aspects of her experience to create herself anew in profoundly significant cultural terms.

She recalls having asked her grandmother, the old man's wife, about her parents, and her grandmother told how the Gussuck storeman traded them bad liquor. The grandmother is the historical voice. Her story and that of the giant bear become linked in the girl's imagination. Once, while listening "to the old man tell the story all night," she senses her grandmother's spirit. "It will take a long time," the old woman tells her, "but the story must be told. There must not be any lies." At first, she thinks that the spirit is referring to the bear story. She "did not know about the other story then" (p. 26).

This "other story" is in truth the conclusion of her grandmother's story, a conclusion that will make it the girl's story. As it stands, in the inaction of civil and religious authorities and in the storeman's continued existence, the story of her parent's death has not been properly told. The story is life and in life it must be completed. And the story of the giant bear "stalking a lone hunter across the Bering Sea ice" tells her how. "She spent days walking on the river," getting to know the ice as precisely as the old man had described it in his story, learning "the colors of ice that would safely hold her" and where the ice was thin. She already knew that the storeman wanted her and thus it is easy for her to lure him out onto the river and to his death. Though he appeared to chase her out onto the ice, it was she who was the bear.

The attorney wants her to change her story, to tell the court that "it was an accident," but she refuses, even though to follow his advice would mean freedom (p. 31). Hers is the "immediate" voice, the voice that carries the old stories into the present and locates the present within the cycle of mythic time. Through the story, life derives purpose and meaning and experience becomes comprehensible; also through the story, and through her fidelity to it, the girl recreates herself from the fragments of her own history.

Her emergence whole and intact from her experience is, in this respect, like Tayo's emergence in Silko's 1977 novel *Ceremony,* a victory for her people;[13] given the immediate context in which the title story is placed in *Storyteller,* it is, like all stories in the oral tradition, a ritual. The girl's role as a culture-bearer, for example, receives significant emphasis from the surrounding material.

Following "Storyteller" there is a picture of Marie Anayah Marmon, Grandma A'mooh, reading to two of her great granddaughters, Silko's sisters. She is reading, apparently, from *Brownie the Bear,* a book, we later learn, she read many times, not only to her great-granddaughters but to Silko's uncles and father. Accompanying this photograph is a reminiscence about Grandma A'mooh, whose name Silko, as a child, deduced from the woman's continual use of "'a'moo'ooh' / . . . the Laguna expression of endearment / for a young child / spoken with great feeling and love" (p. 34). That love is evident on the faces of the old woman and the little girls; it is also clear that although she is not in this

captured moment telling a story from the oral tradition, she has turned the occasion, much as Nora did with the printed version of Silko's coyote poem, into a rich oral storytelling experience.

We come to the title story by way of several other narrative episodes, beginning with Silko's brief reminiscence and history of Aunt Susie, her father's aunt. Aunt Susie

> was of a generation
> the last generation here at Laguna,
> that passed down an entire culture
> by word of mouth
> an entire history
> an entire vision of the world . . . (pp. 4-6).

In its rhythms and repetitions, Silko's telling here assumes the quality of a chant and in this she reinforces not only Aunt Susie's role as culture-bearer but her own as Aunt Susie's cultural heir. Their relationship provides a necessary context within which to consider the girl and the old man in the title story. That relationship is complicated in several ways, but this context, along with the photograph that follows "Storyteller," highlights her role as the storyteller-successor to the old man.

For Silko, how a story is told is inseparable from the story itself. The old man's bear story exerts its hold on the girl's imagination through his intensely precise, chant-like, dramatic telling and retelling of it. Silko recalls a child's story Aunt Susie told about a "little girl who ran away," and she insists that we hear it as Aunt Susie told it: "She had certain phrases, certain distinctive words / she used in her telling. / I write when I still hear / her voice as she tells the story" (p. 7). In her own telling Silko uses poetic form with varying line-lengths, stresses, and enjambment to provide some of the movement and drama of oral storytelling. She also provides several italicized expository passages to evoke the digressive mode of traditional storytellers and the conversational texture of their speech. When the little girl asks for "yashtoah," for example, we are told that

> "Yashtoah" is the hardened crust on corn meal
>   mush
> that curls up.
> The very name "yashtoah" means
> it's sort of curled up, you know, dried,
> just as mush dries on top (p. 8).

"This is the beauty of the old way," Silko has said. "You can stop the storyteller and ask questions and have things explained."[14]

Aunt Susie's story, in some respects, is a sad one about a little girl who, feeling unloved because she does not get what she wants, decides to drown herself. Attempts by a kindly old man and her mother to save her fail and the child drowns. Grieving, the mother returns to Acoma where, standing on a high mesa, she scatters the girl's clothes to the four directions—and "they all turned into butterflies— / all colors of butterflies" (p. 15).

This is a child's story and whatever truths it may teach it should evoke the child's capacity for wonder and delight. Aunt Susie succeeded brilliantly in this respect. She brought the characters to life, the mother's tenderness and the prophetic foreboding of the old man "that implied the tragedy to come":

> But when Aunt Susie came to the place
> where the little girl's clothes turned into
>   butterflies
> then her voice would change and I could hear the
>   excitement
> and wonder
> and the story wasn't sad any longer (p. 15).

The child learns something of pain through such a story, but she learns too of life's perpetuity, that from death itself can emerge beautiful life. She learns of the delicate balance in which all things exist, a balance forever threatened and forever renewed.

But harsh realities, having been delicately yet honestly prepared for by Aunt Susie's story, dominate, appropriately enough, the two recollections leading directly into "Storyteller." The first offers a brief history of Silko's great-grandparents, and we learn that Robert G. Marmon married a Pueblo woman and "learned to speak Laguna"; but "when great-grandpa went away from Laguna / white people who knew / sometimes called him 'Squaw Man'" (p. 16). The second recollection is of the Albuquerque hotel incident in which Marmon's two young sons, because they are Indians, were not permitted in the hotel.

"Storyteller," is fed by the various motifs and concerns of the narratives leading into it and it recasts them in new ways. In that sense it is as much a retelling as an original telling. It is not merely a story of survival but, like the bear story within it, a survival story itself. It is unsparing in its treatment of the nature and consequences of discrimination and unqualified in its vision of the capacity of oral tradition not merely to survive discrimination but to use it as a source of power. However, as the narratives that follow "Storyteller" suggest, the oral tradition is only as strong—or as fragile—as the memories that carry it and the relationships that sustain it.

Silko's remembrance of Grandma A'mooh, which follows "Storyteller," is warm and moving, yet painful as well. Grandma A'mooh, as her name suggests, was love itself to Silko. She loved the land, her people, her granddaughters, and the stories that evolved from them, yet it was thought best, in her later years, to remove her from all that sustained her and have her live with her daughter in Albuquerque. The daughter had to work, so much of the time Grandma A'mooh was alone—"she did not last long," Silko tells us, "without someone to talk to" (p. 35).

"Indian Song: Survival," like the narrative episodes which precede it, concerns what survival is and what is needed to survive, but it considers these ideas from a somewhat different perspective than the others. It is in the first-person and this heightens the intimacy of the sustaining relationship of the individual with the land the poem explores. The poem moves in a sequence of spare yet sensual images which express at once the elemental and regenerating power of this relationship, and Silko's versification, like that of most of the poetry in *Storyteller,* is alive with motion and the subtle interplay of sound and silence. It is a "desperation journey north" (p. 36) she describes, but it is marked by neither panic nor haste.

"Mountain lion," Silko writes, "shows me the way." He is her guide as he has been for Laguna hunters throughout the time, and his presence helps to establish the true nature of this journey. It is a journey to reestablish old ties, ties essential to survival in any meaningful sense. As the journey continues the "I" becomes more inclusive as the speaker becomes increasingly able to merge with the nature around her. Asked at poem's end "if I still smell winter / . . . I answer:"

> taste me
>   I am the wind
> touch me,
>   I am the lean brown deer
> running on the edge of the rainbow (p. 37).

The "desperation journey" has become a journey of self-discovery, of finding one's being entire in the land. Now she can travel spirit roads.

The wholeness of the relationship emerging from "Indian Song: Survival" enhances our understanding of what, precisely, the young girl in "Storyteller" accomplishes. Her life has been a desperate journey and her final awakening involves the reestablishment of a vital, intimate connection to the land. This is what the bear story requires of her. The poem also intensifies further the poignancy of Grandma A'mooh's last days by compelling us to learn again the value of what, for her own "good," had been taken from her.

Silko follows "Indian Song: Survival" with a painfully enigmatic story from Aunt Susie, a Laguna "flood" story in which a little girl and her younger sister return home to their village after a day's play only to find it abandoned except for "the old people / who cannot travel" (p. 40). Their mother and the others went to the high place to escape the coming flood. If "Indian Song: Survival" concerns the establishment of vital relationships, this story tells of their being sundered. There is a beauty in the girl's devotion to her sister as there is pain in their mother's leaving them and these elements, devotion and separation, are central to the short story, "Lullaby," which follows.

If, as Momaday said, the greatest tragedy is to go unimagined, the title of Silko's "Lullaby" is in one sense bitterly ironic. Having been robbed of her grandchildren, Ayah, the old Navajo woman at the heart of the story, sings a song for them, a song that she remembers having been sung by her mother and grandmother. It is a beautiful song expressing with delicate economy the world view in which she was raised, and its closing words doubtlessly provide some consolation:

> We are together always
> We are together always
> There never was a time
> when this
> was not so (p. 51).

But we cannot forget that there are no children to hear it and, though Ayah's "life had become memories," those memories seem dominated now by the loss of children—of her son Jimmie in the war and the babies to the white doctors. For Silko, to go unremembered is to go unimagined, and in that sense Ayah's is a tragic story. Grandma A'mooh, in her last years, was taken from her grandchildren but she does not go unremembered. Such a fate, though, seems likely to befall Ayah, for her babies are taken not simply to make them well, but to make them white.

The "Survival" section, however, does not end on a hopeless note. Ayah's "lullaby" expresses a timeless harmony and peace which are reflected in the photograph which closes the section, taken from the sandhills a mile east of Laguna. The land seems whole and eternal here, and where that is so the people, and the oral tradition, will survive.

III

But today, even the land is threatened. A photograph in what I will call the "Yellow Woman" section of *Storyteller* (pp. 54-99) is of the Anaconda company's open-pit uranium mine (p. 80). "This photograph," Silko tells us, "was made in the early 1960s. The mesas and hills that appear in the background and foreground are gone now, swallowed by the mine" (p. 270). This photograph deepens our understanding of many things in *Storyteller*: of the importance of the photographs to the stories, for one thing, and of Silko's father's love of photography for another. "He is still most at home in the canyons and sandrock," she says, "and most of his life regular jobs/have been a confinement he has avoided" (p. 160). Some might think less of him for this, but Silko stifles this tendency—first by the story of Reed Woman and Corn Woman that precedes the reminiscence about her father (pp. 158-159) and second by his photographs themselves, one of which is that of the now vanished mesas and hills. Moreover, his photography intensified his love of the land and enabled him to relate to it in new and fulfilling ways. We learn, for instance, that

> His landscapes could not be done
> without certain kinds of clouds—
>   some white and scattered like river rock
>   and others
>   mountains rolling into themselves
>   swollen lavender before rainstorms (p. 161).

Clouds, as we know, are a source of life itself to the land, and for Lee H. Marmon they bring to it a profound and varied beauty as well. Essential to the continuity of physical life, the clouds are no less essential to his spirit in that they help him express through his art his particular vision of the land and by so doing, to define himself in terms of it. Equally important, in these times, is that his artistry can help others, be they Indians removed from the land or people who have never known it, to develop a richer, more meaningful sense of the land than is held by such as those who run Anaconda. It is precisely the development of such a relationship—to the land, to the spirits that pervade it, and to the stories that derive from it—that occupies the "Yellow Woman" section of *Storyteller*.

The "Yellow Woman" section, comprised of the short story "Yellow Woman," 4 poems, poetic retellings of two traditional stories, 4 reminiscences, 4 photographs, and 2 "gossip stories,"[15] is framed by "Yellow Woman" and "Storytelling," a poem consisting of six brief vignettes based on the abduction motif of the traditional Yellow Woman stories. As does "Storyteller" in the "Survival" section, "Yellow Woman," and the traditional stories from which Silko's version evolves, establish the primary structural and thematic concerns of this section.

Based on the traditional stories in which Yellow Woman, on her way to draw water, is abducted by a mountain kachina, Silko's "Yellow Woman" concerns the development of the visionary character. This is hinted at in the story's epigram, "What Whirlwind Man Told Kochininako, Yellow Woman":

> I myself belong to the wind
> and so it is we will travel swiftly
> this whole world
> with dust and with windstorms (p. 54).[16]

Whirlwind Man will take her on a journey beyond the boundaries of time and place, a journey alive with sensation and danger which promises a perspective from which she can see the world new and entire. This in effect is what happens in the story. Like the prophets and visionaries of many cultures, Indian and non-Indian, the narrator travels to the mountain where she learns to see beyond the range of mundane experience. She recalls that, at Silva's mountain cabin,

> I was standing in the sky with nothing around me
> but the wind that came down from the blue
> mountain peak behind me. I could see faint
> mountain images in the distance miles across the
> vast spread of mesas and valleys and plains. I
> wondered who was over there to feel the mountain
> wind on those sheer blue edges—who walks on the
> pine needles in those blue mountains.
> "Can you see the pueblo?" Silva was standing
> behind me.
> I shook my head. "We're too far away."
> "From here I can see the world" (p. 57).

The pueblo, which comprised her whole world before, is, from the perspective of the mountain, but a barely discernible part of a much larger whole. With Silva, on the mountain, she has entered the more expansive and truer realm of imagination and myth.

When we can see imaginatively, William Blake has said, when we can see not merely with but through the eye, "the whole creation will appear infinite and holy whereas it now appears finite and corrupt. This will come to pass by an improvement of sensual enjoyment" (*The Marriage of Heaven and Hell,* plate 14).[17] This is the narrator's experience. She follows a strong impulse in running off with Silva; desire moves her to leave the familiar, secure world of the pueblo and her family to walk a new and daring road. She opens her story in the morning, after she and Silva first made love:

> My thigh clung to his with dampness, and I
> watched the sun rising up through the tamaracks
> and willows . . . I could hear the water, almost at
> our feet where the narrow fast channel bubbled
> and washed green ragged moss and fern leaves.
> I looked at him beside me, rolled in the red
> blanket on the white river sand (p. 54).

She does not awaken to the proverbial harsh light of morning awash in guilt, but to a newly, more vibrantly alive world of sensation within and around her. But this is a world which, like Silva himself, is as frightening in its strength and intensity as it is seductive, and when Silva awakens she tells him she is leaving:

> He smiled now, eyes still closed. "You are
> coming with me, remember?" He sat up now with
> his bare dark chest and belly in the sun.
> "Where?"
> "To my place."
> "And will I come back?"
> He pulled his pants on. I walked away from
> him, feeling him behind me and smelling the
> willows.
> "Yellow Woman," he said.
> I turned to face him, "Who are you?" I asked.

Last night, he reminds her, "you guessed my name, and you knew why I had come" (p. 55). Their lovemaking made her intuitively aware of another, more vital level of being, one which had been within her all along, nurtured since childhood by her grandfather's Yellow Woman stories—and she knew she was Yellow Woman and her lover the dangerous mountain ka'tsina who carries her off.

But imaginative seeing on this morning after is threatening to the narrator, for seeing oneself whole demands eradication of those perceptual boundaries which offer the security of a readily discernible, if severely limited, sense of self. The narrator clings to that historical, time-bound sense of self like a child to her mother's skirts on the first day of school. "I'm not really her," she maintains, not really Yellow Woman. "I have my own name and I come from the pueblo on the other side of the mesa" (p. 55). It is not so much "confusion about what is dream and what is fact"[18] that besets her here as it is

the fear of losing that reality which has heretofore defined her—and him. As they walk she thinks to herself:

> I will see someone, eventually I will see
> someone, and then I will be certain that he
> [Silva] is only a man—some man from nearby—and
> I will be sure that I am not Yellow Woman.
> Because she is from out of time past and I live
> now and I've been to school and there are
> highways and pickup trucks that Yellow Woman
> never saw (p. 56).

Jim Ruppert is right, I think, when he says that the narrator "struggles to . . . establish time boundaries and boundaries between objective reality and myths,"[19] and that struggle is part of the learning process she undergoes in the story. Newly awakened to her own imaginative potential, she has yet to discern the proper relationship between experiential reality and the timeless, all-inclusive mythic reality of her grandfather's stories.

Her desire, however, is stronger than her fear. After they reach his cabin, eat, and she looks out over the world from the mountain, Silva unrolls the bedroll and spreads the blankets. She hesitates, and he slowly undresses her. There is compulsion, this time, on his part, and fear on hers, but she is held to him more by her own passion than by his force. When she does leave, during their confrontation with a rancher who, rightly, accuses Silva of stealing cattle, it is at his command. "I felt sad at leaving him," she recalls, and considers going back, "but the mountains were too far away now. And I told myself, because I believe it, that he will come back sometime and be waiting again by the river" (p. 62).

She returns home. Yellow Woman stories usually end that way. And as she approaches her house, A. Lavonne Ruoff tells us, "she is brought back to the realities of her own life by the smell of supper cooking and the sight of her mother instructing her grandmother in the Anglo art of making Jell-O."[20] The details here suggest a world governed more by routine than by passion, a world somewhat at odds with itself, as mother instructing grandmother suggests, and a world no longer receptive to the wonder and wisdom of the old stories. Having sensed this, she "decided to tell them that some Navajo had kidnapped me" (p. 62). But the unnamed narrator here, like the unnamed Eskimo girl in "Storyteller," keeps the oral tradition alive by going on her own journey of self-discovery—a journey born of acknowledging the rightful demands of passion and imagination—and by intuitively accepting the guidance of her grandfather's stories. Her life itself has become part of a visionary drama to be completed by Silva's return, and within that context it has gained fullness and meaning. Her recognition, in the story's final sentence, that hers is a Yellow Woman story—and that she is Yellow Woman—reveals as much. She has come to see herself, in Momaday's words, "whole and eternal"[21] and like Momaday when, on his journey, he came out upon the northern plains, she will "never again . . . see things as [she] saw them yesterday or the day before."[22]

Cottonwood, which follows "Yellow Woman," is in two parts, each a poetic rendering of a Laguna Yellow Woman story; taken together, these poems and Silko's story provide a richer, more inclusive perspective than they do separately on both the relationship between oral tradition and the written word and Silko's use of the Yellow Woman character.

The focus in "Yellow Woman" is on the unnamed woman narrator. She tells her own story, which concerns her evolving consciousness of who she is, and though that story has definite communal implications, its focus is interior and personal. *Cottonwood,* however, though undeniably Silko's creation,[23] derives directly from the oral tradition and retains that tradition's communal perspective. Neither "Story of Sun House" nor "Buffalo Story," the poems that comprise *Cottonwood,* deal with character development or internal conflict any more than do the stories on which they are based. Rather each poem underscores the communal consequences of Yellow Woman's action, and in each case those consequences are positive. Given the narrator's references within "Yellow Woman" to the grandfather's Yellow Woman stories—indeed, Silko's story ends with such a reference—the *Cottonwood* poems, placed where they are, suggest that however offensive her actions may be to conventional morality, the narrator brings from her journey with Silva a boon for her people.

"Story of Sun House" ends as follows: "Cottonwood, / cottonwood. / So much depends / upon one in the great canyon" (p. 67). It is this tree, "among all the others" (p. 63) where Yellow Woman came to wait for the sun. Like the lone cottonwood, Yellow Woman too has been singled out, and much depends upon her as well. She is called by the Sun to journey to Sun House, and this involves the loss of what is familiar and secure and dear:

> She left precise stone rooms
> that hold the heart silently
> She walked past white corn
> hung in long rows from roof beams
> the dry husks rattled in a thin autumn wind.
>
> She left her home
> her clan
> and the people
>   (three small children
>   the youngest just weaned
>   her husband away cutting firewood) (p. 64).

The sacrifice is great, and in the spare yet powerfully evocative images of these lines Silko conveys the intense pain of separation. Her versification here, with "home," "clan," and "people" isolated in separate lines and children and husband further isolated in parentheses to the right, makes such pain almost palpable, as does the southeastward movement of the verse as it mirrors her journey toward the sun. Such "drastic things," however, "must be done / for the world / to continue" (p. 65). Harmony between the people and the spirit powers of the universe is necessary to existence and, through her

marriage to the Sun, Yellow Woman perpetuates this harmony. The "people may not understand" her going (p. 64); the visionary is invariably misunderstood. But that does not deter her, for she goes "out of love for this earth" (p. 65).

The narrator in "Yellow Woman," too, restores an essential harmony through her going—a going which is also likely to be misunderstood. Her experience in living the reality revealed in her grandfather's stories has shown her the oneness of past and present, of historical and mythic time, and of the stories and the people. More, she has given the people another story and that, too, "must be done / for the world / to continue" (p. 65).

Yellow Woman brings about good in "Buffalo Story" as well, and in a sense its link with Silko's short story is even stronger than that of "Story of Sun House." Like "Sun House," it enriches the short story by locating it for the reader within the necessary cultural and communal context, but "Buffalo Story" is itself enriched by the individualistic perspective cast forward upon it by "Yellow Woman." "Buffalo Story" follows the abduction storyline somewhat more closely than does "Story of Sun House" and evokes the sexual aspects of the traditional Yellow Woman stories more insistently. During a time of drought, when game is scarce and crops cannot grow, Yellow Woman, looking for water for her family, comes to a churning, muddy pool. At first she fears that a great animal had fouled the water. Then

> she saw him.
> She saw him tying his leggings
> drops of water were still shining on his chest.
> He was very good to look at
> and she kept looking at him
> because she had never seen anyone like him.
> It was Buffalo Man who was very beautiful (p. 69).

She has ventured far from her village, as has the narrator in "Yellow Woman," and the intense sexual pull Buffalo Man has on her here recalls that of Silva on the narrator. When Arrowboy, her husband, finds her asleep and calls to her to run to him so that they might escape the Buffalo People, to whose country Buffalo Man had abducted her, "She seemed to / get up a little slowly / but he didn't think much of it then" (p. 72). Her slowness here, he later learns, is not due to fatigue. After he kills all the Buffalo People, he tells Yellow Woman to go tell the people that there is meat, but she refuses to come down from the cottonwood which they had climbed to escape the Buffalo People's pursuit. Arrowboy sees that she is crying and asks her why:

> "Because you killed them,"
>   she said.
> "I suppose you love them,"
>   Estoy-eh-muut [Arrowboy] said,
> "and you want to stay with them."
> And Kochininako nodded her head
> and then he killed her too (p. 75).

Paula Gunn Allen, while acknowledging the underlying centrality of oral tradition in the lives of tribal people, nonetheless maintains that "the oral tradition is often deceptive in what it makes of the lives of women." She says that

> so cleverly disguised are the tales of matricide, abduction and humiliation that the Indian woman is likely to perceive consciously only the surface message of the beauty, fragility, and self-sacrificing strength of her sisters though she cannot help but get the more destructive message that is the point of many tribal tales.[24]

Such a "destructive message" is at least potentially present in the "Buffalo Man" story in Boas' *Keresan Texts,* but Silko casts the killing of Yellow Woman in "Buffalo Story" in a much different light. In Boas' version, when Arrowboy explains to Yellow Woman's father why he killed her, the Chief says, "Indeed? . . ." "All right," said he, "never mind." His response seems to justify the killing.[25] In "Buffalo Story" her father, though implicitly accepting the justice of what was done, cries and mourns. Moreover, in Silko's rendering we are told that "It was all because / one time long ago / our daughter, our sister Kochininako / went away with them" that the people were fed and buffalo hunting began (p. 76). Yellow Woman here is not an adultress who deserted her people but rather remains "our daughter, our sister" whose journey, like her journey in "Story of Sun House," brought good to her people.[26]

The context here established by the written word—Silko's short story—is essential in helping us to see Yellow Woman more completely than do the traditional stories alone, just as those stories in turn provide the necessary cultural context for "Yellow Woman." Through the narrator's telling in Silko's story, the individual dimension predominates and personal longings are shown to be as powerful and worthwhile as communal needs. Silko well knows, as the *Cottonwood* poems make clear, that individual sacrifice is at times crucial to community survival. But, as "Yellow Woman" reveals, individual fulfillment can be equally important to a tribal community, especially in the modern world where acculturation pressures are perhaps greater than ever before. Silko shows us, in this opening sequence of the "Yellow Woman" section, that personal and communal fulfillment need not be mutually exclusive—that they in fact enhance each other. And, by extension, the same is true of oral tradition and the written word as ways of knowing and of expression. To attain this harmony requires a powerful and inclusive vision, one receptive both to internal and external demands and the diverse languages which give them meaning. The development of such a vision, and of the network of relationships to the land, the people, the stories, and oneself it fosters, is, as I have said, the controlling idea of what I have called the "Yellow Woman" section of *Storyteller,* and it is expressed in various ways in the narrative episodes that follow.

The five short pieces that follow "Yellow Woman" and the *Cottonwood* poems focus on learning to see the land rightly and developing the proper relationship to it. This learning process is implicit in the narrator's experience in "Yellow Woman," both in her journey with Silva up the mountain and in the precise, evocative detail in which she describes particular aspects of the landscape; it becomes refined and expanded in these brief narratives. In the first one, a poem entitled "The Time We Climbed Snake Mountain," the narrator is a teacher who knows the mountain intimately and knows that "Somewhere around here / yellow spotted snake is sleeping": "So / please, I tell them / watch out, / don't step on the spotted yellow snake / he lives here. / The mountain is his" (p. 77). "Them" are never identified, but that is unimportant because this kind of teaching has been going on for thousands of years. It is a simple lesson in perspective and respect.

What follows is a personal reminiscence which in a different way reinforces this lesson. It is of Silko's girlhood when she first learned to hunt, and through her telling we learn something of how she began to acquire the wisdom she hands down in "The Time We Climbed Snake Mountain." Hunting alone one day Silko saw, or thought she saw, a "giant brown bear lying in the sun below the hilltop. Dead or just sleeping, I couldn't tell" (p. 77). She "knew there were no bears that large on Mt. Taylor; I was pretty sure there were no bears that large anywhere" (p. 78), and she also knew "what hours of searching for motion, for the outline of a deer, for the color of a deer's hide can do to the imagination" (p. 77). Almost paralyzed with caution and curiosity, eager to examine the bear up close but unsure if it is dead or is just sleeping or is at all, she walks, "as quietly and as carefully as I probably will ever move," away from it. As she goes she looks back, still unsure of what she has seen, and "the big dark bear remained there. . . ." "I never told anyone what I had seen," Silko laughingly recalls, "because I knew they don't let people who see such things carry .30-30s or hunt deer with them" (p. 78).

That the bear impressed itself deeply on her imagination, however, is apparent as she recalls another hunting trip which took place two years after the first one. Her uncle had killed a big mule deer, and, as Silko went to help him, she realized that it was the same time of day as when she saw, or thought she saw, the bear:

> I walked past the place deliberately.
> I found no bones, but when a wind moved
>   through the
> light yellow grass that afternoon I hurried
>   around the
> hill to find my uncle.
> Sleeping, not dead, I decided (p. 79).

At this point, there is no longer any doubt in her mind that the bear was real; and her use of poetic form further suggests that this place where she saw the great bear has become part of an inner as well as an outer landscape.

Through an act of imagination she has learned a profound truth from the land which intensifies her bond to it.

The photograph which separates these two reminiscences reinforces this idea. In it, laid out on the porch of the old cabin in which Silko and her hunting party stayed on Mt. Taylor, are five mule deer bucks, prayer feathers tied to their antlers, Silko herself, and her Uncle Polly (p. 78). She and her uncle had just finished "arranging the bucks . . . so they can have their pictures taken" (p. 270). Given the "special significance" of photographs to her family and to the people of Laguna (p. 1), the careful arrangement of the deer, and the prayer feathers, we are prepared for the subtle revelation in her second reminiscence. Her vision of the bear, like the deer, was a gift to help the people survive. It was the intimate expression of the land to her imagination of its own spiritual integrity and that of its creatures. Through the mystery and wonder of her seeing, the land, impressed itself indelibly upon her memory.

Two photographs follow the second bear reminiscence. The first, discussed earlier, is of hills and mesas that no longer exist and, placed where it is in *Storyteller,* the photograph movingly conveys the need, more important now than ever before, for all people to know the land as the place that gives us being and the source of our profoundest wisdom. It reminds us, as does *Storyteller* as a whole, about the oral tradition—of the fragility of what was once thought whole and eternal and of how much all life ultimately depends on imagination and memory. The second photo, taken from the east edge of Laguna looking toward the west, enhances this idea by showing us the place from which the stories in *Storyteller,* old and contemporary, arise. What follows is a series of such stories and reminiscences unified not by subject or theme but by the shared landscape that nurtured them. They express the richness, diversity, playfulness and humor of Laguna oral tradition. Like the first of these two photographs, they also express its fragility.

The first story which follows these photographs is a poetic retelling of a hunting story Silko, when a child of seven, heard from her Aunt Alice. It flows smoothly out of the photograph of Laguna in that it endows a particular portion of the land with mystery and wonder, and by so doing makes it a gift of and to the imagination. Though she heard this story six years before she saw the great bear on a hunting trip, the story flows out of her recollection of this experience as well; and by using cyclic rather than chronological structure, she more strikingly evokes, as with the "Yellow Woman" and *Cottonwood* sequence, the timeless significance of the oral tradition to the understanding of human experience. Told, as are other such stories in the book, in the conversational accents and occasional expository digressions of the traditional storyteller, the story is again of Yellow Woman, here a young girl and a fine hunter who, having gotten seven big rabbits in a morning's hunting, comes upon "a great big animal" who asks for one of her rabbits, which he immediately devours (p. 83).

The animal's demands escalate with his appetite and they are rendered by Silko in a compellingly dramatic sequence as the animal, having demanded and received all the girl's rabbits and weapons, insists upon her clothes as well. Rightly fearful that she herself will be next, little Yellow Woman fools the animal into letting her remove her clothes in a cave too small for him to enter. Knowing, however, that her escape is at best temporary, she calls upon the twin Brothers, Ma'see'wi and Ou'yu'ye'wi, who kill the animal with their flint knives. They then cut the animal open, pull out his heart, and throw it. At this point in the telling the legend melds with contemporary reality, myth enters experience, as we are told that the heart landed "right over here / near the river / between Laguna and Paguate / where the road turns to go / by the railroad tracks / right around / from John Paisano's place— / that big rock there / looks just like a heart, / . . . and that's why / it is called / Yash'ka / which means 'heart'" (pp. 87-88).

By telling this story to her seven-year-old niece, who is disappointed at not having been allowed to join her parents on a hunting trip, Aunt Alice both entertains and teaches. She raises the child's self-esteem by showing her that young girls can be skillful and clever hunters, alerts the prospective young hunter to the unexpected dangers that at times confront a hunter, reassures her that such obstacles, however dangerous, may be overcome, and perhaps most importantly, helps her niece to see the land with the same sense of wonder and joy with which she heard the story. A part of the landscape heretofore ordinary and unremarked has by means of the story been made precious to the child. Six years later, when she sees the giant bear, Silko will have her own hunting story to tell—and Aunt Alice's story will be recalled anew, recreated as it is here, richer and truer than ever.

The story told by a loving aunt of a special place engenders a reminiscence of another place which is special because of the woman who may, or may not, be buried there. With this reminiscence Silko shifts her focus from the land per se to the people—more precisely, to how people get remembered. This reminiscence concerns two women. Silko's great-grandmother, Helen, was born of an old traditional family, and Silko recalls that "even as a very young child / I sensed she did not like children much and so I remember her / from a distance . . . " (p. 88). Much dearer to memory is a woman Silko never knew, old Juana, of whom Silko learned from the stories of Grandma Lillie, one of Helen's daughters. Juana, who "raised Grandma Lillie and her sisters / and brothers" (p. 88), was not born into a "genteel tradition" as was Grandma Helen. A Navajo, "Juana had been kidnapped by slavehunters / who attacked her family . . . " (p. 89). Stripped of her family, of whom no trace remained, her language, and her heritage, Juana "continued with the work she knew" and was eventually hired by Silko's Grandpa Stagner to care for his family. Silko recalls going on Memorial Day with Grandma Lillie to take flowers to Juana's grave. The graveyard where she was buried was old and the "small flat sandstones" which served as grave markers were mostly broken or covered over; as a result Grandma Lillie could never be certain if they found her grave—"but we left the jar of roses and lilacs we had cut anyway" (p. 89). Juana's actual presence, like the giant bear's in the earlier hunting story, is ultimately irrelevant. As the bear lives in Silko's imagination, so Juana lives in her, and in Grandma Lillie's heart, where they have more perfect being.[27] Though orphaned young, Juana is restored through the stories to a family, language, and heritage.

Juana is remembered for her loving kindness, but that is not the only way people get remembered. The tone shifts rather suddenly from the reminiscence about Juana to two "gossip" stories, both of them rich in humor and irony. The first story, of a man caught en flagrante in a cornfield by his wife and her two sisters, and Silko's telling of it—in which she uses the storyteller's conversational tone and shifts the point of view from the two lovers to the wife and sisters and then to the man alone—express a delicious comic blend of conspiracy, anticipation, antagonism and resignation. She dramatically sets the scene: "His wife had caught them together before / and probably she had been hearing rumors again / the way people talk" (p. 89). The lovers planned to meet in the afternoon, when it was so hot that "everyone just rested" until evening, when it was cool enough to return to work. "This man's wife was always / watching him real close at night / so afternoon was / the only chance they had" (p. 90). When they were caught the woman left, and the man had to take the inevitable chastisement alone. His "wife would cry a little," her sisters would comfort her, "and then they would start talking again / about how good their family had treated him / and how lucky he was. / He couldn't look at them / so he looked at the sky / and then over at the hills behind the village" (p. 91). Though the man's inability to look at the women may suggest guilt, his wandering gaze has something of boredom in it, as if he were merely playing a role in an ancient and rather tiresome domestic ritual. His manhood is not spared, as the women are quick to remind him that his lover "had a younger boyfriend / and it was only afternoons that she had any use / for an old man" (p. 92):

> So pretty soon he started hoeing weeds again
> because they were ignoring him
> like he didn't matter anyway
> now that
> that woman was gone (p. 92).

The irony here is rich. The man, it seems, is important to his wife and relatives, and perhaps to the community as a whole, only by virtue of his infidelity. It is this by which he lives in a communal memory, enriches the storytelling life of the people, and gains mythic dimension. Apart from that context he "didn't matter."

"Then there was the night," Silko gleefully continues, whetting our appetite for the story of old man George

who, on a trip to the outhouse, "heard strange sounds / coming from one of the old barns / below" (p. 92). Checking, "just in case some poor animal / was trapped inside," the old man is shocked to discover Frank,

> so respectable and hard-working
> and hardly ever drunk—
> well there he was
> naked with that Garcia girl—
> you know,
> the big fat one.
> And here it was
> the middle of winter
> without their clothes on! (pp. 92-93).

Silko's tone here expresses two points of view simultaneously. George, to say the least, is surprised to find a man like Frank in this situation and Silko, as storyteller, relishes the irony. Further, she creates the proper context here by giving us, through her "you know" aside, a sense of her immediate audience—another young person, perhaps, to whom Frank would be cited by conventional morality as an example to follow. "Poor old man George / he didn't know what to say," and his befuddlement is comically rendered in the story's closing lines: "so he just closed the door again / and walked back home— / he even forgot where he was going / in the first place" (p. 93). But he'll remember Frank and the Garcia girl.

It may at first glance seem strange that these stories are followed by a brief recollection of Grandma A'mooh and the way she read the children's book *Brownie the Bear* to her great-granddaughters, especially since "Storytelling," which follows, consists of six vignettes largely in the same vein as the "gossip" stories. This reminiscence, however, mentioned earlier in another context, is wonderfully appropriate here. Taken in conjunction with the "gossip" stories that surround it, it reminds us again of the variety and inclusiveness of the oral tradition. It also underscores Silko's intent throughout *Storyteller* to convey the dynamic relationship between the oral tradition and the life it expresses. The life of a community, or of an individual, does not arrange itself into precise categories, literary or otherwise, nor does it follow neat, unbroken lines of development; and Silko, by juxtaposing different kinds of narratives and subjects, helps us to see vital, rewarding connections that might otherwise go unnoticed. Remember, too, that her emphasis in the "Grandma A'mooh" reminiscence is on how a story is told. A good story cannot exist apart from a good storyteller. Much of the fun of the "gossip" stories, as we have seen, is in Silko's manner of telling them. Grandma A'mooh

> always read the story with such animation and
>   expression
> changing her tone of voice and inflection
> each time one of the bears spoke—
> the way a storyteller would have told it (p. 93).

Her telling makes the story live, recreates it in effect with each repetition. This is what Silko, in the "gossip" stories as well as in others, tries to do, to give a sense of the flux and immediacy of life lived. Too, it is her telling which links Grandma A'mooh to past generations of storytellers—as it does Silko.

The six vignettes in "Storytelling," all variations on the Yellow Woman abduction stories, bring what I have called the "Yellow Woman" section of *Storyteller* full circle. The first of these is Silko's abbreviated rendering of the opening of the "Buffalo Story," when Yellow Woman goes for water:

> "Are you here already?"
> "Yes," he said.
> He was smiling.
> "Because I came for you."
> She looked into the
> shallow clear water.
> "But where shall I put my water jar?" (p. 95).

In this version Yellow Woman is apparently expecting Buffalo Man, and though coercion might be implied when he says he came for her, her response is willing, even coy and playful. The tone of the fifth vignette is quite similar:

> Seems like
> it's always happening to me.
> Outside the dance hall door
> late Friday night
> in the summertime.
> and those
> brown-eyed men from Cubero,
> smiling.
> They usually ask me
> "Have you seen the way the stars shine
> up there in the sand hills?"
> And I usually say "No. Will you show me?" (p. 97).

Silko alerts us as "Storytelling" begins that we "should understand / the way it was / back then, / because it is the same / even now" (p. 94). The traditional stories, Silko is saying, both here and throughout *Storyteller,* offer profound and necessary insights into contemporary experiences. Specifically, the "Yellow Woman" stories, especially Silko's renderings of them, are among other things open, unqualified expressions of woman's sexuality. This is not to say that, because the traditional stories are abduction stories, Silko is dealing in rape fantasies. Quite the contrary. In her versions the coercive element, though present, is not the controlling one. Yellow Woman is at all times in charge of her own destiny. She understands and accepts her sexuality, expresses it honestly, and is guided by her own strong desire. We see this in Silko's short story, "Yellow Woman," in the *Cottonwood* stories, and again in these two "Storytelling" vignettes. By focusing in these little narratives not on the lovemaking but on the prelude to it, Silko establishes the sexual integrity of both the mythic and contemporary Yellow Woman, and conveys with playful subtlety the charged eroticism between them and Buffalo Man and "those / brown-eyed men from Cubero" respectively.

Yellow Woman's sexual integrity gets a broadly comic touch in the fourth vignette, where Silko inverts the traditional abduction motif. The F.B.I. and state police in the summer of 1967 pursued a red '56 Ford with four Laguna women and three Navajo men inside. A kidnapping was involved, and the police followed a trail "of wine bottles and / size 42 panties / hanging in bushes and trees / all along the road" (p. 96). When they were caught, one of the men explained: "'We couldn't escape them' . . . / 'We tried, but there were four of them and / only three of us'" (p. 96).

But sexual honesty, especially a woman's, is, as we have seen, likely to be misunderstood. In the first *Cottonwood* poem, "Story of Sun House," the Sun tells Yellow Woman that even though their union is necessary for the world to continue, "the people may not understand" (p. 64); and the narrator in "Yellow Woman" must make up a story for her family about being kidnapped by a Navajo. In fact, the abduction motif of the Yellow Woman stories proves useful, or almost so, in a number of situations. "No! that gossip isn't true," says a distraught mother in the third "Storytelling" vignette: "She didn't elope / She was *kidnapped* by / that Mexican / at Seama Feast. / You know / my daughter / isn't / *that* kind of girl" (pp. 95-96). As was stated earlier, however, there cannot be a good story without a good storyteller, as the contemporary Yellow Woman of the sixth vignette learns. "It was / that Navajo / from Alamo, / you know, / the tall / good-looking / one," she tells her husband. "He told me / he'd kill me / if I didn't / go with him." That, rain, and muddy roads, she said, are why "it took me / so long / to get back home." When her husband leaves her, she blames herself: "I could have told / the story / better than I did" (pp. 97-98).

In a *Sun-Tracks* interview, Silko said of "these gossip stories": "I don't look upon them as gossip. The connotation is all wrong. These stories about goings-on, about what people are up to, give identity to a place."[28] What she argues for here is in effect what the "Yellow Woman" section is all about: a new way of seeing. Seen rightly, such stories are neither idle rumor nor trivial chatter, but are rather another mode of expression, a way in which people define themselves and declare who they are. Thus it is fitting that the "Yellow Woman" section, and this essay, conclude with a photograph taken of some of the houses in Laguna (p. 99). Here, after all, is where the people live their lives and it is this sense of life being lived, of life timeless and ongoing, changing and evolving, contradictory and continuous, that Silko expresses with grace and power through her melding of oral tradition and the written word in *Storyteller.*

NOTES

[1] Much of the work for this study was done with the generous support of the University of Kansas General Research Fund.

[2] Larry Evers and Denny Carr, "A Conversation with Leslie Marmon Silko," *Sun Tracks,* vol. 3., no. 1 (Fall 1976), p. 30.

[3] Speaking to students at Laguna-Acoma High School, Silko said, "Our greatest natural resource is stories and storytelling. We have an endless, continuing, ongoing supply of stories." Per Seyersted, "Two Interviews with Leslie Marmon Silko," *American Studies in Scandinavia,* Vol. 13 (1981), p. 21.

[4] New York, N.Y.: Seaver Books, 1981; all quotations from *Storyteller* are taken from this edition.

[5] The Navajo, for example, "believe that the life and power of their mythology depends upon its being retained in the memory of the people and that to record the mythology is . . . to take away its vitality." Sam D. Gill, *Sacred Words: A Study of Navajo Religion and Prayer,* Contributions in Intercultural and Comparative Studies, No. 4 (Westport, Connecticut: Greenwood Press, 1981), p. 49.

[6] Silko mentions this conversation with Nora in Evers and Carr, p. 31.

[7] Priscilla Wald, rev. of Leslie Marmon Silko's *Storyteller, SAIL,* Vol. 6. No. 4 (Fall 1982), p. 19.

[8] *Orality and Literacy: The Technologizing of the Word* (New York: Methuen, 1982), p. 148.

[9] "The Man Made of Words" in *The Remembered Earth,* edited by Geary Hobson (Albuquerque, N.M.: Red Earth Press, 1979), p. 167.

[10] Let me emphasize that the section titles used here and elsewhere in this essay are of my own devise and meant solely to identify with facility the specific groups of narratives I have chosen to consider.

[11] Per Seyersted, *Leslie Marmon Silko,* Boise State University Western Writer's Series, No. 45 (Boise, Idaho: Boise State University Press, 1980), p. 38.

[12] *The Remembered Earth,* p. 170.

[13] *Ceremony* in fact had its genesis in a short story Silko began to write while she was in Alaska. Seyersted, *Leslie Marmon Silko,* pp. 25-26.

[14] Dexter Fisher, ed., *The Third Woman: Minority Women Writers of the United States.* (Boston: Houghton Mifflin Co., 1980), p. 22.

[15] Evers and Carr, 29; Silko at first refers to "these gossip stories," but then quickly rejects this label: "No, I don't look upon them as gossip. The connotation is all wrong. These stories about goings-on, about what people are up to, give identity to a place."

[16] Only in the *Storyteller* version of "Yellow Woman" is this short poem used as an epigram. A. Lavonne Ruoff provides a brief but useful summary, derived from Boas, of the nature and structure of the "Yellow Woman" stories. She also points out the enigmatic nature of Whirlwind Man, "who may be either an evil kachina or who may live among the good kachinas at Wenimatse. . . . " "Ritual and Renewal: Keres Traditions in the Short Fiction of Leslie Silko," *MELUS,* Vol. 5, No. 4 (Winter, 1978), p. 10.

[17] David V. Erdman, ed., *The Complete Poetry and Prose of William Blake* (Garden City, N.Y.: Anchor Press/Doubleday, 1982), p. 39.

[18] Ruoff, p. 13.

[19] "Story Telling: The Fiction of Leslie Silko," *The Journal of Ethnic Studies,* 9:1 (Spring 1981), p. 53.

[20] Ruoff, 14.

[21] *The Way to Rainy Mountain* (Albuquerque, N.M.: University of New Mexico Press, 1969), p. 12.

[22] *The Way to Rainy Mountain,* p. 17.

[23] Karl Kroeber, writing of Dennis Tedlock's "The Spoken Word and the Work of Interpretation in American Indian Religion," says that Tedlock "shows that a Zuni story *continues* precisely because each reciter is a reviser." "An Introduction to the Art of Traditional American Indian Narration," *Traditional American Literatures: Texts and Interpretations,* edited by Karl Kroeber (Lincoln: University of Nebraska Press, 1981), p. 21. The same may be said of the Laguna stories Silko "revises" in *Cottonwood* and elsewhere in *Storyteller.*

[24] "'The Grace That Remains'—American Indian Women's Literature," *Book Forum,* Volume 5, No. 3 (1981), p. 381.

[25] Franz Boas, ed., *Keresan Texts,* Volume VIII (New York: Publications of the American Ethnological Society, 1928), pp. 122-127.

[26] The changes Silko makes, of course, might well derive from a version of the story she herself had heard. In any case, Silko recalls, elsewhere in *Storyteller* that "Aunt Susie and Aunt Alice would tell me stories they had told me before but with changes in details or descriptions. The story was the important thing and little changes here and there were really part of the story." In the oral tradition variants do not constitute a problem, as they often do where writing is concerned. Rather they are renewals which invigorate the tradition. Silko goes on to say, "I've heard tellers begin 'The way I heard it was . . . ' and then proceed with another story purportedly a version of a story just told but the story they would tell was a . . . new story with an integrity of its own, an offspring, a part of the continuing which storytelling must be" (p. 227).

[27] It is as Momaday says of his grandmother and of his need to retrace the Kiowa migration: "Although my grandmother lived out her long life in the shadow of Rainy Mountain, the immense landscape of the continental interior lay like memory in her blood. . . . I wanted to see in reality what she had seen more perfectly in the mind's eye. . . . " *The Way to Rainy Mountain*, p. 7.

[28] Evers and Carr, p. 29.

Carl R. V. Brown

SOURCE: "'Journey to Ixtlan': Inside the American Indian Oral Tradition," in *The Arizona Quarterly*, Vol. 32, No. 2, Summer, 1976, pp. 138-45.

[In the following essay, Brown assesses the embodiment of the Native American oral tradition in don Juan, the Indian sorcerer who figures prominently in Journey to Ixtlan *and other books by Carlos Castaneda.]*

Don Juan Matus, a Yaqui Indian from Sonora, is becoming the Siddhartha of our time. Just as millions read Herman Hesse's *Siddhartha* during the '50s and '60s and believe that they had found in it an enlightenment and charm lacking in their lives, millions are today fascinated with Carlos Castaneda's don Juan series (*Teachings of Don Juan*, 1969; *A Separate Reality*, 1971; *Journey to Ixtlan*, 1972; and now *A Tale of Power*, 1974). These books are supposedly the factual record of the apprenticeship of the author, an anthropologist at U.C.L.A., to don Juan, an aging Yaqui sorcerer living somewhere in the desert of Arizona. I want to direct my attention, here, to *Journey to Ixtlan* because it is a distillation of Castaneda's entire ten-year apprenticeship (1960-1971) and because the author claims that it contains the really central lessons of don Juan gleaned from their numerous encounters. Furthermore, it strikes me that in *Journey to Ixtlan* the "knowledge" of don Juan is in good part explained by analyzing his lessons in the context of his world view being in the American Indian oral tradition.

Contrasted to the esoteric don Juan is his apprentice, a representative of our own literate culture, conditioned, as Marshall McLuhan has pointed out, by a pervasive reliance upon the printed word. The whole conflict of the book is in the clash of two world views, in don Juan's attempts to decondition his apprentice so that he might "see" more clearly. "The world is a mystery," don Juan tells his antagonist. "And it is not at all as you picture it."[1]

Here, seeing more clearly means the ability to perceive the relevance of don Juan's orally conditioned world view and, it must not be overlooked, the world view of a sorcerer. I want to deal with those teachings of don Juan which correspond directly to ways of thinking and perceiving observable in the American Indian oral tradition generally. These lessons lure readers into the sense that they are magical only because the readers are not accustomed to dealing with the world from a strictly orally conditioned perspective.

First, it must be said that language is the key by which we make sense of the world, and there are important differences between the literate and oral traditions in the way language presents reality. Both don Juan and the apprentice bring different perceptual structures to their encounter, conditioned by the very different assumptions about the nature of reality implicit in their cultural backgrounds. Some explanation for this cultural perspectivism was first offered by the German philologist Wilhelm von Humboldt in the early nineteenth century: "The structure of a language expresses the inner life and knowledge of its speakers. . . . Man lives with the world about him principally, indeed . . . exclusively, as language presents it."[2] And Benjamin Lee Whorf, in his famous eight-year study of the Hopi language, found that the structure of a language

> is not merely a reproducing instrument for voicing ideas but rather is itself the shaper of ideas, the program and guide for the individual's mental activity, for his analysis of impressions, for his synthesis of his mental stock in trade. . . . We dissect nature along lines laid down by our native languages.[3]

And don Juan's way of dissecting nature is perceptually and psychologically oblique to our own. Peter Farb, in his essay "How Do I Know You Mean What You Mean?", adds some clarity to the distinction between the oral and literate ways of perceiving:

> Language does more than merely blind its speaker to certain perceptions; by an opposite influence it directs the speaker's attention to certain habitual patterns of thought. In the Arctic, the Eskimo often travels through an environment in which no horizon separates earth from sky, where the winds rise and snow blots out all perspective. Aivilik Eskimos, who live north of Hudson Bay, showed that they sometimes travel for hundreds of miles in such conditions. They can do so because they unconsciously perceive their environment, not as a collection of points and lines that fill a space, but as interrelationships among snow, wind, ice cracks, contours, and so forth.[4]

Why then, are the don Juan books so popular? For one thing, people are always fascinated with what seems like magic. For another, many are dissatisfied and frustrated with their roles in a crowded and complex society and seek the comfort and simplicity of an ascetic mysticism (be it that of an Indian sorcerer or the fundamental Christian church). Or, as George Evans suggests:

> We are developing into an entirely different kind of culture, moving out of the culture of print . . . to a more oral culture conditioned by the telephone, television, the film, and the tape recorder. The oral tradition will, on this assumption regain some of its status within a society not committed so strongly to an almost total reliance on what is printed.[5]

If Evans is correct, the appeal of the don Juan books is the result of our beginning again to find the oral tradition a comfortable habitat. Castaneda's don Juan shows us the human capacity for transcendental and intuitive knowing—a capacity de-emphasized by a rationalistic, print-oriented culture, but one which is crucial in the American Indian world view.

Consider the opposing views in the book on the question of appearance versus reality. For don Juan, reality is "only a description" to be created; it is the appearance he chooses to give it that is important. Don Juan is not solipsistic, though; the world is out there to marvel at. On the other hand, the anthropologist believes in the objectified world, accurately recorded by his senses and reliably described by his language. For him, the world needs explaining. "I told don Juan," says the apprentice, "that my insistence on finding explanations was not something that I had arbitrarily devised myself, just to be difficult, but was something so deeply ingrained in me that it overruled every other consideration" (p. 291). Eventually, the apprentice does come to "see" the world in other terms, but only after he learns to short-circuit this cultural conditioning. And it takes him almost ten years to accomplish it.

One of the major obstacles to the apprentice's progress is the chauvinistic attitude that his literate, civilized perspective is superior to don Juan's, *ab ovo usque ad mala:*

> I was, naturally being condescending [thought the anthropologist] . . . yet I still held in the back of my mind, although I would never voice it, the belief that I, being a university student, a man of the sophisticated Western world, was superior to an Indian. (p. 81)

And he is shocked by don Juan's reply to his offhand comment that the two of them are equals:

> "No," he [don Juan] said calmly, "we are not."
>
> "Why, certainly we are," I protested.
>
> "No," he said in a soft voice. "We are not equals. I am a hunter and a warrior, and you are a pimp." (p. 81)

Albert Lord, appropriately another anthropologist, lends support to this rejection of literate chauvinism in his book, *The Singer of Tales:*

> We assume without thinking that written style is always superior to oral style, even from the very beginning. Actually, this is an error of simple observation of experience, perpetrated alas by scholars who have shunned experience for the theoretical.[6]

Next, consider the place of silence in the literate and oral perspectives. For don Juan, silence is a positive expression; it is *created* at appropriate times to be in harmony with a natural order. Silence is full of meaning.

For the apprentice, however, silence is the void to be filled. It becomes very difficult for him to use silence as a means of touching the mystery of the desert. As Margot Astrov explains in *American Indian Prose and Poetry:*

> One of the reasons why modern man, generally speaking, avoids the silence of solitude and meditation with such circumspection is that he fears to face the emptiness of his world. He rather drugs himself with the opiates of noise, speed and bustle, which render him immune against the giddying sight of this yawning emptiness which is his heaven and his soul.
>
> But to the Indian, there was no such thing as emptiness in the world. There was no object around him that was not alive with spirit, and earth and tree and stone and the wide scope of the heavens were tenanted with numberless supernaturals and the wandering souls of the dead. And it was in the solitude of remote places and in the sheltering silence of the night that the voices of these spirits might be heard.[7]

And it is just this sheltering silence that don Juan teaches his apprentice to seek.

Closely related to the concept of creative silence is don Juan's belief that we are responsible actors in drama with nature. This feeling of being in and with nature is perhaps the most fundamental and pervasive tenet of don Juan's thought:

> For me [don Juan] the world is weird because it is stupendous, awesome, mysterious, unfathomable; my interest has been to convince you that you must assume responsibility for being here, in this marvelous world, in this marvelous desert, in this marvelous time. I wanted to convince you that you must learn to make every act count, since you are going to be here for only a short while, in fact, too short for witnessing all the marvels of it. (p. 107)

Everything in nature is encountered anthropomorphically and accorded respect. "'How can I know who I am when I am all this?' don Juan said, sweeping the surroundings with a gesture of his head. 'So, all in all, the plants and ourselves are even'" (p. 33). "Neither we nor they are more or less important" (p. 43). And concerning a rattlesnake don Juan had killed for food, he said, "I had to apologize to her [the snake] for cutting her life off so suddenly and so definitely; I did what I did knowing that my own life will also be cut off someday in very much the same fashion, suddenly and definitely. So, all in all, we and the snakes are on a par. One of them fed us today." (p. 77)

The world must, according to don Juan, be approached with humility and care; one must be inaccessible to it.

> To be inaccessible means that you touch the world around you sparingly. You don't eat five quail, you eat one. You don't damage the plants just to

make a barbeque pit. You don't expose yourself to the power of the wind unless it is mandatory. You don't use and squeeze people until they have shriveled into nothing, especially the people you love. (p. 94)

One taps the world lightly, according to don Juan, staying for as long as is needed, and then swiftly moves away, leaving hardly a mark. This tenet is very much in consonance with the American Indian oral tradition.

Consider, too, attitudes about time and chronology. For don Juan, the experiential focus is ineluctably on the present. Looking into the past or projecting into the future for synthesis with the present distorts the reality of the moment and inhibits proper action. A continuous mental record of the passage of time is unnecessary. In his view, one simply makes the proper gestures as his intuition and sense of harmony with the world make it appropriate. As the apprentice says, "There had never been an enduring order, in matters of passage of time [with don Juan] . . . and my conclusion was that if I kept myself alert a moment would come when I would lose my order of sequential time." (p. 284)

In his recent book on the subject of chronology in the oral tradition, David P. Henige explains:

Our own conditioning to the exactitude of calendrical measurement of time too often inhibits our ability to appreciate that such precision is not universal. . . . In doing so we often assume that these societies have remembered their past "calendrically," that is, lineally, sequentially, and even chronometrically. In fact, achronicity is one of the concomitants of an oral non-calendrical society.[8]

This achronicity of the oral tradition explains the conflict between don Juan and the apprentice in conversations like this:

"When was the time you were talking about?" [the apprentice asked].

"Once upon a time."

"When? What does 'once upon a time' mean?"

"It means once upon a time, or maybe it means now, today. It doesn't matter. At one time everybody knew that a hunter was the best of men." (p. 79)

The time that something happens or an idea is held to be true is not crucial in this view. Only the existence (as in space) of the act or belief is attended.

Consider dreams. For the American Indian, dreams were real experiences with deep significance. The dreamer was not merely thinking images; he was acting, and his actions were important and capable of bringing him power. "*Dreaming* is real for a warrior," don Juan tells his student, "because in it he can act deliberately, he can choose and reject, he can select from a variety of items those which lead to power. . . . In *dreaming* you

have power; you can change things; you may find out countless concealed facts; you can control whatever you want" (pp. 119-20). This is certainly different from our own belief that dreams are only shades of the imagination, untrustworthy symbols of the mind's concerns. Waking is reality; dreaming is the mind's energy discharged in its compulsion to find equilibrium and rest.

Finally, and particularly compelling for the contemporary reader, is don Juan's anthropomorphic view of death as man's most reliable companion:

Death is our eternal companion. . . . It is always to our left, at an arm's length. . . . The thing to do when you're impatient . . . is to turn to your left and ask advice from your death. . . . Death is the only wise adviser that we have. Whenever you feel, as you always do, that everything is going wrong and you're about to be annihilated, turn to your death and ask if that is so. Your death will tell you that you're wrong, that nothing really matters outside its touch. Your death will tell you, "I haven't touched you yet." (pp. 54-55)

This is a view which recognizes a benefit in death; it is death as the faithful adviser instead of the grim reaper. Death, the unyielding constant, reminds us that we haven't time to be petty, that we must act with courage and humility, "because the art of a warrior is to balance the terror of being a man with the wonder of being a man" (p. 315). When death does touch us, according to don Juan, we should not resist with ignoble screaming and crying at our fate, but should peacefully realize that our time has come as it does for all things, appropriately—the harmony of the world demands it. For me, the most impressively written passage in the book is don Juan's description of how a true warrior dies:

And thus you will dance to your death here, on this hilltop, at the end of the day. And in your last dance you will tell of your struggle, of the battles you have won and of those you have lost; and you will tell of your joys and bewilderments upon encountering personal power. Your dance will tell about the secrets and about the marvels you have stored. And your death will sit here and watch you.

The dying sun will glow on you without burning. . . . The wind will be soft and mellow and your hilltop will tremble. As you reach the end of your dance you will look at the sun, for you will never see it again in waking or in *dreaming,* and then your death will point to the south. To the vastness. (p. 189)

The felicity and charm readers encounter in the alluring pages of this book are very much a recognition of attraction of the American Indian oral tradition, represented in the lessons of don Juan. The fault of *Journey to Ixtlan* is that in it Castaneda casts the Western tradition in the worst possible light, reducing it to a withdrawn assemblage of pseudo-rationalities, easily ridiculed by the wise and implacable don Juan and ineptly defended by the confused apprentice. Castaneda's bias is absolute on the side of the Indian and his oral tradition. This distortingly erases those shades of gray wherein people actually reside. What is not made clear because of the book's absolutist position is that we live partly in the oral tradition and partly in the literate. True, we have become more overwhelmingly impressed by the written tradition out of which come the art and science that describe modern technological society. It is in good part to correct this imbalanced sensitivity that Castaneda presses us to the extremities (and beyond) of the oral culture's way of perceiving. However, we cannot all retreat to the deserts of Arizona; certainly we cannot all become sorcerers; we cannot abandon Western civilization, such as it is. Remember, *Journey to Ixtlan* was not written by a Yaqui Indian from Sonora, but by an anthropologist from U.C.L.A.

Whatever transcendental charm we may find in don Juan's lessons, they are not parochial. We are capable of synthesizing the oral and literate influences into a truly more wholesome world view. That would be a journey to Ixtlan worth traveling.

NOTES

[1] Carlos Castaneda, *Journey to Ixtlan: The Lessons of Don Juan* (New York: Simon and Schuster, 1972), p. 200. The future page references are included in parentheses in the text.

[2] Peter Farb, "How Do I Know You Mean What You Mean?" *Horizon,* 10 (1968), 53.

[3] Ibid.

[4] Ibid., p. 52

[5] George E. Evans, *Where Beards Wag All: The Relevance of the Oral Tradition* (London: Faber & Faber Ltd., 1970), p. 282.

[6] Albert B. Lord, *The Singer of Tales* (Cambridge: Harvard University Press, 1964), p. 134.

[7] Margot Astroy, *The Winged Serpent: American Indian Prose and Poetry* (Greenwich, Connecticut: Fawcett Publications, Inc., 1947), p. 48.

[8] David P. Henige, *The Chronology of Oral Tradition: Quest for a Chimera* (Oxford: Clarendon Press, 1974), p. 14.

William M. Clements

SOURCE: "Folk Historical Sense in Two Native American Authors," in *MELUS: Society for the Study of the Multi-Ethnic Literature of the United States,* Vol. 12, No. 1, Spring, 1985, pp. 65-78.

[*In the following essay, Clements compares the uses of folk history in works by N. Scott Momaday and Leslie Marmon Silko.*]

Most literary artists who are sympathetic to folklore view oral literature and traditional behavior as material useful for incorporation into their poetry, fiction, or drama. Writers have effected such incorporation in several ways and have put folklore to a number of literary uses: as local color embellishment, as source for characterization, as structuring device for plot, and as vehicle for theme among other possibilities.[1] Yet no matter how they exploit folklore in their work, most writers, at least in the mainstreams of Western literary tradition, seem to view the texts and processes of folk culture as distinct from literary texts and processes. For them, written literature and oral literature (as well as the rest of folklore) represent separate traditions.

The writer's involvement in a tradition has been treated by T. S. Eliot. In his well-known essay "Tradition and the Individual Talent," he insists, "the poet must develop or procure the consciousness of the past and . . . he should continue to develop this consciousness throughout his career."[2] Though he rejects both a slavish imitation of past models and a pedantry arising from tedious study of literary history, Eliot suggests that the writer cultivate a "historical sense":

> [T]he historical sense involves a perception, not only of the pastness of the past, but of its presence; the historical sense compels a man to write not merely with his own generation in his bones, but with a feeling that the whole of the literature of his own country has a simultaneous existence and composes a simultaneous order. This historical sense, which is a sense of the timeless and of the temporal together, is what makes a writer traditional.[3]

The "traditional" writer, as Eliot uses the term, builds upon the literary heritage of his culture and thus must know that heritage as a participant, if not as a scholar. His or her works take their place in that heritage as unique creations of an individual talent and as a reflection of the general patterns of the heritage.

When Eliot writes of "tradition," he is thinking in elitist terms, and the historical sense he means derives from an essentially bookish perspective, even for writers who may incorporate folklore into their works in some way. Yet plenty of writers, especially those who are isolated by some factor such as geography, language, or ethnicity from the mainstreams of Western literary culture, have nurtured a historical sense that responds more to the oral lore and literature of their specific heritages than to the academic heritage of the mainstream. Theirs may be denominated a "folk historical sense," which must be appreciated in folkloric terms.[4] The writer who demonstrates a folk historical sense does more than incorporate folklore into his or her work; a writer with an elite historical sense may do that. Instead, the writer using the folk viewpoint perceives his or her work as part of a continuing artistic heritage which begins with his culture's oral literature, owes its primary survival to oral tradition, and continues to, or through, his or her own fiction, poems, plays, or essays. On the other hand, a writer such as Eliot sees his work as part of a heritage that consists of other works of written literature. *The Wasteland,* for example, takes its place within a heritage that also includes the Bible, *The Divine Comedy,* the medieval Grail legend (not oral literature for Eliot),[5] and Shakespearean tragedy. Perhaps these distinctions between folk historical sense and incorporation of folklore and between folk historical sense and elite historical sense will become clearer from another illustration. Eudora Welty is a novelist and short story writer who incorporates elements of Southern American folklore, Black and white, into her fictions. A novel such as *Delta Wedding,* for instance, achieves much of its depth because of the tapestry of folk culture against which the characters act out their comedy. A novel such as *The Robber Bridegroom,* to a large degree, owes its content, structure, and style to traditions of oral storytelling, particularly of Märchen. But these novels as well as Welty's other work, full of folklore as they are, have become primarily a part of the heritage of the novel and the short story in Western literary tradition; apparently Welty does not think of her work as being a continuation of the folk heritage. Yet the Native American writers whom I will treat in this essay have often utilized material from their tribal oral heritages to go beyond mere incorporation of that material and to imply that their own work should actually be considered a part of that oral heritage. When they perceive their literary efforts as extensions of the oral literary tradition, they evince a folk historical sense just as Eliot and Welty reveal an elitest historical sense when they view their works as existing within the continuum of Western written literature.

To manifest a folk historical sense, as I am employing this term, a writer must have contact with oral literature on a specific, concrete level. Thus, even if he or she has accepted the ideas of Northrop Frye or other literary historians and critics who assert that virtually all written literature has a genetic link to oral literature,[6] he or she does not necessarily possess a folk historical sense. While the writer may believe that the comedy he or she writes derives ultimately from fertility choruses performed eons ago, the connection between the (usually hypothetical) oral originals and the writer's work is too vague and too abstract to have a real folkloric meaning. Moreover, the writer most likely goes back to other literary comedies rather than the oral prototype for the immediate source of his or her tradition. The writer with folk historical sense, though, sees his or her work as part of a specific folk tradition which he or she knows as participant and observer. Following the lead of Richard M. Dorson,[7] I would insist that some sort of biographical evidence—or at least strongly developed inference—of a writer's first-hand connection with folklore in its natural contexts should enter the account when

one discusses folk historical sense. Simply put, a writer has a folk sense of an oral literature that he knows orally/aurally. If he has encountered oral literature only in printed sources and feels his own work grows directly out of what he has read, his historical sense, like Eliot's or Welty's, is elitest. Once the evidence has been marshalled to prove a writer's personal involvement with oral literature and traditional behavior, the literary analyst can explore how the writer uses folk historical sense, his or her perception of how his or her works take their place *within* that folk heritage.

It would indeed be difficult to identify a group of writers who have developed historical sense more effectively than the Native American poets, essayists, and novelists who have been active during the last decade and a half.[8] Their work, which gained considerable attention when N. Scott Momaday's novel *House Made of Dawn* won a Pulitzer Prize in 1969,[9] has drawn extensively upon the traditional cultures which comprise the writers' heritages. These cultures provide settings for poems and works of fiction and afford themes and patterns which form the foundations for writings. Even more importantly, the cultural heritages establish modes of perception which distinguish Native American writers from writers of other cultural backgrounds. And most importantly for the present argument, the Native American cultures also include strong oral literary traditions of which the written literature is perceived to be an extension. But these broad generalizations about the relationship of a body of literature to cultural oral traditions are valid only in a gross sense, for each Native American writer conceives of his or her relationship to his or her tribal heritage of oral literature differently. I hope that all the contemporary Native American writers would agree that such a relationship—that is, a folk historical sense—is necessary, but their perceptions of the nature of that relationship may not coincide. For instance, I find marked contrasts in the way folk historical sense is demonstrated by two of the better known Native American writers, N. Scott Momaday and Leslie Marmon Silko. Looking at their works can show how folk historical sense may operate in varying ways but with similar degrees of richness.

Momaday and Silko have much in common. Both have published successfully in several literary genres: poetry, nonfiction, and the novel for Momaday; poetry, short stories, and the novel for Silko.[10] Both have written novels based on the "reluctant return of the native" theme,[11] in which the protagonists come home from World War II to one of the Southwestern pueblos—Jemez in Momaday's *House Made of Dawn,* Laguna in Silko's *Ceremony*—to face problems in readjusting to reservation life. Both Momaday and Silko recognize the impact of Euro-American culture on Native life and embody the resultant culture clash in their works. Both also exhibit a folk historical sense, an awareness of the relationship between their work and tribal oral literatures. Here, though, the two writers seem to differ as their conceptions of how specific tribal oral cultures interact with the lives and art of contemporary Native Americans diverge.

Momaday is a Kiowa, and except for *House Made of Dawn* his work has been informed primarily by his perception of his Kiowa heritage. Having been reared in Hobbs, New Mexico, and at Jemez Pueblo, where his parents were teachers, though, Momaday never experienced Kiowa culture on a day-to-day basis for long periods of time. In fact, he seems to perceive the culture's lifeways as virtually extinct, surviving only in "mythology, legend, lore, and hearsay."[12] Even that is fragmentary and may be rapidly disappearing. Momaday's fear of the loss of the oral record of his culture provided one of the major themes of his address at the first Convocation of American Indian Scholars in 1970. He urged listeners to follow his example, demonstrated by the then recently published *The Way to Rainy Mountain,* by preserving what remained of tribal oral traditions.[13]

In *The Way to Rainy Mountain,* Momaday has articulated his perception of the development and decline of Kiowa culture. In the 1740s, he suggests, the Kiowa descended to the Plains from their ancestral homeland in the Rocky Mountain Plateau region, thus becoming the "last culture to evolve in North America" (p. 6). Befriended by the Crow, who taught them the rudiments of adaptation to their new environment, the Kiowa quickly developed preeminence in warfare and horsemanship. That preeminence, though, was short-lived—less than a century in duration, for Momaday sees several events in the 1830s as signaling the decline of Kiowa culture: in 1832, the Osage stole the Tai-me, the chief sacred object of the Kiowa ("although it was later returned, the loss was an almost unimaginable tragedy" [p. 114]); in 1833, a shower of Leonid meteors "seemed to image the sudden and violent disintegration of an old order" (p. 114); in 1837, the Kiowa signed their first treaty with the United States. The next two decades witnessed four major smallpox and cholera epidemics sweep through the tribe. And by 1880 the vast buffalo herds which had provided the Kiowa's chief livelihood had been significantly depleted. Moreover, the horses of the Kiowa had been confiscated, thus thwarting "their ancient nomadic spirit" (p. 7). In an essay published in *Ramparts,* Momaday encapsulates these events:

> The year the stars fell is among the earliest entries in the Kiowa calendars, and it is permanent in the Kiowa mind. There was symbolic meaning in that November sky. With the coming of natural dawn there began a new and darker age for the Kiowa people; the last culture to evolve on this continent began to decline. Within four years of the falling stars the Kiowas signed their first treaty with the government; within twenty, four major epidemics of smallpox and Asiatic cholera destroyed more than half their number; and within scarcely more than a generation their horses were taken from them and the herds of buffalo were slaughtered and left to waste upon the plains.[14]

Despite these disasters the Kiowa culture had not "withered and died like grass" (p. 1) until its religious essence had been demolished. In 1887, the tribe held its last Sun Dance, the central religious observance. In order to conduct the ritual, a delegation of tribal elders had to beg and haggle for an old buffalo from cattleman Charles Goodnight. Three years later, on 20 July 1890, "the Kiowas came together for the last time as a living Sun Dance culture" (p. 11). But soldiers stationed at Fort Sill, near the tribal territory in southwestern Oklahoma, prevented the performance of "the essential act of their faith" (p. 11). In his *Ramparts* essay, Momaday reflects on the effects of this "deicide":

> The loss of the Sun Dance was the blow that killed the native Kiowa culture. The Kiowas might have endured every privation but that, the desecration of their faith. Without their religion there was nothing to sustain them. Subsequent acceptance of the Ghost Dance, peyote, and Christianity were for the Kiowas pathetic attempts to revive the old deities; they had become a people whose spirit was broken.[15]

The multiple losses suffered by the Kiowa between 1832 and 1890 leads Momaday to an inescapable conclusion about the holistic culture of these master horsemen of the Plains: "The centaur was dead."[16]

The specific tribal tradition from which Momaday operates, then, is one which has ceased to exist as a total way of life, at least as he seems to perceive the situation. His folk historical sense refers back to a memory culture preserved by an oral heritage in which his own work takes its place. Yet, he demonstrates, it is a heritage that can still inform the literary imagination of the late twentieth century effectively. Although Momaday views his ancestral culture as having ceased to evolve, he implies that it has survival and inspirational power in the imaginations of those who participated in the traditional Kiowa way of life, of those who have heard and taken to heart the reminiscences of these participants, and of those who have read written versions of these reminiscences. For instance, the death of the holistic Kiowa culture in 1890 did not bring about the deaths of individual Kiowas. As long as Kiowa men and women who had been living in 1890, endured, they carried with them memories of their way of life. For instance, Pohd-lohk, the old man who gave the infant N. Scott Momaday his Kiowa name, kept a calendar history of Kiowa life with which he reinforced his memory.[17] Mammedaty, N. Scott's grandfather, preserved the culture, especially in his memories of a Gourd Dance during which he was honored by a ceremonial Give-away.[18] Aho, N. Scott's grandmother whose death inspired the pilgrimage which is recalled in *The Way to Rainy Mountain,* retained the Kiowa lifeways in her memory until the 1960s. For these Kiowa, the culture persisted as it had existed in 1890, captured in their imaginations.

For those born after 1890, the culture as a whole has survival potential in one element of it which still exhibits vitality, the reminiscences, legends, folktales, and myths which comprise Kiowa oral literature. Such is the case for Momaday himself, born in 1934. For instance, although he never knew his grandfather, who died in 1932, this ancestor's distinction as a Gourd Dancer and as an individual lives imaginatively in the recollections recounted about him:

> Mammedaty was my grandfather, whom I never knew. Yet he came to be imagined posthumously in the going on of the blood, having invested the shadow of his presence in an object or a word, in his name above all. He enters into my dreams; he persists in his name.[19]

Through their oral literature, the Kiowa of today are able to retain a memory culture. The modern individual Kiowa thus achieves identity as a Kiowa through traditional language; in this sense, he is a "man made of words." Since language represents "the only chance of survival"[20] for Kiowa culture, that survival is tenuous. Momaday has suggested that Kiowa culture, living only in oral tradition and customary behavior, "was always but one generation removed from extinction."[21] As the storytellers who remember the old ways and their listeners died, so would the memory culture. But Momaday's literary work has helped to prevent this disaster in two ways: by establishing a relatively permanent record of the oral literature (for example, myths and legends in *The Way to Rainy Mountain* and reminiscences in *The Names*),[22] and by extending the audience for the oral literature potentially to all readers of English. Thus, the culture of the Kiowa, though ceasing to evolve since 1890, endures in the imaginations of Momaday and all his readers.

As an illustration, Mammedaty's famous Gourd Dance experience has survived in each of the three ways noticed above. The particular Gourd Dance was memorable since Mammedaty received a fine black horse as a ceremonial gift. For Mammedaty that experience endured in his imagination as long as he remembered and spoke of it, presumably until his death. For Momaday, who had not been present at the dance, it survives imaginatively in the oral accounts of it such as that which he records his father as having related:

> In my mind's eye I see him [Mammedaty] in silhouette, at evening in the plain, walking against a copper sunset; so he lives for me in his name. Fifty years ago, more or less, he was given a horse on the occasion of the Gourd Dance. My father says: "Oh, it was a beautiful horse, black and shining. I was just a boy then. . . . Mammedaty, was called out, and he was given that fine horse. Its mane was fixed in braids and ribbons. There was a beautiful blanket on its back."[23]

Those who have not heard the oral account must rely on one of Momaday's written descriptions of the Gourd Dance for its imaginative survival.[24]

Therefore, Momaday's work, like that of all writers who exercise a historical sense, takes its place within a tradition. But the tradition which it embraces is not primarily that of Western belles lettres; instead it is that of Kiowa oral literature. From Momaday's own perspective, his work occupies a unique position in that tradition: the monument which preserves the unchanging values of a cultural heritage that exists holistically only in the past, but endures in the imagination. For Momaday does not perceive his tribal heritage as defunct, though it may no longer exist as a complete way of life for twentieth-century Native Americans. As he notes, "the loss is less important to me than the spirit which informs the remembrance, the spirit that informs that pageantry across all ages and which persists in the imagination of every man everywhere."[25]

The position which Momaday seems to see his work as occupying in relationship to the Kiowa heritage may help to explain why one commentator has regarded him as the most bitter and pessimistic of Native American authors.[26] It also contrasts with the way in which Leslie Marmon Silko seems to view her work, for her historical sense reflects an awareness of an ongoing oral literary heritage, reflecting a still vital way of life, of which her fiction and poetry are natural extensions. At least part of the explanation for Silko's view arises from the experiences of her own Native American group at Laguna Pueblo. Unlike the Kiowa as perceived by Momaday, the people of Laguna still participate in a vital, holistic culture. To maintain the culture's viability, though, they have had to adapt and adjust to the Euro-American influences which became important factors in the Pueblo's history as early as the early 1700s. Although the people of Laguna are regarded as "probably the most acculturated of all the New Mexico Pueblo tribes,"[27] the process of acculturation has not destroyed the traditional heritage; rather it has provided a mechanism whereby that heritage has continued to flourish as a complete entity into the late twentieth century.[28]

This idea that Native American culture can survive if it is flexible enough to accommodate change is reflected in Silko's folk historical sense. Contrasting with Momaday's perception of his work as a monument to and in the imagination, Silko's dynamism manifests itself in her work in several ways: in themes which emphasize the necessity of change and flexibility, in plots and characters which demonstrate how traditional concepts have contemporary valence, and in a comprehensive view of her work as a continuation of traditional and ongoing literary processes within her culture.

The notion that change and flexibility are essential in Native American—or at least Laguna—life provides one of the central themes of Silko's novel *Ceremony*. One of her arguments in this narrative seems to be that slavish adherence to static traditional forms is just as unproductive for Native Americans as total assimilation into Euro-American culture. Tayo, the World War II veteran who serves as the novel's protagonist, returns to Laguna Pueblo sick in mind and spirit. Strictly traditional cures for his malaise fail, as do the treatments of Euro-American specialists. Only when he seeks the aid of Betonie, a healer who perceives that healing must be based on traditional patterns but must adapt these patterns to modern needs, does the ceremony which returns Tayo to health begin. Betonie's philosophy regarding change is nicely articulated when he tells Tayo, "'things which don't shift and grow are dead things.'"[29] As critics have pointed out, the idea of dynamism lies at the heart of *Ceremony*: "Change, which keeps the ceremonies strong, which characterizes life itself, is forever working through order, balancing opposites, restoring itself, 'enclosing the totality' if temporarily, gradually reordering, rebalancing, restoring."[30] In her novel, Silko suggests that culture change ensures health for the individual participant in the culture as well as for the culture itself. She does not dwell upon the destructive aspects of change, such as those felt by Momaday's Kiowa ancestors.

Another dimension of Silko's dynamic folk historical sense emphasizes the persistence of traditional values in a changing world. Although change must occur for these values to endure, elements of the traditional heritage, firmly anchored in the traditional culture, continue to exert their power. For example, in several of her works Silko shows how Coyote, the traditional Laguna Trickster, has assumed modern garb. Her poem, "Toe'osh: A Laguna Coyote Story," strings together folktales about Coyote's trickery and accounts of how contemporary Native Americans have outsmarted Euro-Americans. In the last stanza of the poem, she equates the traditional Toe'osh with fellow poet Simon Ortiz (from Acoma Pueblo):

> Howling and roaring
> Toe'osh scattered white people
> out of bars all over Wisconsin.
> He bumped into them at the door
> until they said
> "Excuse me"
> And the way Simon meant it
> was for 300 or maybe 400 years.[31]

Another modernization of Coyote, this time without the overt culture clash developed in the poem, occurs in the short story "Coyote Holds a Full House in His Hand" (pp. 257-65). Here a Laguna ne'er-do-well poses as a healer in order to trick several Hopi women into letting him massage their thighs. Coyote is not the only element of the traditional heritage to emerge in twentieth-century costume in Silko's poetry and fiction. She also shows the persistence of witchcraft in *Ceremony,* where the forces arrayed against Tayo are identified as "witchery," and in "Tony's Story" (pp. 123-29), where a state policeman is equated in the Native American narrator's consciousness with the traditional witch; of rain magic in "The Man to Send Rain Clouds" (pp. 182-86), where the holy water a priest sprinkles on an old man's grave is interpreted as imitative magic like that which Laguna lore employs to ensure the presence of rain; and of the activity of kachina spirits in "Yellow Woman" (pp. 54-62), where a Pueblo woman has an affair with a mysterious stranger whom she identifies with the supernatural beings whose liaisons with mortal women are frequent subjects for Laguna oral narratives. Like Momaday,

Silko shows how the traditional culture continues to exert its influence on contemporary imaginations, but unlike the Kiowa writer, she implies that the culture must accommodate itself to its twentieth-century context by accepting some of the adaptations engendered by acculturation and syncretism.

For Silko, the most important feature of the traditional heritage which has persisted into the 1970s and 1980s—a feature which points toward a third way in which her folk historical sense manifests itself—is storytelling. She clearly does not regard the oral literature of Laguna Pueblo as something purely of the past, to be memorialized for the imaginative use of future readers of her work. On the contrary, she views her own work as part of a still ongoing literary tradition, once purely oral and now at least partially written. Such is the major point of her book *Storyteller*. A collection of poems, short stories, and vignettes of Laguna life, *Storyteller* is dedicated to "the storytellers as far back as memory goes and to the telling which continues and through which they all live and we with them" (n.p.). Throughout the work she reveals how storytelling has continued to be central in Native American life. For instance, the short story "Storyteller" depicts an Eskimo woman who is inspired by a long tale her dying grandfather is narrating to act out her vengeance against the Euro-Americans, who have tried to exploit her land and her people. In a poetic sketch of her grandmother, Silko shows how the old woman extended the storyteller's art even into the stories she read to her grandchildren:

> She always read the story with such animation
> and expression changing her tone of voice and
> inflection each time one of the bears spoke—the
> way a storyteller would have told it. (p. 93)

She then emphasizes how the stories of the past are a continuing tradition "because it is the same / even now" (p. 94). Silko recognizes that storytelling is a process of development not preservation when she recalls the variations in how her family members narrated stories: "The story was the important thing and little changes here and there were really part of the story" (p. 227). Moreover, Silko shows how her own fiction is a part of that developing process. In "Yellow Woman," the "kachina" figure tells the protagonist: "But someday they will talk about us, and they will say, 'Those two lived long ago when things like that happened'" (p. 57). In other words, stories like those that have persisted from the Laguna past are still being created.

In a recent interview, N. Scott Momaday specifically articulates his folk historical sense: "I think that my work proceeds from the American Indian oral tradition, and I think it sustains that tradition and carries it along. . . . My purpose is to carry on what was begun a long time ago; there's no end to it that I can see."[32] From what he has written about his Kiowa heritage, it is apparent that the way in which he sustains his particular tribal tradition is by memorializing it. Momaday seems to suggest that aspects of Native American culture, unchanged by the processes of modernization and acculturation, retain imaginative vitality which his own writing preserves. Silko, though, indicates that the traditional heritage must be able to accommodate change if it is to survive and grasp twentieth-century imaginations. Momaday and Silko, then, differ in folk historical sense. The Kiowa author recognizes the demise of his tribal way of life except in the literary expressions which he is preserving and in the revivification of such ceremonial forms as the Gourd Dance. But his memorializing allows the Kiowa heritage to continue to evince imaginative vitality. The Laguna writer regards her heritage as a living entity of which her own work is not so much a memorial as a development which introduces the kinds of changes essential for its continued life. Yet both writers share a historical sense that is essentially folk—that is, responsive to the lore and literature of their tribal cultures more than to the tradition of Western letters. Of course, both writers have taken a place in elite tradition,[33] but the major heritage of which their works have become a part is the oral expressive culture of their Native American groups. The fact, though, that their attitudes toward their heritages are quite different underscores the idea that the concept of historical sense, folk or elite, must be applied pluralistically. There exists no set way for the artist to enter into his or her tradition. He or she may, like Momaday, be the memorial link in the chain of tradition, his or her work serving as a monument to what has gone before so that this heritage may continue to inspire. Or he or she may, like Silko, be one of several developmental links in the chain that stretches into the past and probably into the future, his or her work representing the natural growth of what has happened in the past. In either case, the writer does much more than incorporate his or her heritage into written art. When exercising a folk historical sense, the novelist, short story writer, or poet perceives his or her work not as separate from folklore, but as a vital part of the body of oral literature and traditional behavior that constitutes his or her specific cultural background.

NOTES

[1] For example, see the essays included in these two special issues of folklore periodicals: Mary Ellen B. Lewis, ed., "Special Issue: Folklore and Literature," *Journal of the Folklore Institute,* 13, No. 3 (1976), 225-329; and Eleanor Wachs, ed., "Folklore and Literature," *Folklore Forum,* 11, No. 2 (1978), 70-175.

[2] T. S. Eliot, *The Sacred Wood, Essays on Poetry and Criticism,* 7th edition (London: Methuen, 1950), p. 52.

[3] Eliot, p. 49.

[4] In employing the terms, "elite" and "folk," to distinguish two cultural heritages, I am following the conventional usage of folklorists and of students of popular culture. If these terms have negative connotations, such result primarily from a lack of awareness of how scholars

in these fields employ them. Moreover, potential substitutions such as "tribal" for "folk" seem to have just as many negative connotations without possessing the cachet afforded by usage in established academic disciplines. For a brief overview of the usages of "elite" and "folk" in folklore study, see Jan Harold Brunvand, *The Study of American Folklore, An Introduction,* 2nd edition (New York: Norton, 1978), pp. 2-4.

[5] Eliot bases his use of the Grail legend in *The Wasteland* on Jessie L. Weston, *From Ritual to Romance* (Cambridge: University Press, 1920).

[6] Dan Ben-Amos has denominated this view of the relationship between folklore and literature as the "historical approach." See his "Nationalism and Nihilism: The Attitudes of Two Hebrew Authors Towards Folklore," *International Folklore Review,* 1 (1981), 5. Probably the most influential volume expounding this approach has been Northrop Frye, *Anatomy of Criticism, Four Essays* (Princeton: Princeton University Press, 1957).

[7] Richard M. Dorson, *American Folklore and the Historian* (Chicago: University of Chicago Press, 1971), pp. 186-203. A similar view is articulated in Elaine Jahner, "Intermediate Forms Between Oral and Written Literature," in *Studies in American Indian Literature, Critical Essays and Course Designs,* ed. Paula Gunn Allen (New York: Modern Language Association, 1983), pp. 66-74. The authors who create what Jahner calls "intermediate forms" are clearly exercising what I am calling "folk historical sense."

[8] Of course, writing by Native Americans in English extends well back into the seventeenth century. Anthologies which reproduce samplings of the poetry and fiction created by contemporary Native Americans include Duane Niatum, ed., *Carriers of the Dream Wheel, Contemporary Native American Poetry* (San Francisco: Harper and Row, 1975); Kenneth Rosen, ed., *The Man to Send Rain Clouds, Contemporary Stories by American Indians* (New York: Random House/Vintage, 1975); and Kenneth Rosen, ed., *Voices of the Rainbow, Contemporary Poetry by American Indians* (New York: Viking, 1975). For samples of essays which demonstrate how some of these writers *incorporate* folklore into their works, see Nora Baker Barry, "The Bear's Son Folk Tale in *When the Legends Die* and *House Made of Dawn,*" *Western American Literature,* 12, No. 4 (Winter 1978), 275-87; and A. LaVonne Ruoff, "Ritual and Renewal: Keres Traditions in the Short Fiction of Leslie Silko," *MELUS,* 5, No. 4 (Winter 1978), 2-17.

[9] For a discussion of the relevance of the criteria for the Pulitzer Prize to Momaday's novel, see Joseph F. Trimmer, "Native Americans and the American Mix: N. Scott Momaday's *House Made of Dawn,*" *Indiana Social Studies Quarterly,* 28 (1975), 75-91. I have excluded this novel, Momaday's most important single work, from my discussion since it does not reflect to a great degree his perception of how his literary efforts fit into

the heritage of Kiowa oral literature. A Kiowa character does appear in the novel and, in fact, is made to deliver a "sermon," which embodies Momaday's pilgrimage to the roots of his Kiowa heritage as described in *The Way to Rainy Mountain.* But the specific focus of *House Made of Dawn* is primarily on the heritage of the Southwestern Pueblos, which the novel suggests can still provide a viable way of life.

[10] For a bibliography of Momaday's work, see Martha Scott Trimble, *N. Scott Momaday,* Western Writers Series No. 9 (Boise, Idaho: Boise State College, 1973). Major publications by Momaday since 1973 include *The Gourd Dancer* (New York: Harper and Row, 1976) and *The Names, A Memoir* (New York: Harper and Row, 1976). Silko's bibliography may be found in Per Seyersted, *Leslie Marmon Silko,* Western Writers Series No. 45 (Boise, Idaho: Boise State University, 1980).

[11] Charles R. Larson, *American Indian Fiction* (Albuquerque, New Mexico: University of New Mexico Press, 1978), p. 68.

[12] N. Scott Momaday, *The Way to Rainy Mountain* (New York: Ballantine Books, 1970), p. 5. Further references to this edition of the work will be made parenthetically in the text. The book was originally published by the University of New Mexico Press in 1969. Essays on this book include Charles A. Nicholas, *"The Way to Rainy Mountain*; N. Scott Momaday's "Hard Journey Back," *South Dakota Review,* 13, No. 4 (1975), 149-58; and Mick McAllister, "The Topology of Remembrance in *The Way to Rainy Mountain,*" *Denver Quarterly,* 12, No. 4 (1978), 19-31.

[13] N. Scott Momaday, "The Man Made of Words," in *Literature of the American Indians: Views and Interpretations, A Gathering of Indian Memories, Symbolic Contexts, and Literary Criticism,* ed. Abraham Chapman (New York: New American Library, 1975), pp. 96-110. This frequently reprinted essay was originally published in 1970 in the proceedings of the first Convocation of American Indian Scholars. Incidentally, the fear that oral literature was fast disappearing stimulated the efforts of most of its earliest collectors and preservers. In fact, when William J. Thoms coined the word "folklore" in 1846, he urged his readers to hasten to rescue from oblivion the ballads and tales of "the olden time" from inevitable extinction. See the reprint of Thoms's brief essay on "folklore" in Alan Dundes, ed., *The Study of Folklore* (Englewood Cliffs, New Jersey: Prentice-Hall, 1965), pp. 4-6.

[14] N. Scott Momaday, "The Morality of Indian Hating," *Ramparts,* 3 (1964), 30.

[15] Momaday, "Morality," p. 35.

[16] Momaday, "Morality," p. 36.

[17] Momaday, *The Names,* pp. 42-57.

[18] Momaday, *The Names,* pp. 94, 110. Despite Momaday's perception that the Kiowa culture as a total way of life became extinct in 1890, certain elements of it—including the Gourd Dance—have survived well into the 1900s. Consider the following account:

> Even though the last Kiowa sun dance was held in 1890, the gourd dance continued to be held by the original Tai-pe-go members until 1927, when the last dance was held 3 or 4 miles southeast of Carnegie [Oklahoma]. After this, most of the old people died out, and the gourd dance was not held again until Armistice Day in 1946 when it was again performed in Carnegie. There was no formal organization then, as the Tai-pe-go had disbanded, but beginning in September of 1956, some of the descendants of the original members have formed new organizations, and today [1975] the century-old warrior dance is held at least annually for armed forces days and other special occasions, and is enjoyed not only by Kiowas, but also by many other visiting tribes (Tony Isaacs, as quoted in James H. Howard, "The Plains Gourd Dance as a Revitalization Movement," *American Ethnologist,* 3 [1976], 247).

Momaday does not indicate when Mammedaty performed the Gourd Dance at which he was honored, but it most certainly occurred after 1890 when Mammedaty would have been only ten years old. Momaday describes his own participation in the modern-day Gourd Dance in "To the Singing, to the Drums," *Natural History,* February 1975, pp. 39-44.

[19] Momaday, *The Names,* p. 26.

[20] Momaday, "Man Made of Words," p. 110.

[21] Momaday, "Man Made of Words," p. 108.

[22] Actually a good bit of Kiowa oral literature had been collected and published before *The Way to Rainy Mountain* and *The Names* appeared. In *Native American Folklore, 1879-1979: An Annotated Bibliography* (Athens, Ohio: Swallow Press, 1984), William M. Clements and Frances M. Malpezzi list thirty-six books and articles in addition to Momaday's publications which deal with Kiowa oral literature and its contexts.

[23] Momaday, "To the Singing," p. 44.

[24] For instance, see the title poem in *The Gourd Dancer.*

[25] Joseph Bruchac, "N. Scott Momaday: An Interview," *American Poetry Review,* 13, No. 4 (July/August 1984), 16. For an interpretation of Momaday's relationship to his Kiowa oral heritage which parallels my view, see Lorelei Cedarstrom, "Myth and Ceremony in Contemporary North American Native Fiction," *Canadian Journal of Native Studies,* 2, No. 2 (1983), 292-93.

[26] Larson, p. 93. Most commentators on Momaday's work, especially *House Made of Dawn,* do not find the

dark pessimism that Larson reads into the Kiowa author's perspective. For example, see Michael W. Raymond, "Tai-me, Christ, and the Machine: Affirmation Through Mythic Pluralism in *House Made of Dawn*," *Studies in American Fiction*, 11 (1983), 61-71.

[27] Florence Hawley Ellis, "Laguna Pueblo," in *Southwest. Volume 9. Handbook of North American Indians*, ed. Alfonso Ortiz (Washington: Smithsonian Institution Press, 1979), p. 448. Ellis surveys the acculturation history of the Pueblo on pp. 446-48.

[28] That Silko's work represents an extension of Laguna oral tradition is noted in Ambrose Lucero, "For the People: Leslie Silko's *Storyteller*," *Minority Voices*, 5 (1981), 9; and Jim Ruppert, "Story Telling: The Fiction of Leslie Silko," *Journal of Ethnic Studies*, 9 (1981), 56-57.

[29] Leslie Marmon Silko, *Ceremony* (New York: New American Library, 1978), p. 133. The novel had been published the previous year by Viking Press.

[30] Robert C. Bell, "Circular Design in *Ceremony*," *American Indian Quarterly*, 5, No. 1 (February 1979), 52. Bell's essay is part of a special issue of *American Indian Quarterly* devoted to *Ceremony* and edited by Kathleen M. Sands.

[31] Leslie Marmon Silko, *Storyteller* (New York: Seaver, 1981), p. 239. Subsequent references to this book will be made parenthetically in the text. (Most of the poems and short stories in *Storyteller* had been published previously, but this collection provides a handy and unified compendium of Silko's short work.)

[32] Bruchac, p. 17.

[33] For instance, in *Four American Indian Literary Masters: N. Scott Momaday, James Welch, Leslie Marmon Silko, Gerald Vizenor* (Norman: University of Oklahoma Press, 1982), Alan R. Velie shows how Momaday's poetry falls within the tradition of post-symbolism and how his prose is indebted to such writers as Melville and Faulkner (pp. 13-49). He also parallels the action in Silko's *Ceremony* to the medieval Grail legend (pp. 106-21).

AFRICAN-AMERICAN LITERATURE

Bernard W. Bell

SOURCE: An Introduction to *The Folk Roots of Contemporary Afro-American Poetry*, Broadside Press, 1974, pp. 11-15.

[In the following excerpt, Bell discusses the formation of an African-American "high art" in contrast to the literature of the black folk consciousness.]

Groping toward a realization of Afro-American genius, James Weldon Johnson—like W. E. B. DuBois, Alain Locke and other elder statesmen of the Harlem Renaissance—believed that a "demonstration of intellectual parity by the Negro through the production of literature and art"[1] would serve to eliminate racism. History has not vindicated this faith in "high art," Western reason, or American egalitarianism. Yet some of the most impressive poems by Robert Hayden, Gwendolyn Brooks, Melvin Tolson, Mari Evans, Audre Lorde, Etheridge Knight and other Black poets of the 1960's unquestionably fall within the tradition of high art. All art arises more or less in response to vital human needs. To denigrate the literary progenitors of the current Black Arts Movement or to dismiss their artifacts as mediocre tells us more about the politics and sensibilities of the critic than about the aesthetic qualities of specific works.[2] I do not pretend to be above the struggle to define the nature and function of Afro-American literature. I do not intend, however, to become embroiled here in the controversy of whether Black artists and critics of yesteryear were compelled by historical circumstances to go through the stage of affirming their personal and national identity by aspiring to the ideals of high art. Instead, my major purpose is to reveal why and how contemporary Afro-American poetry makes use of folk materials.

It is obviously time to review our thinking on the general differences between high art and folk art and to examine closely the relationship of Afro-American poetry published during 1962-1972 to the differences. Such an examination, to be useful, should emphasize several points: 1) the distinctions between European and American concepts of high art and folk art, 2) the principal theory of folk art that influenced 19th century Anglo-American writers in their quest for an indigenous art, 3) the ideas about folk art that characterized the attempts of DuBois, Locke, Johnson, Wright, Ellison and Baraka to define the relationship of Afro-American art to American culture, and 4) the techniques by which folk materials, especially music, were transformed into art by several well-known contemporary Afro-American poets.

In its broadest sense, high art connotes formal literature as well as music, dance and the graphic arts. But in this study, we will limit our attention to poetry. "Language," as René Wellek and Austin Warren remind us in *Theory of Literature*, "is the material of literature as stone or bronze is of sculpture, paints of pictures, or sounds of music. But one should realize that language is not mere inert matter like stone but is itself a creation of man and is thus charged with the cultural heritage of a linguistic group."[3] No scholar would argue that Afro-Americans and Anglo-Americans do not belong to the same Indo-European linguistic group. By the same token, no serious student of the Black experience would deny the obvious social and psychological differences in the cultural heritage of the two ethnic groups—deeply ingrained differences that have been manipulated by the WASP majority to perpetuate either an Olympian contempt or paternalistic tolerance of Black American character and culture. I shall return to this point later.

But now I shall focus on the Western concept of high art. Though the line between natural genius and madness is sometimes wafer thin and though poetry lovers may not always agree with the political or ethical content of all they hear, those who flock to readings of Ginsberg, McKuen, Yevtushenko, Baraka, and Gwendolyn Brooks are hardly inclined to dismiss these artists as mad or to endorse a policy of political censorship that would stifle the development of the arts. This in part explains the unpopularity of Plato's contempt for poets as expressed in the *Republic* and *Ion.* Critics have found a more viable concept of the art of poetry in Aristotle. It is in the *Poetics* that we find the definition of formal art, in particular tragedy, as "an imitation of an action that is serious, complete, and of a certain magnitude; in language embellished with each kind of artistic ornament, the several kinds being found in separate parts of the play; in the form of action, not of narrative; through pity and fear effecting the proper purgation of these emotions."[4] Basing his observations on the indigenous literature of Greece, Aristotle further expressed the conviction that the truth of poetry is more philosophical or universal than history, which concerns itself with the particular.

Horace, the conservative Roman critic who became the favorite of the Renaissance and Neo-classical periods, rigidly codified many of Aristotle's observations. The *Art of Poetry* reads like a rule book for critics and writers. Rather than imitate Nature, Horace advised the aspiring artist to study the Greek masterpieces, avoid extreme language, adhere to traditional themes, and cultivate moderation and decorum of style at all times. But the charm of poetry, he cautioned, does not necessarily exist for its own sake. The poet must blend the delightful and the useful, for teaching is also his business.[5]

Assuming that the nature and function of literature must be correlative, some modern aestheticians have taken issue with Horace. Much of the misunderstanding about the function of poetry, we are told in *Theory of Literature,* is buried in the Horatian caveat of *dulce et utile:* poetry delights and instructs. "When a work of literature functions successfully," Wellek and Warren argue, "the two 'notes' of pleasure and utility should not merely coexist but coalesce. The pleasure of literature . . . is not one preference among a long list of possible pleasures but is a 'higher pleasure' because pleasure in a higher kind of activity, i.e., non-acquisitive contemplation. And the utility—the seriousness, the instructiveness—of literature is a pleasurable seriousness, i.e., not the seriousness of a duty which must be done or of a lesson to be learned but an aesthetic seriousness, a seriousness of perception."[6] In this reformulation of the Horatian sugar-coated-pill theory of poetry, Wellek and Warren provide the classic arena for the academic defense of art-for-art's sake.

Turning from high art, the cult of beauty and taste, to folk art, we immediately sense the dialectic tension between the two concepts. But it is an oversimplification of the dynamics of this dialectic to reduce it to the mere question of whether the work is the product of a conscious artist. Folk art is the creative expression of the people, by the people, for the people. Aristotle realized that Homer's *Odyssey* and *Iliad* were originally folk epics performed by bards whose purpose was to entertain and instruct their audience while preserving their national heritage. In written form, this oral literature loses its anonymity of authorship and takes on a hybrid character. This transition is not easy to describe and it most certainly defies dogmatic classifications.

High art and folk art are both concerned with the truth of human experience, but the latter—as the early poems of Wordsworth and Scott vividly illustrate—is a more direct, popular evocation of commonplace reality. And while the high seriousness of much of the poetry of Arnold stresses a morbid individualism and enduring sophistication, folk art emphasizes communal modes of perceiving and expressing the vital forces of life. In contrast to the self-conscious sophistication of high art, folk art at its best is characterized by effortless grace in form and style. Its primary appeal—as serious devotees of Yeats or Joyce or Frost will undoubtedly admit—is to a particular ethnic or regional group. Yet it is the artist's fidelity to the particular, the concrete reality, that enables him to achieve the universal. The verities of high art are not more profound, nor are the two kinds of art necessarily mutually exclusive. In fact, as James Weldon Johnson's "O Black and Unknown Bards" and Jean Toomer's "Song of the Son" suggest, high art and folk art when viewed as the antipodes of a single continuum, are inextricably bound to each other. Both of the above poems address themselves to the fundamental question of identity, celebrate the genius of the first New World Blacks, and capture in self-conscious yet felicitous language the soulful nature of the spirituals.

But when talking about the American identity, one must note, as stated earlier, that the WASP majority has manipulated philosophy and science in an attempt to justify its treatment of Afro-Americans. The Puritan legacy with its distorted notion of sex and the arts, the Jeffersonian-Rousseauistic view of natural rights with its ethnocentric egalitarianism, and the hydra-headed system of capitalism are commonly recognized as the cornerstones of the American ethos. Caught in this juggernaut of social forces, Africa and her progeny fell victim to the myth of an ignoble past and were cast by Europeans and Anglo-Americans alike as archetypal scapegoats on a Manichean world stage on which the victims represented evil. Allegorically, Black people were envisioned as the embodiment of absolute spiritual truths—e.g., Rousseau's Noble Savage or Melville's Babo—that graphically confirmed the white man's privileged relationship to his God and his alleged superiority to non-white men. The tensions between Puritan theology and the vested economic interests of the pioneers of the New World galvanized into the cultural matrix for the development of American character.

Houston A. Baker, Jr.

SOURCE: "Black Folklore and the Black American Literary Tradition," in *Long Black Song: Essays in Black American Literature and Culture*, The University Press of Virginia, 1972, pp. 18-41.

[*In the following excerpt, Baker identifies varieties of typology in African-American folklore by examining an array of literary forms ranging from sermons to blues songs.*]

"The existing monuments form an ideal order among themselves," said T. S. Eliot, for whom the ideal order and its modifications constituted a definition of tradition in a somewhat restricted literary sense. In this sense all works in a body of literature combine to form the tradition of that body, and the introduction of a new work modifies the tradition as a whole. When we turn to an exploration of the black literary tradition, we can hardly doubt the applicability of Eliot's definition. The monuments of black American literature constitute an ideal order, and both the critic of this literature and the writer himself must possess what Eliot called "the historical sense"; that is to say, both must recognize and understand the order constituted by existing works, and both must realize where they themselves stand in relationship to that order. At the foundation of the black American literary tradition stands black folklore. To understand the order as a whole, one must first come to terms with its foundation; this is the first step toward a recognition of what is genuinely new in contemporary works of black American literature.

The word *tradition*, however, has another meaning, one that is broader, less literary. This second definition refers to customs, practices, and beliefs that have been handed down from generation to generation by "the folk" or "the group." The word is no less valuable to us in this sense, for surely tradition in a sociohistorical context plays an important role in the writer's development and in the critic's task. As Charles Sainte-Beuve noted:

> Very great individuals rise beyond a group. They themselves make a center, and gather others to them. But it is the group, the association, the alliance and active exchange of ideas that gives to the man of talent all his *participation in what is outside himself*, all his maturing and value.[1]

Since the group provides direction and gives to the artist principles for the conduct of life, Sainte-Beuve felt that it was necessary for the critic to know the group in which the artist had his genesis; in short, he believed an awareness of sociohistorical factors was a necessity for the reader who wished fully to understand a work of art.

In this second sense of the word *tradition*, it is still black folklore that rests at the foundation; for the customs, practices, and beliefs of the black American race (of the group in which the talented black writer has his genesis) are clearly and simply reflected in the folklore. Some initial attention to the lore aids in an evaluation of black expression, and, paradoxically, it is early black expression that provides one of the surest sources of this sociohistorical knowledge.

The value of black folklore in both the literary and the sociohistorical sense of the word *tradition* forces us to come to terms with the concept of "the folk" before we can arrive at some clear idea of what the black literary tradition encompasses. In the most basic sense, the term refers to all black people in America. In a more definitive sense, however, it refers to that "unsophisticated, homogeneous group" of black people in America "living in a politically-bounded advanced culture but isolated from it by such factors as topography, geography, religion, dialect, economics and race."[2] Obviously topography, geography, and religion have not been as influential in the isolation of the black folk as have dialect, economics, and race. Brought to this country for economic reasons, the first black Americans were legally and systematically isolated on the basis of race, and their dialect—a result of acculturation—helped to set them even further apart. The story of the isolation of the black folk has been too well told by such men as Benjamin Quarles, E. Franklin Frazier, John Hope Franklin, Lerone Bennett, and others to need repetition, but it is essential to realize that this isolation was one of the most thorough, brutal, and complete separations that any group has ever endured. The moral implications are not of great concern here, but the implications for a study of black folklore cannot be ignored.

In effect, a race was *created* from the blacks brought to America; their African ties were severed as thoroughly as possible by slave traders, plantation owners, and politicians, and the folk were accorded neither the rights nor the privileges of American citizenship. Richard Wright has expressed the results of these conditions: "Truly, you must now know that the word Negro in America means something not racial or biological, but something purely social, something made in the United States."[3] Just as the black American is a social being composed of racial and cultural traits ranging from African to Irish, so his folklore is a social product composed of elements from many stocks. The thesis of Richard Dorson's *Negro Folktales in Michigan*, therefore, seems applicable:

> United States Negro tales form a distinctive repertoire, separate from the narratives of West Africa, the West Indies, Europe, the British Isles, and white America. Southern Negroes have drawn upon all these lores, and added materials from their own environment and experience to produce a highly diversified and culturally independent folk tradition.[4]

Sterling Brown has set forth the same *sui generis* category for black spirituals that Dorson claims for black folktales, and his explanation seems more desirable than attributing either the songs or the tales of the black American to a specific racial or cultural group on the basis of provenance.[5] Not that black folklore includes none of the elements of other lores; the point is simply that out of a conglomerate of contacts has come a singular body of folk expression which reflects a singular folk experience. The categories are the same—animal tale, religious tale, folk song, ballad, and so forth—but the reflected experience is unique. Moreover, the significance of black folklore is perhaps greater than that of any other lore in a discussion of the literary tradition of the race from which it originated. Even the most recent black American writer is closer to the earliest folk expression of his culture than are the recent writers of most other groups; the contemporary black author is but three hundred odd years removed, a bare modicum of time to the folklorist.

An exploration of the various genres of black folklore, therefore, should reveal the sources of some of the themes and techniques that we find in the work of conscious literary artists from Paul Laurence Dunbar to Ralph Ellison. Moreover, such an exploration should help to explain the significance of these themes and techniques and should carry us toward a further awareness of the presence of the past.

II Animal Tales

One of the most widely known genres of black folklore is the animal tale. The earliest collector and popularizer of black animal tales was Joel Chandler Harris, whose first volume, *Uncle Remus: His Songs and His Sayings,* was published in 1881; subsequent volumes appeared for the rest of the author's life. His work and the work of his immediate followers, however, while it is of undoubted value, does not truly represent black folk values. Harris and his contemporaries adopted an antebellum perspective and put black animal tales in the mouth of a faithful black retainer—a simple, primitive child of nature. It is not surprising that Harris and others depicted white plantation children as this puerile narrator's audience.

In fact, black animal tales are similar in some respects to the animal tales of all other lores. That is to say, they began as etiological stories and accrued meaning as time passed.[6] From the earliest stages of his existence, man has had a keen interest in animals (if not out of intellectual curiosity, at least for self-interest), and his observations of their actions together with his lack of scientific knowledge has led him to evolve tales of explanation. The explanatory nature of the animal tale was ideally suited to the needs of the black folk in America, since the land and its fauna were alien to the founders of the black American race. Moreover, given the lack of sophistication of the black folk in relation to the advanced culture that surrounded them, one would expect to find a high incidence of animal tales in their folklore.

The farther back we go in time, "the more conspicuous becomes the place taken by etiological animal tales."[7]

As time passed, however, black animal tales took on new meaning, moving closer to the fable. They lost part of their explanatory character and came to be employed more for entertainment and instruction. The chief character of the black animal tales, Brer Rabbit, is an entertaining figure who had much wisdom to impart to the black folk. J. Mason Brewer delineates the trickster rabbit as follows:

> The role of the rabbit in the tales of the American Negro is similar to that of the hare in African folk narratives—that of the trickster who shrewdly outwits and gains a victory over some physically stronger or more powerful adversary. The animal tales told by Negro slaves with Brer Rabbit as the hero had a meaning far deeper than mere entertainment. The rabbit actually symbolized the slave himself. Whenever the rabbit succeeded in proving himself smarter than another animal the slave rejoiced secretly, imagining himself smarter than his master.[8]

Black animal tales, therefore, resemble the animal tales of other lores in their employment of the trickster, but the social condition of the folk producing them gives an added dimension, a certain psychical component which the slave narrator surely supplied and which his slave audience readily recognized.

The subliminal component of black animal tales is apparent in the delineation of the trickster as a cunning figure who tricks others into doing his work. The "avoidance of work" situation motivates the action of such tales as "Playing Godfather," "Tar Baby," and "Brer Fox and the Goobers."[9] In each of these tales Brer Rabbit sets out to evade work, and in the process tricks the larger animals, escapes punishment, and even comes away with certain material gains. Both "Playing Godfather" and "Tar Baby" have parallels in other lores,[10] but the very title of "Brer Fox and the Goobers," indicates its proximity to the black folk, since *goober* ("peanut") is an African linguistic survival.

A second trait of the black animal tale—the hero's employment of disguises—reflects what must have been a familiar experience. In both "The Watcher Blinded" and "Why Brer Gator's Hide Is So Horny," Brer Rabbit shows his expertise in deception. After they had killed a stolen ox, "rabbit asked wolf what would he do if some ladies came and asked him for some meat." When the wolf answers that he would give it to them free of charge, the rabbit begins his performance. The stupidity of the wolf is emphasized by the fact that Brer Rabbit assumes four different feminine disguises and receives a portion of the wolf's meat each time. In "Why Brer Gator's Hide Is So Horny," the protagonist conceals his feelings about Brer Gator in order to trick the larger animal into a painful situation, one which alters the gator's perspective as well as his appearance.

A third trait of black animal tales—the ambivalent attitude toward the trickster—is shared by the animal tales of all lores.[11] Brer Rabbit is not always the cunning and successful hero; he is often depicted as a coarse blunderer. "The Watcher Blinded" shows Brer Rabbit jeopardizing himself in an act of lyrical braggadocio; the "Tar Baby" story shows the trickster tricked; and in "Why Brer Rabbit Wears a 'Round-'Bout" the hero is brought to a painful end. In all lores, these stories reflect the fact that while the narrator and the audience admire the trickster's cunning, they also envy his prowess and fear its possible ramifications.

Black animal tales thus contain both the universal aspects of the animal tale genre and certain characteristic aspects that mark them as the product of the black American folk experience. The common traits of the trickster are present, but his identification with the slave makes the tales unique. Like all animal tales, those in black folklore proceed out of a sylvan and agrarian environment, but they also proceed out of a slave experience in which the success or failure of the trickster had a singularly important didactic and wish-fulfillment value.

The agrarianism and didacticism of black animal tales connect this genre with another genre of black folklore, the proverb.[12] Although they are not uniquely black in theme, black proverbs seem to come directly out of the agrarian soil that nourished the black American race, and the idiom in which they are expressed marks them as distinctively black. Proverbs like "Tarrypin walk fast 'nuff fer to go visitin'," or "Rooster makes mo racket dan de hin w'at lay de aig," or "Hongry rooster don't cackle w'en he fine a wum" are obviously close to the black animal tale in many respects, and the psychical element noted in the animal tales may have been present even in these terse reflections.

III The Trickster Slave

In black folklore, the tales surrounding the exploits of the trickster slave are known as the "John Cycle." John or Jack, or whatever name the protagonist may assume, is usually presented as a lazy, affable slave who has a somewhat easy relationship with his master and is incessantly engaged in some contest with him. Although there are stories which present him as the loser and show him in the throes of punishment, in most cases he emerges victorious, sometimes even gaining his freedom. Tales of the trickster slave began to appear after the Civil War, and the degree of impunity enjoyed by the black folk narrator after the war probably helped to account for the substitution of Jack or John for Brer Rabbit. In the days of jubilee and freedom, the black narrator could talk of the black man's subversion and trickery with a reasonable degree of safety. The trickster in the John tales, therefore, became overtly identified with the black slave. Dorson delineates the tales in the following manner:

> Folktale critics who see the Rabbit as the psychic symbol of Negro resentment against the white man cannot know of the crafty slave named John. Seldom printed, the spate of stories involving John and his Old Master provides the most engaging theme in American Negro lore. . . . trickster John directly expresses and illuminates the plantation Negro character. No allegoric or symbolic creation, he is a generic figure representing the antebellum slave who enjoyed some measure of favoritism and familiarity with his owner.[13]

It is not true that the critic who sees Brer Rabbit as a psychic symbol must be ignorant of the John tales; John is a later figure, and attitudes, impossible earlier, had a good deal to do with his appearance.

The action of the trickster slave tales is made possible only by a lowering of the barriers that normally separated the master and the slave. In "A Laugh That Meant Freedom," for example, Nehemiah is free to come in contact with his various masters, and he is allowed the opportunity to jest with them. It is Nehemiah's ability to jest that helps him avoid work and that eventually secures his liberty. In "How Buck Won His Freedom," Buck's opportunity to steal from the master without fear of a whipping (or death) is made possible by the master's tolerance, since many masters felt that the petit larceny of the slave functioned as an escape valve for his aggression. In this tale, it is finally the master's overconfidence, combined with the slave's knowledge of white society's vulnerabilities, that enables Buck to win his freedom. The stupidity of the master is driven home by the fact that after allowing Buck's knowledge to become consummate he is foolish enough to challenge the slave; the results of the contest are predetermined.

The trickster slave, however, is not always presented as the daring, resourceful challenger of the system; at times he is simply a clownish fellow who escapes defeat through crude wit and uncommon luck. The protagonist of "Uncle Israel and the Law" possesses a desire for material gain that almost lands him in jail. "Do you know who I am?" asks the stranger to whom Uncle Israel has told fantastic tales of chicken stealing. "No, sah, Boss, 'ceptin' yuh's a chicken buyah. Who else is Yuh?" "I'm the biggest constable in this county," answers the stranger. The trickster seems trapped, but his quick wit effects his escape. "Sez yuh is, Boss? Wal, Ah'll decla'. An' don' yuh know who Ah is? Ain't Massa and de oberseeah tol' yuh who Ah is? Wal, Ah's de bigges' liah in dis county." In "The Prophet Vindicated," a combination of proverbial wisdom and luck allows Uncle Phimon to triumph. When Phimon, who had claimed he could prophesy the future and see things hidden from ordinary men, is put to a test, he finally admits his frauds with the words, "Wal, Massa, de ol' coon run uh long time, but dey cotch 'im at las.'" His hearers fail to realize that he is making a confession, however, and when the box whose contents he was supposed to divine is turned over, an old coon scampers out.

Beyond their wish-fulfillment value, trickster slave tales also seem to represent a romanticizing of the slave experience, from a black antebellum perspective. The tales appeared immediately after the Civil War, and a general romanticizing of the "Old South" began as soon as the defeat of the Confederacy became apparent. In the "John Cycle," masters are tolerant and kind, and the slave is allowed rights that could not have been "inalienable" in a slave system. Considering the plight of the freedman, however, it is not surprising that some of the wandering, hungry, and jobless folk looked back on slavery as a time of security and happiness. But the sentimental elements of the trickster tales cannot obscure the fact that they are tales of rebellion, tales of the subversion of the slave system by the jester slave.

From this examination it seems as though some redefinition of the traditional feat and contest heroes is in order when we are dealing with black folklore, for when we consider the folk background of the black race, the stakes in the animal and trickster tales are similar to those in the European romances and legendary ballads. The contest or feat hero of European and other lores wages a battle which must result in freedom or gain on one side and death or incarceration on the other. If we consider the subliminal element of black animal tales and the aspect of ego projection in the John Cycle, we can see this same dichotomy. The trickster (although a slave) had as much to lose if he was defeated as Jason—or Pecos Bill. The trickster of black folklore is both a feat and a contest hero, since in his own manner he fights impressive battles and accomplishes impressive feats, given the nature of his environment. An understanding of the experience of the black American folk and of the psychical component of their tales makes it less difficult for us to see how a hero who not only endured but also achieved certain material gains assumes the status of a quest, contest, or feat hero. Thus it is impossible to agree with the limited view of critics who ignore these crucial aspects of the tales: "On reading through the large body of recorded Negro folktales, one is struck by the one-sided preference for trickster heroes as compared to the well-developed tradition of quest and defender heroes found in abundance in the traditions of the Indians and whites living in close contact with the Negroes."[14] There is no striking or one-sided preference apparent in the tales if one sees the trickster as the contest or feat hero that he surely was for the black folk; what is needed is a modification of Orin Klapp's extremely helpful article on the folk hero,[15] a modification that would take full account of what Sainte-Beuve called the "group" that provides the maturing and value for the artist.

Before leaving the initial stages of folk expression, it should be noted that an extensive body of superstitions, ghost stories, witch-riding stories, voodoo tales, and "hant" stories also characterize black folklore. The same lack of detailed knowledge that contributed to the emergence of the animal tale also motivated explanatory tales that were wider ranging. Witches, hants, and ghosts helped to explain unusual happenings—radical changes of personality, mysterious sicknesses, or merely noises in the night. Voodoo, the practice of attempting to control events by the use of charms, spells, or rituals, was similar to magic, but its implications were more ominous, since the voodoo doctor or the conjurer in the tales often inflicted death or injury on his victims. In some communities both voodoo and conjure reached the religious level. "Superstition," as Krappe points out, "in common parlance designates the sum of beliefs and practices shared by other people in so far as they differ from our own. What we believe and practise ourselves is, of course, religion."[16]

IV Religious Tales, Preacher Tales, Sermons, and Testimonials

The church has played a singular role in the development of black American culture. In one sense, it precedes the family as a black cultural institution, for the black family as such did not exist during the days of slavery. The church was the first stable black institution in America; it was the center of religious, social, and political activity and produced many of the most dynamic black leaders. Its importance is adequately reflected in black folklore, where we find an extensive body of religious tales, preacher tales, sermons, and testimonials, all of which are both didactic and entertaining.

One familiar quip characterizes black religion as opposed to white in the following manner:

> White folks go to Chu'ch
> He nevah crack a smile
> Nigguh go to Chu'ch
> You heah 'im laff a mile.[17]

All that is simple, however, is not naive; for this statement contains an essential fact of religious history. From time immemorial preachers, prophets, and religious leaders have recognized the value of entertaining the audience. The effectiveness of the simple, entertaining story is perhaps greatest when basic religious truths are being imparted. The exemplum aided the medieval religious teacher in his dealings with the peasantry of England, and the short, illustrative religious tale occupies some place in the history of most religions of the world.

In black folklore, we find a story like "De Ways of de Wimmens," functioning as an explanatory, didactic, and entertaining tale. Its stated purpose is to explain the nature of femininity—an awesome task in any age—but the tale goes further than this. It provides an explication of the Genesis story, showing man his place in the universe, and it provides more than one laugh. In effect, it renders an exegesis that is sufficiently imaginative to be understood by an unsophisticated audience. The beginning paragraph of the tale perhaps best illustrates why it would appeal to folk listeners: "Most folks say de six day was Satdy, cause on de SEVENTH day didn't de Lawd rest an look his creation over? Now hit MAY be Satdy dat he done de WORK of making man an woman, but from all de signs, he must THOUGHT UP de first man an woman on old unlucky FRIDAY." The body of the tale details how Adam gained strength while Eve gained control of the keys to the kitchen and the bedroom as gifts from "de Lawd." The ending offers memorable humor: "So dat de reason, de very reason, why de mens THINKS dey is de boss and de wimmen KNOWS dey is boss, cause dey got dem two little keys to use in dat slippery wimmen's way. Yas, fawever mo an den some! And if you don't know DAT already, you ain't no married man."

Another type of religious tale stands in antithesis to the exemplum. In black folklore it is known as the preacher tale. The religious leader has been the protagonist of amusing (at times, scandalous) stories for ages, and the black preacher is no exception. Brewer explains that "the preacher has always been the acknowledged leader in the Negro community, and as such he has been the target of many witty stories told by his followers."[18] And Dorson says of the protagonists of preacher tales, "Their alleged pomposity, greed, unchastity, and hypocrisy made fine joke material for the humour of deflation and irreverence."[19]

Narratives such as "The Farmer and G.P.C.," "The Preacher and His Farmer Brother," and "Reverend Carter's Twelfth Anniversary Sermon" display the humor of deflation in abundance. The farmer's willingness to "go preach Christ" is quickly deflated by the more practical woman who reads the initial *G.P.C.*, which the clouds seem to form, as "go pick cotton." The piety of the preacher, which leads him to attribute his brother's fine crops to "de Lawd," is punctured by the brother's timely remark, "Yeah, but you oughta seed hit when de Lawd had it by Hisse'f." And the otherworldly reverence of preachers receives a prick when the spry Reverend Carter dances on Sunday for a fee and promises to do the same every Sunday if a similar reward is forthcoming. In each of these tales, the church leader is pulled down from his godly perch and shown in all his essential humanity.

But if the preacher himself was often the target of humorous abuse, his sermon was a different matter altogether. The sermon was considered "de Word" of God revealed to man, and in its imagery, detail, and sheer poetry, the black sermon is uniquely powerful. The sermons display the same literalness and picturesqueness of speech that Dobie has noted as characteristic of the religious tales;[20] they present a vivid picture of a personal God and a "chosen people" in language that is often startling in its grace. One of the most famous black sermons, John Jasper's "De Sun Do Move," contains striking images: "I don't carry de keys to de Lord's closet and He ain't tell me to peep in and if I did I'm so stupid I wouldn't know it when I see it"; "But I can read de Bible and get de things what lay on de top of de soil"; "Truth is mighty; it can break de heart of stone and I must fire another arrow of truth out of de quiver of de Lord." The imagery of "The Wounds of Jesus," a sermon recorded by Zora Neale Hurston, is equally impressive: "When de blood is lopin thru yo' veins / Like de iron monasters [monsters] on de rail"; "Two thousand years have went by on their rusty ankles"; "From the stroke of the master's axe / One angel took the flinches of God's eternal power / And bled the veins of the earth." Images such as these speak of the vitality, literalness, and closeness to the soil of the people who produced them; they speak, moreover, of a people who believed in the nearness of God, in his personal nature, in his graciousness and his power. Black sermons, in short, constitute some of the finest poetry of belief ever written, and their fusion of the earthly and the abstract makes them pulsate with meaning.

Another form of religious tale is the black testimonial, which displays some of the same techniques seen in the sermons. The imagery of the opening lines of the testimonial, "God Struck Me Dead," for example—"I have always been a sheep. I was never a goat. I was created and cut out and born in the world for Heaven"—is so brilliant that it immediately captures our attention, and using a favorite device of the black preacher, it identifies the speaker from the outset as one of God's company. The testimonial continues by carrying us into a world of significant numbers, dream visions, and miraculous cures, offering an example of mystical writing of the first order. Yet it is distinguished from a more learned mystical tradition in its employment of the most mundane, at times agrarian, imagery. The work conveys the light and dark of the conversion experience and all of its ramifications in a beautifully simple, poetic manner:

> When God struck me dead with His power I was living on 14th Avenue. It was the year of the Centennial. I was in my house alone and I declare unto you when His power struck me I died. I fell out on the floor flat on my back. I could neither speak nor move for my tongue stuck to the roof of my mouth; my jaws were locked and my limbs were stiff.

Such language could not have failed to affect a godly, or even an ungodly, audience.

V Folk Songs

The songs of black folklore can be categorized under two headings—sacred and secular. In the first category we find the black spirituals, and in the second, the work, levee, river, boating, sea, and jubilee songs. The cogency, beauty, and power of the black spirituals, however, put them first in any evaluation of black folk songs. Spirituals were the first items of black folklore to be collected and publicized with a degree of seriousness. Thomas Wentworth Higginson, an early collector, commented on the nature of the spirituals and recorded a number of them in an article in the *Atlantic* (1867) and in the later *Army Life in a Black Regiment* (1870). W. F. Allen and others familiar with the life and songs of the Sea Islanders of South Carolina published in 1867 a collection of spirituals entitled *Slave Songs of the United States*. Allen's introduction to the volume is still valuable as a guide to the songs. A host of other collectors have written about the spirituals, and although they have debated the origins of the songs, they have usually accorded them high praise.

The controversy over the origin of the spirituals, precipitated and nourished by Henry Krehbiel, James Weldon Johnson, and others, seems best resolved by Sterling Brown's comment: "Neither European nor African, but partaking of elements of both, the result is a new kind of music, certainly not mere imitation, but more creative and original than any other American music."[21] Despite the fact that they grow out of and employ the vocabulary, prophecies, and stories of a Protestant tradition, there is nothing in the history of American religious and secular music to equal the poignancy and lyricism of the black spirituals. The songs, in fact, are almost unique in the history of America, as W. E. B. Du Bois has pointed out:

> Little of beauty has America given the world save the rude grandeur of God himself stamped on her bosom; the human spirit in this new world has expressed itself in vigor and ingenuity rather than in beauty. And so by fateful chance the Negro folk-song—the rhythmic cry of the slave—stands today not simply as the sole American music, but as the most beautiful expression of human experience born this side of the seas.[22]

Like all accomplished works of art, the spirituals show many sides; they are as complex and difficult to define as the word *beauty*. On one hand—considering spirituals such as "Go Down Moses," "Mary Don't You Weep," and "Steal Away"—one can see that the black religious folk identified themselves with the chosen people of Israel. Going further, however, we can see a subversive aspect in the spirituals; after all, Pharoah's army did get drowned. To "steal away," moreover, was anything but constructive for the plantation economy, and when freedom's chariot came low, there were normally fewer slaves in the field the next morning.

On the other hand, the spirituals manifest a great and abiding sorrow, as anyone who has heard "Nobody Knows the Trouble I've Seen," "I Know Moonrise," or "Motherless Child" well sung can testify. In these songs, we have "the articulate cry of the slave to the world," and it seems perfectly justifiable to call them "sorrow songs": the element of pathos singled out by early commentators reveals itself again and again.

But there is also joy, vitality, and a sense of black "fused strength" in spirituals like "No More Auction Block," "Deep River," and "God's Gonna Set Dis World on Fire." In these we see the promised joy of salvation and escape, and we witness one illustration of the apocalypse theme that pervades black American literature. In such songs we have both happiness and hope, and the same can be said of songs such as "When the Saints Go Marching In," "Every Time I Feel the Spirit," and "The Virgin Mary Had a Baby Boy."

The spirituals, therefore, form a genre that cannot be easily categorized; through complex rhythm and crafted poetry, these songs range the entire gamut of human experience. They proceed from the heart of humanity, and their simple form—a single line of recitative and a single line of refrain—makes them memorable. A number of collectors have commented on the method of composition of the spirituals, but again it is Sterling Brown who provides one of the most elucidating statements.[23] Brown feels that the vocabulary, the idiom, and the stories of the spirituals were taken from a "folk storehouse," and that as one "leader" had exhausted his stock, another would take up the recitative. In this manner, the spirituals were not merely sung, but actually "composed," and even the simplest incidents could provide motivation for a new spiritual or could be worked into the framework of an existing one. One former slave detailed the method of composition to James McKim as follows:

> I'll tell you; it's dis way. My master call me up and order me a short peck of corn and a hundred lash. My friends see it and is sorry for me. When dey come to de praise meeting dat night dey sing about it. Some's very good singers and know how; and dey work it in, work it in, you know; till dey get it right; and dat's de way.[24]

We may well conclude with McKim that this is "a very satisfactory explanation."

The secular songs of the black folk are largely concerned with the primary activity of the folk experience—work. Black work songs proceed from the chain gang, the cottonfields, the levee, the inland waterways, and the high seas. They were either accompaniments to the work or descriptions of it. Thus we have the rock-smashing rhythms of "Hyah Come de Cap'm" and "Take This Hammer," and we have the humor and subtle protest of "Pick a Bale of Cotton" (it took an able-bodied man a week, not a day as in the song, to pick a bale of cotton). The chain-gang songs protest the treatment accorded prisoners, and they frequently delineate the escaped convict—the man who has defied the system—as a folk hero. The sea and river songs, like "Blow the Man Down," provide the rhythm for work and at the same time describe the nature of the work and the life that accompanies it.[25]

Two groups of secular songs remain: the jubilee songs and, more important, the blues. Jubilee songs were sung by the folk on celebration days, and the name, according to Maud Cuney-Hare, comes from the chief drummer—known as "Juba"—who pounded out the rhythms. The origin of the blues is not quite so simply explained, for they, in a real sense, represent the juncture of many streams of black folk song and experience. The art form of the blues is a distillate of black music and black folk experience.

A song like "See, See Rider" chronicles the promiscuity forced on blacks, male and female, by society: "I'm goin' away, baby, I won't be back till fall. / Lord, Lord,

Lord! / Goin' away, baby, won't be back till fall. / If I find me a good man, I won't be back at all." And "Southern Blues" captures the pain of hard luck and fickle lovers:

> House catch on fire
> And ain't no water around,
> If your house catch on fire,
> Ain't no water around,
> Throw yourself out the window,
> Let it burn on down.
>
> . . . . .
>
> Let me be your ragdoll
> Until your china comes.
> Let me be your ragdoll
> Until your china comes.
> If he keeps me ragged,
> He's got to rag it some.

"Careless Love" chronicles the anguish of the casual love affairs caused by a migratory existence, and in "Good Morning Blues," appears the overall attitude of endurance in the face of despair:

> Good mornin', blues,
> Blues, how do you do?
> Yes, blues, how do you do?
> I'm doing all right,
> Good morning, how are you?

Throughout the genre, songs like "The Midnight Special" express what the railroad meant to the black folk as a means both of escape and of carrying love away or bringing it "back home."

Ralph Ellison's definition of the blues seems the most comprehensive and enlightening one:

> The blues is an impulse to keep the painful details and episodes of a brutal experience alive in one's aching consciousness, to finger its jagged grain, and to transcend it, not by the consolation of philosophy but by squeezing from it a near-tragic, near-comic lyricism. As a form, the blues is an autobiographical chronicle of personal catastrophe expressed lyrically.[26]

Endurance and transcendence by lyricism are two of the most important aspects of the black folk experience, and the blues capture these essential aspects with consummate skill.

VI Ballads

The final genre of black folklore to be considered is the ballad. Black folk ballads are not numerous, but two are quite important in the present discussion because of their popularity and their role in the development of the black folk hero. One of these is the widely known "John Henry," and the other is "Stackolee." "John Henry" has "transcended" its classification as a black folk ballad, since the hero has become a national folk hero; and a recent rendition of "Stackolee" has increased the popularity of that ballad's protagonist.

The reason for the appeal of "John Henry" is not far to seek; the contest of the ballad is between man and machine. The ballad, of course, reflects more than a simple contest; what we have in "John Henry" is the essential dichotomy of the nineteenth-century industrial revolution and the twentieth-century age of technology. The work presents the new industrial laborer who attempts to retain his importance in the face of an awesome technology, and the results of the effort are foreordained—the man is crushed:

> The steam drill was on the right han' side,
> John Henry was on the left,
> Says before I let this steam drill beat me down,
> I'll hammah myself to death,
> I'll hammah myself to death.
>
> . . . . .
>
> The hammah that John Henry swung,
> It weighed over nine poun',
> He broke a rib in his left han' side,
> And his intrels fell on the groun',
> And his intrels fell on the groun'.

Yet the protagonist is a contest or feat hero of note; his daring is not to be denied, and the pathos and sorrow that accompany his death are his just rewards.

The hero of "Stackolee," on the other hand, is anything but a pitiable figure; he is to be feared and respected because of his deviance from accepted codes of conduct:

> One dark and dusty day
> I was strolling down the street.
> I thought I heard some old dog bark,
> But it warn't nothing but Stackolee gambling in the dark.
> Stackolee threw seven.
> Billy said, It ain't that way.
> You better go home and come back another day.
> Stackolee shot Billy four times in the head
> And left that fool on the floor damn near dead.
> Stackolee decided he'd go up to Sister Lou's.
> Said, Sister Lou! Sister Lou, guess what I done done?
> I just shot and killed Billy, your big-head son.
> Sister Lou said, Stackolee, that can't be true!
> You and Billy been friends for a year or two.
> Stackolee said, Woman, if you don't believe what I said,
> Go count the bullet holes in that son-of-a-gun's head.
> Sister Lou got frantic and all in a rage,
> Like a tea hound dame on some frantic gage.
> She got on the phone, Sheriff, Sheriff, I want you to help poor me.
> I want you to catch that bad son-of-a-gun they call Stackolee.
> Sheriff said, My name might begin with an *s* and end with an *f*
> But if you want that bad Stackolee you got to get him yourself.
> So Stackolee left, he went walking down the New Haven track.
> A train come along and flattened him on his back.

He went up in the air and when he fell
Stackolee landed right down in hell.
He said, Devil, devil, put your fork up on the
   shelf
Cause I'm gonna run this devilish place myself.
There came a rumbling on the earth and a
   tumbling on the ground,
That bad son-of-a-gun, Stackolee, was turning
   hell around.
He ran across one of his ex-girl friends down
   there.
She was Chock-full-o'-nuts and had pony-tail
   hair.
She said, Stackolee, Stackolee, wait for me.
I'm trying to please you, can't you see?
She said, I'm going around the corner but I'll be
   right back.
I'm gonna see if I can't stack my sack.
Stackolee said, Susie Belle, go on and stack your
   sack.
But I just might not be here when you get back.
Meanwhile, Stackolee went with the devil's wife
   and with his girl friend, too.
Winked at the devil and said, I'll go with you.
The devil turned around to hit him a lick.
Stackolee knocked the devil down with a big
   black stick.
Now, to end this story, so I heard tell,
Stackolee, all by his self, is running hell.

Stackolee represents the badman hero who stands out-side the law; he is the rebel who uses any means necessary to get what he wants.

Roger Abrahams has characterized the badman hero and distinguished him from the trickster in the following manner: "Where guile and banter are the weapons of the trickster, arrogance and disdain serve the badman. He does not aim to be a god, but rather to be the eternal man in revolt, the devil."[27] Stackolee, however, represents more particularly the folk hero from the lower echelons of city life. Like the protagonists of "Frankie Baker" and "DuPree and Betty Blues," Stackolee comes out of an urban scene—a world of pimps, prostitutes, gambling, drinking, fighting, and death. He is as far removed from the barnyard and the fields as John Henry is from the plough and the scythe. Both are heroes of the black urban and industrial experiences.

VII

Only when we have arrived at some knowledge of the heroes and values that characterize the group in which the black writer has his genesis, can we begin to discuss the work of conscious literary artists with some degree of authority. When we turn to the first black American poet of distinction, the importance of our awareness of the folk background becomes apparent. Paul Laurence Dunbar draws directly from the "folk storehouse" for the majority of his poems and short stories; often working in what has been called the "Plantation Tradition," he produced poems that share the black antebellum perspective seen in the John Cycle. But Dunbar was not all sweetness and light, and at times (in such poems as "An

Ante-Bellum Sermon" and "We Wear the Mask") we see the subversive component of the trickster tales, the protest element of the work songs, and the impudence of the heroes of the badman ballads. Dunbar, the virtual father of black American poetry, was thus in some respects a "folk" poet, and we must know the lore if we are to understand his work.

Again, we must be fully aware of the black folk experience in order to come to terms with the work of the first black American prose writer of distinction, Charles Chesnutt. Chesnutt's first significant volume was a collection of short fiction entitled *The Conjure Woman* (1899). In this work we find the beliefs and practices associated with voodoo, black magic, and superstition. The full import of stories such as "The Goophered Grapevine" and "The Gray Wolf's Ha'nt" can only be grasped when we realize the role that conjure played in the lives of the agrarian black folk. Aunt Peggy, the conjurer of the first story, and Uncle Jube, of the second, virtually determine the fate of all the characters who surround them; this, of course, is possible only because the black folk (and even those who hold them in bondage, e.g., Mars Dugal) place the greatest faith in the powers of voodoo and conjure. Chesnutt, moreover, seems to make a conscious attempt to evoke the sinister mysteriousness of conjure tales, and his carefully-delineated narrator, Uncle Julius, is a storyteller in the best tradition of black expression.

The value of a knowledge of black sermons becomes apparent when we are confronted with James Weldon Johnson's *God's Trombones* (1927), one of the most beautiful volumes of verse ever produced by a black poet. Johnson used the folk sermons as a basis for his work, but modified and altered them until he produced such imaginative and exciting poems as "The Creation," "Listen, Lord—a Prayer," and "Go Down Death—a Funeral Sermon."

Familiarity with the lower-echelon urban hero facilitates our understanding of the literature of the Harlem Renaissance. Edward Margolies has pointed out that a concern for the low-life character of the city was one of the most salient features of black expression during the 1920s,[28] and Stackolee finds his counterparts in characters such as those encountered in Claude McKay's *Home to Harlem* (1928), and even in such recent black protagonists as the narrators of Claude Brown's *Manchild in the Promised Land* and *The Autobiography of Malcolm X.* Between the work of the Harlem Renaissance and that of more recent writers stand the principal figures of Ann Petry's *The Street* (1946), Chester Himes's *If He Hollers Let Him Go* (1945), and Richard Wright's *Native Son* (1940). Wright's Bigger Thomas is a counterpart of the badman hero who subverts white morality by refusing to heed its dictates; his partial victory assures freedom and material gain; but in the end he is destroyed by an inimical environment much like that which makes an early appearance in "Frankie and Johnny" and "Stackolee."

When we turn to one of Wright's later works, *Black Boy* (1945), we can again see the importance of a knowledge of the folk tradition. According to Ralph Ellison, Wright's work is a perfect expression of blues values and techniques. Ellison's statement appears in *Shadow and Act* (1953), and in this volume Ellison himself has a good deal to say about black folklore (particularly the music). One of his predecessors was equally aware of the value of the folk blues. Both the title and the content of Langston Hughes's first volume of poetry, *The Weary Blues* (1926), indicate that perhaps the most influential black poet of this century knew the value of the blues form. And within the last six years, one of black America's most prolific writers, LeRoi Jones, has manifested his concern for the blues form and values in his poetry and in critical works such as *Blues People* (1963) and *Black Music* (1968).

The characters, themes, and techniques of black religious lore have found their finest modern manifestation in James Baldwin's *Go Tell It on the Mountain* (1952). Baldwin, who was a boy preacher in Harlem, has used in his novel the humor of deflation seen in the preacher tales, the vivid imagery of the sermons, the form of the testimonials (with their awesome pictures of the conversion experience), and the themes of the spirituals. The title of the novel, like those of several of Baldwin's essays ("Many Thousands Gone," "The Fire Next Time"), is taken from a black spiritual.

Finally, there is Ralph Ellison's *Invisible Man*. Speaking of the craft of the black novelist in "The Art of Fiction: An Interview," Ellison says:

> For us [black novelists] the question should be, What are the specific *forms* of that [black American] humanity, and what in our background is worth preserving or abandoning. The clue to this can be found in folklore, which offers the first drawings of any group's character. It preserves mainly those situations which have repeated themselves again and again in the history of any given group. It describes those rites, manners, customs, and so forth, which insure the good life, or destroy it; and it describes those boundaries of feeling, thought, and action which that particular group has found to be the limitation of the human condition. It projects this wisdom in symbols which express the group's will to survive; it embodies those values by which the group lives and dies. These drawings may be crude but they are nonetheless profound in that they represent the group's attempt to humanize the world. It's no accident that great literature, the products of individual artists, is erected upon this humble base.[29]

Dryden's comment on Chaucer—"Here is God's plenty"—offers a fitting characterization of *Invisible Man*. Ellison's protagonist is both a trickster and an urban, industrial feat hero, and his adventures carry him through almost every phase of the black folk experience. There is the melancholy and promiscuity of the blues; the humor, pathos, and conversion of religious lore; the

protest spirit of the work songs and the badman ballads; and the subversiveness of the animal tales and spirituals.

To understand the classic works of black literature, a knowledge of the existing monuments and of the group in which the writers had their genesis is a necessity. Black folklore stands at the base of the black literary tradition, and we must first attain a knowledge of the lore; with such knowledge comes a better understanding of the black literary tradition as a whole.

More than fifty years ago James Weldon Johnson asked some of the same questions about the composers of the spirituals that critics today are posing in regard to all major black American writers:

> O black and unknown bards of long ago,
> How came your lips to touch the sacred fire?
> How, in your darkness, did you come to know
> The power and beauty of the minstrel's lyre?

Black folklore provides many of the answers.

NOTES

[1] From "Chateaubriand," *Nouveau Lundis*, July 22, 1862. In *Criticism: The Major Texts*, ed. Walter Jackson Bate (New York, 1952), p. 498. Italics are Sainte-Beuve's.

[2] John Greenway, *Literature among the Primitives* (Hatboro, Pa., 1964), p. xii.

[3] Richard Wright, "The Literature of the Negro in the United States," in *White Man, Listen!* (New York, 1964), p. 80.

[4] Cambridge, Mass., 1956, p. 187.

[5] Sterling Brown, "The Spirituals," in *The Book of Negro Folklore*, ed. Arna Bontemps and Langston Hughes (New York, 1958), pp. 279-89.

[6] Alexander Haggerty Krappe, *The Science of Folklore* (New York, 1930), pp. 60-63.

[7] *Ibid.*, p. 61.

[8] J. Mason Brewer, *American Negro Folklore* (Chicago, 1968), pp. 3-4.

[9] The tales, sermons, testimonials, songs, and ballads used for illustrative purposes in my text may be found in Bontemps and Hughes, *The Book of Negro Folklore*.

[10] Cf. Aurelia Espinosa, "Notes on the Origin and History of the Tar-Baby Story," *Journal of American Folklore*, XLIII (1930), pp. 129-209.

[11] Greenway, p. 72.

[12] Brewer, *American Negro Folklore*, p. 28.

[13] Dorson, p. 49.

[14] Fred O. Weldon, Jr., "Negro Folktale Heroes," in *And Horns on the Toads,* ed. Mody C. Boatwright, Wilson M. Hudson, Allen Maxwell (Dallas, 1959), p. 170.

[15] Orin E. Klapp, "The Folk Hero," *Journal of American Folklore,* LXI (1949), pp. 17-25.

[16] Krappe, p. 203.

[17] Quoted from J. Mason Brewer, *The Word on the Brazos* (Austin, Tex., 1953), p. 12.

[18] *Ibid.,* p. 3.

[19] Dorson, p. 166.

[20] J. Frank Dobie, "A Word on *The Word,*" in Brewer, *The Word on the Brazos,* pp. ix-x.

[21] Brown, p. 284.

[22] W. E. B. Du Bois, "Of the Sorrow Songs," in *The Souls of Black Folk,* in *Three Negro Classics,* ed. John Hope Franklin (New York, 1965), p. 378.

[23] Brown, "The Spirituals," p. 281. Another notable account is James Weldon Johnson's Introduction to *The Book of American Negro Spirituals* (New York, 1969).

[24] James Miller McKim, "Negro Songs," in *The Negro and His Folklore in Nineteenth-Century Periodicals,* ed. Bruce Jackson (Austin, Tex., 1967), pp. 58-59. McKim's article originally appeared in *Dwight's Journal of Music,* XIX (1862), pp. 148-49.

[25] Maud Cuney-Hare assigns part of her study, *Negro Musicians and Their Music* (Washington, D.C., 1936), to black folk songs of the waterways, the levee, and the high seas, and a number of these songs are recorded in Lafcadio Hearn's "Levee Life," in Bontemps and Hughes, *The Book of Negro Folklore,* pp. 211-22.

[26] Ralph Ellison, "Richard Wright's Blues," in *Shadow and Act* (New York, 1966), p. 90.

[27] Roger Abrahams, "The Changing Concept of the Negro Hero," in *The Golden Log,* ed. Mody C. Boatwright, Wilson M. Hudson, Allen Maxwell (Dallas, 1962), p. 124.

[28] Edward Margolies, *Native Sons: A Critical Study of Twentieth-Century Negro American Authors* (New York, 1969), pp. 30-31.

[29] Ralph Ellison, "The Art of Fiction: An Interview," in *Shadow and Act,* p. 172.

Donald A. Petesch

SOURCE: "The Role of Folklore in the Modern Black Novel," in *Kansas Quarterly,* Vol. 7, No. 3, Summer, 1975, pp. 99-110.

[*In the following essay, Petesch explores the recurrence of certain folkloric themes and character types in the works of African-American writers such as Richard Wright, Ralph Ellison, and many others.*]

Popular articles and the impact of such monumental studies as Newbell Niles Puckett's *The Magic and Folk Beliefs of the Southern Negro* have helped to create the belief that black folklore is exclusively Southern and rural. Actually, folklore follows the people, and the people have gone north, west, and some to the Midwest. Richard M. Dorson, for example, has observed that the best storyteller he ever met was James Douglas Suggs, a resident of Calvin Township, a farming settlement in southwestern Michigan.[1] In addition, rural tales have assumed urban form and content. Roger Abrahams' "classic" study of black urban folklore—*Deep Down in the Jungle*—is an examination of folklore in Philadelphia and was published in 1963.

The urban Midwest has figured importantly in both the preservation and the renewal of black folklore. Numerous writers, for example, have discussed the importance of Kansas City during the period from 1927 to 1938. Marshall Stearns quotes drummer Jo Jones as stating, "'The Kansas City influence first spread within a radius from Texas to Oklahoma and into Missouri.'" Ben Sidran, attempting to explain the influence of Kansas City, declared that the primary reason "was that this part of the country, unlike the cities of the urban North, was both geographically and sociologically close to the origins of black oral tradition. While the rest of the country had been moving swiftly toward a more commercial jazz music, this section of America had remained the blues capital of the world."[2]

In this Midwestern region were born some of the leading black writers, including some of those who have been most conscious of the value of the folk materials. Both the first modern black prose writer and the first modern black poet were Midwesterners born in Ohio. Charles Chesnutt was born in Cleveland and lived there most of his life. His *The Conjure Woman,* published in 1899, borrowed heavily from black lore. Paul Lawrence Dunbar was born in Dayton; his *Lyrics of Lowly Life,* published in 1896, portrayed a folk people. Robert E. Hayden, who employs considerable folklore in his poetry, was born in Detroit, and supervised research into local Negro history and folklore for the Federal Writers' Project during the Depression. Gwendolyn Brooks, though born in Topeka, has lived most of her life in Chicago; her poetry often celebrates the folk. Langston Hughes, whose character Jesse B. Semple comes closer to being a folk character than any ever created by an American writer, was born in Joplin, Missouri, lived at various times in Lawrence and Topeka, and graduated from high school in Cleveland.

In this paper I shall be examining the lore available to these and other black writers. I am particularly interested in the ways in which the oral tradition has influenced the literary tradition. For just as the tales have spread geographically, they have mixed with the forms available. Themes, character types, strategies, and milieus derived from the oral lore echo throughout modern black literature. In order to keep the topic manageable, I shall focus on the role of folklore in the modern black novel.[3]

The presence of folkloric elements in written literature makes a knowledge of folklore an extremely useful tool for the reader of modern black literature. Embedded in this literature are blues and spirituals fragments, slave secular verses, aphorisms, dozens verses, toasts, street calls, hoodoo lore, folk tale motifs—one could go on for pages citing the kinds of lore collected by such folklorists as Abrahams, Brewer, Dorson, Hughes and Bontemps, Hurston, Puckett and others that surface in the written literature.[4] And while the folkloric elements sometimes function as simply one more quality of the milieu, they are often centrally related to characterization, themes, setting, tone, and plot.

This active presence of an oral tradition requires some explanation. Historically, the slave was generally barred from any type of education, other than training in work roles. These restrictions were, in fact, often legally codified. Typical of such statutes, according to the historian Gilbert Osofsky, is provision 149 of the Louisiana slave code of 1852: "All persons who shall teach, or permit or cause to be taught, any slave in this State to read or write, shall, on conviction thereof before any court of competent jurisdiction, be imprisoned not less than one month nor more than twelve months."[5] Some slaves, such as Frederick Douglass, used considerable ingenuity and guile to learn to read despite the law. But when one sees Richard Wright in *Black Boy* having to use similar guile in order to borrow books from the Memphis Public Library, one senses for how long access to a written literature could not be taken for granted. Barred from access to the written tradition; restricted to the heavy, onerous labor—such as cotton picking, cane cutting, lumbering and saw-mill operating, railroad building, and levee labor—labor which employed gangs living and working in a communal fashion; kept poor in poor Southern states, so that there was little commercial entertainment; and located geographically where the climate permitted much visiting and gathering on front porches and store fronts—under these conditions folklore flourished. Richard M. Dorson has observed that in America, "Only the Negro, as a distinct element of the English-speaking population, maintained a full-blown storytelling tradition."[6]

In the absence of a written tradition, an oral tradition must play many roles. Alan Dundes describes some of the general functions of folklore as "aiding in the education of the young, promoting a group's feeling of solidarity, providing socially sanctioned ways for individuals to act superior to or to censure other individuals, serving as a vehicle for social protest, offering an enjoyable escape from reality, and converting dull work into play."[7] In the case of black folklore, the racial element is very strong. Within the formalized and stylized structures of such types of lore as folk tales, folk seculars, spirituals, and the blues, the weak can be found triumphant, The Man can be defeated and embarrassed, the righteous can find a home, the tragic sense of life can be shared. A lore that would fill so many needs is both created by the group and has its reality continually tested by the group. Sterling A. Brown has described the creation of spirituals:

> It is unlikely that any group of worshipers and singers, as a group, composed spirituals. Single individuals with poetic ingenuity, a rhyming gift, or a good memory "composed" or "remembered" lines, couplets, or even quatrains out of a common storehouse. The group would join in with the refrain or the longer chorus. When one leader's ingenuity or memory was exhausted, another might take up the "composition." . . . The spirituals are genuinely folk products, regardless of the fact that gifted individuals may have played leading roles in their composition. From the folk storehouse came the ideas, the vocabulary, the idioms, the images. The folk approved the song or rejected it, as it squared with folk knowledge, memory, and vision. The folk changed lines that were not easily understood, inserted new stanzas, sometimes bringing the songs up to date, and transmitted them orally to the next generation.[8]

These qualities of group creation and improvisational delivery are cited as recently as 1963 for so urban a form of folklore as the toasts described by Roger Abrahams: "[the teller] has learned the conventions, the formulas, and the themes (or commonplaces) and by means of these has reconstructed or retold the narrative. The improvisational nature of the toast makes any one text simply a chance rendering of a story highly transitional by nature—a rendering that will probably never be reproduced exactly, even by the same informant."[9]

The use of folkloric elements by modern black novelists often goes unnoticed. For black readers such elements are so much a part of the warp and woof of their experience as to attract little notice. For white readers folkloric elements are, all too often, merely so many more elements in an already unfamiliar landscape.[10] Another barrier to appreciating the presence of folklore is the fact that the folk-life is associated, in the minds of many people, with a way of life that has passed, or is passing. And it is true, of course, that the seemingly ideal conditions for the generation of folklore—a tradition of good talk and storying at country stores, on front porches, away from the background noises and interference of cities and the impact of mass, standardized forms of entertainment—that these seemingly ideal conditions have either passed or are passing.

These ideal conditions are clearly illustrated in Zora Neale Hurston's novel *Their Eyes Were Watching God.* The protagonist, Janie, is first viewed by "the people": "The people all saw her come because it was sundown. The sun was gone, but he had left his footprints in the sky. It was the time for sitting on porches beside the road. It was the time to hear things and talk." The people also sit on the porch of Joe Starks's store. Janie, Joe Starks's wife, is drawn to their talk: "When the people sat around on the porches and passed around the pictures of their thoughts for the others to look at and see, it was nice. The fact that the thought pictures were always crayon enlargements of life even nicer to listen to." These "crayon enlargements" are the comic exaggerations of folk tales, and what follows in the text are ten pages of mule tales. The novel is a literal compendium of folklore. The reader can find verbal duels, much like the medieval *débat,* where, for example, the relative merits of "nature" and "caution" are debated; references to rhyming as part of the courtship rituals; parodies of courtship rituals, with their exaggerations and epic boasts, such as "'It must be uh recess in heben if St. Peter is lettin' his angels out lak dis'" and "'Ah'll take uh job cleanin' out de Atlantic Ocean fuh you'"; the lore of hoodoo and two-headed doctors; boasts that have their origins in the blues, as in "'Ah can look through muddy water and see dry land'" and "'You don't know dat woman uh mine. She got ninety-nine rows uh jaw teeth and git her good and mad, she'll wade through solid rock up to her hip pockets'"; Big John de Conquer stories; and a dozens verse. One chapter concludes with the folkloric flourish of a rhyming couplet, as Janie notes to Phoebe: "'Some of dese mornin's and it won't be long, you gointuh wake up callin' me and Ah'll be gone.'" In addition, the novel contains many aphorisms.

A number of black novels do suggest the adverse impact of the city, or industrial organization, on folklore. In William Attaway's *Blood on the Forge,* three black brothers— Melody, Big Mat, and Chinatown—go from their farm in Kentucky to work in the Homestead steel plant outside Pittsburgh. In Kentucky Melody played blues on his guitar. As early as the third page he is portrayed translating family troubles into the universalizing frame of a blues song. He sings "Hungry Blues": "Done scratched at the hills, / But the 'taters refuse to grow . . . / Done scratched at the hills, / But the 'taters refuse to grow . . . / Mister Bossman, Mister Bossman, / Lemme mark in the book once mo'. . . . " Attaway, in his role as narrator, remarks, "There were more verses like that than any one man knew." And after each verse the refrain: "'Hungry blues done got me listenin' to my love one cry . . . / Put some vittles in my belly, or yo' honey gonna lay down and die.'" His sister-in-law, Hattie, observes, "'Blues sure is a help.'" After leaving Kentucky Melody's response to music changes: "Every now and then his hands started idly over the strings but they did not find much music. He didn't try any slicking. That was for back home and the distances in the hills. Here at the mills it felt right to find quick chords with the fingers—a strange kind of playing for him, but it was right for that new place."

Lutie, the central character in Ann Petry's novel *The Street,* is alone with her son Bub in Harlem. She bemoans the fact that she is alone, and that her Granny— a compound of tales and advice—is not there to tell her what to do. She fears the building superintendent—a realistic fear, as it turns out. She ponders her fears early in the novel:

> That was it, he probably wanted to hear his favorite program and she thought he was filled with the desire to leap upon her. She was as bad as Granny. Which just went on to prove you couldn't be brought up by someone like Granny without absorbing a lot of nonsense that would spring at you out of nowhere, so to speak, and when you least expected it. All those tales about things that people sensed before they actually happened. Tales that had been handed down and down and down until, if you tried to trace them back, you'd end up God knows where—probably Africa. And Granny had them all at the tip of her tongue.

A little later she broods that "There was no explaining away the instinctive, immediate fear she had felt when she first saw the Super. Granny would have said, 'Nothin' but evil, child. Some folks so full of it you can feel it comin' at you—oozin' right out of their skins.'" In her later bewilderment she considers that "Granny could have told her what to do if she had lived."

Thus it is possible for the city or for industrial society to have an adverse effect on either the survival or transmission of folklore, and the literature of cultural change is filled with the bones from the past. But there is also much evidence to indicate that folklore may change its content, even alter its forms, but persist. Brer Rabbit becomes the Signifying Monkey; John of the Master and John tales becomes Shine and Stackolee; and High John the Conqueror becomes Joe Louis and Muhammad Ali. In fact, the twentieth-century fictional creation who embodies, I believe, more folkloric elements than any other is Langston Hughes's Jesse B. Simple, a city man whose views of the country sound very much like those eighteenth-century exemplars of urbanity and wit, Samuel Johnson and James Boswell. This concern for wit and good conversation echoes in Simple's judgment on the country: "'It is too dark in the country at night, and sunrise comes too early. In the daytime you don't see nothing but animals. Horses, pigs, cows, sheep, birds, chickens. Not a one of them animals ever said one interesting word to me. Animals is no company. I like them in zoos better. Trees I like in parks, birds in somebody else's cages, chickens in frozen-food bins, and sunrise in bed. No, daddy-o, I will not go to the country this summer. I like lights too well.'" Like many of the heroes of folklore, Simple is where he is from having traveled there, and in his life-history he has experienced the "great migration" northward that has been one of the great black mass movements of the twentieth century. But Simple's views on the country are not unmixed. He also expresses nostalgia for "down home," but, in the words of the spiritual, he has been "'buked" and "scorned": "'Maybe if it wasn't for white folks, I would've stayed down South where spring comes earlier than it do up here.'"

Hughes's tales of Simple, like Hurston's novel, are filled with folkloric elements. The very form of the collections suggests collections of folk tales. And the reader quickly senses that the contest situation, typical of the folk tale, is present in these tales, though in a more generalized form. It is Simple pitted against The man or society, with the suggestion that the greatest trick of all might be survival with dignity and wit. Almost every sketch ends with the stylistic flourish familiar to readers of folk tales. Like Brer Rabbit or other trickster protagonists, Simple too usually has the last word, in which he sums up the nonsense of the world, or states positively an absurd position, which, in the context of the general absurdity, makes the greater sense; and makes Simple the greater sense-maker for having caught the world's style and held a mirror up to it.

Simple's role as representative folk figure is clear from the first tale of Hughes's *The Best of Simple*. In talking with Boyd, Simple's constant foil, Simple identifies his life with the fate of his feet, which, in the telling, are exaggerated into feet of epic travail:

> "These feet have stood on every rock from the Rock of Ages to 135th and Lenox. These feet have supported everything from a cotton bale to a hongry woman. These feet have walked ten thousand miles working for white folks and another ten thousand keeping up with colored. These feet have stood at altars, crap tables, free lunches, bars, graves, kitchen doors, betting windows, hospital clinics, WPA desks, social security railings, and in all kinds of lines from soup lines to the draft. If I just had four feet, I could have stood in more places longer. As it is, I done wore out seven hundred pairs of shoes, eighty-nine tennis shoes, twelve summer sandals, also six loafers. The socks that these feet have bought could build a knitting mill. The corns I've cut away would dull a German razor. The bunions I forgot would make you ache from now till Judgment Day. If anybody was to write the history of my life, they should start with my feet."

Thus early established as an embodiment of black, folk experience, Hughes's tales exhibit many of the characteristic folkloric forms: the dozens, tales of creation and the acquiring of color, toasts, be-bop as ethnic marker, blues verses, proverbs, even a rhymed ending similar to the signature endings of certain tale tellers.

. . . . .

So lore moves north, into the cities, and into the written literature. The reader, teacher, or critic of black literature will wonder what insights a knowledge of this lore will provide. Although it is difficult to compartmentalize so diverse and vital a field, I believe four general areas can be identified: (1) the group milieu found in much fiction; (2) the persistence of certain themes;

(3) the presence of certain character types; and (4) explanations of events in certain scenes.

(1) THE GROUP MILIEU.

More commonly than in novels by white writers a reader of black novels finds characters interacting, finds groups interacting. The lonely, private ego of either the Puritan or romantic tradition—either examining its conscience or falling upon the thorns of life—is less frequently encountered in black literature. There, ideas, opinions, expressions, and sentiments more commonly grow in interaction. This quality of the milieu has been frequently noted by students of various types of experience. Frequently cited phenomena are the call-response patterns of work songs and church sermons; the group creation of the spirituals; the audience participation when black speakers speak or poets read; the other-directed nature of performance characteristics generally. This group experience, which many writers have traced to the communal organization of West African society, was reinforced by the plantation system, by the later communal organization of work, by the oral tradition, by white oppression, and by poverty.

This quality of the group presence—the folk collectively experiencing—can be found in numerous black novels. In Richard Wright's novel, *Lawd Today*, Jake Jackson and three friends work in the post office. Their boring, mechanical job of sorting mail permits them to talk with each other. Wright eliminates all such tags as "Jake said," leaving only the dialogue. The effect of this choric device is to emphasize the shared quality of their sentiments:

> "A white man wouldn't fight you fair for nothing."
>
> "He gangs you."
>
> "And once they get you down they don't have no mercy."
>
> "Look like it's fun to them to see people suffer."
>
> "That's cause they ain't happy. . . . "
>
> " . . . and they take it all out on you."
>
> "That's the reason why we had to get out of the South. . . . "
>
> " . . . and stop slaving for them white folks from 'kin 'til can't . . . '"
>
> " . . . from sunup to sundown. . . . "
>
> " . . . rain or shine. . . . "
>
> " . . . picking cotton 'till your back feels like it's going to break in two. . . . "
>
> " . . . and that sun so hot you can't even sweat. . . . "
>
> " . . . and hoeing 'til your hands blister. . . . "

" . . . and plowing. . . . "

" . . . shucking corn. . . . "

This dialogue takes up twenty-seven pages, one entire chapter, of *Lawd Today*.

A similar folk-like quality is achieved by Ernest J. Gaines in the "Introduction" to *The Autobiography of Miss Jane Pittman*. Miss Jane is very old. The "editor" states, "When she was tired, or when she just did not feel like talking any more, or when she had forgotten certain things, someone else would always pick up the narration." The intention of the author is clearly stated in the concluding line of the Introduction: "Miss Jane's story is all of their stories, and their stories are Miss Jane's." Thus is the experience generalized to the folk. Gaines's strategy has respectable forebears. The writers of the slave narratives also tended to view their experiences from the perspective of the group—they would tell the reader how it was to be a slave, not how it was to be themselves.

(2) THE PERSISTENCE OF CERTAIN THEMES

AND

(3) THE PRESENCE OF CERTAIN CHARACTER TYPES.[11]

One of the most recurring elements in black folk tales is the theme of conflict: of Brer Rabbit versus either Brer Bear or Brer Fox, or the slave John versus Master. This conflict pattern both mirrors actual conflicts which took place from the earliest days of slave-holding and projects wish-fulfillment fantasies. Increasingly historians such as Kenneth M. Stampp, Herbert Aptheker, Charles H. Nichols, and John Blassingame are making us aware of the considerable amount of resistance put up by the slaves: from malingering to hiding out in the woods to running away to violence and rebellion. The need to extract work from less than docile slaves called forth all the ingenuity of whip and sermon. The slave was forced to adopt an elaborate system of stylized manners when interacting with whites. Bertram Doyle describes some of the conventions: "If . . . the greetings advanced beyond the primary state, so that a conversation was necessary, the slave removed his hat or touched it as if it would be removed, at each sentence, and kept his eye on the ground during the conversation. If, as was the rule in some sections, the slave had no hat, he then proceeded to pull at his forelock while the conversation continued. . . . Once the conversation got under way, the slave replied with 'sir,' or 'ma'am,' as the occasion demanded. . . . The 'sir' or 'ma'am' was stressed as the one important word, says one author."[12] Probably even more disturbing than Doyle's report is the fact that Allison Davis, and Burleigh B. and Mary R. Gardner cited identical patterns of interaction for rural Mississippi in their *Deep South* published in 1941.[13] The point of this comparison is to suggest how persistent has been this unnatural, and rigid, system. In Richard Wright's autobiography, *Black Boy*, Wright's friend, Griggs, lectures him for his insensitivity to the system: "'You act

around white people as if you didn't know that they were white. And they see it. . . . When you're in front of white people, *think* before you act, *think* before you speak. Your way of doing things is all right among *our* people, but not for *white* people. They won't stand for it.'" Wright analyzes his problem: "In my dealing with whites I was conscious of the entirety of my relations with them, and they were conscious only of what was happening at a given moment. I had to keep remembering what others took for granted; I had to think out what others felt. I had begun coping with the white world too late. I could not make subservience an automatic part of my behavior." James Baldwin, also not knowing the signs, feels the immediacy of the threat when he walks into a white restaurant in Montgomery, Alabama, on his first trip "home."[14] The result of this code is the tension often present in interactions between black and white, a tension that freights the commonplace with significance, that overlays the casual with emotions often too heavy to bear.

The persistence of conflict as theme is illustrated in the lore collected by Hughes and Bontemps and Dorson, as well as by the articles collected by Alan Dundes in his *Mother Wit from the Laughing Barrel*. The level of suppressed anger can perhaps be gauged by the fact that Joe Louis's victories over white men are celebrated in novel after novel: *Lawd Today, If He Hollers Let Him Go, Daddy Was a Number Runner, The Autobiography of Miss Jane Pittman*, and so on. And it is probably revealing that whereas G. Legman considers erotic humor to be "far & away the most popular of all types," Arthur J. Prange, Jr. and M. M. Vitols, in their study of jokes told by Negro patients, found a "rather striking number of jokes refer to race relations: 13 of 18 (72 per cent)."[15]

An important sub-type of the conflict relationship in black literature includes the complex set of attitudes and avoidances enjoined on black males in their interaction with white females. Reflecting this theme in the folklore is the often-cited tale in which Master bets with another plantation owner that his John can beat the strongest slave on the other plantation. On the day of the fight John's competition seems so fearsome that John slaps Master's wife and the other fighter runs away. John explains to his angry master, "'Well, Jim knowed if I slapped a white woman I'd a killed him, so he run.'"[16] A joke collected by Hughes and Bontemps, and cited by others, illustrates the avoidance of black male/white female relations:

> They say once there was a Negro at Atlanta who had made up his mind to commit suicide, so one day he went down to the main street and took the freight elevator up to the top of the highest building in town, in fact, the highest skyscraper in Georgia. Negroes could not ride the passenger elevators, but he was so anxious to commit suicide that he did not let Jim Crow stand in the way. He rode as freight. Once at the top of the building, he took off his coat, drew a deep breath, approached the ledge and jumped off. He went hurtling through the air and was just about to hit the sidewalk when

he saw a white woman come around the corner.
He knew he had better not fall on a white woman,
so he curved and went right back up.[17]

Taboos surrounding the white woman are some of the
earliest learned by black boys. And some of the tensest
scenes in black novels occur when black males are
somehow unavoidably close to white females. The situation is experienced as entrapment, calling forth emotional responses similar to the fear physiologists have
identified in the "fight or flight" response. This is the
response of Fishbelly and his friends to the white
woman who bares her breasts in the darkness among the
circus cars in Richard Wright's *The Long Dream*; in the
same novel Chris is lynched because of his relationship
with a white prostitute, and Fishbelly swallows the picture of the white woman he had carried in his wallet
when he is picked up by the police. In *Native Son* Bigger
Thomas is so fearful of being found in Miss Dalton's
room that he smothers her; at his trial, of course, he is
identified as a rapist, killer. Mr. Trueblood in *Invisible
Man* dreams he is in a white woman's room at the time
he is actually seducing his daughter. Bob Jones is
accused of attempted rape by the woman he is trapped
with in the ship's stateroom in Himes's *If He Hollers
Let Him Go*.

Faced with conflict and oppression black characters frequently dissemble, question, run, or fight. The dissem-
bler or trickster figure has been often noted. He appears
early in the literature. Numerous slave narratives note
the usefulness of dissembling and deception. Typical of
these is Henry Bibb's observation: "The only weapon of
self defence that I could use successfully, was that of
deception. It is useless for a poor slave to resist the
white man in a slaveholding state. Public opinion and
the law is [sic] against him; and resistance in many
cases is death to the slave, while the law declares, that
he shall submit or die." Both Brer Rabbit and John must
win by craft and guile and win they usually do. They are
master talkers who often utter the last line. An urban
counterpart is the "signifying monkey." The man of
words—the good talker in the roles of teacher, preacher,
writer, rapper, leader, pimp—has been discussed by
such diverse figures as Abrahams, James Baldwin, H.
Rap Brown, and Dick Gregory. The contemporary man-
of-words-as-hero is best illustrated by Muhammad Ali.

Dissembling usually involves the wearing of masks, a
fact recognized in Paul Laurence Dunbar's verse: "We
wear the mask that grins and lies, / It hides our cheeks
and shades our eyes,— / This debt we pay to human
guile; / With torn and bleeding hearts we smile, / And
mouth with myriad subtleties."[18] The dynamics of masking are clearly illustrated in the interaction of Big Mat
and Mr. Johnston in *Blood on the Forge*:

> "Us'll have a hard time makin' it on our share,
> mule or no—a hard time. . . ."

> Mr. Johnston caught Big Mat with his eyes. He
> came forward. Big Mat looked doggedly into the

hard eyes. For a long second they hung on the
edge of violence.

> Mr. Johnston said, "You ain't kickin', are you,
> Mat?"

> Big Mat's eyes dropped to the bloody entrails. He
> presented a dull, stupid exterior.

> "Nosuh, I ain't kickin'."

Other mask-wearers include Lutie while working at the
Chandlers in *The Street*; Bob Jones interacting with the
union representative in *If He Hollers Let Him Go*;
Fishbelly's father talking with the sheriff in *The Long
Dream*; Max Reddick interacting with various liberals
in John Williams' *The Man Who Cried I Am*—the list
could be very lengthy. One of the most famous of all
mask-wearers, of course, is Ellison's Rinehart: runner,
gambler, briber, lover, Reverend.

Oppression gives rise to questions. Why is the white
man so mean? What did I do to be so black and blue?
Among the folklore tales of origin appear tales "explaining" who got the "good" hair and why, and who got the
"good" color. The negative valuation of black has led to
the valuing of lighter skin and straight hair and to self-
denigration (the frequent use of the term "ugly" illustrates
this tendency). The struggle for an identity in the face
of oppression and negative valuing is central to many
novels: James Weldon Johnson's *The Autobiography of
an Ex-Coloured Man*, Nella Larsen's *Passing*, Wallace
Thurman's *The Blacker the Berry*, and *If He Hollers Let
Him Go*, *Native Son*, *Invisible Man*, *The Man Who
Cried I Am*. The new self-pride characterized by the
black power movement is reflected in a tendency among
black protagonists to find their identity in a heightened
identification with their roots and their people.

A frequent response to oppression is to run from it, or
to a better place. Black folklore abounds with running
figures. A reading of the slave narratives and slave seculars (for example, the song "Run, Nigger, Run" in
which the runner is being pursued by the pater-rollers,
the patrollers, men on horseback who patrolled the plantations at night) will reveal the persistence of the theme.
One followed the drinking gourd, the big dipper, north
to freedom, 'cause "Many thousand gone." In the spirituals one sought a home up there, in Jordan, in the
promised land; "I spread my wings and I fly"; "Sometimes I don't know where to roam, / But I've heard of
a city called heaven / And I've started to make it my
home"; "Tell old Pharaoh / To let my people go";
"Swing low, sweet chariot, / Coming for to carry me
home"; "Steal away, steal away, steal away to Jesus, /
Steal away, steal away home, / I ain't got long to stay
here"; "Deep river, my home is over Jordan, / Deep
river, Lord; I want to cross over into camp ground";
"But I jes' want-a get up inde Promise Lan'"; "The
gospel train's a-comin', I hear it just at hand"; "Rise up,
shepherd, and follow!" The boll weevil, tiny but voracious
protagonist of numerous twentieth-century folksongs, is

a true insect representative of the theme of running—in Leadbelly's version even he is "lookin' fuh uh home, jus lookin fuh uh home." The most superficial examination of modern black novelists encounters running figures: Bigger Thomas in *Native Son,* the protagonist in *Invisible Man,* Lutie in *The Street,* Bob Jones in *If He Hollers Let Him Go,* Big Mat in *Blood on the Forge,* Fishbelly in *The Long Dream,* Miss Jane in *The Autobiography of Miss Jane Pittman.* What happens when, as Claude Brown phrases it, you get to the promised land ("For where does one run to when he's already in the promised land?")? The black power movement of the sixties and seventies is part of the answer. Other answers will inevitably follow.

Another response to oppression is to fight back. Again, the slave narratives are a source for this type of response. Frederick Douglass describes his feelings after beating up the "nigger-breaker," Mr. Covey: "My long-crushed spirit rose, cowardice departed, bold defiance took its place; and I now resolved that, however long I might remain a slave in form, the day had passed forever when I could be a slave in fact. I did not hesitate to let it be known of me, that the white man who expected to succeed in whipping, must also succeed in killing me." Solomon Northrup similarly resisted. Blassingame reports that every large plantation had at least one such resister. These resisters are the forefathers of later figures called "bad" or "uppity" by whites. Blacks will take over the terminology but reverse the terms, so that to call something "ba-a-a-ad" is to praise it. This usage appears in Arna Bontemps' *Black Thunder,* published in 1936: Gabriel Prosser muses over Ditcher's understanding of Gabriel's reputation: "Of course Ditcher knew right well who was the biggest and the baddest nigger in Henrico County, but Gabriel didn't see any reason to talk about it or rub it in." In Louise Meriwether's novel, *Daddy Was a Number Runner,* published thirty-four years after Bontemps' novel, the term is similarly employed. Junior explains the attraction for him of membership in the gang of Ebony Earls: "People see me walking down the street, they say, there goes James Adam Coffin, Junior. He's a bad stud. Everybody respects a bad stud. Don't make no difference whether you're bad or not, just as long as people think you are. And you naturally get a rep by belonging to the Ebony Earls. You automatically become somebody.'" Richard Wright, in his essay "How 'Bigger' Was Born," describes the five Biggers, the "bad niggers," who served for models. He describes the pride experienced by the community. He notes: "The Bigger Thomases were the only Negroes I know of who consistently violated the Jim Crow laws of the South and got away with it, at least for a sweet brief spell."[19] A similar figure is described by Abrahams as the type of the toast hero Stackolee: "Such a personage used to be common in Southern towns' Negro communities and still flourishes in parts of the South. . . . He is a bad man both by nature and in the sense that his acts almost always violate the white man's laws."[20] These rebels are the prototypes for the urban guerrilla fighter of contemporary drama and fiction, who often has the tacit support of the people.

(4) EXPLANATIONS OF EVENTS IN CERTAIN SCENES.

A final purpose, but a not insignificant one, served by a knowledge of folklore is that it alerts the reader to meanings central to certain scenes in black novels. Several examples will have to suffice to suggest the range of possibilities. The protagonist in *Invisible Man* meets with Brother Jack and the other leaders in the Brotherhood following the funeral for Tod Clifton. In a scene that is like a trial Brother Jack asks on whose authority he arranged the funeral and the protagonist replies, "My personal responsibility,'" to which Brother Jack replies, "His personal responsibility. . . . This is astounding, where did you get it?'" The protagonist starts to reply "From your ma—'" but catches himself in time and answers, "From the committee.'" If the reader is ignorant of the lore, he will not know that the protagonist had started to utter, "your mama," which is an opening thrust in the verbal duel of urban folklore known as "the dozens," a game in which you generally insult the other party's female relatives. But the game is only played among peers, and the protagonist's truncating his remark focuses attention on the fact that these are not brothers in any sense. Central to *Invisible Man* is the question of identity. Earlier, in talking to the "plans man," the protagonist realized he once knew the folklore: "I'd known the stuff from childhood, but had forgotten it; had learned it back of school." At the end of the novel he is discarding the symbols of the schools and the other institutions. He is underground (where the roots are?) playing Louis Armstrong records.

James Baldwin's use of blues motifs suggests the deeper implications in his title *Another Country.* Bessie Smith is frequently heard singing in the background of the novel. The first lines of hers we hear are from "Backwater Blues": *"There's thousands of people . . . ain't got no place to go . . . 'cause my house fell down and I can't live there no mo'."* The primacy of these lines should be considered along with the epigraphs to parts one, two, and three. The first is from a folk song sung by the "father of the blues," W. C. Handy: "I told him, easy riders / Got to stay away, / So he had to vamp it, / But the hike ain't far." The second is from Conrad's *Victory:* "Why don't you take me in your / arms and carry me out of this lonely place?" The third is from Shakespeare's Sonnet LXV: "How with this rage shall beauty hold a plea, / Whose action is no stronger than a flower?" These quotations, considered along with the action of the novel, support the interpretation that the title is more than a simple criticism of America, that country, in Cass's terms, of football players, Eagle Scouts, and cowards. Rather, for Baldwin there is a need for another country of the heart, where love, as desperately fragile as it is, has space to grow, and where there is room for the wisdom necessary to cherish it.

I have attempted to suggest some of the larger issues illuminated by a knowledge of black folklore, to suggest how deep and persistent are certain themes in the black experience, themes which continually recur in the literature. At the same time, of course, such a knowledge enables the reader to understand many expressions, gestures, acts, and characters in many small, but cumulatively significant, situations. For a literature so rooted in the oral, folk tradition a knowledge of folklore provides, in the words of Walter Lippmann, one of those invaluable maps for the territory of the mind.

FOOTNOTES

1 Suggs, an almost classic example of the rambler, had lived in thirty-nine states and had a repertory of 175 tales and 25 songs (Richard M. Dorson, *American Negro Folktales* [1958; rpt. New York: Fawcett World Library, 1967], p. 23).

2 Marshall Stearns, *The Story of Jazz* (1956; rpt. New York: The New American Library, Inc., 1958), p. 135; Ben Sidran, *Black Talk* (New York: Holt, Rinehart and Winston, 1971), p. 83.

3 Bernard W. Bell discusses folklore in contemporary poetry (The Folk Roots of *Contemporary Afro-American Poetry* [Detroit: Broadside Press, 1974]). The interested reader would enjoy Stanley Edgar Hyman's "The Folk Tradition" and Ralph Ellison's rejoinder, "Change the Joke and Slip the Yoke," published in *Partisan Review*, 25 (1958), pp. 197-222. Both articles are reprinted in Alan Dundes, ed. *Mother Wit from the Laughing Barrel* (Englewood Cliffs: Prentice-Hall, Inc., 1973), pp. 45-64.

4 Roger Abrahams, *Deep Down in the Jungle* (Chicago: Aldine Publishing Company, 1970, rev. ed.); J. Mason Brewer, ed., *American Negro Folklore* (Chicago: Quadrangle Books, 1968); Dorson, *op. cit.;* Langston Hughes and Arna Bontemps, eds., *Book of Negro Folklore* (New York: Dodd, Mead & Company, 1958); Zora Neale Hurston, *Mules and Men* (1935; rpt. New York: Harper & Row, 1970); Newbell Niles Puckett, *The Magic and Folk Beliefs of the Southern Negro* (1926; rpt. New York: Dover Publications, Inc., 1969).

5 Gilbert Osofsky, *The Burden of Race* (New York: Harper & Row, 1967), p. 20.

6 Dorson, p. 12.

7 Alan Dundes, *The Study of Folklore* (Englewood Cliffs: Prentice-Hall, Inc., 1965), p. 277.

8 Sterling A. Brown, Arthur P. Davis, and Ulysses Lee, eds., *The Negro Caravan* (1941; rpt. New York: Arno Press, Inc., 1970), p. 414.

9 Abrahams, p. 100.

10 It may be, too, that literary training militates against any easy openness to folklore for many students of literature. Their training prepares them to accept literary influences, but not oral influences; and they gain a deep respect for the *true* text, which ill equips them to respect folklore which can change with every teller and user.

11 These topics cannot be practically dealt with in isolation from each other.

12 Bertram Doyle, *The Etiquette of Race Relations* (1937; rpt. New York: Schocken Books, 1971), p. 14.

13 Allison Davis, Burleigh B. Gardner, and Mary R. Gardner, *Deep South* (1941; rpt. Chicago: The University of Chicago Press, 1965), especially pp. 22-23.

14 James Baldwin, *No Name in the Street* (New York: Dell, 1972), pp. 71-74.

15 G. Legman, *Rationale of the Dirty Joke* (New York: Grove Press, Inc., Evergreen Black Cat Edition, 1971), p. 9. Arthur J. Prange, Jr., and M. M. Vitols, "Jokes Among Southern Negroes: The Revelation of Conflict," in Alan Dundes, ed., *Mother Wit from the Laughing Barrel,* p. 630.

16 Dorson, p. 135.

17 Hughes and Bontemps, pp. 504-505.

18 The separation implicit in mask-wearing is sometimes described in terms of veils, walls, curtains, and boundary lines.

19 Richard Wright, "How 'Bigger' Was Born," in Abraham Chapman, ed., *Black Voices* (New York: The New American Library, 1968), p. 542.

20 Abrahams, pp. 129, 130.

Mildred A. Hill

SOURCE: "Common Folklore Features in African and African American Literature," in *Southern Folklore Quarterly*, Vol. 39, No. 2, June, 1975, pp. 111-33.

[*In the following essay, Hill explores themes common to African and African-American folklore through an examination of elements, including storytelling and folk sayings, in novels and other writings.*]

African folklore forms the secular half of those African beliefs which reveals the faith, humor, and adaptability of the Black man's coping with, explaining, and surviving in life. In traditional Africa, religion and folklore merged.[1] It is almost safe to say that the same has been true for Blacks in America. Although there have been attempts to separate religion from folk beliefs, the two are discussed interchangeably. The spirituals and the folk-sermons of the Black ministers are categorized along with the blues, jazz, folk tales, and jokes. Zora Neale Hurston includes voo-doo and magic which combine the two areas of religion and folk beliefs.[2] Ironically, this grouping is made to indicate that this body of material is not literature because it differs from mainstream American literature, and in addition, it also reflects a way of life that is definitely in contrast to white America. Without any doubts, it belongs to Blacks. Consequently, it has to be called the folklore of Blacks.

This material—the spirituals, the blues, the jokes, folksayings, stories—has been part of practically every Black American; yet it has produced a sense of ambivalence because interestingly enough, it is associated with his "Blackness." Because the Black Experience in America has been such an unpleasant and ambiguous one, most often, Blacks who are trying to become more assimilated into western culture will deny that they know anything about Black folklore. The schools, because they have been perpetuators of a monogamous, white culture, have done very little to change this attitude. Significantly enough, however, a great deal of scholarship surrounds Black American folklore, but for the most part it has been by whites.[3] And even the Black writer who has made the most use of incorporating Black folklore into Black literature, Ralph Ellison, attempts to mitigate its importance. He writes,

> My point is that the Negro American writer is also an heir of the human experience which is literature, and this might well be more important to him than his living folk tradition.[4]

However, my purpose is not merely to lament the confused status that Black folklore has held in America, but to maintain that much of this folklore can be traced to its African heritage. Recognizing that there has been considerable controversy surrounding its origin, I wish to investigate those features from the African tradition which recur in Black literature and in the contemporary life of the people and some of those features which appear in Black literature which may suggest a common African heritage because the treatment or philosophy revealed is so similar. In this article, only a few representative literary references will be cited to illustrate the common theme; however, at the end of the article, a selected bibliography listing other works by African and African-American authors will be given for each area discussed.

In both African and African-American life, the oral tradition has been exceedingly strong. Most of the wisdom, wit, history of both groups survive in the stories that have been passed down from generation-to-generation and which are now finding their way into the written literature. In this discussion, let us look at three areas of folklore: magic and superstition, storytelling, and folksayings. In the discussion on storytelling, I shall describe the various types of stories and storytellers and secondly, investigate one element which tends to appear frequently in the narratives, that of humor.

Magic and Superstition.—In African literature and life, one finds tremendous interests and belief in magic and superstition. In contemporary African-American life and literature, these aspects of the Black tradition are not so widespread, but we shall observe that many writers have used them. From all accounts, magic is a force quite similar to religion. In many situations the two overlap because, frequently, the medium who is the handler of the magic may be a priest or priestess for a god or goddess. Also, magic can be either good or bad. The same person or object that can bring good to one individual can do harm to another. Generally, however, medicine-men, priests, diviners are considered good; witches are considered evil. However, the combination of the name witch-doctor for the medicine man or voodoo doctor illustrates how the two have become intertwined. In either case, these people, with the use of special words, charms, rags, figures, roots, herbs, powders, and certain animals have the power to make situations improve for the individual who believes. The essential element is belief. Unless one believes in the powers of these people and their objects, the magic will not work.

In *Things Fall Apart,* a novel by Chinua Achebe on life in pre-colonial Iboland, we have the close association of religion and magic.[5] A good illustration appears in the episode dealing with Ekwefi, one of the wives of the main character, Okonkwo. Ekwefi has lost nine babies and she longs to have children. Therefore, she and Okonkwo consult the medicine man who is also a diviner; he gives them instructions to follow to achieve a successful birth and to remove the evil cycle which was causing the wife to lose her children. Even after Ezinma, the tenth child comes, the medicine man has to be used in order to save her since she is a delicate child. Because her mother has had to pray to the god Agbala to insure her birth, Ezinma is considered the child of this god. If at any time the priestess informs her family that the God wishes to see his daughter, the parents have to obey. Achebe provides us with an episode where the parents go through a terrifying ordeal when the priestess comes for the daughter.

Black Thunder, an African-American novel on slave life by Arna Bontemps, does not reveal the closely knit association of the gods with magic and superstition.[6] However, there is an old slave woman who is regarded as a person with powers. When Gabriel's venture—to produce a slave revolt—is not successful, its failure is blamed on his not "carrying anything" and his disbelief in "conjure," "signs" and charms. The slaves point out that it was because of such superstitions, especially "his drinking the blood of a hog" that Touissant L'Overture was victorious when he overthrew the French in the Haitian slave revolt. Thus, later on when Juba, Gabriel's girl friend, is near the old woman with the powers, she asks to be given "a good hand" to insure Gabriel's safety while he is running.

In Ann Petry's novel *The Street,* a novel of twentieth century African-American life, one of the characters goes to a "root doctor," another name for the medicine-man-witch doctor, to seek his power to prevent her common-law husband from leaving her for another woman.[7] The practitioner used candles, the cross, powders, vials to get assistance for his patients. The novelist also reveals an important characteristic about these "root-doctors" which may possibly have accounted for their popularity. Mrs. Petry shows that these mystical figures worked not only in the physical realm but the psychological as well. The character, Min, says:

> But this man [the root doctor] had listened and seemed interested, and all the time she had talked he had never shifted his gaze, so that when she came out from behind the white curtains, the satisfaction from his attentive listening, the triumph of actually possessing the means of controlling Jones made her face glow.[8]

Another area closely related to magic is superstition. Its manifestation can be the words of the medicine men, specialists, or even the elders, and the signs or taboos which are passed down as group wisdom. In African and African-American literature and life, most superstitions are associated with childbearing, death, love and sex, relations to parents and elders, and to the weather.

A few illustrations from *Things Fall Apart* are:

> Children were warned not to whistle at night for fear of attracting evil spirits (p. 9).

> The thick dregs of palm-wine were supposed to be good for men who were going into their wives (pp. 19-20).

> This man [medicine-man] told him that the child was an *ogbange,* one of those wicked children who, when they died, entered their mother's wombs to be born again (p. 70).

In some African societies twins were considered evil and had to be killed, while with other groups, twins represented good luck. Any abnormal births suggested magical powers. In African-American life, there are similar carryovers of this superstition. There are frequent references to children having special powers if they are born with veils over their faces or "feet first."[9]

In *Black Thunder,* there are numerous examples of superstitious lore on death and the weather:

> Was I you Ben, I'd do just about like Gabriel say do about that when you see him. That is, I'd do it if I didn't want to be pestered by no mean mens. It won't cost nothing to oblige him that little bit on account of his last request." (p. 50).

> He don't even know a tree got a soul same as a man (p. 53).

> "No, not afeared to fight. Scairt of the signs. Scairt of the stars, as you call it. You heard them talking. 'The stars is against us,' they says. 'All this here rain and storm ain't a nachal thing.'" (p. 103).

The bird had evidently come in when he opened the door. It was a bad luck sign and had to be driven out at once (p. 94).

Storytelling.—The telling of tales is a well-known custom in Africa. Most often, storytelling is a form of entertainment; however, looking at the contents of the tales, one concludes that storytelling must have done more than entertain. The tales, quite often, relate the history of the people; some possibly served as control mechanisms to teach the customs and morals of the community, and still others explain events in nature or how certain things come to be. Slaves coming to America brought these tales and the art of storytelling with them. Although these imported narratives later reflect the unique experiences of the African in America, many of them retain their African flavor. One aspect of the African art of storytelling which has survived is the manner in which the stories are told. The storyteller, quite often dramatizes the tales; that is he becomes the characters and assumes a different voice to represent each personality. At other times, he inserts a song or dance, and frequently, he involves his audience. He will permit them to respond with a word or two or he may engage his listeners by giving them the opportunity to suggest answers, especially if the tale belongs to the riddle-type story. The audience is very important in African and African-American storytelling. The narrator expects the listeners to help him out in the storytelling or in any case to answer him to indicate their acceptance, enjoyment, or understanding.

Two other features which have been labeled African, but have stirred a great deal of controversy, are the animal stories and the trickster motif found in many stories of Black people. The controversy exists over whether two characteristics are authentically African since scholars have discovered similar beast stories and the trickster motif in other bodies of folklore. Despite this disagreement, most persons associate the animal tales with Africa and can even give the animal equivalents in African-American folklore:

> In African cycles the heroes were the jackal or fox, the hare, the tortoise, and the spider. The last, a sort of hairy tarantula, is little used in the lore of the southern Negro, but he is hero of the Anansi tales of Jamaica. The African fox, more like our jackal, has become the American fox; the African hare, "Cunnie Rabbit," really a chevrotain, water deerlet, or gazelle, has become the American rabbit with the work cunnie Englished into cunning, and the African tortoise has become the American dry-land turtle or terrapin. In America, Brer Terrapin is a hero second only to Brer Rabbit whom he bests occasionally. Of the hero's victims, the African hyena has become the American wolf, and the American fox and bear have joined the losing side. African animals—lions, leopards, tigers, and monkeys—are still in the cast of characters.[10]

Likewise, the trickster motif is so much a part of African-American literature that one can trace its development.

The trickster, at one point, is the animal, then he becomes John in the John Tales in which John outwits the white master, and finally we get the pimp or the "cat" in African-American urban folklore who attempts to outsmart society. The trickster is quite an intriguing figure in African folklore, for he is the closest one can find to equal the devil. As we have noted, the gods as well as other spirits have the power to do evil or good. Therefore, when the devil appears in African-American folklore, he continues this image of not being such a terrible creature as European or Christian myths make him, but more of the trickster-mischievous character. A contemporary saying of a famous black television comedian will illustrate the point. Any time this comedian does a deed which may violate the community's values, when asked why he did the action, he will reply, "The devil made me do it." Another example to illustrate the place and attitude of African-Americans about the devil may be found in Julius Lester's tale of Stagolee, a folk hero, in African-American literature.[11] When Stagolee dies, because he has been such a Bad nigger, he goes to Hell instead of Heaven and takes over the Devil's kingdom. Here "Bad" in Black folklore acquires two meanings: Stagolee is "bad" in terms of trouble, but he is "bad" because he is able to get away with his "bad" deeds; therefore, he is considered a hero. Herskovits relates that this concept of the devil is more closely akin to the Dahomean-Yoruba god, Legba, who is a divine-trickster, part God, part man, part trickster.[12]

We shall not pursue the argument over the origin of African-folklore, for as Stith Thompson points out, regardless of whether the stories are European or not, when the African finishes modifying them, "it takes the expert eye to discover that they are not actually native."[13] In addition, perhaps the controversy is also part of the myth which wishes to perpetuate the notion that Africans have not contributed anything to the world or that they have no culture. Nevertheless, there have been many collections of both African and African-American folktales. However, I wish here to concentrate on how both African and African-American writers have incorporated storytelling into the body of modern literature.

In all West African literature, there are many, many references to storytelling. Stories are most often told by women, but men also tell the tales. Usually, the men narrate tales of the history of the people and those dealing with adventure and war. One of the most remarkable examples of storytelling is Amos Tutuola's *The Palm Wine Drinkard*; the book itself is one long "story" being told by the author to his reading audience. Besides employing various storytelling techniques, it contains practically every motif or theme found in African and African-American folklore. First, it is a personal story, for it relates the tale of the palm-wine drinkard, who tells of his adventures, triumphs, and encounters to recover his palm-wine tapster who has died; but on a deeper level, it is an allegory of the beliefs and values of an African people.

Secondly, *The Palm Wine Drinkard* has many "how" and "why" stories and even a riddle story in which the author invites the readers to send him answers. There are stories to teach family relationships and values. The best illustration of this latter form of narrative is in the tale of the young girl who follows the "Full-Bodied Gentlemen." The tale gives two morals: one is more closely related to the culture of the Nigerians in that it warns young girls that they should listen to the advice of the fathers or family when contemplating marriage, and the second is more universal because it points out how people should not become attracted to externals because they may be worthless, as the young girl discovered in the case of the full-bodied gentleman who really did not own anything about himself, except his head. Also, there is the trickster motif running throughout the book, with the palm-wine drinkard being the biggest trickster of all. He refers to himself as a "god and juju man."[14] We note his combining the religious and the magic.

In African-American literature, many writers make use of the motifs and themes found in the oral stories of Black people in America. For example, Ralph Ellison's novel *Invisible Man* includes many of the Black folk heroes; the novel could be subtitled, "The Journey of Black People in America."[15] But the inclusion of storytelling itself is very rare in African-American literature, possibly because these writers have been so influenced by western writers and there has been the movement away from storytelling in literature. Another reason is that most African writing is often a writer narrating his own life's story. The autobiographical mode in both African and African-American literature is a most widely used form.[16]

Only a few writers have created a narrator or storyteller. Charles W. Chestnutt in *The Conjure Woman* has a storyteller;[17] Langston Hughes has given us Simple, who is both a narrator and a participant in his stories.[18] The most common forms of the storyteller that we find in the writings of Black Americans are in the storytelling scenes in which young men tell stories to each other for entertainment, the black minister delivering his sermon, and the street orators who make their pitch to Blacks passing on the streets of the cities. Zora Neale Hurston and Richard Wright present accounts of Black men telling jokes or stories. Miss Hurston's men in *Their Eyes Were Watching God* live in the South and Richard Wright's characters in *Lawd Today* reside in the North.[19] In both cases, these men make use of the hyperbole of the tall-tale stories in which one man tries to out-tell the other one. Sometimes, as in *Their Eyes Were Watching God,* the stories involve animals, but most likely the stories are on sex or male-female relationships.

The folk-sermon has been used by many writers, but I suppose James Weldon Johnson in *God's Trombones* has presented the most outstanding use of this form.[20] The folk-sermons combine all the elements of storytelling that we emphasized earlier. Though in the works where they have been incorporated, the audience may be described as participating, a great deal of the effect of this oral form is lost because we do not get the dramatic effects of both the audience and the narrator. The use of these stories is also enlightening because it reveals how the African has taken Christian mythology and changed it to an African tale and, then, the writer adopts it to suit his purpose. Ralph Ellison in his prologue to *Invisible Man* has his narrator recount a time he was under the influence of a reefer and went deep into his past and heard the Black minister preaching:

> "Brothers and sisters, my text this morning is the 'Blackness of Blackness.'"

> And a congregation of voices answered: "That blackness is most black, brother most black . . ."

> "In the beginning . . ."[21]

The sermon continues for a long time, but the above excerpt illustrates synthesis and adaptation. Richard Wright details these transformations also when one of his characters says "Lawd, when I was down South I use' to dream about Chicago / Chicago seemed like the Promised Land!"[22]

Finally, the street orator is really the black minister who has come to the city. However, instead of preaching the gospel or using Christian mythology, he is crying for Black nationalism. Sometimes he combines the religious myth with the cry for nationalism as in *The Autobiography of Malcolm X.*[23] Often the street orator may be peddling a medicine, magic, or special powers as the "Snake Man" in *Lawd Today,* or he may be a separatist, reminding Black people that they must unite or they must return to Africa. The Black man as orator seems to be a definite carry-over. Carter G. Woodson writes that "classification on the basis of values set forth on the printed page would do injustice to scores of Negro orators who without literary equipment have moved multitudes."[24]

> He continues that their effectiveness was in their delivery.

> Their tones were beautiful, and their gestures natural. They could suit the word to action and the action to word. Using skillfully the eye and voice, they reached the souls of man.[25]

In traditional Africa, men were esteemed for their ability to call the crowd to order and to action. Achebe writes in *Things Fall Apart,*

> Okika was a great man and an orator. But he did not have the booming voice which a first speaker must use to establish silence in the assembly of the clan. Onyeka had such a voice; and so he was asked to salute Umuofia before Okika began to speak.[26]

Parallels exist in African literature in which this oratory tradition continues up to the present day. We have the example of the teacher-turned-politician in James Ngugi's *Weep Not, Child.* Another illustration may be seen in Kofi Awoonor's description of the orator-turned-nationalist in *This Earth, My Brother.*[27]

Before concluding this discussion of storytelling, let us examine briefly humor, which is one of the major elements in much of African and African-American folklore, particularly the stories. We have already noted that many of the tales belong to the trickster tradition in which the listener finds himself laughing at the devious methods used by a supposedly weak individual to overpower the stronger opponent. Secondly, exaggeration and hyperbole have been added as features in the stories, particularly the ones told by African-American young men to entertain themselves while sitting around on porches, corners, or in barber shops.

For a long time, hindered by language barriers, we have not been able to understand the humor in African life; consequently, we have been unable to establish parallels in African-American humor, although it has been partially acknowledged that most African-American folklore derives from Africa. With more Africans writing in English, we are now able to see some similarities. These may help to resolve certain questions about the humor of Blacks. For example, why is the "mother" used in "playing the dozens?" In the *History of Negro Humor,* William Schechter writes that research has shown that some people find humor in situations which are involved with smut or obscenity, crippled physical conditions, filth and excrement, unconventional conduct, misery, discomfort, accidents, stupidity, mispronunciations, aliens, magical changes.[28] Similarly, studies of groups of East and South Africans reveal that on certain occasions, obscenity and certain "lewd" behavior were permitted for palliative reasons when at other times these activities were highly forbidden.[29]

The Herskovits tell us at certain times, particularly in Dahomey, groups were given the freedom to satirize each other. In the competition, the ones who made the sharpest improvised verbal or song attacks were honored. This method of verse-song making could extend even to mocking the king, if there was one. Such a license to criticize was set aside ritually so that any repressed ill-will for abuse at the hands of the king could find release and thereby cease to oppress the king's subjects and "infect their souls."[30]

In addition, in many African oral folksongs are examples in which a woman, if provoked by a co-wife, will make up rhymes while she works; these verses lash out at the offending wife. Even in the religious celebrations, there are masks which were designed to produce laughter.

Indirection—"compensation by ridicule, or evasion, feigned stupidity" plays an important role in Black life.[31] We also learn that Africans prize conversation; Achebe writes "skirting around the subject and then finally hitting it" is all a part of the art.[32] All of these factors, plus the philosophy that life is both tragic and comic, suggest that there is a great deal of humor in African life and we find representations of it in the folk literature.

Humor becomes, like indirection, a means of survival. It can be used for relief against oppression, to forge understanding and compassion, and like African music to transform the individual to a better state. Also it can serve the dual function of protest and mask. It may reveal to the listener or in some cases to the speaker, protest, anger, frustration, threat; but it can mask these qualities, too.

Since one of the dominant themes in African life and literature has been attempts to deal with colonialism or the white man's oppression, both Africans and African-Americans have used humor to assist them. They have also had their languages as another means of masking. Africans, when wanting to ridicule whites, could easily do so in their indigenous languages, and Blacks in America have enjoyed a similar privilege because they developed dialects which could only be understood by people within the culture. Much of the humor was transmitted in these dialects. The plural is used because these African-American dialects have changed. We have had the dialects of the slaves—note the spirituals—and more recently, the dialects of the street. The more acculturated a Black becomes, the less of these dialects he knows. However, as a part of growing up most Black men become acquainted with the language of the streets. In addition, this dialect may function as a bridge to unite the masses with the most educated or western-acculturated group. The success of many Black leaders has depended on their ability to operate in both the dialects—that of the street or the people and the dialect of the white society. Dick Gregory is a noteworthy example of a leader who combines the street talk, the preacher rhetoric, and standard English. Therefore, he is able to attract and communicate with a large diversified audience. Martin Luther King, Jr., quite often used a combination of dialects.

Just as conversation is an art in Igbo society, it occupies a high place in African-American life, particularly that of the male. As we have noted, one aspect of storytelling still survives in the stories told by young men. This form of entertainment is highlighted by humorous verbal battles, which as we have observed, is an African tradition.

In African-American literature Zora Neale Hurston provides us with a good example when David and Jim, two characters in *Their Eyes Were Watching God,* are verbally contesting each other over who loves Daisy the most. The encounter goes:

> Dave: Well all right, less prove dis thing right now. We'll prove right now who love dis gal de best. How much time is you willin' tuh make fuh Daisy?
>
> Jim: Twenty yeahs!
>
> Dave: See? Ah told you dat nigger didn't love you. Me, ah'll beg the Judge tuh hang me, and wouldn't take nothin' less than life.[33]

The conversation illustrates humor through exaggeration which is further highlighted by the incongruency of the two images—that of a jail-sentence with that of loving a woman. Although on one level, the scene is funny because of the description; on another level, the laughter is to keep from crying. Every Black male knows the ease with which a white judge can give him time, sometimes for offenses less ridiculous than what has been described.

Another oral form which is popular and quite humorous is the dozens. It is too a verbal-game, played mainly by young men, and usually with an audience. The requirements are verbal insults about one's mother and the players' ability to keep "their cool." Within this framework, the characters may improvise until one is declared the winner. Violence can occur but most often it is checked by certain stylistic devices and frequently with laughter. The audience also maintains some control and acts as critics to determine which individual has outwitted the other. When the winner has "capped" his opponent he receives the applause of the audience. Excellent examples of the writer's use of the dozens are in Richard Wright's *Lawd Today* and his short story "Big Boy Leaves Home." Ralph Ellison uses it also in *Invisible Man.* When the protagonist is asked how he received "his personal responsibility," he answered, "From you ma—."[34] Brother Jack did not understand the verbal slur.

Another comic form which is closely related to the dozens is signifying. It too involves exaggeration, indirection, and verbal assaults. This type of ridicule-humor is found in both African-American and African literature. Richard Wright provides excellent examples in *Lawd Today* and Okot p' Bitek in *Song of Lawino* gives us an East African's version of signifying. Lawino, in describing her competitor, Clementine, says:

> Forgive me, brother
> Do not think I am insulting
> The woman with whom I share my husband![35]

And then she sets out to blast her:

> Her breasts are completely shrivelled up,
> They are all folded dry skins.
> They have made nests of cotton wool
>
> And she folds the bits of cow-hide
> In the nests
> And calls them breasts! (p. 25)

and

> And when she walks
> You hear her bones rattling
> Her waist resembles that of the hornet.
> The beautiful one is dead dry
> Like a stump,
> She is meatless
> Like a shell
> On a dry river bed. (p. 26)

Missing from Bitek's treatment is the audience participation, yet Lawino speaks as if she is addressing an audience. It is also noteworthy to point out here that Okot p' Bitek, an African, and Langston Hughes, an African-American, are two of the writers who use the storyteller as both a narrator and participant in their works.

Folk-Sayings.—The last topic of folklore I shall discuss is folk-sayings. As we have pointed out, Achebe says that conversation is considered an art in the Ibo life. He adds that "proverbs are the palm-oil with which words are eaten."[36] West African literature is replete with proverbs. Austin Shelton has counted the minimum number in the works of Achebe. There are "29 in *Things Fall Apart*, 42 in *No Longer at Ease*, 129 in *Arrow of God*, 27 in *Man of the People* and 11 in his short stories."[37] Many persons have criticized African writers for an excessive use of proverbs which, according to these critics, do not advance the plot. However, one may argue that the proverbs are useful in terms of literary structure and theme, but more than anything, they "Africanize" or "Igboize" the western literary forms.

African-American literature does not have quite as many proverbs as West African literature, but most of the writers who have preserved the African traditions most firmly do include proverbs, aphorisms, or plain folk-sayings. As in the case of the African proverb, these sayings make the literature sound "blacker" but they also do more. They reveal the collective expressions of Black people, their cultural attitudes, system of values, and wisdom gained through the years. Since folklore presents the other half of the beliefs of African people, let us look at a few of the African proverbs and the African-American folk-sayings which have appeared in the literature.

The most important value that the proverbs in Achebe's novels comment upon has to do with human interdependence. A series of proverbs which so adequately reflect the traditional African value are found in this set.

> "We do not ask for wealth because he that has health and children will also have wealth. We do not pray to have more money but to have more kinsmen. We are better than animals because we have kinsmen. An animal rubs its itching flank against a tree, a man ask his kinsman to scratch him."[38]

On another occasion, to provoke his countrymen to action, Okonkwo, Achebe's main character says:

> "Let us not reason like cowards," said Okonkwo. "If a man comes into my hut and defecates on the floor, what do I do? Do I shut my eyes? No! I take a stick and break his head. That is what a man does."[39]

West Africans are not the only ones to use proverbs. Okot p' Bitek has his long narrative poem *Song of Lawino,* packed with proverbs. Most of his chapter headings are in this form:

> The Graceful Giraffe Cannot Become a Monkey
> The Mother Stone Has a Hollow Stomach

The central theme of the work is also stated in a proverb in which Lawino admonishes her husband.

> Let no one
> Uproot the Pumpkin.[40]

What she is emphasizing to her husband is that Africans do have a proud heritage which is quite deep. Therefore, he should not let his western learning or "civilization" uproot him.

In African-American literature one of the most famous folk sayings is the one given by the peddler to the young protagonist in Ellison's *Invisible Man.* He tells him

> All it takes to get along in this here man's town is a little shit, grit, and motherwit.[41]

It reflects the speaker's concern with making it in America. Maya Angelou in *I Know Why the Caged Bird Sings* gives us the African-American version of the proverb of indirection. Her account is:

> If you asked a Nigger where he has been, he'll tell you where he's going.[42]

Also she expresses the African philosophy showing that the major force in the world has the power to do good or evil. The aphorism is: "Anything that works against you can also work for you once you understand the Principle of Reverse."[43]

I will close with two proverbs which may seem somewhat contradictory but with close reading reflect the African philosophy of using all forces to make life meaningful. One is by an African-American and one by an African.

> Life is going to give you just what you put in it. Put your whole heart in everything you do, and pray, then you can wait.[44]

The other:

> You have offended neither the gods nor your fathers. And when a man is at peace with his gods and his ancestors, his harvest will be good or bad according to the strength of his arm . . . Go home and work like a man.[45]

And finally this proverb seems to apply to Africans wherever they have been. They have "hoped for the best, were prepared for the worst, so anything in between didn't come as a surprise."[46] It is true that many of the proverbs in both African and African-American literature are quite often colored by the particular culture of each group. For example, there are many folk sayings in which American Blacks show distrust of each other in contrast to the ones in Africa which stress interdependence. Nevertheless, there seems to be at the root of both of these cultures a basic philosophy which has been best summarized in the African-American statement: "Be prepared to dance to whatever tune life offers you," or in Ezeulu's warning:

> The world is like a Mask dancing. If you want to see it well you do not stand in one place.[47]

SELECTED BIBLIOGRAPHY OF AFRICAN AND AFRICAN-AMERICAN WORKS WITH COMMON FOLKLORE FEATURES[48]

African

Magic and Superstition:

Longer Works:

Achebe, Chinua: *Arrow of God.* Garden City, New York: Doubleday & Company, 1969.

————. *No Longer at Ease.* London: Heinemann Educational Books Ltd., 1960.

————. *Things Fall Apart.* London: Heinemann Educational Books Ltd., 1958.

Aidoo, Ama. *No Sweetness Here.* Garden City, New York: Doubleday &Company, Inc., 1972.

Awoonor, Kofi. *This Earth, My Brother.* Garden City, New York: Doubleday & Company, Inc., 1972.

Bitek, Okot p'. *Song of Lawino: A Lament.* Nairobi: East African Publishing House, 1966.

Konadu, Asare. *A Woman in Her Prime.* Ibadan: Heinemann, 1967.

Mphahlele, Ezekiel. *Down Second Avenue.* Garden City, New York: Doubleday & Company, 1971.

Nwapa, Flora. *Efuru.* London: Heinemann, 1966.

Tutuola, Amos. *The Palm-Wine Drinkard.* New York: Grove Press, Inc., 1953.

Short Story:

Ogot, Grace. "Tekayo," in *African Writing Today.* Edited by Ezekiel Mphahlele, (Baltimore: Penguin Books, 1967), pp. 109-120.

Poetry:

Diop, Birago. "Omen," in *African Poetry for Schools,* edited by W. L. Radford. Nairobi, Kenya: East African Publishing House, 1970.

Karibo, Minji. "Superstition," in *African Poetry for Schools.*

Soyinka, Wole. "Abiku" (Yoruba Myth of Infant Mortality), in *Contemporary African Literature,* edited by Edris Makward and Leslie Lacy. New York: Random House, Inc., 1972.

African-American

Magic and Superstition:

Longer Works:

Bontemps, Arna. *Black Thunder.* Boston: Beacon Press, 1936.

Douglass, Frederick. *Narrative of the Life of Frederick Douglass. Written by Himself.* Garden City, New York: Doubleday & Company, Inc., 1963.

Gaines, Ernest J. *The Autobiography of Miss Jane Pittman.* New York: Dial Press, 1971.

Chestnutt, Charles. *The Conjure Woman and Other Tales.* Boston: Houghton Mifflin, 1899.

Hughes, Langston. *The Best of Simple.* New York: Hill and Wang, 1961.

Hurston, Zora Neale. *Mules and Men.* Philadelphia: J. B. Lippincott and Company, 1935.

————. *Their Eyes Were Watching God.* New York: Negro Universities Press, 1969.

Petry, Ann. *The Street.* Boston: Houghton Mifflin, 1964.

Walker, Margaret. *Jubilee.* Boston: Houghton Mifflin, 1966.

Wright, Richard. *Lawd Today.* New York: Walker and Company, 1963.

Short Stories:

Gaines, Ernest J. "A Long Day in November," in *Bloodline* (New York: The Dial Press, 1968), pp. 3-79.

McClellan, George Marion. "Annette," in *Early Black American Prose,* Ed. William H. Robinson, Jr. (Dubuque: Wm. C. Brown, 1971), pp. 166-71.

Poetry:

Bethune, Lebert. "A Juju of My Own," in *Understanding The New Black Poetry: Black Speech and Black Music as Poetic References,* Ed. Stephen Henderson, (New York: William Morrow, 1973), p. 297.

Brooks, Gwendolyn. *In The Mecca.* New York: Harper and Row, 1968.

Carter, Karl. "Roots," in *Understanding the New Black Poetry.* p. 312.

Fabio, Sarah Webster. "Evil Is No Black Thing," in *Understanding the New Black Poetry,* pp. 241-242.

Hayden, Robert. "Witch Doctor," in *Understanding the New Black Poetry,* pp. 151-153.

————. "Full Moon," in *Black-American Literature.* 1760-Present. Ed. Ruth Miller (Beverly Hills, California: Glencoe Press, 1971).

Neal, Larry. "The Narrative of the Black Magicians," in *Black Fire: An Anthology of Afro-American Writings.* Eds. Le Roi Jones and Larry Neal, (New York: The Morrow Company, 1968), pp. 312-314.

Walker, Margaret. "We Have Been Believers," in *Black-American Literature.*

African

Storytelling in the Literature:

Achebe, Chinua. *Arrow of God.*

————. *Things Fall Apart.*

Bitek, Okot p'. *Song of Lawino.*

Mphahlele, Ezekiel. *Down Second Avenue.*

Ngugi, James. *Weep Not, Child.* New York: Collier Books, 1964.

Tutuola, Amos. *The Palm-Wine Drinkard.*

Street Orator or Minister:

Achebe, Chinua. *Man of the People.* London: Heinemann, 1966.

Awoonor, Kofi, *This Earth, My Brother.* (Chapter 10a).

Bitek, Okot p'. "The Buffaloes of Poverty Knock the People Down," in *Song of Lawino.*

Ekwensi, Cyprian. *Jagua Nana.* Greenwich: Fawcett Premier Book, 1961.

Ngugi, James. *Weep Not, Child.*

Storytelling in Short Stories:

Ogot, Grace. "Tekayo," in *African Writing Today,* pp. 109-120.

Pliya, Jean. "The Fetish Tree," in *African Writing Today,* pp. 226-240.

African-American

Storytelling Among Black Men:

Angelou, Maya. *I Know Why the Caged Bird Sings.* New York: Bantam Books, 1970.

Hughes, Langston. "The Pool Hall," and "The Barber Shop," in *Not Without Laughter.* London: Collier-MacMillan Ltd., 1969.

————. *The Best of Simple.*

Hurston, Zora Neale. *Their Eyes Were Watching God.*

McKay, Claude. "Storytelling," in *Banjo.* New York: Harper and Brothers Publishers, 1929.

Wright, Richard. *Lawd Today.*

The Dozens:

Ellison, Ralph. *Invisible Man.* New York: Vintage Books, 1972.

Gregory, Dick with Loryle, Robert. *Nigger: An Autobiography.* New York: E. P. Dutton & Co., 1969.

Kelley, William M. "Cry For Me," in *American Negro Short Stories.* Ed. John Henrik Clarke. New York: Hill and Wang, 1967.

Wright, Richard. "Big Boy Leaves Home," in *Uncle Tom's Children.* 1938, rpt., New York: Harper, 1947.

————. *Lawd Today.*

Dozens or Signifying in Poetry:

Barrax, Gerald W. "The Dozens: A Small Drama in One Act, One Scene," in *Understanding the New Black Poetry,* pp. 60-61.

Brown, H. Rap. "Rap's Poem," in *Understanding the New Black Poetry,* pp. 187-88.

Ministers as Storytellers:

Angelou, Maya. *I Know Why the Caged Bird Sings.*

Baldwin, James. *Go Tell It On The Mountain.* New York: Alfred Knopf, 1953.

Ellison, Ralph. *Invisible Man.*

Johnson, James Weldon. *The Autobiography of an Ex-Coloured Man.* 1912, rpt., New York: Hill and Wang, 1960.

Johnson, James Weldon. *God's Trombones: Seven Negro Sermons in Verse.* New York: Viking, 1927.

McKay, Claude. "Sister Geter," in *Banjo.*

Meriwether, Louise. *Daddy Was A Number Runner.* Englewood Cliffs, New Jersey: Prentice-Hall, 1970.

Moody, Anne. *Coming of Age in Mississippi.* New York: Dial Press, 1968.

Wright, Richard. *Lawd Today.*

Street Orators:

Ellison, Ralph. *Invisible Man.*

Gaines, Ernest J. *The Autobiography of Miss Jane Pittman.*

Hurston, Zora Neale. *Their Eyes Were Watching God.*

Malcolm X and Haley, Alex. *The Autobiography of Malcolm X.* New York: Grove Press, Inc., 1964.

Wright, Richard. *Lawd Today.*

Storytelling in Short Stories:

Alba, Nanina. "A Scary Story," *Negro Digest,* 15 (July 1966), 65-68.

Crayton, Pearl. "The Day the World Almost Came to an End," in *Tales and Stories for Black Folks,* edited by Toni Cade Bambara. (Garden City, New York: Doubleday and Company, 1971), pp. 60-67.

Gaines, Ernest J. "The Sky Is Gray," in *Tales and Stories for Black Folks,* pp. 68-100.

Hurston, Zora Neale. "High John De Conjure" in *American Mercury,* 62 (1943), 450-458.

Kelley, William M. "Cry For Me," in *American Negro Short Stories,* pp. 248-263.

Murray, Albert. "Train Whistle Guitar," in *American Negro Short Stories,* pp. 209-226.

African

Humor:

Achebe, Chinua. *Arrow of God.*

———. *Things Fall Apart.*

Bitek, Okot p'. *Song of Lawino.*

Tutuola, Amos. *The Palm-Wine Drinkard.*

African-American

Humor:

Angelou, Maya. *I Know Why The Caged Bird Sings.*

Bambara, Toni Cade. *Tales and Stories for Black Folks.*

———. *Gorilla, My Love.* New York: Random House, 1972.

Ellison, Ralph. *Invisible Man.*

Gregory, Dick. *On The Back of the Bus.*

Hughes, Langston. *The Best of Simple.*

———. Ed. *The Book of Negro Humor.* New York: Dodd, Mead, 1966.

Hurston, Zora Neale. *Mules and Men.* Philadelphia: Lippincott, 1935.

———. *Their Eyes Were Watching God.*

Malcolm X and Haley, Alex. *The Autobiography of Malcolm X.*

African

Proverbs:

Achebe, Chinua. *Arrow of God.*

———. *Man of The People.* London: Heinemann, 1966.

———. *No Longer at Ease.*

———. *Things Fall Apart.*

Bitek, Okot p'. *Song of Lawino.*

Folk Sayings:

Konadu, Asare. *A Woman In Her Prime.*

Nwapa, Flora. *Idu.* London: Heinemann, 1970.

African-American

Folk Sayings:

Angelou, Maya. *I Know Why The Caged Bird Sings.*

Baldwin, James. *Go Tell It On The Mountain.*

Bontemps, Arna. *Black Thunder.*

Ellison, Ralph. *Invisible Man.*

———. *The Best of Simple.*

Hurston, Zora Neale. *Their Eyes Were Watching God.*

Walker, Margaret. *Jubilee.*

Wright, Richard. *Lawd Today.*

Children's Rhymes:

Angelou, Maya: *I Know Why The Caged Bird Sings.*

Morrison, Toni. *The Bluest Eyes.* New York: Holt Rinehart and Winston, 1970.

Walker, Margaret. *Jubilee.*

Folk Sayings in Poetry:

Bennett, Bob. "It Is Time For Action," in *Black Fire.*

Hamilton, Bob. "Brother Harlem Bedford Watts Tells Mr. Charlie Where It's At," in *Black Fire,* pp. 447-451.

Children's Rhymes in Poetry:

Ladele (Leslie Powell). "O-o-o-o-ld Miss Liza," in *Understanding the New Black Poetry,* pp. 356-357.

NOTES

[1] John S. Mbiti, *African Religions and Philosophy* (Garden City, New York: Doubleday and Company, Inc., 1970), p. 2.

[2] Zora Neale Hurston, *Mules and Men* (Philadelphia: J. B. Lippincott and Company, 1935), pp. 229-39.

[3] "Folk Tales," *The Negro Caravan* (Sterling Brown, Arthur P. Davis, and Ulysses Lee, Eds. 1941; rpt. New York: Arno Press and the *New York Times,* 1970), p. 432. A few of the white collectors of Black folklore are: Joel Chandler Harris, *Uncle Remus: His Songs and His Sayings* (1880); G. C. Jones, Jr., *Negro Myths From the Georgia Coast* (1888); A. M. H. Christensen, *Afro-American Folk Lore, Told Round Cabin Fires on the Sea Islands of South Carolina* (1892); Elsie Clews Parson, *Folklore of the Sea Islands, South Carolina* (1923); Guy Johnson, *Folk Culture on St. Helena Island* (1930); Newbell Niles Puckett, *Folk Beliefs of the Southern Negro* (1926). More recent white folklorists are Richard M. Dorson, *American Negro Folktales* (1950), *Negro Tales From Pine Bluff, Arkansas and Calvin, Michigan* (1958) and Roger D. Abrahams, *Deep Down in the Jungle* (1963), *Positively Black* (1970). Arthur Huff Fauset, J. Mason Brewer, Zora Neale Hurston, Onah L. Spencer and Charles J. Johnson are early Black folklorists. Sterling Brown, Langston Hughes, Arna Bontemps, Julius Lester, and Toni Cade Bambara are the later collectors.

[4] Ralph Ellison, "Change the Joke and Slip the Yoke," *Shadow and Act* (New York: The New American Library, 1964), p. 73.

[5] Chinua Achebe, *Things Fall Apart* (London: Heinemann Educational Books, Ltd., 1958). Page references in the text are to this edition.

[6] Arna Bontemps, *Black Thunder* (Boston: Beacon Press, 1936). Page references are to this edition.

[7] Ann Petry, *The Street* (Boston: Houghton Mifflin Company, 1946).

[8] Petry, p. 137.

[9] Melville Herskovits, *The Myth of the Negro Past* (Boston: Beacon Press, 1941), pp. 189-190.

[10] Sterling Brown, "Negro Folk Expression," *Black Expression,* Addison Gayle, Jr., ed. (New York: Weybright and Talley, 1969), pp. 5-6.

[11] Julius Lester, *Black Folktales* (New York: Grove Press, 1969), pp. 113-135.

[12] J. Melville and Frances S. Herskovits, *Dahomean Narrative* (Evanston: Northwestern University Press, 1958), pp. 37-38.

[13] Stith Thompson, *The Folktale* (New York: Holt, Rinehart and Winston, Inc., 1946), p. 286.

[14] Amos Tutuola, *The Palm-Wine Drinkard* (New York: Grove Press, Inc., 1953), p. 10.

[15] The edition being cited is Ralph Ellison, *Invisible Man* (New York: Vintage Books, 1972).

[16] See Joseph Bruchac, "Black Autobiography in Africa and America," *Modern Black Literature* (Buffalo: Black Academy Press, Inc., 1971), pp. 61-70.

[17] Reference is to Charles Chestnutt, *The Conjure Woman and Other Tales* (Boston: Houghton Mifflin, 1899).

[18] Reference is to Langston Hughes, *The Best of Simple* (New York: Hill and Wang, 1961). William Melvin Kelley, *A Different Drummer* (New York: Doubleday and Company, 1962) gives a twist by using an old white storyteller, Mr. Harper, to relate the legend of "The African."

[19] The editions I am citing are Zora Neale Hurston, *Their Eyes Were Watching God* (New York: Negro Universities Press, 1969) and Richard Wright, *Lawd Today* (New York: Walker and Company, 1963).

[20] See James Weldon Johnson, *God's Trombones: Seven Negro Sermons in Verse* (New York: Viking Press, 1927).

[21] Ellison, *Invisible Man,* p. 7.

[22] Wright, p. 154.

[23] Malcolm X and Alex Haley, *The Autobiography of Malcolm X* (New York: Grove Press, Inc., 1964).

[24] Carter G. Woodson, *Negro Orators and Their Orations* (Washington, D.C.: The Associated Publishers, Inc., 1925), p. 6.

[25] Woodson, p. 6.

[26] Achebe, p. 182.

[27] See James Ngugi, *Weep Not, Child* (New York: Collier Books, 1964) and Kofi Awoonor, *This Earth, My Brother* (Garden City, New York: Doubleday and Company, Inc., 1972).

[28] William Schechter, *The History of Negro Humor* (New York: Fleet Press Corp., 1970), p. 12.

[29] E. E. Evans-Pritchard, "Some Collective Expressions of Obscenity in Africa," *Position of Women in Primitive Societies and Other Essays in Social Anthropology* (New York: The Free Press, 1965), p. 101.

[30] Herskovits, *Dahomean Narrative,* p. 62.

[31] Herskovits, *The Myth,* p. 154.

[32] Achebe, p. 6.

[33] Hurston, *Their Eyes Were Watching God,* p. 107.

[34] Ellison, *Invisible Man,* p. 350; Wright, pp. 70-71 and 79-81; Richard Wright, "Big Boy Leaves Home," *Uncle Tom's Children: Five Long Stories* (Cleveland: The World Publishing Company, 1943), pp. 25-26.

[35] Okot p'. Bitek, *Song of Lawino* (Nairobi: East African Publishing House, 1966), p. 24. Page numbers in the text are to this edition.

[36] Achebe, p. 4.

[37] Austin J. Shelton, "The Palm-Oil of Language: Proverbs in Chinua Achebe's Novels," *Modern Language Quarterly,* 30 (1969), 87.

[38] Achebe, p. 151.

[39] Achebe, p. 145.

[40] Bitek, p. 63.

[41] Ellison, *Invisible Man,* p. 134.

[42] Maya Angelou, *I Know Why the Caged Bird Sings* (New York: Bantam Books, 1970), p. 164.

[43] Angelou, p. 187.

[44] Angelou, p. 228.

[45] Achebe, p. 16.

[46] Angelou, p. 234.

[47] Chinua Achebe, *Arrow of God* (Garden City: Doubleday and Company, 1969), p. 51.

[48] Full bibliographical information will be given in the first entry. Subsequent references will use short titles.

Bernard Bell

SOURCE: "Folk Art and the Harlem Renaissance," in *PHYLON: The Atlanta University Review of Race and Culture,* Vol. XXXVI, No. 2, December, 1975, pp. 155-63.

[*In the following essay, Bell compares the forging of an African-American literary consciousness in the writings of James Weldon Johnson, Alain Locke, and others, with the development of national identity in the works of European writers.*]

Major attempts by Afro-American academicians and artists to identify the strengths of Afro-American folk art and its potentialities for a black American tradition of high art have been strikingly similar to the spirit if not the letter of Herder's folk ideology. There is more than adequate circumstantial evidence that W. E. B. DuBois, Alain Locke and James Weldon Johnson—the elder statesmen of the Harlem Renaissance—were familiar with Anglo-American interpretations of Herder's theory that folk art laid the base for high art and the corollary concept of folksong as a spontaneous, indigenous expression of the collective soul of a people.

Interpretations of the pronouncements by Herder and the Grimm brothers generated a controversy in Europe between the concepts of group or folk poetry and individual or art poetry. Toward the close of the nineteenth century the group or communal theory was appropriated by America and applied to the ballads. Spearheaded by the scholarship and example of Francis James Child,[1] Francis Barton Gummere,[2] and George Lyman Kittredge,[3] Harvard University became the bastion of communalists. "The orthodox communalist," writes D. K. Wilgus in *Anglo-American Folksong Scholarship Since 1898,* "held that folk poetry is a genre which precedes and is antithetical to the poetry of art, that it springs spontaneously from a people, and that it is composed collectively by the people."[4] Of the three proponents, only Gummere seems to have been orthodox. Child, Wilgus reveals, "explicitly denied three fundamental tenets of the communalists: that ballads were dance songs, that they were of group authorship, and that they originated among the peasantry or in a classless society."[5] What Child actually believed was that "'truly national or popular poetry' developed in a stage of society in which 'there is such a community of ideas and feelings that the whole people form one individual! . . . This community of thought and feeling (not the homogeneous society of his followers) explains why the composition of one man will always be an expression of the mind and heart of a people as an individual and never the personality of individual men.'"[6] Both Gummere and Kittredge were disciples of Child. And while Gummere was the more prolific and ingenious scholar, Kittredge seems to have influenced more communalists,[7] including DuBois, Locke and Johnson.

Modern ballad scholarship is said to have begun with Kittredge. He kept the faith with the assumptions and conclusions of Child and Gummere, but produced a generation of scholars who eventually disproved his statement that ballad-making and ballad-singing were lost arts. It was Kittredge who gave academic validity to the antiquarian (Rousseauistic) revision of Herder's ideas when he wrote in the Introduction to the abridged *English and Scottish Popular Ballads* (1904):

> . . . quite apart from what we call literature, there is a great mass of miscellaneous song and story which circulates among those who have neither books nor newspapers. To this oral literature . . . education is no friend. Culture destroys it, sometimes with amazing rapidity. When a nation learns to read, it begins to disregard its traditional tales; it feels a little ashamed of them; and finally it loses both the will and the power to remember and transmit them. . . . To this oral literature belong the popular ballads, and we are justified, therefore, in calling them 'folk poetry.' They are not, like written literature, the exclusive possession of the cultivated classes in any community. They belonged, in the first instance, to the whole people, at a time when there were no formal divisions of literate and illiterate; when the intellectual interests of all were substantially identical, from the king to the peasant. As civilization advanced, they were banished from polite society, but they lived on among the humble, among shepherds and ploughboys and 'the spinsters and the knitters in the sun,' until even these became too sophisticated to care for them and they were heard no more.[8]

Kittredge also described the characteristic method of ballad composition "as improvisation in the presence of a sympathetic company which may even, at times, participate in the process," but went on to concede:

> It makes no difference whether a given ballad was in fact composed in the manner described, or whether it was composed (or even written) in solitude, provided the author belonged to the folk, derived his material from popular sources, made his ballad under the inherited influence of the method described, and gave it to the folk as soon as he had made it,—and provided, moreover, the folk accepted the gift and subjected it to that course of oral tradition which . . . is essential to the production of a genuine ballad.[9]

Stirred by the vitality of Afro-American folksong, their own ivy league education, travels abroad and quest for a new phase of group development, DuBois, Locke and Johnson—as we shall see—applied the implications of

Herder's theories (as refracted through the prism of Kittredge's pronouncements) to the spirituals, sermons, blues and jazz.

At this point, it is important to remember that most nineteenth century scholars and folklorists rejected the notion of Afro-American culture, paradoxically identifying black American music as African and imitative Anglo-American music.[10] The fact that most early collections of slave songs were spirituals and rarely included ballads also confused white academicians and encouraged them to exclude Afro-American music from the American canon of folksong. Among the first to part the veil of ignorance and celebrate the virtues of the spirituals was DuBois.

William Edward Burghardt DuBois graduated from Fisk University in 1888 and went on to earn his Ph.D. from Harvard in 1895. He also spent two years (1892-4) of rigorous study at the University of Berlin. While in Germany, he visited Strasbourg, where Herder and Goethe began their life-long friendship, Rhernpfalz, where he "had an excellent opportunity to study the peasant life closely and compare it with country life in the South,"[11] and Weimar, where Herder spent his final years in the court of Duke Karl August.[12] Before returning to the United States, DuBois also toured parts of Italy, Venice, Poland and France. Considering his ambitious pursuit of knowledge in several disciplines at a time when William James, Josiah Royce, George Santayana, Francis Child, Albert Bushnell Hart and George Lyman Kittredge were the great minds of Harvard and considering his training and travels on the continent, it is unlikely that DuBois remained untouched by the spirit and thought of Herber, Goethe, and Rousseau.

The Souls of Black Folk, published in 1903, was a history-making collection of essays. It had, as James Weldon Johnson stated, "'a greater effect upon and within the Negro race in America than any other single book published in this country since *Uncle Tom's Cabin.*'"[13] More pertinent to our concern is the affirmation of a spiritual black community revealed in the title, structure and biblical style of the book. Identifying himself in the Forethought as "bone of the bone and flesh of the flesh of them that live within the Veil," DuBois, in fourteen chapters each prefaced by a brief passage of poetry and a bar of the Sorrow Songs, outlines the spiritual world in which black Americans struggle to survive. "They that walked in darkness," he writes in the chapter on folksongs, "sang songs in the olden days— Sorrow Songs—for they were weary at heart. And so before each thought that I have written in this book I have set a phrase, a haunting echo of these weird old songs in which the soul of the black slave spoke to men."[14] Proclaiming Afro-American folksong "the singular spiritual heritage of the nation and the greatest gift of the Negro people," DuBois restates in Afro-American terms Herder's ideas on the importance of folk music as a window into the souls of a people and as the basis of a new nation's formal art. He considers the music essentially African in origin, recognizes its progressive hybridization and describes the creative process of the spirituals in much the same manner as Kittredge does ballad-making: "As in olden times, the words of these hymns were improvised by some leading minstrel of the religious band. The circumstances of the gathering, however, the rhythm of the songs, and the limitations of allowable thought, confined the poetry for the most part to single or double lines, and they seldom were expanded to quatrains or longer tales, although there are some few examples of sustained efforts, chiefly paraphrases of the Bible."[15] The essay "Of the Sorrow Songs" alludes to the existence of secular Afro-American music—including the debased "minstrel" and "coon" songs—but deemphasizes their importance. In later years as editor of the *Crisis* (1910-33) DuBois championed the cause of high art but encouraged black Americans to turn to their usable past for inspiration and originality.

Like DuBois, Alain Leroy Locke was nurtured in high art but had a deep affinity for Afro-American folk art. He, too, was educated at Harvard (A.B., 1907, Ph.D. 1918) and the University of Berlin (1910-11). Trained in philosophy, Locke was the first black Rhodes Scholar (1907-10). During and subsequent to his three years at Oxford University, he became a frequent visitor to the capitals of the world and drank deeply at the fountains of Western Culture. It is reasonable to assume, therefore, that Locke was familiar with the philosophical and folkloristic formulations of Herder and Kittredge. In 1916 Locke began a long, distinguished career as Professor of Philosophy at Howard University. And as editor of the Bronze Booklets and author of numerous articles and books[16] he was among the first to hail the black Americans' spiritual Coming of Age.

The New Negro (1925), edited by Locke, is considered the landmark of the Harlem Renaissance. It not only celebrated what Locke optimistically described as "the attainment of a significant and satisfying new phase of group development" by Americans of African descent, but also revealed a vastly modified form of Herdian folk ideology and cultural pluralism. These include an emphasis on the dignity of oppressed groups (the common man) and on the vitality of folk art; an effort to establish the legitimacy of racial expression and the functional character of Afro-American folksongs as a response to the particular experience of American history, and finally, an attempt to relate the significance of Harlem, as a community of diverse elements and an emerging common consciousness, to its prototypes in the cultures of other nations.

To Locke, Negro youth spoke out of "an unique experience and with a particular representativeness." In the vanguard of a new cultural awakening they embodied the potentiality of bridging the gap between folk and high art. "All classes of a people under social pressure are permeated with a common experience," Locke

writes, "they are emotionally welded as others cannot be. With them, even ordinary living has epic depth and lyric intensity, and this, their material handicap, is their spiritual advantage. So, in a day when art has run to classes, cliques and coteries, and life lacks more and more a vital common background, the Negro artist, out of the depths of his group and personal experience, has to his hand almost the conditions of a classical art."[17] In other words, the elemental nature of the Afro-American folk tradition is the distillation of the black Americans' struggle to survive in an alien and hostile environment. This was the reality behind Locke's observation that the Negroes of his day relied "upon the race-gift as a vast spiritual endowment from which our best developments have come and must come."[18] It is important to remember, however, that race as objectively employed by the younger generation was not, in Locke's view, a provincial *cul de sac,* but "an idiom of experience, a sort of added enriching adventure and discipline, giving subtler overtones to life, making it more beautiful and interesting, even if more poignantly so."[19] In this sense, it means a deepening rather than a narrowing of social vision. Digging "deep into the racy peasant undersoil of the race life" in order to free themselves from the distorted dialect of the minstrel tradition, the poets of the period "carried the folk-gift to the altitudes of art." In short, what Locke sensed in the "flavor of language, flow of phrase, accent of rhythm in prose, verse and music, color and tone of imagery, idiom and timbre of emotion and symbolism" was the ambition and promise of black artists to make a distinctive contribution to the general development of national art.[20]

The most acclaimed product of the race genius in America during the Harlem Renaissance was the spirituals. "But," as Locke points out, "the very elements which make them uniquely expressive of the Negro make them at the same time deeply representative of the soil that produced them. Thus, as unique spiritual products of American life, they become nationally as well as racially characteristic."[21] The creators of these folk songs, he believed "worked them up from the 'shout' and rhythmic elements of the sensuous dance." But out of this humble origin emanates an epic intensity and tragic profundity for which Locke says "the only historical analogy is the spiritual experience of the Jews and the only analogue, the Psalms."[22] On the other hand, he felt that the exquisite combination of Christian sentiment and music found in the spirituals rank them with the Latin hymns, Gregorian tunes and rarest of German chorals.[23] And though he expressed reservations about the spirituals as poetry, Locke maintained that their broken dialect and grammar were invariably the results of an instinctive euphonic sense in following the requirements of the musical rhythm.[24]

With full knowledge of the folksong origins of the European classics, Locke, DuBois, and Johnson were convinced that the black musician who maintained his relationship with the best traditions of the spirituals and organized their distinctive elements in a formal way would be the musical giant of his age. In the past the chief bond between black Americans was a common condition rather than a common consciousness. However, like Garvey and DuBois, Locke saw Afro-Americans as "the advance-guard of the African peoples" and Harlem as the cultural capital of the race. "In Harlem," he declared, "Negro life is seizing upon its first chances for group expression and self-determination. It is—or promises at least to be—a race capital. That is why our comparison is taken with those nascent centers of folk expression and self-determination which are playing a creative part in the world today. Without pretense to their political significance, Harlem has the same role to play for the New Negro as Dublin has had for the New Ireland or Prague for the New Czechoslovakia."[25] Locke, then, was among the first cultural historians to see Harlem as the key community in black America and in his own unique way affirmed Herder's belief that the highest cultural values are to be found in the lowest orders of society.

Equally important for his example as well as his thoughts on folk art during the Harlem Renaissance was James Weldon Johnson. He was imbued with a deep sense of respect for high art by his West Indian background, cosmopolitan tutors and white New England teachers at Atlanta University, where he graduated in 1894.[26] At the same time, he was no stranger to the folk cultures of Georgia, where he taught during his summer recess from college, and of his home town in Jacksonville, Florida, where he was equally inspired by the urbane music of Ebenezer Methodist Episcopal Church, the chanted sermons of revivalist preachers and the African music of "ring-shouters."[27] Curiously enough, of all the books he read as a youth, "the stories by the Brothers Grimm made the deepest effect."[28] In 1900, he wrote the lyrics to "Lift Every Voice," the Negro National Anthem. Then, under the influence of Dunbar and teamed with his brother Rosamond and a friend, Bob Cole, Johnson blossomed into one of the leading writers of musical comedy tunes in dialect. Also about this time, he discovered Whitman's *Leaves of Grass*. "I was engulfed and submerged by the book, and set floundering again,"[29] he wrote. It was the impact that Whitman had on him which triggered the realization of the artificiality of conventionalized Negro dialect poetry. After touring Paris and London, Johnson returned to New York to study dramatic literature and creative writing under Brander Matthews at Columbia University. The main fruit of these early years as a folk art enthusiast, popular song-writer for the theater, and poet was *The Autobiography of an Ex-Colored Man*.

Published anonymously in 1912, *The Autobiography of an Ex-Colored Man* is the story of Negro soul denied. The special genius of Johnson's protagonist—the product of an interracial union who ultimately decides to pass for white—is that he is equally adept at ragtime and Chopin. His unrealized dream was to write symphonic music based on ragtime and the old slave songs.

Johnson's protagonist was, in effect, the fictional embodiment of Herder's folk ideology.

While collecting folk material to transform into formal art, the nameless protagonist—a nominal prototype of Ellison's young hero in Invisible *Man*—encounters two legendary folk types: John Brown, the old preacher, and "Singing Johnson," the creator of spirituals. Both are impressive men, ingenious and eloquent in their respective arts. In the Preface to *God's Trombones*, seven sermons in verse, Johnson outlines the character and art of the folk preacher:

> The old-time Negro preacher of parts was above all an orator, and in good measure an actor. He knew the secret of oratory, that at bottom it is a progression of rhythmic words more than it is anything else. Indeed, I have witnessed congregations moved to ecstasy by the rhythmic intoning of sheer incoherencies. He was a master of all the modes of eloquence. He often possessed a voice that was a marvelous instrument, a voice he could modulate from a sepulchral whisper to a crashing thunder clap. His discourse was generally kept at a high pitch of fervency, but occasionally he dropped into colloquialisms and, less often, into humor. He preached a personal and anthropomorphic God, a sure-enough heaven and a red-hot hell. His imagination was bold and unfettered. He had the power to sweep his hearers before him; and so himself was often swept away. At such times his language was not prose but poetry.[30]

The folk preacher did not preach a formal sermon from a formal text; the text more often than not served as a starting point and frequently had no relation to the development of the sermon, which was intoned in an electrifying, rhythmic manner.

A full description of "Singing Johnson" and the tradition of the black bards of old dominates the Preface to *The Book of American Negro Spirituals* (1925):

> 'Singing' Johnson is one of the indelible pictures on my mind. A small but stocky, dark-brown man was he, with one eye, and possessing a clear, strong high-pitched voice. . . . A maker of songs and a wonderful leader of singing. A man who could improvise lines on the moment. . . . 'Singing' Johnson was of the line of the mightier bards of an earlier day, and he exemplified how they worked and how the Spirituals were 'composed.' These bards, I believe, made the original inventions of story and song, which in turn were influenced or modified by the group in action.[31]

This tradition, as we may recall, has a strong affinity to that advanced by Kittredge for ballad-making.[32]

It is also important to recall that in the Preface to *The Book of American Negro Poetry* (1922) Johnson advocates one of the most challenging approaches to folk art of his day. In an apparent attempt to reconcile the difference between folk art and high art, he argues that Afro-American folksongs represent a vast mine of material to be tapped by some genius of the race. Unlike many of his urbane contemporaries, Johnson affirmed the cultural values of the blues and jazz. By folksongs, he meant sacred and secular music, the spirituals and ragtime. (He seems to have used the latter term to designate a pot-pourri of musical types, including work songs, blues, and jazz.)[33] And the genius he extols is both national and international in character. The music created through the transmuting power of black artists would be not only the soul of their race, but the soul of America. "This power of the Negro to suck up the national spirit from the soil," Johnson writes, "and create something artistic and original, which, at the same time, possesses the note of universal appeal, is due to a remarkable racial gift of adaptability; it is more than adaptability, *it is a transfusive quality. And the Negro has exercised this transfusive quality not only here in America, where the race lives in large numbers, but in European countries, where the number has been almost infinitesimal.*"[34] The apparent contradiction here is resolved if we acknowledge the creative potentialities of the common man and the reality of the socially induced ethnic and nationalistic tensions mirrored in Afro-American poetry. The parallels between these ideas and Herder's cultural democracy and nationalism seem to me stronger than mere coincidence.

Johnson's comments on the significance of an indigenous language are also related to Herder's views. Observing that the new Negro poets were not trying to break away from Negro dialect but from the limitations imposed on it by the plantation and minstrel traditions, Johnson writes:

> What the colored poet in the United States needs to do is something like what Synge did for the Irish; he needs to find a form that will express the racial spirit by symbols from within rather than without, such as the mere mutilation of English spelling and pronunciation. He needs a form that is freer and larger than dialect, but which will still hold the racial flavor; a form expressing the imagery, the idioms, the peculiar turns of thought, and the distinctive humor and pathos, too, of the Negro, but which will also be capable of voicing the deepest and highest emotions and aspirations, and allowing of the widest range of subjects and the widest scope of treatment.[35]

These ideas are by no means an indiscriminate, direct adoption of Herder's linguistic nationalism, but they do highlight the spiritual bond reflected in a distinctive linguistic form and urge its development.

In the preceding paragraphs I have isolated what was common in the thoughts of the elder statesmen of the Harlem Renaissance in order to highlight their points of contact with, and divergence from, Herdian folk ideology. On the basis of their training, travels and writings, it is reasonable to infer that DuBois, Locke and Johnson

were in tune with both the folk spirit of their age and the spirit of Herder's ideas on the relationship between folk art and formal art.

NOTES

[1] See *The English and Scottish Popular Ballads,* 5 vols. (Boston and New York, 1882-1898); reprinted 1956.

[2] See *Old English Ballads* (Boston 1894); *The Beginnings of Poetry* (New York, 1901); and *Democracy and Poetry* (Boston and New York, 1911).

[3] Introduction, *The English and Scottish Popular Ballads,* abridged ed. (Boston, 1904), pp. xi-xxi.

[4] (New Brunswick, 1959), p. 4.

[5] *Ibid.,* p. 7.

[6] *Ibid.*

[7] *Ibid.,* p. 32.

[8] p. xii.

[9] Quoted in Wilgus, *op. cit.,* p. 34.

[10] See Melville J. Herskovits, *The Myth of the Negro Past* (Boston, 1958).

[11] W. E. B. DuBois, *Dusk of Dawn* (New York, 1968), p. 47.

[12] F. M. Barnard, *Herder's Social and Political Thought* (Oxford, 1965), pp. xiii-xiv.

[13] Quoted by Saunders Redding, Introduction, *The Souls of Black Folk* (New York, 1961), p. ix.

[14] DuBois, *The Souls of Black Folk,* p. 181.

[15] *Ibid.* p. 188.

[16] See, for example, *The New Negro* (New York, 1925), *Four Negro Poets* (New York, 1927), *The Negro and His Music* (Washington, 1936), and *The Negro in Art* (Washington, 1940).

[17] Locke, *The New Negro* (New York, 1968), p. 47.

[18] *Ibid.*

[19] *Ibid.,* p. 48.

[20] *Ibid.,* p. 51.

[21] Locke, "The Negro Spirituals," *The New Negro,* p. 199.

[22] Locke, *The New Negro,* p. 200.

[23] *Ibid.,* p. 201.

[24] *Ibid.*, p. 204.

[25] Locke, *The New Negro*, p. 7.

[26] Johnson took considerable pride in his matrilineal West Indian ancestry. It is also interesting to note that one of his tutors was a West Indian cobbler whose command of the English language and classical literature was impeccable. See James Weldon Johnson *Along This Way: The Autobiography of James Weldon Johnson* (New York, 1933), pp. 6-7; 92-93.

[27] Johnson, *Along This Way,* pp. 10-25.

[28] *Ibid.*, p. 13.

[29] *Ibid.*, p. 158.

[30] (New York, 1969), p. 5. Recently, two perceptive studies of the folk preacher have been published. See Henry E. Mitchell, *Black Preaching* (Philadelphia and New York, 1970) and Bruce A. Rosenberg, *The Art of the American Folk Preacher* (New York, 1970).

[31] James Weldon Johnson and J. Rosamond Johnson, *The Book of American Negro Spirituals* (New York, 1969), p. 23.

[32] See Rosenberg, *The Art of the American Folk Preacher* for an intriguing attempt to relate the spirituals and sermons to Albert B. Lord's formulaic theory of oral composition.

[33] Johnson argued that ragtime was originated by colored piano players in the "questionable resorts" along the Mississippi River. "Once the text of all Ragtime songs was written in Negro dialect," he states, "and was about Negroes in the cabin or in the cotton field or on the levee or at a jubilee or on Sixth Avenue or at a ball, and about their love affairs. Today, only a small proportion of Ragtime songs relate at all to the Negro. . . . But that does not abolish in any way the claim of the American Negro as its originator." *The Book of American Negro Poetry*, p. 12.

[34] James Weldon Johnson, ed. *The Book of American Negro Poetry*, rev. ed. (New York, 1959), p. 20. My italics.

[35] *Ibid.*, pp. 41-42.

Leonard Diepeveen

SOURCE: "Folktales in the Harlem Renaissance," in *American Literature,* Vol. 58, No. 1, March, 1986, pp. 64-81.

[*In the following essay, Diepeveen examines the often ambivalent attitudes of Harlem Renaissance writers and thinkers toward the folklore of Africa and, more specifically, of African America.*]

During the Harlem Renaissance, the "rediscovery" of Black culture seemed to promise a celebration of the folktales that Blacks had inherited from Reconstruction and slavery. The earlier rejuvenation of spirituals, the other great component of the Black folk tradition, offered an apparent analogy. Folktales and spirituals were the two most widely known Black folk expressions; both had explicit references to slave culture, and both (perhaps because of these references) initially found little acceptance by Black intellectuals or the Black middle class. But in the years after the successful Fisk Jubilee Singers tours of the northern states and Europe (1871-78), major writers, in their books and in *The Crisis,* gave spirituals universal praise and much attention, so that by the time of the Harlem Renaissance spirituals formed the centerpiece of Black cultural pride. Outward signs encouraged a similarly eager appropriation of the folktale tradition by contemporary writers and critics.

Indeed, as with the spirituals, "rediscovery" may be too strong a word to apply to folktales, for they had never disappeared as a popular oral art form. However, until the Harlem Renaissance they had not received the sort of official sanction that the Black press gave spirituals. The Harlem Renaissance didn't change this situation. Folktales were never highlighted in the pages of *The Crisis* or *Opportunity,* and W. E. B. Du Bois, Alain Locke, and James Weldon Johnson (who as editors, prolific writers, and leaders of the NAACP presented themselves and were accepted as the arbiters of Black taste) did not acknowledge folktales as significant artifacts of Black cultural achievement. Even though reviews of folktale collections sporadically appeared in the Black press, folk tales were not often mentioned outside of these few occasions.[1]

On the other hand, folktales were not limited to the pages of a writer such as Jean Toomer, who incorporated traditional folk motifs into his writing. The Harlem Renaissance saw the publication of many substantial collections of folktales: *With Aesop Along the Black Border* by Ambrose Gonzales (1922); *Negro Folk Rhymes* by Thomas Talley of Fisk (1922); *Folklore of the Sea Islands, South Carolina* by Elsie Clews Parsons (1923); *Congaree Sketches* (1927) and *Nigger to Nigger* (1928) by E. C. L. Adams; *The Tree Named John* by John Sales (1929); Howard Odum's trilogy *Rainbow Round My Shoulder* (1928), *Wings on My Feet* (1929), and *Cold Blue Moon* (1930); and, somewhat later, Zora Neale Hurston's *Mules and Men* (1935).

But for two reasons this impressive list of publications does not signal the acceptance of Black folktales by the major Harlem Renaissance writers. First, the publication of these folktales was one-sided. With the exception of Zora Neale Hurston, the editors of these collections were white.[2] Arthur Huff Fauset was the only other major Black writer to spend significant attention on collecting AfroAmerican folk tales. Second, the Black intellectual elite of Du Bois, Locke, and Johnson did not follow or accompany this publishing boom with the unanimous acceptance they gave to spirituals. Notice not just of these collections but of the entire folktale tradition was limited to short reviews of a few of these collections (most of these reviews were combined with notices of other books) and a sentence or two in capsule histories of Black cultural achievement.

The few reviews of folktale collections in the major Black periodicals of the time (*The Crisis* and *Opportunity*) are a constructive place to begin probing the reasons for this lack of recognition: the bits of praise they contain are jarring when one compares the little notice folktales received to the lavish and repeated praise accorded spirituals. When critics lauded folk collections, the praise had a specific tone and direction. During the Harlem Renaissance, reviews (and any general discussion) of folk materials tended to contain two ideas more revelatory of the reviewers than of the books themselves: an evaluation of the way in which Black characters were portrayed (either in an uplifting or a stereotyped way) and a reference (usually slightly condescending) to the people from whom these folktales sprang. For example, George Schuyler, the only major writer of the Harlem Renaissance to review a particular collection of folktales in detail, discussed the collection *Nigger to Nigger* in this way: "Here is no uppish white writer straining every nerve to present the Negro as a clown and imbecile, but rather the book is a revelation of the humor, wit, intelligence, philosophy, hopes and fears of the humble negro peasant."[3] Thus, for Schuyler this collection has value because it portrays the Black properly, not as a "clown and imbecile." But neither does Schuyler comfortably acknowledge the model for this portrayal: he somewhat patronizingly distances himself (and the Harlem Renaissance) in his reference to "the humble negro peasant."

Ironically, this reference to the source of these folk tales and the praise of the tales themselves signal some of the ambivalences Harlem Renaissance writers had toward folktales. The two concerns apparent in this review—the condescending reference to the Black past and the concern with the way in which Blacks were portrayed—follow naturally from two marked attitudes of the Harlem Renaissance that helped to continue the neglect of the folktale tradition: an uneasy accommodation with the past and past literary tradition, and the campaign for desegregation, a campaign that used artistic expression as one of its main tools.

I

The uneasy accommodation with the past and its implications for folktales find expression in the "New Negro," an idea central to the development of the Harlem Renaissance. In 1923 Charles Johnson articulated a theme that was to become the hallmark of the new Black writers: "The 'dark ages' of Negro poetry are being left behind and along with this period has gone the muddled psychology of a distracted and overwhelmed race. These voices now speaking have caught not only the inspira-

tion of newer ideals but the new spirit of Negro life."[4] The later publication of Alain Locke's anthology *The New Negro* (1925) gave this concept much wider attention. Obviously, to a certain degree Johnson's (and, later, Alain Locke's) emphasis on newness and rejection of the past oversimplifies the Harlem Renaissance. Race pride gave the New Negro his energy, and this pride didn't obliterate the past. For example, the New Negro anthology acknowledged the importance of and contained articles on the African and the folk heritage. Further, in an editorial in the October 1926 *Crisis,* W. E. B. Du Bois explicitly states that one shouldn't be ashamed of the Negro past,[5] and in his preface to *The Second Book of Negro Spirituals* James Weldon Johnson calls for Negro artists to draw fully "on their racial resources and material."[6]

Nevertheless, the Harlem Renaissance did not look nostalgically to the past for its energy. When Harlem Renaissance critics and artists turned to the past it was to transform the past into something useful for the present, such as "rehabilitating the race in world esteem from that loss of prestige for which the fate and conditions of slavery have so largely been responsible."[7] The Harlem Renaissance further used the past as a way to affirm the new "deep feeling of race";[8] for instance, the African heritage became a way of expressing part of the race's psyche.

This general affirmation of his past by the "New Negro" thus encouraged a marked attitude to the way the past should be used—not as nostalgia, but as a tool useful for developing the present. This attitude helps to elucidate many intellectuals' ambivalences towards folktales. The ambivalence first comes from the fact that the New Negro and the Harlem Renaissance were both contemporary urban phenomena, while most of the earlier folktales came from the rural South. Locke emphasized this change: "The migrant masses, shifting from countryside to city, hurdle several generations of experience at a leap, but more important, the same thing happens spiritually in the life-attitudes and self-expression of the Young Negro, in his poetry, his art, his education and his new outlook, with the additional advantage, of course, of the poise and greater certainty of knowing what it is all about."[9] The shift was not just temporal and geographic, but cultural.

Some writers saw the break between the cultures as complete and perhaps larger than it needed to be. In fact, the urban movement and increasing sophistication of Blacks during the Harlem Renaissance caused James Weldon Johnson to question not just the relevance but the future existence of the entire folk tradition. In his preface to *The Second Book of Negro Spirituals* Johnson argues that folk art in general will disappear because of modern inventions and modern consciousness.[10] Most writers were more moderate, and did not go beyond clearly delineating between modern writers and past generations of peasants—hence the tone of Schuyler's review of *Nigger to Nigger*. Black writers might be using materials from their past, but in the Harlem Renaissance at least, the emphasis was on *past*. Blacks had progressed. Consequently, Black writers such as Langston Hughes who used a folk tradition worked with folk materials most familiar to them and their audiences, mainly urban materials like jazz and blues.[11]

Thus, this unofficial literary program of the Harlem Renaissance tended to break completely with folktales. Part of this break was made in order to emphasize the "New Negro": the race had moved on to more contemporary issues. But Black folklore also was peculiarly tied to the past; Black folklore contained many more references to recent (within the past seventy-five years), historically verified oppression and humiliation than did folklores of most other races and cultures. Because reviewers did not usually recognize the sophisticated and various ways in which these folktales treated slavery and white oppression, the perceived topics of these folktales did not seem to promote the type of art the Harlem Renaissance wanted. The association of folktales with these unpleasant aspects of the cultural heritage created a new set of problems.

This cultural heritage had an uneasy place in critical discussions of the evolution of Black art, and the implications for folktales are not hard to extrapolate from these discussions. For example, although she acknowledged the power of contemporary Black art, Charlotte Taussig argued that the oppression present in the cultural heritage ill prepared Black culture for this present explosion of high art: "Professor Kittredge, of Harvard, once said that culture is a by-product. A by-product of what? Surely not of slavery, or oppression or discrimination. And yet in considering Negro art, this race, with a background so little fitted to make for that illusive [sic] quality, has, in this short time prepared a field too broad to cover."[12]

In speaking of the success of her contemporaries, Taussig implies another reason why the past haunted many writers of the Harlem Renaissance and therefore why the folk tradition embarrassed them. Many Black writers found much distasteful not only in their political and social history but also in their cultural history. As a movement, the Harlem Renaissance deliberately tried to break with past social injustices and past artistic misrepresentations of the race—most writers found the two issues impossible to discuss separately. Literature presented an obvious target, and Harlem Renaissance essayists vigorously denounced Thomas Nelson Page and other writers who presented a stereotyped version of the race. As Locke put it, "The day of 'aunties,' 'uncles' and 'mammies' is equally gone. Uncle Tom and Sambo have passed on. . . . "[13] And the expressed counterpart to this denunciation: "In art and letters, instead of being wholly caricatured, he [the Negro] is being seriously portrayed and painted."[14]

As an extension of this program, New Negro writers characteristically avoided or disparaged earlier folk literature because of the abuses and stereotypes of Blacks

that many collections of this literature (like American literature in general) usually had, especially the emphasis on the laughing, subservient darky. Joel Chandler Harris is the key figure to understanding this ambivalence. Harris was seen by both whites and Blacks as the only major editor of Black folk tales. For example, by the time of the Harlem Renaissance Harris' role in the folk tradition was so firmly established that Arthur Huff Fauset's discussion in *The New Negro* of the folktale tradition spends the bulk of its time evaluating the Uncle Remus stories.[15] Further, Harris' Uncle Remus stories sold phenomenally well, both in popular magazines and collections. Sales are purported to have been brisk during the 1920s, and by 1948 various editions of *Uncle Remus: His Songs and His Sayings* (1880) had sold over 500,000 copies.[16] A poll of four hundred high-school and college teachers in 1926 rated it the fifth most important work of American literature to date, and placed it ahead of *Moby-Dick* and *The Portrait of a Lady*.[17]

But Harris had a shaky reputation with all Harlem Renaissance artists and intellectuals. The typical discussion tempered slight praise with strong reservations. Arthur Fauset praised Harris for presenting some of the richness of the Black folktale tradition to the (white) American public: "It simply happens that the one type of Negro story has struck the popular fancy, and becoming better known, blurred out the remaining types. For this result, we are indebted to Joel Chandler Harris, who saw the popular possibilities of the 'B'rer Rabbit' tales, and with his own flair for literature, adapted them with such remarkable skill and individuality that today they rank with the best known and most highly appreciated works of American literature."[18] However, Fauset went on to chastise Harris for his racial stereotypes and inappropriate humor. Along with many writers, Fauset noticed an unmistakable air of nostalgia for the antebellum South in Harris' folktales, especially in the relationship between Uncle Remus and the slave owner's children: "When we find one critic naively suggesting that Uncle Remus 'makes clear to every thoughtful reader that the system of slavery pernicious as it may appear to us now, took the dusky savage from his haunts in the African jungle and made of him a Christian and a gentleman,' we can clearly see that any writing that can be taken as an *apologia* for a social system, or the idealization of the plantation régime, cannot be taken unsuspiciously as the chronicle of a primitive folk lore."[19] Also, because of Harris' overwhelming use of comic elements, up to this time writers almost solely discussed the folk tradition (Harris' being the only widely known version) within the terms of the comic. Because of this distasteful emphasis on the comic in folktales, critical writers from *The Crisis* and *Opportunity*, writers such as Du Bois, Johnson, and Locke, disparaged unequivocal acceptance of the comic element in the folk tradition.

These writers frowned upon accepting the comic and other accompanying aspects of the folk tradition because such acceptance seemed to imply that these motifs were actual traits of the Black race rather than illegitimate stereotypes. For example, equally (or even spectacularly) unacceptable was this nostalgic reference to the folk past by a Southern white editor: "There is, however, a kind of Negro humor that deals in a distinctively racial manner with the Negro's love of music, talk, animals, meetings, dancing, loafing and fishing, and is best exemplified in the poems of Dunbar, Allen, and Davis. In this direction, the Negro is perhaps likely to make a purely racial contribution to American poetry."[20] Responded the reviewer for *Opportunity*: "And there you have it! The compilers of this volume appear to believe that the 'loud guffaw and the wide grin' are the paramount expressions of Negro aesthetics. At this point, I join the company of Johnson, Braithwaite, and Du Bois, and vehemently dissent. The Negro poet has long since forsaken the jester's tatterdemalion. His contribution is more subtle and pregnant; more sensitive to the adventures of his own harassed soul."[21]

These editors' seeing the comic pastoral tradition as the distinctively Black contribution to American literature was given a more dangerous twist by such contemporary popular folk humorists as Octavus Roy Cohen, Irvin Cobb, and E. K. Means, whose many portrayals of the Negro peasant were both inevitably low comedy and distorted versions of the Negro folk tradition. Not only were the typical characters in these stories ignorant yokels who were most happy when indulging their most base desires, the stories implied that these characters were typical of contemporary Negroes. Thus, the embarrassing tradition which Black intellectuals thought they had put behind them was aggressively present—and often perceived as accurate and contemporary by white readers.

A further complication in this uneasy relation to the past and literary tradition hindered the acceptance of folktales. Most critics writing in *Opportunity* and *The Crisis* disliked the omnipresent use of dialect in folktales. Not only folktale compilers like Harris, but earlier Black writers such as Dunbar and Chesnutt invariably used dialect in their presentations of Black folk culture. Because of this historical association dialect was identified with the folk tradition, and dialect automatically formed part of the controversy over folktales. The immense popularity of Harris' Uncle Remus anthologies, which were written in dialect, initiated the identification of folktales with Black dialect in the minds of most writers and readers. Such an association gained strength as new folk collections consistently presented folktales in dialect. Even the few folktales given in the pages of *The New Negro* were written in dialect.

This inevitable mode of presentation created the problem. In his discussion of Negro dialect, Charles S. Johnson argues that many users of dialects (he singles out Harris) provide inaccurate dialect which is used to make Blacks look uneducated and ridiculous.[22] Fauset made essentially the same point about Harris' books, demonstrating the inaccuracy of his dialect.[23] The attention was one-sided—critics generally ignored the use of dialect in those artists who presented it accurately. Only

Hughes dissented from this lambasting of traditional dialect writers and lamented the lack of interest in Chesnutt and Dunbar.[24]

But Hughes's argument had little influence; few writers attempted dialect. (Indeed, even today dialect has these unfavorable connotations, primarily because of the acceptance of "Standard English" as the socially desirable form of communication.) The unstated rationale for most Harlem Renaissance writers was that because of the abuses noted by Johnson and Fauset, any contemporary use of dialect would be immediately associated with the stereotyped Uncle Remus. Writers argued that dialect did not allow one to take literature seriously, that dialect got in the way of true aesthetic appreciation. For example, in the preface to his book *God's Trombones* James Weldon Johnson proudly points out his ability to use folk materials without resorting to the "distraction" of dialect, and Du Bois and Countee Cullen praised the book for the same reason.[25] Johnson reasoned that dialect was limited, capable of expressing only pathos and humor—a point he made in several essays. Dialect thus didn't form part of the New Negro program. According to Johnson, Black poets of his time had discarded dialect and "most of the material and subject matter that went into dialect poetry."[26]

II

For many critics this ambivalent attitude to the past and literary tradition worked alongside the second major contributor to the neglect of the folktale tradition: the campaign for desegregation. The campaign for desegregation was perhaps the major rallying ground against racism in the Harlem Renaissance, and it led to a basic unity in the mainstream aesthetic theories.

To be sure, although all critics disparaged Negro "protest art," in many respects the aesthetic theory of the Harlem Renaissance had little apparent unity. The positions presented in the central debate, the debate between Du Bois and Locke, seemed inextricably opposed. At times, Du Bois made seemingly radical statements about the need for propaganda in art: "Thus all Art is propaganda and ever must be, despite the wailing of the purists. I stand in utter shamelessness and say that whatever art I have been writing has been used always for propaganda for gaining the right of black folk to love and enjoy. I do not care a damn for any art that is not used for propaganda. But I do care when propaganda is confined to one side while the other is stripped and silent."[27] Granted, Du Bois was not advocating the overthrow of formal concerns; rather, he was pointing out that in its inevitable presentation of values, great art must ally itself with Truth and Justice: "The apostle of Beauty thus becomes the apostle of Truth and Right not by choice but by inner and outer compulsion. Free he is but his freedom is ever bounded by Truth and Justice; and slavery only dogs him when he is denied the right to tell the Truth or recognize an ideal of Justice."[28] Locke took exception to this notion that art had bounds, and his insistence on the artist's complete freedom in choosing materials created a polarity in critical discussion.[29] Du Bois and Locke's debates in print accentuated these differences.

The clearest way to come at the underlying unity in these critics' diverse statements is by considering the unified opposition of artists and critics to Marcus Garvey and his program of Black nationalism and separatism. Locke, Du Bois, and others all saw desegregation rather than separatism as the key to social progress. This common opposition had implications that at one level unified critical theory along integrationist ideals: all critical theory assumed that Negro art at this stage in history has a well-defined integrationist function. Thus, as Robert Hayden points out, Locke's anthology *The New Negro* is a document based on integrationist principles.[30] Therefore, although only some critics argued that the artist has complete freedom in choosing his materials, and is not bound to represent just the uplifting aspects of Negro society, all critics agreed that one presents art—even such "pure" art—in order to show that the race is capable of creating quality Western high art. Locke's introductory essay in *The New Negro* uses this assumption and approaches its conclusion with this rhetorical flourish: "The especially cultural recognition they [New Negro artists] win should in turn prove the key to that revaluation of the Negro which must precede or accompany any considerable further betterment of race relationships. But whatever the general effect, the present generation will have added the motives of self-expression and spiritual development to the old and still unfinished task of making material headway and progress."[31] Both Locke and Du Bois reasoned that if whites were to see how creative and intelligent some Black artists were, whites would be forced to change their opinions about the race as a whole. In their performances in predominantly white concert halls and theaters, individual artists such as Roland Hayes and Paul Robeson became ambassadors for the race.

But the many discussions of the important place of art in furthering desegregation never considered folktales as one of the tools that art could use in the campaign. Desegregation in art necessarily meant that Black artists had both a Black and a white audience, with white attention becoming very important. In fact, a standard complaint during the Renaissance was that white audiences had become too important, that many Blacks would not recognize Black artists until whites did. Much of this attention was undoubtedly unfortunate and was based on an unexamined acceptance of white ideas concerning the function of art in society. However, if art was to advance desegregation, Blacks had to watch and evaluate how whites read and used Black art, and to praise those works which could result in the most "useful" reaction. The minstrel tradition might not have been such a problem if whites had reacted to it with anything more than contemptuous laughter. Thus the question of Black folktales frequently modulated into a question of the relationship of whites to Black folktales.

The problem with folktales was obvious—whites too easily accepted Harris' emphasis on the comic and his inaccurate dialect.

Seeing a major purpose of art as advancing desegregation thus made the goal of the artist self-consciously purposeful, and inevitably somewhat constricting. It did not easily allow for pure aestheticism with its lack of concern for the social utility of art. As mentioned earlier, even the aesthete Locke saw the place of art as "rehabilitating the race in world esteem." If folktales were to be used, then, they were to be used because they satisfied this important requirement of all Black art.

This accepted function of art seriously restricted the use of folktales, which could not easily fulfill this task in the way that the other major part of the folk tradition, spirituals, could. Spirituals were part of the New Negro: they had been elevated from the dubious ring shouts (a combination of a simple chant and shuffling circle dance, which after several hours put the participant in a religious frenzy), transported to the concert hall by the Jubilee Singers, and harmonized and sanctified by composer Harry T. Burleigh. Indeed, according to James Weldon Johnson, the rebirth of the spirituals was part of the new race consciousness.[32] In his preface to *The Second Book of Negro Spirituals*, Johnson asked that since all other folk materials had been brought to the public as lesser art forms, why couldn't the spirituals be more seriously developed?[33] To a large degree, Johnson's reasoning was a rhetorical performance—spirituals were being seriously developed and had a wide, enthusiastic following. Arguing that the spirituals were the "finest distinctive artistic contribution" America had given to the world,[34] Johnson gave the by then almost totally accepted opinion that spirituals certainly differed from other folk materials. As a result, most Black writers accepted spirituals as their primary cultural representative in the battle for desegregation.

For several reasons folktales didn't reach the plateau of the spirituals. First, they didn't fit in with white culture as easily as spirituals, which expressed Protestant convictions. More important, it was very difficult to use folk tales for propaganda if propaganda implied racial uplift. The reason lies in the nondogmatic nature of folktales: what George Kent in *Blackness and the Adventure of Western Culture* calls the concept of "isness" in folk materials. Folk materials, according to Kent, simply present the world as it is, without any suggestions for possible transformation.[35] Since Black folktales not only had little explicit striving for justice but also dealt with Blacks who were neither wealthy nor powerful and didn't have "dignity" (a quality seen as vital to the aesthetic success of spirituals), folktales could not be easily appropriated into the Black aesthetic. Du Bois' assessment of a folktale collection, *Congaree Sketches*, strictly follows these criteria: "There is one criticism which applies to the whole book and keeps it from being as sincere a piece of literature as it deserves to be. And that is the fact that the author has carefully cut out from all this folk stuff every reference to Negro ambition, education, aspiration to better earthly things, every suggestion that these people know of a Negro world of education, comfort and success."[36]

Since art was to be used for uplift which could result in desegregation, many writers discussed subject matter very pragmatically. The question that dominated evaluations of art was: "How will the race be perceived as a result of this work?" Hence, subject matter entered the foreground of most aesthetic discussions. The assumption was that if writers tended to concentrate on Black low life, whites would think that all Black life was low. Countee Cullen's unfavourable reaction to what he saw as a contemporary emphasis on sordidness based itself primarily on considerations of racial uplift, not aesthetics or even truthful representation: "There are some things, some truths of Negro life and thought, of Negro inhibitions that all Negroes know, but take no pride in. To broadcast them to the world will but strengthen the bitterness of our enemies, and in some instances turn away the interest of our friends."[37]

Folktales as motifs in literature did not escape this sort of evaluation. In what begins as a favorable review of Julia Peterkin's novel *Black April*, Du Bois soon finds fault with the omnipresent folk subject matter and gives the book a poor review for its atmosphere of "oppression, hopelessness, defeatism, with clouds of suspicion and ill."[38]

This selective portrayal of the race (and its results for folktales) often appeared in the issue of whether the Black artist should use clearly Black materials to show the richness of his African heritage or whether he should concentrate on the similarities between the races. Writers lined up on a spectrum governed by Du Bois' earlier notion of the "double consciousness" (the African and European-American heritages) of the Black race.[39] At one end a very few Black writers such as Langston Hughes and Claude McKay emphasized the African heritage and encouraged showing white audiences how rich the differences of Black culture were. For Hughes and McKay this meant using the contemporary folk tradition which was very well known to whites in the twenties—blues and jazz. Given the spicy origins of these materials, however, many artists and most critics did not accept this use. Other writers of this first group defined more strictly what they meant by the African heritage, and the homely folktales did not seem to fit these criteria. For example, Countee Cullen's poem "Heritage" sees the AfroAmerican heritage as coming directly from Africa and does not mention the intervening two hundred years of history.

Of those positions that emphasized the European-American aspect of Black culture, a desire to emphasize the sameness between Black and white cultures led to George Schuyler's insistence that there were no significant cultural differences between Blacks and whites: "the Aframerican is merely a lamp-blacked Anglo-Saxon."[40] Schuyler's comment may seem overstated, but he was working with the quite perceptive analysis that white audiences tended to patronize or ridicule the differences of Black culture. Other writers followed with muted versions of Schuyler's thesis. Thus, Cullen disliked Hughes's *The Weary Blues* partially because it had too much of an emphasis on purely Black themes.[41] More elegantly stated, perhaps, is James Weldon Johnson's evaluation of Black poets: "In stating the need for Aframerican poets in the United States to work out a new and distinctive form of expression I do not wish to be understood to hold any theory that they should limit themselves to Negro poetry, to racial themes; the sooner they are able to write *American* poetry spontaneously, the better. Nevertheless, I believe that the richest contribution the Negro poet can make to the American literature of the future will be the fusion into it of his own individual artistic gifts."[42] Most writers follow this moderate stance of "distinctive desegregation," but it was a stance that nevertheless did not comfortably allow Black folktales, which obviously revelled in rural, "unsophisticated" Black dialect and culture. To the Harlem Renaissance writers, the differences between these tales and white culture were not flattering or useful to Blacks. On the other hand, some distinctively Black art, like the spirituals, could be celebrated, but only because it had been transformed safely into Western High Art.

Hughes's dissent from this campaign for distinctive desegregation was important, although he stated it in terms of his fight for the freedom to use urban folk materials. Hughes pointed to a characteristic of the debate that hadn't yet been discussed in print but was tied to the problem: the desegregation that Cullen and Du Bois were espousing was tinged with white middle-classhood. Hughes thought the Black writer's dilemma (one also noticed by Johnson in a different context)[43] was to be caught between a white desire for stereotypes and a Black desire for "niceness."[44] In arguing against jazz poetry, for example, Cullen steeps his language in bourgeois values: " . . . in the light of reflection I wonder if jazz poems really belong to that dignified company, that select and austere circle of high literary expression which we call poetry."[45] Undoubtedly, the dialect-ridden and homely folktales would have an equally difficult time fitting in with these values. According to one writer, if artists were to use folk materials, the artist should become a missionary: "It [jazz] has come to stay, and they are wise, who instead of protesting against it, try to lift and divert it into nobler channels."[46]

Even more emphatic is Du Bois' review of *Congaree Sketches*, in which he argues that the collection ultimately fails because " . . . even to the lowest black swamp peasant there are three worlds ever present to his imagination: his own, the world of the risen black man and the world of white folks. No current folk lore can omit any one of these and be true, complete and, therefore, to the fullest, artistic."[47] Du Bois does not mention where one could find this middle-class Black folklore, but it wasn't found in folktales of the time.

The acceptance of middle-class values in the fight for desegregation easily accepted another view of the way artists should use folk materials. Folktales had to be transformed into respectable high art in the way that spirituals had been. James Weldon Johnson and Du Bois consistently use the word "dignity" in their laudatory evaluations of spirituals but never mention folktales in those terms. Further problems surfaced immediately. Folktales were sometimes not even recognized as having a potential for being appropriated as high art—one early reviewer treats a collection solely as a sociological document.[48]

The single reviewer who considered folktales as part of Western High Art did this only with folk materials that came directly from Africa and were part of the Harlem Renaissance's interest in the African heritage: "They [Africans who helped compile this] have come forward with a group of songs and legends, with descriptions and examples of wood-carving and textile designs which must fix once for all the place of the native African high up in the scale of Art and Literature."[49] Perhaps because AfroAmerican folktales were not exotic but merely different, they were never discussed in these terms.

Concerns for desegregation and the uneasy relation with the past—usually accompanied by an acceptance of middle-class values, the language of uplift, and a patronizing tone—thus never left discussions of the usefulness of folk materials. Where, eventually, did these emphases leave the folk tales of the Black American? The lack of serious critical attention and artistic appropriation were most noticeable. For James Weldon Johnson it is the Grimm brothers' folktales that he fondly remembers from his youth, remembering them for their "elusiveness of beauty."[50] Only a few writers such as Arthur Fauset, Ruth Pearson, Newbell Puckett[51] and Langston Hughes wanted these materials to be used, but Hughes was the most prophetic: "Certainly there is, for the American Negro artist who can escape the restrictions the more advanced among his own group would put upon him, a great deal of unused material ready for his art."[52] During the Harlem Renaissance the material was left unused.

NOTES

[1] Bernard Bell's "Folk Art and the Harlem Renaissance" in *Phylon,* 36 (June 1975), 155-63, is the only work that discusses in detail the attitudes of major Harlem Renaissance critics toward folk tales. Bell argues that Du Bois and others followed Herder's idea that folk art lays the foundations for high art, but Bell does not analyze why folk tales did not receive significant attention by these writers. Two recent collections of Black folk tales are J. Mason Brewer, *American Negro Folklore* (New York: *Quadrangle/New York Times,* 1974) and Julius Lester, *Black Folktales* (New York: Grove, 1970).

[2] *The Negro Caravan,* ed. Sterling A. Brown, Arthur P. Davis, and Ulysses Lee (Dryden Press, 1941, rpt. New York: Arno Press and New York Times, 1970), pp. 432-33.

[3] "Our Book Shelf," *Opportunity,* 6 (Dec. 1928), 380.

[4] "Negro Life and Its Poets," *Opportunity,* 1 (Dec. 1923), 355.

[5] "Criteria of Negro Art," pp. 290-97.

[6] (New York: Viking, 1926), p. 22.

[7] Alain Locke, "The New Negro," in *The New Negro,* ed. Alain Locke (New York: Albert and Charles Boni, 1925), p. 14.

[8] Locke, "New Negro," p. 11.

[9] "New Negro," pp. 4-5.

[10] Pp. 20, 21.

[11] Even Newbell Puckett, the critic whose enthusiasm for the folk tale tradition contained the fewest qualifications, sensed the distance that progress had made between the world of the rural folk tales and the Harlem Renaissance. See "Race-Pride and Folk-Lore," *Opportunity,* 4 (March 1926), 82-84.

[12] "The New Negro as Revealed in His Poetry," *Opportunity,* 5 (April 1927), 108.

[13] "New Negro," p. 5.

[14] "New Negro," p. 9.

[15] "American Negro Folk Literature," pp. 238-44.

[16] F. L. Mott, *Golden Multitudes: The Story of Best Sellers in the United States* (New York: Macmillan, 1947), pp. 162-63.

[17] H. W. Lanier, "'Million' Books and 'Best' Books," *Golden Book Magazine,* 4 (Sept. 1926), 382.

[18] "American Negro Folk Literature," p. 238.

[19] P. 241.

[20] Quoted in Frank S. Horne, "Black Verse," *Opportunity,* 2 (Nov. 1924), 330.

[21] Horne, p. 330.

[22] "Negro Dialect," *Opportunity,* 2 (Sept. 1924), 259.

[23] "American Negro Folk Literature," pp. 238-41.

[24] "The Negro Artist and the Racial Mountain," *Nation,* 122 (23 June 1926), 692-94.

[25] "Preface" (New York: Viking Press, 1927), pp. 7-8; "The Browsing Reader," *The Crisis,* 34 (July 1927), 159; "And the Walls Came Tumblin' Down," *The Bookman,* 66 (October 1927), 221-22.

[26] "Preface," *God's Trombones,* p. 8.

[27] "Criteria of Negro Art," p. 296.

[28] "Criteria of Negro Art," p. 296.

[29] For an example, see his "Negro Youth Speaks" in *The New Negro,* pp. 47-53.

[30] "Preface," *The New Negro,* ed. Alain Locke (New York: Atheneum, 1969), p. xiii.

[31] "The New Negro," pp. 15-16.

[32] "Preface," *The Book of American Negro Spirituals,* p. 49.

[33] Pp. 22, 23.

[34] "Preface," *The Book of American Negro Spirituals,* p. 13.

[35] (Chicago: Third World Press, 1972), pp. 53-72.

[36] "The Browsing Reader," *The Crisis,* 34 (Sept. 1927), 227.

[37] "The Dark Tower," *Opportunity,* 6 (March 1928), 90.

[38] "The Browsing Reader," *The Crisis,* 34 (June 1927), 129.

[39] *The Souls of Black Folk* (Chicago: A. C. McClurg, 1903), pp. 1-12.

[40] "The Negro-Art Hokum," *Nation,* 122 (16 June 1926), 662.

[41] "Poet on Poet," *Opportunity,* 4 (Feb. 1926), 74.

[42] "Preface," *The Book of American Negro Poetry,* ed. James Weldon Johnson (New York: Harcourt, Brace, 1922), p. 42.

[43] "Dilemma of the Negro Author," *American Mercury,* 15 (Dec. 1928), 477-81.

[44] "Mountain," p. 693.

[45] "Poet on Poet," p. 73.

[46] J. A. Rogers, "Jazz at Home," *The New Negro,* p. 224.

[47] "The Browsing Reader," *The Crisis,* 34 (Sept. 1927), 227.

[48] B. A. Botkin, "Self-Portraiture and Social Criticism in Negro Folk-Song," *Opportunity,* 5 (Feb. 1927), 38-42.

[49] Jessie Fauset, "On the Bookshelf," *The Crisis,* 22 (June 1921), 64.

[50] *Along This Way* (New York: Viking, 1933), p. 13.

[51] Fauset, "Folk Art," p. 244; Ruth R. Pearson, "The Bookshelf," *Opportunity,* 1 (April 1923), 29; Puckett, "Race-Pride and Folk-Lore," 82-84.

[52] "Mountain," p. 693.

S. Amanor Dseagu

SOURCE: "The Influence of Folklore Techniques on the Form of the African Novel," in *New Literary History,* Vol. 23, No. 3, Summer, 1992, pp. 583-605.

[In the following excerpt, Dseagu explores the influence of folklore on areas such as plot structure and characterization in a number of African novels, including Things Fall Apart *by Chinua Achebe.]*

INTRODUCTION

The African novel has been attracting attention among scholars and publishers only since the publication of Camara Laye's *L'Enfant Noir* and Chinua Achebe's *Things Fall Apart* barely thirty years ago. In contrast with the long existence of the novel form in Europe and also with the long evolution of complex patterns of the novel form in Europe, the relatively new "emergence" of the form in Africa tended to create at about the time of *L'Enfant Noir* and *Things Fall Apart* the notion, first, that the novel form was new to the African continent and, second, that it had been imported from Europe in the baggage of Western colonialists, missionaries, and educators.

Under the circumstances, critics of the African novel have tended to suggest that, all things being equal, an African novelist would not have had as much experience of the novel form within his African cultural setting as, say, a European novelist. Thus, the trend of critical opinion has been to suggest that African novelists are, relatively speaking, at the beginner's stage in their handling of the novel form while the average European novelist is at the advanced stage. That idea seemed to have been in Achebe's mind when he said "Writing of the kind I do is relatively new in my part of the world."[1]

Shatto Arthur Gakwandi expresses the same thought when he states that the novel "is relatively new on the African scene."[2]

Solomon Iyasere, working with the same idea, claims, "The novel as a particular genre has no history in Africa; it is primarily a Western form."[3]

Thus it becomes almost a necessary logical conclusion to argue that, all things being equal, African novels are inferior:

[Even] a superficial scrutiny establishes that the bulk of it [the African novel] is poor in quality and merely satisfies an anthropological fad for Africa that the western world is currently enjoying. West Africans by the score are telling a fascinated public [mainly overseas] about their indigenous way of life, and, doubtless proceeding on the assumption that we all have at least one piece of fiction in us, are calling their efforts "novels." Criticism, unfortunately, allows this term to cover writing which lies at both extremes on the scale of artistic merit, and a masterpiece of Dickens or Jane Austen must shelter beneath the same roof as an offering from Agatha Christie, Ian Fleming, or, in the present context, Flora Nwapa, Obi Egbuna, Elechi Amadi, John Munonye, and a host of others waiting for recognition.[4]

An aspect of this general impression that African novels are inferior is often found in the argument that African novelists have borrowed all their techniques from the West in the course of borrowing the art form of the novel. This argument appears close to the surface when Kofi Awoonor comments thus on the imagery of Tutuola, a writer generally known to have received the bare minimum of formal Western education:

> Tutuola has definitely been aware of traditions other than his own. Even though he was a man of limited formal education, it is possible that, like every child who attended missionary schools in his time, he must have read Bunyan's *Pilgrim's Progress* in its Yoruba translation. The influence of Bunyan on his work, it can be safely said, does not lie in the total impact or in theological position. Tutuola makes [*sic*] no obvious theological position. He emphasizes the moral or ethical systems of a tradition based in mythology and folklore. His debt to Bunyan may be traced to the details of description of creatures, for example, the Redfish in *The Palm-Wine Drinkard* which comes close to that of Appollyon in Bunyan.[5]

Having made up his mind already that Tutuola, even in spite of his limited formal education, could only have borrowed from the West, Kofi Awoonor then forces the evidence to show that Tutuola did certainly borrow from Bunyan in translation.

A great deal of the critical perception of the African novel stems from the view that the novel as an art form originated in the West in the eighteenth century. Ian Watt, in his important work *The Rise of the Novel,* appears to have given currency to this impression by not providing adequate warning that he was confining himself strictly to the novel in England even while generalizing about the early beginnings of the novel.[6] Thus, certain of his arguments pertaining to the social factors behind the rise of the novel in England are often reproduced to evaluate the situation of the African novel. Thus, for instance, Lewis Nkosi argues that the social and cultural factors prevailing in England in the eighteenth century should be regarded as the universal conditions for the fertile germination of the novel everywhere:

> Certain notions inherent in bourgeois society, in particular the greater regard for individual rights over those of the community as a whole, would have been considered a perversion and an evil in a traditional African society; also that competition between individuals was regarded with a great deal of unease as a basis for considerable disharmony in African traditional society. Naturally, the art forms that any society develops are intimately related to the kind of social structures which it has built up. Thus the kind of art which was prized above all others in the Old Africa was the one which promoted *harmonisation* of the potential areas of conflict within the community.[7]

Lewis Nkosi here argues that an essential condition for the rise of the novel in the West was the enshrinement of individualism as a vital principle in society, and that under that principle an a priori justification was made for the fashion of writing about the peculiar habits of individuals even to the extent of glorifying those habits. He goes on to show, however, that in traditional Africa it is precisely that cult of individualism which is most often abhorred. Thus he brings his argument to one of two possible conclusions: either the African novel has taken off on the wrong foot or it does not qualify as a novel since it does not satisfy the conditions for inclusion in the genre.

Adrian Roscoe, using the same argument of the universal conditions as revealed in the Western novel, comes to a similar position: "The modern African novelist, seeking to imitate Western fiction, runs up against a social system whose watchword has always been conformity; which has, indeed, demanded conformity in the interests of social cohesion, and even of survival."[8] Obiajunwa Wali sums it all up when he remarks, "Character in traditional African society does not exist."[9]

Having made a case that the African novel has been imported from the West and then having shown that it does not fit in well with Africa's social and cultural habits, the logical next step for the critics is to suggest that the African novel is ill-written. The African novelists "take stock-in-trade abstractions of human behaviour and look about for a dummy to dress in them, a dummy put together out of prototypes in other people's books rather than from observation of living people. They set these dummies in action, and you watch till they run down; there is no attempt to uncover human motivation, whether of temperament, from within, or social situation, from without. Such writers do not understand the forces which lie behind the human phenomena they observe and are moved to write about."[10]

But the proposition upon which the argument that the African novel is an import rests—that the art form is a Western form—has very little real historical and intellectual basis. The novel did not originate in England or in Europe; neither did it originate in the eighteenth century; nor were the social and cultural conditions of eighteenth-century England reproduced or even identical in all the other geographical regions where this art form is known to have taken root. It stands as a classic example of Eurocentric criticism that critics and scholars of the West have turned the conditions *peculiar* to their races into a universal prerequisite for the emergence of the novel.

History tells us that the novel did not originate in England or in Europe. The novel was already well known in the Far East before A.D. 1000. The first Japanese novel is said to have been written by a Japanese woman, traditionally identified by name as Murasaki Shihitu, who lived during the Heian Age, which dates from about 795 to about 1185. Both in style and in plot structure, that novel has been said to be very different from the usual Western novel:

> It differs from these European masterworks of the art of fiction most notably in the manner of the unfolding of the plot. In this it has been likened to a Japanese scroll. At any time the scroll presents to our view a vast panorama of persons and events which require that the eye devote several chapters, as it were, to taking in simultaneous actions. As the scroll is rolled in at one end and out at the other, formerly prominent persons and events become peripheral and new data assume the focus of attention. Even the novel's hero, who is central through about four-fifths of the thousand pages of the translation, in the last ten chapters yields the stage to his son.[11]

There is also evidence that the novel form had been known in China long before it became established in England and Europe: "The classic Chinese novel spans a long period of European literary history stretching from the late Middle Ages to the nineteenth century. Even judging by its finest titles, it differs from the modern Western novel not only because it shows no comparable concern with form but because it represents a different composition of fiction."[12]

There are also records to show that the novel was already well known in India before A.D. 1000. According to most scholars the Vedic Period was when the best Indian novels appeared. It is reckoned that the Vedic Age extended from about 2500 B.C. to about A.D. 1000.

There is also considerable evidence that the novel was well known in Africa before the coming of the Western races. If the definition of the novel as "an epic in prose" is valid, there is a case to be made for calling the extended prose narratives of Africa which deal with the exploits of hero-men novels or prototypes of novels. Many such narratives are well known among the peoples of Africa. For example, in Southern Africa many narratives are woven around the figure of Masilo. The hero-man first came to the attention of readers in a tale collected by Casalis in 1879. In 1895, Edouard Jacottet devoted more than 180 pages of his book of about 270 pages to the activities of the character. Surely, the length of 180 typed pages compares well with an established novel such as Jane Austen's *Northanger Abbey.*

Callaway also used the same activities of the hero-man Masilo in his collection of Zulu narratives. Similarly, S. H. Edwards, Alice Wesner, Phyllis Sarony, and Minnie Postma have all used basically the same set of material in their handling of the Masilo tale. Going solely by the evidence of the history of the printed narratives, the Masilo tale has been known and appreciated in a fairly standardized form as a full-length narrative for over a hundred years. If we also consider the fact that the first compiler of the tale in written form, Eugene Arnaud Casalis, must certainly have collected it from people who had known it well and had received it down from antiquity, it could in fact be claimed that the Masilo tale has existed in standardized form as a full-length narrative for well over four hundred years—that is, since before the introduction of Western civilization.

History also tells us that the novel did not emerge only in the eighteenth century. As previously noted, the first Japanese novel was written between 795 A.D. and 1185 A.D. The earliest known Chinese novel was *The Romance of the Three Kingdoms* (Sankuo-chih yen-i). According to tradition it was written by Lo Kuan-chung, who lived from about 1330 to about 1400, thus making him a contemporary of Geoffrey Chaucer. *The Romance of the Three Kingdoms* deals with political and military events that occurred in China for a period of one hundred years stretching from A.D. 168 to 265. It is written in a matter-of-fact style in conscious opposition, according to most Chinese scholars, to the heavy didactic style of the traditional Chinese historical narrative.

The next major work of fiction in China after *The Romance of the Three Kingdoms* was *The Water Margin* (Shui-hu chuan). According to tradition, it was first compiled by Shih Nai-an. The text that has survived dates, however, from about 1550, when Kuo Hsun, the marquis of Wu-ting, commissioned Lo Kuan-chung to reproduce the original novel to satisfy popular demand. It is said to be the first major Chinese literary work to have used a colloquial vernacular style. It deals in realistic detail with the adventures of a band of outlaws as they move from one place to another seducing the wives of the local overlords and generally making merry with wine and meat in taverns. The next major work was *A Record of the Journey to the West* (Hsi-yu-chi). It is said to have been written by Wu Ch'engen who lived from about 1506 to about 1582. It is a satirical study of human nature which in many respects anticipates *Gulliver's Travels,* published almost three hundred years later. If one were to insist upon literary influences, one could argue that the English novel might have been influenced in its formation by these Far Eastern novels.

In India too the novel had been established long before the eighteenth century. According to tradition, the first novel in India was written by Visnusarman during the fourth century A.D. The next major novelist was Bana, who lived at the court of the Emperor Harsa in the seventh century A.D. His *Harsacarita* is said to be a full-length study of the life of Harsa as a young man.

Thus before the start of the Middle Ages, when the romances of the West, which are said to mark the early beginnings of the Western novel, were even written, India had already developed a complex novel form.

History also teaches us that the rise of the novel in the other regions of the world was not necessarily conditioned by the rise of individualism, industrialism, and capitalism. The eras of the classic novels of Japan, China, and India corresponded with the medieval epochs of those nations. Indeed, at the time when the novel was becoming well established in Asia, it was rather the communalistic and ascetic religion of Confucius which held sway in those nations. Similarly, the Masilo tale had become established in Southern Africa at a time when the indigenous cultures were still largely intact and were therefore in such an unadulterated state that they favored only the kind of art which, according to Nkosi, "promoted harmonisation of the potential areas of conflict within the community."[13]

PROPOSAL

The issue then is that since the novel form did not originate in the West in the eighteenth century it is fallacious to argue that the African novel must only be seen in relation to the Western novel. There is no doubt that the predominant influence on Africa in the last four hundred years has come from the West; the use of the metropolitan languages of Europe as the lingua franca in Africa is sufficient evidence of that massive influence. As far as the novel is concerned, the influence of Western culture is clearly noticeable in the choice of the metropolitan languages of Europe as the medium of expression. Moreover, the influence of the West is also clear in the advantages which the written medium of expression confers: such advantages as the facility to indulge in extended metaphors or to complicate the plot structure with elaborate digressions without losing the thread.

The proposal then is that we should see the African novel as a pastiche of a variety of separate influences and modes. The influences from the West have until now been the major area of study by critics and scholars. To seek to redress the balance slightly in favor of the other influences, I shall attempt to outline those elements of expression which reflect how the African novel has been influenced by the oral traditions of Africa. I shall concentrate on how techniques of tale narration in Africa have influenced the manner in which the novelists of Africa have generally gone about their narration. The elements of the tale and the novel that I shall be concentrating on are plot structure, characterization, and use of time.

The method of investigation that I shall be using is the formalist approach developed by Vladimir Propp in his *Morphology of the Folktale* and modified by Alan Dundes in his *Morphology of the North American Indian Folk Tales.* The principle that I shall be working with is that which Vladimir Propp set up and used in

his seminal work: that is, that *tales with identical functions can be considered as belonging to one type.* In other words, if it can be demonstrated that features of a variety of tales and narratives follow the same pattern of expression and that they combine with other elements in an identical manner, although they may have been taken from diverse sources, they should be seen as performing the same type of functions and must therefore be grouped together and classified as belonging to the same type. Until Vladimir Propp, the principle had been used mainly in the sciences but is now increasingly used in linguistics and in folklore. It can save several hours of extensive research in the field by allowing the researcher to concentrate solely on the internal evidence.

ANALYSIS

1. Plot Structure

I shall use the following short Ghanaian folktale as the main folktale model:

> One day the Great King called together all his subjects and commanded that he wanted to be amused. He wanted to be told a tale which would not have an end. All the subjects came to try but they could not afford not to end their tales. Since they had wasted his time, the Great King ordered all of them to be beheaded. Soon only Kwaku Ananse was left in the village. He came forward to tell his tale that should not have an end. The story he told the Great King was this. One day a man went to his farm. There he discovered that his corn had matured. So he decided to harvest his corn in bits. He picked one grain from the farm and took it home. He came back, picked a second grain and took it home. He came back, picked another one and took it home. He came back . . . Thereupon the Great King begged Kwaku Ananse to stop because soon it would be nighttime. Kwaku Ananse protested angrily that he had not yet got to the middle of his story. In the end, the Great King had to pacify him with gifts just to stop his tale.

Many, if not all, African folktales involve a movement from home into the forest wilderness and back again to the homestead. The Ghanaian story above is one such story. The tale teller and the audience clearly see the journey motif in allegorical terms as a reflection of a person's progress in life. The point is emphasized by Harold Scheub in his study of Southern African narratives: "As the child prepares for circumcision and purification rites, the artists concentrate on the dramatization of the odyssey that leads the youth from a state of impurity to its opposite, from youth to adulthood, from irresponsibility in the human community to the state of a mature adult. Narratives are now brought together to externalize that spiritual journey, and in Xhosa and Zulu societies that 'journey' seems to be a major preoccupation of the tradition itself."[14]

In thus reflecting the processes of life, narratives become a representation of the life-journey. The episodes in the narratives therefore tend to mark important epochs in the rites of passage of the individual. Among these phases, the most significant are the starting phase representing the birth of the hero; the middle phase representing the adulthood of the hero; and the final phase representing the decline of the hero. In most, if not all, African folktales, the tale is told long after the action has occurred by someone who has matured since the time of the action and is therefore in a position to make ethical recommendations as he narrates the tale. In other words, the tale teller uses the representation of the life-journey to show which actions are good to follow and which actions are bad and must not be followed. The tales therefore not only deal with the motif of a journey, they also set up the polarities of right and wrong.

In the Ananse tale above, the journey motif has been worked into the never-ending mode of the tale. Basically, however, Ananse progresses from an inferior position at the beginning of the tale to the most sought-after position by the end. Although he himself never actually sets out on the journey, he nonetheless uses the element of the journey as the means by which he attains the status of the most highly sought-after person. By so doing he serves, as well, as a contrast to those other citizens who tried and failed to tell the unending tale.

In the case of the African novel, precisely that same passage from birth to adulthood is at the core of the plot structure. For instance, Ihechukwu Madubuike has revealed that the Senegalese novel is structured in three phases—the departure, the initiation, and the return—which closely parallel the rites of passage:

> In general three phases depict the spatial and chronological progression of the protagonist of each of these novels: the happy, innocent period when the hero is in the village, a well-structured universe, with its norms and social values intact; the problematic period when the hero is in an urban setting, in an environment where values and norms are in a state of flux, and where the hero does not know which values to adhere to— the traditional or the modern; and finally, the weak, feeble period which is characterised by the return of the protagonist to the village.[15]

Other novels sharing the same technique of plot structure are *Mission Terminée, Fragments, Why Are We So Blest?, The Palm-Wine Drinkard, My Life in the Bush of Ghosts, Ajaiyi and His Inherited Poverty.* These are novels making use of the physical motif of a journey. But if one were to include novels which, though not dealing with the physical journey, nonetheless use the symbol of the journey as a reflection of the rites of passage, one would come up with the result that more than 75 percent of Africa's novels are based on the plot structure of the folktales.[16]

In many of these the beginning of the novel coincides with the home situation, just as in the folktales. For example, in *Mission Terminée,* Medza sets off from home. In *Fragments,* Onipa Baako sets out from home. Similarly, in *Petals of Blood,* the people of Ilmorog set out to Nairobi from their home in Ilmorog. However, much more similar is the tendency of modern African novelists to see life away from the home as the equivalent of the forest wilderness of the folktale. For example, in *Things Fall Apart,* Chinua Achebe leaves no doubt that outside Umuafia life is led in a chaotic way; at least, that is the impression that the narrator of the novel seeks to convey, especially from the following passage:

> "It was only this morning," said Obierika, "that Okonkwo and I were talking about Abame and Aninta, where titled men climb trees and pound foo-foo for their wives."

> "All their customs are upside-down. They do not decide bride-price as we do, with sticks. They haggle and bargain as if they were buying a goat or a cow in the market."[17]

Similarly, in *Petals of Blood,* Ngugi views the life outside Ilmorog as a chaotic life. The travelers discover that people they come across during the journey to Nairobi tend to behave contrary to home culture. First they come across a priest, a man of God. The man's house is fortified and is being guarded by the local arm of the international security firm of Securicor. Next they come across a leading politician who had fought at their side during the Kenyan Mau Mau resistance struggle. The politician is at a party with friends and singing Mau Mau songs as the travelers approach. The travelers feel relieved and believe they are going to be well received by a comrade. But as it turns out, this "comrade" lets them understand that he has no time for the likes of them. But before he sends them packing, he gives them a "friendly" piece of advice: "Now, I want you to go back to Ilmorog. Get yourselves together. Subscribe money. You can even sell some of the cows and goats instead of letting them die. Dive deep into your pockets. Your businessmen, your shopkeepers, instead of telling stories, should contribute generously. Get also a group of singers and dancers—those who know traditional songs. Gitiro, Muthuu, Ndumo, Mumburo, Muthungucu, Mwomboko—things like that. Our culture, our African culture and spiritual values, should form the true foundation for this nation."[18]

Many of the novelists also tend to equate the ending of the journey with the mature and reflective phase of an individual's life. Amos Tutuola makes that phase the most important part of his structure in the sense that it is that period in which the narrator is able to moralize and comment on the events of the "fiction." For instance, in *My Life in the Bush of Ghosts,* it is stated that the events of the novel occurred at a time when the hero was too young to understand life. Later, after going through the trials and tribulations of the journey, the hero concludes at the end of the journey and also at the end of the "fiction," "This is what hatred did."[19] By the time he was able thus to moralize, the hero had developed sufficiently in maturity so as to be able to distinguish between good and evil and certainly to be able to tell between gunshots and dance music—a distinction which he was not able to make at the beginning of the novel:

> But as we were eating yam inside our mother's room, these two wives who hated us heard information before us that war was nearly breaking into the town, so both of them and their daughters ran away from the town without informing us or taking us along with themselves and all of them knew already that our mother was out of the town.

> Even as we were very young to know the meaning of "bad" and "good" both of us were dancing to the noises of the enemies' guns.[20]

Similarly, in *Mission Terminée,* Mongo Beti equates the end of the journey with the maturity of Medza:

> Yet I remain proud of my mission to Kala—that mission which formed the original subject of my story, though I must apologize for wandering fairly far afield from it at times. Niam got his wife back, even if he didn't exactly thank me for the privilege. Anyway, which of us, when you come to think of it, really owed thanks to the other?

> The more I think about it, the more certain I am that it is I who owe him a debt of gratitude for sending me on a journey which enabled me to discover many truths.[21]

Thus it can be seen that the modern novel in Africa tends to reflect the plot structure of the folktale. The beginning of the fiction almost always takes place in the home because the home tends to function as the place of birth and the place of innocence. As the individual enters puberty, he begins to encounter experiences that involve life away from home. This second stage of the rites of passage is marked in the folktales by a withdrawal from home into the region of the forest wilderness: the world of strange behavior, the world of fantasy. In the novels, this second stage is represented also by a withdrawal from home by the hero; the difference, however, is that here the withdrawal is into the city or large town where the hero loses all sense of identity. In certain novels, such as *No Longer At Ease* or *Why Are We So Blest?,* the withdrawal is further intensified by being made into a completely alien environment of a different country, very often in the West. Finally, having learnt a lesson from those new experiences, the hero might return home a more mature person. . . .

[T]he novels of Africa closely reflect the folktales in plot structure. For the traditional public as well as for the modern public of Africa, the fictive forms of the folktale and the novel tend to function as modes of cultural education: "Stories are, to a certain extent, the mirror of life: they reflect what people do, what they think, how they live and have lived, their values, their joys, and their sorrows."[22]

2. *Characterization*

Characterization in the African novel could be said to have received the greatest attention from critics of the African novel. The general trend of opinion has been that African novelists are weak on this aspect. Nadine Gordimer's views are typical: "They take stock-in-trade abstractions of human behaviour and look about for a dummy to dress in them, a dummy put together out of prototypes in other people's books."

The opinion that has become established is that, since the traditional cultures of Africa promote communalism, group solidarity, and conformity, but since the "novel" is a product of the cult of individualism, it is a contradiction to talk of character in the African novel. Obiajunwa Wali summarizes the theory in these terms: "Character in traditional African society does not exist."

That view has often been used to conclude that the African novel is faulty on precisely that crucial element of the novel form upon which the whole art form stands. For, as most Western critics on the novel suggest, the epicenter of the novel form is character. The views of Henry James are typical in this respect: "When one says picture one says of character, when one says novel one says of incident, and the terms may be transposed at will. What is character but the determination of incident? What is incident but the illustration of character? What is either a picture or a novel that is *not* of character? What else do we seek in it and find in it?"[23]

However, when the African novel is viewed in a more objective way and not necessarily as a by-product of Western culture, it can be seen to serve as a reflection of African mores. Most African novelists, if not *all,* use character, not as a reflection of individualism, but as a reflection of the ideals of communalism, group solidarity, and conformity to emphasize the principles of Africa's morality. The technique most favored by many African novelists is to make character representative and functional. In that respect, Wole Soyinka's *The Interpreters* has been found to be typical: "In its preoccupation with social corruption, *The Interpreters,* like other urban novels, shows a tendency to see characters in terms of the moral positions which they occupy in the scheme."[24] In the same respect, the novels of Ngugi and Sembene are said to be typical: "The characters have a collective rather than an individual hold upon our imagination which is intended to emphasize the strength of their shared responsibility."[25]

To emphasize the functional and representative aspect of characterization, many African novelists assign generic rather than specific names to characters. In *Nomalizo,* Enoch S. Guma has given to his characters such names as suggest what the characters are. The heroine, Nomalizo, whose name is given to the title of the novel, acts with grace, poise, and control throughout the novel. Her name, therefore, in the Xhosa language, means "a mother of gifts and a delight to her parents."

The young man who tries to seduce her by capturing her and keeping her in seclusion is also given a name that clearly identifies his unruly character: he is called Mxabaniso, which in Xhosa means "a quarrelsome fellow." The irresponsible father of Mxabaniso who has not been able to instill any sense of morality in the young man is also given a name that clearly identifies his personality: he is called Mpambani, which means "a person who is confused in his thoughts and actions." The right-hand man of Mxabaniso, who is always seen in his company whenever he is making mischief, also goes by a fitting name: Pindelo, which in Xhosa means "a companion." The young man who wrestles with Mxabaniso and frees Nomalizo from his captivity is also given an appropriate name: Bangela, which in Xhosa means "one who fights in a contest and wins."[26]

On the whole, Ayi Kwei Armah could be said to have turned the generic pattern of character-naming into a system. In his *The Beautyful Ones Are Not Yet Born* his hero does not even bear a name, if by name we mean a specific tag of identification. His hero goes by the very anonymous name of "The Man." Similarly, in *Fragments,* almost all the characters have functional names. Naana, the grandmother, bears a functional name; the term *naana* is an Akan term for "grandmother." *Foli* is the Ewe term for "uncle," which denotes the character's relation to the hero. The hero bears the name Onipa Baako which, to Akans, is an "anonymous" name meaning "a person" or even "a human being." Thus here as well as in *The Beautyful Ones* the names are mainly generic in the sense that they are universals rather than specifics.

Other novels of Ayi Kwei Armah follow the same system of nomenclature. In *Why Are We So Blest?* almost all the names are again generic. Mr. Blanchard, who is in charge of the program in the United States that is dedicated to the education of Africans, is what his satirical name suggests: a whitener. To disguise his true identity, he has adopted the French term for the meaning of his name. Aimee Reitsch, the object of Modin's corrosive love, is also exactly what her two names suggest. As Aimee, she is the female who is given love but who by implication cannot and does not return love. Thus in the novel she is seen to be so frigid that she once had to subject herself to electric stimulation in order to be sexually aroused. As her last name, Reitsch, suggests, in an obvious echo of Adolf Hitler's name for his government, she comes from a stock of the Aryan race and is committed to the supremacy of the white race. The hero, Modin Dofu, bears an "anonymous" name like the Man and Onipa Baako, his elder foster-brothers. The first name, Modin, is a Ga term for "Black" or "black person." The last name, Dofu, is an Akan adjectival participle meaning "filled to excess with love" (*do,* love; *fu,* filled with). Indeed, in the novel he is seen to be madly and corrosively filled with love for Aimee.

Similarly, in *Two Thousand Seasons,* the handsome and attractive young man who enjoys the bounties of nature is given the appropriate name Brafo. *Brafo* is Akan for one who enjoys life to the fullest (*obra,* life; *fo,* owner). The people who provide all the needs of this young man are referred to in the novel by the generic name "Providers." Notable among such "providers" is the character Dovi who is so loving that his center of interest is said by the narrator not to lie in himself but in some other person. Characteristically enough, the name Dovi is Ewe for "one who is filled with love."

This tendency to make character representative is one of the essential links between the modern novel in Africa and the traditional folktale. In the folktales of Africa, the characters more often than not bear generic names that suggest what the characters are. The following tale from Tchad is typical:

> One day Fox, the trickster, met pigeon making a bed for her young pigeons. Fox, who wanted to eat the young birds, began to say nice things to the mother pigeon: that he was their uncle; that he was going to name the young children; and that he would take them to his house to take care of them. When Fox left the scene, Lizard, who all the time was watching the proceedings from high on a tree, came down to warn pigeon that Fox was no uncle but a dangerous fellow trying to kill pigeon and its young. So, pigeon collected her young and took them safely up a tree. When Fox came back, pigeon was gone.[27]

In this tale, the characters are distinguished by function: Fox is the trickster, Lizard is the helper, Pigeon is the dupe. No attempt is made to give any of these characters any extradistinctive personality apart from their functional representation. In all the folktales of Africa the principle is the same: the character is easily identified for what he stands for, and very little or no attempt is made to give this character any psychological specificity.

The extract from Tchadian folklore also illustrates another important principle of characterization that is overwhelmingly observed in the folktales and the novels. Not only are characters made generic, they are also contrasted. Indeed, it appears that the characters are made functional so as to be seen in stark outline as polarities illustrating certain social propositions. For instance, Fox is polarized against Lizard, and thus one is seen as a false and dangerous friend while the other is seen as a reliable friend. Similarly, in the novels, the same polarization for comment is generally made of the characters. In *Nomalizo,* Mxabaniso, the bully, is polarized against Bangela, the rescuer. In *The Beautyful Ones* The Man is polarized against Koomson, on the one hand, and the nameless "visitor," on the other, who comes to The Man's office formally attired in a rich *kente* cloth swathed over an excessively corpulent body. Similarly, in *Fragments,* Onipa Baako in his almost puritan avoidance of ostentation is polarized against George Hudson Brempong who studiously has been shopping on a massive scale all over Europe. In *Things Fall Apart,* Okonkwo is polarized against his father, Unoka, on the one hand and his son, Nwoye, on the other.

The one novelist who seems to have used characterization almost exclusively for the effect of polarization is Thomas Mofolo. The opening statement of *The Traveller of the East* sets the pattern: "In the black darkness, very black, in the times when the tribes were still eating each other like wild beasts, there lived a [humane] man called Fekisi."[28] In this novel, Fekisi, clearly and prominently identified like Chaucer's knight as "a perfect gentleman," is polarized against Phakoane. He has broken all the rules of decent living: he is often so completely drunk that he has to be dragged along the ground to his house; he quarrels and raves; indeed, in one of his bouts of drunkenness, he quarrels with his wife and fatally hits her on the head with an axe.

Thus it can be seen that characterization in the African novel is not a random feature that has been derived—and derived poorly—from the West but is a reflection of what happens in the folktales. Mazisi Kunene has expressed the point well: "Classic African literature takes it as its primary strategy to broaden the base of its characters through mythification and symbolism. Whereas some literatures make the cosmic purpose their goal, African literature begins from the premise that the cosmic setting is the primary basis of all literature."[29]

It is clear, therefore, that African novels have not made use of that intensely personal and psychological aspect of characterization that is so central to the Western pattern. What is at issue is whether African novelists have not used it *because* they cannot use it and use it well. The evidence so far suggests that they have not used it because they have something better to use: they want to use their own pattern to reflect their way of life. As far as that goes, these writers seem to be saying they want to use characters in such a way as to reflect that essential concern for the "harmonization of the potential areas of conflict" in society.

3. Use of Time

In the folktale, the story is narrated long after the actual event. Indeed it appears to be the rule that the time of the actual performance of the action and the time of the narration about the action must always be separated. Thus the action must have been completed before the narration could begin. The narration therefore becomes a telling of a past and complete action. In several cases, however, since the action is known to have been completed in the distant past, and sometimes even in the remote mythical past of a tribe, the narration becomes a *re*telling of a past and complete action.

Thus the grammatical tense that tends to be used predominantly is the simple past. The folktale cited earlier serves as a convenient illustration. The first sentence is all in the past tense: "Great King *called* . . . and *commanded* . . . he *wanted*. . . . " The rest of the tale also presents the events in the same past tense.

It is doubtful, however, whether the traditional African would have been content with just telling or *re*telling a past action that had been completed and finished long before. Indeed critics have argued persuasively that the whole idea of the traditional African going over that long completed action is that he expects to reopen the "case" through his own particular telling or *re*telling: "By its very nature sacred time is reversible in the sense that, properly speaking, it is a primordial mythical time made present. Every religious festival, any liturgical time, represents the reactualization of a sacred event that took place in a mythical past, 'in the beginning.'"[30]

We have already established that for the traditional African the folktale is not just a source of amusement but functions as an objective dramatization of "ideas, the most pervasive of which is the quest for order."[31] As such, many of the tales are capable of being used by trained and professional, traditional "doctors" as elements in serious spiritual and psychological practice. Herskovits's conclusions on the use of folktales among the Fon of Dahomey confirm the analysis: "It is said that each distinctive tale represents a year of human existence on earth, and only after all the stories that can be used for Fa divination are exhausted will the world come to an end."[32]

Thus both the narrator and his audience expect that each specific telling or the *re*telling of the past event will be a reenactment and a performance of the past action. Therefore the *current* interpretation of the event is just as important as the recollection of the completed action. With each reenactment and performance of a tale, the tale teller or *re*teller seeks to draw himself and his public back into that remote time in order to live the experiences being recounted with the actors. Each folktale, strictly speaking, therefore, swings from the past time of the action to the current time of the telling or *re*telling; and at each of the two time zones the experiences of the action are lived and *re*lived. Mircea Eliade has expressed it well thus: "With each periodical festival, the participants find the same sacred time—the same that had manifested in the festival of the previous year or in the festival of a century earlier; it is the time that was created and sanctified by the gods at the period of the *gesta*, of which the festival is precisely a reactualization. In other words the participants in the festival meet in it the first appearance of sacred time, as it appeared *ab origine*, *in illo tempore*."[33]

As past experience is recalled and relived, the traditional African believes that time swings from the past to the present. Since the reliving of the past occurs in current time at only fixed moments during tale-telling sessions or at festivals, the time swing that takes place can more appropriately be described as a swing from the past to the present and back again to the past.

Time, as far as the traditional African is concerned, is therefore not a linear progression but rather a circular progression. This view of time also finds expression in several of the novels. In *Season of Anomy,* Wole Soyinka sees time as a circular pattern. He uses the cycle of the agricultural seasons as the symbol of that circular structure. The novel opens in a period of time that is captioned "seminal." That period corresponds to the season in the agricultural calendar when seeds are prepared for sowing. The next period of the novel is captioned "Buds," in correspondence with the season when the seeds are germinating. The next period of time is called "Tentacles," the rest being called "Harvest" and "Spores" in that order. Clearly Wole Soyinka is using time deliberately in this manner to emphasize his link to his heritage.

In *Petals of Blood,* Ngugi also marks the passage of time in terms of a cycle of events. Here Ngugi even goes to the extent of arguing, in almost the manner of the "past-recovering" traditional person, that the past has to be and must be recalled:

> It seemed to him that history should provide the key to the present, that a study of history should help us to answer certain questions: where are we now? How did we come to be where we are? How did it come about that 75 per cent of those that produce food and wealth were poor and that a small group—part of the non-producing part of the population—were wealthy? History after all should be about those whose actions, whose labour, had changed nature over the years. But how come that parasites—lice, bedbugs, and jiggers—who did no useful work lived in comfort and those that worked for twenty-four hours went hungry and without clothes? How could there be unemployment in a country that needed every ounce of labour? So how did people produce and organise their wealth before colonialism? What lessons could be learnt from that?[34]

What Ngugi is doing here with time confirms an observation that was made in relation to the oral tradition: "When Africans reckon time, it is for a concrete and specific purpose, in connection with events but not just for the sake of mathematics. Since time is a composition of events, people cannot and do not reckon it in a vacuum."[35]

Again, it is Ayi Kwei Armah who manages to turn the practice into a system. In his novels the recoverable nature of time is expressed through the use of the symbol of the stream. In *Two Thousand Seasons* he uses that symbol to demonstrate how the foreign civilizations of Christianity and the Muslim faith have wreaked havoc on the otherwise self-perpetuating civilization of the Africans: "Spring water flowing to the desert, where you flow there is no regeneration. The desert takes. The desert knows no giving. To the giving water of your flowing it is not in the nature of the desert to return anything but destruction."[36]

The reversible nature of time and of event is also well brought out in the use of tense markers. Since most events in the literature describe action that is capable of being reenacted in the retelling, the narrator therefore moves in the course of his narration from the past event of the action to the current event of the reenactment. As he constantly swings back and forth, sometimes within the same grammatical statement, from the past to the present, his grammatical tense markers also make corresponding swings from the past to the present. It is usual to find a tale teller moving in the same grammatical statement from the remote past to the immediate past to the habitual present and then to the actual present. The rule therefore is that tale narrators are flexible in their use of tense markers. This seems to confirm an observation by Mbiti: "The time factor is on the whole ignored, or manipulated at the will of the narrator. For example, at the beginning of a story, the main character may be referred to as a boy, and a few sentences later he is called 'a man' or an 'adult,' or he is made to act like a mature person. Afterwards, he is called a 'boy' once more."[37]

This flexible use of time markers is evident in *Things Fall Apart.* The first chapter begins with a sentence in the simple past. The next sentence is also set in the simple past and acts as an illustration of the first statement. Both sentences describe a time period that is unspecified and vague. However, the rest of the paragraph and the whole of the next paragraph describe a specified situation within the remote past. It deals with the occasion on which Okonkwo's fame, that had been referred to earlier, was firmly established. It deals with the historical present because the events of this situation are used in illustrating how Okonkwo came to be well known all over the land.

A similar use of flexible tenses can be seen in *Fragments.* The novel opens with statements set in the present tense to express general truths and habitual action. The first paragraph ends however on another time scale. It is cast in the future and expresses a strong desire on the part of Naana for Baako to return to validate the ideas expressed in the general remarks made earlier. By the third paragraph, the narrator has switched his tenses from the general present to the immediate past and then to the simple past. Although the time period throughout the first twelve paragraphs remains unspecified and vague, there is a general impression that Naana is reminiscing and reflecting at a moment in time between Baako's departure and his return. It is tempting to suggest that the actual time is closer to the time of return than to that of departure.

However, within this generally unspecified period, the narrative moves from one time scale to another to describe both habitual and specific actions performed in the past. The rest of the narrative action describes a specific moment in time before the period of reminiscence. It deals with the time of Baako's departure, when Uncle Foli was trying to save some of the gin being used for the libation for his own sweet uses.

Indeed, the actual present time of the novel does not start until about a third of the novel is gone. Even as the narrative picks up the thread of events from the time of arrival, it is not always possible to determine the chronological sequence of events. For example, it is clear that after Baako arrived at the airport he took a taxi to Avenida Hotel, where he spent the night. The following day, he took another taxi to the Bank of Ghana to see his friend Fifi Williams. After the visit to the bank, he and Fifi drove in Fifi's car to Kaneshi to the school where his mother was teaching. However, the chronological connection between that last action and the first action in the next chapter, Awo, is not immediately clear. At what stage in time the sudden cry was heard coming from Araba's room is not immediately clear. Again, there is very little indication of how much time has passed between the chapter of Awo and that of the next, Osagyefo. After Osagyefo, there is strong internal evidence that the next chapter, Igya, does not follow the events of the earlier chapter. Indeed a more chronological presentation will put the chapter of Nsu after that of Osagyfo, and then Igya will come after Nsu. Similarly, Iwu will come before Dam in a more chronological account.

Armah has deliberately upset the normal sequence of time to emphasize the fundamental point of the reversibility of time. As he and other novelists suggest, the recording of time is only made meaningful in the constant recall for object lessons of those past events involved. Mbiti sums up the whole point thus: "Actual time is therefore what is present and what is past. It moves 'backward' rather than 'forward'; and people set their minds not on future things, but chiefly on what has taken place."[38]

CONCLUSION

I have merely skimmed the surface of the research necessary to argue that the African novel is not *purely* and *exclusively* a product of Western culture. The influence of the West is clearly discernible in the use of the metropolitan languages as well as in the written mode of expression. For a more scholarly, balanced assessment, I should devote equal attention to the Western factors and the traditional factors. The present essay has clearly not tried to be balanced in that respect for the simple fact that the limited scope of the present forum militates against that balanced presentation. For the present, it suffices to stress that Africa has produced its own form of the extended prose fiction and thus the production deserves to be described for what it is. The honest observer will find that the prose fiction adequately reflects the present state of Africa: a continent of many disparate cultures, some modern and literate and technological, others almost a relic of life in the primitive past—a pastiche of the old and the new.

NOTES

[1] Chinua Achebe, "The Novelist as Teacher," in *African Writers on African Writing*, ed. G. D. Killam (London, 1975), p. 1.

[2] Shatto Arthur Gakwandi, *The Novel and Contemporary Experience in Africa* (London, 1977), p. 3.

[3] Solomon Iyasere, "Oral Tradition and the Criticism of African Literature," *The Journal of Modern African Studies,* 13 (1975), 114.

[4] Adrian Roscoe, *Mother Is Gold: A Study in West African Literature* (Cambridge, 1971), pp. 71-72.

[5] Kofi Awoonor, *The Breast of the Earth: A Survey of the History, Culture, and Literature of Africa, South of the Sahara* (Garden City, N.Y., 1976), pp. 247-48.

[6] See Ian Watt, *The Rise of the Novel* (London, 1957).

[7] Lewis Nkosi, *Tasks and Masks* (London, 1981), p. 58.

[8] Roscoe, *Mother Is Gold,* p. 78.

[9] Obiajunwa Wali, "The Individual and the Novel in Africa," *Transition,* 18 (1965), 32.

[10] Nadine Gordimer, *The Black Interpreters: Notes on African Writing* (Johannesburg, 1973), p. 19.

[11] John D. Yohannan, *A Treasury of Asian Literature* (New York, 1965), p. 58.

[12] C. T. Hsia, *The Classic Chinese Novel: A Critical Introduction* (Bloomington, Ind., 1980), pp. 15-16.

[13] Lewis Nkosi, *Tasks and Masks,* p. 58.

[14] Harold Scheub, "Fixed and Non-fixed Symbols in Xhosa and Zulu Oral Narrative Tradition," *Journal of American Folklore,* 85 (1972), 273.

[15] Ihechukwu Madubuike, "Form, Structure, and Aesthetics of the Senegalese Novel," *Journal of Black Studies,* 4 (1974), 354.

[16] See Appendix C of my "The Nature of Oral Influence on the African Novel," Diss. Wisconsin 1982, pp. 223-24.

[17] Chinua Achebe, *Things Fall Apart* (1958; rpt. London, 1978), p. 51.

[18] Ngugi wa Thiong'o, *Petals of Blood* (New York, 1978), p. 182.

[19] Amos Tutuola, *My Life in the Bush of Ghosts* (New York, 1954), p. 174.

[20] Tutuola, pp. 18-19.

[21] Mongo Beti, *Mission to Kala,* tr. Peter Green (London, 1964), p. 181.

[22] John S. Mbiti, *Akamba Stories* (Oxford, 1966), p. 31.

[23] Henry James, "The Art of Fiction," *Selected Literary Criticism* (Harmondsworth, 1968), p. 88.

[24] Emmanuel Obiechina, *Culture, Tradition and Society in the West African Novel* (Cambridge, 1971), p. 110.

[25] Lewis Nkosi, *Tasks and Masks,* p. 44.

[26] See Dseagu, "The Nature of Oral Influence on the African Novel," Part III.

[27] Mianmbaymarde Negor and Kali Mekongodo, *Conversations et Textes Ngambaye* (Tchad, 1978), p. 47.

[28] Thomas Mofolo, *The Traveller of the East* (London, n.d.), p. 7.

[29] Mazisi Kunene, "The Relevance of African Cosmological Systems to African Literature Today," in *African Literature Today: Myth and History 11,* ed. Eldred Jones (London, 1980), p. 200.

[30] Mircea Eliade, *The Sacred and The Profane* (New York, 1959), pp. 68-69.

[31] Harold Scheub, *The Xhosa Ntsomi* (Oxford, 1975), p. 56.

[32] Melville J. Herskovits, *Dahomean Narrative: A Cross-Cultural Analysis* (Evanston, Ill., 1958), p. 27.

[33] Eliade, *The Sacred and The Profane,* pp. 69-70.

[34] Ngugi wa Thiong'o, *Petals of Blood,* pp. 198-99.

[35] John S. Mbiti, *African Religions and Philosophy* (New York, 1969), p. 19.

[36] Ayi Kwei Armah, *Two Thousand Seasons* (Nairobi, 1973), p. ix.

[37] Mbiti, *African Religions and Philosophy,* p. 28.

[38] Mbiti, *African Religions and Philosophy,* p. 157.

Valerie Gray Lee

SOURCE: "The Use of Folktalk in Novels by Black Women Writers," in *CLA Journal,* Vol. XXIII, No. 3, March, 1980, pp. 266-72.

[*In the following essay, Lee assesses the use of dialect in Zora Neale Hurston's* Their Eyes Were Watching God, *and in works by Toni Morrison and Gayl Jones.*]

The language of any people reflects their thoughts, their values, their culture. Instead of using "conventional English" to express their themes, many black women novelists employ a folktalk that is metaphorical, instructive, and entertaining. Although black novelists often use "conventional English" to carry the narrative voice in their works, they use folk language to capture the more subtle dynamics of black life from testifying to signifying. Ironically (or perhaps naturally), the folktalk that goes on among mothers and daughters in novels by modern black women writers all centers on the menfolk. Significantly, this is in keeping with an increasing trend in modern black literature—many of the writers are turning or returning to one of the oldest of universal themes: love and man/woman relationships. Such representative works as Zora Neale Hurston's *Their Eyes Were Watching God* (1937), Toni Morrison's *Sula* (1973), and Gayl Jones's *Corregidora* (1975) support this thesis.

The grandmother in *Their Eyes Were Watching God* uses the folk idiom to pass down knowledge that she has received from slavery days. She feels that Janie needs an instructive folk sermon on life, love, and men. After affectionately calling Janie to her side, Nanny explains:

> "Honey, de white man is de ruler of everything as fur as Ah been able tuh find out. Maybe it's some place way off in de ocean where de black man is in power, but we don't know nothin' but what we see. So de white man throw down de load and tell de nigger man tuh pick it up. He pick it up because he have to, but he don't tote it. He hand it to his womenfolks. De nigger woman is de mule uh de world so fur as Ah can see. Ah been prayin' fuh it tuh be different wid you. Lawd, Lawd, Lawd!"[1]

Nanny feels that Janie needs a clearer understanding of the role "womenfolks" must play in society. Unquestionably, she loves Janie and feels that she is giving Janie good advice. Nanny merely wants Janie to understand that being black and a woman affects one's lifestyle: because Janie is a woman, she needs "protection," and because she is a black woman, she needs strength. Nanny does not want Janie to marry a "trashy nigger" (p. 15). Temporarily, this discussion between grandmother and granddaughter affects Janie. Her kiss with Johnny Taylor now seems like "a manure pile after a rain" (p. 15).

In the long run, however, Nanny's folk realism only serves to contrast with Janie's romanticism. Janie's ideas of love and men revolve around the image of a pear blossom. After watching a bee pollinate a flower, Janie gets her revelation of marriage:

> She saw a dust-bearing bee sink into the sanctum of a bloom; the thousand sister-calyxes arch to meet the love embrace and the ecstatic shiver of the tree from root to tiniest branch creaming in every blossom and frothing with delight. So this was marriage! She had been summoned to behold a revelation. (p. 13)

Janie, therefore, rejects her first husband, Logan, because he desecrates her vision of the pear tree. She complains that her second husband, Jody, takes the "bloom" off things. Only Tea Cake, her third husband, fulfills the vision, for he represents "sun-up and pollen and blooming trees." Only Tea Cake "wears the sun for a shawl." This very romantic and organic folktalk is consistent with Janie's whole character portrayal throughout the work. Her growth parallels the budding and the bloom of a tree.

With Tea Cake, Janie does attain her vision of love and men. However, she never forgets the folk wisdom that her grandmother passed down to her. This is evidenced by the fact that the novel is told in retrospect and Nanny's remarks are among Janie's most vivid recollections.

Nanny is not the only person in *Their Eyes Were Watching God* with whom Janie discusses the "menfolks." In all of her conversations with her best friend, Phoebe, Janie uses folk sayings and fresh folk metaphors to discuss love and men. Instead of using trite images to describe life, Janie speaks of life as a "mess of corn-meal dumplings" (p. 10). She also speaks of love as a bedquilt (p. 10). This use of folk language, which includes folk foods (corn-meal dumplings) and a folk art (bedquilting), is typical throughout the work.

The general atmosphere of *Their Eyes Were Watching God* generates the folk talk that goes on. *Their Eyes Were Watching God* is a work wherein all the townsfolk, all the "sitters-and-talkers," gather on their porches at dusk when their work is done to gossip and to signify. They want to know "what Janie doin' coming back here in dem overhalls? . . . What dat ole forty year ole 'oman doin' wid her hair swingin' down her back lack some young gal?" (pp. 5-6). Janie, understanding that these sitters-and-talkers will always be sitting and talking, takes time out to explain her life only to her best friend, Phoebe.

In *Their Eyes Were Watching God*, which takes place in an all-black community, we are given a picture of a special kind of relationship between a black man and woman. Janie moves from what she learns from her grandmother to what she resolves for herself and explains to Phoebe. Janie does not live in a world where she has to fear the sexual advances of a white master as her grandmother did. Nor does she live in a world where she has to marry a man like Logan, who tries to add her to the rest of his property. She further does not need a man like Jody, who will not let her mingle with the folk nor talk their language. She finally asserts herself by playing the dozens and telling Jody that "when [he] pull[s] down [his] britches, he looks lak de change uh life" (p. 69). After this episode, Jody literally dies. Janie moves on to Tea Cake, who gives her the special kind of liberation that she needs. It is a kind of liberation that brings her closer to him. From all the discussions that Janie has had with Nanny and Phoebe, she pulls together in the work's conclusion her own philosophy on love and men:

> . . . love ain't something lak uh grindstone dat's de same thing everywhere and do de same thing tuh everything it touch. Love is lak de sea. It's uh movin' thing, but still and all, it takes its shape from de shore it meets, and it's different with every shore. (p. 158)

Just as the folktalk that goes on among the womenfolk (Janie, her grandmother, and her best friend, Phoebe) in *Their Eyes Were Watching God* is primarily about the menfolk, the folktalk among the womenfolk (Sula, her grandmother, and her best friend, Nel) in *Sula* is also about the menfolk. This is particularly ironic, for *Sula* is very much a woman's novel, a novel that women read and can readily identify with. Nonetheless, all of the Peace women, Eva the grandmother, Hannah the mother, and Sula the daughter, spend time discussing and evaluating menfolk. Eva bequeathed a concept called "man-love" to all the Peace women:

> With the exception of BoyBoy, those Peace women loved all men. It was manlove that Eva bequeathed to her daughters. Probably, people said, because there were no men in the house, no men to run it. But actually that was not true. The Peace women simply loved maleness, for its own sake.[2]

As a god-like figure, Eva is "creator and sovereign of [an] enormous house" (p. 30). Each generation of the Peace women believes in the concept that Eva originates. Hannah has a way with men. It is rumored that Sula even sleeps with white men. The Peace women's freedom and nonchalance about men cause everything except peace in the town's community.

Nel, Sula's best friend, challenges the morality of Sula's concept of manlove when Sula has an affair with Nel's husband and then drops him. Nel expects Sula to use lovely college words like *aesthetic* or *rapport* to explain her position (p. 105). However, when Sula explains her sexual-relations theory, instead of using erudite language, she resorts to folk speech, which captures the frankness and simplicity of her vision. On one occasion she speaks about black men:

> "I mean, I don't know what the fuss is about. I mean, everything in the world loves you. White men love you. They spend so much time worrying about your penis they forget their own. The only thing they want to do is cut off a nigger's privates. And if that ain't love and respect I don't know what is. And white women? They chase you all to every corner of the earth, feel for you under every bed. I knew a white woman wouldn't leave the house after 6 o'clock for fear one of you would snatch her. Now ain't that love? They think rape soon's they see you, and if they don't get the rape they looking for, they scream it anyway just so the search won't be in vain. Colored women worry themselves into bad health just trying to hang on to your cuffs. Even little children—white and black, boys and girls—spend all their childhood eating their hearts out 'cause they think you don't love them. And if that ain't enough, you love yourselves. Nothing in this world loves a black man more than another black man. You hear of solitary white men, but niggers? Cant's stay away from one another a whole day. So. It looks to me like you the envy of the world." (pp. 103-04)

Later, Nel realizes that Jude was not such a great husband anyway. She speculates that their love was "like a pan of syrup kept too long on the stove, had cooked out, leaving only its odor and a hard, sweet sludge, impossible to scrape off" (p. 165). Nel realizes that she will always be closer to Sula than to her own husband.

Sula, like Janie, is an independent and unconventional woman. She will not lie to the townspeople nor will she wear underwear to church suppers. Her concept of "manlove" frees her. Both want men in their lives, as their folk speech points out, but they do not want a man to whom they are in bondage.

Finally, Gayl Jones' *Corregidora* is another work by a black woman in which the womenfolk spend their time discussing the menfolk. Whereas the folktalk that Janie uses in discussing men is romantic and Sula's is earthy, Ursa Corregidora's is downright bawdy. The four-letter sexual street language is in keeping with the trials and pathos of Ursa's story. Old Man Corregidora, the Portuguese slavemaster, mated with Ursa's grandmother and great grandmother. All of the flashbacks of the novel, all of Ursa's thoughts, revolve around Corregidora and what he did with his "womens." Ursa's great grandmother passed the story down from generation to generation so that there would always be evidence of what had gone on. According to Great Gram, Old Man Corregidora first "broke his womens in hisself."[3] She explained to Ursa over and over again the situation:

> "He liked his womens black, but he didn't wont us with no black mens. It wasn't color cause he didn't even wont us with no light black mens, cause there was a man down there as light as he was, but he didn't wont us with him . . . cause when he send them white mens in there to me he didn't look like that, cause he be nodding and saying what a fine piece I was, said I was a fine speciment of a woman, finest speciment of a woman he ever seen in his life." (pp. 143-45)

There is nothing in the novel that does not connect to this sexual theme. Ursa has to come to grips with the story passed down by her ancestors before she can produce her own life story. Because of Ursa's hysterotomy, she is not able to make generations in the literal way that grandmothers and mother did. Instead she turns to folk music—the blues. The blues help her to explain what she cannot explain. They are the evidence that she leaves behind.

Just as Janie and Sula have best friends with whom they discuss "the menfolks," so does Ursa. Ursa tries to explain to Catherine ("Cat") some of her present problems with men. Ursa has an ex-husband and a lover who both claim to love her. Her ex-husband, Mutt, unfortunately, does not view her as a whole person, but refers to her in derogatory folk language as his "piece of ass." Ursa does not want to be a piece of anything. She dreams of telling Mutt off in a dirty-dozens duel. Mutt needs to realize that there will have to be some changes before Ursa takes him back.

The recurring question in *Corregidora* is, "What's a husband for?" Is he someone who literally knocks the womb out of his woman? Is he someone who owns her? Is he someone only to take care of her sexual needs? What's a husband for? The bawdy folk language captures, in a way that "conventional English" cannot, the answers to these questions. It does indeed make the work read like an extended blues lyric.[4]

It is refreshing that modern black women writers are using a tool of their culture, folktalk, to express the deepest feelings of their female protagonists. Hurston, Morrison, and Jones have used black folk speech because it is metaphorical, realistic, and lusty. It is interesting, however, that much of the folktalk among the women characters is about men. Janie, Sula, and Ursa live outside of conventional mores and strive to be intensely independent. Yet their independence does not liberate them fully from romantic visions of men as pollinating bees, from concepts of manlove, and from constantly asking the question, "What's a man for?" The women use folktalk not to discuss religion, politics, or art, but to discuss men and love. The theme of male/female relations and love is not peculiar to Hurston, Morrison, and Jones. Other black female writers—Carolyn Rodgers, Stephany, Nikki Giovanni, Gwendolyn Brooks, Sonia Sanchez, and Alice Walker—are increasingly writing about love: family love, romantic love, and sexual love. Perhaps, as Nikki Giovanni says, "Black love is Black Wealth."[5]

NOTES

[1] Zora Neale Hurston, *Their Eyes Were Watching God* (1937; rpt. New York: Fawcett Premier, 1965), p. 16. All further references from this work will be from this edition and cited in the text.

[2] Toni Morrison, *Sula* (1973; rpt. New York: Alfred A. Knopf, 1976), p. 41. All further references to this work will be from this edition and cited in the text.

[3] Gayl Jones, *Corregidora* (1975; rpt. New York: Bantam Books, 1976), p. 11. All further references from this work will be from this edition and cited in the text.

[4] James Baldwin refers to *Corregidora* as an "extended blues lyric about sexual fear and rage" on the back cover of the edition already cited. The statement originally appeared in *Playboy.*

[5] Nikki Giovanni, "Nikki-Rosa," *Black Feeling, Black Talk, Black Judgment* (New York: W. Morrow, 1970), pp. 58-59.

Robert G. O'Meally

SOURCE: "Riffs and Rituals: Folklore in the Work of Ralph Ellison," in *Afro-American Literature: The Reconstruction of Instruction,* edited by Dexter Fisher and Robert B. Stepto, The Modern Language Association of America, 1979, pp. 153-69.

[*In the following essay, O'Meally examines folklore allusions and interpretations both in the fiction of Ralph Ellison—most notably his one novel,* Invisible Man—*and in his nonfiction, including the essays in* Shadow and Act.]

Nothing great or enduring, especially in music, has ever sprung full-fledged and unprecedented from the brain of any master; the best that he gives to the world he gathers from the hearts of the people, and runs it through the alembic of his genius.

—James Weldon Johnson

Discussions of folk tradition and literature which slight the specific literary forms involved seem to me questionable.

—Ralph Ellison

I

It has long been a commonplace that much of Afro-American literature has its sources in folklore, but only recently have critics begun to examine folklore as a literary tool and to analyze the ways in which folklore informs poetic or narrative structure, figurative language, characterization. This interest reflects a changing attitude toward folklore, from viewing it only as a quaint collection of stories, riddles, games—the folklore of artifact—to seeing folklore as a way of communicating, a *process* of speaking and singing under certain circumstances.[1] Folklore is not, to use Jean Toomer's phrase, "passing, soon gone." Rather it is a present and dynamic process that knows no social or racial boundaries. The effective teacher of the Afro-American literary tradition must be something of a folklorist, because some of the most skillful black writers are conscientious students of the lore, and they employ it to give shape and intensity to their work. One black writer whose fiction is steeped in folklore and whose essays place him in the vanguard of critics attempting to define the significance and use of folklore in literature is Ralph Ellison. His involvement in folklore is by no means a recent development.

Ellison has pointed out that Afro-Americans still participate vitally in an oral culture ("we are still not a reading people," he observes). For all his sophistication and insistence that writers grow up not in pool halls or picket lines but in libraries, college dropout Ellison, a kind of Rinehart in his own right, grew up in settings where folklore flourished. This is not to say that Ellison is not a sternly disciplined craftsman and student of literary traditions; he is. And a subject he has studied with great attention to language, form, and theme is black American *folklore.*

Until age nineteen Ellison lived in Oklahoma City, where a "rich babel" of folklore was alive and thriving. At Avery Chapel A.M.E. church he heard spirituals and gospel music along with the standard Methodist hymns. And for several years, as a teenager, he worked as delivery boy and clerk in J. L. Randolph's Drug Store in Oklahoma City's black section, Deep Second. Ellison recalls hearing exalted talk in the idiom as well as tales delivered in high style by older men who gathered at Randolph's on rainy and snowy days. As a youngster, Ellison also played trumpet in pick-up jazz bands in Oklahoma and in Alabama, where he attended college. Thus he heard the talk of the musicians and was immersed in jazz and the poetry of the blues.

In 1938, as a member of the Federal Writers Project in New York, Ellison worked with several other writers on a book never completed dealing with urban folklore. For this Project book, the working title of which was *Chase the White Horse,* Ellison submitted a number of game rhymes and toasts he remembered from Oklahoma City.[2] He also combed Harlem for more material, copying children's songs and sayings as well as stories told to him by the children and adults he interviewed. For *Chase the White Horse* Ellison also kept notes on the functions and the origins of the materials he collected. From 1938 to 1942 Ellison was collecting folklore during the day and writing fiction at night. By continuing to live in Harlem and by maintaining contact—sometimes in hour-long telephone conversations—with certain old friends in the South and Southwest, Ellison has remained in touch with Afro-American idiom and lore. The folkloric ingredient in Ellison's fiction is a major source of his work's enduring popularity and power.

II

In his fiction and essays, Ellison makes clear his view that the folk artist—the skilled singer or speaker in the folk idiom—is a kind of *griot* serving an ancient and vital function for Afro-Americans. During slavery, black folk songs, dances, stories, toasts, sermons, prayers, and other creations were forged from African, European, and Indian elements into distinctive Afro-American forms. Giving shape and perspective to the chaos of the slave experience, these folk art forms were, Ellison says, "what we had in the place of freedom." Through them blacks have been able to recall the past, escape and study the moment, and dream of a brighter future. There were both sacred and secular settings in which the slaves could, to use Albert L. Murray's phrase, "stomp away" the ever numerous blues.[3] These folk creations represented a triumph of the human spirit, says Ellison, through which black men and women humanized their tragic situation. Folklore provided a sense of continuity: In a simple joke was crystallized and affirmed the wisdom of the forefathers, their styles, techniques, and perspectives for survival. Blacks, says Ellison, do not need to go to Kierkegaard or Sartre or Unamuno for a "tragic sense of life" or an existential view of experience: These resound heartily in the poetry of the spirituals and the blues. By the early forties, Ellison recognized that folklore served the function classically attributed to art: It is delightful and instructive; moreover, it is vital to man's soul, for without it he cannot endure. Furthermore, blacks survived in the twentieth-century North, he says, because they transplanted their institutions and they remained conscious of the folklore in which their identity was deeply rooted.[4]

In *Shadow and Act* (1964), critic Ellison has gone so far as to say that *all* great art, from the work of the Benin masters to master works of the present, rests firmly on folk foundations.[5] Picasso, Bearden, Ailey, and Escudero are above all great manipulators of the signs and symbols of folklore. Moreover, art that is not grounded here is subject to be decadent—overly elaborate in theoretical design and false to the "note and trick of life" preserved in folk art. In Ellison's articles on black music he makes a similar point: Black music that strays too far from its folk and ritual sources—black church music, public dance music, and music of the jam session—is bound to be weak, if not in a state of decay.[6]

In 1965 Ellison asserted that folklore is generally more eclectic and complex in its vision than Afro-American fiction or poetry:

> We [blacks] have been exiled in our own land and, as for our efforts at writing, we have been little better than silent because we have not been cunning. I find this rather astounding because I feel that Negro American folklore is very powerful, wonderful, and universal. And it became so by expressing a people who were assertive, eclectic, and irreverent before all the oral and written literature that came within its grasp. It took what it needed to express its sense of life and rejected what it could not use.
>
> But what we've achieved in folklore has seldom been achieved in the novel, the short story, or poetry. In the folklore we tell what Negro experience really is. We back away from the chaos of experience and from ourselves, and we depict the humor as well as the horror of our living. We project Negro life in a metaphysical perspective and we have seen it with a complexity of vision that seldom gets into our writing. . . .[7]

Since the forties, Ellison has maintained that in order to depict the humor and the horror of our living, black writers need to reclaim some of the power locked in their folklore.

In his very first published writing, a review of Waters Turpin's *These Low Grounds* (1937), Ellison called for a greater consciousness of writing techniques and traditions among Afro-American writers.[8] He steadfastly maintained then, as he does now, that black folklore is one of the richest sources for the black writer.

In 1940, Ellison published "Stormy Weather," his longest and most searching critical review up to that time.[9] It was an important, pioneering work in establishing folklore as a criterion for evaluating black literature. Here, while reviewing one of Langston Hughes's

autobiographies, *The Big Sea,* Ellison proclaims that of the New Negroes, only Hughes, much of whose poetry had been based on black speech and the blues, transcended the "bourgeois," imitative wave of black writing in the twenties and survived the shattering impact of the Great Crash. Most black writers of the twenties wrote as if they were unaware of the technical experiments by such writers as Hemingway, Stein, and Joyce; furthermore, they ignored what Ellison termed "the folk source of all Negro art." Hughes, however, emerges from the fray: "declining the ideological world of the Negro bourgeoisie, he gained his artistic soul." In Ellison's words, "Hughes's vision carried him down into the black masses to seek his literary roots. The crystallized folk experience of the blues, spirituals and folk tales became the stuff of his poetry."[10]

Obviously there is a nationalist or proletarian note struck here; there is also one that has to do with diction and rhetoric. Ellison points out that Hughes was among the first writers of the thirties to sense that the black worker spoke a "language of protest," a black urban idiom, and that "the speech pattern of this new language had long been present in Negro life, recorded in the crystallized protest of American Negro folklore." Moreover, Hughes's poetry reflected the transformation of rural folk expression into urban folk expression, which, by the thirties, was fast becoming "the basis of a new proletarian art." His radical perspective and power as a spokesman for the people derived from Hughes's having followed "the logical development of the national folklore sources of his art."[11] In other words, Hughes used the language, tone, and structure of the blues and spirituals in his work; writing from the perspective of the folk, Hughes's radicalism glowed with the energy and irony of the dozens, the toast, and the elaborate, outright lie.

Always short on praise for contemporary writers, Ellison surveys the field of forties black writers, finding most of them weak on his usual two counts: craft and use of folk materials. For example, in William Attaway's *Blood on the Forge,* the "folk" characters fail because, in Ellison's view, they are too poor of spirit. Furthermore, Ellison feels that Attaway, like other realists, is too pessimistic. His "folk" are defeated when they move North:

> Conceptually, Attaway grasped the destruction of the folk, but missed its rebirth on a higher level. The writer did not see that while the folk individual was being liquidated in the crucible of steel, he was also undergoing a fusion of new elements. Nor did Attaway see that the individual which emerged, blended of old and new, was better fitted for the problems of the industrial environment. As a result the author is so struck by the despair of his material that he fails to see any ground for hope in the material. Yet hope is there. . . .[12]

In Ellison's view, the black writer's vision is incomplete without the presence of a folk character whose consciousness is *reborn* in the modern world. The Signifying Monkey has moved North in current lore, and he "wears a box-back coat with a belt in the back."[13]

In his criticism written in the forties, Ellison champions Richard Wright as living testimony to this rebirth and vitality of black folk consciousness. For Ellison, Wright's early novellas, published as *Uncle Tom's Children*, were his best fiction; their protest and existential themes emerged not from overt Marxist or Kierkegaardian theorizing, but from the fiction itself, which was rich in folklore. It was Ellison's view, however, that while *Native Son* and *Black Boy* are monumental achievements, they are stripped of folklore and portray the "folk" in terms that are too sweepingly harsh. Despite this criticism, Ellison wrote in his important review of *Black Boy*, "Richard Wright's Blues" (1945), that *Black Boy* is filled

> with blues-tempered echoes of railroad trains, the names of Southern towns and cities, estrangements, fights and flights, death and disappointments, charged with physical and spiritual hungers and pain. And like a blues sung by such an artist as Bessie Smith, its lyric prose evokes the paradoxical, almost surreal image of a black boy singing lustily as he probes his own grievous wound.[14]

This quality of the autobiography prompted Ellison to fashion his famous definition of the blues in written art:

> The blues is an impulse to keep the painful details and episodes of a brutal existence alive in one's aching consciousness, to finger its jagged grain, and to transcend it, not by the consolation of philosophy but by squeezing from it a near-tragic, near-comic lyricism. As a form, the blues is an autobiographical chronicle of personal catastrophe expressed lyrically. . . . Their attraction lies in this, that they at once express both the agony of life and the possibility of conquering it through sheer toughness of spirit. They fall short of tragedy only in that they provide no solution, offer no scapegoat but the self.[15]

In his criticism of black literature over the last twenty-five years, Ellison has repeatedly emphasized technique and use of folklore as major criteria for evaluating black writers. Small wonder, then, that the only two contemporary black fiction writers winning Ellison's public praise—James Alan McPherson and Leon Forrest—are lauded for their uses of black folklore. McPherson's *Hue and Cry* (1971), says Ellison, "makes use of the very rich folklore which has accumulated through the experience of dining-car and Pullman porters."[16] In his Foreword to Forrest's first novel, *There Is a Tree More Ancient than Eden* (1973), Ellison is especially ecstatic: "How furiously eloquent is this man Forrest's prose, how zestful his jazz-like invention, his parody, his reference to the classics and commonplaces of literature, tall-tale and street-slum jive!"[17]

III

One familiar with Ellison's strong stand on the relationship of folklore to black literature reads Stanley Edgar Hyman's chapter on folklore and *Invisible Man*, published in *The Promised End*, thinking it derivative of Ellison's work. Hyman identifies the "darky entertainer" as a figure from black American lore, one related to the "archetypal trickster figure, originating from Africa." This minstrel man, a professional entertainer who plays dumb, metamorphoses, in Afro-American literature, into such characters as the wily grandfather of *Invisible Man*. This argument offends Ellison by veering toward negritude's claim that all black writing involves idiosyncratic forms traceable to an African homeland, and in "Change the Joke and Slip the Yoke," Ellison issues a sharp rejoinder to Hyman, stating that he "must disagree with him all along the way."[18] Ellison points out that when black writers *do* tap folk sources, they scrupulously avoid the "darky" figures of minstrelsy. Such characters are by no means black folk types, but *white* ones, born of the white American's peculiar psychological and ritual needs. When these white-in-blackface minstrels—like the Nigger Jim—show up in American literature, they are, at best, slightly repulsive to black readers. Furthermore, masking and "playing dumb" are *American* (and universal) games, not just black ones. Trace them to Africa and one makes a political statement, not a literary one, says Ellison. Afro-American folklore has riches indeed, Ellison says, "but for the novelist, of any cultural or racial identity, his form is his greatest freedom and his insights are where he finds them."[19] Interpret all the colors of his palette as folklore, if you change the joke, and thus limit and segregate him—you gently but firmly slip the yoke.

Having in mind Ellison's warnings, one wonders how folklore operates in Ellison's own fiction. How, extrapolating, does folklore function in Afro-American literature generally? To begin with, folklore heightens the creative tension of Ellison's prose. For example, when Mary in *Invisible Man* tells the novel's protagonist that someday he will "move on up a little higher," she quotes the title of Mahalia Jackson's gospel hit by that name.[20] Thus, she identifies herself, at least for the moment, with the values of black church folk as expressed through this song, which clearly partakes of the idiom of sacred black lore. Subtle references to blues (the Invisible Man says that he felt he had to "Open up the window and let the bad air out," quoting a line from "Buddy Bolden's Blues"); a touch of the dozens (when Jack asks, angrily, who gave the Invisible Man the authority to act alone, the Invisible Man answers, "Your ma"); sermons and sermon-like speeches; casual references to the jokes, toasts, and the signifying games of black folklore—all are elements that enrich the texture and resonance of Ellison's prose.

Folklore also influences the structure of Ellison's fiction. Several critics, following Ellison's lead, have said that *Invisible Man* is, in some sense, an extended blues. In one commentator's words,

> *Invisible Man* was *par excellence* the literary extension of the blues. It was as if Ellison had taken an everyday twelve bar blues tune (by a

man from down South sitting in a manhole up North singing and signifying about how he got there) and scored it for full orchestra. . . . It had new dimensions of rhetorical resonance (based on lying and signifying). . . . It was a first rate novel, a blues odyssey, a tall tale. . . . And like the blues, and echoing the irrepressibility of America itself, it ended on a note of promise, ironic and ambiguous, but a note of promise still. The blues with no aid from existentialism have always known that there were no clear-cut solutions for the human situation.[21]

Like a blues man the Invisible Man struggles to cope with predicament after predicament (the "changes") by the magic of his words. In this sense, the young man is not so much an anti-hero (as several critics call him) as a comic hero striving for "blues heroism." In *The Hero and the Blues,* Albert Murray writes that the true "blues hero" personifies certain qualities perfected by the blues (or jazz) soloist:

> Improvisation is the ultimate human (i.e.) heroic endowment. . . . Even as flexibility or the ability to swing (or to perform with grace under pressure) is the key to . . . the charisma of the hero, and even as infinite alertness-become-dexterity is the functional source of the magic of all master craftsmen, so may skill in the art of improvisation be that which both will enable contemporary man to be at home with his sometimes tolerable but never quite certain condition of *not* being at home in the world and will also dispose him to regard his obstacles and frustrations as well as his achievements in terms of adventures and romance.[22]

Like a blues singer, the Invisible Man recounts his story—full of the train whistles, sudden flights, and the bad men and conjure women of the blues—with style, irony, and a sense of absurdity, viewing his trials and very occasional glories in terms of adventure and bedazzled romance. Also, this soloist, playing against and with his tradition and his society, discovers his identity and his freedom, as he finds his "voice" as a solo player or singer: as he finds, if you will, his "literacy."[23]

Blues *lyrics* also float through the pages of Ellison's fiction. These blues fragments often do more than provide a picturesque setting and tone. They sometimes serve a didactic purpose, calling a young or lost black character back to a sense of his identity, which is rooted in folklore. In the factory hospital the Invisible Man is lost until his memory is jarred and he recalls the dirty-dozens and Buckeye the Rabbit. In "Out of the Hospital and under the Bar," a version of the hospital scene that Ellison published ten years after the novel appeared, the Invisible Man is jarred into self-awareness as he hears, in the recesses of his mind, a high voice calling the "How Long Blues."[24] This secular blues voice here serves a sacred function. As an Ellison hero points out in "Night-Talk" (1965), the careful listener often hears prayers and prophecies from the mouths of even quite profane speakers: God's voice "could sing through the

blues and even speak through the dirty-dozens if only the players were rich-spirited and resourceful enough, comical enough, vital enough and enough aware of the disciplines of life. In the zest and richness Thou were there, yes!"[25] For Ellison, folklore is functional; it may be instructive and even *saving.*

If *Invisible Man* is in some sense an extended blues, Ellison's long-awaited second novel, published only in scattered and ill-fitting fragments (of which "Night-Talk" is one), has overtones of the blues's sacred counterpart: spirituals or gospel songs. One piece of the novel, "Juneteenth," released as a story complete in itself, consists of a sermon preached hard on Juneteenth, the anniversary of emancipation day, by two revivalists, the Reverends Hickman and Bliss.[26] Here, then, a form not always recognized as folkloric—the sermon—is used to provide a story with structure. Part of the success of "Juneteenth" derives from the responses of the congregation and of one preacher to another: It is a highly eloquent "dialogue-sermon." Interestingly, too, the story's *subject* is black identity and survival; thus the words and the form, hammered out by black folk, constitute an exuberant affirmation of Afro-American life. Rev. Hickman shouts:

> We know where we are by the way we walk. We know where we are by the way we talk. We know where we are by the way we sing. We know where we are by the way we dance. We know where we are by the way we praise the Lord on high. We know where we are because we hear a different tune in our minds and in our hearts. We know who we are because when we make the beat of our rhythm to shape our day the whole land says, Amen! It smiles, Rev. Bliss, and it moves to our time! Don't be ashamed, my brothern! Don't be cowed. Don't throw what you have away! Continue! Remember! Believe! Trust the inner beat that tells us who we are.[27]

Drawing earlier on the "Dry Bones" folk sermon mentioned by James Weldon Johnson in the Introduction to *God's Trombones,* Rev. Hickman (an ex-jazzman whose nickname is God's Trombone) taps a rich source for waking and stirring up his congregation's spirit.[28] *"Do,"* Rev. Hickman shouts, *"Do these dry bones live?!"*[29]

Like much Afro-American writing, Ellison's novel and his stories often contain entire sermons. In the Prologue to *Invisible Man,* the sermonic topic, "The Blackness of Blackness," echoes the Bible and the Black Belt sermon. Homer A. Barbee's sermon is one of the great "performances" in American literature. And it is here that Ellison consciously parodies the qualities of the hero in history and myth as outlined by Lord Raglan.[30] For instance, Raglan observes that heroes of legend and history are often born mysteriously only to encounter awesome hardship as youths. Likewise, the Founder in *Invisible Man* knew only his slave mother and suffered great trials as a baby. A note of absurdity undercuts this archetypal pattern when blind Barbee says, "I'm sure you have heard of his precarious infancy, his precious life almost destroyed by an insane cousin who splashed the babe with lye and shrivelled his seed and how, a mere babe, he lay nine days in a deathlike coma and then suddenly and miraculously recovered."[31]

Sometimes Ellison's sermons constitute the nucleus of a story. Such is the case in the first published fragment of the new novel "And Hickman Arrives" (1960).[32] In that story, "God's Trombone" preaches death and resurrection over a small coffin, which opens in mid-sermon as the small boy-preacher, Rev. Bliss, sits up in his white linen suit to inquire, innocently, "Lord, Why Hast Thou Forsaken Me?" An inspired piece of showmanship, this sermon is remembered by the delirious Rev. Bliss-become-Senator Sunraider years later, after he has been shot down on the floor of the U. S. Senate. Just as the sermons by the Prologue preacher and by Homer A. Barbee comment on the themes of *Invisible Man,* the Hickman-Blisssermon is an integral part of "And Hickman Arrives." Indeed, the sermon—moaned, stamped, shouted, sung, and enacted—serves to raise the action of the story beyond realism to surrealism, though such "surrealistic" drama may be witnessed in certain black churches on any Sunday. In this story, a boy becomes compared with Christ; his later assassination is a kind of crucifixion. It is vitally important, too, that Bliss, who as a senator is passing for white, seems to come to himself as he recalls his black past, when under hot tents on the revival circuit, the air was tense with sermons and spirituals.

Like Charles Chesnutt, Ellison sometimes erects an entire short story around a folk tale. Such is the case in "Did You Ever Dream Lucky?" (1956) and "Flying Home" (1944). The use of folklore in these stories would satisfy even folklorists like Richard Dorson whose eye is ever vigilant for evidences of *fake*lorists in the field.[33] "Flying Home" contains allusions to the Icarus and Phoenix myths, but some of the main ore here is from the black folk mine. A young black pilot whose plane is felled, significantly, by "jim crows," meets an old black man who tells him a spirited version of "Colored Man in Heaven." This tale (recorded in Richard Dorson's *American Negro Folktales*) is presented as a parable, designed to instruct the headstrong young man in some of the paradoxes and cruelties of black life. Here again folklore soothes, delights, teaches, arms. At the end of the story the young man is able to confront his tragic predicament; he is even able to face, with less self-destructive bitterness or aggression, the vicious whites in Alabama. As in the Sterling Brown poem, "Slim in Hell," which is also based on "Colored Man in Heaven," the young man is able to deal, like Slim, with the limitations of his life in the Deep South. In Brown's version, St. Peter is surprised to learn that Slim did not know that hell was in Dixie:

> . . . Peter say, "You must
> Be crazy, I vow,
> Where'n hell dja think Hell was
>   Anyhow?"[34]

"Did You Ever Dream Lucky" is a contemporary Harlem story about buried treasure, a "fortune" that turns out to be worthless.[35] Several motifs from Afro-American buried treasure folk stories emerge here. Again, too, the folk story, like an Aesop fable, is a parable for delight and instruction. Complete with tale signatures, "Dream Lucky" would be fascinating to folklorists interested in transcribing folklore as performance. Here one watches folk art transmuted into literature. Here is a perplexing message contained in the simple, poetic terms of the Count Basie/Jimmy Rushing blues that give the story its title:

> Did you ever dream lucky,
> And wake up cold in hand?
> Did you ever dream lucky, baby,
> Just to wake up cold in hand?
>
> And you didn't have a dollar,
> Somebody had your woman.[36]

IV

George W. Kent is right on target when he says that Ellison uses "folk characters" in his fiction.[37] These often heroic characters—whether from the North or South, rural or urban milieus—live in a culture that is principally oral. They speak a vernacular language infused with words from toasts and tales, the dozens and blues, spirituals and sermons. Sometimes these characters are singers or preachers—word experts; just as often they are barflies or ordinary men and women who, given the correct setting and listeners, will spin an inspired lie: that is, they will use a folklore process. The catalog of such Ellison characters includes Trueblood, "Petie Wheatstraw," Mrs. Jackson, Brother Tarp, Mary, and the Rev. Alonzo Zuber Hickman, God's Trombone. They are Ellison's strong men and women of charity and vision who have the "toughness of spirit" expressed in the blues. These characters have their feet firmly planted on the ground, and they are able and willing to help others, often through the power of their words. Most of Ellison's stories concern bright young men lost and confused in the danger-and-fun-house of American society. These "folk characters" are their guides; they are the initiators; they are mother and father.

Other "folk characters" in Ellison's prose are those around whom folk characteristics cluster. Sometimes we meet Ellison characters based on the badmen and badwomen of the blues. Also, the Invisible Man, as some critics have observed, does fall into the role of the yokel in the big city. And he acts like the stumbling Brer Bear, out-maneuvered by several Brer Rabbits: Tarp, Jack, Bledsoe. But it is usually overlooked that the Invisible Man is both the bear and the hare: If he is often duped, by the end of the book it is he who has outrun the entire field, leaving one-eyed Jack to play the role of Jack-the-Bear. Jack is also the Dirty Dog and the Marse of black folklore, keeping the "nigger boy running" until he (the Invisible Man) realizes he must stop running and assert himself. The tables are turned when the Invisible Man becomes, to some degree, *John* of the tales, outmaneuvering the Master and escaping with a modicum of freedom.

Allusions to other folk characters abound. "Petie Wheatstraw," the devil's son-in-law, is conjured. High John the Conquerer makes a brief appearance. References to the biblical Jonah, Samson, St. John, and Jesus occur, particularly in the late stories. Also, references—sometimes in blues lyrics—to such popular, if not, strictly speaking, *folk* characters as Louis Armstrong and Joe Louis are made throughout Ellison's work.

These allusions and the other uses of folklore add a dimension to Ellison's earliest fiction that propels it beyond the stark realism of the thirties. One need only compare "The Birthmark" or "Slick Gonna Learn" (realistic Ellison stories) with the Buster-and-Riley stories to see this difference. The use of folklore adds historical dimension, a sense of the past. Also, it provides a magic, a dreamlike quality missing from most social realist fiction. On the wings of folklore Ellison's characters dream of God-become-Touissant L'Ouverture breathing fire and destruction on the Napoleonic soldiers, who prove as helpless as Pharaoh's army before holy wrath. Characters fly to the moon and to heaven; they meditate on the blackness of blackness and on the rebirth of a chosen people. And for Ellison it is vital that this added dimension be grounded not only in his private fantasy world but in the lore of black folk. What some critics have called experimental or surreal in Ellison's work is often merely folk matter, dramatically rendered.

V

In sum, no longer is it enough merely to inquire about an Afro-American poem, short story, or novel:

(1) Does this work upon folkloric sources?

(2) What are those sources?

(3) How authentic are the specific folklore items?

(4) Are the items cataloged by folklorists?

Ellison's fiction and criticism suggest that we begin with a series of other, more literary questions that address directly the relationship between some texts of actual "raw" folklore—transcribed sermons, blues, spirituals, tales, toasts, dozens—and the literary work. For example:

(1) How does each story, rhyme, or song work as an act of language? What is the structure? How are characters presented? How does the figurative language operate?

(2) What are the ritual functions of each folkloric process? What values does each reflect? What sense of life is implied?

With a clear idea of what the black folkloric processes are, we turn to Afro-American novels, short stories, plays, and poems, asking:

(1) What (if any) folkloric processes operate in each work?

(2) How does each literary work's structure, figurative language, or characterization reflect that of Afro-American folklore?

(3) Does the folklore have ritualistic meaning in the literary work?

(4) How do the uses of folkloric processes vary from literary work to literary work?

(5) Is the folklore skillfully integrated into the structure and meaning of a particular literary work?

(6) Does the use of folkloric processes succeed in enriching the fabric of the literary text? Does the folklore add resonance or creative tension to the literature?

Of course, as Ralph Ellison would be the first to say, many more questions remain to be asked about a given Afro-American poem, play, short story, or novel. But these questions are vital ones. For, as Ellison has said, black literature—if not *all* great art—is erected on the firm base of folklore.

NOTES

[1] See Robert Hemenway's "The Function of Folklore in Charles Chesnutt's *The Conjure Woman*," *Journal of the Folklore Institute,* 13 (1976), 283-309.

[2] The manuscript of *Chase the White Horse* is on file in the Library of Congress, Folklore Division.

[3] *Stomping the Blues* (New York: McGraw-Hill, 1976).

[4] See Ellison's "Blues People," *Shadow and Act* (New York: Random, 1964), pp. 247-58.

[5] See "The Art of Fiction: An Interview," *Shadow and Act,* pp. 167-93.

[6] See "Sound and the Mainstream," *Shadow and Act,* pp. 185-258.

[7] "A Very Stern Discipline," *Harper's,* March 1967, p. 80.

[8] "Creative and Cultural Lag," *New Challenge,* 2 (Fall 1937), 90.

[9] "Stormy Weather," *New Masses,* 24 Sept. 1940, pp. 20-21.

[10] "Stormy Weather," p. 20.

[11] "Stormy Weather," p. 20.

[12] "Transition," *Negro Quarterly,* 1 (Spring 1942), 90-91.

[13] See phonograph recordings by Rudi Ray Moore; also Richard Dorson, *America in Legend* (New York: Pantheon, 1973).

[14] "Richard Wright's Blues," *Shadow and Act,* p. 79.

[15] "Richard Wright's Blues," pp. 78-79, 94.

[16] *The Writer's Voice,* ed. George Garrett (New York: Morrow, 1973), p. 226.

[17] Leon Forrest, *There Is a Tree More Ancient than Eden* (New York: Random, 1973), p. 2.

[18] "Change the Joke and Slip the Yoke," *Shadow and Act,* pp. 45-59.

[19] "Change the Joke," p. 59.

[20] *Invisible Man* (New York: Random, 1952), p. 222.

[21] Murray, *The Omni-Americans* (New York: Outerbridge, 1970), p. 167.

[22] *The Hero and the Blues* (St. Louis: Univ. of Missouri Press, 1973), p. 107.

[23] See Robert B. Stepto, "Teaching Afro-American Literature: Survey on Tradition; or, The Reconstruction of Instruction," in this volume.

[24] "Out of the Hospital and under the Bar," *Soon, One Morning,* ed. Herbert Hill (New York: Knopf, 1963), pp. 242-90.

[25] "Night-Talk," *Quarterly Review of Literature,* 16 (1969), 329.

[26] "Juneteenth," *Quarterly Review of Literature,* 3 (1965), 262-76.

[27] "Juneteenth," p. 276.

[28] *God's Trombones* (New York: Viking, 1927).

[29] "Juneteenth," p. 272.

[30] Lord Raglan, *The Hero* (London: Watts, 1936).

[31] *Invisible Man,* p. 107.

[32] "And Hickman Arrives," *Noble Savage,* (1960), 5-49.

[33] Dorson, *Folklore and Fakelore* (Cambridge: Harvard Univ. Press, 1976).

[34] "Slim in Hell," *Folk-Say,* 4 (1932), 249.

[35] "Did You Ever Dream Lucky?" *New World Writing,* 5 (April 1954), 134-45.

[36] Count Basie and Jimmy Rushing, "Blues in the Dark," Decca Record, DXSB-7170, Jan. 1938.

[37] Kent, *Blackness and the Adventure of American Culture* (Chicago: Third World, 1972), pp. 152-63, 184-201.

Jay Mechling

SOURCE: "The Failure of Folklore in Richard Wright's 'Black Boy'," in *Journal of American Folklore,* Vol. 104, No. 413, Summer, 1991, pp. 275-94.

[*In the following essay, Mechling presents Richard Wright's autobiographical* Black Boy *in terms both of the folk traditions that inform the narrative, and of the ways that those traditions ultimately fail the narrator in cross-cultural situations.*]

We are so accustomed to talking and writing about folklore as a human strength, as a personal and community resource for enduring, connecting, and celebrating, that we sometimes overlook those instances when folklore fails. Perhaps it is the streak of romanticism in folklorists that leads them to celebrate humanity and folklore. Perhaps it is the functional bias of most folklore theories that leads to the expectation that traditions persisting across generations must be working somehow. Whatever the cause, our elation at the successes of folklore can use a sobering antidote now and then, for in examining the failures of folklore, we might be able to see dynamics and processes invisible to us when folklore succeeds.

Richard Wright's *Black Boy* (1945), the first of his two autobiographical volumes, provides the folklorist with an elaborate, fixed text for exploring some of the ways folklore can fail the individual.[1] My aim in this essay is to approach this text with the usual stock of the folklorist's questions about folklore in literature and then to pose the questions not often asked: how does folklore fail the protagonist of this autobiography, and why does this failure occur? I believe the answers to these queries draw our attention to the double bind as a structural instrument of cultural hegemony. Understanding the double bind and the limitations of folklore as a resource for resisting the double bind will teach us something about the workings of folklore as a communications strategy.

Black Boy tells the story of Wright's growing up in the segregationist American South of the early 20th century, from his earliest memories (age four, in 1912) to his decision at age 19 (1927) to flee north (as the closing sentence of the book explains),

full of a hazy notion that life could be lived with dignity, that the personalities of others should not be violated, that men should be able to confront other men without fear or shame, and that if men were lucky in their living on earth they might win some redeeming meaning for their having struggled and suffered here beneath the stars. [Wright 1966:285; all subsequent page citations to *Black Boy* are from this edition]

In between, Wright chronicles an unstable life, including his abusive father's desertion, his mother's stoic pragmatism and wrenching death, his upbringing with an assortment of relatives, his discovery of the power of words in books, his troubles with white teachers and employers, the consequences of transgressing the society structured by Jim Crow laws, and more. *Black Boy* resembles Wright's fiction in its realism, in its unflinching portrayal of the numbing violence, brutality, cruelty, and deprivation (especially hunger, a reigning trope in the book) Wright experienced in his youth.

The present moment in both literary criticism and interpretive anthropology reminds us that all narrative texts are "fictions" and that many fictions have ethnographic insight (e.g., Clifford and Marcus 1986). Although there is plenty of truth in *Black Boy,* there is also plenty of evidence that Wright fashioned a fictionalized biography, an artistic memory for his own purposes (Hakutani 1985:71). Even so, a fictionalized autobiography by Wright serves our purpose here. Richard Dorson (1957) and Alan Dundes (1965) laid out the initial terms for the conversation about the relationships between folklore and literature, and since then, folklorists and literary critics pretty much have worked out the practice of the paradigm. We know that demonstrating folklore in American literature, for example, should consist of more than mere lists of items or motifs; that we must look to the details of the artist's uses of the folk texts in context; and that in the finest examples of literature, the author uses folklore not merely for familiarity's sake but also for clear, artistic purposes that advance the fictive world created in the story.

The traditional approach to folklore in *Black Boy* discovers soon enough a wealth of items and genres. At times, Wright's book reads like a folklorist's ethnography. In a letter advising his friend Joe C. Brown to record the black idiom of the South, Wright wrote:

I wonder if you are not walking each day pass [*sic*] some damn good stuff. I heard a record recently called the Dirty Dozens. It consisted of a recital of the little jingles with which you and I heard in our childhood set to boogie woogie music; the dumb folks around New York are eating it up. Boy, why don't you take pencil and paper and hang around the black boys and put on paper what they say, their tall tales, their words, their folk tales, their songs, their jokes? That stuff is some of the best real stuff this country has produced. . . . The life of the Negro in America is right where you are, on the black lips of men, women, and children. [quoted in McClusky 1983:339-340]

Wright followed his own advice. *Black Boy* devotes two pages (pp. 81-82) to a catalog of folk beliefs he learned as a child, listed in parallel construction:

If I pulled a hair from a horse's tail and sealed it in a jar of my own urine, the hair would turn overnight into a snake.

If I passed a Catholic sister or mother dressed in black and smiled and allowed her to see my teeth, I would surely die.

If I walked under a leaning ladder, I would certainly have bad luck.

If I kissed my elbow, I would certainly turn into a girl.

And so on. He tells of six taunts (pp. 70-71) he recalls using with his seven-to nine-year-old friends to torment the Jewish owner of the small grocery store in the small Mississippi town where he lived, taunts such as

Jew, Jew,
 Two for five
That's what keeps
 Jews alive.

and

Bloody Christ killers
 Never trust a Jew
Bloody Christ killers
 What won't a Jew do?

A little older, Wright hangs out with a group of boys and learns from them the lessons of "the talk of black boys who met at the crossroads" (p. 88). Again, he offers something like an ethnography of the black boys' folk group, including their verbal dueling (pp. 89-91), riddle-jokes (p. 92), games (p. 122), and parodies of Sunday school hymns and stories (pp. 92-93). "And the talk," observes Wright,

would weave, roll, surge, spurt, veer, swell, having no specific aim or direction, touching vast areas of life, expressing the tentative impulses of childhood. . . . The culture of one black household was thus transmitted to another black household, and folk tradition was handed from group to group. Our attitudes were made, defined, set, or corrected; our ideas were discovered, discarded, enlarged, torn apart, and accepted. [pp. 91-92]

One evening Wright hears a legend that has a powerful impact on him, a legend about a black woman who, given permission by the four white men who killed her husband to take her husband's body for burial, used a shotgun hidden in the burial sheets to shoot dead her husband's murderers. "I did not know if the story was factually true or not, but it was emotionally true," recalls Wright, "because I had already grown to feel that there existed men against whom I was powerless, men who could violate my life at will. I resolved that I would emulate the black woman if I were ever faced with a white mob. . . . The story of the woman's deception gave form and meaning to confused defensive feelings that had long been sleeping in me" (pp. 83-84). Wright clearly understands the expressive and instrumental functions of this talk, showing how he and the boys used the verbal dueling and stories to construct and sustain meanings in their lives as young black men in the South.

But Wright's autobiography has the structure and texture of a folklore performance far beyond the mere inventory of genres. On one level, *Black Boy* shares with slave narratives a number of motifs listed by Robert Stepto (1977:533): "the violence and gnawing hunger, the skeptical view of Christianity, the portrait of a black family valiantly attempting to maintain a degree of unity, the impregnable isolation, the longing and scheming to follow the North Star resolved by boarding the 'freedom train'." But most of all, argues Stepto, *Black Boy* resembles slave narratives in "the narrator's quest for literacy" (1977:533).

Apart from this decades-old critical approach that looks at traditional texts and formulae in new contexts, some black critics of African-American literature have been pursuing ways to talk about the continuities between ordinary, vernacular African-American discourse and artistic African-American discourse (Baker 1984:104). Houston Baker, for example, criticizes both Stepto and Henry Louis Gates, Jr., for their "reconstructionist" theories that privilege literary discourse and adopt a semiotic view of African-American literature as a closed system of signs. Baker advocates an interdisciplinary, anthropological approach to African-American art, redesigning the approach of Stephen Henderson and other representatives of the "Black Aesthetic" movement of the 1960s and early 1970s. Baker aims "to establish a verbal and musical *continuum of expressive behavior* in Afro-American culture as an analytical category" (1984:103). He argues for a performance theory of literature that requires the critic to "have at least some theoretically adequate notions of the entire array of cultural forces which shape the performer's cognition, allowing him to actualize a 'text' as one instance of a distinct cultural semantics" (1984:104). Criticism in this mode—which Baker calls the "tropological mode," borrowing Hayden White's (1978) neologism—should resemble the blues, as do the African-American texts themselves, such that the "improvisational dynamism" of the criticism matches that of the texts (1984:112). His guiding model for understanding the *continuities* of African-American expressive culture—continuities between vernacular and high art—is the blues matrix, blues as both code and force in the culture. Baker looks to the ways in which African-American writers tap "blues energies" to write, as he puts it, "blues books most excellent" (1984:115).

Other critics have tried to talk about African-American literature as blues performances. Wright himself provided early fuel for this approach in a lecture on "The Literature of the Negro in the United States," which he had given in the mid-1940s but which was not published until the appearance of *White Man, Listen!* in 1956. Wright identifies two different traditions of African-

American expression in literature. The first is the Narcissistic Level, a formal, self-conscious writing that speaks of the alienation of the black middle class and pleads for the recognition of the humanity of blacks. The other tradition, which Wright calls Forms of Things Unknown, is the realm of the oral folk culture of lower-class blacks, and it amounts to a vernacular repertoire from which African-American literature can draw. John McClusky (1983) shows us Wright's ongoing interest in the blues idiom and Ralph Ellison (1945) goes so far as to call *Black Boy* a blues in prose. Henderson revived this notion of the Forms of Things Unknown as he attempted in 1973 to provide a theory for the Black Aesthetic movement, especially within poetry. For Henderson, "blackness" in expressive culture must exist in the structures of the expressive object, structures that reflect the "interior dynamism" or "inner life" of African-American folk. Theme and structure contribute to blackness, but so does what Henderson calls "saturation," a semantic category. "Certain words and constructions," writes Henderson, "seem to carry an inordinate charge of emotional and psychological weight, so that whenever they are used they set all kinds of bells ringing, all kinds of synapses snapping, on all kinds of levels." He calls these "mascon words," words that carry "a massive concentration of Black experiential energy which powerfully affects the meaning of Black speech, Black song, and Black poetry—if one, indeed, has to make such distinctions" (1973:43).

Baker faults the Black Aesthetic movement for its "romantic Marxism," but he builds upon its interdisciplinary anthropology-of-art approach to the continuities and discontinuities between nonliterary and literary forms of African-American expressive culture. Baker takes seriously the attempt to go beyond the thematic similarity between *Black Boy* and a blues song to seek thicker ways to talk about books as blues performances.

Baker proposes a tropological perspective on Wright, the suggestive trope being the physical phenomenon, the black hole. This perspective leads him to read *Black Boy* as a tale of desire, with the narrator as a "black hole" of blues energy consuming books and experiences to "feed" the "hunger" of the black hole for energy. "In the autobiography," writes Baker, "the mother's suffering absence becomes a figure gathering to itself all lineaments of a black 'blues life'" (1984:146). And just as a black hole "squeezes" matter to a zero sum, so Wright "as voracious center of desire—seeking desire's trace as 'point of view'—reduces literary language to zero sum. *Black Boy* is utterly relentless in its representations of what might be termed a 'code of desire' that reduces conventional discourse to zero" (Baker 1984:148-149). Baker cites several examples of Wright's zero-sum reduction of conventional discourse in the autobiography, citing as an example the black boys' parodies of the preacher's sacred hymns:

> When the preacher intoned:
> *Amazing grace, how sweet it sounds*

we would wink at one another and hum under our
breath:
    A bulldog ran my grandma down [p. 93]

For Baker, this folk discourse amounts to Wright's
adopting what Julia Kristeva calls "carnivalesque discourse" (1980:65) as the ultimate linguistic strategy for
challenging the social order.

On a different level, Wright's use of African-American
vernacular language connects in interesting ways with
Gertrude Stein's uses in "Melanctha," the centerpiece of
Three Lives (1909), and in her poetry. It is well known
that Wright was terribly excited about "Melanctha,"
even to the extreme of taking the book to the workplaces
of laboring blacks in order to read to them aloud from
the story. One critic, Eugene Miller (1982, 1983), has
explored the Wright-Stein-blues triangle in a reading of
a relatively obscure Wright short story, "The Man Who
Killed a Shadow." Miller draws upon an unpublished
Wright manuscript, "Memories of My Grandmother," to
show Wright's linking of black folk expression, including the blues, with surrealism.

These attempts to talk about *Black Boy* as a blues performance are, in my view, still tentative and incomplete.
Baker has not yet exploited fully the aesthetic anthropology of Robert Plant Armstrong (1981) or Robert
Farris Thompson (1983), nor has he exploited fully the
ethnographically informed work of folklorists on African-American performance style. Some of the more obvious poetic elements of blues lyrics, such as repetition,
are clear enough in the autobiography. Wright often
renders pages of single sentences in parallel construction (pp. 14-15, 53-55), and even the list of folk beliefs
I cited earlier has this quality; surely these are the passages critics have in mind when they are moved to call
Black Boy a blues poem.

But there is more to be said about this structure. Critics
(e.g., Hodges 1985; Stepto 1977) have likened the structure of *Black Boy* to other well-known formula genres,
such as the slave narrative or *Bildungsroman,* the story
of a boy's quest and character formation. This suggests,
erroneously, I believe, that the aesthetic principle underlying the structure of *Black Boy* is *synthesis*—the familiar Western literary formula in which thesis and antithesis are resolved by synthesis. In contrast, Armstrong
(1981) identifies an aesthetic principle, *syndesis,* which
he finds in Yoruba art and, by extension, in folk arts
generally. Whereas *synthesis* "apprehends and enacts
the world and the self—through a process of oppositions
and eventuations," *syndesis* works "through a process of
accretion" (Armstrong 1981:13). "The synthetic work,"
continues Armstrong,

> owns inherent principles of *development.* It pro-
> ceeds through the execution and resolution of
> opposites. Its successive units are different from
> one another; and insofar as successive phases grow
> out of prior ones, the synthetic work is linear.
> The syndetic work, on the other hand, grows in

accordance with extrinsic principles; its *growth* is
through repetition of the same or of a small
inventory of similar units. It does not *develop*;
there is no entailment of the subsequent to be
found in the prior. [1981:13]

Notwithstanding the illusion of linear synthesis that an
autobiography creates, *Black Boy* is far more a syndetic
than a synthetic work of art, and it is on this structural
principle that it resembles a blues performance. Although Wright presents his dozens of small stories in
roughly chronological order, the meaning of the entire
autobiography would change little if the stories were
rearranged in random order. The stories are variations
on the same theme, and there is no logical order to them
other than the chronological.

This syndetic aesthetic governing the structure of *Black
Boy* is a prime instance of "intertextuality" between
oral and written expression, and critics (Gates 1987:
xxxi, 1988) of African-American literature recognize
intertextuality as a primary feature both of African-
American expression and of so-called postmodern expression (Jameson 1984). Walter Ong's notion of the
"residual orality" in printed and, finally, in electronic
forms of communication is relevant here, as oral traditions of all sorts provide form and content for cultural
texts thought to be far from folklore (1982). This is not
to say that *Black Boy* is a "postmodern text"; rather, the
important point is that the intertextuality between folklore and high cultural forms may be a feature linking
most 20th-century African-American texts.

Thus far I have discussed, in effect, the ways in which
folklore "succeeds" in *Black Boy.* Wright documents in
a thick description of texts and contexts the ways in
which traditional African-American talk served socialization, bonding, and tendentious functions for black
men growing up in the South. Moreover, the very structures of the book, from the sentence level to the paragraph to the chapter, seem to establish a continuity
between African-American vernacular discourse and
African-American literary discourse. What, then, of the
claim of "failure" announced in the title of this essay?

One way to read *Black Boy* as a literary performance
continuous with folk performances is to focus on the
uses of folklore as a way out of double binds and other
paradoxes of communication that fill our everyday lives.
This everyday communications approach alerts the
reader to the tentative, incomplete, and possibly disas-
trous character of every face-to-face encounter. Every
folk encounter has the possibility of failure.

Folklore is one of those classes of healthy human behavior, along with play, humor, and art, that makes it possible to survive communication paradoxes (Mechling
1988). And examining in detail African-American strategies reminds us how much folklore is about surviving
in asymmetrical power relations. The notion of paradoxical communication is central to the ideas that Gregory

Bateson was developing in the mid-1950s. His 1954 essay, "A Theory of Play and Fantasy" (published in 1972), established his use of the Theory of Logical Types to distinguish between logical types of communication, such as between a message and a metamessage (i.e., a message about messages). This, of course, is the key to Bateson's "frame" analysis, which has contributed importantly to symbolic interactionist theories in sociology and to performance theory in folklore. The discontinuity between messages and metamessages makes paradoxical communication inevitable in our everyday lives, as in Epimenides's familiar case of the Cretan liar. Humans learn to cope with these paradoxical communications involving multiple logical types by invoking ritual, art, humor, play, and related genres of metaphorical behavior (Bateson 1972:193).

Bateson developed his ideas about frames and play while working with a team of psychologists interested in developing a communication-based theory of schizophrenia. Bateson later regretted that his ideas about paradoxical communication and double binds became linked so solidly with the schizophrenia research because, for him, the idea of the double bind explained a broad range of "transcontextual phenomena" and did not have to rest on changing ideas about schizophrenia. According to the theory of the double bind, the schizophrenic lacks the normal person's ability to discriminate between levels of messages. Indeed, schizophrenia becomes the actor's primary defense mechanism against the paradox created by the double bind. The elements of the double bind include:

> 1. Two or more persons. . . . 2. Repeated experience. . . . 3. A primary negative injunction. This may have either of two forms: (a) "Do not do so and so, or I will punish you," or (b) "If you do not do so and so, I will punish you." . . . 4. A secondary injuction conflicting with the first at a more abstract level, and like the first enforced by punishments or signals which threaten survival. . . . 5. A tertiary injunction prohibiting the victim from escaping the field. [Bateson et al. 1956:253-254]

P. Watzlawick, J. H. Beavin and D. D. Jackson (1967:149-186) have used these ideas to define an entire field, the pragmatics of communication. Drawing on Bateson, they show how pervasive paradoxical communications are in our interpersonal interactions. They call these "pragmatic paradoxes" and include the category called "paradoxical injunctions," of which the barber paradox is the most famous example. In Hans Reichenbach's (1947) version of this paradox, "the barber is a soldier who is ordered by his captain to shave all the soldiers of the company who do not shave themselves, but no others" (Watzlawick, Beavin and Jackson 1967:194). Does the barber shave himself? Such a barber cannot logically exist, but in the real world of barbers and military officers the order *can* exist. "A person caught in such a situation," write Watzlawick, Beavin and Jackson,

> is in an untenable position. . . . As soon as we begin to look at paradox in interaction contexts, the phenomenon ceases to be merely a fascinating pursuit of the logician and the philosopher of science and becomes a matter of stark practical importance for the sanity of the communicants, be they individuals, families, societies, or nations. [1967:195]

Such is the condition of any person forced to interact with others while assuming the inferior power position in that interaction. In *Black Boy* Wright tells the story of how a child learns to cope with daily pragmatic paradoxes without going crazy. The answer, of course, is that the child learns to distinguish between levels of communication and further learns to use those distinctions as both a defense mechanism and as a tool for taking power whenever possible in the paradoxical situation. Because play, humor, art, ritual, and the entire range of metaphoric behavior are the processes the child learns for coping with pragmatic paradoxes, and because these are recognizable folkloric processes, we are justified in looking at Wright's *Black Boy* as a primer in folklore as communication strategy for the relatively powerless. Let me offer a few salient examples from the autobiography to make my point.

Wright's earliest lesson in the paradoxes of communication involved his father, who worked as a night porter and was barely part of Wright's childhood even before leaving the family. Wright's primary memory was of having to be quiet during the daytime, when his father slept. "He was the lawgiver in our family," says Richard, "and I never laughed in his presence. . . . He was always a stranger to me, always somehow alien and remote" (pp. 16-17).

The episode that was seared in Wright's memory had to do with a stray kitten he and his brother found and befriended. But the kitten's meowing was loud and persistent, which awakened his father. Richard and his brother were ordered to keep the kitten quiet.

> "Kill that damn thing!" my father exploded. "Do anything, but get it away from here!"

> He went inside, grumbling. I resented his shouting and it irked me that I could never make him feel my resentment. How could I hit back at him? Oh, yes. . . . He had said to kill the kitten and I would kill it! I knew that he had not really meant for me to kill the kitten, but my deep hate of him urged me toward a literal acceptance of his word. [p. 17]

And so, much to the horror of his brother, Richard hangs the cat. Upon discovering this, his mother drags him before the father.

> "You know better than that!" my father stormed.

> "You told me to kill 'im," I said.

> "I told you to drive him away," he said.

"You told me to kill 'im," I countered positively.

"You get out of my eyes before I smack you down!" my father bellowed in disgust, then turned over in bed.

I had had my first triumph over my father. I had made him believe that I had taken his words literally. He could not punish me now without risking his authority. I was happy because I had at last found a way to throw my criticism of him into his face. I had made him feel that, if he whipped me for killing the kitten, I would never give serious weight to his words again. I had made him know that I felt he was cruel and I had done it without his punishing me. [pp. 18-19]

This was Wright's first lesson in the power of words, but he also saw that the power he had over his father was the power to move between levels of logical types in his messages. His father had spoken figuratively and counted on Richard's correctly interpreting the message. Richard reversed the power relationship by literally interpreting a figurative message, just as in other circumstances he takes power by interpreting figuratively a literal message. Schizophrenics, according to the double-bind theory, confuse the literal and metaphorical and are victimized by the confusion. The normal person, on the other hand, finds power and creativity in mixing the literal and metaphorical. Humor often works out of that mix, just as play and ritual depend on it. By taking power in his interactions with his father and by willfully mixing the literal and the metaphorical, Richard marks the early stages of his expressive creativity, a sort of protofolklore. Word games with his peers were a lesson of one sort; word games with his father were far more dangerous, but the games paralleled and anticipated the asymmetry of power that Richard would encounter when dealing with white people.[2]

Elsewhere in the autobiography there are clearcut examples of paradoxical injunctions and other pragmatic paradoxes, and the strategies Wright employs for surviving them. But some of the paradoxes prove not to be susceptible to language games, and in those instances Richard sees how the paradoxes themselves work not only to trap their black victims but also to induce the victims into cooperating with their own victimization. One such paradox arises when Richard turns out to be valedictorian of his class. Richard, who had already written a story, "The Voodoo of Hell's Half-Acre," that had been published in a newspaper, looks forward to writing his valedictorian's speech. But the black principal hands Richard a speech to read, and when Richard balks, insisting on writing and reading his own speech, the principal warns him that he "can't afford to just say *anything* before those white people that night" (p. 193). Richard keeps insisting that he should be able to write his own speech, and the principal finally issues the ultimatum:

"You know, I'm glad I talked to you," he said. "I was seriously thinking of placing you in the school system, teaching. But now, I don't think that you'll fit."

He was tempting me, baiting me; this was the technique that snared black young minds into supporting the southern way of life. [p. 194]

Richard realizes that this black principal is just as trapped in the system as he is. "I had been talking to a 'bought man'," muses Richard on the way home, "and he had tried to 'buy' me. I felt that I had been dealing with something unclean" (p. 195). His friend Griggs advises him to go along with the principal, and his uncle Tom reads both speeches and advises Richard to read the principal's—"the better speech." "The principal's speech was simpler and clearer than mine," observes Richard as his uncle departs, "but it did not say anything; mine was cloudy, but it said what I wanted to say" (p. 196). Richard does deliver his own speech and walks away from that world: "The hell with it! With almost seventeen years of baffled living behind me, I faced the world in 1925" (p. 197).

In this episode Richard faces a paradoxical injunction: speak! but don't speak your own words. Your own words are too dangerous. As the culmination of childhood socialization that aimed at teaching Richard the power of words (in the word games with his peers, in the standoff language game with his father), Richard faces a warning that words are dangerous, at least in the presence of white people. Speak, but say nothing. Silence yourself. It made Richard feel "unclean."

A second paradoxical injunction Richard perceives in the South is the prohibition against dishonesty. As opposed to the previous injunction to speak but to say nothing, this injunction asks the black boy to speak, but always speak truthfully. Searching for a job while in school, Richard is interviewed by a "dour white woman" who needs "an honest boy" to do chores around the house.

"Now, boy, I want to ask you one question and I want you to tell me the truth," she said.

"Yes, ma'am," I said, all attention.

"Do you steal?" she asked me seriously.

I burst into a laugh, then checked myself.

"What's so damn funny about that?" she asked.

"Lady, if I was a thief, I'd never tell anybody."

I had made a mistake during my first five minutes in the white world. I hung my head,

"No, ma'am," I mumbled. "I don't steal."

She stared at me, trying to make up her mind.

"Now, look, we don't want a sassy nigger around here," she said.

"No, ma'am," I assured her. "I'm not sassy." [pp. 160-161]

Later, after graduation, Richard works in a hotel as part of his effort to earn enough money to flee the South and become a writer. All around him in the hotel, "Negroes were stealing" (p. 218) and urging him to do the same. Richard observes that the white employers seemed not at all threatened by the theft. "But I," he realizes, "who stole nothing, who wanted to look them straight in the face, who wanted to talk and act like a man, inspired fear in them. The southern whites would rather have had Negroes who stole, work for them than Negroes who knew, however dimly, the worth of their own humanity. Hence, whites placed a premium upon black deceit. . . . " (p. 219). The paradoxical injunction was as clear as could be. Be honest, but don't speak the truth. Be honest, even though your stealing helps confirm your nature.

A third, even more complex example of the paradoxical injunction that becomes a double bind is the fistfight Richard is induced to enter with another black boy, Harrison. Both work for the same optical company and one day Richard's young white foreman, Mr. Olin, sidles up beside Richard for some unexpected conversation: "'Say, Richard, do you believe that I'm your friend?' he asked me. The question was so loaded with danger that I could not reply at once" (p. 256). Richard cautiously acknowledges that he'd like to think Mr. Olin is his friend, and Olin then warns Richard to be careful of "that nigger Harrison," telling him that Harrison is waiting for Richard with a knife. Olin warns Richard not to talk with Harrison, but at lunchtime Richard seeks out Harrison, and the two warily discover that Olin has told each of them the same story. And has given each of them a knife for "protection." The two agree that they have no grudge against one another and that they'll not tell the white foreman they know the truth.

But the white provocation continues for a week until Olin proposes a boxing match to settle the alleged grudge between Richard and Harrison. At first both resist, but on the promise of five dollars Harrison begins to urge Richard to box with him. Each begins to suspect the motives of the other. Harrison thinks they should do it, just for the money.

> "Look, let's fool them white men," Harrison said. "We won't hurt each other. We'll just pretend, see? We'll show 'em we ain't dumb as they think, see?"
>
> "I don't know."
>
> "It's just exercise. Four rounds for five dollars. You scared?"
>
> "No."
>
> "Then come on and fight."
>
> "All right," I said. "It's just exercise. I'll fight." [p. 264]

Of course, the fight turns out to be more than just exercise. "We squared off," recalls Wright, "and at once I knew that I had not thought sufficiently about what I had bargained for. I could not pretend to fight" (p. 265). The feigned punches soon become real enough. Richard fights hard, condensing his shame and his hate into each blow. Finally, the white men pull apart the two young men. "I clutched my five dollars in my fist and walked home," Wright admits. "Harrison and I avoided each other after that and we rarely spoke. . . . I felt that I had done something unclean, something for which I could never properly atone" (p. 266).

By far the most striking example of a double bind in the autobiography is also the one that shows most clearly how folklore ultimately fails Wright.[3] Richard finds work in an optical factory where he is befriended by a white man who wants to teach him that trade. But his fellow white workers, Misters Reynolds and Pease, do not like the idea. At first they simply harass Richard, warning him that he ought not try to act white and saying things like "If I was a nigger, I'd kill myself" (p. 207). But soon Richard faces a genuine double bind. Pease asks Richard if, as Reynolds said, Richard had called him "Pease," meaning that he had failed to call him "Mr. Pease," as a black person ought. While Richard is grasping the question, Reynolds warns him to tell the truth because Reynolds had heard him:

> If I had said: No sir, Mr. Pease, I never called you *Pease,* I would by inference have been calling Reynolds a liar, and if I had said: Yes, sir, Mr. Pease, I called you *Pease,* I would have been pleading guilty to the worst insult that a Negro can offer to a southern white man. I stood trying to think of a neutral course that would resolve this quickly risen nightmare, but my tongue would not move. [p. 209]

Later, when the white shop owner, Mr. Crane, tries to help Richard and asks what went on between him, Pease, and Reynolds, Richard is once more speechless:

> An impulse to speak rose in me and died with the realization that I was facing a wall that I would never breech. I tried to speak several times and could make no sounds. I grew tense and tears burnt my cheeks. [p. 211]

Richard solves this double bind by escaping—that is, by quitting his job. So in this quintessential example of a pragmatic paradox, Richard is unable to summon artistic—that is, folkloric—resources to help him resolve the situation.

The episode warrants closer scrutiny. Actually a version of a formula found in African-American verbal games, the episode helps us to understand how folklore fails some individuals. Gates (1988) puts the folklore figure of "the Signifying Monkey" and the language games of "Signifyin(g)" at the center of his understanding of African-American literature.[4] While acknowledging that folklorists (e.g., Abrahams 1970; Dundes 1973) have long recognized "the Signifying Monkey" as a key black rhetorical trope, Gates gently chides previous critics for interpreting the monkey tales "against the binary opposition between black and white in American society" and for ignoring "the *trinary* forces of the Monkey, the Lion, and the Elephant" (1988:55). "In the narrative poems," explains Gates,

> the Signifying Monkey invariably repeats to his friend, the Lion, some insult purportedly generated by their mutual friend, the Elephant. The Monkey, however, speaks figuratively. The Lion, indignant and outraged, demands an apology of the Elephant, who refuses and then trounces the Lion. The Lion, realizing that his mistake was to take the Monkey literally, returns to trounce the Monkey. It is this relationship between the literal and the figurative, and the dire consequences of their confusion, which is the most striking repeated element of these tales. The Monkey's trick depends on the Lion's inability to mediate between those two poles of signification, of meaning. [1988:55]

The language game in these poems, therefore, relies on the relationships between the three stock characters. The Monkey is the trickster figure and a "rhetorical genius." Unable to match the Lion's physical power, the Monkey bests the Lion by "lyin(g)," that is, by telling a tale with figurative discourse (1988:56).

Wright presents a perversely transformed version of this Signifyin(g) triangle in both the episode between himself, Pease, and Reynolds and the earlier episode of his arranged fight with Harrison. In these versions the white men have turned this African-American language game back on Wright. They have the power to assign roles in the triangle. Pease and Reynolds are the Lion and the Monkey, respectively, casting Richard in the role of the Elephant.[5] But Richard, of course, has none of the real power of the Elephant. Richard cannot stomp Pease to Reynolds's delight. Richard is the victim of a rhetorical device traditionally used by African-Americans to assert power by setting rivals against one another. He is rendered speechless by this episode, a condition uncharacteristic of him when he is among his adolescent peers. Richard may be familiar with the game, but not as the victim.

What are we to make of this reversal? It is unlikely that Wright unconsciously created this strangely transformed version of a traditional African-American oral formula. He was plenty familiar with this rhetorical strategy and, as Gates shows, used Signifyin(g) in several of his stories, including *Lawd Today* and "Big Boy Leaves Home" (1988:96-97, 99-100). Why did Richard Wright, the artist, choose to take an African-American rhetorical formula and transform it thus?

Wright, I believe, is recording here the failure of folklore. Richard's speechlessness in the face of this circumstance stands in stark contrast to the empowering speech

elsewhere in the autobiography. Whereas language games work *within* a folk community and learning the language games may be an important element in the socialization of members of the community, *those same language games may fail in the intercultural encounter*. Gates (1988:77) acknowledges this as Roger Abrahams's (1976:19) point that "intergroup" Signifyin(g) generally fails except as the Signifyin(g) is used by the African-Americans as a form of "masking behavior." But this is Gates's only mention of the extreme difficulty of Signifyin(g) in the intercultural encounter.

Wright's episodes in the optical shop clarify the difference between the double bind and language games, and the difference lies in the power relations between the participants. Bateson (1972) recognized that the double bind is no mere language game. It resembles language games in that both rely on the difference between messages and metamessages, but the double bind is possible only when there is a real asymmetry of power between the participants. The paradox of the double bind can lead in the direction of either creativity or madness, with a thin line separating the two.

Richard's language game worked on his father in the kitten episode. Although Richard was in the inferior power position in that encounter, he was able to resist his father's authority by taking a figurative message literally. But things could have turned out otherwise. Richard could have received a beating from his father for killing the kitten; indeed, he did get a beating from his mother. And certainly one cannot imagine the language game working on a white schoolteacher or employer, for in those situations the double bind is a structural, institutional reality for African-Americans.

True, Richard and Harrison first tried to handle the double bind by stepping outside the frame provided by the white men. Richard and Harrison negotiated an alternative frame for the events and communications they were receiving from the white foreman; in Bateson's terms, they metacommunicated about the frame. They planned a false performance, playing at the white man's frame while preserving their own understanding of the situation. But their plan was undone by three things. First, as Wright says, he knew too little about such things to create a persuasive performance. More important, Richard and Harrison harbored the mutual suspicion that Richard found elsewhere in relations between black people in the South. Creating and sustaining an interpretive frame for an event as delicate and tentative as a play fight requires a strong metarelationship of trust between the participants, and it is this trust that the segregationist system destroys. Third, the planned-for play fight is undone by the real power advantage the white men held in the contest between interpretive frames. They were there to see two "niggers" fight, and it is doubtful that any performance short of "the real thing" would have satisfied them. The result for Richard, again, is shame, an unclean feeling, and speechlessness.

Striking in all these examples of paradoxical injunctions and full double binds in *Black Boy* is the central role of *speech* and *speechlessness* as tropes governing the episode. Wright learned early the power of words and the dangers lurking in that power. In each case, however, all of his training in language games proved useless in dealing with the language games played on him. "Why could I not learn to keep my mouth shut at the right time?" Wright asks himself at the conclusion of one more unsuccessful attempt to work for a white boss:

> I had said just one short sentence too many. My words were innocent enough, but they indicated, it seemed, a consciousness on my part that infuriated white people. . . .
>
> I knew what was wrong with me, but I could not correct it. The words and actions of white people were baffling signs to me. . . .
>
> I had begun coping with the white world too late. I could never make subservience an automatic part of my behavior. . . . While standing before a white man I had to figure out how to perform each act and how to say each word. I could not help it. I could not grin. In the past I had always said too much, now I found it was difficult to say anything at all. I could not react as the world in which I lived expected me to; that world was too baffling, too uncertain. [p. 215]

The Jim Crow South posed a fundamental double bind: either Richard could continue to resist the white's definition of him and likely suffer a physical death, or he could accept that definition and suffer, as Orlando Patterson puts it, the "social death" of the slave, the living death of the nonperson (JanMohamed 1987:248). Of the options available to the potential victim of the double bind, from madness through humor, Wright chooses escape.

Wright's ultimate act in *Black Boy* is to turn his back on orality and to flee to the written word, to literature. Using a forged note to check books out of the library, Richard finds in the essays of Mencken and in the realist novels of Dreiser and Lewis and other writers a way of "fighting with words" (p. 272), but with written words. He resolves to flee north and become a writer. "It had been only through books," he realizes, "that I had managed to keep myself alive in a negatively vital way. Whenever my environment had failed to support or nourish me, I had clutched at books . . . " (p. 282). For Wright, as for other African-Americans, learning to read and learning to write were political acts (Gates 1987:4). Through writing, Wright again took the power of words, a power he more often felt as victim in the oral realm.

Readers and critics naturally wonder why Richard Wright, as depicted in *Black Boy*, was unable to muster the resources of folklore to help him resist the double-bind situations that ensnared him. Doubtless there are biographical facts that contributed to the failure of folklore for him at crucial times. For one thing, Wright's socialization in the African-American community was sporadic and disjointed. Mary Helen Washington (1979) observes in her introduction to an anthology of the writings of Zora Neale Hurston that Zora grew up in the unusually sheltered environment of Eatonville, Florida, without experiencing racial prejudice. Wright, on the other hand, grew up observing the routine brutality of racial oppression. Most biographies emphasize the "childhood trauma" that must have set the tone for the realism, violence, and brutality of Wright's adult fiction (Walker 1988:247). His father's violence, then desertion; the strict religious expectations of his grandmother and aunt; his mother's suffering and death; the Jim Crow violence visited upon family members and acquaintances—all these doubtless had their effects on Wright.

But I believe there is a simpler, better view of why folklore failed Wright. Put simply, his mother actively discouraged conversations of the sort black children must learn in order to acquire Signifyin(g) as a skill for living (Gates 1988:84). Her approach to child rearing and her advice could be called pragmatic, literal. It was his mother who beat Richard for killing the kitten; it was his mother who insisted he fight the gang of boys that waylaid him for his money on the way to the market to buy groceries (pp. 23-25); it was his mother who called him "foolish" for being unwilling to sell his dog to a white girl for a dollar to buy food. (When the dog was crushed a week later under the wheels of a coal wagon, his mother said coldly: "You could have had a dollar. But you can't eat a dead dog, can you?" [p. 81].) And it was his mother who responded angrily and slapped him when, on a train ride that was his first experience with the segregation dictated by Jim Crow laws, he questioned her about the race of his grandmother (who had very light skin) and his father:

> "Then what am I?"
>
> "They'll call you a colored man when you grow up," she said. Then she turned to me and smiled mockingly and asked: "Do you mind, Mr. Wright?"
>
> I was angry and I did not answer. I did not object to being called colored, but I knew that there was something my mother was holding back. She was not concealing facts, but feelings, attitudes, convictions which she did not want me to know; and she became angry when I prodded her. [pp. 57-58]

In Bateson's (1972) terms, Wright's mother was unwilling to communicate with Richard about communication. She entertained no language games. Nor did she entertain the sort of "indirection" in communication that another autobiographer, Maya Angelou, learned from her Momma, the grandmother who raised her (1969:164-165). The child deprived of language games is deprived of metacommunication, and that child may never learn to acquire "normal" defenses against the double bind (Bateson et al. 1956:258).

Of course, Wright had his male peer groups for learning, practice, and perfecting Signifyin(g) and other oral language games, and these may have mitigated somewhat the primary socialization in Wright's home. At least Wright recognized a language game when he heard it. Still, we ought to trust Wright's testimony that he was not like others, that he could not behave as other blacks and as whites wanted him to behave. His reaction to having the tables turned on him in double binds was not that of the adept player who sees he has been outmaneuvered; rather, he reacted consistently with shock and silence. African-American folklore was available to him for motifs and stylistic elements in his later writing, but they were not available to him in his everyday, oral repertoire, as they ought to have been. African-American writers who rely heavily on folklore tend to emphasize community; perhaps Wright's sense of alienation meant he could never find in African-American folklore more than perfunctory material (McClusky 1983:343). Certainly in *Black Boy* there is no sense of African-American folklore as a resource for living.

Blaming the failure of folklore in *Black Boy* upon the eccentricities of Richard Wright's life, however, may mean missing a more general point for folklorists and other culture critics to ponder. Perhaps the source of the failure lies more in the dynamics of folklore in the intercultural encounter. The example of *Black Boy* invites us to consider the following possibilities.

First, we notice in the book that folklore fails an *individual.* We tend to focus our folklore inquiry so much on the group that we often lose the individual in our analysis. Intracultural variation ought to temper our generalizations in any case, but we ought to allow for the individual who is simply not served well by the group's folk culture.

Second, we notice in *Black Boy* that folklore succeeds and works as we expect it should within the folk community, but that it *fails in the intercultural encounter.* Abrahams (1981) is one of the few folklorists who have paid attention to what happens to folklore in the intercultural encounter. (It is Abrahams [1976], recall, who observes that Signifyin(g) across cultural borders is extremely difficult.) Abrahams draws our attention to "display events" at the borders where cultures meet, those planned-for occasions when "private antipathies explode into open antagonism and threaten to become public events" (1981:303). The folklorist's work at this border is politically "'engaged,' because it brings to the fore the antagonisms and inequities of everyday life as perceived by the performance community and as played out within the larger society" (1981:305).

Abrahams is exactly right in observing that to "analyze lore in terms of how the group projects and plays upon its own image, in relation to stereotypes of other groups within a complex society and a pluralistic cultural situation, is to alter significantly the very study of folklore" (1981:305). But Abrahams over-emphasizes successful

versions of such encounters. "If one wishes to find a successful model for cultural pluralism in operation," he writes, "let him or her look to these fairs and festivals—as the folk have for millennia" (1981:304). Fair enough; but what does the folklorist find in looking at a race riot, a "display event" not far removed (analytically) from the fair and festival? And Abrahams's analysis still works at the level of the group as an "ethnosemiotics" of encounters between groups (MacCannell 1979). I would urge, as above, that we not lose the individual in our attention to the "successes" and the "failures" of folklore in the intercultural encounter.

Third, folklore may not be an effective source of resistance against the hegemony enjoyed by the dominant culture. If the double bind is a structural mode of maintaining hegemony, then language games will have no effect on the dominant culture or even in the intercultural encounter with other marginalized groups. "Masking" may be a form of resistance, but it is a form unlikely to change the situation. Folklore, in short, may be a force for *pacification* rather than *resistance,* a prospect that should not come as good news to those inclined to romanticize the folklore of underclasses.[6]

This is an open question, one not often addressed by folklorists but deserving their immediate attention.[7] Abrahams sees display events as ultimately subversive, as having "maintained a counter-culture of far more revolutionary potential than the radical tactics that brought life to a halt and the authorities to their knees in the sixties" (1981:319). And Abdul JanMohamed (1987:247) may be right in arguing that the key moment in resisting hegemony comes when one asserts control over one's own subjectivity, as Richard Wright did. Still, the role of folklore in the collective and individual resistance against cultural hegemony needs further clarification.

An autobiography is not an ethnographic monograph, but *Black Boy* tells more than just "emotionally true" stories about Richard Wright's youth. Folklorists and other culture critics can read his vignettes as rich, "thick descriptions" of the dynamics of the interactions between the individual, the folk group, and "cultural others." In reading the book, as in living a life, perhaps there is more to be learned from the mistakes and failures of folklore than from the successes that we take so much for granted.

NOTES

This is a revised, expanded version of a paper read at the annual meeting of the American Folklore Society, 26-30 October 1988, in Boston.

[1] The original manuscript of Wright's autobiography was entitled *American Hunger.* Upon the advice of editors, his agent, and some friends, Wright divided the manuscript into two separate volumes and published the first, *Black Boy,* in 1945. The second half

of the manuscript was published as *American Hunger* in 1977. Thaddeus (1985) recounts the publishing history of the manuscript.

[2] Feintuch (1987) explores a similar situation in which a hegemonic, totalitarian regime creates a dangerous setting for language games, such as jokes.

[3] As JanMohamed (1987:256) notes, Fabre (1973) fails to mention this episode. "However," writes JanMohamed, "whether or not the occurrence is factually verifiable, it does seem to possess what Wright would call an 'emotional truth'." While JanMohamed recognizes that the episode presents Wright with a classic double bind, he fails to pursue the larger implications of the episode. Walker (1988:37) mentions the episode but without analysis, and Leibowitz (1985, 1989) mentions it not at all.

[4] Gates renders the gerund "signifying" as "Signifyin(g)" to remind himself and readers that the term refers to a vernacular speech form. Moreover, the "bracketed or aurally erased *g,* like the discourse of black English and dialect poetry generally, stands as the trace of black difference in a remarkably sophisticated and fascinating (re)naming ritual graphically in evidence here. Perhaps replacing with a visual sign the *g* erased in the black vernacular shall, like Derrida's neologism, serve both to avoid confusion and the reduction of these two distinct sets of homonyms to a false identity and to stand as the sign of a (black) Signifyin(g) difference itself. The absent *g* is a figure for the Signifyin(g) black difference" (Gates 1988:46).

[5] As an aside here we should note that there is a long tradition in white American folklore of using the elephant as a trope for African-Americans. See Abrahams and Dundes (1969) and Mechling (1987).

[6] This point touches on current "resistance theory" in the study of schooling. See, for example, the excellent discussions by Willis (1977) and Giroux (1983).

[7] This question comes up most often in studies of the folklore of workers in organizations, where minor instances of "folk resistance" actually may pacify dissatisfied and alienated employees. We might say the same of the folklore of college students.

References Cited

Abrahams, Roger D. 1970. *Deep Down in the Jungle: Negro Narrative Folklore from the Streets of Philadelphia.* Chicago: Aldine Publishing.

————. 1976. *Talking Black.* Rowley, Mass.: Newbury House.

————. 1981. Shouting Match at the Border: The Folklore of Display Events. In *"And Other Neighborly Names": Social Process and Cultural Image in Texas Folklore,* eds. Richard Bauman and Roger D. Abrahams, pp. 303-321. Austin: University of Texas Press.

————, and Alan Dundes. 1969. On Elephantasy and Elephanticide. *Psychoanalytic Quarterly* 56:225-241.

Angelou, Maya. 1969. *I Know Why the Caged Bird Sings.* New York: Bantam.

Armstrong, Robert Plant. 1981. *The Powers of Presence: Consciousness, Myth, and Affecting Presence.* Philadelphia: University of Pennsylvania Press.

Baker, Houston A., Jr. 1984. *Blues, Ideology, and Afro-American Literature: A Vernacular Theory.* Chicago: University of Chicago Press.

Bateson, Gregory. 1972. *Steps to an Ecology of Mind.* New York: Ballantine.

————, D. D. Jackson, J. Haley, and J. Weakland. 1956. Toward a Theory of Schizophrenia. *Behavioral Science* 1:251-264.

Clifford, James, and George E. Marcus, eds. 1986. *Writing Culture: The Poetics and Politics of Ethnography.* Berkeley: University of California Press.

Dorson, Richard M. 1957. The Identification of Folklore in American Literature. *Journal of American Folklore* 70:1-8.

Dundes, Alan. 1965. The Study of Folklore in Literature and Culture: Identification and Interpretation. *Journal of American Folklore* 78:136-142.

————, ed. 1973. *Mother Wit from the Laughing Barrel: Readings in the Interpretation of Afro-American Folklore.* Englewood Cliffs, N.J.: Prentice-Hall.

Ellison, Ralph. 1964 [1945]. *Shadow and Act.* New York: Signet/New American Library.

Fabre, Michel. 1973. *The Unfinished Quest of Richard Wright.* New York: William Morrow.

Feintuch, Burt. 1987. The Joke, Folk Culture, and Milan Kundera's *The Joke. Western Folklore* 46:21-35.

Gates, Henry Louis, Jr. 1987. *Figures in Black: Words, Signs, and the "Racial" Self.* New York: Oxford University Press.

————. 1988. *The Signifying Monkey: A Theory of African-American Literary Criticism.* New York: Oxford University Press.

Giroux, Henry A. 1983. *Theory and Resistance in Education: A Pedagogy for the Opposition.* South Hadley, Mass.: Bergin & Garvey.

Hakutani, Yoshinobu. 1985. Creation of the Self in Richard Wright's *Black Boy. Black American Literature Forum* 19:70-75.

Henderson, Stephen. 1973. *Understanding the New Black Poetry, Black Speech and Black Music as Poetic References.* New York: William Morrow.

Hodges, John O. 1985. An Apprenticeship to Life and Art: Narrative Design in Wright's *Black Boy. College Literature Association Journal* 25:415-433.

Jameson, Frederic. 1984. Postmodernism, or the Cultural Logic of Late Capitalism. *New Left Review* No. 146:53-92.

JanMohamed, Abdul R. 1987. Negating the Negation as a Form of Affirmation in Minority Discourse: The Construction of Richard Wright as Subject. *Cultural Critique* No. 7:245-267.

Kristeva, Julia. 1980. *Desire in Language: A Semiotic Approach to Literature and Art.* New York: Columbia University Press.

Leibowitz, Herbert. 1985. Richard Wright's *Black Boy*: Styles of Deprivation. *Southwest Review* 70:71-94.

————. 1989. *Fabricating Lives: Explorations in American Autobiography.* New York: Knopf.

MacCannell, Dean. 1979. Ethnosemantics. *Semiotica* 27-1/3:149-171.

McClusky, John, Jr. 1983. Two Steppin': Richard Wright's Encounter with Blue-Jazz. *American Literature* 55:332-344.

Mechling, Jay. 1987. Alligator. In *American Wildlife in Symbol and Story,* eds. Angus K. Gillespie and Jay Mechling, pp. 73-98. Knoxville: University of Tennessee Press.

————. 1988. Play and Madness in Joseph Heller's *Catch-22. Play & Culture* 1:226-238.

Miller, Eugene E. 1982. Richard Wright and Gertrude Stein. *Black American Literature Forum* 16:107-112.

————. 1983. Folkloric Aspects of Wright's "The Man Who Killed a Shadow." *College Literature Association Journal* 27:210-223.

Ong, Walter J. 1982. *Orality and Literacy: The Technologizing of the Word.* London: Routledge.

Reichenbach, Hans. 1947. *Elements of Symbolic Logic.* New York: Macmillan.

Stein, Gertrude. 1985 [1909]. *Three Lives.* New York: New American Library.

Stepto, Robert B. 1977. I Thought I Knew These People: Richard Wright and the Afro-American Literary Tradition. *Massachusetts Review* 18:525-541.

Thaddeus, Janice. 1985. The Metamorphosis of Richard Wright's *Black Boy. American Literature* 57:199-214.

Thompson, Robert Farris. 1983. *Flash of the Spirit: African and Afro-American Art and Philosophy.* New York: Vintage/Random House.

Walker, Margaret. 1988. *Richard Wright: Daemonic Genius.* New York: Warner Books.

Washington, Mary Helen. 1979. Zora Neale Hurston: A Woman Half in Shadow. In *I Love Myself When I am Laughing . . . ,* ed. Alice Walker, pp. 7-25. New York: Feminist Press at the City University of New York.

Watzlawick, P., J. H. Beavin, and D. D. Jackson. 1967. *Pragmatics of Human Communication.* New York: W. W. Norton.

White, Hayden. 1978. *Tropics of Discourse.* Baltimore: Johns Hopkins University Press.

Willis, Paul. 1977. *Learning to Labor: How Working Class Kids Get Working Class Jobs.* New York: Columbia University Press.

Wright, Richard. 1966 [1945]. *Black Boy.* New York: Harper & Row.

————. 1977. *American Hunger.* New York: Harper & Row.

FOLKLORE AND THE AMERICAN WEST

Michael Cleary

SOURCE: "Finding the Center of the Earth: Satire, History, and Myth in 'Little Big Man'," in *Western American Literature,* Vol. XV, No. 3, Fall, 1980, pp. 195-211.

[*In the following essay, Cleary identifies Thomas Berger's* Little Big Man *as a parody not only of Old West mythology, but of other myths as well.*]

It is a Western to end all Westerns, with all the Western's clichés neatly reversed into something quite new.[1]

It is, of course, a satire on Westerns, told with high humor.[2]

Berger has in some manner put together a variety of techniques and infused them with a spirit so that . . . it is a functional and successful piece of literature. It is one of the best of American Western novels.[3]

If Buster Keaton had been a novelist, he might have written *Little Big Man*.[4]

This sampling of reactions to Thomas Berger's *Little Big Man* indicates the variety of opinions regarding the nature and success of the novel. The one area of agreement is that it has a satiric core; beyond that, criticism splinters off into theories which espouse romantic, mythic, tragic, parodic, historic, and absurdist interpretations. Such a range of responses implies a literary depth which is verified by close examination. While admitting the plausibility of the various interpretations, I will focus upon the satiric dimensions of the novel, examining Berger's parody of Western conventions, and then discussing its non-Western satire. It is this latter area which carries *Little Big Man* beyond the level of mere parody. On one level it is a condemnation of the weaknesses of human nature; on another level, it is a serious indictment of American institutions, culture, values, and even history itself.

One of the subjects of debate for readers of *Little Big Man* is the novel's interweaving of myth and history. These two elements are apparent in the titles of two essays which discuss the novel in detail: Leo E. Oliva's "Thomas Berger's *Little Big Man* as History" and Delbert E. Wylder's "Thomas Berger's *Little Big Man* as Literature." These essays and others draw attention to two facts: first, that the novel is historically accurate, Berger having researched sixty or seventy western historical accounts before starting his book;[5] second, that the coincidences and exaggerations of the picaresque structure distract from the historical reality presented. Brian W. Dippie describes Berger's unique coordination of the opposing elements of western fiction:

> In *Little Big Man,* Berger is faithful to both the West of history and the West of myth. Each contributes in its own way to the aura of plausibility that so enriches the basic tale. . . . The surface accuracy, the correctness of detail, the verisimilitude that he conveys derive from a book-learned, factual knowledge. But *Little Big Man* rests upon a foundation of myth.[6]

The opposing values of history and myth are bound together by Berger's humorous narrative, which has fun with our historical and mythical expectations without denying the validity of either. As Jack Crabb, the one hundred and eleven year-old narrator explains, "I'm telling the truth here, and the truth is always made up of little particulars which sound ridiculous when repeated."[7] Crabb's narrative follows the picaresque format which is the key to understanding its satiric content. As L. L. Lee has noted, "the picaresque, with its wide range of action and of society, is another way of making a microcosm."[8] Berger has chosen his narrative

structure well, for it is sufficiently broad and stylized to accommodate both Western and non-Western themes. Crabb's alternating experiences with white and Indian cultures allow him the perspective to satirize both, and in so doing, to satirize all of mankind. *Little Big Man* thus does more than lampoon the Western formula and myth: it finds fault with mankind itself.

Berger makes good use of the picaresque mode of episodic scenes and a succession of minor characters. Jack Crabb is an excellent model of the picaresque hero defined by Matthew Hodgart: the perennial outsider who "can find no regular occupation or fixed place in a stratified society. He is forced to . . . keep moving both horizontally in the novel and vertically in society."[9] It is hard to imagine a picaro who better satisfies Hodgart's definition. In the twenty-six years covered by the novel, Crabb is buffeted between the Indian and white societies. In the course of the narrative, Crabb assumes a number of familiar Western roles—adopted Indian, muleskinner, prospector, gunfighter, army scout, con man, entrepreneur, buffalo hunter, gambler, and even town drunk. He finds no permanent role in either world. His adventures share the varied nature of the picaresque, and the constant juxtaposition of the customs and values of both societies helps to achieve the tension which is necessary to satire.

Jack Crabb is no romantic Western hero along the lines of the prototype described by Kent Ladd Steckmesser—genteel, possessed of great physical courage, and worthy of epic consideration through comparison to classical heroes.[10] Crabb is only 5'4" and slight; he confesses that "I ain't big, but I'm shrewd" (p. 64). He is well aware of his physical limitations, creating an imposing figure through his choice of apparel: he wears two inch built-up boots and a Mexican sombrero which adds another six inches; he says that in outline he is six feet tall, but most of that is air (pp. 167-68).

Crabb makes up for his meager build by cultivating his cunning beyond the modest level of Western characters such as the Virginian; Crabb's cunning is far more sly and frequently immoral. In the course of his adventures he lies, steals, bluffs, and begs, as these means suit his needs of the moment. At one point he even out-cons a con man, and develops a ring trick to help him cheat consistently at cards. These devious methods occur while in the white society, but such devices are employed against his Indian companions as well. One incident shows the attempts of Cheyenne boys to outdo one another in bravery by piercing their skin with pointed sticks and tearing off the flesh. Jack admits that he never could get very interested in hurting himself, so he devises an illusory feat of even greater stoic proportions. Breaking an arrow in half, he holds the feathered end against his stomach and clenches the protruding arrowhead end between his buttocks. Apparently skewered, he cleverly gains a reputation for bravery and suffering without undergoing the uncomfortable consequences (p. 65).

The preceding scene prompts Crabb's remark that "Indians did not go around expecting to be swindled, whereas they was always ready for a miracle" (p. 66). This observation suggests one of the remarkable traits of Berger's uncommon Western hero—a garrulous nature which delights in offering humorous insights on any variety of subjects. This loquaciousness is at odds with the Western convention noted by John G. Cawelti: the taciturn hero who lets his actions speak for him.[11] Besides spoofing the stereotype, Berger uses Crabb's verbal wit to produce some wonderful aphorisms. The narrative voice of *Little Big Man* is a source of much of the book's humor and has reminded at least one critic of Twain's style, particularly in *Huckleberry Finn*.[12] The comparison is not farfetched; both writers share a delightful comic diction based upon wry understatement. Because even a casual perusal of the novel will exhibit its verbal wit, only a few samples will be given here, constituting what Delbert E. Wylder has described as epigrammatic satire.[13]

> [On sincere curiosity in others:] It is a rare person in the white world who wants to hear what the other fellow says, all the more so when the other fellow really knows what he is talking about. (p. 117)

> [On morality:] If you want to really relax sometime, just fall to rock bottom and you'll be a happy man. Most all troubles come from having standards. (p. 164)

> [On self-preservation:] I might go on for hours relating the incidents of war, but whereas they are every one different in the actual occurrence and never dull when your own life is at stake, they have a sameness in the telling. (p. 101)

The cynical humor of such aphorisms tells us much about the character of Jack Crabb, the sole survivor of the Battle of Little Bighorn. The last example of self-preservation points out a very important characteristic of this atypical Western hero: his main interest is in survival, not advocating a moral position. For Crabb, as Kerry Ahearn has observed, life is not a matter of moral choices, but expediency.[14] Martin Nussbaum points out that the Western hero has long been the arbiter of moral law, even if it opposes judicial law.[15] Jack Crabb suffers no such burden. Granville Hicks has noted that Crabb is really just a fairly ordinary fellow who is placed in extraordinary circumstances and is bright enough and brave enough and lucky enough to survive them.[16] The key word here is "survive," for that is always foremost in Crabb's mind, more important than weighty moral considerations such as those pondered by Shane and other formula heroes. This characteristic is evidenced when, after years of living with and growing to like the Cheyenne, Crabb immediately throws down his weapon during a cavalry charge and turns himself over to the Indians' enemy. And on the eve of Custer's Last Stand, Crabb does give thought to his rightful allegiance, but even such commendable contemplation soon gives way to his concern for his own self-interest: "Well, I have

spoke about my worries for the Indians and then my disinclination to see these soldiers massacred, but I have so far not mentioned my growing concern for my own arse" (p. 387).

In addition to his generous parody of the formula hero in the fictitious Crabb, Berger lampoons a number of historical figures as well. The debunking in *Little Big Man* is aimed at two separate targets: Western figures and literary figures. Berger's treatment is not totally farcical, however, and often his version of historical figures suggests the realm of probability; his creations of Western legends seem every bit as believable as the popular ones. A case in point is Berger's characterization of Wyatt Earp. Following a day of buffalo hunting, Crabb and his companions share the company of other hunters. One of the strangers is Earp, who suddenly confronts Crabb, demanding to know why Jack spoke Earp's name. Jack explains that he hadn't even known Earp's name, all he had done was belch. Kit Carson is bandy-legged and foul-mouthed, capable of unprovoked violence. Calamity Jane is even more foulmouthed, as well as being "the ugliest woman in the world. . . . She had a face like a potato and was built sort of dumpy." Crabb's first glimpse of Calamity Jane is during her resounding victory in a fistfight with Crabb's sister, Caroline (p. 161).

Wild Bill Hickok is an important minor character in the novel. A wary friend of Crabb's, Hickok is reputed to have killed all six members of the McCanles gang in a glorious showdown. Upon hearing this, Crabb reflects on the probability of such an event, and his thoughts tell us much about the mythification of the gunfight in popular fiction and films:

> I immediately reduced that by half in my mind, for I had been on the frontier from the age of ten on and knew a thing or two as to how fights are conducted. When you run into a story of more than three against one and one winning, then you have heard a lie. I found out later I was right in this case: Wild Bill killed only McCanles and two of his partners, and all from ambush. (p. 293)

Hickok is a fanatic on the operation of guns; his conversations revolve around holster types, cartridge loads, barrel length, and other technical matters. Crabb tells us that "Hickok was a marvelous observer of anything which pertained to killing" (p. 298). In direct opposition to Western mythology, Hickok deteriorates into an overweight, jowly owner of a sleazy Wild West Show.

General George Armstrong Custer is an even more important minor character. He is shown to be a foolish tactician whose arrogance demoralizes his troops (they call him Hard Ass). Custer directs the massacre of peaceful Indians and over eight hundred horses. In Crabb's version of the Last Stand, Custer is spared the expected scalping and Crabb assumes that this is in deference to his valor, but he is told that it is only because "the long haired darling" was going bald (p. 372).

The second type of debunking in *Little Big Man* is directed at literary figures; in many ways, this suggests the technique found in reactionary Western satires such as H. Allen Smith's *Return of the Virginian* and John Seelye's *The Kid*, where contemporary writers take potshots at preceding Western writers as well as their peers. In addition to the humorous dimension it allows, this device develops another dimension of character. For instance, Custer's comments on James Fenimore Cooper accurately describe the romantic fantasy of the noble savage which *Little Big Man* spoofs. At the same time, it reveals Custer's mental instability—his remarks are addressed to no one and come while he and his men are being overrun at the Little Bighorn.

Characterization is also revealed in Crabb's opinions of literary figures, disclosing both his sense of propriety and naïveté about literature. He describes learning about his sister Caroline's crush on a male nurse during the Civil War, a genuinely cultivated man who writes poetry of burning passion in his spare time. Unfortunately, Caroline learns that the man's passion is for a drummer boy. Crabb's gentlemanly refusal to name this writer of "robustious verse" only draws attention to Walt Whitman and his sexual preferences.[17] While journeying up the Missouri River on a steamship piloted by a Captain Marsh, Crabb recalls that "there used to be quite a body of legend about riverboating . . . and Marsh was part of it, not having been hurt any by being a friend of an author named Mark Twain who wasn't noted for understatement" (p. 359). In another scene, Jack displays his innate courtesy and desire to please Mrs. Pendrake when she reads some of Alexander Pope's poetry. Young Crabb pretends to be impressed by the verse, but inwardly feels that it sounds like the trotting of a horse. He does not really understand the lines, but what he "did savvy seemed right opinionated, like that fellow had the last word on everything" (p. 133).

This kind of spoofing is directed only to stereotypes of the white world; however, through techniques of exaggeration and reversal, *Little Big Man* mocks Indian stereotypes, too. His all too vivid descriptions of such Indian practices as scalping and mutilation may, in fact, be realistic and not exaggerated, but his objective reporting of the thwacking sounds and oozing gore which accompany these acts results in a sense of absurdity which at least appears to be exaggerated. One example of Indian humor is when Younger Bear, a lifelong rival of Crabb's, offers Jack his hand at the end of a battle. Unfortunately, the gesture is literal, for Younger Bear has pulled his own arm up his sleeve and when he walks away laughing, Jack is left holding the severed hand of a soldier. In another scene, the convention of the uncanny Indian trackers is concealed by an apparently realistic treatment which gradually moves from the believable to the exceptional to the improbable to finally, the ludicrous. The scene Crabb describes is a familiar one—an Indian brave squinting across the plains:

> One time when . . . us boys was out hunting prairie chickens, we saw some moving objects a couple of miles off that I took for buffalo, but Little Horse, with his Indian eyes, said no, they was white men, that one had yellow hair, was armed with a shotgun and rode a bay that was slightly lame in the left forefoot, and the other wore a beard and was mounted on a roan with a saddle sore. Also, they was lost, but he could see that the bay had got the scent of water and shortly they would strike the river and know where they was. (p. 78)

The second technique for parodying Indian stereotypes is reversal, a device that Berger uses to good effect. Readers long accustomed to the inscrutability and quiet menace of the Indian brave are surprised by the initial description of Old Lodge Skins, the Cheyenne chief:

> The fellow in the plug hat was their leader. He wore one of those silver medals that the government give out to principal men at treaty signings; I think his showed the image of President Fillmore. He was older than the others and he carried an ancient musket with a barrel four foot long. (p. 31)

Berger's parody of Indian stereotypes extends beyond the treatment of character traits to include the Indian environment as well. In most cases, the Indian camp suggests a proximity to nature which is lacking in the civilized white world, a view which traces back as far as the *Leatherstocking Tales*. Indians do not intrude upon their environment with permanent dwellings, but live in harmony with it. There has always been something pastoral about the Indian camp in Westerns. Berger discounts our preconceptions, however, through Crabb's revulsion upon seeing his first Indian camp:

> At the first sight of an Indian camp the stoutest heart is likely to quail. . . . You tend to think: well, I see their dump, but where's the town? And the smell alone is very queer, it isn't precisely a stench as white people know one, but a number of stinks melding together into a sort of invisible fog that replaces the air, so that with every breath you draw in all the facts of life concerning mankind and the four-footed animals. Right now it had a principal odor, owing to our pony stalling under us at that very moment. Except in the case of such a particular event nearby, no smells predominated. (p. 50)

Moments later, Crabb discovers that he has not yet suffered the worst. The inside of a teepee is even more unbearable, "like trying to breathe underwater in a swamp" (p. 52).

It is apparent that one of the purposes of *Little Big Man* is to spoof Western conventions which have grown up around both white and Indian societies. However, Berger's novel transcends Western parody alone, encompassing universal human traits. In commenting upon this aspect of the novel, William T. Pilkington says that "while it often depends for its effect on the absurd and the grotesque, it sheds revealing light . . . on the human condition as well."[18] The method that Berger uses to satirize mankind's limitations is to locate the same weakness in both white and Indian societies, thus testifying to its human, not cultural origin.

Perhaps the overriding human weakness attacked in *Little Big Man* is the propensity for violence in both societies. The Indians happily mutilate the bodies of their victims; the whites conduct a dispassionate extermination of an entire race. For the Indians, fighting is an integral part of life; for the whites, it is an expedient solution. This basic difference in the two cultures is complicated by the fact that neither side has any conception of the enemy's motives, nor do they really care to learn. This results in an absurd cycle of violence which is never directed at the guilty party. Crabb explains that the circle of violence commences when some well-meaning but confused Indians come into a fort to apologize for the murderous actions of other Indians. The soldiers proceed to punish those who apologized, never the ones who committed the outrage. The Indians retaliate by revenging themselves on white people who have no connection with the soldiers; and so on. Because neither side is really interested in stopping the cycle, *Little Big Man* is, as Ahearn put it, a testimony to the essential unity in violence of all men.[19] This unity is brutally evident in the parallel massacres at the close of the novel. At the Washita, Custer's troops annihilate an unsuspecting tribe; the situation is then reversed at Little Bighorn.

Man's propensity for violence discloses another universal flaw, one which sometimes accounts for violent acts—both Indians and whites display the commonly tragic flaw of pride. In battle, the Indians' pride is evidenced by the practice of taking scalps and counting coup; one counts coup by engaging with the enemy, but only touching him with a harmless object instead of killing him. This takes great courage and gains considerable glory for the successful brave. Custer shows a different kind of pride in the white man's approach to the violence of war. Custer's mad monologue on the Little Bighorn is in part due to his incredulity that others, especially Indians, could be capable of courage in the high degree. Even as he is being destroyed, Custer praises his ability to compute disparate information coolly and effectively. The dramatic irony of the scene is emphasized by the knowledge that Berger has taken the obnoxious remarks straight from Custer's self-serving autobiography, *My Life on the Plains*.[20] The General's arrogance is both comic and pathetic.

It is Berger's insight into two universal themes which distinguishes this comic novel from novels of pure parody: man's sense of history and the dilemma of modern man in a "civilized" world. In describing the debunking of Western heroes (Wild Bill Hickok, Calamity Jane, etc.) and literary figures (Mark Twain, Alexander Pope, etc.), we saw that in *Little Big Man* the

"legends and the romanticized history of the West are comically disassembled like Hamlets seen from backstage."[21] As Crabb is fond of observing, we have been lied to so often and so well that the facts appear strange and sound ridiculous when we hear them. Besides his assault on our clay-footed heroes, Berger also satirizes the interpretations of historians who have peddled their erroneous theories as fact. Charles B. Harris states that *Little Big Man* thus debunks man's methods of recording and ordering his past. And although Crabb's version of history is not necessarily the correct one, it casts doubt upon the official version.[22] Berger's spoofing of history is mainly directed at white history, but there is evidence that the Indians' approach is every bit as faulty. Cheyenne history is inseparable from its myths, tales, and legends; it is always interpreted in such a way as to make the Cheyenne the handsomest, bravest, and best people on the earth. An example of this subjective history is found in the scene when Crabb, an adopted Indian brave, throws down his weapons and turns himself over to the cavalry. When he returns to the tribe years later, he finds that his actions have become mythologized to the degree that he is now a greater hero than ever.

The white man's history is equally inaccurate. One example of its questionable veracity is found in the historians' insistence on finding ulterior racist motives and a grand scheme in the actions of the buffalo hunters. Crabb, who had been such a hunter, envisions the task as just a job, not some Machiavellian scheme to abolish an entire way of life. Crabb's account is less imaginative than the historians' hindsight, but it rings true. His explanation suggests the simple motives of the daily worker, not those of a mad genius bent on genocide.

The most prominent example of Berger's satire of historical truth is the continuing absorption with solving the mystery of the events at the Little Bighorn, an interest which historians share with novelists, film makers, and television producers.[23] This sustained attention to the Custer legend makes Crabb's simple interpretation somewhat anticlimactic, but nevertheless more plausible than heroic versions: the Seventh Cavalry was destroyed by poor reconnaissance, lack of modern communication methods, and difficult terrain. Custer's madness at the end, his inability to comprehend being outnumbered more than a hundred to one, is only an interesting sidelight to the event which has no bearing on the outcome.

Berger's multi-level attack on claims of absolute historical truth is given another turn of the screw by his initial persona, Ralph Fielding Snell (the middle name is an obvious giveaway of Berger's satiric intent). A self-proclaimed "man of letters," Snell appears in the foreword and epilogue to introduce Crabb and this "major document of the American frontier" (p. 12). In the epilogue, Snell points out historical inaccuracies in Crabb's account which he has checked against available references. He prides himself on being able to personally dispute Crabb's claim that Crazy Horse did not wear a war bonnet. In the tradition that has given us many titleholders to the Brooklyn Bridge, Snell betrays his gullibility and unreliability: "As to Crazy Horses's not wearing feathers, we know that statement to be erroneous—his war bonnet . . . presently reposes in my own collection: the dealer who sold it to me is a man of the highest integrity" (p. 447).

By using Fielding and Crabb as a persona within a persona, Berger adds a new dimension to *Little Big Man.* As narrator of the "frame," Snell is removed in time and space from the nineteenth-century events described by Crabb. Stanley Kauffman contends that the foreword and epilogue only distort Crabb's tale into an unbelievable fantasy.[24] However, when viewed as a satirical representation of twentieth-century America, and even the human condition, the frame device proves to be an effective technique.

L. L. Lee has perceptively suggested that Snell and his father may be caricatures, but they are living symbols of America's changes between the Sunday afternoon of 1876 (Custer's Last Stand) and 1963 (when Snell presents the final manuscript). Although never actually appearing in the story, Snell's father is depicted by his son as a rich, powerful, insensitive figure—an entrepreneur strongly suggestive of the robber barons of the nineteenth and early twentieth centuries. Bold and determined, these men carried the single-mindedness and ambition of a Custer into the battlefields of the corporate world. The next generation finds everything a bit easier, producing offspring such as the younger Snell—an affected intellectual, "a bit of a coward, a fool, an obvious decline from the older type of American."[25] Trundled about like a child by his medical nurse, the morose victim of his loquacious housekeeper, Snell feels compelled to defend his bachelorhood and heterosexuality to the reader, even giving assurances that he does not own a dressing gown (p. 12). Beset by a deviated septum, weak lungs, migraines, and nightmares, incapacitated for ten years by the death of his father and the discovery of a bastard half-brother, Ralph Fielding Snell is a model for the collective neuroses of the twentieth century. In spite of his obvious failings, the dilettante Snell thinks of himself in grander terms. The foreword is filled with his smug recollections of petty victories over the bureaucrats of Crabb's nursing home.

Although Berger illustrates again and again that the Cheyenne and the whites are bound by identical flaws, he does not assess equal guilt to both cultures, an assertion made by Ahearn who maintains that *Little Big Man* exposes the absurdity of both societies. There are, after all, degrees of guilt, and Berger's novel is not simply a nihilistic condemnation of all human potential. In a number of ways, the white society is shown to lack the moral base which supports Indian society. Through ironic contrast, Berger satirizes the "superior" moral standards of white civilization without obscuring the failings of Indian society. An examination of the moral integrity of both cultures will reveal Berger's predilection.

One of the traits which runs through the white society, and not the Indian one, is hypocrisy. The white man's hypocrisy in dealing with his own kind as well as the Indians is shown when Crabb describes the fate of the Hang About the Forts, the Indians tamed into submission by treaty promises. The Indians lie about the fort in a drunken stupor induced by a ready supply of alcohol. They prostitute their women to pay for whiskey, and subsist on government handouts which are half the legal allotment. The other half is withheld by Indian agents who sell it to white settlers or the Army. The Army has need of the Indians' share because its supplies are often embezzled by the Eastern dealers or the officers at the fort. Berger finally ends the cycle of greed and hypocrisy, but not before the reader is aware of the shameful results of the white man's promises to the Indian and to his own people. The Indians fall more easily to the white man's legal trickery and decadence than they do to his bullets. It should be noted that it is in the white culture that Jack Crabb is bankrupted by cheating business partners, rewarded for his gambling dishonesty, and driven to alcoholism.

In describing Berger's satire, Guy Davenport has observed that the "satire, like that of Aristophanes, Rabelais, and Chaucer, needs a hard moral base from which to flail all that wobbles and stinks."[26] It is ironic that one of Berger's prime targets of satire is the white man's arbiter of morality—the preacher. The first religious target encountered in *Little Big Man* is Crabb's father, an illiterate preacher. His religious beliefs are unorthodox: indulging in "a shot or three" of whiskey while conducting services in a saloon, the senior Crabb tolerates gambling and womanizing. In fact, the only evil he recognizes is that which "makes a man into a mean skunk who will cuss and spit and chew and never wash his face" (pp. 25-26). As long as a man was clean, he could indulge in any pursuit he desired. Killed after foolishly giving whiskey to the Indians, Crabb's father dies believing that he could have converted his murderers if he had been able to speak their language—Hebrew.

At the other end of the religious spectrum is the Reverend Pendrake, a staunch clergyman whose doctrine is as stringent as Mr. Crabb's is lenient. Engulfed in religious dogma, the obese Pendrake is comfortable only when devouring enormous quantities of food. Unlike the tolerant Crabb, Reverend Pendrake is very precise in labeling sinful enterprises which consist of all works of the flesh and sundry others: "adultery, fornication, uncleanness, lasciviousness, idolatry, witchcraft, hatred, variance, emulations, wrath, strife, seditions, heresies, envyings, murders, drunkenness, revelings, and such like" (p. 140). So intent is Pendrake on avoiding sexual sins that he abstains from relations with his wife, resulting in her adulterous affair. Of course, Pendrake's colossal gluttony removes any semblance of righteousness from his dictates.

In direct opposition to Pendrake's prohibitive, joyless religion, is the Indian's acceptance of all things human.

There are only two crimes in the Cheyenne culture, and Crabb tells us that they are very seldom committed: adultery and the killing of one's kinsman. This contrast between the Indians' humanity and the white society's stultifying religion is pointed out when Pendrake enumerates the many sins which comprise his faith. Jack remarks that except for envy, the list of faults perfectly describes the character of a successful Indian.

Despite their lack of a structured religion or a legal code such as that of the whites, the Cheyenne gain our admiration in ways that the corrupt white society fails to accomplish. The reason for Berger's preference for Cheyenne values lies in the two overriding principles which rule Indian life—individualism and dignity. L. L. Lee has noted that the major positive theme of the novel is that "the truly worthy man is the individual—individualism, for Berger, meaning to have the courage and strength to live one's own life."[27] This observation is supported by the fact that the only admirable white man in the novel is General Custer, a fiercely determined individual who remains true to his convictions. He is brave and goes his own way—two qualities which would have served him well had he been an Indian.

It is significant that Crabb has no success when he attempts to explain Custer's sense of independent spirit to Old Lodge Skins. The reason for the Indian's lack of comprehension is central to the virtues promoted in *Little Big Man*: to the Cheyenne, independence is the rule, not the exception. Custer is an exception because the white society suppresses independent action. Crabb does admit that this quality in the Cheyenne can sometimes lead to chaotic action, for if "you give an Indian a choice . . . he is sure to take the reckless alternative: he is inclined to let anybody do what they want" (p. 86). Nevertheless, compared to the white man's submission to authority and conformity, we admire the Cheyenne's independence.

In addition to the Cheyennes' high regard for individualism, there is a corresponding concern for the dignity of each person; this quality is expressed in an unbounded loyalty between tribe members, and even in the treatment of their enemies. The fact that there is no concern for the dignity of others in white civilization is evidenced when Crabb recalls his period as a drunk, singing and dancing to a jeering crowd in exchange for a drink of whiskey: "the Cheyenne would have been depressed to see a fellow tribesman gone to rot; they would have believed it reflected discredit upon all Human Beings. On the contrary, an American just loves to see another who ain't worth a damn" (p. 209).

The contrasting regard of the two societies for the individuality and dignity of their members is represented by the Cheyennes' treatment of their homosexuals (heemanehs). They are understanding of the heemanehs and value them as welcome and contributing members of society. The Indians' consideration of human rights is nowhere more obvious than in their treatment of this traditionally abused minority. In a society where dignity is earned, not granted, there is no need for one person to humiliate another. Even in war, the Cheyenne acknowledge the enemy's honor. The purpose of fighting is not to "show him up or make him eat dust, but rather to kill him altogether" (p. 129). This attitude is quite different from Wild Bill Hickok's, whose life is dedicated to finding opportunities to prove that he is a better man than his opponents.

There is little doubt that Berger favors the moral tenets which the Cheyenne represent. However, it is wrong to assume that Berger is therefore launching a crusade for the preservation of the noble savage or a return to primitivism. Rather, he would have us consider what it means to be a decent human being.

In *Little Big Man*, this reconsideration of human values begins with a new awareness of our Western mythology. Berger brilliantly manages to effect this new awareness without romanticizing Old Lodge Skins or the Indian way of life. However, as we get to know both in the course of the novel, our opinions change considerably. This is illustrated by Jack's changing view of Old Lodge Skins. Initially, he sees him as a farcical buffoon; as he gets to know him the image changes to that of a wise, sympathetic man whom he respects and loves. By the time he greets death, Old Lodge Skins has reached epic and tragic dimensions; his blindness, like Tiresias' in Greek tragedy, allows him greater vision than ordinary men. The same shift in perception can be seen in Jack's evaluation of the ambiance of an Indian camp. We have seen his first reaction to the suffocating stench of the Cheyenne camp, an almost physical revulsion. However, he tells us that it soon became his reality, and when he returned to white society, he missed the odor of what seemed life itself (p. 51).

In a similar manner, all aspects of the "savage" way of life are re-evaluated by Jack—and the reader. The picaresque structure allows comparisons between white and Indian societies, showing us the strengths and weaknesses of both. One of the great weaknesses of white culture is, as Max F. Shulz points out, that it is goal oriented, while the strength of Indian culture is that it is identity conscious.[28] One way that this basic ideological difference is shown is that the Indians, unlike the whites, do not wish to gain power over another's spirit, but to achieve self-fulfillment. Old Lodge Skins shows us this dichotomy when he contemplates the victory at the Little Bighorn which he realizes will mark the end of the Indian way of life:

> Yes, my son . . . it is finished now, because what more can you do to an enemy than beat him? Were we fighting red men against red men . . . it would now be the turn of the other side to try to whip *us* . . . that is the *right* way. There is no permanent winning or losing when things move, as they should, in a circle. . . . But white men, who live in straight lines and squares, do not believe as I do. With them it is rather everything

or nothing. . . . And because of their strange beliefs, they are very persistent. They will even fight at night or in bad weather. But they hate the fighting itself. Winning is all they care about, and if they can do that by scratching a pen across paper or saying something into the wind, they are much happier.

They will not be content now to come and take revenge. . . . Indeed, if we all return to the agencies, they probably would not kill anyone. For killing is part of living, but they hate life. (pp. 441-42)

Little Big Man is a comic novel grounded in satire, but the satire is only an instrument by which it measures the limits of human striving. It accomplishes more than other satiric Westerns because it attempts more: *Little Big Man* is a serious consideration of what it means to live well. Crabb tells us that twice while he was with the Cheyenne he was "at the center of the earth," a Cheyenne concept which expresses one's awareness of the circular nature of things, the unending unity of things past and present, life and death. To be at the center of the earth is to be at complete peace with oneself and others. It is the normal condition for the Cheyenne, but it is a unique and extraordinary experience for Crabb. He is thrilled by the sense of tranquility. Berger's satire in *Little Big Man* shows us how white society, ambitiously pursuing the transformation of the world, has forgotten what it is to live, to be a human being at the center of the earth.

NOTES

[1] William James Smith, "In the Vein of Mark Twain," rev. of *Little Big Man*, by Thomas Berger, *Commonweal*, 20 November 1964, pp. 294-96.

[2] Robert Edson Lee, *From West to East: Studies in the Literature of the American West* (Urbana: University of Illinois Press, 1966), p. 156.

[3] Delbert E. Wylder, "Thomas Berger's *Little Big Man* as Literature," in *Literature of the American West*, ed. J. Golden Taylor (Boston: Houghton Mifflin, 1971), p. 74.

[4] Guy Davenport, "Tough Characters, Solid Novels," rev. of *Little Big Man*, by Thomas Berger, *National Review*, 26 January 1965, p. 68.

[5] Max F. Schulz, *Black Humor Fiction of the Sixties: A Pluralistic Definition of Man and His World* (Athens: Ohio University Press, 1973), p. 74.

[6] Brian W. Dippie, "Jack Crabb and the Sole Survivors of Custer's Last Stand," *Western American Literature*, 4 (1969), 202.

[7] Thomas Berger, *Little Big Man* (1964; rpt. New York: Fawcett, n.d.), p. 245. All further references to this work appear in the text.

[8] L. L. Lee, "American, Western, Picaresque: Thomas Berger's *Little Big Man*," *South Dakota Review*, 4, No. 2 (1966), 35.

[9] Matthew Hodgart, *Satire* (New York: McGraw-Hill, 1969), p. 218.

[10] Kent Ladd Steckmesser, *The Western Hero in History and Legend* (Norman: University of Oklahoma Press, 1965).

[11] John G. Cawelti, "The Gunfighter and the Hard-boiled Dick," *American Studies*, 15, No. 21 (1975), p. 50.

[12] Smith, p. 294.

[13] Wylder, p. 73.

[14] Kerry David Ahearn, "Aspects of the Contemporary American Western Novel," Diss. Ohio University 1974, p. 108.

[15] Martin Nussbaum, "Sociological Symbolism of the 'Adult Western,'" *Social Forces*, 39 (1960), p. 27.

[16] Granville Hicks, "Paleface in the Cheyenne Camp," rev. of *Little Big Man*, by Thomas Berger, *Saturday Review*, 10 October 1964, p. 40.

[17] This seems to be a rather vicious attack on Whitman; but there may be another purpose, in light of Berger's extensive research into the topic. Perhaps Berger is so critical of Whitman because of his opportunism. According to Paul A. Hutton ("Custer's Last Stand," *TV Guide*, 26 November 1977, p. 40), within twenty-four hours of receiving news of Custer's defeat, Whitman had mailed his poem, "A Death Song for Custer," to the *New York Tribune* with an enclosed bill for ten dollars.

[18] William T. Pilkington, "Aspects of the Western Comic Novel," *Western American Literature*, 1 (1966), 217.

[19] Ahearn, p. 110.

[20] Dippie, 199.

[21] "Jack Crabb, Oldtimer," rev. of *Little Big Man*, by Thomas Berger, *Time*, 16 October 1964, p. 128.

[22] Charles B. Harris, *Contemporary American Novelists of the Absurd* (New Haven: College and University Press, 1971), pp. 129-31.

[23] The Custer massacre has never lost its intrigue to novelists or filmmakers. There are dozens of novels which take up the subject, perhaps the best being Ernest Haycox's *Bugles in the Afternoon*. As recently as 1976, Douglas C. Jones broached the topic in his "what if" historical novel, *The Court-Martial of George Armstrong Custer*. Television took its turn with the short-lived 1960s series, *Custer*. But the film has been the most significant

contributor to the legend of Custer, portraying him as everything from national hero (Raoul Walsh's powerful *They Died With Their Boots On,* 1940) to mad egocentric (Arthur Penn's screen version of *Little Big Man,* 1970). Still other Custer films include Thomas H. Ince's *Custer's Last Fight* (1912), Louis Weiss' *Custer's Last Stand* (1936), and Robert Siodmak's *Custer of the West* (1968).

[24] Stanley Kauffman, "O'Hara and Others," rev. of *Little Big Man,* by Thomas Berger, *New York Review of Books,* 17 December 1964, p. 21.

[25] Lee, p. 36.

[26] Davenport, p. 68.

[27] Lee, pp. 36-37.

[28] Schulz, p. 77.

Hector H. Lee

SOURCE: "Tales and Legends in Western American Literature," in *Western American Literature,* Vol. 9, No. 4, Winter, 1975, pp. 239-54.

[*In the following essay, Lee explores the distinctions between fact and legend in the literature of the western, and recounts tales that made their way into the lore of the Old West.*]

Without intending any implication regarding contemporary persons of the female gender one might remark that on the American frontier and in the earlier phases of the Old West women were a very valuable asset, particularly those ladies of the so-called respectable variety. Typical of this shortage of a rare commodity is the story told in the old California mining town of Rough and Ready. Back in the 1850's one lucky miner had a wife and several children; the rest of the town had none. Added to the miner's good fortune was the fact that his wife was a gifted cook, and every Sunday afternoon all the other miners would drop in for a visit because they could always count on getting a generous sample of her very tasty pies. But fate took a hand in the game, and the miner died. With proper solemnity his body was carried up the hill to the graveyard, and after a few appropriate words he was duly shoveled in. On the way back to town one of the pallbearers sidled up to the widow and said, "I know it isn't quite seemly of me to mention it now, but would you consider marrying me?" She twitched her black veil a little and said, "I'm sorry but you're too late; the preacher has already asked me."

Such a yarn is native to the West and there were thousands like it—wandering tales which, like tumbleweeds, break loose and roll across the landscape scattering seeds for later yarn spinners to pick up. This is, of course, folklore. There were in fact lonely miners and loggers, sodbusters, cowboys and Indians, cattle rustlers, horse thieves, and fast-draw lawmen in the Old West; but we know them, not in their historical reality but as the folk, the story tellers, and the writers have imagined them to be. It is therefore the tales and legends of the West that give western literature its distinctive characteristics.

If we are to examine the cultural heritage of the American frontier, particularly as it is seen in the literature of the West, we must begin by reviewing our basic assumptions about cultural inheritance and how societal values are transmitted, and about the essential reality of what we call the West. Immediately we discover that we are dealing with traditional matter—the images of reality, the value systems born of both western idealism and pragmatism, and the romantic vision of a land bigger than life where peace and harmony of spirit could be fought for and won from a hostile environment. This is the substance of folklore, and it is from the tales, legends and myths of a region or the societal enclaves within a region that the poet, novelist, or historian must draw if he is to reconcile the bare facts with the human truths that put flesh on the bones and beauty into the face of the image.

In geography, time, and human life styles the Old West is like the amoeba: its form changes, its boundaries flow, its nucleus shifts, and yet it is always a living entity. Writers have declared that the Old West was and still is mainly a state of mind, that it became "a West that never was," except in imagination. Its time span is elastic, dating perhaps from Lewis and Clark who started west in 1804, or the Alamo in 1836, or the gold rush of 1849-50, or the post Civil War expansion of the 1860's; and its climax may have been the death of Custer in 1876 or the birth of the archetypal cowboy hero in Owen Wister's *The Virginian* in 1902. No one cares to say for sure.

Actually, time is of little matter here, for we are dealing with ideas that are timeless. The Frederick Jackson Turner thesis that American history and the new democracy are essentially the story of a westering frontier, while it may be a rather restrictive view of history, gives sanction to the realization so impressively noted later by Henry Nash Smith that there is indeed an American mythos to be found in the historical, geographical, and cultural West.

Myth does not have any less importance simply because historians discover it not to be true. There is always a disparity between assumption and experience. "The frontier did not have a democratizing effect," says Thomas E. Boyle refuting part of the Turner thesis in a recent article in *Western American Literature.*[1] "Rather, it encouraged stump justice and lynch law. It was not the western spirit of cutting loose and faring forth that explains the titanic achievements of the Overland Mail, the telegraph, and the transcontinental railroad, but the loneliness and nostalgia of those isolated west of the frontier, cut off from the East, from home. The true meaning of the West, then," continues Boyle, "resides not in empirical fact nor in myth, but in the conflict between the two, the Greek word for which is *agon,* from which is derived our word *agony.* And, indeed, the dramatization of the agonizing process by which assumption is undercut by experience is the very stuff of literature." A demonstration of this view can be found in Rolvaag's *Giants in the Earth* or more recently in Wallace Stegner's Pulitzer Prize novel, *Angle of Repose.*

But myth is a synchronous complex of attitudes, values, and psychic needs expressed in tales, legends, rituals, and symbols. The mythology of the West, therefore, may include Old World elements as well as indigenous lore and local color. Some western writers using western settings and characters have a thematic thrust that extends beyond the boundaries of localized time and place. Walter van Tilburg Clark is such a writer; his *The Ox-Bow Incident* and *The Track of the Cat,* for instance, and *The Watchful Gods* draw generously from folklore, but it is the lore of the Old Testament, the Greeks, the Tristan legend, and the symbolism of Carl Jung.

Tales and legends not only imported from the Old World but also derived from the American Indian expressive arts and from the mountain men, cattlemen, loggers, sodbusters, and gunfighters are essential matter, therefore, for the western writer. Some authors have taken a major cycle of legends and made them into a single work of literature. Willa Cather's *Death Comes for the Archbishop* is such a story; it tells the composite legend of Acoma. Helen Hunt Jackson's *Ramona* is the legend of cultures in conflict, as is Oliver LaFarge's *Laughing Boy* and *The Enemy Gods.* Zane Grey in *Riders of the Purple Sage* picks up the anti-Mormon legend.[2] Frank Norris uses the anti-railroad legend in *The Octopus,* and Mari Sandoz in *Old Jules* and Vardis Fisher in his *Toilers of the Hills* or *In Tragic Life* pick up the legend of the hard life of the pioneer. It may be argued that these are themes rather than narrative genres, but if so they are themes that would not be as valid or credible coming from other times and places; it is the compacted western legendry that makes them significant.

The folklorist makes a distinction between tale and legend, with due allowance for the overlapping and blending of types. The work of defining still goes on.[3] Simplistically stated, a folk tale is a traditional narrative told primarily for enjoyment or moral precept and set in an indefinite time and place about characters that may be human, super-human, imaginary creatures, or animals; it may include a variety of story elements such as magic objects, transformations, and supernatural knowledge or powers. Except for native Indian tales the literature of the frontier has not picked up this Old World strain in narrative lore to any significant extent, though tall tales and anecdotes do abound.

The legend, on the other hand, is a traditional narrative set in a presumably real time and place about presumably real characters; it should be believable if not actually believed, and is usually told to explain (such as a geographic feature or name), to glorify (such as the exploits of a hero or villain), or to memorialize (such as a noteworthy event). What is important about legend is that although it is rooted in actual times, places, and people it is not confined to historicity. It is therefore a plague to historians, who must validate the facts. But the folk, relying on their memories and their innate sense of what is relevant, apply the artist's selectivity to the actual facts. In the folk process certain features of a story will be retained, others will be borrowed from outside sources, and still other incidents or motifs will be invented. Students of the English and Scottish popular ballads have noted this process also in the traditional metamorphosis of folk songs. The student of legendry finds that the folk have selected for traditional purposes what may not in the real sense be true, but what conveys nevertheless the "essential truth," that is, the basic human values, significance, and taste in narrative art that gives a story its reason for staying alive in the stream of tradition. This was perhaps best expressed by Black Elk, speaking through John G. Neihardt, in telling the story of the supernatural White Woman: "This they tell, and whether it happened so or not I do not know; but if you think about it, you can see that it is true."[4]

The writer of western literature likewise gets to his essential truth, which is perhaps less mystical, by the same processes. In writing *The Preacher and the Slave* Wallace Stegner thoroughly researched the legendry, the songs, and the history of his subject, which is an account of the life and death of the IWW martyr Joe Hill. About this Stegner says, "It has a novel's intentions and takes a novel's liberties. As necessary, I invented characters, scenes, motivations, dialogue, and though Hill's execution gave me the inescapable ending, I bent the approach to that conclusion as seemed to me needful. . . . "[5]

If the essential truth of a legend lies in its theme, it may be a universal truth manifested through local characters and settings. The fact that a man can summon superhuman strength and endurance when fighting for survival is not in any sense uniquely western; the story of Beowulf demonstrates this at the very beginning of Anglo-Saxon literature. But when we come to the legend of Hugh Glass and his inconceivable endurance after a she-bear had reduced him to little more than hamburger and his companions had left him for as good as dead, we see how he dragged himself for thirty-eight days through scorching deserts and impenetrable wilderness, avoiding hostile Indians and living on only what he could catch with his mangled hands until he reached safety at last, and we see then only the ghost of a man kept alive by his obsession for survival and revenge—and this becomes a legend. Or when Jack London tells of the superhuman fight for life in his stories "To Build a Fire," and "Love of Life," they become literature that is western.

The canny cleverness of the New England Yankee has become a stereotype in American literature with characters like Sam Slick or Edward Noyes Westcott's shrewd David Harum, or the real Phineas T. Barnum, or such fast-dealers on the early frontier as Davy Crockett with his trick of selling the same coonskins over and over again—this is a type that the West did not invent, but one that thrives in western literature. Stuart Edward White's thin Dutchman in his story, "A Corner in Horses," or Mark Twain's Jim Smiley in "The Celebrated Jumping Frog of Calaveras County," are transplants of the Yankee fast-dealer, and yet they and their brethren have contributed much to Western literature.

Sometimes it is not the universal theme or the transplanted character that is given a western home, but the very legends themselves that are borrowed from Old World or eastern American sources to be inserted into a western story. In Willa Cather's *Death Comes for the Archbishop,* Father Junipero Serra and Father Andrea are entertained on the desert by a family who give them food and shelter for the night but who have vanished from sight and existence the next day. This is the old folk motif of the revenant hosts and is not at all what we could call western. But as a vignette in a western story it is reborn as a part of western literature.

But if themes, characters, motifs, and vignettes serve to enrich our literature it is because they can take on the natural coloration and blend into the gestalt that is the geography and mythos of the West. They have not shaped the literature but have contributed to it. What, then, have writers found to be the unique ingredient of their western matter? It would seem to be the western hero, too strong to be vanquished by the hostility of nature, too large to be lost in the vastness of prairie or desert space, too devoted to his code to be confused by the psychological complexities of life, and too skilled at his trade to be defeated by an opponent. The villains or anti-heroes are carved from the same stone, and with the aid of time, American sentimentality, and the commercial media they are all gradually being transformed from bad guys into good guys.

When Owen Wister published *The Virginian* he gave the West a hero that has become legend. Professor Kent Steckmesser suggests that the typing process began with an article by George Ward Nichols in *Harper's Magazine* in 1867 about Wild Bill Hickok. "Nichols," he says, "was trying to create a character who would fascinate Eastern readers; he was also trying to create a type-figure of the frontiersman. . . . Although Wild Bill is typed as a scout in this article, the classic components of the gunfighter legend are also discernible. The fight with Dave Tutt in the public square is treated romantically. . . . The duel is fought in chivalric fashion and involves the honor of the participants. This romanticized encounter may in fact have been the source of a similar episode in Owen Wister's *The Virginian* (1902), and the duel in that novel in turn established the 'walkdown' as rigid convention in Western fiction."[6]

An older generation will immediately recognize both the motif and the character in the type-casting of the late Gary Cooper in the western motion picture. The strong, quiet, honorable cowboy or gunfighter who killed only those who deserved killing became an archetypal hero for the West. For the motion picture this motif reached a climax, at least up to now, in *High Noon* and *Shane.* There were indeed a few real people who were like that. Some of them are not remembered in legend because they did not have a Boswell for a biographer or a Ned Buntline (who glorified Wyatt Earp) or an Owen Wister to tell their story, but their deeds were readily absorbed into the growing stories of the Wild Bill Hickoks, Wyatt Earps, or Buffalo Bill Codys who did have press agents. This is what may be called the accretional characteristic of the folk hero; he takes on remarkable exploits, events, and anecdotes that may have happened—but not to him. Such memorabilia are too attractive to be wasted on the unknown local hero, and hence they gain eternal life by attaching themselves to the larger figure; and he in turn is amplified by just that much. The Abraham Lincoln cycle of legendry illustrates this; not everything told about him really happened to him. The same is true of the George Washington cycle, the Brigham Young cycle, the Nez Perce Indian Chief Joseph cycle, and many others.

The real life cowboy or cattleman as recorded by Andy Adams, Will James, and Eugene Manlove Rhodes has become literature, too. His was a hard but romantic life as seen by readers who will always interpret his loneliness as freedom, his chaps and lariat as the accoutrement of knighthood, his bedbug-infested bunk house and the campfire or chuck wagon as King Arthur's Round Table, and his bashful respect for womanhood as the medieval ideal of Courtly Love. Even the honest realism of Rhodes and Adams become part of the romantic mystique of the western frontier. Material that cannot be absorbed into this picture is rejected and lost to all but the historian. A good example of this selectivity is the case of the Negro cowboy. In reality he played an important role in the roundups, cattle drives, bunkhouse life, the so-called code of the West, and the gunfights; yet he has been for the most part dropped from sight in western fiction. The reason is fairly clear; readers could not accept the Black man as a romantic hero, yet he was not a villain nor was he a menial to be caricatured like the Chinese cook or the Mexican wrangler.

The lawman also contributed his legendry to western writers. Wyatt Earp's biographer, Lake, saw him as the "epitomized symbol" of Western America. And yet later scholarship has subtracted much from this eulogy with evidence that he was a tinhorn and a coward who would seldom face an opponent in a fair fight unless the odds were on his side, particularly in the persons of his brothers or Doc Halliday. In one instance, for example, in a San Francisco saloon after he had refereed a prize fight and thrown the decision to the fighter he had himself bet considerable money on, he was "called out" by a Major McLaughlin of Santa Cruz. Earp backed down and walked away without a word. But his literary image is still heroic.

Not all western lawmen have fared so well. According to folk tradition there are two Pat Garretts. As the New Mexico sheriff who tracked down and finally cornered the notorious Billy the Kid, Garrett is seen as the relentless lawman, champion of good over evil. The other view is that he hid behind his badge to ambush and murder the unfortunate, misguided, good-hearted Billy Bonney. This interpretation is gaining in popularity because of the current anti-establishment, anti-law sentiments of the younger American generation which tends to see society as the villain and the lawman as its unscrupulous accomplice. In his excellent story, "Paso por Aqui," Eugene Rhodes has Pat Garrett cling unshakably to the trail of Ross McEwen across half of New Mexico only to rise above his duty in the end and let McEwen go because he sees in the outlaw more good than bad. But this gesture of humanity becomes important in the Rhodes story precisely because Sheriff Garrett was the man who had killed Billy the Kid. If he had allowed Billy to escape for reasons of innate goodness one wonders how the legend of Pat Garrett would have turned out—or of Billy the Kid, for that matter.

The double image in legend is not, of course, limited to lawmen. There are at least two of every culture hero—two Brigham Youngs, the wenching dictator and the omniscient colonizer; two Abraham Lincolns, the rustic bumpkin haunted by melancholy and the wise and witty statesman who became a martyred saint; two John Bidwells, the squawman who exploited the Indians of the Sacramento Valley and the prince of colonizers with unblemished Christian virtue.

Likewise, there are two images of Billy the Kid. In his book *The Western Hero in History and Legend* Kent Steckmesser clearly draws the two interpretations, the one of the outlaw as a homicidal maniac with probably not one redeeming quality, and the other as a saintly Robin Hood. Many motion pictures and even a musical extravaganza have been made of the exploits of Billy the Kid, and with each successive version he becomes more handsome, more generous, and more the misunderstood victim of a cruel society. In this age of the anti-hero, writers will probably lean toward this point of view, and once again legend will lend a shaping hand to our image of the Old West.

The folk have always taken kindly to Butch Cassidy and Black Bart the Po-8. And the California bandit Joaquin Murieta was almost entirely a folk creation, so from the very beginning his was the legend of a Robin Hood. But the metamorphosis of legendry is also at work now on such bloodthirsty villains as Jesse James and more recently Pretty Boy Floyd and Bonnie and Clyde.

The writer who deals with the matter of the Old West has yet another component to draw upon and that is the intrepid breed known as the mountain men. Jim Bridger, Old Bill Williams, and Kit Carson and their kind either in truth or fiction have added much to our picture. Take Kit Carson, for example. This plain, bandy-legged scout, five and a half feet tall and weighing only 135 pounds, speaking in the ungrammatical lingo of the frontier and never learning to read or write grows to epic proportions as his exploits are told. It is true he was a remarkable tracker, guide, Indian strategist, and on occasion a fierce fighter. But it is the legend that writers preferred and amplified. Professor Steckmesser notes that Herman Melville in 1851 compared Kit Carson with Hercules; and a succession of writers, mostly copying each other, have portrayed him in epic terms not only as Hercules but Nestor, Nimrod, Saladin, Hannibal, and Ulysses. He becomes young, handsome and big, and he speaks in perfect Victorian English. All this, of course, meets the approval of the folk.

The western frontier, we must remember, was more than the hero types we have mentioned, or the coyotes, sidewinders, and other assorted varmints. Into its tapestry is also woven the Mexicans, Chinese, and Indians. Unfortunately for the Chinese, Bret Harte's Ah Sin, the "Heathen Chinee," helped to set the pattern and they are remembered as subtly clever but inconsequential background material functioning as railroad builders, ranch cooks, laundrymen, or hatchet men in the iniquitous dens of Chinatown. The legend of the Indian, on the other hand, is rapidly changing. Once seen as a depraved savage, the Native American is emerging as a new and beautiful thread in the warp and woof of the Old West, bringing a hitherto undiscovered symbolic and poetic beauty to the region and to literature.[7]

A New West is growing up. Its legends will be about migrant workers and college riots and the drug culture and minority group leaders, and new writers will take their material from them, but these will no longer be about the frontier This is not to say that the image and literature of the Old West will go out of vogue; on the contrary, it will probably be as enduring as the medieval romances. But to meet the needs and the taste of new generations of folk the mythos will gradually change and the sense of time and perhaps place also will become blurred. Even now the symbolic earth mother, Kitty of the Long Branch saloon in *Gunsmoke,* has zippers in her dresses; Doc in the same saga can patch up minor wounds with a bandaid; a scout in the old series *Wagon Train* can use a flashlight; and the eternal father image, Ben Cartwright of *Bonanza,* is as young in an episode from the 1880's as he was the week before in the 1860's. Such anachronisms do not bother us. Today's folk do not know the difference, and they become irrelevant.

Even the magnificent Paul Bunyan has had to change to stay alive. He has moved from coast to coast and has even been borrowed by the oil drillers of the Southwest. And when such poets as Carl Sandburg and Robert Frost picked him up they made his strength symbolic rather than real, and his soul tender. Professor Richard Dorson has called Paul Bunyan "fakelore" instead of folklore because Paul was at first largely the product of the advertising media. Yet even though Lassen County, California, was the muzzle from which the first volley of the Paul Bunyan cycle of legends was fired by W. B. Laughead, a publicity man for the Red River Lumber Company, who pulled the trigger,[8] the powder and ball came from the big woods country of both the Great Lakes and the Northwest.

But the Old West will still live in the lore of that mythical other world that has passed. While we remarked earlier that the folk tale in its generic Old World form (i.e., about fairies, elves, witches, enchanted princes, and talking animals) was not transplanted to America we must recognize that the tall tale and fabulous anecdote are comfortably western, and writers frequently spice their material with them. Like Davy Crockett, Jim Bridger was a yarn spinner. An endless variety of anecdotes can still be heard—about some fabulous hunt, or how old prospectors happened to find rich lodes of gold or silver, or such chucklers as the one about the logging camp cook's helper, which is not untypical. This logging camp character was sent to town for the week's wagon load of supplies for the cook shack; when he returned he had a load consisting of three loaves of bread and twenty cases of whiskey, and the old lumberjacks helping with the unloading muttered, "What are we goin' to do with all that bread?"

Also likely to turn up in any western situation are anecdotes such as this about frontier justice. The judge, who in this version of the yarn happens to be William B. Ide, the hero of California's Bear Flag Revolt, is holding court in a saloon, and a horse thief is on trial. The judge asks, "How do you plead? Are you guilty?"

The defendant says, "No, Judge, I'll plead that I'm not guilty."

"Well, then, you are entitled to a fair trial. Do you have a lawyer?"

"No, Judge, there ain't a lawyer within a hundred miles of here."

"Well, you've got to have a lawyer," said Judge Ide. Then after a moment's reflection, "I'm a lawyer. I guess I could defend you."

"Fine with me," said the defendant. How could he lose with the judge defending him? But the judge remembered that there was no prosecuting attorney, either, so Judge William B. Ide appointed Will Ide, himself, to prosecute the case. A jury was selected and the case proceeded. Evidence was introduced by the prosecutor, Will Ide, and frequently the defense attorney, W. B. Ide, objected. After hearing the arguments Judge Ide would rule on the objection. Finally the case went to the jury. After deliberating for as long as the liquor lasted the jury brought in the verdict: "Guilty."

So Judge Ide said, "Well, you've had a fair trial. You have been eminently represented by counsel and you've been found guilty. I'll have to sentence you to hang by the neck until you're dead. Our capable sheriff, William Ide, will carry out the sentence." But some time later when Ide got around to the job of foreclosing on the prisoner he found that the Governor had pardoned the man and he was long gone. But Ide didn't care; he was against capital punishment, anyway. Throughout the frontier variations of this yarn are to be found, and whether it ever happened or not nobody cares much.

We might talk at great length and in general terms about legendry in the West and how such material is used by writers of literature and writers of sub-literature whose commercially profitable titillations are more widely read or viewed on the screen. But perhaps the best way to see the Old West in folk literature is to examine one specific legend in detail. In this version the story is more or less true, and its historicity has been studied.[9] Yet it was first collected in oral tradition from informants. It contains most of the ingredients of the western story: the open-space setting, the tensions and prejudices concerning Indians and the plight of the half-breed, the violence of lynch law, the tragic irony of sacrificed innocence, and the moral theme of retribution. This story is called "The Shadows from Lookout Bridge."[10]

The town was old, and withered, and dying. The one street that threaded the town together was swept clean by that steady, dry plateau wind of Northern California. The old grocery store with its high square board front, the remains of a once-shaded blacksmith shop now turned into a makeshift garage, the beer parlor and sporting goods emporium that had once been a saloon, and the four or five skeletons of old houses with bare driveways and front paths that still clung to the road like the bony fingers of a skeleton—this was the town of Lookout. The boards of what had once been a raised sidewalk in front of the store had shrunk, and the paint on the buildings—where there had been paint—had dried and curled and peeled off, and the wood sidewalls had that pale velvety look that comes from years of wind and rain and hot sun. It was a town fighting against death and decay.

At the end of the one-street settlement a single crossroad led to the cemetery. It was surprisingly well kept, that cemetery, with fresh flowers and neatly clipped hedges, the greenest part of town, as if its role had somehow been reversed and here lay the real life of the village. Green, that is, except for one spot in the extreme southwest corner, where the Russian thistle and the cheat grass grew unmolested. Here was a single grave, marked by a small wooden marker which until recent years bore only one name—"Hall." But in this lonesome grave lay the bodies of five men.

The people of Bieber and Adin and Alturas still don't talk much about these five men. Nobody cares to remember. But most of the story has gradually come out, at least as the folk remember it—an eighty-year-old woman who lay in her last sickness in an Alturas hospital; a Bieber woman whose father had lived in Lookout at the time; a man of importance in the county, whose boyhood memories still burned; and the "old-timer" who, like the ancient mariner, lived it again and again, and who swore with the conviction of one who could not be contradicted that, "Of all them fellers that took part in that thing—I can tell you—Hell overtook them, ever' one of 'em."

Calvin Hall had been a soldier at Fort Crook in 1861. He had taken a friendly interest in the Indians, and when he left the Army he married an Indian girl and they moved to Lookout. It was then a rough and ready outpost town for miners and ranchers. Hall had settled on a few acres up in a little draw called Gouger's Neck, and there he and his Indian wife raised a family. The years went by, and Calvin Hall's boys came to suffer the hatred of half-breeds so common in the West. They struck back in the only way they knew, and the word got around that they were a bad lot. People laid the blame on them for a series of petty thefts like raiding chicken coops, stealing harnesses, cutting fences, stealing calves, and in general trespassing on the sacred property of the other ranchers.

After awhile the Hall ranch was known as a stopping place for renegades—desperate men on the run from sheriffs, or lesser offenders who needed a place to hide out until their little crimes were forgotten in the excitement of newer offenses against the peace and security of Northern California.

"An' that ain't all," a man called Shorty was heard to say one day to his fellow loungers in the country store. "That ain't all. Them Hall scum raises the best tomaters in the valley, an' they're a-sellin' em cheaper'n ever'body else. An' that ain't jest right. I ever said, them Halls has got to go!"

Matters went from bad to worse until the summer of 1901. Old Calvin Hall was in his 70's then. His boys Frank and Jim were about grown, and the youngest boy was past thirteen. There was a girl, too, about middlin' size. And staying with them at this time was a questionable character named Dan Yantes. He had been a real bad man sometime, somewhere, and his temporary abode with the Halls only served to kindle the smouldering fires of community indignation. One by one the other citizens of Lookout came around to Shorty's insistent opinion that the Halls must go, one way or another.

Finally in May of that year Frank and Jim Hall and Dan Yantes were arrested for stealing. They were locked in the makeshift jail, and when old Calvin Hall and his youngest boy came down to investigate they were thrown in jail with the others.

"I don't know about this, boys," said the worried town marshal. "You ain't got no evidence that'll stick in court." Doubt, perplexity, and disappointment spread over the faces of Lookout.

"You just let me on the jury and I'll hang it on 'em," muttered a big man wearing a calf-skin vest. He had overlooked the fact that he was also one of the injured parties and was to be a complaining witness.

"It ain't no jury business," the marshal said. "This won't get past the judge, even."

"Can't let 'em go now," Shorty put in. "You let 'em go now, you're just askin' fer trouble. They'll take it out on you. You've got 'em now—just a bunch of half-breeds. They got it comin' and you'll never get 'em again like you got 'em now. I say let's get a rope!"

"I got a rope. I got plenty of rope," said a man with a big nose and a broad mustache."

"An' I say let's take 'em," Shorty yelled with rising emotion. It had been a hot summer, and the dry wind blowing steadily across the lava beds to the north had set the people's nerves on edge. The talk spread, and their smoldering anger leaped into flame. Their annoyance, frustration, and doubt gave way to conviction, purpose, and action. Seven ropes were brought out, five for the men in the jail and two for the mother and daughter who were lurking somewhere on the outskirts of the town. The marshal knew in his heart that he couldn't be a party to such talk, not and remain faithful to his office. But when it was pointed out that what he didn't know couldn't hurt him he agreed to a plan that would subject his conscience only to the pangs of an unfortunate oversight. He would forget and leave the jail unguarded when he went out for supper. After all, a marshal has to eat.

That night the moon shone big and round and golden over the wide valley. The two women, mother and daughter, sensing trouble, hid behind some sagebrush on a hill nearby, watching the moon-lit town and the shadows moving up and down the street. At the agreed moment the marshal left the jail, stepped up on the boardwalk in front of the hotel, and lighted his cigar. This was the signal. He turned and went in to supper, and the waiting mob rushed in to have its feast. The five men were dragged out of jail and up the street to the high log bridge that stretched across the little river at the edge of town.

The ropes were tied at one end to the poles along the top of the bridge. At the other end were hangman's nooses. The two women were forgotten in the excitement, and they crouched on the hillside nearby, watching. Old Calvin Hall, tired and spent, had lived his life. There wasn't enough left to fight for. He tried to reason with them, but no one listened. The noose was fixed, and he was dropped over the bridge. Frank had started to fight, but a vicious blow to the chin by the big man with the calf-skin vest had brought the sweet blessing of unconsciousness, and he went over without knowing. Jim Hall was paralyzed with terror. His legs crumpled. He slobbered and cried. Mumbling incoherent words and trembling with the sick weakness of his fear, he was lifted over and dropped. Dan Yantes, gunman and tough guy, for some strange reason submitted in sullen resignation. Perhaps he knew in his heart that this was his destiny and the time had now come.

But it was the young boy, the thirteen-year-old, big for his age and full of life, who fought back. He screamed and cursed. He bit at the hands that clutched him. He swung his fists wildly and grabbed the throat of the man with the big nose and held on until they had to pry him loose. He kicked another man in the stomach so hard the man turned sick. But after a terrific struggle, he, too, was dropped from the bridge. And the man called Shorty, who had stood back at the edge of the bridge during these proceedings, spat in the water that flowed quietly under him.

The moon shone full and rich and almost warm on the little town that night. And as the shadows of the now quiet citizens moved slowly back into town, to linger in little groups by the hotel or near the blacksmith shop, there were five other shadows that twisted and swung in the moonlight. The river, like a soft beam of glancing blue light, flowed slowly under the bridge. Then a large cloud moved over the moon and spread its broad shadow to darken the town of Lookout.

The next day the Indian woman and her daughter were allowed to come into town and take away the bodies of their men. How the men were buried and by whom is not remembered, except that they were all put in one grave in a neglected corner of the cemetery. Then the women went back to the ranch, took out their old round-topped tin-covered trunk and packed it with all they had worth taking, loaded it into the wagon, and drove to Alturas where during the years that followed the mother worked at jobs of house cleaning for one family or another until she died. What became of the girl no one seems to know or care much.

Some of the men who were involved in the affair were brought to trial. The people came to listen to the testimony, and they thought about it a lot but didn't say much. The jury brought in its verdict of "Not guilty," and the accused men went their way. Some of them left the country and were never seen again. But some of them stayed, and the people watched them carry their guilt on their faces.

The folk in those towns have come to know what became of the men who did this thing. Ask them and they'll tell you, if they feel like talking about it, that all these men came to a tragic or evil end. One walked in front of a train, and it wasn't exactly an accident. One died of cancer of the throat, right where an imaginary noose might have gone or the hand of a wretched boy might have clutched. And one died from a rotting of the stomach, just as if he had been kicked there. And the people will tell you, "Hell overtook 'em, every one of 'em." Even the bridge caught fire one night and burned away.

And if you will go and visit that little cemetery now, in the town of Lookout, you will find that time has brought at least one change to that desolate corner where the lone grave lies. Someone—the sexton can't remember who—has placed a neat, thin stone slab there. It bears the simple inscription: "Calvin Hall, Sergeant, 2nd U.S. Cavalry."

But the final touch of irony is that when Calvin Hall was a soldier at Fort Crook in 1861 he kept a journal in which he described the way of life among the Indians as he knew them. His observations were so accurate and his accounts were written with such clear, objective, scientific detail, that today he is quoted by scholars as one of the best authorities on the Indians of that region. He has left a gift to science that will make his name immortal, and Calvin Hall will have the respect of men who will never know the name of the man with the calf-skin vest, the man with the big nose, or the man called Shorty.

And the new bridge over the river at Lookout is low and thin, and on a moonlight night it hardly casts a shadow.

NOTES

[1] Thomas E. Boyle, "Frederick Jackson Turner and Thomas Wolfe: The Frontier as History and as Literature," *Western American Literature,* IV (Winter, 1970), 276.

[2] For a recent summary of the anti-Mormon cycle see Leonard Arrington and Jon Haupt, "Community and Isolation: Some Aspects of 'Mormon Westerns'," *Western American Literature,* VII (Spring and Summer, 1973), 15-31.

[3] An excellent recent discussion of legendry by folklorists is to be found in Wayland D. Hand, ed., *American Folk Legend: A Symposium* (Berkeley: University of California Press, 1971).

[4] J. G. Neihardt, *Black Elk Speaks* (Lincoln: University of Nebraska Press, 1961), 5.

[5] Wallace Stegner, *The Sound of Mountain Water* (Garden City: Doubleday & Company, 1969), 206.

[6] Kent Steckmesser, *The Western Hero in History and Legend* (Norman: University of Oklahoma Press, 1965), 36-37.

[7] Many anthologies of Native American literature are now emerging. For example, one now popular among college students is Gerald Haslam, *Forgotten Pages of American Literature* (Boston: Houghton Mifflin Company, 1970).

[8] See W. H. Hutchinson, "The Caesarean Delivery of Paul Bunyan," *Western Folklore*, XXII (January, 1963), 1-15.

[9] James O. Souther, *Legend Into History: Facts and Fiction of the Lookout Lynching* (New York: Vantage Press, 1968).

[10] Hector H. Lee, "The Shadows from Lookout Bridge," from a television series, *There Is A Telling* (Chico, California: KHSL/TV, Channel 12, 1960). Also in Hector Lee: *Tales of California* (Logan: Utah State University Press, 1974).

Mody C. Boatwright

SOURCE: "The American Myth Rides the Range: Owen Wister's 'Man on Horseback'," in *Southwest Review*, Vol. XXXVI, No. 3, Summer, 1951, pp. 157-63.

[In the following essay, Boatwright critiques the image of the cowboy as hero, particularly in the works of Owen Wister.]

If, while you were in your neighborhood grocery this morning, or any morning this year, you went to the rack and picked up at random a two-bit novel, the chances are one in five that the novel was a western. If you read the comic strips in your daily paper, in at least one and possibly four you followed the adventures of man on horseback. If you looked over the offering on your magazine stand, you probably saw no fewer than twenty-five of the fifty or more pulpwood magazines and a dozen of the twenty or more comic books devoted exclusively to westerns. If you read all of any issue of the *Saturday Evening Post,* the chances are six out of ten that you read either a western short story or an instalment of a western serial. If you listened to your radio all day, you heard at least one western drama, and if you sat by your television set, you saw one. If you dropped into a movie house at random, the chances are one in four that you saw a horse opera.

One reason why the cowboy is a popular hero is that historically he possesses the qualities of which folk heroes are made. These qualities are two: prowess and cleverness. It is not necessary that both inhere in the same individual, but I know of no hero in any culture who has not exhibited at least one of them. Prowess, when accompanied by the virtues of bravery, skill, and loyalty, is a romantic ideal, aristocratic in its indifference to material gain, and, incidentally, accessible only to those who have economic security or are indifferent to it. An admiration for prowess thus qualified is an evidence of idealism. Cleverness is the defense of the weak against the strong, the practical against the ideal. It is the middle class's weapon against the aristocracy, the slave's weapon against his master. It is realistic and often cynical. In the folklore of the United States prowess is associated with the South, cleverness with the North.

The cowboy in the time of the open range and the over-land drive exhibited both these traits. One of the few safe generalizations that can be made about cowboys is that they had the stamina and the skills necessary to the practice of their trade. They were not afraid of horses and cattle; they were willing to risk their lives in controlling stampedes and in fording rivers, and in protecting their bosses' herds against Indian raiders, Mexican bandits, and Anglo-American rustlers. In these things cleverness was as important as strength: often the best strategy was not to fight your enemy but to outwit him.

But it was not until the heroic age of the cattle industry had closed that the cowboy emerged as a national folk hero. For qualities alone do not create folk heroes. Essential also is a troubadour, or perhaps a number of troubadours. Their function is not merely to publicize the hero. More importantly it is to develop myths about him and to assimilate these myths to the archetypical myths of the culture. A myth cannot flourish without a congenial climate of opinion. In contemporary civilization the troubadours are historians, biographers, journalists, novelists, script writers. Their media are the written and spoken word, sound effects, the visual image. Their instruments are books, magazines, movies, radio, television.

Owen Wister was not the first troubadour of the cowboy, but he was the first to get a national hearing and to make his heroes acceptable to gentility. When Wister's first western story appeared in 1891, Charlie Siringo's realistic biography was being ignored in literary circles. Several dime novelists had discovered the cowboy, but had referred him to a waning mythology. To some, because he was far away from the corrupting influences of civilization and close to nature, he was innocent and good. To some, he was the contemporary knight-errant, wandering through the cattle kingdom righting wrongs with no thought of material reward. Others believed that men removed from the refinements of urban life and the restraints of home life and religion necessarily degenerated. To them the cowboy was essentially a barbarian whose only recreations were physical violence and drunkenness.

Wister attempted a synthesis of all these concepts, throwing the chief emphasis upon chivalry. His cowboys are neither Arcadian innocents nor drunken rowdies. They are natural gentlemen. Looking on the scene of the Medicine Bow saloon, he is moved to write:

> Saving Trampas, there was scarce a face among them that had not in it something very likable. Here were lusty horsemen ridden from the heat of the sun, and the wet of the storm, to divert themselves awhile. Youth untamed sat here for an idle moment, spending easily its hard-earned wages. City saloons rose into my vision, and I instantly preferred this Rocky Mountain place. More of death it undoubtedly saw, but less of vice, than did its New York equivalents. And death is a thing much cleaner than vice. Moreover, it

was by no means vice that was written upon these wild and manly faces. Even where baseness was visible, baseness was not uppermost. Daring, laughter, endurance—these were what I saw upon the countenances of the cow-boys. And this very first day of my knowledge of them marks a date with me. For something about them, and the idea of them, smote my American heart, and I have never forgotten it, nor ever shall, as long as I live. In their flesh our natural passions ran tumultuous; but often in their spirit sat hidden a true nobility, and often beneath its unexpected shining their figures took on heroic stature.

Even the weak-minded and weak-willed Shorty is not without a touch of nobility: he loves horses. Aside from Trampas, the only Wisterian cowboy without some such touch is Hank in "Hank's Woman." "The creature we call a *gentleman,*" Wister observes, "lies deep in the hearts of thousands that are born without the chance to master the outward graces of the type."

But the outward graces are important, and before Wister's cowboys can enter genteel society, they must acquire them. Even the Virginian must undergo a course in self-improvement—by reading Shakespeare and other literary classics—before he is a fit husband for Mollie Wood. And having observed the clothing of Judge Henry's eastern guests, he reaches Bennington properly attired.

The creature that we call a gentleman is above all chivalrous, and in Wister's cowboys is the chivalry of the aristocratic South modified by the West. Good women are not to be mentioned in levity. Public opinion supports the Virginian when he demands that Trampas rise up on his hind legs and admit that he has lied about Mollie Wood. A gentleman does not boast of his exploits with women not so good. The Virginian's relations with the widow of Medicine Bow are to be inferred from circumstantial evidence, not from anything he has said.

But more than gallantry, Wister emphasized the code of honor. After Trampas had threatened to kill the Virginian if he did not leave town by sundown, the mayor offered to put Trampas in the calaboose until the Virginian married and left town, and Lin McLean and Honey Wiggin, feeling that the code might be suspended in view of the extraordinary circumstances, offered to "take this thing off your hands." But of course it could not be. "It had come to that point where there was no way out, save the ancient, eternal way between man and man. It is only the great mediocrity that goes to law in these personal matters."

In spite of a good number of shootings, stabbings, and lynchings, physical violence is not abundant in Wister's works. His cowboys triumph by cleverness more often than by force. The Virginian outwits Trampas at every turn until the final challenge to death. In a typical Wister short story, Scipio LeMoyne recovers the payroll by giving the robber misleading directions concerning a short route to the village. His cowboys are also tricksters for fun. The Virginian got the drummer's bed by pretending that he had fits, and he got rid of the Reverend MacBride by keeping him up all night on the pretense that he was about to be converted to the preacher's religion.

In Wister's cowboys, then, we have both prowess and cleverness. But more important, the Virginian exemplifies the American version of the myth of the faithful apprentice, the Horatio Alger story. Poor and obscurely born, he goes into the world—the West—to seek his fortune. He wanders from Texas to Montana and eventually settles down as a cowhand on the Sunk Creek Ranch in Wyoming. He serves his employer faithfully, never hesitating to risk life or limb, never complaining about injustices done him, but determined to make his master see his worth. He makes his own decisions and accepts the consequences of them. When duty demands, he can hang his own friend. There is no boss's daughter to reward him with; but Mollie Wood has all the qualifications except the fortune, and that is taken care of by a partnership in the firm, which under his management prospers when other ranches are going broke. But just in case drought or snows or adverse markets or cow thieves, or any act of God or man, should interfere with the profits of the ranch, a deposit of coal is found on the Virginian's land. This assures his ability to support Mollie in the style to which she would have been accustomed if the mills hadn't failed.

But Wister went much farther in making the cowboy a suitable hero for an industrial society.

Before Wister entered Harvard, the Great American Dream, the dream of a nation without great extremes of wealth and poverty, a nation in which all men might enjoy a comfortable living, had been shattered by sectionalism, civil war, and the rise of a socially irresponsible plutocracy. In the light of plain fact, the myths that had sustained unregulated business enterprise melted away. Carnegie's attempt to revive in modified form the religious sanction of stewardship was not conspicuously successful, even among his fellow millionaires. And classical economic theory, which made this the best of all possible worlds because it was a self-regulating world, in which, barring human interference, private selfishness would produce public good, was put to a severe strain. It was difficult for the farmers and laborers to understand that their impoverishment was for the greater glory of the nation.

Clearly, a new mythology was needed. It came as soon as the leaders of American opinion had time to turn from war to peace. Its chief prophet was Herbert Spencer, who, even before the publication of *The Origin of Species,* made a travesty of Darwin's biology by applying it to society and arriving at the conclusion that the rich deserved to be rich and the poor deserved to be poor.

The poverty of the incapable [he wrote], the distresses that come upon the imprudent, the starvation of the idle, and those shouldering asides of the weak by the strong, which leave many "in shallows and miseries," are the decrees of a large, far-seeing benevolence.

William Graham Sumner, Spencer's leading American disciple in the field of social theory, insisted that "poverty belongs to the struggle for existence" into which we are all born, and cannot be alleviated by social action. "Let every man be sober, industrious, prudent, and wise, and bring up his children to be so likewise, and poverty will be abolished in a few generations." It is not clear how the general diffusion of these qualities would lessen the intensity of the economic struggle or reduce the number of casualties, for Sumner could not conceive of a time when the contestants would be equal.

> Let it be understood [he said] that we cannot go outside this alternative: liberty, inequality, survival of the fittest; not—liberty, equality, survival of the unfittest. The former carries society forward and favors all its best members; the latter carries society downward and favors all its worst members.

Theodore Roosevelt applied the theory of evolution to history in his *The Winning of the West*; Wister exemplified it in his western fiction. Indeed, a weighty element in his admiration for the culture of the cattle country was his belief that it permitted the law of natural selection to operate freely. The Virginian's comment on Shorty, who did not survive, is pertinent.

> Now back East you can be middling and get along. But if you go to try a thing on in this Western country, you've got to do it *well.* You've got to deal cards *well;* you've got to steal *well;* and if you claim to be quick with your gun, you must be quick, for you're a public temptation, and some man will not resist trying to prove he is the quicker. You must break all the Commandments *well* in this Western country, and Shorty should have stayed in Brooklyn. . . .

And in a passage that Spencer or Sumner might have written, Wister declares:

> All America is divided into two classes,—the quality and the equality. The latter will always recognize the former when mistaken for it. Both will be with us until our women bear nothing but kings.

It was through the Declaration of Independence that we Americans acknowledged the *eternal inequality* of man. For by it we abolished a cut-and-dried aristocracy. We had seen little men artificially held up in high places, and great men artificially held down in low places, and our own justice-loving hearts abhorred this violence to human nature. Therefore, we decreed that every man would henceforth have equal liberty to find his own level. By this very decree we acknowledged and gave freedom to true aristocracy, saying, "Let the best man win, whoever he is." Let the best man win! That is America's word. That is true democracy. And true democracy and true aristocracy are one and the same thing. If anybody cannot see this, so much the worse for his eyesight.

In Wister's fiction the best man wins, but in fairness to him it should be said victory is not the only evidence of the winner's superiority: it is manifest also in his physical appearance, his bearing and manner, and in his native intelligence.

The businessmen who welcomed the new theory as a weapon against social legislation felt under no compulsion of consistency to refuse the bounty of a friendly government; and Wister apparently saw nothing wrong in the cattlemen's free use of the public domain, nor in the Virginian's homesteading known mineral land.

Wister shared the contempt for the masses inherent in the doctrine of social Darwinism. This contempt is implicit in the passage about the Declaration of Independence and in story after story. In "Specimen Jones," for example, Adams has drawn a six-shooter and is making a young tenderfoot dance. "The fickle audience was with him, of course, for the moment, since he was the upper dog and it was a good show; but one in that room was distinctly against him." This one, Specimen Jones, befriends the youth and turns the crowd against Adams. Wister's exaltation of the hero at the expense of the other characters often interferes with the plausibility of his narrative. To cite one example, only the most naïve reader could believe that young Drake in "The Jimmyjohn Boss" actually intimidated the revolting cowhands and brought them to taw. This emphasis on leadership issues from something deeper than literary convention. In actual life, Wister's pathetic search for a leader brought him to the conclusion that Theodore Roosevelt was "the greatest benefactor we people have known since Lincoln."

Wister subscribed wholeheartedly to the myth of Anglo-Saxon racial superiority, which, like laissez-faire economics, had found a new sanction in the theory of social evolution. White Americans had always proclaimed the racial inferiority of Indians and Negroes and, after the frontiers met, of Mexicans. Now the doctrine was extended to all races, vaguely confused with nationalities and other cultural groups; and it was boldly proclaimed by Josiah Strong, among others, that the Anglo-Saxon race, because of its innate superiority as manifest in its genius for politics and its moral purity, was destined, under God, to rule the world. Wister approved Jim Crow legislation, and in *Lady Baltimore* attempted to establish the inferiority of the Negro on the basis of physical anthropology. Contemplating three skulls, one of a Caucasian, one of a Negro, and one of an ape, Augustus exclaims,

> Why, in every respect that the African departed from the Caucasian, he departed in the direction

of the ape! Here was zoölogy mutely but eloquently telling us why there had blossomed no Confucius, no Moses, no Napoleon, upon that black stem; why no Iliad, no Parthenon, no Sistine Madonna, had ever risen from that tropic mud.

Wister's admiration for Moses did not extend to contemporary Jews. His anti-Semitism is obvious in his treatment of the Jew drummers in *The Virginian* and of the Jewish student in *Philosophy Four*. And in comparing Justices Holmes and Brandeis, he wrote:

> I doubt if any gulf exists more impassable than the one which divides the fundamental processes of a Holmes from those of a Brandeis:—"East is East and West is West, and never the twain shall meet." Holmes descends from the English Common Law, evolved by generations of people who have built themselves the greatest nation in a thousand years; Brandeis, from a noble and ancient race which has . . . failed in all centuries to make a stable nation of itself. *Liberty defined and assured by Law* is a principle as alien to the psychology of that race as it is native with Holmes and his ancestors.

There were Negro cowboys and Mexican cowboys, but they were few in the mountain states; and the appeal this region had for Wister was due in no small measure to the relative absence of foreigners, other than Britishers, there. In an article in *Harper's* for September, 1895, he wrote:

> Directly the English nobleman smelt Texas, the slumbering untamed Saxon awoke in him, and mindful of the tournament, mindful of the hunting-field, galloped howling after wild cattle, a born horseman, a perfect athlete, and spite of the peerage and gules and argent, fundamentally kin with the drifting vagabonds who swore and galloped by his side. The man's outcome typifies the way of the race from the beginning. Hundreds like him have gone to Australia, Canada, India, and have done likewise, and in our own continent you may see the thing plainer than anywhere else. No rood of modern ground is more debased and mongrel with its hordes of encroaching alien vermin, that turn our cities to Babels and our citizenship to a hybrid farce, who degrade our commonwealth from a nation into something half pawn-shop, half broker's office. But to survive in the clean cattle country requires spirit of adventure, courage, and self-sufficiency; you will not find many Poles or Huns or Russian Jews in that district; it stands as yet untainted by the benevolence of Baron Hirsch. . . . The Frenchman to-day is seen at his best inside a house; he can paint and he can play comedy, but he seldom climbs a new mountain. The Italian has forgotten Columbus, and sells fruit. Among the Spaniards and the Portuguese no Cortez or Magellan is found to-day. Except in Prussia, the Teuton is too often a tame, slippered animal, with his pedantic mind swaddled in a dressing-gown. But the Anglo-Saxon is still forever homesick for out-of-doors.

Wister admits that "the Mexican was the original cowboy," but says that "the American improved upon him." "Soon he had taken what was good from this small, deceitful alien, including his name, *Vaquero* . . . translated into Cowboy."

Wister makes no direct mention of Frederick Jackson Turner. He may have been familiar with the famous essay of 1893 in which that historian, neglecting the presence of families and larger social units on the frontier and minimizing the mutual help which had made settlement possible, declared that the frontier "promoted a democracy strong in selfishness and individualism," and "produced an antipathy to control," and in so declaring, added, unwittingly, I think, a historical sanction to the dialectic of American business. Spokesmen for business enterprise, accepting the Turner thesis that the frontier had been the most important determinant in American history, and that the frontier was opposed to social control, came to see in the cowboy, the last of the frontier types, a symbol of the American way. Horace Lorimer, who took over the editorship of the *Saturday Evening Post* in 1898 and frankly made it the voice of American business, assembled a stable of western writers, including Owen Wister, and through them kept before his readers the cowboy as a symbol of the rugged individualism that had made America great. Henceforth the exploits of the cowboy would recreate the tired businessman and at the same time strengthen him in his steadfastness.

Wister made his first trip to Wyoming in the summer of 1885, when the cattle business was on the crest of a boom that broke the following winter. By the time Wister got around to writing his first western story six years later, the West he had first known was gone. He never pretended that his stories described the West of the time of their writing: he always maintained that his fiction was historical. While he was writing it, he was sorely beset by three principal fears: the fear of monopoly, the fear of labor unions, and the fear of immigration. Monopolies and unions interfered with the free operation of the law of survival, and immigration threatened the Anglo-Saxon race.

> Three dangers [he wrote in *The Seven Ages of Washington* (1907)] to-day threaten the United States, any one of which could be fatal: unscrupulous Capital, destroying man's liberty to compete; unscrupulous Labor, destroying man's liberty to work; and undesirable Immigration, in which four years of naturalization are not going to counteract four hundred years of heredity. Unless the people check all of these, American liberty will become extinct.

But he had no program for checking them. Socialism, Populism, Free Silver, even the democratic liberalism of Woodrow Wilson, he hated. His social thinking was purely negative, and in his bafflement he turned to the golden age of the cattle West, an age he more created than perceived. It was not a perfect age, he admitted, but it was an uncomplicated one in which relationships were from man to man, and one in which the social myths of America might conceivably work.

There must be popular amusement—release from the tensions of modern life—and the cowboy is a hero with many faces, most of them innocent. But it is not altogether reassuring that in a time of greater complexity and greater insecurity than Wister lived to see, the cowboy with his six-shooter, his simple ethics, and his facility for direct action is our leading folk hero.

MODERN AND POSTMODERN LITERATURE

Tristram P. Coffin

SOURCE: "Real Use and Real Abuse of Folklore in the Writer's Subconscious: F. Scott Fitzgerald," in *New Voices in American Studies,* edited by Ray B. Browne, Donald M. Winkelman, and Allen Hayman, Purdue University Studies, 1966, pp. 102-12.

[*In the following essay, Coffin presents F. Scott Fitzgerald's* The Great Gatsby *as a retelling of an old folk tale with elements similar to those of John Keats's* "La Belle Dame sans Merci."]

The asininity and arrogance of the psychologists and mythographers who have undertaken literary interpretation in the last few decades rages on. I used to think that Erich Fromm's idiotic interpretation of "Little Red Cap" (his loaded name for "Little Red Riding Hood")[1] was a nadir below which this school could not sink, but I was naive. Since that essay, in 1951, a blaze of equally preposterous remarks on everything from *Hamlet* to *The Hamlet* has consumed scholarship. The latest I recall is a dilly—the theory being that Tom Sawyer, when he enters the cave in Twain's novel, is working out his Oedipus complex by means of a symbolic intercourse with Mother Earth.

I just don't understand scholars who think this way. They are well-trained people, coming from the best graduate schools, teaching at the best universities. Generally they hold a deep scorn for inadequate research and sloppy logic. They hate ignorance. But somehow they can't see how they are guilty of these faults themselves. They are quite insensitive to the fact that depth analyses of various cultures have negated many of the superficial similarities fascinating to the comparative mythologists of earlier generations. They fail to recognize that the interpretation of symbolic language in multiple variants of a myth usually creates paradoxes. They don't seem to know that something like

Sophocles' *Oedipus Rex* is a literary reworking of mythological and legendary matter and therefore cannot be treated as folk. They don't recognize that while America has developed a national subliterary lore, its folklore has remained regional, occupational, and ethnic in focus. They seem to have no idea of how old märchen actually are, how long history can survive in oral tradition, or exactly how ritual does persist. They are psychologists, interpreting written and oral literatures about which they know little. They are literary critics, interpreting psychological and anthropological evidence about which they know little. They are scholars who use terms like "archetype," "myth," "reality," "American folk," "fable," and "legend" so loosely and so casually they have made the words almost meaningless.

In my really cynical moments, I explain their behavior this way: (1) each generation of scholars has to have a gimmick so it can rewrite all the articles of the past, build a bibliography of "fresh" interpretations, and deserve its promotions and grants; (2) irrational symbolic language offers an area in which one cannot be proved wrong and in which one can always defend himself by patronizing the attacker; (3) the political atmosphere in the world today encourages the "discovery" of archetypes and other indications that all men are one and the same. And I suppose most people can't resist the opportunity of new frontiers, *cartes blanches,* immunity from error, and the chance to prove Sophocles, the Watusi, and Oscar Wilde brothers under the skin.

When I am cynical, I am probably right, for cynics usually are. But being right is not my present concern. What really bothers me here is the fact that these scholars have made it all but impossible to talk sensibly about the subconscious use of folklore by a literary genius. One either talks in the sweeping generalities of Frazer, Rank, and Raglan or he talks not at all.

I recall trying to publish the article that has been revised to make up the bulk of this paper. It finally appeared in *Midwest Folklore* under the title "Gatsby's Fairy Lover"[2] after it had been rejected by a very prominent journal. The rejection embittered me, not because the article was deemed unworthy, but because of the reader's sole comment—erased, though still legible, on the cover: "I wouldn't accept this; we have published enough of that myth-ritual stuff already." Now I know who the reader was (his name was also not properly erased) and I know he is a prominent Fitzgerald scholar. Assuming he read the article (and I am certain he did), I can only explain his remark as an instance of preconditioning in the sort of scholarship I have been debunking. Evidently the reader could not believe an article about the subconscious use of folklore in *The Great Gatsby* could be anything except another example of what he erroneously labeled "myth-ritualism." That a scholar this prominent can be this confused is really tragic.

For obviously a writer may use folklore, or any other material for that matter, subconsciously, and be doing nothing more than just that. He may simply call on formulas and motifs gathered from his reading and observations, developing them without an awareness that he has used them—and he may do this without mythic association, without psychic symbolism, without sharing his usage with other minds in his or another culture. The fact that the formulas and motifs have complicated histories or even that they can be traced to myth or ritual is often irrelevant. In fact, it is likely that most uses to which writers put folk materials offer thin pickings in a cross-cultural sense and really prove little except a man must write out of those things he has put into his own mind—"experience, the universal Mother of Science," being also the universal Mother of Art.[3]

Fitzgerald was such a writer. He used folklore and matter derived from folklore steadily, always to be sure generalizing it and refocusing it, but nonetheless using it so integrally one needs to know the folk backgrounds to get a full understanding of the works. Broad themes from Celtic fairy lore and the märchen lie behind many of his tales and novels: "the land of no time," "the vanishing lover," "the golden girl in the white palace," "the underdog hero," "the magic power of money," "the reality of happiness-ever-after." Such motifs, tied up more intimately with his private life than with his American culture background, need no symbolic interpretation, disguise no mythic patterns. Certainly, they are unique for Fitzgerald as he develops them. They distinguish him from, rather than bind him to, other peoples, other Irish-Americans, other graduates of Princeton, just as they are meaningless in the works of his contemporaries Hemingway, Eliot, Frost, or Budd Schulberg.

A penetrating discussion by Richard L. Schoenwald entitled "F. Scott Fitzgerald as John Keats"[4] clearly establishes Fitzgerald's debt to the Englishman in matters all the way from vocabulary to overall inspiration. Schoenwald's remarks concentrate heavily on *Tender is the Night,* and he discusses *The Great Gatsby* only in passing. He might well have spent more time on Fitzgerald's masterpiece, for *The Great Gatsby* uses the basic situation of Keats's *La Belle Dame Sans Merci* as its foundation.[5]

Keats's *La Belle Dame Sans Merci* is an idealistic development of the old ballad of Thomas Rymer, itself a retelling of one of the adventures of Thomas of Erceldoune.[6] The tale that lies behind the folksong, and ultimately behind Keats's poem, is that of the Fairy Queen who seduces a mortal away from earth. Although Keats changes the temper of the narrative from country to court and although he idealizes the whole affair—emphasizing the irresistible charm of the woman, the passion of the love, and the loneliness of the lover—he retains the essential relationship of the tale, that of the normal man who longs for the unattainable girl.

The parallel to Gatsby and Daisy Buchanan is immediately obvious. We are introduced to Gatsby as he stands "alone and palely loitering." Through flashbacks we learn the story of the poor boy and his "faery's child," how she lured him, told him she loved him true, and left him. In fact, so closely does the outline of the novel follow the outline of the poem, it is amazing no one noticed the parallel before.

The Celtic Fairy Queen, of whom Keats makes use, is truly a "full beautiful creature." Her dress is grass-green or white; she rides a belled horse, usually white; she has flowing hair, scented, and sometimes decorated with apple-blossoms. It is no wonder Thomas of Erceldoune once mistook her for the Queen of Heaven. Keats sums up her beauty with the phrase "her hair was long, her foot was light, and her eyes were wild." When we allow for the change in setting, we are struck with how fairy-like Daisy seems too. Though the symbol for her presence is a green light,[7] she dresses in white. When we first meet her with Jordan Baker, the two girls are presented through the sensitive eyes of Nick Carraway as being capable of suspension and even flight, until the earthy Tom Buchanan drops then symbolically to the floor.

> The only completely stationary object in the room was an enormous couch on which two young women were buoyed up as though upon an anchored balloon. They were both in white, and their dresses were rippling and fluttering as if they had just been blown back in after a short flight around the house. I must have stood for a few moments listening to the whip and snap of the curtains and the groan of a picture on the wall. Then there was a boom as Tom Buchanan shut the rear windows and the caught wind died about the room, and the curtains and the rugs and the two young women ballooned slowly to the floor.[8]

Daisy, whose maiden name is Fay (an older word for fairy)[9] continues to be associated with white throughout the book. Jordan Baker recalls her in Louisville "dressed in white" and driving a "little white roadster" (75). She wears white on the day of the accident (115).

White is, to be sure, the color of purity, of the Virgin, and of the bride-to-be. As Fitzgerald uses it, it has a good deal of irony associated with it. It is not without irony as one color of the Celtic Fairy Queen either. The Celtic Fairy is a creature with Satanic connections; some legends even described such beings as the angels who fell in the Revolt from Awe. Daisy, too, has her Satanic side. At least within the framework of her society she is considered fast. Jordan remembers that "wild rumors were circulating about her" (76) and Gatsby was excited by the fact "that many men had already loved" her (148). Yet her reputation only serves to increase her charm in an echoing and nostalgic way.

Her voice is particularly haunting. Keats describes the "belle dame" as making "sweet moan" and singing "a faery's song." Fitzgerald develops a similar idea.

It was the kind of voice that the ear follows up and down, as if each speech is an arrangement of notes that will never be played again. Her face was sad and lovely with bright things in it, bright eyes and a bright passionate mouth, but there was an excitement in her voice that men who had cared for her found difficult to forget; a singing compulsion, a whispered "Listen," a promise that she had done gay, exciting things just a while since and that there were gay, exciting things hovering in the next hour [9-10].

Carraway thinks of the voice as "indiscreet," though that isn't really the word he wants. Gatsby is the one who pin-points it.

"She's got an indiscreet voice," I remarked. "It's full of—"I hesitated.

"Her voice is full of money," he said suddenly.

That was it. I'd never understood it before. It was full of money—that was the inexhaustible charm that rose and fell in it, the jingle of it, the cymbals' song of it—High in a white palace the king's daughter, the golden girl. . . . [120]

Daisy shares the indiscretion and magic that Gatsby and others (including Fitzgerald himself) have long associated with wealth. She does what she wants, she is without care, and she promises what money can bring. Gatsby's love for her is a mixture of desire for a woman and fascination for moving beyond himself.

Socially, Daisy is beyond Gatsby, who even in his youth carried out programs of self-betterment, as far beyond him as any fairy is beyond any mortal. With his "romantic readiness" (2) he turns her into a dream—"the latest dream he ever did dream"—but it is of no more avail than the knight's dream of his fairy love. Out of "the foul dust" of modern America that floats in the wake of such hopes, Fitzgerald develops the tragedy of the book. Gatsby is left where the sedge has withered—frustrated, alone—having "paid a high price for living too long with a single dream (162).

He talked a lot about the past, and I gathered that he wanted to recover something, some idea of himself perhaps, that had gone into loving Daisy. His life had been confused and disordered since then, but if he could once return to a certain starting place and go over it all slowly, he could find out what that thing was. . . . (115)

He stretched out his hand desperately as if to snatch only a wisp of air, to save a fragment of the spot that she had made lovely for him. But it was all going by too fast now for his blurred eyes and he knew that he had lost that part of it, the freshest and the best, forever [153].

The knight's frustration rises, of course, from the fact he is mortal and the fairy is not. The frustration of Gatsby is not dissimilar, though things may seem in reverse at first glance. Gatsby is frustrated not because he is mortal, but because the real Daisy is not supernatural—because she cannot unlive five years, because she reacts practically to the death of Myrtle Wilson. However, this real Daisy is but remotely connected with the Daisy that Gatsby loves. He believes in a supernatural girl who can unlive the past, who is capable of the same "intensity" that he is capable of.

Almost five years! There must have been moments even that afternoon when Daisy tumbled short of his dreams—not through her own fault, but because of the colossal vitality of his illusion. It had gone beyond her, beyond everything. He had thrown himself into it with a creative passion, adding to it all the time, decking it out with every bright feather that drifted his way [97].

It is this creation of Gatsby's hope that deceives him and goes from him, beyond, as it were, the mists of actuality. The real Daisy, a person playing a tired, pointless game, is a member of a "secret society" (18) of the born rich. As Gatsby is not of the group, she looks at him "as she did love" and "makes sweet moan." But she renounces him during the War for a member of her own group, and she does it again over a "plate of cold fried chicken . . . and two bottles of ale" (146)—sans merci.

Fitzgerald describes the development of Gatsby's "romantic readiness" in the short story *Absolution*, which was "intended to be a picture of" Gatsby's early life.[10] Here the young boy learns that there is a glittering world where he can exist free from God's moral truths responsible only to the promptings of his own imagination. Jay Gatsby, once James Gatz, entered such a world, for when he gave up his dream of mounting "to a secret place above the trees" and wed "his unutterable visions" to a girl's "perishable breath," he re-created his life as a fairy tale with Daisy as the heroine.

Now no scholar would be bold enough to claim that Fitzgerald consciously conceived of Gatsby's dream in terms of a formal märchen, but that he thought of Gatsby's dream as a sort of fairy-tale version of life is obvious. Carraway's flash of understanding comes when he realizes Gatsby thinks of Daisy as the king's daughter, the golden girl living high in a white palace (120). Moreover, if we reconstruct what Gatsby expects the story of his affair with Daisy to be, and set it up as a märchen, it would go like this:

1. "High in a white palace" the hero meets "the king's daughter, the golden girl."

2. He possesses a magic with which to win this princess—the fact that he is different from the others she has known, that he seems to know a lot because he knows different things from her (150). "One still October night" he takes the girl because he has no real right to touch her hand. To his lower middle-class midwestern mind, he has married her because she is a "nice" girl (149). She will be his forever and a day as soon as he builds her a castle such as princesses inhabit. She will wait.

3. The third person possesses the wife before the hero can build her the needed castle. This man is an ogre, and the princess longs to be free of him.

4. Five years elapse. The hero has obtained a new magic object, money. He is now able to build the castle. He goes to where she has been taken in order to rescue her. His original magic, his difference from her usual acquaintances, and the old love work again. The ogre attempts to destroy this magic, but he fails. Love is too strong; the hero and the heroine live happily ever after—having completely forgotten the events of the intervening years.

Oddly, this märchen proves to be a variant of a widespread tale commonly known as its Aladdin version.[11] Like all märchen, it has no rigid form. However, the general pattern typed by Aarne and Thompson as #561 is strikingly similar to the fairy-tale Gatsby creates to replace reality.

1. The hero finds a magic object which will perform all the wishes of the owner.

2. By means of the object he builds a magic castle and marries the king's daughter.

3. The magic object is stolen by a third person who wants to possess the wife. The castle and the wife are transported to a distant island.

4. The hero recovers the object with the help of a second magic object which transports the hero to the island. The castle and the princess are restored.

Gatsby's variant contains all the major motifs of A-T 561. The order is somewhat different, but that is not unusual among märchen. The only new element added is the ability of the hero and the heroine to eradicate the five unhappy years. Some readers may feel that Gatsby's "difference" is not a magic power, but a careful reading of the novel does show this to be the charm through which he originally wins Daisy and that it still attracts her five years later. There is also the point that Tom does not actually steal this magic when he first "possesses the wife," but he certainly destroys it in the hotel in New York just before the accident (125-35).

Fitzgerald is no fool. *The Great Gatsby* tells, in a way, the story of the author's own dreams about Ginevra King and Zelda Sayre. That Fitzgerald wished his own life to be a märchen, with Zelda as the princess and money as the magic object, in no way prevented his seeing that a love affair similar to his own could not work as fairy tales might and that money has its limits as far as magic goes. In the novel he sees to it that Gatsby's märchen ends wrong. Daisy's little girl by Tom makes it clear that five years cannot be erased; unhappy fate in the form of the auto accident crushes the hero's hopes; the princess forgets her lover and lets the ogre "save her neck"; and the hero breaks "like glass" against the "hard malice" of the villain (148).

So it is that the Daisy of Gatsby's märchen disillusions him because he is forced to deal with her as a real woman and not as a golden girl. He learns as "the knight-at-arms" learns before him, that life is unsentimental, that "belles dames" are "sans merci," and that an America of social and moral traditions is no setting for a märchen. There is much more to the story than this, of course. There is the contrast of midwestern moralism and Eastern insouciance; there is the denounciation of American materialism; there is the obvious religious overtone of the novel in which the man whose mind romped "like the mind of God" finds "what a grotesque thing a rose is." Any study of the book as a whole must treat these points.

However, we are only concerned with the fact that Fitzgerald used folklore, certainly without conscious awareness, as he went about composing his book. He may have been conscious of his debt to Keats, but surely he did not know that Keats had based his poem on a Celtic fairy motif, and his contact with and recollection of A-T 561 was probably about that of John Doe or Uncle Sam.

Nor am I the only folklorist who has seen Fitzgerald in this light. Horace Beck pursued my thoughts about Fitzgerald further and wrote the following about *The Ice Palace.*

> After your remark on *Gatsby* I have re-read *The Ice Palace* and *The Rich Boy* and would like to make some pertinent remarks about the two stories. Sally Carrol in *The Ice Palace* lives in a warm green country under a magnolia tree. She lolls around all day and listens to horns and to music. Physically she is like Mab, beautiful with dark hair and pale skin, and is young, almost immortally young. She meets the troll from the North and goes with him or is lured by him into the north country where she becomes lost in an ice palace with lights and music and almost loses her life. She even slips and spins through the corridors. Her lover fetches her to the troll king's palace with the magic wand of money. After her escape from the troll king's palace she returns to faeryland, where she lives again on milk and honey in the land of always summer.
>
> In *The Rich Boy* Anson Hunter is last seen trailing a lovely girl with a green, excuse me red, hat across the sea to a strange land hoping to find what can never be found and at the same time using the wand of money. Again in *Babylon Revisited* we have the hero trying to get back to the faeryland of yesterday equipped with money. But try as he might, the spell has been broken and he can never regain that place nor the little child he so wants.
>
> Again in a story called *Absolution* the priest has fallen under the faery spell. It is warm and the green grass is all around. Outside in the warm moonlit night the lovely blond girls whisper on the walks and he is fair moonstruck by the

promise of what might be called faeryland. Take a good look. Even glance at *The Freshest Boy* and see what turns up. Maybe it stretches things but it does work.[12]

He might also have mentioned *Winter Dreams.*

Here then is a very real way in which a writer may make use of folklore filtered from the folk in creating his works. The use is integral to an understanding of the author and the works in question—and it should be studied. But it must be studied by scholars who are not preconditioned by the tidal wave of mythic and psychic half-truths that washes about our graduate schools and scholarly journals. We need scholars who will come to Fitzgerald and the rest without a compulsion for monomyths and archetypes, with minds open to the possibility that an author might borrow a technique from folklore just as he might borrow the technique of focusing a novel through Nick Carraway from Henry James. Then we will get some very fine and very needed studies. As it is now, when I start to read some more of that "myth-ritual stuff" I find an old ballad stanza rising from my subconscious,

> The first line that Sir Patrick red,
>   A loud lauch lauched he;
> The next line that Sir Patrick red,
>   The teir blinded his ee.

NOTES

[1] Erich Fromm, *The Forgotten Language* (New York, 1951), 235-41.

[2] "Gatsby's Fairy Lover," *Midwest Folklore,* X (Summer 1960), 79-85.

[3] See Peter A. Motteux's translation of Cervantes' *Don Quixote,* Chapter 7.

[4] Richard L. Schoenwald, "F. Scott Fitzgerald as John Keats," *Boston University Studies in English,* III (1957), 12-21. The footnotes to this article contain many references to Fitzgerald's interest in Keats.

[5] That Fitzgerald knew the poem well is evident not only from the Schoenwald article, but also from his references to it in *This Side of Paradise* (New York, 1920), 45 and in *The Beautiful and Damned* (New York, 1922), III, 8. In the latter, Anthony's girl, Dorothy Raycroft, is called "*la belle dame sans merci* who lived in his heart."

[6] The revised 1820 text of Keats's poem is used for this article. All quotations come from this version. The ballad "Thomas Rymer" is Number 37 in Francis J. Child's *The English and Scottish Popular Ballads,* 5 vols. (Boston and New York, 1882-98). Thomas of Erceldoune, who was frequently referred to as Thomas the Rymer, had an established reputation as a prophet and poet by 1350. Just when he lived is not known, but it was probably in the Thirteenth Century. His prophetic power supposedly came as a gift from the Queen of the Elves.

[7] It would be stretching things a bit to imply that the green of the light at the end of Daisy's dock is related to the green of the Celtic Fairy. Green, which is a lucky color for the Irish, was unlucky in Scotland where Thomas of Erceldoune lived. It certainly is an unlucky color as it applies to Daisy, but that fact does not jibe with Fitzgerald's Irish background. Green, as it concerns Daisy, probably means no more than it does at any crossroads. However, it is interesting to note that the green of the fairies probably derives from their being associated with older vegetation rites. Fitzgerald uses green as a symbol of fertility and promise, and yellow as a color of sterility and despair throughout the novel.

[8] F. Scott Fitzgerald, *The Great Gatsby* (New York: Scribner's Student's Edition, 1925 and 1953), 8. All other quotations from *The Great Gatsby* are from this edition.

[9] Fitzgerald evidently had Father Fay in mind when he gave Daisy her maiden name. On 53, Jordan Baker refers to her aunt, Mrs. Sigourney Howard. Sigourney was Cyril Fay's middle name. The fact that Fay also means fairy and that the daisy is commonly an emblem of both fidelity and deceit may be just a coincidence; if so, it is a happy one.

[10] See Fitzgerald's letter to John Jamison, April 15, 1934, quoted in Arthur Mizener, *The Far Side of Paradise* (Boston, 1951), 172. Also see his notes to Maxwell Perkins on or about April 16, 1934, preserved in the Scribner files.

[11] See Antti Aarne and Stith Thompson, *The Types of the Folktale,* Folklore Fellows Communications #184 (Helsinki, 1961), where Type 561 is entitled "Aladdin" and is considered to be closely related to Type 560, "The Magic Ring."

[12] Horace P. Beck to author, February 17, 1965.

Patrick B. Mullen

SOURCE: "American Folklife And 'The Grapes of Wrath'," in *Journal of American Culture,* Vol. 1, No. 4, Winter, 1978, pp. 742-53.

[*In the following essay, Mullen identifies a variety of folk qualities in John Steinbeck's* The Grapes of Wrath, *varying from elements as obvious as jokes and proverbs to ones as seemingly obscure as the physical stance of characters when conversing.*]

John Steinbeck's *The Grapes of Wrath* has been continuously popular since it was first published in 1939. Although some literary critics dismiss it, the novel remains a unique American social document which strikes a responsive chord in succeeding generations of American readers. One of the reasons for the novel's success, I think, is Steinbeck's ability to incorporate rural southwestern American folklore and folklife into the fabric of his fiction. He is able to use his own observations of folklife to develop character, give a sense of everyday life, and express the major social, political, and philosophical themes of the novel. Since the folklife he drew upon is interwoven with the society and culture of the people he was writing about, a full understanding of the novel can only come from the perspectives of sociology, history, and politics of migrant farm workers of the 1930's. All aspects of their traditional life should be considered, from verbal expressions such as anecdotes and legends to folk dances, music, superstitions, customs, and behavior; and all of it should be viewed within the context of folk performances.[1]

John Steinbeck had a first-hand knowledge of rural southwestern and migrant farm worker folklife which he gained by observing the people of the region over several years. In 1936 Steinbeck visited migrant camps near Salinas and Bakersfield, California. He wrote a series of articles based on his observations for the San Francisco *News* (Oct. 5 and 12, 1936). In the fall of 1937 Steinbeck travelled with the migrants from Oklahoma to California and lived in their camps. A collection of the newspaper articles plus an epilogue based on his experiences was published in 1938 as a pamphlet entitled *Their Blood is Strong.*[2] This pamphlet contains some of the basic material for *The Grapes of Wrath,* and along with Steinbeck's letters from this period show his knowledge of farm and migrant folklife. Steinbeck was not merely an observer; he was also a participant. He may have worked alongside the migrants in the field. In a letter to Lawrence Clark Powell, Steinbeck states,

> I have to write this sitting in a ditch. I'll be home in two or three weeks. I'm not working— may go south to pick a little cotton. All this, needless to say, is not for publication—migrants are going south now and I'll probably go along. I enjoy it a lot.[3]

His method of observation was to live with the migrants and view their lives as closely as possible.[4] His methods were not too different from modern folklorists' who live with their informants to get a complete picture of their lives.

In identifying and interpreting the folklore and folklife in the novel I shall follow Steinbeck's own model of moving from a microcosm to a macrocosm, from the smallest social group, the family, through the migrant community and finally to the entire society.[5] The family unit provides a traditional context for the use of folklore. The Joad family has a strong sense of tradition, and one of the ways this is passed on is through family anecdotes, oral stories about family members and ancestors and exciting or amusing episodes in family history.[6] Steinbeck introduces family anecdotes into the novel

even before we meet the Joads directly. Shortly after Tom Joad and Jim Casy meet on the road to the Joad farm, Tom relates the story of how Pa Joad stole their house (p.38).[7] The story arises in the natural context of the conversation between the two men; they are getting close to the house when Casy asks:

> "Ain't she over that third rise?"
>
> "Sure," said Joad. "Less somebody stole it, like Pa stole it." (pp. 37-38)

The point of the story is less the origin of the house than the character of Pa, which Casy proceeds to describe from his own observation at camp meetings. This in turn reminds Tom of a funny family character anecdote about Uncle John's and Pa's wild antics at a revival baptism (p. 39). One contextual detail indicates a function for the stories:

> Joad's eyes were inward on his memory. He seemed to be laughing inside himself. "Uncle John was a crazy bastard," he said, "Like what he done with that shoat." He chuckled and walked on.
>
> Jim Casy waited impatiently. The story did not continue. Casy gave it a good long time to come out. "Well, what'd he do with that shoat?" he demanded at last, with some irritation. (pp. 39-40)

Tom then tells the story of how Uncle John ate almost an entire pig by himself (p. 40).[8] The context of the story-telling event serves a literary purpose. Anecdotes are often told in a series with one story reminding the performers of another story, and that is what happens here; Tom tells three stories and Casy comments on them. A story-telling formula occurs in this context; an abstract statement about a character ("Uncle John was a crazy bastard,") is followed by a brief image of the entertaining element in the tale ("Like what he done with that shoat."); the concrete narrative then proceeds to illustrate the abstraction. Tom's formulaic statements about Uncle John create an expectation in Casy for the story but Tom does not fulfill his role as performer within the event, and Casy has to demand that he tell it. The key to the meaning of the scene is the reason Tom forgot to tell the story: "Joad's eyes were inward on his memory." Tom has been away from home for four years; the family anecdotes are a vital link to his past as he nears the reunion with his family. After telling a couple of stories, he no longer has the need for verbal expression of them; he can savor them in his memory. In a folklore context, family anecdotes function to give a sense of family identity through the preservation and evocation of memories of characters and events.[9] In the literary context, Steinbeck suggests this same function, but he goes beyond it. The anecdotes and the context in which they occur reveal something about the character of Tom Joad, his strong feelings for his family and his compassionate nature which offsets the reader's knowledge that he has been in prison for killing a man. The anecdotes also introduce us to some of the characteristics of the family members, their individuality and their eccentricities. A knowledge and understanding of the Joads is significant because Steinbeck has them represent the displaced farmers of the 1930s.

Anecdotes also function to instill pride in the family. After Tom and Casy have reached the deserted house, Tom tells a story about Grampa's "Injun pilla." (p. 59) One purpose of the story is to illustrate Grampa's character in a positive way: "Grampa's a tough ol' bastard." Later Tom relates an anecdote about Ma beating a peddler with a live chicken to indicate her toughnesses: "An' Ma ain't nobody you can push aroun', neither." (p. 64) This story takes on additional meaning because of the context. Tom is trying to figure out why the Joads abandoned their farm without a fight: "I wonder Pa went so easy. I wonder Grampa didn' kill nobody. Nobody never tol' Grampa where to put his feet." (p. 64) The anecdote about Ma reinforces Tom's pride in her spirit and makes their abandonment of the farm even more inexplicable. Later when Steinbeck has presented the full picture of the social and economic reasons for leaving the farm, we can see why the Joads had to leave despite the strength, independence and pride exhibited through the family anecdotes. There are other family anecdotes later in the novel. Ma tells about Pa's father (p. 123) and about Ruthie as a small child (p. 187); all the family stories function to show the family as a traditionally unified group.

The significance of the family unit for Steinbeck's overall thematic concerns is expressed not only through verbal forms such as the anecdote but also through traditional behavior and folklife. Much of this comes out in the family council scene early in the novel: "And without any signal the family gathered by the truck, and the congress, the family government, went into session." (p. 135) The family meeting is itself traditional. The role each member plays is determined by tradition; their behavior indicates the hold the past has on them: "They seemed to be part of an organization of the unconscious." (p. 135) Pa, as the head of the family, is the first to take a position:

> . . . he squatted down in the dust and found a stick to draw with. One foot was flat to the ground, the other rested on the ball and slightly back, so that one knee was higher than the other. Left forearm rested on the lower, left, knee; the right elbow on the right knee, and the right fist cupped for the chin. Pa squatted there, looking at the truck, his chin in his cupped fist. (p. 136)

This detailed description reveals that even his body position is part of traditional folk behavior; in Oklahoma, Arkansas and Texas, this position is known as "hunkerin'," and it is one of the usual ways men will gather for a discussion. Uncle John, Grampa, Tom, Connie and Noah also "hunker down" for the family meeting. The women take their traditional places behind the men, and the children are beside the women. Pa, as head of the family, speaks first. Al, since he has become a young man with adult responsibilities, has a chance to

participate. Every character stays within his own traditional role. The mother in the rural farm family may be secondary to the husband in some ways, but she has a great deal of traditional authority as well.[10] Steinbeck recognized this: " . . . Ma was powerful in the group." (p. 140) She makes the final decision on one important matter. Since there is an established family structure and traditionally defined roles within the culture, the family council gives a sense of unity and cooperation thereby holding the family together in times of stress.

One of the decisions that must be made by the council is whether to take Jim Casy with them to California. Superstitious behavior enters into this decision; Grampa says, "Some folks use' ta figger that a preacher was poison luck." (p. 138) It is fitting that a superstition be a part of the decision-making process since they are part of farm folklore. Grampa as the oldest male in the family is the appropriate person to voice traditional wisdom. The response of the others is also traditional; they do not belittle Grampa's superstition because they respect his age and position in the family, but they recognize that more practical matters must be the basis of the final decision. "'They's more to this than is he lucky, or is he a nice 'fella', Pa said. 'We got to figger close.' . . . 'An' kin we feed a extra mouth?'" (pp. 138-9) Pa's comment is also in keeping with the folklore context of superstitions; people will usually practice superstitions only to the point where they begin to interfere with a rational approach to life.[11] Thus, this one episode indicates that Steinbeck not only used traditional superstitions, but he described them within an accurate traditional context and in a traditional style.

There are similarities in the folklore and literary functions of the superstition since an entire folklore event has been transformed into a novel episode. The council scene also serves literary purposes which would not be found in a family meeting within a folk context. Steinbeck wants to show the importance of communal cooperation within the family unit,[12] and he does so with this episode. Later in the novel the theme of cooperation is expanded beyond the family and becomes part of Steinbeck's social philosophy; but here he is using the interaction of the family members in reaching a decision as a microcosm for the importance of social cooperation. The family council is based on tradition, and by showing Grampa's contribution, Steinbeck indicates the importance of tradition and the democratic nature of the process which can even include a senile man's superstition. "Grampa was still the titular head, but he no longer ruled. His position was honorary and a matter of custom." (p. 137) The social and philosophical meaning of Grampa's superstition within the family council might not occur on the folk level, but by accurately describing the superstition and its folk context and placing it within the thematic framework of the novel, Steinbeck can give it new implications.

Steinbeck juxtaposes the family council scene with another example of folklife in order to emphasize another thematic point. The last decision made at the family council is to slaughter and preserve the hogs for their trip. The daily tasks of the farmer and his wife are considered a part of folklife. The five pages of detailed description of the hog slaughter and curing accurately reproduces the traditional method used on farms.[13] On most farms, the hog slaughtering was a family venture and was usually done in the fall when the weather had turned cold to stay. Uncle John points this out, "Wrong time a year for slaughterin'. Meat'll be sof' if it don' chill." (p. 141) Thus, folk knowledge is combined with the folk method to give a clear picture of this scene, but again Steinbeck has an artistic function in mind here. By describing the hog slaughter immediately after the family council, he is reiterating the point about family cooperation. In the meeting, cooperation takes place on a verbal and cognitive level; with the hog slaughter, mental cooperation is put into active practice. All the family members who are able take part in the killing and curing of the pigs; each has his own role to fulfill just as each did within the family meeting. Steinbeck is showing that traditional family cooperation is not merely an abstraction but an active fact.

The family also functions for psychological support, and Steinbeck employs folklore to show this happening. Rosasharn's pregnancy is a constant theme in the novel, and there are traditional folk beliefs associated with it throughout. Most of them are used by Ma Joad or women close to the family to alleviate Rosasharn's fears about pregnancy and childbirth. Shortly after Grampa dies, Rosasharn expresses her fear about the bad things happening to them having an effect on her unborn baby:

> Ma said, "They used to be a sayin', 'A chile born outa sorrow'll be a happy chile.' Isn't that so, Mis' Wilson?"

> "I heard it like that," said Sairy. "An' I heard the other: 'Born outa too much joy'll be a doleful boy.'" (p. 193)

At the actual birth, Mrs. Wainwright puts a knife under the mattress.

> "Maybe it don't do no good," she said apologetically. "Our folks always done it. Don't do no harm anyways."

> Ma nodded. "We used a plow point. I guess anything sharp'll work, long as it can cut birth pains. I hope it ain't gonna be a long one." (pp. 597-598; Brown no. 45)[14]

Here the superstition functions not only to allay Rosasharn's fears but also to relieve the anxieties of the women in attendance. The context provided by Steinbeck is again accurate as folklore; one of the primary functions of superstition is to relieve anxiety, and people often apologize for their superstitions but rationalize them with statements such as Mrs. Wainwright's, "Don't do no harm anyways."[15] The meaning of this incident and the earlier one is that the psychological

support for Rosasharn is coming not only from her mother but also from women outside the family. The superstitious events surrounding pregnancy and birth are symbolic of the Joads' growing dependency on other people. There is one exception to this pattern; one of the religious fanatics in the government camp tells Rosasharn that dancing and playing will cause her to lose the baby (pp. 423-424), but this woman is described as a troublemaker, and she is not part of the communal spirit of the camp. The prevailing pattern was that as the family disintegrated, the communal spirit of the family moved outward to include the other migrant families.[16] This is an important part of the movement from microcosm to macrocosm and in the development of Steinbeck's social philosophy from one that is based on a family community to one that applies to the community of all humankind.

The outward movement of the novel is also paralleled in Steinbeck's use of anecdotes. Besides the family stories there are also local character anecdotes. The two forms are similar in that they both can deal with human eccentricities, but the context of the local character tales is wider; they are known by the entire community. Some of the family stories about Uncle John and Grampa could be told outside the family, but the tale told about Willy Feeley and the heifer must be widely known since Tom introduces it by saying:

> "'Minds me of a story they tell about Willy Feeley when he was a young fella. Willy was bashful, awful bashful. Well, one day he takes a heifer over to Graves' bull. Ever'body was out but Elsie Graves, and Elsie wasn't bashful at all. Willy, he stood there turnin' red an' he couldn't even talk. Elsie says, 'I know what you come for; the bull's out in back a the barn.' Well, they took the heifer out there an' Willy an' Elsie sat on the fence to watch. Purty soon Willy got feelin' purty fly. Elsie looks over an' says, like she don' know, 'What's a matter, Willy?' Willy's so randy he can't hardly set still. 'By God,' he says, 'by God, I wisht I was a-doin' that!' Elsie says, 'Why not. Willy? It's your heifer.'"

> The preacher laughed softly. (p. 94)

This anecdote is about the same man who drove the tractor that took the corner off the Joad house. (p. 62) The fact that Tom can tell this humorous story about him shows that he has no hard feelings toward him. He understands why Willy had to act; he was a victim of the banks along with everybody else. The anecdote shows some of the same personal warmth toward a member of the community as is shown toward a family member in the family anecdotes.

This local anecdote is contrasted to a joke with a similar motif which occurs later in the novel. Steinbeck changes both the text and context to emphasize the contrast. The joke is related in the interchapter describing life on Highway 66. The context is a truck stop cafe where two truck drivers are talking about waitresses.

Seen any new etchin's lately, Bill?

Well, here's one.

Now, you be careful front of a lady.

Oh, this ain't bad. Little kid comes in late ta school. Teacher says, "Why ya late?" Kid says, "Had a take a heifer down—get 'er bred." Teacher says, "Couldn't your ol' man do it?" Kid says, "Sure he could, but not as good as the bull."

Mae squeaks with laughter, harsh screeching laughter. (p. 214)

This is not an anecdote, it is a joke. The anecdote is personal and characteristic of a local community or small group. The joke is impersonal and characteristic of practically all of modern society. Both the anecdote and joke forms of this narrative depend on the image of a man having intercourse with a cow for their humor, but one contains the warmth of a familiar personality (the "awful bashful" Willy Feeley) and the other an anonymous "little kid." The contexts in which the narratives are told are also different. The anecdote is told by one member of a rural community to another and is received with soft laughter. The joke is told by a travelling man to a woman he does not know well and only sees on an irregular basis, and is received with harsh laughter. Neither the driver nor the waitress has any roots with the land or a specific locale. Even though the joke is folklore, the performer and audience are not part of an agrarian folk group. Steinbeck in this interchapter paints a picture of middle-class popular culture that is the antithesis of the regional folk culture he has described to this point:

... the nickel phonograph with records piled up like pies, ready to swing out to the turntable and play dance music, "Ti-pi-ti-pi-tin," "Thanks for the Memory," Bing Crosby, Benny Goodman. At one end of the counter a covered case; candy cough drops, caffeine sulphate called Sleepless, No-Doze; candy, cigarettes, razor blades, aspirin, Bromo-Seltzer, Alka-Seltzer. The walls decorated with posters, bathing girls, blondes with big breasts and slender hips and waxen faces, in white bathing suits, and holding Coca-Cola and smiling—see what you get with a Coca-Cola. (p. 208)

After establishing this popular context, Steinbeck has the truck driver tell his joke, and after the joke is told he has a poverty-stricken migrant family come into the cafe to provide another contrast with the blatant consumerism of American culture. His anger at the starvation of a people in the midst of plenty comes through clearly in this chapter. The joke is just part of this contrast of two cultures within America, but since he makes it so similar to the previous anecdote, there can be no mistake in the purpose of the contrast in form and context.

The contrast of anecdotes and jokes is stated by one of the characters later in the novel. Ma says:

I was thinkin' today how they use' to be jokes. I don' like it, Tom. We don't joke no more. When they's a joke, it's a mean bitter joke, an' they ain't no fun in it. Fella says today, 'Depression is over. I seen a jackrabbit, an' they wasn't nobody after him.'

. . . . .

That's how I mean. Ain't really funny, not funny like that time Uncle John coverted an Injun an' brang him home, an' that Injun ethis way clean to the bottom of the bean bin, an' then backslid with Uncle John's whiskey. (p. 540)

She speaks of jokes, but her example about Uncle John shows she is talking about humorous anecdotes. The absence of personal anecdotes symbolizes the disintegration of the family and their state of poverty at this point. Humor is expressed through bitter jokes rather than warm human anecdotes.

Despite this statement by Ma about the change in their folklore, Steinbeck recognizes that oral storytelling can fulfill important functions for an oppressed group. In an interchapter, he states:

The migrant people, scuttling for work, scrabbling to live, looked always for pleasure, dug for pleasure, manufactured pleasure, and they were hungry for amusement. Sometimes amusement lay in speech, and they climbed up their lives with jokes. And it came about in the camps along the roads, on the ditch banks beside the streams, under the sycamores, that the storyteller grew into being, so that the people gathered in the low firelight to hear the gifted ones. And they listened while the tales were told, and their participation made the stories great.

. . . . .

And the people listened, and their faces were quiet with listening. The storytellers, gathering attention into their tales, spoke in great rhythms, spoke in great words because the tales were great, and the listeners became great through them. (pp. 444-445)

The difference between this and what Ma states is that this is a communal experience; the storytelling takes their minds off their troubles and gives them a sense of unity.

As indicated previously, the downward movement of family disintegration is balanced by an upward movement of communal spirit growth. Steinbeck uses the context of performance of folk music and dance to illustrate this upward movement. Rural people of Oklahoma had a strong music tradition of ballads, lyrics and string band dance music, and the ones who moved to California took their music with them. One need only look at the early career of Woody Guthrie or at the popularity of Western swing music in California to see evidence of this.[17] Steinbeck describes the context of the music as a part of the evening's entertainment in the roadside camps on the way to California:

> And perhaps a man brought out his guitar to the front of his tent. And he sat on a box to play, and everyone in the camp moved slowly in toward him, drawn in toward him. . . . The man played and the people moved slowly in on him until the circle was closed and tight, and then he sang "Ten-Cent Cotton and Forty-Cent Meat." And the circle sang softly with him.

. . . . .

> And now the group was welded to one thing, one unit, so that in the dark the eyes of the people were inward, and their minds played in other times, and their sadness was like rest, like sleep. (p. 272)

The communal effect of folk dancing is described in much the same way:

> These three in the evening, harmonica and fiddle and guitar. Playing a reel and tapping out the tune, and the big deep strings of the guitar beating like a heart, and the harmonica's sharp chords and the skirl and squeal of the fiddle. People had to move close. They can't help it. (p. 449)

There are two interrelated functions for folk music and dance in these descriptions. One is to give a sense of group solidarity, and the other is to establish a link with the past as a means of security. While watching the square dancers at the government camp Ma says, "Makes me think of ol' times," and Steinbeck adds, "And on the faces of the watchers the smiles were of old times." (p. 467) Alan Lomax has called this effect of folk music one of its most important functions:

> . . . the primary effect of music is to give the listener a feeling of security, for it symbolizes the place where he was born, his earliest childhood satisfactions, his religious experience, his pleasure in community doings, his courtship and his work—any or all of these personality-shaping experiences.[18]

The dances at the government camp also function to give the people a sense of pride. "These here dances done funny things. Our people got nothing, but jes' because they can ast their frien's to come here to the dance, sets 'em up an' makes 'em proud." (p. 464)

Steinbeck recognizes all these functions for folk music and dance and uses them to emphasize his theme of the communal spirit of the people. He makes the functions apparent by describing the entire context of performance—the style of the performer, the reaction of the audience, and the interaction of performer and audience. He gives the comments of the people about the music and goes inside their minds to give psychological reactions. Steinbeck places these descriptions of the music and dance performances at a point in the structure of the novel where they

will have a special meaning. The music scene on the road to California shows that despite the loss of home and land and the disruptive forces of moving, the migrant families still have traditions to keep them together and to give them strength. The square dance scene in the government camp is a folk event symbolizing communal cooperation which exists in the camp. The people are welded into a unit by the music, and they can act as one to repel the attempted attack from the outside. Both scenes are a part of the upward movement of the novel's structure and represent the growth of the family solidarity established at the beginning into a community solidarity.

There is another kind of folklore in *The Grapes of Wrath* which does not fit into the usual formal genres; these are folk ideas. Alan Dundes first formulated this concept:

> By "folk ideas" I mean traditional that a group of people have about the nature of man, of the world, and of man's life in the world. Folk ideas would not constitute a genre of folklore but rather would be expressed in a great variety of different genres. . . . However, insofar as folk ideas are the unstated premises which underlie the thought and action of a given group of people, they are not likely to appear consistently in any fixed phrase form.[19]

The Grapes of Wrath contains folk ideas which are expressed through genres such as proverbs, memorates (first or second-hand accounts of personal experiences) and legends, and also through non-generic means. A folk idea about justice and the law is expressed in the series of legends and memorates about Pretty Boy Floyd. Pretty Boy is first mentioned in the context of Tom's return home from prison. Ma is worried about prison's effect on Tom:

> "I knowed Purty Boy Floyd. I knowed his ma. They was good folks. He was full a hell, sure, like a good boy oughta be." She paused and then her words poured out. "I don' know all like this—but I know it. He done a little bad thing an' they hurt 'im, caught 'im an' hurt him so he was mad, an' the nex' bad thing he done was mad, and' they hurt 'im again. An' purty soon he was mean-mad. They shot at him like a varmint, an' he shot back, an' then they run him like a coyote, an' him a-snappin' and a-snarlin', mean as a lobo. An' he was mad. He wasn't no boy or no man no more, he was jus' a walkin' chunk a mean-mad. But the folks that knowed him didn' hurt 'im. He wasn' mad at them. Finally they run him down an' killed 'im. No matter how they say it in the paper how he was bad—that's how it was." (p.103)

The important attitude here is that Pretty Boy as a member of the community is known to have been a "good boy" and that the established system of law and justice made him bad. Ma makes several other references to Pretty Boy throughout the novel and always in the context of her fear that Tom will be affected by the inhuman treatment of the law in the same way. (pp. 381-501)

The folk idea behind the legend is expressed more directly by Pa when Grampa dies and must be buried against the laws of the state.

> "Sometimes the law can't be foller'd no way," said Pa. "Not in decency anways. They's lot a times you can't. When Floyd was loose an' goin' wild, law said we got to give him up—an' nobody give him up. Sometimes a fella got to sift the law. I'm sayin' now I got the right to bury my own pa." (pp. 190-191)

This attitude toward outlaws is expressed in the legends and ballads about Jesse James, Sam Bass and other outlaw heroes. The folk idea is a belief that there is a deeper natural sense of justice and right that sometimes goes against established laws.

This folk idea in *The Grapes of Wrath* has a literary significance as a justification of the migrant's actions against the police and sheriffs. The police are an arm of the establishment forces of agriculture business who are responsible for keeping the migrants in a position of poverty and degradation. In order to effect any change in their situation, the migrant workers must go against established laws. The anti-establishment folk idea is worked out in terms of the link between Pretty Boy Floyd and Tom Joad. Tom's killing of the man who killed Casy is justified by the folk idea. Casy was murdered in the name of established law, but Tom Joad and his people know from their own sense of justice that it was wrong. At the end of the novel Tom Joad has the potential to become an outlaw hero himself. Right before Tom makes his speech about his mystical connection with the oppressed (p. 572), Ma compares him to "young Floyd" again. (p. 571) Steinbeck has established this link throughout the novel in order to emphasize the folk idea of the outlaw which culminates in Tom Joad's final acceptance of Jim Casy's activist mysticism.

The philosophical ideas of the novel also have a direct correlation to folk ideas. Scholars have identified the major ideas in the novel with American literature and philosophy. Frederick I. Carpenter cites Emersonian transcendentalism, Whitman's mass democracy and William James' and John Dewey's pragmatism as major ideas in the novel.[20] Chester E. Eisinger adds Jeffersonian agrarianism.[21] Steinbeck was probably familiar with these ideas through his reading, but he also more than likely heard similar ideas expressed by the migrant workers while he travelled with them. The migrants may have read of some of these authors, but since these ideas are pervasive throughout American culture, the migrants probably received them orally. The assumptions about spirituality, democracy, pragmatism and agrarianism underlie most American's thoughts and actions and thus can be termed folk ideas. They are ideas which exist on all levels of expressive culture in America—folk, popular and elite—and Steinbeck probably absorbed them from all levels.

Steinbeck has been grouped with other American writers who create "imperfectly realized pastoral[s]" because his "vision of simplicity" is not clearly articulated.[22] Undoubtedly Steinbeck romanticized the folklife of the migrants, but this was in keeping with the overall purposes of the novel. He was highly critical of twentieth century urban technological industrial society, and he presented the traditional values of the agrarian folk as an alternative. In doing this he painted an idealized pastoral picture of rural life, but he did not ignore the realities "of the rudeness, roughness, and lack of comfort" of the migrant experience. Steinbeck described in detail the "smells, tastes and feelings" of farmworkers' life from his own observations. Despite the similarities between Steinbeck's approach with that of the folklorist he was primarily a novelist, and the pastoral ideal was simply another part of his craft. In transforming the raw materials of agrarian folklife into literature, Steinbeck brought together realistic elements with pastoral idealism to ground his social philosophy in real human experience.

He transformed folklife events into elements of the novel by describing the entire context of the event; he even commented at times on the function of folklore. He attempted to objectively report the facts of a folklife event, but it was by his artistic placement of a folklife event at a specific point in the novel that gave it new meaning. This novel lends itself to the use of folklife events since each event can exist as a separate scene along the episodic journey structure. Every concrete folklife element has a meaning as a concept of social and political philosophy. The novel develops from microcosm to macrocosm, from the Joads to the oppressed people, from specific folklife events to an overall social meaning.

The folklife descriptions give a sympathetic insight into the lives of the people. The social philosophy would have no impact if Steinbeck were not able to communicate compassion for real human beings in an oppressed condition. The folklore and folklife of the Joads and their people give a sense of the human side of the problem and at the same time provide a framework of ideas for the story. The continuing appeal for readers today for Steinbeck's ideals at least partially explains the widespread popularity of the novel. Americans still have a pastoral vision, still have sympathy for the downtrodden, and still have a resentment toward urban, technological, industrial life. *The Grapes of Wrath* effectively expresses those ideals for the 1930s and for today.

NOTES

[1] The following studies influenced the approach I am using: Alan Dundes, "The Study of Folklore in Literature and Culture: Identification and Interpretation," *Journal of American Folklore*, 78 (1965), 136-42; Roger D. Abrahams, "Folklore and Literature as Performance," *Journal of the Folklore Institute*, 9 (1972), 75-94; Daniel Barnes, "The Bosom Serpent: A Legend in American Literature and Culture," *Journal of American Folklore*, 85 (1972), 111-122; Rosan Jordan

DeCaro, "A Note About Folklore and Literature (The Bosom Serpent Revisited)," *Journal of American Folklore,* 86 (1973), 62-65; Alan Dundes, "Texture, Text and Context," *Southern Folklore Quarterly,* 28 (1964), 251-65; Dan Ben-Amos, "Toward a Definition of Folklore in Context," *Journal of American Folklore,* 84 (1971), 3-15; Roger D. Abrahams, "Personal Power and Social Restraint in the Definition of Folklore," *Journal of American Folklore,* 84 (1971), 16-30; Richard Bauman, "Differential Identity and the Social Base of Folklore," *Journal of American Folklore,* 84 (1971), 31-41; Robert A. Georges, "Toward an Understanding of Storytelling Events," *Journal of American Folklore,* 83 (1969), 313-28.

[2] Warren French, ed., *A Companion to the Grapes of Wrath* (New York: Viking Press, 1963), pp. 51-92.

[3] Elaine Steinbeck and Robert Wallsten, eds. *Steinbeck, A Life in Letters* (New York: Viking Press, 1975), p. 129.

[4] Peter Lisca, *The Wide World of John Steinbeck* (New Brunswick, N.J.: Rutgers Univ. Press, 1958), 146.

[5] Lisca, *Wide World,* pp. 167-8.

[6] Mody C. Boatright, "The Family Saga as a Form of Folklore," in *The Family Saga and other Phases of American Folklore* (Urbana: Univ. of Ill. Press, 1958), p. 1.

[7] All page references are to *The Grapes of Wrath* (New York: Viking Press, 1939).

[8] Motif X931, Stith Thompson, *Motif-Index of Folk Literature* (Bloomington: Ind. Univ. Press, 1955-58).

[9] Patrick B. Mullen, "Folk Songs and Family Traditions," in *Observations and Reflections on Texas Folklore,* ed. Francis Edward Abernethy, Publications of the Texas Folklore Society, No. 37 (Austin: The Encino Press, 1972), 52-53.

[10] Margaret Jarman Hagood, *Mothers of the South, Portraiture of the White Tenant Farm Woman* (Chapel Hill: Univ. of Carolina Press, 1939), pp. 163-4

[11] Patrick B. Mullen, "The Function of Magic Folk Belief Among Texas Coastal Fishermen," *Journal of American Folklore,* 82 (1969), 216.

[12] Peter Lisca, "The Dynamics of Community in *The Grapes of Wrath,*" in *From Irving to Steinbeck,* eds. Motley Deakin and Peter Lisca (Gainesville: Univ. of Fla. Press, 1972), pp. 127-40.

[13] Eliot Wigginton, ed., *The Foxfire Book* (Garden City, New York: Doubleday and Co., 1972), pp. 189-201.

[14] Wayland D. Hand, ed., *Popular Beliefs and Superstitions from North Carolina,* vols. 6 & 7 of *The Frank C. Brown Collection of North Carolina Folklore,* ed., Newman Ivey White (Chapel Hill: Univ. of North Carolina Press, 1961, 1964).

[15] Mullen, "Magic Folk Belief," 219.

[16] Lisca, *Wide World,* p. 172.

[17] Richard A. Reuss, "Woody Guthrie and His Folk Tradition," *Journal of American Folklore,* 83 (1970), 273-303; Bill C. Malone, *Country Music U.S.A.* (Austin: Univ. of Texas Press, 1968), pp. 154-6, 192-3.

[18] Alan Lomax, "Folk Song Style," *American Anthropologist,* 61, (1959), 929.

[19] Alan Dundes, "Folk Ideas as Units of Worldview," *Journal of American Folklore,* 84 (1971), 95-6.

[20] Frederick I. Carpenter, "The Philosophical Joads," *College English,* 2 (1941), 315-25.

[21] Chester E. Eisinger, "Jeffersonian Agrarianism in *The Grapes of Wrath,*" *The University of Kansas City Review,* 14 (1947), 149-54.

[22] French, p. 56.

[23] Abrahams, "Personal Power," 20-21.

[24] John P. Sisk, "American Pastoral," *Thought,* 27 (1952), 373.

George Dekker and Joseph Harris

SOURCE: "Supernaturalism and the Vernacular Style in 'A Farewell to Arms'," in *PMLA,* Vol. 94, No. 2, March, 1979, pp. 311-18.

[*In the following essay, Dekker and Harris find evidence of "second sight" and other ghostly folk notions in Ernest Hemingway's* A Farewell to Arms.]

The doric voice of Hemingway's twenties protagonists, though communally that of the vernacular tradition in American fiction,[1] is so much his own that words like "tradition" and "community" sound foolish or a cheat when applied to it. It creates a fictional world in which, seemingly, there is no place for literary allusions or intimations of a supernatural order. And it does this so successfully that readers coming to his work for the first time may be surprised, even a little annoyed, to be told that "Hemingway's reading is as important to his art as that of Coleridge";[2] that the author of "In Another Country" was a close student of T. S. Eliot and a good friend of Ezra Pound; that a mythic parallelism recalling *The Waste Land* has been discovered in *The Sun Also Rises;* and that Hemingway himself described *A Farewell to Arms* as his "Romeo and Juliet."[3] More experienced readers might agree that the pursuit of such allusions and parallels has sometimes been pressed too hard, but probably they would consider it wiser to go overboard with Carlos Baker in calling Brett a witch, a lamia, a Morgan le Fay "rolled into one, the *femme fatale de trente ans damnée,*"[4] than to suppose that Hemingway implicitly denies the force and point of "Circe" when he attributes the word to the despised literary intellectual (and Jew) Robert Cohn. Brett may not require Cohn's services, but Hemingway does.

For one of Hemingway's major tactical problems in his early fiction is to make such allusions count—and thus place his characters and actions in a timeless perspective—without ruffling the quotidian vernacular surface of his narrative. Sometimes he exercises so much tact or indirection that he nearly defeats his own complex purpose. This, we believe, is true of the submerged folkloristic motifs of second sight and revenants in *A Farewell to Arms,* for though they are important pointers to (and parts of) its total meaning, they have gone unnoticed in previous discussions of the novel.

That they have been ignored is perhaps somewhat surprising, since similar motifs are prominent in *Huckleberry Finn* and other works in the vernacular tradition. After all, ghosts and omens belong to folk literature almost universally, and the vernacular tradition in American literature springs from folk sources. Revenants return to their mothers or lovers most famously, however, in European folk ballads like "Sweet William's Ghost" and "The Wife of Usher's Well" or in literary imitations like Bürger's *Lenore,* while the phenomenon of second sight as a proleptic device in literature is especially associated with Icelandic sagas. We do not wish to suggest that *A Farewell to Arms* is Hemingway's *Njál's Saga* or "Sweet William"; we do suggest that, insofar as their presence is more than merely decorative, the elements that his novel shares with folk literature like ballads and sagas expand its meaning considerably and further justify its vernacular rhetoric.

I

I look for ghosts; but none will force
Their way to me: 'tis falsely said
That there was ever intercourse
Between the living and the dead.
    Wordsworth, "The Affliction of Margaret"

One symptom of Catherine's "craziness" early in her relationship with Frederic is her need to pretend that he is her dead lover, the English boy killed at the Somme:[5]

"Say, 'I've come back to Catherine in the night.'"

"I've come back to Catherine in the night."

"Oh, darling, you have come back, haven't you?"

"Yes."

"I love you so and it's been awful. You won't go away?"

"No. I'll always come back." (p. 31)

Frederic is prepared to accept his role in her fantasy as an opportunity to step into the dead man's boots; she is "a little crazy," but then he inhabits a universe presented increasingly as irrational, structured only, if at all, by games every bit as mad as hers. As their love develops, their games develop into tender and mutually protective rituals; they are able, for instance, to turn a sordid hotel room into their "home." There is plenty of evidence both in his contemporary writing, as in "Hills like White Elephants," and in his retrospective work, as in *A Moveable Feast,* that Hemingway valued such creative make-believe between a man and woman very highly. And yet there is also evidence in *A Farewell to Arms* that what for Frederic is fine make-believe is not only that but something more for Catherine. Embittered by experience, he is complexly skeptical of anything that cannot be tested by the pulse of everyday reality. She is "crazy" and "simple"—simple in ways we may regard as degrading to women, but simple too as Cooper's Hetty Hutter or Wordsworth's Idiot Boy is simple. For her the barriers between before and after, life and death, have no more reality, finally, than her visions of death have for Frederic. When she is dying, she says, and every reader must believe, that she is unafraid:

> Catherine smiled, "No." Then a little later, "You won't do our things with another girl, or say the same things, will you?"
>
> "Never."
>
> "I want you to have girls, though."
>
> "I don't want them."
>
> "You are talking too much," the doctor said. "Mr. Henry must go out. He can come back again later. You are not going to die. You must not be silly."
>
> "All right," Catherine said. "I'll come and stay with you nights," she said. It was very hard for her to talk. (p. 342)

We may choose, as Frederic doubtless would, to take Catherine's statement that she will come and stay with him nights as her queer way of putting the psychological truth that she will "live" in his memory. A variant of this truth is urged by Robert Jordan when, at the end of *For Whom the Bell Tolls,* he persuades Maria that she must not stay behind and share his certain death. But Catherine is not a Hemingway male: hers is Pilar's superstitious world of faith—of omens that prove true.

Bracketed by these two relatively obvious references to a lover's return after death, Catherine and Frederic's love affair develops as an unresolved "dialectic" between female faith and male skepticism. Frederic at first plays the "game" rather cynically, having nothing to lose: "Nobody had mentioned what the stakes were. It was all right with me" (p. 32). Catherine's gift of a good-luck token (" . . . they say a Saint Anthony's very useful") and Frederic's reaction ("I'll take care of him for you") presents the "dialectic" in miniature, together with the uneasy balance between intuitive and empirical views struck by the novel as a whole:

> I felt him in his metal box against my chest while we drove. Then I forgot about him. After I was wounded I never found him. Some one probably got it at one of the dressing stations. (pp. 45-46)

An ambiguous conclusion—after all Frederic survives—but charged with pessimism.

Under the influence of love Frederic seems to move erratically away from the cynicism suggested by his whoring and by his famous linguistic credo and toward Catherine's affirmative view of the possibility of real love and real language, even if intensely private; and of course this dialectic intersects the political themes of the novel as Frederic discovers that a private life is affirmed by exercising skepticism toward the public world to the point of rejection. However, male and female reach no "synthesis": when Catherine offers to cut her hair short to be one with Frederic, we must believe that he is not oblivious to the pathos and futility of that gesture.[6] Frederic's attitude toward life approaches Catherine's most closely during his erotic reveries on the retreat and in the flatcar, but these are "crazy" dream states. His fully conscious attempt to penetrate beyond the surface of life and death in his conversation with Count Greffi is totally frustrated, for from that graceful man of the world he learns that "the great fallacy [is] the wisdom of old men. They do not grow wise. They grow careful" (p. 271). Frederic's probing, an embarrassment to himself, uncovers only the polish of the old diplomat:

> "Would you like to live after death?" I asked and instantly felt a fool to mention death. But he did not mind the word.
>
> "It would depend on the life." (p. 270)

This quite explicit interrogation provides no more certain resolution than the novel itself:

> "I thought 'Mr. Britling' a very good study of the English middle-class soul."
>
> "I don't know about the soul."
>
> "Poor boy. We none of us know about the soul. Are you *Croyant*?"
>
> "At night." (p. 270)

Night is Catherine's time.

When her death comes, she is *croyante,* and even Frederic's mind races "Dear God, don't let her die." But his experience of her death is expressed mainly through images of physical decay and desolation—the dog nosing among "coffee grounds, dust and some dead flowers" (p. 325), the ants on the burning log; afterward "There's nothing to say" (p. 343). Despite her "courage" and their

"nights," their lovers' dialogue on death is suspended, rather than concluded, on a note of disillusionment:

> But after I had got them out and shut the door and turned off the light it wasn't any good. It was like saying good-by to a statue. After a while I went out and left the hospital and walked back to the hotel in the rain. (p. 343)

In this context, then, it would not be surprising if more subtle and specific associations with the revenant ballads presented themselves. Hemingway had been reading Quiller-Couch's *Oxford Book of English Verse,* where he discovered George Peele's "A Farewell to Arms."[7] There he could also have found "To His Coy Mistress" and "Western Wind," both of which are openly alluded to.[8] Of the revenant ballads there, "The Wife of Usher's Well" is fundamentally unlike Hemingway's story, but "Clerk Saunders" offers many parallels.[9] Like Romeo and Juliet, Saunders and Maid Margaret unite, against a background of war or feuding, first in her bower and then in the tomb; Margaret's pathetic words to the slain lover beside her—"'It is time, true love, you were awa'"—offer a tragic parody of Shakespeare's *aubade* and parallel themselves with a dawn song from the tomb: "'Tis time, 'tis time, my dear, Marg'ret, / That you were going away.'" Saunders' wish to break his ties with the living, to retrieve his "faith and troth," may make us think of Catherine's attitude toward her engagement to the British boy and her effort to release Frederic at the end ("I want you to have girls, though"); most strikingly, Catherine's words "You won't do our things with another girl, or say the same things, will you?" recall the revenant Saunders' last words:

> "And fair Marg'ret, and rare Marg'ret,
>   And Marg'ret o' veritie,
> Gin e'er ye love another man,
>   Ne'er love him as ye did me."

Like other revenant ballads, "Clerk Saunders" associates a mysterious wand ("crystal wand," "wand o' bonny birk") with the return of the dead lover's troth or, perhaps, more generally with laying the ghost;[10] in the novel the "toy riding-crop," a memento of the dead fiancé, disappears from the narrative after Frederic begins to play the "game." One is even tempted to see the ballad's approach-avoidance problem in the novel's last scene ("I'm going to die. . . . Don't touch me. . . . Poor darling. You touch me all you want")[11] and something more than coincidence in the ballad heroine's odd question to her dead lover: " . . . what comes o' women, / . . . who die in strong traivelling?" This redaction of "Clerk Saunders" also seems to be the only ballad that, like the novel, combines a Romeo and Juliet situation with the revenant motif.

The circumstantial evidence that Hemingway knew "Clerk Saunders" is as strong as such evidence can be, and the rejected titles for the novel show, at the least, that Hemingway had searched carefully through the Quiller-Couch anthology, jotting down two titles based on traditional ballads (Reynolds, pp. 295-97). Moreover, Hemingway's reading also included Quiller-Couch's companion volume, the *Oxford Book of Ballads,* where he might have found several other treatments of folk beliefs about lovers transcending death.[12] One such ballad, "The Unquiet Grave," is perhaps the best known of all English revenant ballads, and the parallels to *A Farewell to Arms* are striking indeed.[13] There the dead lover is a woman; a withered flower is an explicit symbol of death and its dissolution of love ties; and the approach-avoidance *topos* is expressed in "one kiss of my clay-cold lips." Such parallels with Hemingway's more oblique "dead flowers" and "saying good-by to a statue" may not carry conviction for everybody; but the way this famous lyrical ballad, which is also a suspended debate, associates death and return with an "objective correlative" of rain may well give pause to the most skeptical reader:

> The wind doth blow to-day my love,
>   And a few small drops of rain;
> I never had but one true-love;
>   In cold grave she was lain.

Here, it may be, was what suggested to Hemingway the link between the "small rain" of Frederic's "Western Wind"-inspired revery of return to Catherine and the "big rain," feared by Catherine herself, which washes everything away.

Apparent agreements with two more standard ballad motifs should be mentioned for what they may be worth. (1) Ballad lovers separated by death may pledge what Child calls "austerities"; one of the most frequent "austerities" is leaving the hair uncut or uncombed or cutting it short.[14] (2) One standard mourning period is a twelvemonth and a day.[15] These two *topoi,* which stand side by side in Quiller-Couch's "The Unquiet Grave," may be detected in the novel at the lovers' first meeting (p. 19). Frederic somewhat abruptly compliments Catherine on her "beautiful hair"; she replies: "I was going to cut it all off when he died. . . . I wanted to do something for him"; and we are told on the preceding page that the British boy was killed "last year."

Still less than in Hawthorne can supernatural visitants stalk the pages of Hemingway, and yet what Yvor Winters calls the "formula of alternative possibilities" in *The Scarlet Letter* is also important in *A Farewell to Arms.*[16] At the primary, or realistic, level the action of the novel is relentlessly, almost ostentatiously, diachronic—dictated by the natural, inexorable rhythms of seasonal change and the gestation of Catherine's child. Most readers will recall the opening descriptions of late summer and early fall in Books I and III and of spring at the end of the novel, when Catherine is dying in childbirth. But if Catherine recognizes that her body is caught in the biological "trap," she does not accept that *she* or her lover is thereby to be dissolved into the great *Nada* beyond. Perhaps Henry's is also Hemingway's final word on Catherine's brave belief in her power to return

to her lover, but Hemingway certainly does not ridicule or dismiss Catherine's "crazy" synchronic vision of reality. And it is a key—the only key offered—to her ability to see the future.

II

"'Second-sight' is a flag over disputed ground."

Eliot, *Daniel Deronda*

In *A Farewell to Arms* Hemingway is a master of sagalike rhetoric—especially foreshadowings that, together with an explicit stoicism, create the fated atmosphere of the novel. The most famous of these foreshadowings occurs at the end of Chapter xix, when Catherine admits to a fear of the rain but refuses at first to tell why she is afraid. At last she yields to Frederic's urging:

> "All right. I'm afraid of the rain because sometimes I see me dead in it."
>
> "No."
>
> "And sometimes I see you dead in it."
>
> "That's more likely."
>
> "No, it's not, darling. Because I can keep you safe. I know I can. But nobody can help themselves."
>
> "Please stop it. I don't want you to get Scotch and crazy tonight. We won't be together much longer."
>
> "No, but I am Scotch and crazy. But I'll stop it. It's all nonsense."
>
> "Yes, it's all nonsense."
>
> "It's all nonsense. It's only nonsense. I'm not afraid of the rain. I'm not afraid of the rain. Oh, oh, God, I wish I wasn't." She was crying. I comforted her and she stopped crying. But outside it kept on raining. (pp. 131-32)

The association between rain and death that runs through the novel is made explicit here for the first and only time. Citing this passage, Philip Young describes the association as "really the old 'pathetic fallacy' put to new use . . . a subtle and unobtrusive device for unity. . . ."[17] This reading of Catherine's "Scotch and crazy" experience as a mere psychological projection is very much in line with Henry's way of seeing things, but not with Catherine's. Hemingway does not come down clearly in favor of either way, since the fact that she does die as she foresaw may be purely fortuitous. But the alternative possibility is there, that she has experienced what is known to folklorists as "second sight."

A person with second sight "sees" things that are not visible to ordinary persons; the visions are predictive if properly interpreted, and (folklore being the fatalistic vessel it typically is) most frequently predictive of death.

The visions are usually either of a person's "fetch" or, as they are for Catherine, of the person herself. Second sight is involuntary, not a sought-after power but almost a curse on the individual who has it; future events are foreseen but, of course, not affected. Despite Catherine's claim that she can keep Frederic safe, visionaries suffer from the irony of powerless foreknowledge; they know a person is "fey," or doomed, but cannot avert the destined events. Fate also requires that those who are "fey" not believe that they are. Hence seers who foresee their own deaths cannot interpret the vision, or at least, like other fey persons, cannot take effective action. As Catherine says, " . . . nobody can help themselves."

The phrase "Scotch and crazy" is Hemingway's pointer to this alternative interpretation of Catherine's vision. Throughout the novel she is the "lady English"; in earlier passages she is contrasted with the Scotswoman Ferguson, who likes her, we are told, in spite of her being English. Only in the passage under discussion is Catherine called "Scotch"—and this can be true only in a special sense: in this context the term is a precise signal that she is gifted with second sight. For second sight is popularly associated with Scotland and Scottish folklore.[18] Hemingway's use of "crazy" here is less precise but in general agreement with this interpretation.[19] Persons endowed with second sight are regarded in folklore and real life as "different," in touch somehow with the supernatural, and a Cassandra may easily be thought mad.

Hemingway's interest in prophetic powers and his tendency to associate them with the polar opposites of his Anglo-Saxon males are also evident in *The Sun Also Rises* and especially in *For Whom the Bell Tolls*. As Carlos Baker notes, among the many signs of Brett's paganism is her visit to the gypsy camp outside Pamplona to have her fortune told (*Writer*, p. 89). But apparently there is nothing ominous about the gypsy's oracle, and although the atmosphere of the novel is as sultry as possible, it could scarcely be called doom-laden. In *For Whom the Bell Tolls*, however, the foreshadowings are even heavier and gloomier than in *A Farewell to Arms*. Pilar refuses to tell Jordan what fate she sees in the palm of his hand, but given her demeanor, what reader coming to the novel for the first time can doubt that it is his imminent death? Jordan claims not to believe in fortune-telling; he has his own way of looking into the future:

> " . . . Also, unlike an ordinary rifle, they continue to fire as long as you exert pressure on the trigger."

> "Unless they jam, run out of ammunition or get so hot they melt," Robert Jordan said in English.

> "What do you say?" Anselmo asked him.

> "Nothing," Robert Jordan said. "I was only looking into the future in English."

> "That is something truly rare," the gypsy said. "Looking into the future in *Ingles*. Can you read in the palm of the hand?"[20]

Robert Jordan looks into the future "in English" by means of empirical inference from previously observed data: the gypsy need not have been astonished by Jordan's claim, for this Anglo-Saxon method of looking into the future, based on scientific probability, is as remote as possible from the oracular fatalism of Pilar. At all events, Hemingway's interest in racial or sexual traits is so well known, if not notorious, that the point will perhaps be conceded without further demonstration: Gypsies, Scots, Spaniards—these exotic peoples, especially the women among them, have powers that are opposite and complementary to those of his Anglo-Saxon heroes; and even when his heroines are in fact English, they take on a kind of borrowed racial identity at those moments when he wishes to establish their profound difference from a Jake Barnes or a Frederic Henry. Carlos Baker's claims notwithstanding, there is striking continuity in Hemingway's portrayal of women in his three major novels.[21]

Besides their relation to a transcendent view of life and death, second-sight and revenant motifs have another common denominator: the theme of human suffering beneath the strokes of fate. Life demands impassive courage of both male and female in *A Farewell to Arms*, as in saga and ballad, where ghosts and omens are universal and stoicism the most honored code of conduct. A stylistic correlative of such a view is ascetic understatement, and this association has occasioned at least one, perhaps not widely noticed, juxtaposition of the Icelandic sagas with the "hard-boiled" novel of the twenties.[22] But the tight-lipped saga style is only a heightening of features common to folk literature, including the American vernacular tradition that lies behind Hemingway. It is true that he adopted his poetic mythology from sophisticated European sources, but he appears to have selected and adapted with a nice sense of its appropriateness to the content and style of his native tradition.

That his sources were European and sophisticated should cause no surprise; for as a junior member of the circle of modernist masters—most notably Ford, Joyce, and Eliot—who were friends of Ezra Pound and shared many of Pound's literary ideals and anthropological/folkloristic interests, Hemingway was lavishly provided with such sources and also with imposing models of how to use them:

> In using the myth, in manipulating a continuous parallel between contemporaneity and antiquity, Mr. Joyce is pursuing a method which others must pursue after him. . . . It is simply a way of controlling, of ordering, of giving a shape and a significance to the immense panorama of futility and anarchy which is contemporary history. . . . Psychology (such as it is, and whether our reaction to it be comic or serious), ethnology, and *The Golden Bough* have concurred to make possible what was impossible even a few years ago.[23]

Few, if any, of Joyce's successors attempted to manipulate a parallel so continuous and elaborate as that of

Ulysses, but as Eliot and his *Dial* readers well knew, when he prophesied that the "mythical method" would be pursued by others after Joyce, it had already been used in *The Waste Land* and the early *Cantos.* That the shade of the Homeric and Sophoclean seer Tiresias is present in all these early experiments with the method may remind us that certain motifs—prophesies and returns from the dead among them—are closely and appropriately associated with the method itself.[24] It is in this context of shared interests in myth and the "mythical method" (without concern for who did what first) that we should place the two clearest contemporary parallels to Hemingway's use of revenant and second-sight motifs. These occur in *The Great Gatsby* (1925) and *The Last Post* (1928).

Ford's great novel of postwar England, notable for its complex and superbly integrated use of the Fisher King legend, is also a work in which revenants appear. Ford mentions them specifically in his Dedicatory Letter and again midway through the novel when Marie Leonie fears to walk out at night because of all the ghosts of the war dead. In one of the concluding scenes, Valentine Wannop, great with Christopher's child and a guilty conscience, has a hallucinatory vision of Christopher's wife as an avenging statue, vividly recalling the end of the Don Juan story and the most famous of all revenants in Western literature.[25] Ford's is not a tragic novel, and so the vision fades and both child and mother survive, but the parallels between *The Last Post* and *A Farewell to Arms* suggest that revenants were indeed abroad during the period when the surviving combatants were trying to face, and make fiction of, their experience of the Great War.

Just as Eliot presents Madame Sosostris as a debased twentieth-century avatar of Tiresias (and other, still more exalted visionaries), so Fitzgerald, in keeping with his scheme of parodic parallel and antithesis, makes the unimaginative but superstitious Tom Buchanan claim prophetic gifts ironically analogous to Gatsby's powers of creative romantic vision:

> "You think I'm pretty dumb, don't you?" he suggested. "Perhaps I am, but I have a—almost second sight, sometimes, that tells me what to do. Maybe you don't believe that, but science——"
>
> He paused. The immediate contingency overtook him, pulled him back from the edge of the theoretical abyss.[26]

Frederic's and Catherine's contrasting ways of "seeing" are likewise elements in an elaborate pattern of antithesis and balance, but of course there is no parodic intent implicit in Hemingway's design. Its point is, rather, that the lovers are opposite yet mutually corrective and necessary to each other, since Catherine's naïveté and "craziness" make her terribly vulnerable while Frederic's defensive nihilism eliminates some of the risks but also most of the rewards of living. At the same time, because the antithetical pattern throws such traits into

high relief, Hemingway himself runs a great—and many would say fatal—risk of unintentional exaggeration and parody in his portrayal of the man-woman relationship.

Although our reinterpretation of the Frederic-Catherine relationship takes its bearings not from a study of possible "sources" or "influences" but from actual (though submerged) references to second sight and revenants in the text of the novel, we believe that the parallel appearance of these motifs in the literature that Hemingway was reading during the twenties can guide readers to a more precise understanding of his intentions, formal as well as thematic, in *A Farewell to Arms.* The existence of these motifs in the work of his elder contemporaries in no way subtracts from Hemingway's originality but, rather, directs attention to the unique character of his genius: he alone uses folkloristic materials to mediate between two antagonistic selves—the one literary and intellectual, the other "low-brow" and "vernacular," but both authentic—that find undivided expression in his greatest art.

NOTES

[1] Our discussion of the vernacular tradition in American literature is indebted to Henry Nash Smith, *Mark Twain: The Development of a Writer* (Cambridge: Harvard Univ. Press, 1962), pp. 1-21. Hemingway's place in that tradition is discussed in Harry Levin, *Contexts of Criticism* (Cambridge: Harvard Univ. Press, 1957), pp. 140-67.

[2] Michael S. Reynolds, *Hemingway's First War: The Making of* A Farewell to Arms (Princeton: Princeton Univ. Press, 1976), p. 283. Our essay draws background information about Hemingway's reading not merely from this definitive study of the novel but also from Reynolds' "Hemingway's Reading (1913-40)," a work in progress that the author generously shared with us by letter (5 Sept. 1977).

[3] See Charles R. Anderson, "Hemingway's Other Style," *Modern Language Notes,* 76 (1961), 434-42; Richard P. Adams, "Sunrise out of *The Waste Land,*" *Tulane Studies in English,* 9 (1959), 119-31; Edmund Wilson, *The Wound and the Bow,* rev. ed. (London: Allen, 1952), p. 198. Reynolds discusses skeptically the *Romeo* comparison and cites the relevant critics (pp. 262-63).

[4] Baker, *Hemingway: The Writer as Artist,* 3rd ed. (Princeton: Princeton Univ. Press, 1963), p. 90.

[5] *A Farewell to Arms* was first published in late 1929; there is no definitive edition. Our quotations are from the Modern Standard Authors edition, made important by Robert Penn Warren's Introduction (New York: Scribners, 1949).

[6] For recently published evidence of Hemingway's interest in androgynous relationships and his fetishistic preoccupation with hair styles, see Aaron Latham's "A Farewell to Machismo," *New York Times Magazine,* 16

Oct. 1977, pp. 52-55, 80, 82, 90, 92, 94, 96-99. Latham's interpretations of Hemingway's published and unpublished works are, however, rather simplistically biographical, and they do not take the mediating influence of his reading seriously into account.

[7] See Carlos Baker, *Ernest Hemingway: A Life Story* (New York: Scribners, 1969), pp. 199 and 630. Hemingway used the first edition of Arthur Quiller-Couch, ed., *The Oxford Book of English Verse, 1250-1900* (Oxford: Clarendon, 1900), which is the source of our own citations.

[8] "To His Coy Mistress," referred to on p. 161 (Quiller-Couch, *Verse,* pp. 387-88); "Western Wind," referred to on p. 204 (Quiller-Couch, *Verse,* p. 53). Charles Anderson, in "Hemingway's Other Style" (p. 440), has pointed out a further allusion to Tennyson's "Sweet and Low," but see also the refrain in Quiller-Couch (*Verse,* pp. 5-7).

[9] Cited here, for obvious reasons, from Quiller-Couch's *Verse* (pp. 415-20), but it should be pointed out that this is a dubious version. Quiller-Couch's editorial principles for ballads (*Oxford Book of Ballads* [Oxford: Clarendon, 1910], pp. ix-xii) involved extensive rewriting and reduction of the versions to a single intuitively determined "idea" of the original. Though he does not cite sources, Quiller-Couch's version of "Clerk Saunders" (in both anthologies) must be drawn from Scott; Scott himself cobbled up his version from two different texts in the manuscripts of David Herd, an eighteenth-century collector and editor of Scots songs, and from his own additions, omissions, changes, and three stray traditional stanzas "recovered" from somewhere else (*Minstrelsy of the Scottish Border,* ed. T. F. Henderson [Edinburgh: Blackwood, 1902], III, 220-31). In *The English and Scottish Popular Ballads* ([Boston: Houghton, 1882-98], II, 156-67; IV, 468-69), Francis J. Child printed the two texts from Herd (69 A, B) but considered the revenant ending of A to belong to "Sweet William's Ghost" (as does Henderson) and printed it as 77 B and Scott's "recovered" stanzas as 77 G. Because of Child's decisions, "Clerk Saunders" is not generally considered a revenant ballad today, and yet the Scott-Quiller-Couch text is aesthetically pleasing and has at least some authority in the first of Herd's versions (Child's 69 A plus 77 B) and in Child's 69 G.

[10] See esp. Child, v, 499, (Index, s.v. "Troth") and for discussion L. C. Wimberly, *Folklore in the English and Scottish Ballads* (Chicago: Univ. of Chicago Press, 1928), pp. 255-60, 343-45, and the references there.

[11] See esp. Child, v, 476 (Index, s.v. "The Dead") and L. C. Wimberly, *Death and Burial Lore in the English and Scottish Popular Ballads,* Univ. of Nebraska Studies in Lang., Lit., and Crit., No. 8 (Lincoln: Univ. of Nebraska Press, 1927), pp. 77-79, and Wimberly, *Folklore,* pp. 264-68, 282-91.

[12] Reynolds' letter adds that, while it cannot be proved that Hemingway owned and read Quiller-Couch's books

before writing the novel, "he certainly had read them by the time he finally got the ending." Other evidence of his acquaintance with ballads goes back as far as Oak Park High School and will appear in Reynolds' book on Hemingway's reading.

[13] Quiller-Couch, *Ballads,* pp. 140-41 (Child's 78 A).

[14] A good example is Child's 25 E 8 (I, 506); further references are cited in Child's Index (V, 470). Wimberly discusses the "austerities" as signs of grief (*Death,* pp. 103-05). The fact that in one version of "Clerk Saunders" the girl dreams of "cutting [her] yellow hair" (Child's 69 D 11 [II, 162]) is without significance here, and Quiller-Couch's "Clerk Saunders" lacks the austerity *topos,* though other versions of that ballad have the *topos* in classical form (Child's 69 A 20-22, D 13-15, E 17-20, G 23-25).

[15] Discussed in Wimberly (*Death,* pp. 113-14; *Folklore,* pp. 231-32).

[16] Winters, *Maule's Curse* (Norfolk: New Directions, 1938), pp. 18-19. Winters points out that Hawthorne, in openly suggesting the possibility that various occurrences are supernatural, offers this interpretation "whimsically and apologetically, professing to let you take it or leave it."

[17] Young, *Ernest Hemingway: A Reconsideration* (University Park: Pennsylvania State Univ. Press, 1966), p. 92. Did the ironic inversion of the "natural" association of rain and life originate in the communal war experience of older contemporaries like Edward Thomas ("Blessed are the dead that the rain rains upon")? Whatever its source, such an inversion loses its apparently arbitrary quality in a novel where "life" cycles so irresistibly into "death" (see, e.g., p. 338).

[18] For example, a good general treatment that Hemingway could have known begins: "Though we hear most of the 'second sight' among the Celts of the Scottish Highlands (it is much less familiar to the Celts of Ireland), this species of involuntary prophetic vision, whether direct or symbolical, is peculiar to no people . . . " (Andrew Lang, "Second Sight," *Encyclopædia Britannica,* 1911 ed., p. 570). Within the English-speaking world the special associations with Scotland, which go back at least to the fourteenth century, formed the subject of a good deal of learned interest as early as the seventeenth and eighteenth centuries.

[19] Hemingway's use of "crazy" in the novel generally imitates the loose usage of a modish word, though the word is used of the barman of Stresa in connection with a "prediction" (p. 275); but the barman has his information from eavesdropping (not from second sight) and therefore is believable, not "crazy." The only important collection of folklore from the general area of Hemingway's youthful haunts includes some tales of second sight (Richard Dorson, *Bloodstoppers and*

Bearwalkers: Folk Traditions of the Upper Peninsula [Cambridge: Harvard Univ. Press, 1952], pp. 139-43), one of them, by chance, containing an informant's description of a seer as popularly regarded as "crazy" (p. 142).

[20] *For Whom the Bell Tolls* (New York: Scribners, 1940), p. 27.

[21] "As if Hemingway were looking back for contrast to the Circean figure of his first novel, Rinaldi refers to Catherine as 'your lovely cool . . . English goddess.' But she is a woman, not a goddess" (Baker, *Writer*, p. 112).

[22] Sveinn Bergsveinsson, "Sagaen og den haardkogte roman," *Edda*, 42 (1942), 56-62.

[23] T. S. Eliot, "*Ulysses,* Order, and Myth," *The Dial,* Nov. 1923; rpt. in *James Joyce: Two Decades of Criticism,* ed. Seon Givens (New York: Vanguard, 1948), pp. 201-02.

[24] Tiresias appears prominently in Cantos I and XLVII; *The Waste Land* III ("The Fire Sermon"); and *Ulysses,* the Hades episode.

[25] *The Last Post* (New York: Literary Guild, 1928), pp. vii, 171-72, and 264-70.

[26] *The Great Gatsby* (New York: Scribners, 1925), p. 145.

Leslie Field

SOURCE: "Wolfe's Use of Folklore," in *New York Folklore Quarterly,* Vol. XVI, No. 3, Autumn, 1960, pp. 203-15.

[*In the following essay, Field identifies extensive uses of folklore in Thomas Wolfe's fragmentary novel* The Hills Beyond, *particularly in Wolfe's portrayal of the family's larger-than-life patriarch.*]

For most students of Wolfe, *The Hills Beyond*[1] is a postscript to his total work. Ironically, the plan for this book appears first as an *actual* postscript to a letter which Wolfe wrote his mother in 1934. In the postscript Wolfe asks his mother to "jot down" a brief history of her family.

> I would just like . . . [Wolfe adds] to get a list of the twenty children or more that your grandfather had by his two marriages and what happened to them and where they settled and what parts of the country they moved to, and so forth. . . .
>
> I'm asking you to do this because some day after I get through with these books I'm working on now, I may wind the whole thing up with a book that will try to tell through the hundreds of members of one family the whole story of America.[2]

Wolfe did go on with his plan, but he died leaving behind only ten chapters of his fragmentary novel—a novel which has thus far received little critical attention. Though a fragment, the novel is pregnant with American folklore as none of Wolfe's other works are. Surprisingly, the folklorists have all but ignored this aspect of Thomas Wolfe.

This study, therefore, will attempt to show that in *Hills* Wolfe did draw heavily on folklore material for the purpose of writing his fictional history of America. Moreover, Wolfe's fictional America will be seen emerging from two strong folklore strains: the frontiersman and the Yankee. We have, of course, Constance Rourke's *American Humor* to thank for its pioneering success in detailing and demonstrating a fusion of these traditions in American culture. But Wolfe adds a third dimension: the American utilitarian scholar.

By and large Wolfe's critics do agree that Wolfe is steeped in a native American tradition. But they hasten to add that Wolfe's work is flavored by non-American myths. Furthermore, most students of Wolfe recognize his heavy dependence upon autobiography in his fiction. His work, to be sure, is deeply personal. As a result of this last element in his work, however, Wolfe has been praised by a few and damned by many.

Again, most agree that Wolfe was tending towards more objective, less autobiographical writing as he returned to his native tradition. That *Hills* is the culmination of this movement can be denied by none, although no one has yet ventured a detailed analysis in this area. Perhaps then it may be rewarding to see just what it is that Wolfe has taken from his native tradition for use in *Hills* and how the folk material acted as a controlling image for his "great new plan."

Wolfe's tentative plan we already have in his letter to his mother. But in its more complete form it goes as follows.[3] Now that he has written four large "novels," the last two published posthumously, dealing with his own family history from about the turn of the century, he wants to backtrack to trace his ancestry as it relates to the American pioneer. William (Bear) Joyner, who lived about 1800, is to be the father of America—an American Moses.

In ten chapters of *Hills* Wolfe traces the careers of Bear and those of eight of his children. The children are the offspring of Bear's two marriages. Wolfe does not get around to dealing with the twenty or so children and hundreds of grandchildren and great-grandchildren that his original plan calls for. The children he does develop, in their various occupations—lawyer, politician, teacher, businessman—represent the occupational face of America. They stand as prototypes of a myriad of rural and urban occupations. In the chapter entitled "The Great Schism," as a matter of fact, Bear's huge family does split up, some staying on the farm and others going to the city. In effect, these people are the beginnings of the American heritage as Wolfe sees it in his projected novel.

But just what is their source? What makes their heritage American rather than, say Pakistanian? Their source is the grand old man who fathers this new race of fictional Americans. He is none other than William (Bear) Joyner, the man who fuses the two most powerful strains of American folk tradition, the frontiersman and the Yankee, and the third strain which Wolfe added by way of Crévecoeur, Franklin and later Thoreau and Emerson. This last strain is the American practical or utilitarian scholar, the new American who learns to read so that he can rise above his fellow man, so that he can add to the Crockett-Bunyan type of hero another dimension—book learning. Not only does the content of Wolfe's tales bear a striking resemblance to general American folk tales, but the manner in which they are told is often far too similar to admit coincidence.

It is doubtful that Wolfe drew upon purely regional North Carolina folklore. In *North Carolina Folklore* by Frank C. Brown and the Hendrick's collection of "tar heel tales," for example, little resemblance seems to appear between North Carolina lore and Wolfe's material. More probable sources, however, are Professor Frederick Koch's and Paul Green's works in the folk-lore area. Wolfe and Green were fellow students in Koch's folk play class at Chapel Hill. Furthermore, Wolfe wrote two folk plays, *The Return of Buck Gavin* and *Third Night*. He also acted in several folk plays at the University. Thus in his undergraduate years Wolfe could not escape the influence of Ameri-can folklore as interpreted by Professor Koch. Still another source for Wolfe's filtered through his own immediate family. Wolfe's family, a good "infor-mant," as demonstrated in Hayden Norwood's *The Family of Irrepressible Talkers,* loved to "tell tales." Wolfe's mother, for instance, could, in folklore jargon, be termed a fairly *Marble Man's Wife.*

Again we may ask this question: How specifically does Bear Joyner, our American Moses, relate to folklore? Thanks to the monumental field work done by an army of folklorists, we are able to compare actual folklore tales with the portrait Wolfe paints of Bear Joyner.

Wolfe tells the following of Bear's fighting prowess:

> The stories of his great physical strength, for example, were prodigious, and yet apparently were founded in substantial fact.
>
> He was said to have been, particularly in his earlier years, a man of a hot temper, who liked a fight. There is a story of his fight with a big blacksmith: a quarrel having broken out between them over the shoeing of a horse, the blacksmith brained him with an iron shoe and knocked him flat. As William started to get up again, bleeding and half conscious, the blacksmith came at him again, and Joyner hit him while still resting on one knee. The blow struck the blacksmith's ribs and caved in his side as one would crack a shell. (pp. 213-214)

Bear's powers in and relish for hand to hand combat calls to mind another fighter—Mike Fink. Fink's love of fight-ing and excellence as a fighter are legendary, of course. In Emerson Bennett's version of Mike Fink, the hero roars:

> I can lick five times my own weight in wildcats. I can use up Injens by the cord. I can swallow niggers whole, raw or cooked. I can out-run, out-dance, out-jump, out-dive, out-holler, and out-lick any white things in the shape o' human that's ever put foot within two thousand miles of the big Missassip. . . . Oh, for a fight! . . . O for a fight, boys, to stretch these here limbs, and get the jints to working easy![4]

And, according to Fink legend, Fink did produce the goods on more than one occasion.

A. B. Longstreet has a spectator report the aftermath of a frontier Georgia fight in this way:

> I looked, and saw that Bob had entirely lost his left ear and a large piece from his left cheek. His right eye was a little discolored, and the blood flowed profusely from his wounds. . . . Bill presented a hideous spectacle. About a third of his nose, at the lower extremity, was bit off, and his face was so swelled and bruised that it was difficult to discover in it anything of the human visage. . . . [5]

And in Paulding's *The Lion of the West,* Nimrod Wild-fire says, "My father can whip the best man in old Kaintuck, and I can whip my father." (Lynn, p. 176) Furthermore, Nimrod can prove his contentions.

Surprisingly enough, another very popular frontier hero, Paul Bunyan, was not a fighter in the Bear Joyner-Mike Fink-Nimrod Wildfire sense. Professor Hoffman points out, for example, that he has discovered no oral folklore of a tale in which Paul Bunyan is in a fight.[6]

II

One of the most important folklore episodes concerning William (Bear) Joyner is the one in which he acquired his nickname.

> He was known in his own day to be a mighty hunter; and old men who remembered him used to tell of the time he "chased the dogs the whole way over into Tennessee, and was gone four days and nights, and never knowed how far from home he was."
>
> There is also the story of his fight with a grizzly bear: the bear charged him at close quarters and there was nothing left for him to do but fight. A searching party found him two days later, more dead than living—as they told it, "all chawed up," but with the carcass of the bear: "and in the fight he had bit the nose off the big b'ar and chawed off both of his years, and that b'ar was so tored up hit was a caution." (p. 214)

Professor Dorson comments about the frontier folk: "Legion were the stories that described fierce brushes, grapples, and encounters between a woodsman and a bear."[7] In "A Bear Hunt in Vermont," for instance, there is the following account of a Vermonter's hand to hand encounter with a bear:

> There he was, rolling round on the ground grappling with the fierce animal which was at least four times his weight, and not a weapon about him. . . . Presently he got one hand in the bear's mouth and grappled his tongue. The bear writhed like a serpent, and chawed away on his arm as if it had been a stick. . . . There he was floundering in the mud with a great bear and nothing but his hands to help him." Then the hunter almost effortlessly drowns the bear in a slough of mud and emerges victorious, but "winding his handkerchief round his arm which was horribly mangled . . . " (Dorson, pp. 116-117)

In a similar vein—hand to antler combat—Mike Fink subdues a monstrous moose. (Blair, pp. 210-211)

Note that in all three fights—Vermont bear hunt, Mike Fink and the moose, and Bear Joyner's encounter—the hunters were attacked at close quarters and could make use of no weapons, or for some reason their weapons failed to function so that they had to proceed with the fight in a primitive fashion. This approach to telling the story in each case adds a spark of folk realism.

Perhaps one of the most famous frontier stories concerning a bear fight appears at the tail end of Thorpe's "The Big Bear of Arkansas." This bear hunt differs from Joyner's, of course, in that our Arkansas hero felled his game with a rifle. (Lynn, pp. 122-137)

Bunyan's superman hunting prowess is more closely allied to Joyner's, however:

> There are three [Paul Bunyan] hunting stories; in one, Paul grabs the Timber Wolf by the ears, hollers, and the wolf dies of fright. In another, Paul confronts a Polar Bear; having no railroad spikes for his gun, he rams it full of icicles and kills the bear with them. In the third, he grabs one mountain lion by the tail, and used it to club two others to death. (Hoffman, p. 84)[8]

III

Still another story is told of Bear Joyner in which he outwitted one of his own kin, won a bet, and as a reward "walked off with enough leather on his back to shoe a regiment." After a wager, Bear Joyner's relative, a storekeeper, kept his part of the bargain:

> He pointed to the pile of leather in his store and told William he could take as much as he could carry. Joyner stood there while his companions heaped the leather on, and finally staggered out the door with eight hundred pounds of it on his shoulders. (pp. 214-215)

And Professor Dorson comments on strong men:

> Fact and legend blended in tales of pioneer strong men. Homemaking in the wilderness had stimulated physical performances that more tender generations recalled with awe and retold with relish. Most of these feats had to do with lifting great weights. Benjamin Tarr of Rockfort, Massachusetts, lifted an anchor weighing 800 pounds. (pp. 122-123)

Dorson goes on to cite a number of other strong men folk tales, one being of a man who effortlessly carries 1600 pounds of boom chains on his back. And as Dorson points out, this and other similar tales in the telling always included an eyewitness to verify the deed, just as Bear Joyner's friends at first tried "to dissuade him" but later observed with relish.

Mr. Vance Randolph also records a story of a man who had prodigious strength:

> The old folks say that a big tavern-keeper at Indian Springs, Missouri, could lift more dead weight than any other man in the country. Nearly seven feet tall, this fellow weighed three hundred pounds, and not an ounce of fat in sight. He often toted two sacks of corn to McNatt's mill and carried the meal home under his arm. One day the boys decided to test him, just to see how much weight he could carry. They built a sort of platform, and set it on his great shoulders like a hod. Then they began to pile big rocks and pieces of old iron on the platform. They kept this up until he sank clear to his knees, right in the hard road beside the blacksmith shop. (pp. 167-168)

And Randolph records many other versions as well.[9]

IV

Throughout *Hills* we have samples of the other folklore strain in Bear Joyner's makeup. He was the shrewd trader, the keen Yankee wit, the teller of tall tales, and the Yankee with a wry sense of humor.

His ability to drive a hard bargain, acquire property and then multiply his holdings until the final accumulation of wealth from the deal completely overshadowed his initial gain would do justice to a nineteenth-century Robber Baron.

Nor did Bear's offspring lack their parent's talents. One of Bear Joyner's sons offered to sell a man some land for $200. The man refused, but later bemoans his folly: "And I was such a fool I didn't take it! If I had, I'd have been a rich man today. You couldn't buy it now for a million dollars." (p. 242) And Wolfe adds:

> By the time the Civil War broke out the Joyners were accounted wealthy folk. It was "the big family" of the whole community. Even long before that their position was so generally acknowledged

throughout the western mountains that when the boys began to "make their mark," it occasioned no surprise. (p. 243)

The traditional tales told of the Yankee often emphasized this very thriftiness, shrewdness, and parsimony which made Bear Joyner's people "wealthy folk." But the Yankee was more. He was a conglomeration, often depicted "as a sly and scheming knave . . . regional in projection and design [but a type that] . . . did not differ fundamentally from backward and backwater types throughout the land."[10]

V

Even though Bear Joyner could hold his own in the realm of the tall tale and keen wit, it was really his son Zach Joyner who was "noted for his ready wit, his coarse humor, and his gift of repartee. People would come into the store 'just to hear Zach Joyner talk.'" (p. 247) The townspeople were proud of the "tincture of charlatanism and smooth dealing" in Zach. They told tales of his "superior adroitness and cunning, and men would wag their heads and laugh with envious approval, as though they wished they could do such things themselves, but knew, being merely average men, that they could not make the grade." (p. 248)

As Dorson illustrates, the Yankee was a spinner of yarns. He told land stories, sea stories, fight stories, hunting and fishing stories, almost any kind of story—all tall tales. His repertoire, however, is inexhaustible. (p. 102) Not only did his story telling display the Yankee's versatility and shrewdness, but his trickster nature also confirmed it. More often than not the trickster quirk in the Yankee was turned to profit. In short, Dorson continues, we have a practical joker who delighted in duping the country bumpkin (pp. 78-79), who twinkled as he passed off his glue-factory candidates for good, solid plow horses (pp. 82-85), and who luxuriated in the warm aura of his own yarn spinning (p. 102).

VI

In one respect we can contrast an army of unlettered folk heroes with Bear and Zach Joyner because Wolfe did add the third dimension. And he emphasized this dimension.[11] "It is important, then, to know, [Wolfe points out] that William Joyner 'chawed the b'ar.' But it is even more important to know that William Joyner was a man who learned to read a book." (p. 218) And in the next few pages "learned to read a book" almost becomes a refrain. No unlettered Moses he, Wolfe insists. Our clan must be of the people, close to the land, but it must rise above the land through learning.

At a time when it was the convention for all men in the wilderness to be illiterate, in a place where the knowledge contained in books was of no earthly use, nothing would suit old Bear Joyner but that he must learn to read. . . .

For no one ever really knew where his father came from. And it did not matter. Old Bear Joyner came from the same place, and was of the same kind, as all the other people in the mountains. But he was a man who learned to read. And there is the core of the whole mystery. (p. 221)

If Bear Joyner was the Moses, the beginning of Wolfe's fictional tribe, both his first and second wife shared part of the glory with him. And the second wife especially, who effortlessly bore and reared some fourteen of Bear's twenty children, has some of the frontier tall tale rub off on her. Zach, for instance, has spoken of "the physical sharpness of her sense of smell, which really was amazing, and which all of her children inherited (she is said one time to have 'smelled burning leaves five miles away upon the mountain, long before anyone else knowed there was a fire'). . . . " (p. 232)

And just as our American Moses had a more striking wife than was Zipporah of the traditional biblical patriarch, so did he have in his son Zachariah a man more marked than Gershom. Zach Joyner, one of the oldest sons, is an extension of old Bear himself. Zach becomes a lawyer-politician, a forerunner of the Willie Stark-Huey Long Southern demagogue.

To the people of Catawba Zach was

not only their native Lincoln—their backwoods son who marched to glory by the log-rail route—he was their Crockett and Paul Bunyan rolled in one. He was not alone their hero; he was their legend and their myth. He was, and has remained so to this day, a kind of living prophecy of all that they themselves might wish to be; a native divinity, shaped out of their own clay, and breathing their own air a tongue that spoke the words, a voice that understood and spoke the language, they would have him speak. (p. 223)

And almost as if Wolfe were explaining the evolution of a folk tale or a myth, he goes on to discuss Zach.

They tell a thousand stories about him today. What does it matter if many of the things which they describe never happened? They are true because they are the kind of things he would have said, the kind of things that would have happened to him. Thus, to what degree, and in what complex ways, he was created so in their imaginations, no one can say. How much the man shaped the myth, how much the myth shaped the man, how much Zach Joyner created his ownfolk, or how much his people created him—no one can know, and it does not matter. (pp. 223-224)

And as Wolfe continues to describe Zach Joyner, the folk hero of the people, we hear more echoes of the academic folklorist.

In examining the history of that great man, we have collected more than eight hundred stories, anecdotes, and jokes that are told of him, and of this number at least six hundred have the un-mistakable ring—or *smack*—of truth. If they did not happen—they *should* have! They belong to him: they fit him like an old shoe. (p. 224)

Shades of Professor Koch's Chapel Hill folklore class!

> ... *"Did* they happen?". ... We are not wholly unprepared for these objections. ... We have actually verified three hundred as authentic beyond the shadow of a doubt, and are ready to cite them by the book—place, time, occasion, evidence—to anyone who may inquire. In these stories there is a strength, a humor, a coarseness, and a native originality that belonged to the man and marked his every utterance. They come straight out of his own earth. (p. 224)

But back to the father, the American Moses himself. Is he merely Wolfe's transplant of the Bunyan-Crockett hero? Indeed not. Bear Joyner is at first very much the traditional American hero. He has no background, no parents, no tyrannical father; he overthrows no throne, is no prince in disguise; no one has cursed his birth or set him in the water. Thus he is no Oedipus, Heracles, Apollo, Zeus, Watu, Gunung, Nychang, Sigurd, or Arthur—at first. But from an almost one-dimensional American hero he is changed. The hero-bachelor takes a wife. And the wife begets children. And they beget. And so on.[12]

So we have a patriarch—the clod who starts a clan. Perhaps we may say that we have in Bear Joyner a semi-traditional American hero. Bear does not disappear after his fame-flame has been kindled, as do Bunyan, Crockett, Fink, et al. He stays and becomes the patri-arch—the Moses of the American family.

That Wolfe was conscious of his use of folklore in *Hills* becomes a pedestrian statement in the light of the above evidence. That he bulldozed the site first, with little beforehand attention to the many possible intricate de-signs on the blueprint is, quite naturally, to be regretted.

But there can remain very little doubt concerning Wolfe's overall literary plan, his controlling image. His four huge novels, as has already been mentioned, were autobiographical. In part, *Hills* is also autobiographical. Wolfe's ancestry is so closely knit with the hill folk he discusses in *Hills* that Wolfe becomes folk and folk becomes Wolfe. But his use of the various strains of folklore tradition does help him tone down the personal elements in his characterizations.

Wolfe's novels document a pilgrimage—a pilgrimage which begins in the hills of North Carolina, moves to cosmopolitan New York and then Europe, and finally returns to Old Catawba—the hills beyond—old North Carolina.[13] Furthermore, the journey documents under various names the Joyner-Gant (Westall-Wolfe) life cycle. To be sure, the four novels, the vehicle for the "story," consisted of autobiography, myth, and folklore of a much more imaginative vein than we find in *Hills*.

But in *Hills* Wolfe was moving away from the first two elements and was attempting a story steeped in the last element—folklore.

Hills may have provided an excellent folkloristic ances-try for the Wolfe tribe he had already depicted in his novels. *Look Homeward, Angel* and the other books, however, are complete. *Hills* is a fragment. As such it must be judged. Power it has. Also life and color ex-tracted from the hills of North Carolina and shaped (albeit imperfectly) by Wolfe's own large imagination.

The story—rough, part molded, incomplete. Yet not raw, not shapeless, not merely Bunyan-Crockett episode.

NOTES

[1] Thomas Wolfe, *The Hills Beyond* (Garden City, N.Y.: Sun Dial Press, 1943). Hereafter the abbrevia-tion *Hills* will be used to refer to the ten chapters of the fragment called "The Hills Beyond." Also, hereafter numbers in parentheses in the text with no designa-tion will refer to *Hills*.

[2] Thomas Wolfe, *Thomas Wolfe's Letters to His Mother* (New York: Charles Scribner's Sons, 1951), pp. 292-293.

[3] See also Edward C. Aswell, "A Note on Thomas Wolfe," *Hills,* pp. 351-386.

[4] Walter Blair and Franklin J. Meine, *Half Horse Half Alligator* (Chicago: Univ. Press, 1956), pp. 170-171.

[5] Kenneth S. Lynn (ed.), *The Comic Tradition in America* (New York: Doubleday Anchor, 1958), p. 78.

[6] Daniel G. Hoffman, *Paul Bunyan: Last of the Frontier Demigods* (Philadelphia: Univ. of Penn. Press, 1952), p. 49.

[7] Richard M. Dorson, *Jonathan Draws the Long Bow* (Cambridge, Mass.: Harvard Univ. Press, 1946), p. 116.

[8] See also Vance Randolph, *We Always Lie to Strangers* (New York: Columbia Univ. Press, 1951), pp. 95-130, 168.

[9] See also Lynn, pp. 169-170; Hoffman, "Breaking the Jam," pp. 28-31.

[10] Dorson, p. 69. For more folk parallels of the shrewd trader see Hoffman, "Paul's Cleverality," pp. 43-48; Lynn, Longstreet's "The Horseswap," pp. 81ff.

[11] But see Hoffman, pp. 100-101, who points out that in one popularization of Bunyan, the giant lumberjack is served up as a *student*.

[12] Frazer's *The Golden Bough*, Raglan's *The Hero*, Rank's *The Myth of the Birth of the Hero*, Campbell's *The Hero With a Thousand Faces* taken collectively categorize the European hero of mythology. Rourke, Hoffman, Blair, and Dorson do likewise for the American folklore hero.

[13] See J. M. Maclachlan, "Folk Concepts in the Novels of Thomas Wolfe," *Southern Folklore Quarterly,* IX (Dec. 1945), 175-186. Maclachlan convincingly points out that Wolfe "was a man bound to interpret the culture of an epoch and do it from the vantage-point of his origin in an indigenous and integrated social structure." (p. 177) He further says that when Wolfe returns to his heritage he recognizes value and identity only in his own roots—the hill folk of North Carolina.

Judith Halden

SOURCE: "Barthelme's 'Snow White': The Making of a Modern Fairy Tale," in *Southern Folklore Quarterly,* Vol. 45, 1981, pp. 145-53.

[*In the following essay, Halden looks at Donald Barthelme's* Snow White *both as a traditional fairy tale and as an inversion of established fairy-tale symbolism.*]

A close examination of Donald Barthelme's *Snow White*[1] reveals that, in one sense, his retelling of the traditional fairy tale is nothing new. For centuries storytellers have retold tales in their own ways, embellishing the storyline with details peculiarly representative of both the individual teller and his time.[2] This is precisely what Barthelme does in *Snow White*: he relates the tale of Snow White, her prince, and the seven dwarves in a way which accommodates his own contemporary sensibilities. The novel, contrary to several current analyses, *is* indeed a fairy tale; however, Barthelme's creative license with the tale blurs the fairy tale elements, making them indistinguishable amidst the novel's surreal, psychological landscape. To date, the connections between the oral genre of the fairy tale and this contemporary instance of that genre have not been delineated. Recognition of these basic elements combined with an analysis of Barthelme's manipulation of them, however, will confirm both the traditional and unique features of Barthelme's modern fairy tale.

The few critical treatments of *Snow White* focus on the novel not as a modern instance of a folktale but as an experiment in language. Commenting upon the complexity of the narrative, Betty Flowers claims that "if the reader cannot ground his point of view in either setting or characters, or in one world or another, he looks to language to direct him."[3] However, Barthelme's linguistic "direction" is not easy to follow. Larry McCaffery, revealing his point of view immediately in his article's title "Barthelme's *Snow White*: The Aesthetics of Trash," claims that the author "seeks to exploit the decay of language and literature" because he realizes that "language no longer communicates effectively, that words [have] lost their power to move us [and that] reality is no longer capable of sustaining mythic devices."[4] The subject matter of the novel is art itself, McCaffery asserts, and he goes on to describe Barthelme's artistic strategy of self-consciously incorporating decayed, brutalized elements into his own idiom in order to make a new language part of his "point."[5] The process McCaffery defines here on a linguistic level is paralleled in Barthelme's folkloristic strategy: Barthelme merges his own intents with familiar fairy tale elements to present a modern fantasy. Yet, however cogent in their linguistic assessments of the novel, both Flowers and McCaffery forego discussion of the novel as a fairy tale and instead treat the "mythic" elements of the text. Flowers asserts that the "mythical reality" of the novel—evidenced by boldface "primitive images"[6] such as "the huntsman" and "the steaming knife"—is by far more intense and "real" than those elements of mundane life seen in the narrative. "The novel," she cryptically explains, "points to the myth as a reality beyond itself."[7] Flowers, like McCaffery, never specifically defines her term "myth" in her analysis of *Snow White,* and, according to its folkloristic implications, the use of this term to classify the storyline of *Snow White* seems inappropriate. McCaffery goes so far as to claim that " . . . the book seems to be deliberately mocking Joyce's painstaking efforts at creating mythic parallels, suggesting perhaps that the condition of both language and reality make[s] such devices unavailable to the modern writer."[8] This analogy too easily implies that myth and fairy tale are the same genre; they are not. Joyce and Barthelme are attempting two entirely different literary feats with two distinctively different forms. In the early chapters of *Ulysses,* Joyce may lure the reader into the narrative with a framework of mythic parallels, but midway in the novel he actively employs new structures to create his *own* modern myth without (except for chapter titles) any consistent or particularly rewarding allusions to Homer's *Odyssey.* What Barthelme does is quite different: he stylistically twists the fairy tale elements of an old story to yield a modern re-telling. *Snow White* is indeed satiric, but is hardly a "mock-myth." Richard Gilman points out that in *Snow White*

> the tale is . . . refracted through the prism of a contemporary sensibility so that it emerges broken up into fragments, shards of its original identity, of its historical career in our consciousness . . . and of its recorded or potential uses for sociology and psychology.[9]

Max Lüthi provides the bases for recognizing in the novel traditional fairy tale elements. In *Once Upon a Time: On the Nature of Fairy Tales,* Lüthi offers the first formal discussion of the literary elements apparent in various versions of fairy tales and reciprocally pairs the literary features with a list of key fairy tale characteristics. Barthelme incorporates almost all of these fairy tale characteristics into *Snow White.* Delineation of character and setting—the area of unstable, shifting ground which Flowers explored—is, even in Barthelme's "brutalized" idiom, fully aligned with traditional fairy tale structure.

In defining the depth of character development seen in fairy tales, Lüthi asserts what McCaffery has criticized in *Snow White*: characters are not personally delineated.[10]

If Snow White and her prince Paul are "flat" and "devoid of details,"[11] as McCaffery charges, it is because Barthelme chooses to retain this characteristic feature. These are characters in a fairy tale, not protagonists representative of more "literary" fiction. The only physical characteristics of Snow White the reader knows are her nicely aligned beauty spots, her attractive breasts, and her long ebony hair. But in fairy tale form, this is all the audience *needs* to know. An individual reader's imagination takes over to fill in additional details. Paul, too, is vaguely drawn: he is excessively "princely" (p. 27) and is also called "a frog"[12] (p. 169) by his ambivalent princess Snow White, two descriptions which offer only a connotative sense of Paul's identity. In addition, though, according to Lüthi's definition, Paul does embody another quality indicative of a fairy tale hero, that of a wanderer.[13] Like other fairy tale heroes, he seeks a quest. Barthelme, however, emphasizes Paul's neurotic reluctance to accept a challenge, a twist of Lüthi's wanderer element to be discussed later. Paul aimlessly travels to a Nevada monastery (p. 116) and then ventures into France to speciously explain the "audacity component" which every mind's "amplifier" (p. 114) should have. Paul, like Snow White and the dwarves, wanders amidst an absurd milieu in which damsels hang their long hair out of windows and psychologically disturbed dwarves tend vats of Chinese baby food. The surreal environment of *Snow White* both replaces the supernatural forces which govern many fairy tale settings, and, in this substitution, allows the novel to feature a third fairy tale element: the hero or heroine is not astonished by "magic" but instead accepts it as a matter of course.[14] While Paul and Snow White lament their personal anxieties throughout the tale, neither of them is conscious of or surprised by the absurdity of, for example, such notions as Snow White's sexual encounters in the shower with the seven dwarves or Paul's underground surveillance installation. The strange nature of the protagonists' lives is left to be appreciated solely by the audience, not by the characters.

These first three comparatively superficial fairy tale elements—the flat characterization, the wanderer theme, and the supernatural setting—are surpassed in their presentation within *Snow White* by Barthelme's powerful styling of another märchen quality: the isolation of the characters.[15] Barthelme structures the novel in brief, discrete episodes which for the most part can stand alone. Form here mirrors content: each chapter offers an isolated instance of a character's unusual behavior or his private meditations. None of these descriptions or observations really "hang together" in a linear narrative form, and consequently the novel easily falls prey to accusations of "shapelessness,"[16] yet the intensely cerebral nature of, for example, an exposé on "the psychology of Snow White" (p. 70) or the diagnoses of the individual dwarves concerning their comrade Bill's reluctance to be touched (p. 4) lends to all the characters the quality of being locked in the tower of their own psyches. While traditional fairy tales depict the hero alone facing the dragon, each character in *Snow White* confronts total psychological isolation—quite an existential twist. The novel is an archive of the characters' overheard self-statements, including those of the dwarves. Dwarves in traditional fairy tales are never individually known but instead function together as a unit. Bruno Bettelheim describes dwarves as "pre-oedipal,"[17] pre-individual men free of mental conflicts and solely interested in work. But Barthelme afflicts even the dwarves with a sense of aloneness, describing their individual mental maladies and misunderstandings. The tiny men may tend the vats and please Snow White en masse, but each one suffers individually. No character escapes the isolation upon which Barthelme bases even the episodic structure of the novel. And in depicting the world in which these psyches collide, Barthelme again injects the fairy tale with concentrated doses of neuroses.

Lüthi defines the fairy tale world as a universe in miniature[18] portrayed with certainty and precision,[19] a place where the passage of time is disregarded. Extremes and contrasts mark this realm, and here also objects are sharply defined by distinct shapes and strong colors.[20] Characters externalize their feelings and relationships by identifying with and displaying particular objects. This kind of fairy tale kingdom is embodied in unique form in *Snow White*. First, there is the sense throughout the novel that all of the characters are fitting representatives of their own unusual world. Barthelme creates this sense of a whole, distinctive fairy world by associating his characters with lively images such as the dwarves' bubbling vat (p. 18), Snow White's "long hair streaming from the high window" (p. 80), Bill's dreaded "black horse" (p. 159), and Jane's gift of a poisoned vodka Gibson (p. 174). These both flesh out Barthelme's bizarre kingdom and act as leitmotifs representative of their owners. The imaged objects, like the characters, stand in colorful contrast with each other, such as the "red meat on the rug" (p. 10)—the metaphor for Snow White's erotic poem—in juxtaposition to her "beautiful snow-white arse itself" (p. 101). Characterizations are similarly disparate, with Hogo, for example, portrayed as the violent, passionate beast and Paul as the passive and indecisive blueblood. Characters and their objects exist in a timeless realm. A vehicle for a psychological hothouse, the narrative communicates no sense of conventional or chronological time. Even after the conflict is "resolved," the narrative indicates an on-going pursuit in the final boldface lines, which read like proposed yet unwritten chapter titles:

THE FAILURE OF SNOW WHITE'S ARSE
REVIRGINIZATION OF SNOW WHITE
SNOW WHITE RISES INTO THE SKY
THE HEROES DEPART IN SEARCH OF A NEW PRINCIPLE
HEIGH-HO (P. 181)

The component parts of this timeless world—the characters and their objects—are then, in their own unusual manner, typical of fairy tales. While Barthelme fashions these elements in peculiar ways, they remain distinctive enough to permit identification of the novel as a fairy tale. Retrieval of these elements, however, is hindered by the author: Barthelme distorts the fairy tale's most important quality to undercut, if not overturn, the reader's expectations.

The salient element in traditional fairy tales is action.[21] Each fairy tale episode conventionally depicts the hero committed to *doing* something, but not in *Snow White*. Barthelme's concerns are with the life of the mind, the only reality that individual human beings know. For heroic action Barthelme substitutes within the narrative the ramblings of disturbed minds, and, while this modification certainly makes Barthelme's retelling of the old tale peculiarly his own, it also makes the novel modern. Paul, the princely hero, suffers from a severe case of Prufrockian inertia. While in one sense he is a traditional wanderer-hero, Paul's restlessness arises not from his anticipation of a noble quest but from his avoidance of one. He would prefer to retreat to a monastery or be "discovered" as a new television star; being a hero in this world is hard, he muses:

> "The engaging and wholly charming way I stand in front of this fence here," Paul said to himself, "will soon persuade someone to discover me. Then I will not have to go to the monastery. Then I can be on television or something, instead of going to the monastery. Yet there is no denying it, something is pulling me toward that monastery located in a remote part of Western Nevada." Lanky, generous-hearted Paul! "If I had been born well prior to 1900, I could have ridden with Pershing against Pancho Villa. Alternatively, I could have ridden with Villa against the landowners and corrupt government officials of the time. In either case, I would have had a horse. How little opportunity there is for young men to have personally owned horses in the bottom half of the twentieth century!" (p. 78)

Snow White, too, laments the disappearance of heroism. She is forced to advertise for a charming prince to take her away from her dreary castle by daily hanging her long, black hair out of her tower window, much like Rapunzel.[22] She attracts no takers, only onlookers such as Paul who finds the hair vaguely disturbing: "that long black hair hanging from that window, that I saw today on my way here, from the Unemployment Office. It has made me terribly nervous, that hair. It was beautiful, I admit it. Long black hair of such texture, fineness, is not easily come by. Hair black as ebony! Yet it has made me terribly nervous" (p. 94). Snow White waits, languishing in anticipation:

> Snow White regarded her hair . . . "Paul? Is there a Paul, or have I only projected him in the shape of my longing, boredom, ennui and pain? Have I been trained in the finest graces and arts all my life for nothing but this? Is my richly-appointed body to go down the drain, at twenty-two, in this horribly boresome milieu, which even my worst enemy would not wish upon me, if she knew? Of course, there is a

> Paul! That Paul who was a friend, the family, who had, at that point, not yet assumed the glistening mantle of princeliness. There is a Paul somewhere, but not here. Not under my window. Not yet." (p. 102)

Unfortunately when Paul finally dons his "mantle of princeliness," he overestimates his powers. When Jane, the jilted lover, offers her rival Snow White the poisoned vodka Gibson, Paul—warned of Snow White's impending sip by his underground surveillance system—rushes in and snatches the drink, claiming that

> "It is a good thing I have taken it away from you, Snow White. It is too exciting for you. If you had drunk it, something bad would probably have happened to your stomach. But because I am a man, and because men have strong stomachs for the business of life . . . nothing will happen to me." (p. 175)

Paul gulps down the drink and, in a complete subversion of fairy tale endings, dies a grisly death. The novel is left hero-less and no "happy ending" marriage between prince and princess occurs. Instead, the "efficient brute" (p. 180) Hogo usurps Paul's potential position as Snow White's man of the house.

Hogo inherits the world of *Snow White*; he is the monarch (his real name is "Roy") of this absurd kingdom, carrying with him to the throne his animal passions and gutter slang. In one sense, then, Barthelme remodels the Snow White tale to mourn the modern world's inability to foster romanticism and gallantry. His heroine whimpers in her repression, his hero fails to achieve the tasks "demanded of [him] by history" (p. 55), and only brutes and neurotic dwarves survive in the surreal and often hostile landscape. In addition to this kind of failure, if the fairy tale offers a symbolic expression of a human being's maturation process—as Bettelheim asserts—then the tale also ends with a sense of stunted growth. No character matures in *Snow White*. Barthelme's conclusion denies any chance for the characters to live "happily ever after" in a better kingdom, but by now the reader is aware that such cheery endings are indeed the stuff of fairy tales. When Paul dies, reality invades the narrative at a desperate moment. Fairy tale princes do *not* perish, and thus Paul's death remains as the most unsettling result of Barthelme's splicing of fantasy and reality. The reluctant, if not unpromising, hero cannot develop the facility to succeed. Suddenly all too human, he suffers and dies, a personification of heroism's extreme frailty in the modern world.

But *Snow White* is no moral tract. It is a very funny book. While the reader often struggles with the intricacies of the characters' minds, he also laughs at the zaniness of the novel. What evokes this dual response of puzzlement and pleasure is Barthelme's method of storytelling: he injects traditional fairy tale characters with his own potent brand of truth serum. The truth wrenched from each character is a testament to Barthelme's free-wheeling playfulness. For example, while tainting the pristine image of traditional fairy tale heroines, the graphic details of Snow White's menage à huit sex life engage simultaneously the reader involved only in the superficial plot, the reader reveling in Barthelme's dirty, "inside" joke, and finally the reader who sees beyond the satire to recognize that Barthelme cleverly manipulates all levels of reader involvement to his best advantage. Bantering with his reader at the end of *Snow White*'s first part, Barthelme asks: "Do you feel that the creation of new modes of hysteria is a viable undertaking for the artist today?" (p. 82). This question can be accepted at face value, but it is also an example of Barthelme's quirky fun. The term "viable" is an abused cliche of social science-ese, stretched to qualify virtually any situation; thus, Barthelme poses his inquiry satirically. But beyond satirizing trendy lingo, the question toys with the perceptive reader in another way. Barthelme's sly banter diverts his reader's attention from his trickery. He uses an "old mode," not a new one, to accommodate his modern notion of hysteria: he employs the fairy tale.

This old mode is certainly viable, as time has attested. The fairy tale elements provide stable ground in *Snow White*'s narrative chaos of hysteria. Also, the fairy tale allows Barthelme the "magical" flexibility to explore the combination of unmanageable fears and excessive emotion indicative of hysteria without falling prey to accusations of total illogic. Characters in traditional fairy tales act in strong, inexplicable—perhaps even hysterical—ways, too. For example, Snow Whites's mother feels compelled, after seeing three drops of her own blood fall upon fresh snow, to have a daughter with skin as white as snow, cheeks as red as blood, and hair black enough to match her ebony windowsill. What strong emotions provoke the queen's sudden compulsion? What sort of fearful hysteria drives Snow White's stepmother to seek out torturous ways to destroy her young charge? The fairy tale embodies a powerful expression of intricate human psychology, as Freud himself pointed out.

However, returning to key terms from Barthelme's quiz question, *Snow White* is at its best a "viable" form of entertainment. A representative "artist of today," Barthelme employs a recognizable, traditional mode—the fairy tale—to communicate his modern sensibility. In addition, like any storyteller, he reinvigorates the tale for his audience, making it somehow "real" for them. Thus, as both artist and tale-teller, Barthelme convinces the reader that, while Snow White remains a timeless fairy tale heroine, she may well be alive and living in New York.

NOTES

[1] Donald Barthelme, *Snow White* (New York: Atheneum, 1965). All references are to this edition.

[2] The individual teller and his potential for remodeling the traditional folktale are topics pursued by prominent folklorists such as Linda Degh, Richard Dorson, and Alan Dundes.

[3] Betty Flowers, "Barthelme's *Snow White*: The Reader-Patient Relationship," *Critique,* 16 (1975), No. 3, 38.

[4] Larry McCaffery, "Barthelme's *Snow White*: The Aesthetics of Trash," *Critique,* 16 (1975), No. 3, 19.

[5] McCaffery, p. 20.

[6] Flowers, p. 35.

[7] Flowers, p. 35.

[8] McCaffery, p. 21.

[9] Richard Gilman, "Donald Barthelme," *The Confusion of Realms* (London: Weidenfeld and Nicolson, 1970), p. 45.

[10] Max Lüthi, *Once Upon a Time: On the Nature of Fairy Tales* (New York: Frederick Ungar Publishing Co., 1970), p. 24.

[11] McCaffery, p. 24.

[12] The reference to Paul as a "frog" indicates that Barthelme is manipulating more than just the Snow White fairy tale. Versions of frog-prince and frog-king fairy tales abound, and this tale, like most fairy tales, is rich in Freudian implications, penis envy being a primary interpretive conjecture.

[13] Lüthi, p. 140.

[14] Lüthi, p. 46.

[15] Lüthi, p. 50.

[16] McCaffery, p. 21.

[17] Bruno Bettelheim, *The Uses of Enchantment* (New York: Alfred A. Knopf, 1976), p. 200.

[18] Lüthi, p. 25.

[19] Lüthi, pp. 47-48.

[20] Lüthi, p. 32.

[21] Lüthi, p. 28.

[22] In this reference to yet another fairy tale—the story of Rapunzel—Barthelme merges the elements of modern realism with fantasy to yield a surreal landscape in which men note ebony hair hanging from tower windows on their way to the unemployment office.

David C. Estes

SOURCE: "American Folk Laughter in Robert Coover's 'The Public Burning'," in *Contemporary Literature,* Vol. 28, No. 2, Summer, 1987, pp. 239-56.

[In the following essay, Estes examines Robert Coover's use of folk styles, particularly an unsentimental type of humor, in The Public Burning.*]*

Robert Coover has shown a continuing interest in the sociological significance of folklore and in the techniques of folk narrative. In *The Universal Baseball Association* (1968), the ball players are an occupational folk group complete with legendary heroes and their own ballads, maintaining their sense of identity partly through the folklore Coover has invented for them. In *Pricksongs & Descants* (1969), the retellings of "Hansel and Gretel" and "Little Red Riding Hood" show his interest in the plots, motifs, and narrative strategies of the European *Märchen,* and "The Magic Poker" is an unconventional fairy tale of Coover's own devising from a variety of traditional tale types and motifs.[1] Another piece in the collection, "Quenby and Ola, Swede and Carl," pays some attention to the folk narrator's performance style and the context of a well-told tale. In this case Ola's story about the night her father shot her cat is technically a memorate, one of those narratives of personal happenings that abound in family folklore. By omitting some details from the original experience, she fashions an account ending with a punchline that becomes a family favorite. The final section of Coover's story raises metafictional questions about this traditional form of closure, which is one of many structuring patterns that control the contents of folk narratives and, according to him, may prevent them from encompassing the full mystery of experience and the imagination.

Coover's use of folklore is most extensive in *The Public Burning* (1977), where almost every genre of verbal folklore appears: folk songs and ballads, tall tales, legends, jokes, folk similes, puns, proverbs, superstitions, and even counting-out rhymes. Metafictional considerations, although present in the narrative variations on a folk motif played out in the final scenes, are less important than the use of folklore in context to reflect cultural values. It takes its place in re-creating life during the Eisenhower era alongside references to significant and insignificant historical events; famous—and not so famous—leaders, entertainers, and writers; and artifacts of popular culture. Primarily, the folklore contributes to the novel's humor, which is thoroughly in the American grain. The folk humor on which Coover relies does not evoke nostalgia for an idealized, folksy wit or for bygone days when such innocent humor presumably flourished, because he refuses to sentimentalize or trivialize it. Therefore, it is as powerful within the fictional world of *The Public Burning* as it is within the real world of human relationships.

Like *The Adventures of Huckleberry Finn,* this novel examines the dark underside of the nation uncritically hallowed in its folk and popular culture. Coover focuses on those items and motifs prevalent in American folk laughter that illustrate its power to degrade and dominate. Furthermore, he draws upon previous uses of folk humor in the popular literature written by the humorists of the Old Southwest—those amateur antebellum authors who preceded Mark Twain in the skillful reliance on such oral material—in order to develop his character Uncle Sam as a representation of the frightening maliciousness of frontier individualism and self-reliance which American culture has prized. The topical subject of the novel, a satiric attack against Richard Nixon, incorporates both his representation in contemporary oral humor and Coover's own inventive application of the techniques of folk humor. While the humor in *The Public Burning* accurately reflects what has made Americans laugh throughout the nation's history, Coover does not find American humor to be a laughing matter. For what we continue to find funny as a nation ultimately has the power to force citizens to enjoy participation in inhuman acts. *The Public Burning* might well be considered a man's book—not only because of the prevalence of locker room humor but also because the few women characters, who represent the moral center of human decency and maternal love, are unable to develop successful strategies to resist being manipulated. Yet ironically, the men are also ultimately defenseless. In Coover's view the dehumanizing masculine control that American folk humor glorifies is surprisingly and menacingly self-renewing.

As Coover has commented in an interview, this novel tells "the story of June 9, 1953. On that day, the Rosenbergs are burned in Times Square and all the members of the tribe are drawn to the scene. All that has happened that day happens there, in a way; everything is condensed into one big circus."[2] He builds up to the electrocution, fantastically transformed into a carnival-like variety show, by tracing the last-minute judicial appeals and the mounting public reaction during the three days preceding it. Although at first most interested in the circus qualities of this spectacle, he later "developed the idea of having the Vice President at the time become the first person narrator. The world has its superheroes—figures like Uncle Sam and the Phantom—and Richard Nixon, who wishes to be the incarnation of Uncle Sam . . . , is studying what is going on very carefully, picking up notes."[3] Alternating chapters switch their focus from the national scene to the thoughts of Nixon, who is paralyzed into inaction by obsessive daydreams about the importance of the Rosenberg case to his personal past and his political future. The nearing execution finally spurs him into making an impulsive secret journey to Sing Sing in hopes of winning a confession from Ethel. This private interview moments before her death ensures Nixon's public humiliation in Times Square, when Coover's two emphases converge on the stage erected there.

Several examples of the items of verbal folklore found throughout the novel will serve to show their part in Coover's fictional world as well as the social values he wishes to satirize. The title of the prologue—"Groun'-Hog Hunt"—is also the title of the ballad whose verses alternate with the prose description found there of the Rosenberg case. It is reminiscent of "Bangum and the Boar" (the American version of the English "Sir Lionel"), in which Old Bangum goes into the forest to kill a blood-thirsty wild boar. There is also a similarity to the English historical ballad "Chevy Chase," in which a hunting adventure quickly turns into a battle between political enemies. In Coover's ballad, Senator Joseph McCarthy and Uncle Sam are in pursuit of a groundhog, and the hunt in the lyrics parallels the capture of Julius and Ethel Rosenberg which the prologue recounts:

> Call up yer dog, O call up yer dog,
> Le's go a-huntin' to ketch a groun'-hog!
>
> Whet up ye knife an' loaden up ye gun,
> Away to the hills to have some fun!
>
> They picked up their guns an' went to the brash,
> By dam, Joe, here's the hog sign fraish!
>
> Git away, Sam, an' lemme load my gun,
> The groun'-hog hunt has jist begun!
>
> He's in here, boys, the hole's wore slick!
> Run here, Sam, with ye forkéd stick!
>
> Stand back, boys, an' le's be wise,
> Fer I think I see his beaded eyes!
>
> Up jumped Joe with a ten-foot pole,
> He roused it in that groun'-hog's hole!
>
> Stand back, boys, an' gimme a little air,
> I've got a little o' the groun'-hog's hair!
>
> I heard 'im give a whistle an' a wail,
> I've wound my stick right in his tail!
>
> Stand back, boys, an' lemme git my breath,
> Ketchin' this groun'-hog's might nigh death!
>   To-my-wham-bam-diddle-all-the-day . . . !
>
> They took 'im by the tail an' wagged 'im to a log,
> An' swore by gum! he's a hell-of-a-'hog!
>
> Carried 'im to the house an' skinned 'im out to bile,
> I bet you forty dollars you could smell 'im fifty mile!
>
> So, Sam cocked his gun an' Dave pulled the trigger,
> But the one killed the 'hog was old Joe Digger!
>
> The chil'ren screamed an' the chil'ren cried,
> They love groun'-hog cooked an' fried!
>   *To-my-ring-a-ding-doodle-all-DAY!*[4]

The chase, with its conclusion in violent domination and death, is here a matter for boasting just as in tales both backwoods and city-bred hunters tell of adventures in the wilds. Although the hunters are named and the

context suggests that the groundhog must be the Rosenbergs, the words do not specify the prey. Therefore, it is possible to read the song as foreshadowing the novel's epilogue in which Richard Nixon, presumably one of the men in this hunting party, becomes the unwitting prey who is sodomized by Uncle Sam. The intentional ambiguity of the line "Up jumped Joe with a ten-foot pole" calls to mind the sexual implications of the chase, and Joe's shout of valor that follows—"I've wound my stick right in his tail!"—suggests his sense of ownership of this "weapon." Gershon Legman has written about popular jokes that similarly celebrate penises of comically exaggerated proportions that are able both to dominate women and intimidate other men.[5] Since the pronouns referring to the groundhog are consistently masculine, in this ballad the implied sexual partner, a victim who literally dies as proof of Joe's manliness, is not female. Such homosexual overtones are typical of phallic brags and are consistent with their tone of hostility, according to Legman. Thus the narrative folk song here serves as a frame for interpreting the final sexual encounter in the novel as the manifestation of a deeply rooted cultural trait—the desire for unlimited domination that recognizes no taboos.

While conversing with an embarrassed Nixon about the time the Vice President lost his virginity, Uncle Sam chants a strongly rhythmical folk verse of the sort that might accompany children's games:

> The Virgin Mary stumped her toe
> On the way to Mexico!
> On the way back she broke her back
> Sliding on the railroad track!
> Queevy, quavy, Irish Mary,
> Stingalum, stangalum, *buck!* (344)

As in the previous ballad, the humor here arises from a situation of implied sexual domination which either injures or kills the partner in the female role. The weakness of the groundhog elicits no sympathy; the divinity of Mary, no reverence. Both verse narratives create a sense of jolly good humor in response to the unrestrained use of power—a humor that strikes outsiders as callous.

The jokes in *The Public Burning* told by a Washington cab driver reflect the political and sexual frustrations of the group Nixon termed America's "silent majority." Through the use of such folk narratives in ordinary discourse, many people can articulate social concerns more vividly and forcefully than by means of abstract language and formal logic. The cabbie who has Nixon as his passenger is a proletarian raconteur who knows, as did President Lincoln, the rhetorical impact of a humorous story. Several of his jokes ambivalently condemn the policies of contemporary politicians while simultaneously admiring their symbolic sexual powers. He quips about Eisenhower: "Hey, I hear Mamie's askin' for a divorce! . . . she says she's gettin' sick 'n' tired of him doin' to the country all the time what he oughta be doin' to her!" (264). In another joke during the same slow ride through heavy traffic, he ridicules former President Truman for unmanly impotence:

> I got three little girls, ya know—well, they ain't so little any more, in fact they just got married the other day. All on the same day, a cute idea! . . .
>
> Yeah, and they all spent their first night in my house, see? When they come down to breakfast the next morning, I ask 'em, I says: "Honey, whaddaya think o' married life?" Well, the first one, she says: "Daddy, with my husband it was just like Winston Churchill, all blood, sweat, and tears!" And the second one, she says: "My old man was like Roosevelt, I thought I'd never get him out—four times, before he finally died on me!" . . .
>
> So I asked the third one, "Well, what about you, honey?" And she says, "Well, mine was just like Harry Truman, Daddy. He wanted out before he'd ever got in, then when he did get in, he didn't know what to do there. Finally, he just rolled over and quit, and when I asked him why, he says: 'Lady, the fuck stops here!'" (265-66)

Despite the driver's awareness of the topical political satire in these jokes, he may be unaware of all that they reveal about the values of the group in which they are traditional. In both of them, women judge their men solely on their performance in bed, and the more forceful and violent it is, the better. While neither pictures intercourse as an act of love, the first is particularly startling because of its ambiguity. Precisely what does Mamie want? An intimate relationship modelled after the insensitive political control that the text implies her husband wields? Not far beneath the surface of these jokes lie the sadistic urges Legman has found to be characteristic of sexual humor.[6]

Not surprisingly, there is a malicious streak in this cabbie's sense of humor, which recalls the Bricksville, Arkansas, loafers in *Huckleberry Finn* who pass their time tormenting stray dogs by tying tin pans to their tails or by setting them on fire. His is a modern version of these practical jokes, which derives from deep-seated sexual frustrations:

> Suddenly, the cabbie spotted a pair of copulating dogs in the street—*"Whoopee!"* he cried, took aim, and roared forward . . . yowling like a wild Indian, [he] reeled cross-traffic . . .
>
> . . . and caught the dogs just as they reached the curb, clipping the top one in the butt and sending them both skidding, still locked up, spraddle-legged and yipping wildly. . . . *"Goal!"* the cabbie cried. . . .
>
> . . . "That's one piece o' ass them old houndawgs won't soon fergit!" (267-68)

Nixon, cringing in the back seat, is frightened enough to forget the embarrassment that the jokes about the Presidents have caused him—an embarrassment that the cabbie recognizes and that tempts him to start telling one on Nixon himself, which the Vice President refuses to allow. Readers are at this point also willing to forego another tale since the practical joke has been a glaring revelation that the driver is a satirist lacking moral rectitude. According to what standards does he praise and censure if he is driven to punish such a normal thing as the intercourse of street dogs? Coover's admiration for the satiric sting in folk humor is limited. He is unwilling to idealize the folk and refuses to allow readers to identify with them completely. Thus while some people search naïvely for folk wisdom upon which to construct solutions to complex social problems, Coover is ultimately distrustful and suspicious of the implications in the lore of the broad American masses.

Because most people mistakenly think of American folklore as existing primarily among the poorly educated, the rural, the impoverished, and the ethnic minorities, many readers might be surprised to find that Coover depicts the Senate as an occupational folk group. Among these legislators, Everett Dirksen is the most revered joke teller because of his style of delivery, which is marked by an ability to use his hands and his expressive clown's face (51). In these politicians' folk tales, Lyndon Johnson has become a legendary hero. Nixon recounts one of the legends about him in which his actions conform to the ethics of domination that Coover finds characteristic of American folk humor. The setting is the Senator's private lavatory, which they reach by passing through the room where the reporters congregate:

> According to the legend, the best news sources have always been Senators with "weak bladders and strong minds"—all the more so when the bladders have been weakened by bourbon. . . . It was said that during the debate on the Tidelands Oil Bill, Lyndon Johnson had got trapped by a young socialite reporter and had agreed to an interview provided only she'd come in and hold his pecker for him while he peed—which presumably she did. Scoop of the year. Or, as Lyndon was said to have remarked at the urinal, "Lady, you just struck a gusher!" (52)

Powerful pissing—a folk verification of manliness—is also a motif in the legends about Uncle Sam. While he is using the toilet in Nixon's office, "the crashing roar of his urine drowned out" the thoughts of the Vice President, who recalls that "he'd smashed up more than one solid-marble toilet bowl in this building with that mighty Niagara of his." Unworried about such consequences, Uncle Sam—like LBJ—boasts: "this is the most magnificent movement of all!" Meanwhile, Nixon remembers this tall tale:

> It was said that he could generate enough power with his flow to light up all Latin America, so long as they didn't mind the odor, and that once, to prove he could stop time, had pissed Old Faithful back down its hole, and thereby had created the Hot Springs of Arkansas. (337)

All of the preceding songs, jokes, legends, and tall tales are reflections of the values of mainstream American culture. The national folklore reveres the unrestrained power of the penis and, consequently, mocks all displays of sexual weakness. Praise goes not to the compassionate, but to those who establish their own individual authority by dominating others. It is truly a man's world in the worst sense of the term, as Coover demonstrates through his use of verbal folklore.

The novel's Uncle Sam is the embodiment of the nation's values who apotheosizes himself every four years in the elected President. Readers can easily recognize that he is modelled after a modern hero with unequalled power—Superman. In Uncle Sam's battle against his arch-rival, the Phantom, readers are told, he "has been whipping about his vast domains all morning, struggling against crooks, Commies, and crawfishing backsliders" (169). The night before the execution, the Phantom vandalizes the Death House set in Times Square, and the clean-up crew is unable to repair the dismantled electric chair. Coming to the rescue like Superman, "with one fluid movement, Uncle Sam lifts from the gutter the wrecked chair, light as a matchbox for him, squeezes the splintered wood whole again, and bolts it down on the concrete part of the stage with hammer blows of his powerful fists!" (171). But Coover has incorporated much more than this comic book figure into Uncle Sam. His character, language, and behavior all reflect humorous folk stereotypes and conventions found in antebellum backwoods sketches, thus rooting him in the tradition that Walter Blair calls "native American humor."[7] Through him, then, Coover reveals the unsettling consequences on a national scale of what Americans have historically chosen to consider funny.

Uncle Sam's real name in the novel is Sam Slick, recalling the Yankee peddler about whom Thomas Chandler Haliburton wrote in the 1830s and '40s. In *The Clockmaker* and *The Attache; or Sam Slick in England,* Haliburton captured the qualities of Down East humor in his hero's aphorisms and his tales illustrating truths about human nature. Slick is able to "come the wooden nutmeg" over householders and sell them over-priced clocks they neither need nor want. According to Blair and Hamlin Hill, he remains a humorous regional character and "does not become a criminal" because he acts "without malice and without the injustice and amorality that so often accompany the true con man."[8] Yet Coover views this figure as more sinister. The name is explicated in the first pages of the prologue to mean "'slick . . . as a snake out of a black skin!'" (6), this allusion underscoring the point that the Yankee peddler's widely admired humorous cunning rests on a satanic ability to manipulate others through the power of language.

Uncle Sam talks like the "game-cocks of the wilderness" that James Kirke Paulding popularized on the stage in 1830 through Nimrod Wildfire in his widely successful *The Lion of the West.* This exaggerated boast at the opening of the novel, while mentioning the subtle and selfish Yankee, mimics the style associated with that likable Kentucky braggart:

> I am Sam Slick the Yankee Peddler—I can ride on a flash of lightnin', catch a thunderbolt in my fist, swaller niggers whole, raw or cooked, slip without a scratch down a honey locust, whup my weight in wildcats and redcoats, squeeze blood out of a turnip and cold cash out of a parson, and out-inscrutabullize the heathen Chinee. (7)

Some reviewers of *The Public Burning* have found Uncle Sam's verbose bragging in this tradition to be tedious. Certainly, these boasts do not have the appeal for current readers that they would have had in the first half of the nineteenth century. Antebellum readers found this type of outlandish boasting extremely amusing, and in addition to Wildfire, Mike Fink the keelboatman and the Davy Crockett of the *Crockett Almanacks* became the most popular "ring-tailed roarers." The tall talk of these Westerners seems to have been first recorded in 1810 in *Travels on an Inland Voyage* by Christian Schultz, Jr., who overheard two drunken riverboatmen in Natchez trying to top each other's boasts with such claims as "'I am an alligator, half man, half horse; can whip any man *on the Mississippi,* by G-d.'"[9] Within the next several years the "half-horse half-alligator" stereotype became part of the national folklore. Similar frontier roarers and screamers peopled the sketches that unpaid correspondents primarily from the South and West submitted to the New York *Spirit of the Times,* a weekly antebellum sporting paper that was extremely influential in the development of American humorous literature.

Uncle Sam's comments about his enemy the Phantom specifically call to mind the writings of these earlier humorists, which Coover suggests are the nation's sacred texts: "'That pestifferous varmint may have got us in a drefful sityeation,' he declares in the old style of Holy Writ" (63). Throughout the novel Uncle Sam's comments are peppered with made-up words either drawn directly from or indebted to antebellum humor: "teetotaciously," "slantidicular," "exfluncticate," "progectorated," and "kankarifferous," to name only a few. His hyperbolic description of his enemy also belongs to the frontier world of boasting and brawling: "'They call him Sudden Death and General Desolation, half cousin to the cholera and godfather of the Apocalypse! . . . half wild horse and half cockeyed catamount, and the rest of him is crooked snags and red-hot snappin' turkle!'" (335-36). References to snags and snapping turtles, common dangers on the great waterways of the West, abound in the boasts of scores of antebellum literary characters indebted to folk stereotypes.

Yet this boast alludes to one humorist in particular, the one called "Saint Mark" later in the novel (500). The first sentence comes with only minor revision from Mark Twain's "Frescoes from the Past," in which two boasting keelboatmen ironically avoid the fist fight their verbal confrontation leads readers to expect. In that sketch, originally intended to be a chapter in *Huckleberry Finn* but included in *Life on the Mississippi* instead, Bob exclaims, "Look at me! I'm the man they call Sudden Death and General Desolation! Sired by a hurricane, dam'd by an earthquake, half-brother to the cholera, nearly related to the small-pox on the mother's side! Look at me!"[10] Uncle Sam also quotes the opening and closing formula from the boast of Bob's opponent in these words: "Whoo-*oop!* . . . bow yore necks and spread, . . . the kingdom of sorrow's a-comin' and the Child of Calamity with her" (7). The allusions to "Frescoes" contribute to the novel's sense of continuity with the history of American folk humor and literature. The particular connections they make between Uncle Sam and his literary ancestors are disturbing ones, however, because Twain's boasting keelboatmen are degenerates, able to mimic the speech of heroic figures like Wildfire, Fink, and Crockett but powerless to act out such fantasies.

By using the conventions of frontier humor to characterize Uncle Sam, Coover is able to suggest the source of his pugnacious spirit. Although in the twentieth century golf has become his game, "before that, he'd pretty much limited himself to hunting and fishing, riding, swimming, war, billiards, and the odd cockfight" (89). On the frontier almost every activity could become the proving grounds for manliness, and Uncle Sam's boasts show that the spirit of competition is integral to life: "let us . . . show the whole world that a Freeman, contendin' for Liberty on his own ground, can out-run, out-dance, out-jump, chaw more tobacky and spit less, out-drink, out-holler, out-finagle and out-lick any yaller, brown, red, black, or white thing in the shape of human" (8). His own interpretation of all this activity is that "'bodies in motion just don't age as fast, that's what it boils down to. America, by stayin' off its ass, was stayin' young!'" (205).

Coover indicates that such activity easily becomes malevolent, however. In the prologue, which recounts the groundhog hunt, Uncle Sam issues a general challenge for a backwoods, no-holds-barred fight of the sort conventional in antebellum humor: "'Who—Whoo—*Whoop!* Who'll come gouge with me? Who'll come bite with me? Rowff—Yough—Snort—*YAHOO!*'"(6). He claims, "'a fight I must have, or else I'll have to be salted down to save me from spilin'!'" (7). This sentence is reminiscent of Mike Fink's lament about the dwindling opportunities for fighting as the frontier becomes civilized, which the Louisiana humorist Thomas Bangs Thorpe recorded in "The Disgraced Scalplock." According to Uncle Sam, such fighting is the necessary basis of American freedom: "'Oh, we must fight! . . . those who expects to reap the blessings of freedom must, like men, undergo the fatigue of twistin' noses and scrougin' eyeballs and rib-brakin' and massacreein'!'" (7). The manliness of which Uncle Sam boasts asserts itself through never-ending physical conflict and domination which prohibit sympathy for the plight of common humanity. In this comic boast in the form of a folk verse, he threatens even defenseless women and

children who might come in his way: "'Yippee! I'm wild and woolly and fulla fleas, ain't never been curried below the knees, so if you wish to avoid foreign collision you had better abandon the ocean, women and children first!'" (7). Although Uncle Sam might at times resemble Superman in his concern to punish criminals, he is fundamentally a representation of frontier lawlessness. The Old West, in his words, "'was all about . . . tumult and butchery and wild unsartinty,'" a belief he illustrates by pointing to "'two pollrumptious screamers shootin' it out on a dusty Main Street over a saddlepack fulla gold: now them two fellers is about as alive as anybody's ever *gonna* be!'" (205). The events of the Rosenberg case, in Coover's view, indicate that the spirit of the Old West continues to be played out on new stages even though it does not lead to life as Uncle Sam preaches.

In the sections of the novel devoted to Richard Nixon, Coover deflates the false gentility of the Vice President by relying on the technique of folk humor that Mikhail Bakhtin has labelled "the material bodily principle" because of its reliance predominantly on "images of the human body with its food, drink, defecation, and sexual life."[11] An important example of this emphasis is Nixon's characterization as a modern Ugly Man, a folk stereotype that provoked antebellum laughter in stories about such figures as Davy Crockett and Abraham Lincoln and that even won votes for Presidential candidates who looked the part.[12] The Alabama humorist Johnson Jones Hooper wrote "A Night at the Ugly Man's" in which the person with this distinction is awarded a prize, a common motif in the tradition. And at the time of Lincoln's first inauguration, George Washington Harris of Tennessee made the new President's physical appearance the chief device in his virulent political satire. Coover is able to place Nixon's ugliness into the fiction effectively, as Harris did Lincoln's, because it is an unquestioned part of his folk image in contemporary lore. In the novel, *Time Magazine* verifies the image by commenting on his "'fat cheeks'" and "'duck-bill nose'" (186). Unlike politicians in the last century who used their ugliness to gain the voters' admiration, Nixon is ashamed of his face and hopes that someday when he becomes President he can cover it with a beard as did Lincoln (174). While shaving, he recalls that "people have often registered an odd kind of surprise on first meeting me face-to-face. They tend to stare at my nose as though measuring its breadth, lost there and unable to find my eyes again." Political cartoonists have fun with his face, and "Herblock always showed me as a jowly, wavy-haired, narrow-eyed tough, . . . with suggestions of some bad odor about me, like a little boy who'd just filled his pants or something" (186).

As the reference to his foul smell indicates, Coover uses the techniques of folk humor to push Nixon's characterization beyond the stereotype of the Ugly Man whose appearance can at times arouse positive emotions. The Vice President is particularly susceptible to such humorous attacks because he prides himself on an excessively prudish modesty: "When I have sex I like to do it between the sheets in a dark room. When I take a shit I lock the door. My chest is hairy but I don't show it off. I don't even like to *eat* in public and just *talking* about one's personal life embarrasses me" (526). Refusing to eat where others can watch him, he often suffers from hunger. One day after working very late, he returns home so ravenous that he gorges himself from the refrigerator with a lack of discrimination that belies his image of self-restraint:

> I'd found a rib bone in the refrigerator for Checkers, a bowl of vanilla pudding, three overripe slices of tomato, a french-fried chicken back, a partial tin of Spam, a plate of soft fudge, cole slaw, a Dr. Pepper, some sour gherkins, a peach half in syrup, and a cold hamburger for myself—more or less in that order and eaten as discovered. . . . I'd also cleaned up what was left of a jar of apple sauce, bottle of skimmed milk, bowl of tapioca, and tin can of cold baked beans, followed by caviar and strawberry ice cream, lit up a ceremonial pipeful of Rum and Maple, and sat down in an armchair to digest. (177-78)

The incongruity of the items on this menu and the unconventional order in which they are speedily consumed mark the man as a gross sensualist finally unable to control his body's urges. Lacking any refinement in taste, he flatly declares that "it all tasted good," but indigestion rewards his gluttony with nightmares. References to body odor that mock Nixon's gentility also derive from the techniques of folk humor. He is frequently embarrassed since he sweats "like a stoat" (209) and refuses to shower in public places such as the golf course clubhouse after a game. Setting off for the last-minute interview with Ethel Rosenberg that he hopes will enhance his prestige, he feels "sticky and ugly with sweat," needs a shave, and desperately wants to urinate. Yet he refuses to do so in a public toilet, thereby making readers even more aware of his bodily functions as his discomfort grows (365, 375).

Coover's satire does not omit Nixon's sexual practices. Despite the politically acceptable glamorlessness of his relationship with Pat, his masturbation contradicts the image of middle-class respectability he wishes to project to voters. The morning of the execution, when he is in his office supposedly working on a speech for the festivities, he is instead daydreaming that he is Clark Gable having intercourse with Ethel. Just at that time Uncle Sam enters suddenly through the open window. "'Well, I see that the old flagpole still stands. . . . You know, son, you'll go blind playing with yourself like that,'" Uncle Sam admonishes him with folk superstitions. "'It can make your hair fall out and your brain rot, too!'" (318). Nixon's mortification increases when he tries to yank shut his fly and traps his shirttail deep in the zipper. For the rest of the momentous day it remains open.

Ironically, Nixon is unable to keep the public from sensing that his gentility is only pretense. For example, when he played Aeneas in a high school production, he was nicknamed "Anus" (50). His fellow law students rewarded him for scholarly diligence by calling him "Iron Butt" (117). And after *Time* dubbed him "The Fighting Quaker," he received an anonymous parody titled "The Farting Quacker" poking fun at his flatulence, a subject to which Coover often refers (50). Even the masturbation that Nixon believes he is concealing behind his closed office door, people have already mocked in anonymous caricatures. The Washington cabbie gleefully tells him about these drawings which he has seen on pamphlets at a pro-Rosenberg rally:

> "You shoulda seen the ones they was handin' out last night! Haw! There was some cute ones of you, Nick! You'd be prouda the dong they hung on ya! . . . Of course, I can't say it was gettin' put to the best *use!* . . .
>
> "Easy, Nick, haw, haw, don't let it go to your head! I mean, there was a lot of 'em showin' you with your face smeared with shit, too. Or eatin' it—I gotta admit the shit looked good there, Nick, you'd make a terrific President!" (270)

In the tradition of restroom graffiti, these drawings have been moved from the public toilet into full public view where, like other forms of folklore, they powerfully shape opinion, judging from the cab driver's reaction.

Nixon's final unmasking occurs in the events at Times Square following his attempted rape of Ethel. In the epilogue Uncle Sam, in turn, reveals his true self, but this is a private unmasking to Nixon alone. Coover has modelled these scenes from the range of structural possibilities inherent within the "caught with one's pants down" motif prevalent in sexual folk humor. Narratives employing this motif derive their comic energy from a double reversal: the shift from the private to the public world is accompanied by a movement from a position of relative power and assurance to one of weakness and humiliation. Coover, however, breaks the structural pattern followed by folk narratives in which the opposites in these two categories—world and position of strength—are always linked so that public exposure produces humiliation. Using various situations in which one's pants are taken off, he develops scenarios based on several possible pairings of these binary opposites. The resulting nontraditional unfoldings of the motif's narrative potential provide Coover a structure highly appropriate for attacking both the values implicit in America's folk humor and the larger social consequences to which they lead.

During the private interview at Sing Sing, Nixon foregoes his plan to make Ethel confess and, instead, bumbles through an unsuccessful attempt at raping her. While he is preoccupied with his pants, which are tangled around his ankles, she writes in lipstick across his bare ass: "I am a scamp." Hearing the prison guards approaching the room, Ethel pushes Nixon out a door that surrealistically opens onto the Times Square stage with its working replica of the electrocution chamber.

There he stands before the whole nation with his pants down and the truth about his motivations written for all to read.

While this situation fits into a long tradition of folk and literary sexual humor about surprised lovers, in other ways it recalls the climax of the most popular antebellum humorous sketch—Thomas Bangs Thorpe's "The Big Bear of Arkansas." In it Jim Doggett, the most renowned hunter in the region, devotes himself without success to tracking a bear of mythical proportions, instinct, and endurance. Then one morning when Doggett is, according to his custom, defecating by squatting in the woods with his pants around his ankles, the bear suddenly appears, ready to give himself up. Frantically trying to get off a shot, Doggett is tripped up by his pants in a scene that demonstrates Thorpe's reliance on the spirit of folk humor to undercut human pretensions. That defecation may follow when pants are dropped and, moreover, that one's private business may become public are as important in Coover's novel as in "The Big Bear." Even though there is no longer a taboo against introducing such a subject into literature for the general public, it remains an effective tool for the satirist. Shortly before Nixon's arrival, the Republican elephant standing at the side of the stage decides "to unloose its considerable bowels" (457). Smelling the pile through which the VIPS have already slipped and slid on the way to their seats in the viewing stand, he imagines that he has fouled himself out of fright and desperately tries to direct attention away from himself by beginning his oration with a prayer (470). Like Doggett, Nixon is unprepared when his moment of testing arrives. The pre-execution speech, which he has long been planning in order to enhance his national reputation, must now be delivered extempore under what seem impossible conditions for winning respect, since he is the laughingstock of the drunken, unruly crowd.

Unable to pull up his trousers, he withstands the public humiliation and keeps talking until he hits upon the idea of calling on everyone to "'drop his pants for America!'" (482). By means of a highly aggressive oratorical style, he is able to gain control of the crowd, reversing his situation so that he assumes a position of strength within the public world. Persuaded to participate in and ultimately to approve of his predicament, everyone except Uncle Sam soon is bare-bottomed. When Nixon and the crowd shout together for him to join them, he complains, "'What mad project of national sooeycide *is* this?'" As he pushes down his pantaloons for the crowd, "There was a blinding flash of light, a simultaneous crack of ear-splitting thunder, and then—BLACKOUT!!" (485). Before he can restore the power, the people's sexual desires overwhelm both their patriotism and their fear of the dark. Times Square becomes a chaotic orgy.

Even though Uncle Sam ends the confusion in order to complete the executions, Coover is not finished with his variations on the theme of what can happen when pants are removed. The last possibility is reserved for the epilogue called "Beauty and the Beast." Before the Nixons were married, they used the title of this fairy tale as the name for their innocent lovemaking game in which he made her laugh by pretending to be a frightening beast (173). But there is to be no such playfulness between them at home after the execution. The long-suffering Pat at last angrily tells her husband to "grow up" and slams the bedroom door in his face, forcing him to sleep in the spare room. Alone, he broods over his misfortunes until Uncle Sam, looking "suddenly old and ugly," enters through the window, intent on enjoying what he calls "'onmittygated cornholin' whoopee!'" (530). The situation for this final scenario is homosexual intercourse, or, more precisely stated, a homosexual rape that readers are to find shocking and brutal. Nixon has endured public humiliation and enjoyed public control, but now in private his role has been reversed from aggressor to victim. He is vulnerable and powerless to change his painful situation. Ironically, this is the moment of his eagerly sought annunciation, the proof that he has been selected to incarnate Uncle Sam to the nation as President. Yet he discovers too late that Uncle Sam is wicked, no better than his foe the Phantom. In their brutal foreplay, Uncle Sam pants a final comic boast to his unwilling lover:

> "You wanta make it with me, . . . you gotta love me like I really am: Sam Slick the Yankee Peddler, gun-totin' hustler and tooth-'n'-claw tamer of the heathen wilderness, lusty and in everything a screamin' meddler, novus ball-bustin' ordo seclorum, that's me, boy—and goodnight Mrs. Calabash to any damfool what gets in my way!" (531-32)

Leaving his partner sick and in pain, Uncle Sam "seemed radiant, aglow, almost as though lit from within. His smile was gentle now, and there was a merry twinkle in his blue eyes." He is fully rejuvenated, and Nixon confesses complete acceptance of both him and, through a double entendre, the symbol of his power: "Whatever else he was, he was beautiful (how had I ever thought him ugly?), the most beautiful thing in all the world" (534).

Thus Coover exposes the American spirit that overlooks no opportunity to dominate, dehumanize, and humiliate the vulnerable. These characteristics of unrestrained competition associated with the national frontier experience continue to be reinforced by the folk humor that evokes admiring laughter. The world of *The Public Burning* is particularly horrifying because it contains no hope for reform or renewal. This is not to say that Coover's vision lacks a moral center. It exists in the devotion of the women characters to the ideal of human decency and maternal love, but they are unable to resist domination by the men who are dedicated to competition and displays of power. For example, Nixon knows he is not living the kind of life that his Quaker mother would condone, but occasional thoughts of her disapproval create only sentimental regret, not true repentance. He realizes that he has taken after his father—"a very competitive man, cantankerous even and aggressive"—rather than his mother, who was a peacemaker and taught him "charity and tolerance" (49). Likewise, Pat's will is unable to restrain her husband's. When he ran for Vice President over her objections, she "became thin and haggard" (308). According to him, "she always looked pooped, it was her way of advertising to the world what a joy it was to be married to me" (522). Thus passivity and defeat characterize her. Despite an earlier ability to humiliate Nixon when they were dating and even to laugh at him when he proposed, she has acquiesced to her public function of remaining silent and looking good in pictures as dictated by her husband's position (54-55). Rather than protest, she chooses simply to ignore events. So on the Times Square stage when Nixon finally sits down beside her to watch the burnings, "she'd patted my hand absently and, staring blankly up at the electric chair, had said: 'That was a nice speech, dear'" (522). Pat's decision to act—to close the bedroom door—is a private statement of personal feelings which cannot influence the public consequences of activities she opposes. Ironically, by sending her husband to the spare room for the night as punishment, she allows Uncle Sam to woo and reward him.

Ethel Rosenberg is a sharp contrast to the women in Nixon's family. Upon first seeing her at their interview, he senses that she is "a strong woman, and brave, but there was a hardness as well, a kind of cunning: she struck me as something of an operator" (429). In a scene that is Coover's variation of "the trickster tricked" type of folk tale, she is able to seduce him while he thinks that he is seducing her. Unfortunately, in the broader perspective he is the wrong target to dupe and suffers only momentary embarrassment at her hands. Despite her cunning, Ethel is no less a maternal figure in the novel. Her love for Julius and their two sons expressed in letters from prison is an affirmation of life despite the imminence of her destruction. Able to make her defiance public unlike Pat Nixon, she "walk[s] buoyantly" across the stage with head held high "directly to the electric chair and plumps herself down in it with all the familiarity of a daily commuter taking her seat in the subway" (512-13). While her final strength of will is courageous and even frightening, it cannot save her. Whereas Julius dies meekly, his wife withstands the prescribed dosage of electric current, and after she has been partially unstrapped, the doctors discover that her heart is still beating. In the ensuing confusion Nixon, John F. Kennedy, and all the VIPS rush to pull the switch, sending the current that whips her unbelted limbs "like a sail in a high wind, flapping out at the people . . . , making them scream and duck and pray for deliverance." Her body appears to be "held aloft by her own incandescent will and haloed about by all the gleaming great of the nation" (517) in ineffectual protest against all that has occurred.

Coover does not suggest, as do some theorists, that folk humor serves as a psychological safety valve, releasing potentially harmful tendencies before they can lead to action. In *The Public Burning* the line between humorous fantasies and horrifying realities vanishes. There is no way to stop the dehumanizing aggressiveness American folk humor worships; each conquest refreshes Uncle Sam, readying him to overcome the next unwitting victim.

NOTES

[1] Cristina Bacchilega, "Folktales, Fictions and Meta-Fictions: Their Interaction in Robert Coover's *Pricksongs & Descants,*" *New York Folklore* 6 (1980): 176-77.

[2] Frank Gado, *First Person: Conversations on Writers & Writing* (Schenectady, NY: Union College Press, 1973) 155.

[3] Gado 155.

[4] *The Public Burning* (New York: Viking, 1977) 15-26. Copyright © Robert Coover 1976, 1977. The ballad is reprinted by permission of Georges Borchardt, Inc., agents. All further references to this book are noted parenthetically in the text.

[5] Gershon Legman, *Rationale of the Dirty Joke: An Analysis of Sexual Humor* 1st Ser. (New York: Grove, 1968) 292-302.

[6] Legman 256-318.

[7] See Blair's anthology *Native American Humor* (1937; rpt. San Francisco: Chandler, 1960).

[8] *America's Humor: From Poor Richard to Doonesbury* (New York: Oxford UP, 1978) 184.

[9] *Native American Humor* 30.

[10] *Life on the Mississippi* (Boston: Osgood, 1883) 45.

[11] *Rabelais and His World,* trans. Helene Iswolsky (Cambridge, MA: MIT P, 1968) 18.

[12] Bernard DeVoto, *Mark Twain's America* (New York: Houghton, 1932) 93-94.

FURTHER READING

Secondary Sources

Abrahams, Roger D. "Folklore and Literature as Performance." *Journal of the Folklore Institute* IX, No. 1 (1972): 75-94.

> Argues for a "performance-centered approach to the study of both folklore and literature, through descriptive analysis of performance features and by a consideration of the excesses fostered by the item-centered approach."

Alexander, Alex E. "Stephen King's *Carrie*—A Universal Fairytale." *Journal of Popular Culture* XIII, No. 2 (Fall 1979): 282-88.
> Presents King's horror novel as "a special kind of fairy tale" replete with "*rites de passage,* supernatural powers, magic and rites of sacrifice."

Aubert, Alvin. "Black American Poetry, Its Language, and the Folk Tradition." *Black Academy Review* 2, Nos. 1 and 2 (Spring-Summer 1971): 71-80.
> An examination of African-American poetry in light of both black culture's suppression under slavery and segregation, and of that culture's accelerated evolution beginning in the mid-twentieth century.

Blake, Susan L. "Old John in Harlem: The Urban Folktales of Langston Hughes." *Black American Literature Forum* 14, No. 3 (Fall 1980): 100-104.
> Presents, with a number of examples, the "direct and dynamic" relationship of Hughes's character Simple to the African-American folk tradition.

Brown, Carolyn S. "Bibliography." In *The Tall Tale in American Folklore and Literature,* pp. 153-63. Knoxville: University of Tennessee Press, 1987.
> Combines primary and secondary sources, the latter including writings on folklore, biography, criticism, and the psychology of humor.

Bruce, Dickson D., Jr. "On Dunbar's 'Jingles in a Broken Tongue': Dunbar's Dialect Poetry and the Afro-American Folk Tradition." In *A Singer in the Dawn: Reinterpretations of Paul Laurence Dunbar,* edited by Jay Martin, pp. 94-113. New York: Dodd, Mead, 1975.
> Approaches the often ambiguous attitudes of critics, and of Dunbar himself, toward his use of dialect.

Brunvand, Jan Harold. "Sailors' and Cowboys' Folklore in Two Popular Classics." *Southern Folklore Quarterly* XXIX, No. 4 (December 1965): 266-83.
> Chronicles the use of seafaring imagery in narratives of the Great Plains, and compares Richard Henry Dana's *Two Years Before the Mast* with *The Log of a Cowboy* by Andy Adams.

Buckner, B. Dilla. "Folkloric Elements in Margaret Walker's Poetry." *College Language Association Journal* XXXIII, No. 4 (June 1990): 367-77.
> Presents Walker's *How I Wrote Jubilee* and other works as exemplifying universal, rather than only African American, folklore elements.

Clipper, Lawrence J. "Folkloric and Mythic Elements in *Invisible Man.*" *College Language Association Journal* XIII, No. 3 (March 1970): 229-41.
> Approaches folkloric elements in Ellison's novel not from the quantitative standpoint of a catalogue, but in view of parallels between the plot and motifs typical to folktales.

Davidson, Levette J. "Folk Elements in Midwestern Literature." *The Western Humanities Review* III, No. 3 (July 1949): 187-95.
> Emphasizes the democratic quality of Midwestern literature, from its origins in the 1830s through the work of Carl Sandburg and others.

De Caro, Francis A. "Proverbs and Originality in Modern Short Fiction." *Western Folklore* XXXVII, No. 1 (January 1978): 30-38.
> Makes the case that modern writers, given the stress on originality in the literary mainstream, are largely prevented from employing traditional sayings in their work.

De Weever, Jacqueline. "Toni Morrison's Use of Fairy Tale, Folk Tale and Myth in *The Song of Solomon.*" *Southern Folklore Quarterly* 44 (1980): 131-44.
> Provides an overview of the disparate folk and myth sources employed by Morrison in her novel.

Hendricks, William O. "Folklore and the Structural Analysis of Literary Texts." *Language and Style* III, No. 2 (Spring 1970): 83-121.
> Provides an overview of the structural analysis employed in folklore studies, and recommends the use of similar approaches in literary criticism at large.

Kent, George E. "Ralph Ellison and Afro-American Folk and Cultural Tradition." In *Blackness and the Advent of Western Culture,* pp. 152-63. Chicago: Third World Press, 1972.
> Assesses Ellison's use of folk motifs in *Invisible Man.*

Leach, Macedward. "Folklore in American Regional Literature." *Journal of the Folklore Institute* III, No. 3 (1966): 376-97.
> Chronicles the development of a regional sensibility in American folklore, and the influence of the regions on centers of folk culture including Boston, New Orleans, and other cities.

Lewis, Mary Ellen B. "Why Study Folklore and Literature?" *Folklore Forum* 11, No. 1 (1979): 163-75.
> Makes a case, using a variety of reasons, for the parallel study of oral tradition and written narrative.

Mootry, Maria K. "'Chocolate Mabbie' and 'Pearl May Lee': Gwendolyn Brooks and the Ballad Tradition." *College Language Association Journal* XXX, No. 3 (March 1987): 278-93.
> Identifies the ballad as a recurring motif in Brooks's poetry, and distinguishes her use of it from that of earlier writers.

Smith, Gary. "The Literary Ballads of Sterling A. Brown." *College Language Association Journal* XXXII, No. 4 (June 1989): 393-409.
> Reasserts the image of Brown as a poet, and not only as an anthologist who "restor[ed] and recreat[ed] . . . black American literature."

Stahl, Sandra K. D. "Style in Oral and Written Narrative." *Southern Folklore Quarterly* 43 (1979): 39-62.

Identifies seven pairs of stylistic features common to oral and written narratives, and explores the means by which writers create the "illusion" of speech in the printed word.

Uba, George. "Only a Man: The Folkloric Subtext of Richard Wright's 'Down by the Riverside'." *Essays in Literature* XVII, No. 2 (Fall 1990): 261-69.

Critiques previous attempts to dismiss as unrealistic Wright's short story from *Uncle Tom's Children,* and asserts that other critics have failed to understand the author's purpose in employing plot elements that allegedly strain credulity.

Vitiello, Justin. "Sicilian Folk Narrative versus Sicilian-American Literature: Mangione's '*Mount Allegro*'." *MELUS* 18, No. 2 (Summer 1993): 61-75.

A close reading of Jerry Mangione's *Mount Allegro* in light of Vitiello's own research in Sicily, and of interpretive ideas developed by Wole Soyinka.

Sports and Literature

INTRODUCTION

The representation of sports in literature reflects the changing values and concerns of society and underscores the cultural importance of sports in America. In the early twentieth century, American sporting culture featured predominantly British games—like cricket and hunting—but over time, these games were modified and transformed into sports such as baseball, football, and basketball. Perceived by writers, commentators, and fans alike as a democratic endeavor, these sports were considered a microcosm of American society, where talent and hard work could result in success regardless of social or economic status. For disparate ethnicities and social classes, games such as baseball accelerated the process of assimilation as shared bonds and a sense of community connected many fans of the sport. Regarded as a unique institution representing order and stability amidst the heterogeneity of American life, baseball also came to be viewed as a way in which individuals could learn to function within the larger group according to its established rules, rituals, etiquette, and concept of fair play. Writers utilized the metaphorical significance and mythical qualities of the game and created stories that incorporate recognizable heroes in familiar situations in order to impose stylistic and thematic continuity in their work; for example, Bernard Malamud's *The Natural* exploits Arthurian myth and the events of Philip Roth's *The Great American Novel* parallel the exodus of Jews from Egypt.

As the twentieth century progressed, modernization, urbanization, and worldwide conflict resulted in changing cultural values and as a consequence, society sought a new mythology to fit contemporary times. Reflecting this evolution, the prevalence of baseball literature diminished as commentators and fans realized the game was less of an athletic competition than a business rife with corruption and greed. With the growing popularity of other sports, the football novel in the late 1960s and early 1970s provided new prototypes and myths and as a result, became a significant subgenre of sports literature. More cynical and unsentimental, the sports novels and stories of this time, such as Jim Bouton's *Ball Four* and Dan Jenkins's *Semi-Tough*, explore the confused and disjointed nature of contemporary existence and often stretch the boundaries of social and moral perspectives on sports literature. In the past few decades, there has been an attempt by writers to create an alternative to male-dominated literature focusing on baseball and football. One recent trend is the emergence of a female sports literature that incorporates themes of co-operation and self-discovery.

REPRESENTATIVE WORKS*

Roger Angell
Five Seasons (essays) 1978
Late Innings (essays) 1982

Tony Ardizzone
Heart of the Order, 1986

Jim Bouton
Ball Four (journal) 1970

Gary Cartwright
The Hundred-Yard War, 1968

Pat Conroy
The Lords of Discipline, 1980

Robert Coover
The Universal Baseball Association, J. Henry Waugh, Prop., 1968
Whatever Happened to Gloomy Gus of the Chicago Bears?, 1987

Harry Crews
The Knockout Artist, 1988

Frank Deford
Cut 'n' Run, 1973
Everybody's All-American, 1981

Don Delillo
End Zone, 1972
Underworld, 1997

Frederick Exley
A Fan's Notes (fictional memoir) 1968

Richard Ford
The Sportswriter, 1986

Leonard Gardner
Fat City, 1969

Peter Gent
North Dallas Forty, 1973
Texas Celebrity Turkey Trot, 1978
The Franchise, 1983
North Dallas after 40, 1989

Eric Rolfe Greenberg
The Celebrant, 1983

Pete Hamill
Flesh & Blood, 1977

Mark Harris
The Southpaw, 1953
Bang the Drum Slowly, 1956

Ernest Hemingway
Old Man and the Sea, 1952

John Hough
The Conduct of the Game, 1986

Dan Jenkins
Semi-Tough, 1972
Life Its Ownself, 1984

Owen Johnson
Stover at Yale, 1911

W. P. Kinsella
Shoeless Joe, 1982
The Thrill of the Grass (short stories) 1984
The Iowa Baseball Confederacy, 1986

John Knowles
A Separate Peace, 1966

Ring Lardner
You Know Me Al (short stories) 1960

Jenifer Levin
Water Dancer, 1982

Norman MacLean
A River Runs through It and Other Stories (short stories) 1976

Bernard Malamud
The Natural, 1952

Thomas McGuane
The Sporting Club, 1968
Ninety-Two in the Shade, 1973

Joyce Carol Oates
You Must Remember This, 1987

David Ritz
The Man Who Brought the Dodgers Back to Brooklyn, 1981

Philip Roth
Goodbye, Columbus (novella) 1959
The Great American Novel, 1973

Lawrence Shainberg
One on One, 1970

Alan Sillitoe
The Loneliness of the Long-Distance Runner (short story) 1959

Harry Stein
Hoopla, 1983

Tom Stoppard
Every Good Boy Deserves Favor and Professional Foul: Two Plays (dramas) 1978

David Storey
The Changing Room (drama) 1972
This Sporting Life, 1975

James Whitehead
Joiner, 1971

Herbert Wilner
Dovisch in the Wilderness and Other Stories (short stories) 1968
The Quarterback Speaks to His God, 1987

*All works are novels unless otherwise noted.

OVERVIEWS

James Barbour and William C. Dowling

SOURCE: "The Death of the Game in Contemporary Literature," in *The Midwest Quarterly,* Vol. XXVII, No. 3, Spring, 1986, pp. 341-60.

[*In the following essay, Barbour and Dowling survey the evolution of baseball from game to business in contemporary baseball literature.*]

For reasons that were apparent almost immediately, Jim Bouton's *Ball Four,* an account of his fortunes in the major and minor leagues during the 1969 baseball season, exploded the conventions of the genre in which it was written. For American sports autobiography, always before serving primarily a juvenile audience, had known nothing like this irreverent behind-the-scenes view of major league baseball as players actually experience it in the locker room and on the road. Though Bouton's revelations concerning sex and drugs in the big leagues seem mild enough now in comparison with what one reads daily in the sports pages, they were enough at the time to draw down on him the wrath of the baseball establishment (the controversy created by the book is chronicled in Bouton's sequel *I'm Glad You Didn't Take It Personally*). Before the stir had died down, *Ball Four* had inspired a new breed of sports autobiography and played a significant role in focusing attention on the cultural importance of sports in America.

On one level, the controversy surrounding *Ball Four* when it first appeared must be viewed as a cultural episode, one having more to do with the institutional conservatism of baseball as with any revelations contained in the book. On another level, however, there were specifically literary reasons for its emergence as a *succès de scandale,* the most important doubtless being that Bouton as narrator of *Ball Four* appears as a *naif,* a figure whose literary lineage traces back to Dante in *The Divine Comedy* and Chaucer in *The Canterbury Tales* and whose representatives in American literature include such naive narrators as Huckleberry Finn and Holden Caulfield. Should *Ball Four* survive as a classic of sports literature, as we suspect it will, it will be not least because of the curious limitation of social and moral perspective that enables Bouton to reveal a new truth about the game while simultaneously revealing a truth about himself of which he is totally unaware. Yet any purely literary analysis of *Ball Four* seems to us incomplete unless it then permits some deeper understanding of the way in which such a work comes to occupy a charged space within its cultural field.

For one reads *Ball Four* today, of course, against a background of growing crisis. Since the publication of Bouton's book, sports in American life have become the focus of a steadily increasing cultural anxiety, most often expressed as a lament over the commercialization of the game; "the age of contemporary organization," as Michael Novak puts it, "casts a special pall. The money comes legally enough. But there is too much of it. It drowns the sensibility. It makes the spirit wither. It suffocates the life of sport" (304). This is the context in which we wish to argue, one, that *Ball Four* represents the literary monument to a moment of drastic change in baseball as an American cultural institution, and, two, that commercialization has only incidentally to do with that change. It is doubtless true that baseball will remain as a phenomenon of American life: it will continue, that is, to have players, owners, spectators, clubs rules, and the like. Yet it is equally true, we think, that at a certain moment in the late twentieth century baseball ceased to be a game in another, deeper sense, and that *Ball Four* unwittingly marks the moment of its demise.

In *Late Innings,* Roger Angell's recent collection of his *New Yorker* baseball pieces, there is a meditative interlude that occurs during the summer of 1981, the year of the baseball players' strike. In the empty days of midsummer and the silence of a nation of deserted ballparks, Angell comes to understand what the game has meant to him. With the onset of the strike, it is as if some mighty and slow-moving river had suddenly dried up: "Baseball flows past us all through the summer—it is one of the reasons that summer exists—and . . . the long, unhurrying swirl and down-flowing have their own purpose and direction, that the river is headed, in its own sweet time, toward a downsummer broadening and debouchment and to its end in the estuary of October" (382).

The vision of baseball as a mighty stream flowing through an eternal American summer is typical of what might be called the idyllic strain in Angell's baseball writings, which celebrate the game as a separate pastoral world existing magically apart from the anxieties and frustrations of ordinary life, as a suspension of historical reality and the resumption of another, more innocent reality within the confines of the ballpark and the season, and, finally, as the shared cultural memory of an entire society. Angell's earlier books, *The Summer Game* and *Five Seasons,* embody that idyllic vision in its purest form; what is striking about this moment in *Late Innings* is that it occurs in a context of loss, when baseball viewed in that magical light has temporarily gone out of existence.

A condition of possibility for this idyllic strain in Angell's writings about baseball was isolated over forty years ago in Johan Huizinga's *Homo Ludens,* a work that remains a classic in the philosophy of culture, the argument of which has scarcely been superseded in more recent analyses of what Huizinga called (in the subtitle of his book) "the play-element in culture." Huizinga's great achievement in *Homo Ludens* was to demonstrate that the notion of play or game lies at the very heart of most social and cultural institutions; his analysis begins in the observation that play is formally circumscribed, the game representing a temporary world or alternative reality: "Play is distinct from 'ordinary' life both as to locality and duration. . . . It is 'played out' within certain limits of time and place. It contains its own course and meaning" (9). The game, to summarize Huizinga's main points, is set apart in time—

> Play begins, and then at a certain moment it is 'over.' It plays itself to an end. While it is in progress all is movement, change, alternation, succession, association, separation. . . . Once played, it endures as a new-found creation of the mind, a treasure to be retained by the memory. It is transmitted, it becomes tradition. (9-10)

—and in space:

> More striking even than the limitations as to time is the limitation as to space. All play moves and has its being within a playground marked off beforehand either materially or ideally, deliberately or as a matter of course. . . . The arena, the card-table, the magic circle, the temple, the stage, the screen, the tennis court, the court of justice, etc., are all in form and function playgrounds, i.e., forbidden spots, isolated, hedged round, hallowed, within which special rules obtain. All are temporary worlds within the ordinary world, dedicated to the performance of an act apart. (10)

All this is made possible, in turn, by the purely formal concept of play as activity carried out within a set of constitutive rules: "All play has rules. They determine what 'holds' in the temporary world circumscribed by play. The rules of a game are absolutely binding and allow no doubt. . . . Indeed, as soon as the rules are transgressed the whole play-world collapses" (11).

The game thus summons into existence a temporary world or alternative reality which, in turn, creates within and beyond itself an alternative community: "A play-community generally tends to become permanent even after the game is over. Of course, not every game of marbles or every bridge-party leads to the founding of a club. But the feeling of being 'apart together' in an exceptional situation, of sharing something important, of mutually withdrawing from the rest of the world and rejecting the usual norms, retains its magic beyond the duration of the individual game" (12). In Angell's writings this community expands to include spectators belonging to the company of what he sometimes calls true fans, and is then joined by players as they retire and so to speak become, through memory, the spectators of their own past deeds. The ultimate community in Angell is the community of observers and rememberers.

Insofar as this notion of an extended community coming into existence through and around the game derives from an idea of the spectator as a vicarious participant, the same general claim might be made about the cultural significance of games in any culture. The reason that baseball in America constitutes a unique cultural institution, then, is that it was able to provide a separate sphere of reality within which a complex and heterogeneous nation could discover order and stability and unity, thus making the game a sort of metaphor for order and stability amidst the ethnic, racial, religious, and regional heterogeneity of American life. This is just the aspect of baseball that was so clairvoyantly glimpsed by Virginia Woolf, for instance, in her essay on American fiction in *The Moment and Other Essays.* Woolf had been pondering, bemusedly, the curious fact that this American fiction seems condemned to constantly measuring its distance from England; then she turned with a kind of wonder to Ring Lardner's baseball novel, *You Know Me, Al,* realizing that here she had come upon an America sublimely indifferent to Europe and its stultifying cultural heritage:

> We gaze into the depths of a society which goes its ways intent on its own concerns. There, perhaps, is one of the elements of Mr. Lardner's success. He is not merely himself intent on his own game, but his characters are equally intent on theirs. It is no coincidence that the best of Mr. Lardner's stories are about games, for one may guess that Mr. Lardner's interest in games has solved one of the most difficult problems of the American writer; it has given him a clue, a centre, a meeting place for the divers activities of people whom a vast continent isolates, whom no tradition controls.

More recently Gunther Barth has argued persuasively that baseball was a major element in the complicated, unsteady process through which America absorbed the immigrant masses of Europe and blended them into a new society perceiving itself as distinctively American, that in the crowded, jostling cities in which the immigrants arrived, the ballpark and the ballgame represented not only a unifying experience in which all were free to participate vicariously, but the spectacle of the game itself, in which success is possible only through the strict observance of a set of rules to which every player must consent, constituted a kind of moral metaphor the lesson of which was learned and applied by successive waves of newcomers to America. Whatever the ultimate merits of such an argument, it is at least grounded in the truth that baseball came to be a major American cultural institution precisely because it constitutes a game in Huizinga's sense, a temporary world standing as an island in the complex, often violent historical flow of American life where spectators could discover unanimity in their shared participation in a distinctively American game. Baseball as reported and meditated upon by Angell, or by Roger Kahn in *The Boys of Summer,* is not the game actually played upon the field but the game as cultural institution.

In this sense Angell's writings are less about baseball than about the community that comes into existence through and around the temporary world of baseball, and that by implication expands to become America itself in relation to its national pastime. It is a celebration of this same idea of community that we come upon, for example, in such occasional pieces as "Hub Fans Bid Kid Adieu," John Updike's moving account of Ted Williams's last game at Fenway Park, and perhaps its most memorable expression in Angell occurs in what is surely his most memorable piece of baseball writing, "Agincourt and After," an account of the 1975 World Series between Cincinnati and Boston. The occasion is Carlton Fisk's twelfth-inning home run in the sixth game of the Series:

> I suddenly remembered all my old absent and distant Sox-afflicted friends (and all the other Red Sox fans, all over New England), and I thought of them—in Brookline, Mass., and Brookline, Maine; in Beverly Farms and Mashpee and Presque Isle and North Conway and Damariscotta; in Pomfret, Connecticut and Pomfret, Vermont; in Wayland and Providence and Revere and Nashua, and in both the Concords and all five Manchesters; and in Raymond, New Hampshire (where Carlton Fisk lives), and Bellows Falls, Vermont (where Carlton Fisk was *born*), and I saw all of them dancing and shouting and kissing and leaping about like the fans at Fenway—jumping up and down in their bedrooms and kitchens and living rooms, and in bars and trailers, and even in some boats here and there, I suppose, and on back-country roads (a lone driver getting the news over the radio and blowing his horn over and over, and finally pulling up and getting out and leaping up and down on the cold macadam, yelling into the night), and all of them, for once at least, utterly joyful and believing in that joy—alight with it. (*Five Seasons*)

It is not news, of course, that in recent years this idyllic view of game has been steadily subverted by certain tensions within the institution of baseball, tensions that writers like Angell, speaking for the average fan, invariably associate with the intrusion of economic considerations into the game. The dilemma of the fan, then, becomes the constant attempt to see the game *as a game*: "when I came to know some of the baseball people in this book . . . ," says Angell in his foreword to *Five Seasons,* "I saw the painful, almost excruciating effort with which each of them was attempting to sustain his lifelong attachment to the game. . . . All of us who care about baseball are making this effort now" (8). Yet the dynamics of disillusionment in contemporary baseball literature demand explanation, we want to suggest, in terms far more complex than the simple notion of a game intruded upon by graceless economic concerns allows for. What is mirrored in Angell's dark and troubled musings is actually the national loss of an innocent *perception* of the game, and with the loss of this perception there has occurred the death or annihilation of the game in Huizinga's sense of an alternative reality or temporary world. This gives us in turn the ultimate context within which baseball as the unique cultural institution glimpsed by Virginia Woolf or described by Gunther Barth has simply ceased to exist in American life.

Huizinga's notion of the play-community is limited to the players of a game or sport, participants so aware of their shared experience as inhabitants of a temporary world that even outside the game they constitute themselves a community apart. This is the genesis of the sports club, and in America of the professional sports team with its own traditions, folklore, folkways, and even language. Sports autobiographies such as Jim Brosnan's *The Long Season* and *The Pennant Race,* Pat Jordan's *A False Spring,* Jerry Kramer's *Instant Replay,* Bill Bradley's *Life on the Run,* and even George Plimpton's best efforts like the Mittyesque *Paper Lion,* are essentially explorations from within the play-community viewed in this light, as a full-developed subculture or miniature society taking the game as its center.

As an American institution, however, baseball must always be viewed as including not only the players but the fans watching the game. For baseball as an institution entails not only an almost mystical nexus between the player active on the field and the spectator contemplating the action, but a consciousness that this relation transcends the moment: the player now on the field represents all players in the past and future of the game, and the spectator now in the stands represents a nation of spectators whose collective memory extends back to the very beginnings of the game. This is what makes the game an institution as Angell perceives it; even as a teenager, he says, "I must have sensed . . . that I was now attached in a rather mysterious way to a larger structure, to something deep and rooted, with its own history, customs, records, honored and dishonored warriors, founders, superstitions, and clouded lore" (*Late Innings,* 10).

The notion of a mystical (or, as Angell says, "mysterious") nexus between spectator and player is worth dwelling on precisely because it is through the rupture of this nexus that the death of the game in Huizinga's sense must occur; the illusion that economic reality can

somehow intrude upon the game in a direct way is, however compelling, only an illusion. To grasp this point is simultaneously to see why the significance of *Ball Four* extends so far beyond its cultural moment, for what Bouton allows us to see is that it is only in a sudden separation between the spheres of observation and action, the stands and the playing field, that the game in its innocent or pastoral aspect ceases to exist. The importance of *Ball Four* in more specific terms is that it prefigures this ultimate rupture, this death of the game.

Since *Ball Four* occasioned a great deal of notoriety when it appeared, it might be thought that its subversion of any innocent perception of the game was a straightforward enough affair, a simple exercise in debunkery. But this was not the case. For the revelations contained in *Ball Four* were only such as might have been guessed at by a sensible observer before the book was written: ballplayers drink too much and have sex with groupies ("Baseball Annies") on the road; they take amphetamines ("greenies") to cure their hangovers and improve their performances, or both; they indulge in adolescent high-jinks like the baseball tradition of peeping Tomism known as "beaver-shooting":

> The roof of the Shoreham is important beaver-shooting country because of the way the hotel is shaped—a series of L-shaped wings that make the windows particularly vulnerable from certain spots on the roof. The Yankees would go up there in squads of fifteen or so, often led by Mickey Mantle himself. You needed a lot of guys to do the spotting. Then someone would whistle from two or three wings away, "*Psst!* Hey! Beaver shot. Section D. Five o'clock." And there'd be a mad scramble of guys climbing over skylights, tripping over each other and trying not to fall off the roof. One of the first big thrills I had with the Yankees was joining about half the club on the roof of the Shoreham at two-thirty in the morning. I remember saying to myself, "So this is the big leagues."

None of this, however, threatens a perception of the game as game. If *Ball Four* had consisted entirely of such revelations it would simply be another ballplayer's autobiography, an inside account of professional sports as a genuine American subculture. Nor is such a perception threatened by Bouton's deliberate debunking of what he calls the Neanderthal aspects of the game: the petty-mindedness of managers and coaches, the rudimentary social and political perspectives of the undereducated young men who play the game, a provincialism so complete that any world outside of baseball seems lost in the mists of incomprehension. All this, to anyone who knew sports and paused to reflect, was to be expected.

There is another process of debunkery at work in *Ball Four,* though, one of which Bouton himself is wholly unaware, and which operates at a deeper level to subvert any perception of the game as game. This is Bouton's preoccupation, amounting at times nearly to an obsession, with everything having to do with compensation, contracts, salaries, benefits, expenses, and, in general terms, all levels of negotiation between players and baseball management. To open the pages of *Ball Four* is to enter upon a scene that has since become all too familiar to spectators like Roger Angell. Bouton begins his narrative with a long and detailed account of his salary negotiations in the years when he was first breaking into baseball with the New York Yankees, when he was offered a minimum salary and told to take it or leave it, and ends with a triumphant account of his successful renegotiation of his present contract with the Houston Astros, and in between we hear constantly the details of his and other players' dealings with the general manager and the front office. And in the background are insistent hints of a more general change soon to sweep through baseball: Marvin Miller, representative of the Baseball Players' Association, is an important off-stage presence, and within the story we hear the first stirrings of a heated and continuous debate about such matters as the reserve clause (then, of course, still in effect).

In light of the later disillusionment that surfaces in Angell's writings, then, we might conclude that Bouton at such moments is a wholly representative figure, a prototype of the sort of players-as-paid-performers who were subsequently to emerge generally. Yet the paradox of *Ball Four* is that Bouton alone in its pages reveals this obsession with compensation and player-management negotiations; baseball in its more innocent aspect is still alive in *Ball Four,* and it is only Bouton as an *un*representative figure who is unable to view it in that light. It is in fact Bouton's attitude on this and other matters that places him outside the inner community of the team, and his journal traces in detail the long and often agonizing train of events leading to the moment of repudiation when Bouton, tensions between himself and the rest of the team having been stretched to the breaking point, enters the clubhouse to find his locker destroyed by an anonymous teammate or teammates: "When I got to the clubhouse tonight I found my two pairs of new baseball shoes had been nailed to the clubhouse floor. Used for the operation were square cement nails. They tore huge holes in the soles. Also the bottoms were torn off my sweatshirts, my Yoo-Hoo T-shirts were ripped to shreds and several jockeystraps were pulled permanently out of stretch" (243).

Throughout *Ball Four* we are dealing with Bouton's exclusion from what Huizinga calls the play-community, and to understand the nature of the community from which he has been excluded we need only look at one last feature of Huizinga's analysis of play. A formal quality of play as he describes it, and one that in a sense completes his analysis of the game as game, is "the *disinterestedness* of play. Not being 'ordinary' life it stands outside the immediate satisfaction of wants and appetites, indeed it interrupts the appetitive process. It interpolates itself as a temporary activity satisfying in itself and ending there" (9). It may seem that this notion of disinterestedness is shattered at the very moment one speaks about playing for pay, but in fact it

is not, and understanding the community that rejects Bouton in *Ball Four* involves seeing why the two things are not irreconcilable.

The answer to the seeming paradox is that Huizinga has correctly described the game in purely formal terms in such a way as to isolate it from everything in ordinary life, including the contingent fact that the players are or are not being paid to perform these actions on the field. This is why, for instance, one could not tell just by looking at a baseball game or a basketball game (independent of outside information) whether or not the players were being paid to play—or, if the players were being paid, it is why the action on the field would remain the same even if the players had for some reason agreed to suspend their salaries before the game. The professional athlete is in this context *paid to be disinterested* in Huizinga's sense, to take with utter seriousness a set of rules about such things as strikeouts and stolen bases, and thus to recreate in adult life the child's total absorption in its play.

The community that rejects Bouton in *Ball Four,* then, is a play-community, one sustained by a shared experience of the game as temporary world, play as a disinterested activity separate from the wants and demands of ordinary life. And because of his exclusion from this community and its values, Bouton is compelled to come up with an alternative conception of what it is he actually does as a player on the field. His answer is to conceive of himself as someone who performs a service for a fee, the equivalent in sports of a lawyer or a dentist or a garage mechanic in ordinary life. His obsession with salaries and negotiations, in turn, arises from Bouton's unvarying sense that he is being inadequately rewarded for his services.

Throughout *Ball Four,* Bouton thus inhabits a sort of twilight zone between baseball as a game in Huizinga's sense and the sphere of ordinary life. He is in a manner of speaking inside baseball as an institution but outside baseball as a game, and it is through the anomalousness of his position that there emerges for the first time in American baseball literature an image of the player as someone who perceives himself as a paid performer providing a service in return for a monetary reward. It would remain for the nation as a whole to discover, under the pressure of endless publicity about salaries and strikes and free agent contracts, that every player of the game could be viewed in the same light, initiating the collapse of an entire structure of perception that had been shared by a nation.

In the work published after his death as the *Philosophical Investigations,* Ludwig Wittgenstein made a distinction that has since been much discussed in analytic philosophy—namely, a distinction between "seeing that" (roughly speaking, perceiving the world at the level of brute facts) and "seeing as" (perceiving those same facts as adding up to or constituting another order of reality). In the philosophical literature on the seeing that/seeing as distinction, sports or games are, conveniently enough for our present purposes, often used by way of illustration. A foreigner and an American fan at a baseball game, for example, see an identical spectacle in "seeing that" terms (both see *that* the field is a certain shape and color, *that* it has poles standing in its remote corners, and so on), but only the mode of "seeing as" allows the American to perceive that one thing (the trajectory of object A as impelled by object B, say) is also something else (a foul ball, a double, a sacrifice fly).

Yet when such examples are used in discussions of the seeing that/seeing as distinction, what usually goes unmentioned is the fact that it is only the same mode of "seeing as" operating at a more fundamental level that allows a spectator to perceive a game *as* a game in Huizinga's sense, a separate world constituted by its own rules and existing apart from ordinary life. The most vivid way of experiencing the truth of this, perhaps, would be to be present at a game or contest where something occurred to make the "seeing as" collapse suddenly into a "seeing that," as happened, gruesomely enough, in two televised prize fights in recent memory when Emile Griffith and Ray Mancini killed their opponents in championship bouts. In both instances viewers were brought to a sudden recognition that they were not watching simply an athletic contest but men attempting to batter one another senseless.

Nothing so dramatic is needed to understand the general principle involved here, however; it is simply that the game in Huizinga's sense is not something inhering in the actions of the players on the field or in the arena, but is something that has its true existence in the mind of the spectator, and for the community of spectators in "seeing as" as a shared mode of perception. It is the collapse of this mode or structure of perception that is responsible for the lament heard everywhere in contemporary baseball writing, from the ephemeral level of the sports column in the morning newspaper to Angell's anguish in *Late Innings*:

> what the man [Dave Winfield] is batting against this season is a million and a half dollars. . . . Winfield is no longer a ballplayer but a celebrity. We have lost him, and will lose more and more like him, as the subtle, ancient bonds of imagination and appreciation and expert knowledge that have connected each true fan to each player of this beautiful and difficult sport become frayed or severed by distraction and greed. It is no wonder that ballpark crowds are so angry these days, and so often drunk and violent. The ballplayers we come to see are no longer close to us, no longer part of our team or, by that psychic extension that gives all sport its meaning, part of us.

Every such lament as this assumes that the change that has taken place is a change in the game itself, as though economic considerations had the power somehow to directly intrude in the game taking place on the field. And, given Huizinga's account of the game, this notion

has a certain prima facie plausibility: since the game previously existed as a temporary world standing out or apart from the anxieties and frustrations of ordinary life, and since worries about money or finances are very basic examples of such anxieties and frustrations, it is easy to imagine that in the last twenty years baseball has somehow imploded upon itself, allowing a steady influx of commercial considerations to mix with what occurs on the field. Yet it seems evident on reflection, as we have said, that the game itself could not change in just this way. It is always some perception of the game that must be altered or lost.

This is why, for instance, in the history of baseball as an American pastime the *fact* that players are paid to perform has never threatened anyone's sense of the game as an innocent or pastoral world; so long as a notion of the player as someone paid to be disinterested in Huizinga's sense remained possible, the game remained alive. Nor do the huge amount of recent salaries threaten that perception of the game; in the past, at least, such salaries merely enhanced the mythological dimensions of outstanding players. When in the Depression year of 1930 the Yankees announced that Babe Ruth's salary for the ensuing season would be $80,000, the announcement caused little envy or rancor in a nation where millions had been suddenly thrown out of work.

Yet Huizinga's analysis seems nonetheless to suggest a deeper truth about Angell's disillusion in that moment when he imagines an overpaid Winfield stepping up to the plate, and by extension about the phenomenon we are calling the death of the game. It is that we mislead ourselves when we use such phrases as "perception of the game" to describe baseball in an era of strikes and lockouts and million-dollar salaries, as though the game had some existence independent of our perceptions. For the truth ultimately suggested by Huizinga (and indirectly by Wittgenstein as well) is that what we mean by "game" is nothing other than a perception in the first place, that sports and games have no real existence outside some collective sphere of perception, the "seeing as" that gives them the status of a separate reality in the minds of players and spectators alike. The death of the game can in this context only be the loss or collapse of a collective perception.

To read *Late Innings* in the light of Huizinga's analysis is, by the same token, to begin to see what causes this collective perception to collapse inward upon itself. Indeed, Angell himself, not just in *Late Innings* but in all his earlier writings, has given unmistakable hints of where to look: it is in the rupture of the mystical nexus between spectator and player—"the subtle, ancient bonds of imagination and appreciation and expert knowledge," as Angell put it, "that have connected each true fan to each player of this beautiful and difficult sport"—that perception of the game as a temporary world begins to dissolve, that the "seeing as" that allowed the game to exist in the minds of the spectators *as* a game collapses into a literal and unprivileged "seeing that," and that the Winfield who steps back to knock dirt off his spikes appears not as a disinterested inhabitant of the separate world of sport but as an overpaid young man performing certain actions in return for a certain sum of money.

Yet something even more significant lurks in the background when Angell contemplates Winfield's swollen salary and celebrity status, an unexpected truth that had been there all along but begins to emerge only in such moments of anguish or extremity. It is that the mechanism of rupture in such cases, the actual means through which the nexus between spectator and player comes to be dissolved, is nothing other than a complex phenomenon of double or reflexive perception: it is not, in short, when spectators perceive players as paid performers that the game ceases to exist as a game, but when *spectators perceive players as perceiving themselves that way.* The very complexity of the phenomenon is enough to suggest how far reaching are its implications for an understanding of contemporary American culture, for in this lies the loss of that disinterestedness essential not only to play but to what Huizinga named the play-element in culture itself.

The death of the game in contemporary baseball literature has less to do with the intrusion of economic considerations into the game than with the national loss of an essential capacity to perceive players as dwelling within and existing solely for the game they are playing. The loss of baseball as an innocent world has been brought about not by changes in baseball as an enterprise but through a hidden epistemological drama playing itself out in the national consciousness, the echoes of which are caught in Angell's gloomy brooding over the game on the field that he can no longer see. The game that has vanished from his sight is lost precisely because it never took place on the field in the first place, but only in that abstract field of perception that was the mind of the fan: "the ball-players . . . are no longer close to us," we recall Angell protesting, "no longer . . . by that psychic extension that gives all sport its meaning, part of us."

The ultimate significance of *Ball Four,* then, if we may return to the remarks from which we began, is that it portrays the game at the moment of its vanishing, not simply because Bouton appears in its pages as a player who perceives himself as a paid performer but because his story contains unmistakable intimations of a coming situation in which all players will be perceived as perceiving themselves in identical terms. It is possible to view *Ball Four* not only as a baseball journal but as a moment in the history of American culture from which one can look either forward or backward: backward to a golden age of pastoral innocence in which baseball existed as a separate world within the complex sphere of national life forward to a time in which it could be viewed only as another species of entertainment.

The disillusionment, even the anguish, evident in Angell's latest writings about the game clearly belong to this later time. They do not derive, as he supposes, from the game's loss of innocence, but rather from the nation's loss of a capacity to see innocently: "So baseball, the quiet show, slips away from us, season by season, and, as with so many of our other lost amenities and gifts— our cities, our countryside—we don't seem to know how to reverse what is happening and win back something we had prized and counted on always" (*Late Innings,* 332). So far as it participates in that more general loss of innocence that is the major characteristic of American life in the waning years of the twentieth century, contemporary baseball literature thus holds a mirror up not merely to a game but to the nation as a whole.

BIBLIOGRAPHY

Angell, Roger. *Five Seasons.* New York, 1978.

———. *Late Innings.* New York, 1982.

Barth, Gunther. *City People: The Rise of Modern City Culture in Nineteenth-Century America.* New York, 1980.

Bouton, Jim. *Ball Four.* New York, 1970.

Novak, Michael. *The Joy of Sport.* New York, 1976.

Wittgenstein, Ludwig. *Philosophical Investigations.* 3rd. ed. Trans. G. E. M. Anscombe. New York, 1958.

Woolf, Virginia. *The Moment and Other Essays.* New York, 1948.

Melvin D. Palmer

SOURCE: "The Heyday of the Football Novel," in *Journal of Popular Culture,* Vol. 16, No. 1, Summer, 1982, pp. 48-54.

[*In the following essay, Palmer accounts for the rise of the football novel in the late 1960s and early 1970s.*]

In spite of the fact that F. Scott Fitzgerald disparaged Ring Lardner's preoccupation with baseball and in spite of the fact that a reviewer of Heywood Broun's *Sun Field* failed to understand how anyone could take baseball seriously, the sports novel has matured into a significant subgenre of modern fiction.[1] Sports have attracted writers of the talent of Philip Roth and Bernard Malamud, not to mention such regulars as Nelson Algren, Irwin Shaw and Budd Schulberg, and such up-and-coming novelists as Frederick Exley and Robert Coover. Furthermore, from the time Lardner created the genre in 1914 with *You Know Me Al,* the sports novel has reflected changes in American society.[2]

As anyone could guess, baseball has dominated the sports novel for most of its history, but a curious thing began to happen in the 1960s. First, the major sports novels of the early 1960s were about basketball; and second, the year 1968 marked a transition to football fiction. From 1968 to 1972 there was only one novel about baseball, and it did not have an athlete for a hero. On the other hand, this five-year period saw the publication of six novels which took football players as central characters or the football game as a central metaphor.

There had been random novels about football before 1968, but these did not amount to much, and none was about professional football. For example, Millard Lampell's first novel, *The Hero,* appeared in 1949 (and was made into a film called *Saturday's Hero,* with John Derek). Lampell tells the tale of a poor son of immigrants, Steve Novak, who was offered a number of scholarships to play football in college. He chose a southern university, and that is where the trouble began. He simply could not establish himself in the refined atmosphere of a southern university. In addition, he had a hard time convincing his English professor that he was a serious student, but he did. He fell in love with the daughter of the college's most conservative and influential supporter, and he gradually fell out of love with football when he began to realize that he was little more than a paid performer. Forced to play when injured, he decided to leave the university; and he left with the young woman and the blessings of the English professor. In spite of some realism of incident, this is a rather simple, predictable story, not much more than juvenile fiction served up in an adult package.

Another early attempt at football fiction was Babs Deal's *The Grail* (1963), which did not get very good reviews. This novel—incidentally, the only sports novel written by a woman—was well researched at the University of Alabama, but it did not succeed. Deal ground her axe too loudly. In this story about the eternal triangle, Arthur, the head coach of a fictional college team, has a wife named Jennie, who falls in love with the coach's star quarterback named—alas—Lance. Many readers got no further in the novel. The theme is trite and the symbolism is much too heavy-handed.

In 1968, however, the football novel grew up. In addition to Frederick Exley's *A Fan's Notes,* in which football is a major theme, the year produced the first full-fledged novel about professional football, Gary Cartwright's *The Hundred Yard War.* The only novel about baseball in 1968 was Robert Coover's *Universal Baseball Association. J. Henry Waugh, Prop.,* a much praised piece of fiction but one in which the hero is neither an athlete nor even a fan. Real baseball bores him. Instead of living an outdoor life, he lives alone and has only two acquaintances—both of whom he manages to lose, along with his job as an accountant. He plays a highly complicated game that he had invented. Over the years he had created characters for his game—a whole baseball league, in fact; and he had always kept thorough and accurate records of the league's activities and history. After cheating at his own game in order to get even with a player he did not like,

he loses touch with ordinary reality altogether. He moves into his fictional world, taking his creations as his friends, looking for "some old lost fabric of unity."[3]

In a real sense Coover's novel was the *coup de grace* of the old baseball novel. In a recent review (of something else), Edward Hoagland observed that "Baseball had stood for loyalty to the verities, memories of innocence, patience with ritual; surely no one who cared about baseball could be an opportunist at heart."[4] In 1968 in America the old verities were fast disappearing and new rituals were being created. Because baseball could no longer carry the burden of the time, American needed a new sports myth; and just as baseball lost its number one position in mass popularity (gate receipts and so forth), the old baseball novel gave way to football. Football became the new myth, at least for a while; and this fact is reflected in sports fiction. Let us survey the six football novels that appeared from 1968 to 1972. The first two—Exley's and Cartwright's—established football as the new metaphor of sports fiction. One shows us the sport from the outside, from the point of view of a fan; the other, from the inside, from a player's point of view.

A Fan's Notes details the frustrations and even the mental illness of a kind of anti-hero named Frederick Exley. In spite of the autobiographical implications of the novel, Exley cautions us not to trust the facts and wants the tale to be read as fantasy. The protagonist's frustrations stem from a number of causes, one major cause being the success of his father, an outstanding high school football player. The father had been unable to capitalize on his success, however. Instead of going on to a college that wanted him, he married, worked hard, smoked a lot and died at forty. Because Exley himself cannot seem to find any of the fame that his father had, he lives vicariously through the New York Giants, especially Frank Gifford, who is in fact the same age as Exley. In Gifford, Exley seems to find an idealized version of himself. He goes to games, watches the Giants on television; but his frustrations never end. He moves from job to job, tries to write and suffers an unsuccessful marriage. When Gifford is hurt on the playing field and taken out for the season, Exley's frustrations cause him to pick fights as he comes to realize that his destiny is to be a fan and nothing more.

This disturbed character no doubt reflects the general disturbances of many Americans in the late '60s, a time that saw severe divisions in America. In fact, a recent *New York Times Magazine* feature called 1968 the year the '60s came to "a full boil." In addition to the anti-war, anti-establishment riots and demonstrations at Columbia, Chicago and elsewhere, this was the year of the Tet offensive, the year President Johnson decided not to run again, the year Nixon made his comeback. It was the year Martin Luther King, Jr. and Robert Kennedy were assassinated. In the midst of this irrational violence and turmoil, it was no doubt the efficient, organized violence of football that drew Exley and people like him to the sport.

In Cartwright's *Hundred Yard War*—published also in 1968—the theme of violence, as suggested by the title, is even more prominent than in Exley's tale. The story traces the rise of rookie Regan Glass and the decline of quarterback Rylie Silver, and it does so with realism of language and incident. Our first glimpse of Glass reveals him in the super-luxurious accommodations of a Las Vegas motel, where he is being wooed by the front man of the fictional Dallas Troupers. The organization lavishes money and nude women on the young player. In addition to easy money and abundant sex, however, the story emphasizes the pain and hardship that professional ballplayers endure for their reward. Fame no longer seems to be a motivating factor. Exley hungered for fame and old-fashioned heroism; the actors of Cartwright's novel seem to hunger for little more than easy kicks and a large enough bankroll to underwrite them.

It was largely in Cartwright's world that football fiction was to thrive as it worked through Joseph Pilliteri's *Two Hours on Sunday* and James Whitehead's *Joiner* in 1971, and through Don Delillo's *End Zone* and Dan Jenkins' *Semi-Tough* in 1972. Of these, the first is a potboiler and needs only brief comment.

Pilliteri's *Two Hours on Sunday* is the first person account of a rather self-pitying number two professional quarterback who melodramatically comes to the rescue when number one gets hurt. Then he himself becomes number one as he achieves victory in the closing moment of a big game. Except for the adult characters and diction, there is not a great deal of difference between this novel and the sort of juvenile fiction that Ring Lardner countered with the publication of *You Know Me Al* in the early years of the century. Nevertheless, the novel does attest to the new interest in professional football in fiction and in fact.

The next three novels, however, represent significant advancements in the genre. Whitehead's *Joiner,* another first-person account, jumps around in time as Sonny Joiner—high school, college and professional star—tells his own story. The setting is Mississippi and Texas. Sonny is a lusty intellectual who detests extremes of stupidity and intellect. We see his loves, his politics, his battles against what he conceives to be redneck bigots and uptight liberals. A star student as well as a star athlete, Sonny combines a colloquial style of writing with learned literary and historical allusions. For example, he suggests: "Why not have an updated picture of Cardinal Bessarion—the great Renaissance Humanist. . . . doing laps while reading Cicero?"[6] It is clear that the name *Joiner* is symbolic of Whitehead's attempt to effect a Rabelaisian joining of body and mind, a modern version of the Greek ideal of sound mind in sound body. Delillo's *End Zone* may very well be the genre's outstanding sports novel with a college setting. Like Joiner, Gary, the novel's hero, tells his own story and is a serious student as well as athlete. He is fascinated by nuclear war and football, efficient violence in general. He takes courses in war from the

ROTC Department and discusses various issues with an ROTC major. In the jargon of the day, however, Gary was a sort of fringe hippie trying to get himself together. With humor and pathos, Delillo attacks "clean bombs" and "humane wars." He constantly draws parallels between the game of football and the worlds of war and technology. For him, both football and war are "tests of opposing technologies."[7]

Another important theme of the novel is physical impairment and illness. One by one, several of the novel's characters come down with unspecified afflictions, motor problems, limps and the like; and in the final scene the hero himself has presumably contracted pneumonia. In addition, sex is generally absent from the novel; Gary's one attempt at passion does not succeed. But there is no mystery disease going around; rather, it is the world itself that is getting worse. And therein lies the significance of the title: We are all hovering in the end zone; and in the end zone, in the words of one of the novel's characters, "we don't care much for bravery anymore. It's better to be efficient than brave."[8]

Dan Jenkins's *Semi-Tough* is perhaps the most popular sports novel since Lardner's *You Know Me Al.* It got to number two on the bestseller list and was recently made into a first-run movie. This very funny book explodes almost every myth about professional football. No doubt taking off on the numerous nonfictional portraits of sports stars, Jenkins tells his story through the voice of Billy Clyde Puckett, as that voice speaks into a tape recorder. The intention is for a friend to edit the material into a biography suitable for young readers, but one doubts that such editing would leave even a paragraph suitable for young readers.

With rowdy humor the novel builds through a series of minor orgies (sexual and otherwise) up to a major orgiastic party the night before the Super Bowl. The action of the novel, in fact, focuses on the celebratory atmosphere of Super Bowl mania. The game itself seems to be an afterthought, and because of the wild party on the night before the big game, one is surprised that Billy Clyde's team wins. Indeed, drugs, booze, sex and dissipation in general are so profuse in the novel that one wonders how the game could have been played at all.

After the game, this world of too-much forces Billy Clyde's best friend, a split end, to leave everything behind. Then Billy Clyde is left with the third major character of the book, Barbara Jane Bookman, the pair's hometown, childhood best companion. Since there is no place to go and no further kicks to have, Billy Clyde and Barbara Jane try to cancel out the heady froth and start all over by going out on dates like old-fashioned teenagers. In a sense, Jenkins brings the sports novel full circle. As the earlier baseball novels depicted ambitious, uneducated but skilled young men from the country who make their way to the city and lose their innocence, Jenkins depicts city boys with a college education who try to regain some innocence by going back to less complex and sophisticated activities.

How does one account for the rise of football fiction in the late sixties and early seventies? It does not solve things to say that the world outside fiction had made a similar shift of emphasis, for then we would have to account for that shift.

One popular theory, suggested several times above, is that the conditions of American culture are at the root of the transition of emphasis from baseball to football. As America lost its innocence in the jungles of Vietnam and the riot- and assassination-torn streets back home, the great American game of baseball, with all its nostalgic associations, was simply inadequate structurally, if not too sacred, to reflect America of the '60s. Simon and Garfunkel said goodbye to the old baseball world in 1968 when they asked "Where have you gone, Joe Dimaggio? Our nation lifts its lonely eyes to you." Football's frank acceptance of violence and sex (baseball has no cheerleaders or half-time leg shows) was something foreign to the leisurely, non-contact sport of baseball. But there is more to it than that.

Perhaps television overexposed baseball, a game that cannot stand too close a look or the tyranny of the clock. One can leave the set during a baseball game, make a sandwich and quite possibly not miss a thing. Not so with the tenser, swifter action of football. Marshall McLuhan, perceptive critic and prophet that he was, pointed out that since baseball is "a game of one-thing-at-a-time, TV, as the very image of the new corporate and participant ways of electric living, fosters habits . . . that alienate us from the peculiar style of baseball."[9] McLuhan here points not only to the electronics media as a cause for baseball's losing its number one position; he also alludes to the *corporate* way of life. Mark Twain long ago saw baseball as symbolic of industrial America.[10] With its long strolls to bat, interminable pitcher preparations and individual duels between rugged individualists, baseball was an appropriate metaphor for the American way earlier in the century. Football, on the other hand, is a symbol of corporate, managerial America, with its highly organized ethic of efficient and interlocking systems within systems. One is reminded of the punster's definition of football: a series of committee meetings separated by spasms of violence.

Delillo suggested this explanation when he said:

> Football is a complex of systems. It's like no other sport. When the game is played properly, it's an interlocking of a number of systems. . . . People stress the violence. That's the smallest part of it. Football is brutal only from a distance. In the middle of it there's a calm, a tranquility. The players accept pain. There's a sense of order. . . . When the systems interlock, there's a satisfaction to the game that can't be duplicated. There's a harmony.

If one bears such comments in mind, then one can better understand Richard Nixon's fascination with football. It is hard to imagine the man throwing out the first baseball of the season. Rather, one recalls his sitting in front of a television set watching a professional football game while demonstrators called for an end to the war in Vietnam. It has even been said that "In the Nixon cabinet, if you knew how the Colts were doing, you were hardnosed, you were all right."[12] Maintaining a cool efficiency while "toughing out" the pain was the Nixon way.

This substitution of systems and superstructures for people is what bothered writers like Whitehead, Delillo and Jenkins. In the classic statement on play, *Homo Ludens,* Johan Huizinga maintained that play in the form of sport has become too complicated, commercial and overly serious.[13] It is interesting that Whitehead, Delillo and Jenkins—without sacrificing their love of the sport itself—have attempted to rescue sports from the morass Huizinga spoke of. Whitehead suggests a reunion of head and body. Our mind-body dualism has often pitted the intellectual against the athlete—the "egghead" against the "jock." Whitehead would like to see a humanistic joining of these two parts of our being. Delillo would like to see a revival of the simplest and most basic element of play: fun. At the conclusion of his *End Zone,* his hero and some friends start a pick-up game of football in the snow; and in spite of his coming down with pneumonia, he and his friends have more downright fun than we have seen anywhere else in the novel. Jenkins's *Semi-Tough* seems to suggest that we have gone too far and that it is time for some old-fashioned starting over, as do Billy Clyde Puckett, his friend Shake, and Barbara Jane.

With the relaxation of the tensions in the early '70s, America experienced a near tidal wave of nostalgia—music from the '40s and '50s, television shows and movies about happier days. Baseball shared in this new nostalgia. The year 1973 saw the first baseball novels in over a decade (not counting Coover's unusual novel in 1968). John Graham produced a zany and serious tale about the sport in *Babe Ruth Caught in a Snow Storm,* and Philip Roth published *The Great American Novel,* about the great American sport, baseball. But baseball's monopoly had been broken. The year 1973 also saw a continuation of the new vogue for football stories. Peter Gent published his fictional expose of professional football, *North Dallas Forty.* Frank Deford, of *Sports Illustrated,* published *Cut 'n' Run* in the same year and comically explained the popularity of football in terms of sex, not war or technology. And in terms of sex, one of Deford's characters offered yet another reason for football's overtaking baseball in our changing time: "Baseball was like marriage; it was a regular sort of everyday thing. Football was a good lay. . . . "[14]

NOTES

[1] See Arthur Mizener, *The Far Side of Paradise* (New York: Houghton Mifflin, 1949), p. 158, and the *New York Times,* Oct. 21, 1923, p. 8. Broun's novel appeared in 1923.

[2] Serialized in the *Saturday Evening Post* in 1914; published in book form by Scribner's in 1916.

[3] New York: New American Library, 1968, p. 166.

[4] Review of Roger Angell's *Five Seasons, Harper's* (July, 1977), p. 76.

[5] Nov. 13, 1977, p. 40.

[6] New York: Knopf, 1971, p. 189.

[7] New York: Houghton Mifflin, 1972, p. 84.

[8] P. 84.

[9] *Understanding Media* (New York: Signet, 1966), p. 212.

[10] See R.S. Graber, "Baseball in American Fiction," *English Journal,* 56 (1967), 1107.

[11] P. 199.

[12] Hoagland, *Harper's* p. 76.

[13] Boston: Beacon Press, 1950, p. 197.

[14] New York: Viking, 1973, p. 4.

Richard Alan Schwartz

SOURCE: "Postmodernist Baseball," in *Modern Fiction Studies,* Vol. 33, No. 1, Spring, 1987, pp. 135-49.

[*In the following essay, Schwartz discusses the appeal of baseball as myth and metaphor for many postmodern writers such as Bernard Malamud, Philip Roth, W. P. Kinsella, and Robert Coover.*]

When, in 1835, Abner Doubleday didn't invent the game of baseball in Cooperstown, Ohio, little did he know he was fueling the imaginations of several postmodernist writers. For not only are baseball and its accompanying traditions eminently exploitable for literary purposes, its history, including the dubious accounts of its origin and its unique status as America's pastime, is especially appealing to postmodernist writers who attack conventional perceptions of reality, who challenge accepted versions of history, and who seek to infuse vitality into an uncertain, unknowable world. In this essay I shall discuss how some innovative and imaginative writers have used the world of baseball for these and other ends.

Perhaps the most significant feature of postmodernist thought concerns the limitations on human knowledge of truth and reality, and the realm of uncertainty into which those restrictions place us. These perceived limitations are consistent with such scientific ideas as relativity theory, which insists that no point of view is intrinsically superior to or more accurate than any other, and with quantum theory, which undercuts the idea of

causality, places real limitations on what we can know,[1] and introduces the principle of complementarity (the union in nature of what seem in traditional orientations to be mutually exclusive characteristics: matter, for instance, can now be described in terms of energy). I cite these scientific outlooks to show that the postmodernist attitudes represent more than the skewed perceptions of socially alienated writers and are, in fact, bound up with the mainstream of twentieth-century thought. Postmodernism, then, pictures a subjective, relativistic world full of contradictions and dependent upon individual observers for its definition. Little, if anything, can be known with absolute certainty. To the extent that their books embody these perceptions, postmodernists can be said to be the new "realists," who are simply describing and reflecting a radically different version of reality from that perceived by such writers as James, Balzac, Zola, Flaubert, and Tolstoy during the time when belief in a mechanistic world view was at its apex.

Most, if not all, of these postmodern characteristics apply to modernism as well. Postmodernism distinguishes itself from modernism largely in terms of tone, audience, and political orientation. For writers and readers who grew up in the '30s, '40s, and '50s, the breakdown of the sense of an ordered universe was not a sudden revelation, as it largely had been for the modernists, but simply a normal circumstance of life, much as the possibility of sudden nuclear holocaust is simply a given for those born since 1945. This familiarity with an absurd universe allows postmodern writers to be less despairing, even to be humorous, and to appeal to a broader range of readers, who are more likely than their counterparts of the '20s to be open to the absurdist viewpoint. Moreover, the experience of World War Two revealed fascism to be a completely abhorrent political means of imposing order, and many postmodernists reject entirely the modernists' search for order within chaos, preferring to advocate an acceptance of uncertainty and chance. And to the extent that the rise of big business and big government after World War Two has restricted individual choices and freedoms, those systems are rejected by postmodernist writers. Thus we find an anticapitalist, though not especially a procommunist stance in much postmodernist literature, particularly in literature written during or immediately after the Vietnam War. Still, like their modernist forebears, postmodernist writers accept the challenge of reorienting us in a fundamentally disorienting world.[2] For some of those writers baseball has emerged as a vehicle for effecting this reorientation. The remainder of this discussion will address how Philip Roth, Bernard Malamud, W. P. Kinsella, Harry Stein, and Robert Coover have turned to baseball to promote their postmodernist view of reality and to reorient us within it.

The facet of baseball that comes most readily to mind in this context is its affinity to myth. After all, the game regularly involves moments of heroism: confrontations between forces of good and evil, the individual struggles between pitcher and batter, the possibility of someone's performing a great act that can turn certain defeat into victory, and so on. Bernard Malamud's *The Natural* provides the most conscious and extensive association of myth with baseball. Several critics have commented upon the subtext of the Grail legend, wherein Roy Hobbs plays Percival to Pop Fisher's Fisher King and to the Knights' Waste Land.[3] Of course, Roy proves to be a failed Grail Knight, a fact that Malamud employs to criticize American values. I shall comment upon that more directly below.

Other novels also use specific myths or mythlike structures. Philip Roth's *The Great American Novel* likens the Ruppert Mundys, a team of misfits consigned by their owners' greed to be a permanent visiting team, to the Jews wandering in the desert after the exodus from Egypt. Moreover, all the players bear the names of gods from various cultures: John Baal (son of Spit Baal, grandson of Base Baal), Frenchy Astarte, Wayne Heket, Red Kronos, Chico Mecoatl, and Jolly Cholly Tuminikar. Roland Agni plays out the legend of *Orlando Furioso,* and the greatest pitcher of all time, Gil Gamesh, still haunts the playing field.

W. P. Kinsella employs a fairy tale structure in his recent novel, *Shoeless Joe.* The protagonist, Ray Kinsella, hears a mystical voice of a radio announcer saying that if he builds a baseball field, *he* will come. Without being told, Roy knows *he* is Shoeless Joe Jackson, whose career was cut short because of his participation in the 1919 World Series fix. Ray builds the field and thereby creates an enchanted island where members of that Black Sox team, ghosts from the past, come alive to fulfill the potential they were never able to realize while living. Later, Ray hears the voice instructing him to "ease his pain," and again Ray knows instinctively what this means: he must seek out J. D. Salinger and bring him to the enchanted ballpark. Like a fairy tale hero, Ray Kinsella leaves home and his loving, too-good-to-be-true wife in order to abduct Salinger, bring him to a Red Sox game at Fenway Park, and ultimately return with him, no longer a hostage but an accomplice, to share the magic of the ballpark and help defeat the malicious schemes of an evil, Snideley Whiplash-like brother-in-law who wants to tear down the stadium and use the land for computerized farming. From the dangerous journey to the wise adviser/companion to the flawless, adoring heroine to the evil mother-in-law and terrible villain, *Shoeless Joe* draws upon the basic fairy tale features.

Finally, the most impressive baseball novel to date, Robert Coover's *Universal Baseball Association, Inc.,* not only plays out the struggle between Satan and Christ (who also seems to be a Dionysius figure), but does so in ways that comment on the idea of divine intervention, the uses of myth, the meaning(s) of history, and the development of Western religious and existential thought. Arlen J. Hansen argues convincingly that Coover was inspired by Einstein's remark during his argument with Neils Bohr over whether the universe functions purely according to probabilities (chance) or whether it is ultimately deterministic in some form. Einstein repeatedly asserted that he refused to believe that "God plays dice with the universe." Hansen suggests that Coover, prompted by this statement, set out to depict such a world in the form of a sophisticated baseball game played with dice.

Given the general associations between baseball and myth and the specific applications in the novels above, what, ultimately, do these writers accomplish by emphasizing baseball's mythic qualities? Perhaps this question is best answered by considering what myth itself can offer a society that accepts it. Shared myths establish human bonds, which in turn foster a sense of community. People who possess the same religious beliefs, for instance, automatically have something in common, and if those beliefs are emphatic, believers are likely to identify closely with others who share their enthusiasm. Myths also function as a mechanism by which outsiders can be integrated into a community. Newcomers who participate in a culture's mythology achieve access to the community's network. Moreover, myth makes possible the extension of the past into the present. To the extent that we share mythic impulses or beliefs from earlier eras, we maintain an on-going presence of the past within the present. This continuation of the past offers feelings of continuity and stability, which most of us consider desirable qualities.

In the twentieth century, however, because of industrialization, urbanization, world-wide wars that radically altered social institutions and living patterns, and other such developments, our experiences often seem disjointed, fragmented, and isolated from the past and often from other people's experiences. This observation, of course, is not new; it dominates the literature of our time. Nor is there anything new about writers trying to impose mythic patterns onto modern experience in order to afford feelings of continuity, shared experience, and connections with the past. That strategy lies at the center of Joyce's *Ulysses,* Eliot's *The Waste Land,* Woolf's *The Waves,* much of Yeats's poetry, and much of Faulkner's fiction, to name but a few.

However, though effective as a literary gambit, the imposition of myth onto daily existence fails ultimately to overcome the reader's own sense of discontinuity. In our increasingly secular era, where religious belief also largely fails to provide the stability and community that myth once offered, baseball emerges as at least a partial alternative. For authors who grew up before enthusiasm for baseball declined and football took over as the national sport, baseball does, indeed, provide a shared human experience, especially, but not exclusively, among men. A stranger can walk into a bar or barbershop in virtually any American city or town and begin a conversation, on equal footing, about a given team's prospects, its strengths and weaknesses, a particular player's performance, or a manager's genius or stupidity. Except for national politics, few other subjects provide this immediate mechanism for Americans to communicate as equals.[4] Historically, baseball provided a way for the great immigrant waves of the late nineteenth and early twentieth centuries to integrate into American life. The identification with and celebration of the local team provided some identification with mainstream American culture.

Moreover, the baseball fans' awareness of records and achievements from earlier eras keeps part of the past alive in the present. Also, baseball's essentially rural origins—we think of it as a game played by farm boys in fields—are themselves anachronisms that call forth the past and bring us even closer to the agrarian myths. And its clock, based on innings instead of hours, places us closer to mythic timelessness.

It is understandable, then, why several writers have seized upon baseball as something to fulfill some of the functions that myths could fulfill, but no longer can, in our highly secular age. On the other hand, baseball does not possess the high seriousness of myth, and any application of it in mythic ways will inevitably be colored by a greater or lesser degree of self-parody. Hitting a game-winning home run, after all, is still a far cry from saving a country from drought and pestilence. Parody, however, has long been used by postmodernists as a double-edged sword: these authors offer hope but raise doubts; they expose the emptiness of certain of their societies' values but undercut their own exposés; and they establish order only to rob us of certainty. For writers who believe cognitive truth to be fundamentally unknowable, who think that reality is based on the paradoxical reconciliation of contraries rather than on models of exclusionary Aristotlean logic, who reject a causally oriented world view in favor of one based on chance, this double-edged parody is a valuable tool.

Moving from myth to texts, I shall show how writers have used the subject of baseball to communicate those limitations on what we can know and to suggest how we can function within such an uncertain world. *The Great American Novel*'s concern with these issues is paramount. The book appeared in 1973, the tail-end of the Sixties movement, when women and minority groups were directing considerable attention to their virtual exclusion from history textbooks and other historical accounts. This political phenomenon raised doubts about the possibility of there being such a thing as objective, historical truth. Who writes history? What conscious and unconscious biases of class, race, nationality, and sex do these authors bring to their historical accounts? Which events are included and excluded, emphasized and glossed over? Who gets left in and who is omitted from these historical accounts? These questions were voiced frequently during the Sixties, and they were part of a larger, overall challenge to the authority of white, middle and upper class, male domination not only of American institutions, but also of perceptions of what America is and has been.

The Great American Novel echoes these socio-political concerns. The narrator, Smitty, who may be sane or

senile, rails against a concerted plot by the baseball establishment—not only the American and National Leagues, but also the sportswriters and record-keepers, who also shape the baseball experience. The establishment has, Smitty claims, deliberately and thoroughly eliminated all references to the third baseball league, the Patriot League. Much as Stalin rewrote Russian history to exclude his foes, so has organized baseball excised the records and accomplishments of the Patriot League. Smitty's book, then, is nothing less than revisionist history, his crusade to restore the omissions by establishment chroniclers.

Most of Smitty's narration concerns the exploits of the hapless Rupert Mundys, whose avaricious owners sold their ballpark at considerable profit to the U.S. government for use as a World War Two staging ground. Relegated to permanent visiting team status, the Mundys are a team of over-the-hill cast-offs, misfits, and cripples. In short, they are the homeless and the downtrodden; yet, they too made their contribution to baseball history, and they deserve to have that contribution recorded, much as the homeless and downtrodden throughout American history deserve likewise. In a very basic sense, then, Roth, through Smitty, calls attention to the Sixties' question, "Who gets left out of history?"

Roth intermingles "known facts" with fictions at once to lend credibility to the possible existence of the Patriot League and to undermine our confidence in our ability to distinguish the truth from the whoppers. My research uncovered no authentic Patriot League, but Roth was successful enough in his technique to send me and my students to the library to check it out. Roth initiates this intermingling of fact and fiction early in the novel and continues with it. One of the more effective instances describes a baseball game between two teams in the Negro League, attended by Aunt Jemima. Here, Roth mixes a "real" league that has largely been ignored by official baseball history with a fictitious creation of Madison Avenue. Yet, in the context, both possess about the same level of reality. In fact, for many of us, Aunt Jemima is even more real than the Negro League. Roth also uses a technique that I label the anti-tall-tale by which he makes the real seem fictional. In the Mundy's lineup are a one-armed outfielder and a midget, apparent exaggerations of the team's ragamuffin nature, something that no one could possibly take seriously. However, a midget and a one-armed fielder did actually play major league ball. The former, Eddie Gaedel, appeared once in one of Bill Veeck's publicity stunts, but the latter, Peter Gray, was a player in the St. Louis Browns' regular lineup.

Roth, then, uses the baseball context not only to question how we record history, but also to make us experience directly the uncertainty of our basic, commonplace assumptions about the nature of truth. He shatters our confidence in our ability to sort out incredible reality from probable fiction. Yet, having taken us to a plane of epistemological uncertainty, he paradoxically insists on the importance of remembering history. After several hundred pages of free-wheeling humor and literary parody, Roth turns his sights to the abuses of McCarthyism and the House Un-American Activities Committee (HUAC). Writing at a time when HUAC was investigating and interrogating Vietnam war protesters and leaders of other challenges to the establishment,[5] Roth reminds us of the outrages committed twenty years before. Smitty describes an alleged Communist conspiracy to infiltrate American baseball and corrupt it, thereby undermining our country's moral fiber. The book culminates with a series of HUAC investigations and a Hollywood Ten-like trial. Several Mundy players, the Mundy 13, are implicated in the alleged Communist conspiracy. Some confess and name other names rather than face blacklisting; others go to jail. One commits suicide. The machinations of former Patriot League star pitcher Gil Gamesh are so complex that we can never know if he is a single, double, or triple agent—or for whom; yet his testimony ruins many players. Smitty himself is sentenced to a year in jail for refusing

> to participate in this lunatic comedy in which American baseball players who could not locate Russia on a map of the world—who could not locate *the world* on a map of the world—denounce themselves and their teammates as Communist spies out of fear and intimidation and howling ignorance, or . . . out of incorrigible human perversity and curdled genes. (371)

Smitty's name never again appears on the byline of an American newspaper.

In the face of uncertainty about even basic facts, then, Roth still makes us feel moral outrage over the owners' and politicians' insidious manipulation of the hapless ballplayers. One of the great difficulties with a relativistic world view that questions our certainty about any basic truths is that it makes decisive action problematic, if not impossible. Yet Roth invokes the outrages of the Fifties so we can feel their innate injustice, even if we are never quite sure of the external facts. To a very real extent, *The Great American Novel* is an admonition to remember and learn from history, as well as to be attentive to who is left in charge of history and to who is excluded from it. Yet, it is an admonishment made through parody, a parody that does not undermine the warning but allows us also to be joyous in the face of it.

Harry Stein's *Hoopla* is also revisionist history. It is the story of the 1919 Black Sox scandal and the events leading to it, as told by Buck Weaver, one of the players actually involved, and by Luther Pond, a newspaper reporter and apparently the creation of Stein's literary imagination. Like Roth, then, Stein mingles fact and fiction and makes them indistinguishable: Weaver and Pond claim equal authority as narrators; or, if anything, Pond's polished language makes him initially more credible than the poorly educated Weaver. Most of the events are identifiable as "real history": the Johnson-Jeffries "Great White Hope" prizefight, the Detroit Tigers'

sympathy strike on behalf of Ty Cobb, the worldwide baseball tour of the Chicago White Sox and New York Giants, and, of course, the fixed World Series of 1919 between the White Sox and Cincinnati Reds.

But Stein's representation, very much in the realistic mode, forces a reevaluation of our traditional response to the Black Sox scandal, one that depicts the Chicago 8 as greedy men who sold out their integrity and the national pastime for filthy lucre. Not only does Stein remind us that fixing ball games was very much a tradition within the national pastime prior to 1920, he also reveals the extent to which American professional, major league baseball was shaped by nineteenth-century American industrialism, and he suggests that the fixed Series was more the product of a long history of unfair labor practices by stingy industrialist/owners than the result of the greed of a few players. Weaver repeatedly refers to White Sox owner Charles Comiskey as "The Noble Roman" and reminds us that he was an industrial magnate. We see how Comiskey and other owners take advantage of uneducated, naive farm boys during contract negotiations, and how they even manipulate the King of England to ensure vast profits for their international baseball tour, while underpaying the players and claiming they are incurring great financial losses to make this gesture of American good will. We learn that in 1918 Comiskey had promised pitcher Ed Cicotte a ten thousand dollar bonus if he won thirty games. After Cicotte had won twenty-nine games, with several more remaining in the season, he was removed from the lineup at Comiskey's insistence and denied the opportunity to earn the bonus. Cicotte's share for throwing the Series was ten thousand dollars.

Stein, then, uses baseball to challenge traditional history and to criticize the action of the industrial magnates as being at the heart of other aspects of American corruption. But by using two narrators of different backgrounds, different levels of involvement, and different levels of integrity (Weaver emerges more respectable than Pond), Stein also underscores the relativity of truth. For Pond's view of the fix, which is unsympathetic to the players and which looks at the event as an entity in itself instead of as the culmination of a long string of injustices, also claims validity. There is, finally, no absolute rule by which we can establish the context within which to view a historical event. Can we isolate an event from its indirect causes? If not, how far back must we go before we have adequately accounted for the indirect causes? Our assessment of the corrupt World Series is complicated even further when we recognize that each narrator has a vested interest in his viewpoint. Weaver wants to clear his name, while Pond wishes to sell papers, advance his journalistic career, and please another magnate, his employer, William Randolph Hearst. So, as we find so often in modernist and postmodernist literature, reality seems to absorb contradictory representations.

Bernard Malamud's *The Natural* also addresses the Black Sox, as it culminates with a talented ball player throwing a championship game for money. Malamud uses the Black Sox scandal in a more traditional way than Stein, however. Baseball's status as the national pastime makes the corruption of its most important series a particularly useful metaphor for portraying the failure of the American dream. Like F. Scott Fitzgerald, who alludes in *The Great Gatsby* to the 1919 Series, Malamud also attacks spiritual impoverishment and materialism. To Malamud, writing during the suburbanization of America in the early 1950s, the United States might easily have seemed to possess the resources and talent to lead the world out of its postwar waste land, but instead appeared to be squandering that potential on superficial attractions and material distractions.

Though *The Natural* employs a traditional narrative strategy, reflecting a more or less traditional world view, there is at least one area where uncertainty figures prominently. Ray may have failed to save the kingdom, but he might still put his own lands in order, as does the Fisher King in Eliot's *The Waste Land*. In the modern world, perhaps that is the best we can do. In this respect, if Roy's final thought, "I never did learn anything out of my past life, now I have to suffer again," represents the equivalent of tragic insight, then there is at least some hope (217). The Knights will remain losers, but he can perhaps build a life that does not rely on breaking records, and he can learn to value more substantial things, for instance Iris' love. On the other hand, if those words do not indicate true insight, then he will remain as spiritually empty as before, and the conclusion is bleak indeed. The text can accommodate both possibilities, and so the reader ultimately determines the nature of the outcome by imposing his preference onto the reading experience. Having the reader play such an active role in determining the nature of the book both underscores the relative nature of experience (is *The Natural* uplifting tragedy or despairing pathos?) and embodies the principle found in modern physics that the observer (here, the reader) plays a role in determining the nature of the event.

A third novel to invoke the 1919 World Series is W. P. Kinsella's *Shoeless Joe*. Kinsella's employment of the event differs from both Stein's and Malamud's. Kinsella is interested in the idea of unfulfilled potential, and Shoeless Joe Jackson, a baseball natural who was banished from the game after the Series fix, is Kinsella's primary embodiment of that concept. Kinsella does little to defend Jackson, other than to point out, "It is likely that he did accept money from gamblers. But throw the Series? Never! Shoeless Joe Jackson led both teams in hitting in that 1919 Series. It was the circumstances. The circumstances. The players were paid peasant salaries while the owners became rich" (8). Instead, Kinsella uses Jackson and the other Black Sox players to celebrate dreams, private aspirations, and appreciation of the land, and to attack corporate indifference to these human necessities.

Like Roth and Stein, Kinsella interweaves fact and fiction, this time less to promote uncertainty or to demonstrate the paradoxical nature of reality than to present reality as something that occurs in layers. Author W. P. Kinsella creates narrator and character Ray Kinsella and his brother Richard, who are also minor characters in the fiction of J. D. Salinger, who is both a real person and a character in *Shoeless Joe*. Minor character Archie "Moonlight" Graham is also drawn from the major league record book, though presumably his "biography" is imagined. The levels of reality, then, are several. Character Salinger seems somehow "realer" than character, Ray Kinsella, exists at the same level of reality as character Salinger. Moreover, novelist Kinsella is realer than character Salinger; novelist Salinger is realer than character Kinsella; and novelists Kinsella and Salinger share the same level of reality—or they would if novelist Salinger were not such a mysterious recluse. Baseball, because it is something that they all share, dream about, and love, synthesizes these levels of reality and serves as the medium through which they exist harmoniously and coherently. In this respect, it functions very much like myth.

Moreover, this synthesis occurs in the setting of an enchanted ballpark: only true believers can see the game. Kinsella has created a sort of magical realism because readers have the choice to accept or reject the existence of the phantom ballplayers (that is, we respond to them either as fictional creations on a par with Ray and character Salinger, or less real than Ray and character Salinger). Because some characters can see the phantoms and others cannot, our willingness to accept the phantoms at the same level of reality as the other characters is predicated on a matter of faith. We are probably prejudiced by our greater liking for the believers than the nonbelievers, but that prejudice is balanced by our Western tendency to disbelieve in phantoms. The power of secular faith is a crucial issue in the novel, extending from Annie's faith in her husband, Ray, to Ray's faith in the magic of the ballpark, to Salinger's faith in the entire experience. Their secular faith is challenged by the hard-nosed, scientific materialism of Ray's brother-in-law. Ultimately in this book, believers prevail and nonbelievers do not. By leaving open the question of the phantoms' reality, Kinsella extends the opportunity for experiencing faith to the readers themselves. In so doing, he elevates the novel from mere fairy tale to something more. We cannot ascertain the truth of the phantom players' existence; consequently, our belief in them requires a leap of faith. This requirement places Kinsella in a league with Flannery O'Connor and Isaac Singer. All three insist on faith over attempts for empirical certainty as the way to survive in a hostile and uncertain world.

Robert Coover, like Kinsella, creates a multi-layered reality, one marked by uncertainty. Coover invented J. Henry Waugh, an accountant fascinated with statistics, probabilities, and record-keeping, who in turn invented the players in the Universal Baseball Association. Unless, as some of my students have suggested, the players, in need of a god, created Henry: "I don't know if there's a record-keeper up there or not, Pauch. But even if there weren't, I think we'd have to play the game as though there were" (239). In either case, by the book's conclusion Henry has disappeared; he is either dead or crazy. Only the ballplayers remain, acting out their same rituals, but wondering what they mean.

Essentially, Coover plays out the history of the Western world through baseball, and does so in language that captures the fan's enthusiasm for the sport. Like Roth, he questions the knowability of history; moreover, he uses the baseball vehicle to ask the big existential questions: why are we here? What does it all mean? Is there a God; if so, is He crazy? In passing, Coover also takes a stand against mechanized, sterile, corporate America. Skyscrapers are penis-prisons; buses exhale people; elevators are the urethra of Henry's world prison. And the "real" world of Henry's employment, the firm of Dunkelmann, Zauber & Zifferblatt, is certainly less appealing than the world of the UBA, even if the latter takes over Henry's sanity.

Much of *The Universal Baseball Association* is concerned with how we describe and record reality/history. Henry, for example, retains detailed statistics of each game, but he also makes entries in The Book:

> Into the Book went the UBA, everything from statistics to journalistic dispatches, from seasonal analyses to general baseball theory. Everything, in short, worth keeping. Style varied from the extreme economy of factual data to the overblown idiom of the sportswriter, from the scientific objectivity of the theoreticians to the literary speculations of essayists and anecdotalists. . . . His own moods, often affected by events in the league, also colored the reports. . . . (55-56)

The Book, then, represents both the importance of hard facts and statistics for retaining the past and the inadequacy of such objective, hard data to perform this task alone. The subjective material is also necessary. Elsewhere, Coover goes further by challenging our instinctive notion that history exists as a fixed entity, unalterable by subsequent events. "You know," says Henry, "you can take history or leave it, but if you take it you have to accept certain assumptions or ground rules about what's left in and what's left out" (49). And Henry observes, as only a postmodernist might, that pitcher-hero Damon Rutherford, through his act of perfection, "was not only creating the future, he was doing something to the past, too" (22). It is Damon's extraordinary accomplishments that induce Henry, and then the players in the league, to review the contributions of Damon's father, Brock, and to begin thinking of his playing days as the Brock Rutherford Era. Prior to the achievements of the son, the father had not emerged as a symbol for his generation. While most of the league comes to accept this historical revision, one cynical manager, Rag Rooney, demurs. "He saw those news guys writing it all down, eyes crossing over their own noses, and saw them for what they were—a pack of goddamn leeches, inventing time and place, scared

shitless by the way things really were. History my god. An incurable diarrhea of dead immortals" (82). Elsewhere, Rooney invokes the Crock Rubberturd Era.

The enigmatic nature of the book's last chapter reflects the fluid and enigmatic nature of history itself. Coover shows us how, over time, the struggle between Damon and his killer, Jock Casey, becomes interpreted, reinterpreted, revised, reversed, and ultimately elevated from the realm of historical event to myth. Because this struggle parallels that between another J. C. and a demon from our own mythology, Coover compels us to extrapolate this tale into our own situation. Moreover, he does it with a twist because Damon, who shares both Dionysiac and Christlike qualities, is the hero, whereas Jock Casey is the villain. Coover compels us to wonder if it is possible that our own chroniclers might over time have reversed the roles of Christ and Satan, much as the Caseyites reversed the roles of Damon and Jock, making Casey the true hero.

The entire last chapter depicts frustrated attempts to understand history. Is there a pattern and meaning in the events that followed Casey's death, or are they entirely independent? This question is nothing less than an inquiry into causation, something appropriate to a world in which God plays dice with our fates. We learn that the UBA has undergone a number of socio-political transformations since the great contest, from the Bogglers to the Legalists to the Guildsmen and, finally, to the Universalists, and we are invited to think analogously of human society's own progression of social and governmental structures. Yet, in trying to understand where they are by investigating where they have been, the players discover that they "can't even be sure about the simple *facts*. Some writers even argue that Rutherford and Casey never existed—nothing more than another of the ancient myths of the sun, symbolized as a victim of slaughter by the monster or force of darkness. History: in the end, you can never prove a thing" (223-224).

Yet, despite this promulgation of uncertainty, Coover ends on a note of acceptance and affirmation. Hardy Ingram has been chosen to enact the role of Damon in the league's annual mystery rite. The ritual is indeed a mystery, as no one knows for sure whether the human sacrifice will be real or symbolic. This uncertainty understandably troubles Hardy, but it upsets his friend and battery mate, Paul Trench, even more. As Paul hands Hardy the ball to begin the ritual game, Hardy, now also Damon, sees his pal's anxiety:

> Damon sees, *must see,* because astonishingly he says: "Hey, wait, buddy! You *love* this game, don't you?"
>
> "Sure, but . . ."
>
> Damon grins. Lights up the whole goddamn world. "Then don't be afraid . . ." he says.
>
> And the black clouds break up, and dew springs again to the green grass, and the stands hang on,

and his own [Paul's] oppressed heart leaps alive to give it one last try.

And he doesn't know anymore whether he's a Damonite or a Caseyite, or something else again . . . it's all irrelevant, it doesn't even matter that he's going to die, all that counts is that he is *here* and here's The Man and here's the boys and there's the crowd, the sun, the noise.

"It's not a trial," says Damon. . . . "It's not even a lesson. It's just what it is." (242)

Perhaps, philosophically, this response to an uncertain and absurd universe differs little from traditional existentialism. Camus's Sisyphus, after all, comes to love his rock. Yet, there are some important differences, differences that typically separate postmodern absurdism from existentialism. First, postmodernists are relativists, who insist upon the subjective and fluid nature of reality, whereas existentialists seem to be more absolutist. For the existentialists, the universe may have no implicit meaning, but generally it is a fixed entity, not especially dependent on the nature of the observer. Second, most existentialist fiction projects a tone of high seriousness, whereas postmodern writers, such as Barth, Pynchon, Roth, Vonnegut, Marquez, Stoppard, and even filmmakers like Fellini, create a mood of playfulness. It may be true that the universe is uncertain, with no inherent meaning, but that belief no longer represents a new discovery, and no longer is it necessarily a cause for despair. In fact, our absurd and uncertain condition might just as easily occasion celebration.

Thus, it is no accident that Coover chooses to write about a game. Games, like baseball, or even Henry's dice game, are fun; they can be exhilarating; they can bring out our warmest human feelings; and, like a postmodernist's view of life, they have no implicit meaning that extends beyond themselves. Coover communicates this playfulness extremely well, and in so doing lends vigor to the reading experience. As in *The Great American Novel,* and in the works of such black humorists as Joseph Heller, Lenny Bruce, Bruce Jay Friedman, John Barth, and Thomas Pynchon, the vitality Coover's readers derive from the reading experience *is* the ultimate response to and antidote for an absurd universe. The very process by which Coover establishes uncertainty and our inability to know truth is the same process by which he generates vitality; and that is his great success.

A more complete analysis of the books in this discussion would address their superb use of language to transmit the energy of baseball, as well as to merge the levels of reality within the books.[6] It would also discuss the issue of perfection, the significance of naming things, the sexual energy in the books and in the game, and the balance between power and control. In this discussion, however, it is sufficient for us to recognize that by choosing baseball as their topic, the authors were able to tap the resources of mythology and the energy and playfulness of a game to establish the subjectivity of truth and the uncertainty of reality, as well as to provide a mechanism for dealing with those circumstances.

NOTES

[1] Heisenberg's Uncertainty Principle (sometimes called Indeterminacy Principle) shows that as our knowledge of a subatomic particle's velocity becomes more complete, our knowledge of its location diminishes: we cannot know both simultaneously. This directly contradicts the boast of the nineteenth-century scientist Laplace, who bragged that if he could know the velocity and location of every molecule at any given instant, he could, in principle, calculate every past and future physical event. Of course, Laplace acknowledged that only God could retain such a vast amount of data, but this was the limit to which humans might aspire. The Uncertainty Principle undermines the highly mechanistic, deterministic world view that Laplace describes and that had been in place since Newton. In the 1930s mathematician Goedel demonstrated that all logical systems are necessarily either complete and inconsistent or consistent and incomplete. This represents another limitation on human knowledge.

[2] For further discussion of the reorientation in postmodernism see John Barth.

[3] For a more complete discussion of the Grail legend in *The Natural* see Earl R. Wasserman.

[4] For an excellent discussion of the role baseball played for at least some who grew up in the 1950s, see Howard Senzel.

[5] One reason that activists like Jerry Rubin and Abbie Hoffman were successful in limiting HUAC's effectiveness was that they responded to the investigation like the theater it was, instead of treating it seriously, as did liberals and leftists in the 1950s. By appearing before the committee wearing Revolutionary War outfits, and by otherwise poking fun at the committee, they robbed HUAC of its credibility. Of course, there were other factors too: the mood of the country was different in the Sixties than in the Fifties, but the Yippies' performance was a postmodernist's dream, a scene from Pynchon or Coover being played out in the Capitol.

[6] For instance in *The Universal Baseball Association,* Coover merges two levels of reality. "The dice rattled in Henry's fist, tumbled out on the kitchen table: *Crack!* hard grounder. Craft jumped on it this time, whipped the ball to second, one out" (70). Here, the word "crack" describes both the sound of the dice hitting the table (Henry's level) and the sound of the bat hitting the ball (the players' level). Coover uses this technique elsewhere, most notably when Henry and Brock deter Damon's teammates from killing Casey (76-77).

WORKS CITED

Barth, John. "The Literature of Exhaustion." *Atlantic* Aug. 1967: 29-34.

———. "The Literature of Replenishment." *Atlantic* Jan. 1980: 65-71.

Coover, Robert. *The Universal Baseball Association, Inc.* New York: NAL, 1968.

Hansen, Arlen J. "The Dice of God: Einstein, Heisenberg, and Robert Coover." *Novel* 10 (1976): 49-59.

Kinsella, W. P. *Shoeless Joe.* New York: Ballentine, 1982.

Malamud, Bernard. *The Natural.* New York: Avon, 1952.

Roth, Philip. *The Great American Novel.* New York: Farrar, 1973.

Senzel, Howard. *Baseball and the Cold War.* New York: Harcourt, 1977.

Stein, Harry. *Hoopla.* New York: Knopf, 1983.

Wasserman, Earl R. "*The Natural:* Malamud's World Ceres." *The Centennial Review of Arts and Science* 9 (1965): 438-460.

Christian K. Messenger

SOURCE: "Expansion Draft: Baseball Fiction of the 1980s," in *The Achievement of American Sports Literature: A Critical Appraisal,* edited by Wiley Lee Umphlett, Bucknell University Press, 1991, pp. 62-79.

[*In the following essay, Messenger surveys recent baseball fiction, contending that "the game as a cultural form with referential and aesthetic properties is solidly historical as well as endlessly allusive."*]

More than thirty adult baseball novels have been published since 1980. Such a prolific output comes after the transitional baseball novels of Jay Neugeboren, Jerome Charyn, and others with their links to the flowering of serious baseball fiction since the 1950s in the work of Mark Harris, Bernard Malamud, Philip Roth, and Robert Coover.[1] Here is an unprecedented sports-fiction expansion that brings with it the problems, perhaps only metaphorical, of any sports expansion—a thinning of talent, some ragged games, retread veterans, callow rookies, careers open to talent, a few major surprises, and realignment of the competition.[2] All this expanded activity is more tentatively played out against and in the shadow of the influence of past heroes (novelists) and teams (their works).

The baseball fiction of Harris, Malamud, Roth, and Coover had been informed by these authors' sense of baseball's aesthetic properties and by baseball's resultant bonding with literature. Each of their novels had been very different in intention and style. The fact that baseball could serve so many varied authorial purposes—comic realism, myth, satire, self-reflexive fiction—suggests that the game as a cultural form with referential and aesthetic properties is solidly historical as well as endlessly allusive.

Baseball's deep historical structures relate strongly to its sense of cultural differences. The preoccupation with journeying, returning home, and plumbing national origins is written into baseball's master narrative, one assimilated by players, fans, and readers in endless repetition. The specific historical contextualizations of this narrative are diverse but may be summarized in two large patterns. They are baseball's "Legend of the Fall," as particularized in the Black Sox scandal of 1919 and its resultant banishments and exile, and the exclusion of blacks from major league baseball before 1947. These exiles and exclusions have fostered an entire counterhistory of baseball that has limned America's hypocrisies and prejudices.

Neugeboren's *Sam's Legacy* and Charyn's *The Seventh Babe* contain by far the most imaginative studies of blacks, exiles, and baseball history. The novels do not treat the baseball subject in chronicle or sentiment but rather construct a dialectic in which whiteness and blackness are both damnation and salvation. Both novels have imagined Negro League histories at their center that define their protagonists' dilemma. *The Seventh Babe* ends, as does *Sam's Legacy,* with a baseball reconciliation, bridging decades and recalling teammates to life. Like Neugeboren, Charyn also has taken the suggestive pose of outlawry and exile and made it meaningful in individual historical terms. The history of black exclusion in baseball taps veins of psychodrama (Neugeboren) and inventive mythologizing (Charyn) to provide two of the most satisfying endings in baseball fiction.

The Black Sox remain the primal cautionary tale of American sports' ensnarement by money and greed. Here all the abuses of the economics of sport are in evidence. Baseball since 1919 has regarded itself as an innocent game above all compromising scandal. Yet its fiction writers know how to work its dialectical opposite of experience and rueful knowledge. If innocence is the official baseball myth, then experience is the bitter legacy in baseball fiction. Homelessness (the baseball equivalent is being left on base) is extended to permanent banishment, wandering, and severance, so clearly present in Malamud, Roth, Charyn, and W. P. Kinsella. From being footnotes to history, players slip beneath baseball's official history. Or they wander in shadow leagues so far below the major leagues as to be invisible. This slippage below baseball history frees authors to create mirror baseball worlds that may be parodic, grotesque, or lyrical.

The Black Sox scandal was early utilized by F. Scott Fitzgerald in a famous scene in *The Great Gatsby* where Gatsby proudly points out Meyer Wolfsheim to Nick Carraway as "the man who fixed the World Series in 1919." Though potentially a symbolic center to fictional baseball representation, the Black Sox scandal itself was not addressed in its specific historical moment again until quite recently. Three novels Harry Stein's *Hoopla* (1983), Kinsella's *Shoeless Joe* (1982), and Eric Rolfe Greenberg's *The Celebrant* (1983)—pick up the subject in different ways. Stein is a Lardnerian, Kinsella, a magician after Malamud, while Greenberg writes a legitimate historical baseball novel. *Hoopla* is alternately narrated by a fictional sportswriter, Luther Pond, and by Buck Weaver, the Black Sox third baseman banned for life in 1920. Although Pond is a potential Lardner and Buck Weaver reads *You Know Me Al* and even sounds like a tepid echo of Jack Keefe, Stein's prose never really comes alive. There are set scenes where Pond interacts with historical icons such as John L. Sullivan, Ty Cobb, and William Randolph Hearst, but the novel, while earnest and historically correct, is more of a history designed to flesh out dramatically the life and times of an early twentieth-century sports culture. It is potentially a novel such as E. L. Doctorow's *Ragtime* (1975) in its conception but not in metaphor or execution.

Stein's Shoeless Joe Jackson is illiterate, cantankerous, and dull. In *Shoeless Joe,* Kinsella's Jackson is a dignified shade, as are his teammates, the men for whom Ray Kinsella builds a diamond on his Iowa farm to redeem them from their wandering and give them a place to play. Kinsella does not judge or question the ghostly crew and is satisfied merely to have them there. Neither *Hoopla* nor *Shoeless Joe* is ideologically aware, Stein being more a transmitter of history than a transformer and Kinsella, a baseball mystic of high sentiment. Thus two of the specific addresses to the Black Sox in recent fiction are somewhat thin.

Greenberg's *The Celebrant* is a historical novel that recreates baseball's first two decades of this century, climaxing with the 1919 World Series and Black Sox scandal. *The Celebrant* is narrated by Jackie Kapp, third son of a Jewish family of jewelers in New York City, whose life and work cross the path of New York Giant pitcher Christy Mathewson from 1901 to 1919. Until the scandal in 1919, each section of the book is built around a pivotal big-game moment in Mathewson's career (1901, 1905, 1908, 1912) that defines his greatness for Kapp and that allows Greenberg, like Stein, to describe early modern sports culture, its mores and habitues. The structure of baseball history punctuates Jackie Kapp's narrative and moves it along. In designing jewelry to commemorate events and ceremony, Kapp practices an art that provides Mathewson with keepsake gems while he himself idolizes the pitcher in reserved appreciation. Potentially about a vital, growing immigrant culture and the Giants under the brawling John McGraw, *The Celebrant* nonetheless takes its tone from Greenberg's vision of the refined, college-educated Mathewson and

Jackie Kapp's appropriately dignified response. Almost against its will, *The Celebrant* becomes a sort of school sports novel about an "amateur" hero of great reserve and stature and his worshipful witness. Mathewson quotes Alexander Pope in describing McGraw to Kapp, and speaks in a mannered fashion as in, "You have an aversion to the man, don't you? I sensed it at my apartment" (Greenberg, 90).

Through the Black Sox debacle in 1919, Greenberg is determined to expand Mathewson into a full-fledged Christ figure, but Mathewson comes unhinged at his realization of Black Sox perfidy and shifts from his reserve into a manic keening for his sport. He curses its defilers:

> "I do damn them," he said. "With a mark I damn them. I damn Cicotte. I damn Jackson. I damn Risberg and Gandil and Williams. And if there be others I will damn them as well, I will root them out and damn them for eternity. And I damn the filth that corrupted them, the dicers and the high rollers. They will pay. They will pay in time. I shall not rouse them now, for I will allow them their full portion of loss, and when the corrupters are counting their gains I shall spring upon them and drive them from the temple!" (262)

Here is an Old Testament prophecy wedded to baseball's Fall. Some middle style of energy and wit between the intensity of Mathewson's final mad scene and the genteel representation of Jackie Kapp and his classical pitcher-hero might have allowed Greenberg to succeed more fully in establishing Mathewson as the wounded historical body of American baseball. Nonetheless, for sheer theatrics, *The Celebrant*'s climax will be hard for future baseball fiction to beat.

Along with ballplayers banned or excluded because of crimes, other players in baseball fiction choose to dehistoricize themselves in willed exile. Donald Hays's narrator, Hog Durham, in *The Dixie Association* (1984) drops back in. He is an ex-convict released to play for the Arkansas Reds, a lively but disaffiliated minor league team of stoic Indians, exiled Cubans, and young blacks. Their manager is a one-armed, ex-major leaguer of Communist sympathies who runs a food co-op for the poor and who between innings leaflets the stands with manifestos. The Reds battle a regressive, racist team from Selma, Alabama, display great solidarity, and give positive meaning to the concept "collective." *The Dixie Association* is baseball fiction's ideological counterpart to James Whitehead's *Joiner* (1971) in football fiction.

The majority of baseball novels still take place in the mode of "baseball as education," one solidly established by Mark Harris in his Henry Wiggen novels. Here is where a series of mostly orderly transactions between the individual sports hero and the collective takes place, one in which the protagonist "adjusts to" or "rebels against" this or that social or economic power that the team may represent. Such traditional novels are extant in all periods up to the present.

A very orderly passage is contained in John Hough, Jr.'s *The Conduct of the Game* (1986), which has an umpire as the improbable protagonist. Young Lee Malcolm works his way up to a major league assignment and along the way learns judgment and tolerance, the tools of his trade, as well as the human foibles and weaknesses that skew "conduct." He loses a bad old girlfriend, wins a loyal new one, confronts a black superstar, and defends a gay umpire, Roy Van Arsdale, against prejudice and exposure. When Van Arsdale commits suicide, Lee Malcolm calls his own game on account of the hypocrisy of the baseball establishment and walks away from sports. A quiet maturation novel of personal baseball history is Don J. Snyder's *Veteran's Park* (1987), in which promising pitcher Brad Schaffer spends a minor league summer in Maine learning his craft and deepening his emotional range. All the verities of baseball's geography and history are present: small towns, farms, a good woman, children, staunch old timers. *Veteran's Park* is Kinsella without the hocus-pocus and a good generic example of current neorealistic fictional expression. Actually, the best recent narrative of baseball is Ron Shelton's film *Bull Durham* (1988), a sensual, knowing account of a Lardnerian bumpkin-pitcher, "Nuke" Laloosh (Tim Robbins), and the proud veteran minor league catcher, Crash Davis (Kevin Costner), who teaches him the game. They in turn compete for and are sustained by the captivating "baseball Annie" (Susan Sarandon), who loves them toward their respective triumphs ("Nuke's" call to the major leagues, Crash's resignation to his own accomplishments and baseball future, perhaps with his Annie). *Bull Durham* is ahistorical, with a benign view of organized baseball, and is antithetical to both myth and fantasy.

In the postmodern era, baseball novels still partake deeply from the sense of baseball as education, and extend the legacy of fantasy and myth that Malamud and Roth provided. Veteran literati step up to the plate with wit and style. Roger Kahn turns his considerable sportswriting talents to fiction in the sentimental *The Seventh Game* (1982). George Plimpton's *The Curious Case of Sidd Finch* (1987) is about a New York Met rookie pitcher with a 160-mph fastball, who also is an Eastern mystic. Wilfred Sheed's *The Boys of Winter* (1987) is a wicked comedy of manners about a group of very competitive writers and artists whose summer softball team on Long Island affords them all sorts of plots, both literary and otherwise. Also, current authors on the baseball fiction beat have looked to Coover's baseball treatise (*The Universal Baseball Association*) as ultimate (universal) guide and influence in the sense that he stipulated the making of universes as a proper inquiry and subject matter for fictions of baseball. Be that as it may, with such expert players in the baseball fiction hall of fame, current authors, instilled with the same diamond religion of restoration and search for origins, appear somewhat derivative at this juncture. Steve Kluger's *Changing Pitches* (1984) is a shallow tale of a veteran left-handed pitcher's infatuation with his catcher that strives to be utterly contemporary. The

novel's resolution comes when the pitcher learns that the catcher is really in love with a pro football quarterback. Harris's Henry Wiggen and Bruce Pearson would blush—and then be bored. David Carkeet's *The Greatest Slump of All Time* (1984) has solid baseball action and strives for Coover's metaphysics but has too many interchangeably depressed characters who are articulate without a Damonsday to vivify them.

The baseball history of the Yankees and Dodgers in the 1940s and 1950s has provided the nostalgic material for three recent novels. Two of these novels, Gary Morgenstein's *The Man Who Wanted to Play Centerfield for the Yankees* (1983) and David Ritz's *The Man Who Brought the Dodgers Back to Brooklyn* (1981), are fictional extensions of the current baseball "fantasy camps" where adult males live out their childhood baseball dreams. Morgenstein's Danny Neuman, in early midlife crisis, chases his goal of playing centerfield for the Yankees to the dismay of his wife and others. When the current Yankees call him up from the low minors at the climax of an improbable promotional campaign, he hits a home run in his only at bat and then abruptly and rather pompously walks right out of Yankee Stadium and baseball. The reader is not so fortunate in Ritz's novel, in which a Brooklyn kid from the 1940s, now a Los Angeles tycoon in the 1980s, buys the Dodgers and installs his boyhood pal as manager. They build an exact replica of Ebbets Field and move the team back to Brooklyn. It is a delightful idea (to this lifelong Dodger fan), but Ritz's characters are wooden, his nostalgia unfocused and poorly evoked.

Robert Mayer's *The Grace of Shortstops* (1984) is, however, quite successful in entwining baseball history with the education of his fourth-grade protagonist, Pee Wee Brunig, a Bronx boy who idolizes the 1947 Dodgers and grows in different ways during the season. Mayer utilizes real baseball events—Jackie Robinson's first game, the first regularly televised baseball games, the heartstopping Dodger-Yankee World Series of 1947—to punctuate Pee Wee's growing consciousness of winning, losing, and adult weaknesses as well as adult responsibilities. Pee Wee's idol is Pee Wee Reese, and the boy wants to learn "the way a shortstop becomes what he was" (85). Mayer's adults lead lives of compromise and complexity. Pee Wee's father, a rabbi, worries about his position and debates whether to become involved in running guns to the Hagannah in Palestine. At novel's end, Pee Wee has helped save a tiny neighborhood girl through considerable courage, but as the Dodgers lose the World Series, he must try to summon the "grace" to understand and forgive his mother, whom he has accidentally found out to have been deeply in love with his best friend's father. Such a knowledge of error and loss (the Dodgers', his own) weighs heavily on the young boy at the novel's open-ended conclusion. Where Morgenstein and Ritz use a baseball childhood as stagnant nostalgia, Mayer depicts baseball's seasonal history to be dynamic as it moves ahead with personal history. *The Grace of Shortstops* is about growth, feeling different toward baseball and self, and playing toward the future rather than recovering the past.

In James McManus's *Chin Music* (1985), the narrative journey is a literal coming home of father and son under the grimmest and most moving of circumstances. Ray Zajak, an ace lefthander for the Chicago White Sox, awakens from a coma after being beaned in a World Series game. It is the last morning of earth: nuclear missiles have been launched and Chicago's death sentence can be measured in minutes. Zajak is an amnesiac, but "he assumes without question that he's got some sort of family out there, waiting for him to come home" (McManus, 15). Zajak himself, without memory but with good intentions, has become the awful buzz of apocalypse. He weaves home through a nightmare city, while his son plays a pick-up baseball game at school, falls in love with a girl on the other team, and then moves toward home himself. McManus acknowledges the beanball ("an enormous white blur, eclipsing your view of all else," 143) as baseball's individual analogy to nuclear explosion. However, he is equally interested in baseball's structural rhythms of coming home and fathers and sons who counter death and destruction. Working from the starkest of fictional premises, McManus uses baseball's deep thematics with sentiment and grace.

Two of the most prominent recent baseball novels, Kinsella's *Shoeless Joe* (1982) and *The Iowa Baseball Confederacy* (1986), suffer from what Fredric Jameson has discerned in postmodernism, "a new depthlessness," "a whole new culture of the image or simulacrum."[3] As an heir of Mark Harris, Kinsella weaves tales that are sincere and educative with no complicated plot or thematic devices. He is reverent toward baseball itself: there is no higher ground or authority, no questioning of history, no shaking of fists at the cosmos, no formal subversion into fragments. His novels are static and vivid at the same time. Joe Jackson and his Black Sox mates will patrol Kinsella's farm diamond in *Shoeless Joe* for as long as he can summon them in mind and spirit. Kinsella is all affect and attempts to speak of what endures in baseball, and ends with thin images of players as ghostly copies of historical figures, shades of shades, who fittingly take J. D. Salinger off with them into a sort of baseball twilight zone.

The Iowa Baseball Confederacy strives toward even greater magic and fantastic effects than *Shoeless Joe*. *The IBC* seems both extensively copied and overly magical. The Confederacy is a regional league that might have existed from 1902 to 1908 and is lodged initially only in the minds of father and son, Matthew and Gideon Clarke, who want to keep its memory alive. The IBC itself thus becomes a cross between Roth's Patriot League (*The Great American Novel*) and Coover's UBA. In addition, there are magical events—young lovers at carnivals struck by lightning (Hobbs and Wonderboy, Harriet Bird of *The Natural*), "back to the future" time travel, a fifteen-foot Indian named Drifting Away who is in touch with tribal ancestors who may or may not be in control of all temporality. A movable Black Angel stone monument from an Iowa City cemetery ends up playing right field. Leonardo Da Vinci arrives in a balloon to announce he invented baseball in 1506. There is even a biblical flood. Kinsella tries hard to unfold all events through his baseball frame. A desperate man blows himself up on a baseball field; an isolated old pitcher builds a fence exactly 60' 6" around himself; Matthew Clarke is killed by a line drive. Many characters are notable baseball aestheticians, including the cosmic Indian. There are "cracks in time"; opinions that "life is full of evil jokes" (95); powers that float "suspended in the silk and satin of the darkness" (103).

The center of the novel is a 2,648-inning game that begins on July 4, 1908, between the Chicago Cubs and the IBC All-Stars and that goes on too long in every sense. Kinsella is unsure of what he wants to do with this creation, and the reader sees little of the field action. In about the 1,000th inning, when Gideon Clarke says "I want to see more of this special magic" (220), he may be the only one. Kinsella has run out of magic by this juncture. He is confident that baseball has wondrous associations for the reader, but his own conceptualizations are not tied to larger myth patterns or to any ideology in his baseball historicizing or to substantive issues in the creation of fiction. With the richness of the 1908 season at hand (versus Greenberg's *The Celebrant,* for instance), Kinsella chooses to trick up a history of his own that pays remarkably little attention to the real ballplayers. Nor does Kinsella take a significant interest in creating fictional baseball players, preferring to control the narrative from the standpoint of a magic spectator-historian. It is no mistake, however, that two imagined baseball players are exceptions: Johnny Baron, a boy in the IBC in 1908 and an old man in 1978 in the novel's present, and Stan Rogalski, a 1970s career minor leaguer hurled back into sudden stardom in the IBC-Cubs marathon in 1908, are Kinsella's most winning pair of baseball characters. Kinsella is at his best when he gives his fictional game over to his players, as in *Shoeless Joe,* where Moonlight Graham, Kid Scissons, and Ray Kinsella's father are more interesting than the Black Sox shades and Kinsella's presumptions with "Jerry" Salinger. All the sweetness and solemnity of Matthew and Gideon Clarke's (and Kinsella's) love of baseball cannot compensate for the randomness of the special effects and the absence of much coherence to the general baseball metaphysics in *The IBC*.

Tony Ardizzone's *Heart of the Order* (1986) is a baseball novel of education clothed in magic raiment but glib and preachy in and around its fantasizing. The unpleasantly self-possessed first-person narrator, Daniel Bacigalupo, is a third baseman of considerable promise who as a youngster kills a playmate with a line drive and from then on must deal with enormous guilt that determines his relations with family, peers, and girls. He imagines that the dead boy, Mickey Meenan, comes back to life inside him and becomes an alternate source of control. This ventriloquist act makes the reader a bit queasy, though actually Mickey is a somewhat harmless cut-up. Ardizzone plays for reader sympathy, but his hero is such an egotist that little in his passage appears moving or sincere. Danny's first major league at bat results in a near re-creation of Mickey's death, Mickey perhaps travels to another body, a magical son is found in the bullrushes for Danny, Mickey's father becomes an improbable avenger, and Danny is almost killed. The last page redresses much of the overbearing narrator's line, but Ardizzone has waited too long.

Baseball novels by women have become a flourishing subgenre in recent sports fiction. Women's baseball fiction centers on the mode of cooperation, of interaction and support among teammates. Baseball appears to be the team sport most congenial to women athletes, with its lack of aggressive physical contact and premium on attributes other than size and strength. Competition and heroic striving are present in the fiction but are integrated with the team's other potentials: nurture, family, growth.

The histories involved in this fiction are personal histories. Barbara Gregorich's *She's on First* (1987) takes female participation in baseball to its extreme: "the first woman to play in the major leagues." Gregorich writes very seriously of her heroine, Linda Sunshine, a talented shortstop who is shocked to learn that she is the daughter of her major league team owner and of a great female player from the Women's All-American League of the 1940s. Gregorich isolates her heroine in competition with men against men and thus creates the most excessive male reactions. The "first woman to . . ." paradigm prevents Linda from the affiliative team experience. One suspects that Gregorich's real imaginative task would be to re-create the historical fact of the Women's All-American League in all its relations, but that team history makes only a cameo appearance to help explain the blood lines for her pioneer who is still in thrall to Daddy—progenitor and "owner."

Softball is a thriving team sport for women and the sport of choice in Sara Vogan's *In Shelly's Leg* (1981) and Ellen Cooney's *All the Way Home* (1984). Vogan's team plays fast-pitch softball, and Cooney's team plays slow-pitch. The choices say much about the novels' respective viewpoints. Vogan writes a more intense romantic narrative about a pitcher and catcher on a state championship team who are vying for the same man. The novel is set against a Montana backdrop of open vistas, sentiment, and personal nostalgia. Cooney's women are suburban housewives and mothers who have never played organized ball or competed for anything until they are brought together in a common effort where they slowly learn to exercise their muscles and capabilities. In both *In Shelly's Leg* and *All the Way Home* the female players come to know each other through their sport and its lessons. Baseball as an education is invoked yet again in a new context.

Shelly's Leg is the name of the bar that sponsors the women's softball team. Vogan's heroines Margaret (pitcher) and Rita (catcher) are very different personalities. Margaret is a transplanted easterner; she is all pattern and definition, desiring stability and control after a failed first marriage and two children. Rita is more of a free spirit from a bad childhood on an Indian reservation; she has little plan to her instinctive affiliations, except to keep struggling. Woody, the object of their affections, is a classic western dreamer who wants to go on the road and try for a country-and-western singing career. Woody wants Margaret to go with him; she hesitates and Rita presents herself as an alternative. The softball season for the Shelly's Leg team proceeds along with this central drama.

Vogan does an excellent job of adapting baseball's field aesthetics to the lives and reactions of her central characters without ever forcing the comparisons. Margaret is the star pitcher: she always wants the ball and will never come out of the game. In effect, by her temperament and choices, she "pitches" Woody to Rita, who "catches" him. Yet Vogan gives the women a complex relation to each other with regard to their feelings of cooperation (on the field) and competition (for Woody). Vogan's baseball voices are authentic. She writes a fine scene of Margaret and Rita alone on a ball field at dusk after another Shelly's Leg victory. Margaret's children are off playing in the distance. The pitcher and catcher have it out. Rita takes the initiative and walks with Margaret off the mound toward the plate:

> "Get down here," Rita said. She crouched behind the plate, her knees splayed as if waiting for the pitch. "Things look different from down here."
>
> Margaret knelt next to Rita, looking out at her children on the pitcher's mound and across the still field. From this angle the field looked more rolling, not as flat as Margaret had always assumed. She saw hollows accentuated by the dusk light, rises that looked as if they would lead off into the trees. (200)

Vogan has used the subjective perspectives formed by positions on the diamond to present her characters in relation to each other. To Margaret, choices are flat and either-or; to Rita, from where "things look different," there are "hollows" and "rises," open-ended choices. Vogan does not take sides: both women argue their field of vision. Rita says, "It's being in the prime of life that's so hard for a woman. You don't know whether to lead or be led" (200). They begin to walk the diamond in the dark. To Margaret, "it seemed . . . that women never had anywhere to go and men surely and always did" (203). She resents Woody and Rita as well, who tells her, "You're just starting to make a home here, in a town that *is* my home. We'll know each other long after Woody's made his first million or gone belly-up for the fiftieth time" (203-4). The familiar tension in baseball fiction of leaving home and returning is invoked in a female context. Their heated dialogue flares and subsides as they explain selves and each other. Finally, Margaret "felt the pressure of Rita's hands holding her own" (207); they acknowledge that they are both afraid, that they are both doing what they must. Nurture holds an equal place with competition.

Cooney's *All the Way Home* is less evocative. It is really an anatomy of a team whose women of various ages and circumstances hardly have time for romantic flight, are indeed barely coping with children, spouses, and parents. Cooney's book has its dark touches—a battered wife and child, the trauma of a double parental death that follows a woman into adulthood and mothering of her own. Yet there are warmer moments as well—the pride of a husband in a wife's new sports interest and competence; a family's encouragement of a middle-aged mom's attempt to lose weight and acquire softball skills and confidence. The Spurs' team is coached by the intense Gussie Cabrini, a star athlete now home in Currys Crossing, Massachusetts, after failing to stick with a traveling women's softball team in the Southwest. She has been in a horrible motorcycle accident that has left her scarred and with an all-but-useless leg. Yet her power and authority, almost that of the male ritualist, inspires her team to take shape and each woman to do her best; they, in turn, bring Gussie back to life.

Nancy Willard's *Things Invisible to See* (1984) is a fine example of how to wed the lyrical to the prosaic in baseball fiction. Willard's strategy is to invoke God-play from the outset that is nonetheless absolutely historical:

> In Paradise, on the banks of the River of Time, the Lord of the Universe is playing ball with His archangels. Hundreds of spheres rest like white stones on the bottom of the river, and hundreds rise like bubbles from the water and fly to His hand that alone brings things to pass and gives them their true colors. What a show! He tosses a white ball which breaks into a yellow ball which breaks into a red ball, and in the northeast corner of the Sahara Desert the sand shifts and buries eight camels. The two herdsmen escape, and in a small town in southern Michigan Wanda Harkissian goes into labor with twins. She will name them Ben and Willie, but it's Esau and Jacob all over again. (3)

Everything and everyone, not just baseball, is determined by the same cosmic play; no privileges are reserved for narrators such as those of Kinsella and Ardizzone. Baseball resides within Willard's magic power and is part of the novel's original vision. No rhetorical claims about the sport's special magic need be made. Ben and Willie cut deals with God and Death, Ben paralyzes a girl with a battered ball (a variant of the new favored plot device in recent baseball fiction), and the girl, Clare, receives instruction in her powers from a guardian "ancestress."

Woven in and around this magic is an engagingly American Gothic story of families on the homefront in Ann Arbor, Michigan, during early World War II, the grounding from which Willard repeatedly returns to cosmic play (36, 147, 218, 263). Her subject is the battle

between love and death. The cosmic choice-making occurs when a decision of some grave import is made about a character who nonetheless must carry it forward in courage and love within his or her own history. Clare takes the form of a bird to be shot down for food by the sailors as Ben's raft drifts helplessly in the South Pacific (191); later, she steals into Ben's hospital room in Ann Arbor to metaphorically light the lamps of his body anew (251).

The novel's gravest encounter is the final baseball match proposed by Ben to Death (to stave off Ben's own); it is the most portentous "big game" in baseball fiction since that on Coover's Damonsday. Death sets the terms: Ben's boys' team from Ann Arbor, the South Side Rovers, will play the "Dead Knights," Death's squad of baseball immortals, for three innings. If the Rovers win, they will survive the war; if not, Death takes them. If any of the Rovers now scattered all over the world cannot play, they must be replaced by their next of kin. Death and his client, Willie Harkissian, contrive a bus crash that injures the Rovers. They are replaced by their mothers who "look like they all work in a defense plant" (253), perhaps comparable to Cooney's women from *All the Way Home* now entering the lists with their sons' lives in the balance. This inexperienced "team" faces Mathewson, Gehrig, and other great stars and ultimately wins. Death moans, "Do you think Matty had to walk Mrs. Bacco? They want the living to win. Even the umpire wants the living to win. They remember how it was. All the pain, all the trouble—they'd choose it again—they'd go extra innings into infinity for the chance to be alive again" (261). Clare pitches heroically, her ancestress telling her to put "the stuff of being alive" (258) on the ball.

Willard lets the fantasy go on just long enough (3 innings and 10 pages as opposed to Kinsella's 2,648 innings and 249 pages in *The Iowa Baseball Confederacy*). She reunites Clare and Ben after the final ball toss by the Lord of the Universe: "Clare starts running and Ben runs after her as they round the bases, past the living and the dead, heading at top speed for home" (263). Baseball's finest diamond rhythm is invoked yet again. Willard has charmingly enlisted baseball to play through her magic and mothers to play for their sons in a history coextensive with time itself.

Baseball fiction in the 1980s carries forward all the baseball thematics heretofore mentioned. Stein's *Hoopla* has Kinsella's Black Sox, but only as historical replicas with their historical "image" intact. Kinsella, Willard, and Ardizzone believe in magic, whereas Vogan, Cooney, Herrin, Hays, Hough, Snyder, and Shelton write solidly of baseball as education, in the wake of many baseball novelists and narratives. Jameson writes that "we are condemned to seek History by way of our own pop images and simulacra of that history, which itself remains forever out of reach."[4] The mix of characters in some of the most recent baseball fiction suggests just such a recycling of baseball history and popular culture[5]: *Hoopla* (Cobb, Buck Weaver, John L. Sullivan, Jackson);

The Seventh Babe (Ruth, Landis, Dizzy Dean); *Sam's Legacy* (Ruth); *Suder* (pianist Bud Powell); *Shoeless Joe* (Black Sox, Salinger); *Things Invisible to See* (the "Dead Knights"); *The Celebrant* (Mathewson, McGraw, Hal Chase, Black Sox); *The Iowa Baseball Confederacy* (the 1908 Cubs, Frank Luther Mott); and *Ragtime* (McGraw, Charlie Faust). Such "copying" is not necessarily enervating if delivered in inventive form, with *Ragtime* the primary example of a postmodern treatise on replication and copying.[6] Nonetheless, baseball fiction at present needs a less complacent use of magic and history, a stiffening against the national romance with baseball, without losing its memory and pleasure. A cinematic triumph such as *Bull Durham,* bawdy, wise, and sentimental, while respectful of baseball's passages and rhythms, may signal a narrative return to comic realism, the most enduring baseball fictional mode through Lardner and Harris.

Furthermore, some hard edges need to be beveled around the diamond. They are installed in the baseball frame of William Kennedy's *Ironweed* (1983), which squarely addresses the issues of fantasy and sentimentality in a dialogue with personal history. Kennedy creates this dialogue within the action of the novel itself in the responses of its protagonist, the blasted ex-Washington Senators third baseman, Francis Phelan. For heart-stopping grief, *Ironweed*'s fictional presentation of the father-son relation in baseball is unmatched. Francis Phelan had been a wondrous fielder with great hands, but in 1916, as he is diapering his infant son Gerald, he unaccountably drops him on the floor and the baby suffers a broken neck and dies. Francis flees his family in mortal devastation, condemning himself to a guilty flight of wandering and vagrancy. The novel opens in late 1938 with Francis back in Albany on Halloween night where ghosts are rising.

Kennedy balances Francis's reveries, his visions of his past and his victims, with his unsparing and violent presentation of self. Francis has killed two men as well as Gerald. The first was a strike-breaking trolley-car conductor "with a smooth round stone the weight of a baseball" (Kennedy, 25) in 1901, making him a labor hero and precipitating his first flight from Albany and into organized baseball, for which he left every year. His second murder victim is a bum, "Rowdy Dick" Doolan, who challenges him on the road. After this incident, he runs again as he "reconstituted a condition that was as pleasurable to his being as it was natural: the running of bases after the crack of the bat, the running from accusation . . . the running from family, from bondage, from destitution of the spirit . . ." (75). Francis has colloquy with all his dead spirits in *Ironweed,* including a lovely early summoning of the dead Gerald who redeems Francis through prophesying Francis's "final acts of expiation": "then when these final acts are complete, you will stop trying to die because of me" (19). Francis attempts stewardship of his own meager flock of friends, Albany's male and female vagrants.

For Francis Phelan, his shades are haunting, not summoned as in Kinsella or Ardizzone to magic up baseball art. Kennedy finally has it out with fantasy and the pull of the past when Francis, having returned to his home and to wife Annie, tentatively opens an old trunk of baseball memorabilia and imagines the people of his past: "the bleachers were all up, and men were filing silently into them" and "they kept coming: forty-three men, four boys, and two mutts . . ." (176), when suddenly Kennedy shifts from the mode of "summoning" that had informed *Ironweed* since Gerald's stunning appearance. Francis closes his eyes "to retch the vision out of his head" (176-77), and as the light brightens, "with it grew Francis's hatred of all fantasy, all insubstantiality"; "I am sick of your melancholy histories, your sentimental pieties, your goddamned unchanging faces." He exclaims, "You're all dead, and if you ain't, you oughta be," and concludes, "So get your ass gone," for "I'm the one is livin'. I'm the one who puts you on the map" (177).

Within Francis, Kennedy has fought the battle between the pull of the past, the summoning of shades, the grief-filled magic, and the need for the living man to continue out of his paralysis. Kennedy has the power to "put [Francis] on the map" and the power to draw the map. The "livin'" writer chooses as well, in this case a positive agency in Francis Phelan (what other baseball fantasists lack in their dreaminess), to embrace the patterns his own history makes beyond the fantasies and myths he constructs to keep himself imprisoned in the past. Francis Phelan's internal debate between fantasy and history in representation, his private agony and public torment, are everywhere related through the baseball frame both real and imagined. Such antagonists in debate define the two major modes in the creation of baseball fiction at present. Francis learns that he has more left than just his guilt. He lays to rest his friend Rudy and his beloved Helen, takes a few good bat swings at a gang that comes to break up a hobo encampment, then flees to his own home at last. He forages in the old trunk for his warm-up jacket, not for pictures of ghosts, and thinks perhaps of moving his bed into his grandson Danny's room; a hope of a future bond born of Gerald's memory is held out at last. Kennedy ends with "sure hands" himself, in the rhythms of coming home, an exile ended. As son Gerald had hoped in the graveyard, his father Francis has "stop[ped] trying to die," his "fugitive dance" (215) at least in abeyance.

Further reaction against the control of myth and fantasy in baseball fiction is David Small's *Almost Famous* (1982), a decidedly antisentimental novel in which minor league stand-out Ward Sullivan loses his career and lover in an automobile accident at age twenty-one. Though possessed of a Roy Hobbsian urgency and natural talent, he will not have a mythic rebirth. Instead, half-crippled at age thirty-three, he lives past baseball in his personal history with his pride and sense of order, attempting to shut out a reconnection to his family and an emotional life. He buries his father, becomes a father, breaks a young woman's heart, grudgingly learns to admire an artist brother, and deals unsparingly with a mad and inspired mother. Ward Sullivan painfully comes home, not through victory or revelation but through a slow imperfect education of his own failings. He is still learning at novel's end, one in which his extended family plays a pick-up game in the fields on family property in Maine. Ward yells to his brother, "Get back, kid! I'm going to hit this one a country mile," whereupon "the kid turned and bounded like a gazelle toward the dark trees at the edge of the clearing" (Small, 416). Small's final image (similar to Vogan's diamond at dusk in *In Shelly's Leg*) is of Ward's exultation as well as of the inner diamond (clearing) glossed with the "dark trees," the space beyond where life is always unbeknown, to which he must "turn." Small provides a fitting encapsulation of baseball's geometry and outer possibility.

Recent novelists, alert to forms of myth, ritual, and history, are alive to their rich embodiment in baseball. Coover's metaphor of universe-making in *The Universal Baseball Association* casts the widest net for baseball tropes in fiction. The creation of his Association and the playing of its games are seen to be part of the same function, that of the tension among the familiarization of baseball, the aesthetic roughening of the sport by Coover, and the reader's refamiliarization with baseball and fiction. The reader "comes home." Baseball encapsulates such voyages and returns, yet is still firmly represented in the present as material for a living history. As Coover's Hettie Irden says in a different but wholly complimentary sense after a night in bed with Henry Waugh playing the role of Damon Rutherford, "Oh, that's a game, Henry! That's really a *great* old *game*" (Coover, 31).

NOTES

[1] The seminal novels in baseball fiction are Bernard Malamud's *The Natural* (1952); Mark Harris's *The Southpaw* (1953) and *Bang the Drum Slowly* (1956); Robert Coover's *The Universal Baseball Association* (1968); Philip Roth's *The Great American Novel* (1973); Jay Neugeboren's *Sam's Legacy* (1974); and Jerome Charyn's *The Seventh Babe* (1979).

[2] In contrast, during 1971-78, in what might be called the discovery of football as fictional subject, there were about half as many football novels published as there were baseball novels published during 1980-88. Football fiction has slowed to a very few titles in the 1980s.

[3] Fredric Jameson, "Postmodernism, or the Cultural Logic of Late Capitalism," *New Left Review* 147 (July-August 1984): 58.

[4] Ibid., 71.

[5] Mixed-genre baseball novels have begun to appear. In detective and crime fiction, there is Robert B. Parker, *Mortal Stakes* (1975); James Magnuson, *The Rundown* (1977); Gary Pomeranz, *Out at Home* (1985); and R. D. Rosen, *Strike Three, You're Dead* (1985). The thriller is represented by Charles Brady, *Seven Games in October* (1979); and Daniel Keith Cohler, *Gamemaker* (1980).

[6] Jameson, "Postmodernism," 71.

WORKS CITED

Ardizzone, Tony. *Heart of the Order.* New York: Henry Holt, 1986.

Brady, Charles. *Seven Games in October.* New York: Little Brown, 1979.

Carkeet, David. *The Greatest Slump of All Time.* New York: Harper and Row, 1984.

Charyn, Jerome. *The Seventh Babe.* New York: Arbor House, 1979.

Cohler, David Keith. *Gamemaker.* New York: Doubleday, 1980.

Cooney, Ellen. *All the Way Home.* New York: Putnam, 1984.

Coover, Robert. *The Universal Baseball Association, J. Henry Waugh, Prop.* New York: Signet, 1968.

Doctorow, E. L. *Ragtime.* New York: Random House, 1975.

Everett, Percival L. *Suder.* New York: Viking, 1983.

Greenberg, Eric Rolfe. *The Celebrant.* 1983. New York: Penguin, 1986.

Gregorich, Barbara. *She's on First.* New York: Contemporary Books, 1987.

Harris, Mark. *Bang the Drum Slowly.* 1956. New York: Dell, 1973.

———. *The Southpaw.* Indianapolis: Bobbs-Merrill, 1953.

Hays, Donald. *The Dixie Association.* New York: Simon and Schuster, 1984.

Hough, John Jr. *The Conduct of the Game.* New York: Harcourt Brace Jovanovich, 1986.

Kahn, Roger. *The Seventh Game.* New York: New American Library, 1982.

Kennedy, William. *Ironweed.* New York: Penguin, 1984.

Kinsella, W. P. *The Iowa Baseball Confederacy.* New York: Ballantine, 1986.

———. *Shoeless Joe.* Boston: Houghton Mifflin, 1982.

Kluger, Steve. *Changing Pitches.* New York: St. Martin's, 1984.

Lorenz, Tom. *Guys Like Us.* New York: Viking, 1980.

McManus, James. *Chin Music.* New York: Crown, 1985.

Magnuson, James. *The Rundown.* New York: Dial, 1977.

Malamud, Bernard. *The Natural.* New York: Dell, 1952.

Mayer, Robert. *The Grace of Shortstops.* New York: Doubleday, 1984.

Morgenstein, Gary. *The Man Who Wanted to Play Centerfield for the Yankees.* New York: Atheneum, 1983.

Neugeboren, Jay. *Sam's Legacy.* New York: Holt, Rinehart and Winston, 1974.

Parker, Robert B. *Mortal Stakes.* Boston: Houghton Mifflin, 1975.

Plimpton, George. *The Curious Case of Sidd Finch.* New York: Macmillan, 1987.

Pomeranz, Gary. *Out at Home.* Boston: Houghton Mifflin, 1985.

Ritz, David. *The Man Who Wanted to Bring the Dodgers Back to Brooklyn.* New York: Simon and Schuster, 1981.

Rosen, R. D. *Strike Three, You're Dead.* New York: Signet, 1984.

Roth, Philip. *The Great American Novel.* New York: Holt, Rinehart and Winston, 1973.

Sheed, Wilfred. *The Boys of Winter.* New York: Knopf, 1987.

Small, David. *Almost Famous.* New York: W. W. Norton, 1982.

Snyder, Don J. *Veteran's Park.* New York: Franklin Watts, 1987.

Stein, Harry. *Hoopla.* New York: Knopf, 1983.

Vogan, Sara. *In Shelley's Leg.* St. Paul, Minn.: Graywolf Press, 1985.

Willard, Nancy. *Things Invisible to See.* New York: Knopf, 1984.

George Bowering

SOURCE: "Baseball and the Canadian Imagination," in *Canadian Literature,* No. 108, Spring, 1986, pp. 115-24.

[*In the following essay, Bowering explores the influence of baseball on Canadian literature.*]

When I was a student at the University of British Columbia I got involved in all the arts I could, and for that reason I had a crush on myself, hero of the green room, the newsroom, the muse room, the art gallery, the concert hall, and especially the caf. In the caf you could sit at the special arty-farty table up front, half a scrawled poem in front of you, a mickey of cheap brandy weighing down your benny pocket, cigarette butts spilling over the edge of the gummy ashtray, and impress the newcomers, if you and your friends permitted them a chair. Realizing that there were other aesthetes there, I needed something to mark myself apart from even them. So I would sit with the sports pages in front of me.

"Afgh," I would mumble, "Drysdale pitches a two-hitter, and *still* he loses."

They rose to the bait, the actresses, poets, columnists, dancers. They would always pull sour faces and ask me what the hell a poet was doing looking at the baseball scores. I expected them to be naive because they were only college students after all. I had been out in the world, an air force station in Manitoba, mainly.

Baseball is poetry, you coddled future-dilettantes, I would think behind my serene or more likely goofy smile. I had what I wanted, a kind of uniqueness inside the uniqueness. But I also knew that a great number of the writers I admired shared with me a lifelong interest in baseball. You wrote about it once in a while, as William Carlos Williams did, or you wrote about it all the time, as Grantland Rice did. You also read the scores and knew something late at night as you remembered them. I rather believed that if some raglan-clad semi-Brit campus poet did not know anything about baseball, did not like it, in fact, he probably didn't know that much about poetry, either.

Things haven't changed much. Even though the fashion-conscious are leaping on baseball and baseball books in recent years, I still get lots of writers and especially reviewers tut-tutting me for mentioning baseball in everything I write, whether it is a novel about eighteenth-century mariners or a "translation" of Rilke.

I have finished another historical novel recently. It will be published early in 1987, ninety-eight years after the actions it depicts. It has baseball in it. Let me tell you why.

The setting for the novel is the Thompson Valley in 1889 and 1890. While doing my research, one's favourite part of writing a novel, I found that a Kamloops team, fortified with some American players, won the British

Columbia baseball tournament in 1889. Even though the villain of the novel is an American who shot a French-Canadian ranch hand near Kamloops, I resisted temptation. Then I found out that New Year's Day of 1890 was preternaturally warm and that the Kamloops team played the CPR team in a game that day, and that the game had to be suspended in the fifth inning because of an eclipse of the sun! What was I supposed to do? Refuse a gift from a muse who has been watching over me since my teen-age days when I reported the doings of the Kamloops baseball team for newspapers in the South Okanagan?

In any case, I don't really feel that I have to defend the appearance of baseball in my poems and fiction. As everyone knows, I have been overly-influenced by American writers, and many of my favourite American writers—Fielding Dawson, Joel Oppenheimer, Tom Clark, Jonathan Williams, Jack Spicer—pepper their writings with references to the diamond game. Even the writers I don't particularly like but always read—Philip Roth, Bernard Malamud, etc.—find that they have to pay attention to the great American game, too.

Well, I have always thought that it was the great Canadian game, too. That reflects, in all likelihood, the fact that I was brought up in a part of Canada that was not cold enough for hockey, and too poor for football, games that were popular, I heard from immigrants, on the prairies. Some of my friends got baseball scholarships to U.S. colleges, a few signed minor league baseball contracts, and one left-hander who used to strike me out with a terrifying curve ball went 3-0 against the Yankees after being brought up by Boston late one season while I was toiling in Manitoba, where the people I knew were already sharpening their skates.

So I am not patient with a certain kind of letter I have seen in various newspapers during the recent hullabaloo about the Toronto Blue Jays, the letter from some unknowledgeable malcontent, probably an ex-Brit, who complains about our press leading the excitement about an "imported" Yankee game. Maybe he is the same guy who spent the 1970's trying to keep American poets out of the country. I would direct him to a lovely picture book entitled *Cheering for the Home Team* by William Humber (1983).

Humber points out that in Southern Ontario they were playing baseball a year before the legendary Abner Doubleday was supposed to have invented it down farther south. That was a century and a half ago. It did not take it long to get into the hands of Canadian writers. Humber quotes Nellie McClung, writing about a game in 1882, from *Clearing in the West* (1936):

> The seats from off the wagons were set around the place where the baseball game was played. The ball was a homemade yarn ball, and the bat a barrel stave, sharpened at one end, but it was a lovely game, and everyone got runs.

Humber also quotes this, from Ralph Connor's *The Sky Pilot* (1899):

> He evidently regarded the exchange of the profession of baseball for the study of theology as a serious error in judgement, and in this opinion every inning of the game confirmed him.

Several years ago I went through all the Canadian poetry books I could find at home and at the UBC library, collecting poems about baseball by Canadian and other poets, including the Cuban and Japanese ones I had found. There were enough to fill a thick volume, and I thought of trying to interest a publisher in such a thing. A. J. M. Smith told me I should call the book *Cobb Would Have Caught It,* apparently a piece of doggerel he had long favoured. I don't remember the name of its author, probably American, but I wish I did. Even the baseball poems by Canadians would make a nice hefty and representative anthology.

The first Canadian poet to have any appreciable influence on my own work was Raymond Souster, who has published many fine poems (and some light hitters) about the game. We have even seen pictures of Souster in baseball garb (check the last issue of *Combustion,* a special issue of its successor, *Is,* edited and published by Victor Coleman, a well-known basketball fan). Most of Souster's recent books have baseball titles—*Change Up, Extra Innings,* etc.—an acknowledgement of his sky-pilot-like regret that he switched lineups.

One of my favourite Souster poems has always been a joyful fancy from the 1950's called "The Opener":

> From where I was sitting
> it looked like an easy double-play.
>
> But at that precise moment
> a sloppy looking freighter
> slipped through the Western Gap
> with a clothesline of washing
> half the length of her deck,
>
> and the runner going into second
> took one look at the ship
> and yelled: "Hey, look, they got
> my old lady's black pants
> flying at the masthead."
>
> And when all the infield
> turned around to get a gape,
> he made second, stole third,
> and scored standing up
> the winning run in what otherwise
> was one of the cleanest-played openers
> in a Toronto ball-park.

Souster has always looked for moments of irrational delight that will ease one's necessary observation of normal mortality. He knows that for baseball aficionados opening day is not only the proof of the end of winter (and should thus be made a Canadian national holiday), but a defiance of the end of things.

George Stanley, a poet who lives in northern British Columbia, and whose poetic is much different from Souster's, understands that defiance. In his book entitled *Opening Day* (1983), the title poem ends this way, saying of "every fist, mouth, mother / and mother-to-be down the first base line":

> & I knew they triumphed
>
> not over me, not over my, mine
>
> mind
>
> not over mind
>
> but over darkness, iso-
> lation, as the staring
> of windows, the eyes of cars
> & streetcars
>
> & most of all the Victorians,
> crouched in jealous rows on the hills
>
> tall dark rooms we had stayed in
> too long
>
> now out in the sun!

Of course not only opening day, but any game at all is surcease from grim reality. But baseball is not all escape; it is not all fantasy or marvel. Dwight Gardiner, a poet from the prairies, who moved first to Montreal and then to Vancouver, in search of minor league ball, has in his latest book, *The New York Book of the Dead & Other Poems* (1984), a serial poem called "Double Header," which, among other things, flicks a note at the condition nearly any fan can glimpse in his own condition:

> Max Venables'
> single
> first news
> from Phoenix
> the pathetic leagues
> the almost got close
> enough leagues.

But in baseball we can say what we have learned not to say in our lives: wait till next year! Now in the last innings of the nineteen hundreds we have come to realize that there is not much time left for the twentieth century to belong to Canada.

Baseball, however, is not life, except for a few hundred substitute players in the majors and minors. Baseball is postmodernism. It is just about all signifier, very little signified, at least in a metaphorical sense. We know that football is referential as can be—to war, to business, to sex life, to the years filled more and more with injuries and failing health.

In Canada, most of the poets are baseball fans. Even some of the women poets are playing softball and writing baseball poems. Judith Fitzgerald is already at least a chapbook ahead of Marianne Moore. The only two football fans I know among the Canadian poets are Eli Mandel and John Newlove. A moment's reflection will remind you that they are both from Saskatchewan, the province most often associated with novels of grim naturalism.

In Canada, a lot of the poets are also ball players. If the poets were to play a game against the fiction writers, they would win10-3. In Montreal in the early days of the Expos I played on a team called the York Street Tigers, and we played a double-header every Saturday against the Domtar All-Stars. The All-Stars used to beat us two games out of three, but I think that was because we had so many fiction writers in key positions. On return to Vancouver I joined the Granville Grange Zephyrs (Zeds, it said on our headbands), one of the founding teams of the famous Kosmik League. We were very successful, made up as we were entirely of poets and painters. Now I play for the Bad Backs, an amazingly successful team with poets as its majority. We clean up on the opposition, formed of teams whose rosters are filled with newspaper reporters and booksellers.

Canada's baseball-loving fiction writers are more famous than its poets, at least for loving baseball. But it has been my experience that they are not as good at playing the great Canadian game, by which I mean, in this context, fastball. In the *Crow Journals* (1980), Robert Kroetsch records this observation, Saturday, July 10, 1976, Qu'Appelle Valley, Saskatchewan:

> Hugh Hood here to teach prose writing. He knows by heart all the statistics about baseball and quotes them without provocation. He comes equipped with seven pairs of expensive sneakers, colors various, many sweat suits and baseball caps and a couple of gloves. We went out to play ball. He can't catch or throw or hit. The novelist as amateur. He'll probably write a great sports novel.

In Montreal, we gave a three-game tryout to Clark Blaise, another writer who can quote baseball statistics at the drop of a popup. We put him at first where a guy who cannot run will do the least harm, but we found out that he could not hit the curve ball. Or the fastball. Or the slowball. When W. P. Kinsella, prize-winning author of *Shoeless Joe* and other baseball fictions, announced that he was moving from Calgary to the west coast, we extended him an invitation to come to our beloved Section 9 for the AAA games at Nat Bailey Stadium, and to the sandlot for a tryout. We have not seen him in either place. Well, we know that he goes to big league parks on his summer rambles, but we wonder what his excuse is for not coming to a Bad Backs practise. Of course Kinsella is also famous for his stories about Indians; and we do not expect him to be good at being an Indian, at least not when we find out that he is not.

Of all the Canadian fiction writers I know, the ablest ball player I have seen is Hanford Woods, and his best-known fiction is a novella that won the Fels Award for the best novella in an American little magazine that year. It has since been published with another long piece of fiction in a book, but its title is *The Drubbing of Nesterenko.* That's right—a hockey story.

A few years ago I edited a book of fiction about sports for Oberon Press, though, and was delighted to find out that Canadian novelists and short story writers seem more interested in baseball than in hockey. Every fall and winter the department store book shops are filled with new hockey books, but they are almost always written by newspaper hacks. Baseball attracts the novelists. Blaise has covered the game for *TV Guide* and other slicks, and so has Kinsella. Mordecai Richler has written with his characteristic high low humour about baseball in and outside his novels.

With few exceptions football does not animate the imaginations of our novelists or poets. Only the reporters try to make the CFL into some kind of national mucilage, and tout the Grey Cup weekend as a national holiday. That says, I think, something about football. Let the Americans have football, says the poet. Canada has not been in a shooting war for over thirty years.

Hugh Hood has written two non-fiction books about hockey, and a novel about politics that uses touch football as a motif. He has written more stories with reference to sports than any other Canadian fiction writer, even Morley Callaghan. But in recent years he has referred to baseball more than to any other athletic and aesthetic play. One marvellous story tells of old Jarry Park fans taking their portable radios there rather than attend the game at the Big Owe, until there are bigger crowds at the phantom game than at the corporeal one. Another relates the dream fiction of a middle-aged man who goes to a major league training camp as a walk-on, and enjoys one magical season as a premier pitcher. In his most recent collection of short stories, *August Nights* (1985), the opening story tells of a woman who listens to Expos games on the radio as she follows the adventures of wild birds around and in her summer place, and the title story relates the giddy activities of a couple of female Expos groupies. That first story, "The Small Birds," has a nice moment that offers a kind of theological, anti-utilitarian defence of baseball. Some swallows have nested under the porch, and by mid-July the miraculous young have grown so large that they are in danger of crowding one or another out of the nest:

> On Saturday, 19 July, she was lurking near the nest, thinking she might anticipate some infant attempt at flight, catch the creature if the attempt should go badly. She might retrieve some squeaking Icarus before he hit rock, a basket catch like those the outfielders kept making in National League play as described in the summer-long sequence of Expo broadcasts going on in the swallows' sky. In a bird's mind, the account of the game would seem like the voice of God, superior to the visible order, coming from elsewhere. Something given, a part of pure life.

Those readers familiar with Hood's cycle of novels know that he is interested in the details of earthly life, but that his vision is spiritual, that he sees Wordsworthian spots in time as epiphanic. Referential meaning is converted by a special energy of attention into pure radiated meaning, regard into love. Even when Hood pokes nimble fun at his own religious and literary belief, he means that a most mundane event can hold the news of redemption and grace. It is no wonder (though it is for wonder that he is there) that Hood will be in the grandstand, looking for a perfect game.

Kinsella, too, is after wonder when he looks at baseball, and like Hood, he has an optimistic view of the world. But while Hood is after vision, Kinsella is after magic, the sort of thing Malamud wanted in *The Natural*; and no wonder—Kinsella came up to the majors from the Iowa Workshop. One of Kinsella's stories bears a remarkable likeness to Hood's story about the radio fans in old Jarry Park. In Kinsella's story, "The Thrill of the Grass," the fans take advantage of a baseball strike to sneak into a stadium night after night, gradually replacing the artificial turf with real grass.

Kinsella does tell nifty and dreamy stories about baseball players and especially pure-hearted fans. But one aspect of his prose does not really suit the game. Kinsella loves similes, the easiest of tropes. He seldom lets a thing or event go by without inventing a lush simile. Baseball, though, is not like anything. Similes would work admirably with football.

Baseball is not like anything. But it does seem to be various things for writers. For many writers, as for many fans, it is a stadium for the play of memory. Clark Blaise, at the heart of the North American tradition, has always been interested in telling stories about (his) childhood and youth. Nostalgia, and what in lesser places is called trivia, pervade his fictions. What could be more useful, and in view of his upbringing, more natural than a first-person recollection of boyhood fascination with baseball statistics or the (temporary) home team? Here is Richard Durgin, the epistolary narrator of Blaise's *Lusts* (1983):

> The first time Pittsburgh became entirely mine was when I walked out of the house one summer Saturday and pieced together the various transfers and streetcar routes that would drop me at the Forbes Field parking lot. I was eight. Bliss, when you're eight, is sitting in the bleachers and pitting your knowledge against the beer-swollen platitudes of laid-off steelworkers. The sweetest words in the world come from some hunky downing his Iron City and nodding, "Think so, kid? Yeah, maybe yer right."

Of course he is right. I mean in saying that those are the sweetest words in the world.

(By the way, have you noticed how often the quotations I have made mention Saturday? Do you remember how you felt about Saturday when you were a schoolboy or schoolgirl?)

One of my favourite short stories is a piece called "Losers," by Brian Fawcett, who is also the catcher for the Bad Backs. Fawcett made his reputation as a poet, but in the past four years he has published three books of fiction. I have noticed that since he became a fiction writer his playing skills have diminished. "Losers" is a story about the earlier days of the Kosmik League, and treats the relationships between that (dis) organization and the rest of the Revolution as it altered consciousnesses in the early 1970's. In the Kosmik League it was considered politically incorrect to give way to ambition or to steal against a lefty. Fawcett's story relates the difficulties of a former Little Leaguer who still wants to knock over the second baseman, but who has become socially educated enough to despise aggressive competition.

In the first year the narrator's team has fun, and occasionally a little stylish victory. But

> The next season, unfortunately, the team began to win. For me and a few others, it signalled that The Revolution was over, and that our side had lost. Our baseball skills had grown, which meant that we were all now *good* sandlot ball players, and that if we were willing to go to work for the telephone company or something like that, we could be playing Senior B softball. It got to some of us.

Some of us baseball fans have wondered for a long time how we can admire someone like Ted Williams, who flew U.S. Marine Corps fighters in Korea, and probably voted for Barry Goldwater and Ronald Reagan. But we do admire Ted Williams. He was the Ezra Pound of baseball, an epic maker who would not wear a necktie. In "Losers," Fawcett's narrator says:

> But The Revolution was in trouble too, and it was in trouble with baseball for the same reasons it was in trouble with a lot of fairly basic laws of behavioural physics. For one thing, if people practice anything, they'll get better at it—unless, of course, they get bored with it, or become afraid of it, and quit. Skill has its own unique set of demands, one of which is that it breeds ambition.

The trouble with The Revolution is that it thought baseball was like something, or about something. Since the Kosmik League has gone and been replaced by a bunch of older guys who like to play ball with each other, the softball has got to be more fun, and there is no more competition to see who can be more revolutionary. Not on the field, anyway.

There are still those who think that baseball is a "slow" game because players do not bash one another. To them, I suppose, "survival" is still the main theme in the Canadian character. There are still those who think that we will be polluting the Canadian imagination by playing and following the game usually associated with the Imperialistic Power to the south of us. There are probably still those who think that an interest in baseball is frivolous and therefore not in keeping with an essentially puritanical Canadian ethos. One thinks of the scorn directed Lester Pearson's way when it was reported that he watched the World Series in his office when he might have been meeting with his cabinet members. In that instance, Pearson, a one-time ballplayer with skills resembling those of Raymond Souster, was probably receiving the tut-tutting of both puritans and chauvinists (if they are two distinct groups).

But it would be hard to find anyone more recognizably Canadian than Lester Pearson or Raymond Souster. It should not surprise anyone to look into the trunk of a Canadian writer's car and see a ball and a bat, a glove and some turf shoes, perhaps some elastic knee bandages and *Cheering for the Home Team.*

MAJOR WRITERS AND WORKS

John Dizikes

SOURCE: "Charles Dickens, 'Martin Chuzzlewit', Mark Twain, and The Spirit of American Sports," in *Dickens Studies Annual: Essays on Victorian Fiction,* Volume 16, edited by Michael Timko, Fred Kaplan, and Edward Guiliano, AMS Press, Inc., 1987, pp. 247-56.

[*In the following essay, Dizikes traces the development of American sporting culture as depicted in the works of Charles Dickens and Mark Twain.*]

> "Oh where will you go?"
>
> "I don't know," he said. "Yes, I do. I'll go to America!"
>
> "No, no," cried Tom, in a kind of agony. Don't go there. . . . Don't go to America!"

However dreadful an experience it was for Martin Chuzzlewit to go to America and however arbitrary it was for Dickens the novelist to interrupt his narrative and send him there, we can surely agree that it was a fortunate thing for Dickens' readers, who, as a consequence, were presented with that famous gallery of American grotesques—Jefferson Brick, La Fayette Kettle, Elijah Pogram, General Choke—even if American readers didn't think so at the time. Dickens and Martin visited a culture whose games and whose spirit contrast strikingly with the attitudes towards sport in England. In Jacksonian America there existed an immense tension between the effort to remain free of social restraint, while at the same time strenuously attempting to create forms that would contain that freedom— the contrast, in short, between play and organized games. In Western societies, paradoxically, play flourishes best the more sharply and coherently defined society is; the more open and undefined it is, the more play becomes transformed, perhaps as a kind of compensation, into organized games.

As a visitor, Dickens observed the general cultural situation of the United States in the 1840s not as a case study in the degeneracy or distortion of old forms and ideas and values, but, as it were, anthropologically, as a culture evolving new forms, not necessarily better or worse, but different ones; and he tried to understand what it was in the situation of the culture that made it different. His response to America was profoundly shaped by that cultural situation, and this is one of the explanations for the schizophrenic quality of his response: the exaggerated vehemence of the burlesque; its obsessively repetitive quality; and also, by contrast, a deeper kind of fitful, but profound, exploration—or groping—toward understanding an unfamiliar situation. On top is satire, broad and energetic, but tiresome and overdrawn, satire that is consistently caricature; below it is something else, more interesting and original—and never fully followed up.

For example, Dickens meant it when he had Tom say that going to America was a kind of "agony," agony in the original meaning of the word as a type of game, a contest, an anguish of mind or sore distress which is the result of a struggle. The optimistic young Dickens imagined, as idealistic people do, that the ills of society might be avoided if we could only begin again, could dismantle the old order and return to a state of nature. The trip to America (*American Notes* plus *Chuzzlewit*) is the record of Martin's, and Dickens', agony; here was (almost) the blank page, the new beginning; here was Dickens seeing the future and being appalled at the immense human cost involved in starting over. Something as profound as this is needed to explain the disproportionate anger of the book. That something elemental had been touched in Dickens seems clear from those unforgettable scenes in Eden, that terrific picture of squalor and demoralization for which no one at all, British or American, had been prepared—and for which Charles Dickens was certainly not prepared; the sense of hopeless despair (the same quality is found in the *Notes* as well as *Chuzzlewit*) that is the most memorable, powerful part of the American section of the novel—indeed, of all of it. (There is a striking parallel between Dickens and that group of American frontier writers who were his contemporaries, those tellers of tall tales—particularly Hooper and Harris—whose stories also picture a society on the verge of disintegration from which comes the grimmest of American humor and which in turn gives us a connection with Mark Twain and the deepest visions of *Huckleberry Finn*.)

This view of culture as play, as evolutionary contest, is the basis for a second example of the agonized Dickens in America, and an explanation of an often quoted passage near the end of Chapter 16. Martin has made the acquaintance of Mr. Bevan, who informs him that in America satirists such as Swift or Juvenal could "not breathe the air." What Mr. Bevan means is that such satirists would be slandered and persecuted for telling unpopular truths (Tocqueville's tyranny of the majority, which, if unchecked, leads to intellectual conformity.)

This would appear to be a flicker of awareness from down below, awareness that the playing field for conventional satire has not been laid out. Dickens was in as much danger as Martin was in Eden of sinking into a swamp; or, in less hyperbolic language, American social forms were not sufficiently finished and crystallized to allow for penetrating comedy of manners, though they allowed—invited, in fact—burlesque and parody. American was too abstract. Reality outdid art. It was what, even a century later, Evelyn Waugh felt when confronted with Forest Lawn.

Some of the sporadic, fitful, Dickensian insights in *Martin Chuzzlewit* seem more revealing about the causal factors of institutional modification going on in America than the broader parodies of character types. The first of these comes from Colonel Diver, editor of the New York *Rowdy Journal,* which the colonel describes, much to Martin's surprise, as "the organ of our aristocracy in this city."

> "Oh! there is an aristocracy here, then?" said Martin. "Of what is it composed?"
>
> "Of intelligence, sir," replied the colonel; "of intelligence and virtue."

Perhaps Dickens here was consciously echoing Thomas Jefferson's definition, three decades earlier, of the only kind of elite that would be proper for a democracy—an aristocracy of virtue and talent. Anyway, "intelligence and virtue," Colonel Diver says, adding, "And of their necessary consequence in this republic. Dollars, sir" (Ch. 16).

Here Dickens has provided for us the central factor in the evolution of the American sporting culture; judged by European standards, the top and bottom of the class system were missing. In the United States there was no aristocracy in the traditional sense, that is, one based on name, established rank, land-holding; one that united political and social and economic power and whose position was unchallenged by those below. Nor was there a peasant class, fixed to the land as a rural labor force; a slave class at the bottom of society is not at all the same thing as a peasant class. Instead of aristocrats and peasants, there were plutocrats and farmers. This may seem obvious enough, but it has been the source of great contention and confusion in American social history. It is not that there were no classes—far from it; there were, and are. But the social basis of the American class system was different. Indeed, the reality of the American class system, and the unwillingness of Americans to acknowledge it, is one of the main thrusts of Dickens' satire in *Martin Chuzzlewit*. The coach driver says to Martin about America: "All men are alike in the United States, ain't they? It makes no odds whether a man has a thousand pound, or nothing, there." This is a nice double hit by Dickens: it does, we know, make a difference; yet the real difference is how much money, not whose money, it is. Another objection often made is the opposite one: that there was, or had been, an American aristocracy of the old sort, which existed in some regional clusters—the seacoast South, and in New York.

But even the proponents of this view seem willing to agree that these clusters never formed a coherent national social elite. Anyway, the characteristic of these isolated regional enclaves has been from early on the effort to preserve their social purity by yielding political power, while struggling ferociously to maintain their economic position, not just against the proletariat, but even more against the tidal wave of plutocratic nouveaux riches—the theme of the stories of Edith Wharton and, in our own day, of Louis Auchincloss.

Dickens is, of course, one of the great chroniclers of industrial laissez-faire capitalism colliding with the remnants of the old feudal order, the chronicler of the achievements, and especially of the horrors, of the clash between capitalist utilitarian rationalism and the inherited irrationalism of the past. We take for granted what was rather remarkable: Dickens could imaginatively do justice to the position of both parties. He relished the rich diversity of the chaotic jumble of the old order without romanticizing it, because he saw how it obstructed the quest for human justice; at the same time he was horrified at the inhumane abstractness of utilitarianism while recognizing the progressive power in it. He is the creator of both *Pickwick* and *Hard Times*.

Arriving in the United States when the industrial revolution was well under way, it has usually been assumed that Dickens was the ideal observer, come at the ideal moment for a comparative evaluation. And in some ways he was. Yet it does him a disservice not to see how much more complex his position actually was and how this is related to the lopsided and curious focus of his fictional report. In the American situation there was very little of the old order resisting the new one. This is what complicates Dickens' satirical point of view, complicates by drastically oversimplifying it. In the agonized conditions of Eden, Dickens found himself baffled. He needed the presence of a coherent culture against which to play off the astonishing crudities and brutalities of the new American capitalist order, as something more inward than farce. Where was he to find this? In the slave-owning planter class, with its bogus aristocratic pretensions? No. (An urban version of this is the Norrises, who are antagonists, not allies.) Yet the alternative, the free play of social type, produced that most dreadful of all American grotesques, Mr. Scadder, whose nature is as amoral as that of the natural birds of prey to which he is compared. In Mr. Bevan Dickens tried to imagine the cultural type he needed, with the resulting vapidity and unbelievability that are so obvious. The Bevan type is itself displaced and really as foreign to America as is Martin; that is what they have in common. Dickens had to make up what didn't exist, and even his extraordinary inventive powers were no substitute for a missing social structure.

Dickens did not know or care about the situation of American sportsmen as a group. But in their plight he would have found dramatized what he was up against as observer. More than any other social group, American sportsmen were determined to re-establish the past, to reclaim their British inheritance, not in some mood of hopeless reaction, but as a means of finding some secure and solid ground in a place where everything was forever swampy, like the Edens they so often lived in.

The sports that they tried to transplant were those of the mid nineteenth century: field sports, hunting and fishing; sailing, running, and walking; above all, thoroughbred horse racing. These sports were, of course, rural, close to nature, rooted in custom, not rules; they were also a powerful way in Britain of tying together rural and urban life by means of a settled and orderly round of social/sporting seasons that brought city and country together, something we see most memorably in the works of another of the early Victorian British novelists, Anthony Trollope. The British aristocracy and middle class had evolved the institutions that defined all this: jockey clubs, yacht clubs, gambling houses, seasons, customs, rules. Insofar as rules were needed, they were altered only occasionally and were enforced informally, by the power of a small, intimately connected social elite whose word was law, whether the law was written in words or not. For example, the decisions of the Newmarket Jockey Club about horse racing were adhered to everywhere in the land, though it ostensibly adjudicated only for the one race course at Newmarket. It didn't matter where it was; society was homogeneous, unified.

Even more remarkable was the evolution of the British idea of sportsmanship, an idea closely associated with, but not identical to, the figure of the British gentleman. This idea of true sportsmanship was that of competition—often fierce, grasping, even reckless—but within rules. It was the concept of competition restrained by something larger than rules, beyond rules: fair play. Of course, it was violated in practice, and yet this concept was immensely powerful, shaping not only conduct within the games, but the games and sports themselves. The image of the British sportsman—British equipment; dress; and, most of all, sporting style, laconic, casual, understated—spread throughout the world, where it had a continuing vogue in many countries. The idea of sportsmanship also spread, but it took hold much more superficially. In addition, the British sporting style may best be understood as an immense elaboration of, but retention of, the idea of sport as play, play taken as activity that is to some degree spontaneous, uncontrolled, improvised, free-flowing, pointless. It is an end in itself; essentially, control of the action, so far as control resides within rules, is left to the players.

And how successful were the Americans in recreating these stabilizing British sporting ideas and institutions? They failed. They built their racing courses and gave them the old names and tried to reproduce the old forms and manners and styles. But they could not do it. They went on trying and failing, and everything they did turned into something else. They could not build and nurture and maintain turf courses that in England were the result of decades of adaptation, conforming to the landscape, looping, and meandering. Americans hacked out tracks in the woods and raced their horses on these straight dirt paths; or, when more ambitious, they built ovals of dirt and raced their horses there—nothing permanent, nothing lasting very long. They emphasized speed more than endurance and shortened the length of their races. There was a country landscape, but no country culture in the British sense; in America the only successful tracks were those near cities for there were no aristocratic patrons of racing; in America horse racing was a business, and it had to attract its audience from cities for the business to succeed. And American sportsmen were entrepreneurs, from Andrew Jackson at the Hermitage, to Richard Ten Broek, New York gambler and promoter.

This was also the case in the history of American yachting. Americans took the light, fast, cheaply built, and cheaply discarded vessels built for commerce and contraband-running in the War of 1812 and gradually converted them into the speediest ships afloat—utilitarian, functional, the magnificent clipper ships of the 1840s and 1850s. These were the model of their sailing ships, the kind of ship—the *America*—with which John Cox Stevens challenged the British in 1851, winning the America's Cup. Commerce and sport were united as forms of competition. And, finally, the most important American ball game of the time, cricket—which at first seemed likely to become established as the national game, with playing fields and teams in New York, Philadelphia, Boston, and points west—did not take hold. So dependent on a sense of leisure, of poise, of patience, cricket turned out to be unexportable—to the United States anyway.

Change, not continuity, was the order of the day. So many of these traditional sports and games depended on the steady patronage of a small elite, patronage possible where there was surplus capital to expend—not as business, but as play. There was great potential (and much actual) wealth in America, but most of it was in the form of land. In America one might own vast tracts of land, land on a scale beyond the dreams of European avarice—yet, for all that, one could be poor, "land-poor," that extraordinary, perplexing phrase.

In this respect Dickens' vision of Eden was vivid and acute. Remember that Martin had come over to go into domestic architecture, virtually the last thing needed in the world to which he came, in the East as well as the West. Imagine it in sporting terms. What if Martin Chuzzlewit, in addition to trying to build a plantation house instead of that log cabin, had also wanted to establish a jockey club, build a race course, buy some blood stock, and hold a racing meet? Who, in Eden, was there to do the labor? Where would the capital have come from? Who would have come? How long would it have lasted?

Henry James wrote about Hawthorne's efforts, at this same time, to write his romances: "It takes a great deal of history to produce a little literature." And to paraphrase James further: "the flower of sporting art blossoms

only where the soil is deep." In this early entrepreneurial phase, American capitalism fluctuated between hard, grinding materiality and speculative fantasy. In Mark Twain's novel *The Gilded Age*, Mr. Hawkins, on his deathbed, urges his family to hang on to their "Tennessee acres"—that pie-in-the-sky, acres-in-the-sky dream of a fabulous future:

> I am leaving you in cruel poverty. . . . But courage! A better day is coming. Never lose sight of the Tennessee land. Be wary. There is wealth stored up for you there—wealth that is boundless.

The sales pitch of Mr. Scadder. There was wealth in the Tennessee lands, but it took the TVA and the Atomic Energy Commission to develop it.

But what about the British ideal of good sportsmanship? Surely material and social conditions need not have affected that. Certainly, in the Jacksonian years this ideal is found in all the American sporting literature, in the diaries and letters of American sportsmen. Yet this also was under assault, the victim of the same absence of definition, of boundaries, of defined social structure—victim, too, of the buoyant sense in America that failure really need not be final. Sportsmanship is associated with the idea of shame; beyond rules and laws, beyond winning and losing, the real penalty for the bad sport was embarrassment or shame. But to free oneself from the past, especially a puritan past, was, for Americans, more and more to emerge as unashamed—unashamed of their vulgarity, unashamed of their bankruptcies, of their lowly origins.

It became a cardinal belief of that Prince of American bad sports, P. T. Barnum, that notoriety was an asset, not a liability. When he had become world famous for the utterly shameless delight he took in his frauds and deceptions, Barnum was asked by Madame Tussaud's if he would be willing to be enshrined in wax—or did he shrink from the notoriety? "Willing?" he replied, "Anxious! What's a show without notoriety!" And what were moral and social conventions but a show, an amoral form of entertainment. Barnum believed that those who swallowed his humbug were chumps, not victims, deserving scorn not pity. "It pays to be shifty in a new country," Simon Suggs used to say. It pays to be wary, to be smart. Another of Dickens' insights. Colonel Diver says to Martin: "We are a smart people here, and can appreciate smartness."

> "Is smartness American for forgery?" asked Martin.

> "Well!" said the colonel, "I expect it's American for a good many things that you call by other names. But you can't help yourselves in Europe. We can."

Even Dickens couldn't have imagined a character quite on Barnum's scale of audacity, of shameless gall. Barnum is one of the chief figures in the development of the sporting equivalent of the con man—the gamesman—

who plays against the rules as much as against his opponent. Those who play by the rules perish by them. Rules are vestiges of the past, and the past is a form of tyranny. And if the rules, in addition, are the imported artifacts of another culture, then right and patriotism are united in shaking free of them. Short cuts and waving the flag—how delightful! Thus, good sportsmanship, in its British version, was more and more seen as something to break away from—yet another of those ages-old straitjackets of inhibition and convention. Europeans perhaps had no choice, but Americans could start over.

In the booming, industrializing, reconstructed America of the 1880s and 1890s, the uncertain, unformed sporting culture that Martin Chuzzlewit had struggled to understand was replaced by one that was defined and well established. America moved decisively from play to games, and throughout the power of American nationalism was pervasive. Cricket gave way to baseball; basketball, the one important game invented by Americans, was in its rudimentary stages; American football, a curious mixture of rugby and soccer, was evolving steadily into something very different from each. The impact of the industrial system was everywhere apparent.

Mark Twain could take this sporting culture for granted as offering him one of his most important metaphors in *A Connecticut Yankee in King Arthur's Court* (1889). There it is striking how much the hero-narrator Hank Morgan stands Dickens on his head; he introduces into backward, medieval, Catholic (for Twain these words are synonyms) England some of the very things that Dickens had found most offensive in *Martin Chuzzlewit*, especially the institutions of public relations and the popular press. But Twain's situation is, as satirist, also very complex. The con-man gamesman was a type Twain was profoundly familiar with all his life, had studied all his life, understood inside and out. He was inextricably intertwined with Twain's view of himself; that arch games-playing manipulator, Tom Sawyer, is Twain himself. A satirist who embodies the contradictions that are the subject of his satire strikes one as a volatile state of affairs, with explosive potential. So it was. Twain's most pessimistic view of life and of human nature was one in which the gamesman was fated always finally to be triumphant.

Twain would thus not have been at all surprised by the ever increasing gamesmanship in American sports. Games have become more and more separated from nature, emphasizing man-made surfaces, stressing technique and equipment. The pattern and rhythm of American games are ones of broken sequences, not free-flowing movement. There is a considerable emphasis on position, on control of the field, and on preplanned sequences of plays. Players can be substituted as a series of interchangeable parts; and even time is divided up, manipulated, made a part of the calculations and action. And all this leads inexorably away from the field of play and from the players to control from the sidelines—from off the field. In no other sporting culture is the coach,

the manager, the all-seeing mastermind, so central a figure as in America. And, of course, as play becomes game, game becomes entertainment, not an end in itself, but a part, another product, in a complex industrial commercial system.

And this has led, in turn, to the abandonment of the older notion of fair play as something decisive beyond the rules themselves. The contest is narrowed solely to what is, or is not, within the rules; and with its narrowness there comes at the same time a growing ambiguity about the rules themselves, a greater sense of the rules as entirely part of the game itself, rules to be revised, tinkered with, modified—rules not inherited, but calculated and managed—a way to attract an audience, to ensure advantage for one group or style. The contest has become triangular, against the opponent and against the rules, without contravening them into illegality. A contemporary baseball player, having studied the rule book in spring training, said to his fellow players: "Boys, you've heard the new rules read. Now the question is: what can we do to beat them?"

Christian K. Messenger

SOURCE: "Lardner: The Popular Sports Hero," in *Sport and the Spirit of Play in American Fiction: Hawthorne to Faulkner,* Columbia University Press, 1981, pp. 108-28.

[In the following essay, Messenger views Lardner's humorous portrayal of the athlete as a prototype for American sports fiction.]

The most talented sportswriter was Ring Lardner, the innovative chronicler of American games, comic players, and their foibles. He allied himself to popular sport and the realist tradition while irrevocably fixing the stereotype of the professional athlete for modern fiction. Lardner stands at the center of any discussion of popular sport in modern American literature. He knew professional sport and suburban recreation to be the average citizen's obsessions, and he worked out of a rich Chicago tradition of sports writers and humorists. He had none of the energy and rawness of American Naturalism and he knew little about it. Throughout his career he affected a classic antiintellectual pose, a stance traditionally feigned by American humorists to enhance satiric thrusts; in Lardner's case, the pose became permanently identified as a trait of his characters, specifically his baseball players. His defensive posture against the world of ideas and, indeed, the world of art as well, seems in retrospect to have been genuine. He was a fearful man, suspicious of his own best and worst impulses, mistrustful of the franker, more open life of the 1920s, proud of his craft as he saw it yet ultimately less than candid about his motivations, both in life and in literature.

Lardner's early primary subjects were athletes. He found a perfect environment for humorous realism in the physical world of professional sport. The sports beat gave him his first writing experience in a milieu that shaped his early attempts at delineating character and writing vernacular speech. By the time he left Chicago for New York in 1919, he had created the first minor galaxy of fictional Popular Sports Heroes. While most of his short stories about sports heroes were simple exercises in broad humor, he was at times able to probe into irrational behavior with characters such as Midge Kelly, Buster Elliott, and blustering Jack Keefe.

Like the Southwestern Humorists a half-century before, Lardner presented the athlete or gamester and his environment as representative of society. In his own reticent fashion he was as angry a stern moralist as Longstreet, as skillful at creating vernacular speech as Harris; his characters could be as sly as Hooper's Simon Suggs or, in another vein, as full of comic bombast as any western roarer. Lardner's links to the Southwestern tradition can be seen most clearly in the role of the narrator as social commentator. The Southwesterners had lashed the rural citizens for their manners; Lardner dissected the urban mass man in his ignorance and insensitivity. Like the Southwestern Realists, Lardner participated in a profound social upheaval, in his case, the twentieth-century urbanization of life and letters.

A philologist of sorts and a writer committed to the vernacular, he found his first congenial subject on the ball field, where his deadpan, laconic narrators related the tallest of baseball tales as in "Horseshoes" (1914), "Alibi Ike" (1915), and "Hurry Kane" (1927). He was the first writer to assume a role critical of the sportswriter's position; he introduced women into sports fiction; he scaled the professional sports hero down into a realistic subject, investing him with physical prowess while comically divesting him of judgment, maturity, and self-knowledge.

Did Lardner mean to criticize athletes as a group? The evidence overwhelmingly suggests that he did not. By making White Sox pitcher Jack Keefe a simple young man with a shrewish wife, unpaid bills, and an apartment he could not afford, Lardner suggested that the athletic hero was not much of a heroic figure and not a symbol of anything, certainly not of the crassness and boobery of all baseball players. Many other Lardnerian urban and suburban citizens shared Keefe's blustering vanity and unrealistic self-image. Lardner mistrusted not ballplayers but popular heroes with self-inflated egos. Also, as ballplayers recalled, Lardner was perhaps never happier than when travelling with the Cubs and White Sox, losing himself in team camaraderie, jokes, and songs.[1]

Critics of Lardner's work suggest that he was either a misanthrope, who saw no saving graces in his characters and thus created less than human subjects, or a repressed idealist, placing all mature experience against some idyllic standard, finding it wanting, and creating strong satire in reaction.[2] Those who feel that Lardner was a misanthrope fail to countenance his tender regard for family and close friends and his many wise, if brittle

and cynical, narrators. The idealists cannot come to grips with his rigid censorship of his most personal feelings in print and the paucity of loving, giving characters in his fiction. As a satirist, Lardner felt little responsibility to suggest alternative and more humanizing worlds.

Lardner's achievement remains difficult to assess. Here was a popular artist who constantly professed his desire to attain nothing more lasting than his newspaper columns and stories yet who, almost despite his mistrust of art, created several modern short classics. In the best Southwestern tradition, he debunked his role as author. His consuming ambition was to write for the Broadway musical comedy stage, and his affinity for popular forms remained unbroken until the end of his life. He would have always chosen fame in Tin Pan Alley over a place in the literary pantheon beside Fitzgerald and Hemingway.

At the center of diffuse modern American life, Lardner found a cluster of social games that revealed what passed for reality in social relations. The tensions in this most uncommunicative of men are shown most strongly in his scores of characters who talk past each other in their attempts at finding a link with other human beings. The shallow surface life of his bragging characters is relieved only occasionally by a wise narrator or by their own unconscious hilarity. His work is replete with ballplayers, fans, newsmen, bridge players, and golf caddies, all filling what seemed to be endless days, isolated in one sort of competition or another.

Lardner had a vision of suburban America at play throughout the 1920s, and he wrote that new social freedoms would dictate a widened scope of "games." He saw that the new age's social disorder could be depicted through its games and game players, the roarer sitting in the big league dugout, the con man sitting at the bridge table at a suburban country club, the competitor as a potential menace to the spirit. Lardner was no apologist for organized sport and competition but then he was no advocate of free play either. He discerned no higher American values or common good to come out of a national obsession; he mistrusted obsessions of any kind, communal or personal.

LARDNER AND BASEBALL

Lardner is best known for his baseball stories, specifically those with a vain, bragging hero. "Alibi Ike," once only the title of a thin story, has passed into the general lexicon. *The Busher's Letters,* the continuing saga of Jack Keefe, appeared regularly in *The Saturday Evening Post* from 1914-19. If the American public at this time had any notion of what the average ballplayer sounded like, what he thought about, what he did off the field, the chances are that Lardner's characters provided the clearest image.

After a desultory semester at a second-rate engineering school in Chicago in 1902, Lardner returned to his family's home in Niles, Michigan with little direction or ambition. He read meters for the Niles Gas Company for a year before landing a reporter's job on the South Bend *Times,* where he covered the police station and the courts in the morning and the Central League baseball team in the afternoon. It was there that he first began emulating the styles of some of Chicago's leading sports writers, including Dryden, Hugh Keogh, and Hugh Fullerton of the *Tribune.* Fullerton helped him get his first Chicago job on the *Inter Ocean* in the fall of 1907.

Before his father lost a great deal of money in land transactionsin 1901, the Lardner estate had a baseball diamond, tennis court, and coach house with a stable of horses. Lardner knew baseball as thoroughly as the traditional country gentleman would have known field sports. In later years, Lardner spoke of having figured baseball statistics in the classroom in Niles. In 1908 he began his first major sporting assignment when he covered the White Sox for the *Tribune,* thus following in the footsteps of Dunne, 21 years before on the *News.* After he assumed the column, "In the Wake of the News," in 1913, Lardner perfected the Keefe persona with startling speed. In a few months, he progressed from a parody of the boys' sports hero with one "Verne Dalton" whose adventures were signed by the "Copy Boy," to an account of the 1913 World Series "By an Athlete," to the narrative voice of the Keefe character.[3] In actuality, the entire series of "Busher" tales that made up *You Know Me Al* (1916), plus the baseball stories "Sick 'Em," "My Roomy," and "Horseshoes," were all written in 1914 when he was turning out seven columns per week for the *Tribune.*

A large, muscular man of 6'2", Lardner fit in well with the players, who knew him as shy and private yet ever willing to get into a card game, to drink with them, or to spend hours making up nonsense rhymes and songs. There was a lot of the amateur folklorist about Lardner, who could never hear enough of the ballplayers' speech or their stories. He wrote poems and songs about them, orchestrated the Cubs' barbershop quartet, allowed them guest appearances in his columns, and altogether encouraged their artistic efforts. In "The Wake," Lardner printed outfielder Frank Schulte's poetry (some of which Lardner had written), ghosted his "answers" to imaginary literary critics, and suspended Schulte from his column for poor writing, then reported that Schulte demanded to be traded to other *Tribune* columns such as "Breakfast Food" or "Day Dreams."[4] At one point he had acted as scribe for an illiterate White Sox pitcher by writing letters home to the player's wife. In recording the repetitive small details, Lardner learned the very cadences and phrasing that he would later perfect in Jack Keefe's letters, a triumph of epistolary style.

Jack Keefe, Lardner's first baseball protagonist, grew out of Lardner's association with ballplayers, their speech, and their lives. The vernacular that Keefe uses in writing letters home to his old friend, Al, is the speech of Niles and semiliterate America. Lardner made a clean break with the dialect tradition. His characters

were always representative of the new middle class, suggesting that the new urban and suburban citizen was bound to his neighbor by immersion in the common milieu of the present rather than the linguistic roots and customs of an ethnic past. Baseball, the great unifying force of American popular sport, was a superb choice for creating a bewildered representative of mass man—at once a hero to thousands yet under financial and emotional stress, a character caught in a commercial system against which he blusters with all the instincts of a frontier roarer.

Standing at the center of popular athletic fame in Lardner's work are isolated, ignorant, and frightened men caught in an unreal world of adulation that they could not assimilate into their personal lives. The tension between an individual American athletic hero and his restriction to a commercial team is highlighted in Keefe, the "busher," a young man lacking self-knowledge, control, and tenderness. The role of Keefe suggests not that ballplayers are all braggarts and louts, but that the modern popular hero is an artificial creation fed by the hero's knowledge of his own heroism in the public eye; however, he is mystified by how to transfer this leverage and notoriety into his personal life, which remains a romantic and financial shambles. Nothing in Jack Keefe's life in Bedford has prepared him for the daily stresses of life in Chicago, performance on a major league team, the advances of designing women, and the frustration of his own appetites. He learns nothing; his teammates, manager, and owner alternately write him off as not worth the trouble in spite of his talent.

The epistolary form is here almost that of a diary, a perfect format for a ballplayer's life that moves slowly, day by day and game by game. Jack reports incidents that fix him in the reader's mind while passing over his own head. His run-on quotations and repetitive word choice add to the dreariness of his accounts. He knows nothing of why the joke is so often on him; fully half the remarks made in the novel are beyond him. His own gaffes are seized on by others in derision, causing him to become belligerent and to withdraw further into the shell of his wounded vanity. The recurrence of Jack's crises and his failure to learn from them are exemplified in the account of a New Year's Eve argument in Chicago with his wife Florrie, her sister ̄Marie, and her husband Allen, a left-hander on the White Sox. Jack, always mindful of his money, suggests that they leave an expensive restaurant before running up an enormous bill:

> Then Marie says Oh, shut up and don't be no quitter. I says You better shut up yourself and not be telling me to shut up, and she says What will you do if I don't shut up? And I says I would bust her in the jaw. But you know Al I would not think of busting no girl. Then Florrie says You better not start nothing because you had to much to drink or you would not be talking about busting girls in the jaw. Then I says I don't care if it is a girl I bust or a lefthander. I did not mean nothing at all Al but Marie says I had insulted Allen and

he gets up and slaps my face. Well Al I am not going to stand that from nobody not even if he is my brother-in-law and a lefthander that has not got enough speed to break a pane of glass.[5]

The pitchers fight, and everyone is thrown out of the restaurant. Jack is thoroughly whipped by Allen and does a poor job of concealing the fact in the remainder of the letter. The deadening, repetitive insults, Jack's false chivalry, Florrie's abused femininity, the girls' eagerness to see a fight, and the childish performance of the teammates suggest the endless round of Jack's life, the threats, the bickering, and, finally, the self-serving explanations. His fight with Allen proves in part how utterly Lardner has defused and scaled down the frontier braggart and physical prowess hero. Goaded by their less than attractive wives, the best that these two professional baseball players can do is have a stupid quarrel and get thrown out of the restaurant.

Jack's mouth gets him into trouble, never out of it. He jauntily confronts White Sox owner Charles Comiskey with his threat to jump to the fledgling Federal League if he cannot get his salary increased; Comiskey merely toys with him. Jack acts as if he were a free agent who can come and play with whomever he chooses, yet his boasts are severely circumscribed by the fact that he is a commodity and not worth the aggravation he causes other people. His bragging is hollow; he has no free will; his public performance is controlled by the team; his private life is manipulated by his wife and her relatives. Ostensibly a hero figure, Jack is, in actuality, a little man to whom things happen.[6]

Increasingly after the Civil War, the Popular Sports Hero had to perform in the arena for spectators; he was a diminished figure in relation to the backwoods heroes of the almanacs and Southwestern Humor tales. Natty Bumppo's conflict with Judge Temple had been over substantive issues in American conduct. In contrast, Jack Keefe has no sporting code, no ideals. His only issue is money, and he loses his salary battle with Comiskey, owner of his own "settlement." Jack's only function is to win, and by that criterion alone is he judged. Lardner reinforces the *agon* as the only valid category of play in the modern Popular Sports Hero's experience. There is no higher order of sport than competition.

Lardner loaded Jack's letters with references to actual ballplayers and teams. Their appearances enhanced the realism of Jack's letters and allowed Lardner to rework the consistent theme of Jack's overestimation of his own worth. When the White Sox and Giants are in training for an around-the-world tour, Jack meets Christy Mathewson, then in the last years of a splendid career; Jack writes: "Al this here Mathewson pitched today and honest Al I don't see how he gets by and either the batters in the National League don't know nothing about hitting or else he is such a old man that they feel sorry for him . . . all as he does now is stick the 1st ball right over with 0 on it and pray that they don't hit it out of the park" (196).

Jack goes on to make excuses to Mathewson for his poor showing: "Then I says a bout me haveing a sore arm Sunday and he says I wisht I had a sore arm like yourn and a little sence with it and was your age and I would not never loose a game . . ." (196-97). Christy Mathewson was *the* Merriwellian figure in professional baseball in the first two decades of this century and was greatly admired by both Lardner and Heywood Broun.[7] As a Bucknell graduate, the idol of boys and the general public, he can tell Jack the truth about himself with considerable authority. Jack is unaware that Mathewson is one who made the sport as popular as it is, a player who paved the way for clowns like Jack.

Jack himself is not a hero-worshipper because, in his view, no ballplayer can measure up to his own skills, except by luck or trickery. In an inversion of a conventional pulp fiction ending, Jack throws a ball at a batter's head in extra innings with the bases loaded and the score tied because he has a grudge against him. Jack gets his man, loses the game, and earns a fifty-dollar fine from his manager. Jack then writes, "And how could a man go to 1st base and the winning run be forced in if he was dead which he should ought to of been the lucky left-handed stiff . . ." (139). This violent reaction is stronger because it comes from Jack who is usually all bluster with little real animosity. However, Lardner's most intriguing baseball story, "My Roomy" (1914), ends with Buster Elliott, the disturbed hero, in an asylum for having attempted to murder his girlfriend and her new lover with a baseball bat. Elliott writes to his former roommate, the story's narrator, "Old Roomy: I was at bat twice and made two hits; but I guess I did not meet 'em square. They tell me they are both alive yet, which I did not mean them to be."[8]

The similarities between these two passages, written at approximately the same period, show how Lardner could take comic material and turn it into a personal tragedy. Jack's bragging turns chilling with Elliott's attempted murder of his girl. The pugnacity always lurking in Jack in response to what he feels is a hostile world is carried through by Elliott, who relates, "That's my business, busting things." Whereas Jack is a sometime-success, showing just enough promise to be suffered for years by the White Sox, Elliott is a thorough outsider, a prodigious slugger who refuses even to attempt to catch fly balls. Indeed, Elliott is a modern athletic reincarnation of a Bartleby, albeit with some manic energy. Elliott's antics are so bizarre as to dictate his release by the team because his mockery of procedure digs at unity; there is a submerged terror evinced by the player who does everything backwards, who sees nothing in conventional threats, who relies on personal quirks to dictate his actions at any given moment. The game is mocked by his aberrations. Tension increases between Elliott and his mates. His loneliness is best described by his sympathetic roommate who comments, "What could you say to a guy who hated himself like that?"

The sports frame throws into bold relief every personal peculiarity. Tales of ballplayers' inability to abide by curfew, meal times, train schedules, and simple field procedures are legion. Elliott's disorientations are overwhelming and all the more so since they literally take place in the public eye. He is rejected even by the narrator who is the only player who would finally consent to room with him. The greatest ballplayer of the time, Ty Cobb, manifested serious personality disorders both on and off the field; however, Cobb's performance was of such brilliance that often his frightened teammates put up with his violence and paranoia. During Cobb's career, Lardner had nothing but praise for his brainy play and competitive drive. It is probable that he was glossing over the facts; as his sportswriter learns in "Champion," "the people don't want to see him knocked. . . . " [9]

As a member of the team, the problem of belonging, of performing day after day, defeats Elliott and highlights his isolation. Lardner complicated both a ballplayer's psyche and the question of his fundamental duties and relations. The individual problems of a team member would become a major theme in later sports fiction. The theme chronicled an American social dilemma which far transcended the playing field, but the field served as an excellent microcosm for investigation of American society. What is the cost of personal freedom? What allegiances are owed to the team, the group, the company, the family, or the society?

Lardner raised questions but he did not answer them. A sober insider in the life of the teams he covered as a newspaperman, Lardner was always with them but not of them; he always preserved a solitary core. This could be ascribed to the traditional role of the artist; but since Lardner himself would have rejected that notion, one must say that the distance he kept in all his relations was one of fear of deeper emotions spilling over, of scenes that could not be controlled. Control is what his narrators possess over their feelings and desires, what his rubes and bushers never achieve. A game with rules and rigid logic was most congenial to his need for an external order. So many of his disordered characters are kept at arm's length from the reader, their bizarre or foolish actions filtered through a cool narrator who stands between the reader and their anarchy. However, the narrator of "My Roomy" does stand up for Elliott; Al, we assume, reads, thinks about, and answers his old friend Jack Keefe at some length, trying to help him cope with city life.

Most of Lardner's early baseball fiction is lighter than "My Roomy," but still portrays a variety of characters. In "Horseshoes," an exasperated player-narrator relates the impossible luck of a teammate in staying clear of responsibility for on-the-field blunders; however, the reader perceives that it is the narrator's self-hatred and inferiority complex that keeps him from success. In "Harmony," an older player is credited with scouting a young slugger for his team. In reality, he never saw the youth play but championed him because of his excellent tenor voice; the team was short one member in its barbershop quartet. The "harmony" is extended from a

musical term to the well-being of the team in general. "Alibi Ike" as a title is almost self-evident; it refers to the insufferable player with an excuse for every miscue whom the team razzes but ultimately nurtures. [10]

As early as 1921, Lardner was revealing his disenchantment with the emphasis on the slugger in baseball:

> A couple yrs. ago a ball player named Baby Ruth that was a pitcher by birth was made into an outfielder on acct. of how he could bust them and he begins breaking records for long distance hits and etc. and he become a big drawing card and the master minds that controls baseball says to themselfs that if it is home runs that the public wants to see, why leave us give them home runs, so they fixed up a ball that if you don't miss it entirely it will clear the fence, and the result is that ballplayers which use to specialize in hump back liners to the pitcher is now amongst our leading sluggers when by rights they couldn't take a ball in their hands and knock it past the base umpire. [11]

Along with his dislike of what he felt to be a poor caliber of play, Lardner also criticized the audience: "We don't play because (1) we lack imagination, and because (2) we are a nation of hero worshippers. . . . But hero worship is the disease that does the most to keep the grandstands full and the playgrounds empty." [12] The heart of Lardner's quarrel with baseball can be seen in "Hurry Kane" when the ignorant but amazing young pitcher, a 36-game winner as a rookie, consents to fix the World Series to enable him to obtain the money he needs to impress a showgirl. When he learns she is only stringing him along, he reverses form to win the deciding game, a cynical transformation of the conclusion of "Along Came Ruth" (1919). Such tainted reformations had their bitter irony. Jack Keefe was many things but one could hardly imagine him as a fixer. Elmer Kane's "moral" decision to go against the gamblers did not exist in reality. In "The Battle of the Century" (1921), "The Venomous Viper of the Volga" (1927), and "Greek Tragedy" (1934), Lardner satirized the fans at wrestling and boxing matches even more pointedly than the performers, who at least knew what they were doing. [13]

Lardner did change his views about sport in the 1920s to some extent but he did not regret his years of writing about it. His defects as a writer were, if anything, masked by his early work in an environment in which he was most comfortable. His creation of baseball "boobs" was extended by others, who attributed to ballplayers qualities ranging from limited intellect to utter boorishness. No small amount of the public's conception of the professional athlete today springs directly from Lardner's early success at creating humorous sports characters in his fiction. Lardner's triumph made the professional athlete a subject for comedy for decades. Lardner's prototypes remain both on the field and in the literary imagination where writers have appropriated his comic ballplayers for more sophisticated ends. Lardner's continual mastery of popular sport consisted in part in his doing what any innovative popular artist does, in giving back mass experience through art with a heightened awareness of its meaning. He identified the Popular Sports Hero and shaped the conventions of his presentation.

Lardner returned to the Busher in 1918 after three years and sent him off to war with an account of army camp in *Treat 'Em Rough* (1918) and his overseas adventures in *The Real Dope* (1919). Both collections were somewhat thin because Keefe learned little and returned as a pitcher still up against the weakness of his own nature and those of his wife and friends. The last Keefe stories, written in 1919, are strangely prophetic for the future of major league baseball. In "Along Came Ruth" (*Saturday Evening Post,* 26 July 1919), Jack is home from the war and begins a new season in fine form, but he sees red when Florrie takes a male partner in a beauty shop business and sits with him in the stands while Jack is pitching against the Red Sox. Jack blows sky-high and does not last out the first inning, vanquished by an enormous home run hit by none other than Babe Ruth, then in his last year with Boston before the 1920 trade to the New York Yankees. Ruth and Keefe were both left-handed rookie pitchers in 1914: one destined to become the slugger who changed forever the tight, low-scoring percentage baseball that Lardner loved, the other destined to be the model for professional athletes in fiction for more than half a century, including the adaptations of Ruth. Ruth eclipsed both Keefe and Lardner's brand of baseball in the 1920s, but his own projected image as the most rollicking, out-sized bumpkin of them all secured and validated Lardner's prototype.

The Keefe tales fade out with Jack on the last place Athletics in 1919, the year of the Black Sox scandal in which eight members of a great White Sox team were barred from baseball for life by the new commissioner, Judge Kenesaw Mountain Landis, for throwing the World Series to the Cincinnati Reds. The White Sox had been the team most favored by literary reporters such as Dunne and Lardner. During the 1919 World Series, Lardner wrote a poem commenting on the White Sox collapse and hinting at scandal. To the tune of "I'm Forever Blowing Bubbles," the poem went in part:

> I'm forever blowing ball games
> Pretty ball games in the air.
> I come from Chi.
> I hardly try,
> Just go to bat and fade and die.[14]

In 1920, the experience of watching the criminal indictment of men whom he knew and had admired was not a pleasant one for Lardner, who had written about all of them at one time or another. His 1919 short stories are full of references to the most prominent fixers, Chick Gandil and Eddie Cicotte, of whom Lardner had written, "They ain't a smarter pitcher in baseball."[15] By public record, these Chicago players were the fictional teammates of Jack Keefe as well, a fact that must have

been particularly galling to their creator. However, the mask stayed in place. Not through even one of his narrators did Lardner ever reveal the depth of his feelings about the affair. With his move to New York in the fall of 1919, Lardner's close ties with baseball receded into a past of Niles and Chicago, Pullman cars and clubhouses, and, for the most part, his happiest years.

From 1908, Lardner was experimenting with and adding to his vision of professional baseball. His ballplayers were comic conceptions eagerly embraced by the fans, for in only a few cases were they malicious or destructive. The Keefes and Elliotts were created in a desire to confront an irrationality which was always evident in Lardner's work. Light comedy was as irresistible to Lardner as it had been to Twain and other humorists. However, overriding the conventional Lardnerian ballplayer, the genial boob with some talent and some quirks, was a darker picture of lonely and bewildered men whose sojourn in the public arena exacerbated their difficulties, whose emotional problems were those of every man but whose public lives demanded performance and concealment of the problem.[16]

LARDNER AND SOUTHWESTERN HUMOR TRADITION

No evidence suggests that Lardner was conscious of the Southwestern writers, their realism, experiments in narration, or humorous treatment of sport in society. By 1914, that tradition had been diffused into the work of major authors such as Twain and into dialect tales in subliterature, the repertoires of anecdotal platform humorists, and the work of many early sportswriters with whom Lardner was familiar. However, Lardner drew all the elements together again in a resurrection of the comic realism that had been so effective in portraying sport and games in backwoods society.

Lardner's temperament and aims were, in general outline, similar to those of Longstreet, Thorpe, Hooper, and Harris, while his characters were more akin to the first-generation urban citizens of Dunne and Ade. Lardner's conservatism was evidenced in many ways. He was always slightly out-of-date in the songs he preferred, in the kind of baseball he liked to watch, and in his own writing, in which he eschewed any mention of sex at a time when strictures of presentation were being relaxed. Late in life, he led a quixotic campaign against suggestive lyrics in popular music, a crusade that dismayed both Fitzgerald and Hemingway.

In general, he was capable of real anger at modern society which he saw as shrill and full of braggarts and empty people. He was not alone in this critical stance. However, he spent a career writing of his own distaste without ever posing an alternative world. He knew that the idyllic Niles of the Lardner family childhood could not be overlaid on the brittle new society of urban and suburban wealth and power. He implicitly mourned a passing life by criticizing the new order just as the Southwesterners had criticized backwoods manners and mores to show their distance from that scene. His ballplayers and fans existed in the same social stratum, that of the middle class. Just as surely as Longstreet, Hooper, and Harris, Lardner knew that the social bonds of a community were reported through its games.

One of the ways in which Lardner worked with the elements of comic realism was to highlight the disparity between the almanac physical-prowess hero such as Crockett and Fink and the outcast Southwestern hero such as Ransy Sniffle or Sut Lovingood. The character of Jack Keefe has both a public and private role as he is both Crockett and Sut. He performs feats in the full glare of modern spectacle on the diamond, but in his private life he feels rejected and duped and looks to battle his enemies, real and imagined. Jack is constantly contesting his tormentors off the field. He should have heroic stature because of his public role but he does not.

In "Champion" (1916), Lardner took on an entire society's cherished beliefs about its athletic heroes when he wrote about middleweight champion Midge Kelly. Boxers, managers, fans, sportswriters—no one is spared in this tale in which Lardner created not simply a picture of a brutal fighter but of a character who was nothing more than a thug in love with violence. Midge's personality is well known to all who have the personal misfortune to depend upon or interact with him. Yet the public is force-fed conventional lies by the sportswriters about his upstanding character. The tone is established at the outset: "Midge Kelly scored his first knockout when he was seventeen. The knockee was his brother Connie, three years his junior and a cripple. The purse was a half dollar given to the youngster by a lady whose electric had just missed bumping his soul from his frail little body."[17] This paragraph parodies the line account of a fight by a wire service, giving all essential information as to fighter, opponent, and purse. However, the tone is one of derision and even bemused acceptance of Midge's character. The effect of "frail little body" and "knockee" gives the reader an early gauge to the moral stance of the tale. The narrator already knows the truth about Midge Kelly; the reader learns it brutally at the outset but it takes him longer to realize why the narrator is so cynical.

Two pages before the conclusion, a New York sportswriter is assigned to write a major piece on Midge's life. In his search for facts he runs up against a sickening collection of homilies advanced by Kelly's manager about his fighter's exemplary family life. These "facts" become the core of the sportswriter's story. Even so, Lardner's narrator excuses the reporter's failure to obtain the real facts about Kelly's countless victims during his rise to the top, the managers, wives, and girlfriends he cast aside: "But a story built on their evidence would never have passed the sporting editor. 'Suppose you can prove it,' that gentleman would have said, 'It wouldn't get us anything but abuse to print it. The people don't want to see him knocked. He's champion.'" (258). Lardner directed the brunt of his message in "Champion" at the sportswriting profession rather than solely at Kelly, whom he never really attempts to make into a believable villain. The cartoon monster Kelly is intentionally as unsatisfactory a portrait as the saccharine family man presented in the Sunday sports section. Lardner very neatly balanced these two polarized descriptions to give the reader a chance to be influenced by his final point about the responsibility of the sporting press. In his view, it was a continuing dilemma, one that still rages between those writers who gloss over the peccadilloes of popular heroes and those reporters who sensationalize the men behind the heroic postures or humanize them, all in the name of selling the heroes for the widest possible commercial consumption.

In "The Fight" Longstreet was completely open in his anger against citizens who had patronized the bloody contest fomented by Hansy Sniffle,[18] but in 1916, Lardner is fighting more insidious enemies than official piety, education, or law enforcement. He is exploring a mentality of collusion between fans and a popular press that feeds back the dreams that the fight public wants to believe. Kelly is as violent as any eye-gouger in Longstreet and more unstable than Sut Lovingood; his combativeness burns at a dull heat at all times.

Lardner's conception of American fandom was to become increasingly pessimistic in the 1920s. The atmosphere of hero-worship is criticized in a number of Lardner tales of athletes, usually by the wise narrator, a teammate, roommate, umpire, or writer, who knows the hero behind the scenes. These figures—the sympathetic teammate of "My Roomy"; Al, by implication in *A Busher's Letters*; the narrators of such tales as "Sick 'Em," "Alibi Ike," "Harmony" (1915), "The Holdout" (1917), "The Battle of the Century," "Hurry Kane," "The Venomous Viper of the Volga," and "Take a Walk" (1933)—give testimony to the fact that Lardner's ballplayers were not all dolts and blusterers. The stories are invariably related by a wise, sane, and often kind member of the athletic fraternity whose balance and good humor enable him to characterize the comic hero. "Harmony" includes a touch of pathos in the sportswriter's story of a veteran ballplayer's search for companionship in the team's barbershop quartet. An umpire in "Take a Walk" sympathetically recounts another umpire's lonely life in rented rooms and his fruitless love for a young girl who prefers a vain young slugging third baseman. The manager of "Holdout" stands up for a raise for his first baseman who is about to become a father. The baby is then named after the manager by the grateful player.

Such reporter-narrators were reminiscent of the Southwestern tradition. Longstreet always wrote from the gentleman's viewpoint, a man above the comic action. Thorpe was often the gentleman participant amused by his fellows, be they rustic hunters or yarn-spinners on steamboats. He also satirized the pomposity of this gentleman. Hooper controlled the Suggs stories from formal narration, allowing Simon to give forth an occasional aphorism after a particularly satisfying swindle. Even Harris' Sut was relating all his adventures to "George," the author/confidant, who transcribed Sut's tales just the way he spoke them as one must believe Al has turned over Jack Keefe's letters for publication. The position of reporter is assumed by an insider in Lardner's athletic tales. He functions as an observer of comic heroes, both those of prowess and of wit; he records their boasts, their deeds, and their essential lack of self-control and self-knowledge. However, his status presupposes an alternative world of order and reason within the team itself, a motive force that enables the unit to withstand the stress put on it by the clown or troublemaker. This character has never been given his due by Lardner's critics. This bemused insider, a rejoinder to the stock conception of Lardner's dumb ballplayers, also appears in Lardner's nonsports narratives, most notably as Finch, the put-upon husband in *The Big Town* (1921).

A variation on this narrator is the insider who reveals concrete details as well as his own moral blankness, the best example being the barber of "Haircut" (1925). Although the story is not about sports, it does have links to the tall tale, pulp fiction, and Southwestern prototypes. Not only is Jim Kendall, the town roarer, a relic of frontier humor, but the locale in which the story takes place is a brilliant stroke inasmuch as the barbershop, saloon, and poolroom were the only male preserves left in town life, otherwise a sea of domesticity. Barbershops had the gaudiest magazines and papers in town; they were the chief outlets for *The Police Gazette,* and the seamy little story underlying the plot of "Haircut" would have been a natural for a writeup in it. The perfect environment for the narration of such a story was chosen by Lardner. The barber gradually reveals his own insensitivity as he tells the facts of a murder he does not even recognize *as* a murder. One of his pals is gone; that is the only truth for him. His deathless last line to the man in the chair, the unseen judge possessing moral sensibility, is "Comb it wet or dry?" Lardner was able here to involve his narrators in the moral uncertainties of the story, a complexity of technique that he seldom undertook and one which no Southwestern realist except Thorpe achieved to any extent.

The role of the reporter, so ingrained in Lardner as a newspaperman, was first utilized in his baseball tales and then transferred to his other fiction. Lardner came to the frame narrator in his own way through his newspaper experience, his temperamental role as an observer, and his critical view of modern life. He needed to appropriate a form that would enhance portraits of comic heroes who could only lose force if made the focal point of the narration, since they did not have the depth, moral sense, or self-irony to criticize themselves.

Likenesses to frontier athletes are found in the physical metaphors that Lardner often used to describe his bumpkins:

> Standing six foot three in what was left of his stockings, he was wearing a suit of Arizona store clothes that would have been a fair fit for Singer's youngest midget and looked like he had pressed it with a tractor that had been parked on a river bottom.

> He had used up both the collars that he figured would see him through his first year in the big league. This left you a clear view of his Adam's apple which would make half a dozen pies. You'd have thought from his shoes that he had just managed to grab hold of the rail on the back platform of his train and been dragged from Yuma to Jacksonville. But when you seen his shirt, you wondered if he hadn't rode in the cab and loaned it to the fireman for a washcloth.[19]

The subject of this description, Elmer "Hurry" Kane, is a super player whose prodigious appetites are both more and less than human. Far from being the source of amusement to their teammates, the Keefes, Elliotts, and Kanes are exasperating and are suffered by the team in the hope that their performance will cancel out their personal foibles. The player who drew attention because of his personality or off-the-field affairs might have been the best fictional subject but his performance was the opposite of what Lardner admired, namely smart play and consistency as he carefully explained in a 1915 *American Magazine* series. A definite split existed between the comic athletes of his short stories and the winning players he respected most: those who evinced professionalism in their work.[20]

It is erroneous to see Lardner as a descendant of Twain. His narrators finally lacked the breadth of humanity that characterized so many of Twain's narrators. Whole areas of human pathology which Twain vividly exposed were closed to Lardner, the student of surface manners. In this way, too, Lardner can more truthfully be placed in a direct line from the more provincial Southwestern Humorists. His attitude toward undisciplined ballplayers is analogous to the Southwesterners' jaundiced view of the backwoods athlete and confidence man. Both Lardner and the Southwesterners wrote in a mixture of amusement and dismay at their subjects' vitality and energy. They reproduced with fidelity their speech and habits. Lardner's narrators are the equivalents of the Southwestern gentleman travellers and hunters, raconteurs, collectors of tall tales. He, too, wrote of a society in flux and created the Popular Sports Hero as one of its representative men.

The problem of narration was of great concern to the Southwestern writers who had wished to convey realistically not only the daily life of the society but also their more refined perspective of it. The choice of narration was determined by the perspective from which the author wished to view the life of society. Just as the Southwesterners vacillated from amused gentleman narrator to vernacular comedian, so did Lardner attempt the more objective mask of the gentleman as sportswriter, teammate, and manager, as well as the subjective persona of a Jack Keefe. The general movement in contemporary sports fiction has been for the reporter, player, or player-as-reporter to be the controlling narrator, most often in first person. Lardner's fiction firmly established this convention.

LARDNER AND 1920s POPULAR CULTURE

In the 1920s, Lardner had become the nation's best-known short story writer and had bought a large house on Long Island where he lived with his wife and four sons. By 1925 he seemed condemned to live the life that he satirized so well. The golf dates, the bridge parties, the winter vacations to warm climates—Lardner's fiction made these environments, along with the world of show business, his settings for the first literary investigation of a broad range of suburban life.[21] Virginia Woolf's famous insight into Lardner's subject matter was written in 1925:

> It is no coincidence that the best of Mr. Lardner's stories are about games, for one may guess that Mr. Lardner's interest in games has solved one of the most difficult problems of the American writer; it has given him a clue, a centre, a meeting place for the divers activities of a people whom a vast continent isolates, whom no tradition controls. Games give him what society gives his English brother.[22]

Lardner suggested that the player and the fan were intimately related. The fan was bored, repressed, needing release from the prison of self; the athlete was under the tension created by constant notoriety. In suburbia, these qualities merged in the fans who became players, whose lives fed on the small competitions of their leisure world. These competitions in turn reflected on their larger relations with other people.

The baseball players of Lardner's earlier fiction were replaced in the 1920s by suburbanites who bared their teeth in competition at golf or bridge. The obvious implication of their boorishness and frantic desire to win was that all of the traits brought forth in their leisure-time pursuits were simply the reflections of their daily lives in business or in the family circle. Lardner wrote about the first generation upper middle class with money to spend and no real idea what to buy, whom to meet, or where to go. His fictional vision of the 1920s was of terminal boredom, full of meaningless excursions and empty chatter. Social competition, for Lardner, was most often mean and petty with no redeeming features. In "A Caddy's Diary" (1922), the narrator, generously supplied with advice from a philosophical fellow caddy named Joe, watches poker-faced all summer while bankers, businessmen, and housewives lie, cheat, and urge him to do the same on their behalf for tips. The urge to cheat, to go one up on the competition, is almost a narcotic for the characters. The women are as bad as the men; two of them end up betting on a fifty-dollar dress and using all their wiles to get the caddy to change their "lies," a lovely golfing term that acknowledges their chicanery. Lardner's master stroke was to have Charles Crane, the club champion who never cheated ("That is one of the penaltys [sic] for being a good player, you can't cheat"), flee town with $8,000 he had stolen from the bank in which he worked. In this story, the suburban caddy becomes wiser from experience that matches that of the urban bootblack in the pulp fiction of the late nineteenth century. Human folly and greed pass before him daily. He believes he is untouched and can freely criticize the morals of his patrons until Joe brings him up short by reminding him of the lies he has changed for a one-dollar tip. The complicity of the caddy turns the morality of the tale back on the narrator who represents the moral point of view as in "Champion" and "My Roomy." Joe pronounces judgment on the cheater's world at the country club placed against the theft of Charles Crane: "the bigger it is the less of a sucker the person is that goes after it."

Lardner's characters had been obsessed with money since Jack Keefe and Midge Kelly. For those who have financial security, other conflicts surface. Lardner was able to capitalize on his years of writing sports by turning the competitions of married life into comic contests. In "The Golden Honeymoon" (1922), the flinty old married couple goes south to Florida where they meet the wife's suitor from fifty years before. The husband-narrator then proceeds to enter the lists to prove to his wife that she made the right choice. He loses to his old rival at cards and horseshoes but whips him at checkers. The games revitalize him and put a snap in his step. In "Contract" (1929), Shelton is reluctantly dragged into a social circle by his wife and then is constantly berated by his partners for his poor bridge playing. One night he retaliates by criticizing their manners and grammar, much to the dismay of his wife. Responding to a random statement from his partner that "The itta girl just overslept herself, that's all," Shelton says: "I have no idea who the itta girl is, but I am interested in your statement that she overslept herself. Would it be possible for her, or any other itta girl to oversleep somebody else? If it were a sleeping contest, I should think 'outsleep' would be preferable, but even so I can't understand how a girl of any size outsleeps herself."[23] Shelton is banished from the table in disgrace, for even these dull characters know when they are being insulted. Lardner satirized the excessive insistence on the rules of the game to turn the play back upon the tormentors by having Shelton play the language game, insisting on verbal precision from the less than articulate group. However, the next week finds Shelton playing at the socially respectable Pardees where his name is mispronounced and he is still being chastised for his poor play. His rebellion has been only momentary for he is caught in the web of social games.

During the 1920s Lardner turned his gaze on his readers and showed them to be players as well, though they achieved no more success than his troubled athletes. What both ballplayers and suburbanites had in common was insecurity, competitiveness, and belligerence instead of humanity and tolerance, acquisitiveness instead of love, and a pervasive hollowness. In his ballplayers, these traits were manifested in an inability to handle successfully the pressures that arose from being popular heroes; for the suburbanites, it was a boredom so deep that it could be attained only through leisure pastimes. His picture of a liberated society at play was always rendered from the caustic point of view of the confirmed bourgeois citizen somberly, hilariously reporting on a frivolity foreign to his nature. None of his characters have the romantic vitality and energy of Fitzgerald's flappers, college men, and intense visionaries. They were all a bit tired and found it hard to adapt to the frenetic style of the 1920s.

Lardner's body of work appeared at the outset of a vast revolution in American popular culture. His career spanned the restructuring of baseball as a game of power rather than speed, the rise of tennis and golf personified in heroes such as Bill Tilden and Bobby Jones, the birth of professional football, and, with the careers of Jack Dempsey and Gene Tunney, an unparalleled excitement in boxing. Lardner also saw the birth of radio and the cinema, as well as the flowering of the Broadway musical stage. His enormous interest in popular forms showed itself in areas outside of sport. After years of attempting to write successful plays for Broadway and musical numbers for reviews, he collaborated in 1929-30 with young George S. Kaufmann on *June Moon*, an adaptation of "Some Like Them Cold," which ultimately ran for 273 performances. Hollywood attempted to woo Lardner on several occasions but failed. Much of his humor fit in perfectly with the then reigning comic talents of the screen.[24] His concise dialogue would have been perfect not only for the silent screen but for talkies as well.[25] He had a flair for stand-up comic routines. They were often part of his early baseball stories, in which one teammate plays straight man to another's clown, as in "Alibi Ike" and "Where Do You Get That Noise?" (1915). In his last years, the poker-faced Lardner bore a startling facial resemblance to Buster Keaton, another consummate master of the deadpan.

Lardner returned near the end of his life to baseball as subject matter. Several of his last stories, which retain the framework of his early baseball pieces with a reporter as narrator, show a softening of his feeling toward the ignorant busher. In *Lose with a Smile*, Lardner's 1932 resurrection of the Keefe format, a young Brooklyn outfielder's letters home to his girl in Illinois and her replies are in a more melancholy, sympathetic tone. Danny Warner has only mediocre ability and appears doomed to a minor league career. He is not the defensive, self-inflated Keefe but is rather a good-humored bumpkin. Oddly enough, his best friend on the team is veteran Casey Stengel, a rookie with Brooklyn in 1912 when Lardner had begun on the sports beat. Here he is portrayed as a bulwark of sanity and steadiness in Danny's young life, rather than the eccentric legend he became in his later years. The pathos of the tale lingers when Danny's dejected letter telling of his demotion to Jersey City crosses with his girl's excited announcement that she has convinced her father that she should come to New York to be with her fiancé. In November 1931 Lardner began a final series of reminiscences in *The Saturday Evening Post* in which he fondly recalled his early days as a baseball reporter in South Bend and Chicago. They are among the sunniest pieces he ever wrote.

When Lardner died in 1933, Broun showed his strong appreciation of what Lardner had achieved in American fiction by commenting in "Nature the Copycat," which ran in his daily column "It Seems to Me" in the *New York World Telegram*: "When Lardner limned his famous character [Elmer Kane] no such person existed. . . . The miracle is reserved only for the truly creative artist." Broun went on, "Before there was a Dizzy Dean, Ring knew him from head to pitching cleat." He concluded, that with "divine arrogance," Lardner had said, "'I see it this way. Let Nature catch up with my conception.'"[26] Although it is hard to imagine Lardner as such an Olympian artist, Broun is acknowledging Lardner's originality in creating his sports characters.

Lardner's work was a true triumph of popular writing. He wrote for a middle-class audience eager to read about itself and its pastimes. His initial subject matter sprang from a specifically modern sports culture while his narrative technique was in a vital tradition of spectatorial reporting that had begun in the newspaper sketches of the Southwestern Humorists in the *Spirit of the Times*, even as his own stories had been nurtured in the *Chicago Tribune*. Lardner was another American gentleman commentator who viewed play with dismay. His characters gained no control of their lives through competition, which basically became their imprisonment. No individuals controlled their experience through play for Lardner could not see beyond the collective paradigm of play experience, and this dogged conformist stance doomed him to be a writer of the second rank. As a modern Puritan, he admired order, restraint, and solid achievement through work well done in society. But as a modern humorist, he wrote of disorder, oddly spiritless profligacy, and wasted lives of little or no accomplishment. Given his temperamental preferences, it is ironic that his most lasting creation was the figure of the bumpkin athlete which he perfected with such success that more than a half-century later reporters and authors still see the professional Popular Sports Hero through the amused eyes of Lardnerian narrators and describe that Hero's foibles through Lardnerian language.

NOTES

[1] On taking over the "In the Wake of the News" column in the *Tribune*, Lardner wrote of ballplayers that "some of them are very nice fellows and others not as nice. They're just like any other set of men." Donald Elder, *Ring Lardner* (Garden City, New York: Doubleday, 1956), p. 72. Cub pitcher Ed Reulbach stated, "If he had any faults, we liked him too much to notice them—he was one of us." Elder, *Ring Lardner*, p. 72.

[2] The most famous attack on Lardner for these sentiments was by Clifton Fadiman, "Ring Lardner and the Triangle of Hate," *Nation*, 22 March 1933, pp. 15-17.

[3] Ring Lardner, Jr., *The Lardners: My Family Remembered* (New York: Harper & Row, 1976), pp. 85-86;

Jonathan Yardley, *Ring: A Biography of Ring Lardner* (New York: Random House, 1977), p. 154.

[4] Elder, *Ring Lardner,* p. 109.

[5] Ring Lardner, *You Know Me Al* (New York: Scribner's, 1960), pp. 98-99. Subsequent page references to this edition appear in parentheses in the text.

[6] Another early series character of Lardner's resembled Jack Keefe in his economic circumstances and opinions. He was Chicago police detective Fred Goss, hero of *Own Your Own Home,* a series of four stories begun in 1915 and collected into a novel in 1919. A series character speaking in witty vernacular was the bright narrator, "Gullible," of *Gullible's Travels,* begun in 1916. This narrator is closest to Lardner's "in-character" mask in numerous stories in later years. Walton Patrick, *Ring Lardner* (New York: Twayne, 1963), p. 27.

[7] Broun travelled with the Giants for the *New York Tribune* from 1911 to 1914 and was a close friend of Mathewson. Lardner wrote an admiring portrait entitled "Matty," *American Magazine,* August 1915.

[8] Lardner, "My Roomy," *The Ring Lardner Reader* (New York: Scribner's, 1963), p. 515.

[9] See Lardner, "Tyrus: The Greatest of Them All," *American Magazine,* June 1915. For an account of the last sad years of Cobb's life as a disease-ravaged, paranoid millionaire, see Al Stump, "The Fight to Live," Edward Ehre, Irving T. Marsh, eds., *Best Sports Stories 1962* (New York: E.P. Dutton, 1962), pp. 35-55.

[10] Other early baseball stories include "Sick 'Em," *Saturday Evening Post,* 25 July 1914; "The Poor Simp," *SEP,* 11 September 1915; "The Crook," *SEP,* 24 June 1916; "The Hold Out," *SEP,* 24 March 1917; and "The Yellow Kid," *SEP,* 23 June 1917.

[11] Elder, *Ring Lardner,* p. 170, from a Lardner 17 July 1921 syndicated column.

[12] See Lardner, "Sport and Play," Harold Steams, ed., *Civilization in the United States* (New York: Harcourt, Brace, 1922), p. 461.

[13] Patrick, *Ring Lardner,* pp. 125-26.

[14] Elder, *Ring Lardner,* p. 160.

[15] Ibid., p. 162.

In the 1915 *American Magazine* series, Lardner had put Cicotte on his personal major league All-Star team.

[16] Lardner's only real competitors of any statute in popular sports fiction during the early modern period were Charles Van Loan and Zane Grey. Van Loan had been a sportswriter in both San Francisco and New York. He wrote more than forty stories collected in 1919 in three volumes: *Score by Innings,* containing baseball stories; *Taking the Count,* about boxing; and *Old Man Curry,* comprised of horse-racing tales. Van Loan created a more populous sporting world than Lardner; however, his host of humorous ballplayers, managers, trainers, and hangers-on included few true villains and fewer neurotics. Although Van Loan did not experiment with narration nor satirize his sports subjects, it was he who perceived Lardner's talent and mentioned him in 1914 to George Horace Lorimer, whose *Saturday Evening Post* initially published the six Jack Keefe episodes that became *You Know Me Al.* Zane Grey's enormous successes came in other popular forms but he dabbled in stories of semipro and professional baseball as well as stories with a college hero. For his baseball stories, he drew on his experience as an outfielder for Newark, N.J. in the Atlantic League in 1896. *The Red Headed Outfield and Other Stories* (1915) included plots derived from Van Loan's and Lardner's tales of "rubes," fans, and team life, but his narration was an unsuccessful mix: half-stilted, half-colloquial.

A popular writer on the periphery of early modern sports fiction was Heywood Broun (1888-1939), best known in the 1920s and 1930s as a tireless liberal columnist married to feminist Ruth Hale. Broun began as a New York City sportswriter, joining the 1911 freshman class of Damon Runyon and Grantland Rice, but Broun soon moved from the sports scene to become a star columnist on Herbert Swope's *New York World.* Broun wrote only two novels, *The Boy Grew Older* (1923) and *The Sun Field* (1923). They were the earliest book-length adult fiction about popular sport and sportswriting which Broun viewed with a refined, puckish perspective.

[17] Lardner, "Champion," *The Ring Lardner Reader,* p. 239. Subsequent page references to this story appear in parentheses in the text.

[18] At the conclusion of "The Fight," Longstreet broke from his narrator's role to comment, "Thanks to the Christian religion, to schools, colleges, and benevolent associations, such scenes of barbarism and cruelty as that which I have been just describing are now of rare occurrence, though they may still be occasionally met with in some of the new counties. . . . The peace officers who countenance them deserve a place in the Penitentiary." Longstreet, "The Fight," *Georgia Scenes,* p. 53.

[19] Lardner, "Hurry Kane," *The Ring Lardner Reader,* p. 517.

[20] This theory has been applied explicitly to Lardner's views on baseball with evidence largely from his nonfiction in Leverett Smith, "The Diameter of Frank Chance's Diamond: Ring Lardner and Professional Sports," *Journal of Popular Culture* 6, no. 1 (Summer 1972), pp. 139-44, and incorporated into Smith, *The American Dream and the National Game* (Bowling Green: Bowling Green University Popular Press, 1975), pp. 110-16.

21 Lardner's vision of the new American suburban life was first identified by Rourke, *American Humor,* pp. 291-94.

22 Virginia Woolf, "American Fiction," *Collected Essays* (London: Harcourt, Brace and World, 1966), 2, p. 118.

23 Lardner, "Contract," *The Ring Lardner Reader,* p. 389.

24 Early film comedians filled the screen with their physical skill and grace as well as with their use of sport in their scenarios. Comedians and classic films include Charlie Chaplin, *The Champion* (1916), *Modern Times* (1936); Buster Keaton, *Battling Butler* (1926), *College* (1927); Harold Lloyd, *The Freshman* (1925); The Marx Brothers, *Horsefeathers* (1932); and W. C. Fields, *Never Give a Sucker an Even Break* (1937).

For a look at sport in early cinema, see Cantwell, "Sport Was Box Office Poison," *Sports Illustrated,* 15 September 1969, rpt. Talamini, Page, eds., *Sport and Society,* pp. 441-54.

25 A writer with a penchant for comic dialogue and the depiction of the Broadway scene was Damon Runyon (1880-1946) whose short fiction was as popular in the 1930s, as Lardner's work had been in the 1920s. Runyon was another refugee from the sport beat. He first came to New York City from Denver to write sports for Hearst's *American.* By 1914, like Broun and Lardner, Runyon had his own column, "This Mornin's Mornin," and he wrote on every topic of sporting interest. He made up for his late start in fiction by publishing 55 stories between 1931 and 1939.30

Runyon explored a world of high-rollers, bookmakers, gangsters, their molls and hangers-on. His laconic style attempted to combine a quaint formal diction with understated sarcasm and underworld argot. The peculiar style that resulted, however, was often strained, dull, and flat, in every way inferior to Lardner's narration. Runyon took a number of two-dimensional eccentrics through a series of comic misadventures that most often took place in the sporting world. His Broadway characters were companions to the 1890s "sports," members of the fringe society that lived off wagering and the entertainment business. He was at his best in creating horseplayers, bookies, and hoods, quixotic philosophers of the school of bad tips and the rubout, heavy losers who kept coming back for more action.

26 Heywood Broun, "Nature the Copycat," *It Seems to Me* (New York: Harcourt, Brace, 1935), p. 298.

Kent Cartwright and Mary McElroy

SOURCE: "Malamud's 'The Natural' and the Appeal of Baseball in American Culture," in *Journal of American Culture,* Vol. 8, No. 2, Summer, 1985, pp. 47-55.

[*In the following essay, Cartwright and McElroy examine the mythic and pastoral qualities of Malamud's novel.*]

British novelist Virginia Woolf observed that sport solves one of the American writer's most difficult artistic problems: "It has given him a clue, a centre, a meeting place for the diverse activities of people whom a vast continent isolates."[1] Sport has an almost religious magnetism in America, and its states of higher exaltation have been regarded by some as the last, comic vestiges of American transcendentalism. Indeed, for the novelist, sport offers a curious, American meeting place in time as well as in space. Correspondingly, the athlete's serviceability as an American symbol is enhanced by the innocence that we traditionally attach to him, "a child existing in the idealized world of game," a condition of innocence that is heightened by the athlete's dream of immortality, his "desire to remain forever whole and young."[2] Such innocence furthermore parallels conveniently that which has always adhered to the classic American hero, Cooper's Natty Bumppo, James' Christopher Newman or Fitzgerald's Jay Gatsby. The sport figure, then, is a kind of Americanized *tabula rasa* upon which the novelist can essay an enormous range of controlled encounters, turning them comic, tragic or satiric as he chooses, and developing meaning both in and out of the sporting arena.

While sport is a powerful metaphor that cuts across the differences of American society, no sport is so broadly appealing or so typically American as baseball. Baseball, in fact, is the central theme of a novel that for three decades now has been accepted as a contemporary classic, Bernard Malamud's *The Natural,*[3] a novel which illuminates baseball's compelling appeal for Americans and suggests baseball as a symbol of the national experience. Played by the upper and middle classes, baseball between 1870 and 1910 evolved into America's national pastime. It captures what Michael Oriard describes as "the shared dreams of a culture, those collectively held that are fundamentally important to the way people think and live."[4] For example, the spirit of American individualism is expressed in a game whose very nature guarantees a certain measure of individuality. The players are assigned specific duties and are responsible for a predesignated portion of the field. The batter confronts the pitcher with little support available from his teammates. Individual achievements become the stuff of record books and legends.

Baseball's appeal may also be explained by its relationship to nature. Played on a grassy, diamond-shaped field, the game has been described as a modern day pastoral art form. It creates an atmosphere of studied harmony, an effort achieved by the "controlled openness" of the perspective from home plate, the calm and wholeness evoked by the way players occupy certain positions on the field, and the almost moral connection between success, on the one hand, and offensive or defensive mastery of the field, on the other.[5] The pastoral also transcends time. In baseball, "no one can tell exactly when a game will end. With sufficient inequalities of sides, the game might go on forever as the weaker team tries vainly to retire the side."[6] Baseball conveys the spectator to an idealized world which is yet attuned to the deepest rhythms of nature.

Baseball's Americanism is exemplified by the persistence of the Doubleday myth concerning the game's invention. The claim to American origins for baseball, although debunked in 1947 by Robert Henderson's seminal work, *Ball, Bat and Bishop,*[7] still echoes in the baseball world. The Doubleday myth survives and is embedded in what baseball historian David Voigt describes as "the class of myths reaffirming the driving faith in human ingenuity and creative individualism—to abandon the myth might mean accepting as fact that the game evolved in a haphazard, piecemeal, trial and error fashion."[8] Perhaps one reason baseball needs a "founding father" is that ballplayers themselves are often perceived as self-made, hardworking men of action, characterized by the spirit of American heroes like Teddy Roosevelt, George Washington and John Wayne. Mike Kelly, baseball's first superstar, for example, won the hearts of fans with his personal daring on the basepaths. Particularly during the early part of the twentieth century, the popular imagination, in an attempt to cling to values that were disappearing in a rapidly changing American society, cast baseball players as folk heroes representing traditional American traits such as fair play, sportsmanship and individual sacrifice. Indeed, for Americans, the game seems fundamentally both moral and heroic. "The wonder," exclaims literary critic Earl Wasserman, "is that we do not have a whole library of significant baseball fiction since so much of the American spirit has been seriously poured into the game and its code until it has a life of its own that affects the national temperament."[9]

Baseball stories did achieve wide popularity during the first half of the twentieth century; however, they rarely appealed to a range of emotions and ideals wider than those produced by winning and losing. Ring Lardner's *You Know Me Al,*[10] published in 1916, today recognized as baseball's first significant sport novel, received scant critical attention. Lardner's sport figures, typified by the bumbling baseball player Jack Keefe, attempted to push the sport novel out of the realm of juvenile fiction through "the creation of an unglamorous but very human hero who does not come out on the top of the heap."[11] Even Heywood Broun's mixture of baseball and the "seedy side of American life" in *Sun Field,*[12] published in 1923, was criticized for using "children's games" to comment on the problems in American society. Overall, serious readers and critics generally considered sport literature inconsequential, and disregarded it. In fact, F. Scott Fitzgerald publicly criticized Ring Lardner's interest in sport, characterizing the game and its players as "a few dozen illiterates playing a boy's game . . . a game bounded by walls which kept out novelty or danger, change or adventure."[13] Fitzgerald's skepticism about sport topics as literary material echoed

through literary circles for some time to come, and not until nearly four decades after the publication of *You Knew Me Al* did sport novels finally gain literary acceptance. The growth of mass spectator sports, particularly after World War II, contributed to the production of outstanding sport fiction. Mark Harris' trilogy of pitcher Henry Wiggen, Robert Coover's *The Universal Baseball Association* and, of course, Bernard Malamud's *The Natural* are just a few examples of sport novels heralded for their literary merits.[14] What is central to the growth of the subgenre of sport literature, resulting in the sport novel's increasing literary recognition, is the novelist's desire to examine the complexity of American life *within* the sporting context which literary characters inhabit.

By far the most significant baseball novel in the American literary tradition is Malamud's *The Natural.* It was published in 1952 and received considerable attention, not only as the first novel of a promising writer but also as the most successful American novel to treat baseball as the subject matter for serious fiction. At first glance, however, *The Natural* offers tantalizing but unlikely material for a disquisition into sport. It tantalizes because its incidents are drawn from specific legends and facts of baseball. Roy Hobbs, the novel's hero, is an echo of Babe Ruth: the orphaned childhood; the switch from pitcher to hitter; the home run hit to cheer a sick child who has seemed to lose the will to live; the traumatic bellyache, which like Ruth's in 1925, hospitalizes the hero and endangers the championship. Other baseball personalities and events also find their counterparts in Malamud's novel: Chuck Hostetler's fall between third base and home in the sixth game of the 1945 World Series; Pete Reiser's ruined career from a crash against an outfield wall; Wilbert Robinson's attempt to catch a grapefruit dropped from an airplane; the shooting of Eddie Waitkus in Chicago's Edgewater Beach Hotel in 1949 by a deranged woman; Hilda "The Bell" Chester, a famous Dodger fan of Ebbets Field; the cold-hearted parsimony of Branch Rickey and Charles Comiskey; Arnold Rothstein, the gambler who allegedly fixed the 1919 World Series; and, perhaps most powerfully evoked of all, the sad if apocryphal disillusionment of the young boy crying to "Shoeless" Joe Jackson, "Say it ain't so, Joe."

As a source of insight into specific historic happenings *The Natural* teases but does not satisfy. While many real events are alluded to, none are explored in depth; while the "Golden Age" of baseball is a source of fictional detail, the material remains unsorted in time and place, an alphabet soup of different decades, characters, teams and circumstances. *The Natural* falls short of (or beyond) history; similarly, it is also not what literary critics like to refer to as "naturalistic." The surface glow of the novel does not recreate the surface glow of life as we know it, in contrast to the manner in which, say, the film *Chariots of Fire* does mirror the ambiance of the real Paris Olympiad. First, the characters in our novel have bizarre, comic book names: Red Blow, Goodwill Banner, Max Mercy, Whammer Wambold, Iris Lemon,

Memo Paris. These figures strike us more often as caricatures than as rounded fictional personages. Judge Goodwill Banner, the major owner of the New York Knights baseball team, for example, lives in a dark, greasy tower overlooking the stadium, the floor of his apartment tilting precariously, and the Judge himself wearing a heavy wig and smoking a huge cigar as he sits in the unillumined darkness quoting biblical scriptures and wise maxims to extenuate his stinginess. While such a character does not lack in significance, he does lack in verisimilitude.

Further, while the novel is powerfully psychological, it is not realistically so. Malamud is clearly interested in the mental states of his characters—indeed, the novel is full of dreams, recollections, associations—but, these mental states are not so much reported or analyzed as they are evoked metaphorically and imagistically. Instead of, say, Virginia Woolf's or James Joyce's fictional stream of consciousness reflecting human mental processes, the minds of Malamud's characters are landscapes of surrealistic images and creatures: trains, twisted trees, looming hills, floods, pitches like birds, meteors, circles within circles. Finally, and perhaps most noticeably, the action of the novel lacks the naturalistic, causal logic of events as we perceive them in life. Incidents in the novel are sometimes dreamlike or ridiculous, symbolic or even questionably real. At one point, for example, Roy believes that a car in which he is a passenger runs over a small boy and a dog, yet the victims cannot be discovered on searching. On another occasion Roy suddenly and inexplicably turns magician, raining gold and silver coins from one person's nose, a dear herring from another's mouth, duck eggs from a woman's bosom.

The reader feels, moreover, that Malamud intends such acts to be inexplicable, to confront and violate our sense of realism. For in *The Natural* events proceed by a logic not entirely our own. Things happen not as links in a chain of physical causes and earthly acts, but as expressions, stations, of a symbolic order. The heart of *The Natural* is not behaviorism but mystery.

What possible benefit can this strange novel have, then, for explaining the persistent appeal of baseball in American culture? In answering this question we must examine baseball from three different angles: its anthropological and mythic background, its discrete rituals and characteristics, and its engagement with the social world that surrounds it, all of which help explain the appeal of this classic American game. John Ruskin, the nineteenth century critic, observed that "Great nations write their autobiography in three manuscripts: the book of their deeds, the book of their words, and the book of their art. Not one of these books can be understood unless we read the two others, but of the three the only trustworthy one is the last."[15] What Ruskin suggests is that art, and for our purposes imaginative literature, gives us a kind of irreducible truth. Let us think of such truth, for the moment, as the observation within sport of

historically recurring patterns. And with that, we are able to say something rather startling: Bernard Malamud is the first writer about baseball to have explored in depth the remote anthropological and cultural allusions imbedded in the pastoral rituals of the game. We have for a long time, of course, thought of baseball in terms of the pastoral: it follows the seasonal cycle of the year—spring training, the summer season, the October classic; it is perennially concerned with age and youth and renewal, though it proceeds without clocks or stopwatches; its very geometry is circular like its seasonalism, and it is the only sport where a player's goals follow the circumference of the bases and return "home"; its heroes, the boys of summer, are country folk at heart, farmers and fishermen; its pundits are bumpkinesque, speaking an idiom of fractured, homespun, innocent English; surrounded by concrete and machines, it is played in a meadow that appears, always, unspeakably green. Baseball, we may say, takes it shape, its character, from the processes of nature.

Malamud understood that, it is grist for his novel. But he saw something more. Malamud recognized that the pastoral rituals of baseball recreate a pattern of cultural experience that is many centuries old, a myth that is not only American but descends from the ancient Vegetation rites of the Orient and of Western Europe, a basic myth that is embodied and refashioned incessantly throughout the history of Western culture.[15] Part of baseball's fundamental appeal, Malamud suggests, is its lineal connection, for example, with the Phoenician-Greek cult of Adonis, circa 3000 B.C., with the epic heroes of ancient Greece, and with the legends of Arthurian romance. One source of baseball's enduring popularity, according to Malamud, is not simply its nostalgic, Jeffersonian, agrarian charm but its expression of something fundamental in the Western psyche, the kind of pattern Jung explores in his notion of the "collective unconscious."[16] The first thing that Malamud has to tell us about baseball, then, is that baseball captures a truth, a shape to experience, that is more central to our heritage than we may have expected.

But what is this mythic pattern that baseball's pastoral rituals derive from and recreate? For an answer, we may start with Sir James G. Frazer's *The Golden Bough*,[17] a work of cultural anthropology rather than of literature, which began to appear around the turn of this century. The ancient Oriental and Western cults of mystery and fertility which Frazer studied have in common a mythic hero, a god or king figure, "whose suffering and death are commemorated with the waning of the year and whose ritual resurrection corresponds to and causes the coming of the crops in spring."[18] The most vivid embodiment of the myth is the Quest for the Grail of Arthurian legend, later explored by Jessie L. Weston,[19] and it is to this version of the myth that Malamud most obviously, though far from exclusively, alludes. The basic challenge of the Quest hero—Sir Galahad, Sir Percival, Sir Gawain, or the antecedent heroes of the ancient Vegetation rites—is to restore the sick or maimed

Fisher King to health through the accomplishment of a task and thereby to relieve the Waste Land from infertility, drought, and desolation. It is no coincidence, then, that Roy Hobbs' baseball team is the New York Knights or that their manager is old Pop Fisher, who suffers from athlete's foot on his hands. When the aging Roy Hobbs joins the Knights part way through the season, the team is disunified and rooted in the cellar. The grass of the playing field is "worn scabby," the season is "blasted" and "dry" (p. 45), and even the drinking fountain spouts rusty water. Roy is destined to lead the Knights to the brink of the pennant; suggestively, his first hit brings a deluge of rain. Baseball, as Malamud insists, is perennially concerned with the newcomer. Indeed, the obsession with the spring rookie has always been one of the more eccentric rites of baseball, eccentric because rookies always prove less interesting as performers than they were as subjects of speculation. In Roy Hobbs, Malamud reveals the pattern that lies at the heart of this puzzle, for Roy embodies the ever-present aspiration of the game, concentrated upon the stranger-hero who will redeem the fallen times.

The correspondence between the basic story of the Quest and *The Natural* are achieved in considerable detail. Memo Paris, the *femme fatale* of the novel, for example, parallels the evil enchantress Morgan le Fay, while her opposite, Iris Lemon, plays the beneficent Lady of the Lake. Merlin the Magician has his double in the evil, one-eyed Gus Sands, the Supreme Bookie. Like Sir Galahad, Roy Hobbs is an orphan who appears out of the West with an aging attendant, his surrogate father, Sam Simpson, who dies shortly thereafter. Similarly, the death of Bump Bailey from a crash against the leftfield wall recalls the strange knight of the Quest who dies early in the company of the Quester. Like the hero of the Grail, Roy too is asked a vital question, and, paralleling the Gawain stories, he fails to answer correctly. In myth the hero must seek to know whom the Grail serves; he must, that is, strive altruistically, for "definite benefits to be won for others,"[20] not for himself. Roy Hobbs, as he is questioned by a *duessa* figure early in the novel, fails of the knowledge of this service, and it is for that failure that he is shot and his baseball heroics delayed until he is thirty-five.

In addition to these allusions to chivalric romance. Roy bears interesting resemblances to Achilles, the hero of *The Iliad,* and other characters suggest figures in that epic. Various events in the novel, furthermore, have analogues ranging from the Greek god Zeus' legendary dry-gulching of his father Kronos to the details of F. Scott Fitzgerald's *The Great Gatsby*. Essentially, Roy Hobbs is the aging fertility hero of Western myth. He is rural, of the land; he comes in the dry season; and his task is to renew the king, save his people, and restore the waters. He is winter becoming spring. In Roy Hobbs, Malamud has created not only a novelistic character but an Everyman of the game. This rich and suggestive metaphoric technique raises to new heights the significance of the seasonal ritual and pastoral mythos of base-ball. Carl Jung describes the primal, indeed irrational, power that such archetypal forms have for us when he observes that "They are ineradicable, for they represent the ultimate foundations of the psyche itself."[21] The appeal of baseball is buried in our psyche, far beyond the allure of designated hitters or the boredom of the game's slow pace and indifferent athleticism. What Malamud says about baseball, then, is that its rites are the crystallization of our collective unconscious in far more elaborate and dramatic ways than we have ever recognized before. Baseball's popular contemporary appeal is, ironically, a very old appeal after all. The pastoral nature of baseball has become a subject of increasing interest to critics of the game; it is Malamud's *The Natural* which revealed most thoroughly the emotional power and ancient cultural heritage within baseball's pastoral scheme.

The Natural, furthermore, explores some of the pastoral qualities specific to baseball that we have mentioned earlier. While sports such as football and basketball are time-conscious, regulated by the clock, baseball is not. It is time-free, elapsing only with the completion of a fixed number of fixed events. That quality makes baseball a paradox, because the game is more attuned than other sports to the rhythms and cycles of nature yet simultaneously free from the immediate tyranny of ticking hands. As spectators and fans, we attend not to the clock but to the pattern of events. That fact seems to have fascinated Malamud, for in *The Natural,* mythic time, we might say, overlays chronological time. Mythic time is not extrinsic, imposed from without as an arbitrary movement between abstract intervals; rather it is intrinsic, an emanation of character, of occasion, and of the limited forms of action possible within the game.

In *The Natural,* for example, a player might plausibly age in a moment. Such an instance of baseball's mythic time comes early in the novel. Roy Hobbs, still only a teenager and on his way to his first professional tryout, finds himself in an impromptu duel as pitcher against last year's leading hitter and Most Valuable Player, Whammer Wambold. Though thirty-three years old, the Whammer is at the height of his game. In three pitches, Roy strikes him out. Those pitches are surrealistic and symbolic, vastly longer in experience than the few seconds Roy takes to hurl them. The first reminds the Whammer of "a white pigeon he had kept as a boy" (p. 28), and he is bothered "no end" with the "surprise and strangeness" of it (p. 28). The second pitch appears like a "slow, spinning planet looming toward earth," then a fortuneteller's crystal ball, and finally a "curious combination of circles" (p. 29). The third slithers like "a meteor, the flame swallowing itself" (p. 29). Even as the Whammer swings, commits himself, he hears a sound like a gong and realizes "with sadness that the ball he had expected to hit had long since been part of the past" (p. 30). And what the Whammer most fully realizes is not just the passing of a ball but the passage of a life: as Malamud puts it, "the Whammer understood he was, in the truest sense of it, out. . . . Dropping the bat, he trotted off to the train, an old man" (p. 30). Likewise, for Roy Hobbs, at bats became constant moments of truth, testings in which he experiences fear, confidence, memories, visions, and the restless ebb and flow of his vital energies. In baseball's mythic time, a player may go from the prime of his career to the ruin of it in an instant, because history is signified to us only in choices and acts, hits, runs and outs.

In the Whammer's *agon* Malamud also isolates another quality that is peculiar to the baseball experience. With a missed ball—in going after, say, a fastball that should have been a curve—every batter undergoes an instantaneous moment of recognition that is intrinsic to baseball. That moment is a kind of ironic double vision, the willing of action in the swing and the simultaneous realization of its futility in the passed ball. Such an irony arises from the very contrast between the split-second speed of the pitch and the expansive consciousness of the batter. The ironic double vision, the straining after an event that is already over, is akin to Roy's repeated sense of *deja vu*, of wanting something that he has had in the past but cannot have now because he has already had it. This remarkable, almost existential, confrontation between pitcher and batter colors the whole world of the novel, as it captures for Malamud the essential ambivalence of modernism. If so, mythic time, imaged in the hitter's moment of loss, is a compelling sense of baseball's power to define and communicate our age.

A corollary to mythic time in baseball is a quality that we might call mythic causation, in opposition to naturalistic causation or scientific determinism. In baseball and in myth, certain things happen because they are part of a pattern that must repeat itself. In baseball and in *The Natural,* great hitters seem to be reincarnations of each other. As fans of the game we make comparisons and compile statistics not so much to emphasize differences as to emphasize similarities. Baseball, whoever plays it, entails a certain, describable destiny which must be served. That insight by Malamud is one of the most enjoyable and characteristic aspects of *The Natural.* And here, in fact, the lack of realism in the novel that we have discussed earlier coincides, rather than clashes, with our intuitive appreciation of baseball. In Roy Hobb's world things follow the logic of symbols. But the interesting phenomenon is that we, as readers of the novel and as fans of baseball together, accept without question or reservation the mythic causality of the novel's world. We accept as readers and fans, for example, that Roy's first hit for the Knights brings a three-day deluge of rain to the parched ballfield; we accept as readers and as fans that the redemptive and regenerative powers of Roy make the grass begin to grow, improve the athlete's foot on Pop Fisher's hands, enliven the fielding, hitting and team play of the other professionals. As readers and fans, we never doubt that Roy's misguided pursuit of Memo Paris causes his slump or that the slump ends because Iris Lemon stands up in the bleachers as a sign of love for him. Such events are not only the "reality" of the novel, they are also the "reality" of baseball, and it is one of Malamud's most brilliant insights into the game that his fictional hero has the power to save a dying boy's life with a home run—just like Babe Ruth. A curious quality about *The Natural* is that we are intensely aware of the scientific unreality of events at the same time that we succumb to them utterly. In drawing such a response from us toward his novel. Malamud is really illuminating our response to baseball.

Malamud, then, explores some of the specific qualities of baseball, just as he describes the historical and cultural analogues that validate it. But Malamud's novel also takes us one step further, to a consideration of the relationship between sport and the social and moral context in which it exists. The ambiguous connection between the inner world of myth and the outer world of society is suggested by Frederick Turner: "It is always clear that mythologies are in some ways divorced from the real world, through what they contain may be directives for solving the world's problems."[22] In *The Natural,* Roy Hobbs repeats the scandal of "Shoeless" Joe Jackson and the 1919 Chicago Black Sox: he sells out to Judge Banner and Gus Sands. Why does he do it? Can we understand this fall of a hero in a way that will clarify for us the real sporting encounter of baseball?

Roy Hobbs agrees to fix the playoff game for the pennant for two interdependent reasons: money and a woman. Sick in the hospital, Roy has just been told by a doctor that his baseball career is over, and Memo Paris, the dishonest temptress, has just told him that she is afraid to be poor. The deceased Bump Bailey, her former lover, once tricked Roy and Memo into going to bed together, and now Roy feels the familiar frustration "having first and then wanting what he had had as if he hadn't had it but just heard about it"; a confusing situation. But Memo Paris is, as she later states to Roy, "strictly a dead man's girl" (p. 94). She is the Bitch Goddess, desirable because she is unobtainable, shallow yet beautiful, lonely yet cold, erotic. Judge Banner, who represents for us the corruption of organized authority, offers Roy enough money to retire from baseball and support Memo.[23]

Those are the surface reasons why Roy sells out. But the causes run deep into the sporting myth. Roy Hobbs is a "natural" in several senses. One is, of course, that he is a naturally gifted athlete. But another facet of his naturalness has to do with his own boyhood—always represented in the image of a boy and his dog deep in a green forest, whole, alone and at peace. Roy is, then, a natural in the sense of Sir Percival or Sir Galahad or any pastoral hero: he is innocent and uncorrupted. Roy's need to be a baseball hero, to be as he says the "'best that ever was in the game'" (p. 33) is "natural" as well, not a rational choice but an inner compulsion, a psychic necessity. Similarly, Roy's baseball values are strictly self-referential, self-validating; he sees the game wholly from within its own mythology. When Roy tells Harriet Bird he will be the best player ever, she looks at him with "touched and troubled eyes. 'Is that all?'

He tried to penetrate her question. Twice he had answered it and still she was unsatisfied. He couldn't be sure what she expected him to say. 'Is that all?' he repeated. 'What more is there?'

'Don't you know?' she said kindly. (p. 33)

Later, with Iris Lemon, Roy says, "'I had a lot to give to this game.' 'Life?'" she asks. "'Baseball'" he replies (p. 156). Roy wants to be a statistical legend, a numerical immortal. He tells Iris, "'It's like what you said before. You break the records and everybody else tries to catch up with you if they can. . . . If you leave all those records that nobody else can beat—they'll always remember you. You sorta never die'" (p. 156). To such ideas Iris replies, "'But I don't understand why you should make so much of that. Are your values so—'" (p. 156). Similarly, Harriet had asked, "'Isn't there something over and above earthly things—some more glorious meaning to one's life and activities?'" (p. 33). Before such questions, such "college stuff" (p. 32), Roy persists baffled and confused.

Roy sells out because, as Turner suggests, a hero cannot defend myth from within. When Roy, after an emotional struggle, agrees to fix the play-off game, he already has all the records that he will ever set. He has no larger, more encompassing set of values to fallback on now, to guide him through the temptation to corruption that comes from without. And here we see that Roy is a "natural" in a rather disconcerting sense. He is the perpetual innocent, lacking in the knowledge that comes from experience to resist evil and corruption. He is not so much pure of heart as he is blind and shallow. He is a "natural" in the Elizabethan sense of a fool. Consequently, Roy cannot deal with life, with the real world, on the terms that life presents to him. He cannot fight evil from a bedrock of personal value. We see, then, the double edge of Roy's naturalness: for Sir Galahad, innocence is moral armor; for Roy Hobbs it is moral vulnerability. Roy exists inside the myth, he fulfills its conditions, but it is those same conditions that make his corruption and fall inevitable. Moral discrimination, or its absence, is here, as Earl Wasserman points out, really a kind of pre-condition of the psyche.[24] Malamud is suggesting that the fatal weakness in Roy's character, that weakness whose ultimate potential is to destroy baseball, as it almost did in 1919, is also linked ineluctably to the very pastoral myths that give baseball its compelling power over our imaginations. If baseball is dimmed in the popular mind during the latter part of the century, is it possible that it has dimmed in part because the boys of summer have somehow failed in integrity or moral clarity to live up to the myths of natural harmony and innocence that baseball embodies?

An interesting paradox of baseball is that it seems both spontaneous yet oddly deterministic at the same time. The same, for example, is one of individual heroics within a team context. When Roy first began his meteoric ascent, one of the hotly debated questions among his teammates was whether he played for himself or for the team. As the Knights succeeded, the question no longer seemed to matter. The issue returns, however, when Roy plays in the fatal championship game, the game he has agreed to throw. As Roy goes up to bat for the second time, suddenly the sun emerges above, bathing him in golden light, his feet stand firm upon the ground, his sickness leaves him, and he feels that he can do anything he wants. At that moment a fan, his antagonist, the shrill dwarf Otto Zipp, catches Roy's attention with his catcalls, and Roy decides to go after him. Using all his hitting prowess, Roy bangs foul balls at the hateful Zipp until, finally hitting him, he also injures Iris Lemon, who has, as yet unrecognized, again stood up for Roy. With one strike to go he swings Wonderboy thunderously, creating lightening, splitting the bat, and curving the ball foul. Tragically the gods leave their hero.

Roy will have one more time at bat, but he will fail in this last hurrah, as well. Two only tenuously connected reasons seem behind his downfall. Roy fails, first, because he attempts to use his skill not for the team or for the sport but for his own anger and emotion. He wastes his vital force going after Otto Zipp. For the first time, Roy allows the varying reactions of his fans to affect his play. His act is negative, destructive and self-serving. Like Sir Gawain, he has failed to ask whom the Grail serves, and his fall now will be linked to "his blindness to the communal and reproductive purpose of his vitality."[25] Roy's attack on Otto Zipp is, of course, the frivolous partner to his decision to cheat the team for money and Memo Paris.

But Roy also fails for a second reason: because his time is past. That cause is only obliquely related to his moral capitulation, just as it is also unaltered by the revival of his will to win. For in the final out, Roy is awesome; he has changed his mind and is set on hitting a home run, winning the championship, redeeming himself, and saving Pop Fisher. He is terrifying at the plate, a man consumed by his mission, the greatest hitter in the game at his moment of greatest determination. His very appearance—like a dark, glowing knight mounted on a black charger—frightens the best pitcher in the league, Dutch Vogelman, into a dead faint. But then, with shocking irony, before anything can happen, everything changes.

The rookie reliever, Youngberry, strikes him out with three pitches. In the flick of an instant, Roy turns from actor to witness, suddenly almost a bystander to his own downfall. Youngberry stuns him with the speed of his fastball, which seems to light its own path. Roy does go down swinging—poetically, at a bad pitch—but he has been, for the reader, "out" long before the third strike, out in the same way that he himself had "retired" Whammer Wambold, the youthful hero slaying the aging one in the endless pattern of baseball and of myth.

We may say, of course, that once Roy deserted baseball, the spirits of baseball deserted him, just as the Roman gods are said to have abandoned Marc Antony before the final battle at Actium. But there is something odd and ironic in Roy's fall, for he is robbed of the heroic gesture, robbed of his Homeric *arete,* his final struggle, at the very moment that he is clearly most capable of fulfilling his greatness. Roy's defeat is peculiarly anti-climactic. Although the event bespeaks the inevitable mythic pattern, it seems gratuitous, irrational and absurd. It arrives at this moment for its own internal logic, for there is no proximate cause in the circumstances of the game, Roy's ability, or Youngberry's record to foretell it. Roy's fall happens now only because it must happen sometime.

Is there something illuminating about baseball in this strangely anti-climactic moment of revelation? Have we arrived again at baseball's ironic double vision? Frederick Turner has described the pattern of diminishing satisfaction and accomplishment which he finds in the careers of America's greatest true-life baseball heroes, as if their deeds never quite live up to their expectations.26 Perhaps in this odd duality of baseball, its obvious individualism in tension with the incipient recognition that each player fulfills a destiny not entirely his own, lies the explanation to the final mystification about life and about the sport which seems to gather like a cloud above the boys of summer. When Roy Hobbs steps up to bat for the last time, he does not know that his greatest moments are past, have receded into the clustered numbers of the scorer's sheet and the dark forest of his youth on the train bound perpetually for nowhere. He never knew, he could not, nor could any player.

That sense of anti-climax leads us to the final point in our discussion. Critics of *The Natural* have been troubled by its tone, its yoking of parody and high comedy on the one hand with pathos and tragic failure on the other, in such a manner that expectations in either direction seem frustrated. For all the novel's epic allusions, for example, Roy Hobbs is always less of a hero than Achilles, Percival, David or Gatsby. One reader, Robert Ducharme, argues that the novel is ultimately unsatisfying because of its "inconsistency of tone": Malamud treats Roy so parodically "as to prevent the reader from making the personal identification with him that is necessary for a serious (if not tragic) response to the novel."27 What response does Malamud wish to draw from his reader at the conclusion of his novel, and how might that response be a reflection of our attitudes toward baseball?

First, we must observe that the degree to which Roy Hobbs is heroic, comic or pathetic depends upon the reader's perspective toward him, as that perspective is controlled by the author. Roy Hobbs is both most heroic and most comic when we see him against the backdrop of baseball and its mythic connotations. Conversely, Hobbs is most pathetic when we see him in terms of the sporting encounter, as a shallow and superficial social retard. Within and between these two points of view, Malamud controls the reader's engagement or detachment *vis a vis* our protagonist. As the novel rushes toward its conclusion, for example, the narrator's camera, as it were, pulls away from Hobbs, pulls away from the sympathetic close-ups until we see him as some other, first a caricature, then a broken and grubby old man. When Youngberry approaches the mound, the point of view shifts toward him and away from Roy. Later that night, Roy climbs the Judge's tower to confront the evil troika of Judge Banner, Gus Sands and Memo Paris, which has fixed the play-off game for gambling profits. In an almost surrealistic scene, Roy easily beats and punishes all of them. Yet we see Roy completely from the outside now, as he acts with the undisturbed confidence and effortlessness of a comic book hero, a Superman or Captain Marvel making "zaps" and "pows." Then as he reaches the street, suddenly he is only an unshaven old man, a pathetic failure who "'coulda been a king'" (p. 237) but whose only record will now be the plaint of a disillusioned boy, "'Say it ain't true, Roy'"(p. 237).

We feel in this relationship that the confrontation between the worlds of social reality and baseball myth has somehow diminished our respect for the sport. What we see is not simply an ambivalence of tone within the novel; it is equally an ambivalence, Malamud seems to suggest, pervading the attitudes of Americans toward heroes and toward their customary modern vehicle, athletics. A democratic society, according to Norman Podhoretz, may need both to have its heroes and to debunk them, to have its inspirational figures of solitary greatness, those heroes who set examples of accomplishment and excellence, and yet to deny them at the final moment, to refuse to establish in our persistently rural egalitarianism, kings and princes before us.28 Baseball heroes, because of their pastoral and epic contexts, face this American ambivalence more than any other sport figures. That tension, with its shifting, off-balance representation in *The Natural,* may tell us why baseball seems both idyllic and yet strangely disappointing for its fictional and even real-life personages, may tell us ultimately why baseball heroes hold such sway in our imagination yet why we also have so often declined to lionize them in our literature.

NOTES

[1] Virginia Woolf, *The Moment and Other Essays* (Boston: Little, Brown, 1963), p. 4.

[2] Wiley Lee Umphlett, *The Sporting Myth and the American Experience* (London: Associated Univ. Press, 1975), p. 23.

[3] Bernard Malamud, *The Natural* (New York: Farrar, Straus and Cudahy, 1952). Subsequent page references are to this edition and appear in parentheses in the text.

[4] Michael Oriard, *Dreaming of Heroes: American Sports Fiction, 1868-1980* (Chicago: Nelson-Hall, 1982), p. 9.

[5] Murray Ross, "Football and Baseball in America," in *Sport and Society,* ed. John Talamini and Charles Page (Boston: Little, Brown, 1973), p. 103.

[6] Allen Guttmann, *From Ritual to Record* (New York: Columbia Univ. Press, 1978), p. 107.

[7] Robert Henderson, *Ball, Bat and Bishop* (New York: Rockport Press, 1947).

[8] David Voigt, "Myths After Baseball: Notes on Myths in Sport," *Quest* 30 (Summer 1978), 48.

[9] Earl Wasserman, *"The Natural: World Ceres,"* in *Bernard Malamud and the Critics,* ed. Leslie Field and Joyce Field (New York: New York Univ. Press, 1970), pl. 45; originally published as "*The Natural:* Malamud's World Ceres," *The Centennial Review* 9 (Fall 1965), 438-460.

[10] Ring Lardner, *You Know Me Al* (New York: Scribner, 1916).

[11] Melvin Palmer, "The Sports Novel: Mythic Heroes and Natural Men," *Quest* 29 (Jan. 1973), 50.

[12] Heywood Broun, *The Sun Field* (New York: Putnam, 1923).

[13] F. Scott Fitzgerald, "Ring," in *The Crack-up,* ed. Edmund Wilson (New York: A New Directions Book, 1945), p. 36.

[14] Robert Coover, *The Universal Baseball Association, Inc.* (New York: Random House, 1968); Mark Harris, *Bang the Drum Slowly* (New York: Knopf, 1956); *Southpaw* (Indianapolis: Bobbs-Merrill, 1953); *A Ticket for a Seamstitch* (New York: Knopf, 1957). Examples of other baseball novels include Eliot Asinof, *Man on Spikes* (Hightown, NJ: McGraw-Hill, 1955); Jerome Charyn, *The Seventh Babe* (New York: Arbor House, 1979); Irwin Shaw, *Voices of a Summer Day* (New York: Delacorte Press, 1965).

[15] Cited in *National Endowment for the Arts Annual Report* 1980 (Washington: U.S. Govt. Printing Office, 1980), p. 319.

[15a] Wasserman, *op.cit.,* is the first critic to have explored such mythic resonances in the novel.

[16] Wasserman, p. 45.

[17] Sir James G. Frazer, *The Golden Bough: A Study in Magic and Religion* (New York: Macmillan, 1922).

[18] Robert Ducharme, *Art and Idea in the Novels of Bernard Malamud* (The Hague: Mouton, 1974), p. 8.

[19] Jessie L. Weston, *From Ritual to Romance* (Garden City: Doubleday, 1957); originally published by Cambridge Univ. Press, 1920.

[20] Weston, p. 65.

[21] Carl Jung, *The Undiscovered Self* (Boston: Houghton Mifflin, 1957), p. 49.

[22] Frederick Turner, "Myth Inside and Out: Malamud's *The Natural,"* *Novel,* 1 (Winter 1968), 116.

[23] Wasserman, p. 54.

[24] Wasserman, p. 54.

[25] Wasserman, p. 48.

[26] Turner, p. 119.

[27] Ducharme, pp. 34-35.

[28] Norman Podhoretz, "Achilles in Left Field," *Commentary* (March 1953).

Donald R. Johnson

SOURCE: "The Hero in Sports Literature and Exley's 'A Fan's Notes'," in *Southern Humanities Review,* Vol. 13, No. 3, Summer, 1979, pp. 233-44.

[*In the following essay, Johnson explores the function of hero worship in Frederick Exley's novel* A Fan's Notes.]

Most good sports literature is hardly about sports at all. The ostensible or titular subjects of most sports books merely provide a rich matrix out of which various authors can deal with striking figures along with eternal issues and conflicts. Just as Virgil's *Georgics* deals with agriculture only insofar as it offers a vehicle for the poet's discussion of the proper way to live in a world threatened by chaos, or *Moby Dick* provides details of the hunt as a backdrop for Melville's exploration of the nature of good and evil, so genuine literature about sports focuses on athletics as a fertile field for examination of contemporary man's heroic aspirations and spiritual/ethical inadequacies.

Despite the increasing capacity of the media to demythologize the athlete, sports—barring an increased emphasis on the human element in the space program or the commencement of a popular war—provide almost the only consistently available arena for the performance of the visible heroic enterprises traditionally associated with the *agon* figure in myth and literature. In a period when a literary protagonist is most apt to be a passive weakling or an anti-hero, the athletic figure offers the potential for the active, physical character who in his struggle, temptation, and even failure, can be an avatar of us all.

The athlete-hero makes for an interesting study for various reasons, not the least of which is his vulnerability. For all his strength and prowess he remains in most cases an innocent, a child playing at children's games. But unlike most innocents, he allows his creator a wide range of adult perceptions and mature desires. Roy Hobbs of Malamud's *The Natural* is such a figure. Heroic, even mythical, Hobbs embarks on a blind but wide-eyed quest for glory, material comfort, and success in love. Early in the novel his youthful zeal precludes his understanding of the sinister Harriet Bird's questions about the nature of heroism and the hero's duty to his public. When the *femme fatale,* trying to stop Roy from trying out with the Cubs, resorts to an unequivocal bullet in his stomach, he fails to understand the act as anything but a wild diversion on the part of "some batty dame." And even at thirty-six, Roy ignores the wisdom of Iris Lemon who tells him, "We have two lives, Roy, the life we learn with and the life we live with after that. Suffering is what brings us toward happiness."[1] Infatuated with the spiritually bankrupt Memo Paris, Roy agrees to throw the crucial world series game for a payoff impressive enough to win her over. Only after his corruption is assured does Roy realize that he could never win Memo's love, and his quest for riches and immortality ends in utter failure.

The sports figure's struggle to transcend his mortality and his fans' obsessive determination that his heroic efforts somehow succeed combine to form a dominant theme throughout much sports literature. Thus the aging fathers in James Wright's "Autumn Begins in Martin's Ferry, Ohio" spend their lives "dreaming of heroes," hoping their sons will prevail where they have failed.[2] And the fans in Randall Jarrell's "Say Good-bye to Big Daddy" have difficulty accepting the death of Big Daddy Lipscomb, whom the television audience "stared at— sometimes almost were." Ironically, the man who had seemed invulnerable, "who stood unmoved among the blockers, like the Rock/Of Gibraltar in a life insurance ad," died from an overdose of heroin, apparently afraid to face everyday life. Finally, the speaker in Gregory Corso's "Dream of a Baseball Star" pleads with the Almighty to throw his "merciful pitch" so that a symbolic Ted Williams, who has just been overwhelmed by a barrage of a hundred fiery strikes, can redeem us all.[3]

The speaker's anxiety over Williams' failure and his craving for the "home run" in the duel against the omnipotent Pitcher reflect the desperate investment contemporary man has made in his few remaining heroes. According to Ernest Becker, "What characterizes modern life is the failure of all traditional immortality ideologies to absorb and quicken man's hunger for self-perpetuation and heroism."[4] Further, citing such thinkers as Harvey Cox, Josef Pieper, and Johan Huizinga, he asserts that "the only secure truth men have is that which they themselves create and dramatize; to live is to play at the meaning of life."[5] A clearer, more insightful explanation for our obsession with both real and fictional sporting heroes would be difficult to conceive. Sports may not be a metaphor for life, but the particular games and the struggles of their participants clearly symbolize our own efforts to transcend our limited existences. Michael

Novak in *The Joy of Sports* compares sports to the most traditional immortality ideology, religion, in that they both embody "the nameless dread of daily human life: aging, dying, failure under pressure, cowardice, betrayal, guilt."[6] He views athletic contests as "rituals concerning human survival on this planet: liturgical enactments of animal perfection and struggles of the human spirit to prevail."[7]

While Becker and Novak make clear the potential in athletics for heroic transcendence, they strongly suggest its limitations and evoke the paradox inherent in the glorification of sport which makes it such fascinating material for literary study. The physical triumphs of the athlete-hero can lead us out of ourselves and assure us at least momentarily of our personal claim on immortality. At the same time, however, we recognize the fact that while the game goes on, individual performers succumb to injuries, better competition, and, ultimately, old age. We recognize that they are victims of the very bodies that captivate us. Their heroics are bound to a self-consuming organism destined to die. It should not be surprising, therefore, that the most pervasive theme in all of sports literature has to do with the aging or failing athlete, the washed-up jock.

Whether it is Roy Hobbs, whose plight is especially significant in that he is both a rookie and an "old man," or Christian Darling in Irwin Shaw's "The Eighty-Yard Run," the athlete who struggles to make his body function in the face of the inevitable decay which dogs us all, provides an ever-poignant study. If the contest on the field is a symbolic confrontation between vitality and death, then the aging hero's agony, as Novak points out, "begins to mix the ritual contest with the actual contest; ritual death with the coming of real death. In the aging athlete, the ultimate reality of sports breaks through the symbol, becomes explicit. Death advances on us all. Not even our vitality, not even our beauty of form, not even our heroic acts can hold it back."[8] But we can delude ourselves with the fantasy that mortality only applies to others by creating what Becker calls the "characterological lie," a subterfuge the healthy mind constructs to overcome the universal fear of death. Since our bodies constantly remind us of what Becker has termed our "creatureliness," even though our minds assure us of ties to a more ideal world, we frantically work out strategies to deny that creatureliness and elevate the ideal. In the event that the individual cannot demonstrate his own heroism, cannot forge a link between finite realities and his vision of the infinite, he must attach his aspirations to an heroic figure who can, since heroism, according to Becker, "transmutes the fear of death into the security of self perpetuation."[9]

In this light the applicability of the athlete's life to our own becomes clear, and what I have called the paradox of the self-consuming organism is made doubly apparent. By linking our aspirations for immortality to a sporting hero, we can be temporarily lulled to complacency by his beauty, grace, and exuberance. At the same time we suffer a nagging uneasiness generated by the athlete's susceptibility to physical injury and decay. Though perhaps reluctant to admit it, we know that the object of our admiration, through the nature of his endeavor, epitomizes the very creatureliness we seek to deny.

In contemporary literature the most complete and provocative examination of the sports hero as immortality object occurs in Frederick Exley's *A Fan's Notes,* an autobiographical novel detailing its protagonist's struggle to throw off the influence of his celebrated athlete father and establish his own identity. Although the situation is timeworn, the uniqueness of particular incidents and the intensity of the narrator/author's suffering mark the work as an original. And while Exley has attempted to discourage readers and critics from categorizing his first novel as a "sports book" (a strange desire, given his title), his subject matter in both bulk and emphasis is overwhelmingly sports-oriented, and the theme which emerges from his treatment of the subject is central to agonistic literature in general and sports literature in particular: the individual's attempt to establish, first through identification with heroes and ultimately through his own heroic performance, a claim to immortality.

In an epigraph drawn from Hawthorne's *Fanshawe,* Exley establishes from its outset that the odyssey described in *A Fan's Notes* has as its ultimate goal immortality: "If his inmost heart could have been laid open there would have been discovered that dream of undying fame; which, dream as it is, is more powerful than a thousand realities."[10] The dream is a natural one for Exley (who, although he insists his work is a fantasy, shares his name with the book's narrator). Having grown up in Watertown, New York, the son of Earl Exley, the region's most popular football hero in the thirties, he developed very early in his life a longing for fame, and he attributes this longing directly to his father's influence: "Other men might inherit from their fathers a head for figures, a gold pocket watch all encrusted with the oxidized green of age or an eternally astonished expression; from mine I acquired this need to have my name whispered in reverential tones" (35). Even at the age of twenty-three he recalls, "I suffered myself the singular notion that fame was an heirloom passed on from my father" (30).

The fact that at twenty-three an individual would continue to see his destiny tied to his father's is evidence enough that Exley's road was a difficult and complicated one. Not the least of these complications arose from the elder Exley's efforts to reinforce and embellish his legend by constantly playing to the crowd, sometimes at the expense of his relationship with his son. In one incident the father, having received a nasty cut in a football game, came off the field bleeding profusely from the hand. When the trainer administered iodine to the wound the father "let out a high fierce, almost girlish howl, one that—representing, as he did to me the epitome of strength and courage—immediately induced in me the urge to scream in terror" (32). Only when the

substitutes on the bench and the crowd behind them began to laugh did the young Exley realize that his father, unaware the youngster was watching, was merely entertaining his admirers. He then joined in the laughter, but was caught short when the father suddenly became aware of his presence. In a moment of intense recognition, writes Exley, "my father looked up at me, surprised and not a little upset, recognizing what had transpired. It was the first time the crowd had come between my father and me, and I became aware that other people understood in him qualities I did not—a knowledge that gave them certain claims on him. It is a terrifying thing to have a wedge driven into one's narrow circle of love" (33).

The widening gap in understanding between Earl Exley and his son led directly, if paradoxically, to Frederick Exley's feeling at twenty-three that his potential for fame was still somehow tied to his father. With the crowd always between them, their relationship never developed to a point which could have allowed a confrontation, a separation leading to the son's temporary rejection of the father and the consequent development of his own ego-identity. For as Exley points out, "The denial of one's father, in whatever spirit, requires great sympathy between the denier and the denied, and this my father and I never had" (43).

Any hope that the scenario of rejection and ego development described above could be played out came to an abrupt end with the father's death at the age of forty. Any father's death is a traumatic experience for the son, but, given his physical prowess and apparent immortality, Earl Exley's death was, for his son, tantamount to a betrayal. The man who promised legendary fame, who somehow seemed immune to the exigencies of common life, succumbed to cancer in the prime of life. Weighing only seventy-nine pounds at his death, the "old man" provided a macabre example of the body's frailty. "No," writes Exley, "there was nothing to suggest either the kind of man my father had been or the life he had led. In death he carried with him the aristocratic nicety of drawing rooms, the inane chatter of teacups" (42). The vagaries of fate had denied him even the semblance of that physical form which had been responsible for his fame.

Although the father's death was critical for Exley, it was not the first occasion on which Exley recognized his father's fallibility. The son first began to see his father's limitations when, "somewhere between the ages of eight and eleven," he accompanied his father to New York City. The two had gone to the city in order to arrange a football game between the New York Giants and Watertown's Red and Black, a local semi-professional team which "took on all challengers and invariably defeated them." Earl Exley, the manager of the Watertown team, had hoped to meet with Steve Owen, the Giants' coach. Although he had written to Owen beforehand, the Giants had refused even to consider the idea, so Exley went to New York hoping to force himself on

Owen and make arrangements for the game. In Frederick Exley's words, the trip was "a series of small, debilitating defeats," culminating in Owen's flat rejection of Earl Exley's proposal. The interview took place in the lobby of Owen's hotel, where, after repeated visits and interminable waits, the Exleys had managed to ensnare him. Even before Owen's rebuff, however, the son had begun to sense the absurdity of their mission and had begun to feel embarrassed for his father. Finally even the father recognized the futility of his arguments, and, looking for a graceful way to end the encounter, shoved his son in front of the Giants' coach and introduced him. When Owen, sensing his opportunity to escape, asked, "Are you tough?" Fred could only answer, "I don't know, sir." And when the question was asked of the father, Earl Exley replied, "It's too soon to tell" (53). This serious blow to the boy's pride was diminished only somewhat by Owen's rejoinder, "I'm sure he's tough, Mr. Exley" (54).

Linked as it was to the father's humiliation, Owen's question and the father's unsupportive reply were crucial factors in young Frederick's development. The author writes of the incident: "My father's shadow was so imposing that I had scarcely ever, until that moment, had any identity of my own. At the same time I had yearned to emulate and become my father, I also longed for his destruction. Steve Owen not only gave me identity; he proved to me my father was vulnerable" (57). In Freudian terms this might be seen as the classic Oedipal conflict, with the son emulating the father while simultaneously attempting to destroy him. In Exley's particular case the incident set the foundation for the complex feelings he experienced at his father's death. On the one hand, weakness in the hero figure suggests one could defeat him. On the other hand, that weakness, particularly when it manifests itself in the father, might generate serious misgivings about one's own strength.

That the end result was ambivalence is evidenced by Exley's claiming that at the age of ten or eleven "Steve Owen . . . gave me identity," and then recording that he felt at twenty-three that fame "was an heirloom passed on from my father." It was ambivalence linked with an unexpressed fear of success which crippled Exley in his first assault on the real world. Having graduated with a degree in English after an undistinguished career at U.S.C., he confronted New York City for the second time, dreaming of success in advertising and eventual literary fame. But like his father before him, and perhaps because of his father, he failed. After a series of rejections, abortive interviews gained with the aid of a ludicrously inflated resume, an identity not his own, he finally encountered an executive who humiliated him with a series of remarks about his clothes, his hair and his brashness. At the same time, a man Exley called Cary Grant empathized with him, told him, "you remind me of myself twenty years ago" (50) and was clearly willing to give him a hand up. But Exley rejected him, failed to press his advantage and sulked off to the first of a succession of near-catatonic retreats to various davenports.

It was no accident that Steve Owen, the man who *gave* Exley an identity, indirectly brought about an end to this first withdrawal. Having read that Owen was being forced to retire and was coaching in his final game at the Polo Grounds, Exley left the security of his aunt's sofa and made the first of his many pilgrimages to the home of the Giants. The game marked a curious crossroads for him, a transference of loyalties from the retiring Owen, who, strangely enough came to represent for him not so much heroic potential as "life's hard fact of famelessness" (70), to Frank Gifford, the sports hero who sustained him through years of self-doubt and depression, a failed marriage and three sojourns in mental hospitals.

Gifford's career proved an ironic counterpoint to Exley's. Both men arrived in New York at the same time, but while Exley, after some initial success in business writing, slipped into a long decline, Gifford rose to stardom, becoming a fixture in the sports pantheon of the fifties. For Exley, Gifford became the objective manifestation of what was for him only a dream of fame. "Frank Gifford, more than any single person, sustained for me the illusion that fame was possible," the author writes (131):

> It was all very simple, really. Where I could not, with syntax, give shape to my fantasies, Gifford could, with his superb timing, his great hands, his uncanny faking, give shape to his. It was something more than this: I cheered for him with such inordinate enthusiasm, my yearning became so involved with his desire to escape life's bleak anonymity, that after a time he became my alter ego, that part of me which had its being in the competitive world of men; I came, as incredible as it seems to me now, to believe that I was, in some magical way, an actual instrument of his success (134).

In other words, for this period of Exley's life, Gifford was able to sustain for him that characterological lie, the illusion that we can somehow transcend our physical limitations and establish a claim to immortality. So complete was Exley's identification with his hero that when his fiancée, curious about why he was not simply jealous of the man who had succeeded so well where Exley had failed, said, "I should think you'd despise him. . . . Envy him to the point of disliking him immensely," Exley replied: "Despise him?. . . . But you don't understand at all. Not at all! He may be the only fame I'll ever have!" (232).

But Exley's illusion was short-lived. After a succession of lost jobs, a rejection of the all-American girl (and the dream she epitomized), and a desperate, drunken search throughout the country for meaning and security, he returned home to his mother's farm in upstate New York, a failure, marking time before his commitment to Avalon Valley State Hospital. Exley's illness and alcoholism stemmed from a breakdown in his own immortality ideology. Having left the protection of his father's fame, yet being at the same time unable to sustain his own, he was reduced to experiencing both his own meaninglessness and the ugliness and vapidity of the America around him. His problem was not so much a desire to evade reality as an inability to shield himself from it. As Becker argues, "the essence of normality is the refusal of reality."[11] Mental illness arises from the "miscarriage of clumsy lies about reality."[12]

Fortunately for some of us, this reduction to the truth about ourselves, what José Ortega y Gasset calls the "mentality of the shipwrecked," promotes the construction of stronger, more effective foundations for carrying on. "This is the simple truth," writes Ortega y Gasset, "that to live is to feel oneself lost—he who accepts it has already begun to find himself, to be on firm ground. Instinctively, as do the shipwrecked, he will look around for something to which to cling. . . . "[13] In a very real sense, *A Fan's Notes* is Exley's diary of the shipwrecked. But the work did not come easily. There were many false starts, and Exley once burned an unsatisfactory first draft. At one point the spectre of the father returned to demonstrate once again his hold upon the son. Sitting down to write, Exley began to experience "sudden and excruciating pains in [his] chest and decided that in [his] father's image [he] was dying of lung cancer" (323). The pains proved to be psychosomatic, of course, reactions to guilt feelings associated with the possibility that his solution to the problem of mortality might prove superior to his father's.

A greater impediment to serious work on his own immortality project was Exley's reluctance to recognize the desperate nature of his predicament. Whether surrounded by other seriously ill patients at Avalon Valley or wasting away in a drunken stupor on some friend's davenport, he sought to maintain a posture of ironic detachment. He admits that for fifteen years he had been troubled by a recurrent vision of himself as a linen-suited colonialist seated, cool drink in hand, on the veranda of an elegant English club in black Africa: "My expression was ironical. In it there was a suggestion of amusement, directed, it seems, as much against myself as against anything or anyone about me, as though I were taking myself not quite seriously, *cum grano salis*" (243). In the vision, he could hear, beyond the polite talk around him, the wailing of blacks portending a bloody uprising. Although no one else seemed to hear the cries, he could not bring himself to warn the others. When the frenzied natives appeared, bent on revenging a century of servitude, he expected to confront them by saying, "You see, I am uninvolved, and my posture in life is one of detachment, irony and amusement . . ." (244), knowing even while mouthing the words that the blacks would probably slit his throat anyway.

Clearly, the wailing Exley heard was his own heart of darkness and it finally began to worry him that his vision might be more real than he would have preferred. Actually, he had proved himself less detached, more capable of sympathy, several times early on in his account: he was saddened by the suicide of a young patient at Avalon Valley, and he acted as an advocate for another patient, trying to convince the man's sister she should take him in so that he could be released from the hospital. But somehow these situations failed to hit home. They were seen as through a veil, with Exley unable to relate them directly to his own horror. However, two crucial incidents precipitated a change in his attitude, allowing Exley to comprehend the enormity of his problem and to transform his sympathy into genuine empathy. Both incidents were related to the Giants.

While working on the manuscript he eventually burned, Exley buoyed himself up with the fantasy that it was to be his ticket to fame. For a time he lost interest in the Giants. He recognized that Gifford, after a good career, was slowing down—the victim, perhaps, of too much fame, too many banquet speeches and product endorsements—and he dreamed of supplanting his hero in the public's eye. Following the destruction of his first completed manuscript, however, the fantasy ended abruptly, and once more, according to the narrator, "Gifford and the Giants were all that sustained me, and I lived only from Sunday afternoon to Sunday afternoon" (337). Given the breakdown of his own plan for immortality, he was compelled once again to transfer his aspirations to the hero figure. But even these hopes were shattered when Gifford was seriously injured as Exley looked on from the stands. The fan's reaction to the incident was intense:

> For the first time since the beginning, when so many autumns before we had had the common ground of large hopes, we were in our separate ways, coming round to the most terrible knowledge of all; we were dying. And that was the inescapable truth. Though I was some time in articulating it, in that limp and broken body against the green turf of the stadium, I had had a glimpse of my own mortality (349).

Both men were victims of the old paradox, the body as the self-consuming organism, and the realization for Exley was so painful that he, "in a futile rage against the inevitability of that mortality" (349), provoked a fight with two young men and was severely beaten. That beating led him to articulate what he felt at the time to be the single incontrovertible fact of his existence: " . . . it was my destiny—unlike that of my father whose fate it was to hear the roar of the crowd—to sit in the stands with most men and acclaim others. It was my fate, my destiny, my end, to be a fan" (357).

Although Exley's resignation at being a fan seems final, such was not the case. After he shook off the initial effects of Gifford's injury, its more profound consequence—Exley's recognition of his own mortality—apparently began to gnaw at him, motivating him, although very subtly at first, to pursue his own immortality project, what we have as *A Fan's Notes*. But one more incident was necessary to bring these apparently subliminal yearnings to fruition, and it, too, was related to the Giants. After the Gifford injury, Exley acquiesced in his new role of the fan and took a teaching job at Glacial Falls, New York, dragging himself through each week, pitying the students and hating most of his comfortable colleagues. Once again, his only joy derived from the weekly ritual of watching the Giants game on Sundays. Having agreed when he took the position not to make a drunken spectacle of himself on the streets of Glacial Falls, he returned to Watertown every weekend for "nearly heroic drinking" and the game. There, ensconced in the Parrot Bar, drink in hand, "I gave myself up to the Giants utterly," Exley writes, and "the recompense gained was the feeling of being alive" (8). To Exley, football "smacked of something old, something traditional, something unclouded by legerdemain and subterfuge. It had that kind of power over me, drawing me back with the force of something known, scarcely remembered" (8).

Obviously a conflict exists here. While literally drinking himself into a stupor, Exley was allowing the old lie to lull him once again into a feeling of security—the game, in an historical and mythical sense, argued continuity. But when, just prior to the kick-off in a game between the Giants and the Dallas Cowboys, Exley suffered what he thought at the time to be a heart attack, the lie was irreparably shattered. As it turned out, Exley had not been stricken by a heart attack, but had collapsed from malnutrition engendered by excessive drinking. But the effects were no less striking: "The pain was excruciatingly vivid, and for many moments I was terrified by the fear of death. Illogically, this was one terror I believed I had long since cast off—having cast it off, I thought, with the effortless lunacy of a man putting a shotgun into his mouth and ridding himself of the back of his skull" (1). This was the full, unqualified experience of mortality he sensed but did not fully comprehend at the time of Gifford's injury, and the ultimate consequence of this incident was Exley's honest admission that "the fear of death still owns me," and the realization that this was "in its way, a beginning" (1).

It is obvious by now that the title, *A Fan's Notes,* is ironic, that Exley outgrew the transference of heroism to the athletic hero, and, from the "beginning" generated by his "heart attack" at the Parrot, formulated his own characterological lie, one radically different from his father's, being grounded in the mind, not the body. The novel is Exley's solution to his own anxiety about death, or, in Becker's terms, "the artist's attempt to justify his heroism objectively, in the concrete creation. It is the testimonial to his absolute uniqueness [not an inheritance from a father] and heroic transcendence."[14]

Interestingly enough, *A Fan's Notes* ends not with a tribute to the intellect, but with the protagonist engaged (in dream, at least) in intense physical activity. The dream is clearly intended to contrast with Exley's earlier vision of himself as detached and uninvolved on the veranda of the club in black Africa. In this fantasy, he envisions himself walking along a country road in upstate New York when he is passed by a convertible carrying six college boys "hurling beer cans and anathemas."

The boys are monuments to the homogeneity and indifference of the great American leisure class. They are all six feet two, well-tanned, and expensively, though casually, attired. When their automobile breaks down Exley runs to the group and begins pleading with them to consider "that of itself longevity is utterly without redeeming qualities, that one has to live the contributive, the passionate, life and that this can as well be done in twenty-six . . . as in a hundred and twenty-six years, done in no longer than the time it takes a man to determine whether the answer is yea or nay" (385). Predictably, the young men choose to ignore his entreaties, and when he persists they set upon him and beat him, and the dream ends with his becoming "suddenly engulfed by this new, this incomprehensible America" (385). Since this vision recurs again and again, Exley is compelled to repeat his quixotic gesture. "When the vision comes," he writes, "I find that, ready to do battle, I am running; obsessively, *running*" (385).

Wiley Lee Umphlett in *The Sporting Myth and the American Experience*[15] cites an interesting parallel between the ending of *A Fan's Notes* and the conclusion of another novel which might be read as sports literature, John Updike's *Rabbit, Run*. But Umphlett has misunderstood Exley. Unlike Rabbit Angstrum, who runs to evade responsibility, Exley is running in an attempt to shoulder it, to confront his experience, to convey to others his own hard-won knowledge that man must live with death but need not be dominated by it.

It is not surprising that Exley bridles at classifying *A Fan's Notes* as sports literature. There are those who would consider the designation itself a contradiction in terms. Perhaps one should insist on emphasizing the term "literature" in order to avoid confusion between works which are merely about sports—*Instant Replay, Ball Four* or *North Dallas Forty*—and more serious efforts which use sport because of its applicability to the central concerns of all literature: how to live life, retain love and face death. Faulkner's *The Bear* uses the hunt, "the best game of all," as a medium through which he can discuss the individual's relationship to history.[16] Philip Roth examines the link between American literature and its English antecedents in *The Great American Novel*, a baseball story. And in *The Universal Baseball Association, Inc., Henry J. Waugh, Prop.*, Robert Coover explores the eternal problem of the godhead's responsibility for and obligation to his creation as it manifests itself in an imaginary baseball game created by a meek, frustrated accountant. All three of these examples qualify as "sports books," and represent *literature* of high seriousness and recognizable quality. Exley should be proud to travel in such company.

NOTES

[1] New York: Pocket Books, 1973, p. 143.

[2] *Collected Poems* (Middletown, Connecticut: Wesleyan Univ. Press, 1972).

[3] Both Jarrell's and Corso's poems appear in *The Sporting Spirit,* ed. Robert J. Higgs and Neil Isaacs (New York: Harcourt Brace Jovanovich, 1977).

[4] *The Denial of Death* (New York: The Free Press, 1973), p. 140. I was first made aware of the applicability of Becker's ideas to sports through a paper entitled "The Athlete and the Denial of Death" delivered by Robert J. Higgs at the annual meeting of the Popular Culture Association-South on October 8, 1976.

[5] *Ibid.,* p. 201.

[6] New York: Basic Books, 1976, p. 30.

[7] *Ibid.,* p. 24.

[8] *Ibid.,* p. 48.

[9] *The Denial of Death,* p. 217.

[10] New York: Random House, 1968. Subsequent references appear in the text.

[11] *The Denial of Death,* p. 178.

[12] *Ibid.*

[13] *The Revolt of the Masses* (New York: Norton, 1957), p. 157.

[14] *The Denial of Death,* p. 172.

[15] Lewisburg, Pa.: Bucknell Univ. Press, 1975.

[16] *Go Down Moses* (New York: Random House, 1942), p. 192.

William Hutchings

SOURCE: "The Work of Play: Anger and the Expropriated Athletes of Alan Sillitoe and David Storey," in *Modern Fiction Studies,* Vol. 33, No. 1, Spring, 1987, pp. 35-47.

[*In the following essay, Hutchings regards sport as an escape for working-class fans and as dehumanizing work for the athletes in the fiction of Alan Sillitoe and David Storey.*]

"At the same time that factory work exhausts the nervous system to the uttermost," Karl Marx observed in *Das Kapital,* "it does away with the many-sided play of the muscles, and confiscates every atom of freedom, both in bodily and intellectual activity" (422). Nowhere has this observation been better exemplified than in the English novels of working-class life since the late 1950s. Whether toiling at lathes like Arthur Seaton in

Alan Sillitoe's *Saturday Night and Sunday Morning* and Arthur Machin in David Storey's *This Sporting Life* or at a milling-machine like Smith's in *The Loneliness of the Long-Distance Runner,* the protagonists of such fiction typically find that their actions soon became automatic, reducing them as workers (and, more importantly, as human beings) to mere operative extensions of the factory's machinery in exactly the way that Marx described. For virtually all of these working-class protagonists, the body and its pleasures provide refuge from the workaday monotony, fragmentation, and dreariness of factory-bound life in a class-ridden world. At the end of the week, having received their pay packets, they leave behind the factory with its noise and smells, eager to have "the effect of a week's monotonous graft in the factory . . . swilled out of [their] system[s]" in the "cosy world of pubs and noisy tarts" (Sillitoe, *Saturday Night* 7, 33) for which such novels are renowned. For many, however, sports provide an equally vital source of such pleasure—and, for those who play the pools or frequent the betting-shops, the prospect of supplementary profit or loss as well. To some fans, such as the narrator of Sillitoe's short story "The Match," a team's dismal fortunes on the playing-field even presage a crisis in the day-to-day relationships of family life; to some athletes, such as the narrator of *This Sporting Life,* a team's collective endeavors provide a welcome release for the frustrations and pain that such personal relationships involve. Even to those who no longer play the game, like the middle-aged sportswriter who is the central character of Storey's novel *Present Times* (1984), the world of sport—with its clear rules and its unambiguous outcomes—provides a haven from the various cultural upheavals and controversies that rive the modern family as well as contemporary society as a whole.

For spectators and participants alike, the importance of the "game" extends far beyond the vicarious enjoyment of fans' team-loyalties and the athletes' personal accomplishments. Yet, as characters in Sillitoe's *The Loneliness of the Long-Distance Runner* and Storey's *This Sporting Life* and *The Changing Room* come to recognize, sport, play, and even the body itself have been expropriated by exactly the social "establishment" from which they are alienated. Turned into the "work" of professional rugby for Storey's characters and into officially mandated "games" in Sillitoe's novella, "play" and sport become dehumanizing, no longer fulfilling their original and essential recreational functions in the way that they did in earlier times. Although in both authors' works the characters' participation in sports affords them a certain personal satisfaction and fulfillment that life in the "real" world cannot provide, the fact of the athlete's expropriation not only provides a crucial symbol for the causes of the characters' alienation and anger but also has implications well beyond their particular time, class, and society.

Almost invariably in such fiction, the protagonist is repeatedly described as being *"big"*—a standard image of the worker in twentieth-century art of all forms, of course, from Soviet Socialist Realism to the murals of the W.P.A. Yet, as Sillitoe has pointed out in one of his essays in *Mountains and Caverns,* such a portrayal of a working-class protagonist had particular importance in England in the mid-1950s when

> working men [who were] portrayed in England by the cinema, or on radio and television, or in books were . . . presented in unrealistic terms . . . behaving in the same jokey but innocuous fashion. They lacked dignity in fiction because they lacked depth. (37-38)

In stark contrast to Alfred Doolittle, Andy Capp, Alf Garnett, and countless others, Arthur Seaton and Arthur Machin tower over their parents and over their bosses at work—even though, symbolically, Seaton's "tall frame was slightly round shouldered from stooping day in and day out at his lathe" (*Saturday Night* 58); even Smith in *The Loneliness of the Long-Distance Runner* is *taller* than the other boys, though not specifically described as *big.* For many, such size reinforces an equally sizeable ego: "it makes you feel good," Arthur Machin is told by the woman he loves; "it makes you feel big—you know how you like to feel big" (*This Sporting Life* 147). Through his success at Rugby League football, Arthur Machin finds both recognition and a source of supplementary income, both of which are means by which, he explains, he "kept his head above the general level of crap, and that . . . was the main thing" (18).

Beyond such fundamental considerations, however, the sport also provides an outlet for important emotions that cannot be expressed in his workaday world. Specifically, Storey's protagonist finds particular satisfaction in the arousal of

> a kind of anger, a savageness, that suited the game very well. . . . This wildness was essential to the way I played . . . [and] seemed to correspond to my personality. . . . [It was] a preliminary feeling of power. I was big, strong, and could make people realize it. I could tackle hard, and with the kind of deliberation I took a pride in later, really hurt someone. I was big. Big! It was no mean elation. (20)

Similarly, as Sillitoe's narrator runs across the chilly fields at dawn, he finds both an elation and a release for the anger that he feels for the "In-laws" of ostensibly respectable society:

> Them bastards over us aren't as daft as they most of the time look. . . . They're cunning, and I'm cunning. . . . If only "them" and "us" had the same ideas we'd get on like a house on fire, but they don't see eye to eye with us and we don't see eye to eye with them . . . the pig-faced snotty-nosed dukes and ladies—who can't add two and two together and would mess themselves like loonies if they didn't have slavies to beck-and-call. . . . [But] standing in the doorway in shimmy and shorts . . . I feel like the first bloke in the world. . . . And that makes me feel good, so as

> soon as I'm steamed up enough to get this feeling in me, I take a flying leap out of the doorway, and off I trot. (*Loneliness* 7-9)

Whether, like rugby, a particular sport requires a subordination of self to the collective endeavors of a team, or whether, like long-distance running, it allows free rein to the individual alone, each athlete finds—uniquely, through the experience of sports—an "alternate reality" into which the problems and anxieties of the everyday world no longer intrude.

Yet even though sports allow such outlets for the anger and frustrations that build up in their lives, the athletes in both novels soon find that they themselves—and, indeed, their respective sports as well—have been expropriated by the very same "establishment" that they rail against, so that (as a character in *This Sporting Life* complains) "a great game . . . [is being] spoiled by people who try and make it something else" (185). Specifically, in Storey's works it is being made a business, even an industry—with paid managers and owners whose interests do not necessarily coincide with those of their workers, the players. Before he has even signed his contract, Machin is told that he is now "property of the City" team (*This Sporting Life* 59), and he soon remarks that "they bought and sold players" like any other commodity or product. Consequently, the athletes can no longer be regarded *primarily* as human beings; their success or failure on the field becomes a matter that must be assessed in terms of profit and loss rather than any more "humane" values. Voluntarily co-opted as part of a system of paid performance for commercial entertainment, Machin soon realizes that he has not only been dehumanized but even reduced to the level of an animal:

> I was an ape. Big, awe-inspiring, something to see perform. . . . People looked at me as if I was an ape. Walking up the road like this they looked at me exactly as they'd look at an ape walking about without a cage . . . [a] thing to make them stare in awe, and wonder if after all . . . I might be human. (163-164)

On *and off* the playing field, no less than when he stands at his lathe in the factory, Machin has been dehumanized by the work of play. As a professional athlete—no less than as a factory worker—he is an operative cog in a commercial, mechanistic enterprise whose owner is far removed from the struggles and sufferings of those who toil on his behalf.

Although Smith in *The Loneliness of the Long-Distance Runner* is certainly not a professional athlete like Arthur Machin, he has been expropriated in exactly the same way by the "establishment" that runs the reformatory in which he is confined. The novella's opening line makes this expropriation unmistakably and emphatically clear: "As soon as I got to Borstal *they* made *me* a long-distance cross-country runner" (7; emphasis mine). During the weeks of his training for a championship race, Smith is repeatedly encouraged to "win *them* the Borstal Blue Ribbon Prize Cup for Long Distance Cross Country Running (All England)" by the borstal's governor—an "owner" who, like the capitalists caricatured in any form of agit-prop, is a "pot-bellied pop-eyed bastard" with a grey moustache and "lily-white workless hands" (11, 9). In fact, his relationship with Smith is defined in explicitly contractual terms, a *quid pro quo* befitting an employer and employee:

> "We want hard honest work and we want good athletics," he said as well. "And if you give us both these things you can be sure we'll do right by you and send you back into the world an honest man." (9)

Although Smith receives no remuneration of any kind for his efforts in the race (not even a quid in exchange for all of his *quo*), his running—no less than Arthur Machin's rugby—has clearly been made a form of contractual work rather than play. And like Machin, Smith finds this expropriation dehumanizing and compares himself to an animal (though his chosen simile is less unflattering than Machin's ape metaphor): "They give us a bit of blue ribbon and a cup for a prize after we've shagged ourselves out running or jumping, like race horses, only we don't get so well looked-after as race horses, that's the only thing" (8). Not even the cup and blue ribbon will be Smith's own because they will belong instead to the winning institution—a reform school *qua* factory whose product is "honest men"; its governor/manager never once suggests that the athlete should win for *himself*—that the laborer should receive the reward of his toil—or even that (altruistically) the sport can provide a sense of personal achievement and a satisfaction all its own whether he wins or not. Accordingly, Smith recognizes that the victory, which he is quite capable of achieving, "won't mean a bloody thing to me, only to him, and it means as much to him as it would mean to me if I picked up the racing paper and put my money on a hoss I didn't know, had never seen, and didn't care a sod if I ever did see" (12). Because Smith's athletic endeavors receive no recompense of any kind, whereas Arthur Machin's are at least a professionally contracted and compensated job, Sillitoe's protagonist is seemingly the more wholly expropriated of the two; yet, in cunningly subverting the plans of those who seek to keep him under their control, Smith is also the more defiant and independent of the pair.

Against all such attempts at dehumanization and expropriation, the narrators of both novels affirm the existence of an innately *human* alternative. However successful others may be in "owning" the athlete's body (which, like a factory's machine, is well-maintained, powerful, efficient, and smoothly functional), they can never control his mind, subdue his emotions, quash his spirit, or quell his independent will. Thus, as Smith contends, he retains a vital freedom of thought and feeling—an unsubduable psychological independence—that those around him fail to acknowledge and/or refuse to take into account:

> I'm a human being and I've got thoughts and secrets and bloody life inside me that [the governor] doesn't know is there, and he'll never know what's there because he's stupid. . . . I can see further into the likes of him than he can see into the likes of me . . . and I'll win in the end even if I die in gaol at eighty-two because I'll have more fun and fire out of my life than he'll ever get out of his. (12)

Relying on exactly the same "cunning" and the pleasures of "thinking" that Arthur Seaton cites in claiming "it's a hard life if you don't weaken" (*Loneliness* 7; *Saturday Night* 34, 28, 32), Smith deliberately loses the race that he could easily win; in so doing, he unmistakably asserts a fundamental human freedom not to suborn himself, not to conform, and not to comply.

For Arthur Machin as well, the primacy of powerful and innately human "feelings" abrades against his "professional" obligations as an athlete—though the emotions involved are more adult (and more amatory) than the adolescent rebelliousness that fuels the defiance of Sillitoe's long-distance runner. Although the hard physical contact involved in professional rugby provides an ample outlet for his anger and frustration, and although the perquisites of being a celebrity (an expensive car, ostentatious dinners, public recognition) provide an ego-gratification that exceeds even the salary that he earns, his attempts to express more *tender* emotions cause much of the turmoil in his life. In the rough-and-tumble sometimes brutally violent world of the playing field, Arthur Machin excels and is appropriately rewarded; in the fragile often stormy relationship with the woman he loves, he encounters a pain no less acute—and no less real—than the pain caused by the physical injuries he gives and receives. Paradoxically, the strain that besets his loving relationship with Mrs. Hammond, the widow from whom he rents a room, is caused by the very same personal traits that contribute so much to his success at rugby: aggressiveness, recklessness, ruthlessness, and a certain impervious disregard for whoever or whatever might thwart his attempts to achieve his goals. As he gains more and more acclaim for exhibiting these traits in the game, he becomes increasingly insensitive in seeking an intimate relationship, until, in his frustration, the type of conduct that is appropriate and applauded on the field obtrudes in—and disrupts—the home as a sudden brutal outburst of domestic violence occurs.

Although the nature of his chosen sport itself inherently demands a number of his macho traits, such tendencies are accelerated by the fact that he is a paid *professional* who is economically (as well as socially and psychologically) rewarded for successfully behaving in this way. Accordingly, Arthur admits,

> I was a hero . . . [but also] the big ape again, known and feared for its strength, frightened of showing a bit of soft feeling in case it might be weakness. . . . No feelings. It'd always helped to have no feelings. So I had no feelings. I was paid not to have feelings. It paid me to have none. (*This Sporting Life* 163)

Nevertheless, as his frustrated love for Mrs. Hammond, his anger, and his grief over her death near the end of the novel demonstrate, powerful and vital human "feelings" have not been entirely suppressed despite the dehumanizing pressures that accompany the work of play. Through their resurgence, even in unpredictably and unacceptably explosive ways, such emotions clearly demonstrate that the athlete has not been *wholly* expropriated by the economic system that "owns" him. Rather than merely a well-functioning body that seems impervious to pain, Arthur Machin is a complex and fully *human* being with feelings that—like those of Sillitoe's long-distance runner—are not entirely subject to any form of *control*; he is, accordingly, a man rather than a mechanism, "A. Machin" rather than "a machine."

The fact that the pervasive influence of economics alters even the most fundamental meaning of the word "play" is particularly evident in *The Changing Room* (1972), Storey's ostensibly "plotless" drama. For the play's athletes and nonathletes alike (the players, the trainers, the team's owner, and even its janitor), the sport is a source of supplementary income—a commercial enterprise—rather than the source of enjoyment that "play" is traditionally held to be; the rugby match is a contractual rather than a wholly "voluntary" obligation, a form of *work* rather than *play*. Subtly but surely, the insidious influence of commercial "professionalism" becomes evident: the owner of the team does not watch it play, retiring to the locker room to warm himself and to enjoy a drink and conversation instead; the team's subsequent victory celebration commingles the players' satisfaction at their achievement and their relief that, in miserable weather and despite physical pain, another of their contractual performances has been completed. As Christopher Lasch has observed, economic concerns taint the basic nature of sports as

> the managerial apparatus makes every effort to eliminate the risk and the uncertainty that contributes so centrally to the ritual and dramatic success of any contest. When sports can no longer be played with appropriate abandon, they lose the capacity to raise the spirits of players and spectators, to transport them to a higher realm. Prudence and calculation, so prominent in everyday life but so inimical to the spirit of games, come to shape sports as they shape everything else. ("Corruption" 30)

Among players who can be sold or traded like commodities and retired by a decision of the owners, the whole concept of being a team is (as Lasch suggests) "drained of its capacity to call up local or regional loyalties" and therefore

> reduces itself (like the rivalry among the corporations themselves) to a struggle for shares of the market. The professional athlete does not care whether his team wins or loses (since losers share in the pot), as long as it stays in business. ("Letter" 40)

Although the athletes in Storey's work are "professional" in that they are paid for their participation in the sport, it is *not* their primary occupation (or "profession"); all also hold "regular" jobs in the world "outside." They play intensely and unrestrainedly, but they are by no means obsessed with winning—a subject they hardly mention among themselves; neither is there any concern about "representing" their particular locality. The owner of the team gives a typical pregame speech inciting them on to victory, but he takes little actual interest in the game itself. The players, like workers aggrieved at the policies and practices of management, complain about the stinginess of the owners and want a "more hygienic" system of separate showers to replace the common bath. A distinction between the workers/players and the owners/management is thus clearly evident in *The Changing Room*; the intrusion of economic issues—including charges of corporate ("Club") stinginess, low compensation, and unhygienic conditions—has blurred the age-old distinction between "work" and "play."

Yet regardless of the compensation that any of the characters receive, the "realm" of sport remains vitally separate from their lives in the "outside" world and their jobs there. The essential reason for this is that, as Johan Huizinga remarked in *Homo Ludens,* "Play is not 'ordinary' or 'real' life. It is rather a stepping out of 'real' life into a temporary sphere of activity with a disposition all of its own" (8) wherein specific and binding rules are observed and administered by impartial officials and a definite hierarchy—in which each person is expected to perform a specific role and duty that he knows well—prevails. In fact, as Huizinga points out, "inside the play-ground an absolute and peculiar order reigns. . . . Play . . . creates order, *is* order. Into an imperfect world and into the confusion of life it brings a temporary, a limited perfection" (10). For players and spectators alike, the game offers a ritualistic reenactment of an unending struggle between competing forces; in Storey's play, the central conflict is between "us" and "them," the primary terms used to refer to the teams. Yet, as in *The Loneliness of the Long-Distance Runner,* this fundamental dichotomy provides a metaphor for much larger issues in the world "outside" the realm of games and "play." Within the microcosm that the artificial world of sports provides, such struggles are resolved with a certain finality at the end of the match; yet, paradoxically, there are no *final* victories. As in the macrocosm of the world "outside," the major struggles of self against other and "us" against "them" are never completely and unambiguously resolved; even at world championships and after tournament "finals," one hears "Wait until next year!"

Although their "play" is actually contractual "work," Storey's rugby players find that their experience as members of a team provides a personal satisfaction that their jobs in the "outside world" lack. As Christopher Lasch has pointed out,

> Modern industry having reduced most jobs to a routine, games in our society take on added meaning. Men seek in play the difficulties and

demands—both intellectual and physical—which they no longer find in work. . . . Risk, daring, and uncertainty, important components of play, have little place in industry or in activities infiltrated by industrial methods, which are intended precisely to predict and control the future and to eliminate risk. ("Corruption" 40)

In the workplace, standardization and automation have supplanted individual craftsmanship and personal pride; as work is ever more deprived of personal responsibility and integrity, sports remain a haven in an increasingly mechanized, literally "heartless" world. Specifically, the experience of being a member of a *team* offers Storey's athletes a number of attributes that are seldom if ever found elsewhere in life: a functional and hierarchical "social" order in which each player knows his clearly defined "position"; a role suited to his particular skills, on which others rely and the success of the collective enterprise may well depend; authoritative rules; reliably impartial officials whose decisions are immediate and (usually) irreversible; "a temporary, a limited perfection"; personal autonomy and accountability; the opportunity to display carefully developed skills and individual judgment; and an unambiguous resolution that yet allows the prospect of a different (and, to the loser, more appealing) outcome on another day. All of these attributes share one all-important characteristic: *certainty*—the quality that is most absent in the modern age of doubt, anxiety, alienation, and anomie.

Among the players themselves, therefore, the experience of "belonging to" the team provides a temporary union that is forged through common purpose and shared endeavor. As they change their clothes and prepare to play the game, the athletes must set aside their various differences and the preoccupations of the outside world and assume new responsibilities and interdependencies as members of a team. Confirmed through wholly secular rituals that are unselfconsciously but unfailingly performed, this crucial "change" remains *beyond* the reach of those who have expropriated the game for purposes of their own, transforming it into an economic enterprise and commercial ceremony. Unlike traditional religious rituals, which confirmed a union and a significance lasting beyond the duration of the activity (and sustained the participants until their next involvement in the group), the wholly secular rituals of the changing room perform no such function; nevertheless, the lives of the players would clearly be less satisfying without them. Though the effects are both fleeting and impermanent, the athletes achieve an instance of order and unity that their lives in the outside world cannot provide.

Significantly, *This Sporting Life* ends in the locker-room rather than on the playing field itself because the latter is the site of the devalued commercial ritual that the game has become. As he joins in the players' post-game horseplay as a new team member undergoes an initiation with a ceremonial shower (a secular rite of passage), Arthur Machin achieves—through a renewal and confirmation of the team bond—a brief respite from the still-intense personal grief that he feels over the death of Mrs. Hammond. Like Paul Morel's decision to turn away from his self-absorbing grief at the conclusion of D. H. Lawrence's *Sons and Lovers,* Arthur Machin's action in the novel's final scene does not in any way deny the *intensity*—or the sincerity—of the grief he feels; yet by participating in the collective life of the team and taking part in one of its wholly private rituals, he too has "chosen life" rather than the death, personal isolation, darkness, and despair that are associated with the "outside" world.

Because long-distance running is an individual sport rather than a team effort, Sillitoe's Smith finds no such communal bond in the experience of sports, nor does he seek any such affirmation. Yet for him, too, the sport provides a haven from the factory-like regimentation and routine of borstal life, and it allows him to assert his individuality and self-reliance in a way that his workaday life in the "outside" world seldom affords. Unlike his job at the factory lathe, running allows him complete autonomy; success in the race—like success in his criminal activities—requires careful planning, agility, strategic maneuvering, and the assumption of risk. As Lasch points out, "risk, daring, and uncertainty, important components of play, have little place in industry or in activities infiltrated by industrial methods, which are intended precisely to predict and control the future and to eliminate risk" ("Corruption" 24). Because the sport has been expropriated by the governor and others like him, however, the rewards for taking such risk will not be his own. By deliberately refusing to win the race, Smith reaffirms the importance of daring, risk, unpredictability, and personal autonomy. Just as he was punished for his similar assertion of autonomy in his criminal activity, he is punished for having defied the authorities and violated their social norms—though he becomes a hero to the other boys, who recognize the significance of what he has done and understand the paradox that, under the circumstances of such expropriation that makes work out of play and attempts to dehumanize the worker/athlete into a mere mechanism, deliberately and defiantly to lose is to win.

Whereas Sillitoe's depiction of sports was not derived from any personal experience as an athlete (as he explains in "The Long Piece" in *Mountains and Caverns*), Storey's portrayal of the world of rugby-league football in *This Sporting Life* was based on his own first-hand experience as a member of a team. While a student at the Slade School of Art in London in 1953, Storey returned home each weekend to England's industrial north, where he played professional rugby for Leeds. Thus, he led a dual life, dividing his time between the physically demanding "public life" of a professional athlete and the private creative life of an art student; after each match, he would return to London to resume a type of life quite apart from (and perhaps incomprehensible to) the working-class teammates with whom he was regularly, though temporarily, united on the field of play. Years later, during an interview published in *Sports Illustrated,* he described the experience as follows:

The pleasure to me is in the pitch of endeavor, sustaining it, going beyond it. In many ways I hated rugby, but it allowed people to do marvelous things. Often the real expression occurs at the point of physical and mental exhaustion. I recall one very hard game, played in pouring rain on a pitch that seemed to be 15 feet deep in mud. My relations with the team were at their worst. I should have hated every minute of that match, but suddenly something almost spiritual happened. The players were taken over by the identity that was the team. We were genuinely transported. (Duffy 69)

That the experience was "something *almost* spiritual" is a crucially precise phrase, suggesting Storey's conscious realization that a *truly* "spiritual" (that is, religious) experience cannot by definition arise from a wholly secular activity and cannot occur in a desacralized world.

The same evolution from participation to "spectatorship" shapes the histories of both sport and theater; yet, as Huizinga contended in *Homo Ludens,* so much of the ritual value of sports has been lost in modern times that "however important [the contest] may be for the players or spectators, it remains sterile . . . the old play-factor [having] undergone almost complete atrophy" as a result of "the fatal shift towards overseriousness" in sports "play" (198). Yet notwithstanding the devaluation of sport (and life) by professionalism and the less-than-heroic stature of modern man, the rugby match and related activities *do* manifestly provide something "real" in the players' lives. "The ancient connections between games, ritual, and public festivity," which Lasch described in his essay on "The Corruption of Sports," have been diminished but *not eradicated* because play retains "its capacity to dramatize reality and to offer a convincing representation of the community's values . . . rooted in shared traditions, to which [games] give objective expression" (30). Like the "sacred space" of traditional religions, the playground is, as Huizinga observed, "hallowed, within which special rules obtain. All are temporary worlds within the ordinary world, dedicated to the performance of an act apart" (10).

The fact that these terms are even *more* applicable to the activities of the locker room is fundamental to Storey's works: unlike the commercial public ceremony of the game itself, the "change" is *literally* "an act apart," occurring within a "temporary world within the ordinary world," a wholly secular sanctuary to which only those with proper "credentials" are allowed access and in which the players' particular and binding but nontraditional rituals are unselfconsciously performed. The significant action of the play is the temporary reaffirmation of what Huizinga termed "the feeling of being 'apart together' in an exceptional situation, of sharing something important, of mutually withdrawing from the rest of the world and rejecting the usual norms" (12). Despite his dour conclusion in the final chapter of *Homo Ludens* that the "ritual tie [having] now been completely severed sport has become profane, 'unholy'

in every way, [having] no organic connection whatever with the structure of society" (197-198), Huizinga also maintained (in his first chapter) that vestigial formal elements of ritual and play survive today:

> The ritual act has all the formal and essential characteristics of play . . . particularly in so far as it transports the participants to another world. . . . A closed space is marked out for [play], either materially or ideally, hedged off from the everyday surroundings. . . . Now the marking out of some sacred spot is also the primary characteristic of every sacred act. . . . *Formally speaking, there is no distinction whatever between marking out a space for a sacred purpose and marking it out for sheer play.* The turf, the tennis-court, the chess-court, and pavement hopscotch cannot formally be distinguished from the temple or the magic circle. (18-20; emphasis mine)

Accordingly, the playing field is the profane world's counterpart of the "sacred space" of a theocentric culture. Yet much more than the public arena, the locker room constitutes a secular "holy of holies"—a "closed space" that may be entered only by those who are responsible for the performance of the public ritual that relies to a remarkable degree on "the feeling of being 'apart together'" that is fostered among them. As Lasch has observed, sports constitute the most efficacious modern means whereby both participants and observers may be (in Storey's phrase) "genuinely transported": "Among the activities through which men seek release from everyday life, games offer in many ways the purest form of escape. . . . They obliterate awareness of everyday reality, not by dimming that awareness but by raising it to a new intensity . . ." (Lasch, "Corruption" 24). Though none of the team members could articulate its significance, each finds in the experience of sports a personal renewal through the affirmation of the team bond—and a unity, transcendence, and significance that would be missing from his life otherwise. Storey's meticulous depiction of this event, "invisible" though it is, affords an insight into the athlete's experience *as an athlete* that is unique among the depictions of sports in modern literature.

The expropriation of the athlete is *not* exclusively economic, however, as Sillitoe's works reveal; its basis is more broadly social, having its origins in the power of one person or group to "have the whip-hand over" others (*Loneliness* 13), demanding allegiance to an institution, class, city, or state. Accordingly, in his essay on "Sport and Nationalism" in *Mountains and Caverns,* Sillitoe argued that "The Olympic torch is a flame of enslavement" for exactly this reason (84), expropriating athletes as champions of the state in much the same way that Storey's athletes become "property of the City." Against such dehumanization and what Sillitoe in *Her Victory* termed "the slavery of expectation" (392), both authors assert remarkably similar alternatives, though vaguely defined by both as just "feelings" and "thinking." Implicitly, these are a recognition of individuality and the inner self, persistent and defiant even in a mechanized world. For Arthur Machin, it is the belated recognition of the importance of his love for Mrs. Hammond; for Smith, as for Arthur Seaton, it is an affirmation of the unsubduable "thoughts and secrets and bloody life inside me" (*Loneliness* 12)—including the essential freedoms *not* to conform, *not* to "play along," *not* to win for others' sakes, and *not* to live by others' expectations and desires. Despite Marx's assertion to the contrary, both authors' works demonstrate that *not* "every atom of freedom" has been confiscated by those seeking to expropriate "the many-sided play of the muscles" in play as well as in work. In the anger and defiant self-assertion of their expropriated athletes—rather than in that of their counterparts still in the factories—Sillitoe and Storey alike have found a crucial symbol that not only embodies the predicament of people in a specific time, place, and class but also resonates throughout modern societies as well.

WORKS CITED

Duffy, Martha. "An Ethic of Work and Play." *Sports Illustrated* 5 Mar. 1973: 66-69.

Huizinga, Johan. *Homo Ludens: A Study of the Play Element in Culture.* Boston: Beacon, 1950.

Lasch, Christopher. "The Corruption of Sports." *The New York Review of Books* 28 April 1977: 24-30.

———. Letter/reply in "Corrupt Sports: An Exchange." *The New York Review of Books* 29 Sept. 1977: 40.

Marx, Karl. *Capital: A Critical Analysis of Capitalist Production.* Trans. from the third German ed. by Samuel Moore and Edward Aveling. Ed. Frederick Engels. London: Swan Sonnenschein & Lowery, 1872.

Sillitoe, Alan. *Her Victory.* London: Granada, 1983.

———. *The Loneliness of the Long-Distance Runner.* New York: NAL, 1959. 7-47.

———. "The Match." *The Loneliness of the Long-Distance Runner.* 105-113.

———. *Mountains and Caverns: Selected Essays by Alan Sillitoe.* London: Allen, 1975.

———. *Saturday Night and Sunday Morning.* New York: NAL, 1958.

Storey, David. *The Changing Room.* London: Cape, 1972.

———. *This Sporting Life.* 1960. New York: Avon, 1975.

———. *Present Times.* London: Cape, 1984.

Wiley Lee Umphlett

SOURCE: "'North Dallas Forty' and the Tradition of the American Sporting Myth," in *American Sport Culture: The Humanistic Dimensions,* edited by Wiley Lee Umphlett, Bucknell University Press, 1985, pp. 186-96.

[*In the following essay, Umphlett provides an analysis of the major themes, dramatic conflicts, characterization, and stylistic elements of Peter Gent's football novel.*]

When *The Sporting Myth and the American Experience* first appeared in 1975, I was pleasantly surprised at the critics' warm reception to my rather scholarly but less than exhaustive treatment of a popular subject area. In particular, various sources who reviewed the book called it "a welcome book, the first of its kind," and "a valuable preliminary study of an important theme in American literature," and—even more flattering— "an important archetypal model for further investigations of the subject."[1] Most reviewers seemed to agree that the book's chief virtue was a strikingly original approach to the interpretation of a neglected area of American fiction.

In my attempt to demonstrate that a literary tradition of sporting experience had originated with writers like Washington Irving and James Fenimore Cooper, I contended that its development, beginning with the contrasting but complementary experience of these authors' athletic character types (Brom Bones and his social conflict and Natty Bumppo and his frontier involvement) and evolving through modern variations of these archetypes, has created a symbolic dramatic pattern that I call the "Sporting Myth" in American fiction.[2]

Then when James Michener drew on some of my ideas as the basis for his chapter on the contemporary athlete in *Sports in America* (Random House, 1976), I was pleased, of course, but somewhat taken aback to discover that he had attempted to fit real-life sports heroes like Don Meredith, Hal Greer, and Robin Roberts into the mold of the "Sporting Myth," finding, not surprisingly to me, that they did not fit its fictional behavior pattern.[3] In refutation of Michener's application of the Myth, my research into a large number of serious fictional works controlled and directed by American sports experience had led me to conclude that fictional characters of a sporting background, either in solitary or in team sports, do not parallel real-life models so much as they exhibit pervasive and commonly identifiable characteristics which afford the reader a larger grasp and understanding of the complexities, ambiguities, and contradictions of American experience. In a significant number of novels and stories that I came across, it was increasingly evident that when American writers create characters who are conditioned by sporting endeavor, game competition, or some kind of athletic activity, distinctive, singular behavior traits symbolic of our cultural heritage as a people establish themselves.

In particular, male literary characters conditioned by American sporting experience all seem to espouse an ingrained adulation of the primitive and a preference for the simple as opposed to the complex and sophisticated; accordingly, they assume postures and attitudes that are anti-urban, anti-establishment, anti-social, and anti-feminine (mainly because woman represents socialization). They also exhibit a narcissus complex which makes them antagonistic toward anyone or anything that would undermine their self-esteem or status; and as men in motion who behave instinctively, they come across as basically innocent, childlike figures who dream of remaining forever young while fearing their ultimate adversary—death.

The fictional pattern of the sporting hero—the experience of encounter—finds its most appropriate expression today in the microcosm of competitive team sports whose literary origins can be traced to the archetypal social and frontier experiences of Brom Bones and Natty Bumppo respectively. But in the contemporary literary hero of sporting background these antithetical experiences of confrontation have become intermingled, creating within his emotional makeup an irreconcilable conflict between the natural and the societal. In other words, the psychological tension in the contemporary sporting hero seems to derive from the fact that he exists as a composite of the Brom Bones-Natty Bumppo character makeups which focus on the conflict between the complex or societal and the primitive or natural. Because sporting activity, as both a source and means of individualized expression, has become so much a part of the American way of life, a perceptive writer attuned to the humanistic implications of modern sports can correlate the resources of the Sporting Myth and the oblique fictional process to express an intensely personal vision of life.[4] To illustrate how the Myth has continued to express itself through a writer's intuitive control of its resources, I intend to focus here on Peter Gent's *North Dallas Forty* (William Morrow, 1973), perhaps the finest novel about professional football to appear thus far, but one whose 1979 film version sparked a degree of controversy concerning the supposedly self-destructive life-style of today's pro football player.[5]

The hero (or anti-hero, if you will) of this novel is a naturally talented, but socially disoriented, wide receiver named Phil Elliott who, as we shall see, comes across as a representative character in the tradition of the sporting hero in American fiction, primarily because he personifies all the Myth's characteristics which I have identified above. Whereas most fiction dealing with professional athletes seems to be controlled by a pulp-magazine kind of emphasis on melodramatic situations—for example, an ongoing feud between team players or a former star's comeback in the big game—Gent's work reflects the serious novel's approach to incorporating the organic ingredients of theme, dramatic conflict, characterization, and structure in the sweep of his canvas, thus enhancing his special talent for dramatizing the internal conflict and emotional pain

of his main character. The overall dramatic effect is a highly compelling reading experience, one that transcends the level of pure narrative appeal to get at something seriously wrong with contemporary society—although many readers must have felt that Gent's prime purpose was to expose the Dallas Cowboy organization, since Gent himself had formerly played for Dallas.[6] Such a reaction merely points out what I have previously suggested; that our familiarity with an area of real-life experience may prompt us to interpret fictional experience in a directly representational manner, thus obscuring an author's underlying intent and the fact that his work could be about a great deal more than, in this case, the rather restricted area of professional football. To test my assessment, we need first to look closely at the structural makeup of *North Dallas Forty,* particularly as it defines the experience of the novel's central character.

The pattern of Phil Elliott's encounter experience is structured around eight days during the football season which graphically reveal his growing disillusionment with the overly organized system of professional football. To dramatize this situation, Gent focuses on his hero's frustrated attempts to find himself as an individual both off the field and within the pro football jungle—from the playing field right up to the Dallas front office. For Elliott, playing football has degenerated into merely participating in a finely tuned system wherein "opponents and teammates alike are his adversaries"—a relationship in which there is "no team, no loyalty, no camaraderie; there is only him, alone."[7] Like the traditional sporting hero, Elliott lives according to the integrity of his own personal code of behavior and also according to what he calls a religion of survival, wherein he must rely on his own basic instincts. His is a faith, however, which is naturally mistrustful of institutionalized religious experiences like, for example, the shallow inspirational talks of the team's devotional leader. Significantly, he maintains a close identity with the blacks on the team, whose unsophisticated and natural air of primitive well-being has contributed to Elliott's understanding that they "always seemed to have more fun" in anything they did. But whereas most of the blacks have learned to adapt to the demands of the system to survive, Elliott, in the literary tradition of the sporting hero, is compelled to go his way alone.

The structural form of Elliott's odyssey to discover self is circular, beginning with his instinctively natural, but socially noncommital, outing with teammates on a dove hunt, then moving through a series of events on the field and off, which are highlighted by flashbacks of his broken marriage, a variety of sordid experiences with alcohol, drugs, and sex, and intermittent clashes with the Dallas coaching-managerial establishment, finally ending in tragedy one week later in the ironically natural setting of the ranch house of his most recent girl friend. The cyclical development of the novel underscores Elliott's innate affinity with nature and the outdoors—his true religion and one of the most pervasive characteristics of the Sporting Myth. In fact, throughout the novel, Elliott, like Natty Bumppo, his frontier ancestor, keeps referring to the suburban countryside and what the encroachment of both the city and technology is doing to it, thus establishing a dramatic contrast between the way the natural environment could be and the way it really is. His participation with three drunken teammates in the travesty of a dove hunt at the beginning of the novel is one of Gent's most vivid metaphors for the way in which modern man has abused his natural right to relate meaningfully to his natural surroundings. Instead of abiding by the ritual of the hunt, the players persist in wantonly slaughtering the helpless birds, apparently only for the thrill of the kill. But while the others indulge themselves in the massacre, Elliott passively resigns himself to the role of a disenchanted onlooker until, as he expresses it: "We returned cold, tired, drunk, and empty-handed. Jo Bob had thrown the remaining doves at passing cars" (7).

The ritual of the hunt is ironically presented here as frustrated, sterile experience, not only to emphasize the negative role of the sporting hero in contemporary literature but to set the tone of the story and introduce the reader to Elliott's inner conflict, which pervades the novel. Appropriately, when Elliott meets Charlotte Caulder, an appealingly independent ranch woman who represents the kind of life-style he is strongly attracted to, he reveals to her through hunting imagery why he thinks the quality of contemporary life has declined:

> Hunting used to be the way energy was balanced. A good hunt was a great combination of muscular and emotional energy. But now hunting just degenerates into butchery, which creates more energy rather than depleting it. Almost all human endeavor is that way. That surplus of energy is the cause of crimes of passion and spectator sports. (178)

Spectator sports, Elliott feels, have been created to function as the artificial rendering of modern man's natural heritage while the remaining "natural energy depleter" and the "savior of human sanity" is sexual identification and satisfaction, which he has determined from his self-oriented outlook is the last frontier for achieving the ultimate balance between self and the natural environment. Phil Elliott's story, we may conclude is yet another fictional variation of the contemporary obsession for sexual experience as a substitute for self-realization, this time as it is expressed from the unique viewpoint of the sporting hero.

Even though heterosexual experience plays a major role in Elliott's life-style, both in actual involvement and vicariously through the lurid locker-room tales of sexual prowess shared in by his teammates, his is an ambivalent attitude toward women, as with most sporting heroes in our literature. In fact, Elliott's feelings are instinctively homosexual in nature, especially toward his best friend on the team, quarterback Seth Maxwell. It is a relationship that he himself admits to, though, and one which he attributes to the rash of game injuries both he and Maxwell have endured together over the years—

a "brotherhood of mutilation," which he considers to be "a very large part of [their] strange relationship" and "maybe even a homosexual bond" (140). The fraternity of athletes bound together by their ability to stand up to pain and injuries takes on distinctive sexual overtones in this novel of grown men clinging to the vestiges of waning youth through their common identity with a game. In this sense, and in his casual relationship with women, whose sexual favors offer a way to expand ego and hopefully discover self, Elliott is a brother to John Updike's has-been athlete, Rabbit Angstrom.

Charlotte Caulder, however, is the most exceptional female he has ever encountered, whose independence and purposefulness Elliott sees as malelike, contrasting markedly with the socializing instincts of his former wife, who, like most football wives who make their "special catalyst" particularly evident at post-game parties, had fostered disharmony among the players. In Gent's satirical portrayal of football wives we observe the recurring literary evidence of the female affinity for social constraints which oppose the natural expressiveness of the male sporting-type character. Charlotte, on the other hand, functions as much more than a social force and a sexual object in Phil Elliott's life: She becomes ultimately the one person who offers him the key to finding himself. The ranch scene in which Charlotte castrates a calf while Elliott reluctantly assists her is a pointedly significant and symbolic moment in their understanding of the unique interrelationship of their roles. In this highly graphic account of what is considered by the male mind to be the most repellent and abhorrent physical debilitation, Charlotte asserts her authority naturally enough for Elliott to sense that the ultimate emasculation is not so much a physical condition as it is to be a slave to a system, whether it be marriage or professional football. Significantly, she offers him the freedom to be himself by coming to live on her ranch, an invitation that heightens the conflict within his own mind of whether to continue abiding by the system or to go his way alone.

While sex represents one avenue taken by Elliott in his intense search for self, others are drugs and alcohol. By the end of *North Dallas Forty* the major characters have indulged in a prodigious amount of pills and marijuana, as well as a torrent of alcohol. As Elliott himself puts it: "I was high on something all the time—codeine, booze, grass, speed, fear; in fact, I doubt that during a season I was ever in a normal state of mind . . ."(154). But true to the performance code of the traditional sporting hero, "doing something better than anyone else in front of millions of people" is Elliott's ultimate high, and to maintain his intensity of purpose and the "ability to endure pain" in one of the most violent of sports, Gent suggests through Elliott's experience that the professional football player is greatly dependent on drugs as both a pain deterrent and an emotional stimulant. Within this situation lies the source of much controversy surrounding the film version, but because in both the film and the novel, drugs are used off field as well as on, the oblique fictional process would probably have us believe that their use represents not only a physiological need but, in a larger, more metaphorical sense, a psychological necessity to shield the self against the harsh realities of an apparently indifferent world, as symbolized by the system of professional football. Ultimately, though, it is Elliott's possession of drugs that precipitates both his final clash with the Dallas front office and his decision to break with football by taking up Charlotte's offer to live on her ranch.

Although the coaching staff has labeled Elliott as immature and unable to take the game of football seriously because of his propensity for clowning and joking on the field and off, his attitude persists as yet another buffer to what he sees of the prevailing system around him. In Elliott's own mind his problems with coaches and the front office have been compounded by the injuries he has suffered during his career—"five major operations, plus numerous muscle tears, breaks and dislocations" (49). As a result, Elliott contends that he hasn't had the opportunity to play up to his full potential. Revering the act of quality performance as his sporting hero brothers do, Elliott shares their naturally expressive need to participate meaningfully in the sacrosanct world of the game. But because management now looks upon him as "damaged" property, he knows that he must somehow make his peace soon or the system "would be shopping for a new piece of equipment" (23).

But Elliott's increasingly antagonistic attitude toward management's coldly detached approach to problem solution has created a seemingly irreconcilable emotional conflict between his inherent love for a game and his growing detestation of a system which inhibits the individualistic and freely expressive manner of the prototypal sporting hero. As Elliott instinctively understands involvement in sports,

> There is a basic reality where it is just me and the job to be done, the game and all its skills. And the reward wasn't what other people thought or how much they paid me but how I felt at the moment I was exhibiting my special skill. How I felt about me. That's what's true. (265)

Over the long run, then, Elliott comprehends his participatory role in the special sense that there is really only "the game. Not the end, the winning or losing, but the means: the game." With the sporting hero of American literary tradition, the game or sporting act itself has always been understood in terms of the experience of pursuit and not in the achievement of a goal. Because of his emphasis on game experience as both an end in itself and a means to self-realization, Phil Elliott stands in the direct line of this tradition.

Professional football as it is represented in *North Dallas Forty,* then, exists as a metaphor for a large area of modern experience, suggesting that today there may be many people—and not just professional football play-

ers—who find themselves in a psychological predicament or moral dilemma similar to that of Phil Elliott. At particular points throughout the novel, Elliott observes and comments on events reported in the newspaper or over his car radio—reports of scandals, violence, and murders—asides that inform the reader of serious problems that exist outside the isolated world of the football game, yet suggesting that Elliott's life could be a microcosm of what is happening at large in contemporary society. Occasionally, in the insulated comfort of his late-model car, he observes the malaise of the passing scene, as at one point:

> It was the afternoon rush hour and I was going against the grain of the traffic escaping north to the suburbs. I passed miles of glazed eyes, tight jaws, and hands tensely gripped on steering wheels, people rushing home, dazedly thankful that the world had held together for another day. (61-62)

If there is a sickness that pervades the game of professional football, Gent intimates through his hero's experience that it is perhaps only a reflection of a more widespread and malignant illness within society itself.

Consequently, as a contemporary version of the sporting hero who seeks a symbolic return to his natural heritage but who is frustrated in his quest by both an unfathomable system and frustrating societal demands which entrap rather than free, Phil Elliott is involved in a search that is apparently doomed to failure. From time to time, he can reflect from his vantage point in the city that

> the land was still out there and not that hard to reach. Sometimes I felt that knowledge was what kept me from going totally crazy in Dallas. . . . But lately that fantasy didn't seem to hold. How could I return to the land? I had never been there in the first place. (170)

It is through this denial of his natural heritage, then, that we observe Elliott's encounter experience taking shape as a conflict between trying to realize the romantic identity of his heritage or giving in to the edicts and demands of the Dallas coaching-managerial establishment. Even his best friend, Seth Maxwell, who as the team's quarterback represents the organizational philosophy of his coach, cannot offer Elliott any consolation and in the end cops out on him because in reality he functions as a lackey to management. To Maxwell's attitude that the best way to get along in a system is to join it, Elliott ironically underscores his own theory of the game as an enjoyable end in itself when he remarks, "People don't talk about football teams anymore, they talk about football systems, and the control long ago moved off the field" (263). True to the code of the sporting hero, Elliott maintains his individualistic stance through the novel's climax and even through its tragic denouement.

After the critical New York game, which Dallas loses by one point and in which Elliott ironically enjoys one of his best days, the Dallas coach calls him before a tribunal of club and league officials. It is a powerful scene, one in which intense personal confrontations are staged to spotlight Elliott's ultimate clash with management. Informed that he has been under investigative surveillance for the past week, Elliott is accused of "conduct unbecoming professional football," specifically that of indulging in illegal drugs and carrying on an illicit affair with the fiancée of the team owner's brother. The dramatically charged setting also invites the Dallas coach to make one of the most paradoxically revealing comments in the entire novel when he criticizes Elliott as being "dangerous to organization for the same reason you are desirable" (281). Although he is categorized as a superior athlete, Elliott must pay the ultimate price for trying to be an individual in a system in which the individual must be sacrificed to the good of the organization. It is a familiar theme in American literature, but here it finds unique expression through Gent's skillful application of the resources of the Sporting Myth. Banished from league play, Elliott realizes once again that the "game wasn't on the field, it never had been." The real game had been played by the Dallas coach and his staff, who looked upon the game of football as a complex brand of technology requiring a systems management control. Charlotte had been right, he reasons: "I must have a value to myself and that has to come from inside, not from achievements in the world" (287). Once again the peculiar code of the sporting hero expresses itself through Elliott's awareness that to overcome the personally restrictive forces of the system, he must find a way to be himself.

In spite of the novel's violently shattering ending, Gent manages to convey the basic posture of the sporting hero up to the very last line of his story. Returning to Charlotte's ranch where he has decided his true destiny lies, Elliott confronts the sporting hero's most feared adversary when he discovers that an estranged acquaintance of Charlotte's, having come upon her and her black ranch hand in bed together, has shot them to death in a fit of jealous rage. Elliott's first impulse is to kill the murderer, but his efforts are frustrated, as if to dramatize the literary convention of death's role as the most formidable antagonist of the sporting hero. Thus, for Elliott there can now be only one recourse—self-renewal through nature—and after the police complete their investigation, he walks out of the ranch house to confront the natural force he innately understands by looking "out over the silent rolling pasture . . . [and] listening for sounds of life in the distance" (294). Bringing his hero full circle from the grotesque dove hunt of eight days previous to this final symbolic scene at the ranch, Peter Gent has constructed from both the resources of the American Sporting Myth and the oblique writing technique of the serious novelist a remarkable first novel that transcends the mundane level of a popular sport to tell us a great deal about the identity problems of the individual in contemporary society.

NOTES

[1] The quotations are from *Choice, Journal of Modern Literature,* and *Library Journal* respectively.

[2] In using the term *sporting* as opposed to *sports,* my intent is to suggest an attitude toward a code of behavior or a set of values derived from our frontier heritage. The term *sports,* on the other hand, connotes the system of organized games and contests as affected by societal needs. *Myth* I interpret as a symbolic pattern of action or frame of literary reference representative of and common to a culture, which a writer uses either consciously or subconsciously to give his readers a better understanding of, and a deeper insight into, themselves and their culture.

[3] See Michener, *Sports in America,* 224-68. Michener's assumptions suggest that even reputable and experienced fiction writers may critically misconstrue what ought to be the connotative function of serious fiction. The fictional process, I believe, is not intended to create a *direct* representation of life as the nonfiction writer would attempt it in, say, a biographical work. If such were the case, the experience of reading fiction would be journalistic in nature, akin to looking at the world as a mirror image. Instead, the fictional process ought to be dependent on an *oblique* approach to describing experience so that the reader may perceive nuances of character and insights into human behavior which a mirror representation would overlook by its very directness. In fact, the mirror or visual representation projected by the film version of *North Dallas Forty* may be the major contributory factor to audience misinterpretation of literary intent and the resultant controversy surrounding what this film is probably trying to say.

[4] Hemingway, of course, is the most obvious example of a writer who depended on sporting experience to project an attitude toward life, but one should also note other outstanding examples in the writings of William Faulkner, Nelson Algren, James Jones, Philip Roth, Irwin Shaw, John Updike, and Bernard Malamud, to mention some established writers who have relied on the Myth.

[5] The fact that I ignored this novel in *The Sporting Myth* (Lewisburg: Bucknell University Press, 1975) was not because I underrated it at the time but was rather due to my feeling then that I had reviewed sufficient material to illustrate the major points of my thesis. Because professional football keeps growing in popularity, *North Dallas Forty* is a prime example for updating the Myth, I think.

[6] Note, however, that for obvious reasons the "Cowboy" generic term is never mentioned in this novel.

[7] Peter Gent, *North Dallas Forty* (New York: New American Library, Signet edition, 1974), 24. All subsequent quotations are from this edition, with pagination noted in the text.

David A. Jones and Leverett T. Smith, Jr.

SOURCE: "Jerry Kramer's 'Instant Replay' and Dan Jenkins' 'Semi-Tough': A Cultural Dialogue," in *Journal of Popular Culture,* Vol. XII, No. 1, Summer, 1978, pp. 156-67.

[*In the following essay, Jones and Smith contrast the different representations of American football culture found in* Instant Replay *and* Semi-Tough.]

Our frame of reference for understanding *Instant Replay* and *Semi-Tough* is provided by R. W. B. Lewis in *The American Adam*. Professor Lewis believes, as we do, that a culture defines itself by and through a dialogue of participating voices. Certain issues emerge which capture the attention of large numbers of people, at least "articulate" people—those who write, teach, preach, and so on. Various responses to these issues as felt moral imperatives and ethical realities shape themselves into a dialogue. "Every culture," writes Lewis,

> seems . . . to produce its own determining debate over the ideas that preoccupy it: salvation, the order of nature, money, power, sex, the machine, and the like. The debate, indeed, may be said to *be* the culture, at least on its loftiest levels; for a culture achieves identity not so much through the ascendancy of the one particular set of convictions as through the emergence of its peculiar and distinctive dialogue. . . . Intellectual history, properly conducted, exposes not only the dominant ideas of a period, or of a nation, but more important, the dominant clashes over ideas. Or to put it more austerely: the historian looks not only for the major terms of discourse, but also for major pairs of opposed terms which by their very opposition, carry the discourse forward. . . . As he does so . . . the historian is likely to discover that the development of the culture in question resembles a protracted and broadly ranging conversation: at best a dialogue.[1]

We believe that *Instant Replay* and *Semi-Tough* qualify as dialogic participants in just such a cultural debate as Lewis has described. Sport in America, and especially professional sport, has become a major dimension of our social and cultural life. Our intention here is not to argue whether this is good or bad, but rather to show how *Instant Replay* and *Semi-Tough* reflect that dimension of American culture, and how they represent a "major pair of opposed terms" in a contemporary cultural dialogue.

Admittedly Lewis is talking primarily about what we may designate as "high culture." But we believe that the same kind of "debate," or "conversation," or "dialogue" with which he is concerned at "high" levels, occurs at the level of "popular" culture; and in these two books we have the articulation of strikingly different views about a major cultural phenomenon in contemporary America: professional football.

In *Instant Reply* Jerry Kramer clearly has more in mind than simply describing a football season. He announces his purpose at the very beginning of the book. "Perhaps by setting down my daily thoughts and observations, I'll be able to understand precisely what it is that draws me back to professional football."[2] In explaining why he takes up, again and again, the punishing job of an offensive lineman on a professional football team, Kramer necessarily involves himself in more than just an analysis of himself. He writes about the kind of community in which he finds himself. *Instant Replay* finally describes the shape of a whole culture, not just that of an individual psyche. This second, larger purpose becomes increasingly conscious as the book proceeds, and Kramer best articulates it when he faces the television cameras after throwing his "block felt round the world" in the final seconds of the NFL Championship game with Dallas. In speaking to a national television audience, Kramer, offended by a recent magazine article which suggested that his coach was something of a tyrant, defends his coach's philosophy.[3] This brings him to his reasons for playing football. At the end of the book he concludes:

> I know that for me the main lure of football is the guys, my teammates, the friendship, the fun, the excitement, the incredibly exhilarating feeling of a shared achievement. When I look back upon the 1967 season, before I remember the block on Jethro Pugh, before I remember our victory in the Super Bowl, I remember a very special spirit, a rare camaraderie, something I can't quite define, but something I've tried to capture in this diary (p. 284).

It seems valuable to discover the shape of this "very special spirit."

We can see its shape in the images Kramer associates with the individual players on the team, with the team's coach, Vince Lombardi, and finally with the community the team as a whole constitutes. Each is imaged in four different ways: there are associations with war, with the family, with the business world, and with the machine. They all flow from the figure of Lombardi, the emotional center of the book.

Lombardi the coach is presented as first of all a businessman. Kramer reports early in the book that:

> Lombardi chewed on us again tonight. Sometimes he seems to hate everybody without regard to race, religion, or national origin. First he compared the Packers to a large corporation, like General Motors or IBM or Chrysler, and he said that a large business cannot tolerate mistakes. "We've got seventy people here in camp," he said. "If the ones we have can't do the job, we'll get some more" (p. 30).

Here the Packers are a corporation, a community whose basic characteristic must be their efficiency in working together. Personal relationships claim a rather low priority—in fact, it would be better if none were developed at all. But if the Packers are a business and Lombardi is their manager, they are "a helluva business" (p. 2). to use Lombardi's own phrase. His decision to place Paul Hornung, a player to whom he felt a particular closeness, on a list of players to stock expansion teams shows us at once that Lombardi regards the business dimension of the Packers as the essential one. His sorrow when Hornung is selected—this is our first glimpse of him in the book—shows that the business dimension is not the only important one.

That the players also consider themselves businessmen provides one of the central overt conflicts of the book. Throughout the season, Lombardi continually shouts at players who lack dedication because they spend so much time on interests outside their concerns as football players. Jerry Kramer is among the worst offenders. He describes himself as "not a one-dimensional figure. I'm a businessman much of the time. I own part of the American Archery company in Wisconsin and part of the Packer Diving Company in Louisiana. I'm the host of a syndicated TV show once a week during the football season, and I'm involved in half a dozen advertising ventures. I follow the stock market. I keep looking for new opportunities for investments" (p. xii). These business ventures command some of his attention throughout the season and Lombardi worries about his devotion to the Packers.

Lombardi clearly thinks outside business ventures prevent the machine he wishes to make of the Packer football team from operating smoothly. For as well as being a business, the team is also seen as a machine. Lombardi is the operator, the players the parts. Kramer himself suggests at one point that Lombardi's regimen has reduced him to an automaton.

> A fan gave me a ride this morning up the hill to the dressing room from the practice field, and he asked me what time we practice in the afternoon and I couldn't tell him. All I know is that when everyone else moves, I move, and when everyone else files out of the dorm, I file out, and when everyone else gets on the bus, I get on the bus. I get dressed with everyone else and I leave the locker room with everyone else. I really don't know what time it is, what day it is, what year it is. I don't know anything at all (p. 35).

Lombardi drives his team toward his goal of a perfectly operating machine. Kramer comments:

> Coach Lombardi seemed more disturbed than angry during our meeting this morning. He said there's a general lack of enthusiasm on the club, a lack of desire, something he can't quite put his finger on. He said that sometimes he would rather lose and have everybody play a perfect game than win and have everybody look sloppy. My immediate reaction is to say that's crazy, that's ridiculous, he couldn't really mean that, but, somehow, I suspect he does, at least in theory. His desire for perfection is immense, and he's been very unhappy with our habit of doing only as much as we have to do to win (p. 141-42).

Here Lombardi asks for the machine which operates perfectly, while conceding that he would be happy being beaten by a better team, if only he could get the parts of his own into good working order. This perfectionism actually seems to unite the figure of the businessman with that of the machine operator. Both "pay meticulous attention to detail."

> He makes us execute the same plays over and over, a hundred times, two hundred times, until we do every little thing right automatically. He works to make the kickoff-return team perfect. He ignores nothing. Technique, technique, technique over and over and over, until we feel like we're going crazy. But we win (p. 41).

This business machine is organized along the principles of an army, and its preparations for and games with its opponents are pictured as those of an army preparing for and entering battle, as a look at the section and chapter headings of the book will show. Kramer once describes the team as looking "like a lost army getting ready for battle" (p. 166), and compares Lombardi to the commander in a military movie.

> Bart and Max and I all agreed that Lombardi really prepares us, really pushes us toward perfection. The conversation reminded me of a late-night movie I was watching on TV a few days ago. It was a Navy movie, and the commander was a real Vince Lombardi-type character. He got killed, and one of the men on his ship commented, "He made us all a little better than we thought we could ever be." It sounds corny, but that's the way we feel about Lombardi (p. 181).

The businessman-perfectionist becomes in addition a military hero.

But the image most closely associated with Lombardi is that of the father. He is a patriarch. Kramer tells us early in the book that "Lombardi thinks of himself as the patriarch of a large family, and he loves all his children" (p. 10). Lombardi's treatment of Kramer when he was ill moves Kramer to say that "his players are his children, and he nurses them when they're sick and scolds them when they're bad and rewards them when they're good" (p. 42). Kramer mentions that Lombardi has "a real thing about loyalty" (p. 5). calls him "a child psychologist" (p. 78). and characterizes his relationship with Paul Hornung as that of "the stern father" and "the wild son" (p. 245).

In this scheme, all the players, not just Paul Hornung, are children. They are children in addition to being businessmen, parts of the machine, and warriors. Kramer speaks of his "boyish" play (p. 3) and of being an essentially "undisciplined" person (p. 149). who needs to be a part of Lombardi's patriarchy. The Packers resemble a community of children, characterized by intensity and high pressure to conform. Kramer speaks of the difficulties of socializing with rookies during training camp.

It's not only the newness of the whole system, learning the plays and the players. There's also the attitude among the veterans, the feeling of togetherness that makes the rookie feel like an outsider. He's away from home, away from a familiar setting, and often away from a wife he's just been married to for a little while. It's a miracle that any of them make it. In the past we've had lots of rookies "domino" out on us, just pack up in the middle of the night, sneak out the door and go home. The strain is brutal, going through all the incredible torture we go through and wondering if you're going to make the club (p. 23).

Kramer makes clear that a veteran's loyalties are first to other veterans in describing his relationship to Dick Arndt, a rookie from the same college where Kramer played. Arndt is trying out for positions presently occupied by Kramer's friends. Kramer describes the situation as "touchy" (p. 34). and is quite ambivalent about offering Arndt advice, because of the friendliness he feels for his fellow linemen. This feeling of togetherness not only results in conflicts in relation to rookies, but is easily lost if a veteran's status changes within the community. When Kramer is injured during the Minnesota game, he stands on the sideline, feeling "like an outsider." He finds that he is jealous of the players on the field (p. 157).

In addition Kramer feels this togetherness abolishes, at least temporarily, racial tensions felt by ordinary citizens. He tells us that on the Packers "there's no friction on the field, not even a hint of prejudice. You've got to give Lombardi the credit" (p. 27). This is because "we rarely think in terms of race. The way we look at it, guys like Wood and Herb Adderly and Lionel Aldridge aren't Negroes—they're Packers; they're teammates" (p. 28).

Kramer speculates at various points in the book "about what holds us all together" (p. 58). He says that "there's a sort of mutual respect agreement on the team. Everybody's allowed to have his own feelings, his own preferences, his own way of life, and everybody else's way. Nobody judges anybody else" (p. 58-9). This mutual respect is possible because of "the love we have on our team" (p. 85).

Actually, the Packer mold seems rather narrower than Kramer's description. A minor dimension of the book concerns the adventures of Don Horn as he completes the transformation from rookie to Green Bay Packer. When we first meet him we find Kramer worrying over his (Horn's) spiritual condition:

> He's a little hard to figure out. He's a bachelor, drives a Jaguar, dresses flashy, seems like a cocky kid, not in the Bart Starr-Zeke Bratkowski quiet, unassuming mold. But the other day he walked up to one of the veterans and said he'd heard that some of the veterans thought he was cocky and he didn't want them to get that idea. He's starting to come around (p. 73).

We never learn what is wrong with Horn's attitude; surely he has other options than becoming quiet and unassuming if he wants to become a member of the Packers family. But Kramer does not name any. When we meet Horn again, Kramer is still worried, but optimistic.

> When I went in to get taped, Fuzzy and Don Horn were lying on the tables, and Bud Jorgensen, our trainer, was taping Horn's knee. "What the hell you wasting all that tape for, Horn?" Fuzzy said, needling the kid. "You've been in here half an hour getting taped, and there ain't no way you're gonna get to play, unless Bart and Zeke and three other guys get hurt." Horn laughed. He's coming around. He's lost a little of his cocky attitude, and he's starting to fit the Green Bay Packers mold (p. 131).

We are relieved to learn, toward the end of the book, that Horn does lose his cockiness and becomes a full-fledged Packer.

> Don Horn, the rookie quarterback, came on my TV show tonight, and his answers to a few of my questions showed how far he's come since training camp. He's changed his attitude—he isn't cocky anymore—and, like all the other first-year men he's become a part of the Green Bay Packers (p. 226).

And this seems a genuine accomplishment. The Packers are a closed, brotherly community—like children. It's terribly easy to be an outsider.

Lombardi functions not only as an earthly father in this community, but also as a kind of personal representative of the spiritual father. In fact, the players often confuse him with God. He is certainly a spiritual as well as a political leader: a soldier-priest. This image of Lombardi is conveyed mostly through humor in the book. There is the song Fuzzy Thurston sings, "He's got the whole world, in his hands," with local variations on the words (pp. 40, 87). There is also Kramer's joking comparison of Lombardi to Oral Roberts. Both, Kramer says, are miraculous in their ability to make sick people well (p. 32). But later in the book the references are more serious. When Lombardi insists on holding practices despite inclement weather, Kramer remarks that "I think he's starting to believe he controls the weather" (p. 152). A long discussion of religion concludes with this anecdote.

> Max wouldn't accept Paul's answer, and they argued back and forth and finally, they called over Bill Curry, a deeply religious young man who used to play with us, and presented their cases to him. Bill listened very carefully, then said, "This isn't something between you and me, Paul, or between you and me, Max. This is something between both of you and—"
>
> McGee interrupted. "Oh, no," he said. "Don't bring that Lombardi into this" (p. 146).

This perhaps best testifies to the extent of Lombardi's influence over his players.

Late in the book Kramer finds a myth which makes many of these images cohere into a symbolic structure. His characterization of the Packers as a Camelot forces the military and patriarchal images into the foreground. Community, not the individual, cooperation, not competition, are stressed. "There's a great deal of love for one another on this club," Kramer says to a national television audience. "Perhaps we're living in Camelot." Kramer "was referring to the idea of one for all and all for one, the ideal of King Arthur's Round Table" (p. 281). This makes Lombardi Arthur and his players knights in search of the Holy Grail. Though Kramer has to drag in the Three Musketeers to do it, he has little difficulty accentuating the ideal of brotherhood. Even the militaristic dimension of the image is muted. Later, Kramer elaborates his meaning a little more in response to a reporter's question.

> I told him I felt that Camelot was the ideal situation, the perfect place, the epitome of everything good. For example, I tried to explain to him the attitude of the guys on the club. I mentioned Doug Hart. "He was a starter in '65," I said. "He played the whole year, did a great job, then lost his position to Bob Jeter in 1966. He should be upset. He should be sulking or demanding to be traded. Right? Wrong. Not here. He's one of the best men we have on our special units. He hustles harder than anybody on the club."

> Then I told him about Fuzzy. "When Gill took over this year," I said, "I'm sure it hurt Fuzzy. I'm sure he felt bad about losing his job. But he sat behind Gilly in every movie, he talked with him, he coached him, he was just like a big brother. He did everything he could to make Gilly a better ballplayer. This is why we win, I guess" (p. 265).

And this is what the book finally provides us with: a version of the "ideal situation, the perfect place, the epitome of everything good," a whole community ruled by a patriarch, motivated by brotherly love, in war-like quest of some holy grail.

There seems nothing "whole" or "holy" in Dan Jenkins *Semi-Tough*: its attitude toward everything appears "semi," and nothing if not profane. The book is a novel; it only pretends to be the same kind of book Kramer has produced. But it is easily established that *Semi-Tough* is written in response to Kramer's book. Too many obvious rejoinders to Kramer occur for this to be doubted. And to anyone who has read *Instant Replay* it is immediately clear that *Semi-Tough* is a heavily-humored response.

Jenkins would seem to be responding to Kramer when he has Billy Clyde Puckett say he is writing his book because he "got talked into it." His friend Jim Tom Pinch, a newspaperman from Fort Worth, convinced him that "it might be good for a pro football stud to have a book which might have a healthy influence on kids."[4] Kramer writes his book in order to discover what he is all about, to search out some new meaning in life,

to learn why he incurs the pain and grueling regimentation of a professional football player's life. Billy Clyde, on the other hand, in his own inimitable way, rather knows where he stands. He is easy in relation to his account; he is semi-detached from it and takes it all less seriously than does Kramer.

Semi-Tough is intended to be outrageously funny. Everything sacred in *Instant Replay* is profaned in *Semi-Tough*: the idea of a team as a family; the revered and awful figure of the coach (Vince Lombardi's counterpart in *Semi-Tough* is named Shoat Cooper); the terribly earnest effort which produced Kramer's block "felt round the world" (matched against T. J. Lambert's flatulence which works to something of the same effect). Jerry Kramer takes himself and professional football with absolute seriousness, and Billy Clyde Puckett is something of a flake.

There is one point at which Jenkins especially wants to spoof Kramer. In *Semi-Tough*, the name of Billy Clyde's publisher is "Koming and LaGuerre," which names can be loosely understood as "sex and war." In *Instant Reply*, Kramer simply does not discuss sex. Sexual matters are of considerably more interest to the characters in *Semi-Tough*. It may or may not be true that *Semi-Tough*'s description of sex in the lives of pro football players is more accurate than its monastic absence in *Instant Replay*. What is important is that the role of sex in *Semi-Tough* is as overstated as it is understated in *Instant Replay*. The image of professional football as war works in the same way, although the emphasis is reversed. Kramer perceives football as war in *Instant Replay*, religious war at that. Lombardi can be seen as the Ignatius Loyola of pro football, and the Packers as the Church Militant, striving mightily to transcend time and space and become the Church Triumphant. There is a militant and aggressive Catholic Christianity embodied in Lombardi's approach to the game, as we have it through Kramer's recorded perceptions and experiences. In general, pro football *is* very warlike in its self-understanding and its vernacular.[5] But in *Semi-Tough*, Billy Clyde Puckett transcends conventional notions of *both* sex and war for *his* ultimate meaning, as we shall see.

It is important to move beyond the initial awareness that *Semi-Tough* is a response to Kramer, and beyond the uncritical conclusion that it is *only* a hilarious parody. Obviously this is a funny book, as surely as Kramer's is terribly earnest. But just as obviously Jenkins is softening us up to laugh at ourselves as a culture precisely because he has captured the flavor of excess that *is* America. *Semi-Tough*, then, is far more than a satire, in part because the more one regards it in reflecting on contemporary American culture, the less satirical it appears. More importantly, it is more than satire because besides making fun of *Instant Replay*, it proposes a set of values fundamentally different from Kramer's.

Semi-Tough offers an alternative view of professional football and by implication of sport in general. It does not have to be that way, Jenkins is saying, and in fact Jerry Kramer is a bit of a jerk for putting up with all that pain and suffering. There is, to be sure, in *Semi-Tough,* a genuine appreciation of the camaraderie among men in athletics, an understanding that men may indeed love each other as they engage in the combat we call sport. The relationship between Billy Clyde and Shake Tiller demonstrates this. They have been there together, many times, ever since grammar school. And there is a clear recognition that an athlete is not indifferent to winning. It matters very much. "You can take your wars and your starvation and your fires and your floods," says Shake Tiller, "but there's no heartbreak in life like losing the big game in high school" (p. 102). On these two points, the importance of camaraderie and of winning, Kramer and Jenkins would seem to be in agreement.

Semi-Tough, though, does not take professional football seriously; it rather seems interested in playfulness and fun, and for the moment the context in which this occurs—the wildly extravagant extra-curricular activities of players—is of little importance. What is clear is that the business of football is not everything in life; in fact it becomes almost incidental. The players behave more as flower children are thought to behave; they do not resemble Christian soldiers. *Semi-Tough* is not serious about pro football, and pro football is nothing if not serious, at least in Jerry Kramer's version of it. But the reason it is not serious is that *Semi-Tough* offers an alternative view of meaning and reality. It offers a different vision.

We have in *Semi-Tough* the restoration of play to the game of football, and the restoration of football to a subordinate place in a hierarchy of values. It is quite clear that some young studs who practice the paramartial arts of playing the game do not subordinate themselves to it. They laugh, they fool around, they *play* the game. They are men at play, in football and in life. The game is made for the players and not the players for the game. In that difference and by that distinction we are presented with nothing short of an alternative world view. And the alternative engages Kramer's view in a dialogue of value and meaning for contemporary American culture.

Jenkins is saying that football ought to be regarded as a game, and in fact is by some of the best who play it. Billy Clyde Puckett is not a button-down junior executive type whose "work" happens to take him onto a football field. He is essentially a boy playing a boy's game, but one who grows up in the course of playing it, rather than remaining a boy in the course of working at it. The playfulness and spontaneity of Puckett and his friends on the field and off are apparent. Each is an individual of a sort we do not meet in the disciplined and regimented world of *Instant Replay.*

The social context within which football is played is strikingly different for Billy Clyde Puckett from what it is for Jerry Kramer. In *Semi-Tough,* Big Ed Bookman, a character who combines the worst features of male chauvinism, U.S. Jingoism, and crass materialism, loves to take people to dinner, announcing that "I'm buying." But his daughter Barbara Jane, Billy Clyde, and Shake Tiller are not "buying" him and his world. Jenkins' characterization gives the reader an enlarging view of a clear self-understanding and self-possession by both Billy Clyde and Barbara Jane, and a somewhat lesser one by Shake. We remember that Kramer writes his book to discover himself; these people already know who they are. Each is a person in his/her own right. They are not ciphers, they are not cogs in anybody's machine. While they recognize a certain affection for Big Ed, who functions as a father-figure for Billy Clyde and Shake even as he *is* Barbara Jane's father, they simply do not take him seriously. Obviously Shoat Cooper, the coach of the Billy Clyde Puckett Giants, is a far cry from Jerry Kramer's Vince Lombardi. The *real* father figure in *Semi-Tough* is Big Ed, and he is a father only in a formal sense. *His* children are, in their own fashion, grown up. They are their own persons, doing what *they* want to do, acting on *their* impulses, and generally setting aside the wisdom and prerogative of age. They don't fear him, they don't admire him, they don't obey him; they simply suffer him as a windy old fool is suffered. They go their own way.

The concept and reality of the "family" is strikingly different in the two books. Jerry Kramer's "family" is the Green Bay Packers, and Vince Lombardi is clearly the father. The players, consequently, are *his* children, and in his final pep-talk to them he calls them "boys." We learn virtually nothing about Kramer's own personal family, his wife and children. They do not exist in any meaningful way in his life as a football player. They are not allowed to intrude into his "business," his "professional calling," which is, in part, to be one of Lombardi's children.

Billy Clyde, on the other hand, is very much a part of a family: it is made up of himself, Shake, and Barbara Jane. No father presides over this brood. As we have said, Big Ed is largely endured in good humor, and the three friends become a close-knit family of their own, with a remarkable degree of respect and admiration for each other. Barbara Jane and Shake are "semi" in love, Billy Clyde tells us, but the larger meaning is that the three of them love each other. There is here an egalitarian camaraderie across the lines of sex and status. Shake Tiller's origins are pretty meager, and unlike any other female in the book, Barbara Jane is regarded by the two men as an equal.

The family here is the three-part family referred to, and not another version of Jerry Kramer's team. The coach is largely absent, and hardly dominates anything or anybody when he does appear. We have here children come of age who feel that "kids are the hope of the world" (p 13), rather than a coach who asks his players to endure pain and suffering and loss of identity. In *Semi-Tough* we see the athlete come of age as an individual person in a very different way than in *Instant Replay,* where he is scarcely an individual at all. Another kind of mutual love and regard define the meaning and content of community.

There is much that is racy and saucy in *Semi-Tough*; there is a degree of plain old raunchiness that virtually batters the reader's sensibility into an unbelieving submission. But it should not be allowed to obscure the emergence of genuine persons, namely Billy Clyde Puckett, Shake Tiller, and Barbara Jane Bookman. And not the least human aspect of these genuine persons is a degree of detachment which allows them to take the utterly serious pretensions and professions of others, such as Big Ed Bookman and by implication the sacralizing of professional football, with a few solid grains of salt. The very title of the book tells us this: *Semi-Tough*. It appears that everything for Billy Clyde is "semi" something or other. At one level this is an obvious satire on the toughness and absoluteness of Vince Lombardi and his values, and to some it may represent a transition from the sacred to the profane. For Kramer, even time and the elements are mysteriously transcended by Lombardi's power; the Packers, so long as they do His Will (Lombardi's), are not bound by the limits of ordinary mortals. Lombardi is a man larger than life; he is invested with attributes of divinity. He is, in short, idolized. *Semi-Tough* shows us a casual attention to detail which, compared to Lombardi's demand for perfection, is simply blasphemous. In *Instant Replay* such fundamentals as well-executed power-sweeps take on moral and religious sanctity. There are no tricks, there is no luck. There is, in *Semi-Tough*, a rollicking challenge to the religious world of Vince Lombardi. Championships are decided there not by Kramer's art of precision blocking, but by T. J. Lambert's flatus.

At a deeper level, this "semi" attitude is itself profound, and Jenkins is trying to tell us something about a fundamental stance in life. The "semi" point of view, initially intended to act as a counter to the total seriousness of Lombardi's style, is finally an acknowledgement of finitude and mortality, an awareness that to worship anything—money, a coach, success, the game of football itself—is a form of idolatry which is the end self-defeating. Billy Clyde and his friends do not imagine themselves as unbeatable: they are not idolatrous, that is, they do not apotheosize the coach, the father, the game. Their world is one in which their real meaning derives from the love they share for and with each other. It is this that becomes sacred by the end of *Semi-Tough*. This is Jenkins' alternative to Kramer's "Camelot."

We have said that these two books engage in a cultural dialogue; that Jenkins has responded to Kramer by apparently satirizing Kramer's book; that Jenkins has offered an alternative view of the game of football as perceived by a fictional creation, Billy Clyde Puckett; and that further we see a different world view with a different set of values. Now, finally, it is important to say something about love, because that is where both books lead and that is where a comparison, a listening to the cultural dialogue, must take us.

Much is made in Kramer's book of the sense of family among the Packers, and at the conclusion of their victory over the Dallas Cowboys we are allowed to hear and see overt expressions of the "love" that exists among the Green Bay Packers. This is Camelot, "One for all and all for one," as Kramer puts it with a little literary license. The team has character, says Lombardi, and respect for each other: and love. The father loves his children, the children love their father, and now they love each other too.

Semi-Tough treats us to a very different culmination of movement through the week of the Super Bowl, and along the way through the lives of Shake, Billy Clyde, and Barbara Jane. What we get here is indeed love, but of a quite different sort. Not only does Billy Clyde take a different view of the game than does Jerry Kramer, and not only does he have a world view which departs radically from Kramer's. Now we are carried to a love that is genuine and promising, which is mutual and relational, and whose consummation is proposed by Barbara Jane, in what we take to be a final rejection (in this cultural dialogue) of the male-dominated world of the Vince Lombardi Green Bay Packers.

At the end of *Semi-Tough*, Billy Clyde Puckett meets Barbara Jane in a New York airport. He has been off on the rubber-chicken circuit, and is altogether worn out from it. He has had enough of the glory that was the Super Bowl. Now Barbara Jane declares her love for Billy and, in a manner of speaking, proposes to him. In the end they agree to give it a try. The reader is left with no doubt that Jenkins assumes it will work out.

What is significant about this is that what is involved is indeed love and not sex. The spoof on "sex and war" (Koming and LaGuerre) throughout the book is here clearly transcended. Finally Billy Clyde Puckett and Barbara Jane Bookman find the sum of human meaning in a relational love, a love which is rooted in friendship, mutuality, and congeniality; only *then* does sex enter it. There has been something of a brother-sister aspect to their relationship throughout the book. Now Barbara Jane realizes that such a shared experience is what real love is all about. Love, it has been said, is what you've been through together, and that is what she tells Billy Clyde. Only *then* does it occur to her that sex might be a bonus in this case. The order of priority is very important: first love, then sex—not the other way around. After pouring out her heart and declaring her love, still in the airport terminal, Barbara Jane exclaims:

> "And you know what I suddenly thought this morning?" she said. "I was pining for you, I really was—for all the stuff you mean to me, in so many ways—and I thought Christ-o-mighty, what if Billy C. on top of everything else is a great f[. . .]!" (p. 214)

It seems fair to say, then, that Jenkins has responded in dialogue, as it were, to Kramer's book by joining the issue at a number of levels. In the end, individual personhood conscious of its own limits, which makes possible relational love at all, leads to love between a man and a woman, and the importance and meaning of this love render the world of professional football profane.

NOTES

[1] R. W. B. Lewis, *The American Adam* (Chicago: Phoenix Books, 1958), 1-2.

[2] Jerry Kramer, *Instant Replay* (New York: World Publishing Co., 1968), xiii. Future references to this book will be included, in parenthesis, in the text of the paper.

[3] The article is "The Toughest Man in Pro Football" by Leonard Schecter. It appeared in the January, 1968 *Esquire*.

[4] Dan Jenkins, *Semi-Tough* (New York: Signet Books, 1972), 12-13. Future references to this book will be included, in parentheses, in the text of the paper.

[5] See Eugene Bianchi, "Pigskin Piety," *Christianity and Crisis,* Vol. 32, No. 2 (February 21, 1972).

Gary Storoff

SOURCE: "The Failure of Games in Don DeLillo's 'End Zone'," in *American Sport Culture: The Humanistic Dimensions,* edited by Wiley Lee Umphlett, Bucknell University Press, 1985, pp. 235-45.

[*In the following essay, Storoff determines how the characters in* End Zone *use the language and structure of athletic games to organize and define their existence.*]

Gary Harkness, the protagonist of Don DeLillo's brilliant but enigmatic novel *End Zone,* desperately searches for a game that will provide his life with significance. Having failed at three other schools, he is given his last chance to succeed at Logos College. Here, Harkness tests alternative games designed to organize his life coherently and finds in each instance that the game fails because he perceives too clearly the contrast between man's contrived portrayal of experience in games and the world as it actually is—irrational, disorderly, and ambiguous. In the novel, games assume a much greater significance than the football contests Gary enjoys. A game becomes for Harkness a device for ordering his life, and he discovers that all men use games for the same purpose: to define and order existence. In the end, the game becomes coextensive with civilization itself.[1]

His first experience with game playing is through his father's idea of success, for his father is a salesman who sees personal worth in terms of sales volume. A former football player himself, Harkness's father envisions his job as an athletic contest, with sports language defining his effort to succeed: "Suck in that gut and go harder."[2] He is a successful and ambitious man who cannot understand his son's perpetual failure, but beyond his father's safely circumscribed business-game world, Gary senses only a spiritual vacancy. In Gary's words, "Beyond these honest latitudes lay nothing but chaos" (14).

Like his father, the people Harkness encounters at Logos College all employ game techniques to order their lives. Another father-figure, Coach Emmett Creed—whose name underscores his religious sense of games—is convinced that only through football can one acquire a clear sense of self and a healthy inner life. He also believes that self-transcendence can be achieved by total commitment to the game; self-sacrifice, pain, and hard work result in victory on the field and off. His motto, "It's only a game, but it's the only game" (12), emphasizes his concentrated vision, a vision he imparts to his team through complicated football plays and the private language describing them. Much like God as he stands in his tower watching the patterns he has created, Creed is worshiped by his team because he has become "famous for creating order out of chaos" (8). Indeed, he even extends his influence well beyond the gridiron, for his rules include such social concerns as being courteous, writing home, dressing neatly, and so forth. Although he demands "the maximal effort" (84), he makes the choices for the team, thus lessening for them the burden of choice.

Because Creed reduces the complexity of experience for Harkness ("When the Coach says hit, we hit. It's so simple." [28]), football does offer a reprieve from chaos and uncertainty. As Harkness points out, "the football player travels in the straightest of all lines . . . , his actions uncomplicated by history, enigma, holocaust or dream" (3). Gary feels "reduced in complexity" (24) because as a halfback he enjoys a clear sense of role, a clearly defined function assigned by Creed, and a private language of plays known only to him and his team—a knowledge that brings a pervasive sense of harmony and order. Because Creed is a source of order, *all* the athletes deeply appreciate his effort to provide a structure for their lives, and thereby forgo the responsibility of choice. One player worries that his beard may disrupt Creed's regulated world, while the team's inept quarterback slavishly depends upon Creed's assurance that he has selected the "correct" play. As the team is losing their most important game, a player assures Harkness that they will "come back," that Creed will win for them in the end. Even losing does not shake their almost religious faith in him.

Yet inevitably, Harkness must step outside the realm of game and enter the "end zone," literally the field beyond the playing area but symbolically the full realization of an imponderable reality. When he makes this step, he realizes that the sense of order and rationality assumed by Creed is illusory; that Creed, like his father, has betrayed him with a game and a language that encloses experience more complex and mysterious than a game will allow. In a lengthy report of a game between Logos and West Centrex Tech, their chief rivals, Logos is defeated in a violent, brutal contest that discloses the irrationality masked by the game's rational and orderly rules. Indeed, Centrex's number 62 actually uses the rules to inflict unnecessary pain, thereby suggesting a return to primordial chaos and disorder. At the end of the game, one of the Logos players, Jessup, gives up all pretense of civilized game-playing when he fights with 62. The game with Centrex is doubly ironic because it is so crucial: Although the Logos team has done extremely well that season, the Centrex victory makes their previous triumphs meaningless.

Through DeLillo's description of the game, the two football teams acquire symbolic significance. While Logos College is a liberal arts school, its opponent is named "West Centrex Biotechnical Institute," and the victory of the technical college over Logos suggests the ascendancy of technology over liberal humanist faith in our contemporary culture. Pitted against technology, human limitations seem discouragingly immediate. The players of Centrex Tech are even comparable to machines due to their metallic, silver-and-red uniforms and their well-executed plays. After several Logos players are severely injured during the game, the Centrex team seems more inhumanly invincible. Onan Moley notes that Centrex is "the kind of team that gets stronger and stronger. . . . They'll just keep coming" (100), and the Logos team is utterly exhausted by half-time. The Centrex players are identified only by numbers, except for the quarterback Telcon, whose name implies his computerlike function. Even though Logos plays uninspired and disappointing football, their mistakes and injuries remind us of their essential humanity as opposed to Centrex's mechanical perfection. Also, the Logos colors emphasize the connection of the team with natural life itself. As Bing says, "Our uniforms are green and white. . . . The field itself is green and white—grass and chalk markings. We melt into our environment. We are doubled in the primitive mirror" (112).

This "melting" Bing refers to is repeated with ironic implications in a second football game played later, one clearly intended to parody the Centrex-Logos humiliation. The Logos team spontaneously begins playing in a snow storm and finally becomes almost lost in the snow. As the teams play, they add more and more rules, making the game more predictable and less specialized while denying life's irregular and conditional nature. For these players, even conventional football regulations and rules make life too chaotic. When the game finally ends, their rigid rules permit only one tactic—running the ball. Ironically, however, they have become a static group indistinguishable from one another in the storm. Associated with the snow, the players exemplify the unifying force of death through their deification of order, regularity, and predictability at the expense of life's unpredictable and impulsive nature.

Harkness seeks refuge in football, then, but ultimately discovers that the game cannot prevent the encroachment of the irrational reality he flees. As Bing points out, football paradoxically "harks back" to the primeval. Despite football's intricate player structure and complex rules and plays, its violence recalls an uncivilized era when no games were played. Although Gary says, "My life meant nothing without football" (18), ultimately he must confront the futility of evading the absurd through

games. Indeed, the very shape of a football—unlike the round tennis ball, baseball, or basketball—maximizes chance, for a player cannot possibly anticipate the direction of the bounce. DeLillo concludes that "sport is a benign illusion, the illusion that order is possible" (89), but he has created an ironic novel in which his protagonist penetrates that illusion to the void beneath.

Harkness also tries to find stability from another father-figure, Major Staley, an Air Force ROTC instructor who celebrates modern technology by transforming nuclear war into an elaborate game. "We'll get together with [the enemy] beforehand," Staley assures Harkness, "and there'll be an agreement that if the issue can't be settled . . . we keep our war as relatively humane as possible" (63). In making football analogous to nuclear war, DeLillo is not merely making the facile, popular observation that violent sports are our surrogates for modern war. As "Zap" Zapalac, the professor, says, "I reject the notion of football as warfare. Warfare is warfare. We don't need substitutes because we've got the real thing" (135). Instead, DeLillo communicates a much more profound insight: The nature of civilization demands—even in something so chaotic as war—the regularity, uniformity, and stability that a "game" (however loosely defined) provides. Faced with the utterly unthinkable prospect of nuclear war, our world can do little else than codify and systematize it; transform it into manageable and contained patterns which won't threaten us so much. Finally, we are all runners in the arms race. In the book, Major Staley represents this impulse, and although he is an amusing caricature of the devotee of military technology, he is a frighteningly real element of our modern world.

As such, Harkness is attracted to him, for Staley's game, like Creed's, organizes life with a new language that describes and reduces life's complexity. Like football, war is played according to rules ("we'll use only clean bombs"), complete with game plays using the language of weapons technology ("maximum attack posture," "collateral damage," "x-ray pulse intensity," "interval recognition bombing"). While Creed resembles a god on the football field, Staley believes that "the bombs are a kind of god" (62). Harkness is urged by Staley to join the Air Force "team," "the most self-actualizing branch of the military" (128). In the Air Force as on the gridiron, Harkness would have a specific role and a definite function, and Staley emphasizes that his recruit would also have a unique advantage because of his athletic prowess. Since Harkness would not call his own "plays," choices would be eliminated and guilt would disappear.

But like Creed, Staley ultimately fails to offer a viable game for Harkness. In a lengthy war game Staley plays at the end of the book, the entire world is devastated through "rational and orderly" use of weaponry. The fallacy of Staley's conception of an impersonal and predictable technocratic world order is shattered by a simple instrument of technology: the ringing telephone, which reminds him of his wife and children who would perish in a "rational" war. And in a parody of the technocracy Staley idealizes, Gary's friend Bloomberg imagines the role of "an anguished physicist" who invents "the super-megaroach aerosol bomb" (176). The consequence of Staley's impersonal game theory is revealed by Bloomberg's tongue-in-cheek nihilism: "I came to the realization that one terminal bomb more or less makes small difference in this ever-expanding universe of ours" (177). Once again, Harkness is compelled to step from an illusory ordered world into an "end zone" of fragmentation and chaos.

The "language game," the third pervasive game in the novel, is much more subtle than Creed's or Staley's games, but is nevertheless crucial because all the characters are unconscious players. The notion of DeLillo's "language game" derives from Ludwig Wittgenstein, to whom DeLillo alludes late in the novel. The allusion is embedded in Gary's last visit to Taft, the "mystical" football player:

> Poster of Wittgenstein, I thought. Maybe that's what he'd had up there, or almost had. Dollar ninety-eight poster of philosopher surrounded by Vienna Circle. Two parts to that man's work. What is written. What is not written. The man himself seemed to favor second part. Perhaps Taft was a student of that part. (192)

DeLillo's allusion is adopted without quotation marks from a letter Wittgenstein wrote to his publisher Ludwig von Ficker in 1919 in which he comments on his intentions in his book *Tractatus Logico-Philosophicus*:

> The book's point is an ethical one. I once meant to include in the preface a sentence which is not in fact there now but which I will write out for you here, because it will perhaps be a key to the work for you. What I meant to write, then, was this: My work consists of two parts: the one presented here plus all that I have *not* written. And it is precisely this second part that is the important one. My book draws limits to the sphere of the ethical from the inside as it were, and I am convinced that this is the ONLY *rigorous* way of drawing those limits. In short, I believe that where *many* others today are just *gassing,* I have managed in my book to put everything firmly into place by being silent about it.[3] (Emphasis Wittgenstein's)

Wittgenstein emphasizes in the *Tractatus* the limits of language and its inability to communicate the nature of the ethical, mystical, and transcendental realm of meanings. In his letter to Ficker, he scorns those metaphysicians who are just "gassing" about transcendental reality, which to him *does* exist but is ineffable and "unthinkable."[4] He therefore cannot write about the mystical sphere but acknowledges its reality by his silence. Indeed, the last sentence of the *Tractatus*—"What we cannot speak about we must pass over in silence"[5]—insists upon the existence of the mystical realm that Taft meditates upon in *End Zone*. Also, Billy Mast's course in "the untellable" is yet another hidden allusion to Wittgenstein's

philosophy; both Taft and Mast are trying to find meaning in their lives by embracing Wittgenstein's concept of a unified—but unthinkable and unsayable—Ideal.

Wittgenstein himself abandons this quest for unity in his *Philosophical Investigations,* the book in which he develops his famous theory of "language games."[6] In attempting to explain language's purpose, he argues that language is not a *picture* of reality, nor does it *depict* the world. Instead, there are diverse types or families of language "games"—some describing the world, but others which assert or report or command. There are countless "language games," then, each having its own set of "rules." The conviction that a word actually communicates accurately or completely the "reality" it designates is a delusion. Thus Wittgenstein argues that the meaning of a word depends entirely upon its function and its context (its "game"); it is like a tool with countless uses.[7]

DeLillo ingeniously incorporates Wittgenstein's doctrines into his narrative by having his characters constantly speak at cross-purposes, never noticing that they are indeed speakers in different contexts, players in different language games. For instance, Dennis Smee wonders about the proper role, the "function" of captains on a football team. Billy Mast immediately supplies a precise mathematical definition of the word *function*: "A rule of correspondence between two sets related in value and nature to the extent that there is a unique element in one set assigned to each element in the corresponding set, given the respective value difference" (122). Clearly, neither concept of "function" is the complete or total one. This divergent use of a word occurs many times throughout the novel, as in the football game when Jessup and Gary differ in their use of the word *black*:

> "Fee-uck, man. This game is still on. I get that sixty-two yet. I get his ass and whip it into shape. Damn right. I get that shitpiss sixty-two and beat his black ass into the ground."
>
> He's white," I said.
>
> "I know he's white. They're all white. Everybody's white. Those black fucks" (112).

Jessup's racist use of the word *black* differs completely from Gary's racial identification. Jessup's meaning is intimately connected to his actions, particularly his aggressive nature, and to the racist and profane hazing typical in collegiate and professional sports. DeLillo demonstrates artistically Wittgenstein's thesis: that the "meaning" of a word is not constant and unyielding but is entirely relative to its purpose in a particular context, to the multifarious forms of human activity in the world.

The implications of the language game are enormous for Harkness, who wants to abandon appearances in favor of an essential and basic reality. But he recognizes that since any word can convey only a *partial* "reality" rather than a totality of experience, man's inadequacy must be as basic as his language: he can never know "truth." Knowledge must necessarily be fragmentary and incomplete because of the inevitable "failure" of language games themselves. In a deceptively humorous incident, Gary attempts to "know" a pile of manure he sees in the desert, but realizes the inability of language to express the object's ontological reality:

> It was overwhelming, a terminal act, nullity in the very word, shit, as of dogs squatting near partly eaten bodies, rot repeating itself; defecation as of old women in nursing homes fouling their beds; feces, as of specimen, sample, analysis, diagnosis, bleak assessments of disease in the bowels; dung, as of dry straw erupting with microscopic eggs; excrement, as of final matter voided, the chemical stink of self discontinued; offal, as of butchered animals' intestines slick with shit and blood; shit everywhere. . . . (70)

In some contexts, or games, the object is "shit"; in others, "feces," "dung," "excrement," or "offal"—and each word leads Gary to the inevitability of death. Even this seemingly simply defined object becomes enigmatic and unknowable—Harkness ponders "shit's infinite treachery," "this whisper of inexistence"—for it cannot escape the chaos of the verbal context. "Perhaps it was easier to die than admit that words could lose their meaning," Gary says (42); but even at *Logos* College no one has discovered words adequate to picture a shifting and impalpable world.

Harkness's dilemma is mirrored by the other characters in the novel, all of whom formulate games of varying complexity to rid themselves of a sense of the absurd. Wally Pippich, for example, uses "a little word-play" (124) to construct a public relations game which totally falsifies reality. The enthusiastic teacher "Zap" Zapalac uses "ploys and counterploys" (173) against his students, who are themselves playing games with him when they create an imaginary student named "Robert Reynolds." Myna, Gary's girl friend, wears bizarre costumes and gains weight to avoid "the responsibility of beauty"; presumably, "beauty" would force her to play yet another game not to her liking. Esther and Vera Chalk play a game in which certain words are forbidden. Many of the characters also play games in order to hide from the horror of a sudden, meaningless death. Norgene, for instance, is given his strange first name to ward off bad luck, but we see the futility of his game when he is killed in a tragic car accident. Bloomberg devises a history game—"Who was the greater man?"—to escape history, but is continually reminded of his own horrible past: his mother's murder by a lunatic. Finally, Coach Tom Cook Clark plays the part of a sophisticated, suave, eloquent man who seems to have everything in control—until he kills himself early one morning. Cook's funeral becomes an elaborate game in which the team evades the true meaning of Cook's suicide: The players comment on "how good the embalmed corpse looked" and Creed praises him as "a fine inter-denominational example of all those fortunate enough to have

been associated with him" (55). Throughout the book, then, we are made to see the futility of people's games in the face of the absurd.

Indeed, DeLillo's novel itself could be seen as a perverse "antigame," an artistic refutation of the popular, nonserious college football novel.[8] Unlike the teams usually celebrated in this genre, Gary's team not only loses the "big game," it plays sloppy football. No all-American, Gary smokes pot and evades the draft. The mythical football hero on college campuses always dates the Homecoming Queen, but Gary self-consciously selects the heaviest, worst-dressed girl on campus. Football players supposedly take the simplest courses to graduate, but DeLillo's players quote Wittgenstein, argue theology, enroll in bizarre "exobiology" courses, and study "the untellable." DeLillo satirizes all the black athletes named after U.S. presidents (e.g., Roosevelt Grier) through sleek and fast "Taft" Robinson—named, presumably, after America's only three-hundred pound president. DeLillo, then, consistently reverses the "rules" of one of the most familiar novelistic forms of popular culture, sport fiction. In so doing, he artistically acknowledges the idea of failed rules that his novel so emphatically inculcates.

But the character who finally convinces Harkness of the futility of games is Taft Robinson, the extraordinary fullback who renounces football. Renowned for his speed, Taft opts for "stasis" and silence as he retreats to a solipsistic world of the "smoky languid dream" (192). Although Taft has been enticed to enroll at Logos College because Creed told him that football would lead to self-transcendence, to passing limits of "mind and body" (195), Taft chooses a mystic existence where the only reality is his own thoughts and perceptions. Inexplicably, he escapes from all game playing and merely sits alone in his room meditating, silent and still. Unable to accept such a solution for himself, Gary desperately tells Taft, "There must be something we can do" (199). But he finally accepts that there is no game, no rules, which will impose absolute order and confer unambiguous meaning. With this realization, he stops playing games too. But more than this—he stops eating and drinking. For in the "end zone," to refuse to play the game is to welcome death.

Despite its comic tone, DeLillo's novel veers perilously close to a tragic vision, a sense that even if essential "truth" were accessible, it would be too painful to bear. *End Zone* does not allow us our comfortable conception of a game as frivolous play, inconsequential and profitless, set against a background of the stable, coherent, and meaningful though mundane "reality" of our everyday world. Instead, DeLillo makes us see that the fundamental character of civilization is the game: that we are continually caught up in playing with appearances of our own making—appearances designed to conceal our own metaphysical barrenness. In the "end zone" which we all inhabit, DeLillo makes us see that our games are at best evasions, unconscious methods of escaping the void, but that for the truly thoughtful person these strategies must inevitably fail.

NOTES

[1] This essay was influenced by the concept of games discussed in Johan Huizinga's ground-breaking book *Homo Ludens: A Study of the Play Element in Culture* (London: Temple Smith, 1970). However, Huizinga's definition of "game" limits it to an activity "standing quite consciously outside of 'ordinary' life" proceeding "within its own proper boundaries of time and space according to fixed rules . . ." (32). As I argue in my paper, DeLillo makes no such qualifications. Also, I am greatly indebted to Jacques Ehrmann's essay *"Homo Ludens* Revisited," *Yale French Studies* 41 (1968): 31-57; cf. ". . . play in the fullest sense is coextensive with culture" (44).

[2] Don DeLillo, *End Zone* (New York: Simon & Schuster, 1973), 13. All quotations are from this edition, with pagination noted in the text.

[3] *Letters from Ludwig Wittgenstein, With a Memoir,* Paul Engelmann, ed. (New York: Horizon Press, 1968), 143.

[4] *Tractatus Logico-Philosophicus,* trans. D. F. Pears and B. F. McGuinness (New York: Humanities Press, 1961), 53.

[5] Ibid., 151.

[6] Perhaps *End Zone* itself was inspired by Wittgenstein's injunction in *Philosophical Investigations,* trans. G. E. M. Anscombe (New York: Macmillan Co., 1953):

> Consider for example the proceedings that we call "games." I mean board-games, card-games, ball-games, Olympic games, and so on. What is common to them all?—Don't say: "There *must* be something common, or they would not be called 'games'"—but *look and see* whether there is anything common to all.—For if you look at them you will not see something that is common to *all,* but similarities, relationships, and a whole series of them at that. To repeat: don't think, but look! (No. 66, p. 31e, emphasis Wittgenstein's)

[7] Ibid., no. 11, p. 6e.

[8] DeLillo published part of this novel in *Sports Illustrated,* a fact that demonstrates his wry sense of humor.

Neil Berman

SOURCE: "Coover's 'Universal Baseball Association': Play as Personalized Myth," in *Modern Fiction Studies,* Vol. 24, No. 2, Summer, 1978, pp. 209-22.

[*In the following essay, Berman explores the roles of myth, ritual, and reality in Coover's novel.*]

A striking development in recent American fiction is the extraordinary number of novels written in the past seven or eight years by serious young writers which use sports as their dominant theme.[1] The range of recent sports novels vary widely in technique and in some assumptions, from the stark naturalism of Leonard Gardner's *Fat City* and Peter Gent's *North Dallas Forty* to the more fantastic, surreal visions of Lawrence Shainberg's *One on One* and Robert Coover's *The Universal Baseball Association.* But they all share the same startling vision of a world that is actively hostile to the essential elements of play: human joy, freedom, and creativity.[2] Play, often specifically manifested as sport, offers the possibility, real or apparent, of achieving some liberation and hence self-definition, however minimal, in a reductive world.

The player seeks escape from an environment he finds uninteresting at best, intolerable at worst. Play is never opposed to reality or seriousness, but all recent sports novels *do* suggest a dualism between play and the modern world; a repressive, technological society is constantly challenging the more liberating values of play. In order to exist in the modern world, and certainly in order to become a transforming reality, play *must* be internalized. Thus, in the highly naturalistic novel *Fat City,* play exists only as an ironic illusion. In *North Dallas Forty* there is some potential for play, but the tantalizing glimpses of liberation here are constantly undercut and finally destroyed by an antagonistic emphasis on computer technology and vicarious experience. Don Delillo's *End Zone* is similar to *North Dallas Forty* insofar as the literal description of a college football season is itself unplayful. But play is partially recovered in the novel. Spontaneous, primitive games and verbal foreplay which exemplify the essential characteristics of play begin to appear as alternatives to the threatening world of imminent nuclear holocaust.

At the opposite extreme to these fictions stands Robert Coover's *Universal Baseball Association,* in which Henry Waugh's game-world has been so completely internalized that it creates its own course and meaning, creates its own myths and rituals, entirely cut off from such established mythic traditions as are employed in Malamud's *The Natural* or Roth's *The Great American Novel.* Henry Waugh's baseball game is so fertile in metaphorical significance that there is virtually no activity in his life upon which the game does not impinge. There is nothing the game cannot include. Henry Waugh is the only character in all of recent sports fiction who can bear the full weight of Eugen Fink's ontological definition of play: "The player experiences himself as the lord of the products of his imagination—because it is virtually unlimited, play is an eminent manifestation of human freedom."[3] In The *Universal Baseball Association* imagination is so truly protean that it becomes an end in itself. The final vision of the novel is of a complete play-world, personalized and separated as myth, art, and religion.

John Steinbeck once said of baseball that "There is no way to explain that baseball is not a sport or a game or a contest. It is a state of mind, and you can't learn it."[4] For Henry Waugh, and for Robert Coover playing with his protagonist, baseball surely has the force of an idea. It is an abstraction to be played with and explored as the focus of Henry's imaginative universe. Real baseball always bored Henry. What initially attracted him to the game was "the records, the statistics, the peculiar balances. . . . And no other activity in the world had so precise and comprehensive a history, so specific an ethic, and at the same time, strange as it seemed, so much ultimate mystery" (p. 38).[5] Even the most traditional of game accoutrements, the playing board, has been eliminated. At one time Henry used "a mock-up of a ball park, but it only got in the way" (p. 131); instead, he uses the more abstract statistics to create the game as a product of his imagination.

The remarkable richness and vitality of Henry Waugh's Association mark it as a self-enclosed world. Indeed, the ascription "Universal Baseball Association" forewarns the reader that nothing as petty or parochial as "American" or "National" is intended. The Association has its own metaphysics and must be seen as the product of a godlike creative act. Henry's initials—J. H. W.—identify him with the Hebrew god Yahweh. He has created the eight teams in his Association, all the personnel of those teams, and the physical and biographical data of his players. The tiresome, naturalistic world of Henry's accounting job is trivial beside his Association, but both worlds exist and exert some influence over Henry's being. When Henry decides to return to work after the exhausting game in which Damon Rutherford is killed, we see his own confusion about which world is more real and vital as he buys a newspaper, "obeying some old impulse which, he realized, he'd nearly forgotten, the giving of the coin, the snapping up of the paper, taking the world to heart and mind, or some world anyway" (p. 96). *The Universal Baseball Association* confronts the reader with a vision of play and reality as radically interdependent. In addition to the figure of Henry Waugh, who plays with the actors in his game-world, the reader is never allowed to forget for long that Robert Coover is playing with Henry Waugh, with numbers, with language, and with myth. Even the players in the Association play baseball and act out rituals. The playfulness of the book thus exists on several levels simultaneously and shatters the idea that reality must be played out against a fixed and stable background.

One of the most important aspects of the game—and a sure sign of Coover's delight in playing games—is the naming of players. The inspiration for a player's name often comes from a sign Henry happens to see, but any words that happen to catch Henry's attention are played with, possibly recombined, until the sound is right for a ballplayer's name. Once a rookie has a name, his actual accomplishments on the field begin to give the name a certain character and fill out its appropriateness, but the initial act is the creative one. Henry knows the weight of what he is about; the artistry of naming has consequences: "name a man and you make him what he is. Or something can go wrong. Lots of nicknames invented as a result of Rookie-year surprises. But the basic stuff is

already there. In the name. Or rather: in the naming" (p. 40). Coover may be trying to show the consistency (or limitedness?) of Henry's imagination, or it may be sheer playful perversity on the author's part, but in fact almost every player in the Association has an Anglo/Irish name. The only obvious exceptions are some parodic names—including Yip Yick Ping, Bruiser Brusatti, and Agapito Bacigalupo—none of whom figures very prominently in the novel. Perhaps the best explanation is that since names form the emotional center of the game, Henry is wary of those which may be too eccentric: "Henry was always careful about names, for they were what gave the league its sense of fulfillment and failure, its emotion. The dice and charts and other paraphernalia were only the mechanics of the drama, not the drama itself. Names had to be chosen, therefore, that could bear the whole weight of perpetuity" (p. 39).

The last phrase gives some indication as to the scope of Henry's essentially historical imagination. Because of its long tradition as the national pastime, and because of the accessibility of its records and statistics, baseball is a fine metaphor for history, process, and order. It is history and continuity which most fascinate Henry, and that is why he has always been somewhat anxious about the gratuitousness of the Association's beginnings:

> In spite of the almost excessive warmth he felt toward those first ballplayers, it always troubled him that their life histories were so unavailable to him: What had a great player already in his thirties been doing for the previous ten years? It was much better once a kind of continuity had been established, and when new players had taken over the league who had their whole careers still ahead of them. It was, in fact, when the last Year I player had retired that Henry felt the Association had come of age, and when, a couple of years ago, the last veteran of Year I, old ex-Chancellor Barnaby North, had died, he had felt an odd sense of relief: the touch with the deep past was now purely "historic," its ambiguity only natural. Luckily, all the first-year records had been broken. And soon there would be no more living veterans born before Year I. (pp. 38-39)

Once all of those first-year records have been broken, all the game's hallmarks are products of a historical continuum and can thus be explained with the same kind of logic that orders the playing of the game.

Briefly, the game is played by tossing three dice; the numbers determine what happens on the playing field. If certain combinations come up, reference must be made to a special "Stress Chart." And the very unlikely possibility of rolling 1-1-1 twice in a row necessitates the use of the "Extraordinary Occurrences Chart" where another roll may result in a hitter killing a pitcher with a line drive or a batter being killed by a beanball. Every contingency has been accounted for; even the eventual demise of players is tabulated with the aid of Henry's actuarial tables. While Henry is the creator of his game, his power is limited by the rules and forms of the game itself. His only real choice—at least initially—is whether or not to actuate the game by throwing the dice. Henry religiously records the records and statistics of the Association, but the substance of the game is determined by the dice, "three ivory cubes, heedless of history yet makers of it" (p. 18).

There would appear to be a strong measure of dispassionate logic about all this; the game contains within itself an order which seems unshakeable. If Henry himself were a dispassionate god, the history which he records would be as mechanical as the tossing of the dice. But Henry is not at all detached. Those names he has created mean something to him. The historical relationships developed over many seasons transcend the mere statistical accounts of games recorded in the Book, the bible of the game-world. The game-world is so engaging that even a local bartender named Pete becomes the embodiment of Jake Bradley, a former Association great, and Henry cannot forbear referring to the place as "Jake's." When Henry's actuarial tables inform him that Jake Bradley has died, the reality of the play-world demands that Henry can no longer inhabit Pete's bar, since Pete *cum* Jake is dead. While the dice may be heedless of history, Henry is not. Even the Association's fielding statistics must be faithfully recorded, although they are dull and make few discriminations among ballplayers. Here again, Henry's commitment is to history as a source of order and continuity: "He had thought of giving them up altogether, they took a lot of time and didn't seem worth it, but there were all those fielding records already established, and what would they mean if they had no challengers?" (p. 44).

The novel opens, appropriately, as Damon Rutherford, a star rookie pitcher in the Association, is in the process of pitching a history-making perfect game. Damon also happens to be the son of Brock Rutherford, the central figure in the Association's first great era. From the outset one sees the dangerous involvement of the creator in the world of his game. Henry *is* aware, at this point in the novel, that there is some difference between the game and external reality: Coover emphasizes that Henry is "sweating with relief and tension all at once, unable to sit, unable to think, *in* there, *with* them" (p. 9). But the game is surely the more compelling reality, so much so that when Henry wants to get a snack his impulse *must* coincide with the traditional seventh inning stretch which marks a break in the action of the game. And when in his mind's eye he sees the warm-up pitches for the next inning, Henry knows he must hurry back to the game with his food. We know that the game cannot continue until Henry throws the dice again, but Henry's sense of urgency indicates that the game has its own momentum.

Henry's engagement with his play-world, although dangerous, is not surprising. Robert E. Neale, in his excellent book on play, psychology, and religion, has aptly described the mature player in terms which closely fit Henry Waugh and his imaginative universe: "He does

not alternately fight the world and escape from it . . . nor does he usefully and abusively covenant with it. . . . Rather, the full adult adventurer is in communion with the world, demonstrating the love that is identical to that expressed by the gods in their creation of the world in the beginning."[6] Henry's communion with his Association is so complete that the game dominates all of his routine activities. Even some casual sex with a B-girl is only possible insofar as Henry can correlate the metaphors of sex with those of baseball and identify completely with his heroic creation of Damon Rutherford. The scene in which Henry and Hettie have intercourse is one of the book's most dazzling examples of verbal playfulness. Henry is as much a part of his own game as his players, and, furthermore, both Henry and the Association are parts of a larger game being played by still another god figure—Robert Coover. The significance of that manipulation is brilliantly pointed up by Jacques Ehrmann's critique of the seminal play theories of Johan Huizinga and Roger Caillois, who "erred principally in never doubting . . . that the player is the subject of play; in believing that, present in the game, at the center of play, they dominated it. They forgot that players may be played; that, as an object in the game, the player can be its stakes (*enjeu*) and its toy (*jouet*)."[7] The implication is that unless Henry realizes that he and the game are part of the same stakes, that both he and the game are subject *and* object of play, he is destined for a severe blow, which comes swiftly enough in the death of Damon Rutherford.

The game-world has always had the apparent means for dealing with death but always in the abstract form of statistics; older, retired ballplayers are "sorted out" of the Association on the basis of Henry's actuarial tables. But death in the impalpable form of mere statistics is an evasion. The death of Damon Rutherford marks the introduction of something new and significant into the game-world and makes death, for the first time, a concrete reality. Henry is more deeply committed to Damon than any other player in the Association, and that personal involvement, which as I have already noted even manifests itself in Henry's sexual activity, makes him more vulnerable than a god-figure should be. After Damon's historic perfect game, Henry builds dramatic significance around his next pitching assignment, which holds the possibility of further perfection and, thus, even more historic importance. The day of the game is turned into Brock Rutherford Day, a tribute to Damon's father as the central figure in the history of the Association. But Henry's involvement goes much further than this. Both Henry and Brock are fifty-six years old, and their complete identification with the game-world is pointed up by the fact that the Association is also in its fifty-sixth season. Additionally, since Henry has always had both a deep admiration for Brock's skills and a profound respect for his values, the identification of Henry and Brock is almost complete. Since Damon is the son of Brock, Henry's affection toward Damon is fatherly; Damon, by extension, is, after all, the son of god. Damon's opponent in this central game is Jock Casey, another star rookie pitcher, and one whose ancestry may be traced back to Fancy Dan Casey, one of the greats of Year I of the Association. The struggle between Damon and Casey thus has a doubly historic significance even before Henry turns the events of that game into ritual: there is the commemoration of the Brock Rutherford Era with Brock and all the great personages of his time in attendance; and there is the duel between Damon and Casey, with the possibility of extending Damon's perfect game into a second. As Henry muses before the game, "It was *more* than history, it was, it was: fulfillment!" (p. 52).

The introduction of death into the game is eventually positive because it makes the game more profound; it projects the game, and Henry's conception of the game, into a more serious stature by bridging the gap between the game and external reality. More than any other recent novel, Coover's book directly challenges the reader's tendency to dichotomize play and seriousness, game and reality, by portraying a game-world which becomes increasingly integrative and whole. The dice dictate that Damon is killed by one of Casey's pitches. Henry feels powerless to do anything about the gratuitous act of the dice, and so he invents a corresponding gratuitousness in Casey to account for his loss. Suddenly, Casey becomes a villain, who after shaking off several signs from his catcher, threw a pitch which he wanted to hit Damon. While Henry may arrange the circumstances of Damon's death and thus make them slightly more manageable, or superficially explicable, he is incapable of changing the verdict of the dice. Casey must, therefore, share the responsibility for Damon's death with the unthinking and heedless dice. Henry realizes that integrity is essential to the freedom of play and understands that a violation of the rules destroys the play-attitude, the whole reality which is the game. His commitment to the game demands an adherence to its rules because the game is real to him and, like all play, has final consequences. Henry's response is, therefore, not that of a detached observer, but of an engaged and fatherly participant: "The Proprietor of the Universal Baseball Association, utterly brought down, brought utterly to grief, buried his face in the heap of papers on his kitchen table and cried for a long bad time" (p. 59). As Jacques Ehrmann had predicted, Henry has become both an object of his own play-world as well as the subject of Coover's. The seriousness of Henry's response represents the profundity of his play-world. "Play," Ehrmann writes, "cannot therefore be isolated as an activity without *consequences*. Its integrity, its gratuitousness are only apparent, since the very freedom of the expenditure made in it is part of a circuit which reaches beyond the spatial and temporal limits of play."[8]

The extent to which Damon's death reaches beyond the spatial and temporal limits of the Association is manifested in Henry's complete inability to function outside the play-world and the overwhelming influence which the Association begins to have on Henry's external relationships. At first Henry is so immobilized by Damon's death that he cannot bring himself to face the tiresome columns of figures he is responsible for at his accounting job. That evening he visits his friend and co-worker, Lou Engel, but before he actually arrives he is already imagining Lou's apartment as the scene of Damon's funeral. Lou's apartment is transformed in Henry's imagination into a musty Gothic cathedral. Lou infers that Henry is in mourning, never of course suspecting that the deceased is a player in a game-world, and he plays, at Henry's insistence, a series of classical recordings which should be appropriate for a funeral. But the intended solemnity of the occasion is crushed by irreverence. Henry becomes drunk, Lou is constantly bumping into things, including the record player, and the "players" Henry has assembled for the funeral are making fun of their creator's sentimentality. In the midst of a funeral piece by Purcell, Henry, drinking sherry, bourbon, and whiskey, turns the record player to a higher speed and irreverently reduces the funeral to a shambles.

After the funeral, Coover further reinforces the play-world as real and serious by paraphrasing the most common of clichés about death with the diction of play. And so "Play resumed. It always resumes . . ." (p. 71). Play, like life, must go on. But the problem for Henry is *how* to go on. The order which once seemed so natural a part of the game has become a source of dread both for Henry and for the players in the Association. Sycamore Flynn, Casey's manager, thinks about calling off the rest of the season but wonders "what would all the past mean then without the present process? Nothing at all, but so what? No answers: only dread. . . . Finally, he supposed, it would resume, and he would simply have to play out his part. But he dreaded that, too" (p. 88).

Above even Henry is the impersonal force of fate, physically represented by the dice but more interestingly conceived of as Robert Coover. The coincidence of Casey killing Damon precisely on Brock Rutherford Day is an authorial machination, a contrivance designed to point up the limitations of Henry's commitment to the dice. Henry himself begins to see that commitment as a sign of his own impotence. He vows revenge on Casey, who increasingly comes to haunt his imagination and around whom he builds an aura of rebelliousness and defiance. The very first description of Casey emphasizes that he "Played the game his own way, threw everything except what the catcher ordered, got along with no one . . ." (p. 52) and foreshadows Casey's killing Damon when he shakes off the catcher's signal twice before beaning his rival, then stands "oddly aloof" on the mound as Damon's teammates murderously charge him. When play resumes, Casey's every move is unpredictable, some even contradict his manager's signals, but as if in defiance of Henry's will, everything Casey does is successful. Henry does everything in his power to defeat Casey; he even goes so far as to roll the dice for the first hitter before writing Casey's name into the lineup. But Henry's limited and partial measures are of little consequence. Casey continues to win ballgames and Henry walks the streets "possessed by impotence. . . . If he didn't know better, he'd suspect the dice of malevolence, rather than mere mindlessness. And it was Henry, not Casey, who was losing control" (pp. 111-112).

Henry sees his apparent loss of control as part of "the new and wearisome order" of the game. But the order of the game has not changed at all, only Henry's understanding of his increasing identification with the play-world and his personal involvement with its players. He tries to rationalize his growing sense of impotence in a meditation about Casey, which once again shows the inseparability of the creator and his creation:

> Impotent? Not really. . . . Supposing he just shipped Casey to the minors and to hell with the rules . . . ? Could explain it in the Book. It wasn't impotence. Still, it might cause trouble. What trouble? The players . . . What players? *Some kind* of limit there, all right, now that he thought about it. He might smash their resistance, but he couldn't help *feeling* that resistance all the same. Their? mine; it was all the same. (p. 115)

Henry cannot in any meaningful way separate his own reality from that of the play-world. The order of the game—the rules of whimsy by which it is run—is just as relative as its ontology. In the monologue above, Henry begins to see himself as Coover has always intended the reader to see him: as both the subject and object of play, as player and toy, as creator and participant.

As a way of infusing new life and meaning into the game, as a way of restoring its faltering order, Henry attempts to share it with Lou Engel. But Lou only contributes to the further dissolution of the game and Henry's control of it, because he cannot possibly understand the magnitude of the creative act which produced the game in the first place. Since the play-world is a product of Henry's imagination—and Lou, of course, is not—Lou must be seen as an intruder. The play-world is a manifestation of the sacred, but Lou can only conceive of it in profane terms; he cannot, for example, imagine what Henry's stacks of paper (records, charts, the Book) have to do with a "mere" game. And while Henry approaches the play-sphere with respect, by washing his hands, Lou "absently" wipes *his* hands on his pants. Lou's presence in the game proves to be truly disruptive. He cannot, or will not, understand the intricacies of strategy because he can *only* understand the game metaphor in terms of victory. Lou's intrusion into the game-world emphasizes that it is radically individual and cannot be shared. With his beer and pizza, Lou upsets the balance and order which make Henry's play-world so vivid and real and thus reinforces our sense that Henry's proprietorship over a play-world is an intensely lonely one.

The chaos which Lou brings to the game culminates in his spilling beer all over the Association and its records. With the game almost a complete shambles, Henry seriously and for the first time contemplates sacking it. But the magnitude of the power which Henry might use to destroy the game implies the godlike act which engendered it. Henry begins to see a way of saving the game but only if he reasserts that power and transgresses the rules to which he has felt so committed. He realizes that all the seemingly chaotic influences on the game reduce to one central fact—Damon Rutherford is dead. The solution, in a word, is murder.

After Lou leaves, Henry cheats and changes 2-6-6 on the dice to 6-6-6 and thus moves the game over to the Extraordinary Occurrences Chart. Another roll of 6-6-6 would mean that Royce Ingram, the batter, would kill Casey, the pitcher, with a line drive. Henry has several, anxious second thoughts about the consequences of what he feels he must do: "Do you really *want* to save it? Wouldn't it be better just to drop it now, burn it, go on to something else, get working regularly again, back into the swing of things, see movies, maybe copyright that Intermonop game and try to market it, or do some traveling, read books . . . ?" (p. 144). None of the alternatives here is reasonable because none is as real and compelling as the Association. And so Henry murders Casey by controlling the dice instead of submitting to them. The horror of the act is appropriately emphasized by Henry's spasmodic vomiting which convulses him "with the impact of a smashing line drive . . ." (p. 145). The implications of this scene go beyond the use of violence in any other recent sports fiction. Henry, acting as a participant-god in the play sphere, has introduced murder as a means of saving the play-world. In *Fat City* and *North Dallas Forty,* the violence of the game is never seen as playful. It is pure hostility without any of the harmony essential to play. The snow football game in *End Zone* and playground basketball in *One on One* are examples of how violence may be tolerated in the play-world, perhaps even be made somehow essential to it. However, the separation of the play-world is complete in *The Universal Baseball Association,* not partial as it is, for example, in *One on One.* And once the play-world is seen as total, self-enclosed, one might properly ask, why not death? It gives that world still more completeness than even its creator—Waugh—had anticipated but surely no less profundity than Waugh's creator intended the reader to see.

The self-sufficiency and completeness of Henry's Association are emphasized by the startling vision of the last chapter of the novel, in which the tragic deaths of Damon Rutherford and Jock Casey have been transmuted into the full mature play of ritual. Henry's violation of the rules of the game, his assertion of his superior personality, paradoxically confirms those rules and establishes the primacy of the game over his personality. The world of the Association has been sealed off: every character who appears in Chapter 8 of *The Universal Baseball Association* is a descendant of a previous player. Perhaps the most striking aspect of the play-world here is that Henry Waugh has ceased to appear as a character. The harmony of play has evidently become so complete that there is not even enough conflict to insure survival. Henry's identification with the Association is so total that, to paraphrase Robert E. Neale, all play and no work have made no Henry.[9] The imaginative recreation of sport as play has become the world. There is not the slightest sign here of any other reality; even the existence of a creator external to the play-world may now only be inferred.

The subject of the last chapter is the annual reenactment of the Parable of the Duel. The Parable is a mythic condensation of the deaths of Damon and Casey into a single game, and each season the Association's top rookies must assume the roles of their forebears and play out the story. The ritual has distinctly religious overtones: it is played on Damonsday of each season, which, like Doomsday, is a day of judgment for the rookies, an initiation ceremony for each new crop of innocents. The events surrounding the Damon-Casey duel are now 101 seasons old, and so like all mythic stories the Parable of the Duel and its ritual enactment are subject to interpretation. Damon has come to represent the power of tradition and conservatism, an image which is foreshadowed very early in the novel when Henry identifies Damon's "total involvement, his oneness with the Universal Baseball Association" (p. 13). Casey, the original villain in Henry's imagination, has become an existential hero whose isolation, "essential freedom," and "uniqueness" are emphasized by his partisans.

The Parable of the Duel must, therefore, be seen as the central myth of the Universal Baseball Association. The creation of a myth is essential to full mature play,[10] and so the Parable is also Henry's playful response to the threat of chaos in the play-sphere. Coover has foreshadowed the very idea of turning the history of the Association into myth even before Damon's death. He has Henry see with uncanny irony that the pitcher's duel between Damon and Casey is "Not just a duel of dynasties, but a *real* duel, a duel to the death between Jock Casey and Damon Rutherford . . ." (p. 55). Henry, clearly nervous about what for him is the real possibility of death, sees the two great rookie pitchers "waiting for this awful rite to be played out" (p. 55). And after Damon's death, Henry is already thinking about turning the fact into legend. The inspiration for treating Damon's death as folklore is prepared for as early as the post-funeral party at Jake's at which Sandy Shaw, folk-balladeer of the Association, creates a maudlin ballad about Damon's death to the tune of "Tom Dooley."

Rather than relying on some established tradition of myth as, for example, Malamud's use of the Grail legend and vegetation myths in *The Natural,* Coover allows Henry to find a new order for his play-world by creating his own myth out of the history of that world. Given the overwhelming concern with history, order, and process in the Association, the Parable of the Duel as myth and ritual seems natural. Henry is implicated in Casey's death; his personal involvement in the play-world makes him guilty of murder. The transformation of history into myth provides the distance necessary to mitigate and contain the crime. It allows for a playful response to climactic events which must be transcended

to maintain order but which, also to maintain continuity in the play-world, may not be excluded.

What *is* excluded from the play-world is anything that is not essential to it. The initial movement of the novel was to pose a dualism between the literal world of Dunklemann, Zauber and Zifferblatt, the world of work; and the imaginative and playful world of Henry's Association. But by the last chapter of the novel, the low-mimetic world of accounting firms has vanished; it simply does not exist any more. The only world that exists is the one that has been imaginatively recreated. The separation of this world is so total that it has finally given rise to its *own* dualism: the players in the Association are now trying to distinguish between the reality of their own world and the ritual they are about to perform, a play-form within the play-world. The conflict necessary to insure survival no longer comes from Henry's vacillation between two worlds but from within the play-world itself.

The source of that conflict is epitomized by the ritual, the meaning of which is unclear since over 100 seasons have elapsed since the original Damon-Casey duel. There are those like Cuss McCamish who treat the ritual with profanity. McCamish goes so far as to suggest irreverently that Casey, like Christ, returns in the flesh each year to act his part in the ritual. However, the profaners are all characters who think their roles in the ritual will not personally involve them in the tragedy, and so they feel removed from the central action of the rite. Others, like Paul Trench and Hardy Ingram, who must play the roles of Royce Ingram and Damon Rutherford, are deeply troubled by the potential consequences of their participation. Hardy Ingram is actually a Caseyite and cannot quite believe that by some ironic twist he must play the role of Damon Rutherford. Yet he has a vivid premonition of the reality and truth of his role, a premonition which is pointed up when he "feels a tingling just behind his left ear" (p. 160). Skeeter Parsons advises Hardy in all earnestness to step back from the fatal pitch when it comes: "Maybe . . . maybe, Hardy, they're gonna kill you out there today!" (p. 163). Hardy curses in response, but his gruffness is clearly a way of hiding his fear.

Paul Trench, who must play the role of the Avenger, is so anxious about his participation that he is led to the following rumination: "He wants to quit—but what does he mean, 'quit'? The game? Life? Could you separate them?" (p. 171). The answer which Coover is clearly pushing us toward is "No." But the dread which Trench feels is in keeping with the character of all sacred rites. As Huizinga points out, "The function of the rite . . . is far from being merely imitative; it causes the worshippers to participate in the sacred happening itself."[11]

Indeed, the self-enclosed, mythic play-world at the end of *The Universal Baseball Association* has all the characteristics which Huizinga identified as essential to play: joy, creativity, freedom, tension, and isolation. Huizinga's only major error, and the one which later play theorists have continually taken him to task for, is his failure to see that play, while it may be separated from the literal world, may never be divorced from its potential consequences. He failed to see that there is no necessary dichotomy between play and seriousness or play and reality.

The final vision of the eighth chapter is strikingly indeterminate. There are no final answers for the players in the game world, for even the mythic order of the Association is only one possibility among many. As Hardy Ingram says of the ritual, "It's not a trial. . . . It's not even a lesson. It's just what it is" (p. 174). The ritual is not played out; a ninth chapter would have implied the perfection of a completed baseball game, an orderliness and tidiness which the novel argues can never be absolute. What makes the Association universal, the only absolute in the game-world, is the play-attitude. Play encompasses the joy, creativity, and freedom which engendered the Association; play produced the story which became its central myth; and play is the essence of ritual, through which the myth is acted out. Of all the play-worlds in recent sports fiction the Universal Baseball Association is the most supremely playful imaginative recreation of sport, and, since it is mythic, and thus timeless, it partakes not so much of "real time" as "significant time" (p. 155).

NOTES

[1] In addition to Coover's *The Universal Baseball Association, Inc.—J. Henry Waugh, Prop.,* other prominent examples include Don Delillo's *End Zone* (1972), Leonard Gardner's *Fat City* (1969), Lawrence Shainberg's *One on One* (1970), Philip Roth's *The Great American Novel* (1973), James Whitehead's *Joiner* (1972). Peter Gent's *North Dallas Forty* (1973), and Sam Koperwas's *Westchester Bull* (1976).

[2] Although there are almost as many definitions of play as there are writers on the subject, these three qualities are almost universally accepted, regardless of whether the play theorist is a psychologist, philosopher, anthropologist, or sociologist. See, for example, Johan Huizinga's *Homo Ludens* (1950), Roger Caillois' *Man and the Sacred* (1959), David Miller's *Gods & Games: Toward a Theology of Play* (1973), Robert E. Neale's *In Praise of Play: Toward a Psychology of Religion* (1969), Susanna Millar's *The Psychology of Play* (1968). A particularly valuable resource is volume 41 (1968) of *Yale French Studies,* which is entitled "Game, Play, Literature."

[3] Eugen Fink, "The Oasis of Happiness: Toward an Ontology of Play," *Yale French Studies,* 41 (1968), 24-25.

[4] Quoted in Howard S. Slusher, *Man, Sport, and Existence* (Philadelphia, PA: Lea & Febiger, 1967), p. 9.

[5] All page references are to the Signet edition, New York: New American Library, 1969.

[6] Robert E. Neale, *In Praise of Play: Toward a Psychology of Religion* (New York: Harper & Row, 1969), p. 172.

[7] Jacques Ehrmann, "Homo Ludens Revisited," *Yale French Studies,* 41 (1968), 55.

[8] Ehrmann, pp. 42-43.

[9] Neale, p. 104.

[10] See Robert E. Neale, "Full mature play creates the type of story defined as myth" (p. 135).

[11] Johan Huizinga, *Homo Ludens* (Boston, MA: Beacon, 1955), p. 15.

David Lamoreaux

SOURCE: "'Stover at Yale': and the Gridiron Metaphor," in Journal *of Popular Culture,* Vol. XI, No. 2, Fall, 1977, pp. 330-44.

[*In the following essay, Lamoreaux emphasizes the significance of the football metaphor in Owen Johnson's novel* Stover at Yale, *and places it within societal and historical context.*]

Owen Johnson's *Stover at Yale* (1911) inevitably brings to mind an image of an energetic young man with tousled hair, lofty brow, sparking eyes and ruddy cheeks, a football tucked securely under his thick-blue-turtle-neck-sweatered arm.[1] Confining his scholastic activities to the athletic field, he adroitly threads his way through ranks of befuddled adversaries—invariably scoring the game-winning touchdown in the waning seconds of play for the collective glory of God, Country, and Yale (though not necessarily in that order).

While this indeed may have been the story of Frank Merriwell, Young Fred Fearnot, or a host of other less prominent "college novel" heroes, it is not the story—at least not the whole story—of John Humperdink Stover. This popular misconception of *Stover at Yale* is unfortunate, because it effectively obscures the purpose for which the book was written. In fact, once Stover completes his freshman year at New Haven there is little additional mention of athletics at all, except a couple of brief asides to indicate that, yes, our hero has once again demonstrated his gridiron prowess by leading the Yale eleven on to hitherto unknown pinnacles of greatness. The author's real intention in writing *Stover* is suggested by a letter which Theodore Roosevelt sent to Abbott Lawrence Lowell, the then President of Harvard University:

> This will introduce to your Mr. Owen Johnson, the son of the editor of the *Century,* a Yale man . . . who is now writing about Yale a story dealing especially with the club and society problems of which you and I have so often talked, and which have so puzzled us. I really wish you would talk freely with Johnson, who can be entirely trusted,

and will not quote you in any way if you do not wish, and who sees us as we do both the evils of the club or society system and the difficulties in the way of doing away with these difficulties. That is, he is what in politics I would call a sane progressive! . . . Johnson is taking this matter up from the National point of view, the point of view of all the universities and not merely Harvard and Yale.[2]

Contrary to popular impression, then, and despite the fact that his hero is a football All-American, Johnson wrote *Stover at Yale* not as a sports story for juveniles but as an attack on what he regarded as the growth of snobbery at American universities. As such it shares the general tone of the muckraking exposes which flourished at about the time that *Stover* was written (although it was perhaps somewhat more reserved than most of them). It also employs all the standard conventions of that genre, including trusts, machines, corruption, and whole-souled reformers. In order to supplement his critique—and to make sure there could be no misunderstanding of his purpose in writing it—Johnson published in May and June of 1912 a series of five articles in *Collier's Magazine* entitled "The Social Usurpation of Our Colleges," in which he documented his charges against the universities.[3] The first of these dealt with snobbery as a general feature of student life, while the remaining four unmasked the agencies of undergraduate exclusiveness—the social clubs and senior societies of Harvard, Yale, and Princeton, as well as the nationwide fraternity system. Hence it is not surprising that Johnson's Stover is more preoccupied with campus politics than he is with intercollegiate football.

The problems with which Stover is obliged to contend are outlined for us immediately upon his arrival at New Haven, where he is befriended by an upperclassman whom he had encountered briefly once before, when they had lined up against each other in a Lawrenceville-Andover game. "'I'm frankly aristocratic in my point of view,'"[4] proclaims ex-Andover luminary Hugh Le Baron, who, consistent with both his surname and philosophy, exuded "a certain finely aristocratic quality that won rather than provoked."[5] Le Baron's rationale is based primarily on the inability of the common man to manage his own affairs. "'This college is made up of all sorts of elements,'" he explains. "'And it is not easy to run it. Now, in every class there are just a small number of fellows who are able to do it and who will do it. They form the real crowd. All the rest don't count.'"[6]

This "small number of fellows" to which Le Baron referred was composed largely of former prep school students, who tended to be wealthier than their classmates, and came from "better" homes. Their power derived from the monopoly they exercised over the "graduated system of authority"[7] which characterized the social organization of the undergraduate community. Specifically, they dominated the senior society system, which technically included only the three senior social fraternities—Skull and Bones, Scroll and Key, and Wolf's Head—but whose influence actually extended to every

aspect of student life. In theory these societies existed only as "an honest attempt to reward the best in the college life, a sort of academic legion of honor, formed not on social cleavage, but given as a reward of merit."[8] In fact they functioned as an interlocking directorate, controlling the access to social prestige through feeder groups of junior and sophomore societies, whose membership in each case was determined by those who had been inducted the previous year. They had even managed to convert undergraduate activities into client organizations, since students participated in them primarily as a means of securing election to a social fraternity. The implications of this development were not lost on Stover's more sensitive classmates. As one of them complained, "'We are like a beef trust, with every by-product organized, down to the last possibility.'"[9] Johnson's own conclusion was even more emphatic: Yale College, he claimed, was "perhaps the most perfectly organized trust in operation. . . ."[10]

Having envisioned the organization of the student body from the top down as a monopoly or trust of the social elite, Johnson proceeded to examine it from the bottom up. What he discovered was a political machine which functioned in opposition to the established system of senior societies, and which was patronized by ambitious undergraduates whose lack of wealth, family background, or productive contacts with upperclassmen precluded any chance of social mobility within the limits imposed by the fraternity system. The embodiment of these nonsociety men—the "spokesman for an unsuspected proletarian opposition"[11]—is Ray Gimbel, like Le Baron an Andover graduate, but without his connections and pull. Why don't I "heel" a society? he asks: "'I couldn't make 'em anyway.'"[12] With the traditional avenues of power closed off to him, Gimbel organizes the remaining six-sevenths of his class in a determined effort to do away with the society system altogether. He does so (much to Johnson's consternation) by setting himself up as a political boss, fielding candidates for every class election in opposition to the society candidates and overwhelmingly electing them. I like "'the organizing, pulling wires, all that sort of thing,'" he admits, and brags: "'I've got the whole thing organized sure as a steel trap.'"[13] Nor is he any more concerned with the merits of the candidates he stands for office than are the leaders of the society crowd. As he tells a couple of potential recruits:

> "See here, there's a combination being gotten up . . . a sort of slate for our class football managers . . . If you fellows weren't out for football, we'd put one of you up for secretary and treasurer. You can name him if you want. I've got a hundred votes already, and we're putting through a deal with a Sheff crowd for vice-president that will give us thirty or forty more."[14]

Though distressed by Gimbel's tactics, Johnson was not altogether unsympathetic to his point of view. His chief concern, however, was the aura of secrecy with which the society system had managed to endow itself, and the morbid fascination which it exercised over the minds of the Yale undergraduates. "The freshman who arrives unprepared is amazed to find the college in the grip of a mystic bugaboo," Johnson confided. At every step he is confronted by sudden mysterious tomb-like structures, padlocked and without visible windows, with the general atmosphere of a dungeon. He is told that the cabalistic words denoting the different societies must never be pronounced in the presence of a member. If by any unfortunate coincidence he should be passing a tomb when a society member should be coming out, he must avoid a distressing direct confrontation. Returning across the campus about midnight, he sees a solemn line emerging two by two in impenetrable silence back from the society building. Usually at first he is struck by the ridiculousness of the whole proceeding, but inevitably he yields to the all-pervading awe.[15]

Johnson does not want to do away with the society system altogether—he refers specifically to "the poppycock that has been thrown around a good central idea. . . ."[16] And he wants to "retain the privilege any club has of excluding outsiders. . . ."[17] But he insists the societies "drop the secrecy" which surrounds them, a secrecy of such formidable attractive force that even Gimbel's undergraduate wardheelers are not entirely immune from its influence.[18] Like his fellow muckrakers, Johnson hoped that exposing secrecy in high places would eventually lead to social reform. The society system, which at present served as an upper-class sinecure, would be transformed under the press of public scrutiny into a "reward of merit" for Yale's natural aristocrats.

And so the duty of our hero is clear: Stover must discover some way to rejuvenate college life as "a battle in the open where courage and a thinking mind must win."[19] Initially he forages around for an alternative, discovering it in the form of a debating society "drawing from every element of the class, to meet for the sole purpose of doing a little thinking and getting to know other crowds."[20] The most intriguing aspect of the scheme, however, is how clearly it typifies the New Freedom's approach to reform: in essence the debating society is little more than a miniature version of the "parliament of the people," which Woodrow Wilson proposed in order "to restore the processes of common counsel, and to substitute them for the processes of private arrangement."[21] Yet for all Stover's good intentions the debating society is only a temporary success, largely because it relies too heavily on the voluntary cooperation of his fellow students. "Once the edge of novelty had worn off, there were too many diverting interests to throng in and deplete the ranks."[22] Its declension impels Stover to lay an increased emphasis on the necessity for enlightened leadership, a change of heart which established him firmly among the votaries of Teddy Roosevelt's cult of personality. "'I'm going out to lead because I can do it,'" he proclaims, subsequent to his conversion, "'and because I believe in the right things.'"[23] By the end of his junior year he is well on his way to achieving his goal. How do we know this? Because Stover, who has

battled the injustices of the senior society system for the better part of his college career, is ultimately tapped for Skull and Bones.

Machines and trusts and the secret dealings by which such institutions are maintained—these are the negative images which inform the novel, and provide the background of Stover's reform activities. And yet, if people remember Stover at all, they invariably recall him as an athlete rather than as an incipient Progressive. Why should this be?

In order to answer this question, it is necessary to distinguish between the argument (or didactic function) of the book and the narrative (or entertainment function). *Stover at Yale* was originally conceived as a "novel with a purpose," a kind of secular tract intended to draw a moral for the reader.[24] The argument, in this case, arose from the discussion of issues relating directly to Stover's political endeavors, while the narrative involved the use of local color (football and other undergraduate activities) which Johnson recorded primarily to amuse his readers. Yet in certain key respects the narrative is often skew, and sometimes even at cross-purposes to the argument itself. For instance, though Johnson considered "overemphasized sport"[25] a factor in the relative decline of the English universities during this period, and cast aspersions on his own alma mater for upholding "the standards of the gladiatorial arena,"[26] he himself wrote of football with a relish that belies his reservations. In this sense the narrative may indicate as much about Johnson's actual convictions as his conscious attempts to state them in the argument. Perhaps the real reason why Stover is remembered as a football player rather than as a reformer was the capacity of the football game, conceived as a metaphor of society as a whole, to express better than Johnson could do himself the social ideals of his readership. The relation between the football game and the Progressive's utopia was a conjugate one: each embodied a common point of view. This would explain why so many reformers were inclined to exploit the "game" metaphor as a symbolic description of their beliefs—it was a positive counterpart to the images of the political machine and the trust which were so frequently anathematized in Progressive rhetoric.

This is made clear at the outset of the novel, as Stover journeys to New Haven for the start of his freshman year. What excites him most is "the free struggle for leadership that was now opening to his joyful combative nature," a struggle which he approaches "as if the idea were something that could be pursued, tackled, and thrown headlong to the ground."[27] To Stover, already calculating his chances of captaining the Yale varsity in his senior year, the football team represents this free struggle for leadership in its highest form: it is an aristocracy of talent, selected through the impartial procedure of the intrasquad scrimmage, and its members are among the acknowledged representatives of the school. Membership is prima facie evidence of personal success.

From this perspective, the football metaphor expresses a belief in equal opportunity at a time when it was thought that personal autonomy was being hedged about with institutional confinements and restraints. It reflects a desire to maintain the fluidity of society in order that life might still be envisioned as a contest, the outcome of which was decided according to the ability, training, and determination of the participants. Although a man's success or failure might be to some extent dependent on the calibre of his associates, the metaphor clearly implies that it did not depend on his social or economic background, but simply on the degree to which he possessed those qualities which the "game" itself elicited. As Theodore Roosevelt once put it, "Athletics are good . . . because they encourage a true democratic spirit; for in the athletic field the man must be judged not with reference to outside and accidental attributes, but to that combination of bodily vigor and moral quality which go to make up prowess."[28] Success, in short, was not a matter of social ascription but of personal achievement, and therefore a reflection of character.

The aptness of the metaphor was reinforced during this period by the manner in which football was thought to function as a ladder of social mobility for graduates of the public school system.[29] As such, it represented "one democratic solution to the increasing number of rich men's sons on the American campus." And the spirit which it engendered (in the words of President Hadley of Yale) captured "the emotions of the student body in such a way as to make class distinctions relatively unimportant."[30]

Hence the idea of a controlled scrimmage provided a perfect analogue for the selection of those natural leaders who Johnson felt were indispensable to the eventuation of social reform. The individual players, chosen for their ability from among the student body at large, and directed by a captain in whom they reposed absolute trust, comprised an elite which "carried the ball" for its less vigorous brethren. Significantly, this metaphorical elite was university-trained. Like many other Progressives, Johnson viewed the university as a critically important institution. Its essential function was to sanction his natural aristocracy by transforming members of the "society crowd" into useful citizens while serving as a ladder of social mobility for nonsociety men.[31]

At the same time the football metaphor redefined the relationship between the leaders and the led. It implied that the actual physical participation in public affairs by the great mass of citizens was either unnecessary or not to be expected. This mirrored the shift of political attention from the local to the national level which occurred at the turn of the century, a shift of which Theodore Roosevelt's accession to the presidency was the most conspicuous symbol.[32] As a result, politics became a far more "spectatorial" form of activity, since individuals could not hope to have the same political impact on national affairs as they had in their own communities. The spectator, furthermore, was conscious of the contest being waged before his eyes; as such, he was in a position to evaluate the actions of his representatives on the field. There was no allowance for secrecy here: the leaders' abilities (or lack of them) would be clearly apparent to everyone.[33]

But there is another sense in which the "game" is used by Johnson, as when Le Baron admonishes Stover to "'Play the game as others are playing it.'"[34] To make a senior society and emerge as a leader of his class, Le Baron counsels him, Stover must abide by the rigid pattern of behavior which the society system imposes on those who compete for membership. This, Stover discovers, is no less true on the football field. What he finds there is not only "the joyful shock of bodies in fair combat," but a "stern discipline . . . subordinating everything to the one purpose, eliminating the individual factor, demanding absolute subordination to the whole, submerging everything into the machine—that was not a machine only, when once accomplished, but an immense idea of sacrifice and self-abnegation." This, too, becomes a metaphor of his relationship to the college. "Directly, clearly visualized, he perceived, for the first time, what he was to perceive in every side of his college career, that a standard had been fashioned to which, irresistibly, subtly, he would have to conform; only here, in the free domain of combat, the standard that imposed itself upon him was something bigger than his own."[35] Football, obviously, was not merely the personal drama to which Stover had initially looked forward. It was a matter of social accommodation as well.

The corresponding emphasis on the proper functioning of the team, and on team spirit, is perhaps the most important aspect of the football metaphor. For by the time Johnson matriculated at Yale (1869), team play had become the essence of the game. Though football was opened up somewhat by the legalization of the forward pass in 1906 (five years before *Stover at Yale* was published), it is clear from his descriptions of the game that Johnson had in mind the close-ordered formations characteristic of the sport in the 1890's, when he himself was a student.[36] At that time the line of scrimmage, which previously had extended the entire width of the field, had been "contracted until the players stood shoulder to shoulder as they do today. The backs were drawn in and also stationed close to the line."[37] As a result, open field running had virtually disappeared, to be replaced by a heavy-handed, unimaginative mass and momentum attack characterized by line plunges executed behind heavy interference.[38] As a player of the time noted, the most important feature of the game was *"clock-like regularity."* It was far better, he added, "to expect moderately rapid work with *system,* than fast play which savors of individuality and is confused."[39] Johnson himself seemed to share something of this attitude, as he revealed in the following observation: "about the big tackle was always a feeling of confidence, of rugged, immovable determination that perhaps in its steadying influence had built up the team more than his own [Stover's] individual brilliancy."[40] "'That's grandstand playing, my boy; good for you, rotten for the team,'" barks a coach after Stover has performed a spectacular feat of personal heroics. "'You're one of eleven men, not a newspaper phenomenon—get that in your head.'"[41]

In football, then, each player must submit his own ego to the will of the team. He does not have to repress his aggressive impulses, however, but merely redirect them. This was perhaps why football was so attractive to Progressives: it glorified purposeful activity and social restraint at the same time. Indeed, American educators clearly promoted the sport as a means of sublimating the anti-social tendencies of their budding scholars.[42] Its appeal reflects an increased concern with the mechanics of law and order in an era saturated with the worship of brute strength, and thus unwilling to abandon the putative moral influence of competitive strife. Competition, in fact—both within groups and among them—became more intense, because individual self-assertion is less restrained where it can be rationalized as a contribution to the welfare of others. Stover, for instance, is a little appalled by the ferocity of his first football practice. "Something sharp went through him at the thought of the man for whose position, ruthlessly, fiercely, he was beginning to fight." Victory, he sensed, "was built on the broken hopes of a comrade."[43] This tendency becomes even more pronounced as the team prepares for the big game against Princeton, when the substitutes become mere cannon fodder for the first string:

> No one paid any attention to the scrubs, fighting desperately with the same loyalty against the odds of weight and organization, without hope of distinction, giving every last ounce of strength in futile, frantic effort, rejoicing when flung aside and crushed under the victorious rush of the varsity, who alone counted. . . . The first feeling of sympathy [Stover] had felt so acutely for those who bore all the brunt of the punishment, unrewarded, was gone. He no longer felt any pity, but a brutal joy at the incessant smarting, grinding shock of the attack of which he was part and the touch of prostrate bodies under his rushing feet.[44]

Stover's competitive instincts are proportionally liberated as he submerges his own identity in that of the group. To win a starting berth, i.e., to achieve a position of leadership on the team, becomes not a manifestation of self-love but a grave responsibility, recognized even by the scrubs, who rejoice at their own pulverization.[45]

This emphasis on the importance of team work is comprehensible only in terms of the burgeoning attack during these years on the excesses of laissez-faire capitalism, and on its philosophical counterpart—individualism. Conversely, it must also be understood as a response to the various challenges to personal liberty which arose in the late nineteenth century. On the one hand, rapacious competition seemed to threaten the very fabric of society; on the other, the monopolistic power of social institutions—especially the trusts and the political machines—appeared as a permanent restriction on human freedom. In this situation, as William Appleman

Williams has pointed out, "Americans came increasingly to see their society as one composed of groups—farmers, workers, and businessmen—rather than of individuals and sections."[46] What is significant here is that the group as an aspect of social theory emerged in the form of a compromise between unregenerate individualism and unrestrained collectivism. This involved little deviation from the traditional norms by which most Americans conceived of social dynamics—what had previously been thought of as the province of the individual was now identified with the group. Americans, in short, merely extended the mental habits associated with laissez faire into a corporate milieu. Where competition (which was still regarded as contributing ultimately to the public good) had previously been envisioned as a pitting of one man against his fellows, it was now understood as a contest of one group against all other groups. Where success had once been regarded as the culmination of a "race" in which victory went to the fleetest of foot, it was now a "game" in which one's own activities were circumscribed not merely by the members of opposing groups but by members of one's own group as well. (It was no accident that G. Stanley Hall observed at this time that games of chase had given way to team sports.)[47] By the same token, leadership was also conceptualized as a team effort, and thus redefined as a manifestation of social responsibility rather than of personal ambition. Here we have the basis for the ideology of social service which became the rallying cry of the Progressive movement, as well as of succeeding generations of liberals.

For the individual, this shift in emphasis implied a need for social adjustment: it is the ability to respond to the demands of a common enterprise that signifies one's own true worth. Hence football is described as a school for character, much as it is today. "The test [Stover] had gone through," Johnson writes, "had educated him to self-control in its most difficult form."[48] Though Johnson heartily despised the disciplined, self-controlled personalities who spent their time heeling a social fraternity, he is drawn to football in good measure because it evokes these same traits. Football, however, is never a matter of pure self-interest. While self-control—subordinating every impulse to one overriding purpose—is of fundamental importance, it is no longer exclusively tied to the pursuit of private ambition.[49] This is clearly reflected in the development of Stover's own character under the impact of collective necessity: he sacrifices his chances of making the All-American team when his services are required at a position for which he is less well suited, and relinquishes the captaincy when his opposition to the society system threatens to undermine the unity of his team. In each case the self-discipline he has learned on the field contributes to the good of the whole. Once again the social dynamics of laissez faire—the rational pursuit of self-interest through self-control—have been modified in order to advance the cause of the group rather than the individual.

Progressive social ideals based on group conflict are inherent in the very structure of the game. At a time when the frontier's viability as a safety valve was being widely questioned, national consolidation became the animating vision of the reformers. This is why Progressives placed so much emphasis on the rule of law, and devoted so much energy to the problem of defining the values and purposes of their society: hence the appeal of football, where boundaries and objectives were clearly marked out beforehand. While individuals might contend against each other, might strive toward entirely different goals, each was expected to adhere to a prescriptive code of personal behavior, a code which, like the rules of a football game, could not be abrogated without incurring a penalty of some sort. The concept of society as a game, then, conditions the ends sought by establishing preclusive goals and defining the boundaries of the contest; it conditions the manner in which they are pursued by subjecting them to rules and regulations. The responsibility for enforcing the rules did not devolve on the participants themselves, however, for society was no longer regarded as self-regulating. Instead, Progressives tended to agree with Teddy Roosevelt that "we must have government supervision,"[50] though the state was only to function as a "referee" or "umpire," as a neutral third party whose purpose it was to resolve the various claims among the conflicting interest groups. As such it would serve to maintain social stability in the absence of Adam Smith's "invisible hand." That political organization should be construed in this manner reflects a certain distrust of concentrated authority which had always been characteristic of liberalism—the government's function would be essentially a negative one, and power (at least in theory) would still be juxtaposed against equal and opposite power in order to maintain an equilibrium of force.

Football, moreover, was a perfect expression of the pragmatic temperament which had fastened itself upon the country. The very image of corporate instrumentalism, football was emblematic of a society in which the individual was increasingly defined in terms of his functional relationship to a group or series of groups within it. The goal of the individual is indistinguishable from the goal of his team; the mobility of the individual up and down the field is a function of the mobility of those with whom he is playing. Even the procedure of the game reflects an instrumental approach to the problems faced by the group. The goals of the team are implicit, and there is a consequent emphasis on technique. Once a modus operandi has been decided upon, it is executed in the form of a play. The team's decision is then reassessed in the light of experience, the validity of which is determined by reference to its practical consequence. Based on this reassessment a new modus operandi is arrived at, and the team returns to the line of scrimmage in order to experiment on the strength of its latest conclusions. The parallel to the development of pragmatic philosophy is clear. Ideas were merely plans of action. And in the reformulation of pragmatist thinking by Progressives like John Dewey, action was admissible only insofar as it accorded with the general interests of the group.

These plans of action encompassed both long- and short-range goals, an aspect of play embodied primarily in the down system, which allows a team to retain possession of the ball if it can make a limited number of yards in a finite number of plays. Hence the game encourages not only concern with an ultimate purpose (the touchdown) but with a series of intermediate steps as well (first downs). Even the touchdown is in a sense an intermediate goal, since it does not in and of itself bring victory; and victory is merely the prelude of another fray. Such an arrangement is an exact representation of what Teddy Roosevelt meant by "practical idealism," by his injunction not "to put your ideals so high that you feel that there is no use in trying to live up to them, because you cannot do it."[51] Not only was idealism limited to the concrete and the credible by the structure of the game's objectives; it did not extend beyond the group itself.

Clearly, then, the emotional thrust of Johnson's rhetoric as reflected in the narrative rather than in the strictly didactic portions of the novel indicates that he was far more ambivalent about the social situation at Yale than he would have cared to admit. Though he defended the autonomy of the individual against the imperatives of organization as embodied in the trust and the political machine, he was equally alive to the possibilities inherent in mechanization and efficiency, and to a purely functional view of the individual as a member of a "team" or social group. A determined critic of the anti-intellectualism which flourished on the Yale campus, he admired the man of action who accepted the premises of the contest in which he participated. In short, though Johnson was an avowed opponent of what he called "over-organization" in all its various guises, he was simultaneously searching for a concept which would reconcile the advantages of organization with traditional values of personal freedom. Football became for him the very image of this synthesis. When Johnson claimed that football at Yale had been undermined by "the business ideal," that it was "one of the most perfectly organized business systems for achieving a required result—success," he indicated how well the development of football mirrored the growth of corporated organization.[52] Nevertheless, football was fundamentally different from trusts and political machines, where individuals used organization for their own selfish purposes. Football was idealistic—there were no material rewards involved, and efficiency was a natural result of group loyalty achieved through the emotional involvement of its individual members. Defeats invariably resulted from a lack of team spirit, and in fact the Princeton varsity, whose efficient, well-coordinated attack resembles nothing so much as the "perfected, grinding surge of the complete machine,"[53] is hard pressed by an inferior Yale squad spiritually welded together beyond thought of their separate selves. Nothing much has happened to change their relationship with each other except in their own minds—but that is all-important.

It is apparent that Johnson and his readers resented the growth of an organized society yet simultaneously understood its advantages and accepted its inevitability. In this situation football had an immense appeal to them, for it caricatured the highly structured activity which increasingly defined American life, while it denied the sense of estrangement which so many people feared would result from it. Above all else, it was the "spirit of the game" which appealed to them, the subjective aspect of voluntary personal sacrifice in the interest of group harmony. The fact that Stover's audience would recall his football exploits rather than his reform activities attests not merely its imperviousness to serious argument, but to the irrelevance of many of Johnson's arguments. Only in the narrative was he able to capture something of the new spirit which was overtaking the nation. And it was that, of course, which his readers remembered.

NOTES

[1] The writer would like to thank Louis Galambos, Naomi R. Lamoreaux, William R. Taylor, and R. Jackson Wilson for their help in formulating this essay.

[2] Elting E. Morison, ed., *The Letters of Theodore Roosevelt* (Cambridge, Mass.: Harvard University Press, 1954), VII, 433-434.

[3] The five articles appeared on May 18, May 25, June 8, June 15, and June 22. Each article will hereafter be cited by Roman numeral in the order of its appearance in the series.

[4] Owen Johnson, *Stover at Yale* (1911; rpt. New York: Collier-Macmillan, 1968), p. 20.

[5] Ibid., p. 7.

[6] Ibid., p. 20.

[7] Ibid., p. 14.

[8] Ibid., p. 269.

[9] Ibid., p. 196. The student who makes this statement (he is called "Brockhurst" in the novel, and is the spokesman for many of Johnson's ideas) is modeled after Henry T. Hunt, reform mayor of Cincinnati, and one of Johnson's classmates at Yale. It was Hunt who as county prosecutor in the spring of 1911 succeeded in returning the indictments which ended the political career of Boss Cox.

[10] Johnson, "Social Usurpation," III, 13. Though Johnson had been elected chairman of the *Yale Literary Magazine,* and had been admitted to a junior fraternity, he had missed out in his bid for Skull and Bones. Whether this had anything to do with the publication in the *Yale Literary Magazine* of an editorial mildly critical of the society system one month prior to elections is, of course, impossible to say, but it would help to explain a good deal about Johnson's attitude toward the system. In any event, Johnson claimed that "Forty years ago the senior society membership was preponderatingly intellectual; the orators, scholars, writers—the intellectual leaders— were almost certain of election. To-day this element has dwindled, constantly yielding to a social note." (*New York Times,* May 1, 1913).

[11] Johnson, *Stover,* p. 41.

[12] Ibid.

[13] Ibid., p. 40

[14] Ibid., p. 32. "Sheff" refers to the Sheffield Scientific School, founded in 1854 in order to provide an undergraduate program in science.

[15] Johnson, "Social Usurpation," III, 23.

[16] Johnson, *Stover,* p. 275.

[17] Ibid., p. 274.

[18] This is the conclusion to which Johnson leads Stover by the end of the novel. "'. . . I've come to the point where I believe secrecy is un-American, undemocratic, and stultifying; and, as I say, totally unnecessary,'" he declares. "'I should always be against it.'" (p. 300).

[19] Johnson, *Stover,* p. 5.

[20] Ibid., p. 253. Johnson himself formed an organization very similar to this during his undergraduate days, called the Wigwam.

[21] Woodrow Wilson, *The New Freedom* (1913; rpt. Englewood Cliffs, N.J.: Spectrum-Prentice-Hall, 1961), p. 65.

[22] Johnson, *Stover,* p. 261.

[23] Ibid., p. 252. Johnson, for instance, specifically criticized both the nature and handling of the reforms which Wilson attempted to introduce as President of Princeton, though he sympathized with Wilson's intentions.

[24] Quoted in *Current Literature,* July 1912, p. 95. According to Johnson, "The novel with a purpose may not be the best kind of novel, but it is the best vehicle for the expression of ideas."

[25] Johnson, "Social Usurpation," I, 10.

[26] Johnson, "Social Usurpation," III, 25.

[27] Johnson, *Stover,* p. 4.

[28] Theodore Roosevelt, "The Strenuous Life," in *Citizenship, Politics and the Elemental Virtues,* ed. Hermann Hagedorn (New York: Charles Scribner's Sons, 1925), p. 484.

[29] This theme (with particular reference to immigrant groups) is stressed in David Riesman and Reuel Denney, "Football in America: A Study in Cultural Diffusion," *American Quarterly,* 3 (Winter 1951), 309-325. For a dissenting, "Marxist" view, see Paul Hoch, *Rip Off the Big Game* (Garden City, N.Y.: Anchor-Doubleday, 1972).

[30] Frederick Rudolph, *The American College and University* (1962; rpt. New York: Vintage-Random House, 1965), p. 378. Johnson himself admitted that athletics, "whatever may be urged against it for over-accentuation, at least serves as a democratic leaven . . ." ("Social Usurpation," II, 36).

[31] Far from being an expression of rank anti-intellectualism, Johnson is quite clear that football is as much a game of "brains" as it is of force. This is perhaps best indicated by the fact that Stover weighs in at only 141 pounds for the Big Game. For a similar judgment, cf. Walter Camp and Lorin F. Deland's *Football* (Boston: Houghton, Mifflin and Company, 1896), pp. iii-iv: "The great lesson of the game may be put into a single line: *it teaches that brains will always win over muscle!*"

[32] The best description of this development is in Robert H. Wiebe, *The Search for Order: 1877-1920* (New York: Hill and Wang, 1967).

[33] In a sense, however, football *does* make provision for secrecy: this is what happens every time members of a team huddle and accede to a course of action unknown to anyone but themselves, though the agreed-upon strategy (communicated by recourse to a secret code, or signals) quickly becomes apparent once the play gets under way. On the one hand, football is conspiratorial; on the other, the "plot" is always speedily and completely revealed. Hence football substantiated the image which Progressives had of their society, yet simultaneously exploded it—a comforting image. For a description of the use of signals and the huddle in the early game, see Amos Alonzo Stagg and Wesley Winans Stout, *Touchdown!* (New York: Longmans, Green and Co., 1927), pp. 119, 127.

[34] Johnson, *Stover,* p. 22.

[35] Ibid., pp. 5, 55.

[36] The one contest which Johnson describes in any detail is clearly based on the Yale-Princeton game of 1896. Cf. *Stover,* pp. 102-111 with Caspar Whitney's weekly "Amateur Sport" column in *Harper's Weekly,* 28 November 1896, p. 1182. The parallel suggests that Stover's football exploits are modeled after those of Frank Hinkey, Yale's great All-American end.

[37] Parke H. Davis, "Walter Camp, Father of American Football," in *Oh, How They Played the Game: The Early Days of Football and the Heroes Who Made It Great,* ed. Allison Danzig (New York: Macmillan, 1971), p. 20.

[38] The innovation which apparently prompted this change was the low tackle, originated by Walter Camp in 1888. As described by Parke Davis: "from the fall of 1876, tackling had been of the classic Rugby fashion, waist high . . . In the convention of March 3, 1888, Mr. Camp introduced a resolution allowing tackles to be made as low as the knees. Prior to that year formations had found the line of scrimmage stretching widely across the field, with the backs far out, the ball being passed to them always by a long pass. This was the beautiful old open game, so loved and lamented by the oldtimers. And now came the low tackle. It apparently was only a slight change in the rule, but a slight change in the rule can make a profound alteration in the practice of play. Against the sure and deadly low tackle the best of backs no longer could gain consistently in an open field." ("Walter Camp," pp. 19-20). Hence the logic of the mass play.

[39] James R. Church, "Foot-Ball Generally Considered," in *University Foot-Ball: The Play of Each Position Treated by a College Expert,* ed. James R. Church (New York: Charles Scribner's Sons, 1893), p. 9.

[40] Johnson, *Stover,* p. 177.

[41] Ibid., p. 62.

[42] Oscar and Mary F. Handlin, *Facing Life: Youth and the Family in American History* (Boston: Little, Brown, 1971), p. 202.

[43] Johnson, *Stover,* pp. 60, 63.

[44] Ibid., p. 91.

[45] This celebration of the primitive is in part an attempt by Progressives such as Johnson to dissociate themselves from the genteel reformers of the late nineteenth century, who (as Roosevelt was later to recall them) were "very nice, very refined, who shook their heads over political corruption and discussed it in drawing-rooms and parlors, but who were unable to grapple with real men in real life." (*Autobiography,* ed. Wayne Andrews [New York: Charles Scribner's Sons, 1958], p. 56).

[46] William Appleman Williams, *The Contours of American History* (Cleveland: World, 1961), p. 358. Johnson, for example, placed heavy emphasis on the autonomy and cohesion of the college class. One of his chief objections to the society system was that it undermined class unity.

[47] G. Stanley Hall, *Youth* (New York: D. Appleton, 1906), pp. 84-85.

[48] Johnson, *Stover,* p. 115. The transformation of football into a school for character is well described by Donald B. Meyer in his "Early Football," which he delivered in Boston on April 17, 1975, at the Annual Meeting of the Organization of American Historians. Professor Meyer was kind enough to make a copy available to me.

[49] This is evident in the structure of the game. Players are assigned to specific positions whose tasks are defined by reference to the purpose of the team as a whole. There is also a formalized division of labor between the backfield and the line, which clearly subordinates the latter to the former. All this is vastly different, say, from the freer and more open style of Rugby.

[50] Theodore Roosevelt, *The New Nationalism* (1910; rpt. Englewood Cliffs, N.J.: Spectrum-Prentice-Hall, 1961), p. 28.

[51] Ibid., pp. 140-141.

[52] Johnson, *Stover,* pp. 192,195. It is interesting to note that the reforms of the game which Theodore Roosevelt demanded in 1905 were essentially attempts to suppress the less savory aspects of this "ideal" as they manifested themselves on the playing field: football was coming too closely to resemble the trusts and political machines for which it was supposed to provide a moral equivalent. Thus Roosevelt resolved: 1) to modify the mass brutality of the sport at the same time that he strove to protect the average citizen from the power of the trusts; and 2) to discourage the ranker forms of professionalism ("graft") that had crept into the game.

[53] Ibid., p. 105.

Richard J. Buhr

SOURCE: "The Philosophy Game in Tom Stoppard's 'Professional Foul'," in *The Midwest Quarterly*, Vol. XXII, No. 4, Summer, 1981, pp. 407-15.

[In the following essay, Buhr explores Stoppard's use of the game-life analogy and assesses its linguistic implications.]

In his television play *Professional Foul* Tom Stoppard creates a tightly unified structure through the use of the popular analogy that life is like a game. The professional foul of the title refers not only to Roy Broadbent's intentional football foul in the play's offscreen English-Czech match but also to Professor Anderson's own professional foul—the violation of his code of ethical principles. In contrasting football and ethics, Stoppard is not merely presenting a convenient and clever analogy to capture the interest of the popular audience. Just as he examines the implications of the stage-life metaphor in *Rosencrantz and Guildenstern Are Dead* and the epistemological assumptions of the detective genre in *The Real Inspector Hound* and *After Magritte*, Stoppard examines the widely-accepted philosophic analogy between games and life through the structure of *Professional Foul*. By questioning whether the game-life analogy is a valid or useful analogy for philosophic argument,

Stoppard also critiques the methods and conclusions of the British language analysts who frequently use the analogy.

In *Professional Foul* Stoppard first employs the play's title as a cue for the viewer to consider the similarities between football and ethical fouls, and then he forces the viewer to examine the two professional fouls even more closely by holding both fouls up to the criticism of the play's characters. Anderson, a professor of moral philosophy, is himself the questioning critic of his own foul. Early in the play, Anderson takes the stand that moral principles should be obeyed absolutely and that individuals who engage in promises or contracts have an absolute moral obligation to honor those promises and contracts. Anderson later breaks what he considers to be his own contract with the Czechoslovakian government when he smuggles a former student's thesis on human rights out of Prague and delivers an unscheduled paper on human rights at the Prague philosophy colloquium. Anderson commits this "professional foul" after learning that the Czech government has arrested his former student Pavel Hollar on trumped-up currency-crimes charges and after witnessing the suffering of Hollar's wife and son. Through these experiences, Anderson reluctantly comes to the position that basic human rights and emotions must take precedence over the institutional rules of promising and contracts. While Anderson ponders the ethical dimensions of his own professional foul, it is his drunken colleague Bill McKendrick who is the critic of Roy Broadbent's intentional football foul and of the entire football milieu that encourages the expediency of rule breaking, or even of bone breaking, for utilitarian ends. McKendrick comments:

> Roy here is sensitive because he gave away a penalty today, by a deliberate foul. To stop a certain goal he hacked a chap down. After all, a penalty might be saved and broken legs are quite rare. . . . It's perfectly all right—you [Broadbent] were adopting the utilitarian values of the community, for the good of the team, for England! But I'm not talking about particular acts of expediency. No, I'm talking about the whole *ethos*. (p. 106)

In comparing the two professional fouls, Stoppard compels the viewer to examine whether football rules and ethical principles are similar or different and whether football fouls and ethical violations are justifiable or not.

The questions Stoppard raises are similar to those a reader confronts when surveying many of the major philosophy journals, where he is soon struck by the many discussions of games—philosophers such as John R. Searle discoursing on baseball, R. M. Hare on fox hunting, and Mary Midgley on football, chess, and tennis. Philosophers have long employed games in their discussions of society's most important institutions—such as language, law, and ethics—because games provide apparently closed systems of constitutive rules similar to those of institutions. In *Professional Foul* Stoppard is attempting to clarify the issues and implications involved in the debates of the ethical philosophers who employ the analogy. In particular Stoppard is concerned with the game analogy as it is used or assumed by the philosophers of the linguistic tradition, such as Wittgenstein, R. M. Hare, and P. H. Nowell-Smith. In the *Philosophical Investigations,* probably the most important seminal work in the linguistic tradition, Wittgenstein initially proposes and explores what he considers to be the important similarities between games and language. Working within this tradition of the *Investigations,* linguistic philosophers such as Hare and Nowell-Smith have based their discussions on Wittgenstein's belief that language is a compilation of different types of language games. These language analysts perceive philosophic confusions as the result of the confusions between the rules of the various language games, and the goal of these philosophers is to clarify philosophic issues through the examination of philosophic language.

Of the various implications involved in the assumption that philosophy is the study of language games, Stoppard objects most to the implication that when life's institutions are compared to games, these institutions are often perceived as being intrinsically unimportant or optional: since games are normally perceived as closed systems of rules with little or no overlap with actual life, institutions such as law or ethics are often viewed in the same manner when they are compared to games. Nor is Stoppard alone in his concern about these implications of the game-life analogy. Stoppard's strategy and conclusions are very similar to those of philosopher Mary Midgley in "The Game Game," an article which begins with a quotation from Bill Shankly, manager of a Liverpool football club; Shankly's quote humorously echoes Stoppard's concerns about the relationship between football and life: "Some people talk about football as if it were life or death itself, but it is much more serious than that" (p. 231). Midgley's purpose in "The Game Game" is to examine the validity and appropriateness of the game-life analogy as it is used in philosophy, and a look at her discussion will cast light on the issues that Stoppard is exploring in *Professional Foul.*

Midgley's examination was particularly occasioned by R. M. Hare's article "The Promising Game" in which Hare reduces the supposed moral obligation entailed in promises to a confusion between language games. Midgley takes issue with the assumption, which Hare and other philosophers make, that "a Game is a self-contained system, an enclave which can be dropped without upsetting the surrounding scenery, an activity discontinuous with the life around it" (p. 234). Midgley believes that these philosophers use the game concept carelessly and inaccurately. Games, she explains, are not closed systems—they involve strong and specific motivations which cause them to "flow over in a perfectly recognized way into the rest of life" (p. 236). The philosopher need only look at such figures as the chess champion Bobby Fischer or the fans of a football club to see how central games can be to people's lives:

> If you say to Bobby Fischer, "Calm down, chess is only a game" your point will be obscure. Chess is the business of his life; he has no other; his only outside interest is in seeing the other fellow's nerve crack. . . . Similarly, when Rangers play Celtic, not only may people get killed, but the event is central to the lives of many people present. (See the report of the *Observer* man interviewing boys from the Gorbals, who asked them, "Which is the best of these four things: Drink, Sex, Fighting and Celtic?" and got the answer, "Celtic every time." (p. 237)

Besides arguing that games flow over into life, Midgley further argues that games are also much more amorphous in terms of rules than the concept implies in many philosophical discussions. Game rules are not clear and comprehensive. Rule books mislead those who expect to find the whole truth about a game: "Books take obvious points for granted. For instance, the book does not mention spectators, nor the reasons for playing and the kind and degree of friendliness called for between players: nor do they mention the choice of teams and opponents, but every game makes quite complicated demands here" (p. 237).

The overall point of Midgley's game analysis is that a great number of terms and analogies are employed in moral and political philosophy without attempts by the philosophers to define their terms or to search for underlying unities among their analogies. Without attempts to define the underlying structure of a concept such as games or of other concepts such as "exploitation, oppression, sanity, disease, pollution, fulfillment, justice, freedom, art form, escapism, obscurity, sexual, serious, [or] normal," the concepts fall apart. It is with the analysis of such concepts that Midgley believes moral philosophy must begin (p. 252-53).

In *Professional Foul* Stoppard's purpose in using the game-life structure is very similar to Midgley's purpose, which in itself shares the same goals and methodology as the linguistic philosophic tradition; all are attempting to clarify mistakes in the philosophic use of language. Stoppard and Midgley are, however, critical of the language analysts' own use of language, particularly their use of the game analogy. By structuring his play around a comparison between Anderson's violation of his moral code and Broadbent's intentional football foul, Stoppard criticizes the use of the game-life analogy by ironically reversing its usual implications. Normally a comparison between moral principles and game rules could imply two things: that moral principles should be obeyed just as the rules of a game should be obeyed by those playing (see Searle) or that moral principles cannot be very important anyway since they are similar to the rules of a game (see Hare). Stoppard, however, reverses the tenor of the analogy in *Professional Foul* by cleverly illustrating that ethics is both as complicated and as important as a football game can be to the players and fans. In the play Professor Anderson is an ardent football fan, and he never assumes, as the naive McKendrick does, that football is a closed system of absolute rules. Whereas McKendrick criticizes Roy Broadbent on moral grounds for violating the institutional rules of football in his attempt to stop his opponent's goal, Anderson knows that the professional foul is one of the unwritten rules of the game. McKendrick fails, moreover, to understand that football flows over into life; the game is part of the emotional lives of a large body of the world's population, and intentional fouls, self-congratulations, and even broken bones are accepted parts of the intense emotional nature of the game. Although Anderson never questions the emotional element of football, he does ironically refuse to admit the emotional element into his own system of ethical rules when he attempts to create a closed system of explicitly stated rules to order his moral life. It takes the brutal realities of Prague politics to force Anderson to a delayed awareness that human emotions share as great a part in life's institutions as they do in a football match. The play illustrates that neither a game nor ethics is a closed system—both have emotional natures that cannot be contained by a system of explicit rules. It is with this realization that Anderson alters his ethical principles and intentionally breaks the rules of the Czech government to aid Hollar's cause, the cause of human rights.

Through the structure of *Professional Foul,* Stoppard wittily beats the language analysts at their own game. By examining one of their predominant rhetorical devices—the game-life analogy—and detecting its misleading implications, Stoppard illustrates certain criticisms of linguistic philosophy that Anderson himself explicitly states. As early as the play's very first scene, Stoppard uses Anderson to develop his views on the subject. On the plane to Prague, Anderson demonstrates condescension toward the language analysts as he explains to McKendrick his habit of making notes of linguistic oddities: "Yes, I like to collect little curiosities for the language chaps. It's like handing round a bag of licorice allsorts. They're terribly grateful" (p. 46). This tone is similar to that of Stoppard's own statements in a *New York Times* interview where he comments that linguistic philosophers occupy a position similar to those persons who enthusiastically collect and trade "the labels off triangular pieces of cheese." While neither activity does "anybody any harm," according to Stoppard, both label collecting and linguistic philosophy are too esoteric to have much practical value for everyday life (p. 36). The problem that Stoppard finds with linguistic philosophy is that in its obsession with detecting the linguistic confusions of traditional ethical and political philosophy, it has avoided directly confronting the ethical and political problems themselves. Stoppard implies that by reducing problems to language games, linguistic philosophy reduces motivation for individual action. Although an analysis of the linguistic confusions of a political issue, such as human rights, might clarify the issue and indeed even show that there is no logically correct answer to the question, the problem itself, Stoppard believes, still exists; the language analysts' position is incorrect when they conclude that ethical and

political issues are merely the creations of language. Anderson expresses Stoppard's own opinion near the end of the play when he explains:

> In our own time linguistic philosophy proposes that the notion of, say, justice has no existence outside the ways in which we choose to employ the word, and indeed *consists* only of the ways we employ it. In other words, that ethics are not the inspiration of our behavior but merely the creation of our utterances. . . . And yet common observation shows us that this view demands qualification. . . . We must see that natural justice, however illusory, does inspire many people's behavior much of the time. As an ethical utterance it seems to be an attempt to define a sense of rightness which is not simply derived from some other utterance elsewhere. (p. 117-18)

Anderson argues that the "importance of language is overrated" by the language analysts, and his criticism of the ridiculous Professor Stone nicely summarizes Stoppard's views: "[Language] allows me and Professor Stone to show off a bit, and it is very useful for communicating detail—but the important truths are simple and monolithic" (p. 75).

In *Professional Foul* Stoppard affirms a belief in a cognitive, intuitive truth and morality. As Anderson asserts, "There is a sense of right and wrong which precedes utterance. It is individually experienced and it concerns one person's dealings with another person. From this experience we have built a system of ethics which is the sum of individual acts of recognition of individual right" (p. 118). Stoppard's belief in intuitive truths is a stand against both the linguistic philosophers, who believe that ethics are merely the result of linguistic confusions, and the Marxist relativists, who believe that epistemology is dependent on ideology. Although Stoppard is critical of the tradition of language analysis because he feels that it ignores simple intuitive truths, he implies through his own critique of the game-life analogy that the examination of language can be a valuable aid to approaching truth. As Anderson remarks, "language is as capable of obscuring the truth as of revealing it" (p. 75). By structuring his play around the game-life analogy, Stoppard discloses how the linguistic philosophers have, ironically, obscured the truth with their own careless use of language.

WORKS CITED

Gussow, Mel. "*Jumpers* Author Is Verbal Gymnast," *New York Times,* 23 April 1974, p. 36.

Hare, R. M. "The Promising Game," *Revue Internationale de Philosophie,* 18 (1964), 398-412.

Midgley, Mary. "The Game Game," *Philosophy,* 49 (1974), 231-53.

Nowell-Smith, P. H. *Ethics.* Baltimore: Penguin, 1954.

Searle, John R. "How to Derive 'Ought' from 'Is,'" *Philosophical Review*, 73 (1964), 43-58.

Stoppard, Tom. "But for the middle classes," *Times Literary Supplement* (London), 3 June 1977, p. 677.

————. *Every Good Boy Deserves Favor* and *Professional Foul: Two Plays*. New York: Grove Press, 1978.

Wittgenstein, Ludwig. *Philosophical Investigations*. 3rd ed. Trans. G. E. M. Anscombe. New York: Macmillan, 1958.

C. Harold Hurley

SOURCE: "The Facts Behind the Fiction: The 1950 American League Pennant Race and 'The Old Man and the Sea'," in *Hemingway's Debt to Baseball in 'The Old Man and the Sea'*, The Edwin Mellen Press, 1992, pp. 77-93.

[*In the following essay, Hurley determines the extent to which the actual events of the 1950 American League pennant race correspond to episodes in Hemingway's novel, asserting that the relationship lends thematic unity to the story.*]

When *The Old Man and the Sea* first appeared in the September 1, 1952 issue of *Life*, fans and critics alike, caught up in the excitement of the current major league pennant races, undoubtedly smiled when reading of Hemingway's allusions to America's national pastime. Although the references to baseball's "older days" (22) and to the exploits of Luque, Gonzalez, and McGraw[1] were obscure even then, the factual events behind the fictional account of the 1950 season—removed from one another by the space of only two Septembers[2]—would have lingered still in the memories of knowledgeable fans. But now, separated by forty-two summers from the season chronicled there, even the most inveterate follower of the game fails to comprehend the extent to which the actual historical events of the American League pennant race correspond to Hemingway's fictional account of the aged fisherman. Only with the knowledge that Hemingway, working directly from contemporary accounts, sets Santiago's encounter with the big fish against the backdrop of crucial contests staged during the second full week of September in the 1950 season are we able to catch a glimpse of a world beyond that encompassed by the story. Against the games of baseball's "September Stretch," Santiago's ordeal at sea achieves temporal and thematic synchronism with the larger order of a sport whose contests seem to many a paradigm of the human condition.

That the action of the story unfolds during the second full week of September 1950—specifically Tuesday, September 12 through Saturday, 16 September—can be determined from isolated references to baseball interspersed throughout the novel and from Manolin and Santiago's constant bantering about the sport.

The year 1950 can be deduced from the exchange stemming from the young boy's request of the old man to be told about "the baseball" (17). After predicting that "the great DiMaggio" (17) will lead the New York Yankees to the pennant in the American League, Santiago indicates "in the other league [the National League] between Brooklyn and Philadelphia I must take Brooklyn" (21), even though he fears the prowess of Philadelphia's Dick Sisler.

Widely known to readers of the novel is the fact that Dick Sisler's dramatic home run on the last day of the season and in extra innings against the Brooklyn Dodgers secured the flag for Philadelphia's "Whiz Kids" in the National League and that Joe DiMaggio's hitting heroics led the New York Yankees to the championship over the Detroit Tigers in the American League, with the Yankees sweeping the Phillies in four straight games in the 1950 Series.

That the month is September of that year is made apparent in several instances beginning early in the book with Manolin's advice to the old man to "Keep warm. . . . Remember we are in September" (18) and ending with the narrator's statement on Santiago's second day at sea: "It was dark now as it becomes dark quickly after the sun sets in September" (74).

The actual dates in September, not so readily apparent as the year and the month and never before identified, can be derived from the combination of several different allusions to specific games being played in the major leagues—games that as we shall see momentarily not only establish a context for the baseball dialogue but also clarify the larger significance of baseball's place in the inner stitching of the novel.

The first indication of the actual dates stems from Santiago's account of his struggle with the great fish on his second day at sea:

> He felt very tired now and he knew the night would come soon and he tried to think of other things. He thought of the Big Leagues, to him they were the *Gran Ligas*, and he knew the Yankees of New York were playing the *Tigres* of Detroit.
>
> This is the second day now that I do not know the results of the *juegos*, he thought (67-68).

Since the Yankees and the Tigers, locked in a long struggle for first place, played only a single series in the final month of the 1950 season—Thursday, September 14 through Saturday, September 16—Santiago's second day at sea and second day without the results of the games must, of necessity, correspond with one of those three days. That Santiago, on his second day out, is in fact alluding to the first game of the series, played on

Thursday, September 14, can be deduced from several exchanges between the old fisherman and his young apprentice as they prepare two days earlier for Santiago's fishing expedition. Upon returning with the old man's supper, Manolin and his friend engage in conversation:

> "Your stew is excellent," the old man said.
>
> "Tell me about the baseball," the boy asked him.
>
> "In the American League it is the Yankees as I said," the old man said happily.
>
> "They lost today," the boy told him.
>
> "That means nothing. The great DiMaggio is himself again."
>
> "They have other men on the team."
>
> "Naturally. But he makes the difference" (21). . . .

On the day prior to Santiago's putting to sea, Manolin's comment in the above exchange that "They [the Yankees] lost today" (21), when coupled with Santiago's lament two days later that the "Yankees of New York were playing the *Tigres* of Detroit" (68) and for "the second day now I do not know the results of the *juegos,*" (68) places Santiago and Manolin's exchange about the Yankees losing on Tuesday, September 12, 1950.

Historically, just prior to their three-game series with Detroit—to which Santiago alludes at sea—the Yankees were playing a two-game set with the Cleveland Indians, winning the second game on Wednesday, September 13 after losing the first game on Tuesday, September 12. It is to this loss on September 12—the Yankees had won their previous games earlier in the week—that Manolin refers. In short, Manolin and Santiago's references to major league baseball games enable the reader to detail as follows the novel's chronology against the backdrop of the American League baseball schedule for Tuesday, September 12 through Saturday, September 16, 1950:

Day 1, Tuesday, September 12 (pp. 1-25 of the novel): Having gone 84 days without a catch but with his hope and confidence still intact, the old man, firm in his belief that "tomorrow is going to be a good day with this current" (14), determines to go "far out [on the Gulf] to come in when the wind shifts" (14). Before reading about baseball in "yesterday's paper" (17)—but more on that later—Santiago discusses with Manolin their concerns about the major league pennant races. Although Manolin fears the Indians of Cleveland and the Tigers of Detroit, Santiago seeks to allay the boy's concern by assuring him that the Yankees, led by the great DiMaggio, "cannot lose" (17). Later that same day, Santiago, having read yesterday's paper about "the baseball" (21) while Manolin has gone for bait and supper, indicates that "in the American League it is the Yankees as I said" (21). Even though the boy has returned with news of the Yankees' loss to Cleveland—"They lost

today" (21), the boy told him—Santiago, emphasizing that the great DiMaggio is himself again and that "he makes the difference" (21), predicts for the second time a pennant for the Yankees.

Day 2, Wednesday, September 13 (pp. 25-50): Rising early, Santiago walks up the road to the young boy's house and awakens him. Together they drink coffee from condensed milk cans at an early morning place that serves fishermen. Manolin, providing Santiago with sardines and bait prepared the day before and wishing him good luck, watches as the old man rows out of the harbor in the dark. At noon, his lines set with precision and saddened that he is not one of "the rich [who] have radios to talk to them in their boats and to bring them the baseball" (39), Santiago sets his hook into a very large fish, which for the remainder of the first day and night at sea tows the old man and his skiff east and then north away from Havana and into the Gulf. Unaware of the results of the games played that day and with his right hand bleeding, Santiago seeks to demonstrate to the biggest fish he has ever seen just "what a man can do and what a man endures" (66).

Day 3, Thursday, September 14 (pp. 50-86): At sea for the second day, Santiago, his left hand almost as stiff as rigor mortis, catches sight of the great fish—nearly two feet longer than the skiff and with a sword as long as a baseball bat. Exhausted and turning his thoughts to other things, Santiago again reflects on the Big Leagues and on the Yankees of New York playing against the Tigers of Detroit. Not knowing for the second day the results of the *juegos* but sustained by the thoughts of the great DiMaggio and of his own arm wrestling match many years ago against the great negro dockworker from Cienfuegos, himself a fine athlete, Santiago, with the setting of the sun, braces himself for his second night at sea with the great fish.

Day 4, Friday, September 15 (pp. 86-117): On his final day at sea and his third with the fish, Santiago, confused, faint, and sick, succeeds nonetheless in harpooning his worthy opponent and lashing him beside the skiff for the long journey home, content that the great DiMaggio would have been proud of him that day. But then the sharks strike. Seeking consolation from thoughts of baseball and defending his catch until nothing remains but the head and tail and skeleton, Santiago, destroyed but not defeated, catches at last the reflected glare of the lights of the city at ten o'clock that night and sails into the harbor in the early hours of Saturday morning.

Day 5, Saturday, September 16 (pp. 117-127 [end]): Secure in his shack, the old fisherman, asleep on his bed and with his arms out straight on the newspapers and the palms of his hands up, is discovered some hours later by Manolin. Overwhelmed by what Santiago has obviously endured, the boy, amidst plans to rejoin Santiago at sea, prepares for his sleeping friend a pot of hot coffee. As Manolin leaves to bring the old man something to eat and a clean shirt, Santiago's lone request is for "any of the papers of the time that I was gone" (126). When the young boy returns, the old fisherman is asleep and dreaming about the lions.

Hemingway, in his allusions to the actual events transpiring in the American League pennant race during the second full week of September, not only invites readers to date the events within the story but also encourages them to consider the significance of the external events to the internal events of the novel. On several occasions, for example, Hemingway has Santiago read the newspaper to follow the progress of the Yankees' pennant drive. Never once stating explicitly the actual dates of the papers, Hemingway nonetheless enables the reader to determine precisely the accounts of Santiago's reading. More than idle baseball chatter, these accounts serve to gloss passages in the text that might otherwise prove problematic and, more significantly, to place Santiago's private confrontations with the great fish against the public struggles of individual men like Joe DiMaggio whose teams during baseball's September stretch are engaged in contests of their own.

With "yesterday's paper" in hand, Santiago, in the first instance, plans to bask in the sun in the doorway of his shack and read of the games while Manolin, in preparation for the old man's venture the next day, leaves to get the sardines and casting net:

> "I'll get the cast net and go for sardines. Will you sit in the sun in the doorway?"
>
> "Yes. I have yesterday's newspaper and I will read the baseball."
>
> The boy did not know whether yesterday's paper was a fiction too [as were the pot of yellow rice with fish (16)]. But the old man brought it out from under the bed.
>
> "Perico gave it to me at the *bodega*," he explained.
>
> "I'll be back when I have the sardines. I'll keep yours and mine together on ice and we can share them in the morning. When I come back you can tell me about the baseball" (16-17).

The reader who is aware as a result of Hemingway's allusions that this conversation takes place on Tuesday, September 12 and that "yesterday's paper," dated Monday, September 11, recounts the activities of the preceding day, Sunday, September 10, will discover that Sunday was a momentous day for Joe DiMaggio and his Yankees. On that day, the sports headlines, box score, and team standings reveal that the Yankees, led by Jolting Joe's record-breaking three home runs in spacious Griffith Stadium, have beaten the lowly Washington Senators (currently in fifth place, twenty-five games off the pace) by a score of 8-1.[3] After a sluggish start for the team and its aging star, the Yankees, with eight wins in their last eleven games, recorded their 84th victory against 49 defeats to move into second place, one-half

game behind the first-place Detroit Tigers, with the Boston Red Sox in third place, just one game back and the Cleveland Indians in fourth place, seven games behind the frontrunners but still in contention.

Inspired by the Yankee Clipper's assault on the record books and armed with the two-fold awareness that the Yankees' 84th victory coincides numerically with his own 84th day of defeat and, furthermore, that the Yankees—should they record at least one victory against Washington in their scheduled doubleheader on Monday, September 11—would with their 85th victory secure a tie with the idle Detroit Tigers for the American League lead, the superstitious Santiago ["he knew that if you said a good thing it might not happen" (43)] is doubly sure that his 85th day at sea will itself prove momentous.

When the boy returns with the net and the bait, Santiago, having just read of DiMaggio's exploits and of the Yankees' good fortunes, responds joyously to Manolin's request to be told of "the baseball"—a response that in light of Sunday, September 10's game makes perfect sense:

> "In the American League it is the Yankees as I said" the old man said happily. [Santiago has learned that the Yankees have beaten the Senators to record their 84th victory and to move within a half-game of first place Detroit.]
>
> "They lost today," the boy told him. [Manolin, having left to make preparations for the old man's fishing trip, has apparently heard on the radio the results of the Yankees' loss to Cleveland earlier in the day (Tuesday September 12).[4] The boy obviously does not share Santiago's confidence in the Yankees' prospects of winning the pennant.]
>
> "That means nothing. The great DiMaggio is himself again." [Santiago is well aware of recent newspaper accounts detailing DiMaggio's "early and midseason slump" (*New York Times*, Monday September 4) that prompted the press to call for his retirement. "Playing despite injuries that have beset nearly his entire body" (*Times*, September 4), the 35-year-old DiMaggio, having found it necessary in late August to "rest strained ligaments in both knees" (*Times*, September 1), returned to the lineup in early September and proved that he "still is one of the most feared batters in the game" (*Times*, September 4), as again attested to by his recent home run spree against the Senators.]
>
> "They have other men on the team." [Manolin, a young but knowledgeable fan, knows on a roster that includes the likes of Rizzuto, Berra, Mize, Woodling, Bauer, Coleman and Henrick that the Yankees are more than a one-man team.]
>
> "Naturally. But he makes the difference." [In the heat of the pennant race, Santiago seems to suggest, the skill and experience of DiMaggio, renowned for his individual skills and his team-play, will help carry the Yankees to victory.]

The close correspondence of Hemingway's fictional account to the actual events of baseball's proceedings, though of great thematic significance, also serves as a gloss to the following sometimes-misunderstood-exchange between Santiago and Manolin earlier in the day:

> "The Yankees cannot lose." [Santiago is confident that his team, on a hot streak since the middle of August, will ultimately prevail.]
>
> "But I fear the Indians of Cleveland." [Manolin, aware that the Yankees are playing Cleveland in a two-game series, fears that a sweep by the Indians, currently in fourth place just seven-and-a-half games behind the Yankees, would pull them up within five-and-a-half games of his team with seventeen games remaining in the season.]
>
> "Have faith in the Yankees my son. Think of the great DiMaggio." [Even prior to reading of the Yankees' win against the Senators and of Joe DiMaggio's heroics, Santiago, the seasoned baseball follower, is convinced that the Yankees, having righted themselves in the standings, will go on to win the championship.]
>
> "I fear both the Tigers of Detroit and the Indians of Cleveland." [Not easily consoled, Manolin knows that after the Yankees complete their series with the contending Indians their next opponent will be the first-place Tigers. If the Yankees are to prevail, they must do well against both teams.]
>
> "Be careful or you will fear even the Reds of Cincinnati and the White Sox of Chicago" (17).[5] [The hapless White Sox, Santiago teases, currently in sixth place and thirty-four games out in the American League race, are no more a threat to win the championship than are the Cincinnati Reds, mired, as they both know, in sixth place in the other league.]

Hemingway's second reference to Santiago's reading of the newspaper—"yesterday's paper," Monday, September 11, was the first—occurs, significantly, on the next-to-last page of the novel upon Santiago's return home. Working elliptically as before, Hemingway invites the reader to consider the significance of the external events recorded in the sports section to the internal events delineated in the novel. This time, however, the newspaper accounts serve less as a gloss to the dialogue than as a backdrop to Santiago's lonely ordeal on the Gulf.

Santiago, having left in the early morning of Wednesday, September 13, knows only that the Yankees have lost their first game in the series with Cleveland. Without a radio, Santiago does not know the score of the second game with Cleveland nor the outcome of the first game between the Yankees and Detroit, prompting the lament that for two consecutive days now he does not know the results of the games—a lament that would extend until his return to shore early Saturday, September 16, after three grueling days with the fish.

As Manolin leaves the old fisherman's shack early on the morning of his return to port to bring the old man a clean shirt and something to eat, Santiago's only request, as previously indicated, is for "any of the papers of the time that I was gone" (126)—not to read of the front-page headlines of the day, but to learn of the great DiMaggio and the fate of his beloved Yankees.

We do not know, of course, the dates of the papers that Manolin will provide. Unless an early-morning edition of Saturday's paper is available, Friday's paper (September 15) will report that the Yankees won both the final game against Cleveland (played on Wednesday, September 13) and the first game against Detroit (played on Thursday, September 14) to move into first place by half-a-game. With Friday's sports headlines proclaiming that "Yanks Regain League Lead by Downing Tigers" as "DiMaggio Blasts no. 29" (*Times,* September 15), Santiago is doubtless pleased to learn that in the three days he was doing battle with the greatest foe of his long career, alone on the Gulf Stream, the great DiMaggio and his Yankees, in one of the most exciting weeks of the season, were before thousands of jubilant fans in Yankee Stadium proving themselves victors in contests of another sort.[6]

Running parallel to the internal action of the novel, the games of baseball's "September Stretch" serve not only to heighten and intensify Santiago's heroic encounter with the great marlin and the sharks, but also to place that encounter against the heroes of a sport that in the mythic sense is emblematic of humanity's struggle to endure and prevail. For Santiago it is the constant measuring of self against the yardstick of the incomparable DiMaggio that sustains him in the agony of his ordeal, and his thoughts of the game itself that console and divert him when that agony becomes too great.

From the outset, Santiago and Manolin, by sharing their countrymen's passion for baseball, discover in their bantering about the exploits of Sisler and Durocher, Luque and Gonzalez, but especially of DiMaggio, topics of mutual interest that not only solidify the bond between the old master and the aspiring apprentice but also strengthen the resolve of the aged fisherman when after 84 days without a catch he struggles with the biggest fish "he had ever seen and bigger than he had ever heard of" (63).

Frequently comparing himself with the great DiMaggio, whose father was also a fisherman, Santiago repeatedly conjures up the image of the Yankee Clipper to win, despite the limitations imposed by infirmity, age, and pain, a hard-fought victory, first over the great fish itself and then over the sharks that would strip him of his record-breaking prize. It is small wonder that the beleaguered old man, buoyed by the newspaper accounts of the ballplayer's own record-breaking feats, longs "to take the great DiMaggio fishing" (22) with him. DiMaggio, the old fisherman implies, is the kind of man who in the batter's box or in an open boat "makes the difference" (21). When on his first day at sea, Santiago, rather than drift and sleep and put a bight around his toe to awaken him, determines that today, the eighty-fifth, he will fish well, not only to assure his success but also to make the great DiMaggio proud of him.

To increase his strength and confidence in his efforts to land the fish and to defend it from its attackers, Santiago, though he clearly knows the facts from following the newspaper accounts, purposely perpetuates the fiction that DiMaggio is still hampered by a painful bone spur on his right heel that cut short his play in the preceding season. Plagued himself by a traitorous left hand, Santiago sets himself in fictive competition with the great DiMaggio "who does all things perfectly even with the pain of the bone spur in his heel" (68). Although he does not know if the pain in his "hands were as great a handicap as bone spurs" (104), Santiago's suffering is such that he wonders whether "the great DiMaggio would stay with a fish as long as I will stay with this one" (68).[7]

But if it is Santiago's fictional competition with the skilled but injured DiMaggio that sustains him when "the bad time" (103) comes, it is his thoughts of the game itself which comfort and distract the old fisherman when those hard times test the limits of his endurance. Joined with the fish since noon of the first day and with no one to help him, Santiago turns repeatedly to thoughts of the Big Leagues and to the results of the games, thoughts that along with those of the boy and the lions serve him well until such time that his pain and confusion make it increasingly difficult to "think about something cheerful" (104).

Far more, then, than providing small talk, comic relief or a foreign amusement, Hemingway's allusions to baseball set Santiago's efforts at sea against the larger world of the game's September stretch to achieve for the novel a single, thematic whole. Santiago and Manolin's musings about baseball, its heroes, and their achievements, when examined within the framework of an old fisherman's solitary struggle, serve not only to make understandable certain passages of dialogue and to date the internal events of the book, but, more importantly, to allow that struggle to achieve both temporal and thematic resonance with a world of sport whose contests for many seem a paradigm of the human condition. Whether for an aged fisherman alone in an open boat testing his skill and endurance against marlin and sharks on the Gulf Stream or for an aging baseball player measuring his strength and courage against the Indians of Cleveland or the Tigers of Detroit in Yankee Stadium, the contest is the same; and in the application of skill and strength, endurance and courage lie man's only hope for victory, short-lived though it may be.

NOTES

[1] In the novel, Hemingway refers directly or indirectly to the following major league players and managers: Joe

DiMaggio (844), Leo Durocher (859), Mike Gonzalez (928), Adolpho Luque (1774-75), John J. McGraw (1138-39), Dick Sisler (1330-31) and George Sisler (1331). For a statistical overview of their careers, see the pages cited parenthetically above after each player's name in *The Baseball Encyclopedia, Bicentennial Edition: The Complete and Official Record of Major League Baseball.*

[2] The date of the novel's composition is open to debate. Baker indicates, however, that Hemingway, "after the holiday hubbub [of late December 1950 and early January 1951] began to tell the story of the old Cuban fisherman and the giant marlin that Carlos Gutierrez had told him in 1935"—see "On the Blue Water," Esquire 5 (April 1936), pp. 31, 184-185—and "by January 17th, his manuscript stood at 6,000 words, about a quarter of the whole." . . ."Working like a bulldozer, averaging a thousand words a day for sixteen days . . . by February 17th it stood virtually finished" (*Life Story* 489-490).

Drawn from the recently completed season, many of Hemingway's references to baseball were, consequently, fewer than six months old.

[3] *The New York Times* sports headline for Monday, September 11 proclaims that on the previous day "DiMaggio Wallops 3 Homers as Yankees Rout Senators." After subheadlines indicating "DiMaggio Sets a Record" and "First Player to Hit 3 Homers in One Game at Griffith Stadium—Also Doubles," the ensuing article provides the following account: "The opener [the second scheduled game was rained out], during which DiMaggio drove his three circuit clouts into the distant left field bleachers, went to Casey Stengel's Bombers, 8-1. It marked the third time in his career that the Clipper had clubbed three in one game and the first time any batter, left or right handed, had been able to gain this distinction in the 30-year history of the present arena. All three clouts traveled well over 400 feet" (31).

[4] Hemingway at this point alters the facts slightly. Although the Yankees indeed lost to the Indians as Manolin reports, the game was played on the night of Tuesday, September 12, not during the day, as called for in the story.

[5] Manolin's fears for the Tigers and the Indians are well justified, not that they were the respective winners of the 1946 and 1948 pennants as Richard Allan Davison alleges but that they were currently contending for the championship and playing the Yankees in consecutive series that very week. Davison is right to remind us, however, that "both the Reds and the White Sox were firmly second division clubs between 1947 and 1951" (13) though wrong to conclude that Hemingway errs in having the old fisherman refer to "the Cincinnati Reds as if they were in the American League" (11).

George Monteiro, in response to Davison's observations about the Reds, interprets the passage correctly when he states: "The joke is, one supposes, that even a mediocre team in the other league has as much of a chance at beating the Yankees to the American League championship as do the hapless White Sox of Chicago" ("The Reds" 8).

The feared Indians, interestingly enough, helped the idle Yankees "clinch" the 1950 pennant by eliminating the Tigers on Friday, September 29.

[6] The Yankees, with an 84-49 record, began the week of September 10 in second place one-half game behind the Tigers and one-half game ahead of third-place Boston. The Indians were seven games back. By winning six of eight games during that crucial week, the Yankees finished the span with a slim half-game edge over the Tigers and a two-game lead over the Red Sox. In a week that saw the American League leadership change hands no fewer than five times, Joe DiMaggio hit six home runs, drove in his hundredth run of the season, and raised his batting average from .287 to .297.

Although tied with the Tigers for first place as late as Thursday, September 21, the Yankees went on to win the pennant by three games over Detroit, with Boston in third place four games back, and Cleveland in fourth place six games off the pace. DiMaggio finished the season with a .301 average, 32 home runs, and 122 runs-batted-in.

[7] Carlos Baker is mistaken in his belief that even then the great DiMaggio was suffering from a bone spur (*Writer as Artist*, 305, n. 28). George Monteiro, although aware that DiMaggio had recovered from the painful right heel by the middle of the preceding season, is also mistaken is his belief that "it is essential to Hemingway's handling of the theme of endurance that Santiago not know of this [recovery]" ("Santiago" 277). But Santiago, as we have seen, has carefully followed DiMaggio's progress in the newspapers and for reasons of his own purposely sets himself in competition with the ailing ballplayer.

WORKS CITED

Baker, Carlos. *Ernest Hemingway: A Life Story.* New York: Scribner's, 1969.

———. *Hemingway: The Writer as Artist.* 2nd. ed. Princeton, N.J.: Princeton UP, 1956.

The Baseball Encyclopedia, Bicentennial Edition: The Complete and Official Record of Major League Baseball. 3rd. ed. New York: Macmillan, 1976.

Davison, Richard A. "Carelessness and the Cincinnati Reds in *The Old Man and the Sea.*" *Notes on Contemporary Literature* 1.1 (1971): 11-13.

Hemingway, Ernest. "On the Blue Water: A Gulf Stream Letter." *Esquire* 5 (April 1936): 31, 184-185.

Monteiro, George. "The Reds, the White Sox, and *The Old Man and the Sea.*" *Notes on Contemporary Literature* 4.3 (1974): 7-9.

———. "Santiago, DiMaggio, and Hemingway: The Aging Professionals of *The Old Man and the Sea.*" *Fitzgerald/Hemingway Annual 1974:* 273-80.

New York Times (Sports) 1 September 1950, p. 24; 4 September 1950, p. 12; 11 September 1950, p. 31; 15 September 1950, p. 32.

Ira Berkow

SOURCE: "Farrell and Sports," in *Twentieth Century Literature,* Vol. 22, No. 1, February, 1976, pp. 105-10.

[*In the following essay, Berkow discusses the influence of sports on the life and work of James Farrell.*]

When I called for James T. Farrell at his mid-Manhattan apartment to drive to the baseball game on a late afternoon last August, he answered the door wearing, most strikingly, a red tie and a light-blue summer sport jacket, buttoned. He was ready to go. He was seventy-one years old but I was reminded of his description in *My Baseball Diary* of how at age thirteen he went to his first World Series game and waited impatiently in line in the early morning for the ticket window to open.

He says he still goes to games on an average of once a week. It seems always an event. Our talk while driving on the parkway was solely baseball. He was genuinely concerned with the recent inductees into the Baseball Hall of Fame and whether they deserved to be so anointed. (He remains adamant that some of his favorite "Black Sox" players, such as "Shoeless" Joe Jackson and Buck Weaver, should not be excluded from the Hall because of the infamous scandal.) Farrell enjoys collecting and sharing esoteric facts. He recalled that Ty Cobb practiced stealing bases more than entire teams would, and that Cobb actually studied the grains of wood before choosing his custom-made bats. And Eddie Collins, a White Sox second baseman of Farrell's youth, had an interesting superstition: At the plate he would touch the chewing gum stuck on the peak of his cap.

While doing research for an article for "Park East," his neighborhood newspaper in which he writes a column, Farrell discovered a great fact about Joe Jackson. Jackson, in the seven recorded full seasons he played in the big leagues (from 1913 through 1920—with one year out for injury), struck out only 158 times. Farrell found that this statistic aptly depicts the gifted batting eye of Jackson.

At the batting cage now before the game at Shea Stadium, Farrell mingled with the society of ballplayers and sportswriters. Over the years he has grown friendly with the latter group particularly. And he is treated with almost courtly respect (many of the writers call him "Mr. Farrell," though some call him "Jim"). I believe they view him as a venerable man of letters and are flattered by his enthusiasm and knowledge of baseball.

Farrell asked several if they knew how many times Joe Jackson struck out in his career. It came as a surprising, somewhat pleasant and rather odd question, bordering on the irrelevant. He waited and rocked in place, as is his custom in a standing conversation—a heel-and-toe rock. The stadium lights glinted in his thick glasses. No one knew the answer. He told them happily. Red Foley of the New York *Daily News* countered, "All right, but how many strikeouts does Millan have so far this season?" (Felix Millan is the Mets' second baseman.) Farrell replied, "About twenty." Foley nodded, with a little smile.

Before coming to the game, I happened to re-read the short story, "The Fastest Runner on Sixty-First Street," the first Farrell work I'd ever read. The passion with which Farrell described the Runner running epitomizes the joys that may be first experienced from the legitimate triumphs of an athletic skill. Farrell went on in that story to paint the youthful dreams and delicious possibilities of life as seen in the fourteen-year-old runner, Morty Aiken:

> He had gained his second wind. He felt himself running, felt the movement of his legs and muscles, felt his arms, felt the sensation of his whole body as he raced. . . . Never had he run so swiftly. . . .
>
> He gained the reputation of being the best runner, for his age, on the South Side of Chicago. . . . Although he was outwardly modest, Morty had his dreams. . . . He was impatient to go to high school and get into high school track meets. . . . He dreamed that he would be called the Human Streak of Lightning. . . . and the most beautiful girl in the world would marry him. . . .

I first read that story when I was about fourteen, while at Sullivan High School on the north side of Chicago, only several miles and several years away from Farrell's scene. It made a deep impact. I was involved in schoolboy sports, primarily baseball and basketball. And the delights and strengths and mysteries of physical growth (and of burgeoning inner visions) as described by Farrell in the story struck an emphatic chord within me—the dramatic, sudden, tragic murder of the boy-runner notwithstanding.

Later, I would read Farrell's baseball diary; a book of reminiscences; selections from his fiction and from magazine stories; *Studs Lonigan,* in which there was a cruel park football game and a wistful baseball pickup game; and a goodly number of magazine articles and short stories (such as the boxing piece, "Twenty-five Bucks"). Most if not all contain the symbiotic qualities of romance and disaster that I first found in "The Fastest Runner on Sixty-First Street" and which, it seems, is a thread through Farrell's work generally.

Farrell uses sports in his writing more than many "important" or "serious" writers. "Sports," Farrell told me, "is an integral part of the American way of life, and of the dreams of boys. It was for me when I was growing up. I determined when I first began writing that I was going to include in my work aspects of sports, particularly baseball."

The integration of sport into the lives of his most important characters, such as Danny O'Neill (who may most resemble Farrell himself), was noted by Edgar M. Branch: "[Danny's] increasing interest in baseball is a good example of Farrell's use of common materials to suggest the dynamics of growth." In "Father and Son," a novel in the Danny O'Neill pentalogy, the fifteen-year-old Danny writes a disguised letter to Connie Mack, manager of the Philadelphia A's baseball club. It reads in part: "Dear Mr. Mack: I am writing this letter to tip you off about a kid named O'Neill who is to be seen playing ball in Washington Park in Chicago all of the time. . . . You can pick this kid up for nothing and you will never regret it." It was signed, "A baseball fan, a real one—T. J. Walker." Farrell, when he was fifteen and a sandlot player, wrote just such a letter to Connie Mack. Neither O'Neill nor Farrell was signed by Mack. The dream unfulfilled did not destroy O'Neill. Nor did it Farrell. The actual attempt to realize a dream, regardless how outrageous, demonstrated a sense of character development for both. That each survived this small crisis and other personal and artistic blows of various magnitudes shows a strengthening of character. This kind of progression and balance is what the lessons of sport are ideally about.

Growing up, Farrell was a devoted baseball fan, particularly of the Chicago White Sox. It stirred his imagination. His dreams of one day playing in White Sox park before roaring fans was, he wrote, "describable as [being in] a walking coma." The players, for the most part, were "living legends," including Ed Walsh, whose no-hitter Farrell thrillingly witnessed in 1911 and wrote about years later in *A World I Never Made.*

Young Farrell would hang around the park after games. Once, a White Sox pitcher named Doc White got on a streetcar with Jim and his brother Earl. White recognized the boys.

> "The two kids," White told the conductor, paying their fare.
>
> When Jim arrived home, he burst into his apartment and loudly announced:
>
> "Doc White paid my carfare."
>
> "And who is he, Son?" asked his grandmother.
>
> "A baseball player."
>
> She replied, "He must be a nice man."

In a few years a certain section of his world would come crashing down on Farrell. One August day in 1920 he picked up the newspaper and read the headlined story that eight of the White Sox players had been charged with intentionally losing the previous fall's World Series to the Cincinnati Reds. "Shoeless" Joe Jackson was one of those sullied heroes. Shortly after the announcement of the alleged "fix," Farrell attended a game. The trial had not yet been set and the charged fixers were still playing. Farrell waited after the game under the stands. He watched the men come out of the dressing room. When Jackson appeared, "sportively" dressed in gray silk shirt, white duck trousers, and white shoes, his face "masked by impassivity," Farrell heard a fan call out, "It ain't true, Joe." And again, hauntingly, "It ain't true, Joe." Big Joe Jackson drove out in his "sportive" roadster, through a double file of silent fans, including Jim Farrell.

"My interest in baseball changed after this," Farrell wrote. "I was growing up [he was now 16] and this marked the end of my days of hero-worshiping baseball players. Many fans felt betrayed. I didn't. I felt sorry. I wished it weren't true."

Today, Farrell says that the "fix" did not destroy his faith in humanity, or anything else like that. "It was a great surprise and disappointment to learn of the events," said Farrell, "but I knew by this time that of course there was crookedness in the world."

Yet the crookedness exposed in this heretofore sacrosanct little world may have contributed to Farrell's sense of "reality," and in the way the Fastest Runner, the boxer of Twenty-five Bucks, Jewboy Schwartz in the football game in *Studs Lonigan,* had their dreams dashed.

For the next several years, Farrell "had no favorite team." Also, he was growing into another stage, one in which he developed a heightened interest in academics. His concern for sports appears to have somewhat abated. This may have had less to do with "the scandal" than with the normal maturing process of a bright and intellectually stimulated young man. Yet when Farrell began writing seriously for publication in his mid- and late-twenties, he wrote about the world he knew. It included sports.

The writing style itself was influenced by sportswriters, most importantly Ring Lardner. Lardner was sports columnist in the years that paralleled Farrell's discovery and involvement in sports as a youngster. Farrell says today that he read Lardner avidly and there is evidence of Farrell directly and unabashedly aping Lardner's colloquial style. Lardner captured the nuances of the highly individualized speech of ballplayers, many of whom came from small towns and retained also their parochial patois.

In Farrell's third year at St. Cyril High School he had printed in the school magazine a rather strained parody with the attempt at a Lardner touch. The piece was called, "Julius Caesar," and signed "by William Shakespeare and James Farrell." It began: "Caesar is the toughest guy in Rome, which has cleaned up all the bad eggs in the surrounded country. The last bird he socked, which is Cassius, spent two months in the hospital; the only reason he didn't visit the undertaker was, that guy wouldn't take him; and after he kissed the hospital a sad ado, he spent two weeks in a beauty parlor trying to get his mush to look something like a face. . . . "

Today, Farrell believes he was fortunate to have a writer of the stature of Lardner to read daily. He felt Lardner's influence was significant in developing his own ear for the vernacular. A few years ago, in discussing a novel dealing with the Black Sox scandal on which he was working (and still is), Farrell said of the dialogue: "Baseball players don't say 'bingle' for base hit or 'twin killing' for double play. But they do say things like 'soupbone' for pitching arm. And one once said to me, 'I didn't have much zip or zum on the ball today.'" (Interestingly, Ernest Hemingway, who was five years older than Farrell and who grew up in the Chicago area, also credited his early writing influence to reading Lardner's sports columns; he also imitated Lardner's style while writing for his high school paper.)

Farrell says that he is sometimes asked, "When will the great novel about baseball be written?" "Such answers," he wrote in a New York *Times Sunday Book Review* piece on sports books (August 10, 1958), "are unanswerable—or rather, answers are meaningless. Great books are like accidents, and their subject-matter cannot be predicted. But it may well be that the great, or at least the definitive, work of fiction on baseball has already been written and that readers keep forgetting about it or keep paying mere lip service. I refer, of course, to Ring Lardner's *You Know Me, Al.* And later in the same review Farrell quotes Virginia Woolf on Lardner's baseball novel: "Games give him [Lardner] what society gives his English brother." That is, the most penetrating insights into the indigenous qualities of the people of each country.

Although Farrell's interests continued to broaden in middle age, he continued to keep abreast of sports. He still does.

In the press box at the game Farrell and I attended together last August, he noted the wind conditions and how the outfielders adjusted their positions accordingly, and observed the pitching strategies. He noted, for example, that the pitchers throw Dave Kingman, slugger of the Mets, "more fastballs than they ought to. I don't think they understand." One sports writer brought a paperback copy of *Studs Lonigan* to the game with the hope of seeing Farrell and getting his autograph for his wife, "who is a big fan of yours." Earl Lawson, a Cincinnati sportswriter covering this game between the Reds and Mets, recalled the first time he had ever seen a copy of *Studs Lonigan.* "It was in a foxhole in

Guadalcanal," Lawson told Farrell. "One of the men in the line ahead of us left it behind. Then I'd see others reading it from time to time. But it wasn't the biggest book of the war. *Forever Amber* was. That was the spiciest novel of the day. Our one copy was all ripped out and each guy in the company would read one page and then pass it on to the next guy." Farrell enjoyed listening to that very much.

Farrell said that he likes baseball still because it is a beautiful game to watch, because it is relaxing, and because it has such nostalgic appeal. "It's the part of your boyhood you want to remember," he said. "You see games now and you remember the games you used to see. It's a dream that lingers, and retains a hold on us from boyhood through maturity and into adulthood.

"For some, the hold is stronger than for others. I wrote in one of my Danny O'Neill novels that we are a nation of frustrated ballplayers."

I asked if he was.

"No, my frustration eventually sank away," he said. "I did dream of being a big-league star when I was young, the way Freddie Lindstrom went from playing in knickers in Washington Park to the big leagues in the early '20s. I remember him when he was a kid in Chicago. I was a pretty good player. And the last time up in high school I hit a terrific wallop. But I realized after awhile that my eyes were bad—I'm far-sighted—and I really couldn't see the ball well enough to hit consistently. And once in a high school game I struck out three times with the bases loaded." (Danny O'Neill, at age eighteen, also struck out in a tight situation. Farrell wrote: "Yes, after kidding himself about his destiny, and having the nerve to think that he would be a star like Ty Cobb and Eddie Collins, he was a miserable failure. He was a bust, a flat tire. . . . ")

"And sometimes," continued Farrell now, "the frustration recurs. It's spasmodic. But I'm quite satisfied with what I do do. If I weren't, it would be just too damn bad at my age.

"But, you know, I went down to spring training to do a magazine story when I was fifty-four and I got into the batting cage and hit some balls. Paul Waner, who is in the Hall of Fame, said he liked my swing.

"Nowadays, one of the most useful things baseball provides for me is when I go home after a game. I think about some of the plays and how they looked and how the game went. It transports me, calms me and puts me to sleep."

A. James Memmott

SOURCE: "Wordsworth in the Bleachers: The Baseball Essays of Roger Angell," in *Journal of American Culture,* Vol. 5, No. 4, Winter, 1982, pp. 52-56.

[In the following essay, Memmott explores the major themes of Angell's baseball essays and compares his work to the poems of William Wordsworth.]

Since 1962 Roger Angell has written more than thirty essays on baseball for *The New Yorker* magazine, and these essays have been gathered into two collections: *The Summer Game* (1972) and *Five Seasons: A Baseball Companion* (1977). Angell, a fiction writer and editor, is not a sports reporter, and *The New Yorker* is hardly *The Sporting News,* but Angell's essays are, without question, the best writing on baseball that has been produced in recent years. Explaining his discovery of baseball's mystery and beauty, Angell writes in the introduction to *A Summer Game,* "how could I have guessed . . . that baseball, of all team sports anywhere, should turn out to be so complex, so rich and various in structure and aesthetics and emotion, as to convince me, after ten years as a [baseball] writer and forty years as a fan, that I have not yet come close to its heart."[1] This statement neatly categorizes Angell's interest in baseball. Structure, aesthetics and emotion—how the game works, appears and feels—form the themes of his baseball writings; they are, in a sense, the three bases which lead toward home plate, the mysterious heart of the game itself. To get near to home plate Angell uses a method quite different from that of the typical baseball writer. He notes that he writes "at length for a leisurely and most generous weekly magazine" (*SG,* p. x), and that he is not hard pressed by deadline or by space limitation. While the sports writer for a daily newspaper must strike his lead and fix his view of the game before the fans have left the stadium, Angell has the time to sit and think awhile, to replay the game within his mind until its telling images fix themselves upon his memory. These images in turn become the lyrical passages within the essays, spots of inspiration amidst the reportage. They seem to stop and bring back not only the game but time itself and to achieve, fleetingly, the victory of time which Angell finds latent in the structure of baseball itself.

Roger Angell's prefatory account of his themes and his methods in *The Summer Game* echoes another introduction, the landmark "Preface to the Second Edition of Lyrical Ballads" (1800) of William Wordsworth. The Lake Country would seem a long way from Shea Stadium, and Wordsworth an unlikely denizen of the press box, but the resemblance is too clear to be ignored. Like Wordsworth, Angell finds emblematic images, "spots of time," which break down the distinction between the present and the past and restore the feeling that had been lost. And like Wordsworth, Angell achieves this restoration of emotion by the paradoxical technique of getting away from the event in order that he can bring the event back. In the "Preface" Wordsworth outlines his theory and his method: "poetry is the spontaneous overflow of powerful emotions: it takes its origin from emotion recollected in tranquility: the emotion is contemplated till, by a species of reaction, the tranquility gradually disappears, and an emotion, kindred to that which was before the subject of contemplation, is gradually produced, and does itself actually exist in the mind."[2] As outlined by Wordsworth, the movement is from event, to tranquil contemplation of the emotional reaction to the event, to the appearance of an emotion similar to the original emotion. Upon the page, within the poem, the recalled experience stands as what Wordsworth called a "spot of time" in which the past is recalled as if it were present. The spot of time records not so much the details of the experience as the feeling felt during the experience. In *The Prelude* (1850) Wordsworth distinguishes between "mere memory," the intellectual recollection of what happened, and the soul's memory, the recollection of what was felt: "the soul / Remembering how she felt, but what she felt / Remembering not."[3] Like Wordsworth, Angell seeks to recall and recreate emotions; he writes, "my main job, as I conceived it, was to continue to give the feel of things—to explain the baseball as it happened to me, at a distance and in retrospect" (*SG*, p. x.).

It can be seen that Angell imitates Wordsworth's technique of getting away in time and space from the experience in order to understand it, as he seeks to recreate his emotional response, what he calls "the feel of things." Angell does not attempt to describe how the player felt while playing, though often he will let the players do this themselves, and he will record their comments. Many sportswriters do try to see the game through the player's eye, or at least they imply that they are on the field and not in the press box. But Angell makes his vantage point clear; he stresses the fact that he sees the game from the stands at a self-imposed distance. Watching the game from afar and then recollecting it in tranquility, Angell achieves a sense of the whole process. Steve Blass, the former Pittsburgh pitcher, endorses Angell's perspective, telling him, "'Hey, you really see how it *works* from here, can't you? . . . Down there, you've got to look at it all in pieces. No wonder it's so hard to play this game right'."[4] How baseball works, its structure, can be perceived from afar with the help of an optical trick. In the last two paragraphs of "The Interior Stadium," the concluding essay of *The Summer Game,* Angell instructs the reader to "sit quietly in the upper stand and look at the field. Half close your eyes against the sun, so that the players recede a little, and watch the movements of baseball. The pitcher, immobile on the mound, holds the inert white ball, his little lump of physics. Now, with abrupt gestures, he gives it enormous speed and direction, converting it suddenly into a line, a moving line. The batter wielding a plane, attempts to intercept the line and acutely alter it, but he fails; the ball, a line again, is redrawn to the pitcher, in the center of this square, the diamond" (*SG*, p. 302). The trick of half closing the eyes offers one a view of baseball's substructure, the permanent forces and immutable laws which govern it. But the structure is only the first part of Angell's trinity of structure, aesthetics and emotions, and the game as seen through half-closed eyes is not the whole game, for it is baseball rendered abstract and

dehumanized; it resembles a Saul Steinberg drawing such as the one which accompanied "The Interior Stadium" in its *New Yorker* publication. The half-closed eye views a game which is, in Angell's words, "neat, pretty and satisfying" (*SG*, p. 303), something akin to a mathematical equation, but the fully-opened eye allows one to see players upon the field and to witness the game in three dimensions. It is this game which Angell recalls in his soul's memory, which he recreates in arrested images which are to his essays what the "spots of time" are to Wordsworth's poetry.

In "The Interior Stadium" Angell recalls moments which have remained in his father's memory and his own memory: "Sixty-seven years have gone by, yet Nat Lajoie is in plain view, and the ball still floats over to Terry Turner. Well, my father is eighty-one now, and old men are great rememberers of the distant past. But I am fifty and I also bring things back: Lefty Gomez, skinny-necked and frighteningly wild, pitching his first game at Yankee Stadium. . . . Old John McGraw, in a business suit and a white fedora, sitting lumpily in a dark corner of the dugout at the Polo Grounds and glowering out at the field. Babe Ruth, wearing a new, bright yellow glove, trotting out to right field—a swollen ballet dancer, with those delicate, almost feminine feet and ankles" (*SG*, pp. 293-294). One cannot read this and similar passages without appreciating Angell's ability to strike the right phrase and his ability to add humanizing details, not to bring heroes down to size but rather to give them their individual and unique attributes. McGraw sits "lumpily"; Ruth trots to right field, almost preening with his "new, bright yellow glove." If one read these descriptions in a novel, he would conclude that the details served as indexes of character, signs of the inner self of the individual described. And it seems safe to argue that Angell, like the novelist, intends these descriptions as economical explanations of McGraw and Ruth. As in these images, Angell's spots of time often show the player on the brink of play or immediately after the action has taken place. Consequently, Angell's suspended spots of time, his verbal images, are themselves images of suspended or potential moments.

But if the image captures the player's inner character, his potential, the description of the action itself is technically redundant for, at least in Angell's essays, character predicts action. Consequently, Angell, in his reports on the World Series, will often condense the historical elements of the game—who won, who lost—and enlarge what might be called the peripheral moments. It is as if to say that Roberto Clemente could be understood by closely watching him take batting practice, as Angell did come to understand Clemente in 1971. Angell's verbal spots of time are often images of men alone, players on a team who are separated from their teammates by the literal space of the playing field and by the game's existential requirements that the player act alone, that he hit by himself and catch the ball in his own hand. Angell writes: "what is certain in baseball is that someone, perhaps several people, will fail. They will be searched out, caught in the open, and defeated, and there will be no confusion about it or sharing of the blame. This is sure to happen, because what baseball requires of its athletes, of course, is nothing less than perfection, and perfection cannot be eased or divided. Every movement of every game, from first pitch to last out, is measured and recorded against an absolute standard, and thus each success is also a failure" (*SG*, p. 296). Angell seldom speaks to baseball's social lessons, perhaps because he seems the game as an individual and not a communal experience, and exercise which tests the player and not the team. Other sports, especially football, lend themselves more easily to sociology because they demand that the team act as a unit. The baseball player is forever in an existential predicament; he is vulnerable, exposed and alone, and his prior good deeds and great plays do not help him much at all in meeting the demands of the present. As Gilbert Sorrentino argues, baseball is essentially unfair: "No matter how good the pitcher has been, he must get the last out. . . . What he *has done* has no effect on the batter he must face next. The eight men who assist him can only assist him after the ball is released."[5]

Angell's images of solitary men at play contain implicit assumptions about human nature and the human predicament. They suggest that the baseball player is to be admired because he faces difficult tasks with courage, a courage which he often disguises with the very grace with which he performs his role. And though player and spectator are separated by space and by task, both are alike in their essential isolation and in their vulnerability to change, their susceptibility to accident. Though the spectator cannot feel *with* the player he can feel *for* the player, especially because the player's act can take the spectator outside of the "real" world for a few minutes. The spectator can extend sympathy to the player for he understands the difficulty of the player's tasks, and watching the game can involve a sympathetic, imaginative connection between spectator and player. Consequently, though the very space and nature of baseball reinforce the view that men are isolated from one another, the game also provides the opportunity for men to be brought together through shared feelings, feelings which are irresistible and spontaneous and potentially recollectable. Angell implies that while watching and playing a sport are inevitably different actions, they are similar experiences in that they temporarily liberate man from reality and place him in a different kind of space and time. As Angell points out, baseball's time is different from clock time; the action is measured by outs and not by minutes. Conceivably the game could go on forever: "Since baseball time is measured only in outs, all you have to do is succeed utterly; keep hitting, keep the rally alive, and you have defeated time. You remain forever young. The players below us—Mayes, DiMaggio, Ruth, Snodgrass—swim and blur in memory, the ball floats over to Terry Turner, and the end of this game may never come" (*SG*, p. 303).

Of course the other side of the coin is that the end of the game must come if the game is to have an existence separate from ordinary reality. Roger Callois recognizes this when he argues that games are separate, "circumscribed within limits of space and time which are precise and fixed in advance."[6] The end of a baseball game—the last out—is a fixed and inflexible end, however long it may be in coming. But here I am speaking of the real game, and Angell may refer to the game of baseball in the mind, the game in which Mays and Snodgrass can take the field at once. It is this game which seems to break down history and connect the present with the past. Significantly, it joins Angell with his father, as the father's memories are passed on like a legacy to the son. The virtues of the mental game are shown forth in another of Angell's essays, an article on Steve Blass, a former major league pitcher who inexplicably lost his control. Angell begins his account of Blass' fall from glory with a detailed description of a photograph. The description of the picture is a microcosm of Angell's themes and techniques:

> The photograph shows a perfectly arrested moment of joy. On one side—the left, as you look at the picture—the catcher is running toward the camera at full speed, with his upraised arms spread wide, his body is tilting toward the center of the picture, his mask is held in his right hand, his big glove is still on his left hand, and his mouth is open in a gigantic shout of pleasure. Over on the right, another player, the pitcher, is just past the apex of an astonishing leap that has brought his knees up to his chest and his feet well up off the ground. Both of his arms are flung wide, and he, too, is shouting. His hunched, airborne posture makes him look like a man who has just made a running leap over a sizable object—a kitchen table, say. By luck, two of the outreaching hands have overlapped exactly in the middle of the photograph, so that the pitcher's bare right palm and fingers are silhouetted against the catcher's glove, and as a result the two men are linked and seemed to be executing a figure in a manic and difficult dance. There is a further marvel—a touch of pure fortune—in the background, where a spectator in dark glasses, wearing a dark suit, has risen from his seat in the grandstand and is lifting his arms in triumph. This, the third and central Y in the picture, is immobile. It is directly behind the overlapping hand and glove of the dancers, and it binds and recapitulates the lines of force and the movements and the themes of the work, creating a composition as serene and well ordered as a Giotto. The subject of the picture, of course, is classical—the celebration of the last out of the seventh game of the World Series (*FS*, pp. 223-224)

Angell appreciates the picture because it shows a "perfectly arrested moment of joy"; as a maker of verbal images which attempt to capture a moment and arrest time, he praises the camera's ability to stop the action at a perfectly emblematic moment. And while Angell did not take the picture of Sanguillen and Blass running, leaping toward each other, the picture becomes his as he interprets it and stresses those elements which he finds important. He is, first of all, taken by its aesthetic, structural qualities. The catcher's outspread arms are reflected by the pitcher's arms, and both figures are recapitulated and bound by the spectator in the middle of the frame whose upraised and immobile arms form the Central Y. The Roger Angell who discovers this internal symmetry within the picture is the same man who squints his eyes and discovers the interweaving lines of force upon the baseball field. But, as always, structure is only part of the story, and it is not the picture's arrangement which captures Angell's heart. He writes: "I am not a Pittsburger, but looking at this photograph never fails to give me pleasure, not just because of its aesthetic qualities but because its high-bounding happiness so perfectly brings back that eventful World Series and that particular gray autumn afternoon in Baltimore and the wonderful and inexpungible expression of joy that remained on Steve Blass's face after the game ended" (*FS,* p. 224). Consequently, the image brings back a moment of joy, an inexpungible expression that Angell witnessed and shared. In a sense, Angell becomes the spectator in the center of the picture who reflects the player's motions and emotions.

But while the union between Sanguillen, Blass and the spectator is recorded and recalled, Angell suggests in his description that the union is also a physical illusion, though it may have been, and may still be, a spiritual reality. The camera's elimination of spatial distance brings the background and foreground of the picture together so that Sanguillen and Blass *seem* to touch and dance, though the reality is that they are apart. The spectator, too, is further away from the players than he seems to be. Furthermore, Angell finds embedded within the picture a suggestion that the moment of joy is lost as soon as it is gained. The picture catches Blass just after the moment of his greatest triumph and at the beginning of his decline. He is "just past the apex" of his astonishing leap, and he will never reach such a height again. But the fact of the decline was not known at the time of the victory, and Angell or I may impose the present upon the past by looking at the picture as a premonition of Blass's fall. The picture's primary message is not that Blass is about to go down but that he has succeeded and that he has reacted to his success with a joyous leap. The leap reveals Blass' open, responsive temperament, a temperament which will remain unchanged throughout the testing times that are to follow the World Series victory. The point of "Down the Drain" becomes not that Blass has lost his control but that he has reacted with grace and humility to the loss of his control.

To prove that Blass's decline is unusual, even extraordinary, Angell offers extensive statistical data to establish how good Blass was and how bad he became. Angell writes, "of all the mysteries that surround the Steve Blass story, perhaps the most mysterious is the fact that his collapse is unique. There is no other player in recent baseball history—at least none with Blass's record and credentials—who has lost his form in such a sudden and devastating fashion and been totally unable to recover" (*FS,* p. 249). Having made this generalization, Angell turns to case histories, dismissing the ever wild Rex Barney as a man who had no control to lose and the suddenly wild Dick Radatz as a player who let himself get out of shape. The case histories are supplemented by oral testimonies to Blass's control and loss of control from his teammates, coaches and friends. Everyone seems to have a theory about the decline of Steve Blass, but the most convincing of the explanations is that which Blass offers himself: "'There's one possibility nobody has brought up. . . . I don't think anybody's ever said that maybe I just lost my control. Maybe your control is something that can just go. It's no big thing, but suddenly it's gone'" (*FS,* p. 256). Again we are given a non-rational, but convincing testimony to baseball's complexity and difficulty. Blass and Angell imply that statistics and science will only carry one so far, that there are some things that one cannot know and probably should not even question. But if Blass's control is lost on the real playing field it is not gone for good upon the imaginary turf of the interior stadium; it can be recreated just as Angell can call back his remembrances of baseball past. Angell tells how he used Blass to pitch an imaginary game against the Cincinnati Reds. Warmed to the task, Blass narrates his pitches and Angell calls the balls and strikes. The imaginary game then shifts parks and Blass is once again pitching against the 1971 Baltimore Orioles. Sanguillen catching; Angell umpiring; in full control Blass strikes out Boog Powell; the ball floats toward the plate and the end of the game may never come.

But retreats into the interior stadium are more and more difficult for Angell because baseball itself seems more and more threatened by the real world. In his introduction to *Five Seasons,* Angell writes, "we have begun to understand at last that baseball is most of all an enormous and cold-blooded corporate enterprise, and as such is probably a much more revelatory and disturbing part of our national psyche than we had supposed. . . . Most grown-ups, I believe, will find little pleasure now if they try to isolate the game—simply to sit in the stands as before and smile upon the familiar patterns and adventures on the bright lawns below" (*FS,* p. 8). Discussions of free agent negotiations, players' strikes and owners' lockouts weigh down an essay and a heart, but they also serve to set off and make more special the times when the patterns and adventures on the field are exhilarating and joyous. If rarer, the spots of time in *Five Seasons* seem brighter than those in *The Summer Game,* and perhaps the brightest of them is Angell's account of Carlton Fisk's winning home run in the sixth game of the 1975 World Series.

Again, as in the case of Steve Blass's marvelous leap, Angell has to describe something he did not see, for while he was in the park watching the ball, the television cameras caught Fisk "waving wildly, weaving and writhing and gyrating along the first-base line, as he wished the ball fair, *forced* it fair with his entire body." But if he did not see Fisk's dance, the home run did lead Angell to think of other dancers, Boston fans throughout New England, "jumping up and down in their bedrooms and kitchens and living rooms, and in bars trailers, and even in boats here and there, I suppose, on the back-country roads (a lone driver getting the news over the radio and blowing his horn over and over, and finally pulling up and getting out and leaping up and down on the cold macadam, yelling in to the night), and all of them, for once at least, utterly joyful and believing in that joy—alight with it" (*FS,* p. 305). Here Angell creates an image of something he did not see; at this moment he may be more Milton than Wordsworth, though a cheerful Milton to be sure. The image of the lone driver leaping up and down on the cold macadam connected in joy with Carlton Fisk, with Roger Angell, and with the reader of the essay recreates and affirms the joy that was felt and, for a moment, comes close to the heart of baseball and to the heart itself.

NOTES

[1] New York: Viking, 1972, p. x. Subsequent references to *The Summer Game (SG)* will be cited in the text.

[2] *The Poetical Works of William Wordsworth,* ed. Ernest De Selincourt (Oxford: Clarenden, 1944), pp. 400-401.

[3] *The Prelude,* ed. Ernest De Selincourt (London: Oxford, 1928), II, 315-17.

[4] Roger Angel, *Five Seasons: A Baseball Companion* (New York: Simon and Schuster, 1977), p. 240. Subsequent references to *Five Seasons (FS),* will be cited in the text.

[5] "Baseball," in *IQ: Baseball Issue,* 10, p. 94.

[6] As quoted in "Homo Ludens Revisited," by Jacques Ehrmann, in *Game, Play and Literature,* edited by Ehrmann (Boston: Beacon, 1968), p. 35.

SPORTS, LITERATURE, AND SOCIAL ISSUES

Robert W. Cochran

SOURCE: "The Bench Warmer with a Thousand Faces: Sports Fiction and the Democratic Ideal," in *The Achievement of American Sports Literature: A Critical Appraisal,* edited by Wiley Lee Umphlett, Bucknell University Press, 1991, pp. 80-99.

[*In the following essay, Cochran analyzes the emergence of the common citizen, or everyman, as protagonist in recent baseball literature.*]

Having paved the way for the favorable critical reception of sports fiction in America, baseball fiction deserving of consideration as serious literature is now being practiced by its third generation of authors. Ring Lardner, the patriarch and a generation unto himself, was followed rather directly by Mark Harris, though perhaps scarcely at all by Bernard Malamud, Robert Coover, and Philip Roth, all authors of the very first rank, each of whom has written just one baseball novel. To these four second-generation worthies must be added Eliot Asinof, for both his novel *Man on Spikes* (1955) and his study of the Black Sox scandal, *Eight Men Out* (1963). Distinguished offspring of *Eight Men Out* are W. P. Kinsella's *Shoeless Joe* (1982), Eric Rolfe Greenberg's *The Celebrant* (1983), and Harry Stein's *Hoopla* (1983), as well as an Off-Broadway play, Lawrence Kelley's *Out!*

Now, with splendid contributions from an ever-growing list of authors that includes—in addition to Kinsella, Greenberg, and Stein—Barry Beckham, David Carkeet, Donald Hays, John Hough, Jr., Robert Mayer, Philip O'Connor, George Plimpton, and Nancy Willard, novels and short stories with baseball as an ingredient have emerged in great profusion but not so much that at least some meaningful patterns may be discerned.

As sports fiction—baseball fiction, especially—has come of age in the 1970s and '80s, the worth of the common citizen has emerged as a major theme. It is as though several authors had anticipated a pronouncement Thomas Boswell made as a Parthian shot in a syndicated column released during the summer of 1988: "One reason that baseball films and fiction almost always fail is that hyperbole rarely works except in reality." Realizing before the appearance of Boswell's column that the point is sound, many serious authors of sports fiction have concentrated on protagonists who are not star athletes and on plots that do not follow a pennant drive or a Super Bowl week as ready-made scaffolds for organization.

Sport no doubt initially does invite a literary treatment of extremes, since the sports world of action on the field affords on the one hand a realm of heroes and hero worship, of romantic promise and of pastoral setting, and on the other, of worn-out arms, torn-up knees, and careers that at best are brief when compared to a lifespan, which in its turn is altogether too brief. And, since both literature for juveniles, whether past or present, and moving pictures for a mass audience, even to the present day, continue to supply a presumably yearned-for, literal, scoreboard victory, it follows that a sobering, corrective sense of tragedy would seem to be the remaining line to be followed in serious literature. Or, if not precisely tragedy, then certainly the high road of elevated significance and cosmic proportion. And so it is with Malamud's *The Natural,* Coover's *Universal Baseball Association,* and Roth's mock-heroic *The Great American Novel.* It is all the more heartening, then, that what today has been arrived at is a settled sense of coexistence between sport and art, born of a confidence that the honest pursuit of accomplishment in whatever human endeavor, and of fidelity to self under whatever sorts of pressures, need offer no apology for themselves.

Of the many trends and themes emerging from the extraordinarily rich sports fiction of the last two decades, a pronounced emphasis has been given to expressions of faith in democracy. Such a faith is not likely to attach to the star athlete, or at any rate certainly not to the star athlete while he or she is on the playing field, living life "all the way up," as Hemingway's Jake Barnes says of bullfighters. From a competitive realm that features Tom Boswell's "hyperbolic" reality—a realm of potential soaring heroes and Casey-at-the-Bat goats—several authors of fine fiction have created protagonists who occupy an intermediate position between the star on the field and the fan in the bleachers—a coach, an umpire, a sportswriter—in the service of large democratic themes. Eschewing the literary equivalents of Ruth and DiMaggio, these authors concentrate on the journeyman ballplayer, or the professional player as exploited chattel, or the successful high school player become big-league umpire, or the unsuccessful prep school player become sportswriter—or the boy on the sandlot—in a demonstration that sports (and again, especially baseball) supply sustaining threads in the fabric of American life. The upshot of this emphasis is the clear implication that the outlook of Arthur Miller in "Tragedy and the Common Man," as the playwright titled his celebrated companion-piece to *Death of a Salesman,* can be revised; that perhaps in the present generation the Willy Lomans of the Republic can be helped to recognize in themselves the carpenters and farmers they are meant to be and can learn to take pride and pleasure in their work, so that further tragic waste can be averted. The fathers will no longer need to fill their sons "so full of hot air [that the sons] could never stand taking orders from anybody," as Biff Loman so accurately describes his condition, having fallen from the perilous heights of stardom as a high school quarterback. Perhaps with the proper perspective the Biff Lomans of America can derive solid satisfaction from being "a dime a dozen" and can come to assess their personal value in less-demeaning figures of speech. In a nation still largely gauged to the Waterman and Peters model of a "search for excellence" as the only lifetime pursuit that can lead to authentic success, these authors of sports fiction assert that a place must be found for the ordinary achievements and enjoyments of the average citizen.

It may be instructive to return to Boswell's 1988 column, and in conjunction with it, drop back in time to the 1984 movie *The Natural,* starring Robert Redford, and to Bernard Malamud's 1952 novel, *The Natural.* In his essay composed on the occasion of the one-hundredth anniversary of the popular favorite "Casey at the Bat," Donald Hall reminds us that we are the Mudville crowd, first cheering on our hero and then agonizing over his failure. In that same position, the reader of Malamud's novel hopes along with the character Iris

Lemon that Roy will break out of his slump, as for a time, with Iris's encouragement, he does. But of course Roy does not succeed finally in the novel, just as of course he must be made to succeed in the movie version, happy endings remaining *de rigueur* in sports films.

Malamud's title should be appreciated for its ambiguity: Roy Hobbs not only has a natural, God-given talent for baseball—first as a pitcher whiffing the Whammer and then as a major league hitter—but Roy *(roi)* Hobbs *(habitants)* also is emphatically and perhaps even particularly susceptible to human error. Still, Roy is one of the select few superb athletes for whom Harriet Bird reserves her silver bullets. Unlike Robert Redford's Hobbs, Malamud's does not (cannot) slug a dramatic game- and pennant-winning home run. Malamud's Roy has erred, has failed to learn a valuable lesson from his personal history, and so has been condemned to repeat that error. Having undergone the torture of being gutshot by Harriet Bird, Roy nonetheless becomes an enthralled New York Knight for a second time, this time enthralled by the "sick-breasted" Memo Paris. Hobbs is a tragic figure, and he gains tragic stature by recognizing that he has failed to learn. The prideful Roy Hobbs considers it beneath his dignity to settle for and to settle down with Iris Lemon, very pointedly because Iris is a thirty-three-year-old grandmother. The only bride acceptable to the great Roy Hobbs is a veritable Marilyn Monroe. Malamud sees his audience as a society bedazzled by beauty contests, a society where wives are chosen for a surface pulchritude that can enhance their husbands' images and further their husbands' careers.

Malamud's keen interest in this topic is shown also in his short story "The Girl of My Dreams," in which the protagonist early in the story admits that he prefers a "looker." Eventually he learns enough to save his soul and his writing career by embracing his plump and middle-aged but doting and supportive landlady. And Mark Harris shares this concern of Malamud's in the third of his Henry Wiggen novels, *A Ticket for a Seamstitch.*

Since athletic-star talent and movie-star beauty are not vouchsafed many of us, what evaluation of self is possible in a star-struck, media-hype, personality-cult society, authors of the third generation of American sport fiction seem to be asking and answering. In this undertaking they are following the lead of Malamud and Harris but with a more positive approach and a more firm, because longer developed, outcome. The topical approaches are essentially two in number: first, the removal of belittling stereotypes—those handy putdowns so frequently seized upon in a young and diverse nation of immigrants, whatever the arrival date, but now to be overcome through efforts at consciousness raising. A special subheading here features the upgrading of the reputation of have-nots through revision of accepted history of the Black Sox scandal of 1919, from the stunned condemnation of the players during the 1920s and beyond to the more recent identification of owner greed as the root cause of betrayal of the public trust. In addition to the attempt to remove blinding stereotypes, a second pronounced approach has been the explicit celebration of ordinariness. Ordinariness is, of course, by definition the normal human condition; it is also, or so it might be argued, a basic tenet of our Founding Fathers' ringing declaration. If the self sung by Richard Ford in *The Sportswriter* is no exuberant Walt Whitman, Ford is no less the celebrant of the democratic "word *En-Masse*" than was the good gray poet of a century and more ago.

The first image of the protagonist in respectable baseball fiction is that which is referred to familiarly today as the "dumb jock," ironically revealing in his own self and voice his coarseness, ignorance, and even stupidity. This style-setting protagonist is patronized by the reader, who cannot match the narrator's accomplishments on the field but who can share a laugh with the author at the character's expense and so cut the mighty down to size, whether hero or goat. In avoiding extravagant praise of the literary pioneer on the one hand and condescension toward him on the other, it is to be noted that Ring Lardner initiated with his busher, Jack Keefe, a tradition of the athlete as narrator that has been followed with distinction by Mark Harris with his "author" Henry Wiggen—and in altered but still indebted form by, among others, Jay Neugeboren with his chapters of "slave" narration by Mason Tidewater in *Sam's Legacy,* Harry Stein with his fictional George (Buck) Weaver of the historical Black Sox in *Hoopla,* and John Hough, Jr., with his umpire, Lee Malcolm, in *The Conduct of the Game.*

In assessing reader reaction to Lardner's character, Walton R. Patrick is surely correct when he says, ". . . the Keefe stories . . . had the appeal of humor to one class of readers and of satire to another . . ." (47). That is, some readers saw but others failed to notice the extent to which Lardner distanced himself from his busher by means of the epistolary technique, just as patently as the Southern-gentleman authors in the tradition of Old Southwest humor identified themselves with—indeed, virtually *as*—the narrator-observers within their stories. Formal and articulate, these narrators relayed to their audiences, in cacographic spelling and fractured grammar, entertaining tales of ring-tailed roarers and latter-day Mrs. Malaprops. In founding the literary tradition of the athlete who as first-person narrator was often made to look decidedly foolish, Lardner fixed in print the stereotype of the athlete as limited in experience, education, intelligence—any or all of the above.

In his novel *Hoopla,* from the vantage point of the 1980s, Harry Stein assigns his fictional character George D. Weaver an attitude that humanizes and upgrades in perceived intelligence and sensitivity one of the infamous Black Sox of 1919 (even if not the greatest player among them—Shoeless Joe Jackson had a doubly great grievance against Charles Comiskey, the skinflint owner, and the pitcher Eddie Cicotte was a heavily-mortgaged farmer). Stein's choice of the historical

Weaver for a fictional role rests on Weaver's having been aware of the World Series fix but having been unable to bring himself finally to participate in it; yet he was banned all the same by the inflexible and self-righteous first commissioner of baseball, Judge Kenesaw Mountain Landis. And so Stein's Weaver is emphatically a character with whom the reader can sympathize, warily at first and then ever more fully as Weaver's moral decency is seen both in and of itself and in marked contrast to the opportunism and amorality of the novel's alternating narrator, columnist Luther Pond. What Stein has his George Weaver say of baseball reporters in general and of the author of *You Know Me Al* in particular can well be imagined to be the opinion held by an athlete of whatever era:

> Us ballplayers did not call him Ring, but Old Owl Eyes. . . . When that book came out, there was all kinds of gas about how Old Owl Eyes was a great genius, and how fine it was that for the first time us ballplayers were not made out to be heroes, but just regular guys, and that in the book was what we were really like. Well, we did not ask to be heroes in the first place, but only got that way on account of the scribes themselves. . . . But this is how it always was with the writers, anyway. They were the ones that were really simple-minded, not us. (160-61)

A particularly well-contrived playing upon negative stereotypes is a story by W. P. Kinsella entitled "The Valley of the Schmoon." The story is not so incidentally a tribute to the comic genius Al Capp, whose "Li'l Abner" comic strip lends the story its title and whose unhappy final years contribute to the story's point. That point is delayed until the final sentence, in a switch reminiscent of Mark Twain's early work "The Dandy Frightening the Squatter," reminiscent even though Kinsella doubles the twist of the Twain reversal of expectations. What the two stories have in common is that in each the relatively elitist figure gets his comeuppance from the supposedly unsophisticated, apparently outclassed bumpkin. In "The Valley of the Schmoon" the joke is played on the highly educated, well-paid rookie ballplayer who is the increasingly alarmed passenger in the narrator's car; the joke is even more on the reader, however, who may grow a bit uneasy at the improbability of the story's premises but who is forced to admit that he or she has been outfoxed by Kinsella—a realization delayed until the reader has encountered the twist revealed in the final, uncompleted sentence.

Once the reader has finished the story and has viewed it in retrospect, he will appreciate how shrewdly the old coach must have maneuvered the rookie into what the rookie comes to fear is a potential death seat. Reminiscing about the old days, pretending to think he may be repeating himself, and explaining that he intends to commit suicide one day by crashing his car into an interstate overpass, the old-timer frightens the rookie into jumping from the car at his first opportunity and running off up the highway, away from what he regards as a despairing has-been whose life has degenerated into meaninglessness. But Kinsella has skillfully planted in the old coach's monologue three salient details. First is the story of how Babe Ruth as a rookie pitcher was victimized by Red Sox veterans into sleeping with his pitching arm in a sling to strengthen the arm before his pitching debut. Second is the information that in addition to being highly paid, the Mariners rookie is a college graduate, the fiancé of a psychologist and the son of a Shell Oil executive—in short, enviably well connected. And third is the narrator's assertion that his wife Lucy, whom he admits he still loves and toward whom he says he bears no grudge, divorced him to marry an owner of "six Ace Hardware stores." Then, as the rookie streaks down the highway in the story's penultimate moments, the narrator imperturbably follows up his "Geez, was it somethin' I said?" with words that demonstrate that the narrator is well aware that it was and that Kinsella has tricked the reader:

> Rookies. They never learn. Hell, I'd been in the majors for three years before I ever heard the word *sophisticated.* Let's see, by the time I get to Seattle it will be four A.M. That'll be seven in the East. I can phone Lucy before she goes to work. . . . (118)

Lucy is still the coach's wife, it dawns on the reader; the coach's tale of woe is an elaborate fabrication; and the coach's excuse for stopping here poses a threat to the rookie only because the coach has cunningly counted on the rookie to be attentive to the details of the coach's announced plans to commit the perfect, undetected suicide. Thus Kinsella shows the reader up as the true rookie, hooked on the stereotype of the old-time ballplayer as a maudlin and nostalgic recaller of the good old days and as a hopelessly naive revealer of his own considerable shortcomings.[1]

Readers. Maybe now they'll learn.

A second image of baseball fiction after that of the dumb jock is perhaps, properly speaking, not an image but rather an issue, at least once one proceeds beyond Malamud's Roy Hobbs and into characters created by the third generation of writers. This second image or issue is the hero, best exemplified in the words assigned by Eric Rolfe Greenberg to his fictional adaptation of the real-life sportswriter Hugh Fullerton, words about the hero Christy Mathewson that Fullerton addresses to the protagonist of *The Celebrant,* Jackie Kapp:

> "Have you ever considered what he is to himself? What it's like to be Christy Mathewson? . . . The world makes you a god and hates you for being human, and if you plead for understanding it hates you all the more. Heroes are never forgiven their success, still less their failure. . . . I want him to throw a no-hit game tomorrow, not for his sake but for mine. And don't you want the same, so you can cover him in glory? We're the worms that eat at the bodies of the great." (196)

Once readers have progressed beyond these two isolating conceptions of the performer on the field—conceptions of the stupid, self-absorbed athlete and of the supposedly superhuman hero—once the ground is cleared or raked smooth and level, one can read the current stage of some of the best sports fiction, where the human subjects are more nearly you and me (our name is Legion) and the topic our relationship to the game rather than the game itself. Among many of the works of the third generation of sports fiction, the protagonists are not the spotlighted stars. Even apparent exceptions, the fictional Buck Weaver of Harry Stein's *Hoopla* and the slugger Hog Durham of Donald Hays's *The Dixie Association,* for instance, are Ishmaels—outcasts whose survival as self-respecting human beings derives from their acceptance of figurative Queequegs and hence of themselves.

In this second but foremost of the two games involved in sports fiction—the game of literature—the reader is not mere spectator. He or she is invited to identify so closely with the protagonist as to be a virtual participant. Perhaps the most remarkable feature of Hough's *The Conduct of the Game* is that even while Hough pays tribute to the fictional tradition preceding him—and especially to Harris—he lets his protagonist, emphatically a common man, exhibit his decency and his intelligence as the teller of his own tale. Hough has carried the implications of the theme of faith in democracy to its logical conclusion, whereas in earlier decades, first Lardner and then Harris distanced themselves from their characters.

A most influential figure in the shift away from author conspiring with his reader to laugh at the athlete is Eliot Asinof, himself once a professional baseball player. Both in fiction, with *Man on Spikes,* and in nonfiction, with what Harry Stein authoritatively calls the "seminal" *Eight Men Out,* Asinof began what has amounted to a revisionist interpretation of baseball history. From this perspective, the inherent dignity of the individual in a democratic society is emphasized in the playing off of the protagonists against baseball executives and even exalted commissioners. Thus the reader's identification with the main character is twofold. First, athletic identification with the protagonist feeds, and feeds upon, beguiling dreams of stardom that the reader has carried over from childhood. Next is a far more realistic political and economic identification with the fictionalized Buck Weaver or Joe Jackson or the wholly fictional Mike Kutner, in these novels set in an era when professional athletes were poorly paid. Just as the Black Sox figures provide instances of the underdogs exploited by a power-drunk owner, so is Asinof's Kutner of *Man on Spikes* as surely a man on a bed of spikes as he is an athlete wearing spiked shoes.

A second gain that Hough makes over Lardner and Harris is in the low-key but deep-rooted way he finds for relating Lee Malcolm's experience to the reader's experience. The national pastime is very often touted for its broad appeal, an appeal that cuts across levels of income and taste. Hough's appeal is different, but it is as surely democratic and also less suspect as an instance of shared experience:

> Now Pam and I sat down in the dark, cool grass along the first base line, exactly where I'd plunked down after a ball game with Joey and Howie Gladding and Robert Nailer and the rest. When had it ended? What day in our lives had we played here for the last time? There had been one final game, one last swing of a bat, one last out made, and we'd mounted our bikes and pedaled home in a spring dusk for the last time ever, without knowing it. I wished I could remember that time. (57-58)

Hough carries the protagonist out of any team lineup and into a role in the game that the reader might be able to learn to perform, the role of arbiter. And then that protagonist is also victimized by the members of baseball's power structure.

In *The Conduct of the Game,* Hough brings to life not a major league ballplayer (Lee Malcolm's older brother Joey, dead at age 18 in a car crash, is the Dimaggio-like "natural" athlete) but rather a quite good (all-conference) high school outfielder who becomes for a brief period a major league umpire. This is not the stuff of romantic dreams. The story Lee Malcolm tells of himself concerns not the materials of boyhood fantasies, but instead the requisites for solid achievement. Lee's career choice is not the goal of starry-eyed, red-white-and-blue-blooded American boys; it is not to be sneered at, however—most readers (fans), at one time or another, probably here agreed with the outraged fan who screams "Kill the umpire." Hough's novel is not set on the plane of tragedy, but Lee Malcolm qualifies as a hero of sorts, a hero of properly scaled-down democratic proportions. In trying to qualify as a major league umpire and succeeding, and in fulfilling his obligations to the game of baseball and his responsibilities to others and to himself, Lee Malcolm remains true to his own better nature.

Hough exhibits a marked awareness of themes developed by his predecessors in this literary subgenre. The most obvious indebtedness is to Harris and his *Bang the Drum Slowly.* From the treatment of Lucinda Fragosi in the opening chapter of *Conduct of the Game*—the hapless butt of school bus joking until Lee's brother Joey, the star athlete, calls a halt to the youthful callousness—the practice of "ragging" is condemned, in a clear echoing of Henry Wiggen's final utterance in *Bang the Drum Slowly*: "From here on in I rag nobody." The list of underdogs not to be ragged is long, if not absolutely exhaustive. In addition to Lucinda of the novel's prelude section, it includes alcoholics in the person of Lee's father, Frank; little guys like Eddie Snyder, a would-be umpire; jocks assumed to be stereotypically stupid ("[Pam] said Coach Maretta was dumb. He wasn't." [47]); blacks (baseball star Ron Chapman); gays—a former English teacher who is now Lee Malcolm's

umpiring partner, Roy Van Arsadle; and, most importantly, just plain Janes and Bills like Lee's girl friend Vicky Vadnais and the first-person narrator himself. No reader will fail to see this stress pattern, and no reader of Mark Harris will fail to recognize it as an expansion on the lesson Henry Wiggen learned from coming to see Bruce Pearson's human worth during Bruce's final playing season, before he died of Hodgkin's disease.

Hough makes Lee Malcolm life size rather than the mythic larger than life. Nor does Hough invert the heroic; he does not reduce his protagonist to feckless cosmic pawn. Malamud's Roy Hobbs fails, both publicly as a hero and privately as a man. And Lee Malcolm would seem to a public within the novel to fail (were any public reaction included by Hough, which it is not)—for Lee is forced to resign after just his rookie year as a big-league umpire. Knowing the "inside story," however, which no newspaper reporter will ever even try to dig out, the reader sees Lee as unquestionably a successful human being. If the stage of *The Conduct of the Game* is not elevated and if the style is less than pyrotechnic, neither are the forces of temptation and manipulation at all distant for the reader. No translation is required: the character Pam Rogers recalls to the reader his own physically toothsome but ultimately undesirable high school crush, and the commissioner behaves like the reader's own high-handed, image-protecting boss.

The ultimate villain of *The Conduct of the Game* is not greed, as represented in the Black Sox novels and, rather allegorically, in *The Natural* by the team owner Judge Goodwill Banner and the one-eyed gambler Gus Sands. The ultimate villain of Hough's work is respectability, particularly in the person of the commissioner of baseball. The commissioner appears in a cameo role also facilitated by the revisionist view of the Black Sox scandal. The commissioner as a kind of latter-day unyielding Judge Landis represents society in hounding Van Arsdale to his death (whether that death is suicide or accident) and in requesting Malcolm's resignation. Thus Hough, like Asinof, Kinsella, Stein, and Greenberg, exposes immorality on what passes for the high road of integrity in representations made in print to hoodwink the public.

For all his championing of the common man, Hough does not emerge as a sentimentalist. Vicky Vadnais's father, the owner of a neighborhood bar, is a particularly well-drawn working stiff, utterly convincing in his love for his daughter and in his hope that Lee will become his daughter's husband. If Lee does not, Mr. Vadnais knows that Vicky will in all probability marry a longtime suitor who simply is not worthy of her.

The protagonist's fundamental decency as depicted in *The Conduct of the Game* is in essence an adult version of the cloyingly didactic school-sports novel written for a juvenile audience. But for that very reason, in these secular, iconoclastic and dry-eyed times, the portrayal of such decency places enormous demands on the author, since, without constant application of taste and vigilance, wholesomeness readily turns saccharine and silly.

In "K-Mart," like "The Valley of the Schmoon," one of the best of several fine stories in Kinsella's collection *The Further Adventures of Slugger McBatt,* the first-person narrator raises the besetting question of where the line is to be drawn between sports fiction and fiction that is not to be so categorized:

> Jamie Kirkendahl [the narrator when he was a boy] would say this is not a story about baseball. Perhaps I [the narrator as an adult and a professional writer] should let you [the reader] be the judge of that. (78)

The reader has little difficulty in judging, thanks to such passages as the following:

> I suppose it was sometime in my twenties when I realized that my *baseball days,* those three summers I spent in Northside, had so far been the best days of my life. That time when baseball was like the sun lighting my days. . . . My suspicions, shadows, gray, disturbing, like animals skulking about the edge of a camp, came in the form of disturbing thoughts about Cory, mixed with pleasant reveries about baseball. I dreamed of the long, sunny afternoons on the field where our endless game went on from the time the dew left the grass until it was too dark to see the ball. . . .
>
> I loved those times, the tense, uncaring heat of August, the air thick, sweat drizzling into my eyebrows. I remember grabbing the bottom of my damp T-shirt, pulling it up and wiping my forehead, drying my eyes before heading for the plate. I remember squinting through a haze of perspiration from my spot in right field, the earth aerated by cheeky prairie dogs who peeked and chittered all the long, lazy afternoons. (85)

The question with respect to this story, and often elsewhere, may be debatable; yet what matters is not whether the answer given is that this is or is not a story about baseball but how one qualifies the response. In any case, the reader is forever, and properly so, in the presence of a passage from Wright Morris's *The Huge Season,* which Mark Harris chose as the epigraph for *Bang the Drum Slowly:*

> He wiped his face with the towel again. "Old man, a book can have Chicago in it, and not be about Chicago. It can have a tennis player in it without being about a tennis player. . . . "

Kinsella's "K-Mart" both is and is not a sports story, which is but another way of saying that although third-generation writers of sports fiction may profitably tantalize with the question, any strict division between "life" and sport as provinces for fictional treatment would represent precisely that benighted attitude which the current generation of authors has striven to overcome. In "K-Mart," Kinsella uses sandlot participation in

baseball as a reference point for poignant recollection of the narrator's adolescent years. The result is a nicely understated preference for a sandlot ball field over the same acreage after it has become a site of commercial development. The story also produces, more personally, a well-modulated tribute to Corrina Mazeppa, the daughter of immigrants and a high school dropout. The spiritual business that the story transacts is the restoration in retrospect of Cory's teenage virtue, whereupon her life is viewed as sadly wasted even well before her untimely death.

Many readers will wish to raise Kinsella's "K-Mart" question about Richard Ford's excellent novel *The Sportswriter.* Indeed, it is probably fair to say that many will argue that *The Sportswriter* is not a sports novel at all. To those readers, the relatively slight attention paid directly to sports in the novel, and that almost exclusively from the angle of reportage and commentary, will buttress the position that Ford's novel does not fall within the purview of sport literature. But *The Sportswriter* has something to say about the place of sport in American life and about the function of sport in personal relationships. Still more valuable are its periodic definitions of sportswriting as opposed to what first-person narrator Frank Bascombe terms "real writing." Even more particularly, in Frank Bascombe's insistence on his own (and the reader's own) ordinariness, *The Sportswriter* takes its place very comfortably in the company of the work of Harris, Stein, Kinsella, and Hough, to name just a few of the authors whose works are indubitably to be labeled sports fiction.

Ford does not attempt to analyze athletic events in close, technical fashion. Such a feature is unlikely in a present-day sports novel. In calling *The Celebrant* "simply the best baseball novel ever written," Kinsella presumably expresses his admiration for Greenberg's rather astonishing success in interweaving illuminating and evocatively detailed accounts of action on the field (although these are re-creations of actual major league games) with *The Celebrant's* further intricacies. Among Greenberg's accomplishments are his impressive handling of social, economic, and sports history; his establishing of the mutual admiration between the fictional Christy Mathewson and the totally fictional protagonist of the novel, Jackie Kapp; and his paralleling of Mathewson's sports performance "gems" with Jackie Kapp's artistic designing and rendering of gemstones in the creation of celebratory jewelry.

The experience of reading *The Sportswriter* is one of anticipating developments that would tidy up Frank Bascombe's life, or at least some significant part of it, only to have those anticipations checked by what does or, more accurately, does not develop. The experience is nonetheless remarkably free of frustration for the reader, even though Frank Bascombe is such a convincingly decent fellow that the reader hopes time and again for some solution or resolution of Frank's state. It is a state that one is tempted to call suspended, but that temptation must be withstood. The reader of *The Sports-writer* may call to mind John Ciardi's invitation to honor twentieth-century poets because, unlike the fire-side poets of an earlier day, they "won't tell us what they don't know."

Two literary parallels to *The Sportswriter* that suggest themselves are first, the Book of Job, Job's prime virtue being not the patience traditionally ascribed to him but rather a scrupulous intellectual honesty; and second, the distinction Eric Greenberg draws between baseball and life by having his fictional Christy Mathewson disagree with attempts to find analogies between the game of baseball and life:

> "After all, baseball isn't anything like life. . . . In truth, nothing in the game appealed to me as much as its unreality. Baseball is all clean lines and clear decisions. Wouldn't life be far easier if it consisted of a series of definitive calls: safe or out, fair or foul, strike or ball. Oh, for a life like that, where every day produces a clear winner and an equally clear loser, and back to it the next day with the slate wiped clean and the teams starting out equal." (86-87)

Like life, *The Sportswriter* is inconclusive, although Ford's novel ends inevitably; ends, that is, in a fashion absolutely consistent with its meaning. While Frank Bascombe would also reject the help offered Job by the comforters and while Ford will not say what he does not know, what he does know more than suffices. Indeed, it positively rewards.

Accustomed as the reader of modern literature is to sto-ries of the unlived life, Ford's very title—*The Sports-writer*—will recall to many the Walker Percy title *The Moviegoer*. Ford's title, like Percy's, will at first sug-gest some such generic title as *The Bystander*. The story, the reader supposes, is to be one of a lack of commitment recognized too late (Joyce's "The Dead" or "A Painful Case," James's "The Beast in the Jungle") or providentially reversed by love (*The Moviegoer*). This latter expectation is particularly strong, and particularly well counteracted, in the novel's Easter chapter, chapter 9, which ends with Frank's feeling himself "saved in the only way I can be (*pro tempore*)" (238).

Each of several solutions to a predicament of personal isolation appears to be a distinct possibility in *The Sportswriter*. Each time Frank Bascombe thinks of the death at age nine of his beloved son Ralph, and more especially each time Frank hears sounds of grief ema-nating from the cemetery beside his house, the likeli-hood seems great that Ford will have Frank profit from another's moving exhibition of genuine grief, just as Henry James had his cold and withdrawn John Marcher learn true emotion. But Ford's recurrent use of Ralph's death at the age of nine ends with Frank's saying, ". . . I realized that my own mourning is finally over. . . . Grief, real grief, is relatively short, though mourning can be long" (374). Forewarned as he has been by Frank's

belief that Joyce's conception of epiphanies is "a good example of [literary] falsehood" (119), readers have only themselves to blame for their mistaken assumption.

The possibility that love will provide a release from what the reader may regard as Frank's emotional pre-dicament is never the issue in Frank's relationship with the Lebanese woman Selma Jassim, neither while he teaches for a term at Berkshire College nor when he calls her on the telephone during what seems to be his time of crisis late in the novel. Much more likely is a reconciliation with "X", as Frank regularly refers to her, the ex-wife he still loves and who still loves him. X is a fine golfer, though, and has returned to serious play following her divorce from Frank. Once he has com-bined a working definition of what it means to be a sportswriter according to Frank's lexicon with the detail that Frank as a teenager was unable to develop into a competent first baseman, Ford can slip in as unobtrusive symbolism the fact that X plays golf so well. A gentler hint at the incompatibility of two people who once were married and who still love one another is hard to imag-ine. And so when Frank missteps with X after Walter Luckett's suicide, the reader understands that a recon-ciliation is not possible.

Among the other many women in Frank's life, only Vicki Arcenault and Catherine Flaherty require com-ment. Vicki looks particularly promising: she has the same first name as Vicky Vadnais of Hough's *The Con-duct of the Game* and, similarly, a French last name; she has the same physical attractiveness, straightfor-ward speech, and self-possession as Hough's Vicky; and her father, although he has graduated from Texas A&M with a degree in engineering, now works as a toll-taker in a booth on the New Jersey Turnpike. Present in only one scene in the novel, Wade Arcenault wins the respect of Frank Bascombe and of the reader in very much the same manner and to the same considerable degree as Mr. Vadnais does in *The Conduct of the Game*.

Catherine Flaherty is the late arrival in *The Sports-writer*. At last report she is trying on medical school for size and seeing Frank from time to time, while he, too, in an even more unhurried way, is deciding what he'll do next, and even whether he'll do something other than what he is now doing, which by accepted American standards is not very much. Among the fringe benefits of Frank's current sojourn in Florida is his meeting and enjoying the company of several pleasant, respectable but quite undistinguished relatives (Buster Bascombe, for one self-explanatory name) from both his father's and his mother's sides of his family. It is significant that these Florida retirees are presented more sympa-thetically than are X's affluent parents in Michigan.

This preference for prototypical retirees, at ease with themselves, over X's parents, who effect a late reconcili-ation only because they are afraid of dying alone, is but a very minor detail contributing to the major theme of *The Sportswriter*: the celebration of the ordinary and

Frank's calm but repeated insistence on his own ordinariness. Very early, Frank describes human experience as "the normal applauseless life of us all" (10). A characteristic observation later in the novel is "for my lights they thought too little of themselves and didn't realize how much all of us are in the very same boat, and how much it is an imperfect boat" (220). Or again, "We've all felt that way, I'm confident, since there's no way that I could feel what hundreds of millions of other citizens haven't" (375). Frank does acknowledge that "None of our lives is really ordinary; nothing humdrum in our delights or our disasters" (107). Still, Frank does not simply insist upon but he wholeheartedly and even cheerfully accepts the notion that "Anyone could be anyone else in most ways. Face facts" (81). In Frank's particular case, this sense of self is in no wise a diminished sense. Even though the reader will wish to rate Frank higher than he rates himself, Frank's refusal to be self-congratulatory is one of his great virtues.

Again, in Frank's case his sense of his own ordinariness seems to others to prevent his developing his literary career beyond the single collection of short stories he has published and the one novel he loses. Branding "transcendent themes in life" a "lie of literature and the liberal arts" (16), Bascombe disappoints those well-wishers, mostly academics, who expect more from him. But Bascombe speaks somewhat ambiguously of those he considers "real writers." While he respects them, he is mistrustful of their tendentiousness.

Bascombe derives genuine satisfaction from his sportswriting, although here again Ford plays upon reader expectation by arousing conventional pieties and then methodically confounding them. Early in the novel the plot builds toward an interview Frank is to conduct with Herb Wallagher, a former professional football lineman who is now a paraplegic. Well after the unproductive interview has occurred, an interview during which Frank learns that Herb is no longer retained by the Detroit Lions as a source of inspiration and comes to see that Herb is, quite simply, "crazy" and no inspiration to anyone, the sportswriter toys briefly with trying to salvage the story that he was sent to get from Herb. But Frank's professional judgment is sound; there is no story here. Unquestionably, Frank knows his trade: his description of how to compose a good sports story,

> . . . put together some useful ideas, . . . just a detail or two to act as magnets for what else will occur to me in the next days, which is the way good sportswriting gets done (208)

would hold true for any successful piece of writing. It is hardly incidental that when the sportswriter must leave Haddam, New Jersey, doing so with no sense of where he is headed, he winds up in his office at the sports magazine's headquarters in New York City. The importance lies in his not finding himself by getting caught up (lost) in work but rather in his finding at his place of work—or being found at work by—Catherine Flaherty,

a magazine apprentice who is an admirer of Frank's published sportswriting. That is, Frank does not take charge of his own fate, which is consistent with his belief that life does not allow anyone to do so, no matter how hard the struggle.

Including the predictable recognition of sports as "the perfect *lingua franca* for . . . crablike advances between successive boyfriends and husbands" (135) and as "always a good distraction from life at its dreariest" (186), Ford goes well beyond a consideration of the function of sports in American society. Introduction of *The Sportswriter*'s theme comes very early in the novel, in a sentence fragment among enumerations by his ex-wife of "mistakes" she believes Frank makes in concentrating his life too narrowly: "Sportswriting and being an ordinary citizen." (13) If that moment comes too early for more than speculation, the reader need not be tentative for very long; for *The Sportswriter* as a whole says that sportswriting, as opposed to sports performance at some high level of competition, is a very valuable enterprise for coming to grips with impermanence: "(Muslims, let me tell you, are a race of people who understand impermanence. More so even than sportswriters.)" (224) Frank judges that when he was still an aspiring "real writer" he had become

> . . . stuck in bad stereotypes. All my men were too serious, too brooding and humorless, characters at loggerheads with imponderable dilemmas, and much less interesting than my female characters, who were always . . . free spirited and sharpwitted. (46)

Now, as a sportswriter, Frank studies athletes, people he regards as typically "within themselves," by which he means that they are self-possessed but also that that admirable confidence in their own ability is confidence only within a severely circumscribed arena.

This progress from "bad stereotypes" to emancipation from the tendency to pigeonhole others is given summary statement in a passage midway in the novel, in which virtually all the chief recommendations of the work are included:

> At least as a stranger to almost everyone and a sportswriter to boot, I have a clean slate almost every day of my life,[2] a chance not to be negative, to give someone unknown a pat on the back, to recognize courage and improvement, to take the battle with cynicism head-on and win. (152)

When Walter Luckett, a character who also strongly rejects cynicism as a *modus vivendi*, embraces suicide as his only recourse after he has disappointed himself by engaging in a homosexual relationship, Frank's honest curiosity (which leads him to inspect Walter's living quarters after the suicide) and firm refusal to assume a guilt that another might readily have assumed are typical of the man and are saving graces. The inclusion of Walter and his suicide are the author's dismissal of that desperate "alternative" for Frank. Well after Walter's suicide has been reported, Frank provides an analogy between sport and life that is based on Frank's common sense and on his common experience as one of life's bench warmers:

> It takes a depth of character as noble and enduring as willingness to come off the bench to play a great game knowing full well that you'll never be a regular; or as one who chooses not to hop into bed with your best friend's beautiful wife. Walter Luckett could be alive today if he knew that. (341)

One reservation must be expressed. The poet John Berryman once said that one is gripped by Hamlet because Hamlet is a "poet." The critical point is well taken, surely, telling because of its paradoxical nature. With Richard Ford's Frank Bascombe, a kind of additional turn has been given this screw of the voice that an author gives to his or her character. Any character who argues so eloquently the point of his own ordinariness is, in Berryman's terms, too much a poet to be ordinary. But Frank Bascombe's ordinariness has, in the late twentieth century, a salutary effect startlingly similar to the effect of Hamlet's tragic stature. In either instance, the reader or viewer, common or uncommon, can only feel elevated by the shared humanity that such a revealed human being compels the thankful reader to acknowledge. And finally, it is well to remember what Frank Bascombe has thought, "The world is a more engaging and less dramatic place than writers ever give it credit for being." The sentence immediately preceding this literary accolade to the world is a warning against the tendency to stereotype: "But that is a man of bad stereotype, the kind my ["real"] writing career foundered over and probably should have" (261).

In creating Lee Malcolm, his first-person narrator, John Hough, Jr., breaks free from the distancing of Ring Lardner from his "busher," Jack Keefe; from the self-muzzling that Mark Harris felt to some extent he underwent in speaking through his "author," Henry Wiggen; and from the respectable and realistic voice of the fictional George Weaver as imagined by Harry Stein. Malcolm organizes his story precisely as his author organizes it (or vice versa)—no gap exists between the two, to be exploited for the reader's amusement—so that *The Conduct of the Game* is a thoroughly impressive work and a work devoid of the slightest hint of condescension of the author toward his character. Still, the words of Lee Malcolm are not very memorable or highly quotable. In this characteristic lies a descriptive distinction between two fine sports novels, *The Conduct of the Game* and *The Sportswriter,* each celebrating human ordinariness. One is written in a style the reader may think he or she could achieve, although he or she emphatically could not; the other in a style not soon to be equaled by any writer, no matter how accomplished. The voice of one illustrates the worth of the common citizen; the voice of the other accepts and champions that worth. Each celebrates it.

NOTES

[1] The old catcher's nickname, "Comic Book," recalls the story of Yogi Berra's looking up from his comic books to ask his road-trip roommate, Bobby Brown, how the plot of the book Brown was reading—Gray's *Anatomy*—turned out. In the days of such apocryphal stories, it was assumed that Yogi stumbled onto his many Yogi-isms. That was before Yogi managed and coached, and decidedly before he reviewed not just game films but feature films, in mufti and in front of audiences.

[2] That is, Bascombe achieves precisely what Greenberg's Mathewson yearns for: a transference from sport to life in general.

WORKS CITED

Ford, Richard. *The Sportswriter.* New York: Vintage, 1986.

Greenberg, Eric Rolfe. *The Celebrant.* 1983. New York: Penguin, 1986.

Harris, Mark. *Bang the Drum Slowly.* 1956. New York: Dell, 1973.

Hough, John, Jr. *The Conduct of the Game.* San Diego: Harcourt Brace Jovanovich, 1986.

Kinsella, W. P. *The Further Adventures of Slugger McBatt.* Boston: Houghton Mifflin, 1988.

Malamud, Bernard. *The Natural.* New York: Noonday, 1952.

Patrick, Walton R. *Ring Lardner.* New York: Twayne, 1963.

Stein, Harry. *Hoopla.* New York: St. Martin's, 1983.

John Limon

SOURCE: "Diversions: A Theory of the Vietnam Sports Novel," in *Writing After War: American War Fiction from Realism to Postmodernism,* Oxford University Press, 1994, pp. 154-82.

[*In the following essay, Limon examines the manner in which several postmodern American sports novels relate to and reflect attitudes toward the Vietnam War.*]

"Why not a smooth, orderly arc from war to peace?"

Tim O'Brien, *Going After Cacciato*

PLAY, PART I

(1955) Among the things that Vladimir Nabokov disdained, according to his introduction to *Bend Sinister,* were atomic warfare and the entire Orient,[1] which makes it unsurprising that the Korean War, fought on the sub-nuclear level and on only one Asian peninsula, left him cold. *Lolita* (whose action takes place between 1947 and 1952) hardly mentions the war (1950-53).[2] The war years are more or less the blank years of the novel (1949-52), the interlude of "Dolorès Disparue" (*L*, 231). When the action resumes, Humbert tracks Lolita to Dick, who—Humbert notes unsympathetically—is hard of hearing, the result of an injury in "a remote war" (*L*, 249), probably Korea, though his friend Bill lost his arm in World War II. And when Humbert returns to Ramsdale, on the scent of Quilty, he is pointedly unmoved by the news that Charlie Holmes, old summer camp debaucher, was killed in Korea—the place and the war named for the first and only time. It would be easy to assert that the casualty is admitted into the book to stand for everything to which Nabokov is "supremely indifferent"[3]—except that Nabokov (even if identical with the author of the introduction to *Bend Sinister*) is not identical with Humbert Humbert. If Korea is merely the contingent token of all that Nabokov does not condescend to aestheticize, at least it serves in that capacity in a book that displays the consequences of a murderous aesthetic solipsism.

(1966) In *The Crying of Lot 49*, Thomas Pynchon alludes to Vietnam, in passing, twice. This seems short shrift in a book (a) published in 1966, and (b) much interested in the Civil War, World War I, and World War II.[4] Nevertheless, the book might have been called *Why Are We in Vietnam?*, on Norman Mailer's principle that a book on that war might be better off barely naming it. The clue to discovering Vietnam in—or Vietnam out of—*Lot 49* is observing, first of all, that the war between Squamuglia and Faggio illustrates no cunning rationality in history: both sides are devastated. Centuries later, during World War II, a company of Americans is wiped out by Germans on the Italian coast. One side loses the war, the other side—"cut off without communication"—loses the battle with such extravagance that no member of the company lives to celebrate the ultimate victory to which he contributed so negligibly. The Americans disappear "without a trace or a word"[5]—which certainly elicits the question of how anybody knows about them. Only one thing connects these two bits of catastrophic absurdity. Bones of combatants in the first war are used by Tristero for charcoal in pens, and bones of the dead GIs are used by Pierce Inverarity for charcoal in cigarettes. The plot of *Lot 49* imitates the plot of history; death is only the raw material of marketing and marking. The book's impossible project is to inscribe Vietnam only insofar as it leaves no trace or word.

(1968) John Barth's *Lost in the Funhouse* is the Ultima Thule of self-reflexive metafiction.[6] The mythic preoccupation is *The Odyssey*, the postmodernist Ulysses is communication itself, whose arrival at any destination is always in peril. Nevertheless, the absence of an *Iliad* is on Barth's mind. ("Anonymiad" is the culminating story

of a poet who invents writing while on an eventless adventure away from Troy during the Trojan War.) In the title story, Ambrose, too young to go to war (born, presumably, in 1930), visits Ocean City and its funhouse around 1943; there are signs everywhere of the war on, but the narrator, Ambrose/Barth, wonders: "What relevance does the war have to the story?" (*LF*, 92). The answer seems to be: it mirrors it.

> On account of German U-boats, Ocean City was "browned out": streetlights were shaded on the seaward side; shop windows and boardwalk amusement places were kept dim, not to silhouette tankers and Liberty-ships for torpedoing. In a short story about Ocean City, Maryland, during World War II, the author could make use of the image of sailors on leave in the penny arcades and shooting galleries, sighting through the crosshairs of toy machine guns at swastika'd subs, while out in the black Atlantic a U-boat skipper squints through his periscope at real ships outlined by the glow of penny arcades. (*LF*, 82)

This is, however, too treacherous a passage to use as an emblem: the author does not in fact write this mirror story, except insofar as he floats its scenario. It would be a silly story to write, but that does not prevent it so much as its self-importance. The funhouse of the story that does get written is disturbing not in its ludic contagiousness (its fictionality projected dangerously— browned out arcades somehow aglow—into the historical mirror), rather in its grim infectedness. The Barthian/Ambrosian narrative voice laments: "How much better it would be to be that common sailor! A wiry little Seaman 3rd, the fellow squeezed a girl to each side and stumbled hilarious into the mirror room, closer to Magda in thirty seconds than Ambrose had got in thirteen years" (*LF*, 89). Banal reality—a military-sexual complex—informs the funhouse.

Nabokov first dreamt the proto-*Lolita* in France, just before it was invaded, redreamt and rewrote *Lolita* during Korea. Pynchon wrote *The Crying of Lot 49* in the first year of significant anti-Vietnam protests (Oedipa, walking through Berkeley, breathes the radicalized air). Barth's collection of stories is high-Vietnam art. Nabokov mentions Korea once and there is one sad reminder of World War II; Pynchon alludes to Vietnam twice; Barth does not mention Vietnam at all. Is the Nabokovian moment of the American novel averse to combat fiction (1) because high-international postmodernism is superbly ahistorical, or (2) because history is the prey of textuality, or (3) because history is so hauntingly an apparition in the text itself that every formal gesture is a historical gesture?

Sports

If Nabokov is the pre-eminent advocate of the ludic novel, of literary creation as the word's superiority to history, then he ought to be the furthest thing possible from war novelist. Pynchon and Barth provide only two examples of the impossibility of writing Vietnam in the Nabokovian tradition: Donald Barthelme, in the metafictional questionnaire of *Snow White,* asks of presumably bored readers, "Would you like a war?"[7] Not all American postmodernism, of course, is Nabokovian (or Borgesian, international, rarefied) postmodernism. Nevertheless, though there were already something like 130 Vietnam novels by 1987, none to that or this moment has made a convincing claim to being the final, extensive, satisfying treatment of the war. Even Vietnam novelists themselves, at a conference dedicated to establishing and publicizing the vitality of the subgenre, "agreed that *the* Vietnam novel is yet to be written,"[8] despite the fact that through the 1980s *the* Vietnam film was released at approximately the rate of one every two years. The Vietnam film is sensuous bombardment diagrammatically framed; the postmodern Vietnam novel can be neither so crude nor so orderly. Such diversely excellent Vietnam novels as *Going After Cacciato, Why Are We in Vietnam?,* and *In Country* are combat writing by indirection: to transport us to Vietnam, they transport Vietnam to Paris, Alaska, and Kentucky.

Still—America makes available, between play and war, a compromise formation. American sports are oxymoronic to begin with—what is sport but beautiful belligerence?—and the American sports novel has served the impossible necessity of making Vietnam available to the postmodern novel. Bernard Malamud's *The Natural* and John Updike's *The Centaur* are pre-Vietnam, but taken together they illustrate the formal possibilities sport offers to Vietnam-era literature that is obsessed with the war it despairs of representing.

The Natural (written during Korea) concerns two peace-time eras, without the war dividing them.[9] But for a book about baseball, it is unduly violent; most of the crippling is just prior to the moment Roy Hobbs, the "natural" whose potentially brilliant career had been cut short fifteen years before by a nearly successful assassination, reappears on the scene. Walking into the equipment room to get his new uniform, Roy is addressed by the chatty equipment manager: "Caught me at an interesting moment. . . . I was reading about this catcher that got beaned in Boston yesterday. Broke the side of his skull." Then the equipment manager acknowledges his own team's desiderata: "Yeah, we been one man short on the roster for two weeks. One of our guys went and got himself hit on the head with a fly ball and both of his legs are now paralyzed." And "just before that our regular third baseman stepped on a bat and rolled down the dugout steps. Snapped his spine in two places" (*TN,* 42). A string of bad luck? This is more brutal misfortune than major league baseball will suffer in decades.

Granted that on one level of the allegory, what we have here is nothing historically specifiable, rather the seasonal confrontation of Parsifal and Death. (Going to bat, Roy swears that he will "murder" the ball; as he approaches the plate, the manager says, "Keep us alive" [*TN,* 210].) One of the athlete's functions is to play out

the spectacular confrontation of life and death prematurely, when heroic exemptions are still possible; baseball players start fending off death around the age of thirty, which is why the book is framed by Roy's humiliation of "The Whammer" (aged 33) and his own humiliation (aged 34), and why the book turns out to be a meditation on another summer confrontation of Parsifal and Death, *The Great Gatsby,* in which Gatsby's martyrdom allegorizes Nick's thirtieth birthday. The two books are based on the same vision of green West and Eastern Waste, on the same paradox of Western pioneers moving East again, apparently in the direction of the past and rebirth but in fact toward decay. The shared vision, which almost necessarily turns men into boys and their fate over to murderous women, will place two separate infantalized heroes in two cars driving between Long Island and New York City, and will manage to have two separate women take over the steering and two homicides as the result (possibly imaginary in *The Natural*).

Finally, the analogy of the books involves the same allusion to baseball history: the fixing of the 1919 World Series, just before the action of *The Great Gatsby* and its historical correlative, is the climactic event of *The Natural,* transported three decades. After Roy is corrupted by the gamblers and the pennant is lost, a newspaper boy pleads, "Say it ain't so, Roy," because an apocryphal newspaper boy had implored, "Say it ain't so, Joe" to Joe Jackson after the 1919 scandal. If you throw Jordan Baker's cheating at golf into a consideration of *The Great Gatsby,* you get two powerful novels that stake their ironic grandiosity not merely on the decline of the athletic body toward death but also on the corruption of sport itself. Why should the mortification of American athletics appear to Fitzgerald—and to Malamud in turn—as necessary to their Arthurian-Eliotic parables of the decline of cultures?

The answer gets us to the relation of sport and war; the so-called Black Sox scandal, model for Malamud's climax, occurred at a crucial allegorical moment. We entered the war in 1917, we won the war in 1918, we belatedly suffered the degradation of the war in 1919. The bitterness of inheriting a bankrupt patrimony came to Americans a year late: the world war was fun for Gatsby and Nick, but the World Series made it possible for *Gatsby* to rewrite *The Waste Land.* As in Huizinga, what is at risk in modern civilization is the agon, the play-principle of civilization; it survives the Great War, but professional sport (as in Huizinga) is a more insidious enemy. When Malamud came to write his own allegory of war and waste land, the Black Sox scandal was simply transformed into the belatedly culminating event of the *next* world war—hence the rash of casualties just prior to Hobbs's return.

War is never mentioned in *The Natural,* but World War II intervenes nevertheless. A simple calculation puts this into relief. Sam Simpson, the scout who discovers Roy Hobbs, was a ballplayer from 1919 to 1921, a full-time scout in 1925. By the time he discovers Hobbs, however, he is only a scout insofar as he wanders the country looking for ballplayers on his own. Assume that a decade more or less has passed since 1925. Then he discovers Hobbs, who shows his genius by winning a baseball duel with the legendary Whammer, clearly Babe Ruth, who retired in 1935; but Hobbs is shot, not to complete his odyssey back to the majors, Malamud specifies, for another fifteen years. World War II is what, conspicuously, intervenes and disappears, like the Revolutionary War in the missing twenty years of "Rip Van Winkle," like Korea in the missing three years of *Lolita.*

Its intervention, though invisible, is unmistakable, because the vision that the antebellum Hobbs represents is a pastoral, romantic, Aryan affair: Sam's dream as a scout, which only Hobbs ever promises to realize, is of "twelve blond-bearded players," farmers, athletes, and supermen, playing titanic baseball on an unscouted farm (*TN*, 10). The corruption of Roy Hobbs is a fortunate fall, insofar as we do not buy into Sam's Aryan, agrarian, prelapsarian vision, or, to return to *The Great Gatsby,* Tom Buchanan's. Whether or not the fall is fortunate, the baseball story will be about, is virtually required to be about, the war that brought us to our urban, ethnic, mercenary present. The war that did that is every war; the baseball novel is our perpetual combat novel for novelists who missed the war, but got the parable.

The suspense of *The Natural* is whether it will be seduced by baseball's aesthetics of return: from adulthood to innocence, city to country, representation (legends and statistics) to history; basketball glamorizes the body in perpetual transition (history never solidifies, urban frenzy never relaxes, adolescence is eternal). In Updike's *The Centaur,* the emblematic sport of which is basketball, antitheses of the sort that Malamud's novel depends on keeping antithetical always mingle and refuse to detach.[10] It is unclear whether the book's Hebraic element (the Presbyterian, Hawthornean speculation) and the Hellenic element (the mythic frame) can be untangled. It is uncertain whether Updike's men are little lower than gods or little higher than animals: the centaur is a not wholly integrated but not wholly disintegrated (*half*-natural) monster, part god, human, and beast. The book chronicles the relation of a child-man and man-child, mutually compromised and inseparable.

Accordingly, Updike can make no Malamudian distinction of innocence and degradation, separable in principle even in a fallen world, or of war and peace. Both confusions come out at the basketball game, whose climactic vividness I hope justifies my taking *The Centaur* as a basketball novel. The basketball game is a monolith of Updikean sexuality—because of the closeness of the spectators to the exposed bodies on the court, the hot-house excitement of the packed bodies in the stands, the suggestiveness of the ball and skirted basket. The description of the game is suffused with sex: a player "drives in past the West Alton defender, and in a rapt

moment of flight drops the peeper" (*TC*, 172). We register the "rape" in "rapt," the penetration, as they say, of the drive, the play of driving and flying, terms not only of transportation but of sexual transport, and the erotic vibrations of "drops the peeper." During the game, the centaur's son Peter decides to initiate himself into the truths of his girlfriend's body. He is anxious because his body is marred by psoriasis: not every body is a god's body, and Updike as intimately as Mark Twain knows that one truth of the human body is that it itches.

Penny's love, however, surmounts this difficulty, which I take it is responsible for the startling purity and grotesqueness of the vision immediately following the peace-in-war of the game. Caldwell père and fils leave the gymnasium; it is snowing outside, and Peter believes that "the multitude of flakes seems to have been released by a profanation" (*TC*, 190). How does a profanation entail a vision as consoling as the paraclete (of "an entire broadening wing of infinitesimal feathers")? The answer is that we have heard previously about a falling multitude of white flakes, as Peter scratches his decomposing skin. The universe magnifies and glorifies Peter's disease. If this is as sanctified a rottenness as can be imagined, it is an emblem of Updike's book.

So the novel, unlike Malamud's, has no before and after, prelapsarian and fallen: it lapses. There is no place for the American designation of war as fall, despite the fact that the book, written at the beginning of the 1960s, locates itself as a post-war novel. It takes place, more precisely dated than *The Natural,* in 1947, when post-war prosperity has begun: "The Esso and Mobil gas chains had both built service stations a few blocks away from the pike, and now that the war was over, and everybody could buy new cars with their war-work money, the demand for repairs had plummeted" (*TC*, 12). This is misleading, however, since *Caldwell's* demand for repairs of his car (and life) does not plummet, but increases to infinity during the course of *The Centaur*— the car that keeps needing repairs is a '36 Buick. And the war spills into post-war. A student named Ache (Achilles) survives the war but is killed in a plane crash after it: "Isn't that funny? To go all through the war without a scratch and then get nailed in peacetime" (*TC*, 167).

The inference is that the war has negligible impact on the events of the novel. Caldwell, asked how long he has been a teacher, answers, "Fourteen years. . . . I was laid off late in '31 and was out of work the whole year the kid was born. In the summer of '33, Al Hummel . . . came up to the house and suggested [getting a teaching job]" (*TC*, 101). The war, which began when Caldwell was forty-five, merely represents four of the fourteen years of his pedagogical futility in a world of "living corpses." In Roy Hobbs's experience, the fallen world has replaced his agonistic Eden. For all we know of it, he may as well have slept through the rupture, World War II, as Rip Van Winkle slept through the Revolution, to awaken to newly perfected venalities. Caldwell's world, on the other hand, is a perpetual falling: "From Sky to Earth, they said, an anvil would fall nine days and nights. . . . Perhaps now it was more, perhaps—the thought deepened his sickness—an anvil could fall forever from Sky and never strike Earth" (*TC*, 218). He has been falling from 1933 to 1947, while Roy Hobbs was entombed, and the war did not deflect his course.

The Natural does not mention war, but war is the subject of its allegory. *The Centaur* purports to register the effects of war, but finds war and peace, like hate and love, mixed or compounded in every human gesture, hence inappropriate as a special concern or referent of referents. A theory of the sports novel needs to establish under what conditions it is crypto- or pseudo-war literature, and to observe distinctions, war equally invisible in either case, in the patterns of invisibility. A theory of the *Vietnam* sports novel needs to do more. It needs to show how Updike's and Malamud's quite particular purposes—after all, World War II did produce its candidates for *the* combat novel, *The Naked and the Dead*, *From Here to Eternity*, *Catch-22*, *Gravity's Rainbow*— required techniques of indirection that would be useful generally during Vietnam. And it must show how those techniques were manipulated by novelists who could not be so confident as Malamud that the war was sufficiently distanced from their prose as to be available for allegory, or share Updike's confidence (in *The Centaur*, at least) that the war sufficiently informs life on the home front as to be absorbed. *The Natural* and *The Centaur* are in control of their paradoxes; during Vietnam, sports novelists seem as much victimized as energized by the problematics of representing war in terms of peace.

TENNIS, BASEBALL

The sports novel inherits its specific force from the ambiguities of sport itself—the gift of anthropology to sports novelists is that there is no anthropological consensus as to what sport is. The problem begins with the anomaly that sport seems conceptually halfway between play and work; sport makes a continuum of what is, in our purest, pre-industrial dreams, a polarity. There is a riskier, more indispensable mediation that sport performs: it figures the relationship of art and war, a trickier function, since art and war are not antonyms.

What sport shares with art is the assertion of a quasi-sacred value free from utility and productivity.[11] On the other hand is the anaesthetic belligerence of the competition:

> Manifestations of the predatory temperament are all to be classed under the head of the exploit. They are partly simple and unreflected expressions of an attitude of emulative ferocity, partly activities deliberately entered upon with a view to gaining repute for prowess. Sports of all kind are of the same general character, including prizefights, bullfights, athletics, shooting, angling, yachting, and games of skill, even where the element of destructive

physical efficiency is not an obtrusive feature. Sports shade off from the basis of hostile combat, through skill to cunning and chicanery, without its being possible to draw a line at any point.[12]

Thorstein Veblen's family likening is in Hemingwayesque increments, except that Veblen is unconcerned to find, migrating through the spectrum, a separate peace for literature. The inference is that sport is perfectly positioned for the aestheticizing of war and the militarization of art.

Even amateur tennis? Suppose that a character in a work of literature is identified as a tennis devotee (like Humbert Humbert, say); is it likely that its author wants us to think of him as a paragon of martial virtues? When the Dauphin sends Henry V a present of tennis balls, presumably he believes that thus to metonymize Henry is to disqualify him as a warrior or King. The simplest way to understand what ensues is to find evidence in Agincourt that Henry is no longer Hal, the boy at play. But that would be to make a simple distinction of sport and war that is not only invalid per se; to believe it would invalidate the drama.

The reason that tennis is instrumental is that Shakespeare is defensive, in the wake of realist skepticism, about the susceptibility of war to theatre;[13] if war cannot be represented by play, can it be represented by plays? In the Prologue to Act IV, for example, Shakespeare is confessedly unequal to the task of putting combat on stage:

> And so our scene must to the battle fly,
> Where—oh, for pity!—we shall much disgrace
> With four or five most vile and ragged foils,
> Right ill-disposed in brawl ridiculous,
> The name of Agincourt. Yet sit and see,
> Minding the things by what their mockeries be.
> (*CW*, IV. Prologue. 48-53)

All that Shakespeare can rely on is the cooperation of his audience, which is doubly tested: even a realistic representation would be a weak representation. But Shakespeare does more than apologize and beseech. The challenge to his audience is built into his play, so as to make criticism unpatriotic. The Englishmen at Agincourt look little worthier, according to the drama, than their dramatic mockeries. Henry's lament is like a boast:

> We are but warriors for the working day.
> Our gayness and our gilt are all besmirched
> With rainy marching in the painful field.
> There's not a piece of feather in our host—
> Good argument, I hope, we will not fly—
> And time hath worn us into slovenry.
> (*CW*, IV. iii. 109-114)

That the English army will not fly is of course desirable, but it would have seemed to the French more likely that their unfledgedness signified "flat unraisèd spirits" (*CW*, I. Prologue. 9), a phrase that does not, however, refer to them, but to the play's own strategic modesty. When the arrogant French "behold yon poor and starvèd band" (*CW*, IV. ii. 16) and see such pathetic details—as if from the prop department—as the horsemen sitting "like fixèd candlesticks,/ With torch staves in their hand" (*CW*, IV. ii. 45-46), they may as well be the spectators of Henry's cavalry or Shakespeare's cast, mockers of mockeries.

If the audience scorns the play, they are equal in superficiality to the Dauphin and his entourage. What the French lack, the audience is manipulated to value: an imagination that is both productive ("Piece out the imperfections with your thoughts") and susceptible ("let us . . . on your imaginary forces work" [*CW*, I. Prologue. 23,18]). Between Shakespeare and his audience is an imaginary co-dependency, a community with reciprocal obligations: Shakespeare makes his own art the field of patriotism. In these terms, the tennis ball insult is not so much pointed as imaginatively flat. The French perceive, apparently, no relation between play and war, despite their own dedication to martial splendor. Henry sees a metaphorical relation:

> When we have matched our rackets to these balls,
> We will in France, by God's grace, play a set
> Shall strike his father's crown into the hazard.
> Tell him he hath made a match with such a
> > wrangler
> That all the courts of France will be disturbed
> With chaces.
>
> (*CW*, I. ii. 261-266)

The conceit is not merely improvised for the occasion; Henry *believes* it. At the siege of Harfleur, Henry proclaims that "the game's afoot" (*CW*, III. i. 32). Justifying the execution of Bardolph for stealing, he pronounces that "when lenity and cruelty play for a kingdom, the gentler gamester is the soonest winner" (*CW*, III. vi. 118-120). If Henry had turned out to be no warrior, then the insistent metaphor would conclusively prove that a talent for tennis is congruent with a talent for poetry. Since he is victorious, the equation is as follows: to suspect nothing serious in Harry is to find nothing daunting in the English army is to conceive nothing belligerent in play is to consider nothing in *a* play to be adequate to war. The progression is from tennis court to royal court to Agincourt, and back from battleground to playground to playhouse.

I have not prejudged whether in fact tennis is sufficiently violent—or Agincourt sufficiently agonistic—to justify Harry's metaphorical, metamorphic leap. The case is best put as a rolling conditional: if tennis prepares for combat, then boyhood is preparation for adulthood, then a play can represent Agincourt. A standard supposition about sport, of course, even such a brutal one as boxing, is that whatever relation it has to war works precisely to make war less necessary or attractive. Was Henry V wasting his manhood on boyish pursuits like tennis, or was he preparing himself for conquest? Shakespeare's answer—it depends on the power of metaphor—is my answer also, that is, sport, like war on the one hand and literature on the other, is an aspect of the symbolic expression of a culture. The relationship of the three cannot be worked out in advance of cultural interpretation: the French at Waterloo will again fail to realize that specifically English imperialism is practiced on playing fields. The duplicity of sport, its prefiguration of violence and regimentation as against its descent from ludic joy, makes it an eternal shifter in the grammar of a culture, as this review of the anthropological scholarship gravely, hilariously, implies:

> The literature on athletics and violence generally suggests one of two things; [sic] that sports either lower violence levels in society by providing a significant cathartic experience for both participants and spectators [list of five studies follows] or conversely that they increase the incidence of such unstructured aggression [list of eight studies follows].[14]

"Like any other form of sacrificial prophylaxis," René Girard says, "prohibitions can on occasion turn against their users": if sports are meant to replace unstructured violence with violence against a scapegoat, how could they ever fully succeed, given the nearly perfect indiscernibility of the players or teams, and the impossibility of any final sacrifice of the outsider who looks exactly like an insider? "In the end the kudos mean nothing," Girard writes of the unsatisfying condition. "It is the prize of a temporary victory, an advantage no sooner won than challenged."[15] Contests are contests and not duels. Sport participates in the quasi-catharsis of pornography and the remembered nightmare: its double force is that it produces or exacerbates what it quashes or contains. The novelist who comes to the sports theme may do so exclusively to claim for art a moral equivalence to war, or exclusively to subject war to the moral superiority of the book, but no sports novel can avoid doing some of both.

The peculiar difficulty of sorting out which relationship to war the sports novelist favors—which way he reads the relationship of art and combat in his culture—is most vivid in the baseball novel.[16] Though it has its own resemblance to combat writing, the most striking fact about baseball literature is how arty it is. Even as moralistic a book as *Bang the Drum Slowly* glides from morals to metafiction with athletic ease: the book is unassuming yet persistent in its self-reference. The narrator (and fictional author) is a character named Author; he refers occasionally to his previous book, as well as to the present one; the book we are reading has two time frames, the time it is describing and the time of its writing, and within the latter frame we hear about the submission of early chapters, which we have read, to a literature professor for a critique.

Philip Roth gets involved much more flamboyantly in the labyrinths of fictionality in *The Great American Novel,* the narrator/fictional author of which is the sportswriter Word Smith, a concise amalgam of Red Smith, William Shakespeare, William Wordsworth, and Henry Wadsworth Long-fellow, author of "The Village Blacksmith." The narrator discusses the "Great American Novel" in *The Great American Novel* with Hemingway; a discussion of the competition between Word Smith's attempt at the "GAN" and other candidates for the title follows. Unexpectedly, the book is comparable to Robert Coover's *The Universal Baseball Association,* in which Coover creates a fictional demiurge named J. Henry Waugh who sub-creates a fictional baseball league (which he also chronicles) which itself has a fictionalizing league historian.

It is not surprising that baseball, the most self-absorbed and literary of all sports, should produce metafiction almost naturally. But why should writers with referential ambitions, like Harris and Roth, have turned to baseball for its metafictional suitability? And why should Roth have done so in 1973—or, for that matter, why Coover in 1968—when the continuing war in Southeast Asia might have shattered any incipient self-reflexive baseball fantasy? Why was *Bang the Drum Slowly* turned into a movie in 1973, almost two decades after publication?

I do not mean that, in their self-conscious intricacies, these baseball novels have no contact with reality, or with war, at all. In every baseball novel, as in *The Natural,* there is too much bloodshed for anyone to assume that baseball is the entire subject. There are two ballfield murders in *The Universal Baseball Association,* and a wide assortment of diamond murders and maimings in *The Great American Novel.* (Roth's book takes place in 1943 and 1944—the war accounts for much of the weirdness of Patriot League pennant races.) War is a minor theme of *Bang the Drum Slowly*: we hear of the hero Bruce Pearson's incompetence in World War II, and the book's central metaphor is the card game TEGWAR (The Exciting Game Without Any Rules), the Shermanesque pastime that stands for the lawless cruelty that claims the Georgian Bruce Pearson's life.

On the one hand, we have the bookishness of metafiction, on the other, the paradigmatic extra-referentiality of the war novel, in every baseball book. At least part of the key to the paradox is provided by the advertising on the first page of *Bang the Drum Slowly* when it was republished, following the movie, in 1973: "Remember the 50s, when ballplayers were gods and the major leagues seemed like heaven? *Bang the Drum Slowly* is about those golden years." One should not need to commit all one's intellectual force to controverting bookjacket copy. I merely note that the ballplayers of *Bang the Drum Slowly* are not gods, the major leagues do not seem like heaven, and what the "golden years" amount to is the attenuation, cut off finally by Pearson's death, of pre-World War II America when a hick was still a hick. Still—there *is something* nostalgic about *Bang the Drum Slowly* that would be attractive in 1973—the bookjacket is correct despite itself. Despite Harris: as if a Borges parable, the novel published in 1973 is nostalgic exactly where the 1956 book was cynical. The players are mainly white, and mainly country boys. They have colorful nicknames. They are childish. Money is discussed, but rather small sums.

The antebellum baseball ethos is similarly, almost unwillingly, preserved in *The Great American Novel* and *The Universal Baseball Association.* This means that the baseball novel—even in the hands of writers like Coover and Roth, who are sardonic and antic, respectively, about the pastoral, prelapsarian pretensions of baseball and who are capable of concerning themselves with the football-loving President whose administration lasted from just after Coover's baseball novel to just after Roth's—is inevitably an exercise in mixed, but not mock, nostalgia. Roth's book takes place during a war, and his baseball season mimics it; Coover's is apocalyptic; neither book flees war to a pure pastoral utopia. This would have been bad faith in 1968 or 1973. But they have the war wrong. If Roth's book is set in World War II and Coover's in a numerological Armageddon, then what they both avoid is the war planted uncomfortably in every imagination without ordinal specification between the second world war and the third and final one—the anti-literary war that was fought while they wrote.

Vietnam was not absolute enough for their purposes; it was anaesthetic in its irrationality, impersonality, shapelessness, beginninglessness, endlessness. But it is missing—it is the thing not being written about—in every withdrawal from referentiality to signification. Roth's meta-picaresque follows a single hapless team, the Ruppert Mundys, whose ballfield has been turned over to the government for war use. To make them feel more at home wherever they have to play their games—since the whole season is "away"—an official at each park has been given a statement to announce by the league president's office: "Welcome Ruppert Mundys, welcome to _____, your home away from home! (PAUSE)." The "pause" is to allow an interval for neighborly cheering, but each official inevitably reads the word; the Mundys get to like it, and when an official at one park actually pauses, they are offended. Finally, a judicious ballplayer tries to calm everyone down. "A word," he says, "don't mean a thing that I could ever see. A whole speech is just a bunch of words from beginning to end, you know, that didn't fool nobody yet what's got half a brain in his head" (*GAN,* 137). Earlier, the league president had worried about the pernicious implications of radio broadcasts of games: "Why, the game might just as well not be happening, for all [listeners] knew! The whole thing might even be a hoax, a joke. . . . Furthermore, you could not begin to communicate through *words,* either printed or spoken, what this game was all about" (text's emphasis, *GAN,* 88). What the league president dreads is *The Great American Novel,* itself a hoax and a joke.

That literature was by its nature a hoax and a joke seemed to be the discovery of the 60s. But suppose Roth and Coover to be stymied by a repellent war; then conceivably we are led by the crazy bloodiness of these baseball books to conjure the unrepresented and anti-literary ghost itself. We might defend these books and their nostalgia by arguing that Vietnam, as endlessness, as inscrutability, as the final lapse of the agonistic element in war, was unavailable to the formal intelligence, so that allusions to other wars were a stratagem to make Vietnam appear (like an apparition) as what has been lost to beautiful play. In these terms I admire the courage of writers who admit—the admission is in the nostalgia for reference veiled by metafiction—that the central event of their time, for all their high literacy, belonged to others—because of their high literacy it belonged to others—and so admire metafiction as the publication and sly redemption of their failure.

The violence of these baseball books indicates Vietnam—or at least prevents their inability to represent Vietnam directly from turning into the positive invocation of a pastoral Utopia. The violence of baseball metafiction is a locally necessary paradox: football brutality infecting even baseball and even the most academic of literary forms in the 60s. What nags at this rationalization is that metafiction does not merely represent violence contingently or dutifully, but enacts it gleefully. In this respect, the violence of pacific baseball, almost as peaceful as pacific tennis, in the hands of metafictionists is token of the violence that metafiction does to reality. Non-representational, self-congratulatory fabulation emblematized by its own violence to resistant reality was the *appropriate* technique of the Nixon era.[17] The Vietnam baseball novel resembles Malamud's *The Natural* in importing violence into the text the source of which it cannot name; but in the Vietnam book, as opposed to Malamud's, the violence is in the textuality.

BASKETBALL

All basketball novels—like *The Centaur*—take betweenness as their aesthetic principle—they are entirely transition.[18] First, the basketball novel is the adolescent novel between the protracted innocence of the baseball book and the corruption of the football book. (Updike's Rabbit is a perpetual adolescent; the basketball players of Lawrence Shainberg's *One on One*, Jeremy Larner's *Drive, He Said*, and Coover's *The Origin of the Brunists* have unjettisoned late adolescent fantasies, anxieties, and dreams.) Second, it is most often the 50s book, in spirit, between the spiritually antebellum baseball book and the football book at home in the 60s. (*Drive, He Said*, just further than *Rabbit, Run* into the 60s—the rebel *almost* has a cause—assists Updike's book in attaching the basketball component to the Beat pun of car drive and sexual drive.) Finally, the basketball novel, situated between meta-literary baseball art and anti-literary football art, portrays the passing of mimesis.

Shainberg's *One on One* (not even distantly related to the silly movie of that name) is the classic case: as basketball is turned first into writing (the star center, Elwood Baskin, dreams about the newspaper accounts of his upcoming game almost to the point of missing it) and second into art (the hero fantasizes about a cement casting of the entire basketball scene, himself to be cast

and never released, at the moment of one of his own jump shots), the passage of time brings Elwood back from verbal and plastic fancies to the game that has almost been fully supplemented. Meanwhile, predictably, onanism threatens to supplement intercourse: when Baskin imagines the moment when "suddenly you and the ball and the hoop are *together,* all of one piece" (*OO*, 38), the displaced congress is descended from that of Romero and the bull in *The Sun Also Rises*. The object of basketball like bullfighting is sex that does not notice what is missing. The subjective overcoming of limits and absences might be called onanism, and it might be called transcendence; when Baskin's fantasy psychoanalyst has an epiphany—"Internal and external will merge into a continual rhythmic flow!" (*OO*, 211)—he approximates what Emerson called "spirit." The question is whether the book reduces Vietnam to a solipsist's fantasy or whether the hero's subjectivity is capable of expanding its circle to include the geography of Southeast Asia.

For thirteen of its fourteen chapters, *One on One* never mentions Vietnam, though the book was published in 1970 and is set just before. *Love,* as in Barth's *Lost in the Funhouse* in general, and "The Meneliad" in particular, is the missing referent of the substitutions that begin with onanism. In a series of displacements from love to sex to art, where can war appear—is Vietnam the unrealizable reality that requires us to take *One on One* as nothing but Baskin's Barthian microcosm? Not entirely. The fourteenth chapter reveals retrospectively that Vietnam is a repressed pressure on the book, which finally becomes intolerable. In the cab ride to the game, the radio is on, and the news keeps referring to Vietnam—five separate times. It interrupts the novel as slavery breaks into transcendentalist testimony: the historical fact that defines the necessity and impossibility of individual ideal transcendence.

When Vietnam finally enters the book as its repressed subject, it is only revealed by means of radio reports of succinct meaninglessness: "the Marines were battering an outpost west of Hue"; "in Vietnam today American Marines report the killing of four hundred thirteen Communists"; "the Johnson peace offensive is continuing" (*OO*, 202, 205, 207). Vietnam appears only as the moment in the book's dialectic when reality has been most displaced by words, when you might as well call a war offensive a peace offensive. If the sports novel exists to make a continuum from art to war, then what basketball as a subject can primarily do for the subgenre is allude to war as the defeat of that mimesis on which the basketball novel depends. The basketball book simply lacks the power of the baseball book to make the missing reality itself its metaliterary impetus. If the basketball novel is the transcendentalist novel of sports literature, if it tracks the progress of the subject from private to public, then Vietnam can only make its appearance as what cannot be assimilated, as what is beyond the possibility of intercourse, as bad publicity.

John Updike cannot afford to submit to this inevitability without a struggle—Updike believes in "the irrepressible combinations of the real!"[19] This sounds Stephen Dedalian but is more Thoreauvian: Updike's books attempt to reconstruct Thoreau's "realometer," in order to measure the true meanness of the world and publish it, or else graph the world's evolution from ants to God. The problem is that between *Rabbit, Run* and *Rabbit Redux*, the world does not merely get meaner—it gets lost. *Present* Vietnam reality in *Rabbit Redux* is as irrecoverable as Rabbit's *past* basketball stardom in *Rabbit, Run.*

The first two Rabbit novels are a parenthesis around the 60s: *Rabbit, Run,* published in 1960, precedes its sequel by eleven years. From the first words of the novel, it looks two ways. It begins with kids at play, kids who will grow up into the 60s but who remind Rabbit of his high school basketball stardom in the 50s. "Boys are playing basketball around a telephone pole with a backboard bolted to it. Legs, shouts. The scrape and snap of Keds on loose alley pebbles seems to catapult their voices high into the moist March air blue above the wires" (*Run,* 7). No wonder that the founding gesture of the book is a description of basketball, the sport of the body panting to be soul. Fundamental reality exactly observed (Keds sneakers) and heard (on loose pebbles) is already elevated by tropes (seems to catapult their voices) toward firmamental reality (into the moist air blue). Rabbit joins the game, and can still *play*: "Then the ball seems to ride up the right lapel of his coat and comes off his shoulder as his knees dip down, and it appears the ball is not going toward the backboard. It was not aimed there. It drops into the circle of the rim, whipping the net with a ladylike whisper. 'Hey!' he shouts in pride" (*Run,* 8).[20] This sets off Rabbit's quest to fill the gap between memory and presence, desire and satisfaction, earth and heaven, by a series of sexual conquests modeled on this first one—both sadistic (whipping the net) and genteel (with a ladylike whisper)—on behalf of Updike's desire for representational fullness.

Rabbit, Run culminates with Rabbit's flight from the cemetery into the woods, which he conceives of as an emptiness to be filled: "He arrives between the arms of the woods and aims for the center of the crescent." This begins a long passage of dense Updikean description, mimicking the enveloping natural density: "Rocks jut up through the blanket of needles, scabby with lichen; collapsed trunks hold intricate claws across his path." Everywhere there are gaps—"places where a hole has been opened up in the roof of evergreen"—but everywhere the gaps are being filled: "berrying bushes and yellow grass grow in a hasty sweet-smelling tumble" into every hole. Rabbit's final vision, it is true, is that he has confronted the abyss and the abyss is Rabbit. "He feels his inside as very real suddenly, a pure blank space in the middle of a dense net" (*Run,* 245-246, 254). The net toward which he has been shooting (the phrase registers ballistic violence) is himself. Perhaps Rabbit can eke a moment of transcendence out of resignation to vacancy—to what Jeremy Larner calls, in a similar dis-

play of the invariant basketball metaphor, the "void of freedom" (*DHS,* 186). But the book has depended on continually filling it in—the book lives to the extent that Rabbit can reclaim his basketball prowess.

In *Rabbit Redux,* first paragraph, Updike is still filling in: "the granite curbs starred with mica and the row houses differentiated by speckled bastard sidings and the hopeful small porches with their jigsaw brackets and gray milk-bottle boxes and the sooty gingko trees and the baking curbside cars wince beneath a brilliance like a frozen explosion" (*Redux,* 13). Rabbit will not walk down a street in *Rabbit Redux* without the street getting described, serially, gaplessly, reality turning by means of a crystalline violence, a frozen explosion, into literature. But there is a crisis. *Rabbit Redux* is published in 1971, takes place in 1969; uncrystallized Vietnam is the context.

The problem is considerable, so long as Vietnam comes into the novel the way it comes into *One on One*: Rabbit watches the news. Rabbit has his hawk opinions, Charlie Stavros, lover of Rabbit's wife, has his dove opinions—the war is elsewhere. So Updike determines to "Bring the War Home" (*Redux,* 240). Rabbit has an early vision of his young lover Jill burned "like a napalmed child" by his semen (*Redux,* p. 142); when, finally, Rabbit's illiberal neighbors burn his house (in which he has been harboring not only drop-out Jill but the messianic black man, Skeeter), and Jill is killed, it is no surprise that Skeeter senses that the "war is come home" half-literally (*Redux,* 290). The lesson, as in *The Centaur,* is that sex and war, or sex as war, inhabits every human gesture.

This is, however, facile. Updike knows that for all the Angstrom family proficiency at killing children (one baby drowned, one girl incinerated in two books), they are no Viet Cong or Green Berets. So he introduces a character—Skeeter—who has been in Vietnam; this maneuver brings the war in so baldly that it seems an admission of failure. "Tell us about Vietnam, Skeeter," Rabbit says, at the beginning of Skeeter's informal, familial lecture series. Even this strategy—the novel turning into pseudo-memoir and pseudo-essay, as if granting its generic ineptitude—does not get the job done. The war resists verbal representation: "there is no word" for the peacefulness of the dead; Skeeter realizes, "I'm not doing it justice, I'm selling it short" (*Redux,* 223, 228). Vietnam is an orifice that cannot be filled, rather spews out of itself: when Skeeter begins to describe the war, it is as if "colored fragments pour down toward him through the hole in the ceiling." If the frozen explosion is a lovely metaphor for Clausewitz's absolute war, then the point about Vietnam is that it was all chance and politics and friction. The pouring fragmentation, the unwillingness of the explosion to freeze, is an affront to Updike's mimesis. "It was very complicated, there isn't any net," Skeeter says, "to grab it all in" (*Redux,* 227). Which means it is not susceptible to a pure shooter's prowess, that is, Updike's.

Updike's attempt to get the war integrated into the novel seems increasingly desperate—"to bring the war home," he resorts to purely verbal methods. The name Charlie multiplies. It is the nickname of the Cong, the designation of Skeeter's company in Vietnam, Skeeter's term of abuse for all whites including Rabbit, and the name of Rabbit's wife's Greek lover: it applies to Asians, blacks, mainstream Protestant whites, and ethnic whites, from Vietnam to America. But the war, for Rabbit, is what he has irrevocably missed. For Updike, consequently, it is a sign of the Protestant God—everything that Updike cannot contain. His purely verbal methods for bringing the war into literature fail to the extent that they are purely verbal. Vietnam falsifies his theorem that war is not essentially different from peace.

Vietnam is what Updike wants sport to represent, but the metaphor is always in trouble. The competition of Rabbit and Charlie Stavros for Rabbit's wife is described alternately, as if indifferently, in basketball and war terms. Basketball terms: "Now [Rabbit] sees [Charlie] as a type he never liked, the competitor. The type that sits on the bench doing the loudmouth bit until the coach sends him in with a play or with orders to foul" (*Redux*, 160). War terms: Rabbit says, "You intervened, not me." Charlie replies, "I didn't intervene, I performed a rescue." Rabbit rejoins, "That's what all us hawks say" (*Redux*, 161). The idea is that the two metaphors interchangeably render the mortal competition of daily life; if this is true, then doves are closet hawks. On the other hand, sport is precisely what prevents daily life from always replicating war. "In a room obliquely off the main room, a pool table: colored boys all arms and legs spidering around the idyllic green felt. The presence of a game reassures Rabbit. Where any game is being played a hedge exists against fury" (*Redux*, 107). Scared Rabbit is a closet dove.

Updike's funhouse menagerie of hawks, doves, rabbits, and spiders—Updike's mobile taxonomy of the ambiguity of sport—permits him to pretend he has a way of bringing the war home and to acknowledge that he does not. As basketball fades from this novel along with Rabbit's skill (all that is left of his prowess is his ludicrously old-fashioned set shot), Updike's confidence that his technique is adequate to the world fades pari passu. Sport had been his way of making contact with middle-American reality; but indescribable Vietnam *is* America. "Man don't like Vietnam, he don't like America," Skeeter says, and Rabbit seconds it, in rare agreement (*Redux*, 232). The full extent of the tragedy is that for Updike mortality is the inability to describe. He feels reality slipping from him the way Rabbit feels the diminution of his basketball skills: as death. If the baseball novel portrays Vietnam as what is masked in the turn to self-referentiality, the basketball novel is suited for a passing reference. For writers like Updike, that was the sort of dying they could do during Vietnam.

FOOTBALL, THE HUNT

Lewis Mumford's comparison of mass sports to war by virtue of their regimentation, non-spontaneity, and nationalism seems peculiarly fitted to football;[21] mass

sports, he believes, rank only above war among the "least effective reactions against the machine"—which is to say that the reaction may be so weak as to constitute replication.[22] A black football player in Peter Gent's *North Dallas Forty* who seems to have been reading Mumford posts this sign: "MODERN MAN NO LONGER FEELS, HE MERELY REACTS. CREATIVITY HAS BEEN REPLACED BY CONFORMITY. LIFE HAS LOST ITS SPONTANEITY: WE ARE BEING MANIPULATED BY OUR MACHINES. THE INDIVIDUAL IS DEAD" (*NDF*, 158). Football—with its long bombs, blitzes, trenches, etc.—is a verbal compendium of twentieth-century war, so that the football novel ought to be the noncombatant's Vietnam novel.

The neat symmetry of the sports metaphor in terms of literary effects is simple to complete. If the baseball novel is meta-literary, the basketball novel anxiously literary, then the football novel is anti-literary. Language is in retreat: Billy Clyde Puckett, in Dan Jenkins' *Semi-Tough*, speaks of his "palatial apartment" until the adjective means as little to us as it does to him. Gary Harkness, the narrator of Don DeLillo's *End Zone*, stares at the phrase "When the going gets tough the tough get going" until "all meaning faded. . . . It was a sinister thing to discover at such an age, that words can escape their meaning" (*EZ*, 17). The football novel ought not to be quite a novel. *Semi-Tough* is supposedly spoken into a tape recorder, and *Why Are We In Vietnam?*, the apotheosis of the football novel, partly pretends to be a tape-recording of its narrator DJ's "brain in the deep of its mysterious unwindings" (*IV*, 24). Apparently the football anti-novel sacrifices its own literariness to capture the Vietnam era.

And yet—for all the despair of the finest football novelist, Don DeLillo, that words are losing their meaning, nevertheless he refuses the available series of equations above: football = war = the death of language. Rather, he presents as the problem of novelists the appalling purchase that football and war in fact have on language. They are simultaneously the arenas in which (1) obsolete language is revived, and (2) contemporary language is invented. In facing this scandal, DeLillo brings all the dilemmas of the 60s sports novel to an extreme paradoxical acuteness.

The first point recalls Fussell: war and football still cannot get along without the vocabulary World War I should have outmoded. When a football player gets killed in an automobile accident, "a local minister called him a fallen warrior"—the pre-World War I name for a military corpse. "Death is the best soil for cliché," Harkness explains (*EZ*, 69-70); he might have added that wartime clichés are superior for all irruptions of death. Nor can we conclude that the obsolete vocabulary of ancient wars is inappropriate to modern wars, so long as it is dead language that men are dying for: "It was easier to die than admit that words could lose their meaning" (*EZ*, 54).

More insidiously, war diction is not merely passé (though revived) but also à la mode. The field of atomic war generates its own vocabulary, which is not without aesthetic charm. "I became fascinated," Harkness confesses, "by words and phrases like thermal hurricane, overkill, circular error probability, post-attack environment, stark deterrence, dose-rate contours, kill-ratio, spasm war. Pleasure in these words" (*EZ,* 21). The pleasure is uniquely satisfying because the language refers, at once, to the grossest conceivable eventuality and to no referent at all—thus Derrida characterizes nuclear language as "fabulously textual." (The aesthetic pleasure might well be in the vertiginous confrontations of hard, often Anglo-Saxon and immaterial, often Latinate, terms: stark deterrence, kill-ratio.) Football coaches have the same Adamic power as generals: the coach is the "maker of plays, the name-giver. We were his chalk-scrawls" (*EZ,* 118, 135). Generals and football coaches, together, "reinvent the language" (*EZ,* 85). It is not an irony that the Texas football school of this novel is Logos College.

Observe the darker reason that football books have to be anti-novels: not so much in imitation of the death of language in football and war—in wargames—as in obeisance to the preemption of language, traditional and contemporary, by wargames. The question is how a novelist can maneuver with respect to an invasive diction. DeLillo's preliminary answer is a 250-page allusion to silence. When we first hear about the late President of Logos College, who "was a man of reason," "who cherished the very word," we assume it is a joke that "unfortunately he was mute" (*EZ,* 7). Not entirely. Harkness's project is a sort of non-verbal oneness with the Texas environment, which, toward the end of the novel, he glimpses: "Beyond the window was that other world, unsyllabled, snow lifted in the wind, swirling up, massing within the lightless white day, falling toward the sky" (*EZ,* 189). Thirty-eight syllables, as it happens, to suggest zero.

At least one of the things DeLillo leaves to the silence must be suspected. DeLillo never mentions Vietnam, never names it directly. One player's girlfriend spends a night with a soldier on leave (from "Nam"), and the black star of the team explains why his barren room must have a radio: "The place where words are recycled. The place where villages are burned. That's my Indochina" (*EZ,* 239). Vietnam only exists in the novel as recycled words, twice nicknamed in this book about naming.

Has it been haunting *End Zone*—burning villages veiled in prose—or has the book successfully evaded it? What is the quality of the silence about Vietnam? If readers of this chapter have been seduced to conclude that it is unnecessary to mention Vietnam because football allegorizes it, they have been misled in just the way that DeLillo's readers may be. DeLillo does the reader the courtesy of clarifying the matter twice, in the words of the book's two most convincing theorists. First, Harkness himself: "The exemplary spectator is the person who understands that sport is a benign illusion, the illusion

that order is possible. . . . The exemplary spectator has his occasional lusts, but not for warfare, hardly at all for that. No, it's detail he needs—impressions, colors, statistics, patterns, mysteries, numbers, idioms, symbols. Football, more than other sports, fulfills this need. . . . Here is not just order but civilization." And the eccentric Professor Zapalac, pure left-wing, is nevertheless attracted to General Sherman's tautology: "I reject the notion of football as warfare. Warfare is warfare" (*EZ,* 111-112, 164). Football has been aligned with nuclear wargames—the naming of the patterns of apocalypse—not war.

Quite as much as the baseball novelist who writes during Vietnam about World War II, and exactly like the baseball novelist who writes during Vietnam about an interior Armageddon, DeLillo avoids the war he might have invoked—though as a football novelist rather than a baseball novelist, he does not reinvoke the war as what he has eschewed. His position as a football novelist turns out to be unique not because he can approach nearer to Vietnam through the nature of his sport, rather because he cannot gauge the passing of reference or replace description with self-reference: the assumption among baseball and basketball novelists but not permitted among football novelists is that reality had formerly belonged to novelists like themselves. The football novelist, DeLillo suggests, is not allowed this belief or the consequent nostalgia or panic.

DeLillo is so admirably determined not to claim that he feels all the death of Vietnam in the death of his own art (as metaphorized, elsewhere, by the demise of pre-war baseball and 50s white basketball) that he makes the surprise gesture of identifying football *with* art—with impressions, patterns, mysteries, idioms, symbols—though not with representation. At the belligerent end of the spectrum from art to war that sport makes available, DeLillo tries to win it all back—football, sport, and at least imaginary war—though not Vietnam. His anti-novel is poised to assimilate the imaginary order of football and wargames into the passion for silence that their racket had seemed to inspire: the book's final twist is that their verbal inventiveness seems like DeLillo's a tribute to an unspeakable ideal, Clausewitz's absolute war, war removed from time. In the process, however, Vietnam, which baseball and basketball novelists manage paradoxically to display, paradoxically disappears. DeLillo accepts literary complicity in football and World War III but not Vietnam.

Norman Mailer's *Why Are We in Vietnam?* begins in Texas—which is the setting of every football novel I have named—and features as the father of the narrator one Rusty Jethroe, third-string football All-American in 1936 and 1937, current member of the Gridiron Club, the Dallas Cowboy Turtle Creek Cheering and Chowder, the TCU Boosters, and the SMU Boosters, who challenges son DJ to his first Oedipal showdown by means of a head-to-head running-tackling competition, and who takes DJ on the Alaskan adventure that is the subject of the book and the scene of their second Oedipal duel, on the premise that "the great white athlete is being superseded by the great black athlete" (*IV*, 110). *Why Are We in Vietnam?* starts where football novels leave off, and heads for Indochina.

Does it get there? On the final page of the anti-novel, Vietnam is mentioned twice, and the title seems decisive. If the title indicates that the Alaskan bear hunt is an allegory of Vietnam, then we learn that the war is a product of patricidal filial devotion, homoerotic homophobia, Negrophile Negrophobia, pious diabolism—each oxymoron indicative of white masculinity defeated and enraged—and the love of technology serving bestiality and anal aggressiveness turning into phallic aggression. That summary will have to serve as all the diagnosis Vietnam can get in this essay. The point here is that by virtue of these contradictions, the book portrays Vietnam as the quintessence of football—patricidal and filial, homophobic and homoerotic, Negrophile and Negrophobe, mechanical and primeval—as portrayed in all football novels.

But the book is not unambiguously an allegory of Vietnam, nor is the hunt unambiguously an extension of sport. Vietnam satisfies urges not satisfied by the hunt, which satisfies hungers not assuaged by football. The relation of the three activities might still be simple enough: they might be charted as increasingly hysterical attempts of white men to discharge primal instincts when the most sacred rituals of masculinity are conducted by blacks. If this were true, we could have the mediation of the football novel and the Vietnam novel accomplished neatly enough. At the last moment of *Why Are We in Vietnam?*, however, something peculiar happens. DJ announces that Tex and he are "off to see the Wizard in Vietnam"—first mention of that country and war. DJ immediately adds: "Unless, that is, I'm a black-ass cripple Spade and sending from Harlem" (*IV*, 208). This remark adverts to one of the book's occasional counter-suggestions: that Mailer is not ventriloquizing a WASP adventure inspired by fantasies about blacks but a black analysis or fantasy concerning WASPs. Deduce that Vietnam was generated out of the fictions that whites and blacks produce about each other—what would that mean? The crippled black—not only not going off to Vietnam but apparently not a daunting sexual threat—is inventing a white paranoia about blacks that only Vietnam can pacify?

It is not clear—and Mailer in an introduction admits he is not sure about his intention. We do not know what we need to know: is the bear hunt a white adventure or black fantasy of a white adventure? Will the bear hunt and Vietnam differ in the magnitude or the quality of their violence? A deeper obscurity, perhaps, is why the novel seeks to explain Vietnam in terms of the hankering of two white kids to fight, when white kids mainly did not volunteer. The book does not culminate in Rusty's love of Vietnam on behalf of the corporation (only DJ and Tex crave it) or any black's going off to

the war (since if DJ is a black, he is a crippled black). The book was originally intended, Mailer tells us, not as preliminary to DJ and Tex's volunteering for Vietnam but to their metamorphosis into Mansonesque terrorists in Provincetown. It cannot be assumed that the switch has been successfully made.

The best reading of Mailer is that the book was not written to represent Vietnam, rather, in his introductory terms, as "a diversion in the fields of dread" (*IV*, 5). This might mean that it is not so much about Vietnam as against it—that the hunt, which culminates in the pursuit of the bear by DJ and Tex without rifles, is not at all what leads them to Vietnam, but should have prevented that outcome. One mystery of the book's construction is the two-year blank interval between the hunt and the narration of the story followed by the decision to go to the war—possibly the solution is that it is not so much the hunt as the impossibility of reabsorption into Dallas society after the hunt, the paucity of appropriate Texan rituals rather than the Alaskan ritual, that drives DJ and Tex to war. The hunt might very well precede Vietnam not as a preface to it but as an inadequate prophylactic against it, as ritual violence that fails to ward off unleashed and unsanctified violence. The book might be taken as an attempt to redeem that failure: DJ and Tex are sent to Vietnam by mailer not as a realistic appraisal of who went to Vietnam and why, but as a symbolic sacrifice the homeopathic power of which is intended to prevent our technological, anti-metaphoric, profane commitment to the war.

Can it be said that the allegory of the book is precisely *not* of Vietnam?

> We will never know if primitive artists painted their caves to show a representation, or whether the moving hand was looking to placate the forces above and the forces below. Sometimes, I think the novelist fashions a totem just as much as an aesthetic, and his real aim, not even known necessarily to himself, is to create a diversion in the fields of dread, a sanctuary in some of the arenas of magic. . . . By such logic, the book before you is a totem, not empty of amulets for the author against curses, static, and the pervasive malignity of our electronic air. (*IV*, 4-5)

And against Vietnam, of which Mailer does not "show a representation." If Veblen is right that predatory activity shades off from war to the hunt to games seamlessly, then this essay exists to reverse the perspective and climb from (tennis to) baseball to basketball to football to the hunt back to war. But the misdirection of the 60s sports novel provides that the closer you get to Vietnam the more it is distanced and withheld: people die violently in baseball novels all the time, almost never in football novels. We grasp Vietnam in sports novels, if at all, as the thing that made novels seem less powerful, less representative, than ever before. On the other hand, we might value the Vietnam sports novel as verbal homeopathy. As postmodernist novels incline toward the (modernist) "sanctuary" (as mailer says) of textuality, textuality itself expands, so that the world is threatened, as if by book-burning. Mailer's Vietnam book reads the sports novel tradition that arrives at DeLillo, in which verbal bliss shadows the ecstasy of the contemplation of nuclear Armageddon. The homeopathic method is the converse of the metonymic method: by adding death to baseball as the formula of the baseball novel, and literary life to football as the formula of the football novel, sports novelists of the 60s brought the play of signifiers as near as possible to wargames as a diversion in the fields of dread.

PLAY, PART II

(1938-1939) "A happier age than ours once made bold to call our species by the name of *Homo Sapiens*."[23] So wrote Huizinga, in Leyden, in June 1938. The sentence, the first one of his distinguished study, *Homo Ludens*, makes sense in its own terms; the problem is that it comes close to making nonsense of the rest of the book. It might seem equally appropriate to open the book with the declaration, "Only a happier age than ours would make bold to call our species by the name of *Homo Ludens*," in which case the book would last one sentence before folding. What would justify, in 1938, a book on Homo Ludens any better than a book on Homo Sapiens? The answer seems to be that by 1938 no one could claim that we had ever been, essentially, sapient; in 1938, Huizinga proposes that we had always been ludic.

The hypothesis makes the urgency of the book comprehensible. That the book was personally pressing is unmysterious: Huizinga was writing it while Hitler was preparing his assault on Europe; Huizinga was translating it into English and adding material after Hitler had invaded Poland; he was in fact killed in the invasion of Holland. But the book feels historically and politically urgent: "To fill in all the gaps in my knowledge beforehand was out of the question for me. I had to write now, or not at all. And I wanted to write" (*HL*, foreword). The sense of crisis in the early prose is despite the conceivable reservation that nothing could be more irrelevant to Hitler's Europe than a scholarly, humane, civilized, generous study of the play principle in civilization. Huizinga believed, however, that Nazism was attractive precisely because its brutality was masked as play.

The two elaborations of play that Huizinga cares most about are poetry and war. Play is so thoroughly beautiful that aesthetics represents the single threat to the autonomy of the category (*HL*, 7). And poetry is still, of all human activities including all other arts, the one that "remains fixed in the play-sphere where it was born" (*HL*, 119). The detecting of play in war is more difficult and controversial. Nevertheless: "who can deny that in all these concepts—challenge, danger, contest, etc.—we are very close to the play-sphere" (*HL*, 40). Shakespeare's Agincourt—a sacred event (this is indicated but not defined by its dedication to St. Crispin and St. Crispian), ruled off in time and space, where an insult is rejoined

and glory is an object—might have been Huizinga's best demonstration that "Play is battle and battle is play" (*HL*, 41). It was the centrality to chivalric culture of tournaments and jousting that inspired *Homo Ludens* in the first place (*HL*, 104).

War is injuring and war is contest; clearly what is playful about war is exclusively the latter aspect. War is "very close to the play-sphere" insofar as it is "challenge, danger, contest." It is life conceived agonistically that best brings war into contact with play and hence with art: "On numerous Greek vases we can see that a contest of armed men is characterized as an agon by the presence of the flute-players who accompany it. At the Olympic games there were duels fought to the death" (*HL*, 49). If Burckhardt believed that a civilization, like the Greek, had no need of games if it had war, then Huizinga endeavors, on a Greek inspiration, to make the Scarrian idea plausible that a civilization has no particular need of war if every aspect of peace is thoroughly agonized.

Huizinga, however, was writing at the worst moment for proving that theorem. History seemed, in fact, to be moving in the contrary direction: civilization as play reached its summit in the eighteenth century, Huizinga comes to judge, and has been in decline ever since. This is doubtless the reason his book can seem zealous and strained. Huizinga is forced to be militant in his defense of play in this degraded and sobering epoch. The book is intellectually, politely aggressive and expansive. Play takes over, in successive chapters, law and war and metaphysics and poetry and myth and philosophy and art, until Huizinga finally surveys all of "Western civilization *Sub Specie Ludi*." I of course do not mean to identify Huizinga with the brutal expansionism that killed him. Nevertheless, he seems obliged to write as if conquering all the territory, domain by domain, that Nazism was devastating from the opposite side.

Another way to say it is that the conceptual uniting of war, play, and art is homeopathically close to what the Nazis were doing. In skirting that possibility, Huizinga is admittedly confused. As against German political theory, which describes the progression from peace to war as "the serious development of an emergency" (*HL*, 208), Huizinga argues that "it is not war that is serious, but peace." He immediately adds, "War and everything to do with it remains fast in the daemonic and magical bonds of play" (*HL*, 209). But that cannot be precisely put, because to nominate something as play, in this book, had never been to dismiss it as unserious. Yet: "we cannot deny that modern warfare has lapsed into the old agonistic attitude of playing at war for the sake of prestige and glory" (*HL*, 210). From sentence to sentence, it is not clear where Huizinga is going to come out.

Huizinga resorts to a desperate stratagem. The Nazis are not playful after all; they are puerile. In some ways this demarcation makes perfect sense. War is ludic insofar as it is rule-bound (countries should declare war before invading other countries [*HL*, 208]), agonistic insofar as the enemy is respected (*HL,* 209), aesthetic if the political motive is secondary (*HL,* 210). In all these respects the Nazis were not playing. Yet Hitler's preference for the gamble is reminiscent of the play spirit (*HL,* 210). Huizinga might also have mentioned other facets of his appeal, like the excessiveness of his demagoguery. The only solution is to assert that the Nazis were playing at play, playing the "play-concept of war false" (*HL,* 210). The play element must not "be a false seeming, a masking of political purposes behind the illusion of genuine play-forms" (*HL,* 211).

This seems to me *ad hoc*: Huizinga admits that the "puerilism" of contemporary life had once seemed to him a "play-function."

> I have now come to a different conclusion. . . . [I]f our modern puerilism were genuine play we ought to see civilization returning to the great archaic forms of recreation where ritual, style and dignity are in perfect unison. The spectacle of a society rapidly goose-stepping into helotry is, for some, the dawn of the millennium. We believe them to be in error. (*HL,* 206)

The criterion of playfulness seems to me unmeetable: to rule out Nazis, you would have to rule out everything. In another context, the goose-step would not have seemed a despicable emblem; it would have seemed a genuine play element itself.

Huizinga has been playing a dangerous game. The game is intellectual homeopathy, and taken in enormous doses, the cure makes acquaintance with the disease. Huizinga wanted to carry sacred art into the domain of war, partly to condemn modern war for its apostasy. The line proved impossible to draw cleanly. Possibly Huizinga should have stuck by an earlier formulation, rather atypical of him, but typical at least of the dilemma war causes him.

> The noble life is seen as an exhilarating game of courage and honour. Unfortunately, even in archaic surroundings war with its grimness and bitterness offers but scant occasion for this noble game to become a reality. Bloody violence cannot be caught to any great extent in truly noble form; hence the game can only be fully experienced and enjoyed as a social and aesthetic fiction. That is why the spirit of society ever again seeks escape in fair imaginings of the life heroic, which is played out in the ideal sphere of honour, virtue, and beauty. (*HL,* 101)

That war is contest does not mean that war is beautiful, because war is injuring. The play-spirit does not really connect art and war; art *imagines* that the play-spirit connects art and war. The last two sentences of Huizinga's passage add up to this: because war is not beautiful, society fancies that war is beautiful. The beauty of war is a fiction, Homer's Athena's illusion. But to admit that is to concede that the book is less powerful than it had seemed; insofar as it made war

beautiful it played playing false; the play-spirit does not provide a measure against which to condemn Nazi warfare, because the play-spirit had never really informed war. Homeopathy can endorse Nazi hypocrisy if it imports the play spirit where it does not naturally belong. If, on the other hand, war had ever been playful, it might, to that extent, be play for Nazis also.

(1984) The most sensational and influential section of Jacques Derrida's "No Apocalypse, Not Now (full speed ahead, seven missiles, seven missives)"[24] is the third missive, in which Derrida describes nuclear warfare as "fabulously textual" (*D,* 23), by which he primarily indicates that it exists only, until it occurs, as literature. (No actual war has ever been so out of proportion to previous wars as to make anticipation thoroughly imaginary; no other anticipated war ever inspired so much imagining.) Derrida of course is not attempting to make the phenomenon (the imagining) harmless: "For the 'reality' of the nuclear age and the fable of nuclear war are perhaps distinct, but they are not two separate things" (*D,* 23). This means that the voluminous literature of nuclear warfare—in the absence of any previous war that helpfully foreshadows it—is the sole guide of the actual diplomatic, technological, and military gamesmanship that has real and immediate as well as hypothetical effects.

This is the fullest textualization of warfare in history—possibly the textualization prevents anything beyond it. Derrida goes on to show how it is not merely that military affairs have been textualized; textuality has always, prefiguratively, been approaching nuclear war (*D,* 26-28). Since the seventeenth century, since the opening of the Age of Reason, literature has apprehended its own contingency; because its relationship to any referent is always creative, literature is exactly what could not survive a nuclear war. The reasoning here is a little odd, since Derrida has been considering *total* nuclear war, the thing that *nothing* human could survive; and he is not sure that literature's relation to the referent is peculiar. The tactic of positing a nuclear remainder that discriminates literature from non-literature is a thought experiment that might be restated this way. Suppose that only two people, a man and a woman of childbearing age, survived the war. It would be possible to fancy, in the next pulse of human history, Archimedean, Newtonian, and Einsteinian physics, but not Dante, Shakespeare, or Tolstoy. This may or may not be true; but since the seventeenth century, literature has conceived it to be true, that is, considered that it was uniquely contingent, susceptible to absolute annihilation.[25]

Though you might assume that this eventuality would be literature's horror, Derrida suspects that literature, like Hawthorne's Coverdale, longs for apocalypse: "Who can swear that our unconscious is not expecting this? dreaming of it, desiring it?" (*D,* 23). This is not, however, as necessary to his argument as the theorem that we (humanists) have been *depending* on it, at least insofar as we cherish literature, distinct from science, for its freedom.

Derrida brings war to literature and literature to war, thus his running series of meta-tropes: what "weapons of irony" are appropriate to a conference on "nuclear criticism"? What would be its characteristic "arguments and its armaments, its modes of persuasion or intimidation" (*D,* 21)? The title—"seven missiles, seven missives"—turns out to be a kind of Heideggerian analogy, with overtones from Revelation, of the way that writing and weaponry are projected into the world.

What is the point of this assimilation? It is not to domesticate the possibility of absolute holocaust; it is not to create a bad conscience among humanists; it is not to win a Hellish glamour for literary theory. The answer emerges from three passages of Derrida's text that adumbrate his surprise ending.

First:

> For the "reality" of the nuclear age and the fable of nuclear war are perhaps distinct, but they are not two separate things. It is the war (in other words the fable) that triggers this fabulous war effort, this senseless capitalization of sophisticated weaponry, this speed race in search of speed, this crazy precipitation which, through techno-science, through all the techno-scientific inventiveness that it motivates, structures not only the army, diplomacy, politics, but the whole of the human *socius* today, everything that is named by the old words culture, civilization, *Bildung, scholè, paideia.* "Reality," let's say the encompassing institution of the nuclear age, is constructed by the fable. . . . (*D,* 23)

This is a fabulator's absolutism (like DeLillo's) in the image of absolute war, a step beyond Huizinga's imperial playfulness in the image of imperialistic puerilism. Nevertheless, it is perhaps less absolute than it appears. Derrida first declares that civilization is "structured" by the fable, then that "reality" is "constructed" by the fable, which is not quite to say that there is only the fable. Otherwise, the words "senseless" and "crazy" would be impossible. It is not clear to me how the words are possible in a civilization even only "structured" by the fable, unless it is licit to say that a thesis structures its antithesis. I doubt that that is what Derrida means either.

Second:

> No, nuclear war is not *only* fabulous because one can *only* talk about it, but because the extraordinary *sophistication* of its technologies—which are also the technologies of delivery, sending, dispatching, of the missile in general, of mission, missive, emission, and transmission, like all *technè*—the extraordinary sophistication of these technologies coexists, cooperates in an essential way with sophistry, psycho-rhetoric, and the most cursory, the most archaic, the most crudely opinionated psychagogy, the most vulgar psychology. (*D,* 24)

What makes nuclear war fabulous here is its combination of sophistication and vulgarity, but I am not certain why. Derrida goes on to explicate the passage as if he had only

said that technology has to be mixed with *doxa,* with opinion and opinion about opinion. In the passage itself, "missiles" is aligned with "missives" in the technology part of the equation—Derrida's missive is *all* sophistication—and is distinguished from not merely *doxa* but vulgar *doxa.* Once again, terms of opprobrium imply that there is a structural principle in the culture (distinguishing sophistication from vulgarity) after nuclear warfare (which does not recognize the distinction) has totally structured it.

Third:

> I am thus choosing, as you have already observed, the genre or rhetorical form of tiny atomic nuclei (in the process of fission or division in an uninterruptible chain) which I shall arrange or rather which I shall project toward you, like tiny inoffensive missiles: in a discontinuous, more or less haphazard fashion. (*D,* 21)

If the text is itself a fission bomb, why "inoffensive"? This is all the more surprising in that a later passage, again associating missives and missiles, is careful not to suggest that that association reduces bombs "to the dull inoffensiveness that some would naively attribute to books. It recalls (exposes, explodes) that which, in writing, always includes the power of a death machine" (*D,* 29). If Derrida's paper was inoffensive merely insofar as no one was killed by it, he has made the rhetorical mistake of exculpating literature just on the brink of implicating it. I am tempted to believe that Derrida means "the opposite of offensive," that is, "defensive." But he does not say "defensive," nor does his essay care about any offensive-defensive distinction in the discourse of nuclear strategy. Perhaps he is being modest.

Why does Derrida keep exposing the attraction of nuclear war and textuality and then keep, in effect, denying it? The answer comes, at long last, in the movement from the fourth to the fifth missive. In the fourth, Derrida isolates the "destruction" in "deconstruction" (*D,* 27); he reveals deconstruction to be the theory of the nuclear age, which is equal to the epoch of literature. "Literature belongs to the nuclear age by virtue of the performative character of its relation to the referent." Then comes the surprise of the apothegm of the fifth missive: *"But we do not believe, such is the other version or the other side of the same paradox, in any thing except the nuclear referent"* (*D,* 28).

The referent repressed by literary history, repressed in order that literature might have a history, is absolute disappearance. Insofar as we had thought of deconstruction as attention to the free play of signfiers forming links with signifieds that turn into signifiers, we had thought of writing as unbounded. Even death could be absorbed into this formulation, since death can be denigrated to a significant event by survivors. But insofar as literature is essentially contingent, it always points to annihilation, the singularity at the end of signification: "The only 'subject' of all possible literature, of all possible criticism, its only ultimate and a-symbolic referent, unsymbolizable, even unsignifiable; this is, if not the nuclear age, if not the nuclear catastrophe, at least that toward which nuclear discourse and the nuclear symbolic *are still beckoning*: the remainderless and a-symbolic destruction of literature." In making annihilation the referent of literature, Derrida does not bring it into or up against literature: it is literature's only referent because it is "that unassimilable wholly other"; the relation is one of "incommensurability" (*D*, 28).

From this vantage, we have to return to all Derrida's puns of Ars and Mars and reread them. Literature is said to depend on "a project of stockpiling, of building up an objective archive over and above any traditional oral base," as well as on the legalities of authorship (*D*, 26). These two conditions define contingency: literary history is a development that moves not by closer approximations of the world but by the accumulation of unrepeatable, individually authored, events. What one picks out of this particular formulation, of course, is the term "stockpiling." It is not immediately clear what to make of it—until the revelation that literature aims at what it can never, by accumulation, annihilate: annihilation. "Stockpiling" indicates something outside of literature, more powerful than literature, wholly incommensurable with it, unsignifiable by it, but undermining it so definitively that you might as well say it is underwriting it. Literature stockpiles texts because it is radically vulnerable to destruction by stockpiled weapons. Derrida's logic is the logic of homeopathy ("strategic maneuvers to assimilate the unassimilable" [*D*, 28]): every move of deconstruction, as the theory best adapted to the precariousness of literature, is an attempt to reveal the resemblance of health and illness, up to and including the end of death and life at once. Derrida calls nuclear catastrophe the "absolute *pharmakon*" (*D*, 24). The logic of homeopathy turns poison into cure.

Stockpiling is the condition, Derrida says, of literature—that is, of writing—"over and above any traditional oral base"; epic is always excluded from what Derrida means by "literature" as such, not participating in its radical historical contingency. This book began with the insufficiency of oral poetry to modern, post-Trojan, war; literature is not so much sufficient to it as a progressive admission of its own ineptitude. At the near end of this epoch, the most admired literature has so lost the world as to resemble atechnology for sacrificing it, just as the nuclear technology for sacrificing it almost dissolves entirely into literature. That is only to assert that literature as play, as beautiful contingency in the fields of fate, seeks to resemble what threatens it infinitely.

NOTES

1 Vladimir Nabokov, *Bend Sinister* (New York: McGraw-Hill, 1947), vi.

2 Vladimir Nabokov, *Lolita* (New York: Berkley, 1955). All further references to this edition, abbreviated *L*, will be inserted parenthetically in the text.

3 *Bend Sinister*, vi.

4 Thomas Pynchon, *The Crying of Lot 49* (New York: Bantam, 1966). I have been told several times that 1966 is too early to expect much on Vietnam. But it was in February 1965 that Johnson began bombing North Vietnam; the April demonstration in Washington attracted 20,000 people. Between December 1964 and October 1965, SDS membership increased from 2,500 to 10,000. In the spring of 1966, sit-ins began at universities across the country. And one of the key events in shaking American consciences, the self-immolation of Buddhists, is recorded in *Lot 49*. See Allen J. Matusow, *The Unraveling of America: A History of Liberalism in the 1960s* (New York: Harper & Row, 1984), 319-21.

5 Pynchon, 42.

6 John Barth, *Lost in the Funhouse* (New York: Bantam, 1968). All further references to this edition, abbreviated *LF*, will be inserted parenthetically in the text.

7 Donald Barthelme, *Snow White* (New York: Bantam, 1967), 82.

8 Timothy J. Lomperis, *"Reading the Wind": The Literature of the Vietnam War* (Durham: Duke Univ. Press, 1987), 42; the count of Vietnam novels comes from Lomperis.

9 Bernard Malamud, *The Natural* (New York: Pocket Books, 1952); all further references to this edition, abbreviated *TN*, will be inserted parenthetically in the text.

10 John Updike, *The Centaur* (Greenwich, Conn.: Fawcett, 1963); all further references to this edition, abbreviated *TC*, will be inserted parenthetically in the text.

11 See Richard Carlton, "Sport as Art—Some Reflections on Definitional Problems in the Sociology of Sport," in David F. Lancy and B. Allan Tindall, eds., *The Anthropological Study of Play: Problems and Prospects* (Cornwall, N.Y.: Leisure Press, 1976), 25-26.

12 Thorstein Veblen, "Modern Survivals of Prowess," in John T. Talamini and Charles H. Page, eds., *Sport & Society* (Boston: Little, Brown, 1973), 47.

13 G. B. Harrison, ed., *Shakespeare: The Complete Works* (New York: Harcourt, Brace & World), 1968), 734. All further references to this edition, abbreviated *CW*, will be inserted parenthetically in the text.

14 Kendall Blanchard, "Team Sports and Violence: An Anthropological Perspective," in Lancy and Tindall, 95.

15 René Girard, *Violence and the Sacred*, trans. Patrick Gregory (Baltimore: The Johns Hopkins Univ. Press, 1977), 154, 219.

[16] I consider the following books under this heading. Mark Harris, *Bang the Drum Slowly* (New York: Dell, 1956). Robert Goover, *The Universal Baseball Association, Inc.: J. Henry Waugh, Prop* (New York: New American Library, 1968). Philip Roth, *The Great American Novel* (New York: Holt, Rinehart and Winston, 1973); all further references to this edition, abbreviated *GAN,* will be inserted parenthetically in the text.

[17] For an analysis of Nixon (in association with Mailer and Herr) as a kind of New Journalist, see Susan Jeffords, *The Remasculinization of America: Gender and the Vietnam War* (Bloomington: Indiana Univ. Press, 1989), 22-35.

[18] I consider Robert Coover, *The Origin of the Brunists* (London: Arthur Baker, 1966); Lawrence Shainberg, *One on One* (New York: Holt, Rinehart and Winston, 1970), references to which, abbreviated *OO,* will be inserted parenthetically in the text; Jeremy Larner, *Drive, He Said* (New York: Delacorte, 1964), references to which, abbreviated *DHS,* will be inserted parenthetically in the text; John Updike, *Rabbit, Run* (Greenwich, Conn.: Fawcett, 1960) and *Rabbit Redux* (Greenwich, Conn.: Fawcett, 1971), references to which, abbreviated *Run* and *Redux,* respectively, will be inserted parenthetically in the text.

[19] John Updike, *Roger's Version* (New York: Knopf, 1986), 56.

[20] See *The Origin of the Brunists* for an example of the invariance of metaphorics within sports: the aging star, wearing a coat, is "Tiger" not "Rabbit," but he intrudes on a kids' game in March, his muscles seem to remember what to do, and his shot touches only net, at which moment he shouts with sexual pride.

[21] Under the heading "football novel," I consider Dan Jenkins, *Semi-Tough* (New York: New American Library, 1972); Peter Gent, *North Dallas Forty* (New York: William Morrow, 1973), references to which, abbreviated *NDF,* will be inserted parenthetically in the text; Norman Mailer, *Why Are We in Vietnam?* (New York: Holt, Rinehart and Winston, 1967, preface 1977), references to which, abbreviated *IV,* will be inserted parenthetically in the text; Don DeLillo, *End Zone* (New York: Pocket Books, 1973), references to which, abbreviated *EZ,* will be inserted parenthetically in the text.

[22] Lewis Mumford, "Sport and the 'Bitch Goddess,'" in Talamini and Page, 65.

[23] Johan Huizinga, *Homo Ludens: A Study of the Play Element in Culture* (Boston: Beacon, 1955), foreword. All further references to this edition, abbreviated *HL,* will be inserted parenthetically in the text.

[24] Jacques Derrida, "No Apocalypse, Not Now (full speed ahead, seven missiles, seven missives)," *Diacritics,* 14 (1984). All further references to this volume, abbreviated *D,* will be inserted parenthetically in the text.

[25] Clausewitz believes that actual battle is to all other belligerent operations what cash payment is to credit, or gold to money. This causes Raymond Aron, in his book on Clausewitz, to wonder whether cold war might cause "permanent inflation," i.e., escalating threats of complete destruction, or, on the other hand, "permanent warfare." That writing has no backing on the model of gold is a premise of post-structuralism (I am necessarily thinking here of the work of Walter Michaels); by this similar route nuclear war meets "the text." See Raymond Aron, *Clausewitz: Philosopher of War,* trans. Christine Booker and Norman Stone (Englewood Cliffs, N.J.: Prentice-Hall, 1985).

Allen Guttmann

SOURCE: "Out of the Ghetto and onto the Field: Jewish Writers and the Theme of Sport," in *American Jewish History,* Vol. LXXIV, No. 3, March, 1985, pp. 274-86.

[In the following essay, Guttmann assesses the contribution of Jewish writers to the development of the American sports literature.]

It is now a commonplace of literary criticism that Jewish writers emerged in the 1940's and 1950's as a major force in American letters. It is less widely realized that Jewish writers have also contributed disproportionately to the development of sport as a theme for novels, plays, poems, and stories. The explanation for both phenomena lies in the complex processes by which immigrants to the United States have become Americans. If we want to understand why Jews seemed in the postwar period almost to dominate American literature and why Jewish writers seemed especially fascinated by baseball and other sports, we must be students of history and sociology before we can be psychologists or textual analysts. To say this is not to denigrate psychological or linguistic approaches to literature; it is merely to insist that such themes as "the son's search for the father" are best understood when one realizes who these fathers and sons were and what kind of a world they inhabited.[1]

I have argued elsewhere, at some length, that Jewish writers seemed to dominate the postwar literary scene because they were obsessed by the theme of Americanization. As they became assimilated into American society, they began to ask themselves, often with searing intensity, how is it possible to be simultaneously a Jew and an American?[2] Not *is* it possible, which might have seemed a reasonable question before the process of assimilation had begun, but *how* is it possible. In other words, assimilation and the resultant crisis of identity fueled the fires of literary ambition. From the need to understand the self came the ability to show others the complexity of modern identity. Obviously, Jews were not the only people to arrive at Ellis Island and experience culture shock, but Jewish immigrants from the ghettos and *shtetlach* of Eastern Europe can be distinguished by two facts: first, their journey to America was a more nearly total cultural transformation than was, for example, the immigration of Protestants arriving from the British Isles; second, they already possessed a highly developed literary tradition. While Catholic immigrants driven from the peasant villages of Ireland or Italy and Black Americans uprooted from the tribal societies of Africa also suffered intense dislocation and cultural disorientation, they did not very often, at least not until rather recently, turn their anguished experiences into literature. The *Ostjuden* did. (It is significant that German Jews arriving in the United States during the nineteenth century were seldom moved to dramatize the experience of assimilation in fiction or poetry. They had the requisite verbal skills but not the psychological need.)

The Americanization of East European Jews was characterized by another important factor. While most immigrants, even the Afro-Americans, who were scarcely "immigrants" in the ordinary sense, tended to linger for at least a generation in a cultural twilight zone between the old homeland and the New World, first-generation Jews frequently rejected the rich but burdensome traditions of their Orthodox ancestors in order to survive and succeed in America. The dilemma of the Orthodox Jew was poignantly described by the hero of Abraham Cahan's novel, *The Rise of David Levinsky*:

> If you are a Jew of the type to which I belonged when I came to New York and you attempt to bend your religion to the spirit of your new surroundings, it breaks. It falls to pieces. The very clothes I wore and the very food I ate had a fatal effect on my religious habits. A whole book could be written on the influence of a starched collar and a necktie on a man who was brought up as I was. It was inevitable that, sooner or later, I should let a barber shave my sprouting beard.[3]

For Russian or Polish Jews like Levinsky, the culture shock was intense. And the literary response was equally intense. But what does this have to do with sport? A great deal. Sport, an increasingly important modern institution, became a central metaphor for the entire process of Americanization of which it was a small but vital part. Since sport had never been a significant aspect of Orthodox tradition, it was an especially powerful metaphor of contrast.

For Jews as for others, the relative freedom of modern sport from the ascriptive limitations of race, religion, nationality, gender, and social class made it an especially attractive embodiment of democratic ideals. Of course Jews, like other disadvantaged groups, were aware of the all too numerous betrayals of the ideal, in sport as elsewhere, but sport seemed nonetheless the domain where the ideal was most closely approached. Since sport also provided opportunities for what Johan Huizinga, following Friedrich Schiller, called "the play-instinct," its appeals were all but irresistible.

These generalizations, inevitably simplified, can be exemplified by a scene from Cahan's first novel, *Yekl: A Tale of the New York Ghetto* (1896). The novel opens in a sweatshop in which Yekl, now renamed Jake, boasts to his fellow immigrants that he is a real American because he understands the mysteries of sport. He tells the others all about John L. Sullivan. Indicating that Yekl communicates mainly in Yiddish, Cahan uses italics for interspersed English terms, many of which refer to sport.

> Jimmie Corbett *leaked* him, and Jimmie *leaked* Cholly Meetchel, too. *You can betch you bootsh!* Johnnie could not leak Chollie, *becaush* he is a big *bluffer*, Chollie is . . . But Jimmie *pundished* him. *Oh, didn't he knock him out of shight!*

When the other workers, simultaneously impressed and appalled, point out that boxing is a brutal and brutalizing activity, unsuited for an educated and civilized person, Yekl has a ready answer.

> *Alla right,* let it be as you say; the *fighters* are not *ejecate*. No, not a bit! But what will you say to *baseball*? All *college boys* and *tony peoplesh* play it.

The others admit to the truth of these assertions. That "college boys" were actually more likely to play football rather than baseball is irrelevant. Baseball was the national game. To know baseball was to be a real American.

Cahan never did write an entire novel in which sport was a central theme, but one should note that the protagonist of his longest and best work, David Levinsky, falls in love with a Russian-born girl whose Americanization has reached the point where she, like Philip Roth's Brenda Patimkin, plays a mean game of tennis.

The two sports which attract Yekl, baseball and boxing, were the first sports to fascinate American writers, Jews and non-Jews alike. It is possible that Jewish writers turned to these two sports because they seemed to represent the attractive and the unattractive aspects of Americanization. If baseball, despite its urban origins and popularity, carried with it pastoral connotations (hence the myth of Abner Doubleday and the cow pasture), boxing was unmistakably associated with the rough and tumble of city streets. Baseball was the fair promise of a place in the sun; boxing was the grim reality of survival of the fittest. Jewish writers tended to ignore the fact, well recognized by Robert Coover in *The Universal Baseball Association,* that baseball was also a very modern game characterized by a myth of "scientific play" and an obsession for quantified, measurable achievement.[5]

In the generation of Jewish writers that followed Cahan, sport remained a minor metaphor. Ludwig Lewisohn's fictionalized autobiography, *The Island Within* (1928), is a passionate polemic against assimilation and for the concept of Jewish peoplehood. Lewisohn's reference to the national game is part of his Menckenesque dismissal of American society as a mob of halfwits:

The state is an image—brazen, remote, implacable except by stealthy magnates; the augurs, fat-paunched, bellow at each other on the public roads; the gates of the land are sealed; the duped and stupefied populace . . . dances about fundamentalist preachers, baseball pitchers and a Rumanian queen . . ."[6]

Few writers have been as negative about sport as Lewisohn was.

In the best of his numerous novels, *The Old Bunch* (1937), Meyer Levin tells the story of a group of second-generation Chicago Jews whose determined drive for Americanization makes of them doctors, lawyers, teachers, union-organizers, businessmen, criminals, artists. There is no rabbi among them, but one of the bunch becomes a passionate bicycle racer. Why Levin did not choose a more typically representative sport, baseball or boxing, is puzzling, but Sol Meisel's races are dramatically and positively presented.

When Clifford Odets wrote *Golden Boy* (1937), he had more than simply the process of assimilation in mind. Although there are several Jewish characters in the play, Odets chose to make his hero an Italian American—a technique of displacement that he was by no means the last to employ. Odets concentrated not on the abandonment of religious orthodoxy but on the conflict between the concert stage and the boxing arena. Joe Bonaparte plays the violin, which is a stereotyped link to the musical culture of the old country; he is good with his fists as well as with his fingers, which draws him toward the new environment. It is not much of a play; the situation is implausible, the characters are flat, the dialogue is stilted, and the conclusion, in which Joe is killed in an automobile crash, is melodramatic. Nonetheless, *Golden Boy* is one of the earliest exploitations of sport as a metaphor for Americanization.

Budd Schulberg, a much better writer than Odets, was drawn like Odets to sport as well to the workers' struggle for unionization. (Schulberg's *On the Waterfront* can be compared to Odets' *Waiting for Lefty*). *The Harder They Fall* (1947) is a landmark in the literary use of sport. The story of Argentine heavyweight boxer El Toro Molino is of far more than historical importance. One can still read it for insight into the penumbra of subterfuge, deceit, and criminality which surrounded the ring. It is not, in the words of one of Schulberg's characters, about "violinists with brittle hands"[7] No more than Odets, however, did Schulberg focus upon the Jewish boxers who were then vastly overrepresented in the profession. He chose to model El Toro Molino on the Italian heavyweight Primo Carnera, whose career certainly had its comic and its tragic moments. Schulberg concentrates on the tragic. Boxing is "a genuinely manly art, dragged down through the sewers of human greed" (p. 281). The writer-narrator is asked, "Mr. Lewis, what is it that turned a fine sport into a dirty business?" "Money," he replies (p. 7). In this case, the money is made by a cabal of crooks who build the untalented giant's reputation

with a series of fixed fights and then, when he is battered and hospitalized in the aftermath of his one genuine bout, cheat him of his earnings and abandon him. His owner's heartless comment? "Did you ever see a worse bum?" (p. 334).

A Stone for Danny Fisher (1951) is not in the same aesthetic class with *The Harder They Fall,* but Harold Robbins deserves mention as one of the very few authors to have created a Jewish boxer. Driven by poverty, Danny Fisher ignores his father's vehement, horrified, religiously motivated opposition and begins to make a name for himself as a fighter. Unlike Schulberg's innocent, victimized Argentine, Robbins' hero double-crosses his gangster owner and wins a fight he'd been paid to lose. He compounds his sins by winning the love of the owner's girl friend and repeatedly mauling the hitmen who attempt—over the next several years—to mete out gangland justice. In the end, inevitably, the mob gets its revenge and the moral is plain. There are better roads to success than the crooked street of the fight business. (In subsequent best-sellers, Robbins seems to have explored most of them.)

The year after Robbins' *A Stone for Danny Fisher* appeared, Bernard Malamud published his first novel, *The Natural* (1952). Although the novel's glory has faded somewhat, it too has historical importance. Not yet aware that his true vocation as a writer was to create a mythical ghetto peopled with cobblers, bakers, tailors, marriage-brokers, and storekeepers who might just as well have lived in Warsaw or Vilna as in New York, Malamud attempted a fantasy of sport and religious myth. Malamud's real interest lies less in baseball than in the vegetation myths of divine death and rebirth which are a main theme of Sir James Frazier's *The Golden Bough* and form the central structure of T. S. Eliot's poem, *The Waste Land.* Roy Hobbs is a version of the Grail Knight questing after the cup from which Jesus drank at the Last Supper, and Roy's manager, Pop Fisher, is a version of the mysteriously wounded "Fisher King" whose impotence has made the wasteland, in this case the baseball field, arid and infertile. In many ways, the book is an erudite literary spoof.

Malamud's hero comes from the Far West rather than from the slums of Baltimore or the sidewalks of New York. When he arrives in the city, the grass of the outfield turns green and he "romped in it like a happy calf in its pasture."[8] The pastoral elements are heightened to myth. Roy's magic bat, Wonderboy, is also his "foolproof lance" (p. 9), with which he terrorizes luckless pitchers. The ancient goddesses—Ishtar, Isis, Aphrodite—appear in the guise of the mysterious Harriet Bird, referred to as "a snappy goddess" (p. 25). The first part of the novel ends when Roy is shot by Harriet Bird in his Chicago hotel room. The scene mingles memories of the dead gods—Tammuz, Osiris, Adonis, Jesus—with less mythical resemblances to the sad fate of Eddie Waitkus.

The stage is set for the second part of the novel, in which Malamud introduces his version of Eliot's mythic poem. The wounded Fisher King, who rules over the sterile land, appears as Pop Fisher, manager of the New York Knights, a man afflicted with itchy hands. He waits vainly for the life-giving rain: "It's been a blasted dry season. No rains at all. The grass is worn scabby in the outfield and the infield is cracking. My heart feels as dry as dirt for the little I have to show for all my years in the game" (pp. 34-35). Hobbs brings rain to the parched land and an end to the team's slump. The first time he comes to bat a tremendous noise cracks the sky and "a few drops of rain spattered to the ground" (p. 63). Moments later comes the deluge, which turns the grass green at last. Pop Fisher's hands heal. Unfortunately, Roy demonstrates a selfish pride which finally renders him unfit for the task of the grail knight. His obstinate love of wicked Memo Paris, rather than earth-motherly Iris Lemon, dooms him. His recognition comes too late. The novel concludes not with the resurrection of the fertility god but with recollections of the Black Sox. Roy changes his mind about throwing the playoff game, but his beloved Wonderboy splits in two, he strikes out impotently, and the newspapers expose his past and present misdeeds. "Say it ain't true, Roy," begs the newsboy, and Roy cannot (p. 190). Malamud has exploited the possibilities of baseball as a rite of spring in order to moralize about ambition and ingratitude. While the baseball buff might enjoy the allusions to Eddie Waitkus or Shoeless Joe Jackson, no American is liable to confuse Malamud's wacky descriptions with anything that actually happens on a baseball diamond. The point is, finally, that Malamud realized that baseball was a perfect vehicle for an *American* version of a universal myth.

Bernard Malamud and Philip Roth arrived almost simultaneously on the literary scene and have long been recognized as leading literary exponents of peoplehood (Malamud) and assimilation (Roth). In his first collection of stories, *Goodbye, Columbus,* Roth, despite his own enthusiasm for sport, beautifully expressed in an essay entitled "My Baseball Years," satirized its worship by assimilated American Jews. The title story opens with the brilliant evocation of two worlds:

> The first time I saw Brenda she asked me to hold her glasses. Then she stepped out to the edge of the diving board and looked foggily into the pool; it could have been drained, myopic Brenda would never have known it. She dove beautifully, and a moment later she was swimming back to the side of the pool, her head of short-clipped auburn hair held up, straight ahead of her, as though it were a rose on a long stem. She glided to the edge and then was beside me. "Thank you," she said, her eyes watery though not from the water. She extended a hand for her glasses but did not put them on until she turned and headed away. I watched her move off. Her hands suddenly appeared behind her. She caught the bottom of her suit between thumb and index finger and flicked what flesh had been showing back where it belonged. My blood jumped.

That night before dinner, I called her.

"Who are you calling?" my Aunt Gladys asked.

"Some girl I met today."

"Doris introduced you?"

"Doris wouldn't introduce me to the guy who drains the pool, Aunt Gladys."

"Don't criticize all the time. A cousin's a cousin. How did you meet her."

"I didn't really meet her. I saw her."

"Who is she?"

"Her last name is Patimkin."

"Patimkin I don't know."[9]

Neil Klugman wants desperately, too desperately it turns out in the end, to move from the working-class ghetto of Newark to the airy expanse of suburban Short Hills. Brenda can make it possible. He meets Brenda at the pool. He sees her again in the middle of a tennis match. When he visits Short Hills, he enters a ludic fantasy:

> Outside, through the wide picture window, I could see the back lawn with its twin oak trees. I say oaks, though fancifully, one might call them sporting-goods trees. Beneath their branches, like fruit dropped from their limbs, were two irons, a golf ball, a tennis can, a baseball bat, basketball, a first-baseman's glove, and what was apparently a riding crop (pp. 21-22).

When Brenda suggests he begin running, he goes to the track and runs, "and always at the end there was the little click of the watch and Brenda's arms" (p. 73). He plays table tennis and basketball with her younger sister (who must always be allowed to win). He attempts conversation with sport-obsessed Ron Patimkin, his prospective brother-in-law, whose mind (what there is of it) remains forever caught somewhere back on the basketball courts of Ohio State University. If there is a single criticism to be made of Roth's use of sport as a symbol of Americanization, it is that the symbolism is probably too obvious.

It was probably inevitable that Roth write a novel about baseball. Unlike Malamud, whose relationship to baseball seems wholly literary, Roth was a passionate baseball fan before he was a writer. Of this passion for the game, Eric Solomon writes, "For Melville, whaling, for Twain, the river, for Hemingway, war, for Roth, baseball."[10] His baseball fiction, *The Great American Novel* (1973), is no more realistic than *The Natural,* but *its* combination of literary parody ("Call me Smitty" is the Melvillean first sentence), baseball allusion, and mythic highjinks has turned out to be more durable. The book traces the comic adventures of the Ruppert Mundys, a team in the mythical Patriot League. Their story is told sympathetically by the loquacious baseball writer, Word Smith. With characters like Gil Gamesh (identified, in case anyone missed the reference, as a Babylonian), Roth seems to have a wonderful time. Certainly most readers do, if they have a taste for rollicking satire and hyperbolic burlesque. Throughout, Roth makes the most of ethnic humor. Frenchy Astarte, for instance, has played for Latin American and Japanese teams and now fears sale to India, where he would be "playing ball next with a bunch of guys talking it up in Hindi and running around the bases in bedsheets."[11] Jews figure in the novel as owners rather than as players. They are proud of their role, which they see as the final certification of their Americanization. "Only in America . . . could a Jew rise to such heights! Only in America could a Jew ever hope to become the owner of a major league baseball team!" (p. 272). True enough. Where else can Jews own baseball teams?[12]

There is little in Roth's novel that one can point to as a sign of the author's Jewishness. There is even less in the baseball stories of Mark Harris. Indeed, it is a question whether or not *The Southpaw* (1953) and *Bang the Drum Slowly* (1956) are in any significant way *Jewish*. Harris himself has rather heatedly insisted that they *are*, but it is doubtful that readers unfamiliar with Harris' autobiography have been aware that he is a Jew. His protagonist, Henry Wiggen, is a twentieth-century version of Mark Twain's vernacular heroes. He is a modern Huck Finn, telling his own story in his own wonderfully vivid, and wonderfully ungrammatical, language. Henry Wiggen is Everyman on the mound, the ordinary person with a special talent, pitching. The best part of the novel is not the plot, which is minimal, but the characterization, which is a delight.

The Southpaw is a good novel; *Bang the Drum Slowly* is a great one, the only baseball novel to rival Robert Coover's brilliant *The Universal Baseball Association*. In this second novel, Henry Wiggen has comic difficulties with the Bureau of Internal Revenue, but the book is not about *his* problems at all. The book is about Bruce Pearson, of Bainbridge, Georgia, a country boy who functions as a symbol of rural simplicity and an emblem of man in nature. He learned to play baseball in a pre-Jimmy-Carter field of peanut hay; he was astonished to learn that the New York Mammoths intended to pay him money to continue at the game. The big leagues are a mixture of urban and rural types, but Henry's advice to Bruce, who lacks confidence in his own abilities, is suggestive: "Half the pitchers you face are only country boys like yourself, and the other half are only country boys from the city."[13]

The plot of the novel is a pastoral version of the Lou Gehrig story. Bruce calls Henry from the Mayo Clinic in Minnesota and tells him that he has been given only a few months to live. His speech is comical: "It means I am doomded" (p. 12), but the novel is a strange combination of comedy and tragedy. Henry and Bruce spend the time just before spring training in Bainbridge, Georgia,

where Bruce's family welcomes the two of them to sit on the front porch, to talk of crops and hogs, to comment on the sultry weather, to reminisce in a slow country way. The countryside is full of memories for Bruce, who overcomes his taciturnity enough to tell a few stories and give Henry a sense of the place.

The baseball season is a contrast, partly comic, partly grim. There is rough-and-tumble competition, the grate of personalities against each other as men travel and live together under tension; there is hostility and meanness as well as prankish camaraderie. Henry finds himself changed by the knowledge of Bruce's illness: "When your roomie is libel to die any day on you you do not think about bonus clauses, and that is the truth whether anybody happens to think so or not" (p. 139). When the rest of the team learns about Bruce's fate, there is an extraordinary moment of harmony and reconciliation that begins when one of the players sings Bruce's favorite song:

> O bang the drum slowly and play the fife lowly
> Play the dead march as they carry me on,
> Put bunches of roses all over my coffin,
> Roses to deaden the clods as they fall
>
> (p. 212).

"It made me feel very sad," writes Henry. "Yet I knew that some of the boys felt the same, and knowing it made me feel better" (p. 212). He goes on to express love in the awkward, touching way appropriate to the situation:

> you felt warm towards them, and you looked at them, and them at you, and you were both alive, and you might as well said, "Ain't it something? Being alive, I mean! Ain't it really quite a great thing at that?" and if they would of been a girl you would of kissed them, though you never said such a thing out loud but only went on about your business (p. 212).

Alas, when Bruce dies, Henry is the only member of the club to be present at the burial. Pastoral harmony is never more than momentary. Harris has written sequels to these first two Henry Wiggen novels, but he has not yet matched the greatness of *Bang the Drum Slowly*.

What Malamud, Roth, and Harris all leave fairly implicit in their novels about baseball, none of which has a Jewish protagonist, Irwin Shaw has made quite explicit. In *Voices of a Summer Day* (1965), baseball has become a traditional way to claim an American identity. Israel Federov "was made into an American catching behind the plate bare-handed in the years between 1895 and 1910."[14] His son Benjamin, the novel's protagonist, played baseball in his youth. Taking *his* son Michael to a game, Benjamin thinks of the Jews as an "uprooted people" who have abandoned their "tribal paraphernalia." He goes with Michael to the Polo Grounds, because "when *he* was six *his* father had taken him to the Polo Grounds" (pp. 152-153). Watching Michael play, years later, Benjamin realizes even more deeply what the game means to him:

The sounds were the same through the years—the American sounds of summer, the tap of bat against ball, the cries of the infielders, the wooden plump of the ball into catchers' mitts, the umpires calling "Strike three and you're out." The generations circled the bases, the dust rose for forty years as runners slid in from third, dead boys hit doubles, famous men made errors at shortstop, forgotten friends tapped the clay from their spikes with their bats as they stepped up to the batter's box, coaches' voices warned, across the decades, "Tag up, tag up!" on fly balls. The distant, mortal innings of boyhood and youth (p. 12).

In addition to having made the symbolic nature of sport wholly and vividly explicit, Shaw is also the only Jewish writer (to my knowledge) to have explored the world of the risk-intoxicated downhill skier and sport parachutist. Michael Storrs, the neurotic protagonist of *The Top of the Hill* (1979), is a WASP banker when he is not seeking to break his bones. He finally overcomes his suicidal impulses, which suggests perhaps that Shaw had begun to feel his age.

Malamud, Roth, Harris, and Shaw are all established writers with international reputations. They are by no means the only Jewish writers to have written baseball fiction. Charles Einstein's *The Only Game in Town* is a youthful effort and best forgotten, but Eliot Asinof's *Man on Spikes* (1955) is a fine account of a young player (possibly but probably not Jewish) who spends years in the minor leagues and then, given one last chance to make the majors, fails. On the other hand, the protagonist of Roger Kahn's *The Seventh Game* (1982) is successful enough professionally to pitch in the World Series, but he has lost his way morally. His punishment is to lose the seventh game, but Kahn grants him insight and a second chance to recoup the moral failure. Don Kowet's novel, also called *The Seventh Game* (1977), is a thriller (the pitcher's daughter is kidnapped and the blackmailers want him to lose the game for them) of some literary substance. Jerome Charyn's *The Seventh Babe* (1979) is a grotesque fantasy in the tradition of *The Natural* and *The Great American Novel*. The younger writers seem to have moved beyond the point where baseball functions symbolically as a metaphor of Americanization. They take it for granted that they *are* Americans and that baseball is, of course, their national game.

One reason for lessened symbolic emphasis is the fact that baseball can no longer claim to be the undisputed national game. If it has not lost that cherished position to football, it must, at the very least, share the limelight (and the television screen) with football and basketball. Jews have been comparatively hesitant about football as a metaphor. Most of the many football novels which have appeared in the last decade have been by written by gentiles (or by Jews who have changed their names and escaped identification as Jews). Since Jews have not neglected boxing as a subject for fiction, it is difficult to imagine that football's violence is the reason for the relative lack of interest.

The neglect is not total. Dorian Fliegel and Sam Koperwas are among the exceptional Jews who have dramatized football. Fliegel's book, *The Fix* (1978), belongs in the tradition of Sherwood Anderson and Ernest Hemingway. In "I Want to Know Why" and "My Old Man" Anderson and Hemingway told of the disillusionment of boys who realized that their fathers were dishonest sportsmen; in *The Fix,* Fliegel's narrator Jack Rose learns to his dismay that the coach whom many have idealized worked hand in glove with assorted mobsters to fix a whole series of games. Fliegel explores the dishonesty of commercialized sport but, while indicating a sharp eye for the ethnic relationships in modern sport, he has no point to make about ethnicity. Koperwas, however, revels in the theme of ethnicity and creates a Jewish running back who loves the violent aspects of the game and fights like an animal for a place on a semi-pro team dominated by black athletes.

Jake, the hero of Koperwas' *Westchester Bull* (1976), prays to the God of the Chosen People to choose him. "Ace of Aces, Make me fast. In the end zone I will sing your praises. I swear it." If chosen, he promises to be "your little Jewboy forever."[15] His mother sits shiva because she considers Jake ritually dead, but his brother offers him tasteless encouragement: "Score touchdowns for the Six Million. Gain yardage for the religion that's been around" (p. 9). It is just as well that Ludwig Lewisohn did not live long enough to discover this debased form of assimilation through sport.

For reasons that escape detection, Jewish writers have begun to publish novels about basketball now that Black players have replaced the Jews who were among the great names of the 1940's and 1950's. Indeed, Jay Neugeboren's *Big Man,* which explores a point-fixing scandal and its consequences, has a Black protagonist. Neugeboren's empathy is remarkable, and the book deserved the enthusiastic reviews it received. Jeremy Larner's *Drive, He Said* (1964) concerns the erotic and athletic adventures of one Hector Bloom. The novel, a somewhat surrealistic rendering of college life, was awarded the first Delta Prize by Walter van Tilburg Clark, Leslie Fiedler, and Mary McCarthy. The hero of Charles Rosen's *Have Jump Shot Will Travel* (1975) is probably not a Jew, but Robert Greenfield's *Haymon's Crowd* (1978) and Bob Levin's *The Best Ride to New York* (1978) are novels about Jewish basketball players. All three of these more recent novels depict a world of fast talk and hard knocks. They dramatize racial tension, which is scarcely surprising in a sport where Black players have ousted whites from stardom, and in Greenfield's novel the tension erupts into violence. In this way too, sadly, sport is a useful metaphor.

One can well end with Jenifer Levin's fine novel, *Water Dancer* (1982). It is a book that is nearly unique on two counts: it is a work of serious sports fiction written by a woman; it is about a female athlete. That the swimmer Dorey Thomas is indeed the central character is not entirely certain because much of the novel concerns

David "Sarge" Olsen and his wife Ilana, both of whom withdrew from the world and from each other after their son, trained by Sarge for the feat, froze to death attempting to swim the San Antonio Strait. Dorey Thomas persuades Sarge to train her for the same hazardous swim. The two grow to love each other. He becomes totally absorbed in her effort:

> "You'll be"—he fished for her wrist and held it, rubbed the sponge along her arm—"the strongest lady on earth. Tear things down a little, they grow back stronger."[16]

The reference is clearly to his psychic wound as well as to her muscles. Levin foregoes the conventionally expected adultery. The book, psychologically as well as physiologically subtle, concludes with the heroic accomplishment of the impossible task. The exhausting physical feat, carried out in defiance of the bitterly cold water, heals the psychic wounds and ends the coldness between Sarge and his wife. No doubt it is a romantic novel, but some kinds of romanticism are more effective than others.

Generalizations about three generations of writers, some major, some minor, are not easy, but it is reasonable to repeat that Jewish writers have been unusually frequent among those who have turned to sports. Originally, one motive was clearly the writers' realization that sport was a central institution and, in its high ideals and its sometimes low practices, a perfect symbol for Americanization. In the passage of nearly a century, however, sport has tended gradually to become a metaphor not for an *American* but for a *human* identity. When the contemporary writer is pessimistic about the human condition, as many are, dramatization of the violent side of sport suggests a larger disillusionment. When, on the other hand, the writer clings to the notion that life is a game that can be won as well as lost, then self-realization becomes the theme. Whether one thinks of the gloom of Greenfield's *Haymon's Crowd* or the glory of Levin's *Water Dancer,* sport seems as good a metaphor as it ever was.

NOTES

[1] For the fathers-and-sons approach, see Irving Malin, *Jews and Americans* (Carbondale, Illinois: 1965).

[2] See my book, *The Jewish Writer in America: Assimilation and the Crisis of Identity* (New York: 1971).

[3] Abraham Cahan, *The Rise of David Levinsky* (New York: 1917), p. 110.

[4] Abraham Cahan, *Yekl* (New York: 1896), pp. 4, 10.

[5] Allen Guttmann, *From Ritual to Record* (New York: 1978), pp. 92-114.

[6] Ludwig Lewisohn, *The Island Within* (New York: 1928), p. 5.

[7] Budd Schulberg, *The Harder They Fall* (New York: 1947), p. 8.

[8] Bernard Malamud, *The Natural* (New York: 1952), p. 66.

[9] Philip Roth, *Goodbye, Columbus* (Boston: 1959), pp. 3-4.

[10] Eric Solomon, "Jews, Baseball, and the American Novel," in *Arete,* 1, 2 (Spring, 1984), 65.

[11] Philip Roth, *The Great American Novel* (New York: 1973), p. 98.

[12] Max Apple's Novel, *Zip* (1978), is a variant of the theme of Jewish sports ownership; Ira Goldstein inherits a junkyard and becomes the backer of a Hispanic fighter whose adventures include a fight in Havana arranged by Fidel Castro and Lyndon Johnson, reported by Howard Cosell, and witnessed by J. Edgar Hoover, suspended over the ring in a basket.

[13] Mark Harris, *Bang the Drum Slowly* (New York: 1956), p. 73.

[14] Irwin Shaw, *Voices of a Summer Day* (New York: 1965), p. 142.

[15] Sam Koperwas, *Westchester Bull* (New York: 1976), p. 223.

[16] Jenifer Levin, *Water Dancer* (New York: 1982), p. 145.

Michael Oriard

SOURCE: "From Jane Allen to 'Water Dancer': A Brief History of the Feminist (?) Sports Novel," in *Modern Fiction Studies,* Vol. 38, No. 1 Spring, 1987, pp. 9-20.

[*In the following essay, Oriard chronicles the history of female sports fiction, contending that only recently have women articulated a credible alternative to predominantly masculine sports literature.*]

I am interested here in an obvious fact: that women have written very few sports novels in America for the equally obvious reason that from the 1920s until the 1970s they were largely excluded from what seemed an essentially masculine world of sport. They were not excluded from sport itself, of course, but from that sporting world in which sport mattered as more than physical health, that world where sport was viewed as a training ground, where sport was thought to teach valuable lessons for conduct in life generally, where sport embodied a cultural myth and ideology. In this world, not only did boys and men play athletic games, but men wrote books for boys to read that made the moral lessons of the playing field clear, and occasionally a male author transformed these masculine athletic experiences into a novel that the world welcomed as "literature." Women neither played the same games nor wrote about them in the same way, when they wrote at all. This essay examines the fiction they did write.

More particularly, I want to make a case for Jenifer Levin's novel about marathon swimming, *Water Dancer* (1982), as a major breakthrough in the genre of sports fiction. In the first place, it is a fine novel, but, more important here, it offers a feminist alternative to the masculine sports myth, the first important novel to do so that I am aware of. *Water Dancer* counters that long literary tradition, from Jack London and Ring Lardner to Malamud, Coover, Roth, and beyond, in which women have been adjuncts to the hero's achievements at best, major obstacles at worst: a fundamental antagonism between the athlete and his women as a staple of American male sports fiction for a century. Women simply have not established an alternative literary tradition. Among the relative handful of novels by women in this century there may exist an undiscovered masterpiece, but our cultural history makes such a possibility unlikely.

The position of women who would write of sports in this country is revealed in particularly interesting ways by the example of the few who have written juvenile fiction. From Gilbert Patten, Ralph Henry Barbour, and other early writers on, men have written thousands of sports novels for boys with a single plot: a story about achievement in the face of severe competition, with fair play and other virtues conspicuously promoted but with heroic action and triumph overwhelming all other concerns. Women have contributed at most one or two percent of the novels in this genre. Before the 1920s, girls' athletics offered a potentially rich subject for fiction. Describing athletic competition at women's colleges at the turn of the century, Helen Lefkowitz Horowitz has written that "college women played rough, competed keenly, and cheered passionately" (159). A handful of writers created fiction out of such competition. One of Grace Margaret Gallaher's *Vassar Stories,* published in 1899, described how in the fury of a game one young woman on her class basketball team "broke her nose, and jumped up shouting, 'Come on, I've only blacked my eye'" (227). Another player in the same story dislocates her knee, flinging herself between an opponent and a bench in a mad scramble for the ball. The rivalry is fierce, the emotions unladylike, the ethics of the players not always exemplary. In another story from the same era, one of Julia Augusta Schwartze's *Vassar Studies* (1899), a student steals away from the infirmary, risking additional injury to win the hurdles race for the honor of her class on Field Day. Gilbert Patten, Ralph Henry Barbour, and other writers told the same story over and over about their boy heroes, and their successors have continued the tradition to our own time, but as such competition for girls and women disappeared in the 1920s, opportunities for women writers to develop a feminine sports myth disappeared as well.

In the 1910s, Jessie Graham Flower, Gertrude Morrison, and Edith Bancroft wrote series books about female athletes, after which women seem to have dropped from the field altogether until the 1940s and '50s when Amelia Elizabeth Walden and a few others began again to write for young people about girls in sports. Flower in her Grace Harlowe novels and Morrison with her Girls of Central High books took sport for granted as a part of their characters' school lives without developing any distinctive ideology from it. Sport was an activity without an underlying code, easily replaceable by, say, high school theatricals as a focus for the girls' interests. Bancroft explored the subject of girls' athletics more fully, but her five Jane Allen novels, written between 1917 and 1922, finally refuse to take sport seriously. In this refusal, the novels offer a fascinating commentary on those years during which women finally won the vote then paradoxically retreated from political self-assertion back into glorified motherhood to prevent what the culture feared as imminent race suicide.

In the first of the series, *Jane Allen of the Scrub Team* (1917), Bancroft seems initially to follow the model of the boys' books. Jane arrives alone at a proper women's college from her home in Montana to become the center of a circle of good friends and the hated rival of not one but three snobbish antagonists. She withstands early adversity, develops a crush on a junior who reminds her of her dead mother, participates in typical mild pranks, rescues a classmate after a fall from her horse, wins the admiration of two of her three adversaries while vanquishing the third, and stars in the Big Game against the sophomores—modestly accepting the accolades of her teammates. All of this comes straight from Patten and Barbour. In other important ways, however, it is clear that Bancroft did not simply appropriate the boys'-story formula as the proper one for girls. Jane's father, though no snob, is extremely wealthy, contrary to the middle-class emphasis of boys' books, and he and his dead wife play a much more prominent role in Jane's life than is customary in the juvenile formula, where separation from family is a prerequisite for triumph. Moreover, although the story culminates in the usual Big Game (described very briefly), basketball occupies the girls' attention only during the last half of the novel and receives a much reduced and different emphasis in their lives. The competition is strictly intraschool, between the freshman and sophomore teams; the juniors and seniors do not play because they have more important activities. Basketball is termed an "outlet for stored-up energy" (185); for Jane in particular its primary function is to teach her the value of friendship and appreciation of qualities in her sophisticated Eastern schoolmates that run counter to her Western upbringing. The boy hero, if tainted by either excess of money or overrefined manners, is purged of these false marks of status as a prerequisite to genuine achievement. Jane, on the other hand, learns to value the trappings of social hierarchy within a democratic framework; whereas the boys' story, we might say, moves psychologically westward in search of Frederick Jackson Turner's seedbed of Americanism, the girls' story moves eastward.

Basketball also offers Jane the opportunity to prove the importance of "being true to herself": she wins the right to play in the Big Game without telling tales against the girl who unfairly holds Jane's position. The values of family, conventional virtue, and propriety hover over the novel; competition is downplayed and personal triumph minimized. Whereas the boy hero is severed from his family to be thrust into an unfamiliar and challenging athletic environment as a proving ground for success in the larger world of adult males awaiting him, Jane physically leaves one family to discover another, but emotionally and psychologically never leaves at all.

In the second of the series, *Jane Allen: Right Guard* (1918), this fundamental difference from the boys' story continues. Jane increasingly appears to be a conventional adolescent heroine rather than a representative of the competitive new woman winning a place in the world of men. Her sentimental attachment to father and dead mother (called "Dearest" throughout) opens the second volume as it did the first, as Jane returns to Wellington to more haughty adversaries but even less basketball. A sophomore now, Jane is to participate in three games against the freshmen, but the third game never takes place: there is no Big Game at all but rather a climatic scene in which Jane wins the friendship of two of her three enemies, while the mystery that has tarnished Jane's and her best friend's reputation is finally solved. In the few pages given over to the first two basketball games, there is no description of the action, only of the uniforms:

> Both teams made a fine appearance on the floor. Neither team had adhered to class colors that year in choosing their basketball-suits. The freshmen wore suits of navy blue decorated with an old rose "F" on the front of the blouse. A wide rolling sailor collar of the same color further added to the effect. The sophomores had elected to be patriotic, and wore khaki-colored suits, unrelieved by a contrasting color. It was a decided innovation of its kind and they liked it. (224-225)

Jane, we are told, "played with a dash and skill that was noticeable even above the good work of the other players" (225)—faint praise in the world of juvenile sports fiction. Jane is more decisively declared the star of the second game; her teammates play out a familiar ritual as they march her around the gym to the cheering cry, "Who's Jane Allen? Right, right right Guard!" But at this moment of heroic apotheosis so crucial to the boys' story, the narrator draws a moral very different from mere personal triumph:

> Jane never forgot that stirring cry of "Right Guard!" It conveyed to her a higher meaning than mere basketball glorification. It fell upon her ears as an admonition to do well. To do right, to be right, and to stay right. It was almost as if she had been elected of her own soul to be a guardian of right. (225-226)

This is the high point in Jane's basketball career. In *Jane Allen: Center* (1920), the girls compete against teams from other schools, but basketball plays a decidedly subordinate role to the unraveling of a mystery—this time the identity of a beautiful Polish musician pursued by evil Bolshevists. More puzzling identities, exotic villainesses, and frantic activity mark *Jane Allen: Junior* (1921) and *Senior* (1922). Jane befriends two freshmen and instructs them in the importance of popularity and good times. This abrupt shift in values, accompanied by snappy Jazz-Age dialogue (Dozia: "How's the Wild and Woolly?" Jane: "Almost ready to shear. There are whiskers on the moon, and the sun has a pompadour" [*Center* 124]), raises the possibility that a new "Edith Bancroft" has assumed the series. But a deeper consistency emerges in the portrait of gender relations and the place of sport in them. Basketball is debunked or ignored in these final two volumes. Jane and her chum feel "a little too grown up" to play in the game when there are perplexing mysteries to be solved. A Big Dance takes the place of the Big Game, and in the final volume basketball has disappeared altogether. Here, on the brink of her entry into the outside world, Jane commits herself to social service as her future profession (unknown to Jane, her wealthy father chooses her trial case and monitors it closely to reduce his daughter's contamination by the wrong kind of people). In this concluding story (a sixth, *Jane Allen: Graduate,* is announced at the end but never appeared), the kind of woman Jane has grown to be is made quite clear. Against a background of boyfriends, proms, and hope chests, Jane works on her case to restore a family's emotional and financial stability, in so doing preparing for her own wife- and motherhood. When circumstances lead her to bring two small children to her dorm room for the night, she and her friends discover firsthand the joys of mothering. "That's what the whole, wide world has been raving about since creation," says Dozia to an agreeing Jane (66). And at the end of the novel, Jane assumes toward her chosen male the too familiar woman's stance: "Then he smiled down at her and she felt small—he was so tall and so protective" (308). After five volumes and some 1600 pages Jane Allen, the Frank Merriwell of female athletes, has become the woman her Victorian grandmother must have been.

Jane Allen's circumscribed athletic role was repeatedly played out by the scant handful of heroines who appeared in the following decades (see, for example, Amelia Elizabeth Walden's *My Sister Mike* and *Queen of the Courts*). Until the 1970s, the decade of Title IX, girls competed in juvenile novels less seriously than they dated or pursued other interests. The change was not abrupt or complete: Walden's later *Basketball Girl of the Year* (1970) and Evelyn Lunemann's *Tennis Champ* continued to subordinate athletic triumph to traditional "feminine" values. But in other '70s novels such as Elizabeth Levy's *The Tryouts* and Isabella Taves' *Not Bad for a Girl* the fact of girls' admission to Little League and school teams for the first time produced realistic—not mythic—stories of girls in athletics.

By distinguishing the realistic from the mythic I point to the larger function that boys' books have served in articulating a myth of success in a competitive world and for which women writers have offered no alternative until very recently. This is not to say that women have left no distinctive gender mark on juvenile sports fiction: they have, but in a "subversive" way. A number of women, Eleanor Clymer and Marion Renick for example, in writing about *boys* rather than girls, have subtly altered the Patten-Barbour formula. By placing greater emphasis than male authors typically did on family, moral values, and gender relations, they abridged the prevailing masculine ethos of personal achievement. Particularly fascinating in this context is a handful of women who wrote under male pseudonyms. Sandra Gilbert and Susan Gubar have described why such nineteenth-century women novelists as "George Sand," "George Eliot," "Currer," "Ellis," and "Acton Bell" wrote under masculine names in order to circumvent the bias against writers of their sex. How much more prejudice faced women in the overwhelmingly masculine genre of juvenile sports fiction—not from critics but from readers. Based on my own typical childhood attitudes, I am certain that boys were more likely to read a novel by John Prescott Earl or Jack Wright than by Beth Bradford Gilchrist or Elsie Wright, the authors' true names. C. H. Frick, B. J. Chute, M. G. Bonner, and H. D. Francis would have seemed safe enough, their boy readers unaware that the C. stood for Constance, B. for Beatrice, M. for Mary, and H. for Helen. These double-agents writing for poor unsuspecting boys undermined in subtle ways the genre in which they worked. Earl (Gilchrist) was typical. In *On the School Team* (1908), contrary to the Frank Merriwellian tradition, the hero yields his starring position at the crucial point in a football game to a rival less worn down by training. Later, he achieves his greatest triumph not by his own exploits on the track but by coaching a former cripple to victory and self-respect, then sacrifices his pride to compete in the unfamiliar discus throw, tying for fourth place to gain crucial points for his team. All of these pseudonymous writers worked against the formula of competition and individualistic achievement central to the boys' sports novel. Indirectly, they encouraged boy readers to imagine a world of heroic possibility that could accommodate the politically weak.

It was not until the 1970s, however, that a woman developed a myth of feminine athletic achievement to compete with the deep-rooted male tradition. In the decade that saw such books as Boslooper and Hayes's *The Femininity Game* and Harragan's *Games Mother Never Taught You*—arguing that women were disadvantaged in the corporate world by their exclusion from competitive team games as girls—R. R. Knudson in such novels as *Zanballer* (1972) and *Zanbanger* (1977) brought Betty Friedan's type of feminism to the juvenile sports novel. Knudson offered no *alternative* to the boys' story but appropriated the male myth intact, allowing her heroines the same sort of impossible athletic triumphs fictional boys had been enjoying for decades.

Knudson's feminist juvenile fiction suggests one possible response by the contemporary woman writer to the masculine sporting myth. If we distinguish two basic kinds of feminism—the kind that demands equal rights for women and the kind that envisions an alternative feminine mode of being—then Knudson's novels provide a feminist sporting myth of the first type. Anything boys can do, girls can do, too, if not better, Knudson's novels insist. As a model for adult behavior, Knudson's books tell their young readers: men have power; women are entitled to an equal share of the power and are fully competent to have it. The alternative, which I associate with Mary Daly or Marilyn French rather than Betty Friedan, says essentially: we reject male power as inherently destructive; we have no interest in simply seizing our share of that power in order to participate equally in the destruction of our world; we want to envision an alternative feminine way of being that renounces death-dealing power for something more life-giving. This is the sort of vision Jenifer Levin develops in *Water Dancer*.

Water Dancer appeared at a time when a number of women writers were dealing with sport, more or less incidentally, for the first time. Although nearly every major male novelist of the century—from Fitzgerald, Faulkner, and Hemingway to Updike, Mailer, and Malamud—has dealt with sport either briefly or extensively, women writers until recently have been largely silent on the subject. The extraordinary flourishing of women's fiction since the 1960s has ended that silence, but the majority of women writers have acknowledged sport's importance in American culture only to denounce it. A notable exception, Joyce Carol Oates in her first novel, *With Shuddering Fall* (1964), and in the story "Golden Gloves" in her most recent collection, *Raven's Wing* (1986), has dealt impressively with traditional male sporting themes without casting them in any distinctively feminine light (Oates' just-published *On Boxing* deals with the most "masculine" of all sports). But Oates writes against the current of contemporary fiction by women. In varying degrees more clearly feminist in their perspective, Alix Kates Shulman in *Memoirs of an Ex-Prom Queen* (1972), Lisa Alther in *Kinflicks* (1976), Mary Gordon in *Final Payments* (1978), and Ellen Gilchrist and Bobbie Ann Mason in a few stories have either attacked or satirized various elements of the masculine sports world. Shulman and Gilchrist have both dealt with girls' exclusion from it, Shulman finding in playground grade-school games a metaphor for the male appropriation of the larger world, as her protagonist, Sasha Davis, recalls:

> Before and after school, the boys would fan out over the school grounds and take over the ball fields, the apple orchard, the skating pond, the "Mountain" for king-of-the castle, while we stayed in the concrete playground in the shadow of the school building. There we played girls' games under the teacher's protective eyes. (20)

Davis wants to play touch football but must instead cultivate her prettiness as her only means of acceptance.

In the story "Revenge," Gilchrist's ten-year-old Rhoda similarly is kept on the sidelines while her brothers and cousins train at track and field events, until one evening, sneaking away from a wedding, she flies down the runway, pole in hand, to soar over the bar and into the sawdust pit before she is dragged back to her girl's life. The story ends with Rhoda's words: "Sometimes I think whatever has happened since has been of no real interest to me" (124).

Gordon, Alther, and Mason have parodied or otherwise deflated the masculine sporting myth through humor. In Mason's "The Rookers," the estrangement of male and female is symbolized by the women playing cards while a husband, a man bewildered by nearly everything in his life, watches a football game on television. One of the women cackles, "Did ya'll hear what Erma Bombeck said? She said that any man who watches more than a hundred and sixty-eight football games in one year ought to be declared legally dead" (20). In Gordon's *Final Payments,* an ambitious, overbearing man, successful at both sports and politics, talks about his underlings as a "team" and himself as "captain," eliciting this bitter mockery from his wife: "Everyone in the office wears football helmets. . . . Except the secretaries. They wear little cheerleading skirts. It's all such a great deal of *fun.* And it's not winning or losing, it's how you play the *game*" (92). (Mary Daly has termed such language the "jockocratic 'ethical' jargon" of "jockdom" [217, 226]). In *Kinflicks,* finally, Alther exposed this antagonism with a full-scale burlesque on that paragon of the masculine sporting world, the "stud" football player. Ginny Babcock as an adolescent is a "flag swinger on the sidelines of Joe Bob's triumphs," Joe Bob being the star high school halfback with the "modest shrug," "moronic smile," and a response to anything he doesn't understand: "Do whut?" (30-32). He says it a lot. Ginny, too, loves to play football, but at thirteen she is forced to exchange her "shoulder pads for a sanitary pad and elastic belt" as society requires (33). High-school for Ginny and Joe Bob means hand jobs in back seats; the Teen Team for Jesus inspired by a former NFL lineman who ran into a goal post and woke up to hear the Lord call him, "Ah got plans for you on *mah* team, fella!" (39); backseat passion interrupted by Joe Bob's bolting upright from his exertions to announce, "Trainin'," and to fly for home (47); trips to the drive-in where every high school jock honks his horn at the moment of ecstasy "to indicate to his teammates that he had scored" (62). The comic foolishness of this adolescent sporting ethos darkens as Ginny grows older and meets its grown-up practitioners. The bitterness of Alther's feelings comes through in a counterpoint that runs through much of the novel's second half: Ginny's mother painfully dying in a hospital room, next door to Joe Bob's old coach, now utterly deranged, crying out repeatedly to some remembered team, "You run until you drop, and then you pick yourself up and run some more! Do you understand what I'm saying, men?" (340). No "wisdom" could be less useful for the real problems of the real world, Alther implied.

Against this tide of debunking, Jenifer Levin's *Water Dancer* stands as a crucial document, appropriating the athletic arena to women's experience in a wholly original way. As sport has become less closed off to women writers, Levin alone seems to me to have fully imagined it as a female activity. In *Things Invisible to See* (1985), Nancy Willard writes lovingly of baseball in what might be considered a gender-free way. Among other books that might be considered women's sports novels, Sara Vogan's *In Shelly's Leg* (1981) offers wise and beautiful writing about many things, but softball is only incidental to her characters' lives; and the plotting and prose of Rita Mae Brown's *Sudden Death* (1983), her roman à clef about the women's tennis circuit, are worthy only of *The National Enquirer.* A fourth novel, Silvia Tennenbaum's *Rachel, the Rabbi's Wife* (1978), concerns a woman as baseball *fan,* not athlete. *Water Dancer,* on the other hand, is both a novel with a female athlete as protagonist and a novel emphatically about sport and gender. It is the story of a marathon swimmer, Dorey Thomas, who trains under a male coach, Sarge Olssen, to swim the until now unconquered San Antonio Strait in the state of Washington: a grueling, dangerous swim that killed Sarge's own son two years earlier. In her interest in sport and gender, Levin assembles a number of representative types. Sarge, the coach, a former world-class marathon swimmer himself, is fiercely competitive, needing to master and control—whether the water he swims in or the people in his life. Sarge's feminine antithesis is his wife Ilana, a cliff diver who has given up her own public life to be wife, mother, and godmother to the young men Sarge has trained since his own swimming career ended. The death of their son has devastated both domineering Sarge and nurturing Ilana, driving them apart, until Dorey Thomas arrives at Sarge's swimming camp, asking to be trained. Dorey seems neither masculine nor feminine, less androgynous than asexual, a young woman who appears uncomfortable on land but beautifully natural in the water. A more sensitive male friend of Sarge's; another woman swimmer, Anne, who is both more "feminine" and more "masculine" than Dorey, a combination of cheerleader and tomboy, as she's described; and Anne's weaker, more "feminine" boyfriend complete the cast of main characters. Levin refuses to define "male" and "female" in absolute ways. Both Rita Mae Brown in *Sudden Death* and Patricia Nell Warren in *The Front Runner* (1964) have used the homosexual as the marginal person of the sporting world; Levin moves beyond this obvious point. Dorey discovers her lesbianism during the course of the novel, but Anne is emphatically heterosexual—Levin clearly intending no equation of female athleticism with homosexuality. Dorey's partner, Ilana, finds nurturant rather than erotic pleasure in their relationship. Levin's point throughout the novel is that masculinity and femininity are traits not limited to either gender, while sexuality is larger than lust. Levin's world is filled with individual beings who must find their own element. Dorey seems natural in the water and in bed with Ilana. For others, what's natural lies elsewhere.

In the context of these larger interests, Levin convincingly suggests an alternative to the masculine sporting myth. In the first place, in writing of marathon swimming Levin uses a sport in which men and women compete as equals. She shows men beating women and women beating men, but she is interested in much more than the equality of competition in the sport. For one thing, Levin makes the sport itself excruciatingly real to nonswimming readers. Having read the novel—with its women swimmers enduring twenty-four hours and more of freezing water, tossing waves, opposing currents, boredom, chafing, swelling, stinging, vomiting, begging, surviving—no reader can doubt women's "toughness" or "courage," those preeminently "masculine" sporting virtues. But Levin is not interested in an adult version of R. R. Knudson's all-conquering heroine. Rather, she submits competition itself to close scrutiny. In her earlier swimming career, before the novel opens, Dorey had felt the need to be what she calls a "giant," one who dominated the water, one who was invincible in it. "I'd worked up an image of myself," she explains to Ilana, "big, bad giant, taller than the men and taller than the waves." But in a practice swim one day, her world changed:

> I was doing well, I felt fine. Then there was one wave and I caught it right at the critical point and I just stopped. Everything seemed to stop. All I felt was my body, all of the sudden it wasn't much of a giant's body for sure. . . . I got very small. Very human. (186)

With this crushing revelation Dorey leaves the sport, returning as the novel opens to attempt a comeback. But Dorey has changed. In her discussions with Anne their different attitudes toward competition appear. Anne drives herself to win, loving most to beat men, whereas Dorey competes only against the water. But in the novel's climactic swim, she surrenders that last competitive feeling as well. At the point where the swim becomes most grueling, she gives up forever trying to be a giant, seeing herself now as a "water dancer." Dorey gives up on time (she had always counted her strokes as a way to distract herself), gives up thinking about the distant shore as her goal. "The only goal left her—if it could indeed be called a goal—was the rhythmic continuation of strokes through water" (349). The giant proved fragile; in surrendering herself to the water, in *dancing* in her element, Dorey discovers a different kind of strength, an intense feeling of being alive. Not competition or mastery but surrender becomes a new kind of freedom. Yet this surrender has nothing in it of "masochism," that supposedly typical feminine neurosis that feminist psychoanalysts struck from the psychiatric vocabulary just a few months ago. To be a water dancer is neither to dominate nor to be dominated but to live in one's body in the world.

Levin does not present this alternative vision as specifically "feminine." Anne, after all, competes in the same way that Sarge has done, and Levin's vision has been shared by a number of male writers from Henry Thoreau to Robert Pirsig. But in the context of the masculine sporting myth and of contemporary feminist writing, it seems appropriate to consider this vision a "feminist" one. As such it is unique, to my knowledge, in American sports fiction. This is not to suggest that *Water Dancer* alone has broken through to discover the truth about gender in America, that it describes *the* feminist vision, or that it reveals the foundation on which women's sports should develop. More simply, the novel successfully articulates a credible alternative to the masculine sports myth that has been virtually the only sports myth embedded in American sports fiction. For the first time another possibility has been powerfully imagined.

WORKS CITED

Alther, Lisa. *Kinflicks.* New York: Knopf, 1976.

Bancroft, Edith. *Jane Allen: Center.* New York: Cupples, 1920.

——. *Jane Allen: Junior.* New York: Cupples, 1921.

——. *Jane Allen of the Sub Team.* New York: Cupples, 1917.

——. *Jane Allen: Right Guard.* Akron: Saalfield, 1918.

——. *Jane Allen: Senior.* New York: Cupples, 1922.

Boslooper, Thomas, and Marcia Hayes. *The Femininity Game.* New York: Stein, 1973.

Brown, Rita Mae. *Sudden Death.* New York: Bantam, 1983.

Daly, Mary. *Pure Lust: Element Feminist Philosophy.* Boston: Beacon, 1984.

Flower, Jessie Graham. *Grace Harlowe's Junior Year at High School.* Philadelphia: Altemus, 1911.

——. *Grace Harlowe's Senior Year at High School.* Philadelphia: Altemus, 1911.

Gallaher, Grace Margaret. *Vassar Stories.* 1899. Freeport: Books for Libraries, 1970.

Gilbert, Sandra M., and Susan Gubar. *The Madwoman in the Attic: The Woman Writer and the Nineteenth-Century Literary Imagination.* New Haven: Yale UP, 1979.

Gilchrist, Ellen. *In the Land of Dreamy Dreams.* Boston: Little, 1981.

Gordon, Mary. *Final Payments.* New York: Random, 1978.

Harragan, Betty. *Games Mother Never Taught You: Corporate Gamesmanship for Women.* New York: Rawson, 1977.

Horowitz, Helen Lefkowitz. *Alma Mater: Design and Experience in the Women's Colleges from Their Nineteenth-Century Beginnings to the 1930s.* New York: Knopf, 1984.

Knudson, R. R. *Zanballer.* New York: Delacorte, 1972.

———. *Zanbanger.* New York: Harper, 1977.

Levin, Jenifer. *Water Dancer.* New York: Poseidon, 1982.

Levy, Elizabeth. *The Tryouts.* New York: Winds, 1979.

Lunemann, Evelyn. *Tennis Champ.* Westchester: Benefic, 1972.

Mason, Bobbie Ann. *Shiloh and Other Stories.* New York: Harper, 1982.

Morrison, Gertrude W. *The Girls of Central High at Basketball.* Cleveland: Goldsmith, 1914.

———. *The Girls of Central High on Track and Field.* Cleveland: World Syndicate, 1914.

Oates, Joyce Carol. *On Boxing.* New York: Dolphin-Doubleday, 1987.

———. *Raven's Wing.* New York: Dutton, 1986.

———. *With Shuddering Fall.* New York: Vanguard, 1964.

Schwartze, Julia Augusta. *Vassar Studies.* New York: Putnam's, 1899.

Shulman, Alix Kates. *Memoirs of an Ex-Prom Queen.* New York: Knopf, 1972.

Taves, Isabella. *Not Bad for a Girl.* New York: Evans, 1972.

Tennebaum, Silvia. *Rachel, the Rabbi's Wife.* New York: Morrow, 1978.

Vogan, Sara. *In Shelly's Leg.* New York: Knopf, 1981.

Walden, Amelia Elizabeth. *Basketball Girl of the Year.* New York: McGraw, 1970.

———. *My Sister Mike.* New York: Whittlesey House, 1956.

———. *Queen of the Courts.* Philadelphia: Westminster, n.d.

Warren, Patricia Nell. *The Front Runner.* 1964. New York: Bantam, 1975.

Willard, Nancy. *Things Invisible to See.* New York: Knopf, 1985.

Brooke K. Horvath and Sharon G. Carson

SOURCE: "Women's Sports Poetry: Some Observations and Representative Texts," in *The Achievement of American Sports Literature: A Critical Appraisal,* edited by Wiley Lee Umphlett, Bucknell University Press, 1991, pp. 116-31.

[*In the following essay, Horvath and Carson offer an overview of the subjects and major themes of contemporary women's sports poetry.*]

As readers of this volume should be aware, the past several years have seen sport literature emerge from the ghetto of subliterature to critical respectability. Critical esteem no longer depends on the extent to which one can make the case that a "sports" poem or novel is not really about sports, or is worthwhile despite the fact that it has sport as its subject. Today, discussions of sport literature's aesthetic success can drop the qualifying adjective and judge a text in terms of the expectations and evaluative criteria brought to bear on it while recognizing that sport literature does retain a claim to an area of experience that is this literature's business to explore fully.

Yet despite this growing critical interest, women's sport literature—especially women's sports poetry—continues to suffer neglect. The reasons for this situation are not so hard to fathom. Most critics attracted to sport literature are men, women poets have written fewer sports poems than have male poets, and sports poems feature women less often than men, partly because women have been excluded from those sports—professional baseball, football, basketball, boxing—which have most often received poetic treatment and which most interest the majority of critics (principally because these sports, especially baseball, have been most often and most successfully treated in fiction). In literature as in life, sports remain primarily a male enterprise. Thus, as Michael Oriard says in his "Brief History" of the feminist sport novel,

> from the 1920s until the 1970s [women] were largely excluded from what seemed an essentially masculine world of sport. They were not excluded from sport itself, of course, but from that sporting world in which sport mattered as more than physical health, that world where sport was viewed as a training ground, where sport was thought to teach valuable lessons for conduct in life generally, where sport embodied a cultural myth and ideology. (9)

Moreover, women's sport literature has doubtless been ignored in part because the feminists, literary and otherwise, have paid scant attention to sport. There is, for example, no full-scale work of feminist theory treating women and sport, despite the American society's obsession with sport, despite sport's significance as a locus of those societal values and attitudes of which Oriard writes.

All of which is not to deny a wealth of relevant material—in the biographies and autobiographies of successful female athletes, in the pages of *Ms., Women's Sport and Fitness,* and general-interest magazines as well as in scholarly journals such as *The Journal of Sport Psychology, The Journal of Sport and Social Issues,* and *The Journal of Sport Behavior,* among others. Yet with the focus of attention elsewhere, little of this material is immediately useful to the would-be critic of women's sports poetry. Consequently, in the space allotted here, we cannot offer, as we might wish, anything like a complete theoretical foundation upon which to erect readings of individual poems.

Given, then, our space limitations and our principal desire—to introduce readers to some very good sports poems by women—we will, as a sort of prolegomenon to a proper study of the subject, simply draw upon a few provocative comments for insights into what might be said to characterize a female response to sport, a set of sporting values forming an alternative to the habitual ones espoused and/or embodied in male writing about sport, to see if these ideas provide a useful lens through which to view a handful of poems by women that deserve to be better known and more often taught, poems that ought to be taken into account in any effort to grasp what is happening in sport literature today.

Let us begin with Bonnie Beck's 1980 essay, "The Future of Women's Sport: Issues, Insights, and Struggles." The bit of verse with which Beck opens her essay succinctly reveals her orientation:

> PERHAPS,
> Before there were Gods there were Goddesses;
> Before there was Man there was Woman;
> Before there was Sport there was Play;
> Before Roboticized-Automatons there were Life-Living/Loving-Free-Spirited/Joyful Humans-Be-ing,
> and PERHAPS, there will be again.
>
> (401)

In brief, Beck sees sport as it exists today—which she labels "NowSport" or "ManSport"—to be a product of a male mindset and as such "reflect[ing] the dominant values of both patriarchy and capitalism" (401). "Male-dominated" and "for-profit," ManSport fosters "sexism, racism, ageism, and classicism" (402), creating a sporting world "hellbent on a Death-March at the end of which lies robotocized existence and nonSelves . . ." (405). With its unhealthy commitment to violence, competition, ends over means, and thanatos over eros, ManSport "contribute[s] strongly and effectively to the gradual but persistent demise of Living/Loving, Free-Spirited, Joyful, Creatively energized Humans Being" (406), and for Beck, women appear all too eager to plug into this male-defined sports world, to join in this nation's "Death-March (with NowSport leading the way)" (407) rather than seeking to realize the alternative she calls "NewSport" or "JoySport": a playful, communal "abandon/reunion of comtesting . . . that is, playing with others in the quest for Self-Knowing, Self-Being, Self-Creation, universal Spiraling, Spinning, Con-

necting . . ." (401). Valuing the life-affirmative beauty that springs from creative energy employed "to create new patterns of movement/forms of moving/ways of moving that emphasize Wholeness/Integration/Connectedness" (409), Beck's vision is one of play as an end in itself with cooperation replacing agon, "life-energizing" activity replacing competitive violence both physical and psychological, participation for all regardless of ability replacing selection on the basis of talent: "play for the enjoyment of playing, with winning and extrinsic rewards being only incidental to the experience of playing hard, sweating profusely, scoring a goal, [and] bond-ing with other women" in "an environment conducive to healthy com-testing . . ." (406).

Having taught Beck in several college sport literature classes, we know that her essay will strike many readers as outrageous (her aggressively hostile and divisive language, so at odds with her ostensible message, is in large part to blame), giving voice not to a truly female alternative conception of sport but to hopelessly idiosyncratic wishful thinking to which few others will want to pledge allegiance. Yet consider the following pairs of poems, chosen more or less at random from those available in Tom Dodge's *A Literature of Sports*: Maxine Kumin's "Morning Swim" and Robert Francis's "Swimmer"; James Dickey's "In the Picket" and May Swenson's "Watching the Jets Lose to Buffalo at Shea."

Kumin's poem describes a solitary swim in a quiet foggy lake at dawn. Opening with the speaker's account of how, "oily and nude," she gives herself trustingly to the unknown, to the misty uncertainty of the lake, "Morning Swim" evokes memories that come to fill her "empty head" with thoughts that despite the "fuzzy" dark, arrive with all the domestic comfort and familiar warmth of a terry cloth robe (feelings echoed by the poem's rhythmic tetrameter couplets):

> Into my empty head there come
> A cotton beach, a dock wherefrom
>
> I set out, oily and nude
> Through mist, in chilly solitude.
>
> There was no line, no roof or floor
> To tell the water from the air.
>
> Night fog thick as terry cloth
> Closed me in its fuzzy growth.
>
> I hung my bathrobe on two pegs.
> I took the lake between my legs.

Although the next stanza briefly introduces a note of potential hostility ("invaded and invader"), this attitude is quickly diluted in the smoothing immersion of the swimmer's body into the lake, to which she soon acclimates herself. Her swim becomes both a source of erotic pleasure ("I took the lake between my legs"); and later: "water fell / Through all my doors") and a means of establishing communion with nature:

Invaded and invader, I
Went overhand on that flat sky.

Fish twitched beneath me, quick and tame.
In their green zone they sang my name
And in the rhythm of the swim
I hummed a two-four-time slow hymn.

With this last line, the religious dimension of the swimmer's activity breaks the poem's surface as a romantic transcendence through union with nature, a sensual-spiritual experience healing the split between body and soul and giving rise to thoughts of God. This becomes the poem's dominant mood to its conclusion, her sense of oneness and harmony emphasized by the mingling of her breath with the lake water and by her conviction that her bones "drank water" even as she feels herself that water's source:

I hummed *Abide With Me.* The beat
Rose in the fine thrash of my feet,

Rose in the bubbles I put out
Slantwise, trailing through my mouth.

My bones drank water; water fell
Through all my doors. I was the well

That fed the lake that met the sea
In which I sang *Abide With Me.*

In "Morning Swim," in short, are depicted many of those characteristic attitudes and values attributed by Beck and others to a female (if not strictly feminist) perspective: a dilution of egotism and absence of competition and violence; an affirmation of joy, health, self, and communion; the portrayal of a positive body image; a freedom from stifling regimens or fears of failure; a peaceful coexistence with and love for the other (here, the lake and its fish). Indeed, one might conclude that "Morning Swim" is not finally a sports poem at all (insofar as it does not involve rule-governed competition) but rather a poem celebrating seriously playful physical activity as an end in itself whose end is joy. To this point we will return.

By way of contrast, consider Robert Francis's "Swimmer":

Observe how he negotiates his way
With trust and the least violence, making
The stranger friend, the enemy ally.
The depth that could destroy gently supports him.
With water he defends himself from water.
Danger he leans on, rests in. The drowning sea
Is all he has between himself and drowning.

Although the poem speaks of "trust and the least violence," of gentle support, it is the potential for violence, the imminence of death by drowning, that dominates the scene. Emphasizing the disharmony between man and sea (a more threatening locale than a lake) through the irregular rhythm and the absence of rhyme, the poem stands at a distance from its subject ("Observe how

he . . .") as though objectivity and a correct reading of the lesson to be learned matter more than a subjective re-creation of the experience itself. Success here lies in turning the sea's powers against it, in learning to inhabit danger, a strategy giving the lie to the speaker's description of the sea as "friend" and "ally." The achievement here is not communion with nature, not erotic-spiritual ecstasy, but a sense of triumph in danger overcome through pure mind and self-control, of disaster outwitted through skill and courage, of that invigoration which comes from successfully flirting with and cheating death. (For a discussion of the relation of sport to death, see Howard Slusher.)

The second set of poems may be addressed more briefly. In James Dickey's "In the Pocket," the same preoccupation with danger overcome through skillful confrontation and controlled violence that informs "Swimmer" appears once more. Plugging directly into one of the most familiar of football truisms—that football is metaphoric warfare—"In the Pocket" is a highly successful evocation through form and content of that chancy and chaotic moment when a quarterback drops back to pass.

. . . my arm is looking
Everywhere and some are breaking
In   breaking down
And out   breaking
Across, and one is going deep   deeper
Than my arm. Where is Number One hooking
Into the violent green alive
With linebackers? I cannot find him he cannot beat
His man   I fall back more
Into the pocket   it is raging and breaking . . .

Conflict, violence, destruction (of poetic line as of the offensive line), impending threat and death are clearly foregrounded; the poem speaks for itself:

. . . my friends are crumbling
Around me the wrong color
Is looming   hands are coming
Up and over between
My arm and Number Three: throw it hit him in the middle
Of his enemies   hit move scramble
Before death and the ground
Come up LEAP STAND KILL DIE STRIKE
Now

In "Watching the Jets Lose to Buffalo at Shea," May Swenson perceives the same literal/symbolic violence and danger of which Dickey writes (and that are, after all, difficult to ignore) but turns immediately to the action's allegorical possibilities in a fashion quite distinct from Dickey's (who worked his own variation of sorts on this theme in "The Bee"). Here, the ball becomes a baby, the runner a father, the field life's dangers, and the endzone a cradle of safety:

Sent aloft by a leather toe,
a rugged leather baby
dropped from the sky and slammed
into the sling of your arms.

Oh, the feel of that leather bundle.
Oh, what a blooper and fumbler
you are, that you couldn't nest it,

that you lost and couldn't nurse it,
long enough to lay it
in the cradle of grass at the goalposts.

We leave it to the reader to make what he or she will of the runner-father's failure and of the implications of a man's lavishing such solicitude upon a "leather baby"; regardless, what is striking is Swenson's perception of the scene in such familial terms.[1] If nothing else, the poem would seem to urge readers to keep their priorities straight—that a player's failure finally matters less than a father's—and to see sport not only as a metaphor for war and aggression but, in the face of such unpleasantries, as a reminder of the need for similar care and concern in the world beyond the endzones.

Readers may feel that we have stacked the deck in our choice of poems, and no amount of protesting on our part is likely to alter this opinion. (Actually juxtaposing these poems was a happy moment of serendipity when our sport literature students turned in disgust from Beck to test her ideas against whatever poems they could find in their text.) It is therefore worth noting that Beck's contentions are corroborated elsewhere—for instance, in Marcia Westkott and Jay J. Coakley's "Women in Sport: Modalities of Feminist Social Change." Summarizing and synthesizing the answers forwarded in response to the question of why women should want to gain access to sporting activities and organizations that have excluded them, the authors present as one of two principal responses what they designate "the critical argument."[2] This response

> rejects patriarchal institutions and their activities. In particular, it rejects the values and attitudes associated with male defined behavior: competition, aggression, inflexibility, and egotism. According to this argument, the goals of feminist social change are not to have girls and women emulate "macho" behavior, nor to encourage females to participate in the institutions that require such behavior for survival or success. Those who reject male dominated institutions and behavior endorse the creation of alternative institutions that permit the freedom for women to define their own goals and modes of operating. . . . (32)

Briefly, the critical argument rejects the present sports world again because of its negative effects on participants (and, one imagines, on spectators as well). It fosters a set of distorted values that "often turn individuals into anxiety-ridden failures or cynical, egotistical sport specialists" (37). Further, sport's unhealthy emphasis on winning—"on the quality of performance and the outcome of contests" (38)—transforms what should be a playful, life-enhancing activity into an overly rigid, work-oriented chore and devalues "the goals of improved health, self-esteem, and [positive] body image" (39) while wrongheadedly translating success on the field into an

index of one's worth as a human being. Finally, with the pressure to win joining hands with the present coaching practices, sport encourages not assertiveness and autonomy but "responsiveness, dependence, and self-doubt . . ." (39). As Harry Edwards has remarked, advocates of the critical argument would, all things considered, prefer to see women's athletics not mirror existing programs but develop real alternatives wherein "the younger generation can be socialized with values stressing cooperation rather than antagonism, participation and self-actualization rather than confrontation and domination" (cited by Westkott and Coakley, 39).

From these brief summaries of Beck and of Westkott and Coakley—to which could be added others[3]—a set of alternative values and attitudes can readily be extrapolated. In addition to those suggested already, these values include self-identity and a self-awareness that specifically *includes* others rather than *excludes* them, as do the "rules" or the "game plan" of organized sport. This may be a strong theme because the rules of sport, like many of the rules of life, have so often excluded women. Other poems stress the pure joy of play and reveal an obvious preference for play as a more self-affirming and other-affirming activity than sport. And a final and recurrent theme in this poetry is a life-and-love-expanding coexistence with nature.[4] This key theme clearly implies that the natural world is superior to the human-made environment of sports, games, and "life by the rules," and suggests that an understanding of life involves not a struggle against it but cooperation with it. As Oriard remarks in his essay on Jenifer Levin's *Water Dancer*: "Not competition or mastery but surrender becomes a new kind of freedom. . . . To be a water dancer is neither to dominate nor be dominated but to live in one's body in the world" (18). Jenifer Levin's swimmer in *Water Dancer* becomes the prototype for all players who would achieve harmony and balance in the element of life.

Judith Wright's poem "Sports Field" illustrates the theme of self-identity that includes rather than excludes others. The poem's playing field functions as a clear metaphor for the duality of the natural and the artificial environment. As the poem opens, the reader sees the field at night, "naked . . . breathing its dew," and it is marked and controlled for the forthcoming game only by the appearance of the sun, "the great gold ball of day," which springs from the "dark hill." Wright emphasizes the autonomy of the natural world and its rhythms by using the sun as the golden ball "that no one ever catches." The children who come to play the game are born equally into the day with each other being all at first "gilt by the sun." However, this equality is soon shattered by the artificial provisions of the race, requiring that the children "shoulder one another; / crouch at the marks." The game divides and pits player against player, rather than achieving a union of children "gilt by the sun." For this activity, the field itself is "ruled": "measured and marked, its lanes and tapes are set." It becomes clear that this is a race, the race of life, and because of the rules, not everyone can win, so the children must be separated:

the children pledged and matched,
and built to win or lose,
who grow, while no one watches,

the selves in their sidelong eyes.

Thus, the "rules of the game" have become a substitute for the players' experience of themselves. They are watched in vain by spectators who love an illusion, because the only things that are real are the rules: "What's real here is the field, / the starter's gun, the lane, / the ball dropped or held."

Set toward the future, the children "run like running water," their pride and pain to be won only out of a "measured field," but the night and the field continue to glitter, "naked and perilous," a continuous reminder of the futility and transience of their games in contrast to the enduring rhythms of the sun and the night.

In stark contrast to Wright's "Sports Field" is Elizabeth Spires's poem "The Playground," wherein she eloquently captures the joy and pleasure of play for its own sake. Here the speaker is "drawn by shouts / of the children playing tug-of-war and crack-the-whip." Their joy becomes for both children and speaker a lifeline: "the lines alive, *taut.*" The children demand entrance into this play, this life, through her body, and as she stretches her arms to grasp a child on each side, she becomes a link in the chain. The chain grows as DNA grows, becoming a line of time:

> caught in a line
> snaking backward and forward
> until it joins, like time, at either end
> and mends invisibly,
> the face of the child on either side of me
> pale as a star
> as each holds my hand tightly
> begging to enter the world and live a little while,
> my body the instrument of passage.

Here Spires captures the innocent grace and symmetry of the threads of life, weaving all into a single pattern, a pattern of patterns, which overrides human-made rules, even the rules of time itself:

> We play
> as the clock strikes
> *one,* then *two,* then *three,*
>
> . . . . .
>
> no thought to the waning moon.

Spires pictures the joy of childhood play as a dream—a state of grace that cannot last—and like Wright, she grieves that it is ultimately lost in the rush toward the future:

> . . . the world inverted
> like a dream I'll wake alone from in the
> morning, the bed's cold sheets
> thrown off like so many obligations,
> as they pull me toward them and I pull away,
> the future bearing down so quickly upon us.

Jan Mordenski's "For Athletes, Poets, and Lovers" carries this key theme of separation from the self and from others because of rules over into adult love relationships, again in the context of a football game. There is a gender division at the first line of scrimmage:

> After the draft, there is
> the line of scrimmage, the moment
> that stretches long white arms to the left
> and the right dividing the world in half.

Unknowingly, all have "padded ourselves with elaborate protections" against the other—a ritual of isolation. Here the reader imagines not only football pads but the more impenetrable garments of "masculinity" and "femininity." And once people have insulated themselves, and step out on the field, they are on their own:

> There is no cheering from the stands;
> the air stands still and green
> as a referee from training while we
> try to read the opposition, the strategies,
> the strengths, the potential for effectual pain.

Unlike those of an actual football game, the signals for this game come to the players like the shadows of Plato's cave—never direct, always heard from behind, always futile:

> Somewhere from behind I hear signals being
>   called,
> a litany of attempts that have failed or half-failed

Although none of the signals makes sense, the reader keeps hoping for one that does: "a new number, a number that will work." Amid this confusion, people keep trying: "in order to catch, / take hold, and run with the one small thing / that still matters in this game." Here Mordenski uses the image of the football to suggest that the large things that should matter—such as love, tenderness, and communication—don't, and the small things that shouldn't matter—such as power, status, and wealth—do.

Finally, even the goal becomes an illusion, and just as the signals for the game have been heard only vaguely, so the goal is seen only as an abstraction, "not the goal, / but a picture of the goal," and in the player's attempts to seize this goal he sees only "a picture of my hands as they stretch to meet it." Here the sport imagery emphasizes the distance and isolation of the players, even lovers, from one another, and the futility of human relationships played by "the rules of the game."

Linda Mizejewski's poem "Season Wish" is an even more poignant statement about the arbitrary rules of human relationships. This time, however, the game is between a father and daughter. The daughter is reminiscent of the little left out Sasha Davis in Alix Kate Shulman's *Memoirs of an Ex-Prom Queen.* Oriard notes that Shulman finds in "playground grade-school games a metaphor for the male appropriation of the larger world" (15).

"Season Wish" brings home the whole history of the female as an offering, an object to be traded, bought, purchased, exchanged, bartered, stolen, or sacrificed for some artificial social or material gain. Like Rapunzel, the little girl in "Season Wish" is also "traded to the gods for wheat or rain." Every spring, her father takes her "out at dusk, to lots the boys had left," to see if she could become the "missing son." The father hopes that there might be some "magic in the glove or sneakers or wooden bat." The little girl understands very painfully her father's attempt to transform her through some mystical baseball alchemy:

> The cap, perhaps, might keep my hair
> forever clipped; holding the glove
> against my chest might stop
> my breasts; and if I learned
> the grip and stance, perhaps my wrists
> would thicken, hard, around the bat.

The father becomes the priest in this ritual of sacrifices and transformation, as he "made the diamond out of stones he piled like altars into three small mounds."

Year by year, the father continues this ceremony in other ways. Just as he tries to make her fit into the sandlot where she knows she does not belong, he tries to make her fit into the "real" world, from which she has also been excluded:

> Year by year he built for me
> the things he thought
> a man one day would want me for:
> investments, a name
> the family business—stock
> to insure a fair exchange
> for a man who might try
> to be a son.

But her father always fails at the spring trades, and is never able to transform her:

> I always came back being
> still a girl who couldn't play
> the way he'd hoped. . . .

Being "still a girl," she is denied access to any game. Read the rules.

But if left to herself this same little girl would play for all she was worth, and this is the message of Alice Fulton's "Fierce Girl Playing Hopscotch." This poem is a celebration of the value of play above and around and beyond and between all rules, play that carries people into the future, with messages about who they are. The speaker in the poem looks into the past at herself as a girl:

> I am what you made to live in
> from what you had: hair matted as kelp, bad
>   schools.

Unlike the adult speaker observing her past, the girl is so engrossed in play that she is oblivious to her future:

> Oh you will never know me. I wave and you go
> on playing in the clouds
> boys clap from erasers.

Playmates are gone from this future without play:

> Where's the kid called Katydid? The moonfaced
> Kewpiedoll? The excitable pouting
> Zookie? The somber O-Be-Joyful?

But the "lost girl" of the speaker's memory continues to play hopscotch, while the adult fulfills the promise of the child, but now believing in the anagrams and magic chants that once led her down the walk: "Name of father, son, ghost. Cross my heart and hope." The hopscotch ritual of childhood becomes the social ritual of self-identity and survival in adulthood as the sea of chalk changes to "loam and gold."

The little lost girl of hopscotch dancing in a sea of chalk, the players in tug-of-war, and the children "gilt by the sun" keep resurfacing with a central message already noted in Maxine Kumin's "Morning Swim." It is the idea that a peaceful cooperation among people and a faith in the natural world will expand and redeem loves. This is once again the theme of our final poem, Linda McCarriston's "Riding Out at Evening." The poem begins quietly, with a feeling of companionship between horse and rider, moves into a life-affirming love for particular others, and rises mystically into a love-expanding affirmation of the whole world. Dusk at the beginning of the poem is pictured as a sanctified time when "everything blurs and softens." As the fields and hills pull up "the first slight sheets of evening" and the rider "on horseback takes it in" she becomes one with the dusk—not an intruder, "but kin passing, closer and closer to night." It is in this peaceful union with the evening that the rider begins her blessing of her surroundings, "alone, wishing, or praying for particular good to particular beings."

The horse at once becomes a symbol of the rider and a vehicle of transcendence carrying her into flight:

> The horse bears me along, like grace,
> making me better than what I am,
> and what I think or say or see
> is whole in these moments, is neither
>
> small nor broken. For up
> out of the inscrutable earth, have come my body
> and the separate body of the mare:
> flawed and aching and wronged.

Horse and rider experience the power of their weakness and the strength of their separateness. And "we, as one, might course over the entire valley, over all valleys, as a bird in a great embrace of flight." Like the myth of Bellerophon and the winged horse Pegasus who triumph over the monster of havoc, they triumph over the grief of the world with tenderness:

as a bird in a great embrace
of flight, who presses against her breast,
in grief and tenderness,
the whole weeping body of the world. . . .

It was by way of a similarly tender image that Kenneth Patchen once described art as a pair of magic shoes that take one where one has never been before. If not all sports poems by women exhibit the alternative values about which we have been speaking, if some seem indistinguishable from poems written by men insofar as attitudes toward and perceived significance of sport are concerned,[5] women's sports poetry nonetheless continually offers itself as a pair of magic shoes, as a strong and graceful horse, ready to carry the reader into regions of experience he or she may never have visited before. We hope this essay proves useful en route.

NOTES

[1] A positive focus on family values was one early modification of the traditional male sporting myth made by women writers in the years before a fully female alternative began to assert itself, according to Oriard (11-14). Indeed, an emphasis on family—fathers and daughters, mothers and their children, husbands and wives (as well as other male-female relationships and dreams of such potentially familial relationships)—accounts for the subject matter of many sports poems by women. In addition to several of the poems discussed here, see, for example, Betty Adcock's "The Sixth Day," Nancy Jones's "Running Blind," Mabel M. Kuykendall's "Baseball Pitcher," and Louise Glück's "The Racer's Widow," all in Tom Dodge's *A Literature of Sports.*

[2] The other response discussed by Westkott and Coakley is "the assimilationist argument," according to which "feminist change is defined in terms of women gaining access to culturally valued spheres of action rather than changing those cultural values and actions" (32).

[3] Here is not the place to offer a working bibliography of useful sources for the further study of women and sport. Beyond the bibliography in this volume, we would direct the reader's attention to Oriard, whose essay deserves to be read in its entirety; to the work of feminists Mary Daly and Marilyn French; and to the extensive lists of references appended to the Beck and Westkott and Coakley essays.

[4] A feature of a number of women's sports poems we have not considered at length but that deserves mention at this point is the direct criticism of male-defined sport behavior. See, for instance, Babette Deutsch's "A Bull," Louise Glück's "The Racer's Widow," and Barbara Howes's "In Autumn," among others, in Tom Dodge's *A Literature of Sports.*

[5] From Beck's perspective, such nonalterative poems would be the products of women who have fully assimilated male values and attitudes. Also of interest in this respect are the recently reconceptualized Jungian notions of anima and animus as discussed, for instance, in Bettina Knapp's *Women in Twentieth-Century Literature,* which applies a number of Jungian concepts to a spectrum of literary works. As Knapp explains, the anima (or female principle of all personalities, female and male), once characterized as the source of emotionalism, helplessness, vanity, and the like, is now described positively as nurturing, caring, feeling, creative, and life enhancing (with the animus representing intellect, rationality, heroism). Such concepts might help, among other things, in positing a female perspective on sport not exclusively the possession of women and thereby in accounting for masculine values and attitudes in certain sports poems by women as well as feminine characteristics in sports poems by men.

WORKS CITED

Beck, Bonnie. "The Future of Women's Sport: Issues, Insights, and Struggles." In *Sport in Contemporary Society,* edited by D. Stanley Eitzen, 401-14. 2d ed. New York: St. Martin's, 1984.

Dickey, James. "In the Pocket." In *A Literature of Sports,* edited by Tom Dodge, 389-90. Lexington, Mass.: Heath, 1980.

Dodge, Tom, ed. *A Literature of Sports,* Lexington, Mass.: Heath, 1980.

Francis, Robert. "Swimmer." In *A Literature of Sports,* edited by Tom Dodge, 416. Lexington, Mass.: Heath, 1980.

Fulton, Alice. "Fierce Girl Playing Hopscotch." *Poetry,* March 1985, 340.

Knapp, Bettina. *Women in Twentieth-Century Literature: A Jungian View.* University Park: Pennsylvania State University Press, 1987.

Kumin, Maxine. "Morning Swim." In *A Literature of Sports,* edited by Tom Dodge, 413-14. Lexington, Mass.: Heath, 1980.

McCarriston, Linda. "Riding Out at Evening." *Poetry,* June 1982, 153-54.

Mizejewski, Linda. "Season Wish." In *Baseball Diamonds: Tales, Traces, Visions & Voodoo from a Native American Rite,* edited by Kevin Kerrane and Richard Grossinger, 37-38. Garden City, N.Y.: Anchor-Doubleday, 1980.

Mordenski, Jan. "For Athletes, Poets, and Lovers." *Arete: The Journal of Sport Literature* 4, no. 1 (1986): 56.

Oriard, Michael. "From Jane Allen to *Water Dancer:* A Brief History of the Feminist (?) Sports Novel." *Modern Fiction Studies* 33 (1987): 9-20.

Slusher, Howard S. "Sport and Death." In *Sport Inside Out: Readings in Literature and Philosophy,* edited by David L. Vanderwerken and Spencer K. Wertz, 752-55. Fort Worth: Texas Christian University Press, 1985.

Spires, Elizabeth. "The Playground." *Poetry,* October 1983, 33.

Swenson, May. "Watching the Jets Lose to Buffalo at Shea." In *A Literature of Sports,* edited by Tom Dodge, 410-11. Lexington, Mass.: Heath, 1980.

Westkott, Marcia, and Jay J. Coakley. "Women in Sport: Modalities of Feminist Social Change." *Journal of Sport and Social Issues* 5, no. 1 (1981): 32-45.

Wright, Judith. "Sports Field." In *A Literature of Sports,* edited by Tom Dodge, 425-26. Lexington, Mass.: Heath, 1980.

FURTHER READING

Anthologies

Vanderwerken, David L., and Wertz, Spencer K. *Sport Inside Out: Readings in Literature and Philosophy.* Fort Worth: Texas Christian University Press, 1985, 782 p.

> Compilation of fiction, poetry, essays, and philosophical meditations focusing on the relationship between sports and life.

Secondary Sources

Epstein, Joseph. "A Boy's Own Author." *Commentary* 84, No. 6 (December 1987): 50-6.

> Profiles John Tunis, author of sports novels for young boys.

Fotheringham, Richard. *Sport in Australian Drama.* Cambridge: Cambridge University Press, 1992, 268 p.

> Full-length critical discussion of the relationship between sports and Australian drama, film, and literature.

Hammer, Adam. "Kidsport: The Works of John T. Tunis." *Journal of Popular Culture* 17, No. 3 (Winter 1983): 146-49.

> Offers a laudatory assessment of Tunis's sports novels for young boys.

Harrington, Henry R. "Charles Kingsley's Fallen Athlete." *Victorian Studies* 21, No. 1 (Autumn 1977): 73-86.

> Explores the function of sport, violence, and sexuality in the work of Charles Kingsley.

Higgs, Robert J. *Laurel & Thorn: The Athlete in American Literature.* Lexington: University Press of Kentucky, 1981, 196 p.

> Catalogs several types of athletic heroes and interprets these models as symbols of American culture.

Modern Fiction Studies 33, No. 1 (Spring 1987): 1-194.

> Special issue devoted to historical, mythical, and critical discourse on sports and games as represented in and by literature.

Moore, Jim, and Vermilyea, Natalie. *Ernest Thayer's 'Casey at the Bat': Background and Characters of Baseball's Most Famous Poem.* Jefferson, N.C.: McFarland & Company, 1994, 360 p.

> Biographical and critical study of Thayer.

Shideler, Ross. "Putting Together the Puzzle in Per Olov Enquist's *Sekonden.*" *Scandinavian Studies* 49, No. 3 (Summer 1977): 311-29.

> Provides a stylistic and thematic analysis of Enquist's novel.

Westbrook, Deeanne. *Ground Rules: Baseball & Myth.* Urbana: University of Chicago Press, 1996, 348 p.

> Examines the role of myth in baseball literature.

Wise, Suzanne. *Sports Fiction for Adults: An Annotated Bibliography of Novels, Plays, Short Stories, and Poetry with Sporting Settings.* New York: Garland Publishing, 1986, 203 p.

> Annotated primary bibliography.

Twentieth-Century Literary Criticism

Cumulative Indexes
Volumes 1-86

How to Use This Index

The main references

> Calvino, Italo
> 1923–1985 .... CLC 5, 8, 11, 22, 33, 39,
> 73; SSC 3

list all author entries in the following Gale Literary Criticism series:

BLC = *Black Literature Criticism*
CLC = *Contemporary Literary Criticism*
CLR = *Children's Literature Review*
CMLC = *Classical and Medieval Literature Criticism*
DA = *DISCovering Authors*
DAB = *DISCovering Authors: British*
DAC = *DISCovering Authors: Canadian*
DAM = *DISCovering Authors: Modules*
    DRAM: *Dramatists Module;* *MST*: *Most-Studied Authors Module;*
    MULT: *Multicultural Authors Module;* *NOV*: *Novelists Module;*
    POET: *Poets Module;* *POP*: *Popular Fiction and Genre Authors Module*
DC = *Drama Criticism*
HLC = *Hispanic Literature Criticism*
LC = *Literature Criticism from 1400 to 1800*
NCLC = *Nineteenth-Century Literature Criticism*
PC = *Poetry Criticism*
SSC = *Short Story Criticism*
TCLC = *Twentieth-Century Literary Criticism*
WLC = *World Literature Criticism, 1500 to the Present*

The cross-references

> See also CANR 23; CA 85-88;
>   obituary CA116

list all author entries in the following Gale biographical and literary sources:

AAYA = *Authors & Artists for Young Adults*
AITN = *Authors in the News*
BEST = *Bestsellers*
BW = *Black Writers*
CA = *Contemporary Authors*
CAAS = *Contemporary Authors Autobiography Series*
CABS = *Contemporary Authors Bibliographical Series*
CANR = *Contemporary Authors New Revision Series*
CAP = *Contemporary Authors Permanent Series*
CDALB = *Concise Dictionary of American Literary Biography*
CDBLB = *Concise Dictionary of British Literary Biography*
DLB = *Dictionary of Literary Biography*
DLBD = *Dictionary of Literary Biography Documentary Series*
DLBY = *Dictionary of Literary Biography Yearbook*
HW = *Hispanic Writers*
JRDA = *Junior DISCovering Authors*
MAICYA = *Major Authors and Illustrators for Children and Young Adults*
MTCW = *Major 20th-Century Writers*
NNAL = *Native North American Literature*
SAAS = *Something about the Author Autobiography Series*
SATA = *Something about the Author*
YABC = *Yesterday's Authors of Books for Children*

See Prado (Calvo), Pedro
Angelique, Pierre
See Bataille, Georges
Angell, Roger 1920- .... **CLC 26**
See also CA 57-60; CANR 13, 44, 70; DLB 171, 185
Angelou, Maya 1928-**CLC 12, 35, 64, 77; BLC 1; DA; DAB; DAC; DAM MST, MULT, POET, POP; WLCS**
See also Johnson, Marguerite (Annie)
See also AAYA 7, 20; BW 2; CA 65-68; CANR 19, 42, 65; CLR 53; DLB 38; MTCW 1; SATA 49
Anna Comnena 1083-1153 .... **CMLC 25**
Annensky, Innokenty (Fyodorovich) 1856-1909 **TCLC 14**
See also CA 110; 155
Annunzio, Gabriele d'
See D'Annunzio, Gabriele
Anodos
See Coleridge, Mary E(lizabeth)
Anon, Charles Robert
See Pessoa, Fernando (Antonio Nogueira)
Anouilh, Jean (Marie Lucien Pierre) 1910-1987 **CLC 1, 3, 8, 13, 40, 50; DAM DRAM; DC 8**
See also CA 17-20R; 123; CANR 32; MTCW 1
Anthony, Florence
See Ai
Anthony, John
See Ciardi, John (Anthony)
Anthony, Peter
See Shaffer, Anthony (Joshua); Shaffer, Peter (Levin)
Anthony, Piers 1934- .... **CLC 35; DAM POP**
See also AAYA 11; CA 21-24R; CANR 28, 56; DLB 8; MTCW 1; SAAS 22; SATA 84
Anthony, Susan B(rownell) 1916-1991 **T C L C 84**
See also CA 89-92; 134
Antoine, Marc
See Proust, (Valentin-Louis-George-Eugene-) Marcel
Antoninus, Brother
See Everson, William (Oliver)
Antonioni, Michelangelo 1912- .... **CLC 20**
See also CA 73-76; CANR 45
Antschel, Paul 1920-1970
See Celan, Paul
See also CA 85-88; CANR 33, 61; MTCW 1
Anwar, Chairil 1922-1949 .... **TCLC 22**
See also CA 121
Apess, William 1798-1839(?)**NCLC 73; DAM MULT**
See also DLB 175; NNAL
Apollinaire, Guillaume 1880-1918**TCLC 3, 8, 51; DAM POET; PC 7**
See also Kostrowitzki, Wilhelm Apollinaris de
See also CA 152
Appelfeld, Aharon 1932- .... **CLC 23, 47**
See also CA 112; 133
Apple, Max (Isaac) 1941-................**CLC 9, 33**
See also CA 81-84; CANR 19, 54; DLB 130
Appleman, Philip (Dean) 1926- .... **CLC 51**
See also CA 13-16R; CAAS 18; CANR 6, 29, 56
Appleton, Lawrence
See Lovecraft, H(oward) P(hillips)
Apteryx
See Eliot, T(homas) S(tearns)
Apuleius, (Lucius Madaurensis) 125(?)-175(?) **CMLC 1**
Aquin, Hubert 1929-1977 .... **CLC 15**
See also CA 105; DLB 53
Aragon, Louis 1897-1982 .. **CLC 3, 22; DAM NOV, POET**
See also CA 69-72; 108; CANR 28, 71; DLB

72; MTCW 1
Arany, Janos 1817-1882 .... **NCLC 34**
Arbuthnot, John 1667-1735 .... **LC 1**
See also DLB 101
Archer, Herbert Winslow
See Mencken, H(enry) L(ouis)
Archer, Jeffrey (Howard) 1940- ..... **CLC 28; DAM POP**
See also AAYA 16; BEST 89:3; CA 77-80; CANR 22, 52; INT CANR-22
Archer, Jules 1915- .... **CLC 12**
See also CA 9-12R; CANR 6, 69; SAAS 5; SATA 4, 85
Archer, Lee
See Ellison, Harlan (Jay)
Arden, John 1930-**CLC 6, 13, 15; DAM DRAM**
See also CA 13-16R; CAAS 4; CANR 31, 65, 67; DLB 13; MTCW 1
Arenas, Reinaldo 1943-1990 . **CLC 41; DAM MULT; HLC**
See also CA 124; 128; 133; DLB 145; HW
Arendt, Hannah 1906-1975 .... **CLC 66, 98**
See also CA 17-20R; 61-64; CANR 26, 60; MTCW 1
Aretino, Pietro 1492-1556 .... **LC 12**
Arghezi, Tudor 1880-1967 .... **CLC 80**
See also Theodorescu, Ion N.
See also CA 167
Arguedas, Jose Maria 1911-1969 **CLC 10, 18**
See also CA 89-92; DLB 113; HW
Argueta, Manlio 1936- .... **CLC 31**
See also CA 131; DLB 145; HW
Ariosto, Ludovico 1474-1533 .... **LC 6**
Aristides
See Epstein, Joseph
Aristophanes 450B.C.-385B.C.**CMLC 4; DA; DAB; DAC; DAM DRAM, MST; DC 2; WLCS**
See also DLB 176
Arlt, Roberto (Godofredo Christophersen) 1900-1942 ....
TCLC 29; DAM MULT; HLC
See also CA 123; 131; CANR 67; HW
Armah, Ayi Kwei 1939- . **CLC 5, 33; BLC 1; DAM MULT, POET**
See also BW 1; CA 61-64; CANR 21, 64; DLB 117; MTCW 1
Armatrading, Joan 1950- .... **CLC 17**
See also CA 114
Arnette, Robert
See Silverberg, Robert
Arnim, Achim von (Ludwig Joachim von Arnim) 1781-1831 ...... **NCLC 5; SSC 29**
See also DLB 90
Arnim, Bettina von 1785-1859 .... **NCLC 38**
See also DLB 90
Arnold, Matthew 1822-1888**NCLC 6, 29; DA; DAB; DAC; DAM MST, POET; PC 5; WLC**
See also CDBLB 1832-1890; DLB 32, 57
Arnold, Thomas 1795-1842 .... **NCLC 18**
See also DLB 55
Arnow, Harriette (Louisa) Simpson 1908-1986
CLC 2, 7, 18
See also CA 9-12R; 118; CANR 14; DLB 6; MTCW 1; SATA 42; SATA-Obit 47
Arouet, Francois-Marie
See Voltaire
Arp, Hans
See Arp, Jean
Arp, Jean 1887-1966 .... **CLC 5**
See also CA 81-84; 25-28R; CANR 42
Arrabal
See Arrabal, Fernando
Arrabal, Fernando 1932- .... **CLC 2, 9, 18, 58**
See also CA 9-12R; CANR 15
Arrick, Fran .... **CLC 30**

See also Gaberman, Judie Angell
Artaud, Antonin (Marie Joseph) 1896-1948
TCLC 3, 36; DAM DRAM
See also CA 104; 149
Arthur, Ruth M(abel) 1905-1979 ...... **CLC 12**
See also CA 9-12R; 85-88; CANR 4; SATA 7, 26
Artsybashev, Mikhail (Petrovich) 1878-1927 **TCLC 31**
Arundel, Honor (Morfydd) 1919-1973**CLC 17**
See also CA 21-22; 41-44R; CAP 2; CLR 35; SATA 4; SATA-Obit 24
Arzner, Dorothy 1897-1979 .... **CLC 98**
Asch, Sholem 1880-1957 .... **TCLC 3**
See also CA 105
Ash, Shalom
See Asch, Sholem
Ashbery, John (Lawrence) 1927-**CLC 2, 3, 4, 6, 9, 13, 15, 25, 41, 77; DAM POET**
See also CA 5-8R; CANR 9, 37, 66; DLB 5, 165; DLBY 81; INT CANR-9; MTCW 1
Ashdown, Clifford
See Freeman, R(ichard) Austin
Ashe, Gordon
See Creasey, John
Ashton-Warner, Sylvia (Constance) 1908-1984
CLC 19
See also CA 69-72; 112; CANR 29; MTCW 1
Asimov, Isaac 1920-1992 **CLC 1, 3, 9, 19, 26, 76, 92; DAM POP**
See also AAYA 13; BEST 90:2; CA 1-4R; 137; CANR 2, 19, 36, 60; CLR 12; DLB 8; DLBY 92; INT CANR-19; JRDA; MAICYA; MTCW 1; SATA 1, 26, 74
Assis, Joaquim Maria Machado de
See Machado de Assis, Joaquim Maria
Astley, Thea (Beatrice May) 1925- ... **CLC 41**
See also CA 65-68; CANR 11, 43
Aston, James
See White, T(erence) H(anbury)
Asturias, Miguel Angel 1899-1974 **CLC 3, 8, 13; DAM MULT, NOV; HLC**
See also CA 25-28; 49-52; CANR 32; CAP 2; DLB 113; HW; MTCW 1
Atares, Carlos Saura
See Saura (Atares), Carlos
Atheling, William
See Pound, Ezra (Weston Loomis)
Atheling, William, Jr.
See Blish, James (Benjamin)
Atherton, Gertrude (Franklin Horn) 1857-1948
TCLC 2
See also CA 104; 155; DLB 9, 78, 186
Atherton, Lucius
See Masters, Edgar Lee
Atkins, Jack
See Harris, Mark
Atkinson, Kate .... **CLC 99**
See also CA 166
Attaway, William (Alexander) 1911-1986
CLC 92; BLC 1; DAM MULT
See also BW 2; CA 143; DLB 76
Atticus
See Fleming, Ian (Lancaster); Wilson, (Thomas) Woodrow
Atwood, Margaret (Eleanor) 1939-**CLC 2, 3, 4, 8, 13, 15, 25, 44, 84; DA; DAB; DAC; DAM MST, NOV, POET; PC 8; SSC 2; WLC**
See also AAYA 12; BEST 89:2; CA 49-52; CANR 3, 24, 33, 59; DLB 53; INT CANR-24; MTCW 1; SATA 50
Aubigny, Pierre d'
See Mencken, H(enry) L(ouis)
Aubin, Penelope 1685-1731(?) .... **LC 9**
See also DLB 39
Auchincloss, Louis (Stanton) 1917-**CLC 4, 6,**

See also CA 102; DLB 13

Barker, Pat(ricia) 1943- .... **CLC 32, 94**
See also CA 117; 122; CANR 50; INT 122

Barlach, Ernst 1870-1938 .... **TCLC 84**
See also DLB 56, 118

Barlow, Joel 1754-1812 .... **NCLC 23**
See also DLB 37

Barnard, Mary (Ethel) 1909- .... **CLC 48**
See also CA 21-22; CAP 2

Barnes, Djuna 1892-1982 **CLC 3, 4, 8, 11, 29; SSC 3**
See also CA 9-12R; 107; CANR 16, 55; DLB 4, 9, 45; MTCW 1

Barnes, Julian (Patrick) 1946- **CLC 42; DAB**
See also CA 102; CANR 19, 54; DLB 194; DLBY 93

Barnes, Peter 1931- .... **CLC 5, 56**
See also CA 65-68; CAAS 12; CANR 33, 34, 64; DLB 13; MTCW 1

Baroja (y Nessi), Pio 1872-1956 **TCLC 8; HLC**
See also CA 104

Baron, David
See Pinter, Harold

Baron Corvo
See Rolfe, Frederick (William Serafino Austin Lewis Mary)

Barondess, Sue K(aufman) 1926-1977 **CLC 8**
See Kaufman, Sue
See also CA 1-4R; 69-72; CANR 1

Baron de Teive
See Pessoa, Fernando (Antonio Nogueira)

Baroness Von S.
See Zangwill, Israel

Barres, (Auguste-) Maurice 1862-1923 **TCLC 47**
See also CA 164; DLB 123

Barreto, Afonso Henrique de Lima
See Lima Barreto, Afonso Henrique de

Barrett, (Roger) Syd 1946- .... **CLC 35**

Barrett, William (Christopher) 1913-1992 **CLC 27**
See also CA 13-16R; 139; CANR 11, 67; INT CANR-11

Barrie, J(ames) M(atthew) 1860-1937 **TCLC 2; DAB; DAM DRAM**
See also CA 104; 136; CDBLB 1890-1914; CLR 16; DLB 10, 141, 156; MAICYA; SATA 100; YABC 1

Barrington, Michael
See Moorcock, Michael (John)

Barrol, Grady
See Bograd, Larry

Barry, Mike
See Malzberg, Barry N(athaniel)

Barry, Philip 1896-1949 .... **TCLC 11**
See also CA 109; DLB 7

Bart, Andre Schwarz
See Schwarz-Bart, Andre

Barth, John (Simmons) 1930- **CLC 1, 2, 3, 5, 7, 9, 10, 14, 27, 51, 89; DAM NOV; SSC 10**
See also AITN 1, 2; CA 1-4R; CABS 1; CANR 5, 23, 49, 64; DLB 2; MTCW 1

Barthelme, Donald 1931-1989 **CLC 1, 2, 3, 5, 6, 8, 13, 23, 46, 59, 115; DAM NOV; SSC 2**
See also CA 21-24R; 129; CANR 20, 58; DLB 2; DLBY 80, 89; MTCW 1; SATA 7; SATA-Obit 62

Barthelme, Frederick 1943- .... **CLC 36**
See also CA 114; 122; DLBY 85; INT 122

Barthes, Roland (Gerard) 1915-1980 **CLC 24, 83**
See also CA 130; 97-100; CANR 66; MTCW 1

Barzun, Jacques (Martin) 1907- .... **CLC 51**
See also CA 61-64; CANR 22

Bashevis, Isaac
See Singer, Isaac Bashevis

Bashkirtseff, Marie 1859-1884 ...... **NCLC 27**

Basho
See Matsuo Basho

Bass, Kingsley B., Jr.
See Bullins, Ed

Bass, Rick 1958- .... **CLC 79**
See also CA 126; CANR 53

Bassani, Giorgio 1916- .... **CLC 9**
See also CA 65-68; CANR 33; DLB 128, 177; MTCW 1

Bastos, Augusto (Antonio) Roa
See Roa Bastos, Augusto (Antonio)

Bataille, Georges 1897-1962 .... **CLC 29**
See also CA 101; 89-92

Bates, H(erbert) E(rnest) 1905-1974 **CLC 46; DAB; DAM POP; SSC 10**
See also CA 93-96; 45-48; CANR 34; DLB 162, 191; MTCW 1

Bauchart
See Camus, Albert

Baudelaire, Charles 1821-1867 . **NCLC 6, 29, 55; DA; DAB; DAC; DAM MST, POET; PC 1; SSC 18; WLC**

Baudrillard, Jean 1929- .... **CLC 60**

Baum, L(yman) Frank 1856-1919 ... **TCLC 7**
See also CA 108; 133; CLR 15; DLB 22; JRDA; MAICYA; MTCW 1; SATA 18, 100

Baum, Louis F.
See Baum, L(yman) Frank

Baumbach, Jonathan 1933- .... **CLC 6, 23**
See also CA 13-16R; CAAS 5; CANR 12, 66; DLBY 80; INT CANR-12; MTCW 1

Bausch, Richard (Carl) 1945- .... **CLC 51**
See also CA 101; CAAS 14; CANR 43, 61; DLB 130

Baxter, Charles (Morley) 1947- **CLC 45, 78; DAM POP**
See also CA 57-60; CANR 40, 64; DLB 130

Baxter, George Owen
See Faust, Frederick (Schiller)

Baxter, James K(eir) 1926-1972 .... **CLC 14**
See also CA 77-80

Baxter, John
See Hunt, E(verette) Howard, (Jr.)

Bayer, Sylvia
See Glassco, John

Baynton, Barbara 1857-1929 .... **TCLC 57**

Beagle, Peter S(oyer) 1939- .... **CLC 7, 104**
See also CA 9-12R; CANR 4, 51; DLBY 80; INT CANR-4; SATA 60

Bean, Normal
See Burroughs, Edgar Rice

Beard, Charles A(ustin) 1874-1948 **TCLC 15**
See also CA 115; DLB 17; SATA 18

Beardsley, Aubrey 1872-1898 .... **NCLC 6**

Beattie, Ann 1947- **CLC 8, 13, 18, 40, 63; DAM NOV, POP; SSC 11**
See also BEST 90:2; CA 81-84; CANR 53; DLBY 82; MTCW 1

Beattie, James 1735-1803 .... **NCLC 25**
See also DLB 109

Beauchamp, Kathleen Mansfield 1888-1923
See Mansfield, Katherine
See also CA 104; 134; DA; DAC; DAM MST

Beaumarchais, Pierre-Augustin Caron de 1732-1799 .... **DC 4**
See also DAM DRAM

Beaumont, Francis 1584(?)-1616 **LC 33; DC 6**
See also CDBLB Before 1660; DLB 58, 121

Beauvoir, Simone (Lucie Ernestine Marie Bertrand) de 1908-1986 **CLC 1, 2, 4, 8, 14, 31, 44, 50, 71; DA; DAB; DAC; DAM MST, NOV; WLC**
See also CA 9-12R; 118; CANR 28, 61; DLB 72; DLBY 86; MTCW 1

Becker, Carl (Lotus) 1873-1945 ..... **TCLC 63**
See also CA 157; DLB 17

Becker, Jurek 1937-1997 .... **CLC 7, 19**

See also CA 85-88; 157; CANR 60; DLB 75

Becker, Walter 1950- .... **CLC 26**

Beckett, Samuel (Barclay) 1906-1989 **CLC 1, 2, 3, 4, 6, 9, 10, 11, 14, 18, 29, 57, 59, 83; DA; DAB; DAC; DAM DRAM, MST, NOV; SSC 16; WLC**
See also CA 5-8R; 130; CANR 33, 61; CDBLB 1945-1960; DLB 13, 15; DLBY 90; MTCW 1

Beckford, William 1760-1844 .... **NCLC 16**
See also DLB 39

Beckman, Gunnel 1910- .... **CLC 26**
See also CA 33-36R; CANR 15; CLR 25; MAICYA; SAAS 9; SATA 6

Becque, Henri 1837-1899 .... **NCLC 3**
See also DLB 192

Beddoes, Thomas Lovell 1803-1849 **NCLC 3**
See also DLB 96

Bede c. 673-735 .... **CMLC 20**
See also DLB 146

Bedford, Donald F.
See Fearing, Kenneth (Flexner)

Beecher, Catharine Esther 1800-1878 **NCLC 30**
See also DLB 1

Beecher, John 1904-1980 .... **CLC 6**
See also AITN 1; CA 5-8R; 105; CANR 8

Beer, Johann 1655-1700 .... **LC 5**
See also DLB 168

Beer, Patricia 1924- .... **CLC 58**
See also CA 61-64; CANR 13, 46; DLB 40

Beerbohm, Max
See Beerbohm, (Henry) Max(imilian)

Beerbohm, (Henry) Max(imilian) 1872-1956 **TCLC 1, 24**
See also CA 104; 154; DLB 34, 100

Beer-Hofmann, Richard 1866-1945 **TCLC 60**
See also CA 160; DLB 81

Begiebing, Robert J(ohn) 1946- .... **CLC 70**
See also CA 122; CANR 40

Behan, Brendan 1923-1964 **CLC 1, 8, 11, 15, 79; DAM DRAM**
See also CA 73-76; CANR 33; CDBLB 1945-1960; DLB 13; MTCW 1

Behn, Aphra 1640(?)-1689 **LC 1, 30; DA; DAB; DAC; DAM DRAM, MST, NOV, POET; DC 4; PC 13; WLC**
See also DLB 39, 80, 131

Behrman, S(amuel) N(athaniel) 1893-1973 **CLC 40**
See also CA 13-16; 45-48; CAP 1; DLB 7, 44

Belasco, David 1853-1931 .... **TCLC 3**
See also CA 104; 168; DLB 7

Belcheva, Elisaveta 1893- .... **CLC 10**
See also Bagryana, Elisaveta

Beldone, Phil "Cheech"
See Ellison, Harlan (Jay)

Beleno
See Azuela, Mariano

Belinski, Vissarion Grigoryevich 1811-1848 **NCLC 5**
See also DLB 198

Belitt, Ben 1911- .... **CLC 22**
See also CA 13-16R; CAAS 4; CANR 7; DLB 5

Bell, Gertrude (Margaret Lowthian) 1868-1926 **TCLC 67**
See also CA 167; DLB 174

Bell, J. Freeman
See Zangwill, Israel

Bell, James Madison 1826-1902 ... **TCLC 43; BLC 1; DAM MULT**
See also BW 1; CA 122; 124; DLB 50

Bell, Madison Smartt 1957- ..... **CLC 41, 102**
See also CA 111; CANR 28, 54

Bell, Marvin (Hartley) 1937- **CLC 8, 31; DAM POET**

See also AITN 1; CA 41-44R; 151; CANR 37; DAM POET; MTCW 1

Brodsky, Joseph 1940-1996 **CLC 4, 6, 13, 36, 100; PC 9**
See also Brodskii, Iosif; Brodsky, Iosif Alexandrovich

Brodsky, Michael (Mark) 1948- .... **CLC 19**
See also CA 102; CANR 18, 41, 58

Bromell, Henry 1947- .... **CLC 5**
See also CA 53-56; CANR 9

Bromfield, Louis (Brucker) 1896-1956 **TCLC 11**
See also CA 107; 155; DLB 4, 9, 86

Broner, E(sther) M(asserman) 1930- **CLC 19**
See also CA 17-20R; CANR 8, 25, 72; DLB 28

Bronk, William 1918- .... **CLC 10**
See also CA 89-92; CANR 23; DLB 165

Bronstein, Lev Davidovich
See Trotsky, Leon

Bronte, Anne 1820-1849 .... **NCLC 71**
See also DLB 21, 199

Bronte, Charlotte 1816-1855 **NCLC 3, 8, 33, 58; DA; DAB; DAC; DAM MST, NOV; WLC**
See also AAYA 17; CDBLB 1832-1890; DLB 21, 159, 199

Bronte, Emily (Jane) 1818-1848 **NCLC 16, 35; DA; DAB; DAC; DAM MST, NOV, POET; PC 8; WLC**
See also AAYA 17; CDBLB 1832-1890; DLB 21, 32, 199

Brooke, Frances 1724-1789 .... **LC 6**
See also DLB 39, 99

Brooke, Henry 1703(?)-1783 .... **LC 1**
See also DLB 39

Brooke, Rupert (Chawner) 1887-1915 **TCLC 2, 7; DA; DAB; DAC; DAM MST, POET; PC 24; WLC**
See also CA 104; 132; CANR 61; CDBLB 1914-1945; DLB 19; MTCW 1

Brooke-Haven, P.
See Wodehouse, P(elham) G(renville)

Brooke-Rose, Christine 1926(?)- .... **CLC 40**
See also CA 13-16R; CANR 58; DLB 14

Brookner, Anita 1928- **CLC 32, 34, 51; DAB; DAM POP**
See also CA 114; 120; CANR 37, 56; DLB 194; DLBY 87; MTCW 1

Brooks, Cleanth 1906-1994 **CLC 24, 86, 110**
See also CA 17-20R; 145; CANR 33, 35; DLB 63; DLBY 94; INT CANR-35; MTCW 1

Brooks, George
See Baum, L(yman) Frank

Brooks, Gwendolyn 1917- **CLC 1, 2, 4, 5, 15, 49; BLC 1; DA; DAC; DAM MST, MULT, POET; PC 7; WLC**
See also AAYA 20; AITN 1; BW 2; CA 1-4R; CANR 1, 27, 52; CDALB 1941-1968; CLR 27; DLB 5, 76, 165; MTCW 1; SATA 6

Brooks, Mel .... **CLC 12**
See also Kaminsky, Melvin
See also AAYA 13; DLB 26

Brooks, Peter 1938- .... **CLC 34**
See also CA 45-48; CANR 1

Brooks, Van Wyck 1886-1963 .... **CLC 29**
See also CA 1-4R; CANR 6; DLB 45, 63, 103

Brophy, Brigid (Antonia) 1929-1995 **CLC 6, 11, 29, 105**
See also CA 5-8R; 149; CAAS 4; CANR 25, 53; DLB 14; MTCW 1

Brosman, Catharine Savage 1934- ..... **CLC 9**
See also CA 61-64; CANR 21, 46

Brossard, Chandler 1922-1993 .... **CLC 115**
See also CA 61-64; 142; CAAS 2; CANR 8, 56; DLB 16

Brother Antoninus
See Everson, William (Oliver)

The Brothers Quay
See Quay, Stephen; Quay, Timothy

Broughton, T(homas) Alan 1936- ..... **CLC 19**
See also CA 45-48; CANR 2, 23, 48

Broumas, Olga 1949- .... **CLC 10, 73**
See also CA 85-88; CANR 20, 69

Brown, Alan 1950- .... **CLC 99**
See also CA 156

Brown, Charles Brockden 1771-1810 **NCLC 22**
See also CDALB 1640-1865; DLB 37, 59, 73

Brown, Christy 1932-1981 .... **CLC 63**
See also CA 105; 104; CANR 72; DLB 14

Brown, Claude 1937- **CLC 30; BLC 1; DAM MULT**
See also AAYA 7; BW 1; CA 73-76

Brown, Dee (Alexander) 1908- .. **CLC 18, 47; DAM POP**
See also CA 13-16R; CAAS 6; CANR 11, 45, 60; DLBY 80; MTCW 1; SATA 5

Brown, George
See Wertmueller, Lina

Brown, George Douglas 1869-1902 **TCLC 28**
See also CA 162

Brown, George Mackay 1921-1996 **CLC 5, 48, 100**
See also CA 21-24R; 151; CAAS 6; CANR 12, 37, 67; DLB 14, 27, 139; MTCW 1; SATA 35

Brown, (William) Larry 1951- .... **CLC 73**
See also CA 130; 134; INT 133

Brown, Moses
See Barrett, William (Christopher)

Brown, Rita Mae 1944- **CLC 18, 43, 79; DAM NOV, POP**
See also CA 45-48; CANR 2, 11, 35, 62; INT CANR-11; MTCW 1

Brown, Roderick (Langmere) Haig-
See Haig-Brown, Roderick (Langmere)

Brown, Rosellen 1939- .... **CLC 32**
See also CA 77-80; CAAS 10; CANR 14, 44

Brown, Sterling Allen 1901-1989 **CLC 1, 23, 59; BLC 1; DAM MULT, POET**
See also BW 1; CA 85-88; 127; CANR 26; DLB 48, 51, 63; MTCW 1

Brown, Will
See Ainsworth, William Harrison

Brown, William Wells 1813-1884 ... **NCLC 2; BLC 1; DAM MULT; DC 1**
See also DLB 3, 50

Browne, (Clyde) Jackson 1948(?)- .... **CLC 21**
See also CA 120

Browning, Elizabeth Barrett 1806-1861 **NCLC 1, 16, 61, 66; DA; DAB; DAC; DAM MST, POET; PC 6; WLC**
See also CDBLB 1832-1890; DLB 32, 199

Browning, Robert 1812-1889 **NCLC 19; DA; DAB; DAC; DAM MST, POET; PC 2; WLCS**
See also CDBLB 1832-1890; DLB 32, 163; YABC 1

Browning, Tod 1882-1962 .... **CLC 16**
See also CA 141; 117

Brownson, Orestes Augustus 1803-1876 **NCLC 50**
See also DLB 1, 59, 73

Bruccoli, Matthew J(oseph) 1931- ... **CLC 34**
See also CA 9-12R; CANR 7; DLB 103

Bruce, Lenny .... **CLC 21**
See also Schneider, Leonard Alfred

Bruin, John
See Brutus, Dennis

Brulard, Henri
See Stendhal

Brulls, Christian
See Simenon, Georges (Jacques Christian)

Brunner, John (Kilian Houston) 1934-1995 **CLC 8, 10; DAM POP**
See also CA 1-4R; 149; CAAS 8; CANR 2, 37; MTCW 1

Bruno, Giordano 1548-1600 .... **LC 27**

Brutus, Dennis 1924- **CLC 43; BLC 1; DAM MULT, POET; PC 24**
See also BW 2; CA 49-52; CAAS 14; CANR 2, 27, 42; DLB 117

Bryan, C(ourtlandt) D(ixon) B(arnes) 1936- **CLC 29**
See also CA 73-76; CANR 13, 68; DLB 185; INT CANR-13

Bryan, Michael
See Moore, Brian

Bryant, William Cullen 1794-1878 . **NCLC 6, 46; DA; DAB; DAC; DAM MST, POET; PC 20**
See also CDALB 1640-1865; DLB 3, 43, 59, 189

Bryusov, Valery Yakovlevich 1873-1924 **TCLC 10**
See also CA 107; 155

Buchan, John 1875-1940 ..... **TCLC 41; DAB; DAM POP**
See also CA 108; 145; DLB 34, 70, 156; YABC 2

Buchanan, George 1506-1582 .... **LC 4**
See also DLB 152

Buchheim, Lothar-Guenther 1918- .... **CLC 6**
See also CA 85-88

Buchner, (Karl) Georg 1813-1837 . **NCLC 26**

Buchwald, Art(hur) 1925- .... **CLC 33**
See also AITN 1; CA 5-8R; CANR 21, 67; MTCW 1; SATA 10

Buck, Pearl S(ydenstricker) 1892-1973 **CLC 7, 11, 18; DA; DAB; DAC; DAM MST, NOV**
See also AITN 1; CA 1-4R; 41-44R; CANR 1, 34; DLB 9, 102; MTCW 1; SATA 1, 25

Buckler, Ernest 1908-1984 .... **CLC 13; DAC; DAM MST**
See also CA 11-12; 114; CAP 1; DLB 68; SATA 47

Buckley, Vincent (Thomas) 1925-1988 **CLC 57**
See also CA 101

Buckley, William F(rank), Jr. 1925- **CLC 7, 18, 37; DAM POP**
See also AITN 1; CA 1-4R; CANR 1, 24, 53; DLB 137; DLBY 80; INT CANR-24; MTCW 1

Buechner, (Carl) Frederick 1926- **CLC 2, 4, 6, 9; DAM NOV**
See also CA 13-16R; CANR 11, 39, 64; DLBY 80; INT CANR-11; MTCW 1

Buell, John (Edward) 1927- .... **CLC 10**
See also CA 1-4R; CANR 71; DLB 53

Buero Vallejo, Antonio 1916- ..... **CLC 15, 46**
See also CA 106; CANR 24, 49; HW; MTCW 1

Bufalino, Gesualdo 1920(?)- .... **CLC 74**
See also DLB 196

Bugayev, Boris Nikolayevich 1880-1934 **TCLC 7; PC 11**
See also Bely, Andrey
See also CA 104; 165

Bukowski, Charles 1920-1994 **CLC 2, 5, 9, 41, 82, 108; DAM NOV, POET; PC 18**
See also CA 17-20R; 144; CANR 40, 62; DLB 5, 130, 169; MTCW 1

Bulgakov, Mikhail (Afanas'evich) 1891-1940 **TCLC 2, 16; DAM DRAM, NOV; SSC 18**
See also CA 105; 152

Bulgya, Alexander Alexandrovich 1901-1956 **TCLC 53**
See also Fadeyev, Alexander
See also CA 117

Bullins, Ed 1935- **CLC 1, 5, 7; BLC 1; DAM DRAM, MULT; DC 6**

See Hunter, Evan

Cao, Lan 1961- .... **CLC 109**
See also CA 165

Cape, Judith
See Page, P(atricia) K(athleen)

Capek, Karel 1890-1938 ... **TCLC 6, 37; DA; DAB; DAC; DAM DRAM, MST, NOV; DC 1; WLC**
See also CA 104; 140

Capote, Truman 1924-1984 **CLC 1, 3, 8, 13, 19, 34, 38, 58; DA; DAB; DAC; DAM MST, NOV, POP; SSC 2; WLC**
See also CA 5-8R; 113; CANR 18, 62; CDALB 1941-1968; DLB 2, 185; DLBY 80, 84; MTCW 1; SATA 91

Capra, Frank 1897-1991 .... **CLC 16**
See also CA 61-64; 135

Caputo, Philip 1941- .... **CLC 32**
See also CA 73-76; CANR 40

Caragiale, Ion Luca 1852-1912 ..... **TCLC 76**
See also CA 157

Card, Orson Scott 1951- **CLC 44, 47, 50; DAM POP**
See also AAYA 11; CA 102; CANR 27, 47; INT CANR-27; MTCW 1; SATA 83

Cardenal, Ernesto 1925- .... **CLC 31; DAM MULT, POET; HLC; PC 22**
See also CA 49-52; CANR 2, 32, 66; HW; MTCW 1

Cardozo, Benjamin N(athan) 1870-1938 **TCLC 65**
See also CA 117; 164

Carducci, Giosue (Alessandro Giuseppe) 1835-1907 ....
TCLC 32
See also CA 163

Carew, Thomas 1595(?)-1640 .... **LC 13**
See also DLB 126

Carey, Ernestine Gilbreth 1908- .... **CLC 17**
See also CA 5-8R; CANR 71; SATA 2

Carey, Peter 1943- .... **CLC 40, 55, 96**
See also CA 123; 127; CANR 53; INT 127; MTCW 1; SATA 94

Carleton, William 1794-1869 .... **NCLC 3**
See also DLB 159

Carlisle, Henry (Coffin) 1926- .... **CLC 33**
See also CA 13-16R; CANR 15

Carlsen, Chris
See Holdstock, Robert P.

Carlson, Ron(ald F.) 1947- .... **CLC 54**
See also CA 105; CANR 27

Carlyle, Thomas 1795-1881 . **NCLC 70; DA; DAB; DAC; DAM MST**
See also CDBLB 1789-1832; DLB 55; 144

Carman, (William) Bliss 1861-1929 **TCLC 7; DAC**
See also CA 104; 152; DLB 92

Carnegie, Dale 1888-1955 .... **TCLC 53**

Carossa, Hans 1878-1956 .... **TCLC 48**
See also DLB 66

Carpenter, Don(ald Richard) 1931-1995 **C L C 41**
See also CA 45-48; 149; CANR 1, 71

Carpentier (y Valmont), Alejo 1904-1980 **CLC 8, 11, 38, 110; DAM MULT; HLC**
See also CA 65-68; 97-100; CANR 11, 70; DLB 113; HW

Carr, Caleb 1955(?)- .... **CLC 86**
See also CA 147

Carr, Emily 1871-1945 .... **TCLC 32**
See also CA 159; DLB 68

Carr, John Dickson 1906-1977 .... **CLC 3**
See also Fairbairn, Roger
See also CA 49-52; 69-72; CANR 3, 33, 60; MTCW 1

Carr, Philippa
See Hibbert, Eleanor Alice Burford

Carr, Virginia Spencer 1929- .... **CLC 34**
See also CA 61-64; DLB 111

Carrere, Emmanuel 1957- .... **CLC 89**

Carrier, Roch 1937- **CLC 13, 78; DAC; DAM MST**
See also CA 130; CANR 61; DLB 53

Carroll, James P. 1943(?)- .... **CLC 38**
See also CA 81-84

Carroll, Jim 1951- .... **CLC 35**
See also AAYA 17; CA 45-48; CANR 42

Carroll, Lewis ..... **NCLC 2, 53; PC 18; WLC**
See also Dodgson, Charles Lutwidge
See also CDBLB 1832-1890; CLR 2, 18; DLB 18, 163, 178; JRDA

Carroll, Paul Vincent 1900-1968 ...... **CLC 10**
See also CA 9-12R; 25-28R; DLB 10

Carruth, Hayden 1921- **CLC 4, 7, 10, 18, 84; PC 10**
See also CA 9-12R; CANR 4, 38, 59; DLB 5, 165; INT CANR-4; MTCW 1; SATA 47

Carson, Rachel Louise 1907-1964 .. **CLC 71; DAM POP**
See also CA 77-80; CANR 35; MTCW 1; SATA 23

Carter, Angela (Olive) 1940-1992 **CLC 5, 41, 76; SSC 13**
See also CA 53-56; 136; CANR 12, 36, 61; DLB 14; MTCW 1; SATA 66; SATA-Obit 70

Carter, Nick
See Smith, Martin Cruz

Carver, Raymond 1938-1988 **CLC 22, 36, 53, 55; DAM NOV; SSC 8**
See also CA 33-36R; 126; CANR 17, 34, 61; DLB 130; DLBY 84, 88; MTCW 1

Cary, Elizabeth, Lady Falkland 1585-1639 **LC 30**

Cary, (Arthur) Joyce (Lunel) 1888-1957 **TCLC 1, 29**
See also CA 104; 164; CDBLB 1914-1945; DLB 15, 100

Casanova de Seingalt, Giovanni Jacopo 1725-1798 .... **LC 13**

Casares, Adolfo Bioy
See Bioy Casares, Adolfo

Casely-Hayford, J(oseph) E(phraim) 1866-1930 **TCLC 24; BLC 1; DAM MULT**
See also BW 2; CA 123; 152

Casey, John (Dudley) 1939- .... **CLC 59**
See also BEST 90:2; CA 69-72; CANR 23

Casey, Michael 1947- .... **CLC 2**
See also CA 65-68; DLB 5

Casey, Patrick
See Thurman, Wallace (Henry)

Casey, Warren (Peter) 1935-1988 ..... **CLC 12**
See also CA 101; 127; INT 101

Casona, Alejandro .... **CLC 49**
See also Alvarez, Alejandro Rodriguez

Cassavetes, John 1929-1989 .... **CLC 20**
See also CA 85-88; 127

Cassian, Nina 1924- .... **PC 17**

Cassill, R(onald) V(erlin) 1919- .... **CLC 4, 23**
See also CA 9-12R; CAAS 1; CANR 7, 45; DLB 6

Cassirer, Ernst 1874-1945 .... **TCLC 61**
See also CA 157

Cassity, (Allen) Turner 1929- .... **CLC 6, 42**
See also CA 17-20R; CAAS 8; CANR 11; DLB 105

Castaneda, Carlos 1931(?)- .... **CLC 12**
See also CA 25-28R; CANR 32, 66; HW; MTCW 1

Castedo, Elena 1937- .... **CLC 65**
See also CA 132

Castedo-Ellerman, Elena
See Castedo, Elena

Castellanos, Rosario 1925-1974 **CLC 66; DAM MULT; HLC**

See also CA 131; 53-56; CANR 58; DLB 113; HW

Castelvetro, Lodovico 1505-1571 .... **LC 12**

Castiglione, Baldassare 1478-1529 ..... **LC 12**

Castle, Robert
See Hamilton, Edmond

Castro, Guillen de 1569-1631 .... **LC 19**

Castro, Rosalia de 1837-1885 **NCLC 3; DAM MULT**

Cather, Willa
See Cather, Willa Sibert

Cather, Willa Sibert 1873-1947 **TCLC 1, 11, 31; DA; DAB; DAC; DAM MST, NOV; SSC 2; WLC**
See also AAYA 24; CA 104; 128; CDALB 1865-1917; DLB 9, 54, 78; DLBD 1; MTCW 1; SATA 30

Catherine, Saint 1347-1380 .... **CMLC 27**

Cato, Marcus Porcius 234B.C.-149B.C. **CMLC 21**

Catton, (Charles) Bruce 1899-1978 .. **CLC 35**
See also AITN 1; CA 5-8R; 81-84; CANR 7; DLB 17; SATA 2; SATA-Obit 24

Catullus c. 84B.C.-c. 54B.C. .... **CMLC 18**

Cauldwell, Frank
See King, Francis (Henry)

Caunitz, William J. 1933-1996 .... **CLC 34**
See also BEST 89:3; CA 125; 130; 152; INT 130

Causley, Charles (Stanley) 1917- .... **CLC 7**
See also CA 9-12R; CANR 5, 35; CLR 30; DLB 27; MTCW 1; SATA 3, 66

Caute, (John) David 1936- ..... **CLC 29; DAM NOV**
See also CA 1-4R; CAAS 4; CANR 1, 33, 64; DLB 14

Cavafy, C(onstantine) P(eter) 1863-1933 **TCLC 2, 7; DAM POET**
See also Kavafis, Konstantinos Petrou
See also CA 148

Cavallo, Evelyn
See Spark, Muriel (Sarah)

Cavanna, Betty .... **CLC 12**
See also Harrison, Elizabeth Cavanna
See also JRDA; MAICYA; SAAS 4; SATA 1, 30

Cavendish, Margaret Lucas 1623-1673 **LC 30**
See also DLB 131

Caxton, William 1421(?)-1491(?) .... **LC 17**
See also DLB 170

Cayer, D. M.
See Duffy, Maureen

Cayrol, Jean 1911- .... **CLC 11**
See also CA 89-92; DLB 83

Cela, Camilo Jose 1916- **CLC 4, 13, 59; DAM MULT; HLC**
See also BEST 90:2; CA 21-24R; CAAS 10; CANR 21, 32; DLBY 89; HW; MTCW 1

Celan, Paul .... **CLC 10, 19, 53, 82; PC 10**
See also Antschel, Paul
See also DLB 69

Celine, Louis-Ferdinand **CLC 1, 3, 4, 7, 9, 15, 47**
See also Destouches, Louis-Ferdinand
See also DLB 72

Cellini, Benvenuto 1500-1571 .... **LC 7**

Cendrars, Blaise 1887-1961 ..... **CLC 18, 106**
See also Sauser-Hall, Frederic

Cernuda (y Bidon), Luis 1902-1963 **CLC 54; DAM POET**
See also CA 131; 89-92; DLB 134; HW

Cervantes (Saavedra), Miguel de 1547-1616 **LC 6, 23; DA; DAB; DAC; DAM MST, NOV; SSC 12; WLC**

Cesaire, Aime (Fernand) 1913- . **CLC 19, 32, 112; BLC 1; DAM MULT, POET**
See also BW 2; CA 65-68; CANR 24, 43;

MTCW 1

Chabon, Michael 1963- .... **CLC 55**
See also CA 139; CANR 57

Chabrol, Claude 1930- .... **CLC 16**
See also CA 110

Challans, Mary 1905-1983
See Renault, Mary
See also CA 81-84; 111; SATA 23; SATA-Obit 36

Challis, George
See Faust, Frederick (Schiller)

Chambers, Aidan 1934- .... **CLC 35**
See also AAYA 27; CA 25-28R; CANR 12, 31, 58; JRDA; MAICYA; SAAS 12; SATA 1, 69

Chambers, James 1948-
See Cliff, Jimmy
See also CA 124

Chambers, Jessie
See Lawrence, D(avid) H(erbert Richards)

Chambers, Robert W(illiam) 1865-1933
TCLC 41
See also CA 165; DLB 202

Chandler, Raymond (Thornton) 1888-1959
TCLC 1, 7; SSC 23
See also AAYA 25; CA 104; 129; CANR 60; CDALB 1929-1941; DLBD 6; MTCW 1

Chang, Eileen 1920-1995 .... **SSC 28**
See also CA 166

Chang, Jung 1952- .... **CLC 71**
See also CA 142

Chang Ai-Ling
See Chang, Eileen

Channing, William Ellery 1780-1842 **NCLC 17**
See also DLB 1, 59

Chaplin, Charles Spencer 1889-1977 **CLC 16**
See also Chaplin, Charlie
See also CA 81-84; 73-76

Chaplin, Charlie
See Chaplin, Charles Spencer
See also DLB 44

Chapman, George 1559(?)-1634 **LC 22; DAM DRAM**
See also DLB 62, 121

Chapman, Graham 1941-1989 .... **CLC 21**
See also Monty Python
See also CA 116; 129; CANR 35

Chapman, John Jay 1862-1933 .... **TCLC 7**
See also CA 104

Chapman, Lee
See Bradley, Marion Zimmer

Chapman, Walker
See Silverberg, Robert

Chappell, Fred (Davis) 1936- ...... **CLC 40, 78**
See also CA 5-8R; CAAS 4; CANR 8, 33, 67; DLB 6, 105

Char, Rene(-Emile) 1907-1988 **CLC 9, 11, 14, 55; DAM POET**
See also CA 13-16R; 124; CANR 32; MTCW 1

Charby, Jay
See Ellison, Harlan (Jay)

Chardin, Pierre Teilhard de
See Teilhard de Chardin, (Marie Joseph) Pierre

Charles I 1600-1649 .... **LC 13**

Charriere, Isabelle de 1740-1805 .. **NCLC 66**

Charyn, Jerome 1937- .... **CLC 5, 8, 18**
See also CA 5-8R; CAAS 1; CANR 7, 61; DLBY 83; MTCW 1

Chase, Mary (Coyle) 1907-1981 .... **DC 1**
See also CA 77-80; 105; SATA 17; SATA-Obit 29

Chase, Mary Ellen 1887-1973 .... **CLC 2**
See also CA 13-16; 41-44R; CAP 1; SATA 10

Chase, Nicholas
See Hyde, Anthony

Chateaubriand, Francois Rene de 1768-1848
NCLC 3

See also DLB 119

Chatterje, Sarat Chandra 1876-1936(?)
See Chatterji, Saratchandra
See also CA 109

Chatterji, Bankim Chandra 1838-1894 **NCLC 19**

Chatterji, Saratchandra .... **TCLC 13**
See also Chatterje, Sarat Chandra

Chatterton, Thomas 1752-1770 . **LC 3; DAM POET**
See also DLB 109

Chatwin, (Charles) Bruce 1940-1989 **CLC 28, 57, 59; DAM POP**
See also AAYA 4; BEST 90:1; CA 85-88; 127; DLB 194

Chaucer, Daniel
See Ford, Ford Madox

Chaucer, Geoffrey 1340(?)-1400 **LC 17; DA; DAB; DAC; DAM MST, POET; PC 19; WLCS**
See also CDBLB Before 1660; DLB 146

Chaviaras, Strates 1935-
See Haviaras, Stratis
See also CA 105

Chayefsky, Paddy .... **CLC 23**
See also Chayefsky, Sidney
See also DLB 7, 44; DLBY 81

Chayefsky, Sidney 1923-1981
See Chayefsky, Paddy
See also CA 9-12R; 104; CANR 18; DAM DRAM

Chedid, Andree 1920- .... **CLC 47**
See also CA 145

Cheever, John 1912-1982 **CLC 3, 7, 8, 11, 15, 25, 64; DA; DAB; DAC; DAM MST, NOV, POP; SSC 1; WLC**
See also CA 5-8R; 106; CABS 1; CANR 5, 27; CDALB 1941-1968; DLB 2, 102; DLBY 80, 82; INT CANR-5; MTCW 1

Cheever, Susan 1943- .... **CLC 18, 48**
See also CA 103; CANR 27, 51; DLBY 82; INT CANR-27

Chekhonte, Antosha
See Chekhov, Anton (Pavlovich)

Chekhov, Anton (Pavlovich) 1860-1904 **TCLC 3, 10, 31, 55; DA; DAB; DAC; DAM DRAM, MST; DC 9; SSC 2, 28; WLC**
See also CA 104; 124; SATA 90

Chernyshevsky, Nikolay Gavrilovich 1828-1889
NCLC 1

Cherry, Carolyn Janice 1942-
See Cherryh, C. J.
See also CA 65-68; CANR 10

Cherryh, C. J. .... **CLC 35**
See also Cherry, Carolyn Janice
See also AAYA 24; DLBY 80; SATA 93

Chesnutt, Charles W(addell) 1858-1932
TCLC 5, 39; BLC 1; DAM MULT; SSC 7
See also BW 1; CA 106; 125; DLB 12, 50, 78; MTCW 1

Chester, Alfred 1929(?)-1971 .... **CLC 49**
See also CA 33-36R; DLB 130

Chesterton, G(ilbert) K(eith) 1874-1936
TCLC 1, 6, 64; DAM NOV, POET; SSC 1
See also CA 104; 132; CDBLB 1914-1945; DLB 10, 19, 34, 70, 98, 149, 178; MTCW 1; SATA 27

Chiang, Pin-chin 1904-1986
See Ding Ling
See also CA 118

Ch'ien Chung-shu 1910- .... **CLC 22**
See also CA 130; MTCW 1

Child, L. Maria
See Child, Lydia Maria

Child, Lydia Maria 1802-1880 ... **NCLC 6, 73**
See also DLB 1, 74; SATA 67

Child, Mrs.

See Child, Lydia Maria

Child, Philip 1898-1978 .... **CLC 19, 68**
See also CA 13-14; CAP 1; SATA 47

Childers, (Robert) Erskine 1870-1922 **T C L C 65**
See also CA 113; 153; DLB 70

Childress, Alice 1920-1994 **CLC 12, 15, 86, 96; BLC 1; DAM DRAM, MULT, NOV; DC 4**
See also AAYA 8; BW 2; CA 45-48; 146; CANR 3, 27, 50; CLR 14; DLB 7, 38; JRDA; MAICYA; MTCW 1; SATA 7, 48, 81

Chin, Frank (Chew, Jr.) 1940- .... **DC 7**
See also CA 33-36R; CANR 71; DAM MULT

Chislett, (Margaret) Anne 1943- ...... **CLC 34**
See also CA 151

Chitty, Thomas Willes 1926- .... **CLC 11**
See also Hinde, Thomas
See also CA 5-8R

Chivers, Thomas Holley 1809-1858 **NCLC 49**
See also DLB 3

Chomette, Rene Lucien 1898-1981
See Clair, Rene
See also CA 103

Chopin, Kate **TCLC 5, 14; DA; DAB; SSC 8; WLCS**
See also Chopin, Katherine
See also CDALB 1865-1917; DLB 12, 78

Chopin, Katherine 1851-1904
See Chopin, Kate
See also CA 104; 122; DAC; DAM MST, NOV

Chretien de Troyes c. 12th cent. - . **CMLC 10**

Christie
See Ichikawa, Kon

Christie, Agatha (Mary Clarissa) 1890-1976
CLC 1, 6, 8, 12, 39, 48, 110; DAB; DAC; DAM NOV
See also AAYA 9; AITN 1, 2; CA 17-20R; 61-64; CANR 10, 37; CDBLB 1914-1945; DLB 13, 77; MTCW 1; SATA 36

Christie, (Ann) Philippa
See Pearce, Philippa
See also CA 5-8R; CANR 4

Christine de Pizan 1365(?)-1431(?) .... **LC 9**

Chubb, Elmer
See Masters, Edgar Lee

Chulkov, Mikhail Dmitrievich 1743-1792 **LC 2**
See also DLB 150

Churchill, Caryl 1938- ..... **CLC 31, 55; DC 5**
See also CA 102; CANR 22, 46; DLB 13; MTCW 1

Churchill, Charles 1731-1764 .... **LC 3**
See also DLB 109

Chute, Carolyn 1947- .... **CLC 39**
See also CA 123

Ciardi, John (Anthony) 1916-1986 . **CLC 10, 40, 44; DAM POET**
See also CA 5-8R; 118; CAAS 2; CANR 5, 33; CLR 19; DLB 5; DLBY 86; INT CANR-5; MAICYA; MTCW 1; SAAS 26; SATA 1, 65; SATA-Obit 46

Cicero, Marcus Tullius 106B.C.-43B.C.
CMLC 3

Cimino, Michael 1943- .... **CLC 16**
See also CA 105

Cioran, E(mil) M. 1911-1995 .... **CLC 64**
See also CA 25-28R; 149

Cisneros, Sandra 1954- **CLC 69; DAM MULT; HLC; SSC 32**
See also AAYA 9; CA 131; CANR 64; DLB 122, 152; HW

Cixous, Helene 1937- .... **CLC 92**
See also CA 126; CANR 55; DLB 83; MTCW 1

Clair, Rene .... **CLC 20**
See also Chomette, Rene Lucien

Clampitt, Amy 1920-1994 ..... **CLC 32; PC 19**
See also CA 110; 146; CANR 29; DLB 105

Clancy, Thomas L., Jr. 1947-
  See Clancy, Tom
  See also CA 125; 131; CANR 62; INT 131;
    MTCW 1
Clancy, Tom .. CLC 45, 112; DAM NOV, POP
  See also Clancy, Thomas L., Jr.
  See also AAYA 9; BEST 89:1, 90:1
Clare, John 1793-1864 NCLC 9; DAB; DAM
    POET; PC 23
  See also DLB 55, 96
Clarin
  See Alas (y Urena), Leopoldo (Enrique Garcia)
Clark, Al C.
  See Goines, Donald
Clark, (Robert) Brian 1932- .... CLC 29
  See also CA 41-44R; CANR 67
Clark, Curt
  See Westlake, Donald E(dwin)
Clark, Eleanor 1913-1996 .... CLC 5, 19
  See also CA 9-12R; 151; CANR 41; DLB 6
Clark, J. P.
  See Clark, John Pepper
  See also DLB 117
Clark, John Pepper 1935-.. CLC 38; BLC 1;
    DAM DRAM, MULT; DC 5
  See also Clark, J. P.
  See also BW 1; CA 65-68; CANR 16, 72
Clark, M. R.
  See Clark, Mavis Thorpe
Clark, Mavis Thorpe 1909- .... CLC 12
  See also CA 57-60; CANR 8, 37; CLR 30;
    MAICYA; SAAS 5; SATA 8, 74
Clark, Walter Van Tilburg 1909-1971 CLC 28
  See also CA 9-12R; 33-36R; CANR 63; DLB
    9; SATA 8
Clark Bekederemo, J(ohnson) P(epper)
  See Clark, John Pepper
Clarke, Arthur C(harles) 1917- CLC 1, 4, 13,
    18, 35; DAM POP; SSC 3
  See also AAYA 4; CA 1-4R; CANR 2, 28, 55;
    JRDA; MAICYA; MTCW 1; SATA 13, 70
Clarke, Austin 1896-1974 .... CLC 6, 9; DAM
    POET
  See also CA 29-32; 49-52; CAP 2; DLB 10, 20
Clarke, Austin C(hesterfield) 1934-CLC 8, 53;
    BLC 1; DAC; DAM MULT
  See also BW 1; CA 25-28R; CAAS 16; CANR
    14, 32, 68; DLB 53, 125
Clarke, Gillian 1937- .... CLC 61
  See also CA 106; DLB 40
Clarke, Marcus (Andrew Hislop) 1846-1881
    NCLC 19
Clarke, Shirley 1925- .... CLC 16
Clash, The
  See Headon, (Nicky) Topper; Jones, Mick;
    Simonon, Paul; Strummer, Joe
Claudel, Paul (Louis Charles Marie) 1868-1955
    TCLC 2, 10
  See also CA 104; 165; DLB 192
Clavell, James (duMaresq) 1925-1994CLC 6,
    25, 87; DAM NOV, POP
  See also CA 25-28R; 146; CANR 26, 48;
    MTCW 1
Cleaver, (Leroy) Eldridge 1935-1998CLC 30;
    BLC 1; DAM MULT
  See also BW 1; CA 21-24R; 167; CANR 16
Cleese, John (Marwood) 1939- .... CLC 21
  See also Monty Python
  See also CA 112; 116; CANR 35; MTCW 1
Cleishbotham, Jebediah
  See Scott, Walter
Cleland, John 1710-1789 .... LC 2
  See also DLB 39
Clemens, Samuel Langhorne 1835-1910
  See Twain, Mark
  See also CA 104; 135; CDALB 1865-1917; DA;
    DAB; DAC; DAM MST, NOV; DLB 11, 12,

    23, 64, 74, 186, 189; JRDA; MAICYA; SATA
    100; YABC 2
Cleophil
  See Congreve, William
Clerihew, E.
  See Bentley, E(dmund) C(lerihew)
Clerk, N. W.
  See Lewis, C(live) S(taples)
Cliff, Jimmy .... CLC 21
  See also Chambers, James
Clifton, (Thelma) Lucille 1936- CLC 19, 66;
    BLC 1; DAM MULT, POET; PC 17
  See also BW 2; CA 49-52; CANR 2, 24, 42;
    CLR 5; DLB 5, 41; MAICYA; MTCW 1;
    SATA 20, 69
Clinton, Dirk
  See Silverberg, Robert
Clough, Arthur Hugh 1819-1861 ... NCLC 27
  See also DLB 32
Clutha, Janet Paterson Frame 1924-
  See Frame, Janet
  See also CA 1-4R; CANR 2, 36; MTCW 1
Clyne, Terence
  See Blatty, William Peter
Cobalt, Martin
  See Mayne, William (James Carter)
Cobb, Irvin S. 1876-1944 .... TCLC 77
  See also DLB 11, 25, 86
Cobbett, William 1763-1835 .... NCLC 49
  See also DLB 43, 107, 158
Coburn, D(onald) L(ee) 1938- .... CLC 10
  See also CA 89-92
Cocteau, Jean (Maurice Eugene Clement) 1889-
    1963
    CLC 1, 8, 15, 16, 43; DA; DAB; DAC; DAM
    DRAM, MST, NOV; WLC
  See also CA 25-28; CANR 40; CAP 2; DLB
    65; MTCW 1
Codrescu, Andrei 1946-CLC 46; DAM POET
  See also CA 33-36R; CAAS 19; CANR 13, 34,
    53
Coe, Max
  See Bourne, Randolph S(illiman)
Coe, Tucker
  See Westlake, Donald E(dwin)
Coen, Ethan 1958- .... CLC 108
  See also CA 126
Coen, Joel 1955- .... CLC 108
  See also CA 126
The Coen Brothers
  See Coen, Ethan; Coen, Joel
Coetzee, J(ohn) M(ichael) 1940- CLC 23, 33,
    66; DAM NOV
  See also CA 77-80; CANR 41, 54; MTCW 1
Coffey, Brian
  See Koontz, Dean R(ay)
Cohan, George M(ichael) 1878-1942TCLC 60
  See also CA 157
Cohen, Arthur A(llen) 1928-1986 . CLC 7, 31
  See also CA 1-4R; 120; CANR 1, 17, 42; DLB
    28
Cohen, Leonard (Norman) 1934- CLC 3, 38;
    DAC; DAM MST
  See also CA 21-24R; CANR 14, 69; DLB 53;
    MTCW 1
Cohen, Matt 1942- .... CLC 19; DAC
  See also CA 61-64; CAAS 18; CANR 40; DLB
    53
Cohen-Solal, Annie 19(?)- .... CLC 50
Colegate, Isabel 1931- .... CLC 36
  See also CA 17-20R; CANR 8, 22; DLB 14;
    INT CANR-22; MTCW 1
Coleman, Emmett
  See Reed, Ishmael
Coleridge, M. E.
  See Coleridge, Mary E(lizabeth)
Coleridge, Mary E(lizabeth) 1861-1907TCLC

    73
  See also CA 116; 166; DLB 19, 98
Coleridge, Samuel Taylor 1772-1834NCLC 9,
    54; DA; DAB; DAC; DAM MST, POET;
    PC 11; WLC
  See also CDBLB 1789-1832; DLB 93, 107
Coleridge, Sara 1802-1852 .... NCLC 31
  See also DLB 199
Coles, Don 1928- .... CLC 46
  See also CA 115; CANR 38
Coles, Robert (Martin) 1929- .... CLC 108
  See also CA 45-48; CANR 3, 32, 66, 70; INT
    CANR-32; SATA 23
Colette, (Sidonie-Gabrielle) 1873-1954TCLC
    1, 5, 16; DAM NOV; SSC 10
  See also CA 104; 131; DLB 65; MTCW 1
Collett, (Jacobine) Camilla (Wergeland) 1813-
    1895 ....
    NCLC 22
Collier, Christopher 1930- .... CLC 30
  See also AAYA 13; CA 33-36R; CANR 13, 33;
    JRDA; MAICYA; SATA 16, 70
Collier, James L(incoln) 1928-CLC 30; DAM
    POP
  See also AAYA 13; CA 9-12R; CANR 4, 33,
    60; CLR 3; JRDA; MAICYA; SAAS 21;
    SATA 8, 70
Collier, Jeremy 1650-1726 .... LC 6
Collier, John 1901-1980 .... SSC 19
  See also CA 65-68; 97-100; CANR 10; DLB
    77
Collingwood, R(obin) G(eorge) 1889(?)-1943
    TCLC 67
  See also CA 117; 155
Collins, Hunt
  See Hunter, Evan
Collins, Linda 1931- .... CLC 44
  See also CA 125
Collins, (William) Wilkie 1824-1889NCLC 1,
    18
  See also CDBLB 1832-1890; DLB 18, 70, 159
Collins, William 1721-1759 . LC 4, 40; DAM
    POET
  See also DLB 109
Collodi, Carlo 1826-1890 .... NCLC 54
  See also Lorenzini, Carlo
  See also CLR 5
Colman, George 1732-1794
  See Glassco, John
Colt, Winchester Remington
  See Hubbard, L(afayette) Ron(ald)
Colter, Cyrus 1910- .... CLC 58
  See also BW 1; CA 65-68; CANR 10, 66; DLB
    33
Colton, James
  See Hansen, Joseph
Colum, Padraic 1881-1972 .... CLC 28
  See also CA 73-76; 33-36R; CANR 35; CLR
    36; MAICYA; MTCW 1; SATA 15
Colvin, James
  See Moorcock, Michael (John)
Colwin, Laurie (E.) 1944-1992CLC 5, 13, 23,
    84
  See also CA 89-92; 139; CANR 20, 46; DLBY
    80; MTCW 1
Comfort, Alex(ander) 1920-CLC 7; DAM POP
  See also CA 1-4R; CANR 1, 45
Comfort, Montgomery
  See Campbell, (John) Ramsey
Compton-Burnett, I(vy) 1884(?)-1969CLC 1,
    3, 10, 15, 34; DAM NOV
  See also CA 1-4R; 25-28R; CANR 4; DLB 36;
    MTCW 1
Comstock, Anthony 1844-1915 ...... TCLC 13
  See also CA 110
Comte, Auguste 1798-1857 .... NCLC 54
Conan Doyle, Arthur

Devkota, Laxmiprasad 1909-1959. **TCLC 23**
See also CA 123
De Voto, Bernard (Augustine) 1897-1955
TCLC 29
See also CA 113; 160; DLB 9
De Vries, Peter 1910-1993 **CLC 1, 2, 3, 7, 10, 28, 46; DAM NOV**
See also CA 17-20R; 142; CANR 41; DLB 6; DLBY 82; MTCW 1
Dexter, John
See Bradley, Marion Zimmer
Dexter, Martin
See Faust, Frederick (Schiller)
Dexter, Pete 1943- ... **CLC 34, 55; DAM POP**
See also BEST 89:2; CA 127; 131; INT 131; MTCW 1
Diamano, Silmang
See Senghor, Leopold Sedar
Diamond, Neil 1941- .... **CLC 30**
See also CA 108
Diaz del Castillo, Bernal 1496-1584 .... **LC 31**
di Bassetto, Corno
See Shaw, George Bernard
Dick, Philip K(indred) 1928-1982 **CLC 10, 30, 72; DAM NOV, POP**
See also AAYA 24; CA 49-52; 106; CANR 2, 16; DLB 8; MTCW 1
Dickens, Charles (John Huffam) 1812-1870
NCLC 3, 8, 18, 26, 37, 50; DA; DAB; DAC; DAM MST, NOV; SSC 17; WLC
See also AAYA 23; CDBLB 1832-1890; DLB 21, 55, 70, 159, 166; JRDA; MAICYA; SATA 15
Dickey, James (Lafayette) 1923-1997 **CLC 1, 2, 4, 7, 10, 15, 47, 109; DAM NOV, POET, POP**
See also AITN 1, 2; CA 9-12R; 156; CABS 2; CANR 10, 48, 61; CDALB 1968-1988; DLB 5, 193; DLBD 7; DLBY 82, 93, 96, 97; INT CANR-10; MTCW 1
Dickey, William 1928-1994 .... **CLC 3, 28**
See also CA 9-12R; 145; CANR 24; DLB 5
Dickinson, Charles 1951- .... **CLC 49**
See also CA 128
Dickinson, Emily (Elizabeth) 1830-1886
NCLC 21; DA; DAB; DAC; DAM MST, POET; PC 1; WLC
See also AAYA 22; CDALB 1865-1917; DLB 1; SATA 29
Dickinson, Peter (Malcolm) 1927- **CLC 12, 35**
See also AAYA 9; CA 41-44R; CANR 31, 58; CLR 29; DLB 87, 161; JRDA; MAICYA; SATA 5, 62, 95
Dickson, Carr
See Carr, John Dickson
Dickson, Carter
See Carr, John Dickson
Diderot, Denis 1713-1784 .... **LC 26**
Didion, Joan 1934- **CLC 1, 3, 8, 14, 32; DAM NOV**
See also AITN 1; CA 5-8R; CANR 14, 52; CDALB 1968-1988; DLB 2, 173, 185; DLBY 81, 86; MTCW 1
Dietrich, Robert
See Hunt, E(verette) Howard, (Jr.)
Difusa, Pati
See Almodovar, Pedro
Dillard, Annie 1945- .. **CLC 9, 60, 115; DAM NOV**
See also AAYA 6; CA 49-52; CANR 3, 43, 62; DLBY 80; MTCW 1; SATA 10
Dillard, R(ichard) H(enry) W(ilde) 1937-
CLC 5
See also CA 21-24R; CAAS 7; CANR 10; DLB 5
Dillon, Eilis 1920-1994 .... **CLC 17**
See also CA 9-12R; 147; CAAS 3; CANR 4,

38; CLR 26; MAICYA; SATA 2, 74; SATA-Obit 83
Dimont, Penelope
See Mortimer, Penelope (Ruth)
Dinesen, Isak .... **CLC 10, 29, 95; SSC 7**
See also Blixen, Karen (Christentze Dinesen)
Ding Ling .... **CLC 68**
See also Chiang, Pin-chin
Disch, Thomas M(ichael) 1940- .... **CLC 7, 36**
See also AAYA 17; CA 21-24R; CAAS 4; CANR 17, 36, 54; CLR 18; DLB 8; MAICYA; MTCW 1; SAAS 15; SATA 92
Disch, Tom
See Disch, Thomas M(ichael)
d'Isly, Georges
See Simenon, Georges (Jacques Christian)
Disraeli, Benjamin 1804-1881 .... **NCLC 2, 39**
See also DLB 21, 55
Ditcum, Steve
See Crumb, R(obert)
Dixon, Paige
See Corcoran, Barbara
Dixon, Stephen 1936- .... **CLC 52; SSC 16**
See also CA 89-92; CANR 17, 40, 54; DLB 130
Doak, Annie
See Dillard, Annie
Dobell, Sydney Thompson 1824-1874 **NCLC 43**
See also DLB 32
Doblin, Alfred .... **TCLC 13**
See also Doeblin, Alfred
Dobrolyubov, Nikolai Alexandrovich 1836-1861
NCLC 5
Dobson, Austin 1840-1921 .... **TCLC 79**
See also DLB 35; 144
Dobyns, Stephen 1941- .... **CLC 37**
See also CA 45-48; CANR 2, 18
Doctorow, E(dgar) L(aurence) 1931- **CLC 6, 11, 15, 18, 37, 44, 65, 113; DAM NOV, POP**
See also AAYA 22; AITN 2; BEST 89:3; CA 45-48; CANR 2, 33, 51; CDALB 1968-1988; DLB 2, 28, 173; DLBY 80; MTCW 1
Dodgson, Charles Lutwidge 1832-1898
See Carroll, Lewis
See also CLR 2; DA; DAB; DAC; DAM MST, NOV, POET; MAICYA; SATA 100; YABC 2
Dodson, Owen (Vincent) 1914-1983 **CLC 79; BLC 1; DAM MULT**
See also BW 1; CA 65-68; 110; CANR 24; DLB 76
Doeblin, Alfred 1878-1957 .... **TCLC 13**
See also Doblin, Alfred
See also CA 110; 141; DLB 66
Doerr, Harriet 1910- .... **CLC 34**
See also CA 117; 122; CANR 47; INT 122
Domecq, H(onorio) Bustos
See Bioy Casares, Adolfo; Borges, Jorge Luis
Domini, Rey
See Lorde, Audre (Geraldine)
Dominique
See Proust, (Valentin-Louis-George-Eugene-) Marcel
Don, A
See Stephen, Sir Leslie
Donaldson, Stephen R. 1947- **CLC 46; DAM POP**
See also CA 89-92; CANR 13, 55; INT CANR-13
Donleavy, J(ames) P(atrick) 1926- **CLC 1, 4, 6, 10, 45**
See also AITN 2; CA 9-12R; CANR 24, 49, 62; DLB 6, 173; INT CANR-24; MTCW 1
Donne, John 1572-1631 **LC 10, 24; DA; DAB; DAC; DAM MST, POET; PC 1**
See also CDBLB Before 1660; DLB 121, 151
Donnell, David 1939(?)- .... **CLC 34**
Donoghue, P. S.

See Hunt, E(verette) Howard, (Jr.)
Donoso (Yanez), Jose 1924-1996 **CLC 4, 8, 11, 32, 99; DAM MULT; HLC**
See also CA 81-84; 155; CANR 32; DLB 113; HW; MTCW 1
Donovan, John 1928-1992 .... **CLC 35**
See also AAYA 20; CA 97-100; 137; CLR 3; MAICYA; SATA 72; SATA-Brief 29
Don Roberto
See Cunninghame Graham, R(obert) B(ontine)
Doolittle, Hilda 1886-1961 **CLC 3, 8, 14, 31, 34, 73; DA; DAC; DAM MST, POET; PC 5; WLC**
See also H. D.
See also CA 97-100; CANR 35; DLB 4, 45; MTCW 1
Dorfman, Ariel 1942- ...... **CLC 48, 77; DAM MULT; HLC**
See also CA 124; 130; CANR 67, 70; HW; INT 130
Dorn, Edward (Merton) 1929- ... **CLC 10, 18**
See also CA 93-96; CANR 42; DLB 5; INT 93-96
Dorris, Michael (Anthony) 1945-1997 .. **C L C 109; DAM MULT, NOV**
See also AAYA 20; BEST 90:1; CA 102; 157; CANR 19, 46; DLB 175; NNAL; SATA 75; SATA-Obit 94
Dorris, Michael A.
See Dorris, Michael (Anthony)
Dorsan, Luc
See Simenon, Georges (Jacques Christian)
Dorsange, Jean
See Simenon, Georges (Jacques Christian)
Dos Passos, John (Roderigo) 1896-1970 **C L C 1, 4, 8, 11, 15, 25, 34, 82; DA; DAB; DAC; DAM MST, NOV; WLC**
See also CA 1-4R; 29-32R; CANR 3; CDALB 1929-1941; DLB 4, 9; DLBD 1, 15; DLBY 96; MTCW 1
Dossage, Jean
See Simenon, Georges (Jacques Christian)
Dostoevsky, Fedor Mikhailovich 1821-1881
NCLC 2, 7, 21, 33, 43; DA; DAB; DAC; DAM MST, NOV; SSC 2; WLC
Doughty, Charles M(ontagu) 1843-1926
TCLC 27
See also CA 115; DLB 19, 57, 174
Douglas, Ellen .... **CLC 73**
See also Haxton, Josephine Ayres; Williamson, Ellen Douglas
Douglas, Gavin 1475(?)-1522 .... **LC 20**
See also DLB 132
Douglas, George
See Brown, George Douglas
Douglas, Keith (Castellain) 1920-1944 **T C L C 40**
See also CA 160; DLB 27
Douglas, Leonard
See Bradbury, Ray (Douglas)
Douglas, Michael
See Crichton, (John) Michael
Douglas, (George) Norman 1868-1952 **T C L C 68**
See also CA 119; 157; DLB 34, 195
Douglas, William
See Brown, George Douglas
Douglass, Frederick 1817(?)-1895 **NCLC 7, 55; BLC 1; DA; DAC; DAM MST, MULT; WLC**
See also CDALB 1640-1865; DLB 1, 43, 50, 79; SATA 29
Dourado, (Waldomiro Freitas) Autran 1926-
CLC 23, 60
See also CA 25-28R; CANR 34
Dourado, Waldomiro Autran
See Dourado, (Waldomiro Freitas) Autran

Eastlake, William (Derry) 1917-1997 **CLC 8**
See also CA 5-8R; 158; CAAS 1; CANR 5, 63;
DLB 6; INT CANR-5

Eastman, Charles A(lexander) 1858-1939
TCLC 55; DAM MULT
See also DLB 175; NNAL; YABC 1

Eberhart, Richard (Ghormley) 1904- **CLC 3,
11, 19, 56; DAM POET**
See also CA 1-4R; CANR 2; CDALB 1941-
1968; DLB 48; MTCW 1

Eberstadt, Fernanda 1960- .... **CLC 39**
See also CA 136; CANR 69

Echegaray (y Eizaguirre), Jose (Maria Waldo)
1832-1916 .... **TCLC 4**
See also CA 104; CANR 32; HW; MTCW 1

Echeverria, (Jose) Esteban (Antonino) 1805-
1851 .... **NCLC 18**

Echo
See Proust, (Valentin-Louis-George-Eugene-)
Marcel

Eckert, Allan W. 1931- .... **CLC 17**
See also AAYA 18; CA 13-16R; CANR 14, 45;
INT CANR-14; SAAS 21; SATA 29, 91;
SATA-Brief 27

Eckhart, Meister 1260(?)-1328(?) ... **CMLC 9**
See also DLB 115

Eckmar, F. R.
See de Hartog, Jan

Eco, Umberto 1932- **CLC 28, 60; DAM NOV,
POP**
See also BEST 90:1; CA 77-80; CANR 12, 33,
55; DLB 196; MTCW 1

Eddison, E(ric) R(ucker) 1882-1945 **TCLC 15**
See also CA 109; 156

Eddy, Mary (Morse) Baker 1821-1910 **T C L C
71**
See also CA 113

Edel, (Joseph) Leon 1907-1997 .. **CLC 29, 34**
See also CA 1-4R; 161; CANR 1, 22; DLB 103;
INT CANR-22

Eden, Emily 1797-1869 .... **NCLC 10**

Edgar, David 1948- ... **CLC 42; DAM DRAM**
See also CA 57-60; CANR 12, 61; DLB 13;
MTCW 1

Edgerton, Clyde (Carlyle) 1944- ...... **CLC 39**
See also AAYA 17; CA 118; 134; CANR 64;
INT 134

Edgeworth, Maria 1768-1849 .... **NCLC 1, 51**
See also DLB 116, 159, 163; SATA 21

Edmonds, Paul
See Kuttner, Henry

Edmonds, Walter D(umaux) 1903-1998 **C L C
35**
See also CA 5-8R; CANR 2; DLB 9; MAICYA;
SAAS 4; SATA 1, 27; SATA-Obit 99

Edmondson, Wallace
See Ellison, Harlan (Jay)

Edson, Russell .... **CLC 13**
See also CA 33-36R

Edwards, Bronwen Elizabeth
See Rose, Wendy

Edwards, G(erald) B(asil) 1899-1976 **CLC 25**
See also CA 110

Edwards, Gus 1939- .... **CLC 43**
See also CA 108; INT 108

Edwards, Jonathan 1703-1758 .... **LC 7; DA;
DAC; DAM MST**
See also DLB 24

Efron, Marina Ivanovna Tsvetaeva
See Tsvetaeva (Efron), Marina (Ivanovna)

Ehle, John (Marsden, Jr.) 1925- .... **CLC 27**
See also CA 9-12R

Ehrenbourg, Ilya (Grigoryevich)
See Ehrenburg, Ilya (Grigoryevich)

Ehrenburg, Ilya (Grigoryevich) 1891-1967
CLC 18, 34, 62
See also CA 102; 25-28R

Ehrenburg, Ilyo (Grigoryevich)
See Ehrenburg, Ilya (Grigoryevich)

Ehrenreich, Barbara 1941- .... **CLC 110**
See also BEST 90:4; CA 73-76; CANR 16, 37,
62; MTCW 1

Eich, Guenter 1907-1972 .... **CLC 15**
See also CA 111; 93-96; DLB 69, 124

Eichendorff, Joseph Freiherr von 1788-1857
NCLC 8
See also DLB 90

Eigner, Larry .... **CLC 9**
See also Eigner, Laurence (Joel)
See also CAAS 23; DLB 5

Eigner, Laurence (Joel) 1927-1996
See Eigner, Larry
See also CA 9-12R; 151; CANR 6; DLB 193

Einstein, Albert 1879-1955 .... **TCLC 65**
See also CA 121; 133; MTCW 1

Eiseley, Loren Corey 1907-1977 .... **CLC 7**
See also AAYA 5; CA 1-4R; 73-76; CANR 6;
DLBD 17

Eisenstadt, Jill 1963- .... **CLC 50**
See also CA 140

Eisenstein, Sergei (Mikhailovich) 1898-1948
TCLC 57
See also CA 114; 149

Eisner, Simon
See Kornbluth, C(yril) M.

Ekeloef, (Bengt) Gunnar 1907-1968 **CLC 27;
DAM POET; PC 23**
See also CA 123; 25-28R

Ekelof, (Bengt) Gunnar
See Ekeloef, (Bengt) Gunnar

Ekelund, Vilhelm 1880-1949 .... **TCLC 75**

Ekwensi, C. O. D.
See Ekwensi, Cyprian (Odiatu Duaka)

Ekwensi, Cyprian (Odiatu Duaka) 1921- **CLC
4; BLC 1; DAM MULT**
See also BW 2; CA 29-32R; CANR 18, 42; DLB
117; MTCW 1; SATA 66

Elaine .... **TCLC 18**
See also Leverson, Ada

El Crummo
See Crumb, R(obert)

Elder, Lonne III 1931-1996 .... **DC 8**
See also BLC 1; BW 1; CA 81-84; 152; CANR
25; DAM MULT; DLB 7, 38, 44

Elia
See Lamb, Charles

Eliade, Mircea 1907-1986 .... **CLC 19**
See also CA 65-68; 119; CANR 30, 62; MTCW
1

Eliot, A. D.
See Jewett, (Theodora) Sarah Orne

Eliot, Alice
See Jewett, (Theodora) Sarah Orne

Eliot, Dan
See Silverberg, Robert

Eliot, George 1819-1880 **NCLC 4, 13, 23, 41,
49; DA; DAB; DAC; DAM MST, NOV; PC
20; WLC**
See also CDBLB 1832-1890; DLB 21, 35, 55

Eliot, John 1604-1690 .... **LC 5**
See also DLB 24

Eliot, T(homas) S(tearns) 1888-1965 **CLC 1, 2,
3, 6, 9, 10, 13, 15, 24, 34, 41, 55, 57, 113;
DA; DAB; DAC; DAM DRAM, MST,
POET; PC 5; WLC**
See also CA 5-8R; 25-28R; CANR 41; CDALB
1929-1941; DLB 7, 10, 45, 63; DLBY 88;
MTCW 1

Elizabeth 1866-1941 .... **TCLC 41**

Elkin, Stanley L(awrence) 1930-1995 **CLC 4,
6, 9, 14, 27, 51, 91; DAM NOV, POP; SSC
12**
See also CA 9-12R; 148; CANR 8, 46; DLB 2,
28; DLBY 80; INT CANR-8; MTCW 1

Elledge, Scott .... **CLC 34**

Elliot, Don
See Silverberg, Robert

Elliott, Don
See Silverberg, Robert

Elliott, George P(aul) 1918-1980 .... **CLC 2**
See also CA 1-4R; 97-100; CANR 2

Elliott, Janice 1931- .... **CLC 47**
See also CA 13-16R; CANR 8, 29; DLB 14

Elliott, Sumner Locke 1917-1991 ..... **CLC 38**
See also CA 5-8R; 134; CANR 2, 21

Elliott, William
See Bradbury, Ray (Douglas)

Ellis, A. E. .... **CLC 7**

Ellis, Alice Thomas .... **CLC 40**
See also Haycraft, Anna
See also DLB 194

Ellis, Bret Easton 1964- .. **CLC 39, 71; DAM
POP**
See also AAYA 2; CA 118; 123; CANR 51; INT
123

Ellis, (Henry) Havelock 1859-1939 **TCLC 14**
See also CA 109; DLB 190

Ellis, Landon
See Ellison, Harlan (Jay)

Ellis, Trey 1962- .... **CLC 55**
See also CA 146

Ellison, Harlan (Jay) 1934- ... **CLC 1, 13, 42;
DAM POP; SSC 14**
See also CA 5-8R; CANR 5, 46; DLB 8; INT
CANR-5; MTCW 1

Ellison, Ralph (Waldo) 1914-1994 . **CLC 1, 3,
11, 54, 86, 114; BLC 1; DA; DAB; DAC;
DAM MST, MULT, NOV; SSC 26; WLC**
See also AAYA 19; BW 1; CA 9-12R; 145;
CANR 24, 53; CDALB 1941-1968; DLB 2,
76; DLBY 94; MTCW 1

Ellmann, Lucy (Elizabeth) 1956- ..... **CLC 61**
See also CA 128

Ellmann, Richard (David) 1918-1987 **CLC 50**
See also BEST 89:2; CA 1-4R; 122; CANR 2,
28, 61; DLB 103; DLBY 87; MTCW 1

Elman, Richard (Martin) 1934-1997 **CLC 19**
See also CA 17-20R; 163; CAAS 3; CANR 47

Elron
See Hubbard, L(afayette) Ron(ald)

Eluard, Paul .... **TCLC 7, 41**
See also Grindel, Eugene

Elyot, Sir Thomas 1490(?)-1546 .... **LC 11**

Elytis, Odysseus 1911-1996 **CLC 15, 49, 100;
DAM POET; PC 21**
See also CA 102; 151; MTCW 1

Emecheta, (Florence Onye) Buchi 1944- **C L C
14, 48; BLC 2; DAM MULT**
See also BW 2; CA 81-84; CANR 27; DLB 117;
MTCW 1; SATA 66

Emerson, Mary Moody 1774-1863 **NCLC 66**

Emerson, Ralph Waldo 1803-1882 . **NCLC 1,
38; DA; DAB; DAC; DAM MST, POET;
PC 18; WLC**
See also CDALB 1640-1865; DLB 1, 59, 73

Eminescu, Mihail 1850-1889 .... **NCLC 33**

Empson, William 1906-1984 **CLC 3, 8, 19, 33,
34**
See also CA 17-20R; 112; CANR 31, 61; DLB
20; MTCW 1

Enchi, Fumiko (Ueda) 1905-1986 ..... **CLC 31**
See also CA 129; 121

Ende, Michael (Andreas Helmuth) 1929-1995
CLC 31
See also CA 118; 124; 149; CANR 36; CLR
14; DLB 75; MAICYA; SATA 61; SATA-
Brief 42; SATA-Obit 86

Endo, Shusaku 1923-1996 **CLC 7, 14, 19, 54,
99; DAM NOV**
See also CA 29-32R; 153; CANR 21, 54; DLB
182; MTCW 1

See also BEST 89:4; CA 85-88; CANR 38, 62;
DLB 87; MTCW 1

Forten, Charlotte L. .... TCLC 16; BLC 2
See also Grimke, Charlotte L(ottie) Forten
See also DLB 50

Foscolo, Ugo 1778-1827 .... **NCLC 8**

Fosse, Bob .... CLC 20
See also Fosse, Robert Louis

Fosse, Robert Louis 1927-1987
See Fosse, Bob
See also CA 110; 123

Foster, Stephen Collins 1826-1864 **NCLC 26**

Foucault, Michel 1926-1984 . **CLC 31, 34, 69**
See also CA 105; 113; CANR 34; MTCW 1

Fouque, Friedrich (Heinrich Karl) de la Motte
1777-1843 .... **NCLC 2**
See also DLB 90

Fourier, Charles 1772-1837 .... **NCLC 51**

Fournier, Henri Alban 1886-1914
See Alain-Fournier
See also CA 104

Fournier, Pierre 1916- .... **CLC 11**
See also Gascar, Pierre
See also CA 89-92; CANR 16, 40

Fowles, John (Philip) 1926- **CLC 1, 2, 3, 4, 6,
9, 10, 15, 33, 87; DAB; DAC; DAM MST**
See also CA 5-8R; CANR 25, 71; CDBLB 1960
to Present; DLB 14, 139; MTCW 1; SATA
22

Fox, Paula 1923- .... **CLC 2, 8**
See also AAYA 3; CA 73-76; CANR 20, 36,
62; CLR 1, 44; DLB 52; JRDA; MAICYA;
MTCW 1; SATA 17, 60

Fox, William Price (Jr.) 1926- .... **CLC 22**
See also CA 17-20R; CAAS 19; CANR 11; DLB
2; DLBY 81

Foxe, John 1516(?)-1587 .... **LC 14**
See also DLB 132

Frame, Janet 1924- **CLC 2, 3, 6, 22, 66, 96; SSC
29**
See also Clutha, Janet Paterson Frame

France, Anatole .... **TCLC 9**
See also Thibault, Jacques Anatole Francois
See also DLB 123

Francis, Claude 19(?)- .... **CLC 50**

Francis, Dick 1920- **CLC 2, 22, 42, 102; DAM
POP**
See also AAYA 5, 21; BEST 89:3; CA 5-8R;
CANR 9, 42, 68; CDBLB 1960 to Present;
DLB 87; INT CANR-9; MTCW 1

Francis, Robert (Churchill) 1901-1987 **C L C
15**
See also CA 1-4R; 123; CANR 1

Frank, Anne(lies Marie) 1929-1945 **TCLC 17;
DA; DAB; DAC; DAM MST; WLC**
See also AAYA 12; CA 113; 133; CANR 68;
MTCW 1; SATA 87; SATA-Brief 42

Frank, Bruno 1887-1945 .... **TCLC 81**
See also DLB 118

Frank, Elizabeth 1945- .... **CLC 39**
See also CA 121; 126; INT 126

Frankl, Viktor E(mil) 1905-1997 ...... **CLC 93**
See also CA 65-68; 161

Franklin, Benjamin
See Hasek, Jaroslav (Matej Frantisek)

Franklin, Benjamin 1706-1790 .. **LC 25; DA;
DAB; DAC; DAM MST; WLCS**
See also CDALB 1640-1865; DLB 24, 43, 73

Franklin, (Stella Maria Sarah) Miles (Lampe)
1879-1954 .... **TCLC 7**
See also CA 104; 164

Fraser, (Lady) Antonia (Pakenham) 1932-
...... **CLC 32, 107**
See also CA 85-88; CANR 44, 65; MTCW 1;
SATA-Brief 32

Fraser, George MacDonald 1925- ...... **CLC 7**
See also CA 45-48; CANR 2, 48

Fraser, Sylvia 1935- .... **CLC 64**
See also CA 45-48; CANR 1, 16, 60

Frayn, Michael 1933- **CLC 3, 7, 31, 47; DAM
DRAM, NOV**
See also CA 5-8R; CANR 30, 69; DLB 13, 14,
194; MTCW 1

Fraze, Candida (Merrill) 1945- .... **CLC 50**
See also CA 126

Frazer, J(ames) G(eorge) 1854-1941 **TCLC 32**
See also CA 118

Frazer, Robert Caine
See Creasey, John

Frazer, Sir James George
See Frazer, J(ames) G(eorge)

Frazier, Charles 1950- .... **CLC 109**
See also CA 161

Frazier, Ian 1951- .... **CLC 46**
See also CA 130; CANR 54

Frederic, Harold 1856-1898 .... **NCLC 10**
See also DLB 12, 23; DLBD 13

Frederick, John
See Faust, Frederick (Schiller)

Frederick the Great 1712-1786 .... **LC 14**

Fredro, Aleksander 1793-1876 .... **NCLC 8**

Freeling, Nicolas 1927- .... **CLC 38**
See also CA 49-52; CAAS 12; CANR 1, 17,
50; DLB 87

Freeman, Douglas Southall 1886-1953 **T C L C
11**
See also CA 109; DLB 17; DLBD 17

Freeman, Judith 1946- .... **CLC 55**
See also CA 148

Freeman, Mary Eleanor Wilkins 1852-1930
TCLC 9; SSC 1
See also CA 106; DLB 12, 78

Freeman, R(ichard) Austin 1862-1943 **T C L C
21**
See also CA 113; DLB 70

French, Albert 1943- .... **CLC 86**
See also CA 167

French, Marilyn 1929- **CLC 10, 18, 60; DAM
DRAM, NOV, POP**
See also CA 69-72; CANR 3, 31; INT CANR-
31; MTCW 1

French, Paul
See Asimov, Isaac

Freneau, Philip Morin 1752-1832 ... **NCLC 1**
See also DLB 37, 43

Freud, Sigmund 1856-1939 .... **TCLC 52**
See also CA 115; 133; CANR 69; MTCW 1

Friedan, Betty (Naomi) 1921- .... **CLC 74**
See also CA 65-68; CANR 18, 45; MTCW 1

Friedlander, Saul 1932- .... **CLC 90**
See also CA 117; 130; CANR 72

Friedman, B(ernard) H(arper) 1926- **CLC 7**
See also CA 1-4R; CANR 3, 48

Friedman, Bruce Jay 1930- ...... **CLC 3, 5, 56**
See also CA 9-12R; CANR 25, 52; DLB 2, 28;
INT CANR-25

Friel, Brian 1929- . **CLC 5, 42, 59, 115; DC 8**
See also CA 21-24R; CANR 33, 69; DLB 13;
MTCW 1

Friis-Baastad, Babbis Ellinor 1921-1970 **C L C
12**
See also CA 17-20R; 134; SATA 7

Frisch, Max (Rudolf) 1911-1991 **CLC 3, 9, 14,
18, 32, 44; DAM DRAM, NOV**
See also CA 85-88; 134; CANR 32; DLB 69,
124; MTCW 1

Fromentin, Eugene (Samuel Auguste) 1820-
1876 .... **NCLC 10**
See also DLB 123

Frost, Frederick
See Faust, Frederick (Schiller)

Frost, Robert (Lee) 1874-1963 **CLC 1, 3, 4, 9,
10, 13, 15, 26, 34, 44; DA; DAB; DAC;
DAM MST, POET; PC 1; WLC**

See also AAYA 21; CA 89-92; CANR 33;
CDALB 1917-1929; DLB 54; DLBD 7;
MTCW 1; SATA 14

Froude, James Anthony 1818-1894 **NCLC 43**
See also DLB 18, 57, 144

Froy, Herald
See Waterhouse, Keith (Spencer)

Fry, Christopher 1907- **CLC 2, 10, 14; DAM
DRAM**
See also CA 17-20R; CAAS 23; CANR 9, 30;
DLB 13; MTCW 1; SATA 66

Frye, (Herman) Northrop 1912-1991 **CLC 24,
70**
See also CA 5-8R; 133; CANR 8, 37; DLB 67,
68; MTCW 1

Fuchs, Daniel 1909-1993 .... **CLC 8, 22**
See also CA 81-84; 142; CAAS 5; CANR 40;
DLB 9, 26, 28; DLBY 93

Fuchs, Daniel 1934- .... **CLC 34**
See also CA 37-40R; CANR 14, 48

Fuentes, Carlos 1928- **CLC 3, 8, 10, 13, 22, 41,
60, 113; DA; DAB; DAC; DAM MST,
MULT, NOV; HLC; SSC 24; WLC**
See also AAYA 4; AITN 2; CA 69-72; CANR
10, 32, 68; DLB 113; HW; MTCW 1

Fuentes, Gregorio Lopez y
See Lopez y Fuentes, Gregorio

Fugard, (Harold) Athol 1932- **CLC 5, 9, 14, 25,
40, 80; DAM DRAM; DC 3**
See also AAYA 17; CA 85-88; CANR 32, 54;
MTCW 1

Fugard, Sheila 1932- .... **CLC 48**
See also CA 125

Fuller, Charles (H., Jr.) 1939- **CLC 25; BLC 2;
DAM DRAM, MULT; DC 1**
See also BW 2; CA 108; 112; DLB 38; INT 112;
MTCW 1

Fuller, John (Leopold) 1937- .... **CLC 62**
See also CA 21-24R; CANR 9, 44; DLB 40

Fuller, Margaret .... **NCLC 5, 50**
See also Ossoli, Sarah Margaret (Fuller
marchesa d')

Fuller, Roy (Broadbent) 1912-1991 **CLC 4, 28**
See also CA 5-8R; 135; CAAS 10; CANR 53;
DLB 15, 20; SATA 87

Fulton, Alice 1952- .... **CLC 52**
See also CA 116; CANR 57; DLB 193

Furphy, Joseph 1843-1912 .... **TCLC 25**
See also CA 163

Fussell, Paul 1924- .... **CLC 74**
See also BEST 90:1; CA 17-20R; CANR 8, 21,
35, 69; INT CANR-21; MTCW 1

Futabatei, Shimei 1864-1909 .... **TCLC 44**
See also CA 162; DLB 180

Futrelle, Jacques 1875-1912 .... **TCLC 19**
See also CA 113; 155

Gaboriau, Emile 1835-1873 .... **NCLC 14**

Gadda, Carlo Emilio 1893-1973 .... **CLC 11**
See also CA 89-92; DLB 177

Gaddis, William 1922- **CLC 1, 3, 6, 8, 10, 19,
43, 86**
See also CA 17-20R; CANR 21, 48; DLB 2;
MTCW 1

Gage, Walter
See Inge, William (Motter)

Gaines, Ernest J(ames) 1933- **CLC 3, 11, 18,
86; BLC 2; DAM MULT**
See also AAYA 18; AITN 1; BW 2; CA 9-12R;
CANR 6, 24, 42; CDALB 1968-1988; DLB
2, 33, 152; DLBY 80; MTCW 1; SATA 86

Gaitskill, Mary 1954- .... **CLC 69**
See also CA 128; CANR 61

Galdos, Benito Perez
See Perez Galdos, Benito

Gale, Zona 1874-1938 **TCLC 7; DAM DRAM**
See also CA 105; 153; DLB 9, 78

Galeano, Eduardo (Hughes) 1940- ... **CLC 72**

See also CA 29-32R; CANR 13, 32; HW
Galiano, Juan Valera y Alcala
See Valera y Alcala-Galiano, Juan
Galilei, Galileo 1546-1642 .... **LC 45**
Gallagher, Tess 1943- ...... **CLC 18, 63; DAM POET; PC 9**
See also CA 106; DLB 120
Gallant, Mavis 1922- ... **CLC 7, 18, 38; DAC; DAM MST; SSC 5**
See also CA 69-72; CANR 29, 69; DLB 53; MTCW 1
Gallant, Roy A(rthur) 1924- .... **CLC 17**
See also CA 5-8R; CANR 4, 29, 54; CLR 30; MAICYA; SATA 4, 68
Gallico, Paul (William) 1897-1976 ..... **CLC 2**
See also AITN 1; CA 5-8R; 69-72; CANR 23; DLB 9, 171; MAICYA; SATA 13
Gallo, Max Louis 1932- .... **CLC 95**
See also CA 85-88
Gallois, Lucien
See Desnos, Robert
Gallup, Ralph
See Whitemore, Hugh (John)
Galsworthy, John 1867-1933**TCLC 1, 45; DA; DAB; DAC; DAM DRAM, MST, NOV; SSC 22; WLC 2**
See also CA 104; 141; CDBLB 1890-1914; DLB 10, 34, 98, 162; DLBD 16
Galt, John 1779-1839 .... **NCLC 1**
See also DLB 99, 116, 159
Galvin, James 1951- .... **CLC 38**
See also CA 108; CANR 26
Gamboa, Federico 1864-1939 .... **TCLC 36**
See also CA 167
Gandhi, M. K.
See Gandhi, Mohandas Karamchand
Gandhi, Mahatma
See Gandhi, Mohandas Karamchand
Gandhi, Mohandas Karamchand 1869-1948 **TCLC 59; DAM MULT**
See also CA 121; 132; MTCW 1
Gann, Ernest Kellogg 1910-1991 ...... **CLC 23**
See also AITN 1; CA 1-4R; 136; CANR 1
Garcia, Cristina 1958- .... **CLC 76**
See also CA 141
Garcia Lorca, Federico 1898-1936**TCLC 1, 7, 49; DA; DAB; DAC; DAM DRAM, MST, MULT, POET; DC 2; HLC; PC 3; WLC**
See also CA 104; 131; DLB 108; HW; MTCW 1
Garcia Marquez, Gabriel (Jose) 1928-**CLC 2, 3, 8, 10, 15, 27, 47, 55, 68; DA; DAB; DAC; DAM MST, MULT, NOV, POP; HLC; SSC 8; WLC**
See also AAYA 3; BEST 89:1, 90:4; CA 33-36R; CANR 10, 28, 50; DLB 113; HW; MTCW 1
Gard, Janice
See Latham, Jean Lee
Gard, Roger Martin du
See Martin du Gard, Roger
Gardam, Jane 1928- .... **CLC 43**
See also CA 49-52; CANR 2, 18, 33, 54; CLR 12; DLB 14, 161; MAICYA; MTCW 1; SAAS 9; SATA 39, 76; SATA-Brief 28
Gardner, Herb(ert) 1934- .... **CLC 44**
See also CA 149
Gardner, John (Champlin), Jr. 1933-1982 **CLC 2, 3, 5, 7, 8, 10, 18, 28, 34; DAM NOV, POP; SSC 7**
See also AITN 1; CA 65-68; 107; CANR 33; DLB 2; DLBY 82; MTCW 1; SATA 40; SATA-Obit 31
Gardner, John (Edmund) 1926-**CLC 30; DAM POP**
See also CA 103; CANR 15, 69; MTCW 1
Gardner, Miriam

See Bradley, Marion Zimmer
Gardner, Noel
See Kuttner, Henry
Gardons, S. S.
See Snodgrass, W(illiam) D(e Witt)
Garfield, Leon 1921-1996 .... **CLC 12**
See also AAYA 8; CA 17-20R; 152; CANR 38, 41; CLR 21; DLB 161; JRDA; MAICYA; SATA 1, 32, 76; SATA-Obit 90
Garland, (Hannibal) Hamlin 1860-1940 **TCLC 3; SSC 18**
See also CA 104; DLB 12, 71, 78, 186
Garneau, (Hector de) Saint-Denys 1912-1943 **TCLC 13**
See also CA 111; DLB 88
Garner, Alan 1934-**CLC 17; DAB; DAM POP**
See also AAYA 18; CA 73-76; CANR 15, 64; CLR 20; DLB 161; MAICYA; MTCW 1; SATA 18, 69
Garner, Hugh 1913-1979 .... **CLC 13**
See also CA 69-72; CANR 31; DLB 68
Garnett, David 1892-1981 .... **CLC 3**
See also CA 5-8R; 103; CANR 17; DLB 34
Garos, Stephanie
See Katz, Steve
Garrett, George (Palmer) 1929-**CLC 3, 11, 51; SSC 30**
See also CA 1-4R; CAAS 5; CANR 1, 42, 67; DLB 2, 5, 130, 152; DLBY 83
Garrick, David 1717-1779 ....**LC 15; DAM DRAM**
See also DLB 84
Garrigue, Jean 1914-1972 .... **CLC 2, 8**
See also CA 5-8R; 37-40R; CANR 20
Garrison, Frederick
See Sinclair, Upton (Beall)
Garth, Will
See Hamilton, Edmond; Kuttner, Henry
Garvey, Marcus (Moziah, Jr.) 1887-1940 **TCLC 41; BLC 2; DAM MULT**
See also BW 1; CA 120; 124
Gary, Romain .... **CLC 25**
See also Kacew, Romain
See also DLB 83
Gascar, Pierre .... **CLC 11**
See also Fournier, Pierre
Gascoyne, David (Emery) 1916- .... **CLC 45**
See also CA 65-68; CANR 10, 28, 54; DLB 20; MTCW 1
Gaskell, Elizabeth Cleghorn 1810-1865**NCLC 70; DAB; DAM MST; SSC 25**
See also CDBLB 1832-1890; DLB 21, 144, 159
Gass, William H(oward) 1924-**CLC 1, 2, 8, 11, 15, 39; SSC 12**
See also CA 17-20R; CANR 30, 71; DLB 2; MTCW 1
Gasset, Jose Ortega y
See Ortega y Gasset, Jose
Gates, Henry Louis, Jr. 1950-**CLC 65; BLCS; DAM MULT**
See also BW 2; CA 109; CANR 25, 53; DLB 67
Gautier, Theophile 1811-1872 .. **NCLC 1, 59; DAM POET; PC 18; SSC 20**
See also DLB 119
Gawsworth, John
See Bates, H(erbert) E(rnest)
Gay, Oliver
See Gogarty, Oliver St. John
Gaye, Marvin (Penze) 1939-1984 ..... **CLC 26**
See also CA 112
Gebler, Carlo (Ernest) 1954- .... **CLC 39**
See also CA 119; 133
Gee, Maggie (Mary) 1948- .... **CLC 57**
See also CA 130
Gee, Maurice (Gough) 1931- .... **CLC 29**
See also CA 97-100; CANR 67; SATA 46, 101

Gelbart, Larry (Simon) 1923-.... **CLC 21, 61**
See also CA 73-76; CANR 45
Gelber, Jack 1932- .... **CLC 1, 6, 14, 79**
See also CA 1-4R; CANR 2; DLB 7
Gellhorn, Martha (Ellis) 1908-1998 **CLC 14, 60**
See also CA 77-80; 164; CANR 44; DLBY 82
Genet, Jean 1910-1986**CLC 1, 2, 5, 10, 14, 44, 46; DAM DRAM**
See also CA 13-16R; CANR 18; DLB 72; DLBY 86; MTCW 1
Gent, Peter 1942- .... **CLC 29**
See also AITN 1; CA 89-92; DLBY 82
Gentlewoman in New England, A
See Bradstreet, Anne
Gentlewoman in Those Parts, A
See Bradstreet, Anne
George, Jean Craighead 1919- .... **CLC 35**
See also AAYA 8; CA 5-8R; CANR 25; CLR 1; DLB 52; JRDA; MAICYA; SATA 2, 68
George, Stefan (Anton) 1868-1933**TCLC 2, 14**
See also CA 104
Georges, Georges Martin
See Simenon, Georges (Jacques Christian)
Gerhardi, William Alexander
See Gerhardie, William Alexander
Gerhardie, William Alexander 1895-1977 **CLC 5**
See also CA 25-28R; 73-76; CANR 18; DLB 36
Gerstler, Amy 1956- .... **CLC 70**
See also CA 146
Gertler, T. .... **CLC 34**
See also CA 116; 121; INT 121
Ghalib .... **NCLC 39**
See also Ghalib, Hsadullah Khan
Ghalib, Hsadullah Khan 1797-1869
See Ghalib
See also DAM POET
Ghelderode, Michel de 1898-1962**CLC 6, 11; DAM DRAM**
See also CA 85-88; CANR 40
Ghiselin, Brewster 1903- .... **CLC 23**
See also CA 13-16R; CAAS 10; CANR 13
Ghose, Aurabinda 1872-1950......... **TCLC 63**
See also CA 163
Ghose, Zulfikar 1935- .... **CLC 42**
See also CA 65-68; CANR 67
Ghosh, Amitav 1956- .... **CLC 44**
See also CA 147
Giacosa, Giuseppe 1847-1906 .... **TCLC 7**
See also CA 104
Gibb, Lee
See Waterhouse, Keith (Spencer)
Gibbon, Lewis Grassic .... **TCLC 4**
See also Mitchell, James Leslie
Gibbons, Kaye 1960-**CLC 50, 88; DAM POP**
See also CA 151
Gibran, Kahlil 1883-1931 . **TCLC 1, 9; DAM POET, POP; PC 9**
See also CA 104; 150
Gibran, Khalil
See Gibran, Kahlil
Gibson, William 1914- .. **CLC 23; DA; DAB; DAC; DAM DRAM, MST**
See also CA 9-12R; CANR 9, 42; DLB 7; SATA 66
Gibson, William (Ford) 1948- ... **CLC 39, 63; DAM POP**
See also AAYA 12; CA 126; 133; CANR 52
Gide, Andre (Paul Guillaume) 1869-1951 **TCLC 5, 12, 36; DA; DAB; DAC; DAM MST, NOV; SSC 13; WLC**
See also CA 104; 124; DLB 65; MTCW 1
Gifford, Barry (Colby) 1946- .... **CLC 34**
See also CA 65-68; CANR 9, 30, 40
Gilbert, Frank

Gosse, Edmund (William) 1849-1928 **TCLC 28**
See also CA 117; DLB 57, 144, 184
Gotlieb, Phyllis Fay (Bloom) 1926- .. **CLC 18**
See also CA 13-16R; CANR 7; DLB 88
Gottesman, S. D.
See Kornbluth, C(yril) M.; Pohl, Frederik
Gottfried von Strassburg fl. c. 1210- **CMLC 10**
See also DLB 138
Gould, Lois .... **CLC 4, 10**
See also CA 77-80; CANR 29; MTCW 1
Gourmont, Remy (-Marie-Charles) de 1858-1915 .... **TCLC 17**
See also CA 109; 150
Govier, Katherine 1948- .... **CLC 51**
See also CA 101; CANR 18, 40
Goyen, (Charles) William 1915-1983 **CLC 5, 8, 14, 40**
See also AITN 2; CA 5-8R; 110; CANR 6, 71; DLB 2; DLBY 83; INT CANR-6
Goytisolo, Juan 1931- . **CLC 5, 10, 23; DAM MULT; HLC**
See also CA 85-88; CANR 32, 61; HW; MTCW 1
Gozzano, Guido 1883-1916 .... **PC 10**
See also CA 154; DLB 114
Gozzi, (Conte) Carlo 1720-1806 .... **NCLC 23**
Grabbe, Christian Dietrich 1801-1836 **NCLC 2**
See also DLB 133
Grace, Patricia 1937- .... **CLC 56**
Gracian y Morales, Baltasar 1601-1658 **LC 15**
Gracq, Julien .... **CLC 11, 48**
See also Poirier, Louis
See also DLB 83
Grade, Chaim 1910-1982 .... **CLC 10**
See also CA 93-96; 107
Graduate of Oxford, A
See Ruskin, John
Grafton, Garth
See Duncan, Sara Jeannette
Graham, John
See Phillips, David Graham
Graham, Jorie 1951- .... **CLC 48**
See also CA 111; CANR 63; DLB 120
Graham, R(obert) B(ontine) Cunninghame
See Cunninghame Graham, R(obert) B(ontine)
See also DLB 98, 135, 174
Graham, Robert
See Haldeman, Joe (William)
Graham, Tom
See Lewis, (Harry) Sinclair
Graham, W(illiam) S(ydney) 1918-1986 **CLC 29**
See also CA 73-76; 118; DLB 20
Graham, Winston (Mawdsley) 1910- **CLC 23**
See also CA 49-52; CANR 2, 22, 45, 66; DLB 77
Grahame, Kenneth 1859-1932 **TCLC 64; DAB**
See also CA 108; 136; CLR 5; DLB 34, 141, 178; MAICYA; SATA 100; YABC 1
Grant, Skeeter
See Spiegelman, Art
Granville-Barker, Harley 1877-1946 **TCLC 2; DAM DRAM**
See also Barker, Harley Granville
See also CA 104
Grass, Guenter (Wilhelm) 1927- **CLC 1, 2, 4, 6, 11, 15, 22, 32, 49, 88; DA; DAB; DAC; DAM MST, NOV; WLC**
See also CA 13-16R; CANR 20; DLB 75, 124; MTCW 1
Gratton, Thomas
See Hulme, T(homas) E(rnest)
Grau, Shirley Ann 1929- . **CLC 4, 9; SSC 15**
See also CA 89-92; CANR 22, 69; DLB 2; INT CANR-22; MTCW 1

Gravel, Fern
See Hall, James Norman
Graver, Elizabeth 1964- .... **CLC 70**
See also CA 135; CANR 71
Graves, Richard Perceval 1945- .... **CLC 44**
See also CA 65-68; CANR 9, 26, 51
Graves, Robert (von Ranke) 1895-1985 **CLC 1, 2, 6, 11, 39, 44, 45; DAB; DAC; DAM MST, POET; PC 6**
See also CA 5-8R; 117; CANR 5, 36; CDBLB 1914-1945; DLB 20, 100, 191; DLBD 18; DLBY 85; MTCW 1; SATA 45
Graves, Valerie
See Bradley, Marion Zimmer
Gray, Alasdair (James) 1934- .... **CLC 41**
See also CA 126; CANR 47, 69; DLB 194; INT 126; MTCW 1
Gray, Amlin 1946- .... **CLC 29**
See also CA 138
Gray, Francine du Plessix 1930- ..... **CLC 22; DAM NOV**
See also BEST 90:3; CA 61-64; CAAS 2; CANR 11, 33; INT CANR-11; MTCW 1
Gray, John (Henry) 1866-1934 ...... **TCLC 19**
See also CA 119; 162
Gray, Simon (James Holliday) 1936- **CLC 9, 14, 36**
See also AITN 1; CA 21-24R; CAAS 3; CANR 32, 69; DLB 13; MTCW 1
Gray, Spalding 1941- **CLC 49, 112; DAM POP; DC 7**
See also CA 128
Gray, Thomas 1716-1771 **LC 4, 40; DA; DAB; DAC; DAM MST; PC 2; WLC**
See also CDBLB 1660-1789; DLB 109
Grayson, David
See Baker, Ray Stannard
Grayson, Richard (A.) 1951- .... **CLC 38**
See also CA 85-88; CANR 14, 31, 57
Greeley, Andrew M(oran) 1928- ..... **CLC 28; DAM POP**
See also CA 5-8R; CAAS 7; CANR 7, 43, 69; MTCW 1
Green, Anna Katharine 1846-1935 **TCLC 63**
See also CA 112; 159; DLB 202
Green, Brian
See Card, Orson Scott
Green, Hannah
See Greenberg, Joanne (Goldenberg)
Green, Hannah 1927(?)-1996 .... **CLC 3**
See also CA 73-76; CANR 59
Green, Henry 1905-1973 .... **CLC 2, 13, 97**
See also Yorke, Henry Vincent
See also DLB 15
Green, Julian (Hartridge) 1900-
See Green, Julien
See also CA 21-24R; CANR 33; DLB 4, 72; MTCW 1
Green, Julien .... **CLC 3, 11, 77**
See also Green, Julian (Hartridge)
Green, Paul (Eliot) 1894-1981 **CLC 25; DAM DRAM**
See also AITN 1; CA 5-8R; 103; CANR 3; DLB 7, 9; DLBY 81
Greenberg, Ivan 1908-1973
See Rahv, Philip
See also CA 85-88
Greenberg, Joanne (Goldenberg) 1932- **CLC 7, 30**
See also AAYA 12; CA 5-8R; CANR 14, 32, 69; SATA 25
Greenberg, Richard 1959(?)- .... **CLC 57**
See also CA 138
Greene, Bette 1934- .... **CLC 30**
See also AAYA 7; CA 53-56; CANR 4; CLR 2; JRDA; MAICYA; SAAS 16; SATA 8, 102
Greene, Gael .... **CLC 8**

See also CA 13-16R; CANR 10
Greene, Graham (Henry) 1904-1991 **CLC 1, 3, 6, 9, 14, 18, 27, 37, 70, 72; DA; DAB; DAC; DAM MST, NOV; SSC 29; WLC**
See also AITN 2; CA 13-16R; 133; CANR 35, 61; CDBLB 1945-1960; DLB 13, 15, 77, 100, 162, 201; DLBY 91; MTCW 1; SATA 20
Greene, Robert 1558-1592 .... **LC 41**
See also DLB 62, 167
Greer, Richard
See Silverberg, Robert
Gregor, Arthur 1923- .... **CLC 9**
See also CA 25-28R; CAAS 10; CANR 11; SATA 36
Gregor, Lee
See Pohl, Frederik
Gregory, Isabella Augusta (Persse) 1852-1932 **TCLC 1**
See also CA 104; DLB 10
Gregory, J. Dennis
See Williams, John A(lfred)
Grendon, Stephen
See Derleth, August (William)
Grenville, Kate 1950- .... **CLC 61**
See also CA 118; CANR 53
Grenville, Pelham
See Wodehouse, P(elham) G(renville)
Greve, Felix Paul (Berthold Friedrich) 1879-1948
See Grove, Frederick Philip
See also CA 104; 141; DAC; DAM MST
Grey, Zane 1872-1939 .. **TCLC 6; DAM POP**
See also CA 104; 132; DLB 9; MTCW 1
Grieg, (Johan) Nordahl (Brun) 1902-1943 **TCLC 10**
See also CA 107
Grieve, C(hristopher) M(urray) 1892-1978 **CLC 11, 19; DAM POET**
See also MacDiarmid, Hugh; Pteleon
See also CA 5-8R; 85-88; CANR 33; MTCW 1
Griffin, Gerald 1803-1840 .... **NCLC 7**
See also DLB 159
Griffin, John Howard 1920-1980 ..... **CLC 68**
See also AITN 1; CA 1-4R; 101; CANR 2
Griffin, Peter 1942- .... **CLC 39**
See also CA 136
Griffith, D(avid Lewelyn) W(ark) 1875(?)-1948 **TCLC 68**
See also CA 119; 150
Griffith, Lawrence
See Griffith, D(avid Lewelyn) W(ark)
Griffiths, Trevor 1935- .... **CLC 13, 52**
See also CA 97-100; CANR 45; DLB 13
Griggs, Sutton Elbert 1872-1930(?) **TCLC 77**
See also CA 123; DLB 50
Grigson, Geoffrey (Edward Harvey) 1905-1985 **CLC 7, 39**
See also CA 25-28R; 118; CANR 20, 33; DLB 27; MTCW 1
Grillparzer, Franz 1791-1872 .... **NCLC 1**
See also DLB 133
Grimble, Reverend Charles James
See Eliot, T(homas) S(tearns)
Grimke, Charlotte L(ottie) Forten 1837(?)-1914
See Forten, Charlotte L.
See also BW 1; CA 117; 124; DAM MULT, POET
Grimm, Jacob Ludwig Karl 1785-1863 **NCLC 3**
See also DLB 90; MAICYA; SATA 22
Grimm, Wilhelm Karl 1786-1859 .... **NCLC 3**
See also DLB 90; MAICYA; SATA 22
Grimmelshausen, Johann Jakob Christoffel von 1621-1676 .... **LC 6**
See also DLB 168
Grindel, Eugene 1895-1952

See Eluard, Paul
See also CA 104
Grisham, John 1955- .... **CLC 84; DAM POP**
See also AAYA 14; CA 138; CANR 47, 69
Grossman, David 1954- .... **CLC 67**
See also CA 138
Grossman, Vasily (Semenovich) 1905-1964
CLC 41
See also CA 124; 130; MTCW 1
Grove, Frederick Philip .... **TCLC 4**
See also Greve, Felix Paul (Berthold Friedrich)
See also DLB 92
Grubb
See Crumb, R(obert)
Grumbach, Doris (Isaac) 1918-**CLC 13, 22, 64**
See also CA 5-8R; CAAS 2; CANR 9, 42, 70;
INT CANR-9
Grundtvig, Nicolai Frederik Severin 1783-1872
NCLC 1
Grunge
See Crumb, R(obert)
Grunwald, Lisa 1959- .... **CLC 44**
See also CA 120
Guare, John 1938- . **CLC 8, 14, 29, 67; DAM**
DRAM
See also CA 73-76; CANR 21, 69; DLB 7;
MTCW 1
Gudjonsson, Halldor Kiljan 1902-1998
See Laxness, Halldor
See also CA 103; 164
Guenter, Erich
See Eich, Guenter
Guest, Barbara 1920- .... **CLC 34**
See also CA 25-28R; CANR 11, 44; DLB 5,
193
Guest, Judith (Ann) 1936- **CLC 8, 30; DAM**
NOV, POP
See also AAYA 7; CA 77-80; CANR 15; INT
CANR-15; MTCW 1
Guevara, Che .... **CLC 87; HLC**
See also Guevara (Serna), Ernesto
Guevara (Serna), Ernesto 1928-1967
See Guevara, Che
See also CA 127; 111; CANR 56; DAM MULT;
HW
Guild, Nicholas M. 1944- .... **CLC 33**
See also CA 93-96
Guillemin, Jacques
See Sartre, Jean-Paul
Guillen, Jorge 1893-1984 .... **CLC 11; DAM**
MULT, POET
See also CA 89-92; 112; DLB 108; HW
Guillen, Nicolas (Cristobal) 1902-1989 **C L C**
48, 79; BLC 2; DAM MST, MULT, POET;
HLC; PC 23
See also BW 2; CA 116; 125; 129; HW
Guillevic, (Eugene) 1907- .... **CLC 33**
See also CA 93-96
Guillois
See Desnos, Robert
Guillois, Valentin
See Desnos, Robert
Guiney, Louise Imogen 1861-1920 **TCLC 41**
See also CA 160; DLB 54
Guiraldes, Ricardo (Guillermo) 1886-1927
TCLC 39
See also CA 131; HW; MTCW 1
Gumilev, Nikolai (Stepanovich) 1886-1921
TCLC 60
See also CA 165
Gunesekera, Romesh 1954- .... **CLC 91**
See also CA 159
Gunn, Bill .... **CLC 5**
See also Gunn, William Harrison
See also DLB 38
Gunn, Thom(son William) 1929-**CLC 3, 6, 18,**
32, 81; DAM POET

See also CA 17-20R; CANR 9, 33; CDBLB
1960 to Present; DLB 27; INT CANR-33;
MTCW 1
Gunn, William Harrison 1934(?)-1989
See Gunn, Bill
See also AITN 1; BW 1; CA 13-16R; 128;
CANR 12, 25
Gunnars, Kristjana 1948- .... **CLC 69**
See also CA 113; DLB 60
Gurdjieff, G(eorgei) I(vanovich) 1877(?)-1949
TCLC 71
See also CA 157
Gurganus, Allan 1947- . **CLC 70; DAM POP**
See also BEST 90:1; CA 135
Gurney, A(lbert) R(amsdell), Jr. 1930- . **C L C**
32, 50, 54; DAM DRAM
See also CA 77-80; CANR 32, 64
Gurney, Ivor (Bertie) 1890-1937 ... **TCLC 33**
See also CA 167
Gurney, Peter
See Gurney, A(lbert) R(amsdell), Jr.
Guro, Elena 1877-1913 .... **TCLC 56**
Gustafson, James M(oody) 1925- ... **CLC 100**
See also CA 25-28R; CANR 37
Gustafson, Ralph (Barker) 1909- ..... **CLC 36**
See also CA 21-24R; CANR 8, 45; DLB 88
Gut, Gom
See Simenon, Georges (Jacques Christian)
Guterson, David 1956- .... **CLC 91**
See also CA 132
Guthrie, A(lfred) B(ertram), Jr. 1901-1991
CLC 23
See also CA 57-60; 134; CANR 24; DLB 6;
SATA 62; SATA-Obit 67
Guthrie, Isobel
See Grieve, C(hristopher) M(urray)
Guthrie, Woodrow Wilson 1912-1967
See Guthrie, Woody
See also CA 113; 93-96
Guthrie, Woody .... **CLC 35**
See also Guthrie, Woodrow Wilson
Guy, Rosa (Cuthbert) 1928- .... **CLC 26**
See also AAYA 4; BW 2; CA 17-20R; CANR
14, 34; CLR 13; DLB 33; JRDA; MAICYA;
SATA 14, 62
Gwendolyn
See Bennett, (Enoch) Arnold
H. D. .... **CLC 3, 8, 14, 31, 34, 73; PC 5**
See also Doolittle, Hilda
H. de V.
See Buchan, John
Haavikko, Paavo Juhani 1931- .. **CLC 18, 34**
See also CA 106
Habbema, Koos
See Heijermans, Herman
Habermas, Juergen 1929- .... **CLC 104**
See also CA 109
Habermas, Jurgen
See Habermas, Juergen
Hacker, Marilyn 1942- **CLC 5, 9, 23, 72, 91;**
DAM POET
See also CA 77-80; CANR 68; DLB 120
Haeckel, Ernst Heinrich (Philipp August) 1834-
1919 ....
TCLC 83
See also CA 157
Haggard, H(enry) Rider 1856-1925**TCLC 11**
See also CA 108; 148; DLB 70, 156, 174, 178;
SATA 16
Hagiosy, L.
See Larbaud, Valery (Nicolas)
Hagiwara Sakutaro 1886-1942**TCLC 60; PC**
18
Haig, Fenil
See Ford, Ford Madox
Haig-Brown, Roderick (Langmere) 1908-1976
CLC 21

See also CA 5-8R; 69-72; CANR 4, 38; CLR
31; DLB 88; MAICYA; SATA 12
Hailey, Arthur 1920-**CLC 5; DAM NOV, POP**
See also AITN 2; BEST 90:3; CA 1-4R; CANR
2, 36; DLB 88; DLBY 82; MTCW 1
Hailey, Elizabeth Forsythe 1938- ..... **CLC 40**
See also CA 93-96; CAAS 1; CANR 15, 48;
INT CANR-15
Haines, John (Meade) 1924- .... **CLC 58**
See also CA 17-20R; CANR 13, 34; DLB 5
Hakluyt, Richard 1552-1616 .... **LC 31**
Haldeman, Joe (William) 1943- .... **CLC 61**
See also CA 53-56; CAAS 25; CANR 6, 70,
72; DLB 8; INT CANR-6
Haley, Alex(ander Murray Palmer) 1921-1992
CLC 8, 12, 76; BLC 2; DA; DAB; DAC;
DAM MST, MULT, POP
See also AAYA 26; BW 2; CA 77-80; 136;
CANR 61; DLB 38; MTCW 1
Haliburton, Thomas Chandler 1796-1865
NCLC 15
See also DLB 11, 99
Hall, Donald (Andrew, Jr.) 1928- **CLC 1, 13,**
37, 59; DAM POET
See also CA 5-8R; CAAS 7; CANR 2, 44, 64;
DLB 5; SATA 23, 97
Hall, Frederic Sauser
See Sauser-Hall, Frederic
Hall, James
See Kuttner, Henry
Hall, James Norman 1887-1951 ..... **TCLC 23**
See also CA 123; SATA 21
Hall, (Marguerite) Radclyffe 1886-1943
TCLC 12
See also CA 110; 150
Hall, Rodney 1935- .... **CLC 51**
See also CA 109; CANR 69
Halleck, Fitz-Greene 1790-1867 .... **NCLC 47**
See also DLB 3
Halliday, Michael
See Creasey, John
Halpern, Daniel 1945- .... **CLC 14**
See also CA 33-36R
Hamburger, Michael (Peter Leopold) 1924-
CLC 5, 14
See also CA 5-8R; CAAS 4; CANR 2, 47; DLB
27
Hamill, Pete 1935- .... **CLC 10**
See also CA 25-28R; CANR 18, 71
Hamilton, Alexander 1755(?)-1804 **NCLC 49**
See also DLB 37
Hamilton, Clive
See Lewis, C(live) S(taples)
Hamilton, Edmond 1904-1977 .... **CLC 1**
See also CA 1-4R; CANR 3; DLB 8
Hamilton, Eugene (Jacob) Lee
See Lee-Hamilton, Eugene (Jacob)
Hamilton, Franklin
See Silverberg, Robert
Hamilton, Gail
See Corcoran, Barbara
Hamilton, Mollie
See Kaye, M(ary) M(argaret)
Hamilton, (Anthony Walter) Patrick 1904-1962
CLC 51
See also CA 113; DLB 10
Hamilton, Virginia 1936- .... **CLC 26; DAM**
MULT
See also AAYA 2, 21; BW 2; CA 25-28R;
CANR 20, 37; CLR 1, 11, 40; DLB 33, 52;
INT CANR-20; JRDA; MAICYA; MTCW 1;
SATA 4, 56, 79
Hammett, (Samuel) Dashiell 1894-1961 **C L C**
3, 5, 10, 19, 47; SSC 17
See also AITN 1; CA 81-84; CANR 42; CDALB
1929-1941; DLBD 6; DLBY 96; MTCW 1
Hammon, Jupiter 1711(?)-1800(?) .. **NCLC 5;**

Horovitz, Israel (Arthur) 1939-CLC 56; DAM
DRAM
See also CA 33-36R; CANR 46, 59; DLB 7
Horvath, Odon von
See Horvath, Oedoen von
See also DLB 85, 124
Horvath, Oedoen von 1901-1938 ... TCLC 45
See also Horvath, Odon von
See also CA 118
Horwitz, Julius 1920-1986 .... CLC 14
See also CA 9-12R; 119; CANR 12
Hospital, Janette Turner 1942- .... CLC 42
See also CA 108; CANR 48
Hostos, E. M. de
See Hostos (y Bonilla), Eugenio Maria de
Hostos, Eugenio M. de
See Hostos (y Bonilla), Eugenio Maria de
Hostos, Eugenio Maria
See Hostos (y Bonilla), Eugenio Maria de
Hostos (y Bonilla), Eugenio Maria de 1839-
1903 .... TCLC 24
See also CA 123; 131; HW
Houdini
See Lovecraft, H(oward) P(hillips)
Hougan, Carolyn 1943- .... CLC 34
See also CA 139
Household, Geoffrey (Edward West) 1900-1988
CLC 11
See also CA 77-80; 126; CANR 58; DLB 87;
SATA 14; SATA-Obit 59
Housman, A(lfred) E(dward) 1859-1936
TCLC 1, 10; DA; DAB; DAC; DAM MST,
POET; PC 2; WLCS
See also CA 104; 125; DLB 19; MTCW 1
Housman, Laurence 1865-1959 .... TCLC 7
See also CA 106; 155; DLB 10; SATA 25
Howard, Elizabeth Jane 1923- ..... CLC 7, 29
See also CA 5-8R; CANR 8, 62
Howard, Maureen 1930- .... CLC 5, 14, 46
See also CA 53-56; CANR 31; DLBY 83; INT
CANR-31; MTCW 1
Howard, Richard 1929- .... CLC 7, 10, 47
See also AITN 1; CA 85-88; CANR 25; DLB 5;
INT CANR-25
Howard, Robert E(rvin) 1906-1936 TCLC 8
See also CA 105; 157
Howard, Warren F.
See Pohl, Frederik
Howe, Fanny (Quincy) 1940- .... CLC 47
See also CA 117; CAAS 27; CANR 70; SATA-
Brief 52
Howe, Irving 1920-1993 .... CLC 85
See also CA 9-12R; 141; CANR 21, 50; DLB
67; MTCW 1
Howe, Julia Ward 1819-1910 .... TCLC 21
See also CA 117; DLB 1, 189
Howe, Susan 1937- .... CLC 72
See also CA 160; DLB 120
Howe, Tina 1937- .... CLC 48
See also CA 109
Howell, James 1594(?)-1666 .... LC 13
See also DLB 151
Howells, W. D.
See Howells, William Dean
Howells, William D.
See Howells, William Dean
Howells, William Dean 1837-1920TCLC 7, 17,
41
See also CA 104; 134; CDALB 1865-1917;
DLB 12, 64, 74, 79, 189
Howes, Barbara 1914-1996 .... CLC 15
See also CA 9-12R; 151; CAAS 3; CANR 53;
SATA 5
Hrabal, Bohumil 1914-1997 .... CLC 13, 67
See also CA 106; 156; CAAS 12; CANR 57
Hroswitha of Gandersheim c. 935-c. 1002
CMLC 29

See also DLB 148
Hsun, Lu
See Lu Hsun
Hubbard, L(afayette) Ron(ald) 1911-1986
CLC 43; DAM POP
See also CA 77-80; 118; CANR 52
Huch, Ricarda (Octavia) 1864-1947TCLC 13
See also CA 111; DLB 66
Huddle, David 1942- .... CLC 49
See also CA 57-60; CAAS 20; DLB 130
Hudson, Jeffrey
See Crichton, (John) Michael
Hudson, W(illiam) H(enry) 1841-1922T C L C
29
See also CA 115; DLB 98, 153, 174; SATA 35
Hueffer, Ford Madox
See Ford, Ford Madox
Hughart, Barry 1934- .... CLC 39
See also CA 137
Hughes, Colin
See Creasey, John
Hughes, David (John) 1930- .... CLC 48
See also CA 116; 129; DLB 14
Hughes, Edward James
See Hughes, Ted
See also DAM MST, POET
Hughes, (James) Langston 1902-1967CLC 1,
5, 10, 15, 35, 44, 108; BLC 2; DA; DAB;
DAC; DAM DRAM, MST, MULT, POET;
DC 3; PC 1; SSC 6; WLC
See also AAYA 12; BW 1; CA 1-4R; 25-28R;
CANR 1, 34; CDALB 1929-1941; CLR 17;
DLB 4, 7, 48, 51, 86; JRDA; MAICYA;
MTCW 1; SATA 4, 33
Hughes, Richard (Arthur Warren) 1900-1976
CLC 1, 11; DAM NOV
See also CA 5-8R; 65-68; CANR 4; DLB 15,
161; MTCW 1; SATA 8; SATA-Obit 25
Hughes, Ted 1930- CLC 2, 4, 9, 14, 37; DAB;
DAC; PC 7
See also Hughes, Edward James
See also CA 1-4R; CANR 1, 33, 66; CLR 3;
DLB 40, 161; MAICYA; MTCW 1; SATA
49; SATA-Brief 27
Hugo, Richard F(ranklin) 1923-1982 CLC 6,
18, 32; DAM POET
See also CA 49-52; 108; CANR 3; DLB 5
Hugo, Victor (Marie) 1802-1885NCLC 3, 10,
21; DA; DAB; DAC; DAM DRAM, MST,
NOV, POET; PC 17; WLC
See also DLB 119, 192; SATA 47
Huidobro, Vicente
See Huidobro Fernandez, Vicente Garcia
Huidobro Fernandez, Vicente Garcia 1893-
1948 .... TCLC 31
See also CA 131; HW
Hulme, Keri 1947- .... CLC 39
See also CA 125; CANR 69; INT 125
Hulme, T(homas) E(rnest) 1883-1917 T C L C
21
See also CA 117; DLB 19
Hume, David 1711-1776 .... LC 7
See also DLB 104
Humphrey, William 1924-1997 .... CLC 45
See also CA 77-80; 160; CANR 68; DLB 6
Humphreys, Emyr Owen 1919- .... CLC 47
See also CA 5-8R; CANR 3, 24; DLB 15
Humphreys, Josephine 1945- ..... CLC 34, 57
See also CA 121; 127; INT 127
Huneker, James Gibbons 1857-1921TCLC 65
See also DLB 71
Hungerford, Pixie
See Brinsmead, H(esba) F(ay)
Hunt, E(verette) Howard, (Jr.) 1918- CLC 3
See also AITN 1; CA 45-48; CANR 2, 47
Hunt, Kyle
See Creasey, John

Hunt, (James Henry) Leigh 1784-1859N C L C
70; DAM POET
See also DLB 96, 110, 144
Hunt, (James Henry) Leigh 1784-1859N C L C
1; DAM POET
Hunt, Marsha 1946- .... CLC 70
See also BW 2; CA 143
Hunt, Violet 1866(?)-1942 .... TCLC 53
See also DLB 162, 197
Hunter, E. Waldo
See Sturgeon, Theodore (Hamilton)
Hunter, Evan 1926-. CLC 11, 31; DAM POP
See also CA 5-8R; CANR 5, 38, 62; DLBY 82;
INT CANR-5; MTCW 1; SATA 25
Hunter, Kristin (Eggleston) 1931- .... CLC 35
See also AITN 1; BW 1; CA 13-16R; CANR
13; CLR 3; DLB 33; INT CANR-13;
MAICYA; SAAS 10; SATA 12
Hunter, Mollie 1922- .... CLC 21
See also McIlwraith, Maureen Mollie Hunter
See also AAYA 13; CANR 37; CLR 25; DLB
161; JRDA; MAICYA; SAAS 7; SATA 54
Hunter, Robert (?)-1734 .... LC 7
Hurston, Zora Neale 1903-1960CLC 7, 30, 61;
BLC 2; DA; DAC; DAM MST, MULT,
NOV; SSC 4; WLCS
See also AAYA 15; BW 1; CA 85-88; CANR
61; DLB 51, 86; MTCW 1
Huston, John (Marcellus) 1906-1987CLC 20
See also CA 73-76; 123; CANR 34; DLB 26
Hustvedt, Siri 1955- .... CLC 76
See also CA 137
Hutten, Ulrich von 1488-1523 .... LC 16
See also DLB 179
Huxley, Aldous (Leonard) 1894-1963 CLC 1,
3, 4, 5, 8, 11, 18, 35, 79; DA; DAB; DAC;
DAM MST, NOV; WLC
See also AAYA 11; CA 85-88; CANR 44;
CDBLB 1914-1945; DLB 36, 100, 162, 195;
MTCW 1; SATA 63
Huxley, T(homas) H(enry) 1825-1895 N C L C
67
See also DLB 57
Huysmans, Joris-Karl 1848-1907TCLC 7, 69
See also CA 104; 165; DLB 123
Hwang, David Henry 1957- ... CLC 55; DAM
DRAM; DC 4
See also CA 127; 132; INT 132
Hyde, Anthony 1946- .... CLC 42
See also CA 136
Hyde, Margaret O(ldroyd) 1917- ..... CLC 21
See also CA 1-4R; CANR 1, 36; CLR 23; JRDA;
MAICYA; SAAS 8; SATA 1, 42, 76
Hynes, James 1956(?)- .... CLC 65
See also CA 164
Ian, Janis 1951- .... CLC 21
See also CA 105
Ibanez, Vicente Blasco
See Blasco Ibanez, Vicente
Ibarguengoitia, Jorge 1928-1983 ..... CLC 37
See also CA 124; 113; HW
Ibsen, Henrik (Johan) 1828-1906 TCLC 2, 8,
16, 37, 52; DA; DAB; DAC; DAM DRAM,
MST; DC 2; WLC
See also CA 104; 141
Ibuse, Masuji 1898-1993 .... CLC 22
See also CA 127; 141; DLB 180
Ichikawa, Kon 1915- .... CLC 20
See also CA 121
Idle, Eric 1943- .... CLC 21
See also Monty Python
See also CA 116; CANR 35
Ignatow, David 1914-1997 .. CLC 4, 7, 14, 40
See also CA 9-12R; 162; CAAS 3; CANR 31,
57; DLB 5
Ihimaera, Witi 1944- .... CLC 46
See also CA 77-80

59; DLB 157

King, Francis (Henry) 1923-**CLC 8, 53; DAM NOV**
See also CA 1-4R; CANR 1, 33; DLB 15, 139; MTCW 1

King, Kennedy
See Brown, George Douglas

King, Martin Luther, Jr. 1929-1968 **CLC 83; BLC 2; DA; DAB; DAC; DAM MST, MULT; WLCS**
See also BW 2; CA 25-28; CANR 27, 44; CAP 2; MTCW 1; SATA 14

King, Stephen (Edwin) 1947-**CLC 12, 26, 37, 61, 113; DAM NOV, POP; SSC 17**
See also AAYA 1, 17; BEST 90:1; CA 61-64; CANR 1, 30, 52; DLB 143; DLBY 80; JRDA; MTCW 1; SATA 9, 55

King, Steve
See King, Stephen (Edwin)

King, Thomas 1943- ... **CLC 89; DAC; DAM MULT**
See also CA 144; DLB 175; NNAL; SATA 96

Kingman, Lee .... **CLC 17**
See also Natti, (Mary) Lee
See also SAAS 3; SATA 1, 67

Kingsley, Charles 1819-1875 .... **NCLC 35**
See also DLB 21, 32, 163, 190; YABC 2

Kingsley, Sidney 1906-1995 .... **CLC 44**
See also CA 85-88; 147; DLB 7

Kingsolver, Barbara 1955-**CLC 55, 81; DAM POP**
See also AAYA 15; CA 129; 134; CANR 60; INT 134

Kingston, Maxine (Ting Ting) Hong 1940-**CLC 12, 19, 58; DAM MULT, NOV; WLCS**
See also AAYA 8; CA 69-72; CANR 13, 38; DLB 173; DLBY 80; INT CANR-13; MTCW 1; SATA 53

Kinnell, Galway 1927- **CLC 1, 2, 3, 5, 13, 29**
See also CA 9-12R; CANR 10, 34, 66; DLB 5; DLBY 87; INT CANR-34; MTCW 1

Kinsella, Thomas 1928- .... **CLC 4, 19**
See also CA 17-20R; CANR 15; DLB 27; MTCW 1

Kinsella, W(illiam) P(atrick) 1935-**CLC 27, 43; DAC; DAM NOV, POP**
See also AAYA 7; CA 97-100; CAAS 7; CANR 21, 35, 66; INT CANR-21; MTCW 1

Kipling, (Joseph) Rudyard 1865-1936 **TCLC 8, 17; DA; DAB; DAC; DAM MST, POET; PC 3; SSC 5; WLC**
See also CA 105; 120; CANR 33; CDBLB 1890-1914; CLR 39; DLB 19, 34, 141, 156; MAICYA; MTCW 1; SATA 100; YABC 2

Kirkup, James 1918- .... **CLC 1**
See also CA 1-4R; CAAS 4; CANR 2; DLB 27; SATA 12

Kirkwood, James 1930(?)-1989 .... **CLC 9**
See also AITN 2; CA 1-4R; 128; CANR 6, 40

Kirshner, Sidney
See Kingsley, Sidney

Kis, Danilo 1935-1989 .... **CLC 57**
See also CA 109; 118; 129; CANR 61; DLB 181; MTCW 1

Kivi, Aleksis 1834-1872 .... **NCLC 30**

Kizer, Carolyn (Ashley) 1925-**CLC 15, 39, 80; DAM POET**
See also CA 65-68; CAAS 5; CANR 24, 70; DLB 5, 169

Klabund 1890-1928 .... **TCLC 44**
See also CA 162; DLB 66

Klappert, Peter 1942- .... **CLC 57**
See also CA 33-36R; DLB 5

Klein, A(braham) M(oses) 1909-1972 **CLC 19; DAB; DAC; DAM MST**
See also CA 101; 37-40R; DLB 68

Klein, Norma 1938-1989 .... **CLC 30**
See also AAYA 2; CA 41-44R; 128; CANR 15, 37; CLR 2, 19; INT CANR-15; JRDA; MAICYA; SAAS 1; SATA 7, 57

Klein, T(heodore) E(ibon) D(onald) 1947-**CLC 34**
See also CA 119; CANR 44

Kleist, Heinrich von 1777-1811 **NCLC 2, 37; DAM DRAM; SSC 22**
See also DLB 90

Klima, Ivan 1931- .... **CLC 56; DAM NOV**
See also CA 25-28R; CANR 17, 50

Klimentov, Andrei Platonovich 1899-1951
See Platonov, Andrei
See also CA 108

Klinger, Friedrich Maximilian von 1752-1831 **NCLC 1**
See also DLB 94

Klingsor the Magician
See Hartmann, Sadakichi

Klopstock, Friedrich Gottlieb 1724-1803 **NCLC 11**
See also DLB 97

Knapp, Caroline 1959- .... **CLC 99**
See also CA 154

Knebel, Fletcher 1911-1993 .... **CLC 14**
See also AITN 1; CA 1-4R; 140; CAAS 3; CANR 1, 36; SATA 36; SATA-Obit 75

Knickerbocker, Diedrich
See Irving, Washington

Knight, Etheridge 1931-1991 **CLC 40; BLC 2; DAM POET; PC 14**
See also BW 1; CA 21-24R; 133; CANR 23; DLB 41

Knight, Sarah Kemble 1666-1727 .... **LC 7**
See also DLB 24, 200

Knister, Raymond 1899-1932 .... **TCLC 56**
See also DLB 68

Knowles, John 1926- . **CLC 1, 4, 10, 26; DA; DAC; DAM MST, NOV**
See also AAYA 10; CA 17-20R; CANR 40; CDALB 1968-1988; DLB 6; MTCW 1; SATA 8, 89

Knox, Calvin M.
See Silverberg, Robert

Knox, John c. 1505-1572 .... **LC 37**
See also DLB 132

Knye, Cassandra
See Disch, Thomas M(ichael)

Koch, C(hristopher) J(ohn) 1932- .... **CLC 42**
See also CA 127

Koch, Christopher
See Koch, C(hristopher) J(ohn)

Koch, Kenneth 1925- ..... **CLC 5, 8, 44; DAM POET**
See also CA 1-4R; CANR 6, 36, 57; DLB 5; INT CANR-36; SATA 65

Kochanowski, Jan 1530-1584 .... **LC 10**

Kock, Charles Paul de 1794-1871 . **NCLC 16**

Koda Shigeyuki 1867-1947
See Rohan, Koda
See also CA 121

Koestler, Arthur 1905-1983 **CLC 1, 3, 6, 8, 15, 33**
See also CA 1-4R; 109; CANR 1, 33; CDBLB 1945-1960; DLBY 83; MTCW 1

Kogawa, Joy Nozomi 1935- .. **CLC 78; DAC; DAM MST, MULT**
See also CA 101; CANR 19, 62; SATA 99

Kohout, Pavel 1928- .... **CLC 13**
See also CA 45-48; CANR 3

Koizumi, Yakumo
See Hearn, (Patricio) Lafcadio (Tessima Carlos)

Kolmar, Gertrud 1894-1943 .... **TCLC 40**
See also CA 167

Komunyakaa, Yusef 1947-**CLC 86, 94; BLCS**
See also CA 147; DLB 120

Konrad, George
See Konrad, Gyoergy

Konrad, Gyoergy 1933- .... **CLC 4, 10, 73**
See also CA 85-88

Konwicki, Tadeusz 1926- .... **CLC 8, 28, 54**
See also CA 101; CAAS 9; CANR 39, 59; MTCW 1

Koontz, Dean R(ay) 1945- ..... **CLC 78; DAM NOV, POP**
See also AAYA 9; BEST 89:3, 90:2; CA 108; CANR 19, 36, 52; MTCW 1; SATA 92

Kopernik, Mikolaj
See Copernicus, Nicolaus

Kopit, Arthur (Lee) 1937-**CLC 1, 18, 33; DAM DRAM**
See also AITN 1; CA 81-84; CABS 3; DLB 7; MTCW 1

Kops, Bernard 1926- .... **CLC 4**
See also CA 5-8R; DLB 13

Kornbluth, C(yril) M. 1923-1958 .... **TCLC 8**
See also CA 105; 160; DLB 8

Korolenko, V. G.
See Korolenko, Vladimir Galaktionovich

Korolenko, Vladimir
See Korolenko, Vladimir Galaktionovich

Korolenko, Vladimir G.
See Korolenko, Vladimir Galaktionovich

Korolenko, Vladimir Galaktionovich 1853-1921 .... **TCLC 22**
See also CA 121

Korzybski, Alfred (Habdank Skarbek) 1879-1950 .... **TCLC 61**
See also CA 123; 160

Kosinski, Jerzy (Nikodem) 1933-1991 **CLC 1, 2, 3, 6, 10, 15, 53, 70; DAM NOV**
See also CA 17-20R; 134; CANR 9, 46; DLB 2; DLBY 82; MTCW 1

Kostelanetz, Richard (Cory) 1940- .. **CLC 28**
See also CA 13-16R; CAAS 8; CANR 38

Kostrowitzki, Wilhelm Apollinaris de 1880-1918
See Apollinaire, Guillaume
See also CA 104

Kotlowitz, Robert 1924- .... **CLC 4**
See also CA 33-36R; CANR 36

Kotzebue, August (Friedrich Ferdinand) von 1761-1819 .... **NCLC 25**
See also DLB 94

Kotzwinkle, William 1938- ..... **CLC 5, 14, 35**
See also CA 45-48; CANR 3, 44; CLR 6; DLB 173; MAICYA; SATA 24, 70

Kowna, Stancy
See Szymborska, Wislawa

Kozol, Jonathan 1936- .... **CLC 17**
See also CA 61-64; CANR 16, 45

Kozoll, Michael 1940(?)- .... **CLC 35**

Kramer, Kathryn 19(?)- .... **CLC 34**

Kramer, Larry 1935-**CLC 42; DAM POP; DC 8**
See also CA 124; 126; CANR 60

Krasicki, Ignacy 1735-1801 .... **NCLC 8**

Krasinski, Zygmunt 1812-1859 .... **NCLC 4**

Kraus, Karl 1874-1936 .... **TCLC 5**
See also CA 104; DLB 118

Kreve (Mickevicius), Vincas 1882-1954 **TCLC 27**

Kristeva, Julia 1941- .... **CLC 77**
See also CA 154

Kristofferson, Kris 1936- .... **CLC 26**
See also CA 104

Krizanc, John 1956- .... **CLC 57**

Krleza, Miroslav 1893-1981 .... **CLC 8, 114**
See also CA 97-100; 105; CANR 50; DLB 147

Kroetsch, Robert 1927-**CLC 5, 23, 57; DAC; DAM POET**
See also CA 17-20R; CANR 8, 38; DLB 53;

MTCW 1

Kroetz, Franz
See Kroetz, Franz Xaver

Kroetz, Franz Xaver 1946- .... **CLC 41**
See also CA 130

Kroker, Arthur (W.) 1945- .... **CLC 77**
See also CA 161

Kropotkin, Peter (Aleksieevich) 1842-1921
TCLC 36
See also CA 119

Krotkov, Yuri 1917- .... **CLC 19**
See also CA 102

Krumb
See Crumb, R(obert)

Krumgold, Joseph (Quincy) 1908-1980 **C L C
12**
See also CA 9-12R; 101; CANR 7; MAICYA;
SATA 1, 48; SATA-Obit 23

Krumwitz
See Crumb, R(obert)

Krutch, Joseph Wood 1893-1970 ...... **CLC 24**
See also CA 1-4R; 25-28R; CANR 4; DLB 63

Krutzch, Gus
See Eliot, T(homas) S(tearns)

Krylov, Ivan Andreevich 1768(?)-1844 **N C L C
1**
See also DLB 150

Kubin, Alfred (Leopold Isidor) 1877-1959
TCLC 23
See also CA 112; 149; DLB 81

Kubrick, Stanley 1928- .... **CLC 16**
See also CA 81-84; CANR 33; DLB 26

Kumin, Maxine (Winokur) 1925- **CLC 5, 13,
28; DAM POET; PC 15**
See also AITN 2; CA 1-4R; CAAS 8; CANR 1,
21, 69; DLB 5; MTCW 1; SATA 12

Kundera, Milan 1929- ... **CLC 4, 9, 19, 32, 68,
115; DAM NOV; SSC 24**
See also AAYA 2; CA 85-88; CANR 19, 52;
MTCW 1

Kunene, Mazisi (Raymond) 1930- .... **CLC 85**
See also BW 1; CA 125; DLB 117

Kunitz, Stanley (Jasspon) 1905- **CLC 6, 11, 14;
PC 19**
See also CA 41-44R; CANR 26, 57; DLB 48;
INT CANR-26; MTCW 1

Kunze, Reiner 1933- .... **CLC 10**
See also CA 93-96; DLB 75

Kuprin, Aleksandr Ivanovich 1870-1938
TCLC 5
See also CA 104

Kureishi, Hanif 1954(?)- .... **CLC 64**
See also CA 139; DLB 194

Kurosawa, Akira 1910- **CLC 16; DAM MULT**
See also AAYA 11; CA 101; CANR 46

Kushner, Tony 1957(?)- **CLC 81; DAM DRAM**
See also CA 144

Kuttner, Henry 1915-1958 .... **TCLC 10**
See also Vance, Jack
See also CA 107; 157; DLB 8

Kuzma, Greg 1944- .... **CLC 7**
See also CA 33-36R; CANR 70

Kuzmin, Mikhail 1872(?)-1936 ...... **TCLC 40**

Kyd, Thomas 1558-1594 **LC 22; DAM DRAM;
DC 3**
See also DLB 62

Kyprianos, Iossif
See Samarakis, Antonis

La Bruyere, Jean de 1645-1696 .... **LC 17**

Lacan, Jacques (Marie Emile) 1901-1981
CLC 75
See also CA 121; 104

Laclos, Pierre Ambroise Francois Choderlos de
1741-1803 .... **NCLC 4**

Lacolere, Francois
See Aragon, Louis

La Colere, Francois

See Aragon, Louis

La Deshabilleuse
See Simenon, Georges (Jacques Christian)

Lady Gregory
See Gregory, Isabella Augusta (Persse)

Lady of Quality, A
See Bagnold, Enid

**La Fayette, Marie (Madelaine Pioche de la
Vergne Comtes** 1634-1693 .... **LC 2**

Lafayette, Rene
See Hubbard, L(afayette) Ron(ald)

Laforgue, Jules 1860-1887 **NCLC 5, 53; PC 14;
SSC 20**

Lagerkvist, Paer (Fabian) 1891-1974 **CLC 7,
10, 13, 54; DAM DRAM, NOV**
See also Lagerkvist, Par
See also CA 85-88; 49-52; MTCW 1

Lagerkvist, Par .... **SSC 12**
See also Lagerkvist, Paer (Fabian)

Lagerloef, Selma (Ottiliana Lovisa) 1858-1940
TCLC 4, 36
See also Lagerlof, Selma (Ottiliana Lovisa)
See also CA 108; SATA 15

Lagerlof, Selma (Ottiliana Lovisa)
See Lagerloef, Selma (Ottiliana Lovisa)
See also CLR 7; SATA 15

La Guma, (Justin) Alex(ander) 1925-1985
CLC 19; BLCS; DAM NOV
See also BW 1; CA 49-52; 118; CANR 25; DLB
117; MTCW 1

Laidlaw, A. K.
See Grieve, C(hristopher) M(urray)

Lainez, Manuel Mujica
See Mujica Lainez, Manuel
See also HW

Laing, R(onald) D(avid) 1927-1989 . **CLC 95**
See also CA 107; 129; CANR 34; MTCW 1

Lamartine, Alphonse (Marie Louis Prat) de
1790-1869 ....
NCLC 11; DAM POET; PC 16

Lamb, Charles 1775-1834 ..... **NCLC 10; DA;
DAB; DAC; DAM MST; WLC**
See also CDBLB 1789-1832; DLB 93, 107, 163;
SATA 17

Lamb, Lady Caroline 1785-1828 ... **NCLC 38**
See also DLB 116

Lamming, George (William) 1927- **CLC 2, 4,
66; BLC 2; DAM MULT**
See also BW 2; CA 85-88; CANR 26; DLB 125;
MTCW 1

L'Amour, Louis (Dearborn) 1908-1988 **C L C
25, 55; DAM NOV, POP**
See also AAYA 16; AITN 2; BEST 89:2; CA 1-
4R; 125; CANR 3, 25, 40; DLBY 80; MTCW
1

Lampedusa, Giuseppe (Tomasi) di 1896-1957
TCLC 13
See also Tomasi di Lampedusa, Giuseppe
See also CA 164; DLB 177

Lampman, Archibald 1861-1899 ... **NCLC 25**
See also DLB 92

Lancaster, Bruce 1896-1963 .... **CLC 36**
See also CA 9-10; CANR 70; CAP 1; SATA 9

Lanchester, John .... **CLC 99**

Landau, Mark Alexandrovich
See Aldanov, Mark (Alexandrovich)

Landau-Aldanov, Mark Alexandrovich
See Aldanov, Mark (Alexandrovich)

Landis, Jerry
See Simon, Paul (Frederick)

Landis, John 1950- .... **CLC 26**
See also CA 112; 122

Landolfi, Tommaso 1908-1979 .... **CLC 11, 49**
See also CA 127; 117; DLB 177

Landon, Letitia Elizabeth 1802-1838 **N C L C
15**
See also DLB 96

Landor, Walter Savage 1775-1864 **NCLC 14**
See also DLB 93, 107

Landwirth, Heinz 1927-
See Lind, Jakov
See also CA 9-12R; CANR 7

Lane, Patrick 1939- ... **CLC 25; DAM POET**
See also CA 97-100; CANR 54; DLB 53; INT
97-100

Lang, Andrew 1844-1912 .... **TCLC 16**
See also CA 114; 137; DLB 98, 141, 184;
MAICYA; SATA 16

Lang, Fritz 1890-1976 .... **CLC 20, 103**
See also CA 77-80; 69-72; CANR 30

Lange, John
See Crichton, (John) Michael

Langer, Elinor 1939- .... **CLC 34**
See also CA 121

Langland, William 1330(?)-1400(?) ... **LC 19;
DA; DAB; DAC; DAM MST, POET**
See also DLB 146

Langstaff, Launcelot
See Irving, Washington

Lanier, Sidney 1842-1881 ..... **NCLC 6; DAM
POET**
See also DLB 64; DLBD 13; MAICYA; SATA
18

Lanyer, Aemilia 1569-1645 .... **LC 10, 30**
See also DLB 121

Lao-Tzu
See Lao Tzu

Lao Tzu fl. 6th cent. B.C.- .... **CMLC 7**

Lapine, James (Elliot) 1949- .... **CLC 39**
See also CA 123; 130; CANR 54; INT 130

Larbaud, Valery (Nicolas) 1881-1957 **TCLC 9**
See also CA 106; 152

Lardner, Ring
See Lardner, Ring(gold) W(ilmer)

Lardner, Ring W., Jr.
See Lardner, Ring(gold) W(ilmer)

Lardner, Ring(gold) W(ilmer) 1885-1933
TCLC 2, 14; SSC 32
See also CA 104; 131; CDALB 1917-1929;
DLB 11, 25, 86; DLBD 16; MTCW 1

Laredo, Betty
See Codrescu, Andrei

Larkin, Maia
See Wojciechowska, Maia (Teresa)

Larkin, Philip (Arthur) 1922-1985 **CLC 3, 5, 8,
9, 13, 18, 33, 39, 64; DAB; DAM MST,
POET; PC 21**
See also CA 5-8R; 117; CANR 24, 62; CDBLB
1960 to Present; DLB 27; MTCW 1

Larra (y Sanchez de Castro), Mariano Jose de
1809-1837 .... **NCLC 17**

Larsen, Eric 1941- .... **CLC 55**
See also CA 132

Larsen, Nella 1891-1964 .... **CLC 37; BLC 2;
DAM MULT**
See also BW 1; CA 125; DLB 51

Larson, Charles R(aymond) 1938- ... **CLC 31**
See also CA 53-56; CANR 4

Larson, Jonathan 1961-1996 .... **CLC 99**
See also CA 156

Las Casas, Bartolome de 1474-1566 ... **LC 31**

Lasch, Christopher 1932-1994 .... **CLC 102**
See also CA 73-76; 144; CANR 25; MTCW 1

Lasker-Schueler, Else 1869-1945 ... **TCLC 57**
See also DLB 66, 124

Laski, Harold 1893-1950 .... **TCLC 79**

Latham, Jean Lee 1902-1995 .... **CLC 12**
See also AITN 1; CA 5-8R; CANR 7; CLR 50;
MAICYA; SATA 2, 68

Latham, Mavis
See Clark, Mavis Thorpe

Lathen, Emma .... **CLC 2**
See also Hennissart, Martha; Latsis, Mary J(ane)

Lathrop, Francis

See Leiber, Fritz (Reuter, Jr.)
Latsis, Mary J(ane) 1927(?)-1997
See Lathen, Emma
See also CA 85-88; 162
Lattimore, Richmond (Alexander) 1906-1984
CLC 3
See also CA 1-4R; 112; CANR 1
Laughlin, James 1914-1997 .... **CLC 49**
See also CA 21-24R; 162; CAAS 22; CANR 9,
47; DLB 48; DLBY 96, 97
Laurence, (Jean) Margaret (Wemyss) 1926-
1987 .. **CLC 3, 6, 13, 50, 62; DAC; DAM
MST; SSC 7**
See also CA 5-8R; 121; CANR 33; DLB 53;
MTCW 1; SATA-Obit 50
Laurent, Antoine 1952- .... **CLC 50**
Lauscher, Hermann
See Hesse, Hermann
Lautreamont, Comte de 1846-1870 **NCLC 12;
SSC 14**
Laverty, Donald
See Blish, James (Benjamin)
Lavin, Mary 1912-1996 **CLC 4, 18, 99; SSC 4**
See also CA 9-12R; 151; CANR 33; DLB 15;
MTCW 1
Lavond, Paul Dennis
See Kornbluth, C(yril) M.; Pohl, Frederik
Lawler, Raymond Evenor 1922- .... **CLC 58**
See also CA 103
Lawrence, D(avid) H(erbert Richards) 1885-
1930 **TCLC 2, 9, 16, 33, 48, 61; DA; DAB;
DAC; DAM MST, NOV, POET; SSC 4, 19;
WLC**
See also CA 104; 121; CDBLB 1914-1945;
DLB 10, 19, 36, 98, 162, 195; MTCW 1
Lawrence, T(homas) E(dward) 1888-1935
TCLC 18
See also Dale, Colin
See also CA 115; 167; DLB 195
Lawrence of Arabia
See Lawrence, T(homas) E(dward)
Lawson, Henry (Archibald Hertzberg) 1867-
1922 .... **TCLC 27; SSC 18**
See also CA 120
Lawton, Dennis
See Faust, Frederick (Schiller)
Laxness, Halldor .... **CLC 25**
See also Gudjonsson, Halldor Kiljan
Layamon fl. c. 1200- .... **CMLC 10**
See also DLB 146
Laye, Camara 1928-1980 **CLC 4, 38; BLC 2;
DAM MULT**
See also BW 1; CA 85-88; 97-100; CANR 25;
MTCW 1
Layton, Irving (Peter) 1912- **CLC 2, 15; DAC;
DAM MST, POET**
See also CA 1-4R; CANR 2, 33, 43, 66; DLB
88; MTCW 1
Lazarus, Emma 1849-1887 .... **NCLC 8**
Lazarus, Felix
See Cable, George Washington
Lazarus, Henry
See Slavitt, David R(ytman)
Lea, Joan
See Neufeld, John (Arthur)
Leacock, Stephen (Butler) 1869-1944 **TCLC 2;
DAC; DAM MST**
See also CA 104; 141; DLB 92
Lear, Edward 1812-1888 .... **NCLC 3**
See also CLR 1; DLB 32, 163, 166; MAICYA;
SATA 18, 100
Lear, Norman (Milton) 1922- .... **CLC 12**
See also CA 73-76
Leautaud, Paul 1872-1956 .... **TCLC 83**
See also DLB 65
Leavis, F(rank) R(aymond) 1895-1978 **CLC 24**
See also CA 21-24R; 77-80; CANR 44; MTCW

1
Leavitt, David 1961- ..... **CLC 34; DAM POP**
See also CA 116; 122; CANR 50, 62; DLB 130;
INT 122
Leblanc, Maurice (Marie Emile) 1864-1941
TCLC 49
See also CA 110
Lebowitz, Fran(ces Ann) 1951(?)- **CLC 11, 36**
See also CA 81-84; CANR 14, 60, 70; INT
CANR-14; MTCW 1
Lebrecht, Peter
See Tieck, (Johann) Ludwig
le Carre, John .... **CLC 3, 5, 9, 15, 28**
See also Cornwell, David (John Moore)
See also BEST 89:4; CDBLB 1960 to Present;
DLB 87
Le Clezio, J(ean) M(arie) G(ustave) 1940-
CLC 31
See also CA 116; 128; DLB 83
Leconte de Lisle, Charles-Marie-Rene 1818-
1894 .... **NCLC 29**
Le Coq, Monsieur
See Simenon, Georges (Jacques Christian)
Leduc, Violette 1907-1972 .... **CLC 22**
See also CA 13-14; 33-36R; CANR 69; CAP 1
Ledwidge, Francis 1887(?)-1917 .... **TCLC 23**
See also CA 123; DLB 20
Lee, Andrea 1953- .... **CLC 36; BLC 2; DAM
MULT**
See also BW 1; CA 125
Lee, Andrew
See Auchincloss, Louis (Stanton)
Lee, Chang-rae 1965- .... **CLC 91**
See also CA 148
Lee, Don L. .... **CLC 2**
See also Madhubuti, Haki R.
Lee, George W(ashington) 1894-1976 **CLC 52;
BLC 2; DAM MULT**
See also BW 1; CA 125; DLB 51
Lee, (Nelle) Harper 1926- .. **CLC 12, 60; DA;
DAB; DAC; DAM MST, NOV; WLC**
See also AAYA 13; CA 13-16R; CANR 51;
CDALB 1941-1968; DLB 6; MTCW 1;
SATA 11
Lee, Helen Elaine 1959(?)- .... **CLC 86**
See also CA 148
Lee, Julian
See Latham, Jean Lee
Lee, Larry
See Lee, Lawrence
Lee, Laurie 1914-1997 **CLC 90; DAB; DAM
POP**
See also CA 77-80; 158; CANR 33; DLB 27;
MTCW 1
Lee, Lawrence 1941-1990 .... **CLC 34**
See also CA 131; CANR 43
Lee, Li-Young 1957- .... **PC 24**
See also CA 153; DLB 165
Lee, Manfred B(ennington) 1905-1971 **CLC 11**
See also Queen, Ellery
See also CA 1-4R; 29-32R; CANR 2; DLB 137
Lee, Shelton Jackson 1957(?)- .... **CLC 105;
BLCS; DAM MULT**
See also Lee, Spike
See also BW 2; CA 125; CANR 42
Lee, Spike
See Lee, Shelton Jackson
See also AAYA 4
Lee, Stan 1922- .... **CLC 17**
See also AAYA 5; CA 108; 111; INT 111
Lee, Tanith 1947- .... **CLC 46**
See also AAYA 15; CA 37-40R; CANR 53;
SATA 8, 88
Lee, Vernon .... **TCLC 5**
See also Paget, Violet
See also DLB 57, 153, 156, 174, 178
Lee, William

See Burroughs, William S(eward)
Lee, Willy
See Burroughs, William S(eward)
Lee-Hamilton, Eugene (Jacob) 1845-1907
TCLC 22
See also CA 117
Leet, Judith 1935- .... **CLC 11**
Le Fanu, Joseph Sheridan 1814-1873 **NCLC 9,
58; DAM POP; SSC 14**
See also DLB 21, 70, 159, 178
Leffland, Ella 1931- .... **CLC 19**
See also CA 29-32R; CANR 35; DLBY 84; INT
CANR-35; SATA 65
Leger, Alexis
See Leger, (Marie-Rene Auguste) Alexis Saint-
Leger
**Leger, (Marie-Rene Auguste) Alexis Saint-
Leger** 1887-1975 . **CLC 4, 11, 46; DAM
POET; PC 23**
See also CA 13-16R; 61-64; CANR 43; MTCW
1
Leger, Saintleger
See Leger, (Marie-Rene Auguste) Alexis Saint-
Leger
Le Guin, Ursula K(roeber) 1929- **CLC 8, 13,
22, 45, 71; DAB; DAC; DAM MST, POP;
SSC 12**
See also AAYA 9, 27; AITN 1; CA 21-24R;
CANR 9, 32, 52; CDALB 1968-1988; CLR
3, 28; DLB 8, 52; INT CANR-32; JRDA;
MAICYA; MTCW 1; SATA 4, 52, 99
Lehmann, Rosamond (Nina) 1901-1990 **CLC 5**
See also CA 77-80; 131; CANR 8; DLB 15
Leiber, Fritz (Reuter, Jr.) 1910-1992 **CLC 25**
See also CA 45-48; 139; CANR 2, 40; DLB 8;
MTCW 1; SATA 45; SATA-Obit 73
Leibniz, Gottfried Wilhelm von 1646-1716 **LC
35**
See also DLB 168
Leimbach, Martha 1963-
See Leimbach, Marti
See also CA 130
Leimbach, Marti .... **CLC 65**
See also Leimbach, Martha
Leino, Eino .... **TCLC 24**
See also Loennbohm, Armas Eino Leopold
Leiris, Michel (Julien) 1901-1990 ..... **CLC 61**
See also CA 119; 128; 132
Leithauser, Brad 1953- .... **CLC 27**
See also CA 107; CANR 27; DLB 120
Lelchuk, Alan 1938- .... **CLC 5**
See also CA 45-48; CAAS 20; CANR 1, 70
Lem, Stanislaw 1921- .... **CLC 8, 15, 40**
See also CA 105; CAAS 1; CANR 32; MTCW
1
Lemann, Nancy 1956- .... **CLC 39**
See also CA 118; 136
Lemonnier, (Antoine Louis) Camille 1844-1913
TCLC 22
See also CA 121
Lenau, Nikolaus 1802-1850 .... **NCLC 16**
L'Engle, Madeleine (Camp Franklin) 1918-
CLC 12; DAM POP
See also AAYA 1; AITN 2; CA 1-4R; CANR 3,
21, 39, 66; CLR 1, 14; DLB 52; JRDA;
MAICYA; MTCW 1; SAAS 15; SATA 1, 27,
75
Lengyel, Jozsef 1896-1975 .... **CLC 7**
See also CA 85-88; 57-60; CANR 71
Lenin 1870-1924
See Lenin, V. I.
See also CA 121; 168
Lenin, V. I. .... **TCLC 67**
See also Lenin
Lennon, John (Ono) 1940-1980 . **CLC 12, 35**
See also CA 102
Lennox, Charlotte Ramsay 1729(?)-1804

NCLC 23
See also DLB 39

Lentricchia, Frank (Jr.) 1940- .... **CLC 34**
See also CA 25-28R; CANR 19

Lenz, Siegfried 1926- .... **CLC 27**
See also CA 89-92; DLB 75

Leonard, Elmore (John, Jr.) 1925-**CLC 28, 34, 71; DAM POP**
See also AAYA 22; AITN 1; BEST 89:1, 90:4; CA 81-84; CANR 12, 28, 53; DLB 173; INT CANR-28; MTCW 1

Leonard, Hugh .... **CLC 19**
See also Byrne, John Keyes
See also DLB 13

Leonov, Leonid (Maximovich) 1899-1994 **CLC 92; DAM NOV**
See also CA 129; MTCW 1

Leopardi, (Conte) Giacomo 1798-1837**NCLC 22**

Le Reveler
See Artaud, Antonin (Marie Joseph)

Lerman, Eleanor 1952- .... **CLC 9**
See also CA 85-88; CANR 69

Lerman, Rhoda 1936- .... **CLC 56**
See also CA 49-52; CANR 70

Lermontov, Mikhail Yuryevich 1814-1841 **NCLC 47; PC 18**

Leroux, Gaston 1868-1927 .... **TCLC 25**
See also CA 108; 136; CANR 69; SATA 65

Lesage, Alain-Rene 1668-1747 .... **LC 28**

Leskov, Nikolai (Semyonovich) 1831-1895 **NCLC 25**

Lessing, Doris (May) 1919-**CLC 1, 2, 3, 6, 10, 15, 22, 40, 94; DA; DAB; DAC; DAM MST, NOV; SSC 6; WLCS**
See also CA 9-12R; CAAS 14; CANR 33, 54; CDBLB 1960 to Present; DLB 15, 139; DLBY 85; MTCW 1

Lessing, Gotthold Ephraim 1729-1781 . **LC 8**
See also DLB 97

Lester, Richard 1932- .... **CLC 20**

Lever, Charles (James) 1806-1872 **NCLC 23**
See also DLB 21

Leverson, Ada 1865(?)-1936(?) ...... **TCLC 18**
See also Elaine
See also CA 117; DLB 153

Levertov, Denise 1923-1997**CLC 1, 2, 3, 5, 8, 15, 28, 66; DAM POET; PC 11**
See also CA 1-4R; 163; CAAS 19; CANR 3, 29, 50; DLB 5, 165; INT CANR-29; MTCW 1

Levi, Jonathan .... **CLC 76**

Levi, Peter (Chad Tigar) 1931- .... **CLC 41**
See also CA 5-8R; CANR 34; DLB 40

Levi, Primo 1919-1987 . **CLC 37, 50; SSC 12**
See also CA 13-16R; 122; CANR 12, 33, 61, 70; DLB 177; MTCW 1

Levin, Ira 1929- .... **CLC 3, 6; DAM POP**
See also CA 21-24R; CANR 17, 44; MTCW 1; SATA 66

Levin, Meyer 1905-1981 . **CLC 7; DAM POP**
See also AITN 1; CA 9-12R; 104; CANR 15; DLB 9, 28; DLBY 81; SATA 21; SATA-Obit 27

Levine, Norman 1924- .... **CLC 54**
See also CA 73-76; CAAS 23; CANR 14, 70; DLB 88

Levine, Philip 1928-... **CLC 2, 4, 5, 9, 14, 33; DAM POET; PC 22**
See also CA 9-12R; CANR 9, 37, 52; DLB 5

Levinson, Deirdre 1931- .... **CLC 49**
See also CA 73-76; CANR 70

Levi-Strauss, Claude 1908- .... **CLC 38**
See also CA 1-4R; CANR 6, 32, 57; MTCW 1

Levitin, Sonia (Wolff) 1934- .... **CLC 17**
See also AAYA 13; CA 29-32R; CANR 14, 32; CLR 53; JRDA; MAICYA; SAAS 2; SATA

4, 68

Levon, O. U.
See Kesey, Ken (Elton)

Levy, Amy 1861-1889 .... **NCLC 59**
See also DLB 156

Lewes, George Henry 1817-1878 ... **NCLC 25**
See also DLB 55, 144

Lewis, Alun 1915-1944 .... **TCLC 3**
See also CA 104; DLB 20, 162

Lewis, C. Day
See Day Lewis, C(ecil)

Lewis, C(live) S(taples) 1898-1963**CLC 1, 3, 6, 14, 27; DA; DAB; DAC; DAM MST, NOV, POP; WLC**
See also AAYA 3; CA 81-84; CANR 33, 71; CDBLB 1945-1960; CLR 3, 27; DLB 15, 100, 160; JRDA; MAICYA; MTCW 1; SATA 13, 100

Lewis, Janet 1899- .... **CLC 41**
See also Winters, Janet Lewis
See also CA 9-12R; CANR 29, 63; CAP 1; DLBY 87

Lewis, Matthew Gregory 1775-1818**NCLC 11, 62**
See also DLB 39, 158, 178

Lewis, (Harry) Sinclair 1885-1951. **TCLC 4, 13, 23, 39; DA; DAB; DAC; DAM MST, NOV; WLC**
See also CA 104; 133; CDALB 1917-1929; DLB 9, 102; DLBD 1; MTCW 1

Lewis, (Percy) Wyndham 1882(?)-1957**TCLC 2, 9**
See also CA 104; 157; DLB 15

Lewisohn, Ludwig 1883-1955 .... **TCLC 19**
See also CA 107; DLB 4, 9, 28, 102

Lewton, Val 1904-1951 .... **TCLC 76**

Leyner, Mark 1956- .... **CLC 92**
See also CA 110; CANR 28, 53

Lezama Lima, Jose 1910-1976**CLC 4, 10, 101; DAM MULT**
See also CA 77-80; CANR 71; DLB 113; HW

L'Heureux, John (Clarke) 1934- .... **CLC 52**
See also CA 13-16R; CANR 23, 45

Liddell, C. H.
See Kuttner, Henry

Lie, Jonas (Lauritz Idemil) 1833-1908(?) **TCLC 5**
See also CA 115

Lieber, Joel 1937-1971 .... **CLC 6**
See also CA 73-76; 29-32R

Lieber, Stanley Martin
See Lee, Stan

Lieberman, Laurence (James) 1935- **CLC 4, 36**
See also CA 17-20R; CANR 8, 36

Lieh Tzu fl. 7th cent. B.C.-5th cent. B.C. **CMLC 27**

Lieksman, Anders
See Haavikko, Paavo Juhani

Li Fei-kan 1904-
See Pa Chin
See also CA 105

Lifton, Robert Jay 1926- .... **CLC 67**
See also CA 17-20R; CANR 27; INT CANR-27; SATA 66

Lightfoot, Gordon 1938- .... **CLC 26**
See also CA 109

Lightman, Alan P(aige) 1948- .... **CLC 81**
See also CA 141; CANR 63

Ligotti, Thomas (Robert) 1953-**CLC 44; SSC 16**
See also CA 123; CANR 49

Li Ho 791-817 .... **PC 13**

Liliencron, (Friedrich Adolf Axel) Detlev von 1844-1909 .... **TCLC 18**
See also CA 117

Lilly, William 1602-1681 .... **LC 27**

Lima, Jose Lezama
See Lezama Lima, Jose

Lima Barreto, Afonso Henrique de 1881-1922 **TCLC 23**
See also CA 117

Limonov, Edward 1944- .... **CLC 67**
See also CA 137

Lin, Frank
See Atherton, Gertrude (Franklin Horn)

Lincoln, Abraham 1809-1865 .... **NCLC 18**

Lind, Jakov .... **CLC 1, 2, 4, 27, 82**
See also Landwirth, Heinz
See also CAAS 4

Lindbergh, Anne (Spencer) Morrow 1906- **CLC 82; DAM NOV**
See also CA 17-20R; CANR 16; MTCW 1; SATA 33

Lindsay, David 1878-1945 .... **TCLC 15**
See also CA 113

Lindsay, (Nicholas) Vachel 1879-1931 **TCLC 17; DA; DAC; DAM MST, POET; PC 23; WLC**
See also CA 114; 135; CDALB 1865-1917; DLB 54; SATA 40

Linke-Poot
See Doeblin, Alfred

Linney, Romulus 1930- .... **CLC 51**
See also CA 1-4R; CANR 40, 44

Linton, Eliza Lynn 1822-1898........ **NCLC 41**
See also DLB 18

Li Po 701-763 .... **CMLC 2**

Lipsius, Justus 1547-1606 .... **LC 16**

Lipsyte, Robert (Michael) 1938-**CLC 21; DA; DAC; DAM MST, NOV**
See also AAYA 7; CA 17-20R; CANR 8, 57; CLR 23; JRDA; MAICYA; SATA 5, 68

Lish, Gordon (Jay) 1934- ... **CLC 45; SSC 18**
See also CA 113; 117; DLB 130; INT 117

Lispector, Clarice 1925(?)-1977 .... **CLC 43**
See also CA 139; 116; CANR 71; DLB 113

Littell, Robert 1935(?)- .... **CLC 42**
See also CA 109; 112; CANR 64

Little, Malcolm 1925-1965
See Malcolm X
See also BW 1; CA 125; 111; DA; DAB; DAC; DAM MST, MULT; MTCW 1

Littlewit, Humphrey Gent.
See Lovecraft, H(oward) P(hillips)

Litwos
See Sienkiewicz, Henryk (Adam Alexander Pius)

Liu, E 1857-1909 .... **TCLC 15**
See also CA 115

Lively, Penelope (Margaret) 1933-...**CLC 32, 50; DAM NOV**
See also CA 41-44R; CANR 29, 67; CLR 7; DLB 14, 161; JRDA; MAICYA; MTCW 1; SATA 7, 60, 101

Livesay, Dorothy (Kathleen) 1909-**CLC 4, 15, 79; DAC; DAM MST, POET**
See also AITN 2; CA 25-28R; CAAS 8; CANR 36, 67; DLB 68; MTCW 1

Livy c. 59B.C.-c. 17 .... **CMLC 11**

Lizardi, Jose Joaquin Fernandez de 1776-1827 **NCLC 30**

Llewellyn, Richard
See Llewellyn Lloyd, Richard Dafydd Vivian
See also DLB 15

Llewellyn Lloyd, Richard Dafydd Vivian 1906-1983..

CLC 7, 80
See also Llewellyn, Richard
See also CA 53-56; 111; CANR 7, 71; SATA 11; SATA-Obit 37

Llosa, (Jorge) Mario (Pedro) Vargas
See Vargas Llosa, (Jorge) Mario (Pedro)

Lloyd, Manda

See Heinlein, Robert A(nson)

Macdonald, Cynthia 1928- .... **CLC 13, 19**
See also CA 49-52; CANR 4, 44; DLB 105

MacDonald, George 1824-1905 .... **TCLC 9**
See also CA 106; 137; DLB 18, 163, 178;
MAICYA; SATA 33, 100

Macdonald, John
See Millar, Kenneth

MacDonald, John D(ann) 1916-1986 **CLC 3, 27, 44; DAM NOV, POP**
See also CA 1-4R; 121; CANR 1, 19, 60; DLB
8; DLBY 86; MTCW 1

Macdonald, John Ross
See Millar, Kenneth

Macdonald, Ross .... **CLC 1, 2, 3, 14, 34, 41**
See also Millar, Kenneth
See also DLBD 6

MacDougal, John
See Blish, James (Benjamin)

MacEwen, Gwendolyn (Margaret) 1941-1987
CLC 13, 55
See also CA 9-12R; 124; CANR 7, 22; DLB
53; SATA 50; SATA-Obit 55

Macha, Karel Hynek 1810-1846 .... **NCLC 46**

Machado (y Ruiz), Antonio 1875-1939 **T C L C 3**
See also CA 104; DLB 108

Machado de Assis, Joaquim Maria 1839-1908
TCLC 10; BLC 2; SSC 24
See also CA 107; 153

Machen, Arthur .... **TCLC 4; SSC 20**
See also Jones, Arthur Llewellyn
See also DLB 36, 156, 178

Machiavelli, Niccolo 1469-1527 **LC 8, 36; DA; DAB; DAC; DAM MST; WLCS**

MacInnes, Colin 1914-1976 .... **CLC 4, 23**
See also CA 69-72; 65-68; CANR 21; DLB 14;
MTCW 1

MacInnes, Helen (Clark) 1907-1985 **CLC 27, 39; DAM POP**
See also CA 1-4R; 117; CANR 1, 28, 58; DLB
87; MTCW 1; SATA 22; SATA-Obit 44

Mackay, Mary 1855-1924
See Corelli, Marie
See also CA 118

Mackenzie, Compton (Edward Montague)
1883-1972 .... **CLC 18**
See also CA 21-22; 37-40R; CAP 2; DLB 34,
100

Mackenzie, Henry 1745-1831 .... **NCLC 41**
See also DLB 39

Mackintosh, Elizabeth 1896(?)-1952
See Tey, Josephine
See also CA 110

MacLaren, James
See Grieve, C(hristopher) M(urray)

Mac Laverty, Bernard 1942- .... **CLC 31**
See also CA 116; 118; CANR 43; INT 118

MacLean, Alistair (Stuart) 1922(?)-1987 **C L C 3, 13, 50, 63; DAM POP**
See also CA 57-60; 121; CANR 28, 61; MTCW
1; SATA 23; SATA-Obit 50

Maclean, Norman (Fitzroy) 1902-1990 **C L C 78; DAM POP; SSC 13**
See also CA 102; 132; CANR 49

MacLeish, Archibald 1892-1982 **CLC 3, 8, 14, 68; DAM POET**
See also CA 9-12R; 106; CANR 33, 63; DLB
4, 7, 45; DLBY 82; MTCW 1

MacLennan, (John) Hugh 1907-1990 **CLC 2, 14, 92; DAC; DAM MST**
See also CA 5-8R; 142; CANR 33; DLB 68;
MTCW 1

MacLeod, Alistair 1936- **CLC 56; DAC; DAM MST**
See also CA 123; DLB 60

Macleod, Fiona

See Sharp, William

MacNeice, (Frederick) Louis 1907-1963 **C L C 1, 4, 10, 53; DAB; DAM POET**
See also CA 85-88; CANR 61; DLB 10, 20;
MTCW 1

MacNeill, Dand
See Fraser, George MacDonald

Macpherson, James 1736-1796 .... **LC 29**
See also Ossian
See also DLB 109

Macpherson, (Jean) Jay 1931- .... **CLC 14**
See also CA 5-8R; DLB 53

MacShane, Frank 1927- .... **CLC 39**
See also CA 9-12R; CANR 3, 33; DLB 111

Macumber, Mari
See Sandoz, Mari(e Susette)

Madach, Imre 1823-1864 .... **NCLC 19**

Madden, (Jerry) David 1933- .... **CLC 5, 15**
See also CA 1-4R; CAAS 3; CANR 4, 45; DLB
6; MTCW 1

Maddern, Al(an)
See Ellison, Harlan (Jay)

Madhubuti, Haki R. 1942- **CLC 6, 73; BLC 2; DAM MULT, POET; PC 5**
See also Lee, Don L.
See also BW 2; CA 73-76; CANR 24, 51; DLB
5, 41; DLBD 8

Maepenn, Hugh
See Kuttner, Henry

Maepenn, K. H.
See Kuttner, Henry

Maeterlinck, Maurice 1862-1949 ... **TCLC 3; DAM DRAM**
See also CA 104; 136; DLB 192; SATA 66

Maginn, William 1794-1842 .... **NCLC 8**
See also DLB 110, 159

Mahapatra, Jayanta 1928- .... **CLC 33; DAM MULT**
See also CA 73-76; CAAS 9; CANR 15, 33, 66

Mahfouz, Naguib (Abdel Aziz Al-Sabilgi)
1911(?)-
See Mahfuz, Najib
See also BEST 89:2; CA 128; CANR 55; DAM
NOV; MTCW 1

Mahfuz, Najib .... **CLC 52, 55**
See also Mahfouz, Naguib (Abdel Aziz Al-
Sabilgi)
See also DLBY 88

Mahon, Derek 1941- .... **CLC 27**
See also CA 113; 128; DLB 40

Mailer, Norman 1923- **CLC 1, 2, 3, 4, 5, 8, 11, 14, 28, 39, 74, 111; DA; DAB; DAC; DAM MST, NOV, POP**
See also AITN 2; CA 9-12R; CABS 1; CANR
28; CDALB 1968-1988; DLB 2, 16, 28, 185;
DLBD 3; DLBY 80, 83; MTCW 1

Maillet, Antonine 1929- .... **CLC 54; DAC**
See also CA 115; 120; CANR 46; DLB 60; INT
120

Mais, Roger 1905-1955 .... **TCLC 8**
See also BW 1; CA 105; 124; DLB 125; MTCW
1 .

Maistre, Joseph de 1753-1821 .... **NCLC 37**

Maitland, Frederic 1850-1906 .... **TCLC 65**

Maitland, Sara (Louise) 1950- .... **CLC 49**
See also CA 69-72; CANR 13, 59

Major, Clarence 1936- **CLC 3, 19, 48; BLC 2; DAM MULT**
See also BW 2; CA 21-24R; CAAS 6; CANR
13, 25, 53; DLB 33

Major, Kevin (Gerald) 1949- .. **CLC 26; DAC**
See also AAYA 16; CA 97-100; CANR 21, 38;
CLR 11; DLB 60; INT CANR-21; JRDA;
MAICYA; SATA 32, 82

Maki, James
See Ozu, Yasujiro

Malabaila, Damiano

See Levi, Primo

Malamud, Bernard 1914-1986 **CLC 1, 2, 3, 5, 8, 9, 11, 18, 27, 44, 78, 85; DA; DAB; DAC; DAM MST, NOV, POP; SSC 15; WLC**
See also AAYA 16; CA 5-8R; 118; CABS 1;
CANR 28, 62; CDALB 1941-1968; DLB 2,
28, 152; DLBY 80, 86; MTCW 1

Malan, Herman
See Bosman, Herman Charles; Bosman, Herman
Charles

Malaparte, Curzio 1898-1957 .... **TCLC 52**

Malcolm, Dan
See Silverberg, Robert

Malcolm X .... **CLC 82; BLC 2; WLCS**
See also Little, Malcolm

Malherbe, Francois de 1555-1628 .... **LC 5**

Mallarme, Stephane 1842-1898 **NCLC 4, 41; DAM POET; PC 4**

Mallet-Joris, Francoise 1930- .... **CLC 11**
See also CA 65-68; CANR 17; DLB 83

Malley, Ern
See McAuley, James Phillip

Mallowan, Agatha Christie
See Christie, Agatha (Mary Clarissa)

Maloff, Saul 1922- .... **CLC 5**
See also CA 33-36R

Malone, Louis
See MacNeice, (Frederick) Louis

Malone, Michael (Christopher) 1942- **CLC 43**
See also CA 77-80; CANR 14, 32, 57

Malory, (Sir) Thomas 1410(?)-1471(?) **LC 11; DA; DAB; DAC; DAM MST; WLCS**
See also CDBLB Before 1660; DLB 146; SATA
59; SATA-Brief 33

Malouf, (George Joseph) David 1934- **CLC 28, 86**
See also CA 124; CANR 50

Malraux, (Georges-)Andre 1901-1976 **CLC 1, 4, 9, 13, 15, 57; DAM NOV**
See also CA 21-22; 69-72; CANR 34, 58; CAP
2; DLB 72; MTCW 1

Malzberg, Barry N(athaniel) 1939- ... **CLC 7**
See also CA 61-64; CAAS 4; CANR 16; DLB
8

Mamet, David (Alan) 1947- **CLC 9, 15, 34, 46, 91; DAM DRAM; DC 4**
See also AAYA 3; CA 81-84; CABS 3; CANR
15, 41, 67, 72; DLB 7; MTCW 1

Mamoulian, Rouben (Zachary) 1897-1987
CLC 16
See also CA 25-28R; 124

Mandelstam, Osip (Emilievich) 1891(?)-1938(?)
TCLC 2, 6; PC 14
See also CA 104; 150

Mander, (Mary) Jane 1877-1949 ... **TCLC 31**
See also CA 162

Mandeville, John fl. 1350- .... **CMLC 19**
See also DLB 146

Mandiargues, Andre Pieyre de .... **CLC 41**
See also Pieyre de Mandiargues, Andre
See also DLB 83

Mandrake, Ethel Belle
See Thurman, Wallace (Henry)

Mangan, James Clarence 1803-1849 **NCLC 27**

Maniere, J.-E.
See Giraudoux, (Hippolyte) Jean

Mankiewicz, Herman (Jacob) 1897-1953
TCLC 85
See also CA 120; DLB 26

Manley, (Mary) Delariviere 1672(?)-1724 **L C 1**
See also DLB 39, 80

Mann, Abel
See Creasey, John

Mann, Emily 1952- .... **DC 7**
See also CA 130; CANR 55

Mann, (Luiz) Heinrich 1871-1950 ... **TCLC 9**

CANR 21, 50; DLB 6, 173; MTCW 1; SATA 27

Maturin, Charles Robert 1780(?)-1824 NCLC 6
See also DLB 178

Matute (Ausejo), Ana Maria 1925- .. CLC 11
See also CA 89-92; MTCW 1

Maugham, W. S.
See Maugham, W(illiam) Somerset

Maugham, W(illiam) Somerset 1874-1965 CLC 1, 11, 15, 67, 93; DA; DAB; DAC; DAM DRAM, MST, NOV; SSC 8; WLC
See also CA 5-8R; 25-28R; CANR 40; CDBLB 1914-1945; DLB 10, 36, 77, 100, 162, 195; MTCW 1; SATA 54

Maugham, William Somerset
See Maugham, W(illiam) Somerset

Maupassant, (Henri Rene Albert) Guy de 1850-1893 ....
NCLC 1, 42; DA; DAB; DAC; DAM MST; SSC 1; WLC
See also DLB 123

Maupin, Armistead 1944- CLC 95; DAM POP
See also CA 125; 130; CANR 58; INT 130

Maurhut, Richard
See Traven, B.

Mauriac, Claude 1914-1996 .... CLC 9
See also CA 89-92; 152; DLB 83

Mauriac, Francois (Charles) 1885-1970 CLC 4, 9, 56; SSC 24
See also CA 25-28; CAP 2; DLB 65; MTCW 1

Mavor, Osborne Henry 1888-1951
See Bridie, James
See also CA 104

Maxwell, William (Keepers, Jr.) 1908- CLC 19
See also CA 93-96; CANR 54; DLBY 80; INT 93-96

May, Elaine 1932- .... CLC 16
See also CA 124; 142; DLB 44

Mayakovski, Vladimir (Vladimirovich) 1893-1930 .... TCLC 4, 18
See also CA 104; 158

Mayhew, Henry 1812-1887 .... NCLC 31
See also DLB 18, 55, 190

Mayle, Peter 1939(?)- .... CLC 89
See also CA 139; CANR 64

Maynard, Joyce 1953- .... CLC 23
See also CA 111; 129; CANR 64

Mayne, William (James Carter) 1928- CLC 12
See also AAYA 20; CA 9-12R; CANR 37; CLR 25; JRDA; MAICYA; SAAS 11; SATA 6, 68

Mayo, Jim
See L'Amour, Louis (Dearborn)

Maysles, Albert 1926- .... CLC 16
See also CA 29-32R

Maysles, David 1932- .... CLC 16

Mazer, Norma Fox 1931- .... CLC 26
See also AAYA 5; CA 69-72; CANR 12, 32, 66; CLR 23; JRDA; MAICYA; SAAS 1; SATA 24, 67

Mazzini, Guiseppe 1805-1872 .... NCLC 34

McAuley, James Phillip 1917-1976 .. CLC 45
See also CA 97-100

McBain, Ed
See Hunter, Evan

McBrien, William Augustine 1930- .. CLC 44
See also CA 107

McCaffrey, Anne (Inez) 1926- CLC 17; DAM NOV, POP
See also AAYA 6; AITN 2; BEST 89:2; CA 25-28R; CANR 15, 35, 55; CLR 49; DLB 8; JRDA; MAICYA; MTCW 1; SAAS 11; SATA 8, 70

McCall, Nathan 1955(?)- .... CLC 86
See also CA 146

McCann, Arthur
See Campbell, John W(ood, Jr.)

McCann, Edson
See Pohl, Frederik

McCarthy, Charles, Jr. 1933-
See McCarthy, Cormac
See also CANR 42, 69; DAM POP

McCarthy, Cormac 1933- CLC 4, 57, 59, 101
See also McCarthy, Charles, Jr.
See also DLB 6, 143

McCarthy, Mary (Therese) 1912-1989 CLC 1, 3, 5, 14, 24, 39, 59; SSC 24
See also CA 5-8R; 129; CANR 16, 50, 64; DLB 2; DLBY 81; INT CANR-16; MTCW 1

McCartney, (James) Paul 1942- CLC 12, 35
See also CA 146

McCauley, Stephen (D.) 1955- .... CLC 50
See also CA 141

McClure, Michael (Thomas) 1932- CLC 6, 10
See also CA 21-24R; CANR 17, 46; DLB 16

McCorkle, Jill (Collins) 1958- .... CLC 51
See also CA 121; DLBY 87

McCourt, Frank 1930- .... CLC 109
See also CA 157

McCourt, James 1941- .... CLC 5
See also CA 57-60

McCoy, Horace (Stanley) 1897-1955 TCLC 28
See also CA 108; 155; DLB 9

McCrae, John 1872-1918 .... TCLC 12
See also CA 109; DLB 92

McCreigh, James
See Pohl, Frederik

McCullers, (Lula) Carson (Smith) 1917-1967 CLC 1, 4, 10, 12, 48, 100; DA; DAB; DAC; DAM MST, NOV; SSC 9, 24; WLC
See also AAYA 21; CA 5-8R; 25-28R; CABS 1, 3; CANR 18; CDALB 1941-1968; DLB 2, 7, 173; MTCW 1; SATA 27

McCulloch, John Tyler
See Burroughs, Edgar Rice

McCullough, Colleen 1938(?)- CLC 27, 107; DAM NOV, POP
See also CA 81-84; CANR 17, 46, 67; MTCW 1

McDermott, Alice 1953- .... CLC 90
See also CA 109; CANR 40

McElroy, Joseph 1930- .... CLC 5, 47
See also CA 17-20R

McEwan, Ian (Russell) 1948- .... CLC 13, 66; DAM NOV
See also BEST 90:4; CA 61-64; CANR 14, 41, 69; DLB 14, 194; MTCW 1

McFadden, David 1940- .... CLC 48
See also CA 104; DLB 60; INT 104

McFarland, Dennis 1950- .... CLC 65
See also CA 165

McGahern, John 1934- CLC 5, 9, 48; SSC 17
See also CA 17-20R; CANR 29, 68; DLB 14; MTCW 1

McGinley, Patrick (Anthony) 1937- . CLC 41
See also CA 120; 127; CANR 56; INT 127

McGinley, Phyllis 1905-1978 .... CLC 14
See also CA 9-12R; 77-80; CANR 19; DLB 11, 48; SATA 2, 44; SATA-Obit 24

McGinniss, Joe 1942- .... CLC 32
See also AITN 2; BEST 89:2; CA 25-28R; CANR 26, 70; DLB 185; INT CANR-26

McGivern, Maureen Daly
See Daly, Maureen

McGrath, Patrick 1950- .... CLC 55
See also CA 136; CANR 65

McGrath, Thomas (Matthew) 1916-1990 CLC 28, 59; DAM POET
See also CA 9-12R; 132; CANR 6, 33; MTCW 1; SATA 41; SATA-Obit 66

McGuane, Thomas (Francis III) 1939- CLC 3, 7, 18, 45
See also AITN 2; CA 49-52; CANR 5, 24, 49; DLB 2; DLBY 80; INT CANR-24; MTCW

McGuckian, Medbh 1950- ..... CLC 48; DAM POET
See also CA 143; DLB 40

McHale, Tom 1942(?)-1982 .... CLC 3, 5
See also AITN 1; CA 77-80; 106

McIlvanney, William 1936- .... CLC 42
See also CA 25-28R; CANR 61; DLB 14

McIlwraith, Maureen Mollie Hunter
See Hunter, Mollie
See also SATA 2

McInerney, Jay 1955- CLC 34, 112; DAM POP
See also AAYA 18; CA 116; 123; CANR 45, 68; INT 123

McIntyre, Vonda N(eel) 1948- .... CLC 18
See also CA 81-84; CANR 17, 34, 69; MTCW 1

McKay, Claude TCLC 7, 41; BLC 3; DAB; PC 2
See also McKay, Festus Claudius
See also DLB 4, 45, 51, 117

McKay, Festus Claudius 1889-1948
See McKay, Claude
See also BW 1; CA 104; 124; DA; DAC; DAM MST, MULT, NOV, POET; MTCW 1; WLC

McKuen, Rod 1933- .... CLC 1, 3
See also AITN 1; CA 41-44R; CANR 40

McLoughlin, R. B.
See Mencken, H(enry) L(ouis)

McLuhan, (Herbert) Marshall 1911-1980 CLC 37, 83
See also CA 9-12R; 102; CANR 12, 34, 61; DLB 88; INT CANR-12; MTCW 1

McMillan, Terry (L.) 1951- CLC 50, 61, 112; BLCS; DAM MULT, NOV, POP
See also AAYA 21; BW 2; CA 140; CANR 60

McMurtry, Larry (Jeff) 1936- CLC 2, 3, 7, 11, 27, 44; DAM NOV, POP
See also AAYA 15; AITN 2; BEST 89:2; CA 5-8R; CANR 19, 43, 64; CDALB 1968-1988; DLB 2, 143; DLBY 80, 87; MTCW 1

McNally, T. M. 1961- .... CLC 82

McNally, Terrence 1939- .... CLC 4, 7, 41, 91; DAM DRAM
See also CA 45-48; CANR 2, 56; DLB 7

McNamer, Deirdre 1950- .... CLC 70

McNeile, Herman Cyril 1888-1937
See Sapper
See also DLB 77

McNickle, (William) D'Arcy 1904-1977 CLC 89; DAM MULT
See also CA 9-12R; 85-88; CANR 5, 45; DLB 175; NNAL; SATA-Obit 22

McPhee, John (Angus) 1931- .... CLC 36
See also BEST 90:1; CA 65-68; CANR 20, 46, 64, 69; DLB 185; MTCW 1

McPherson, James Alan 1943- ... CLC 19, 77; BLCS
See also BW 1; CA 25-28R; CAAS 17; CANR 24; DLB 38; MTCW 1

McPherson, William (Alexander) 1933- CLC 34
See also CA 69-72; CANR 28; INT CANR-28

Mead, Margaret 1901-1978 .... CLC 37
See also AITN 1; CA 1-4R; 81-84; CANR 4; MTCW 1; SATA-Obit 20

Meaker, Marijane (Agnes) 1927-
See Kerr, M. E.
See also CA 107; CANR 37, 63; INT 107; JRDA; MAICYA; MTCW 1; SATA 20, 61, 99

Medoff, Mark (Howard) 1940- ... CLC 6, 23; DAM DRAM
See also AITN 1; CA 53-56; CANR 5; DLB 7; INT CANR-5

Medvedev, P. N.
See Bakhtin, Mikhail Mikhailovich

Meged, Aharon
See Megged, Aharon
Meged, Aron
See Megged, Aharon
Megged, Aharon 1920- .... **CLC 9**
See also CA 49-52; CAAS 13; CANR 1
Mehta, Ved (Parkash) 1934- .... **CLC 37**
See also CA 1-4R; CANR 2, 23, 69; MTCW 1
Melanter
See Blackmore, R(ichard) D(oddridge)
Melies, Georges 1861-1938 .... **TCLC 81**
Melikow, Loris
See Hofmannsthal, Hugo von
Melmoth, Sebastian
See Wilde, Oscar (Fingal O'Flahertie Wills)
Meltzer, Milton 1915- .... **CLC 26**
See also AAYA 8; CA 13-16R; CANR 38; CLR
13; DLB 61; JRDA; MAICYA; SAAS 1;
SATA 1, 50, 80
Melville, Herman 1819-1891NCLC **3, 12, 29,
45, 49; DA; DAB; DAC; DAM MST, NOV;
SSC 1, 17; WLC**
See also AAYA 25; CDALB 1640-1865; DLB
3, 74; SATA 59
Menander c. 342B.C.-c. 292B.C. .... **CMLC 9;
DAM DRAM; DC 3**
See also DLB 176
Mencken, H(enry) L(ouis) 1880-1956 **T C L C
13**
See also CA 105; 125; CDALB 1917-1929;
DLB 11, 29, 63, 137; MTCW 1
Mendelsohn, Jane 1965(?)- .... **CLC 99**
See also CA 154
Mercer, David 1928-1980CLC **5; DAM DRAM**
See also CA 9-12R; 102; CANR 23; DLB 13;
MTCW 1
Merchant, Paul
See Ellison, Harlan (Jay)
Meredith, George 1828-1909 . **TCLC 17, 43;
DAM POET**
See also CA 117; 153; CDBLB 1832-1890;
DLB 18, 35, 57, 159
Meredith, William (Morris) 1919-CLC **4, 13,
22, 55; DAM POET**
See also CA 9-12R; CAAS 14; CANR 6, 40;
DLB 5
Merezhkovsky, Dmitry Sergeyevich 1865-1941
TCLC 29
Merimee, Prosper 1803-1870NCLC **6, 65; SSC
7**
See also DLB 119, 192
Merkin, Daphne 1954- .... **CLC 44**
See also CA 123
Merlin, Arthur
See Blish, James (Benjamin)
Merrill, James (Ingram) 1926-1995CLC **2, 3,
6, 8, 13, 18, 34, 91; DAM POET**
See also CA 13-16R; 147; CANR 10, 49, 63;
DLB 5, 165; DLBY 85; INT CANR-10;
MTCW 1
Merriman, Alex
See Silverberg, Robert
Merriman, Brian 1747-1805 .... **NCLC 70**
Merritt, E. B.
See Waddington, Miriam
Merton, Thomas 1915-1968 CLC **1, 3, 11, 34,
83; PC 10**
See also CA 5-8R; 25-28R; CANR 22, 53; DLB
48; DLBY 81; MTCW 1
Merwin, W(illiam) S(tanley) 1927- CLC **1, 2,
3, 5, 8, 13, 18, 45, 88; DAM POET**
See also CA 13-16R; CANR 15, 51; DLB 5,
169; INT CANR-15; MTCW 1
Metcalf, John 1938- .... **CLC 37**
See also CA 113; DLB 60
Metcalf, Suzanne
See Baum, L(yman) Frank

Mew, Charlotte (Mary) 1870-1928 .. **TCLC 8**
See also CA 105; DLB 19, 135
Mewshaw, Michael 1943- .... **CLC 9**
See also CA 53-56; CANR 7, 47; DLBY 80
Meyer, June
See Jordan, June
Meyer, Lynn
See Slavitt, David R(ytman)
Meyer-Meyrink, Gustav 1868-1932
See Meyrink, Gustav
See also CA 117
Meyers, Jeffrey 1939- .... **CLC 39**
See also CA 73-76; CANR 54; DLB 111
Meynell, Alice (Christina Gertrude Thompson)
1847-1922 .... **TCLC 6**
See also CA 104; DLB 19, 98
Meyrink, Gustav .... **TCLC 21**
See also Meyer-Meyrink, Gustav
See also DLB 81
Michaels, Leonard 1933- CLC **6, 25; SSC 16**
See also CA 61-64; CANR 21, 62; DLB 130;
MTCW 1
Michaux, Henri 1899-1984 ....CLC **8, 19**
See also CA 85-88; 114
Micheaux, Oscar 1884-1951 .... **TCLC 76**
See also DLB 50
Michelangelo 1475-1564 .... **LC 12**
Michelet, Jules 1798-1874 .... **NCLC 31**
Michener, James A(lbert) 1907(?)-1997 **C L C
1, 5, 11, 29, 60, 109; DAM NOV, POP**
See also AAYA 27; AITN 1; BEST 90:1; CA 5-
8R; 161; CANR 21, 45, 68; DLB 6; MTCW
1
Mickiewicz, Adam 1798-1855 .... **NCLC 3**
Middleton, Christopher 1926- .... **CLC 13**
See also CA 13-16R; CANR 29, 54; DLB 40
Middleton, Richard (Barham) 1882-1911
TCLC 56
See also DLB 156
Middleton, Stanley 1919- .... **CLC 7, 38**
See also CA 25-28R; CAAS 23; CANR 21, 46;
DLB 14
Middleton, Thomas 1580-1627 **LC 33; DAM
DRAM, MST; DC 5**
See also DLB 58
Migueis, Jose Rodrigues 1901- .... **CLC 10**
Mikszath, Kalman 1847-1910 .... **TCLC 31**
Miles, Jack .... **CLC 100**
Miles, Josephine (Louise) 1911-1985CLC **1, 2,
14, 34, 39; DAM POET**
See also CA 1-4R; 116; CANR 2, 55; DLB 48
Militant
See Sandburg, Carl (August)
Mill, John Stuart 1806-1873 .... **NCLC 11, 58**
See also CDBLB 1832-1890; DLB 55, 190
Millar, Kenneth 1915-1983 ....CLC **14; DAM
POP**
See also Macdonald, Ross
See also CA 9-12R; 110; CANR 16, 63; DLB
2; DLBD 6; DLBY 83; MTCW 1
Millay, E. Vincent
See Millay, Edna St. Vincent
Millay, Edna St. Vincent 1892-1950 **T C L C 4,
49; DA; DAB; DAC; DAM MST, POET;
PC 6; WLCS**
See also CA 104; 130; CDALB 1917-1929;
DLB 45; MTCW 1
Miller, Arthur 1915-CLC **1, 2, 6, 10, 15, 26, 47,
78; DA; DAB; DAC; DAM DRAM, MST;
DC 1; WLC**
See also AAYA 15; AITN 1; CA 1-4R; CABS
3; CANR 2, 30, 54; CDALB 1941-1968;
DLB 7; MTCW 1
Miller, Henry (Valentine) 1891-1980CLC **1, 2,
4, 9, 14, 43, 84; DA; DAB; DAC; DAM
MST, NOV; WLC**
See also CA 9-12R; 97-100; CANR 33, 64;

CDALB 1929-1941; DLB 4, 9; DLBY 80;
MTCW 1
Miller, Jason 1939(?)- .... **CLC 2**
See also AITN 1; CA 73-76; DLB 7
Miller, Sue 1943- .... CLC **44; DAM POP**
See also BEST 90:3; CA 139; CANR 59; DLB
143
Miller, Walter M(ichael, Jr.) 1923-CLC **4, 30**
See also CA 85-88; DLB 8
Millett, Kate 1934- .... **CLC 67**
See also AITN 1; CA 73-76; CANR 32, 53;
MTCW 1
Millhauser, Steven (Lewis) 1943-CLC **21, 54,
109**
See also CA 110; 111; CANR 63; DLB 2; INT
111
Millin, Sarah Gertrude 1889-1968 ... **CLC 49**
See also CA 102; 93-96
Milne, A(lan) A(lexander) 1882-1956TCLC **6;
DAB; DAC; DAM MST**
See also CA 104; 133; CLR 1, 26; DLB 10, 77,
100, 160; MAICYA; MTCW 1; SATA 100;
YABC 1
Milner, Ron(ald) 1938-CLC **56; BLC 3; DAM
MULT**
See also AITN 1; BW 1; CA 73-76; CANR 24;
DLB 38; MTCW 1
Milnes, Richard Monckton 1809-1885N C L C
61
See also DLB 32, 184
Milosz, Czeslaw 1911- CLC **5, 11, 22, 31, 56,
82; DAM MST, POET; PC 8; WLCS**
See also CA 81-84; CANR 23, 51; MTCW 1
Milton, John 1608-1674 LC **9, 43; DA; DAB;
DAC; DAM MST, POET; PC 19; WLC**
See also CDBLB 1660-1789; DLB 131, 151
Min, Anchee 1957- .... **CLC 86**
See also CA 146
Minehaha, Cornelius
See Wedekind, (Benjamin) Frank(lin)
Miner, Valerie 1947- .... **CLC 40**
See also CA 97-100; CANR 59
Minimo, Duca
See D'Annunzio, Gabriele
Minot, Susan 1956- .... **CLC 44**
See also CA 134
Minus, Ed 1938- .... **CLC 39**
Miranda, Javier
See Bioy Casares, Adolfo
Mirbeau, Octave 1848-1917 .... **TCLC 55**
See also DLB 123, 192
Miro (Ferrer), Gabriel (Francisco Victor) 1879-
1930 ....
TCLC 5
See also CA 104
Mishima, Yukio 1925-1970CLC **2, 4, 6, 9, 27;
DC 1; SSC 4**
See also Hiraoka, Kimitake
See also DLB 182
Mistral, Frederic 1830-1914 .... **TCLC 51**
See also CA 122
Mistral, Gabriela .... **TCLC 2; HLC**
See also Godoy Alcayaga, Lucila
Mistry, Rohinton 1952- .... CLC **71; DAC**
See also CA 141
Mitchell, Clyde
See Ellison, Harlan (Jay); Silverberg, Robert
Mitchell, James Leslie 1901-1935
See Gibbon, Lewis Grassic
See also CA 104; DLB 15
Mitchell, Joni 1943- .... **CLC 12**
See also CA 112
Mitchell, Joseph (Quincy) 1908-1996CLC **98**
See also CA 77-80; 152; CANR 69; DLB 185;
DLBY 96
Mitchell, Margaret (Munnerlyn) 1900-1949
TCLC 11; DAM NOV, POP

See also AAYA 23; CA 109; 125; CANR 55; DLB 9; MTCW 1

Mitchell, Peggy
See Mitchell, Margaret (Munnerlyn)

Mitchell, S(ilas) Weir 1829-1914 ... **TCLC 36**
See also CA 165; DLB 202

Mitchell, W(illiam) O(rmond) 1914-1998**CLC 25; DAC; DAM MST**
See also CA 77-80; 165; CANR 15, 43; DLB 88

Mitchell, William 1879-1936 .... **TCLC 81**

Mitford, Mary Russell 1787-1855 ... **NCLC 4**
See also DLB 110, 116

Mitford, Nancy 1904-1973 .... **CLC 44**
See also CA 9-12R; DLB 191

Miyamoto, Yuriko 1899-1951 .... **TCLC 37**
See also DLB 180

Miyazawa, Kenji 1896-1933 .... **TCLC 76**
See also CA 157

Mizoguchi, Kenji 1898-1956 .... **TCLC 72**
See also CA 167

Mo, Timothy (Peter) 1950(?)- .... **CLC 46**
See also CA 117; DLB 194; MTCW 1

Modarressi, Taghi (M.) 1931- .... **CLC 44**
See also CA 121; 134; INT 134

Modiano, Patrick (Jean) 1945- .... **CLC 18**
See also CA 85-88; CANR 17, 40; DLB 83

Moerck, Paal
See Roelvaag, O(le) E(dvart)

Mofolo, Thomas (Mokopu) 1875(?)-1948 **TCLC 22; BLC 3; DAM MULT**
See also CA 121; 153

Mohr, Nicholasa 1938-**CLC 12; DAM MULT; HLC**
See also AAYA 8; CA 49-52; CANR 1, 32, 64; CLR 22; DLB 145; HW; JRDA; SAAS 8; SATA 8, 97

Mojtabai, A(nn) G(race) 1938- **CLC 5, 9, 15, 29**
See also CA 85-88

Moliere 1622-1673 . **LC 28; DA; DAB; DAC; DAM DRAM, MST; WLC**

Molin, Charles
See Mayne, William (James Carter)

Molnar, Ferenc 1878-1952 .. **TCLC 20; DAM DRAM**
See also CA 109; 153

Momaday, N(avarre) Scott 1934- **CLC 2, 19, 85, 95; DA; DAB; DAC; DAM MST, MULT, NOV, POP; WLCS**
See also AAYA 11; CA 25-28R; CANR 14, 34, 68; DLB 143; 175; INT CANR-14; MTCW 1; NNAL; SATA 48; SATA-Brief 30

Monette, Paul 1945-1995 .... **CLC 82**
See also CA 139; 147

Monroe, Harriet 1860-1936 .... **TCLC 12**
See also CA 109; DLB 54, 91

Monroe, Lyle
See Heinlein, Robert A(nson)

Montagu, Elizabeth 1720-1800 .... **NCLC 7**

Montagu, Mary (Pierrepont) Wortley 1689-1762 .... **LC 9; PC 16**
See also DLB 95, 101

Montagu, W. H.
See Coleridge, Samuel Taylor

Montague, John (Patrick) 1929- **CLC 13, 46**
See also CA 9-12R; CANR 9, 69; DLB 40; MTCW 1

Montaigne, Michel (Eyquem) de 1533-1592 **LC 8; DA; DAB; DAC; DAM MST; WLC**

Montale, Eugenio 1896-1981**CLC 7, 9, 18; PC 13**
See also CA 17-20R; 104; CANR 30; DLB 114; MTCW 1

Montesquieu, Charles-Louis de Secondat 1689-1755 .... **LC 7**

Montgomery, (Robert) Bruce 1921-1978

See Crispin, Edmund
See also CA 104

Montgomery, L(ucy) M(aud) 1874-1942 **TCLC 51; DAC; DAM MST**
See also AAYA 12; CA 108; 137; CLR 8; DLB 92; DLBD 14; JRDA; MAICYA; SATA 100; YABC 1

Montgomery, Marion H., Jr. 1925- .... **CLC 7**
See also AITN 1; CA 1-4R; CANR 3, 48; DLB 6

Montgomery, Max
See Davenport, Guy (Mattison, Jr.)

Montherlant, Henry (Milon) de 1896-1972 **CLC 8, 19; DAM DRAM**
See also CA 85-88; 37-40R; DLB 72; MTCW 1

Monty Python
See Chapman, Graham; Cleese, John (Marwood); Gilliam, Terry (Vance); Idle, Eric; Jones, Terence Graham Parry; Palin, Michael (Edward)
See also AAYA 7

Moodie, Susanna (Strickland) 1803-1885 **NCLC 14**
See also DLB 99

Mooney, Edward 1951-
See Mooney, Ted
See also CA 130

Mooney, Ted .... **CLC 25**
See also Mooney, Edward

Moorcock, Michael (John) 1939-**CLC 5, 27, 58**
See also AAYA 26; CA 45-48; CAAS 5; CANR 2, 17, 38, 64; DLB 14; MTCW 1; SATA 93

Moore, Brian 1921- **CLC 1, 3, 5, 7, 8, 19, 32, 90; DAB; DAC; DAM MST**
See also CA 1-4R; CANR 1, 25, 42, 63; MTCW 1

Moore, Edward
See Muir, Edwin

Moore, George Augustus 1852-1933**TCLC 7; SSC 19**
See also CA 104; DLB 10, 18, 57, 135

Moore, Lorrie .... **CLC 39, 45, 68**
See also Moore, Marie Lorena

Moore, Marianne (Craig) 1887-1972**CLC 1, 2, 4, 8, 10, 13, 19, 47; DA; DAB; DAC; DAM MST, POET; PC 4; WLCS**
See also CA 1-4R; 33-36R; CANR 3, 61; CDALB 1929-1941; DLB 45; DLBD 7; MTCW 1; SATA 20

Moore, Marie Lorena 1957-
See Moore, Lorrie
See also CA 116; CANR 39

Moore, Thomas 1779-1852 .... **NCLC 6**
See also DLB 96, 144

Morand, Paul 1888-1976 .... **CLC 41; SSC 22**
See also CA 69-72; DLB 65

Morante, Elsa 1918-1985 .... **CLC 8, 47**
See also CA 85-88; 117; CANR 35; DLB 177; MTCW 1

Moravia, Alberto 1907-1990**CLC 2, 7, 11, 27, 46; SSC 26**
See also Pincherle, Alberto
See also DLB 177

More, Hannah 1745-1833 .... **NCLC 27**
See also DLB 107, 109, 116, 158

More, Henry 1614-1687 .... **LC 9**
See also DLB 126

More, Sir Thomas 1478-1535 .... **LC 10, 32**

Moreas, Jean .... **TCLC 18**
See also Papadiamantopoulos, Johannes

Morgan, Berry 1919- .... **CLC 6**
See also CA 49-52; DLB 6

Morgan, Claire
See Highsmith, (Mary) Patricia

Morgan, Edwin (George) 1920- .... **CLC 31**
See also CA 5-8R; CANR 3, 43; DLB 27

Morgan, (George) Frederick 1922- .. **CLC 23**
See also CA 17-20R; CANR 21

Morgan, Harriet
See Mencken, H(enry) L(ouis)

Morgan, Jane
See Cooper, James Fenimore

Morgan, Janet 1945- .... **CLC 39**
See also CA 65-68

Morgan, Lady 1776(?)-1859 .... **NCLC 29**
See also DLB 116, 158

Morgan, Robin (Evonne) 1941- .... **CLC 2**
See also CA 69-72; CANR 29, 68; MTCW 1; SATA 80

Morgan, Scott
See Kuttner, Henry

Morgan, Seth 1949(?)-1990 .... **CLC 65**
See also CA 132

Morgenstern, Christian 1871-1914 . **TCLC 8**
See also CA 105

Morgenstern, S.
See Goldman, William (W.)

Moricz, Zsigmond 1879-1942 .... **TCLC 33**
See also CA 165

Morike, Eduard (Friedrich) 1804-1875**NCLC 10**
See also DLB 133

Moritz, Karl Philipp 1756-1793 .... **LC 2**
See also DLB 94

Morland, Peter Henry
See Faust, Frederick (Schiller)

Morren, Theophil
See Hofmannsthal, Hugo von

Morris, Bill 1952- .... **CLC 76**

Morris, Julian
See West, Morris L(anglo)

Morris, Steveland Judkins 1950(?)-
See Wonder, Stevie
See also CA 111

Morris, William 1834-1896 .... **NCLC 4**
See also CDBLB 1832-1890; DLB 18, 35, 57, 156, 178, 184

Morris, Wright 1910-1998**CLC 1, 3, 7, 18, 37**
See also CA 9-12R; 167; CANR 21; DLB 2; DLBY 81; MTCW 1

Morrison, Arthur 1863-1945 .... **TCLC 72**
See also CA 120; 157; DLB 70, 135, 197

Morrison, Chloe Anthony Wofford
See Morrison, Toni

Morrison, James Douglas 1943-1971
See Morrison, Jim
See also CA 73-76; CANR 40

Morrison, Jim .... **CLC 17**
See also Morrison, James Douglas

Morrison, Toni 1931-**CLC 4, 10, 22, 55, 81, 87; BLC 3; DA; DAB; DAC; DAM MST, MULT, NOV, POP**
See also AAYA 1, 22; BW 2; CA 29-32R; CANR 27, 42, 67; CDALB 1968-1988; DLB 6, 33, 143; DLBY 81; MTCW 1; SATA 57

Morrison, Van 1945- .... **CLC 21**
See also CA 116; 168

Morrissy, Mary 1958- .... **CLC 99**

Mortimer, John (Clifford) 1923-**CLC 28, 43; DAM DRAM, POP**
See also CA 13-16R; CANR 21, 69; CDBLB 1960 to Present; DLB 13; INT CANR-21; MTCW 1

Mortimer, Penelope (Ruth) 1918- .... **CLC 5**
See also CA 57-60; CANR 45

Morton, Anthony
See Creasey, John

Mosca, Gaetano 1858-1941 .... **TCLC 75**

Mosher, Howard Frank 1943- .... **CLC 62**
See also CA 139; CANR 65

Mosley, Nicholas 1923- .... **CLC 43, 70**
See also CA 69-72; CANR 41, 60; DLB 14

Mosley, Walter 1952- . **CLC 97; BLCS; DAM**

MULT, POP
See also AAYA 17; BW 2; CA 142; CANR 57

Moss, Howard 1922-1987 **CLC 7, 14, 45, 50; DAM POET**
See also CA 1-4R; 123; CANR 1, 44; DLB 5

Mossgiel, Rab
See Burns, Robert

Motion, Andrew (Peter) 1952- .... **CLC 47**
See also CA 146; DLB 40

Motley, Willard (Francis) 1909-1965 **CLC 18**
See also BW 1; CA 117; 106; DLB 76, 143

Motoori, Norinaga 1730-1801 .... **NCLC 45**

Mott, Michael (Charles Alston) 1930- **CLC 15, 34**
See also CA 5-8R; CAAS 7; CANR 7, 29

Mountain Wolf Woman 1884-1960 .. **CLC 92**
See also CA 144; NNAL

Moure, Erin 1955- .... **CLC 88**
See also CA 113; DLB 60

Mowat, Farley (McGill) 1921- **CLC 26; DAC; DAM MST**
See also AAYA 1; CA 1-4R; CANR 4, 24, 42, 68; CLR 20; DLB 68; INT CANAR-24; JRDA; MAICYA; MTCW 1; SATA 3, 55

Moyers, Bill 1934- .... **CLC 74**
See also AITN 2; CA 61-64; CANR 31, 52

Mphahlele, Es'kia
See Mphahlele, Ezekiel
See also CA 125

Mphahlele, Ezekiel 1919-1983 **CLC 25; BLC 3; DAM MULT**
See also Mphahlele, Es'kia
See also BW 2; CA 81-84; CANR 26

Mqhayi, S(amuel) E(dward) K(rune Loliwe) 1875-1945 ....
TCLC 25; BLC 3; DAM MULT
See also CA 153

Mrozek, Slawomir 1930- .... **CLC 3, 13**
See also CA 13-16R; CAAS 10; CANR 29; MTCW 1

Mrs. Belloc-Lowndes
See Lowndes, Marie Adelaide (Belloc)

Mtwa, Percy (?)- .... **CLC 47**

Mueller, Lisel 1924- .... **CLC 13, 51**
See also CA 93-96; DLB 105

Muir, Edwin 1887-1959 .... **TCLC 2**
See also CA 104; DLB 20, 100, 191

Muir, John 1838-1914 .... **TCLC 28**
See also CA 165; DLB 186

Mujica Lainez, Manuel 1910-1984 ... **CLC 31**
See also Lainez, Manuel Mujica
See also CA 81-84; 112; CANR 32; HW

Mukherjee, Bharati 1940- **CLC 53, 115; DAM NOV**
See also BEST 89:2; CA 107; CANR 45, 72; DLB 60; MTCW 1

Muldoon, Paul 1951- **CLC 32, 72; DAM POET**
See also CA 113; 129; CANR 52; DLB 40; INT 129

Mulisch, Harry 1927- .... **CLC 42**
See also CA 9-12R; CANR 6, 26, 56

Mull, Martin 1943- .... **CLC 17**
See also CA 105

Mulock, Dinah Maria
See Craik, Dinah Maria (Mulock)

Munford, Robert 1737(?)-1783 .... **LC 5**
See also DLB 31

Mungo, Raymond 1946- .... **CLC 72**
See also CA 49-52; CANR 2

Munro, Alice 1931- .... **CLC 6, 10, 19, 50, 95; DAC; DAM MST, NOV; SSC 3; WLCS**
See also AITN 2; CA 33-36R; CANR 33, 53; DLB 53; MTCW 1; SATA 29

Munro, H(ector) H(ugh) 1870-1916
See Saki
See also CA 104; 130; CDBLB 1890-1914; DA; DAB; DAC; DAM MST, NOV; DLB 34, 162;

MTCW 1; WLC

Murasaki, Lady .... **CMLC 1**

Murdoch, (Jean) Iris 1919- **CLC 1, 2, 3, 4, 6, 8, 11, 15, 22, 31, 51; DAB; DAC; DAM MST, NOV**
See also CA 13-16R; CANR 8, 43, 68; CDBLB 1960 to Present; DLB 14, 194; INT CANR-8; MTCW 1

Murfree, Mary Noailles 1850-1922 ... **SSC 22**
See also CA 122; DLB 12, 74

Murnau, Friedrich Wilhelm
See Plumpe, Friedrich Wilhelm

Murphy, Richard 1927- .... **CLC 41**
See also CA 29-32R; DLB 40

Murphy, Sylvia 1937- .... **CLC 34**
See also CA 121

Murphy, Thomas (Bernard) 1935- ... **CLC 51**
See also CA 101

Murray, Albert L. 1916- .... **CLC 73**
See also BW 2; CA 49-52; CANR 26, 52; DLB 38

Murray, Judith Sargent 1751-1820 **NCLC 63**
See also DLB 37, 200

Murray, Les(lie) A(llan) 1938- **CLC 40; DAM POET**
See also CA 21-24R; CANR 11, 27, 56

Murry, J. Middleton
See Murry, John Middleton

Murry, John Middleton 1889-1957 **TCLC 16**
See also CA 118; DLB 149

Musgrave, Susan 1951- .... **CLC 13, 54**
See also CA 69-72; CANR 45

Musil, Robert (Edler von) 1880-1942 **T C L C 12, 68; SSC 18**
See also CA 109; CANR 55; DLB 81, 124

Muske, Carol 1945- .... **CLC 90**
See also Muske-Dukes, Carol (Anne)

Muske-Dukes, Carol (Anne) 1945-
See Muske, Carol
See also CA 65-68; CANR 32, 70

Musset, (Louis Charles) Alfred de 1810-1857 **NCLC 7**
See also DLB 192

My Brother's Brother
See Chekhov, Anton (Pavlovich)

Myers, L(eopold) H(amilton) 1881-1944 **TCLC 59**
See also CA 157; DLB 15

Myers, Walter Dean 1937- . **CLC 35; BLC 3; DAM MULT, NOV**
See also AAYA 4, 23; BW 2; CA 33-36R; CANR 20, 42, 67; CLR 4, 16, 35; DLB 33; INT CANR-20; JRDA; MAICYA; SAAS 2; SATA 41, 71; SATA-Brief 27

Myers, Walter M.
See Myers, Walter Dean

Myles, Symon
See Follett, Ken(neth Martin)

Nabokov, Vladimir (Vladimirovich) 1899-1977 **CLC 1, 2, 3, 6, 8, 11, 15, 23, 44, 46, 64; DA; DAB; DAC; DAM MST, NOV; SSC 11; WLC**
See also CA 5-8R; 69-72; CANR 20; CDALB 1941-1968; DLB 2; DLBD 3; DLBY 80, 91; MTCW 1

Nagai Kafu 1879-1959 .... **TCLC 51**
See also Nagai Sokichi
See also DLB 180

Nagai Sokichi 1879-1959
See Nagai Kafu
See also CA 117

Nagy, Laszlo 1925-1978 .... **CLC 7**
See also CA 129; 112

Naidu, Sarojini 1879-1943 .... **TCLC 80**

Naipaul, Shiva(dhar Srinivasa) 1945-1985 **CLC 32, 39; DAM NOV**
See also CA 110; 112; 116; CANR 33; DLB

157; DLBY 85; MTCW 1

Naipaul, V(idiadhar) S(urajprasad) 1932- **CLC 4, 7, 9, 13, 18, 37, 105; DAB; DAC; DAM MST, NOV**
See also CA 1-4R; CANR 1, 33, 51; CDBLB 1960 to Present; DLB 125; DLBY 85; MTCW 1

Nakos, Lilika 1899(?)- .... **CLC 29**

Narayan, R(asipuram) K(rishnaswami) 1906- **CLC 7, 28, 47; DAM NOV; SSC 25**
See also CA 81-84; CANR 33, 61; MTCW 1; SATA 62

Nash, (Frediric) Ogden 1902-1971 . **CLC 23; DAM POET; PC 21**
See also CA 13-14; 29-32R; CANR 34, 61; CAP 1; DLB 11; MAICYA; MTCW 1; SATA 2, 46

Nashe, Thomas 1567-1601(?) .... **LC 41**
See also DLB 167

Nashe, Thomas 1567-1601 .... **LC 41**

Nathan, Daniel
See Dannay, Frederic

Nathan, George Jean 1882-1958 ... **TCLC 18**
See also Hatteras, Owen
See also CA 114; DLB 137

Natsume, Kinnosuke 1867-1916
See Natsume, Soseki
See also CA 104

Natsume, Soseki 1867-1916 .... **TCLC 2, 10**
See also Natsume, Kinnosuke
See also DLB 180

Natti, (Mary) Lee 1919-
See Kingman, Lee
See also CA 5-8R; CANR 2

Naylor, Gloria 1950- **CLC 28, 52; BLC 3; DA; DAC; DAM MST, MULT, NOV, POP; WLCS**
See also AAYA 6; BW 2; CA 107; CANR 27, 51; DLB 173; MTCW 1

Neihardt, John Gneisenau 1881-1973 **CLC 32**
See also CA 13-14; CANR 65; CAP 1; DLB 9, 54

Nekrasov, Nikolai Alekseevich 1821-1878 **NCLC 11**

Nelligan, Emile 1879-1941 .... **TCLC 14**
See also CA 114; DLB 92

Nelson, Willie 1933- .... **CLC 17**
See also CA 107

Nemerov, Howard (Stanley) 1920-1991 **CLC 2, 6, 9, 36; DAM POET; PC 24**
See also CA 1-4R; 134; CABS 2; CANR 1, 27, 53; DLB 5, 6; DLBY 83; INT CANR-27; MTCW 1

Neruda, Pablo 1904-1973 **CLC 1, 2, 5, 7, 9, 28, 62; DA; DAB; DAC; DAM MST, MULT, POET; HLC; PC 4; WLC**
See also CA 19-20; 45-48; CAP 2; HW; MTCW 1

Nerval, Gerard de 1808-1855 **NCLC 1, 67; PC 13; SSC 18**

Nervo, (Jose) Amado (Ruiz de) 1870-1919 **TCLC 11**
See also CA 109; 131; HW

Nessi, Pio Baroja y
See Baroja (y Nessi), Pio

Nestroy, Johann 1801-1862 .... **NCLC 42**
See also DLB 133

Netterville, Luke
See O'Grady, Standish (James)

Neufeld, John (Arthur) 1938- .... **CLC 17**
See also AAYA 11; CA 25-28R; CANR 11, 37, 56; CLR 52; MAICYA; SAAS 3; SATA 6, 81

Neville, Emily Cheney 1919- .... **CLC 12**
See also CA 5-8R; CANR 3, 37; JRDA; MAICYA; SAAS 2; SATA 1

Newbound, Bernard Slade 1930-

Pancake, Breece D'J .... **CLC 29**
See also Pancake, Breece Dexter
See also DLB 130
Panko, Rudy
See Gogol, Nikolai (Vasilyevich)
Papadiamantis, Alexandros 1851-1911**T C L C 29**
See also CA 168
Papadiamantopoulos, Johannes 1856-1910
See Moreas, Jean
See also CA 117
Papini, Giovanni 1881-1956 .... **TCLC 22**
See also CA 121
Paracelsus 1493-1541 .... **LC 14**
See also DLB 179
Parasol, Peter
See Stevens, Wallace
Pardo Bazan, Emilia 1851-1921 .... **SSC 30**
Pareto, Vilfredo 1848-1923 .... **TCLC 69**
Parfenie, Maria
See Codrescu, Andrei
Parini, Jay (Lee) 1948- .... **CLC 54**
See also CA 97-100; CAAS 16; CANR 32
Park, Jordan
See Kornbluth, C(yril) M.; Pohl, Frederik
Park, Robert E(zra) 1864-1944 ...... **TCLC 73**
See also CA 122; 165
Parker, Bert
See Ellison, Harlan (Jay)
Parker, Dorothy (Rothschild) 1893-1967**C L C 15, 68; DAM POET; SSC 2**
See also CA 19-20; 25-28R; CAP 2; DLB 11, 45, 86; MTCW 1
Parker, Robert B(rown) 1932-**CLC 27; DAM NOV, POP**
See also BEST 89:4; CA 49-52; CANR 1, 26, 52; INT CANR-26; MTCW 1
Parkin, Frank 1940- .... **CLC 43**
See also CA 147
Parkman, Francis, Jr. 1823-1893 .. **NCLC 12**
See also DLB 1, 30, 186
Parks, Gordon (Alexander Buchanan) 1912-**CLC 1, 16; BLC 3; DAM MULT**
See also AITN 2; BW 2; CA 41-44R; CANR 26, 66; DLB 33; SATA 8
Parmenides c. 515B.C.-c. 450B.C. **CMLC 22**
See also DLB 176
Parnell, Thomas 1679-1718 .... **LC 3**
See also DLB 94
Parra, Nicanor 1914- ...... **CLC 2, 102; DAM MULT; HLC**
See also CA 85-88; CANR 32; HW; MTCW 1
Parrish, Mary Frances
See Fisher, M(ary) F(rances) K(ennedy)
Parson
See Coleridge, Samuel Taylor
Parson Lot
See Kingsley, Charles
Partridge, Anthony
See Oppenheim, E(dward) Phillips
Pascal, Blaise 1623-1662 .... **LC 35**
Pascoli, Giovanni 1855-1912 .... **TCLC 45**
Pasolini, Pier Paolo 1922-1975 . **CLC 20, 37, 106; PC 17**
See also CA 93-96; 61-64; CANR 63; DLB 128, 177; MTCW 1
Pasquini
See Silone, Ignazio
Pastan, Linda (Olenik) 1932- **CLC 27; DAM POET**
See also CA 61-64; CANR 18, 40, 61; DLB 5
Pasternak, Boris (Leonidovich) 1890-1960 **CLC 7, 10, 18, 63; DA; DAB; DAC; DAM MST, NOV, POET; PC 6; SSC 31; WLC**
See also CA 127; 116; MTCW 1
Patchen, Kenneth 1911-1972 ... **CLC 1, 2, 18; DAM POET**

See also CA 1-4R; 33-36R; CANR 3, 35; DLB 16, 48; MTCW 1
Pater, Walter (Horatio) 1839-1894 .. **NCLC 7**
See also CDBLB 1832-1890; DLB 57, 156
Paterson, A(ndrew) B(arton) 1864-1941 **TCLC 32**
See also CA 155; SATA 97
Paterson, Katherine (Womeldorf) 1932-**C L C 12, 30**
See also AAYA 1; CA 21-24R; CANR 28, 59; CLR 7, 50; DLB 52; JRDA; MAICYA; MTCW 1; SATA 13, 53, 92
Patmore, Coventry Kersey Dighton 1823-1896 **NCLC 9**
See also DLB 35, 98
Paton, Alan (Stewart) 1903-1988 **CLC 4, 10, 25, 55, 106; DA; DAB; DAC; DAM MST, NOV; WLC**
See also AAYA 26; CA 13-16; 125; CANR 22; CAP 1; DLBD 17; MTCW 1; SATA 11; SATA-Obit 56
Paton Walsh, Gillian 1937-
See Walsh, Jill Paton
See also CANR 38; JRDA; MAICYA; SAAS 3; SATA 4, 72
Patton, George S. 1885-1945 .... **TCLC 79**
Paulding, James Kirke 1778-1860 ... **NCLC 2**
See also DLB 3, 59, 74
Paulin, Thomas Neilson 1949-
See Paulin, Tom
See also CA 123; 128
Paulin, Tom .... **CLC 37**
See also Paulin, Thomas Neilson
See also DLB 40
Paustovsky, Konstantin (Georgievich) 1892-1968 .... **CLC 40**
See also CA 93-96; 25-28R
Pavese, Cesare 1908-1950 ... **TCLC 3; PC 13; SSC 19**
See also CA 104; DLB 128, 177
Pavic, Milorad 1929- .... **CLC 60**
See also CA 136; DLB 181
Payne, Alan
See Jakes, John (William)
Paz, Gil
See Lugones, Leopoldo
Paz, Octavio 1914-1998**CLC 3, 4, 6, 10, 19, 51, 65; DA; DAB; DAC; DAM MST, MULT, POET; HLC; PC 1; WLC**
See also CA 73-76; 165; CANR 32, 65; DLBY 90; HW; MTCW 1
p'Bitek, Okot 1931-1982 .... **CLC 96; BLC 3; DAM MULT**
See also BW 2; CA 124; 107; DLB 125; MTCW 1
Peacock, Molly 1947- .... **CLC 60**
See also CA 103; CAAS 21; CANR 52; DLB 120
Peacock, Thomas Love 1785-1866 . **NCLC 22**
See also DLB 96, 116
Peake, Mervyn 1911-1968 .... **CLC 7, 54**
See also CA 5-8R; 25-28R; CANR 3; DLB 15, 160; MTCW 1; SATA 23
Pearce, Philippa .... **CLC 21**
See also Christie, (Ann) Philippa
See also CLR 9; DLB 161; MAICYA; SATA 1, 67
Pearl, Eric
See Elman, Richard (Martin)
Pearson, T(homas) R(eid) 1956- .... **CLC 39**
See also CA 120; 130; INT 130
Peck, Dale 1967- .... **CLC 81**
See also CA 146; CANR 72
Peck, John 1941- .... **CLC 3**
See also CA 49-52; CANR 3
Peck, Richard (Wayne) 1934- .... **CLC 21**
See also AAYA 1, 24; CA 85-88; CANR 19,

38; CLR 15; INT CANR-19; JRDA; MAICYA; SAAS 2; SATA 18, 55, 97
Peck, Robert Newton 1928- ..... **CLC 17; DA; DAC; DAM MST**
See also AAYA 3; CA 81-84; CANR 31, 63; CLR 45; JRDA; MAICYA; SAAS 1; SATA 21, 62
Peckinpah, (David) Sam(uel) 1925-1984**C L C 20**
See also CA 109; 114
Pedersen, Knut 1859-1952
See Hamsun, Knut
See also CA 104; 119; CANR 63; MTCW 1
Peeslake, Gaffer
See Durrell, Lawrence (George)
Peguy, Charles Pierre 1873-1914 .. **TCLC 10**
See also CA 107
Peirce, Charles Sanders 1839-1914 **TCLC 81**
Pena, Ramon del Valle y
See Valle-Inclan, Ramon (Maria) del
Pendennis, Arthur Esquir
See Thackeray, William Makepeace
Penn, William 1644-1718 .... **LC 25**
See also DLB 24
PEPECE
See Prado (Calvo), Pedro
Pepys, Samuel 1633-1703 **LC 11; DA; DAB; DAC; DAM MST; WLC**
See also CDBLB 1660-1789; DLB 101
Percy, Walker 1916-1990**CLC 2, 3, 6, 8, 14, 18, 47, 65; DAM NOV, POP**
See also CA 1-4R; 131; CANR 1, 23, 64; DLB 2; DLBY 80, 90; MTCW 1
Percy, William Alexander 1885-1942**TCLC 84**
See also CA 163
Perec, Georges 1936-1982 .... **CLC 56**
See also CA 141; DLB 83
Pereda (y Sanchez de Porrua), Jose Maria de 1833-1906 .... **TCLC 16**
See also CA 117
Pereda y Porrua, Jose Maria de
See Pereda (y Sanchez de Porrua), Jose Maria de
Peregoy, George Weems
See Mencken, H(enry) L(ouis)
Perelman, S(idney) J(oseph) 1904-1979 **C L C 3, 5, 9, 15, 23, 44, 49; DAM DRAM; SSC 32**
See also AITN 1, 2; CA 73-76; 89-92; CANR 18; DLB 11, 44; MTCW 1
Peret, Benjamin 1899-1959 .... **TCLC 20**
See also CA 117
Peretz, Isaac Loeb 1851(?)-1915 ... **TCLC 16; SSC 26**
See also CA 109
Peretz, Yitzhok Leibush
See Peretz, Isaac Loeb
Perez Galdos, Benito 1843-1920 .... **TCLC 27**
See also CA 125; 153; HW
Perrault, Charles 1628-1703 .... **LC 2**
See also MAICYA; SATA 25
Perry, Brighton
See Sherwood, Robert E(mmet)
Perse, St.-John
See Leger, (Marie-Rene Auguste) Alexis Saint-Leger
Perutz, Leo 1882-1957 .... **TCLC 60**
See also DLB 81
Peseenz, Tulio F.
See Lopez y Fuentes, Gregorio
Pesetsky, Bette 1932- .... **CLC 28**
See also CA 133; DLB 130
Peshkov, Alexei Maximovich 1868-1936
See Gorky, Maxim
See also CA 105; 141; DA; DAC; DAM DRAM, MST, NOV
Pessoa, Fernando (Antonio Nogueira) 1898-

1935 .... **TCLC 27; HLC; PC 20**
See also CA 125
Peterkin, Julia Mood 1880-1961 .... **CLC 31**
See also CA 102; DLB 9
Peters, Joan K(aren) 1945- .... **CLC 39**
See also CA 158
Peters, Robert L(ouis) 1924- .... **CLC 7**
See also CA 13-16R; CAAS 8; DLB 105
Petofi, Sandor 1823-1849 .... **NCLC 21**
Petrakis, Harry Mark 1923- .... **CLC 3**
See also CA 9-12R; CANR 4, 30
Petrarch 1304-1374 **CMLC 20; DAM POET; PC 8**
Petrov, Evgeny .... **TCLC 21**
See also Kataev, Evgeny Petrovich
Petry, Ann (Lane) 1908-1997 ... **CLC 1, 7, 18**
See also BW 1; CA 5-8R; 157; CAAS 6; CANR 4, 46; CLR 12; DLB 76; JRDA; MAICYA; MTCW 1; SATA 5; SATA-Obit 94
Petursson, Halligrimur 1614-1674 .... **LC 8**
Peychinovich
See Vazov, Ivan (Minchov)
Phaedrus 18(?)B.C.-55(?) .... **CMLC 25**
Philips, Katherine 1632-1664 .... **LC 30**
See also DLB 131
Philipson, Morris H. 1926- .... **CLC 53**
See also CA 1-4R; CANR 4
Phillips, Caryl 1958- ..**CLC 96; BLCS; DAM MULT**
See also BW 2; CA 141; CANR 63; DLB 157
Phillips, David Graham 1867-1911 **TCLC 44**
See also CA 108; DLB 9, 12
Phillips, Jack
See Sandburg, Carl (August)
Phillips, Jayne Anne 1952- **CLC 15, 33; SSC 16**
See also CA 101; CANR 24, 50; DLBY 80; INT CANR-24; MTCW 1
Phillips, Richard
See Dick, Philip K(indred)
Phillips, Robert (Schaeffer) 1938- .... **CLC 28**
See also CA 17-20R; CAAS 13; CANR 8; DLB 105
Phillips, Ward
See Lovecraft, H(oward) P(hillips)
Piccolo, Lucio 1901-1969 .... **CLC 13**
See also CA 97-100; DLB 114
Pickthall, Marjorie L(owry) C(hristie) 1883-1922 ....
TCLC 21
See also CA 107; DLB 92
Pico della Mirandola, Giovanni 1463-1494**LC 15**
Piercy, Marge 1936- **CLC 3, 6, 14, 18, 27, 62**
See also CA 21-24R; CAAS 1; CANR 13, 43, 66; DLB 120; MTCW 1
Piers, Robert
See Anthony, Piers
Pieyre de Mandiargues, Andre 1909-1991
See Mandiargues, Andre Pieyre de
See also CA 103; 136; CANR 22
Pilnyak, Boris .... **TCLC 23**
See also Vogau, Boris Andreyevich
Pincherle, Alberto 1907-1990 ... **CLC 11, 18; DAM NOV**
See Moravia, Alberto
See also CA 25-28R; 132; CANR 33, 63; MTCW 1
Pinckney, Darryl 1953- .... **CLC 76**
See also BW 2; CA 143
Pindar 518B.C.-446B.C. .... **CMLC 12; PC 19**
See also DLB 176
Pineda, Cecile 1942- .... **CLC 39**
See also CA 118
Pinero, Arthur Wing 1855-1934 ... **TCLC 32; DAM DRAM**
See also CA 110; 153; DLB 10
Pinero, Miguel (Antonio Gomez) 1946-1988

CLC 4, 55
See also CA 61-64; 125; CANR 29; HW
Pinget, Robert 1919-1997 .... **CLC 7, 13, 37**
See also CA 85-88; 160; DLB 83
Pink Floyd
See Barrett, (Roger) Syd; Gilmour, David; Mason, Nick; Waters, Roger; Wright, Rick
Pinkney, Edward 1802-1828 .... **NCLC 31**
Pinkwater, Daniel Manus 1941- .... **CLC 35**
See also Pinkwater, Manus
See also AAYA 1; CA 29-32R; CANR 12, 38; CLR 4; JRDA; MAICYA; SAAS 3; SATA 46, 76
Pinkwater, Manus
See Pinkwater, Daniel Manus
See also SATA 8
Pinsky, Robert 1940-**CLC 9, 19, 38, 94; DAM POET**
See also CA 29-32R; CAAS 4; CANR 58; DLBY 82
Pinta, Harold
See Pinter, Harold
Pinter, Harold 1930-**CLC 1, 3, 6, 9, 11, 15, 27, 58, 73; DA; DAB; DAC; DAM DRAM, MST; WLC**
See also CA 5-8R; CANR 33, 65; CDBLB 1960 to Present; DLB 13; MTCW 1
Piozzi, Hester Lynch (Thrale) 1741-1821
NCLC 57
See also DLB 104, 142
Pirandello, Luigi 1867-1936**TCLC 4, 29; DA; DAB; DAC; DAM DRAM, MST; DC 5; SSC 22; WLC**
See also CA 104; 153
Pirsig, Robert M(aynard) 1928-**CLC 4, 6, 73; DAM POP**
See also CA 53-56; CANR 42; MTCW 1; SATA 39
Pisarev, Dmitry Ivanovich 1840-1868 **NCLC 25**
Pix, Mary (Griffith) 1666-1709 .... **LC 8**
See also DLB 80
Pixerecourt, (Rene Charles) Guilbert de 1773-1844 ....
NCLC 39
See also DLB 192
Plaatje, Sol(omon) T(shekisho) 1876-1932
TCLC 73; BLCS
See also BW 2; CA 141
Plaidy, Jean
See Hibbert, Eleanor Alice Burford
Planche, James Robinson 1796-1880**NCLC 42**
Plant, Robert 1948- .... **CLC 12**
Plante, David (Robert) 1940- **CLC 7, 23, 38; DAM NOV**
See also CA 37-40R; CANR 12, 36, 58; DLBY 83; INT CANR-12; MTCW 1
Plath, Sylvia 1932-1963 **CLC 1, 2, 3, 5, 9, 11, 14, 17, 50, 51, 62, 111; DA; DAB; DAC; DAM MST, POET; PC 1; WLC**
See also AAYA 13; CA 19-20; CANR 34; CAP 2; CDALB 1941-1968; DLB 5, 6, 152; MTCW 1; SATA 96
Plato 428(?)B.C.-348(?)B.C.... **CMLC 8; DA; DAB; DAC; DAM MST; WLCS**
See also DLB 176
Platonov, Andrei .... **TCLC 14**
See also Klimentov, Andrei Platonovich
Platt, Kin 1911- .... **CLC 26**
See also AAYA 11; CA 17-20R; CANR 11; JRDA; SAAS 17; SATA 21, 86
Plautus c. 251B.C.-184B.C..**CMLC 24; DC 6**
Plick et Plock
See Simenon, Georges (Jacques Christian)
Plimpton, George (Ames) 1927- .... **CLC 36**
See also AITN 1; CA 21-24R; CANR 32, 70; DLB 185; MTCW 1; SATA 10

Pliny the Elder c. 23-79 .... **CMLC 23**
Plomer, William Charles Franklin 1903-1973
CLC 4, 8
See also CA 21-22; CANR 34; CAP 2; DLB 20, 162, 191; MTCW 1; SATA 24
Plowman, Piers
See Kavanagh, Patrick (Joseph)
Plum, J.
See Wodehouse, P(elham) G(renville)
Plumly, Stanley (Ross) 1939- .... **CLC 33**
See also CA 108; 110; DLB 5, 193; INT 110
Plumpe, Friedrich Wilhelm 1888-1931**T C L C 53**
See also CA 112
Po Chu-i 772-846 .... **CMLC 24**
Poe, Edgar Allan 1809-1849**NCLC 1, 16, 55; DA; DAB; DAC; DAM MST, POET; PC 1; SSC 1, 22; WLC**
See also AAYA 14; CDALB 1640-1865; DLB 3, 59, 73, 74; SATA 23
Poet of Titchfield Street, The
See Pound, Ezra (Weston Loomis)
Pohl, Frederik 1919- .... **CLC 18; SSC 25**
See also AAYA 24; CA 61-64; CAAS 1; CANR 11, 37; DLB 8; INT CANR-11; MTCW 1; SATA 24
Poirier, Louis 1910-
See Gracq, Julien
See also CA 122; 126
Poitier, Sidney 1927- .... **CLC 26**
See also BW 1; CA 117
Polanski, Roman 1933- .... **CLC 16**
See also CA 77-80
Poliakoff, Stephen 1952- .... **CLC 38**
See also CA 106; DLB 13
Police, The
See Copeland, Stewart (Armstrong); Summers, Andrew James; Sumner, Gordon Matthew
Polidori, John William 1795-1821 . **NCLC 51**
See also DLB 116
Pollitt, Katha 1949- .... **CLC 28**
See also CA 120; 122; CANR 66; MTCW 1
Pollock, (Mary) Sharon 1936-**CLC 50; DAC; DAM DRAM, MST**
See also CA 141; DLB 60
Polo, Marco 1254-1324 .... **CMLC 15**
Polonsky, Abraham (Lincoln) 1910- **CLC 92**
See also CA 104; DLB 26; INT 104
Polybius c. 200B.C.-c. 118B.C. ...... **CMLC 17**
See also DLB 176
Pomerance, Bernard 1940- .... **CLC 13; DAM DRAM**
See also CA 101; CANR 49
Ponge, Francis (Jean Gaston Alfred) 1899-1988
CLC 6, 18; DAM POET
See also CA 85-88; 126; CANR 40
Pontoppidan, Henrik 1857-1943 .... **TCLC 29**
Poole, Josephine .... **CLC 17**
See also Helyar, Jane Penelope Josephine
See also SAAS 2; SATA 5
Popa, Vasko 1922-1991 .... **CLC 19**
See also CA 112; 148; DLB 181
Pope, Alexander 1688-1744**LC 3; DA; DAB; DAC; DAM MST, POET; WLC**
See also CDBLB 1660-1789; DLB 95, 101
Porter, Connie (Rose) 1959(?)- .... **CLC 70**
See also BW 2; CA 142; SATA 81
Porter, Gene(va Grace) Stratton 1863(?)-1924
TCLC 21
See also CA 112
Porter, Katherine Anne 1890-1980**CLC 1, 3, 7, 10, 13, 15, 27, 101; DA; DAB; DAC; DAM MST, NOV; SSC 4, 31**
See also AITN 2; CA 1-4R; 101; CANR 1, 65; DLB 4, 9, 102; DLBD 12; DLBY 80; MTCW 1; SATA 39; SATA-Obit 23
Porter, Peter (Neville Frederick) 1929-**CLC 5,**

13, 33
See also CA 85-88; DLB 40

Porter, William Sydney 1862-1910
See Henry, O.
See also CA 104; 131; CDALB 1865-1917; DA; DAB; DAC; DAM MST; DLB 12, 78, 79; MTCW 1; YABC 2

Portillo (y Pacheco), Jose Lopez
See Lopez Portillo (y Pacheco), Jose

Post, Melville Davisson 1869-1930 **TCLC 39**
See also CA 110

Potok, Chaim 1929- ... **CLC 2, 7, 14, 26, 112; DAM NOV**
See also AAYA 15; AITN 1, 2; CA 17-20R; CANR 19, 35, 64; DLB 28, 152; INT CANR-19; MTCW 1; SATA 33

Potter, (Helen) Beatrix 1866-1943
See Webb, (Martha) Beatrice (Potter)
See also MAICYA

Potter, Dennis (Christopher George) 1935-1994 **CLC 58, 86**
See also CA 107; 145; CANR 33, 61; MTCW 1

Pound, Ezra (Weston Loomis) 1885-1972
CLC 1, 2, 3, 4, 5, 7, 10, 13, 18, 34, 48, 50, 112; DA; DAB; DAC; DAM MST, POET; PC 4; WLC
See also CA 5-8R; 37-40R; CANR 40; CDALB 1917-1929; DLB 4, 45, 63; DLBD 15; MTCW 1

Povod, Reinaldo 1959-1994 .... **CLC 44**
See also CA 136; 146

Powell, Adam Clayton, Jr. 1908-1972 **CLC 89; BLC 3; DAM MULT**
See also BW 1; CA 102; 33-36R

Powell, Anthony (Dymoke) 1905- **CLC 1, 3, 7, 9, 10, 31**
See also CA 1-4R; CANR 1, 32, 62; CDBLB 1945-1960; DLB 15; MTCW 1

Powell, Dawn 1897-1965 .... **CLC 66**
See also CA 5-8R; DLBY 97

Powell, Padgett 1952- .... **CLC 34**
See also CA 126; CANR 63

Power, Susan 1961- .... **CLC 91**

Powers, J(ames) F(arl) 1917- **CLC 1, 4, 8, 57; SSC 4**
See also CA 1-4R; CANR 2, 61; DLB 130; MTCW 1

Powers, John J(ames) 1945-
See Powers, John R.
See also CA 69-72

Powers, John R. .... **CLC 66**
See also Powers, John J(ames)

Powers, Richard (S.) 1957- .... **CLC 93**
See also CA 148

Pownall, David 1938- .... **CLC 10**
See also CA 89-92; CAAS 18; CANR 49; DLB 14

Powys, John Cowper 1872-1963 **CLC 7, 9, 15, 46**
See also CA 85-88; DLB 15; MTCW 1

Powys, T(heodore) F(rancis) 1875-1953
TCLC 9
See also CA 106; DLB 36, 162

Prado (Calvo), Pedro 1886-1952 ... **TCLC 75**
See also CA 131; HW

Prager, Emily 1952- .... **CLC 56**

Pratt, E(dwin) J(ohn) 1883(?)-1964 **CLC 19; DAC; DAM POET**
See also CA 141; 93-96; DLB 92

Premchand .... **TCLC 21**
See also Srivastava, Dhanpat Rai

Preussler, Otfried 1923- .... **CLC 17**
See also CA 77-80; SATA 24

Prevert, Jacques (Henri Marie) 1900-1977
CLC 15
See also CA 77-80; 69-72; CANR 29, 61; MTCW 1; SATA-Obit 30

Prevost, Abbe (Antoine Francois) 1697-1763
LC 1

Price, (Edward) Reynolds 1933- **CLC 3, 6, 13, 43, 50, 63; DAM NOV; SSC 22**
See also CA 1-4R; CANR 1, 37, 57; DLB 2; INT CANR-37

Price, Richard 1949- .... **CLC 6, 12**
See also CA 49-52; CANR 3; DLBY 81

Prichard, Katharine Susannah 1883-1969
CLC 46
See also CA 11-12; CANR 33; CAP 1; MTCW 1; SATA 66

Priestley, J(ohn) B(oynton) 1894-1984 **CLC 2, 5, 9, 34; DAM DRAM, NOV**
See also CA 9-12R; 113; CANR 33; CDBLB 1914-1945; DLB 10, 34, 77, 100, 139; DLBY 84; MTCW 1

Prince 1958(?)- .... **CLC 35**

Prince, F(rank) T(empleton) 1912- .. **CLC 22**
See also CA 101; CANR 43; DLB 20

Prince Kropotkin
See Kropotkin, Peter (Aleksieevich)

Prior, Matthew 1664-1721 .... **LC 4**
See also DLB 95

Prishvin, Mikhail 1873-1954 .... **TCLC 75**

Pritchard, William H(arrison) 1932- **CLC 34**
See also CA 65-68; CANR 23; DLB 111

Pritchett, V(ictor) S(awdon) 1900-1997 **C L C 5, 13, 15, 41; DAM NOV; SSC 14**
See also CA 61-64; 157; CANR 31, 63; DLB 15, 139; MTCW 1

Private 19022
See Manning, Frederic

Probst, Mark 1925- .... **CLC 59**
See also CA 130

Prokosch, Frederic 1908-1989 ...... **CLC 4, 48**
See also CA 73-76; 128; DLB 48

Prophet, The
See Dreiser, Theodore (Herman Albert)

Prose, Francine 1947- .... **CLC 45**
See also CA 109; 112; CANR 46; SATA 101

Proudhon
See Cunha, Euclides (Rodrigues Pimenta) da

Proulx, Annie
See Proulx, E(dna) Annie

Proulx, E(dna) Annie 1935- ... **CLC 81; DAM POP**
See also CA 145; CANR 65

Proust, (Valentin-Louis-George-Eugene-) Marcel 1871-1922 **TCLC 7, 13, 33; DA; DAB; DAC; DAM MST, NOV; WLC**
See also CA 104; 120; DLB 65; MTCW 1

Prowler, Harley
See Masters, Edgar Lee

Prus, Boleslaw 1845-1912 .... **TCLC 48**

Pryor, Richard (Franklin Lenox Thomas) 1940-
CLC 26
See also CA 122

Przybyszewski, Stanislaw 1868-1927 **TCLC 36**
See also CA 160; DLB 66

Pteleon
See Grieve, C(hristopher) M(urray)
See also DAM POET

Puckett, Lute
See Masters, Edgar Lee

Puig, Manuel 1932-1990 **CLC 3, 5, 10, 28, 65; DAM MULT; HLC**
See also CA 45-48; CANR 2, 32, 63; DLB 113; HW; MTCW 1

Pulitzer, Joseph 1847-1911 .... **TCLC 76**
See also CA 114; DLB 23

Purdy, A(lfred) W(ellington) 1918- **CLC 3, 6, 14, 50; DAC; DAM MST, POET**
See also CA 81-84; CAAS 17; CANR 42, 66; DLB 88

Purdy, James (Amos) 1923- **CLC 2, 4, 10, 28, 52**

See also CA 33-36R; CAAS 1; CANR 19, 51; DLB 2; INT CANR-19; MTCW 1

Pure, Simon
See Swinnerton, Frank Arthur

Pushkin, Alexander (Sergeyevich) 1799-1837
NCLC 3, 27; DA; DAB; DAC; DAM DRAM, MST, POET; PC 10; SSC 27; WLC
See also SATA 61

P'u Sung-ling 1640-1715 .... **LC 3; SSC 31**

Putnam, Arthur Lee
See Alger, Horatio, Jr.

Puzo, Mario 1920- **CLC 1, 2, 6, 36, 107; DAM NOV, POP**
See also CA 65-68; CANR 4, 42, 65; DLB 6; MTCW 1

Pygge, Edward
See Barnes, Julian (Patrick)

Pyle, Ernest Taylor 1900-1945
See Pyle, Ernie
See also CA 115; 160

Pyle, Ernie 1900-1945 .... **TCLC 75**
See also Pyle, Ernest Taylor
See also DLB 29

Pyle, Howard 1853-1911 .... **TCLC 81**
See also CA 109; 137; CLR 22; DLB 42, 188; DLBD 13; MAICYA; SATA 16, 100

Pym, Barbara (Mary Crampton) 1913-1980
CLC 13, 19, 37, 111
See also CA 13-14; 97-100; CANR 13, 34; CAP 1; DLB 14; DLBY 87; MTCW 1

Pynchon, Thomas (Ruggles, Jr.) 1937- **CLC 2, 3, 6, 9, 11, 18, 33, 62, 72; DA; DAB; DAC; DAM MST, NOV, POP; SSC 14; WLC**
See also BEST 90:2; CA 17-20R; CANR 22, 46; DLB 2, 173; MTCW 1

Pythagoras c. 570B.C.-c. 500B.C. . **CMLC 22**
See also DLB 176

Q
See Quiller-Couch, SirArthur (Thomas)

Qian Zhongshu
See Ch'ien Chung-shu

Qroll
See Dagerman, Stig (Halvard)

Quarrington, Paul (Lewis) 1953- ..... **CLC 65**
See also CA 129; CANR 62

Quasimodo, Salvatore 1901-1968 ..... **CLC 10**
See also CA 13-16; 25-28R; CAP 1; DLB 114; MTCW 1

Quay, Stephen 1947- .... **CLC 95**
Quay, Timothy 1947- .... **CLC 95**

Queen, Ellery .... **CLC 3, 11**
See also Dannay, Frederic; Davidson, Avram; Lee, Manfred B(ennington); Marlowe, Stephen; Sturgeon, Theodore (Hamilton); Vance, John Holbrook

Queen, Ellery, Jr.
See Dannay, Frederic; Lee, Manfred B(ennington)

Queneau, Raymond 1903-1976 **CLC 2, 5, 10, 42**
See also CA 77-80; 69-72; CANR 32; DLB 72; MTCW 1

Quevedo, Francisco de 1580-1645 .... **LC 23**

Quiller-Couch, SirArthur (Thomas) 1863-1944
TCLC 53
See also CA 118; 166; DLB 135, 153, 190

Quin, Ann (Marie) 1936-1973 .... **CLC 6**
See also CA 9-12R; 45-48; DLB 14

Quinn, Martin
See Smith, Martin Cruz

Quinn, Peter 1947- .... **CLC 91**

Quinn, Simon
See Smith, Martin Cruz

Quiroga, Horacio (Sylvestre) 1878-1937
TCLC 20; DAM MULT; HLC
See also CA 117; 131; HW; MTCW 1

51; DAM NOV; SSC 21
  See also CA 25-28R; 85-88; CANR 35, 62;
    CDBLB 1945-1960; DLB 36, 117, 162;
    MTCW 1
Ribeiro, Darcy 1922-1997 .... **CLC 34**
  See also CA 33-36R; 156
Ribeiro, Joao Ubaldo (Osorio Pimentel) 1941-
    CLC 10, 67
  See also CA 81-84
Ribman, Ronald (Burt) 1932- .... **CLC 7**
  See also CA 21-24R; CANR 46
Ricci, Nino 1959- .... **CLC 70**
  See also CA 137
Rice, Anne 1941- .... **CLC 41; DAM POP**
  See also AAYA 9; BEST 89:2; CA 65-68; CANR
    12, 36, 53
Rice, Elmer (Leopold) 1892-1967 **CLC 7, 49;**
    DAM DRAM
  See also CA 21-22; 25-28R; CAP 2; DLB 4, 7;
    MTCW 1
Rice, Tim(othy Miles Bindon) 1944- **CLC 21**
  See also CA 103; CANR 46
Rich, Adrienne (Cecile) 1929-**CLC 3, 6, 7, 11,**
    18, 36, 73, 76; DAM POET; PC 5
  See also CA 9-12R; CANR 20, 53; DLB 5, 67;
    MTCW 1
Rich, Barbara
  See Graves, Robert (von Ranke)
Rich, Robert
  See Trumbo, Dalton
Richard, Keith .... **CLC 17**
  See also Richards, Keith
Richards, David Adams 1950- **CLC 59; DAC**
  See also CA 93-96; CANR 60; DLB 53
Richards, I(vor) A(rmstrong) 1893-1979**C L C**
    14, 24
  See also CA 41-44R; 89-92; CANR 34; DLB
    27
Richards, Keith 1943-
  See Richard, Keith
  See also CA 107
Richardson, Anne
  See Roiphe, Anne (Richardson)
Richardson, Dorothy Miller 1873-1957**TCLC**
    3
  See also CA 104; DLB 36
Richardson, Ethel Florence (Lindesay) 1870-
    1946
  See Richardson, Henry Handel
  See also CA 105
Richardson, Henry Handel .... **TCLC 4**
  See also Richardson, Ethel Florence (Lindesay)
  See also DLB 197
Richardson, John 1796-1852**NCLC 55; DAC**
  See also DLB 99
Richardson, Samuel 1689-1761**LC 1, 44; DA;**
    DAB; DAC; DAM MST, NOV; WLC
  See also CDBLB 1660-1789; DLB 39
Richler, Mordecai 1931-**CLC 3, 5, 9, 13, 18, 46,**
    70; DAC; DAM MST, NOV
  See also AITN 1; CA 65-68; CANR 31, 62; CLR
    17; DLB 53; MAICYA; MTCW 1; SATA 44,
    98; SATA-Brief 27
Richter, Conrad (Michael) 1890-1968**CLC 30**
  See also AAYA 21; CA 5-8R; 25-28R; CANR
    23; DLB 9; MTCW 1; SATA 3
Ricostranza, Tom
  See Ellis, Trey
Riddell, Charlotte 1832-1906 .... **TCLC 40**
  See also CA 165; DLB 156
Riding, Laura .... **CLC 3, 7**
  See also Jackson, Laura (Riding)
Riefenstahl, Berta Helene Amalia 1902-
  See Riefenstahl, Leni
  See also CA 108
Riefenstahl, Leni .... **CLC 16**
  See also Riefenstahl, Berta Helene Amalia

Riffe, Ernest
  See Bergman, (Ernst) Ingmar
Riggs, (Rolla) Lynn 1899-1954 ..... **TCLC 56;**
    DAM MULT
  See also CA 144; DLB 175; NNAL
Riis, Jacob A(ugust) 1849-1914 ..... **TCLC 80**
  See also CA 113; 168; DLB 23
Riley, James Whitcomb 1849-1916**TCLC 51;**
    DAM POET
  See also CA 118; 137; MAICYA; SATA 17
Riley, Tex
  See Creasey, John
Rilke, Rainer Maria 1875-1926**TCLC 1, 6, 19;**
    DAM POET; PC 2
  See also CA 104; 132; CANR 62; DLB 81;
    MTCW 1
Rimbaud, (Jean Nicolas) Arthur 1854-1891
    NCLC 4, 35; DA; DAB; DAC; DAM MST,
    POET; PC 3; WLC
Rinehart, Mary Roberts 1876-1958**TCLC 52**
  See also CA 108; 166
Ringmaster, The
  See Mencken, H(enry) L(ouis)
Ringwood, Gwen(dolyn Margaret) Pharis
    1910-1984 .... **CLC 48**
  See also CA 148; 112; DLB 88
Rio, Michel 19(?)- .... **CLC 43**
Ritsos, Giannes
  See Ritsos, Yannis
Ritsos, Yannis 1909-1990 .... **CLC 6, 13, 31**
  See also CA 77-80; 133; CANR 39, 61; MTCW
    1
Ritter, Erika 1948(?)- .... **CLC 52**
Rivera, Jose Eustasio 1889-1928 ... **TCLC 35**
  See also CA 162; HW
Rivers, Conrad Kent 1933-1968 .... **CLC 1**
  See also BW 1; CA 85-88; DLB 41
Rivers, Elfrida
  See Bradley, Marion Zimmer
Riverside, John
  See Heinlein, Robert A(nson)
Rizal, Jose 1861-1896 .... **NCLC 27**
Roa Bastos, Augusto (Antonio) 1917-**CLC 45;**
    DAM MULT; HLC
  See also CA 131; DLB 113; HW
Robbe-Grillet, Alain 1922-**CLC 1, 2, 4, 6, 8, 10,**
    14, 43
  See also CA 9-12R; CANR 33, 65; DLB 83;
    MTCW 1
Robbins, Harold 1916-1997 ..... **CLC 5; DAM**
    NOV
  See also CA 73-76; 162; CANR 26, 54; MTCW
    1
Robbins, Thomas Eugene 1936-
  See Robbins, Tom
  See also CA 81-84; CANR 29, 59; DAM NOV,
    POP; MTCW 1
Robbins, Tom .... **CLC 9, 32, 64**
  See also Robbins, Thomas Eugene
  See also BEST 90:3; DLBY 80
Robbins, Trina 1938- .... **CLC 21**
  See also CA 128
Roberts, Charles G(eorge) D(ouglas) 1860-1943
    TCLC 8
  See also CA 105; CLR 33; DLB 92; SATA 88;
    SATA-Brief 29
Roberts, Elizabeth Madox 1886-1941 **T C L C**
    68
  See also CA 111; 166; DLB 9, 54, 102; SATA
    33; SATA-Brief 27
Roberts, Kate 1891-1985 .... **CLC 15**
  See also CA 107; 116
Roberts, Keith (John Kingston) 1935-**CLC 14**
  See also CA 25-28R; CANR 46
Roberts, Kenneth (Lewis) 1885-1957**TCLC 23**
  See also CA 109; DLB 9
Roberts, Michele (B.) 1949- .... **CLC 48**

  See also CA 115; CANR 58
Robertson, Ellis
  See Ellison, Harlan (Jay); Silverberg, Robert
Robertson, Thomas William 1829-1871**NCLC**
    35; DAM DRAM
Robeson, Kenneth
  See Dent, Lester
Robinson, Edwin Arlington 1869-1935**T C L C**
    5; DA; DAC; DAM MST, POET; PC 1
  See also CA 104; 133; CDALB 1865-1917;
    DLB 54; MTCW 1
Robinson, Henry Crabb 1775-1867**NCLC 15**
  See also DLB 107
Robinson, Jill 1936- .... **CLC 10**
  See also CA 102; INT 102
Robinson, Kim Stanley 1952- .... **CLC 34**
  See also AAYA 26; CA 126
Robinson, Lloyd
  See Silverberg, Robert
Robinson, Marilynne 1944- .... **CLC 25**
  See also CA 116
Robinson, Smokey .... **CLC 21**
  See also Robinson, William, Jr.
Robinson, William, Jr. 1940-
  See Robinson, Smokey
  See also CA 116
Robison, Mary 1949- .... **CLC 42, 98**
  See also CA 113; 116; DLB 130; INT 116
Rod, Edouard 1857-1910 .... **TCLC 52**
Roddenberry, Eugene Wesley 1921-1991
  See Roddenberry, Gene
  See also CA 110; 135; CANR 37; SATA 45;
    SATA-Obit 69
Roddenberry, Gene .... **CLC 17**
  See also Roddenberry, Eugene Wesley
  See also AAYA 5; SATA-Obit 69
Rodgers, Mary 1931- .... **CLC 12**
  See also CA 49-52; CANR 8, 55; CLR 20; INT
    CANR-8; JRDA; MAICYA; SATA 8
Rodgers, W(illiam) R(obert) 1909-1969**CLC 7**
  See also CA 85-88; DLB 20
Rodman, Eric
  See Silverberg, Robert
Rodman, Howard 1920(?)-1985 .... **CLC 65**
  See also CA 118
Rodman, Maia
  See Wojciechowska, Maia (Teresa)
Rodriguez, Claudio 1934- .... **CLC 10**
  See also DLB 134
Roelvaag, O(le) E(dvart) 1876-1931**TCLC 17**
  See also CA 117; DLB 9
Roethke, Theodore (Huebner) 1908-1963**CLC**
    1, 3, 8, 11, 19, 46, 101; DAM POET; PC 15
  See also CA 81-84; CABS 2; CDALB 1941-
    1968; DLB 5; MTCW 1
Rogers, Samuel 1763-1855 .... **NCLC 69**
  See also DLB 93
Rogers, Thomas Hunton 1927- .... **CLC 57**
  See also CA 89-92; INT 89-92
Rogers, Will(iam Penn Adair) 1879-1935
    TCLC 8, 71; DAM MULT
  See also CA 105; 144; DLB 11; NNAL
Rogin, Gilbert 1929- .... **CLC 18**
  See also CA 65-68; CANR 15
Rohan, Koda .... **TCLC 22**
  See also Koda Shigeyuki
Rohlfs, Anna Katharine Green
  See Green, Anna Katharine
Rohmer, Eric .... **CLC 16**
  See also Scherer, Jean-Marie Maurice
Rohmer, Sax .... **TCLC 28**
  See also Ward, Arthur Henry Sarsfield
  See also DLB 70
Roiphe, Anne (Richardson) 1935- .. **CLC 3, 9**
  See also CA 89-92; CANR 45; DLBY 80; INT
    89-92
Rojas, Fernando de 1465-1541 .... **LC 23**

Sadoff, Ira 1945- .... CLC 9
  See also CA 53-56; CANR 5, 21; DLB 120
Saetone
  See Camus, Albert
Safire, William 1929- .... CLC 10
  See also CA 17-20R; CANR 31, 54
Sagan, Carl (Edward) 1934-1996CLC 30, 112
  See also AAYA 2; CA 25-28R; 155; CANR 11,
    36; MTCW 1; SATA 58; SATA-Obit 94
Sagan, Francoise .... CLC 3, 6, 9, 17, 36
  See also Quoirez, Francoise
  See also DLB 83
Sahgal, Nayantara (Pandit) 1927- .... CLC 41
  See also CA 9-12R; CANR 11
Saint, H(arry) F. 1941- .... CLC 50
  See also CA 127
St. Aubin de Teran, Lisa 1953-
  See Teran, Lisa St. Aubin de
  See also CA 118; 126; INT 126
Saint Birgitta of Sweden c. 1303-1373 C M L C
    24
Sainte-Beuve, Charles Augustin 1804-1869
    NCLC 5
Saint-Exupery, Antoine (Jean Baptiste Marie
    Roger) de 1900-1944TCLC 2, 56; DAM
    NOV; WLC
  See also CA 108; 132; CLR 10; DLB 72;
    MAICYA; MTCW 1; SATA 20
St. John, David
  See Hunt, E(verette) Howard, (Jr.)
Saint-John Perse
  See Leger, (Marie-Rene Auguste) Alexis Saint-
    Leger
Saintsbury, George (Edward Bateman) 1845-
    1933 .... TCLC 31
  See also CA 160; DLB 57, 149
Sait Faik .... TCLC 23
  See also Abasiyanik, Sait Faik
Saki .... TCLC 3; SSC 12
  See also Munro, H(ector) H(ugh)
Sala, George Augustus .... NCLC 46
Salama, Hannu 1936- .... CLC 18
Salamanca, J(ack) R(ichard) 1922-CLC 4, 15
  See also CA 25-28R
Sale, J. Kirkpatrick
  See Sale, Kirkpatrick
Sale, Kirkpatrick 1937- .... CLC 68
  See also CA 13-16R; CANR 10
Salinas, Luis Omar 1937- ...... CLC 90; DAM
    MULT; HLC
  See also CA 131; DLB 82; HW
Salinas (y Serrano), Pedro 1891(?)-1951
    TCLC 17
  See also CA 117; DLB 134
Salinger, J(erome) D(avid) 1919-CLC 1, 3, 8,
    12, 55, 56; DA; DAB; DAC; DAM MST,
    NOV, POP; SSC 2, 28; WLC
  See also AAYA 2; CA 5-8R; CANR 39; CDALB
    1941-1968; CLR 18; DLB 2, 102, 173;
    MAICYA; MTCW 1; SATA 67
Salisbury, John
  See Caute, (John) David
Salter, James 1925- .... CLC 7, 52, 59
  See also CA 73-76; DLB 130
Saltus, Edgar (Everton) 1855-1921 . TCLC 8
  See also CA 105; DLB 202
Saltykov, Mikhail Evgrafovich 1826-1889
    NCLC 16
Samarakis, Antonis 1919- .... CLC 5
  See also CA 25-28R; CAAS 16; CANR 36
Sanchez, Florencio 1875-1910........ TCLC 37
  See also CA 153; HW
Sanchez, Luis Rafael 1936- .... CLC 23
  See also CA 128; DLB 145; HW
Sanchez, Sonia 1934-.. CLC 5; BLC 3; DAM
    MULT; PC 9
  See also BW 2; CA 33-36R; CANR 24, 49; CLR

18; DLB 41; DLBD 8; MAICYA; MTCW 1;
    SATA 22
Sand, George 1804-1876NCLC 2, 42, 57; DA;
    DAB; DAC; DAM MST, NOV; WLC
  See also DLB 119, 192
Sandburg, Carl (August) 1878-1967CLC 1, 4,
    10, 15, 35; DA; DAB; DAC; DAM MST,
    POET; PC 2; WLC
  See also AAYA 24; CA 5-8R; 25-28R; CANR
    35; CDALB 1865-1917; DLB 17, 54;
    MAICYA; MTCW 1; SATA 8
Sandburg, Charles
  See Sandburg, Carl (August)
Sandburg, Charles A.
  See Sandburg, Carl (August)
Sanders, (James) Ed(ward) 1939- .... CLC 53
  See also CA 13-16R; CAAS 21; CANR 13, 44;
    DLB 16
Sanders, Lawrence 1920-1998CLC 41; DAM
    POP
  See also BEST 89:4; CA 81-84; 165; CANR
    33, 62; MTCW 1
Sanders, Noah
  See Blount, Roy (Alton), Jr.
Sanders, Winston P.
  See Anderson, Poul (William)
Sandoz, Mari(e Susette) 1896-1966 .. CLC 28
  See also CA 1-4R; 25-28R; CANR 17, 64; DLB
    9; MTCW 1; SATA 5
Saner, Reg(inald Anthony) 1931- .... CLC 9
  See also CA 65-68
Sannazaro, Jacopo 1456(?)-1530 .... LC 8
Sansom, William 1912-1976 CLC 2, 6; DAM
    NOV; SSC 21
  See also CA 5-8R; 65-68; CANR 42; DLB 139;
    MTCW 1
Santayana, George 1863-1952 .... TCLC 40
  See also CA 115; DLB 54, 71; DLBD 13
Santiago, Danny .... CLC 33
  See also James, Daniel (Lewis)
  See also DLB 122
Santmyer, Helen Hoover 1895-1986 . CLC 33
  See also CA 1-4R; 118; CANR 15, 33; DLBY
    84; MTCW 1
Santoka, Taneda 1882-1940 .... TCLC 72
Santos, Bienvenido N(uqui) 1911-1996 . C L C
    22; DAM MULT
  See also CA 101; 151; CANR 19, 46
Sapper .... TCLC 44
  See also McNeile, Herman Cyril
Sapphire 1950- .... CLC 99
Sappho fl. 6th cent. B.C.- .... CMLC 3; DAM
    POET; PC 5
  See also DLB 176
Sarduy, Severo 1937-1993 .... CLC 6, 97
  See also CA 89-92; 142; CANR 58; DLB 113;
    HW
Sargeson, Frank 1903-1982 .... CLC 31
  See also CA 25-28R; 106; CANR 38
Sarmiento, Felix Ruben Garcia
  See Dario, Ruben
Saro-Wiwa, Ken(ule Beeson) 1941-1995C L C
    114
  See also BW 2; CA 142; 150; CANR 60; DLB
    157
Saroyan, William 1908-1981CLC 1, 8, 10, 29,
    34, 56; DA; DAB; DAC; DAM DRAM,
    MST, NOV; SSC 21; WLC
  See also CA 5-8R; 103; CANR 30; DLB 7, 9,
    86; DLBY 81; MTCW 1; SATA 23; SATA-
    Obit 24
Sarraute, Nathalie 1900-CLC 1, 2, 4, 8, 10, 31,
    80
  See also CA 9-12R; CANR 23, 66; DLB 83;
    MTCW 1
Sarton, (Eleanor) May 1912-1995CLC 4, 14,
    49, 91; DAM POET

See also CA 1-4R; 149; CANR 1, 34, 55; DLB
    48; DLBY 81; INT CANR-34; MTCW 1;
    SATA 36; SATA-Obit 86
Sartre, Jean-Paul 1905-1980CLC 1, 4, 7, 9, 13,
    18, 24, 44, 50, 52; DA; DAB; DAC; DAM
    DRAM, MST, NOV; DC 3; SSC 32; WLC
  See also CA 9-12R; 97-100; CANR 21; DLB
    72; MTCW 1
Sassoon, Siegfried (Lorraine) 1886-1967C L C
    36; DAB; DAM MST, NOV, POET; PC 12
  See also CA 104; 25-28R; CANR 36; DLB 20,
    191; DLBD 18; MTCW 1
Satterfield, Charles
  See Pohl, Frederik
Saul, John (W. III) 1942-CLC 46; DAM NOV,
    POP
  See also AAYA 10; BEST 90:4; CA 81-84;
    CANR 16, 40; SATA 98
Saunders, Caleb
  See Heinlein, Robert A(nson)
Saura (Atares), Carlos 1932- .... CLC 20
  See also CA 114; 131; HW
Sauser-Hall, Frederic 1887-1961 ...... CLC 18
  See also Cendrars, Blaise
  See also CA 102; 93-96; CANR 36, 62; MTCW
    1
Saussure, Ferdinand de 1857-1913 TCLC 49
Savage, Catharine
  See Brosman, Catharine Savage
Savage, Thomas 1915- .... CLC 40
  See also CA 126; 132; CAAS 15; INT 132
Savan, Glenn 19(?)- .... CLC 50
Sayers, Dorothy L(eigh) 1893-1957 TCLC 2,
    15; DAM POP
  See also CA 104; 119; CANR 60; CDBLB 1914-
    1945; DLB 10, 36, 77, 100; MTCW 1
Sayers, Valerie 1952- .... CLC 50
  See also CA 134; CANR 61
Sayles, John (Thomas) 1950- . CLC 7, 10, 14
  See also CA 57-60; CANR 41; DLB 44
Scammell, Michael 1935- .... CLC 34
  See also CA 156
Scannell, Vernon 1922- .... CLC 49
  See also CA 5-8R; CANR 8, 24, 57; DLB 27;
    SATA 59
Scarlett, Susan
  See Streatfeild, (Mary) Noel
Schaeffer, Susan Fromberg 1941- CLC 6, 11,
    22
  See also CA 49-52; CANR 18, 65; DLB 28;
    MTCW 1; SATA 22
Schary, Jill
  See Robinson, Jill
Schell, Jonathan 1943- .... CLC 35
  See also CA 73-76; CANR 12
Schelling, Friedrich Wilhelm Joseph von 1775-
    1854 ....
NCLC 30
  See also DLB 90
Schendel, Arthur van 1874-1946 ... TCLC 56
Scherer, Jean-Marie Maurice 1920-
  See Rohmer, Eric
  See also CA 110
Schevill, James (Erwin) 1920- .... CLC 7
  See also CA 5-8R; CAAS 12
Schiller, Friedrich 1759-1805 . NCLC 39, 69;
    DAM DRAM
  See also DLB 94
Schisgal, Murray (Joseph) 1926- .... CLC 6
  See also CA 21-24R; CANR 48
Schlee, Ann 1934- .... CLC 35
  See also CA 101; CANR 29; SATA 44; SATA-
    Brief 36
Schlegel, August Wilhelm von 1767-1845
    NCLC 15
  See also DLB 94
Schlegel, Friedrich 1772-1829 .... NCLC 45

Shamlu, Ahmad 1925- .... **CLC 10**

Shammas, Anton 1951- .... **CLC 55**

Shange, Ntozake 1948-**CLC 8, 25, 38, 74; BLC 3; DAM DRAM, MULT; DC 3**
See also AAYA 9; BW 2; CA 85-88; CABS 3; CANR 27, 48; DLB 38; MTCW 1

Shanley, John Patrick 1950-.............. **CLC 75**
See also CA 128; 133

Shapcott, Thomas W(illiam) 1935- .. **CLC 38**
See also CA 69-72; CANR 49

Shapiro, Jane .... **CLC 76**

Shapiro, Karl (Jay) 1913- ... **CLC 4, 8, 15, 53**
See also CA 1-4R; CAAS 6; CANR 1, 36, 66; DLB 48; MTCW 1

Sharp, William 1855-1905 .... **TCLC 39**
See also CA 160; DLB 156

Sharpe, Thomas Ridley 1928-
See Sharpe, Tom
See also CA 114; 122; INT 122

Sharpe, Tom .... **CLC 36**
See also Sharpe, Thomas Ridley
See also DLB 14

Shaw, Bernard .... **TCLC 45**
See also Shaw, George Bernard
See also BW 1

Shaw, G. Bernard
See Shaw, George Bernard

Shaw, George Bernard 1856-1950**TCLC 3, 9, 21; DA; DAB; DAC; DAM DRAM, MST; WLC**
See also Shaw, Bernard
See also CA 104; 128; CDBLB 1914-1945; DLB 10, 57, 190; MTCW 1

Shaw, Henry Wheeler 1818-1885 .. **NCLC 15**
See also DLB 11

Shaw, Irwin 1913-1984 **CLC 7, 23, 34; DAM DRAM, POP**
See also AITN 1; CA 13-16R; 112; CANR 21; CDALB 1941-1968; DLB 6, 102; DLBY 84; MTCW 1

Shaw, Robert 1927-1978 .... **CLC 5**
See also AITN 1; CA 1-4R; 81-84; CANR 4; DLB 13, 14

Shaw, T. E.
See Lawrence, T(homas) E(dward)

Shawn, Wallace 1943- .... **CLC 41**
See also CA 112

Shea, Lisa 1953- .... **CLC 86**
See also CA 147

Sheed, Wilfrid (John Joseph) 1930-**CLC 2, 4, 10, 53**
See also CA 65-68; CANR 30, 66; DLB 6; MTCW 1

Sheldon, Alice Hastings Bradley 1915(?)-1987
See Tiptree, James, Jr.
See also CA 108; 122; CANR 34; INT 108; MTCW 1

Sheldon, John
See Bloch, Robert (Albert)

Shelley, Mary Wollstonecraft (Godwin) 1797-1851**NCLC 14, 59; DA; DAB; DAC; DAM MST, NOV; WLC**
See also AAYA 20; CDBLB 1789-1832; DLB 110, 116, 159, 178; SATA 29

Shelley, Percy Bysshe 1792-1822 . **NCLC 18; DA; DAB; DAC; DAM MST, POET; PC 14; WLC**
See also CDBLB 1789-1832; DLB 96, 110, 158

Shepard, Jim 1956-............................. **CLC 36**
See also CA 137; CANR 59; SATA 90

Shepard, Lucius 1947- .... **CLC 34**
See also CA 128; 141

Shepard, Sam 1943-**CLC 4, 6, 17, 34, 41, 44; DAM DRAM; DC 5**
See also AAYA 1; CA 69-72; CABS 3; CANR 22; DLB 7; MTCW 1

Shepherd, Michael

See Ludlum, Robert

Sherburne, Zoa (Morin) 1912- .... **CLC 30**
See also AAYA 13; CA 1-4R; CANR 3, 37; MAICYA; SAAS 18; SATA 3

Sheridan, Frances 1724-1766 .... **LC 7**
See also DLB 39, 84

Sheridan, Richard Brinsley 1751-1816**NCLC 5; DA; DAB; DAC; DAM DRAM, MST; DC 1; WLC**
See also CDBLB 1660-1789; DLB 89

Sherman, Jonathan Marc .... **CLC 55**

Sherman, Martin 1941(?)- .... **CLC 19**
See also CA 116; 123

Sherwin, Judith Johnson 1936- ....**CLC 7, 15**
See also CA 25-28R; CANR 34

Sherwood, Frances 1940- .... **CLC 81**
See also CA 146

Sherwood, Robert E(mmet) 1896-1955**TCLC 3; DAM DRAM**
See also CA 104; 153; DLB 7, 26

Shestov, Lev 1866-1938 .... **TCLC 56**

Shevchenko, Taras 1814-1861 .... **NCLC 54**

Shiel, M(atthew) P(hipps) 1865-1947**TCLC 8**
See also Holmes, Gordon
See also CA 106; 160; DLB 153

Shields, Carol 1935- .... **CLC 91, 113; DAC**
See also CA 81-84; CANR 51

Shields, David 1956- .... **CLC 97**
See also CA 124; CANR 48

Shiga, Naoya 1883-1971 ...... **CLC 33; SSC 23**
See also CA 101; 33-36R; DLB 180

Shilts, Randy 1951-1994 .... **CLC 85**
See also AAYA 19; CA 115; 127; 144; CANR 45; INT 127

Shimazaki, Haruki 1872-1943
See Shimazaki Toson
See also CA 105; 134

Shimazaki Toson 1872-1943 .... **TCLC 5**
See also Shimazaki, Haruki
See also DLB 180

Sholokhov, Mikhail (Aleksandrovich) 1905-1984 ....**CLC 7, 15**
See also CA 101; 112; MTCW 1; SATA-Obit 36

Shone, Patric
See Hanley, James

Shreve, Susan Richards 1939-........... **CLC 23**
See also CA 49-52; CAAS 5; CANR 5, 38, 69; MAICYA; SATA 46, 95; SATA-Brief 41

Shue, Larry 1946-1985**CLC 52; DAM DRAM**
See also CA 145; 117

Shu-Jen, Chou 1881-1936
See Lu Hsun
See also CA 104

Shulman, Alix Kates 1932- .... **CLC 2, 10**
See also CA 29-32R; CANR 43; SATA 7

Shuster, Joe 1914- .... **CLC 21**

Shute, Nevil .... **CLC 30**
See also Norway, Nevil Shute

Shuttle, Penelope (Diane) 1947- .... **CLC 7**
See also CA 93-96; CANR 39; DLB 14, 40

Sidney, Mary 1561-1621 .... **LC 19, 39**

Sidney, Sir Philip 1554-1586 **LC 19, 39; DA; DAB; DAC; DAM MST, POET**
See also CDBLB Before 1660; DLB 167

Siegel, Jerome 1914-1996 .... **CLC 21**
See also CA 116; 151

Siegel, Jerry
See Siegel, Jerome

Sienkiewicz, Henryk (Adam Alexander Pius) 1846-1916 ....
TCLC 3
See also CA 104; 134

Sierra, Gregorio Martinez
See Martinez Sierra, Gregorio

Sierra, Maria (de la O'LeJarraga) Martinez
See Martinez Sierra, Maria (de la O'LeJarraga)

Sigal, Clancy 1926-............................... **CLC 7**
See also CA 1-4R

Sigourney, Lydia Howard (Huntley) 1791-1865
NCLC 21
See also DLB 1, 42, 73

Siguenza y Gongora, Carlos de 1645-1700**LC 8**

Sigurjonsson, Johann 1880-1919 ... **TCLC 27**

Sikelianos, Angelos 1884-1951 .... **TCLC 39**

Silkin, Jon 1930- .... **CLC 2, 6, 43**
See also CA 5-8R; CAAS 5; DLB 27

Silko, Leslie (Marmon) 1948-**CLC 23, 74, 114; DA; DAC; DAM MST, MULT, POP; WLCS**
See also AAYA 14; CA 115; 122; CANR 45, 65; DLB 143, 175; NNAL

Sillanpaa, Frans Eemil 1888-1964 ... **CLC 19**
See also CA 129; 93-96; MTCW 1

Sillitoe, Alan 1928- ... **CLC 1, 3, 6, 10, 19, 57**
See also AITN 1; CA 9-12R; CAAS 2; CANR 8, 26, 55; CDBLB 1960 to Present; DLB 14, 139; MTCW 1; SATA 61

Silone, Ignazio 1900-1978 .... **CLC 4**
See also CA 25-28; 81-84; CANR 34; CAP 2; MTCW 1

Silver, Joan Micklin 1935- .... **CLC 20**
See also CA 114; 121; INT 121

Silver, Nicholas
See Faust, Frederick (Schiller)

Silverberg, Robert 1935- **CLC 7; DAM POP**
See also AAYA 24; CA 1-4R; CAAS 3; CANR 1, 20, 36; DLB 8; INT CANR-20; MAICYA; MTCW 1; SATA 13, 91

Silverstein, Alvin 1933- .... **CLC 17**
See also CA 49-52; CANR 2; CLR 25; JRDA; MAICYA; SATA 8, 69

Silverstein, Virginia B(arbara Opshelor) 1937-
CLC 17
See also CA 49-52; CANR 2; CLR 25; JRDA; MAICYA; SATA 8, 69

Sim, Georges
See Simenon, Georges (Jacques Christian)

Simak, Clifford D(onald) 1904-1988**CLC 1, 55**
See also CA 1-4R; 125; CANR 1, 35; DLB 8; MTCW 1; SATA-Obit 56

Simenon, Georges (Jacques Christian) 1903-1989 .. **CLC 1, 2, 3, 8, 18, 47; DAM POP**
See also CA 85-88; 129; CANR 35; DLB 72; DLBY 89; MTCW 1

Simic, Charles 1938-.... **CLC 6, 9, 22, 49, 68; DAM POET**
See also CA 29-32R; CAAS 4; CANR 12, 33, 52, 61; DLB 105

Simmel, Georg 1858-1918 .... **TCLC 64**
See also CA 157

Simmons, Charles (Paul) 1924- .... **CLC 57**
See also CA 89-92; INT 89-92

Simmons, Dan 1948- ...... **CLC 44; DAM POP**
See also AAYA 16; CA 138; CANR 53

Simmons, James (Stewart Alexander) 1933-
CLC 43
See also CA 105; CAAS 21; DLB 40

Simms, William Gilmore 1806-1870 **NCLC 3**
See also DLB 3, 30, 59, 73

Simon, Carly 1945- .... **CLC 26**
See also CA 105

Simon, Claude 1913-1984 ..**CLC 4, 9, 15, 39; DAM NOV**
See also CA 89-92; CANR 33; DLB 83; MTCW 1

Simon, (Marvin) Neil 1927-**CLC 6, 11, 31, 39, 70; DAM DRAM**
See also AITN 1; CA 21-24R; CANR 26, 54; DLB 7; MTCW 1

Simon, Paul (Frederick) 1941(?)- ..... **CLC 17**
See also CA 116; 153

Simonon, Paul 1956(?)- .... **CLC 30**

Sommer, Scott 1951- .... **CLC 25**
See also CA 106
Sondheim, Stephen (Joshua) 1930- . **CLC 30, 39; DAM DRAM**
See also AAYA 11; CA 103; CANR 47, 68
Song, Cathy 1955- .... **PC 21**
See also CA 154; DLB 169
Sontag, Susan 1933-**CLC 1, 2, 10, 13, 31, 105; DAM POP**
See also CA 17-20R; CANR 25, 51; DLB 2, 67; MTCW 1
Sophocles 496(?)B.C.-406(?)B.C. ... **CMLC 2; DA; DAB; DAC; DAM DRAM, MST; DC 1; WLCS**
See also DLB 176
Sordello 1189-1269 .... **CMLC 15**
Sorel, Julia
See Drexler, Rosalyn
Sorrentino, Gilbert 1929-**CLC 3, 7, 14, 22, 40**
See also CA 77-80; CANR 14, 33; DLB 5, 173; DLBY 80; INT CANR-14
Soto, Gary 1952- **CLC 32, 80; DAM MULT; HLC**
See also AAYA 10; CA 119; 125; CANR 50; CLR 38; DLB 82; HW; INT 125; JRDA; SATA 80
Soupault, Philippe 1897-1990 .... **CLC 68**
See also CA 116; 147; 131
Souster, (Holmes) Raymond 1921-**CLC 5, 14; DAC; DAM POET**
See also CA 13-16R; CAAS 14; CANR 13, 29, 53; DLB 88; SATA 63
Southern, Terry 1924(?)-1995 .... **CLC 7**
See also CA 1-4R; 150; CANR 1, 55; DLB 2
Southey, Robert 1774-1843 .... **NCLC 8**
See also DLB 93, 107, 142; SATA 54
Southworth, Emma Dorothy Eliza Nevitte 1819-1899 ....
NCLC 26
Souza, Ernest
See Scott, Evelyn
Soyinka, Wole 1934-**CLC 3, 5, 14, 36, 44; BLC 3; DA; DAB; DAC; DAM DRAM, MST, MULT; DC 2; WLC**
See also BW 2; CA 13-16R; CANR 27, 39; DLB 125; MTCW 1
Spackman, W(illiam) M(ode) 1905-1990**CLC 46**
See also CA 81-84; 132
Spacks, Barry (Bernard) 1931- .... **CLC 14**
See also CA 154; CANR 33; DLB 105
Spanidou, Irini 1946- .... **CLC 44**
Spark, Muriel (Sarah) 1918-**CLC 2, 3, 5, 8, 13, 18, 40, 94; DAB; DAC; DAM MST, NOV; SSC 10**
See also CA 5-8R; CANR 12, 36; CDBLB 1945-1960; DLB 15, 139; INT CANR-12; MTCW 1
Spaulding, Douglas
See Bradbury, Ray (Douglas)
Spaulding, Leonard
See Bradbury, Ray (Douglas)
Spence, J. A. D.
See Eliot, T(homas) S(tearns)
Spencer, Elizabeth 1921- .... **CLC 22**
See also CA 13-16R; CANR 32, 65; DLB 6; MTCW 1; SATA 14
Spencer, Leonard G.
See Silverberg, Robert
Spencer, Scott 1945- .... **CLC 30**
See also CA 113; CANR 51; DLBY 86
Spender, Stephen (Harold) 1909-1995**CLC 1, 2, 5, 10, 41, 91; DAM POET**
See also CA 9-12R; 149; CANR 31, 54; CDBLB 1945-1960; DLB 20; MTCW 1
Spengler, Oswald (Arnold Gottfried) 1880-1936
TCLC 25

See also CA 118
Spenser, Edmund 1552(?)-1599**LC 5, 39; DA; DAB; DAC; DAM MST, POET; PC 8; WLC**
See also CDBLB Before 1660; DLB 167
Spicer, Jack 1925-1965 **CLC 8, 18, 72; DAM POET**
See also CA 85-88; DLB 5, 16, 193
Spiegelman, Art 1948- .... **CLC 76**
See also AAYA 10; CA 125; CANR 41, 55
Spielberg, Peter 1929- .... **CLC 6**
See also CA 5-8R; CANR 4, 48; DLBY 81
Spielberg, Steven 1947- .... **CLC 20**
See also AAYA 8, 24; CA 77-80; CANR 32; SATA 32
Spillane, Frank Morrison 1918-
See Spillane, Mickey
See also CA 25-28R; CANR 28, 63; MTCW 1; SATA 66
Spillane, Mickey .... **CLC 3, 13**
See also Spillane, Frank Morrison
Spinoza, Benedictus de 1632-1677 .... **LC 9**
Spinrad, Norman (Richard) 1940- ... **CLC 46**
See also CA 37-40R; CAAS 19; CANR 20; DLB 8; INT CANR-20
Spitteler, Carl (Friedrich Georg) 1845-1924
TCLC 12
See also CA 109; DLB 129
Spivack, Kathleen (Romola Drucker) 1938-
CLC 6
See also CA 49-52
Spoto, Donald 1941- .... **CLC 39**
See also CA 65-68; CANR 11, 57
Springsteen, Bruce (F.) 1949- .... **CLC 17**
See also CA 111
Spurling, Hilary 1940- .... **CLC 34**
See also CA 104; CANR 25, 52
Spyker, John Howland
See Elman, Richard (Martin)
Squires, (James) Radcliffe 1917-1993**CLC 51**
See also CA 1-4R; 140; CANR 6, 21
Srivastava, Dhanpat Rai 1880(?)-1936
See Premchand
See also CA 118
Stacy, Donald
See Pohl, Frederik
Stael, Germaine de 1766-1817
See Stael-Holstein, Anne Louise Germaine Necker Baronn
See also DLB 119
Stael-Holstein, Anne Louise Germaine Necker Baronn 1766-1817 .... **NCLC 3**
See also Stael, Germaine de
See also DLB 192
Stafford, Jean 1915-1979**CLC 4, 7, 19, 68; SSC 26**
See also CA 1-4R; 85-88; CANR 3, 65; DLB 2, 173; MTCW 1; SATA-Obit 22
Stafford, William (Edgar) 1914-1993 **CLC 4, 7, 29; DAM POET**
See also CA 5-8R; 142; CAAS 3; CANR 5, 22; DLB 5; INT CANR-22
Stagnelius, Eric Johan 1793-1823 . **NCLC 61**
Staines, Trevor
See Brunner, John (Kilian Houston)
Stairs, Gordon
See Austin, Mary (Hunter)
Stannard, Martin 1947- .... **CLC 44**
See also CA 142; DLB 155
Stanton, Elizabeth Cady 1815-1902**TCLC 73**
See also DLB 79
Stanton, Maura 1946- .... **CLC 9**
See also CA 89-92; CANR 15; DLB 120
Stanton, Schuyler
See Baum, L(yman) Frank
Stapledon, (William) Olaf 1886-1950 **TCLC 22**

See also CA 111; 162; DLB 15
Starbuck, George (Edwin) 1931-1996**CLC 53; DAM POET**
See also CA 21-24R; 153; CANR 23
Stark, Richard
See Westlake, Donald E(dwin)
Staunton, Schuyler
See Baum, L(yman) Frank
Stead, Christina (Ellen) 1902-1983 **CLC 2, 5, 8, 32, 80**
See also CA 13-16R; 109; CANR 33, 40; MTCW 1
Stead, William Thomas 1849-1912 **TCLC 48**
See also CA 167
Steele, Richard 1672-1729 .... **LC 18**
See also CDBLB 1660-1789; DLB 84, 101
Steele, Timothy (Reid) 1948- .... **CLC 45**
See also CA 93-96; CANR 16, 50; DLB 120
Steffens, (Joseph) Lincoln 1866-1936 **TCLC 20**
See also CA 117
Stegner, Wallace (Earle) 1909-1993**CLC 9, 49, 81; DAM NOV; SSC 27**
See also AITN 1; BEST 90:3; CA 1-4R; 141; CAAS 9; CANR 1, 21, 46; DLB 9; DLBY 93; MTCW 1
Stein, Gertrude 1874-1946**TCLC 1, 6, 28, 48; DA; DAB; DAC; DAM MST, NOV, POET; PC 18; WLC**
See also CA 104; 132; CDALB 1917-1929; DLB 4, 54, 86; DLBD 15; MTCW 1
Steinbeck, John (Ernst) 1902-1968 **CLC 1, 5, 9, 13, 21, 34, 45, 75; DA; DAB; DAC; DAM DRAM, MST, NOV; SSC 11; WLC**
See also AAYA 12; CA 1-4R; 25-28R; CANR 1, 35; CDALB 1929-1941; DLB 7, 9; DLBD 2; MTCW 1; SATA 9
Steinem, Gloria 1934- .... **CLC 63**
See also CA 53-56; CANR 28, 51; MTCW 1
Steiner, George 1929- ... **CLC 24; DAM NOV**
See also CA 73-76; CANR 31, 67; DLB 67; MTCW 1; SATA 62
Steiner, K. Leslie
See Delany, Samuel R(ay, Jr.)
Steiner, Rudolf 1861-1925 .... **TCLC 13**
See also CA 107
Stendhal 1783-1842**NCLC 23, 46; DA; DAB; DAC; DAM MST, NOV; SSC 27; WLC**
See also DLB 119
Stephen, Adeline Virginia
See Woolf, (Adeline) Virginia
Stephen, SirLeslie 1832-1904 .... **TCLC 23**
See also CA 123; DLB 57, 144, 190
Stephen, Sir Leslie
See Stephen, SirLeslie
Stephen, Virginia
See Woolf, (Adeline) Virginia
Stephens, James 1882(?)-1950.......... **TCLC 4**
See also CA 104; DLB 19, 153, 162
Stephens, Reed
See Donaldson, Stephen R.
Steptoe, Lydia
See Barnes, Djuna
Sterchi, Beat 1949- .... **CLC 65**
Sterling, Brett
See Bradbury, Ray (Douglas); Hamilton, Edmond
Sterling, Bruce 1954- .... **CLC 72**
See also CA 119; CANR 44
Sterling, George 1869-1926 .... **TCLC 20**
See also CA 117; 165; DLB 54
Stern, Gerald 1925- .... **CLC 40, 100**
See also CA 81-84; CANR 28; DLB 105
Stern, Richard (Gustave) 1928- ....**CLC 4, 39**
See also CA 1-4R; CANR 1, 25, 52; DLBY 87; INT CANR-25
Sternberg, Josef von 1894-1969 .... **CLC 20**

See also CA 81-84

Sterne, Laurence 1713-1768**LC 2; DA; DAB; DAC; DAM MST, NOV; WLC**
See also CDBLB 1660-1789; DLB 39

Sternheim, (William Adolf) Carl 1878-1942
TCLC 8
See also CA 105; DLB 56, 118

Stevens, Mark 1951- .... **CLC 34**
See also CA 122

Stevens, Wallace 1879-1955 **TCLC 3, 12, 45; DA; DAB; DAC; DAM MST, POET; PC 6; WLC**
See also CA 104; 124; CDALB 1929-1941; DLB 54; MTCW 1

Stevenson, Anne (Katharine) 1933-**CLC 7, 33**
See also CA 17-20R; CAAS 9; CANR 9, 33; DLB 40; MTCW 1

Stevenson, Robert Louis (Balfour) 1850-1894
NCLC 5, 14, 63; DA; DAB; DAC; DAM MST, NOV; SSC 11; WLC
See also AAYA 24; CDBLB 1890-1914; CLR 10, 11; DLB 18, 57, 141, 156, 174; DLBD 13; JRDA; MAICYA; SATA 100; YABC 2

Stewart, J(ohn) I(nnes) M(ackintosh) 1906-1994 .... **CLC 7, 14, 32**
See also CA 85-88; 147; CAAS 3; CANR 47; MTCW 1

Stewart, Mary (Florence Elinor) 1916-**CLC 7, 35; DAB**
See also CA 1-4R; CANR 1, 59; SATA 12

Stewart, Mary Rainbow
See Stewart, Mary (Florence Elinor)

Stifle, June
See Campbell, Maria

Stifter, Adalbert 1805-1868**NCLC 41; SSC 28**
See also DLB 133

Still, James 1906- .... **CLC 49**
See also CA 65-68; CAAS 17; CANR 10, 26; DLB 9; SATA 29

Sting 1951-
See Sumner, Gordon Matthew
See also CA 167

Stirling, Arthur
See Sinclair, Upton (Beall)

Stitt, Milan 1941- .... **CLC 29**
See also CA 69-72

Stockton, Francis Richard 1834-1902
See Stockton, Frank R.
See also CA 108; 137; MAICYA; SATA 44

Stockton, Frank R. .... **TCLC 47**
See also Stockton, Francis Richard
See also DLB 42, 74; DLBD 13; SATA-Brief 32

Stoddard, Charles
See Kuttner, Henry

Stoker, Abraham 1847-1912
See Stoker, Bram
See also CA 105; 150; DA; DAC; DAM MST, NOV; SATA 29

Stoker, Bram 1847-1912**TCLC 8; DAB; WLC**
See also Stoker, Abraham
See also AAYA 23; CDBLB 1890-1914; DLB 36, 70, 178

Stolz, Mary (Slattery) 1920- .... **CLC 12**
See also AAYA 8; AITN 1; CA 5-8R; CANR 13, 41; JRDA; MAICYA; SAAS 3; SATA 10, 71

Stone, Irving 1903-1989 ..**CLC 7; DAM POP**
See also AITN 1; CA 1-4R; 129; CAAS 3; CANR 1, 23; INT CANR-23; MTCW 1; SATA 3; SATA-Obit 64

Stone, Oliver (William) 1946- .... **CLC 73**
See also AAYA 15; CA 110; CANR 55

Stone, Robert (Anthony) 1937-**CLC 5, 23, 42**
See also CA 85-88; CANR 23, 66; DLB 152; INT CANR-23; MTCW 1

Stone, Zachary

See Follett, Ken(neth Martin)

Stoppard, Tom 1937-**CLC 1, 3, 4, 5, 8, 15, 29, 34, 63, 91; DA; DAB; DAC; DAM DRAM, MST; DC 6; WLC**
See also CA 81-84; CANR 39, 67; CDBLB 1960 to Present; DLB 13; DLBY 85; MTCW 1

Storey, David (Malcolm) 1933-**CLC 2, 4, 5, 8; DAM DRAM**
See also CA 81-84; CANR 36; DLB 13, 14; MTCW 1

Storm, Hyemeyohsts 1935- ...... **CLC 3; DAM MULT**
See also CA 81-84; CANR 45; NNAL

Storm, (Hans) Theodor (Woldsen) 1817-1888
NCLC 1; SSC 27
See also DLB 129

Storni, Alfonsina 1892-1938 . **TCLC 5; DAM MULT; HLC**
See also CA 104; 131; HW

Stoughton, William 1631-1701 .... **LC 38**
See also DLB 24

Stout, Rex (Todhunter) 1886-1975 ..... **CLC 3**
See also AITN 2; CA 61-64; CANR 71

Stow, (Julian) Randolph 1935- .. **CLC 23, 48**
See also CA 13-16R; CANR 33; MTCW 1

Stowe, Harriet (Elizabeth) Beecher 1811-1896
NCLC 3, 50; DA; DAB; DAC; DAM MST, NOV; WLC
See also CDALB 1865-1917; DLB 1, 12, 42, 74, 189; JRDA; MAICYA; YABC 1

Strachey, (Giles) Lytton 1880-1932 **TCLC 12**
See also CA 110; DLB 149; DLBD 10

Strand, Mark 1934- **CLC 6, 18, 41, 71; DAM POET**
See also CA 21-24R; CANR 40, 65; DLB 5; SATA 41

Straub, Peter (Francis) 1943- . **CLC 28, 107; DAM POP**
See also BEST 89:1; CA 85-88; CANR 28, 65; DLBY 84; MTCW 1

Strauss, Botho 1944- .... **CLC 22**
See also CA 157; DLB 124

Streatfeild, (Mary) Noel 1895(?)-1986**CLC 21**
See also CA 81-84; 120; CANR 31; CLR 17; DLB 160; MAICYA; SATA 20; SATA-Obit 48

Stribling, T(homas) S(igismund) 1881-1965
CLC 23
See also CA 107; DLB 9

Strindberg, (Johan) August 1849-1912**TCLC 1, 8, 21, 47; DA; DAB; DAC; DAM DRAM, MST; WLC**
See also CA 104; 135

Stringer, Arthur 1874-1950 .... **TCLC 37**
See also CA 161; DLB 92

Stringer, David
See Roberts, Keith (John Kingston)

Stroheim, Erich von 1885-1957 ..... **TCLC 71**

Strugatskii, Arkadii (Natanovich) 1925-1991
CLC 27
See also CA 106; 135

Strugatskii, Boris (Natanovich) 1933-**CLC 27**
See also CA 106

Strummer, Joe 1953(?)- .... **CLC 30**

Stuart, Don A.
See Campbell, John W(ood, Jr.)

Stuart, Ian
See MacLean, Alistair (Stuart)

Stuart, Jesse (Hilton) 1906-1984**CLC 1, 8, 11, 14, 34; SSC 31**
See also CA 5-8R; 112; CANR 31; DLB 9, 48, 102; DLBY 84; SATA 2; SATA-Obit 36

Sturgeon, Theodore (Hamilton) 1918-1985
CLC 22, 39
See also Queen, Ellery
See also CA 81-84; 116; CANR 32; DLB 8;

DLBY 85; MTCW 1

Sturges, Preston 1898-1959 .... **TCLC 48**
See also CA 114; 149; DLB 26

Styron, William 1925-**CLC 1, 3, 5, 11, 15, 60; DAM NOV, POP; SSC 25**
See also BEST 90:4; CA 5-8R; CANR 6, 33; CDALB 1968-1988; DLB 2, 143; DLBY 80; INT CANR-6; MTCW 1

Su, Chien 1884-1918
See Su Man-shu
See also CA 123

Suarez Lynch, B.
See Bioy Casares, Adolfo; Borges, Jorge Luis

Suckow, Ruth 1892-1960 .... **SSC 18**
See also CA 113; DLB 9, 102

Sudermann, Hermann 1857-1928 .. **TCLC 15**
See also CA 107; DLB 118

Sue, Eugene 1804-1857 .... **NCLC 1**
See also DLB 119

Sueskind, Patrick 1949- .... **CLC 44**
See also Suskind, Patrick

Sukenick, Ronald 1932- .... **CLC 3, 4, 6, 48**
See also CA 25-28R; CAAS 8; CANR 32; DLB 173; DLBY 81

Suknaski, Andrew 1942- .... **CLC 19**
See also CA 101; DLB 53

Sullivan, Vernon
See Vian, Boris

Sully Prudhomme 1839-1907 .... **TCLC 31**

Su Man-shu .... **TCLC 24**
See also Su, Chien

Summerforest, Ivy B.
See Kirkup, James

Summers, Andrew James 1942- .... **CLC 26**

Summers, Andy
See Summers, Andrew James

Summers, Hollis (Spurgeon, Jr.) 1916-**CLC 10**
See also CA 5-8R; CANR 3; DLB 6

Summers, (Alphonsus Joseph-Mary Augustus) Montague 1880-1948 .... **TCLC 16**
See also CA 118; 163

Sumner, Gordon Matthew .... **CLC 26**
See also Sting

Surtees, Robert Smith 1803-1864 .. **NCLC 14**
See also DLB 21

Susann, Jacqueline 1921-1974 .... **CLC 3**
See also AITN 1; CA 65-68; 53-56; MTCW 1

Su Shih 1036-1101 .... **CMLC 15**

Suskind, Patrick
See Sueskind, Patrick
See also CA 145

Sutcliff, Rosemary 1920-1992**CLC 26; DAB; DAC; DAM MST, POP**
See also AAYA 10; CA 5-8R; 139; CANR 37; CLR 1, 37; JRDA; MAICYA; SATA 6, 44, 78; SATA-Obit 73

Sutro, Alfred 1863-1933 .... **TCLC 6**
See also CA 105; DLB 10

Sutton, Henry
See Slavitt, David R(ytman)

Svevo, Italo 1861-1928 . **TCLC 2, 35; SSC 25**
See also Schmitz, Aron Hector

Swados, Elizabeth (A.) 1951- .... **CLC 12**
See also CA 97-100; CANR 49; INT 97-100

Swados, Harvey 1920-1972 .... **CLC 5**
See also CA 5-8R; 37-40R; CANR 6; DLB 2

Swan, Gladys 1934- .... **CLC 69**
See also CA 101; CANR 17, 39

Swarthout, Glendon (Fred) 1918-1992**CLC 35**
See also CA 1-4R; 139; CANR 1, 47; SATA 26

Sweet, Sarah C.
See Jewett, (Theodora) Sarah Orne

Swenson, May 1919-1989**CLC 4, 14, 61, 106; DA; DAB; DAC; DAM MST, POET; PC 14**
See also CA 5-8R; 130; CANR 36, 61; DLB 5; MTCW 1; SATA 15

Swift, Augustus
See Lovecraft, H(oward) P(hillips)
Swift, Graham (Colin) 1949- ...... **CLC 41, 88**
See also CA 117; 122; CANR 46, 71; DLB 194
Swift, Jonathan 1667-1745 **LC 1; DA; DAB; DAC; DAM MST, NOV, POET; PC 9; WLC**
See also CDBLB 1660-1789; CLR 53; DLB 39, 95, 101; SATA 19
Swinburne, Algernon Charles 1837-1909 **TCLC 8, 36; DA; DAB; DAC; DAM MST, POET; PC 24; WLC**
See also CA 105; 140; CDBLB 1832-1890; DLB 35, 57
Swinfen, Ann .... **CLC 34**
Swinnerton, Frank Arthur 1884-1982 **CLC 31**
See also CA 108; DLB 34
Swithen, John
See King, Stephen (Edwin)
Sylvia
See Ashton-Warner, Sylvia (Constance)
Symmes, Robert Edward
See Duncan, Robert (Edward)
Symonds, John Addington 1840-1893 **N C L C 34**
See also DLB 57, 144
Symons, Arthur 1865-1945 .... **TCLC 11**
See also CA 107; DLB 19, 57, 149
Symons, Julian (Gustave) 1912-1994 **CLC 2, 14, 32**
See also CA 49-52; 147; CAAS 3; CANR 3, 33, 59; DLB 87, 155; DLBY 92; MTCW 1
Synge, (Edmund) J(ohn) M(illington) 1871-1909 ... **TCLC 6, 37; DAM DRAM; DC 2**
See also CA 104; 141; CDBLB 1890-1914; DLB 10, 19
Syruc, J.
See Milosz, Czeslaw
Szirtes, George 1948- .... **CLC 46**
See also CA 109; CANR 27, 61
Szymborska, Wislawa 1923- .... **CLC 99**
See also CA 154; DLBY 96
T. O., Nik
See Annensky, Innokenty (Fyodorovich)
Tabori, George 1914- .... **CLC 19**
See also CA 49-52; CANR 4, 69
Tagore, Rabindranath 1861-1941 **TCLC 3, 53; DAM DRAM, POET; PC 8**
See also CA 104; 120; MTCW 1
Taine, Hippolyte Adolphe 1828-1893 . **N C L C 15**
Talese, Gay 1932- .... **CLC 37**
See also AITN 1; CA 1-4R; CANR 9, 58; DLB 185; INT CANR-9; MTCW 1
Tallent, Elizabeth (Ann) 1954- .... **CLC 45**
See also CA 117; CANR 72; DLB 130
Tally, Ted 1952- .... **CLC 42**
See also CA 120; 124; INT 124
Tamayo y Baus, Manuel 1829-1898 **NCLC 1**
Tammsaare, A(nton) H(ansen) 1878-1940 **TCLC 27**
See also CA 164
Tam'si, Tchicaya U
See Tchicaya, Gerald Felix
Tan, Amy (Ruth) 1952- **CLC 59; DAM MULT, NOV, POP**
See also AAYA 9; BEST 89:3; CA 136; CANR 54; DLB 173; SATA 75
Tandem, Felix
See Spitteler, Carl (Friedrich Georg)
Tanizaki, Jun'ichiro 1886-1965 **CLC 8, 14, 28; SSC 21**
See also CA 93-96; 25-28R; DLB 180
Tanner, William
See Amis, Kingsley (William)
Tao Lao
See Storni, Alfonsina

Tarassoff, Lev
See Troyat, Henri
Tarbell, Ida M(inerva) 1857-1944 . **TCLC 40**
See also CA 122; DLB 47
Tarkington, (Newton) Booth 1869-1946 **TCLC 9**
See also CA 110; 143; DLB 9, 102; SATA 17
Tarkovsky, Andrei (Arsenyevich) 1932-1986 **CLC 75**
See also CA 127
Tartt, Donna 1964(?)- .... **CLC 76**
See also CA 142
Tasso, Torquato 1544-1595 .... **LC 5**
Tate, (John Orley) Allen 1899-1979 **CLC 2, 4, 6, 9, 11, 14, 24**
See also CA 5-8R; 85-88; CANR 32; DLB 4, 45, 63; DLBD 17; MTCW 1
Tate, Ellalice
See Hibbert, Eleanor Alice Burford
Tate, James (Vincent) 1943- ..... **CLC 2, 6, 25**
See also CA 21-24R; CANR 29, 57; DLB 5, 169
Tavel, Ronald 1940- .... **CLC 6**
See also CA 21-24R; CANR 33
Taylor, C(ecil) P(hilip) 1929-1981 .... **CLC 27**
See also CA 25-28R; 105; CANR 47
Taylor, Edward 1642(?)-1729 ..... **LC 11; DA; DAB; DAC; DAM MST, POET**
See also DLB 24
Taylor, Eleanor Ross 1920- .... **CLC 5**
See also CA 81-84; CANR 70
Taylor, Elizabeth 1912-1975 ..... **CLC 2, 4, 29**
See also CA 13-16R; CANR 9, 70; DLB 139; MTCW 1; SATA 13
Taylor, Frederick Winslow 1856-1915 **T C L C 76**
Taylor, Henry (Splawn) 1942- .... **CLC 44**
See also CA 33-36R; CAAS 7; CANR 31; DLB 5
Taylor, Kamala (Purnaiya) 1924-
See Markandaya, Kamala
See also CA 77-80
Taylor, Mildred D. .... **CLC 21**
See also AAYA 10; BW 1; CA 85-88; CANR 25; CLR 9; DLB 52; JRDA; MAICYA; SAAS 5; SATA 15, 70
Taylor, Peter (Hillsman) 1917-1994 **CLC 1, 4, 18, 37, 44, 50, 71; SSC 10**
See also CA 13-16R; 147; CANR 9, 50; DLBY 81, 94; INT CANR-9; MTCW 1
Taylor, Robert Lewis 1912- .... **CLC 14**
See also CA 1-4R; CANR 3, 64; SATA 10
Tchekhov, Anton
See Chekhov, Anton (Pavlovich)
Tchicaya, Gerald Felix 1931-1988 .. **CLC 101**
See also CA 129; 125
Tchicaya U Tam'si
See Tchicaya, Gerald Felix
Teasdale, Sara 1884-1933 .... **TCLC 4**
See also CA 104; 163; DLB 45; SATA 32
Tegner, Esaias 1782-1846 .... **NCLC 2**
Teilhard de Chardin, (Marie Joseph) Pierre 1881-1955 .... **TCLC 9**
See also CA 105
Temple, Ann
See Mortimer, Penelope (Ruth)
Tennant, Emma (Christina) 1937- **CLC 13, 52**
See also CA 65-68; CAAS 9; CANR 10, 38, 59; DLB 14
Tenneshaw, S. M.
See Silverberg, Robert
Tennyson, Alfred 1809-1892 ... **NCLC 30, 65; DA; DAB; DAC; DAM MST, POET; PC 6; WLC**
See also CDBLB 1832-1890; DLB 32
Teran, Lisa St. Aubin de .... **CLC 36**

See also St. Aubin de Teran, Lisa
Terence 195(?)B.C.-159B.C. **CMLC 14; DC 7**
Teresa de Jesus, St. 1515-1582 .... **LC 18**
Terkel, Louis 1912-
See Terkel, Studs
See also CA 57-60; CANR 18, 45, 67; MTCW 1
Terkel, Studs .... **CLC 38**
See also Terkel, Louis
See also AITN 1
Terry, C. V.
See Slaughter, Frank G(ill)
Terry, Megan 1932- .... **CLC 19**
See also CA 77-80; CABS 3; CANR 43; DLB 7
Tertullian c. 155-c. 245 .... **CMLC 29**
Tertz, Abram
See Sinyavsky, Andrei (Donatevich)
Tesich, Steve 1943(?)-1996 .... **CLC 40, 69**
See also CA 105; 152; DLBY 83
Teternikov, Fyodor Kuzmich 1863-1927
See Sologub, Fyodor
See also CA 104
Tevis, Walter 1928-1984 .... **CLC 42**
See also CA 113
Tey, Josephine .... **TCLC 14**
See also Mackintosh, Elizabeth
See also DLB 77
Thackeray, William Makepeace 1811-1863 **NCLC 5, 14, 22, 43; DA; DAB; DAC; DAM MST, NOV; WLC**
See also CDBLB 1832-1890; DLB 21, 55, 159, 163; SATA 23
Thakura, Ravindranatha
See Tagore, Rabindranath
Tharoor, Shashi 1956- .... **CLC 70**
See also CA 141
Thelwell, Michael Miles 1939- .... **CLC 22**
See also BW 2; CA 101
Theobald, Lewis, Jr.
See Lovecraft, H(oward) P(hillips)
Theodorescu, Ion N. 1880-1967
See Arghezi, Tudor
See also CA 116
Theriault, Yves 1915-1983 .... **CLC 79; DAC; DAM MST**
See also CA 102; DLB 88
Theroux, Alexander (Louis) 1939- **CLC 2, 25**
See also CA 85-88; CANR 20, 63
Theroux, Paul (Edward) 1941- **CLC 5, 8, 11, 15, 28, 46; DAM POP**
See also BEST 89:4; CA 33-36R; CANR 20, 45; DLB 2; MTCW 1; SATA 44
Thesen, Sharon 1946- .... **CLC 56**
See also CA 163
Thevenin, Denis
See Duhamel, Georges
Thibault, Jacques Anatole Francois 1844-1924
See France, Anatole
See also CA 106; 127; DAM NOV; MTCW 1
Thiele, Colin (Milton) 1920- .... **CLC 17**
See also CA 29-32R; CANR 12, 28, 53; CLR 27; MAICYA; SAAS 2; SATA 14, 72
Thomas, Audrey (Callahan) 1935- **CLC 7, 13, 37, 107; SSC 20**
See also AITN 2; CA 21-24R; CAAS 19; CANR 36, 58; DLB 60; MTCW 1
Thomas, D(onald) M(ichael) 1935- . **CLC 13, 22, 31**
See also CA 61-64; CAAS 11; CANR 17, 45; CDBLB 1960 to Present; DLB 40; INT CANR-17; MTCW 1
Thomas, Dylan (Marlais) 1914-1953 **TCLC 1, 8, 45; DA; DAB; DAC; DAM DRAM, MST, POET; PC 2; SSC 3; WLC**
See also CA 104; 120; CANR 65; CDBLB 1945-1960; DLB 13, 20, 139; MTCW 1; SATA 60

Thomas, (Philip) Edward 1878-1917 . **T C L C 10; DAM POET**
See also CA 106; 153; DLB 19

Thomas, Joyce Carol 1938- .... **CLC 35**
See also AAYA 12; BW 2; CA 113; 116; CANR 48; CLR 19; DLB 33; INT 116; JRDA; MAICYA; MTCW 1; SAAS 7; SATA 40, 78

Thomas, Lewis 1913-1993 .... **CLC 35**
See also CA 85-88; 143; CANR 38, 60; MTCW 1

Thomas, Paul
See Mann, (Paul) Thomas

Thomas, Piri 1928- .... **CLC 17**
See also CA 73-76; HW

Thomas, R(onald) S(tuart) 1913- **CLC 6, 13, 48; DAB; DAM POET**
See also CA 89-92; CAAS 4; CANR 30; CDBLB 1960 to Present; DLB 27; MTCW 1

Thomas, Ross (Elmore) 1926-1995 ... **CLC 39**
See also CA 33-36R; 150; CANR 22, 63

Thompson, Francis Clegg
See Mencken, H(enry) L(ouis)

Thompson, Francis Joseph 1859-1907**TCLC 4**
See also CA 104; CDBLB 1890-1914; DLB 19

Thompson, Hunter S(tockton) 1939- **CLC 9, 17, 40, 104; DAM POP**
See also BEST 89:1; CA 17-20R; CANR 23, 46; DLB 185; MTCW 1

Thompson, James Myers
See Thompson, Jim (Myers)

Thompson, Jim (Myers) 1906-1977(?)**CLC 69**
See also CA 140

Thompson, Judith .... **CLC 39**

Thomson, James 1700-1748 ... **LC 16, 29, 40; DAM POET**
See also DLB 95

Thomson, James 1834-1882 **NCLC 18; DAM POET**
See also DLB 35

Thoreau, Henry David 1817-1862**NCLC 7, 21, 61; DA; DAB; DAC; DAM MST; WLC**
See also CDALB 1640-1865; DLB 1

Thornton, Hall
See Silverberg, Robert

Thucydides c. 455B.C.-399B.C. .... **CMLC 17**
See also DLB 176

Thurber, James (Grover) 1894-1961 . **CLC 5, 11, 25; DA; DAB; DAC; DAM DRAM, MST, NOV; SSC 1**
See also CA 73-76; CANR 17, 39; CDALB 1929-1941; DLB 4, 11, 22, 102; MAICYA; MTCW 1; SATA 13

Thurman, Wallace (Henry) 1902-1934**T C L C 6; BLC 3; DAM MULT**
See also BW 1; CA 104; 124; DLB 51

Ticheburn, Cheviot
See Ainsworth, William Harrison

Tieck, (Johann) Ludwig 1773-1853 **NCLC 5, 46; SSC 31**
See also DLB 90

Tiger, Derry
See Ellison, Harlan (Jay)

Tilghman, Christopher 1948(?)- .... **CLC 65**
See also CA 159

Tillinghast, Richard (Williford) 1940-**CLC 29**
See also CA 29-32R; CAAS 23; CANR 26, 51

Timrod, Henry 1828-1867 .... **NCLC 25**
See also DLB 3

Tindall, Gillian (Elizabeth) 1938- ...... **CLC 7**
See also CA 21-24R; CANR 11, 65

Tiptree, James, Jr. .... **CLC 48, 50**
See also Sheldon, Alice Hastings Bradley
See also DLB 8

Titmarsh, Michael Angelo
See Thackeray, William Makepeace

Tocqueville, Alexis (Charles Henri Maurice Clerel Comte) 1805-1859 ... **NCLC 7, 63**

Tolkien, J(ohn) R(onald) R(euel) 1892-1973 **CLC 1, 2, 3, 8, 12, 38; DA; DAB; DAC; DAM MST, NOV, POP; WLC**
See also AAYA 10; AITN 1; CA 17-18; 45-48; CANR 36; CAP 2; CDBLB 1914-1945; DLB 15, 160; JRDA; MAICYA; MTCW 1; SATA 2, 32, 100; SATA-Obit 24

Toller, Ernst 1893-1939 .... **TCLC 10**
See also CA 107; DLB 124

Tolson, M. B.
See Tolson, Melvin B(eaunorus)

Tolson, Melvin B(eaunorus) 1898(?)-1966 **CLC 36, 105; BLC 3; DAM MULT, POET**
See also BW 1; CA 124; 89-92; DLB 48, 76

Tolstoi, Aleksei Nikolaevich
See Tolstoy, Alexey Nikolaevich

Tolstoy, Alexey Nikolaevich 1882-1945**T C L C 18**
See also CA 107; 158

Tolstoy, Count Leo
See Tolstoy, Leo (Nikolaevich)

Tolstoy, Leo (Nikolaevich) 1828-1910**TCLC 4, 11, 17, 28, 44, 79; DA; DAB; DAC; DAM MST, NOV; SSC 9, 30; WLC**
See also CA 104; 123; SATA 26

Tomasi di Lampedusa, Giuseppe 1896-1957
See Lampedusa, Giuseppe (Tomasi) di
See also CA 111

Tomlin, Lily .... **CLC 17**
See also Tomlin, Mary Jean

Tomlin, Mary Jean 1939(?)-
See Tomlin, Lily
See also CA 117

Tomlinson, (Alfred) Charles 1927-**CLC 2, 4, 6, 13, 45; DAM POET; PC 17**
See also CA 5-8R; CANR 33; DLB 40

Tomlinson, H(enry) M(ajor) 1873-1958**TCLC 71**
See also CA 118; 161; DLB 36, 100, 195

Tonson, Jacob
See Bennett, (Enoch) Arnold

Toole, John Kennedy 1937-1969 **CLC 19, 64**
See also CA 104; DLBY 81

Toomer, Jean 1894-1967**CLC 1, 4, 13, 22; BLC 3; DAM MULT; PC 7; SSC 1; WLCS**
See also BW 1; CA 85-88; CDALB 1917-1929; DLB 45, 51; MTCW 1

Torley, Luke
See Blish, James (Benjamin)

Tornimparte, Alessandra
See Ginzburg, Natalia

Torre, Raoul della
See Mencken, H(enry) L(ouis)

Torrey, E(dwin) Fuller 1937- .... **CLC 34**
See also CA 119; CANR 71

Torsvan, Ben Traven
See Traven, B.

Torsvan, Benno Traven
See Traven, B.

Torsvan, Berick Traven
See Traven, B.

Torsvan, Berwick Traven
See Traven, B.

Torsvan, Bruno Traven
See Traven, B.

Torsvan, Traven
See Traven, B.

Tournier, Michel (Edouard) 1924-**CLC 6, 23, 36, 95**
See also CA 49-52; CANR 3, 36; DLB 83; MTCW 1; SATA 23

Tournimparte, Alessandra
See Ginzburg, Natalia

Towers, Ivar
See Kornbluth, C(yril) M.

Towne, Robert (Burton) 1936(?)- ..... **CLC 87**
See also CA 108; DLB 44

Townsend, Sue .... **CLC 61**
See also Townsend, Susan Elaine
See also SATA 55, 93; SATA-Brief 48

Townsend, Susan Elaine 1946-
See Townsend, Sue
See also CA 119; 127; CANR 65; DAB; DAC; DAM MST

Townshend, Peter (Dennis Blandford) 1945-**CLC 17, 42**
See also CA 107

Tozzi, Federigo 1883-1920 .... **TCLC 31**
See also CA 160

Traill, Catharine Parr 1802-1899 .. **NCLC 31**
See also DLB 99

Trakl, Georg 1887-1914 .... **TCLC 5; PC 20**
See also CA 104; 165

Transtroemer, Tomas (Goesta) 1931-**CLC 52, 65; DAM POET**
See also CA 117; 129; CAAS 17

Transtromer, Tomas Gosta
See Transtroemer, Tomas (Goesta)

Traven, B. (?)-1969 .... **CLC 8, 11**
See also CA 19-20; 25-28R; CAP 2; DLB 9, 56; MTCW 1

Treitel, Jonathan 1959- .... **CLC 70**

Tremain, Rose 1943- .... **CLC 42**
See also CA 97-100; CANR 44; DLB 14

Tremblay, Michel 1942- **CLC 29, 102; DAC; DAM MST**
See also CA 116; 128; DLB 60; MTCW 1

Trevanian .... **CLC 29**
See also Whitaker, Rod(ney)

Trevor, Glen
See Hilton, James

Trevor, William 1928- . **CLC 7, 9, 14, 25, 71; SSC 21**
See also Cox, William Trevor
See also DLB 14, 139

Trifonov, Yuri (Valentinovich) 1925-1981 **CLC 45**
See also CA 126; 103; MTCW 1

Trilling, Lionel 1905-1975 ...... **CLC 9, 11, 24**
See also CA 9-12R; 61-64; CANR 10; DLB 28, 63; INT CANR-10; MTCW 1

Trimball, W. H.
See Mencken, H(enry) L(ouis)

Tristan
See Gomez de la Serna, Ramon

Tristram
See Housman, A(lfred) E(dward)

Trogdon, William (Lewis) 1939-
See Heat-Moon, William Least
See also CA 115; 119; CANR 47; INT 119

Trollope, Anthony 1815-1882**NCLC 6, 33; DA; DAB; DAC; DAM MST, NOV; SSC 28; WLC**
See also CDBLB 1832-1890; DLB 21, 57, 159; SATA 22

Trollope, Frances 1779-1863 .... **NCLC 30**
See also DLB 21, 166

Trotsky, Leon 1879-1940 .... **TCLC 22**
See also CA 118; 167

Trotter (Cockburn), Catharine 1679-1749**L C 8**
See also DLB 84

Trout, Kilgore
See Farmer, Philip Jose

Trow, George W. S. 1943- .... **CLC 52**
See also CA 126

Troyat, Henri 1911- .... **CLC 23**
See also CA 45-48; CANR 2, 33, 67; MTCW 1

Trudeau, G(arretson) B(eekman) 1948-
See Trudeau, Garry B.
See also CA 81-84; CANR 31; SATA 35

Trudeau, Garry B. .... **CLC 12**
See also Trudeau, G(arretson) B(eekman)
See also AAYA 10; AITN 2

Truffaut, Francois 1932-1984 .. **CLC 20, 101**
See also CA 81-84; 113; CANR 34
Trumbo, Dalton 1905-1976 .... **CLC 19**
See also CA 21-24R; 69-72; CANR 10; DLB 26
Trumbull, John 1750-1831 .... **NCLC 30**
See also DLB 31
Trundlett, Helen B.
See Eliot, T(homas) S(tearns)
Tryon, Thomas 1926-1991 . **CLC 3, 11; DAM POP**
See also AITN 1; CA 29-32R; 135; CANR 32; MTCW 1
Tryon, Tom
See Tryon, Thomas
Ts'ao Hsueh-ch'in 1715(?)-1763 .... **LC 1**
Tsushima, Shuji 1909-1948
See Dazai Osamu
See also CA 107
Tsvetaeva (Efron), Marina (Ivanovna) 1892-1941 .... **TCLC 7, 35; PC 14**
See also CA 104; 128; MTCW 1
Tuck, Lily 1938- .... **CLC 70**
See also CA 139
Tu Fu 712-770 .... **PC 9**
See also DAM MULT
Tunis, John R(oberts) 1889-1975 ...... **CLC 12**
See also CA 61-64; CANR 62; DLB 22, 171; JRDA; MAICYA; SATA 37; SATA-Brief 30
Tuohy, Frank .... **CLC 37**
See also Tuohy, John Francis
See also DLB 14, 139
Tuohy, John Francis 1925-
See Tuohy, Frank
See also CA 5-8R; CANR 3, 47
Turco, Lewis (Putnam) 1934- ...... **CLC 11, 63**
See also CA 13-16R; CAAS 22; CANR 24, 51; DLBY 84
Turgenev, Ivan 1818-1883 .... **NCLC 21; DA; DAB; DAC; DAM MST, NOV; DC 7; SSC 7; WLC**
Turgot, Anne-Robert-Jacques 1727-1781 **L C 26**
Turner, Frederick 1943- .... **CLC 48**
See also CA 73-76; CAAS 10; CANR 12, 30, 56; DLB 40
Tutu, Desmond M(pilo) 1931-**CLC 80; BLC 3; DAM MULT**
See also BW 1; CA 125; CANR 67
Tutuola, Amos 1920-1997**CLC 5, 14, 29; BLC 3; DAM MULT**
See also BW 2; CA 9-12R; 159; CANR 27, 66; DLB 125; MTCW 1
Twain, MarkTCLC 6, 12, 19, 36, 48, 59; SSC 6, 26; WLC
See also Clemens, Samuel Langhorne
See also AAYA 20; DLB 11, 12, 23, 64, 74
Tyler, Anne 1941- . **CLC 7, 11, 18, 28, 44, 59, 103; DAM NOV, POP**
See also AAYA 18; BEST 89:1; CA 9-12R; CANR 11, 33, 53; DLB 6, 143; DLBY 82; MTCW 1; SATA 7, 90
Tyler, Royall 1757-1826 .... **NCLC 3**
See also DLB 37
Tynan, Katharine 1861-1931 .... **TCLC 3**
See also CA 104; 167; DLB 153
Tyutchev, Fyodor 1803-1873 .... **NCLC 34**
Tzara, Tristan 1896-1963 ...... **CLC 47; DAM POET**
See also CA 153; 89-92
Uhry, Alfred 1936- ... **CLC 55; DAM DRAM, POP**
See also CA 127; 133; INT 133
Ulf, Haerved
See Strindberg, (Johan) August
Ulf, Harved
See Strindberg, (Johan) August

Ulibarri, Sabine R(eyes) 1919-**CLC 83; DAM MULT**
See also CA 131; DLB 82; HW
Unamuno (y Jugo), Miguel de 1864-1936 **TCLC 2, 9; DAM MULT, NOV; HLC; SSC 11**
See also CA 104; 131; DLB 108; HW; MTCW 1
Undercliffe, Errol
See Campbell, (John) Ramsey
Underwood, Miles
See Glassco, John
Undset, Sigrid 1882-1949**TCLC 3; DA; DAB; DAC; DAM MST, NOV; WLC**
See also CA 104; 129; MTCW 1
Ungaretti, Giuseppe 1888-1970**CLC 7, 11, 15**
See also CA 19-20; 25-28R; CAP 2; DLB 114
Unger, Douglas 1952- .... **CLC 34**
See also CA 130
Unsworth, Barry (Forster) 1930- ..... **CLC 76**
See also CA 25-28R; CANR 30, 54; DLB 194
Updike, John (Hoyer) 1932-**CLC 1, 2, 3, 5, 7, 9, 13, 15, 23, 34, 43, 70; DA; DAB; DAC; DAM MST, NOV, POET, POP; SSC 13, 27; WLC**
See also CA 1-4R; CABS 1; CANR 4, 33, 51; CDALB 1968-1988; DLB 2, 5, 143; DLBD 3; DLBY 80, 82, 97; MTCW 1
Upshaw, Margaret Mitchell
See Mitchell, Margaret (Munnerlyn)
Upton, Mark
See Sanders, Lawrence
Upward, Allen 1863-1926 .... **TCLC 85**
See also CA 117; DLB 36
Urdang, Constance (Henriette) 1922-**CLC 47**
See also CA 21-24R; CANR 9, 24
Uriel, Henry
See Faust, Frederick (Schiller)
Uris, Leon (Marcus) 1924- **CLC 7, 32; DAM NOV, POP**
See also AITN 1, 2; BEST 89:2; CA 1-4R; CANR 1, 40, 65; MTCW 1; SATA 49
Urmuz
See Codrescu, Andrei
Urquhart, Jane 1949- .... **CLC 90; DAC**
See also CA 113; CANR 32, 68
Ustinov, Peter (Alexander) 1921- .... **CLC 1**
See also AITN 1; CA 13-16R; CANR 25, 51; DLB 13
U Tam'si, Gerald Felix Tchicaya
See Tchicaya, Gerald Felix
U Tam'si, Tchicaya
See Tchicaya, Gerald Felix
Vachss, Andrew (Henry) 1942- .... **CLC 106**
See also CA 118; CANR 44
Vachss, Andrew H.
See Vachss, Andrew (Henry)
Vaculik, Ludvik 1926- .... **CLC 7**
See also CA 53-56; CANR 72
Vaihinger, Hans 1852-1933 .... **TCLC 71**
See also CA 116; 166
Valdez, Luis (Miguel) 1940- .. **CLC 84; DAM MULT; HLC**
See also CA 101; CANR 32; DLB 122; HW
Valenzuela, Luisa 1938- **CLC 31, 104; DAM MULT; SSC 14**
See also CA 101; CANR 32, 65; DLB 113; HW
Valera y Alcala-Galiano, Juan 1824-1905 **TCLC 10**
See also CA 106
Valery, (Ambroise) Paul (Toussaint Jules) 1871-1945 ....
TCLC 4, 15; DAM POET; PC 9
See also CA 104; 122; MTCW 1
Valle-Inclan, Ramon (Maria) del 1866-1936 **TCLC 5; DAM MULT; HLC**
See also CA 106; 153; DLB 134

Vallejo, Antonio Buero
See Buero Vallejo, Antonio
Vallejo, Cesar (Abraham) 1892-1938**TCLC 3, 56; DAM MULT; HLC**
See also CA 105; 153; HW
Vallette, Marguerite Eymery
See Rachilde
Valle Y Pena, Ramon del
See Valle-Inclan, Ramon (Maria) del
Van Ash, Cay 1918- .... **CLC 34**
Vanbrugh, Sir John 1664-1726 **LC 21; DAM DRAM**
See also DLB 80
Van Campen, Karl
See Campbell, John W(ood, Jr.)
Vance, Gerald
See Silverberg, Robert
Vance, Jack .... **CLC 35**
See also Kuttner, Henry; Vance, John Holbrook
See also DLB 8
Vance, John Holbrook 1916-
See Queen, Ellery; Vance, Jack
See also CA 29-32R; CANR 17, 65; MTCW 1
Van Den Bogarde, Derek Jules Gaspard Ulric Niven 1921-
See Bogarde, Dirk
See also CA 77-80
Vandenburgh, Jane .... **CLC 59**
See also CA 168
Vanderhaeghe, Guy 1951- .... **CLC 41**
See also CA 113; CANR 72
van der Post, Laurens (Jan) 1906-1996**CLC 5**
See also CA 5-8R; 155; CANR 35
van de Wetering, Janwillem 1931- ... **CLC 47**
See also CA 49-52; CANR 4, 62
Van Dine, S. S. .... **TCLC 23**
See also Wright, Willard Huntington
Van Doren, Carl (Clinton) 1885-1950 **T C L C 18**
See also CA 111; 168
Van Doren, Mark 1894-1972 ....**CLC 6, 10**
See also CA 1-4R; 37-40R; CANR 3; DLB 45; MTCW 1
Van Druten, John (William) 1901-1957**TCLC 2**
See also CA 104; 161; DLB 10
Van Duyn, Mona (Jane) 1921- **CLC 3, 7, 63; DAM POET**
See also CA 9-12R; CANR 7, 38, 60; DLB 5
Van Dyne, Edith
See Baum, L(yman) Frank
van Itallie, Jean-Claude 1936- .... **CLC 3**
See also CA 45-48; CAAS 2; CANR 1, 48; DLB 7
van Ostaijen, Paul 1896-1928 .... **TCLC 33**
See also CA 163
Van Peebles, Melvin 1932- **CLC 2, 20; DAM MULT**
See also BW 2; CA 85-88; CANR 27, 67
Vansittart, Peter 1920- .... **CLC 42**
See also CA 1-4R; CANR 3, 49
Van Vechten, Carl 1880-1964 .... **CLC 33**
See also CA 89-92; DLB 4, 9, 51
Van Vogt, A(lfred) E(lton) 1912- .... **CLC 1**
See also CA 21-24R; CANR 28; DLB 8; SATA 14
Varda, Agnes 1928-............................. **CLC 16**
See also CA 116; 122
Vargas Llosa, (Jorge) Mario (Pedro) 1936-**CLC 3, 6, 9, 10, 15, 31, 42, 85; DA; DAB; DAC; DAM MST, MULT, NOV; HLC**
See also CA 73-76; CANR 18, 32, 42, 67; DLB 145; HW; MTCW 1
Vasiliu, Gheorghe 1881-1957
See Bacovia, George
See also CA 123
Vassa, Gustavus

Wallace, Irving 1916-1990 **CLC 7, 13; DAM NOV, POP**
  See also AITN 1; CA 1-4R; 132; CAAS 1; CANR 1, 27; INT CANR-27; MTCW 1
Wallant, Edward Lewis 1926-1962**CLC 5, 10**
  See also CA 1-4R; CANR 22; DLB 2, 28, 143; MTCW 1
Walley, Byron
  See Card, Orson Scott
Walpole, Horace 1717-1797 .... **LC 2**
  See also DLB 39, 104
Walpole, Hugh (Seymour) 1884-1941**TCLC 5**
  See also CA 104; 165; DLB 34
Walser, Martin 1927- .... **CLC 27**
  See also CA 57-60; CANR 8, 46; DLB 75, 124
Walser, Robert 1878-1956 **TCLC 18; SSC 20**
  See also CA 118; 165; DLB 66
Walsh, Jill Paton .... **CLC 35**
  See also Paton Walsh, Gillian
  See also AAYA 11; CLR 2; DLB 161; SAAS 3
Walter, Villiam Christian
  See Andersen, Hans Christian
Wambaugh, Joseph (Aloysius, Jr.) 1937-**CLC 3, 18; DAM NOV, POP**
  See also AITN 1; BEST 89:3; CA 33-36R; CANR 42, 65; DLB 6; DLBY 83; MTCW 1
Wang Wei 699(?)-761(?) .... **PC 18**
Ward, Arthur Henry Sarsfield 1883-1959
  See Rohmer, Sax
  See also CA 108
Ward, Douglas Turner 1930- .... **CLC 19**
  See also BW 1; CA 81-84; CANR 27; DLB 7, 38
Ward, Mary Augusta
  See Ward, Mrs. Humphry
Ward, Mrs. Humphry 1851-1920 .. **TCLC 55**
  See also DLB 18
Ward, Peter
  See Faust, Frederick (Schiller)
Warhol, Andy 1928(?)-1987 .... **CLC 20**
  See also AAYA 12; BEST 89:4; CA 89-92; 121; CANR 34
Warner, Francis (Robert le Plastrier) 1937-
CLC 14
  See also CA 53-56; CANR 11
Warner, Marina 1946- .... **CLC 59**
  See also CA 65-68; CANR 21, 55; DLB 194
Warner, Rex (Ernest) 1905-1986 ...... **CLC 45**
  See also CA 89-92; 119; DLB 15
Warner, Susan (Bogert) 1819-1885 **NCLC 31**
  See also DLB 3, 42
Warner, Sylvia (Constance) Ashton
  See Ashton-Warner, Sylvia (Constance)
Warner, Sylvia Townsend 1893-1978 **CLC 7, 19; SSC 23**
  See also CA 61-64; 77-80; CANR 16, 60; DLB 34, 139; MTCW 1
Warren, Mercy Otis 1728-1814 ..... **NCLC 13**
  See also DLB 31, 200
Warren, Robert Penn 1905-1989**CLC 1, 4, 6, 8, 10, 13, 18, 39, 53, 59; DA; DAB; DAC; DAM MST, NOV, POET; SSC 4; WLC**
  See also AITN 1; CA 13-16R; 129; CANR 10, 47; CDALB 1968-1988; DLB 2, 48, 152; DLBY 80, 89; INT CANR-10; MTCW 1; SATA 46; SATA-Obit 63
Warshofsky, Isaac
  See Singer, Isaac Bashevis
Warton, Thomas 1728-1790 ..... **LC 15; DAM POET**
  See also DLB 104, 109
Waruk, Kona
  See Harris, (Theodore) Wilson
Warung, Price 1855-1911 .... **TCLC 45**
Warwick, Jarvis
  See Garner, Hugh
Washington, Alex

See Harris, Mark
Washington, Booker T(aliaferro) 1856-1915
TCLC 10; BLC 3; DAM MULT
  See also BW 1; CA 114; 125; SATA 28
Washington, George 1732-1799 .... **LC 25**
  See also DLB 31
Wassermann, (Karl) Jakob 1873-1934**T C L C 6**
  See also CA 104; DLB 66
Wasserstein, Wendy 1950- ... **CLC 32, 59, 90; DAM DRAM; DC 4**
  See also CA 121; 129; CABS 3; CANR 53; INT 129; SATA 94
Waterhouse, Keith (Spencer) 1929- **CLC 47**
  See also CA 5-8R; CANR 38, 67; DLB 13, 15; MTCW 1
Waters, Frank (Joseph) 1902-1995 ..**CLC 88**
  See also CA 5-8R; 149; CAAS 13; CANR 3, 18, 63; DLBY 86
Waters, Roger 1944- .... **CLC 35**
Watkins, Frances Ellen
  See Harper, Frances Ellen Watkins
Watkins, Gerrold
  See Malzberg, Barry N(athaniel)
Watkins, Gloria 1955(?)-
  See hooks, bell
  See also BW 2; CA 143
Watkins, Paul 1964- .... **CLC 55**
  See also CA 132; CANR 62
Watkins, Vernon Phillips 1906-1967 **CLC 43**
  See also CA 9-10; 25-28R; CAP 1; DLB 20
Watson, Irving S.
  See Mencken, H(enry) L(ouis)
Watson, John H.
  See Farmer, Philip Jose
Watson, Richard F.
  See Silverberg, Robert
Waugh, Auberon (Alexander) 1939- .. **CLC 7**
  See also CA 45-48; CANR 6, 22; DLB 14, 194
Waugh, Evelyn (Arthur St. John) 1903-1966
CLC 1, 3, 8, 13, 19, 27, 44, 107; DA; DAB; DAC; DAM MST, NOV, POP; WLC
  See also CA 85-88; 25-28R; CANR 22; CDBLB 1914-1945; DLB 15, 162, 195; MTCW 1
Waugh, Harriet 1944- .... **CLC 6**
  See also CA 85-88; CANR 22
Ways, C. R.
  See Blount, Roy (Alton), Jr.
Waystaff, Simon
  See Swift, Jonathan
Webb, (Martha) Beatrice (Potter) 1858-1943
TCLC 22
  See also Potter, (Helen) Beatrix
  See also CA 117
Webb, Charles (Richard) 1939- .... **CLC 7**
  See also CA 25-28R
Webb, James H(enry), Jr. 1946- .... **CLC 22**
  See also CA 81-84
Webb, Mary (Gladys Meredith) 1881-1927
TCLC 24
  See also CA 123; DLB 34
Webb, Mrs. Sidney
  See Webb, (Martha) Beatrice (Potter)
Webb, Phyllis 1927- .... **CLC 18**
  See also CA 104; CANR 23; DLB 53
Webb, Sidney (James) 1859-1947 .. **TCLC 22**
  See also CA 117; 163; DLB 190
Webber, Andrew Lloyd .... **CLC 21**
  See also Lloyd Webber, Andrew
Weber, Lenora Mattingly 1895-1971 **CLC 12**
  See also CA 19-20; 29-32R; CAP 1; SATA 2; SATA-Obit 26
Weber, Max 1864-1920 .... **TCLC 69**
  See also CA 109
Webster, John 1579(?)-1634(?) ... **LC 33; DA; DAB; DAC; DAM DRAM, MST; DC 2; WLC**

See also CDBLB Before 1660; DLB 58
Webster, Noah 1758-1843 .... **NCLC 30**
Wedekind, (Benjamin) Frank(lin) 1864-1918
TCLC 7; DAM DRAM
  See also CA 104; 153; DLB 118
Weidman, Jerome 1913- .... **CLC 7**
  See also AITN 2; CA 1-4R; CANR 1; DLB 28
Weil, Simone (Adolphine) 1909-1943**TCLC 23**
  See also CA 117; 159
Weininger, Otto 1880-1903 .... **TCLC 84**
Weinstein, Nathan
  See West, Nathanael
Weinstein, Nathan von Wallenstein
  See West, Nathanael
Weir, Peter (Lindsay) 1944- .... **CLC 20**
  See also CA 113; 123
Weiss, Peter (Ulrich) 1916-1982**CLC 3, 15, 51; DAM DRAM**
  See also CA 45-48; 106; CANR 3; DLB 69, 124
Weiss, Theodore (Russell) 1916-**CLC 3, 8, 14**
  See also CA 9-12R; CAAS 2; CANR 46; DLB 5
Welch, (Maurice) Denton 1915-1948**TCLC 22**
  See also CA 121; 148
Welch, James 1940- ..... **CLC 6, 14, 52; DAM MULT, POP**
  See also CA 85-88; CANR 42, 66; DLB 175; NNAL
Weldon, Fay 1931- . **CLC 6, 9, 11, 19, 36, 59; DAM POP**
  See also CA 21-24R; CANR 16, 46, 63; CDBLB 1960 to Present; DLB 14, 194; INT CANR-16; MTCW 1
Wellek, Rene 1903-1995 .... **CLC 28**
  See also CA 5-8R; 150; CAAS 7; CANR 8; DLB 63; INT CANR-8
Weller, Michael 1942- .... **CLC 10, 53**
  See also CA 85-88
Weller, Paul 1958- .... **CLC 26**
Wellershoff, Dieter 1925- .... **CLC 46**
  See also CA 89-92; CANR 16, 37
Welles, (George) Orson 1915-1985**CLC 20, 80**
  See also CA 93-96; 117
Wellman, John McDowell 1945-
  See Wellman, Mac
  See also CA 166
Wellman, Mac 1945- .... **CLC 65**
  See also Wellman, John McDowell; Wellman, John McDowell
Wellman, Manly Wade 1903-1986 .... **CLC 49**
  See also CA 1-4R; 118; CANR 6, 16, 44; SATA 6; SATA-Obit 47
Wells, Carolyn 1869(?)-1942 .... **TCLC 35**
  See also CA 113; DLB 11
Wells, H(erbert) G(eorge) 1866-1946**TCLC 6, 12, 19; DA; DAB; DAC; DAM MST, NOV; SSC 6; WLC**
  See also AAYA 18; CA 110; 121; CDBLB 1914-1945; DLB 34, 70, 156, 178; MTCW 1; SATA 20
Wells, Rosemary 1943- .... **CLC 12**
  See also AAYA 13; CA 85-88; CANR 48; CLR 16; MAICYA; SAAS 1; SATA 18, 69
Welty, Eudora 1909- **CLC 1, 2, 5, 14, 22, 33, 105; DA; DAB; DAC; DAM MST, NOV; SSC 1, 27; WLC**
  See also CA 9-12R; CABS 1; CANR 32, 65; CDALB 1941-1968; DLB 2, 102, 143; DLBD 12; DLBY 87; MTCW 1
Wen I-to 1899-1946 .... **TCLC 28**
Wentworth, Robert
  See Hamilton, Edmond
Werfel, Franz (Viktor) 1890-1945 ... **TCLC 8**
  See also CA 104; 161; DLB 81, 124
Wergeland, Henrik Arnold 1808-1845**N C L C 5**
Wersba, Barbara 1932- .... **CLC 30**

See also AAYA 2; CA 29-32R; CANR 16, 38; CLR 3; DLB 52; JRDA; MAICYA; SAAS 2; SATA 1, 58

Wertmueller, Lina 1928- .... **CLC 16**
See also CA 97-100; CANR 39

Wescott, Glenway 1901-1987 .... **CLC 13**
See also CA 13-16R; 121; CANR 23, 70; DLB 4, 9, 102

Wesker, Arnold 1932- .... **CLC 3, 5, 42; DAB; DAM DRAM**
See also CA 1-4R; CAAS 7; CANR 1, 33; CDBLB 1960 to Present; DLB 13; MTCW 1

Wesley, Richard (Errol) 1945- .... **CLC 7**
See also BW 1; CA 57-60; CANR 27; DLB 38

Wessel, Johan Herman 1742-1785 .... **LC 7**

West, Anthony (Panther) 1914-1987 **CLC 50**
See also CA 45-48; 124; CANR 3, 19; DLB 15

West, C. P.
See Wodehouse, P(elham) G(renville)

West, (Mary) Jessamyn 1902-1984 **CLC 7, 17**
See also CA 9-12R; 112; CANR 27; DLB 6; DLBY 84; MTCW 1; SATA-Obit 37

West, Morris L(anglo) 1916- .... **CLC 6, 33**
See also CA 5-8R; CANR 24, 49, 64; MTCW 1

West, Nathanael 1903-1940 **TCLC 1, 14, 44; SSC 16**
See also CA 104; 125; CDALB 1929-1941; DLB 4, 9, 28; MTCW 1

West, Owen
See Koontz, Dean R(ay)

West, Paul 1930- .... **CLC 7, 14, 96**
See also CA 13-16R; CAAS 7; CANR 22, 53; DLB 14; INT CANR-22

West, Rebecca 1892-1983 ... **CLC 7, 9, 31, 50**
See also CA 5-8R; 109; CANR 19; DLB 36; DLBY 83; MTCW 1

Westall, Robert (Atkinson) 1929-1993 **CLC 17**
See also AAYA 12; CA 69-72; 141; CANR 18, 68; CLR 13; JRDA; MAICYA; SAAS 2; SATA 23, 69; SATA-Obit 75

Westlake, Donald E(dwin) 1933- **CLC 7, 33; DAM POP**
See also CA 17-20R; CAAS 13; CANR 16, 44, 65; INT CANR-16

Westmacott, Mary
See Christie, Agatha (Mary Clarissa)

Weston, Allen
See Norton, Andre

Wetcheek, J. L.
See Feuchtwanger, Lion

Wetering, Janwillem van de
See van de Wetering, Janwillem

Wetherald, Agnes Ethelwyn 1857-1940 **TCLC 81**
See also DLB 99

Wetherell, Elizabeth
See Warner, Susan (Bogert)

Whale, James 1889-1957 .... **TCLC 63**

Whalen, Philip 1923- .... **CLC 6, 29**
See also CA 9-12R; CANR 5, 39; DLB 16

Wharton, Edith (Newbold Jones) 1862-1937 **TCLC 3, 9, 27, 53; DA; DAB; DAC; DAM MST, NOV; SSC 6; WLC**
See also AAYA 25; CA 104; 132; CDALB 1865-1917; DLB 4, 9, 12, 78, 189; DLBD 13; MTCW 1

Wharton, James
See Mencken, H(enry) L(ouis)

Wharton, William (a pseudonym) **CLC 18, 37**
See also CA 93-96; DLBY 80; INT 93-96

Wheatley (Peters), Phillis 1754(?)-1784 **LC 3; BLC 3; DA; DAC; DAM MST, MULT, POET; PC 3; WLC**
See also CDALB 1640-1865; DLB 31, 50

Wheelock, John Hall 1886-1978 .... **CLC 14**
See also CA 13-16R; 77-80; CANR 14; DLB 45

White, E(lwyn) B(rooks) 1899-1985 **CLC 10, 34, 39; DAM POP**
See also AITN 2; CA 13-16R; 116; CANR 16, 37; CLR 1, 21; DLB 11, 22; MAICYA; MTCW 1; SATA 2, 29, 100; SATA-Obit 44

White, Edmund (Valentine III) 1940- **CLC 27, 110; DAM POP**
See also CA 45-48; CANR 3, 19, 36, 62; MTCW 1

White, Patrick (Victor Martindale) 1912-1990 **CLC 3, 4, 5, 7, 9, 18, 65, 69**
See also CA 81-84; 132; CANR 43; MTCW 1

White, Phyllis Dorothy James 1920-
See James, P. D.
See also CA 21-24R; CANR 17, 43, 65; DAM POP; MTCW 1

White, T(erence) H(anbury) 1906-1964 **C L C 30**
See also AAYA 22; CA 73-76; CANR 37; DLB 160; JRDA; MAICYA; SATA 12

White, Terence de Vere 1912-1994 ... **CLC 49**
See also CA 49-52; 145; CANR 3

White, Walter F(rancis) 1893-1955 **TCLC 15**
See also White, Walter
See also BW 1; CA 115; 124; DLB 51

White, William Hale 1831-1913
See Rutherford, Mark
See also CA 121

Whitehead, E(dward) A(nthony) 1933- **CLC 5**
See also CA 65-68; CANR 58

Whitemore, Hugh (John) 1936- .... **CLC 37**
See also CA 132; INT 132

Whitman, Sarah Helen (Power) 1803-1878 **NCLC 19**
See also DLB 1

Whitman, Walt(er) 1819-1892 . **NCLC 4, 31; DA; DAB; DAC; DAM MST, POET; PC 3; WLC**
See also CDALB 1640-1865; DLB 3, 64; SATA 20

Whitney, Phyllis A(yame) 1903- ..... **CLC 42; DAM POP**
See also AITN 2; BEST 90:3; CA 1-4R; CANR 3, 25, 38, 60; JRDA; MAICYA; SATA 1, 30

Whittemore, (Edward) Reed (Jr.) 1919- **CLC 4**
See also CA 9-12R; CAAS 8; CANR 4; DLB 5

Whittier, John Greenleaf 1807-1892 **NCLC 8, 59**
See also DLB 1

Whittlebot, Hernia
See Coward, Noel (Peirce)

Wicker, Thomas Grey 1926-
See Wicker, Tom
See also CA 65-68; CANR 21, 46

Wicker, Tom .... **CLC 7**
See also Wicker, Thomas Grey

Wideman, John Edgar 1941- **CLC 5, 34, 36, 67; BLC 3; DAM MULT**
See also BW 2; CA 85-88; CANR 14, 42, 67; DLB 33, 143

Wiebe, Rudy (Henry) 1934- .. **CLC 6, 11, 14; DAC; DAM MST**
See also CA 37-40R; CANR 42, 67; DLB 60

Wieland, Christoph Martin 1733-1813 **N C L C 17**
See also DLB 97

Wiene, Robert 1881-1938 .... **TCLC 56**

Wieners, John 1934- .... **CLC 7**
See also CA 13-16R; DLB 16

Wiesel, Elie(zer) 1928- **CLC 3, 5, 11, 37; DA; DAB; DAC; DAM MST, NOV; WLCS 2**
See also AAYA 7; AITN 1; CA 5-8R; CAAS 4; CANR 8, 40, 65; DLB 83; DLBY 87; INT CANR-8; MTCW 1; SATA 56

Wiggins, Marianne 1947- .... **CLC 57**
See also BEST 89:3; CA 130; CANR 60

Wight, James Alfred 1916-1995

See Herriot, James
See also CA 77-80; SATA 55; SATA-Brief 44

Wilbur, Richard (Purdy) 1921- **CLC 3, 6, 9, 14, 53, 110; DA; DAB; DAC; DAM MST, POET**
See also CA 1-4R; CABS 2; CANR 2, 29; DLB 5, 169; INT CANR-29; MTCW 1; SATA 9

Wild, Peter 1940- .... **CLC 14**
See also CA 37-40R; DLB 5

Wilde, Oscar (Fingal O'Flahertie Wills) 1854(?)-1900 ....
TCLC 1, 8, 23, 41; DA; DAB; DAC; DAM DRAM, MST, NOV; SSC 11; WLC
See also CA 104; 119; CDBLB 1890-1914; DLB 10, 19, 34, 57, 141, 156, 190; SATA 24

Wilder, Billy .... **CLC 20**
See also Wilder, Samuel
See also DLB 26

Wilder, Samuel 1906-
See Wilder, Billy
See also CA 89-92

Wilder, Thornton (Niven) 1897-1975 **CLC 1, 5, 6, 10, 15, 35, 82; DA; DAB; DAC; DAM DRAM, MST, NOV; DC 1; WLC**
See also AITN 2; CA 13-16R; 61-64; CANR 40; DLB 4, 7, 9; DLBY 97; MTCW 1

Wilding, Michael 1942- .... **CLC 73**
See also CA 104; CANR 24, 49

Wiley, Richard 1944- .... **CLC 44**
See also CA 121; 129; CANR 71

Wilhelm, Kate .... **CLC 7**
See also Wilhelm, Katie Gertrude
See also AAYA 20; CAAS 5; DLB 8; INT CANR-17

Wilhelm, Katie Gertrude 1928-
See Wilhelm, Kate
See also CA 37-40R; CANR 17, 36, 60; MTCW 1

Wilkins, Mary
See Freeman, Mary Eleanor Wilkins

Willard, Nancy 1936- .... **CLC 7, 37**
See also CA 89-92; CANR 10, 39, 68; CLR 5; DLB 5, 52; MAICYA; MTCW 1; SATA 37, 71; SATA-Brief 30

Williams, C(harles) K(enneth) 1936- **CLC 33, 56; DAM POET**
See also CA 37-40R; CAAS 26; CANR 57; DLB 5

Williams, Charles
See Collier, James L(incoln)

Williams, Charles (Walter Stansby) 1886-1945 **TCLC 1, 11**
See also CA 104; 163; DLB 100, 153

Williams, (George) Emlyn 1905-1987 **CLC 15; DAM DRAM**
See also CA 104; 123; CANR 36; DLB 10, 77; MTCW 1

Williams, Hank 1923-1953 .... **TCLC 81**

Williams, Hugo 1942- .... **CLC 42**
See also CA 17-20R; CANR 45; DLB 40

Williams, J. Walker
See Wodehouse, P(elham) G(renville)

Williams, John A(lfred) 1925- **CLC 5, 13; BLC 3; DAM MULT**
See also BW 2; CA 53-56; CAAS 3; CANR 6, 26, 51; DLB 2, 33; INT CANR-6

Williams, Jonathan (Chamberlain) 1929- **CLC 13**
See also CA 9-12R; CAAS 12; CANR 8; DLB 5

Williams, Joy 1944- .... **CLC 31**
See also CA 41-44R; CANR 22, 48

Williams, Norman 1952- .... **CLC 39**
See also CA 118

Williams, Sherley Anne 1944- **CLC 89; BLC 3; DAM MULT, POET**
See also BW 2; CA 73-76; CANR 25; DLB 41;

Literary Criticism Series
Cumulative Topic Index

This index lists all topic entries in Gale's *Classical and Medieval Literature Criticism, Contemporary Literary Criticism, Literature Criticism from 1400 to 1800, Nineteenth-Century Literature Criticism,* and *Twentieth-Century Literary Criticism.*

Topic Index

Topic Index

Twentieth-Century Literary Criticism
Cumulative Nationality Index

AMERICAN

Adams, Andy **56**
Adams, Brooks **80**
Adams, Henry (Brooks) **4, 52**
Addams, Jane **76**
Agee, James (Rufus) **1, 19**
Anderson, Maxwell **2**
Anderson, Sherwood **1, 10, 24**
Anthony, Susan B(rownell) **84**
Atherton, Gertrude (Franklin Horn) **2**
Austin, Mary (Hunter) **25**
Baker, Ray Stannard **47**
Barry, Philip **11**
Baum, L(yman) Frank **7**
Beard, Charles A(ustin) **15**
Becker, Carl (Lotus) **63**
Belasco, David **3**
Bell, James Madison **43**
Benchley, Robert (Charles) **1, 55**
Benedict, Ruth (Fulton) **60**
Benet, Stephen Vincent **7**
Benet, William Rose **28**
Bierce, Ambrose (Gwinett) **1, 7, 44**
Biggers, Earl Derr **65**
Black Elk **33**
Boas, Franz **56**
Bodenheim, Maxwell **44**
Bourne, Randolph S(illiman) **16**
Bradford, Gamaliel **36**
Brennan, Christopher John **17**
Bromfield, Louis (Brucker) **11**
Burroughs, Edgar Rice **2, 32**
Cabell, James Branch **6**
Cable, George Washington **4**
Cahan, Abraham **71**
Cardozo, Benjamin N(athan) **65**
Carnegie, Dale **53**
Cather, Willa Sibert **1, 11, 31**
Chambers, Robert W(illiam) **41**
Chandler, Raymond (Thornton) **1, 7**
Chapman, John Jay **7**
Chesnutt, Charles W(addell) **5, 39**
Chopin, Kate **5, 14**
Cobb, Irvin S. **77**
Cohan, George M(ichael) **60**
Comstock, Anthony **13**
Cotter, Joseph Seamon Sr. **28**
Cram, Ralph Adams **45**
Crane, (Harold) Hart **2, 5, 80**
Crane, Stephen (Townley) **11, 17, 32**
Crawford, F(rancis) Marion **10**
Crothers, Rachel **19**
Cullen, Countee **4, 37**
Darrow, Clarence (Seward) **81**
Davis, Rebecca (Blaine) Harding **6**
Davis, Richard Harding **24**
Day, Clarence (Shepard Jr.) **25**
Dent, Lester **72**

De Voto, Bernard (Augustine) **29**
Dreiser, Theodore (Herman Albert) **10, 18, 35, 83**
Dulles, John Foster **72**
Dunbar, Paul Laurence **2, 12**
Duncan, Isadora **68**
Dunne, Finley Peter **28**
Eastman, Charles A(lexander) **55**
Eddy, Mary (Morse) Baker **71**
Einstein, Albert **65**
Erskine, John **84**
Faust, Frederick (Schiller) **49**
Fields, W. C. **80**
Fisher, Rudolph **11**
Fitzgerald, F(rancis) Scott (Key) **1, 6, 14, 28, 55**
Fitzgerald, Zelda (Sayre) **52**
Flecker, (Herman) James Elroy **43**
Fletcher, John Gould **35**
Ford, Henry **73**
Forten, Charlotte L. **16**
Freeman, Douglas Southall **11**
Freeman, Mary Eleanor Wilkins **9**
Futrelle, Jacques **19**
Gale, Zona **7**
Garland, (Hannibal) Hamlin **3**
Gilman, Charlotte (Anna) Perkins (Stetson) **9, 37**
Glasgow, Ellen (Anderson Gholson) **2, 7**
Glaspell, Susan **55**
Goldman, Emma **13**
Green, Anna Katharine **63**
Grey, Zane **6**
Griffith, D(avid Lewelyn) W(ark) **68**
Griggs, Sutton Elbert **77**
Guiney, Louise Imogen **41**
Hall, James Norman **23**
Harper, Frances Ellen Watkins **14**
Harris, Joel Chandler **2**
Harte, (Francis) Bret(t) **1, 25**
Hartmann, Sadakichi **73**
Hatteras, Owen **18**
Hawthorne, Julian **25**
Hearn, (Patricio) Lafcadio (Tessima Carlos) **9**
Henry, O. **1, 19**
Hergesheimer, Joseph **11**
Higginson, Thomas Wentworth **36**
Holly, Buddy **65**
Holmes, Oliver Wendell Jr. **77**
Hopkins, Pauline Elizabeth **28**
Horney, Karen (Clementine Theodore Danielsen) **71**
Howard, Robert E(rvin) **8**
Howe, Julia Ward **21**
Howells, William Dean **7, 17, 41**
Huneker, James Gibbons **65**
James, Henry **2, 11, 24, 40, 47, 64**
James, William **15, 32**

Jewett, (Theodora) Sarah Orne **1, 22**
Johnson, James Weldon **3, 19**
Johnson, Robert **69**
Kornbluth, C(yril) M. **8**
Korzybski, Alfred (Habdank Skarbek) **61**
Kuttner, Henry **10**
Lardner, Ring(gold) W(ilmer) **2, 14**
Lewis, (Harry) Sinclair **4, 13, 23, 39**
Lewisohn, Ludwig **19**
Lewton, Val **76**
Lindsay, (Nicholas) Vachel **17**
Locke, Alain (Le Roy) **43**
London, Jack **9, 15, 39**
Lovecraft, H(oward) P(hillips) **4, 22**
Lowell, Amy **1, 8**
Mankiewicz, Herman (Jacob) **85**
Markham, Edwin **47**
Marquis, Don(ald Robert Perry) **7**
Masters, Edgar Lee **2, 25**
McCoy, Horace (Stanley) **28**
McKay, Claude **7, 41**
Mencken, H(enry) L(ouis) **13**
Micheaux, Oscar **76**
Millay, Edna St. Vincent **4, 49**
Mitchell, Margaret (Munnerlyn) **11**
Mitchell, S(ilas) Weir **36**
Mitchell, William **81**
Monroe, Harriet **12**
Muir, John **28**
Nathan, George Jean **18**
Nordhoff, Charles (Bernard) **23**
Norris, (Benjamin) Frank(lin Jr.) **24**
O'Neill, Eugene (Gladstone) **1, 6, 27, 49**
Oskison, John Milton **35**
Park, Robert E(zra) **73**
Patton, George S. **79**
Peirce, Charles Sanders **81**
Percy, William Alexander **84**
Phillips, David Graham **44**
Porter, Gene(va Grace) Stratton **21**
Post, Melville Davisson **39**
Pulitzer, Joseph **76**
Pyle, Ernie **75**
Pyle, Howard **81**
Rawlings, Marjorie Kinnan **4**
Reed, John (Silas) **9**
Reich, Wilhelm **57**
Rhodes, Eugene Manlove **53**
Riggs, (Rolla) Lynn **56**
Riis, Jacob A(ugust) **80**
Riley, James Whitcomb **51**
Rinehart, Mary Roberts **52**
Roberts, Elizabeth Madox **68**
Roberts, Kenneth (Lewis) **23**
Robinson, Edwin Arlington **5**
Roelvaag, O(le) E(dvart) **17**
Rogers, Will(iam Penn Adair) **8, 71**
Roosevelt, Theodore **69**

Nationality Index

ISBN 0-7876-2747-X

90000